Teacher's
Introduction and
Answer Key

Annotated Edition

Our
American
Government

Stanley E. Dimond
Elmer F. Pflieger

J. B. LIPPINCOTT COMPANY   Philadelphia, New York

ISBN–0–397–40217–1

TABLE OF CONTENTS

INTRODUCTION

Developing responsible citizens is a primary task of the American schools. The authors of *Our American Government* believe that the high school government course makes a major contribution to this citizenship goal. The understandings gained, the new knowledge acquired, the thought processes refined, the appreciations deepened, and the interest aroused assist youth on the road to mature citizenship.

The use of the *Our* in the title of the book symbolizes the faith we have in American institutions. We hope it helps you as the teacher to get across the idea in the government class that this is a joint enterprise in which you as the teacher and we as the authors are joining forces with the students in a common endeavor.

This edition of the manual has been made in the same spirit. From our personal experiences as teachers plus varied experiences with hundreds of classroom teachers, we have assembled those ideas which might help you teach the course in American government more effectively.

PRESENT EMPHASES IN TEACHING GOVERNMENT

From our visits to government classes and from a review of the literature of government teaching, the following more or less distinct points of emphasis have been noted.

EMPHASIS ON UNDERSTANDING AND GENERALIZATION

Government was once taught chiefly from the point of view of the acquisition of detailed information. Rote memory of factual information was the rule. Disappointment with results was common among teachers; boredom was common among pupils. With the advent of the eighteen-year-old vote, the trend has been to arrange facts into patterns that support broad generalizations. As a result logical organization, stress on relationships, study of the whole as well as the parts have become more common. *Our American Government* presents facts in organized ways, in proper relationships, so that concepts and generalizations can be learned.

CONCERN FOR AROUSING INTEREST

At one time it was taken for granted that high school students would automatically be interested in American government because they were American citizens growing up in the American culture. That assumption is no longer held. Some young people are intensely interested in the study of government. But for others interest must be created. Their major interests lie in other areas: athletics, movies, dancing, science, English, the opposite sex. So the trend in American government classes has been to do a better job of arousing interest. Human-interest stories, anecdotes, visual aids, greater participation through a range of methods have been employed to increase the number who leave the government course with an enduring interest in our government.

STRESS ON THE RELATION OF GOVERNMENT AND CONTEMPORARY LIFE

A considerable portion of the time given to the study of government in the past was devoted to the historical evolution of government. The overlapping with American history was recognized, but repetition was thought desirable. Major emphasis was on the analysis of the Constitution. Much of this has changed. The trend today is to deal with these matters in a summary review fashion and to increase the study of practical, present-day civic, economic, and social questions that confront the public. The enduring historical values are stressed through a constant comparison of the past with the present. Understanding of the Constitution is gained by applying its principles to present-day situations. Learning is enhanced with this approach because there is application of knowledge.

SOLICITUDE FOR THOUGHT PROCESSES

While the terminology is varied and sometimes ambiguous, an increased concern for teaching thought processes is apparent. Problem solving, inquiry, and discovery have received much emphasis in the newer efforts to upgrade the social studies curriculum. The effort is to get students to put information to use in rational ways and not merely to emphasize memory.

DEDICATION TO DEMOCRATIC IDEALS

Until fairly recently it was generally believed that the ideals of democracy were well understood and were almost self-taught. Growing up in a democratic society was believed to result in the automatic acquisition of democratic ideals. The skepticism of youth centering on the long Vietnam war has underlined the need for more effective teaching of our way of life. As a result, three trends are apparent: (1) a more careful study of the operation of democracy through a better analysis of the factors that comprise democratic living; (2) efforts to give students opportunities to practice democratic ideas in school and in the community; (3) the basing of loyalty on intellectual understanding and thoughtful comparative analysis.

CLEAR RECOGNITION OF BASIC OBJECTIVES

During recent years there has been a trend toward a clearer recognition of the basic objectives in the teaching of government. At one time, textbooks and courses of study neglected objectives. Later, elaborate statements of detailed objectives became popular. Today both of these extremes are avoided. The trend is toward a simple statement of guiding principles from which the individual teacher, or the teacher and the class, determine the objectives for the work to be done. Without some basic goals there is no direction, but with too complicated and too numerous goals direction is lost through diffusion and confusion.

In keeping with this trend the authors, in the Preface, state four purposes for *Our American Government:*

1. To stimulate interest in our government.
2. To provide students with an essential understanding of the operations of our government.
3. To promote careful thinking about government problems.
4. To encourage active participation in governmental activities.

4

UNIT ORGANIZATION

In keeping with these purposes *Our American Government* is organized into eight units with thirty-three chapters. Teachers have always tried to organize their instruction in a manner that will aid learning. This has been our endeavor too. The eight units have been carefully planned. They are based on the experiences of many teachers and many classes. These units are flexible and permit teaching by a variety of methods. There is no one best method of teaching; teaching seems to be personal to the individual teacher. A text should assist and not interfere with the teaching method.

The unit organization employed is designed to help teachers with the type of teaching they desire to use. In our work with teachers we have observed that there are three general types of unit teaching which have many followers. We shall call them the *daily-assignment method,* the *group method,* and the *study-group method.* Briefly these methods operate as follows:

DAILY-ASSIGNMENT METHOD

The first step in this method is the *introduction* of the unit. There follow *daily assignments* focused on the ideas of the unit. The unit is brought to a close with a period for *summary or culmination and evaluation.* Diagrammatically this procedure for a 15-20 day unit is shown in figure 1 below.

THE GROUP METHOD

Again the first step in this method is the *introduction* of the unit, but, in addition to emphasizing the nature of the unit, *groups or committees* are organized to work on various phases of the unit. During the second step these groups undertake study and research on the phases selected. At the third step the groups *present to the total group* the results of their work. Fourth, the unit is closed with a period for *summary or culmination and evaluation.* Diagramed, this procedure for a 15-20 day unit is as shown in figure 2.

THE STUDY-GROUP METHOD

The first step again is the *introduction* of the unit. But some teachers feel that before pupils select committee or individual activities, they need to have some understanding of the information of the unit. So, the second step of this method is a period of

Figure 1: Daily-Assignment Method

Introduction	Daily assignments	Summary and evaluation
1-2 days	13-17 days	1-3 days

Figure 2: The Group Method

Introduction	Group or committee work	Group presentations	Summary and evaluation
1-2 days	5-9 days	4-6 days	1-3 days

Figure 3: The Study-Group Method

Introduction 1-2 days	Intense study period 4-5 days	Period for activities 3-7 days	Presentation 3-5 days	Summary and evaluation 1-3 days

highly concentrated study in which all pupils study the chapters of the unit in a short, intense period. Third, the class then engages in a period of *work on individual or group projects.* Fourth, the *presentation* of the projects is made. Fifth, there is a period of *summary or culmination and evaluation.* The diagram for this study-group method is shown in figure 3.

Adaptations of these three unit procedures seem to encompass most of the high school government teaching done today.

For example, some teachers seem to prefer a *textbook method* in which the organization of the textbook is followed with considerable care. Basically this seems to be an adaptation of the daily-assignment method. Other teachers like to use a *problem-solving or inquiring method* in which students select problems or topics for intensive study. This method carries the study-group method one step further. Following the introduction and the period of intensive study, instead of using activities and presentations, the class states the problem or problems, suggests solutions, seeks supporting evidence, and attempts to reach agreement on solutions. Again, topics for inquiry and research may be chosen after which investigation and research are undertaken by individuals or teams.

Each of these methods has merits, and which one to use depends to a great extent on the nature of the class and the general background of the teacher. Regardless of which method is employed, the *introduction* and the *summary or culmination and evaluation* are common. Ways of getting started and means of bringing learnings to a fruitful end are earmarks of good teaching.

INTRODUCTION OF A UNIT

The purpose of the introduction is to give students an overview of the unit.

There are many ways by which teachers introduce units. A common practice is for the teacher to take considerable time for an informal lecture in which the nature of the unit is described. Movies, filmstrips, and other audio-visual aids are sometimes employed. The reading and discussion of the unit introduction is another common practice. In using *Our American Government* this plan is suggested as having considerable merit when it is supplemented by a student discussion or by the pooling of experiences in relation to the ideas of the unit. Other teachers like to raise the question of what the main ideas are that students would like to learn about the unit. By listing these on the blackboard, the major desirable directions for the study of the unit can be ascertained.

SUMMARY OR CULMINATION AND EVALUATION

At the end of each unit of the book, teachers try to pull the unit together, regardless of which plan of unit teaching they have employed. The purpose is to provide an opportunity to put information to use. This final look at the totality of the unit contributes to the learning by "overlearning" in a new situation in which thinking becomes a primary objective. To assist with this overview process, *Our American Government* contains suggested cases or discovery episodes at the end of each unit. These cases provide opportunities to apply learning in real situations.

In addition to using the case at the end of the unit, teachers usually wish to do some of their own evaluating. Because this evaluation often includes an objective test, the authors have prepared the booklet *Tests for Our American Government*. In addition to giving an objective test, some teachers like to use essay tests, student self-evaluation, group evaluation, or peer evaluation devices. Others like to raise such questions as: Did we accomplish our objectives? Was our unit planned wisely? Did we work effectively? How could our learning have been improved? The values in all of these procedures are that future improvement for students and the teacher depends upon a careful appraisal of what has been done.

WORKING ON THE UNIT

As noted in descriptions of the three general types of unit teaching, the variations between the *introduction* and the *summary or culmination and evaluation* are numerous. In spite of the differences, however, there are several common features. Teachers want students to learn certain specifics. To help this process, each chapter begins with a section on *The language of government*. At the end of each chapter are *Study questions* which help students review and apply basic learnings.

Teachers want students to think, to compare present-day events with ideas of the text, and to discuss public issues intelligently. To assist the teacher in achieving these goals, each chapter contains a section called *Ideas for discussion*.

Teachers want to care for individual differences by providing a range of activities for individuals or groups. To this end the *Things to do* have been included at the end of each chapter.

To extend the range of reading, a brief list of *Further readings* (bibliography) of valuable readings has been supplied.

The use of these end-of-chapter materials is discussed in more detail below.

USING THE SPECIAL FEATURES IN A CHAPTER

The special features of each chapter are tools to assist the teacher. They have grown from study, analysis, and discussion with many teachers.

THE LANGUAGE OF GOVERNMENT

These lists provide a helpful study device. Most students should be able to define and use these words and phrases. They are placed at the start of each chapter to assist the students when they encounter the words later in the chapter. The words also appear in the *Glossary* at the end of the book. The number of items in this list has been kept small to give emphasis to the most important terms. While recognizing the necessity for developing a civic vocabulary, the authors have also tried to avoid the danger of turning the teaching of government into primarily a process of translating unfamiliar words and phrases. These lists can be used for aiding daily assignments, for locating the words in daily newspapers, for holding definition "spelldowns," for sparking classroom discussions, and reviewing for tests. Probably most students should be expected to understand these words and phrases.

SPECIAL BOXES

Each chapter contains two types of special boxes: a pertinent quotation and some type of special interest account. Each box provides a springboard for discussion or inquiry. The teacher may launch these discussions or inquiries by asking: Do you agree or disagree? What are the results of this point of view? Do people act any differently because of this statement? Sometimes it is wise strategy not to say anything about a box and wait until students raise questions or make comments.

CONCEPTS AND GENERALIZATIONS

Each chapter ends with a list of concepts and generalizations which the authors have employed in the chapter. These are not to be considered fixed and unchangeable. Teachers and students could and should challenge them and develop others if these, too, have resulted from their study. They do, however, represent some of the fundamental ideas of political science and as such are deserving of special emphasis. In effect, they supply a useful summary of the chapter.

STUDY QUESTIONS

These questions are designed to assist the student in reviewing learning. The questions have been selected to provide direction to the central ideas of each chapter. They can be used in several ways: to make daily assignments for the whole class, for committees, or for individuals; to provide reviews before tests; to provide the basis for classroom checkup on lesson preparation. Most students should be able to answer the bulk of these questions.

IDEAS FOR DISCUSSION

The items in these lists come from a great variety of sources. They are intended to help in the application of civic knowl-edge to current situations. They represent the type of material which all citizens are required to discuss in ordinary civic life. Teachers use them for classroom discussion by assigning one or two to individuals, to committees, or to the entire class. In the latter case, one or two students can be designated to start the discussion by presenting a personal point of view. In most cases there are no "correct" answers. The intent is to give students a chance to put ideas to work in a socialized recitation or class discussion.

Some teachers divide the class into small groups of six or seven students. One group discusses one item, another group discusses another item, another group a third item. The number of groups depends on the size of the class. After short discussions of six to ten minutes, a designated chairman for each group reports the results of the group's thinking to the entire class. This technique is commonly called the "buzz session" or the "66 technique."

Some of the most lively classroom sessions occur during informal debating of these *Ideas for discussion*. Probably only a few items will be used.

THINGS TO DO

The great individual differences in senior high school government classes require some variety in activities. The slower student needs an opportunity for success. The brighter student needs the chance to go beyond the usual work of the class. *Things to do* provides a reservoir of activities for caring for individual differences. The items are used in several ways. Under the daily-assignment method, individuals are asked to do certain activities for supplementary work. Under either group method, the items provide opportunities for groups to decide what they wish to do.

Some teachers have devised a point system by which students are required to earn a certain number of points for each unit by doing one or more of the activities. Again, in most cases not all the *Things to do* will be used. Their use depends on the nature of the class and the nature of the teaching.

FURTHER READINGS

Every student will benefit from further readings; but not every student will be so inclined. Some students will examine all of the references at the end of each chapter, some only one or two, and some none at all. The broadly varied lists of readings at the end of each chapter were chosen to provide subject matter that would appeal to almost every interest level.

TIME SCHEDULES

Government is taught in American high schools under either a semester plan or a year plan. About 75 per cent of the schools teach the course for one semester. *Our American Government,* because of the rich variety of end-of-chapter materials, and the unit endings, is used successfully with either plan. Time schedules are at best rough approximations because classes may develop intense interest in some phase and

show less interest in another phase. Some classes may need to devote more time to one particular unit than to others. Workable schemes (for a semester and also for a year) based on an 18-week semester are shown in the chart below.

Teachers of government have varying ideas on the content they wish to emphasize in their government classes. Some teachers devote time to a study of the form and functions of government and also to the problems of government. The eight units of *Our American Government* treat both of these phases, and the suggested time schedule above shows how a portion of the course may be devoted to each.

However, *Our American Government* may also be used effectively by teachers who wish to devote the whole course, or most of it, to one or the other phase. A teacher wishing to develop a course around the study of the form and functions of government will use Units One through Six primarily, devoting one or two additional weeks to each of these units in the suggested time schedule. The material in Units Seven and Eight may then be used to supplement various topics studied in the first five units.

The teacher who wishes to develop a course around various topics and problems will find the content of Units Seven and

	UNIT	SEMESTER PLAN	YEAR PLAN
I	Principles and practices of our government	2 weeks	3 weeks
II	The political processes	2 weeks	3 weeks
III	National government	4 weeks	6 weeks
IV	State government	2 weeks	5 weeks plus 1 week for review and examination
V	Local government	2 weeks	5 weeks
VI	Taxation and finance	1 week	2 weeks
VII	The United States and world affairs	2½ weeks	5 weeks
VIII	Government and the life of our people	2½ weeks	5 weeks plus 1 week for review and examination

Eight especially well suited to this type of content emphasis. Certain chapters (for example, 18 and 22) in the other units are also rich in content for this type of treatment. Units One to Six may then be used for additional topics and as resource and reference material for the topics and problems studied.

UNFINISHED BUSINESS

With the 1971 edition a new feature was added to *Our American Government*—a chapter on "Unfinished Business," which summarized the unresolved issues before the nation in December 1970. With the 1973 revision this chapter has been rewritten. By calling attention to the issues unresolved after the 1972 elections, it is hoped that students will be able to determine what will happen concerning these matters. Will the issues persist? Will they be resolved? Will these headlines be replaced in the public mind by new developments? By means of special reports, inquiry exercises, and discussion, the dynamic character of American government will be underlined for readers of this book.

USING THE ANNOTATED EDITION

This annotated edition of *Our American Government* provides supplementary information and suggestions useful for teaching government to high school youth. All suggestions are based upon classroom experience in the presentation of the subject and are of aid in emphasizing major concepts as well as in meeting immediate problems inherent in the teaching-learning process.

The teacher who wishes to make fullest use of the annotated edition will make additional notes in the margin and at the ends or beginnings of chapters or units. According to individual classroom situations, adjustments in the presentation of subject matter and projects proposed to the students will vary.

Most annotations have been related to specific portions of the text, indicated by a large dot (●). If there are two dots on a page, the first dot refers to the annotation at the top of the page and the second dot refers to the annotation at the bottom of the page.

GOVERNMENT PUBLICATIONS

LOCAL GOVERNMENT REPORTS. From the city or county clerk or secretaries of other agencies of local government, it is usually possible to obtain the following:
1. Annual reports
2. Charters
3. Departmental reports
4. Financial reports

CONGRESSIONAL DIRECTORY. Government Printing Office, Washington, D. C. Congressional biographies, committee assignments, maps of congressional districts, officials of executive and judicial branches. Issued biennially for each Congress.

STATE BLUEBOOK OR MANUAL. (Write to your state Secretary of State.) In most states an annual report is published containing the state constitution, biographies of officials, descriptions of agencies and commissions.

STATISTICAL ABSTRACT OF THE UNITED STATES. Government Printing Office, Washington, D. C. Published annually. Summarizes important statistics on governmental, economic, and social data.

UNITED STATES GOVERNMENT ORGANIZATION MANUAL. Government Printing Office, Washington, D. C. Published annually. Describes the agencies of the federal government. This official handbook is the best source for up-to-date, factual information on the federal government.

GENERAL REFERENCE BOOKS

THE AMERICAN YEARBOOK: A RECORD OF EVENTS AND PROGRESS. Thomas Nelson and Sons. Published annually. Summarizes important developments in American governmental and economic life.

THE BOOK OF THE STATES. Council of State Governments. Published biennially. Supplies accurate information about each of the state governments.

ECONOMIC ALMANAC. Industrial Conference Board. A handbook of trustworthy statistical data on current economic life.

INFORMATION PLEASE ALMANAC. The Macmillan Co. An annual compilation of pertinent information on numerous subjects. Much useful governmental data.

THE MUNICIPAL YEARBOOK. International City Managers' Association. Published annually. Summarizes activities and statistics of American cities.

THE STATESMAN'S YEARBOOK. The Macmillan Co. Published annually. Statistical and political information about all nations and international organizations.

THE WORLD ALMANAC AND BOOK OF FACTS. New York World-Telegram. An annual compilation of pertinent information on numerous subjects. Much useful governmental data.

YEARBOOK OF THE UNITED NATIONS. Columbia University Press. Published annually. Summarizes activities of the UN and its agencies.

OTHER SELECTED REFERENCES

Adler, Mortimer, THE COMMON SENSE OF POLITICS. Holt, Rinehart and Winston, Inc., 1971.

Adrian, Charles R., and Press, Charles, GOVERNING URBAN AMERICA. McGraw-Hill Book Company, 1972.

Alvarez, Joseph A., FROM RECONSTRUCTION TO REVOLUTION. Atheneum Publishers, 1971.

Ambrose, Stephen E., and Barber, James Alden, Jr., THE MILITARY AND AMERICAN SOCIETY. The Free Press, 1972.

Barber, James A., Jr., SOCIAL MOBILITY AND VOTING BEHAVIOR. Rand McNally & Company, 1971.

Barker, Lucius J., and Barker, Twiley, Jr.,

FREEDOM, COURTS, POLITICS: STUDIES IN CIVIL LIBERTIES. Prentice-Hall, Inc., 1972.

Bernstein, Irving, TURBULENT YEARS: A HISTORY OF THE AMERICAN WORKER, 1933-1941. Houghton-Mifflin Company, 1970.

Bonsal, Philip W., CUBA, CASTRO, AND THE UNITED STATES. University of Pittsburgh Press, 1971.

Brown, Stuart Gerry, THE PRESIDENCY ON TRIAL: ROBERT KENNEDY'S 1968 CAMPAIGN AND AFTERWARDS. University of Hawaii Press, 1972.

Buechner, John C., STATE GOVERNMENT IN THE TWENTIETH CENTURY. Houghton Mifflin Company, 1967.

Campbell, Angus, et al, THE AMERICAN VOTER. John Wiley & Sons, Inc., 1964.

———, ELECTIONS AND THE POLITICAL ORDER. John Wiley & Sons, Inc., 1966.

Campbell, Angus, and Converse, Philip E., eds., HUMAN MEANING OF SOCIAL CHANGE. Russell Sage Foundation, 1971.

Carter, Gwendolen M., and Herz, John H., MAJOR FOREIGN POWERS: THE GOVERNMENT OF GREAT BRITAIN, FRANCE, GERMANY, AND THE SOVIET UNION. Harcourt Brace Jovanovich, Inc., 1967.

Chafe, William H., THE AMERICAN WOMAN: HER CHANGING SOCIAL, ECONOMIC, AND POLITICAL ROLES, 1920-1970. Oxford University Press, Inc., 1972.

Citizens Conference on State Legislatures, THE SOMETIME GOVERNMENTS. Bantam Books, Inc., 1971.

Cohen, Carl, ed., COMMUNISM, FASCISM, AND DEMOCRACY: THE THEORETICAL FOUNDATIONS. Random House, Inc., 1972.

Committee for Economic Development, GUIDING METROPOLITAN GROWTH. The Committee, 1966.

———, IMPROVING THE PUBLIC WELFARE SYSTEM. The Committee, 1970.

———, MAKING CONGRESS MORE EFFECTIVE. The Committee, 1970.

———, MODERNIZING LOCAL GOVERNMENT. The Committee, 1966.

———, MODERNIZING STATE GOVERNMENT. The Committee, 1967.

———, REDUCING CRIME AND ASSURING JUSTICE. The Committe, 1972.

Cortner, Richard C., THE APPORTIONMENT CASES. W. W. Norton & Company, Inc., 1972.

Corwin, E. S., THE CONSTITUTION AND WHAT IT MEANS TODAY. Princeton University Press, 1958.

Cox, Edward F., et al, THE NADER REPORT ON THE FEDERAL TRADE COMMISSION. Richard W. Baron Publishing Co., Inc., 1969.

Crassweller, Robert D., THE CARIBBEAN COMMUNITY: CHANGING SOCIETIES AND U.S. POLICY. Praeger Publishers, Inc., 1972.

Crossman, Richard H. S., THE MYTHS OF CABINET GOVERNMENT. Harvard University Press, 1970.

Curtis, Richard, THE LIFE OF MALCOLM X. Macrae Smith Company, 1971.

Cushman, Robert E., ed., LEADING CONSTITUTIONAL DECISIONS. Appleton-Century-Crofts, 1971.

Dahl, Robert A., DEMOCRACY IN THE UNITED STATES: PROMISE AND PERFORMANCE. Rand McNally & Company, 1972.

David, Paul T., PARTY STRENGTH IN THE UNITED STATES, 1872-1970. The University Press of Virginia, 1972.

Davis, David Brian, ed., THE FEAR OF CONSPIRACY: IMAGES OF UN-AMERICAN SUBVERSION FROM THE REVOLUTION TO THE PRESENT. Cornell University Press, 1971.

Downie, Leonard, Jr., JUSTICE DENIED: THE CASE FOR REFORM IN THE COURTS. Penguin Books Inc., 1972.

Due, John F., STATE AND LOCAL SALES TAX: STRUCTURE AND ADMINISTRATION, rev. ed. Public Administration Service, 1971.

Eddy, Elizabeth M., BECOMING A TEACHER: THE PASSAGE TO PROFESSIONAL STATUS. Teachers College Press, 1971.

Elton, G. R., POLITICAL HISTORY: PRINCIPLES AND PRACTICE. Basic Books, Inc., Publishers, 1970.

Farkas, Suzanne, URBAN LOBBYING: MAYORS IN THE FEDERAL AREA. New York University Press, 1971.

Fleming, Alice, and Meltzer, Milton, eds., IDA TARBELL: FIRST OF THE MUCKRAKERS. Thomas Y. Crowell Company, 1971.

Fleming, Thomas J., THOMAS JEFFERSON. Grosset & Dunlap, Inc., 1971.

Fried, Joseph P., HOUSING CRISIS U.S.A. Praeger Publishers, Inc., 1971.

Goodspeed, Stephen S., THE NATURE AND FUNCTION OF INTERNATIONAL ORGANIZATION. Oxford University Press, Inc., 1967.

Graham, Frank, Jr., MAN'S DOMINION: THE STORY OF CONSERVATION IN AMERICA. M. Evans & Co., Inc., 1971.

Green, Mark J., et al, WHO RUNS CONGRESS? Bantam Books, Inc., 1972.

Halacy, D. S., NOW OR NEVER: THE FIGHT AGAINST POLLUTION. Four Winds Press, 1971.

Handler, Joel F., and Hollingsworth, Ellen Jane, DESERVING POOR: A STUDY OF WELFARE ADMINISTRATION. Markham Publishing Company, 1972.

Harlan, Louis R., BOOKER T. WASHINGTON: THE MAKING OF A BLACK LEADER, 1856-1901. Oxford University Press, Inc., 1972.

Harris, Richard, DECISION. E. P. Dutton & Co., Inc., 1971.

Huntington, Samuel P., and Moore, Clement H., eds., AUTHORITARIAN POLITICS IN MODERN SOCIETY. Basic Books, Inc., Publishers, 1970.

Johnson, Lyndon Baines, THE VANTAGE POINT: PERSPECTIVE OF THE PRESIDENCY, 1963-1969. Holt, Rinehart and Winston, Inc., 1971.

Jones, Edward H., BLACKS IN BUSINESS: PROBLEMS AND PROSPECTS. Holt, Rinehart and Winston, Inc., 1971.

Kallenbach, Joseph E., THE AMERICAN CHIEF EXECUTIVE. Harper & Row, Publishers, 1966.

Kaplan, Lawrence S., RECENT AMERICAN FOREIGN POLICY: CONFLICTING INTERPRETATIONS, rev. ed. Dorsey Press, 1972.

Kautsky, John H., THE POLITICAL CONSEQUENCES OF MODERNIZATION. John Wiley & Sons., Inc., 1972.

Kennedy, John F., PROFILES IN COURAGE. Pocket Books, 1964.

Key, V. O., and Cummings, M. C., Jr., THE RESPONSIBLE ELECTORATE: RATIONALITY IN PRESIDENTIAL VOTING, 1936-1960. Harvard University Press, 1966.

Kimball, Penn T., THE DISCONNECTED. Columbia University Press, 1972.

Kohn, Hans, POLITICAL IDEOLOGIES OF THE TWENTIETH CENTURY. Harper & Row, Publishers, 1966.

Kristol, Irving, ON THE DEMOCRATIC IDEA IN AMERICA. Harper & Row, Publishers, 1972.

Kolkowicz, Roman, et al, THE SOVIET UNION AND ARMS CONTROL: A SUPERPOWER DILEMMA. The Johns Hopkins University Press, 1970.

Ladd, Everett C., Jr., IDEOLOGY IN AMERICA: CHANGE AND RESPONSE IN A CITY, A SUBURB, AND A SMALL TOWN. Cornell University Press, 1969.

Lasswell, Harold D., THE FUTURE OF POLITICAL SCIENCE. Atherton Press, 1963.

———, POLITICS: WHO GETS WHAT, WHEN, AND HOW. Peter Smith, 1936.

Levy, Mark R., and Kramer, Michael S., THE ETHNIC FACTOR: HOW AMERICA'S MINORITIES DECIDE ELECTIONS. Simon and Schuster, Inc., 1972.

Lineberry, Robert L., and Sharkansy, Ira, URBAN POLITICS AND PUBLIC POLICY. Harper & Row, Publishers, 1971.

Lippman, Theo, Jr., SPIRO AGNEW'S AMERICA: THE VICE PRESIDENT AND THE POLITICS OF SUBURBIA. W. W. Norton & Company, Inc., 1972.

Liston, Robert A., PRESIDENTIAL POWER: HOW MUCH IS TOO MUCH. McGraw-Hill Book Company, 1971.

McCloskey, Robert G., THE MODERN SUPREME COURT. Harvard University Press, 1972.

Mills, Edwin S., URBAN ECONOMICS. Scott, Foresman and Company, 1972.

Mitau, G. Theodore, STATE AND LOCAL GOVERNMENT: POLITICS AND PROCESS. Charles Scribner's Sons, 1966.

Mitchell, William, THE AMERICAN POLICY. Glencoe Press, 1962.

Morgan, David, SUFFRAGISTS AND DEMOCRATS: THE POLITICS OF WOMAN SUFFRAGE IN AMERICA. Michigan State University Press, 1971.

Murphy, Paul L. THE CONSTITUTION IN CRISIS TIMES, 1918-1969. Harper & Row, Publishers, 1972.

Myrdal, Gunnar, ASIAN DRAMA: AN INQUIRY INTO THE POVERTY OF NATIONS. Pantheon Books, Inc., 1972.

Nadel, Mark V., THE POLITICS OF CONSUMER PROTECTION. The Bobbs-Merrill Co., Inc., 1971.

National Geographic Society, AS WE LIVE AND BREATHE: THE CHALLENGE OF OUR ENVIRONMENT. National Geographic Society, 1971.

Neilands, J. B., et al, HARVEST OF DEATH: CHEMICAL WARFARE IN VIETNAM AND CAMBODIA. The Free Press, 1972.

Neustadt, Richard E., PRESIDENTIAL POWER. John Wiley & Sons, Inc., 1964.

Northedge, F. S., and Grieve, M. J., A HUNDRED YEARS OF INTERNATIONAL RELATIONS. Praeger Publishers, Inc., 1972.

Oates, Wallace E., FISCAL FEDERALISM. Harcourt Brace Jovanovich, Inc., 1972.

Ottensoser, Milton, and Sigall, Michael W., eds., THE AMERICAN POLITICAL REALITY. Random House, Inc., 1972.

Pechman, Joseph A., FEDERAL TAX POLICY. The Brookings Institution, 1966.

Perloff, Harvey S., ed., THE FUTURE OF THE

UNITED STATES GOVERNMENT TOWARD THE YEAR 2000. George Braziller, Inc., 1971.

Polsby, Nelson W., ed., REAPPORTIONMENT IN THE 1970's. University of California Press, 1971.

Porter, Kirk H., and Johnson, Donald S., NATIONAL PARTY PLATFORMS, 1840-1964. University of Illinois Press, 1966.

Pye, Lucian W., WARLORD POLITICS: CONFLICT AND COALITION IN THE MODERNIZATION OF REPUBLICAN CHINA. Praeger Pubishers, Inc., 1971.

Reedy, George E., THE TWILIGHT OF THE PRESIDENCY. W. W. Norton & Company, Inc., 1970.

Rees, John, EQUALITY. Praeger Publishers, Inc., 1972.

Rakove, Milton L., ed., ARMS AND FOREIGN POLICY IN THE NUCLEAR AGE. Oxford University Press, 1972.

Robottom, John, MODERN RUSSIA. McGraw-Hill Book Company, 1971.

Robson, William A., and Regan, D. E., eds., GREAT CITIES OF THE WORLD. Sage Publications Inc., 1971.

Rogers, David, THE MANAGEMENT OF BIG CITIES: INTEREST AND SOCIAL CHANGE STRATEGIES. Sage Publications, Inc., 1971.

Rose, Arnold M., THE POWER STRUCTURE: POLITICAL PROGRESS IN AMERICAN SOCIETY. Oxford University Press, Inc., 1967.

Rosenbloom, David H., FEDERAL SERVICE AND THE CONSTITUTION: THE DEVELOPMENT OF THE PUBLIC EMPLOYMENT RELATIONSHIP. Cornell University Press, 1971.

Rossiter, Clinton, PARTIES AND POLITICS IN AMERICA. Cornell University Press, 1960.

Rothberg, Abraham, THE HEIRS OF STALIN: DISSIDENCE AND THE SOVIET REGIME, 1953-1970. Cornell University Press, 1972.

Sargent, L. T., CONTEMPORARY POLITICAL IDEOLOGIES: A COMPARATIVE ANALYSIS, rev. ed. Dorsey Press, 1972.

Sayre, Wallace S., and Parris, Judith H., VOTING FOR PRESIDENT: THE ELECTORAL COLLEGE AND THE AMERICAN POLITICAL SYSTEM. The Brookings Institution, 1970.

Seashore, Stanley E., and McNeill, Robert J., MANAGEMENT OF THE URBAN CRISIS. The Free Press, 1971.

Secretary of State, UNITED STATES FOREIGN POLICY. Department of State Publication 8634, 1972.

Shick, Allen, BUDGET INNOVATION IN THE STATES. The Brookings Institution, 1971.

Shulman, Colette, ed., WE THE RUSSIANS: VOICES FROM RUSSIA. Praeger Publishers, Inc., 1971.

Smith, Judith G., ed., POLITICAL BROKERS: PEOPLE, ORGANIZATIONS, MONEY, AND POWER. Liveright, 1972.

Snider, Clyde F., and Gove, S. K., AMERICAN STATE AND LOCAL GOVERNMENT. Appleton-Century-Crofts, 1965.

Sparks, Will, WHO TALKED TO THE PRESIDENT LAST? W. W. Norton & Company, Inc., 1971.

Stanley, David T., MANAGING LOCAL GOVERNMENT UNDER PRESSURE. The Brookings Institution, 1972.

Sterne, Gelders, HIS WAS THE VOICE: THE LIFE OF W. E. DUBOIS. The Macmillan Company, 1971.

Taylor, General Maxwell D., SWORDS AND PLOWSHARES. W. W. Norton & Company, Inc., 1972.

Thorp, Willard L., THE REALITY OF FOREIGN AID. Praeger Publishers, Inc., 1971.

Tolchin, Martin, and Tolchin, Susan, TO THE VICTOR. Random House, Inc., 1971.

Travis, Walter E., ed., CONGRESS AND THE PRESIDENT. Teachers' College Press, 1971.

Tullock, Gordon, TOWARD A MATHEMATICS OF POLITICS. The University of Michigan Press, 1972.

Vinyard, Dale, CONGRESS. Charles Scribner's Sons, 1972.

Walker, Patrick G., THE BRITISH CABINET. Basic Books, Inc., Publishers, 1970.

Wellington, Harry H., and Winter, Ralph K., Jr., THE UNIONS AND THE CITIES. The Brookings Institution, 1972.

Whale, John, JOURNALISM AND GOVERNMENT: A BRITISH VIEW. University of South Carolina Press, 1972.

White, Theodore H., THE MAKING OF THE PRESIDENT—1960. Atheneum Publishers, 1961.

———, THE MAKING OF THE PRESIDENT—1964. Atheneum Publishers, 1964.

———, THE MAKING OF THE PRESIDENT—1968. Atheneum Publishers, 1969.

Wilcox, Francis O., CONGRESS, THE EXECUTIVE, AND FOREIGN POLICY. Harper & Row, Publishers, 1971.

Williams, Oliver P., METROPOLITAN POLITICAL ANALYSIS. The Free Press, 1971.

Ziegler, L. Harmon, and Peak, G. Wayne, INTEREST GROUPS IN AMERICAN SOCIETY. Prentice-Hall, Inc., 1972.

AUDIO-VISUAL MATERIALS

UNIT I
PRINCIPLES AND PRACTICES OF OUR GOVERNMENT

SOUND FILMS

THE BILL OF RIGHTS OF THE UNITED STATES. 19 min, b & w. Encyclopaedia Britannica Educational Corp. A description of the first ten amendments to the Constitution. Highlights the struggle for personal liberty through the ages.

CHICANO. 22 min, color. BFA Educational Media. Shows examples of bias, oppression, and discrimination affecting Mexican-Americans.

CIVIL RIGHTS MOVEMENT: THE PERSONAL VIEW. 25 min, b & w. Encyclopaedia Britannica Educational Corp. Importance of personal attitudes in the development of mass prejudice. Case study of a Negro family living in an integrated neighborhood.

CONFRONTED. 60 min, b & w. NET Film Service. The reactions of Negroes and whites to integration in several Northern communities.

THE CONSTITUTION: GUARDIAN OF LIBERTY. 20 min, color. McGraw-Hill Text-Films. Many constitutional safeguards to our existing civil rights are illustrated and traced to their historical origins.

DATE WITH LIBERTY. 20 min, b & w. Cassyd Productions. Presents five sequences illustrating key concepts of liberty safeguarded by law.

DEFINING DEMOCRACY. 18 min, b & w. Encyclopaedia Britannica Educational Corp. Democracy defined in terms of shared respect and shared power and showing how communities rate on a scale from democracy to despotism.

FREEDOM OF THE PRESS. 20 min, b & w. United World Free Film Service. A U. S. Army film that shows the importance of a free press through the work of major press services and local papers.

JUSTICE, LIBERTY AND LAW. 22 min, color. Churchill Films. Film shows how government provides justice and maximum freedom to individuals while still enforcing order.

LOUISIANA DIARY. 59 min, b & w. NET Film Service. A documentary film on the efforts of CORE to assist Negroes to register in Louisiana.

THE NEGRO AND THE AMERICAN PROMISE. 60 min, b & w. NET Film Service. Martin Luther King, Malcolm X, Kenneth Clark, and James Baldwin discuss the movement for social and racial equality.

NEW MOOD. 30 min, b & w. NET Film Service. Reviews historical moments in the civil rights struggle.

OUR LIVING CONSTITUTION. 11 min, b & w or color. Coronet Films. Shows the manner in which the Constitution has adapted to changing times.

FILMSTRIPS

THE AMERICAN NEGRO: QUEST FOR EQUALITY. B & w. Current Affairs Films. Shows the progress of the Civil Rights movement.

BENJAMIN FRANKLIN: SYMBOL OF THE AMERICAN REVOLUTION. Color. Guidance Associates. Based largely on Franklin's own writings, his career is traced both here and abroad.

BOOKER T. WASHINGTON. B & w. Encyclopaedia Britannica Educational Corp. Sketches the life of an historic Negro leader.

EXPLODING THE MYTHS OF PREJUDICE. Color. Social Studies School Service. Dr. Ethel J. Alpenfels attempts to answer such questions as: What is prejudice? Are there pure stocks of people? What causes dark and light skin? Is the white race smarter than others?

GHETTOS OF AMERICA. Color. Social Studies School Service. Presents ghetto life in Harlem and Watts through the everyday relationships and experiences of a teen-age boy, his family and the people in their neighborhood.

MINORITIES HAVE MADE AMERICA GREAT. Color. Social Studies School Service. Filmstrips trace the story of a different ethnic group from early in American history to the present time, relating their accomplishments, struggles and obstacles faced.

PEOPLE OF RUSSIA. Color. *Life* Magazine. Work and play in Russia under the Communist party discipline.

TO SECURE THESE RIGHTS. B & w. Anti-Defamation League of B'nai B'rith. Illustrations based on the report of the President's Committee on Civil Rights.

THE SHADOW OF THE KREMLIN. B & w. New York *Times*. Describes the power and weakness of the Russian communist system and its relation with Communist China and other satellite countries.

STRENGTH OF A DEMOCRACY. B & w. Current Affairs Films. Explains the nature of democracy, how it operates, and the responsibility of citizenship.

THEY HAVE OVERCOME. Color. Social Studies School Service. Four prominent Negroes tell how they achieved their present distinguished status in spite of enduring almost insurmountable odds.

WE ARE ALL BROTHERS. Color. Social Studies School Service. A basic introduction to the problems of racial prejudice.

ZENGER AND THE FREEDOM OF THE PRESS. B & w. Heritage Filmstrips. Presents Zenger's life in relationship to the struggle for freedom of the press; shows the crucial Zenger trial and its far-reaching effects.

CHARTS

Dimond, Stanley E., and Beamer, Miles E. CITIZENSHIP FOR DEMOCRACY CHARTS. A. J. Nystrom & Co.

CD2   The United States, a Good Place to Live.
CD9   Living in a Democratic Country.
CD10   Living in a Totalitarian Country.
CD31   Our American Heritage of Freedom.
CD32   Symbols of Freedom.

RECORDINGS

THE CONSTITUTION OF THE UNITED STATES. 78 and 33⅓ rpm. National Association of Secondary School Principals. Reproductions of broadcasts on the Constitution from "Cavalcade of America" series.

THE LOYALIST. 30-minute tape recording. University of Michigan Audio-Visual Service. Story of the way the Declaration of Independence was delivered to England and the manner of its reception by King George III.

"TOWN MEETING" RECORD ALBUM. Long-play recording. Town Hall, Inc. Famous discussions from "Town Meeting of the Air" programs of the past twenty years.

UNIT II
THE POLITICAL PROCESSES

SOUND FILMS

HOW WE ELECT OUR REPRESENTATIVES. 10 min, b & w. Coronet Films. The election of representatives is followed from the registration procedure to the final counting of ballots; shown are the primary election, the campaign, and the voting.

NOMINATIONS AND ELECTIONS. 25 min, b & w. University of Wisconsin. Shows scenes from national conventions, giving information regarding delegates, committee work, and general procedures.

PROPAGANDA TECHNIQUES. 11 min, b & w. Coronet Films. Illustrates seven basic propaganda techniques in campaign posters, broadcasts, and campaign movies.

PRESSURE GROUPS. 20 min, b & w. Encyclopaedia Britannica Educational Corp. Explains what pressure groups are and reveals that, when democratically used, they are a necessary instrument for decision-making in a democracy. Illustrates methods used by a representative democratic pressure group to bring about legislation for a desirable civic project. Contrasts these methods with the underhanded, behind-the-scenes manipulation employed by a group attempting to prevent the passage of a bill.

THE YOUNG VOTES: POWER, POLITICS, AND PARTICIPATION. 15 min, color. BFA Educational Media. The film raises questions about values and attitudes of youth related to voting, politics, and democracy. It presents alternative responses and examples of behavior.

FILMSTRIPS

AMERICAN PARTIES IN POLITICS. B & w. New York *Times.* The story of the rise of political parties in America.

THE U.S. PRESIDENCY IN AN ELECTION YEAR—1964. Color. Current Affairs Films. Describes the role of the President as the head of his political party in an election year.

WHAT'S HAPPENED TO PATRIOTISM? B & w with recording. New York Times. Differing views on patriotism, using historical and contemporary sources.

CHARTS

CD7   Immigration and Naturalization.

RECORDINGS

INHERITANCE. 30 min, 33⅓ rpm. Social Studies School Service. Portrays the struggles and social progress of the late 19th- and 20th-century immigrants and the growth of trade unionism. Includes the arrival on Ellis Island, sweatshops, 53-hour work weeks, lockouts, sit-down strikes, violence and collective bargaining.

UNIT III
NATIONAL GOVERNMENT

SOUND FILMS

BASIC COURT PROCEDURES. 13½ min, b & w or color. Coronet Films. Two high school students learn from a practicing lawyer the function of the courts and how our law operates. Many specialized legal terms are defined, and the audience sees the roles played by the various courtroom figures. The film teaches the function of the courts and the place of the judicial system in a democracy.

THE CONGRESS. 21 min, b & w. Encyclopaedia Britannica Educational Corp. Describes the powers of Congress as expressly provided in the Constitution and as developed by applying the principle of implied powers. Explains the relationship between Congress and other branches of government and shows procedures by which Congress enacts laws and directs federal policies.

THE CONGRESS. 10 min, b & w. McGraw-Hill Text-Films. Shows the functions of the two houses of Congress—how a bill is introduced, considered, and acted upon. The problem of relationship of the Congress to the Presidency and to the Supreme Court is explored.

CONGRESSMAN AT WORK. 22 min, b & w. Encyclopaedia Britannica Educational Corp. Case studies of duties, activities and problems of a member of Congress with suggestions for improvements.

CRISIS OF PRESIDENTIAL SUCCESSION. 48 min, b & w. Carousel Films. Depicts problems which arise with the death or disability of a President —from Harrison to Kennedy.

THE FEDERAL GOVERNMENT. 13 min, b & w or color. Coronet Films. Outlines the primary divisions of responsibility in the government. The reasons for this division and the problems that arise from the many quasi-legislative and quasi-judicial boards and agencies are also shown.

FEDERAL RESERVE SYSTEM. 20 min, b & w. Encyclopaedia Britannica Educational Corp. Explains the purpose and functions of the Federal Reserve System. Shows how the system was devised to meet certain economic conditions. Covers the period from the money panic of 1907 through World War II, emphasizing high spots in the system's development.

FREEDOM TO SPEAK (People of New York vs. Irving Feiner). 23 min, b & w. Encyclopaedia Britannica Educational Corp. Case study in the area of individual liberty.

JOHN FITZGERALD KENNEDY. 25 min, b & w. Twentieth Century Fox. Highlights in the life of President Kennedy from boyhood to asassination.

MAKING OF THE PRESIDENT 1960, AND 1964. 80 min, each, b & w. Xerox. The presidential campaigns of 1960 and 1964 each depicted in dramatic episodes.

NATION'S CAPITAL. 15 min, b & w. McGraw-Hill Text-Films. Shows the daily life of a congressman in Washington and the many complex departments and bureaus of the federal government. Includes scenes of important monuments and inside views of the White House.

POWERS OF CONGRESS. 10 min, b & w. Coronet Films. A fantasy is employed in this film to define and explain the powers of Congress. Mr. Williams drops off to sleep for a few minutes to find himself confronted with a world in which Congress has been suspended and federal authority dissolved. When he awakes from his dream, he has a better understanding of his own responsibility in the selection of that body.

THE PRESIDENCY: SEARCH FOR A CANDIDATE. 29 min, b & w. Shows the ways a candidate becomes his party's choice and how compromise is essential in decision-making.

THE PRESIDENT. 17 min, b & w. Encyclopaedia Britannica Educational Corp. Dramatizes the major historical events which established the present power and influence of the Presidency, and shows how the office has grown because of actions of strong Presidents in times of crisis.

STORM OVER THE SUPREME COURT, PART I, 1790-1932; PART II, 1933—PRESENT. 21 min & 31 min, b & w. Carousel Films. Part I deals with early history of the court through Taney. Part II begins with Roosevelt's effort to change the court and features philosophical differences of recent justices.

SUPREME COURT. 18 min, b & w. Encyclopaedia Britannica Educational Corp. Discusses the history and function of the Supreme Court. Shows how the welfare of Americans is affected by the Supreme Court's decisions and the procedures for making its decisions.

VICE PRESIDENCY. 51 min, b & w. McGraw-Hill Text-Films. Describes the rights and duties of the Vice President of the United States, and presents a study of the men who served in this office from John Adams to Richard Nixon. Explains the original concept of the Vice Presidency.

WASHINGTON, D.C., CAPITAL CITY, U.S.A. 26 min, color. Films, Inc. Government buildings and shrines of our nation's capital; shows the historic shrines, monuments, and major points of interest.

AMERICAN PRESIDENCY—THE OFFICE OF THE PRESIDENT. B & w. Current Affairs Films. Traces the origin of presidential powers and duties from the Constitution. Describes the expansion of the executive branch and consequent pressure on the President.

OUR CONSTITUTION SERIES. Color. McGraw-Hill Text-Films. This series includes these three filmstrips:

    THE LEGISLATIVE BRANCH.
    THE EXECUTIVE BRANCH.
    THE JUDICIAL BRANCH.

The work of each of these three branches of government is explained.

GOVERNMENT IN ACTION. B & w. Encyclopaedia Britannica Educational Corp. This series includes the following separate filmstrips:

    THE PRESIDENT.
    THE CONGRESS.
    THE FEDERAL COURTS.
    EXECUTIVE DEPARTMENTS AND AGENCIES.

The organization and work of our national government is explained.

PORTRAIT OF A FRESHMAN CONGRESSMAN. Color. Guidance Associates. Two filmstrips narrated by Chet Huntley describe the activities of a new member of Congress.

YOUR FEDERAL GOVERNMENT SERIES. Color. Young America Films. This series includes the following separate filmstrips:

    THE FEDERAL GOVERNMENT.
    THE EXECUTIVE BRANCH.
    HOW A BILL BECOMES A LAW.
    THE LEGISLATIVE BRANCH.
    THE JUDICIAL BRANCH.
    OUR CAPITAL CITY.

These filmstrips illustrate the following features of our federal government: its structure and function, its system of checks and balances, the nature of the three branches, the steps in making a law. Includes a tour of Washington.

FILMSTRIPS

AMERICAN GOVERNMENT SERIES. B & w. McGraw-Hill Text-Films. The following filmstrips in this series describe certain functions of federal government:

    FEDERAL SYSTEM, parts I and II.
    CONGRESS: ORGANIZATION AND PROCEDURE.
    THE PRESIDENT: OFFICE AND POWERS.
    FEDERAL COURTS AND LAW ENFORCEMENT.
    PUBLIC ADMINISTRATION AND CIVIL SERVICE.

CHARTS

Dimond, Stanley E., and Beamer, Miles E. CITIZENSHIP FOR DEMOCRACY CHARTS. A. J. Nystrom & Co.

    CD15 How the Social Security Administration Works.
    CD19 How a Law is Made.
    CD20 Federal and State Courts.
    CD21 Organization of the National Government.

RECORDINGS

AMERICAN HERITAGE, VOL. 2. Long-play recording. Folkways. Includes two speeches which illustrate certain phases of government: Washington's Farewell Address and Daniel Webster in the Senate.

THE ELECTORAL COLLEGE. 30 min, dual tape 3¾. Social Studies Service. A full explanation of the electoral system in the United States, beginning with the Constitutional Convention of 1787. Includes a dramatic presentation of the day electoral votes are cast in Washington, D.C.

UNIT IV
STATE GOVERNMENT

SOUND FILMS

BASIC COURT PROCEDURES. 14 min, b & w. Coronet Films. Two high school students learn from a lawyer the functions and operations of the courts. Helps with special legal terms.

CENTRALIZATION AND DECENTRALIZATION. 18 min, b & w. Encyclopaedia Britannica Educational Corp. Deals with the problem of the gradual transfer of decision-making from local communities to state and national levels.

ENGLISH CRIMINAL JUSTICE. 21 min, b & w. British Information Services. Describes criminal court procedure as carried on in England.

GOVERNOR. 27 min, b & w. McGraw-Hill Text-Films. Governor's duties in relation to legislation, ceremonial events, communication, and political leadership.

INTERROGATION AND COUNSEL. 20 min, color. Churchill. Raises questions such as: When should a person be entitled to have a lawyer? Does justice work differently for the indigent?

JUSTICE UNDER LAW. 35 min, b & w. Teaching Film Custodians. Emphasizes the duty of the prosecutor to protect the innocent. Shows the legal steps in a murder case.

JUSTICE UNDER LAW—THE GIDEON CASE. 23 min, b & w. Encyclopaedia Britannica Educational Corp. Issue centers around the right of counsel despite race or financial ability.

THE LEGISLATIVE PROCESS. 28 min, color. Indiana University. Uses the actual scenes from the Indiana legislature to describe the lawmaking process.

OHIO RIVER: BACKGROUND FOR SOCIAL STUDIES. 11 min, color. Coronet Films. This great inland waterway from colonial times to present including problems of floods and water pollution.

OHIO RIVER: LOWER VALLEY, UPPER VALLEY. 11 min each, b & w. Academy Films. Features of the Ohio River and the river's important influence on the development of Louisville, Pittsburgh, and Cincinnati are shown. The functions of the river for transportation, waste removal, and water supply are described.

OUR BASIC CIVIL RIGHTS. 14 min, b & w. Coronet Films. Three high school students attend a trial of a man charged with distributing handbills illegally.

SEARCH AND PRIVACY. 20 min, color. Churchill. Two episodes of search are treated in different ways. Viewers are asked to consider questions raised.

STATE LEGISLATURE. 21 min, b & w. Academy Films. The steps in passing a law through a state legislature are described.

WHY WE RESPECT THE LAW. 14 min, b & w. Coronet Films. High school boys accused of stealing are helped by a lawyer to appreciate the importance of law.

FILMSTRIPS

LEGISLATIVE PROCESS IN MICHIGAN. B & w. University of Michigan. Depicts the passage of a law in the Michigan legislature.

MICHIGAN STATE GOVERNMENT. Color. Associated Educators. This series deals with various functions and services related to state government. It includes these separate filmstrips:
> THE CITIZEN PARTICIPATES.
> LEGISLATIVE AND EXECUTIVE BRANCHES.
> EDUCATION.
> PUBLIC HEALTH.
> STATE FUNCTIONS, HIGHWAYS, CONSERVATION, AND AGRICULTURE.
> LAW ENFORCEMENT, COURTS, AND CORRECTION.

STATE GOVERNMENT. B & w. Encyclopaedia Britannica Educational Corp. Explains the organization and work of state government.

CHARTS

Dimond, Stanley E., and Beamer, Miles E. CITIZENSHIP FOR DEMOCRACY CHARTS. A. J. Nystrom & Co.

CD1 Uncle Sam Grows Up.
CD19 How a Law Is Made.
CD20 Federal and State Courts.
CD22 Types of Administration of State and Local Governments.

RECORDINGS

MICHIGAN STATE POLICE AIR WING. 15-minute tape recording. University of Michigan, Audio-Visual Service. Reviews the operations of the air force of the state police including a pickup in the police communications center.

UNIT V
LOCAL GOVERNMENT

SOUND FILMS

ARTERIES OF NEW YORK CITY. 10 min, b & w. Encyclopaedia Britannica Educational Corp. Analyzes transportation facilities of New York City. Calls attention to distribution of residential and business districts and daily flow of people between them.

BIG CITY, 1980. PARTS I AND II. 54 min, b & w. Carousel Films. The story of what the big city in America will be in the future. Problems and prospects of city development.

THE CITIES AND THE POOR: PARTS I AND II. 60 min, b & w. NET Film Service. These two films portray poverty in urban areas and the effects of discontent on the poverty programs.

COMMUNITY GOVERNMENTS: HOW THEY FUNCTION. 13½ min, b & w. Coronet Films. The citizens of Riverside, dissatisfied with their community, look into the advantages and disadvantages of the mayor-council, city manager, and commission forms of government, and learn that the active particpation of the people and their co-operation in solving problems of local government are an integral part of community progress.

COUNTY GOVERNMENT. 22 min, b & w. Progressive Pictures. How county governments came into being, the function and duties of each county department, and the need and value of modernization of this form of government.

ON GUARD. 22 min, color. Byron. Varied services of a county health department.

PORTRAIT OF THE INNER CITY. 18 min, b & w. McGraw-Hill Text-Films. The streets, schools, and living quarters in the inner city and the citizens who serve as models for youth.

STORY OF ANYBURG, USA. 10 min, color. Walt Disney Productions. Animated cartoon of a town overrun with traffic hazards and ways to overcome the problems.

TOMORROW'S GOVERNMENT TODAY. 27 min, color. International Film Bureau. How trained personnel and teamwork between local governments can meet today's complex problems.

URBAN SPRAWL. 15 min, color. Arthur Barr. Explains the characteristics of urban growth, the problems created by it, and the necessity for urban planning.

FILMSTRIPS

BY AND FOR THE PEOPLE. Color. Curriculum Films. The government of Fairtown insures each citizen certain benefits such as fire protection and civic improvements. The responsibility for the services rests with the average citizen.

LOCAL GOVERNMENT. Color. Encyclopaedia Britannica Educational Corp. Drawings explain the organization and work of a local government.

MUNICIPAL GOVERNMENT. Color. Encyclopaedia Britannica Educational Corp. Drawings explain the functions of the executive, legislative, and judicial departments of municipal government.

CHARTS

Dimond, Stanley E., and Beamer, Miles E. CITIZENSHIP FOR DEMOCRACY CHARTS. A. J. Nystrom & Co.
    CD22 Types of Administration of State and Local Governments.

UNIT VI
TAXATION AND FINANCE

SOUND FILMS

FEDERAL TAXATION. 10 min, b & w and color. Coronet Films. Outlines federal personal and corporation income taxes and taxes on luxuries and special services. Has a graphic presentation of the federal government's efforts to support the many projects connected with our national economy.

PROPERTY TAXATION. 11 min, b & w. Encyclopaedia. Britannica Educational Corp. Portrays the social usefulness of property taxation, the types of government expenditures supported by property levies, public financing through bond issues, and procedures of levying taxes on property.

THE POWER TO TAX. B & w. Encyclopaedia Britannica Educational Corp. Title 41225. Considers the problems of concurrent powers of taxation of federal and state governments.

YOUR STATE BUDGET. 26 min, color. Virginia Board of Education. A presentation of the governor's budget and an explanation of the two types of state funds, special and general. The film shows the sources from which the state of Virginia collects its revenues and the many services on which these revenues are expended.

FILMSTRIPS

DEPARTMENT OF THE TREASURY. B & w. Creative Arts Studios. Presents the work of the eleven major divisions of the Department of the Treasury. Includes customs and government purchasing.

MONEY AND GOVERNMENT. Color. Encyclopaedia Britannica Educational Corp. Part of the series *Basic Economics* which discusses the economics of an imaginary primitive community.

TAXES—YOUR CITY'S INCOME. B & w. Current Affairs Films. Shows the great expense involved in running a city, how a typical city budget is prepared, and where the money comes from to finance the budget.

CHARTS

Dimond, Stanley E., and Beamer, Miles E. CITIZENSHIP FOR DEMOCRACY CHARTS. A. J. Nystrom & Co.

    CD16   Division of United States Income
    CD17   Taxation
               United States Income and Expenses
    CD18   Growth of Our National Debt

UNIT VII
THE UNITED STATES AND WORLD AFFAIRS

SOUND FILMS

ALASKA—THE STORY OF A FRONTIER. 18 min, b & w. Films, Inc. The history and development of Alaska.

AMERICAN FOREIGN POLICY: CHALLENGES OF CO-EXISTENCE. 23 min, b & w. Encyclopaedia Britannica Educational Corp. Nuclear war, changes in East, West leadership and containment policies.

AMERICAN FOREIGN POLICY: CONTAINMENT IN ASIA. 31 min, b & w. Encyclopaedia Britannica Educational Corp. Fundamental principles of Far East policies based on case study of Vietnam War.

AMERICAN FOREIGN POLICY: FOUNDATION. 32 min, b & w. Encyclopaedia Britannica Educational Corp. The nature of American foreign policy throughout its history is described. Twentieth century policies are emphasized.

ANATOMY OF AGGRESSION. 25 min, b & w. Norwood Films. Reviews communist activities and emphasizes conflicts between democracy and totalitarianism.

ARCHITECTS OF PEACE. 28 min, b & w. U.S. Dept. of Defense. This film depicts how in our offices and embassies around the world American diplomats continue their efforts toward satisfactory peaceful settlement of all issues.

THE ARCHIVES. 10 min, b & w. Teaching Film Custodians. The Archives Building in Washington, D.C.

ATOMIC RESEARCH AREAS AND DEVELOPMENT. 14 min, b & w. Coronet Films. Surveys application of nuclear fission, the structure of the atom, and by-products of fission.

THE CHALLENGE OF IDEAS. 31 min, b & w. United World Films. The basic values and differences between communist and democratic governments are analyzed and discussed.

CHARTER OF THE UNITED NATIONS. 15 min, b & w. British Information Services. Describes the basic structure and purposes of the United Nations.

CHINA. RISE OF COMMUNIST POWER, 1941-1967. 29 min, b & w. Encyclopaedia Britanica Educational Corp. Documents the rise to power of Mao Tse-tung.

COMMUNISM. 31 min, b & w. Castle Films. History, characteristics, and operation of communism as portrayed in a U.S. Army film.

THE F.B.I. 17 min, b & w. McGraw-Hill Text-Films. Describes the methods and techniques of this organization.

GENERAL MARSHALL. 30 min, b & w. Association. The life of General George C. Marshall spotlighting his leadership as Chief of Staff, Secretary of State, Secretary of Defense and the conception of the plan that hastened Europe's economic recovery.

THE GROWTH OF AMERICAN FOREIGN POLICY. 20 min, b & w. McGraw-Hill Text-Films. This historical film traces the development of our foreign policy from Washington's time to the present. Major steps such as the Monroe Doctrine, the Marshall Plan, the Truman Doctrine, Point IV are emphasized.

MAN IN THE BLUE HELMET. 28 min, b & w. Contemporary Films or United Nations. How the UN emergency force was formed to stop uprisings and keep the peace.

MAO TSE-TUNG. 26 min, b & w. McGraw-Hill Text-Films. History of the rise of Mao Tse-tung and his present control of China.

MIDDLE EAST, THE POWDER KEG ON THE RIM OF THE COMMUNIST WORLD. 25 min, b & w. March of Time-TV (McGraw-Hill Text-Films). Explains the major interests of the Middle East countries.

A MISSION OF DISCOVERY. 28 min, b & w. Wilding. Representative Peace Corps activities around the world are depicted, and the philosophy of involving local inhabitants in activities is expounded.

OUR MONROE DOCTRINE. 21 min, b & w. Academic Films. Describes the conditions which led to the declaring of the Monroe Doctrine and the contributions of the leaders.

PLANNING OUR FOREIGN POLICY. 21 min, b & w. Encyclopaedia Britannica Educational Corp. Describes the procedure by which foreign policy is developed, using the Middle East as the example.

TECHNIQUES AND OBJECTIVES OF AMERICAN FOREIGN POLICY. 30 min, b & w. Encyclopaedia Britannica Educational Corp. An interview with Harland Cleveland, Assistant Secretary of State, brings out some of the little-known aspects of the problems and the handling of foreign relations.

VERSUS. 11 min, color. United States Department of State. The need for collective security through NATO is described by contrasting man's desire for a tranquil world with the problem of human conflict.

WHAT ARE THE MILITARY SERVICES? 10 min, b & w. Coronet Films. General structure and functions of each of the services are explained.

WHO INVITED US. 60 min, b & w. NET Film Service. Reviews history of United States military intervention from the take-over of the Philippines to the Vietnam War.

WORKSHOP FOR PEACE. 28 min, b & w. United Nations. Describes facilites and activities at the New York United Nations headquarters.

WORLD WITHOUT END. 40 min, b & w. UNESCO (Brandon Films). Shows how UN agencies have aided Thailand and Mexico in medicine, agriculture, and education.

THE YEARS OF DECISION. 21 min. March of Time. Documents the origin of the Marshall Plan and shows its effects on families in various countries.

FILMSTRIPS

AGE OF MEGATON. Color, with recording. Doubleday and Company. Presents issues involving nuclear weapons and superiority.

ALASKA. B & w. *Life Magazine.* Describes the development of Alaska.

THE ANATOMY OF COMMUNISM (with records). Color. Linda Atchinson. This series includes the following separate filmstrips:
  THE NATURE AND MEANING OF COMMUNISM: THE BEGINNINGS.
  KARL MARX AND FREIDRICH ENGELS: THE PHILOSOPHY OF MARXIAN SOCIALISM.
  LENIN: LEGACY OF LENIN.
  COMMUNISM IN PRACTICE: COMMUNIST TACTICS AND TECHNIQUES.
  COMMUNISM IN THE UNITED STATES.

ASPIRATION STATEHOOD. B & w. New York Times. Arguments for and against statehood for Alaska and Hawaii.

ATOMIC ENERGY. B & w. United Nations. Deals with problems of international control.

COMMUNISM—WHAT YOU SHOULD KNOW ABOUT IT AND WHY. Color. McGraw-Hill Text-Films. This series is designed to help students understand the challenge of communism to the free world. The separate titles are:
  WHY STUDY COMMUNISM?
  WHAT COMMUNISM IS.
  HISTORY OF COMMUNISM: MARX TO LENIN.
  HISTORY OF COMMUNISM: STALIN TO KHRUSHCHEV.

COMMUNISM AS PRACTICED IN THE U.S.S.R.
COMMUNIST EXPANSION IN EUROPE.
COMMUNIST EXPANSION IN ASIA.
MEETING THE CHALLENGE OF COMMUNISM.

FOREIGN RELATIONS. B & w. McGraw-Hill Text-Films. Describes the development of foreign relations policies.

NATURAL RESOURCES. B & w. New York *Times*. Shows that natural resources are the key to America's strength.

OUR UNDERWATER DEFENSE. B & w. *Life* Magazine. Describes the efforts to provide national security below the oceans.

PROFILE OF COMMUNISM. Color. Carousel Films. The two separate filmstrips in this series are:
THE GROWTH OF COMMUNISM.
THE U.S.S.R. TODAY.

THE SOVIET UNION TODAY (with records). Color. Jam Handy Organization. The separate titles in this series are:
THE DEVELOPMENT OF THE SOVIET UNION.
THE GEOGRAPHY OF THE SOVIET UNION.
FARMING AND RURAL LIFE IN THE SOVIET UNION.
EUROPEAN RUSSIA AND THE UKRAINE.
THE CAUCASUS AND SOVIET CENTRAL ASIA.
CITY LIFE IN THE SOVIET UNION.

THERE SHALL BE PEACE. B & w. United Nations. Underlines the basic purpose of the United Nations.

UNITED NATIONS ORGANIZATION. B & w. *Life* Magazine. The history, purposes, and structure of the United Nations.

UNIVERSAL DECLARATION OF HUMAN RIGHTS. B & w. United Nations.

CHARTS

Dimond, Stanley E., and Beamer, Miles E. CITIZENSHIP FOR DEMOCRACY CHARTS. A. J. Nystrom & Co.

CD8 How Crowded Are the Countries of the World?
CD11 How Communists Gain Control of Non-Communist Governments
CD13 Energy of the United States
CD23 How the United Nations Is Organized
CD24 How the United Nations Deals with International Disputes
CD25 International Trade

RECORDINGS

THE UNDEFENDED BORDER. 78 or 33⅓ rpm. National Association of Secondary School Principals. Reproduction of a "Cavalcade of America" broadcast on the peaceful relations between the United States and Canada. Written by Stephen Vincent Benét and starring Raymond Massey.

UNIT VIII
GOVERNMENT AND THE LIFE OF OUR PEOPLE

SOUND FILMS

APPOINTMENT WITH YOUTH. 26 min, b & w. McGraw-Hill Text-Films. Dramatizes the work of a teacher, deals with his problems, his satisfactions, and his opportunities.

THE BALTIMORE PLAN. 20 min, b & w. Encyclopaedia Britannica Educational Corp. Documents a plan in which municipal agencies and citizens groups cooperated in a program for neighborhood renewal. Reveals the success of this plan in Baltimore in raising the quality of housing.

BARGAINING COLLECTIVELY. 10 min, b & w. Teaching Film Custodians. An excerpt from the film "An American Romance" produced by MGM. Presents arguments of labor and management for and against union recognition.

BEGINNINGS AND GROWTH OF INDUSTRIAL AMERICA. 11 min, b & w. Coronet Films. The development of American manufacturing from a system of home crafts to an industrialized factory system is explained.

CONSERVATION OF NATURAL RESOURCES. 11 min, b & w. Encyclopaedia Britannica Educational Corp. Shows results of the waste of natural resources and describes how such waste can be prevented. Discusses depletion of forests, effects of wind and water erosion, waste of mineral resources, and wasteful killing of wildlife.

CONSERVING OUR FORESTS TODAY. 11 min, color. Coronet Films. Emphasizes advances in forest conservation and shows values of forests for lumber, grazing, water, and recreation.

CONSERVING OUR SOIL TODAY. 11 min, color. Coronet Films. Shows latest techniques and experiments in soil conservation.

COUNTY AGENT. 17 min, b & w. United World Films. Illustrates some of the activities of the county agent and his services to farmers, such as giving information on soil conservation.

CURRENT EVENTS: UNDERSTANDING AND EVALUATING THEM. 11 min, b & w. Coronet Films. Standards for analyzing current events using newsreel footage to show reliability of information.

DESIGN OF AMERICAN PUBLIC EDUCATION. 16 min, b & w. McGraw-Hill Text-Films. Contrasts decentralized control of education as we have it with a system controlled centrally.

INJUSTICE ON TRIAL. 20 min, b & w. AFL-CIO. Presents labor's viewpoint on right-to-work laws in the form of a trial.

LABOR COMES OF AGE. 19 min, b & w. Encyclopaedia Britannica Educational Corp. Growth of labor unions and strengthening of collective bargaining.

MAGIC HIGHWAY, U.S.A. 29 min, color. Walt Disney Productions. The story of our highways from early times into the future. Construction methods and vital role of highways are stressed.

THE PROBLEM WITH WATER IS PEOPLE. 30 min, color. McGraw-Hill Text-Films. Potential crises in the water supply are depicted through scenes along the Colorado River and in cities and farm areas.

PROBLEMS OF HOUSING. 11 min, b & w. Encyclopaedia Britannica Educational Corp. Shows standards for pleasant and healthful housing.

RIGHTS OF AGE. 28 min, b & w. International Film Bureau. Contrasts old people who have maximum benefits of Social Security with those who suffer from illness and deprivation.

SAFE AS YOU THINK. 30 min, b & w. General Motors Corporation. Stresses the need and importance of being conscious of safety at all times—at home, at school, at work, or in the street. Shows how we often take foolish chances just to save a few seconds.

SECURE THE BLESSINGS. 26 min, b & w. National Education Association. Dramatizes the role of the public school in a democracy. Shows that the manner in which people solve their problems is determined, to a large extent, by the education they have received.

SOIL AND WATER CONSERVATION. 10 min, b & w. United World Films. Shows how conservation farming may prevent further destruction of our soil and water resources. Demonstrates several good practices, such as contouring, terracing, strip-cropping, rotation, and tree and grass planting.

WHO'S DELINQUENT? 16 min, b & w. McGraw-Hill Text-Films. Causes of delinquency in a community are investigated by the newspaper of a typical town; the townspeople meet to solve the problems and eliminate the causes.

WITNESS TO AN ACCIDENT. 11 min, color. Indiana University. Describes activities of a police officer investigating an automobile accident. Shows the extensive laboratory facilities available to him.

WORKING TOGETHER. 23 min, b & w. Encyclopaedia Britannica Educational Corp. The story of how labor and management adjusted their interests in the case of the American Lead Pencil Company and the local unit of the Textile Workers Union.

FILMSTRIPS

CITY WITHIN A CITY. B & w. American Council on Education. Pictures a privately financed housing project in a large city and indicates its possibilities in providing good housing in congested areas.

CONSERVATION IS EVERYBODY'S BUSINESS. Color. McGraw-Hill Text-Films. A series of four filmstrips pointing up the vital importance of conservation. The titles are:
PEOPLE, OUR MOST VALUABLE RESOURCE.
SAVING THE SOIL.
USING OUR FORESTS WISELY.
NOTHING CAN LIVE WITHOUT WATER.

CONSERVING OUR NATURAL RESOURCES. Color. Encyclopaedia Britannica Educational Corp. This series discusses various aspects of our conservation program. The titles in the series are:
WHAT IS CONSERVATION?
SAVING OUR SOIL.
ENOUGH WATER FOR EVERYONE.
IMPROVING OUR GRASSLANDS.
USING OUR FORESTS WISELY.
GIVING OUR WILDLIFE A CHANCE.
USING OUR MINERALS WISELY.

CRIME—EVERYBODY'S PROBLEM. B & w. Current Affairs Films. Presents various ways to solve our crime problem: punishment, rehabilitation of criminals, and preventive measures.

FARM PROBLEM. B & w. Current Affairs Films. Presents the farmer's problem of rising production costs and lower market prices for his products.

FOCUS ON CHANGE. Color. National Education Association. Deals with education; presents ideas as a guide to better schools.

GROWTH OF AMERICAN EDUCATION. B & w. Yale University Press. Discusses the growth of America's schools and the struggle for a free public school system; shows the influence of various leaders in education.

INDUSTRY HARMONY THROUGH L.M.C. B & w. Current Affairs Films. Discusses the operation of a labor-management-citizens committee; presents the efforts of a community to get industrial harmony.

LABOR CLOSES RANKS. B & w. New York *Times*. Examines the role of the workers in the United States; traces the development of unions, including the merger of the Congress of Industrial Organizations and the American Federation of Labor.

LAND OF THE FREE. Color. Museum Extension Service. Traces the history of American agriculture and depicts its present status.

THE NATION'S HEALTH—PROBLEMS AND PROGRESS. Color. Current Affairs Films. Deals with problems the individual faces in providing adequate protection in case of illness: health insurance plans; also deals with health problems faced by the community.

NATURAL RESOURCES. B & w. New York *Times*. Shows the importance of our natural resources of water, soil, forests, and minerals.

OUR NATION'S HEALTH. B & w. Current Affairs Films. Surveys the various public and private health agencies, presents arguments of various groups as to how a higher national health standard may be achieved.

OUR NATION'S RESOURCES—NATURAL GAS. B & w. Visual Education Consultants. Shows location of gas fields in the United States and gives the story of bringing natural gas to homes and industries.

GAMES AND SIMULATIONS

THE AMERICAN CONSTITUTIONAL CONVENTION. Science Research Associates, Inc., Chicago. Problems and processes in the drafting of the U. S. Constitution.

BUDGETARY POLITICS AND PRESIDENTIAL DECISION-MAKING. Science Research Associate, Inc., Chicago. The federal budget as the focal point of political activities.

THE CANDIDATE. Lincoln Filene Center and *Newsweek*, New York. Information and commentary on the 1972 political conventions.

DECISION-MAKING IN CONGRESSIONAL COMMITTEES. Science Research Associates, Inc., Chicago. The procedures necessary to enact a federal law.

THE TRAP. Color. Social Studies School Service. A dramatic picture of the immediate and long-range effects of poverty in an affluent society.

YOU AND LABOR. Sound and color. Seminar Films. Has three parts with disc recordings. Part 1 tells why we have labor laws and shows how they evolved. Parts 2 and 3 explain the provisions of the Taft-Hartley Act.

CHARTS

Dimond, Stanley E., and Beamer, Miles E. CITIZENSHIP FOR DEMOCRACY CHARTS. A. J. Nystrom & Co.

CD15   How the Social Security Administration Works
CD26   Education for Democracy
CD29   Man's Battle Against Disease

RECORDINGS

FREE EDUCATION. 14½-minute tape recording. The Junior League of Albany, N. Y. Tells the development of public education in New York from small beginnings to today's large organization.

STORY OF AGRICULTURE. 14½-minute tape recording. The Junior League of Albany, N. Y. Tells the development of agriculture in New York State.

THEY CAN'T WAIT. 26-minute tape recording. American Jewish Committee. How we can get the best education for our children; the problems which face public education.

DEMOCRACY. Western Publishing Co., New York. Political decision-making in a democracy.

ELECTION '72: THE NEW POLITICS. Lincoln Filene Center and *Newsweek*, New York. Data on the election and the electoral college.

NINTH-JUSTICE. Ginn and Co., Lexington, Mass. Choosing a new justice of the Supreme Court.

PLANS. Simili II, La Jolla, California. Methods of interest groups and lobbyists.

THE PROPAGANDA GAME. WFF'N Proof Publishers, New Haven, Conn. The techniques professionals use to mold public opinion.

PRESIDENTIAL ELECTION CAMPAIGNING. Science Research Associates, Inc., Chicago. The complex decisions of presidential candidates during the campaigns.

AUDIO-VISUAL SOURCES

Academic Films, 445 West 86 Street, New York, New York, 10036

Academy Films, 748 North Seward Street, Hollywood, California 90038

AFL-CIO Department of Education, Film Division, 815 16th Street, N.W., Washington, D.C. 20006

American Council on Education, 1785 Massachusetts Avenue, N.W., Washington, D.C. 20036

American Forest Products Industries, 2 West 45 Street, New York, New York 10036

American Jewish Committee, 165 East 56 Street, New York, New York 10022

Anti-Defamation League of B'nai B'rith, 315 Lexington Avenue, New York, New York 10016

Associated Educators, Box 11, Kalamazoo, Michigan 49001

Association Films, Inc., 600 Madison Avenue, New York, New York 10022

Linda Atchinson, Instructional Materials Service, 2333 Monroe, Dearborn, Michigan 48214

Arthur Barr Productions, 1029 North Allen Avenue, Pasadena, California 91104

BFA Educational Media, 2211 Michigan Avenue, Santa Monica, California 90404

Brandon Films, Inc., 221 West 57 Street, New York, New York 10019

British Information Services, 845 Third Avenue, New York, New York 10019

Byron Motion Pictures, Inc., 1226 Wisconsin Avenue, Washington, D.C. 20007

Carousel Films, Inc., 1501 Broadway, New York, New York 10036

Cassyd Productions, 917 Tremaine Avenue South, Los Angeles, California 90019

Castle Films, 221 Park Avenue South, New York, New York 10003

Chamber of Commerce of the United States, 1615 H Street, N.W., Washington, D.C. 20006

Churchill Films, 662 North Robertson Blvd., Los Angeles, California 90069

Columbia Records, 545 Madison Avenue, New York, New York 10022

Contemporary Films, Inc., 267 West 25 Street, New York, New York 10001

Cornell University Tape Library, Roberts Hall, Ithaca, New York 14850

Coronet Films, 65 East South Water Street, Chicago, Illinois 60601

Creative Arts Studio, 814 H Street, N.W., Washington, D.C. 20001

Current Affairs Films, 527 Madison Avenue, New York, New York 10022

Curriculum Films, 10031 Commerce Avenue, Tujunga, California 91042

Doubleday & Company, Inc., 277 Park Avenue, New York, New York 10017

Educational Film Library Association, Inc., 250 West 57 Street, New York, New York 10019

Encyclopaedia Britannica Education Corp., Educational Services Department, 425 North Michigan Avenue, Chicago, Illinois 60611

Enrichment Records, 20 East 8 Street, New York, New York 10003

Films, Inc., 1150 Wilmette Avenue, Wilmette, Illinois 60091

Folkways Records and Service Corporation, 117 West 46 Street, New York, New York 10036

General Motors Corporation, Public Relations Staff, General Motors Building, Detroit, Michigan 48202

Ginn and Company, 191 Spring Street, Lexington, Massachusetts 02173

Guidance Associates, Pleasantville, New York 10570

Heritage Filmstrips, 89-11 63rd Drive, Rego, New York 10074

Indiana University, Audio-Visual Center, Bloomington, Indiana 47401

International Film Bureau, 332 South Michigan Avenue, Chicago, Illinois 60604

International Film Foundation, Inc., 475 Fifth Avenue, New York, New York 10017

International Ladies Garment Workers' Union, Education Department, 1710 Broadway, New York, New York 10019

Iowa State University, Visual Instruction Service, Iowa City, Iowa 52240

Jam Handy Organization, 2821 East Grand Blvd., Detroit, Michigan 48211

The Junior League of Albany, Albany, New York 12201

Life Magazine, Filmstrip Division, Time & Life Building, New York, New York 10019

McGraw-Hill Book Co., Text-Film Division, 330 West 42 Street, New York, New York 10036

March of Time, 369 Lexington Avenue, New York, New York 10017

Modern Learning Aids, 315 Springfield Ave., Summit, New Jersey 07901

Modern Talking Picture Service, 1212 Avenue of the Americas, New York, New York 10036

Museum Extension Service, 80 West 40 Street, New York, New York 10036

Museum of Modern Art Film Library, 11 West 53 Street, New York, New York 10019

National Association of Manufacturers, Film Division, 277 Park Avenue, New York, New York 10017

National Association of Secondary School Principals, 1201 16th Street, N.W., Washington, D.C. 20006

National Education Association, Press and Radio Section, 1201 16th Street, N.W., Washington, D.C. 20006

National Education Films, Inc., 420 Lexington Avenue, New York, New York 10036

National Film Board of Canada, 680 Fifth Avenue, New York, New York 10019

NET Film Service, Indiana University Audio-Visual Center, Bloomington, Indiana 47401

New York Times, Office of Educational Activities, 229 West 43 Street, New York, New York 10036

Norwood Film Studios, Inc., 926 New Jersey Avenue, N.W., Washington, D.C. 20001

A. J. Nystrom & Co., 3333 North Elston Avenue, Chicago, Illinois 60618

Popular Science Publishing Co., Inc., Audio-Visual Department, 355 Lexington Avenue, New York, New York 10017

Progressive Pictures, 6351 Thornhill Drive, Oakland, California 94611

Science Research Associates Inc., 259 East Erie Street, Chicago, Illinois 60611

Seminar Films, 480 Lexington Avenue, New York, New York 10017

Simili II, P.O. Box 1023, La Jolla, California 92037

Social Studies School Service, 4455 Lennox Blvd., Inglewood, California 90304

Society for Visual Education, 1345 Diversey Parkway, Chicago, Illinois 60614

Teaching Film Custodians, Inc., 25 West 43 Street, New York, New York 10036

Tennessee Valley Authority, Film Services, Knoxville, Tennessee 37902

Town Hall, Inc., 123 West 43 Street, New York, New York 10036

Twentieth Century Fox, Educational Films, Beverly Hills, California 90210

UNESCO Publications Center, 801 Third Avenue, New York, New York 10022

United Nations, Office of Public Information, Film Service, New York, New York 10017

United States Department of Agriculture, Motion Picture Service, Washington, D.C. 20025

United States Department of Defense, Directorate for Defense Information, Washington, D.C. 20301

United States Department of the Interior, Washington, D.C. 20025

United States Soil Conservation Service, South Agriculture Building, Washington, D.C. 20025

United World Free Film Service, 221 Park Avenue South, New York, New York 10003

University of Michigan, Audio-Visual Education Center, Ann Arbor, Michigan 48104

University of Wisconsin, Audio-Visual Service, Madison, Wisconsin 53706

Virginia Board of Education, Richmond, Virginia 23216

Visual Education Consultants, 2066 Helena Street, Madison, Wisconsin 53704

Walt Disney Productions, 800 Sonora Avenue, Glendale, California 91201

Wayne State University, Audio-Visual Materials Consultation Bureau, 438 Ferry Street, Detroit, Michigan 48202

Western Publishing Company, Inc., 850 Third Avenue, New York, New York 10022

Wilding, Inc., 1345 West Argyle Street, Chicago, Illinois 60640

Xerox Corp., Rochester, New York 14603

Yale University Press, Film Service, New Haven, Connecticut 06520

Young America Films, 330 West 42 Street, New York, New York 10036

ANSWERS TO CHAPTER-END QUESTIONS

Page numbers listed below refer to the pages in the textbook on which answers may be found to the *Study Questions* and to the key ideas for *Ideas for discussion.*

CHAPTER 1 (PP. 15-16)

Study questions

1. Encourage pupils to express ideas. Use the last paragraph, col. 1, p. 14 as a discussion primer. *2.* pp. 4 and 6-7. *3.* p. 8. *4.* pp. 6-7. *5.* p. 10. *6.* p. 13. *7.* pp. 13 and 14. *8.* p. 12.

Ideas for discussion

1. p. 7. *2.* Compare with discussion on pp. 14-15. *3.* p. 13. *4.* Compare with p. 3. *5.* pp. 11-12. *6.* p. 6. *7.* p. 14.

CHAPTER 2 (PP. 32-34)

Study questions

1. p. 18. *2.* pp. 18-19. *3.* pp. 19-20. *4.* pp. 20-23. *5.* pp. 23-24. *6.* pp. 24-25. *7.* pp. 25-26. *8.* pp. 26-27. *9.* pp. 27-28. *10.* pp. 28-29. *11.* p. 29.

Ideas for discussion

1. Any part of the chapter may be used. See also p. 83. *2.* Any part of the chapter may be used. *3.* Any part of the chapter may be used. *4.* p. 22. *5.* p. 29. *6.* pp. 28-29. *7.* p. 27. *8.* p. 28. *9.* p. 19. *10.* p. 28. *11.* pp. 31-32. *12.* p. 32.

CHAPTER 3 (PP. 53-54)

Study questions

1. pp. 36 and 37. *2.* pp. 37-38 and Appendix (Articles of Confederation). *3.* p. 40. *4.* p. 41. *5.* p. 41. *6.* pp. 41 and 43. *7.* Constitution, Article VII. *8.* p. 44. *9.* p. 46. *10.* p. 48. *11.* p. 48. *12.* pp. 47-48. *13.* pp. 48-49. *14.* pp. 48-49. *15.* pp. 50-51. *16.* p. 50. *17.* All amendments have originated in Congress. All but the Twenty-first (repeal of prohibition) have been ratified by state legislatures. *18.* pp. 51-52. *19.* pp. 52-53. The Louisiana Purchase and the Social Security Act are examples. *20.* p. 52.

Ideas for discussion

1. p. 40. *2.* p. 40. *3.* p. 41. *4.* pp. 51 and Appendix (Constitution—Amendments—XXII). *5.* pp. 51-52. *6.* p. 41 and quote on p. 43. *7.* pp. 51-52. *8.* pp. 51-52. *9.* pp. 36-37. *10.* p. 41. *11.* pp. 51 and Appendix (Constitution—Amendments—XXV).

CHAPTER 4 (PP. 74-75)

Study questions

1. p. 57. *2.* pp. 58-59. *3.* Kennedy stressed economic aspects; King stressed ideals. *4.* pp. 59-60. *5.* p. 60. *6.* p. 60. *7.* p. 61. *8.* pp. 61-62; 69-70. *9.* pp. 61-62; 69-70. *10.* p. 62. *11.* pp. 62-68. *12.* p. 60 and pp. 62-63. *13.* p. 67. *14.* pp. 67-69 and pp. 72-73. *15.* p. 67. *16.* pp. 69-70. *17.* pp. 70-71. *18.* pp. 72-73. *19.* pp. 69-70.

Ideas for discussion

1. pp. 69-73. *2.* pp. 69-73. *3.* pp. 62-63. *4.* pp. 72-73. *5.* p. 69. *6.* pp. 72-73. *7.* pp. 58-59, 70-72. *8.* pp. 60, 63, and 67. *9.* p. 71.

CHAPTER 5 (PP. 94-96)

Study questions

1. p. 81. *2.* pp. 83-85. *3.* pp. 85-87. *4.* pp. 85-88. *5.* p. 86. *6.* pp. 87-88. *7.* pp. 87-88. *8.* p. 88. *9.* p. 89. *10.* p. 89. *11.* pp. 91-92. *12.* p. 90. *13.* p. 92. *14.* p. 93. *15.* pp. 93-94.

Ideas for discussion

1. p. 90. *2.* pp. 91-93. *3.* pp. 91-93. *4.* pp. 90-93. *5.* p. 92. *6.* p. 94. *7.* p. 84.

CHAPTER 6 (PP. 120-121)

Study questions

1. pp. 98-99. *2.* Appendix (Table 1). *3.* pp. 100-101. *4.* pp. 100-101. *5.* pp. 101-106 plus individual investigation. *6.* pp. 106-108 plus individual investigation. *7.* pp. 102-103. *8.* pp. 108-109. *9.* individual investigation. *10.* p. 110. *11.* pp. 110-114. *12.* pp. 115-119 plus individual investigation. *13.* p. 106. *14.* pp. 117-119.

Ideas for discussion

1. pp. 98-100. *2.* p. 100. *3.* p. 101. *4.* p. 106. *5.* pp. 105-106. *6.* pp. 113-114. *7.* pp. 106, 108.

CHAPTER 7 (P. 144)

Study questions

1. pp. 131-135. *2.* p. 126. *3.* pp. 128-129. *4.* p. 127. *5.* pp. 130, 127, 130, 130-131. *6.* pp. 131, 132. *7.* pp. 132-135. *8.* p. 134. *9.* p. 136. *10.* See *World Almanac.* *11.* pp. 134 and 138. *12.* p. 136. *13.* pp. 138-139. *14.* pp. 139-141. *15.* p. 141. *16.* pp. 141-142. *17.* pp. 125-126.

Ideas for discussion

1. pp. 124-127. *2.* pp. 127-129. *3.* pp. 128-129 and 131-132. *4.* pp. 128-129 and 131-132. *5.* pp. 131-132. *6.* pp. 124 and 133. *7.* pp. 135-139. *8.* p. 139. *9.* pp. 141-142. *10.* p. 142. *11.* pp. 138-139. *12.* p. 135. *13.* pp. 137; 138. *14.* pp. 137 and 164.

CHAPTER 8 (PP. 166-167)

Study questions

1. p. 146. *2.* p. 147. *3.* p. 147. Placement of highway is one example. *4.* p. 147. Reaction to calling of a strike is one example. *5.* pp. 148-151. *6.* pp. 151-152. *7.* pp. 152-155. *8.* pp. 155-159. *9.* p. 155. *10.* p. 156. *11.* pp. 156-158 and 158-159. *12.* p. 159. *13.* pp. 161-162. *14.* p. 163. *15.* pp. 155-159. *16.* p. 164. *17.* p. 165.

Ideas for discussion

1. p. 135. *2.* pp. 161-162. *3.* pp. 152-155. *4.* pp. 148-151. *5.* pp. 155-159. *6.* p. 153. *7.* pp.

152-153. *8.* pp. 163-166. *9.* p. 159. *10.* pp. 148-149. *11.* pp. 159-161.

CHAPTER 9 (PP. 198-200)

Study questions

1. pp. 178-180. *2.* pp. 181-183. *3.* p. 183. *4.* pp. 183-184. *5.* p. 186. *6.* pp. 186-187. *7.* p. 187. *8.* p. 187. *9.* pp. 187-188. *10.* pp. 188-190. *11.* p. 188. *12.* p. 191. *13.* pp. 194-195. *14.* pp. 195-196. *15.* pp. 196-197. *16.* pp. 197-198. *17.* p. 191. *18.* p. 184 (map).

Ideas for discussion

1. pp. 179-180. *2.* p. 181. *3.* pp. 181-183. *4.* pp. 190-191. *5.* p. 191. *6.* p. 191. *7.* p. 181. *8.* pp. 181-183. *9.* p. 183. *10.* pp. 186-187. *11.* p. 188. *12.* p. 190.

CHAPTER 10 (PP. 228-230)

Study questions

1. pp. 203-213. *2.* pp. 211-214. *3.* pp. 204-205. *4.* p. 206. *5.* p. 208. *6.* p. 209. *7.* p. 209. *8.* pp. 209-211. *9.* pp. 211-212. *10.* Answers will vary. *11.* pp. 212-213. *12.* pp. 214-216. *13.* pp. 216-217. *14.* pp. 217-222. *15.* p. 220. *16.* pp. 221-222 and 226. *17.* p. 222. *18.* pp. 223-225. *19.* pp. 225-227.

Ideas for discussion

1. pp. 201-202. *2.* p. 209. *3.* pp. 204 and 218. *4.* p. 222. *5.* p. 219. *6.* pp. 211-213. *7.* p. 205. *8.* pp. 226-227. *9.* pp. 223-225. *10.* pp. 205-206.

CHAPTER 11 (P. 252)

Study questions

1. pp. 232-234. *2.* pp. 234-235. *3.* pp. 234-235. *4.* pp. 235-236. *5.* p. 236. *6.* pp. 236-237. *7.* pp. 237-238. *8.* p. 238. *9.* Varies with states. *10.* p. 239. *11.* pp. 240-241. *12.* p. 241. *13.* p. 241. *14.* pp. 242-243. *15.* pp. 243-248. *16.* p. 248. *17.* p. 248. *18.* pp. 248-250.

Ideas for discussion

1. pp. 238-240. *2.* p. 241. *3.* pp. 241-242. *4.* p. 247. *5.* p. 238. *6. a)* part of system of checks and balances. *b)* to avoid removal for political reasons or for minor differences with congressmen.

Chapter 12 (pp. 274-276)

Study questions

1. p. 254. *2.* pp. 254-255. *3.* pp. 255-257. *4.* pp. 257-259. *5.* pp. 259-260. *6.* p. 261. *7.* pp. 263-264. *8.* pp. 265-266. *9.* pp. 267-268. *10.* p. 268. *11.* pp. 268-269. *12.* p. 270. *13.* p. 272. *14.* p. 272. *15.* p. 273. *16. a)* p. 263 (Treasury). *b)* pp. 259-260 (State). *c)* pp. 265-266 (Justice). *d)* p. 267 (Interior). *e)* pp. 271-272 (Health, Education, and Welfare). *f)* pp. 258-259 (State). *g)* p. 261 (Treasury). *h)* p. 268 (Agriculture). *i)* p. 264 (Defense-Army). *j)* p. 265 (Justice). *k)* p. 273 (Transportation). *l)* p. 268 (Interior). *m)* p. 270 (Labor). *n)* pp. 268-269 (Commerce). *o)* p. 271 (Health, Education, and Welfare). *p)* p. 269 (Commerce). *q)* p. 269 (Commerce). *r)* pp. 270-271 (Health, Education, and Welfare). *s)* pp. 267-268 (Interior). *t)* p. 272 (Housing and Urban Development). *u)* p. 273 (Transportation).

Ideas for discussion

1. p. 256. *2.* p. 257. *3.* p. 263. *4.* pp. 263-265. *5.* p. 255. *6.* pp. 263-265. *7.* pp. 271-272.

Chapter 13 (pp. 294-296)

Study questions

1. p. 278. *2.* p. 278. *3.* p. 279. *4.* p. 280. *5.* pp. 280-281. *6.* pp. 282-284. *7.* p. 284. *8.* p. 285. *9.* p. 285. *10.* p. 286. *11.* p. 287. *12.* p. 288. *13.* p. 288. *14.* p. 288. *15.* p. 288. *16.* p. 289. *17.* p. 290. *18.* p. 291. *19.* pp. 291-292. *20.* pp. 292-293. *21.* p. 294.

Ideas for discussion

1. pp. 279-280. *2.* pp. 290-291. *3.* p. 288. *4.* pp. 287, 289, and 292. *5.* p. 294. *6.* pp. 286-287. *7.* p. 291.

Chapter 14 (pp. 313-315)

Study questions

1. pp. 298-299. *2.* p. 298. *3.* pp. 298-301. *4.* p. 299. *5.* pp. 301-302. *6.* p. 302. *7.* p. 299. *8.* pp. 303-305. *9.* p. 305. *10.* p. 305. *11.* pp. 307-309, 310. *12.* pp. 308-310. *13.* pp. 308-309. *14.* pp. 311-313. *15.* p. 313.

Ideas for discussion

1. pp. 308-309. *2.* pp. 303 and 311-312. *3.* p. 302. *4.* p. 303. *5.* p. 303. *6.* p. 302. *7.* p. 299. *8.* pp. 307-311. *9.* pp. 301-302. *10.* pp. 308-309. *11.* p. 308. *12.* p. 312.

Chapter 15 (pp. 343-345)

Study questions

1. p. 325. *2.* pp. 326-327. *3.* p. 327. *4.* p. 327. *5.* pp. 327-328. *6.* pp. 328-330. *7.* Consult your state manual. *8.* Appendix Table 3 and state manual. *9.* p. 333. *10.* p. 333. *11.* Appendix Table 3. *12.* p. 334. *13.* p. 335. *14.* pp. 339-342 and state legislative manual. *15.* p. 339. *16.* p. 340. *17.* Consult your state manual. *18.* pp. 342-343.

Ideas for discussion

1. pp. 327-330. *2.* p. 326. *3.* pp. 326-327. *4.* p. 333. *5.* p. 336. *6.* p. 340. *7.* p. 336. *8.* pp. 341-342. *9.* pp. 342-343. *10.* p. 340. *11.* p. 334 and state manual.

Chapter 16 (pp. 362-363)

Study questions

1. pp. 346-347. *2.* p. 347. *3.* p. 347. *4.* pp. 347-348. *5.* p. 348. *6.* p. 348. *7.* p. 348. *8.* pp. 351-352. *9.* pp. 354-355. *10.* p. 355. *11.* p. 355. *12.* pp. 355-357. *13.* pp. 357-358. *14.* p. 359. *15.* pp. 359-360. *16.* pp. 360-361. *17.* p. 361.

Ideas for discussion

1. p. 348. *2.* pp. 348 and 361. *3.* pp. 354-355. *4.* pp. 347-348. *5.* p. 348. *6.* pp. 348 and 361. *7.* Consult your state manual and p. 355. *8.* p. 355.

Chapter 17 (pp. 380-382)

Study questions

1. pp. 365-368 and your state manual. *2.* pp. 365-367. *3.* pp. 365-367. *4.* p. 367. *5.* pp. 368-369. *6.* Consult your state manual. *7.* pp. 368-369 and 372-376. *8.* pp. 371-372. *9.* pp. 373-374. *10.* pp. 373-374. *11.* pp. 374-376. *12.* p. 375. *13.* pp. 376-380.

Ideas for discussion

1. p. 366. *2.* p. 377. *3.* pp. 378-379. *4.* pp. 365-367. *5.* p. 376. *6.* p. 380. *7.* p. 380. *8.* p. 379. *9.* pp. 373-374. Fraud in the sale of a stock would be an example.

CHAPTER 18 (PP. 400-401)

Study questions

1. pp. 383-384. *2.* pp. 384-387. *3.* pp. 386-387. *4.* p. 390. *5.* pp. 391-392. *6.* pp. 392-394. *7.* pp. 394-395. *8.* p. 396. *9.* p. 397. *10.* p. 397 and *The Book of the States*. *11.* pp. 397-398. *12.* pp. 398-399. *13.* p. 399. *14.* p. 399.

Ideas for discussion

1. pp. 383-384, 393, 395. *2.* Consult your telephone directory and state manual. *3.* pp. 396; 398. *4.* pp. 383-384. *5.* pp. 383-384. *6.* p. 393. *7.* p. 395. *8.* pp. 388, 391.

CHAPTER 19 (PP. 424-426)

Study questions

1. p. 409. *2.* pp. 409-410. *3.* pp. 410-412. *4.* pp. 412-414. *5.* p. 414. *6.* p. 414. *7.* p. 414. *8.* p. 414. *9.* pp. 415-422. *10.* pp. 415-420. *11.* pp. 417-420. *12.* pp. 416-420. *13.* p. 420. *14.* pp. 420-421. *15.* Discuss; see p. 421. *16.* p. 421. *17.* p. 422. *18.* pp. 423-424. *19.* pp. 423-424. *20.* pp. 423-424.

Ideas for discussion

1. p. 414; also see pp. 459-460. *2.* p. 414; also see p. 470. *3.* pp. 417-418. *4.* p. 420; also see pp. 138-139. *5.* p. 416; chart p. 417. *6.* pp. 420-421. *7.* p. 421. *8.* pp. 421-422. *9.* pp. 423-424.

CHAPTER 20 (PP. 442-443)

Study questions

1. p. 427. *2.* pp. 427-428. *3.* p. 428. *4.* p. 429. *5.* p. 429. *6.* p. 430. *7.* p. 432. *8.* pp. 432-433. *9.* pp. 433-434. *10.* p. 434. *11.* p. 434. *12.* p. 435. *13.* Encourage discussion on this question; see p. 435. *14.* p. 435. Discuss reasons. *15.* p. 436. *16.* Discuss this question; see p. 437. *17.* pp. 439-440. List reasons for both sides. *18.* p. 439.

Ideas for discussion

1. pp. 431-432, 439-440. *2.* pp. 440-441; see also pp. 463-464. *3.* pp. 433-434. *4.* pp. 438 and 441. *5.* pp. 438-493. *6.* p. 441. *7.* p. 441. *8.* pp. 438-442.

CHAPTER 21 (PP. 455-456)

Study questions

1. p. 444. *2.* p. 445. *3.* p. 445. *4.* pp. 445-447. *5.* p. 447. *6.* pp. 447 and 448-449. *7.* p.

447. *8.* pp. 447-448. *9.* p. 449. *10.* pp. 449-451. *11.* pp. 451-453. *12.* p. 452. *13.* pp. 453-454. *14.* p. 454. *15.* pp. 454-455.

Ideas for discussion

1. pp. 446-447; also see Chapter 19. *2.* p. 448. *3.* pp. 451-452. *4.* p. 453. *5.* pp. 453-455. *6.* pp. 449, 453. *7.* pp. 451-452, 453.

CHAPTER 22 (PP. 475-477)

Study questions

1. pp. 458-459. *2.* pp. 459-460. *3.* p. 459. *4.* p. 460. *5.* p. 460. *6.* p. 460. *7.* p. 461. *8.* p. 462. *9.* pp. 462-463. *10.* pp. 463-464. *11.* pp. 464-465. *12.* p. 465. *13.* pp. 465-467. *14.* p. 467. *15.* p. 468. *16.* p. 469. *17.* pp. 469-470. *18.* pp. 470-471. *19.* p. 471. *20.* p. 472. *21.* pp. 473-474. *22.* p. 475.

Ideas for discussion

1. pp. 460-462. *2.* p. 462. *3.* p. 469. *4.* pp. 468-475. *5.* p. 473. *6.* pp. 474-475. *7.* pp. 464-468. *8.* pp. 468-469.

CHAPTER 23 (PP. 500-501)

Study questions

1. pp. 484-485. *2.* pp. 485-486. *3.* p. 488. *4.* pp. 488 and 489. *5.* p. 490. *6.* p. 490. *7.* p. 489. *8.* p. 490. *9.* pp. 491-492. *10.* p. 491. *11.* p. 493. *12.* See pp. 493, 494, but check with your local government. *13.* pp. 485, 494-495, and 496. *14.* p. 495. *15.* pp. 496-499. *16.* pp. 497-499. *17.* p. 499.

Ideas for discussion

1. pp. 485, 486-488, and 490. *2.* pp. 488, 489. *3.* p. 488. *4.* p. 490. *5.* pp. 496-499. *6.* p. 499. *7.* p. 490.

CHAPTER 24 (PP. 517-518)

Study questions

1. pp. 503-504. *2.* p. 504; Appendix (Constitution—Article I, Section 8, paragraph #1) and (Constitution—Amendments—XIV). *3.* pp. 504-505. *4.* p. 505. *5.* p. 505. *6.* p. 505 (table). *7.* p. 507. *8.* p. 506. *9.* pp. 508-509. *10.* pp. 509-510. *11.* p. 510. *12.* pp. 510-511. *13.* pp. 511-512. *14.* p. 512. *15.* pp. 512-514. *16.* pp. 515-516. *17.* pp. 516-517.

Ideas for discussion

1. p. 505. *2.* p. 506. *3.* pp. 508-509. *4.* pp. 508-509. *5.* pp. 512-514. *6.* p. 515. *7.* pp. 516-517. *8.* pp. 505-517.

CHAPTER 25 (PP. 551-553)

Study questions

1. p. 528. *2.* pp. 529-530. *3.* p. 530. *4.* p. 531. *5.* p. 532. *6.* p. 532. *7.* p. 533. *8.* p. 534. *9.* p. 534. *10.* pp. 534-535. *11.* p. 535. *12.* p. 536-539. *13.* pp. 539-542. *14.* p. 542. *15.* pp. 542, 546, 547, 550, 548, 549, 551, 547-548. *16.* pp. 544-545.

Ideas for discussion

1. p. 533. *2.* pp. 536 and 539. *3.* p. 541. *4.* pp. 540-541. *5.* p. 530. *6.* pp. 535-536. *7.* pp. 542-551. *8.* p. 534. *9.* p. 530.

CHAPTER 26 (P. 577)

Study questions

1. p. 555. *2.* p. 556. *3.* pp. 557-558. *4.* pp. 558-559. *5.* pp. 559-560. *6.* pp. 561-563. *7.* pp. 564-565. *8.* p. 561. *9.* pp. 567-569. *10.* p. 567. *11.* p. 567. *12.* pp. 568-569. *13.* p. 570. *14.* pp. 571-576. *15.* pp. 573-574. *16.* p. 575.

Ideas for discussion

1. p. 555. *2.* p. 556. *3.* p. 560. *4.* p. 560. *5.* p. 561. *6. a)* pp. 565-566. *b)* p. 567. *c)* p. 556. *7.* pp. 565; 569-570. *8.* pp. 573-576. *9.* pp. 557-559. *10.* pp. 571-572.

CHAPTER 27 (PP. 596-598)

Study questions

1. p. 580. *2.* pp. 580-581. *3.* pp. 581-582. *4.* p. 582. *5.* p. 582. *6.* p. 583. *7.* pp. 583-585. *8.* p. 585. *9.* p. 586. *10.* pp. 586-587. *11.* p. 590. *12.* pp. 590-591. *13.* p. 594. *14.* p. 592. *15.* pp. 591-592. *16.* pp. 595-596.

Ideas for discussion

1. pp. 579-580. *2.* p. 581. *3.* p. 580. *4.* pp. 583 and Appendix (Constitution—Preamble). *5.* pp. 583-590. *6. a)* p. 583. *b)* p. 583. *c)* p. 588. *d)* p. 590. *7.* pp. 585-586; 591. *8.* pp. 586-587. *9.* pp. 592, 595-596. *10.* p. 593. *11.* p. 594. *12.* pp. 595-596. *13.* p. 588.

CHAPTER 28 (PP. 614-616)

Study questions

1. p. 600. *2.* p. 600. *3.* pp. 601-602. *4.* p. 602. *5.* pp. 602-604. *6.* pp. 600 and 602; 604-606. *7.* p. 605. *8.* p. 607. *9.* pp. 608-609. *10.* p. 608. *11.* p. 609. *12.* p. 610. *13.* pp. 611-612. *14.* p. 612. *15.* pp. 612-614.

Ideas for discussion

1. p. 600. *2.* p. 611. *3.* pp. 611-612. *4.* pp. 612-614. *5.* pp. 604-606. *6.* pp. 604-606. *7.* p. 604.

CHAPTER 29 (PP. 642-644)

Study questions

1. p. 625. *2.* p. 625. *3.* pp. 627-628. *4.* p. 628. *5.* p. 629. *6.* p. 629. *7.* pp. 630-631. *8.* pp. 631-633. *9.* p. 634. *10.* p. 634. *11.* p. 636. *12.* p. 636. *13.* pp. 637-638. *14.* pp. 639-641. *15.* p. 641.

Ideas for discussion

1. p. 625. *2.* pp. 629-631. *3.* pp. 630-633; 637-638. *4.* pp. 631-636. *5.* pp. 636-638. *6.* p. 641. *7.* pp. 636-642. *8.* pp. 629-630. *9.* pp. 631-633. *10.* pp. 639-640.

CHAPTER 30 (PP. 661-663)

Study questions

1. pp. 646-647. *2.* p. 647. *3.* p. 647. *4.* pp. 647-648. *5.* p. 648. *6.* pp. 648-650. *7.* p. 650. *8.* pp. 650-652. *9.* p. 651. *10.* p. 652. *11.* pp. 652-653. *12.* p. 653. *13.* p. 654. *14.* pp. 654-656. *15.* p. 656. *16.* pp. 656-657. *17.* p. 657. *18.* p. 658. *19.* p. 659. *20.* p. 659. *21.* pp. 659-660 and check recent laws. *22.* pp. 660-661.

Ideas for discussion

1. pp. 646-647; see also pp. 128-129. *2.* pp. 647-648. *3.* pp. 650-653. *4.* p. 657. *5.* pp. 647 and 653. *6.* pp. 654-658; see also pp. 290-291. *7.* p. 661. *8.* pp. 654-656. *9.* pp. 658-661. *10.* pp. 647-648. *11.* p. 661.

CHAPTER 31 (PP. 681-683)

Study questions

1. p. 666. *2.* p. 666. *3.* p. 666. *4.* p. 667. *5.* pp. 666-667. *6.* pp. 669-670. *7.* pp. 670-671. *8.* pp. 671-672. *9.* pp. 672-673. *10.* p. 673. *11.* pp. 673-674. *12.* p. 674. *13.* p. 674. *14.* pp. 674-676. *15.* pp. 676-679. *16.* p. 677. *17.* pp.

678-679. *18.* p. 679. *19.* p. 679. *20.* p. 679. *21.* pp. 679-680. *22.* p. 680. *23.* pp. 680-681. *24.* p. 681.

Ideas for discussion
1. pp. 666-667. *2.* pp. 666-667. *3.* p. 673. *4.* p. 672. *5.* p. 673. *6.* p. 673. *7.* pp. 674-676; see also p. 271. *8.* pp. 679-680. *9.* pp. 680-681.

CHAPTER 32 (PP. 699-701)

Study questions
1. p. 684. *2.* p. 685. *3.* p. 685. *4.* pp. 685-686. *5.* pp. 686-687. *6.* pp. 686-687. *7.* p. 687-688. *8.* pp. 688-689. *9.* p. 689. *10.* pp. 689-691. *11.* p. 691. *12.* p. 691. *13.* pp. 691-692. *14.* p. 692. *15.* p. 693. *16.* p. 693. *17.* p. 694. *18.* p. 694. *19.* pp. 694-695. *20.* p. 695. *21.* p. 696. *22.* p. 696. *23.* p. 698.

Ideas for discussion
1. pp. 686-689. *2.* pp. 686-687. *3.* p. 690. *4.* p. 690; see also p. 272. *5.* pp. 689-691. *6.* p. 692. *7.* pp. 698-699. *8.* pp. 686-687; see also state manual. *9.* p. 695.

ANSWERS TO SEPARATE UNIT TESTS

These tests accompany the text *Our American Government* and are published by J. B. Lippincott Company as separate booklets.

Designed to measure the learning taking place during this course, these tests should take the students approximately 30 minutes, except for the final examination which will require 40-45 minutes. The score on each test is the total number of correct items.

UNIT ONE

PRINCIPLES AND PRACTICES OF OUR GOVERNMENT

1. b	*13.* b	*25.* a	*37.* false	*49.* false
2. a	*14.* d	*26.* e	*38.* true	*50.* true
3. c	*15.* a	*27.* false	*39.* true	*51.* Bill of Rights
4. a	*16.* c	*28.* true	*40.* false	*52.* Third (III)
5. a	*17.* c	*29.* true	*41.* true	*53.* Jefferson
6. d	*18.* c	*30.* true	*42.* true	*54.* death
7. a	*19.* d	*31.* false	*43.* false	*55.* political scientists
8. d	*20.* b	*32.* true	*44.* true	*56.* Puerto Ricans
9. a	*21.* e	*33.* false	*45.* true	*57.* *ex post facto*
10. b	*22.* d	*34.* true	*46.* false	*58.* nonviolence
11. b	*23.* a	*35.* false	*47.* true	*59.* Jim Crow law
12. a	*24.* d	*36.* true	*48.* false	*60.* cloture

UNIT TWO

THE POLITICAL PROCESSES

1. a	13. c	25. false	37. false	49. platform
2. d	14. d	26. false	38. false	50. short
3. c	15. a	27. true	39. true	51. Lincoln
4. a	16. c	28. false	40. true	52. rural
5. c	17. a	29. false	41. true	53. boss
6. b	18. b	30. false	42. true	54. office-block (Mass.)
7. a	19. e	31. true	43. false	55. residence
8. c	20. b	32. false	44. true	56. bureaucrat
9. b	21. c	33. false	45. aliens	57. sample
10. a	22. a	34. false	46. social class	58. urban
11. c	23. b	35. false	47. suffrage (or franchise)	59. FCC
12. a	24. d	36. false	48. straight-ticket	60. preference

UNIT THREE

NATIONAL GOVERNMENT

1. b	18. b	35. c	52. true	69. NASA
2. c	19. c	36. d	53. true	70. 435
3. d	20. c	37. e	54. true	71. vote
4. c	21. b	38. e	55. true	72. sessions
5. d	22. c	39. a	56. false	73. cloture
6. a	23. e	40. b	57. true	74. lobbying
7. a	24. c	41. true	58. true	75. Supreme Court
8. c	25. d	42. false	59. true	76. district
9. b	26. a	43. false	60. true	77. civil
10. d	27. c	44. true	61. false	78. parliamentarian
11. a	28. d	45. false	62. false	79. pigeonholing
12. c	29. c	46. true	63. true	80. dark horse
13. d	30. b	47. true	64. thirty-five	81. security
14. a	31. d	48. false	65. the Speaker of the House	82. tariff
15. d	32. d	49. false	66. Congress	83. *persona non grata*
16. c	33. b	50. true	67. pocket veto	84. bankruptcy
17. a	34. a	51. true	68. ICC	85. inauguration

UNIT FOUR

STATE GOVERNMENT

1. c	13. b	25. b	37. true	49. false
2. b	14. c	26. c	38. false	50. false
3. a	15. a	27. true	39. false	51. extradition
4. a	16. c	28. false	40. true	52. auditor
5. b	17. b	29. false	41. true	53. bicameral
6. c	18. d	30. true	42. false	54. (answers vary)
7. b	19. a	31. true	43. true	55. referendum
8. a	20. c	32. true	44. true	56. see text pp. 742-743
9. c	21. b	33. true	45. true	57. veto
10. d	22. a	34. false	46. true	58. civil
11. b	23. c	35. false	47. true	59. Hoover (Little Hoover)
12. c	24. e	36. false	48. false	60. grant-in-aid

MID-COURSE TEST (OPTIONAL)

1. b	17. b	33. true	49. true	64. party whips
2. d	18. c	34. false	50. true	65. anarchist
3. b	19. c	35. false	51. true	66. charter
4. a	20. a	36. true	52. false	67. boycotting
5. d	21. b	37. false	53. false	68. patronage
6. d	22. d	38. true	54. false	69. a conference committee
7. b	23. a	39. false	55. minority groups	70. a monopoly
8. c	24. d	40. false	(Negroes)	71. appellate jurisdiction
9. c	25. e	41. false	56. two houses	72. commutation
10. b	26. a	42. true	57. model	73. trial
11. c	27. false	43. false	58. guaranteed	74. filibustering (debate)
12. d	28. false	44. true	59. parents	75. ambassador
13. c	29. false	45. false	60. absentee voting	
14. c	30. false	46. true	61. school	
15. a	31. false	47. true	62. lobbyist	
16. b	32. true	48. false	63. Civil Service Commission	

UNIT FIVE

Local Government

1. a	13. c	25. true	37. false	49. Texas
2. b	14. a	26. false	38. true	50. inquest
3. a	15. e	27. false	39. true	51. charter
4. d	16. a	28. true	40. false	52. commission
5. c	17. c	29. true	41. true	53. selectman
6. a	18. a	30. true	42. false	54. home rule
7. d	19. c	31. false	43. false	55. deed
8. c	20. e	32. true	44. true	56. real
9. c	21. a	33. true	45. true	57. county seat
10. b	22. e	34. false	46. true	58. birth
11. a	23. b	35. false	47. false	59. ordinance
12. b	24. false	36. true	48. true	60. election

UNIT SIX

Taxation and Finance

1. b	7. c	13. d	19. true	25. false
2. d	8. c	14. false	20. false	26. taxes
3. d	9. d	15. true	21. false	27. exemption
4. c	10. c	16. true	22. true	28. reciprocal
5. d	11. e	17. true	23. true	29. earmarking
6. a	12. a	18. true	24. true	30. pay-as-you-go

UNIT SEVEN

The United States and World Affairs

1. a	13. b	25. c	37. false	49. true
2. c	14. d	26. d	38. true	50. true
3. d	15. b	27. false	39. true	51. Internal Security
4. b	16. b	28. true	40. true	52. IV (Four)
5. b	17. b	29. false	41. false	53. executive agreement
6. d	18. c	30. false	42. true	54. stockpiling
7. a	19. d	31. false	43. false	55. deferment
8. d	20. c	32. false	44. false	56. Secretary-General
9. c	21. e	33. true	45. true	57. marketplace
10. c	22. d	34. true	46. false	58. *status quo*
11. b	23. c	35. false	47. true	59. common law
12. c	24. a	36. true	48. false	60. free enterprise

UNIT EIGHT

Government and the Life of Our People

1. b	14. d	27. false	40. true	53. monopoly
2. d	15. b	28. false	41. true	54. Interstate Commerce
3. b	16. c	29. false	42. false	Commission
4. c	17. b	30. true	43. false	55. land-grant
5. b	18. b	31. true	44. false	56. vital
6. c	19. b	32. false	45. true	57. agriculture
7. c	20. e	33. true	46. true	58. Slums
8. a	21. a	34. true	47. true	59. probation
9. d	22. d	35. true	48. false	60. common
10. c	23. d	36. true	49. false	
11. a	24. a	37. false	50. true	
12. c	25. true	38. true	51. REA	
13. b	26. true	39. true	52. Contour (plowing)	

FINAL TEST

1. b	17. c	33. e	49. false	65. false
2. b	18. c	34. a	50. true	66. true
3. b	19. b	35. e	51. true	67. false
4. b	20. d	36. b	52. true	68. false
5. c	21. b	37. a	53. true	69. Madison
6. a	22. a	38. c	54. false	70. Australian
7. b	23. c	39. d	55. false	71. judicial review
8. c	24. b	40. true	56. true	72. parliamentary
9. c	25. c	41. true	57. false	73. criminal
10. c	26. d	42. false	58. true	74. whip
11. d	27. c	43. false	59. false	75. full faith and credit
12. c	28. c	44. false	60. false	76. defense (military security)
13. a	29. a	45. false	61. false	77. pure
14. d	30. a	46. false	62. true	78. irrigation
15. c	31. d	47. false	63. false	79. ambassadors
16. c	32. a	48. false	64. false	80. Prime Minister

OUR
AMERICAN
GOVERNMENT

OUR
AMERICAN
GOVERNMENT

Stanley E. Dimond, Elmer F. Pflieger

J. B. LIPPINCOTT COMPANY
Philadelphia, New York

THE LIPPINCOTT SOCIAL STUDIES PROGRAM
SUPERVISED BY STANLEY E. DIMOND

STANLEY E. DIMOND

Dr. Dimond has been a civics teacher at Monmouth High School, Illinois; a government teacher and chairman of the Social Studies Department at Redford High School in Detroit; Director of the Detroit Citizenship Education Study; Divisional Director of the Department of Social Studies for the Detroit Public Schools; and Professor of Education at the University of Michigan at Ann Arbor. He is a past president of the National Council for the Social Studies; author of *Schools and the Development of Good Citizens;* and co-author of *Civics for Citizens.*

ELMER F. PFLIEGER

Dr. Pflieger has been a teacher in Utica, Madison Heights, and Detroit, Michigan; Evaluation Director of the Detroit Citizenship Education Study; Director of the Television Teaching Project and Divisional Director of the Department of Social Studies for the Detroit Public Schools; a staff member of the Civic Education Project; and a former member of the Board of Directors of the National Council for the Social Studies. He is co-author of *Emotional Adjustment: A Key to Good Citizenship, Promising Practices in Civic Education,* and *Civics for Citizens.*

Design: Ann Atene
Maps and graphs: Ann Atene and Alan Young
Layout: Bill Hamilton Associates

Copyright © 1973, 1971, 1969 by J. B. LIPPINCOTT COMPANY

Printed in the United States of America

ISBN–0–397–40216–3

PREFACE

The authors of *Our American Government* have been guided by three major social and educational changes that have taken place recently. First, recognition has been made of the new ideas and new acceptance of political science as a scholarly, academic field. Second, the emergence of civil rights as the crucial testing ground for ideas about democratic government has been incorporated throughout the text. Third, voting by eighteen-year-olds and the demands of youth for the democratic system to operate effectively has been reflected.

The original purposes that caused us to plan and to write *Our American Government* continue to guide us. The authors believe that developing good citizens is a primary obligation of American schools. As high school teachers, research workers, authors, and curriculum leaders we have devoted our lives to the improvement of education for citizenship. We recognize that building responsible citizens is a complicated process, but surely one important aspect of responsible citizenship is to appreciate, to understand, and to be interested in American government.

OUR AMERICAN GOVERNMENT. We chose the title of this book deliberately because we wanted to include the idea of the pronoun *our*. *Our* expresses the faith citizens have in American institutions. Government in this country belongs to you, to other students, to your teacher, to all of us. It does not belong to any one person alone or to any one group. Our government belongs to the people. It is *ours*.

One of the things we all have in common is *our* government. In your school and neighborhood there may be Democrats, Republicans, independent voters, and members of minority parties, but the federal, state, and local governments are still our common heritage. This heritage gives us a real responsibility. If our government is to be effective, there must be constant, intelligent citizen interest and participation. Each generation must understand our system of government and assist in the complicated process of making the system work. In this process the high school government course plays an important part.

High school students, as citizens, already know much about government. They have had many governmental experiences. They have formed definite attitudes toward government. The high school government course provides one more opportunity to add to this knowledge, to rethink previous learnings, and to modify or confirm attitudes in the light of new experience.

In this common endeavor, *Our American Government* has been written to accomplish four purposes: (1) to stimulate interest in our government, (2) to provide essential understandings of the operations of our government, (3) to promote careful thinking about governmental problems, and (4) to encourage participation in governmental activities.

The writing in this book has been designed to appeal to a great variety of high school students. The high school government course rightfully includes all types of students: good readers and poor, those with rich experiences and those with limited backgrounds, those with special interests in government and those who have primary interests in science or art or music or athletics. But all are citizens and all deserve a book that is interesting, readable, and thought-provoking. We hope this is such a book.

The writing has been done around concepts and generalizations. Research has shown that detailed facts are forgotten quite rapidly but that generalizations tend to endure. So while this book has many facts, these facts are used to develop, support, and highlight major ideas. These generalizations and concepts are important, for they provide a framework for future learning. Government changes so rapidly that the details of what is written today may be out of date tomorrow. Hence, no book on government can be completely up to date. But generalizations and concepts do not change rapidly, so they provide a framework for more permanent learning. Of course, this book needs to be supplemented by the use of current materials from magazines, newspapers, television, and radio.

Our former students have urged us "to tell it like it is." This we have tried to do. The great ideals which have made our society are here. So are the short-comings and inadequacies. The basic theory of our government is presented, but alongside are the practices which men employ to get their way. The world of practical politics is not neglected, but neither are the aspirations and dreams of our people. The present generation continues the struggle of our forefathers to make the dreams of democracy come true. The results and the struggle are here.

ORGANIZATION. The unit organization for this book has been carefully planned and is based on the experiences of many teachers and many classes. Each unit provides a complete wholeness in itself, yet each unit makes a contribution to other units. Each unit begins with a brief summary of what the unit is about and ends with a case or episode which provides an opportunity to put the learnings of the unit to work in an actual situation.

Each chapter contains a section on "The Language of Government" which provides a handy reference to the special governmental words used in the chapter. These words from all the chapters have been compiled into a glossary at the end of the book. Each chapter also has a special feature story about some idea which can provide a springboard for discussion. Each chapter ends with a proposed list of concepts and generalizations which have been developed in the chapter.

The pictures and charts have been selected to help develop important ideas. A careful search was made for the best available illustrations to add meaning to the text. Charts were made to explain and expand ideas. There is a planned unity of the written text, illustrations, and charts. Students and teachers have, therefore, a rich resource for study and investigation.

The materials at the end of each chapter have also been carefully planned. The "Study Questions" not only focus attention on the important ideas of a chapter but also include questions that require use of the factual information presented. These questions provide a convenient review of basic understandings. The "Ideas for Discussion" are designed to enable students to test their thoughts against the ideas of others. They provide stimulation for thinking. Frequently these items present a thought-provoking idea or a challenging statement that requires careful thought on the part of students.

The "Things To Do" provide a wide range of activities. The individual interests and talents in any government class are extremely varied. The suggested activities enable each student to find some activity at which he can be successful. It is not intended, however, that any one class will use all these activities. Flexibility and choice are desirable.

The authors of this book believe in our form of government. They recognize its weaknesses and failures but think that it can and does respond to the needs of people and to changes in social and economic conditions. They recognize that the future of all mankind may depend on the understanding and appreciation that this generation of youth has for our form of government and the loyalty that is developed to ideas of freedom. *Our American Government* was written to foster understanding, appreciation, and loyalty in thoughtful citizens.

The authors are indebted to many people for help with this book. We are grateful to the teachers, colleagues, students, friends, and members of our families who have aided us in this major revision of this book. Their criticisms, suggestions, and encouragement have been of great help.

CONTENTS

2

THE
POLITICAL
PROCESSES
Page 78

3

NATIONAL GOVERNMENT
Page 176

4

STATE GOVERNMENT
Page 322

5

LOCAL GOVERNMENT
Page 406

6

TAXATION AND FINANCE
Page 482

7

THE
UNITED STATES
AND
WORLD AFFAIRS
Page 526

8

GOVERNMENT AND THE LIFE OF OUR PEOPLE
Page 622

1
PRINCIPLES AND PRACTICES OF OUR GOVERNMENT

"Theory and practice usually differ in any human activity . . ." Other than the treatment of minorities in our society, point out areas in our system where theory and practice are closer together or diverging.

Introduce *Our American Government* by calling the student's attention to some of the special features included in this text.

The language of government: This section at the beginning of each chapter introduces the students to the new terms which they will be meeting. This may also be used as a study list for the students to determine their ability to define and use these terms.

Charts: Many charts appear throughout the book. These can be used effectively to aid the student in visualizing practical applications of the mechanics of government explained in each chapter.

Concepts and generalizations: Each chapter includes this feature. This can be employed by the students as a general review of each chapter. Students should be encouraged to recognize the relationship between these concepts and the practical aspects of government.

Appendix: Show the Appendix and point out the fact that it contains the text of some of the early documents of American history and many useful tables. At this point it will be helpful to explain how these tables are to be read, when to refer to the footnotes included in each table, and to mention their usefulness in doing work on various aspects of American government.

Glossary: This section, following the Appendix, is a compilation of the words in the language of government sections. The Glossary may be used as a quick reference should a student meet a term which he has forgotten or with which he is not familiar.

Index: This is the final section of the book; however, its importance cannot be overlooked. Explain the mechanics of using this section, emphasizing "why" and "how." Conduct an oral drill finding information by using the Index. Explain to the students that the italic type refers to charts, illustrations, or tables. This will aid them in finding factual material to support their statements.

Quotations and feature stories: Note throughout the book the quotations (like those on page 7 and 31 from Learned Hand and Abraham Lincoln) and the special feature stories (like "The Political Scientist" on page 13 and "Plato's Republic" on page 20). Plan, before introducing units, ways to utilize these special features—as a means of illustrating major ideas of the text; as the basis for further reading of resource materials; as subjects for class discussions or debates.

This unit presents the basic principles on which our government was founded and under which we have lived since the adoption of the United States Constitution in 1789. This is the *theory* of our government. The unit also presents the *practices* of our system in one area—the treatment of a minority. Theory and practice usually differ in any human activity, so the intent of this unit is to bring practice into closer harmony with theory.

The unit is based on a belief that high school students know a great deal more about government than they, or their friends, or their parents recognize. Growing up in a democratic country means that everyone is exposed to ideas about government and has experiences with govern-ment. The newspaper, the traffic light, the football game, television and radio, previous schooling, experiences with prejudice, and conversations with friends teach us many things about government. These learnings may not be organized, but they exist. They are the basis of this unit.

Chapter 1 describes the basic idea that men can govern themselves.

Chapter 2 traces the source of these ideas from early religions to great historic documents.

Chapter 3 describes the fundamental framework of our government, the Constitution.

Chapter 4 presents the effects on one minority group, the Negroes, of these principles in practice.

DEMOCRACY—government by direct participation of the people.

FREE ENTERPRISE—the economic system in which first reliance is placed on private business operating in competitive markets.

GENERAL WELFARE—the state of well-being of the public as a whole; the common good.

LIBERTY—freedom from arbitrary or despotic choice.

MAJORITY RULE—the political principle that the greater number (usually one more than 50 per cent) shall have the power to make decisions.

MINORITY—less than half; a group that is a small but important portion of the total population.

REPRESENTATIVE GOVERNMENT—the system by which government operates through elected officials.

REPUBLIC—government by the people through elected representatives.

UNALIENABLE—cannot be taken away; belongs to each human being by right of birth; inalienable.

Each chapter of *Our American Government* is introduced by a word list, "the language of government." Understanding of these words should be stressed as basic to an understanding of the chapter. Point out, from the beginning, that students should refer to these lists while reading the chapters. Introduce also at this time the Glossary (pages 760-768), that contains important terms belonging to the language of government. Encourage students to refer to the Glossary while reading the text and discuss with them the significance of understanding words and phrases frequently used in discussions of government.

THE LANGUAGE OF GOVERNMENT

Discuss with the students the importance of reading the introduction of each chapter as it is an important part of the text and serves to state the main ideas which will be discussed in the chapter.

1

The Fundamental Ideas of a Free People

This book is built on a belief that the government of the United States is based on some fundamental ideas that are important for all mankind. These ideas influence the lives of each one of us. They can make a difference in the future of the world if they are accepted by more people and nations.

These fundamental ideas have been expressed in great documents of our past—the Declaration of Independence and the Constitution of the United States. Presidents, starting with George Washington, have spoken about these great ideas. Wars have been fought to preserve these ideas. And each generation of Americans has faced the problem of getting more of our people to live up to the ideals contained in these fundamental ideas.

Political leaders, judges, clergymen, editors, teachers—thoughtful people from all walks of life—have pleaded that young people be helped to understand and appreciate these ideas. These leaders urge that the ideas be understood, in order that they

Ask "how" and "why" if you wish to teach students to think. Ask "who" and "what" if you wish to teach facts or determine whether they have studied the lesson.

Basic ideas of self-government are expressed in the Declaration of Independence. In this mural, Jefferson is shown presenting the famous document to John Hancock. (The National Archives)

can be honored, practiced, analyzed, criticized, improved. The ideas deserve to be compared honestly with the basic ideas of other countries. They deserve, also, to be the standards by which one judges the effectiveness of governments.

THE FUNDAMENTAL IDEAS

Although these ideas are not simple, we, as a people, have come to use simple terms to express them. Democracy is commonly used as a good, brief descriptive word to explain our system of fundamental ideas. President Woodrow Wilson during World War I used the phrase, ". . . to make the world safe for democracy." The Constitution of the United States uses the phrase, ". . . a republican form of government. . . ." A famous historian called these ideas "the American dream." Freedom, liberty, representative government are other similar terms in constant use. Probably the most widely used expression for these ideas is Abraham Lincoln's famous phrase, ". . . government of the people, by the people, and for the people. . . ."

But the frequent use of these simple words and phrases often means that pro-found ideas are dulled by thoughtless usage. Sometimes, too, those who do not believe in the ideas use the words to cloak their real intentions. It is important, therefore, that students of government examine these ideas which have influenced our nation throughout its history.

THE BASIC IDEA. The basic idea in the government of our country is that *men can govern themselves.* In the Declaration of Independence our forefathers stated that governments obtain their powers "from the consent of the governed."

The opposite of this idea of self-government sometimes is that one man (a king, a dictator, a military general) rules over other men. Sometimes the opposite of this idea of self-government is found when a small group (the Communist party, a gang, the aristocrats) rules over other people. One-man rule or rule by a small group destroys the basic idea for which our country stands because by these means some persons lose their right to share in the governmental process.

But this basic idea that men can govern themselves is so profound and complex that great statesmen throughout our history have constantly worked to understand and to explain it. This book, and especially this chapter, is another attempt to explain the big ideas that have undergirded our way of life.

The idea that men can govern themselves means one test can determine the quality of a government: Do the people have the opportunity to make the final decisions? Our system of government is based on the principle that the people must make the final decisions. This principle is expressed in the opening words of the Constitution of the United States, "We the people of the United States. . . ."

In applying this test of self-government, differences of opinion sometimes arise over whether to describe our system as a *democracy* or a *republic*. The word *democracy* emphasizes the idea of participation by all people in government. The word *republic* emphasizes the idea of governing through representatives elected by the people. A republic is often called an indirect democracy. The important point is that the people make the final decisions.

OTHER FUNDAMENTALS. To have self-government certain other fundamentals are necessary. Four of these have been selected for special attention here. They are: (1) liberty; (2) concern for the general welfare; (3) majority rule; and (4) respect for the rights of minorities.

In our country these fundamentals have existed and have been developed throughout our history. They are the fundamentals that each citizen should understand well enough to explain his form of government to others who may have different opinions about the nature of government.

LIBERTY The first of these fundamental ideas, *liberty*, means freedom. The free man is able to think, write, and speak his own thoughts. He is free to attend the church

The men who met in Independence Hall bequeathed to us our heritage of liberty. Shown here is Independence Mall and Independence Hall in Philadelphia. (Girard Trust Bank)

of his choice, to pray, to read his holy book. He cannot be made a slave, unjustly imprisoned, or forced to do the will of another. He is entitled to a fair trial. He is able to protest, to petition, to defend what he thinks is right.

Liberty is one of the words used often by those who have tried to describe our way of life. Patrick Henry said, "Give me *liberty* or give me death." The Declaration of Independence states that men "are endowed by their Creator with certain unalienable rights; that among these are life, *liberty*, and the pursuit of happiness." The Preamble to the Constitution speaks of "the blessings of *liberty*." The Pledge of Allegiance to the Flag ends with the words "with *liberty* and justice for all."

THE BILL OF RIGHTS. The liberties of free men are guaranteed to each citizen in the Bill of Rights—the first ten amendments to the United States Constitution. These rights are also guaranteed in most state constitutions. They include freedom of speech, freedom of worship, freedom of the press, trial by jury, the right of assembly, and the right to be free from unreasonable search or seizure.

Using the text of the Declaration of Independence (Appendix), discuss the philosophical concepts upon which the colonists based their fight for liberty.

SOME FUNDAMENTAL RIGHTS OF THE BILL OF RIGHTS

FREEDOM OF RELIGION
FREEDOM OF SPEECH
FREEDOM OF THE PRESS
RIGHT TO ASSEMBLE

Congress shall make no law respecting an establishment of religion, or prohibiting the free exercise thereof; or abridging the freedom of speech, or of the press; or the right of the people peaceably to assemble. . . .

FREEDOM FROM UNREASONABLE
SEARCHES AND SEIZURES

The right of the people to be secure . . . against unreasonable searches and seizures shall not be violated. . . .

RIGHT TO DUE PROCESS OF LAW

. . . nor be deprived of life, liberty, or property, without due process of law. . . .

RIGHT TO TRIAL BY JURY

. . . the accused shall enjoy the right to a speedy and public trial, by an impartial jury. . . .

FREEDOM FROM CRUEL PUNISHMENT

. . . nor cruel and unusual punishments inflicted.

AND THE RIGHT TO FREEDOM FOR ALL —
THE CONTINUING BILL OF RIGHTS

NEITHER SLAVERY NOR
INVOLUNTARY SERVITUDE . . .

THIRTEENTH AMENDMENT

Neither slavery nor involuntary servitude . . . shall exist within the United States. . . .

THE RIGHT TO VOTE

FOURTEENTH AMENDMENT

All persons born or naturalized in the United States, and subject to the jurisdiction thereof, are citizens. . . .

EQUAL PROTECTION
OF THE LAWS

FIFTEENTH AMENDMENT

The right of citizens of the United States to vote shall not be denied . . . on account of race, color, or previous condition of servitude.

THE RIGHT TO VOTE

NINETEENTH AMENDMENT

The right of citizens of the United States to vote shall not be denied . . . on account of sex.

TWENTY-THIRD AMENDMENT

The District of Columbia shall elect . . . a number of electors of President and Vice President. . . .

TWENTY-SIXTH AMENDMENT

The right of citizens of the United States, who are eighteen years of age or older, to vote shall not be denied . . . on account of age.

These rights were won from the tyrants of the Middle Ages and from the British kings over a period of many hundreds of years. In this twentieth century some people have taken these rights for granted. But these rights have been lost in some countries of the world in this generation.

They were lost in Italy under Mussolini, in Germany under Hitler, in Russia under Stalin, and in China under Mao Tse-tung. They have been lost in some countries of Latin America, in Africa, in Asia, and in the Middle East. This century has become one of mankind's great periods of struggle to keep man's essential freedoms.

THE INDIVIDUAL. The concern for each individual is an important element of liberty. Each person, regardless of mental ability, physical condition, age, color, sex, or religion, is a person of great worth under our system of government.

Many examples of the value placed on

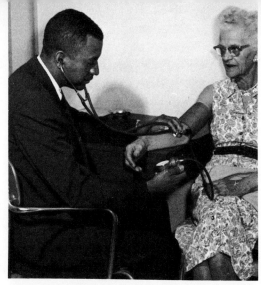

Concern for the individual is one of the most important of our fundamental ideas. Here a public health doctor treats a senior citizen. (Health Services and Mental Health Administration)

each individual human life could be given. A boy is caught in a well. The resources of an entire community are mobilized to try to rescue the boy. The whole nation by newspaper, radio, and television waits anxiously to learn whether this child will be saved.

In Asia, during one battle, a United States pilot was not able to fly his plane back to his navy ship. As dusk arrived, he radioed that he would have to land at sea. Instantly all the resources of the army, the navy, and the air force in that vicinity were ordered to assist in his rescue. Thousands of dollars were spent to locate this one pilot, because we believe that each person is important. No man should drown at sea if we can prevent it.

A Negro, James H. Meredith, was denied admission to the University of Mississippi in 1962. He was not the first Negro to be denied the chance for a good education. But his was the first case in which the federal government used its massive power to guarantee a Negro citizen his right to a college education. It took 15,000 troops and millions of tax dollars to put and keep James

GRIN AND BEAR IT   BY LICHTY

"You sure that's all it says, Otis? . . There MUST be something about an allowance in the Bill of Rights!"

Grin and Bear It *by George Lichty, reprinted by permission of Publishers-Hall Syndicate.*

Meredith in his state university. To protect him, federal marshals lived with him and attended classes with him. The troops had to be called out to put down violent rioting by a mob that included some students but mostly townspeople and outside agitators—violence stemming primarily from Governor Ross Barnett's open defiance of federal court orders. The federal government demonstrated that it would use whatever resources were necessary to guarantee the freedom of one man.

It is in this spirit of the importance of each individual that rescues are made, that the poor are helped, that education is made available to all. Where does this concern for the individual come from? What is the source of this fundamental idea? While the idea is recorded in many famous documents, this belief in the worth and dignity of each individual comes from deep-seated religious beliefs. It is part of our inheritance from Christian and Jewish religions.

FREE ENTERPRISE. Because man has freedom, another important element in liberty is *free enterprise*—the economic system in which first reliance is placed on private business operating in competitive markets. Under this system a man is free to start a business if he wishes. Another man is free to buy or sell a farm. Each man is free to be "a butcher, a baker, a candlestick-maker." No one in our country says, "Tom, you are to be a waiter," or "Jim, you are to be a lawyer," or "Mary, you are to be a nurse." Each person is free to pick his own occupation—or to decide not to seek employment. In contrast, under other systems, men are told what job to hold, where to work, and when to work. The government owns and operates major industries and controls any private business.

The idea of free enterprise in a land of great resources like the United States has helped produce the great factories and businesses of our times. When man is free to invest his money or his time in any way that he desires, he becomes creative. New ideas get tried. New products are made. When one inventor realized that his invention would work, he exclaimed, "I have found a better way!" He had caught this spirit of free enterprise. Finding a better way is part of liberty.

LIBERTY IS NOT UNLIMITED. Liberty, however, does not mean "the right to do as I please." Liberty has limits. Freedom of speech does not mean that one has the right to lie about another person. Free enterprise does not mean that one man can

This is another example of our concern for the individual. James Meredith's right to study at the University of Mississippi was protected by federal marshals and troops. (UPI photo)

Liberty lies in the hearts of men and women. When it dies there, no constitution, no law, no court can save it.

—LEARNED HAND, a widely respected judge of the the U.S. Court of Appeals from 1924 to 1951.

Belief in private enterprise is part of our basic concept of liberty. On the floor of this stock exchange, shares in many different companies are bought and sold. (American Stock Exchange)

steal another man's invention. Respect for the worth of each individual does not mean that a parent can insist that his child be free to destroy a neighbor's flower garden.

When President Abraham Lincoln spoke to a Baltimore audience in 1864, he explained the limits on liberty in this way: "The shepherd drives the wolf from the sheep's throat, for which the sheep thanks the shepherd as his liberator, while the wolf denounces him for the same act, as the destroyer of liberty. . . . Plainly the sheep and the wolf are not agreed upon the definition of the word liberty."

Just as the sheep and the wolf do not agree on the meaning of liberty, there are differences of opinion about how far one person's liberty can go without interfering with the liberty of others. If each person were free to do exactly as he pleased, there could not be real liberty, there could only be great confusion. One function of government is "to keep liberty within law." But governments must be limited too. Individual liberty cannot survive if a government is able to do anything it pleases. The strength of our form of government is that we have found ways to keep a balance between the individual's "doing as he pleases" and the government's "doing as it pleases."

CONCERN FOR THE GENERAL WELFARE

One of the fundamental ideas which limits liberty is "concern for the general welfare." The Preamble to the Constitution says that government exists "to promote the general welfare." Sometimes this idea of the general welfare is referred to as "the common good."

In some ways this idea of the general welfare is exactly the opposite of individual liberty. A worker muttered that his liberty was taken from him because he had to join a labor union in order to work in a certain factory. A businessman groaned that his liberty was destroyed because he could not dismiss an employee without the union steward's approval. A farmer complained that his liberty was gone because he couldn't plant all the cotton he wanted. A homeowner objected because he was not permitted to sell his corner lot for use as a gas station.

The situations that caused these com-

With respect to the importance of the individual and the welfare of the group, describe how this issue has been resolved in the communist world.

Training individuals in the skills they need is part of our concern for the general welfare. Shown here is a scene from a federal vocational education program. (Courtesy of the Office of Economic Opportunity)

plaints developed because the general welfare was considered to be more important than the liberty of the individual. The good of all was thought by the framers of the Constitution to be superior to the rights of the individual.

GENERAL WELFARE IS NOT NEW. Some people seem to think that the idea of general welfare is a new, modern, twentieth-century idea. They say the concern for the general welfare is the result of modern industry with its many factories and of new methods of communication. It is well, therefore, to recall that the words *general welfare* even appeared in the Articles of Confederation, which preceded the Constitution. (The complete texts of the Articles of Confederation and of the Constitution are in the Appendix.) The writers of the Constitution borrowed the phrase and used it not only in the Preamble but also in the

first article of the Constitution under the taxing clause. The idea of general welfare is certainly not new.

The colonies and later the states had laws which were designed to help the sick, the poor, the unfortunate. Cities and states have always tried to help the needy. Today suffering, ill-health, slums, poverty, working conditions, agriculture, and trade are looked upon as matters about which government may need to do something. Why? Because of concern for the general welfare.

Kept within proper bounds, the general welfare idea is good. Fire protection, police protection, highways, food inspection, social security, schools, employment services, regulation of public utilities, guarantees for bank deposits—all are helpful and necessary. But the concept of general welfare could be evil.

DANGERS OF GENERAL WELFARE. A newspaper account told of a small country in which the "president" (really a dictator) made some new laws for the inspection of factories. He told his people that these laws were to protect their welfare. But the businessman who owned this factory told the reporter that he feared the real purpose of the law was to permit inspectors to find fault with enough little things, until the dictator could find an excuse to seize his factory.

This news item is only one sample of what has happened throughout the world. Dictators have risen to power by saying they were working for the common good. Build a new highway, but take away the right to travel freely. Operate the railroad more efficiently, but live in fear that the secret police may board the train and take father away to jail. Take food from the farmers to feed the poor in the cities, but steal the right to trial by jury. These are the ways of the dictators. They use general welfare as an excuse to destroy liberty.

Using Article VIII of the Articles of Confederation (Appendix), discuss how the concept of general welfare has changed from colonial to present times.

Believing as we do that the general welfare is an important part of our way of life, how can we keep this good idea from destroying liberty? This is a question of balance. What is the proper balance between liberty and general welfare? How far shall we limit one and increase the other? No one has found a perfect answer to these questions. But in our country we have a system that works very well.

MAJORITY RULE

When liberty and the general welfare conflict, we say that the majority shall rule. Those who get the most votes will win. Ideally, under our system, the decision is not left to the person with the most power. It is not left to the person with the most money, or to the biggest mob, or to the loudest talker. The decision is left to the votes of the people or to the votes of those they have chosen to represent them. In our country the majority rules.

This faith in the majority is another of our fundamental ideas. And it requires tremendous faith. This faith says that in the long run the people can be trusted. Give them the information; show them the issue; trust them to select the best answer.

There are dangers in this faith. There are examples in our history when the system did not work. Citizens may be selfish. They may be ignorant. They may seem lazy. They may be indifferent. They may not be able to understand the issues. They may be deceived by propaganda. But in spite of all these dangers, it is better to trust the people than it is to trust one person or a small group with the powers of government.

Three elements of majority rule are worthy of special mention here: (1) representative government, (2) equality of all, and (3) education.

REPRESENTATIVE GOVERNMENT. Representative government is the system by which "we the people" choose persons to exercise power for us. These representatives speak for us. They vote in our place. If we do not like their speeches or their votes, we can protest in several ways. We can write letters, send telegrams, and even make a personal visit to our representatives. We can organize groups to oppose their ideas. We can write letters to the editor. We can switch off the radio or television set or turn to another station. Finally, we can vote for someone else at the next election.

If we like the actions of our elected officials we can use these same means and methods to praise instead of blame. Our point of view may not always win, but history is full of cases where today's lost cause becomes the winner a few years later.

Not all government is by the representative system. In a pure democracy, as in some New England town meetings, the people vote directly for all of their officials and on all matters of public policy. This system works well in small communities and when there are not too many issues. The system has been extended in some states by having citizens vote on amendments to state constitutions and to city charters. In some states and cities they may also vote to pass certain laws. Most of our governing, however, is done through our elected representatives.

EQUALITY OF ALL. Rule by the majority, under our governmental system, requires that each person be the equal of any other person. In the words of the Declaration of Independence, ". . . all men are created equal. . . ." Since men are not equal in height, weight, intelligence, or color of the eyes, hair, or skin, in what sense are they equal? First, they are equal before the law, and second they are entitled to equal opportunity.

take it from them, but to inform their discretion by education."

EQUALITY BEFORE THE LAW has two important aspects. The first, the "one man . . . one vote" principle, emphasizes the importance of equality of each voter in choosing representatives. Without this principle, majority rule becomes a farce. In the case of *Reynolds* v. *Sims,* 1964, the United States Supreme Court stated the principle in this way,

> . . . if a State should provide that the votes of citizens in one part of the State should be given two times, or five times, or ten times the weight of votes of citizens in another part of the State, it could hardly be contended that the right to vote of those residing in the disfavored areas had not been effectively diluted. . . .
> . . . all voters, as citizens of a State, stand in the same relation regardless of where they live. . . .
> . . . the basic principle of representative government remains, and must remain, unchanged—the weight of a citizen's vote cannot be made to depend on where he lives.

A second aspect of *equality before the law* is that each person is entitled to "equal justice under the law." This principle means that in our courts each person is to be treated the same as every other person. A good example to illustrate this principle is that of Clarence E. Gideon, a poor man, who was arrested for breaking into a poolroom in Florida. He was too poor to employ a lawyer to defend him and asked the state court to appoint a lawyer for him. The court refused and Gideon had to defend himself. He was found guilty, but an appeal was taken to the Supreme Court of the United States. All nine Justices agreed that no man should have to defend himself against a charge of stealing. How could he base his defense on earlier cases of which he had never heard? Or explain laws that

he had never read? The Supreme Court ruled that if a defendant has no money for a lawyer, the state must appoint one. Gideon was granted a second trial in Florida and was freed. In this and other cases the Court has defined "equal justice under law" to mean that the poor are entitled to the same treatment as the rich.

EQUALITY OF OPPORTUNITY is important under our system of permitting the majority to rule. Each person must be free to make the most of his abilities. It is not wrong for one individual to do better than another, if his superiority is based on effort or ability. It is wrong if one person's success is based on unfairness or dishonesty, or on lack of a reasonable chance for the other person.

The President's Committee on Civil Rights in 1947 stated this principle this way:

> This concept of equality, which is so vital a part of the American heritage, knows no kinship with notions of human uniformity or regimentation. We abhor the totalitarian arrogance which makes one man say that he will respect another man only if he has '*my* race, *my* religion, *my* political views, *my* social position.' In our land men are equal, but they are free to be different. From these very differences among our people has come the great human and national strength of America.
>
> Thus, the aspirations and achievements of each member of our society are to be limited only by the skills and energies he brings to the opportunities equally offered to all Americans.

EDUCATION. Education is a necessity whenever the majority is to rule. Schools are democracy's way of getting a well-informed body of citizens. Free public education in our country is no accident. The leaders of our country saw clearly that if

An opportunity to receive a good education is the right of all our people. Have we ever denied this right to any of our minority groups? (Du Pont, Better Living Magazine)

man was to govern himself "schools and the means of education shall forever be encouraged."

Some effects of this policy are worthy of note. There is a larger percentage of young people between the ages of fifteen and eighteen in school in the United States than in all the rest of the world put together. The United States has more newspapers and more radio and television stations than any other nation in the world. Majority rule requires that people be educated and well informed.

DANGERS OF MAJORITY RULE. There are some dangers to the rule of the majority. Just because the majority has reached a decision does not necessarily make it good. Majority rule can be harsh and evil. The majority may have the most votes, but it may not always be right.

Great wrongs have been done by majorities. Just as mobs have hurt innocent persons, the majority has sometimes harmed the innocent too.

Slavery was approved by the majority in our country for many years, but this did not make slavery right. For years child labor was not regulated by the majority, but this did not make long hours of hard work good for children. For years the mentally ill and the poor were sent to jail, but this did not make a jail sentence the proper treatment.

The writers of the Constitution feared "an unjust combination of the majority." They tried to protect the people from the possible despotism of the majority by having officials elected for terms of office of different lengths. They divided powers between the nation and the state. They gave some responsibilities to the President, other responsibilities to the Congress, and still others to the courts. This system of checks and balances is discussed in Chapter 3.

The final protection against the majority, however, was given by establishing certain rights which cannot be taken from the people. These rights are guaranteed in our Bill of Rights.

MINORITY
RIGHTS   The idea that the majority cannot deprive the minority of fundamental rights has become in recent years the real testing ground for self-government. A generation now living knows that millions of people were killed in gas chambers because they were a minority group in Germany. The expression "You'll get sent to Siberia" is commonplace because the Russian government sent those who disagreed with the Communist system to prison camps in Siberia.

In a South American country, a great newspaper was put out of business because it dared to speak out against the dictator who controlled the country. In our own country there has been a long struggle by racial, religious, economic, and nationality groups to achieve their rights as minority groups.

Are these "minority rights" any different from the "essential freedoms" discussed under the idea of liberty earlier in this chapter? No, they are the freedoms guaranteed under the Bill of Rights. They are singled out here for special emphasis because in our time the real test of government by the *consent of the governed* has been in this realm of majority-minority relations. Freedom of speech, freedom of worship, freedom of the press, and our other fundamental rights assume a new importance when we insist that they exist for others as well as for ourselves.

A great French thinker two hundred years ago said, "I disapprove of what you

THE POLITICAL SCIENTIST

Those individuals who specialize in the study of political, especially governmental, processes are known as *political scientists*. They devote their lives to the study of government, political behavior, decision-making in public bodies, international relations, constitutional law, political leadership, and many other related matters.

Most political scientists are teacher-scholars in colleges and universities, but some political scientists are employed in governmental agencies. To become a political scientist it is necessary to be a college graduate and to continue graduate work in the field of political science. Most political scientists hold the degree of Doctor of Philosophy in political science. About 300 such degrees are earned each year in American universities. The professional organization of these scholars is the American Political Science Association with a membership of approximately 18,000.

The research methods used by political scientists are not unique to their field. They employ the methods of historians and social scientists. They attempt to describe accurately, to weigh evidence, to arrive at verifiable conclusions. Political scientists rely on documents, newspaper reports, official state papers, personal accounts. They also use interviews, questionnaires, observation. They make analyses of the opinions and decisions of our courts. Some spend much time in the library; others use as their laboratory the meeting places of politicians including government officials.

While some people maintain that the political scientist is not a man of science in the same sense as a chemist, a physicist, or a biologist, he is entitled to use the label scientist because he is a seeker after truth in his chosen field.

This is a parade celebrating the Chinese New Year in San Francisco's Chinatown. Have we always been conscious of our obligation to protect the rights of our minority groups? (San Francisco Convention and Visitors Bureau)

say, but I will defend to the death your right to say it." It is this willingness to permit criticism and to accept the other person's right to have different ideas that helps democracy to succeed. The majority rules, but the right of the minority to criticize must be respected.

The right of the other person to have an idea that differs from yours is a concept that is very important for high school students to understand. Several studies have been made of the opinions and ideas of students toward our system of government. These studies have shown that many students think about their rights as being personal rights. Most students give little thought to the idea that these rights belong also to others and that each person has responsibilities that go along with these rights.

The idea that the majority cannot tyrannize the minority may not have occurred to some of these students. The idea of minority rights, however, is fundamental in our system of government.

There is an old expression often used: "We have gone around the circle." This means that we are back where we started. In a sense this is what we have done in describing our system based on the idea that men can govern themselves. We started with liberty. We described the relation of the Bill of Rights, the individual, and free enterprise to liberty. We showed that liberty is not unlimited and sometimes conflicts with the general welfare. We said that to keep liberty and general welfare in proper balance we use majority rule. We stated that representative government, equality of all, and education were important to rule by the majority. Then we returned to the fundamental of liberty by showing that the majority cannot take away the basic rights of the minority.

We believe in these ideas. We think they are important today and will be important in the future. In Asia, in Africa, in the Middle East, in Europe, in South America, and in the United States, men and women are struggling with these ideas.

We have fought two world wars in the first half of this century over these ideas. The world today is divided into armed camps over these ideas. The alternative to our way is not a pleasant one. Does our way seem important to you?

STUDY QUESTIONS

1. This chapter has tried to describe what we believe to be the essential ideas of our system of government. People do not always agree on these features. You may wish to express your ideas in a different way. Do you agree with the main ideas of this chapter? Are there other ideas you would add? Are there any of these ideas with which you do not agree?

2. How does *liberty* differ from doing as one pleases? What are three basic elements of *liberty*?

3. Give an example of one way your liberty is limited in order to protect the welfare of others.

4. Give an example of the great value the American people place on one human life. Could this example have happened in a dictatorship?

5. What are two important elements of majority rule?

6. How have minority rights been protected in the United States Constitution?

7. Must the rights of members of minority groups be assured if our system of government is to endure? Why?

8. What are the dangers of majority rule?

IDEAS FOR DISCUSSION

1. Some critics of the movies, television, and radio believe that too much murder, fighting, and brutality is displayed. They think such

CONCEPTS AND GENERALIZATIONS

1
The government of the United States is based on ideas that are important for all mankind.

2
Men can govern themselves.

3
Liberty is an unalienable human right.

4
Each individual is a person of worth.

5
Free enterprise is an essential element of liberty.

6
Liberty is not unlimited; neither the individual nor the government has "the right to do as I please."

7
Liberty is limited by concern for the general welfare.

8
"Majority rule" is used to settle differences in our system of government.

9
All persons are equal before the law.

10
Diversity develops from equal opportunity.

11
The majority cannot deprive the minority of fundamental rights.

programs may be destroying the American belief in the value of each human being. Do you think these programs have decreased the respect of young people for the worth of each human being? What type of programs would you think could be produced to replace them?

2. An editorial in *Life* quotes this definition of democracy: "Democracy means personal worth, freedom, equality, rule of law, public morality, individual opportunity, and individual responsibility." How do these ideas compare with the ideas of this chapter?

3. A writer says that "governmental policy should be made by men who are free to inquire, to compare, to experiment, to debate, and to complain." Do you agree? Why?

4. Some writers refer to the "fundamental ideas" of this chapter as myths; others refer to them as ideals. Which do you think they are? What distinctions are being made by the "myths vs. ideals" controversy?

5. Walter Lippman, in a March 1967 article for the *Washington Post* on the operation of American government, stated, "The fundamental assumption in the American system is that the individuals concerned—the officials, voters, newspapermen—understand and believe in the system and mean to make it work. This is the great consensus by which the republic operates."[1] Do you agree or disagree? Why?

6. The last time the summer Olympic games were held in the United States was in 1932 at Los Angeles, California. On that occasion a distance runner from a foreign nation fell far behind the other runners. Finally all the other runners passed him. When they had finished the race, he still had a lap to go. Nevertheless he made the final circle around the track and finished the race. When he crossed the finish line, the crowd gave him a tremendous cheer. Was this cheer a symbol of democracy? Is an essential feature of democracy involved?

7. Do high school students today emphasize their responsibilities as well as their rights?

THINGS TO DO

1. Interview three adults by asking each one, "What do you think are four essential ideas for which America stands?" Have a committee put these ideas together into one list. Compare these ideas with the ideas expressed in this chapter.

2. Clip newspaper items to illustrate the main ideas discussed in this chapter.

3. Select what you believe to be the six most important countries in the world. Using major ideas from this chapter, prepare a checklist, showing how each country rates on a democracy-dictatorship scale.

4. Organize the class into four groups. Assign each group one of the four fundamental ideas discussed in this chapter. Have each group discuss the question "Do people in our community have the benefits of this fundamental idea?" A spokesman for the group should summarize the group's answer and present it to the entire class.

5. Imagine that you have a friend in another country who has asked you to explain your system of government to him because he has to make a report on the United States to his class in school. Write a letter in which you try to tell the most important features.

6. Hold a panel discussion on this statement: "Liberty is always dangerous, but it is the safest thing we have."

FURTHER READINGS

Adler, Mortimer J., COMMON SENSE OF POLITICS. Holt, Rinehart and Winston, Inc., 1971.

Emerson, Thomas L., TOWARD A GENERAL THEORY OF THE FIRST AMENDMENT. Random House, Inc., 1966.

Ferguson, John H., and McHenry, Dean E., THE AMERICAN SYSTEM OF GOVERNMENT. McGraw-Hill Book Co., 1967. Chapter 2.

Lasswell, Harold D., THE FUTURE OF POLITICAL SCIENCE. Atherton Press, 1963.

Lippman, Walter, THE PUBLIC PHILOSOPHY. Mentor, 1955. (Paperback edition)

Mitchell, William C., THE AMERICAN POLITY. Free Press of Glencoe, 1962.

Niebuhr, Reinhold, and Sigmund, Paul E., THE DEMOCRATIC EXPERIENCE: PAST AND PROSPECTS. Praeger Publishers, Inc., 1970.

Ranney, Austin, THE GOVERNING OF MEN. Holt, Rinehart and Winston, Inc., 1966.

Thomson, David, ed., POLITICAL IDEAS. Basic Books, Inc., 1967.

Trueblood, Elton, THE LIFE WE PRIZE. Harper & Row, Publishers, Inc., 1951. Pages 188-214.

Woll, Peter, and Binstock, Robert, AMERICA'S POLITICAL SYSTEM. Random House, Inc., 1972. (Paperback edition)

---

[1]*The Washington Post.* Reprinted by permission.

BOYCOTT—to join with others to stop buying certain products.

CHARTER—a written document similar to a constitution; a statement of the rules and regulations and the source of power.

COMPACT—an agreement between two or more parties.

CONFEDERATION—a joining of independent nations or states by a treaty or alliance for joint action (as for common defense). In a confederation each nation or state retains sovereign power; in a federation the nations or states give up some power to the new union.

FEDERAL SYSTEM—a union of nations or states under a central government; a federation.

LIMITED MONARCHY—a form of government in which the supreme power of a hereditary ruler is limited by laws or a constitution.

PREAMBLE—an introduction to a constitution which gives the reasons or purposes for writing the constitution.

PROPRIETOR—the owner; the one who has the final right or title to something.

THE LANGUAGE OF GOVERNMENT

2

The Origins of Our Fundamental Ideas

The idea that men can govern themselves is a heritage from the past. But men have not always been free. Majority rule with respect for minorities has not always been practiced. Equal opportunity has been denied often in the world's history. Men have struggled for these ideas for thousands of years, and the struggle continues to the present day.

Our fundamental ideas of government developed slowly over a long period of time. They have roots deep in the past. These ideas about self-government are an important part of our history. To understand these basic ideas it helps to know about their origins.

The fundamental ideas on which our government is based are the product of many different sources. Some of these ideas developed from ancient religions and cultures, and these ideas have been refined and adapted to modern times. Some of these ideas are inherited from England and the traditions which the English developed. Some of these ideas are the gifts of our forefathers who settled this land and founded our nation. From their efforts at government and their struggles for liberty, we have developed our present-day institutions. A better understanding of government today can be obtained by reviewing some aspects of this past history.

RELIGION   Religion is certainly one of the most important sources of our fundamental ideas. More than two thousand years ago, the great Hebrew religious leaders were teaching that the individual was of supreme importance. The Jewish religion helped spread a system of moral law among mankind. The Ten Commandments of Moses are one example of an early code by which people lived. These ideas from an ancient religion influenced men as they struggled for better ways to govern.

The Christian religion is, of course, a chief contributor to our way of life. Jesus, through his teachings and those of his disciples, spread the idea that each individual is a person of great worth. During the early history of the Christian church thousands were persecuted for these beliefs. Men died because of their faith in Christianity. Over the centuries their struggles for Christian ideas have been rewarded. Today these ideas of justice, charity, brotherhood, and equality are fundamental to the democratic way of life. Our ideas of individual liberty and of concern for the general welfare have been undergirded by the Christian religion.

Other great religious leaders holding similar ideas have strengthened the grip of these ideas on the peoples of the world. Confucius, the great Chinese philosopher, also emphasized the importance of the individual. Although he lived five hundred

years before Christ, his ideas are similar to those believed today. Buddha, founder of a major religion of Asia, lived 2,500 years ago. He taught that a secret of life is brotherly love and that selfishness is the chief cause of man's troubles.

Mohammed taught the Arab world to believe in the brotherhood of man. Living five hundred years after Christ, he stressed the ideas of simplicity, the unity of mankind, and the importance of the individual. Since democratic ideas are being challenged in Asia today, it is important to note that the religious ideas of the great Asiatic religious prophets do not conflict with democratic ideas. Rather, they give support to our democratic faith.

The religions of the world help man to think about himself, his destiny, and his relations with other men. From the writings, teachings, and beliefs about the great religions our forefathers evolved their concepts of man and of government.

ANCIENT
CIVILIZATIONS   The ancient civilizations of Greece and Rome were also sources for our basic ideas. The word democracy comes from two Greek words, *demos* (people) and *kratos* (rule of). Freely translated they mean "rule by the people." The Greeks believed that governmental power belonged to all citizens rather than to one person.

Although masses of people in ancient Athens were held in slavery and could not become citizens, an assembly of male citizens discussed and decided the important public questions of the times. Courts of law existed to determine right and wrong. Citizens testified under oath. Trials were held before very large juries of several hundred persons. Public officials were selected by a vote of the citizens. The freedom of

The Acropolis, the center of ancient Athens' political and religious life, symbolizes our heritage of democracy. (Wolfe Worldwide Films)

citizens was protected. Citizen participation in government was so common that Athens can rightfully be called the birthplace of democracy.

The ideas of Greek thinkers, like Socrates, Plato, and Aristotle, have influenced political thought up to the present time. Socrates emphasized the importance of the individual in his most famous phrase "Know thyself." Plato, a student of Socrates, wrote about government, religion, and justice. For him Truth, Beauty, and Justice were the great ideas. Aristotle wrote that man is basically a political animal and that governments arise from the nature of man himself. Aristotle also thought that the best government was by a middle class—not too rich and not too poor.

Rome, too, contributed to our fundamental ideas. The Romans were excellent organizers. Early in their history they collected, classified, and published their laws. This law system provided the basis for the law of many nations of the Western world. Since the Romans ruled the world for several centuries, they had to be skilled in government. They developed efficient departments of government which provided a model for later rulers.

In the early Roman period, before the tyrannical emperors gained power, Rome was governed by elected officials or representatives. The Latin word describing this system is *republic,* a word and an idea which is part of our representative system today.

The Greeks and the Romans helped originate the idea that men can govern themselves through majority rule.

As the Roman Empire declined, the world entered into a thousand-year period called the Middle Ages (about A.D. 500 to 1500). The *feudal system* was the central feature during this period. People were

Our concept of a government of organized laws comes to us from the Romans, many of whose laws were formulated in the famous Forum shown above. (Pan American Airways)

Plato (427-347 B.C.) would not be classified as a political scientist, for he is considered to be one of the world's great philosophers. Philosophers, however, think and write about a great variety of subjects and one of Plato's greatest books, the *Republic*, describes his ideas of an ideal government.

Plato wrote in the form of dialogues or conversations between his teacher, Socrates, and his listeners. The *Republic* is one of the longest and greatest of these dialogues (one edition contains over 400 pages).

The *Republic* is this young man's dream of what the ideal city-state would be. Plato believed there were three chief virtues: wisdom, courage, and moderation. His government would be ruled by men who had these virtues; he called them philosopher-kings. He thought only the wisest men should have the power to govern. In addition to this group of wise men, he thought there should

be two other classes: the military and the industrial. The military possessed the virtue of courage; the industrial possessed moderation—particularly self-discipline.

In this ideal republic, men would be divided into these three classes, not based upon the circumstances of birth or wealth, but upon their abilities as developed through education. There would be no slaves. Justice was to be the basic principle which would unite the three classes and hold the government together.

Political scientists in all ages have read the *Republic*. Plato, in a time of slavery and of crude knowledge, dared to ask and attempt to answer important questions. For example, he asked, who are to be the rulers? His brief answer was, "Those men who in their whole life show the greatest eagerness to do what is good for their country, and the greatest repugnance to do what is against her interests."

divided into classes: nobles, peasants, clergy, and common people. Except for some of the nobles, life was not too happy for the people. Most of the peasants were serfs of the nobles, who gave them protection. In return the serfs gave up their freedom and served the noblemen.

But underneath this system was a smoldering striving for the rights of individuals. As the Middle Ages came to an end, this striving showed itself in the breakdown of the feudal system. Towns began to grow, feudal nobles began to be overthrown, more individuals began to strive for freedom and personal rights. To escape the tyranny of petty feudal barons, rulers of small territories sought the protection of a stronger ruler. Kings came into power. The first great nation-states of Europe emerged, and in the last centuries of the feudal period powerful kingdoms existed. One of these kingdoms, England, has been a chief contributor to our democratic ideas.

THE ENGLISH DOCUMENTS OF LIBERTY Three great documents from English history provide the foundation stones for our government today. These documents are the Great Charter of 1215, the Petition of Right of 1628, and the Bill of Rights of 1689.

To understand the importance of these documents, it must be realized that for hundreds of years in England strong, powerful kings had absolute control. They ruled by terror; their word was law. One of these ruthless men was William the Conqueror, who crossed the English Channel from France and defeated the English king at the Battle of Hastings in 1066. William was a strong ruler who forced his own feudal system on the land. But, in doing so, he established one precedent which later led to the great documents. Upon seizing the throne, he stated *in writing* that he would govern by the laws of an earlier English king. To him, this was a mere ges-

Emphasize the long historical evolutionary development of English democracy over a period of centuries.

ture. He intended to do as he pleased, but kings who followed him continued this practice of giving the people a written charter. Notice, however, that the kings *of their own free will* decided to sign these agreements. The people did not have the power; the king did.

THE GREAT CHARTER. Five generations after William the Conqueror, the nobles were struggling for power with another ruler, King John. Many barons were dissatisfied with his rule. He was cruel. He threw subjects into jail without trial. Law violators bought their freedom by giving him gifts. The barons finally revolted. In 1215, they forced the king to sign *their* agreement.

This agreement has come to be known as the Great Charter (Magna Carta). It was no charter given by the king. *It was a charter forced upon the king.* A power superior to that of the king had been won. A step had been taken toward the idea of men governing themselves.

The Great Charter deserves its name. While it applied only to the barons and did not help the common people, nevertheless it was a step forward from one-man rule. Its sixty-three articles contained the promise of many freedoms. Among them:

- *No freeman was to be imprisoned except by the judgment of his peers.*
- *The king was not to sell, delay, or refuse justice to anyone.*
- *No grain or other property was to be taken without proper payment.*
- *No church property was to be taken by the king.*
- *Before laying special taxes, the king was to call a meeting of the barons and the churchmen to receive their permission. (This was the beginning of the concept of "no taxation without representation.")*

- *Towns and villages were not to be oppressed.*

The Great Charter established the idea that the king was to rule by law instead of by personal whim. The idea of limited monarchy, a kingdom based on law, was born with the Great Charter. Some of our own ideas about liberty and minority rights can be traced to this document.

But the continued growth of self-government was a slow process. Generation after generation had to struggle against rulers who wanted to keep or regain power. In this struggle the idea of a lawmaking body developed. The British Parliament gradually became a recognized part of the English government.

Starting as a kind of "king's council" to review the king's request for special taxes, as provided in the Great Charter, the members gradually gained more power. They discovered that if a king wanted money badly enough he would grant them additional rights. By the process of refusing to give money to the king, Parliament won the right to make laws, even to know how money was spent, and claimed the right to name the new king when a king died. The idea of majority rule was being developed.

THE PETITION OF RIGHT. The struggles of Parliament to gain control over the kings and to be more representative of the people lasted for more than 400 years after the signing of the Great Charter. A climax was reached in 1628, when Parliament exerted its power and forced King Charles I to sign the famous Petition of Right. Again the representatives of the people had won in a dispute with the king.

The Petition of Right dealt with practical questions which had been argued with the king. It repeated the rights won under the Great Charter. The king agreed not to repeat certain acts of which he had been

The British Parliament Building is bordered by the Thames River in London. It took years of struggle and gradual change before Parliament developed into the democratic institution the world knows today. (Wolfe Worldwide Films)

guilty. Most important of all, the signing of the Petition showed again that the representatives of the people could force their will upon a stubborn king. Charles I was forced to recognize the fundamental rights of the people. England was becoming a *limited monarchy*, a term used to describe a kingdom in which the power of the king is reduced.

The struggles with Charles I continued for twenty more years. Finally, in 1649, a high court of justice, appointed by Parliament, held a trial and ordered the king put to death. For the next eleven years there was no king. In succession Parliament, Oliver Cromwell, and the army ruled. We would today call Cromwell a dictator. In the space of a few years England changed from a limited monarchy to a republic to a dictatorship and back to a limited monarchy.

THE ENGLISH BILL OF RIGHTS. The people were weary, unhappy, seeking stable government. They were so tired of rulers seeking absolute powers that in 1688, Parliament selected a new king and queen, William and Mary, from the Netherlands. This action settled for all time that Parliament had the supreme power in England.

This right of Parliament to name the king was won after years and years of struggle. The people did not want ever to lose their rights again. So in 1689 the third of the great English documents was adopted, the Bill of Rights.

The Bill of Rights of 1689 provided the basis for the freedoms guaranteed by the first ten amendments to our Constitution which we also call the Bill of Rights. By the English Bill of Rights:

- *The king was forbidden to put aside acts of Parliament.*
- *The king was not allowed to levy taxes without the consent of Parliament.*
- *An army could not be maintained in times of peace without permission of Parliament.*
- *Freedom of speech and debate in Parliament could not be taken away.*
- *Excessive punishments, fines, or bail were prohibited.*
- *The right to petition was guaranteed.*
- *The elections to Parliament were to be free.*
- *Parliaments were to meet frequently.*

The Bill of Rights of 1689, the Petition of Right of 1628, and the Great Charter of 1215 are the three fundamental documents which determine the form of English government. England does not have a written constitution. Its form of government depends upon custom, tradition, and laws passed by Parliament. The three great documents, therefore, provide a foundation for the protection of the rights of individuals.

While the last two of these great documents were being won from reluctant kings, the colonies in America were established and starting to grow. Jamestown, Virginia, was founded in 1607 and Plymouth, Massa-

54.

ſ[et]o by them done (this their condition considered) might be as firme as any patent; and in some respects more sure The forme was as followeth.

In y name of god Amen. we whose names are underwriten, the loyall subiects of our dread soueraigne Lord king Iames by y grace of god, of great Britaine, franc, & yreland king; defendor of y faith, &c

Haueing vndertaken, for y glorie of god, and aduancemente of y christian faith, and honour of our king & countrie, a voyage to plant y first colonie in y Northerne parts of Virginia. doe by these presents solemnly & mutualy in y presence of god, and one of another, couenant, & combine our selues togeather into a Ciuill body politick; for y better ordering, & preseruation & furtherance of y ends aforesaid: and by vertue hearof to Enacte,

An early manuscript copy of the Mayflower Compact. (Library of Congress)

chusetts, in 1620. How much did these struggles in England influence our forefathers?

THE DOCUMENTS OF LIBERTY IN AMERICA The time from the founding of Jamestown until today (more than 360 years) can be divided into two parts: (1) the period of colonization and (2) the period of independent government. The colonists were under the rule of England for nearly 170 years. For more than 190 years we have had an independent government. During the beginning years of our history, therefore, English political ideas were predominant.

THE MAYFLOWER COMPACT. The Mayflower Compact illustrates this influence. The Pilgrims, before landing at Plymouth, made some important decisions. While the Mayflower was at anchor off the Atlantic coast, this group drew up a document that has become sacred in our history.

These men had crossed the ocean in search of freedom. They were a weary group, and some members were boasting how they would use "their own liberty" when they landed. Others talked of "discontent" and made "mutinous speeches." Some simple kind of organization was needed if their colony was to be successful.

So before landing they reached an agreement that all would abide by the will of the majority. By formal written agreement signed on November 11, 1620, they promised to "frame just and equal laws . . . for the general good of the Colony," and to give "due submission and obedience to these laws."

The Mayflower Compact showed that these forty-one men could rule themselves. They put their desire into written form. It would have been easy for them to pick one of their strong leaders and give him the power to rule. But their past experience taught them to use a system of majority rule. They put their faith in each other and not in one-man rule.

The distinguished Harvard historian, Samuel Eliot Morison, says of the Mayflower Compact,

It is the earliest known case in American history of people establishing a government for themselves by mutual agreement. Significant, also, is the opening

23

Discuss how the substance of these American documents is related to man's earlier democratic achievements and ideas as described by the authors.

THE MAYFLOWER COMPACT

In the name of God Amen. We whose names are underwriten, the loyall subjects of our dread soveraigne Lord King James by the grace of God, of great Britaine, Franc, & Ireland king, defender of the faith, &c.

Haveing undertaken, for the glorie of God, and advancements of the Christian faith and honour of our king & countrie, a voyage to plant the first colonie in the Northerne parts of Virginia, doe by these presents solemnly & mutualy in the presence of God, and one of another, covenant & combine our selves togeather into a civill body politick; for our better ordering, & preservation & furtherance of the ends aforesaid; and by vertue hearof to enacte, constitute, and frame shuch just & equall lawes, ordinances, Acts, constitutions, & offices, from time to time, as shall be thought most meete & convenient for the generall good of the Colonie: unto which we promise all due submission and obedience.

In witnes whereof we have hereunder subscribed our names at Cap-Codd the ·11· of November, in the year the raigne of our soveraigne Lord King James of England, France, & Ireland the eighteenth and of Scotland the fiftie fourth. An°: Dom. 1620.

John Carver	William Mullins	Thomas Rogers	John Billington	Richard Britterige
William Bradford	William White	Thomas Tinker	Moses Fletcher	George Soule
Edward Winslow	Richard Warren	John Rigdale	John Goodman	Richard Clarke
William Brewster	John Howland	Edward Fuller	Degory Priest	Richard Gardiner
Isaac Allerton	Stephen Hopkins	John Turner	Thomas Williams	John Allerton
Myles Standish	Edward Tilley	Francis Eaton	Gilbert Winslow	Thomas English
John Alden	John Tilley	James Chilton	Edmund Margeson	Edward Doty
Samuel Fuller	Francis Cooke	John Crakston	Peter Brown	Edward Leister
Christopher Martin				

invocation, indicating that these men believed Almighty God to be the author of all government. Moreover, their promise of 'all due submission and obedience' to the laws they themselves would pass and the authorities they would elect indicates their belief that political liberty is fundamental to all liberty; that without it religion cannot flourish or social order be maintained.[1]

THE COLONIAL AGREEMENTS. The colonies at Plymouth and at Jamestown were based on agreements with commercial companies which had been granted rights

to colonize by the king. The other eleven of the thirteen original colonies, over the next century and a quarter, were also established by written agreements between the colonists and those who had granted them the right to colonize. These colonial agreements provided for three different forms of colonial government: royal, proprietary, and charter.

The royal colonies were ruled directly by the king of England, who appointed the governor and a council, or upper house, of a legislature. A lower house, or popular assembly, was elected by the colonists. The governor, subject to orders from the king, tended to be the strong influence, although the lower house provided a forum for com-

[1] Morison, Samuel Eliot. "The Mayflower Compact," in Boorstin, Daniel J. ed., *An American Primer.* University of Chicago Press. ©1966 by The University of Chicago.

plaints and opposition. Much of the dissent which led to the American Revolution arose in the popular assemblies of the royal colonies.

There were seven royal colonies: Georgia, New Hampshire, New Jersey, New York, North Carolina, South Carolina, and Virginia.

The proprietary colonies were private ownership colonies ruled by individuals who had been given the right of ownership by a grant from the king. The *proprietor* received a grant of land from the king with the right to rule almost as he saw fit. The three proprietary colonies were Delaware, Maryland, and Pennsylvania. Lord Baltimore and William Penn were the original proprietors of Maryland and Pennsylvania. Delaware was part of the Penn family domain until the American Revolution.

The proprietor appointed the governor, authorized a legislature, established courts, and created local governments. The first assembly in Maryland forced Lord Baltimore to accept its laws and became a real legislative body. In Pennsylvania, William Penn, as a Quaker, believed in the equality of men and considered his colony to be a "holy experiment." In a document, *The Frame of Government,* the colony was granted a system of government with more power for the colonists than was customary.

The charter colonies were governed by the "freemen" under a charter granted by the king to the colonists as a group. Connecticut, Massachusetts, and Rhode Island were the charter colonies, although Massachusetts was forced in 1691 to take a new charter which made it a royal colony.

In the charter colonies the governor was elected by the colonists, as were the members of the legislature. The governor had no veto over the acts of the legislature.

Both Rhode Island and Connecticut were started by Puritans who had decided to leave the original Massachusetts colony. Their charters, based on government by the consent of the governed, were so advanced that they served as their state constitutions after the American Revolution. Connecticut has been credited with having the first written constitution in history that truly created a government. This document, the *Fundamental Orders of Connecticut,* written in 1639, continued the main features of the Massachusetts charter but provided that a governor could not serve successive terms and that there should be no religious test for citizenship.

TRENDS IN COLONIAL GOVERNMENTS. Under these colonial agreements, the king and his ministers expected the colonists, as British subjects,.to be loyal to the king; but, in turn, the colonists expected to have the same rights as the people in native England. Over the years, because of the great distance and the slow communication between England and the colonies, four general trends arose from these colonial governments.

The *first* trend was for colonial governors to be unpopular. The governors, as the king's representatives, had to enforce unpopular laws. The governors opposed the legislatures when their acts were against British policy. As the conflicts between England and the colonists increased, the dislike and even hatred of the governors grew. After the American Revolution, the powers of governors of the new states were reduced because of these earlier experiences with colonial governors.

The *second* trend was the result of the first: The colonial legislatures became the popular branch of government. Representative government had started with the earliest colony. In 1619 the House of Burgesses had been established in the Virginia colony. This was the first representative assembly

in this country. Gradually legislatures, with the lower house elected by the citizens, were established in other colonies. These legislatures passed many laws on local affairs. They were the protectors of the rights of the colonists.

Arguments were frequent with the governor as to whether an issue was a local matter or whether it concerned England too. These disputes, especially those on tax-ation and the spending of tax money, caused much ill-feeling. They caused bitter feeling toward the governors, but the popularity of the legislatures continued to grow. After the American Revolution, the legislatures were respected and received the greatest powers in the state governments.

A *third* trend was that the courts of the colonial period set the pattern for our court system of today. The colonial courts were

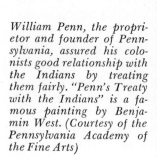

William Penn, the proprietor and founder of Pennsylvania, assured his colonists good relationship with the Indians by treating them fairly. "Penn's Treaty with the Indians" is a famous painting by Benjamin West. (Courtesy of the Pennsylvania Academy of the Fine Arts)

copies of those in England. Judges decided cases on the basis of decisions in earlier English cases. Trial by jury was used in the colonies. Methods of examining witnesses, the rules for admitting evidence, the idea of "being innocent until proven guilty" were used in the colonial courts. The judges were usually appointed by the governors. Final appeals were made to the king.

Since the courts tended to follow English laws, the people looked to their legislatures for correction of fundamental wrongs, for they did not trust courts completely. Some court decisions, however, helped establish freedom of religion, press, and speech.

One famous case was that of John Peter Zenger. Zenger was a brave newspaper editor. He printed criticisms of the governor of New York. The governor had Zenger arrested and kept him in prison for several months. Finally, he was brought to trial in 1735 and the jury found him not guilty. This trial is one of the great trials in history because it helped establish a free press.

EFFORTS TOWARD UNITY. A *fourth* trend from this colonial period was the opportunity for the individual colonies and their leaders to explore the possibilities of joint action. Long before the writing of the United States Constitution the colonies had experiences with working together.

The New England Confederation was the first attempt to unite. In 1643 the Massachusetts Bay, Plymouth, Connecticut, and New Haven colonies formed a "league of friendship" for mutual defense against attacks. The colonies agreed in writing to provide money and soldiers in case of war. This essentially was a business arrangement to protect themselves from the Indians, the Dutch on the west, and the French to the

The Capitol Building at Williamsburg was the site of the Virginia House of Burgesses. The House was established in 1619 and was the earliest form of representative government in the colonies. (Colonial Williamsburg, Williamsburg, Virginia)

north. Massachusetts Bay dominated the confederation, but ten years after the agreement, that colony refused to fight the Dutch and the confederation declined as a result. It was finally disbanded in 1684.

Twelve years later, 1696, William Penn suggested a plan for the colonies to cooperate on matters dealing with trade and with crime. The scheme was elaborate and was never tried.

In the middle of the next century, 1754, Benjamin Franklin proposed the Albany Plan. This plan for cooperation among the colonies was presented at a conference in Albany, New York, attended by delegates from seven colonies. The conference had been called to deal with problems of trade and attacks by French and Indians. Franklin suggested the formation of a council of delegates, chosen by each of the thirteen colonies, which would meet annually to regulate Indian affairs, maintain military forces, and levy taxes for the common defense. Adopted by the conference, the plan was rejected by the individual colonies because they were not ready to give up their individual powers over these matters.

Eleven years later, the conflicts with England over tax and trade policies led to the *Stamp Act Congress* of 1765. Nine colonies with twenty-seven delegates met in New York City and prepared a Declaration of Rights and Grievances protesting that the king and Parliament did not have the right to tax them. One clause stated that it was an "undoubted right of Englishmen, that no taxes be imposed on them but with their own consent, given personally or by their representatives." The four colonies not represented—New Hampshire, Virginia, North Carolina, and Georgia—later approved this Declaration.

In the next decade resistance to the British policies increased the cooperation among the colonies. *Committees of Correspondence* were initiated in 1772 by Samuel Adams in Boston. Within a year almost every town in Massachusetts had a committee, and within another year similar committees had spread throughout the colonies. These committees provided a network for spreading information and the beginnings of organized political opposition.

In early September, 1774, the *First Continental Congress* was held in Philadelphia, with every colony except Georgia represented. For almost two months the delegates discussed ways to safeguard the rights of the colonies and ideas for settling their differences with England. A Declaration of Rights was sent to George III. A trade boycott against England was planned, with committees named in every town to see that the boycott was enforced. When the Congress adjourned in late October, it was agreed that a second meeting of the Continental Congress would be held the following May if the British government had not satisfied their demands. All the colonies, including Georgia, approved these actions.

THE DECLARATION OF INDEPENDENCE

The demands of the colonists were not met. The differences continued and in Massachusetts a British army under General Gage tried to coerce the people to accept Britain's regulations. In an effort to seize stores of munitions and to arrest Samuel Adams and John Hancock, the British marched on Lexington and Concord, where on April 19, 1775, the first armed conflict of the American Revolution took place.

Adams and Hancock with the help of Paul Revere escaped and proceeded to Philadelphia, where the Second Continental Congress began meeting on May 10, 1775, in Independence Hall. Hancock was selected president of this Congress and

George Washington was appointed commander-in-chief of the continental army. For nearly five years this Second Continental Congress was the government—the first really national government. Legislative power was held by the assembly with each colony having one vote. Executive power was carried on through appointed committees.

Efforts to arrive at peaceful compromises were tried for a year and failed. Increasingly there were demands for independence. On May 15, 1776, the Congress authorized the colonies to set up state governments. All the states, except Rhode Island and Connecticut, adopted written state constitutions. In those two charter colonies, which the citizens already controlled, the wording of the charters was slightly changed; and then the charters were used as state constitutions.

On July 4, 1776, the Congress adopted the Declaration of Independence. The Declaration begins with two paragraphs stating beliefs about the nature of man and the nature of government. These paragraphs are considered to be among the most eloquent and influential ever written. One sentence is probably one of the best known in all the writings of mankind. This sentence is: "We hold these truths to be self-evident: that all men are created equal; that they are endowed by their Creator with certain unalienable rights; that among these are life, liberty, and the pursuit of happiness." (The complete text of the Declaration of Independence is in the Appendix.)

After the two opening paragraphs there is a long list of wrongs committed by the king and Parliament against the colonists. These wrongs formed the campaign document, or the political platform, for the American Revolution. They showed the world why independence was demanded.

The original writing of the Declaration of Independence was done by Thomas Jefferson. After changes were made, the Declaration was signed by "the Representatives of the United States of America in General Congress Assembled." The Declaration became the birth certificate of our nation.

THE ARTICLES OF CONFEDERATION

A small group of thirteen states was at war with the great English nation. Troops were trained. Money was raised. Many difficult political problems had to be solved while the war was going on. Could the thirteen new states do all the things that would need to be done? Would the revolt of the colonies end in rule by a dictator, as had happened in England during the civil war when Cromwell came into power?

The Continental Congress, which was the emergency government, gave thought to these matters. Busy as the representatives were with the conduct of the war, they found time to develop a plan for strengthening the union which was adopted on November 15, 1777. This plan, the Articles of Confederation, is usually not listed as one of the great documents of our history. The plan had many defects, as will be discussed in the next chapter. Yet in some respects the Articles belong with our list of great documents because this plan of government took one more step toward representative government.

War pressures could have led the Continental Congress to move back to one-man rule. Instead the colonies chose to form "a firm league of friendship." They decided on a "perpetual union" for "common defense, the security of their liberties," and their "mutual and general welfare." Citizenship was not lost when a person moved

Thomas Jefferson, author of the Declaration of Independence, was all his life a staunch defender of liberty and the rights of the common man. (White House Historical Association)

The Continental Congress adopted the Declaration of Independence in this room in Independence Hall, Philadelphia. Do Americans today agree with the fundamental ideas expressed in this document? For example, how many people would sign a statement that "it is the right of the people to alter or abolish" their government? (National Park Service photo)

His Excell GEORGE WASHINGTON, Esq*
GENERAL and COMMANDER in CHIEF of the Allied Armies,
Supporting the Independence *of* AMERICA.

George Washington is revered by his countrymen because the respect and esteem he commanded, both here and abroad, played a vital role in the successful launching of the young nation. This engraving by John Norman was after a painting by Benjamin Blyth in 1782. (The Free Library of Philadelphia)

from one state to another—the first step toward national citizenship. The defects of the Articles of Confederation were too many; a stronger constitutional government had to arise. But the Constitution of the United States is the direct result of eight years of experience with government under the Articles. The Articles of Confederation were one of the stepping-stones to our government today.

AN APPRECIATION Before examining the greatest document in all our history, the *Constitution of the United States,* a pause to express gratitude for our inheritance is in order. By accident of birth, most of us are citizens of the United States.

Because we were fortunate in our ancestry, we are privileged to live in one of the places in the world where each human being is entitled to respect. Freedom, self-government, the right to "life, liberty and the pursuit of happiness" are guaranteed.

Why? Because those who lived before us cared about these things. From religious institutions we have gained moral ideas that are basic to all free government. From Greece, from Rome, from England, from

I have never had a feeling, politically, that did not spring from the sentiments embodied in the Declaration of Independence.

—ABRAHAM LINCOLN, Speech in Independence Hall, February 22, 1861.

the colonies we have inherited ideas that make our lives better.

The writing of a few great documents in past centuries has preserved for us a way of life by which "equal opportunity" is open to all. Millions of people in other parts of the world are still struggling to gain the freedom which we have.

The silent prayer of most of mankind might well be like that of one high school student who ended his Constitution Day speech by saying, "My prayer is that my generation may be equal to the task of preserving, protecting, and improving the free government under which we live."

No one can predict the future. The miracles of invention in the next few decades may be as strange to us as airplanes, television, atomic energy, and space flight would have been to our great-grandfathers. Our past history shows that our governmental institutions can be adapted to these great changes.

Democracy frees the creative ability of people. Democracy is a starter and mobilizer of human energy. Our system of government has been a powerful factor in the industrial, scientific, and cultural growth of our country. While perfection has certainly not been achieved, progress has been made.

Our future strength lies in correcting weaknesses in our country and helping peoples in other parts of the world understand and gain freedom. We have inherited great ideas from the past. Our job is to help these ideas work in today's world and to pass them on to the next generation.

THE FREEDOM TIMELINE

1971	Twenty-sixth Amendment
1961	Twenty-third Amendment
1920	Nineteenth Amendment
1870	Fifteenth Amendment
1868	Fourteenth Amendment
1865	Thirteenth Amendment
1863	Emancipation Proclamation
1791	Bill of Rights
1787	Constitution of the United States
1777	Articles of Confederation
1776	Declaration of Independence
1772	Committees of Correspondence
1765	Stamp Act Congress
1754	Albany Plan of Union
1735	Trial of John Peter Zenger
1696	William Penn's Plan of Cooperation
1689	ENGLISH BILL OF RIGHTS
1643	New England Confederation
1639	Fundamental Orders of Connecticut
1628	PETITION OF RIGHT (ENGLAND)
1620	Mayflower Compact
1215	THE GREAT CHARTER (ENGLAND)

STUDY QUESTIONS

1. What have religious groups contributed to the American way of life?

2. What were the special contributions of the Greeks to our system of government? What were the special contributions of the Romans?

3. What conditions show that man had lost his freedom during the feudal period?

4. What were the conditions that caused the writing of the Great Charter? The Petition of Right? The Bill of Rights of 1689? What were the more important ideas in each of these documents?

5. Why was the Mayflower Compact written? Why is it still important?

6. How did the royal, proprietary, and charter colonies differ?

7. Why did colonial legislatures become popular with the people? Why did the popularity of the governors decline?

CONCEPTS AND GENERALIZATIONS

1
The fundamental ideas about self-government have evolved over a long period of time.

2
Beliefs about the nature of man, including the worth of each individual, have been derived from the great religions.

3
Greece was the birthplace of democracy, while Rome adapted this idea to the republican system of government by representative officials.

4
The liberties we have are built on those which were wrested from English kings over a period of hundreds of years.

5
Governors were unpopular while legislatures rose in popularity during colonial times.

6
Written constitutions, court systems, cooperation among states were developed in the pre-revolutionary period.

7
Among the great documents in the world's history are: the Great Charter, the Petition of Right, the Bill of Rights, the Mayflower Compact, the Fundamental Orders of Connecticut, the colonial agreements, the Declaration of Independence, the Articles of Confederation, and the Constitution of the United States.

8. How did the courts of the colonial period contribute to our judicial system today?

9. How did the experiences of the colonies in working together help in the later years of the American Revolution?

10. What are the chief features of the Declaration of Independence?

11. Why did the colonists form a confederation rather than a system in which some popular colonial leader would have had great power?

IDEAS FOR DISCUSSION

1. Does the history of the growth of democratic ideas prove the truth of the statement "Eternal vigilance is the price of liberty"?

2. Writers have stated that our government is "one of rules and not of rulers." Why is it important to have basic ideas recorded in writing?

3. The head of a famous law school has said, "In the long run ideas are more powerful than weapons." Test this belief by the main ideas of this chapter.

4. The Fifth Amendment to the United States Constitution states that "no person shall . . . be deprived of life, liberty, or property without due process of law." From which of the great documents of English liberty is this idea taken?

5. Do you think it was necessary for our forefathers to try a confederation before they tried a federal system? Why?

6. An air force major, after his return from fighting in Korea, said at a Flag Day anniversary celebration: "Men in battle have to have a belief, else they couldn't fight, because in battle there is always fear. It is only a belief in what they are fighting for that enables men to overcome that fear. Night fighting is a lonely and fearful existence. You're alone in an alien sky. Why doesn't a pilot just drop his bombs anywhere and return? What makes a rifleman move ahead when every impulse is to pull back? It is a simple, strong belief in American traditions." How does one develop "a simple, strong belief in American traditions"? Does this quotation express the feelings of those who fought in Vietnam?

7. There is a saying that "liberty is always dangerous, but it is the safest thing that we have." What does this mean?

8. Anthony Eden, a British prime minister, said in a speech in the United States, "Democracy is a university in which we learn from one another. It can never be a barracks where blind obedience is the first essential." Do you agree with this statement? What does it mean in terms of your education?

9. Do you agree with Aristotle's ideas of who should rule? Why?

10. The Declaration of Independence has been described as "a radical and revolutionary document." Do you agree? Could such a document be written in the United States today? When is revolution justified?

11. Astronaut John H. Glenn, Jr., speaking before a joint session of Congress, a few days after his space flight, said, "I still get a hard-to-define feeling inside when the flag goes by—and I know you do, too. Today as we rode up Pennsylvania Avenue from the White House and saw the tremendous outpouring of feeling on the part of so many thousands of our people I got this same feeling all over again. Let us hope none of us ever loses it." What would you call the "feeling" Glenn mentions? How do you think he got this feeling?

12. How can you show gratitude for the "blessings of liberty," our heritage from previous generations?

THINGS TO DO

1. Rewrite the Preamble to the Constitution, or the first few sentences of the Declaration of Independence, in words that you would use today.

2. Keep a record of the times you use, hear, or see the words *democracy* and *republic* as descriptions of our system of government. Which word is more commonly used?

3. Prepare a special report on one of the world's great religions.

4. Use the pattern of a television quiz game for a part of one class period in which students try to find out which great document you are representing.

5. Write a 300-word essay describing the contributions to American life of one of the following: Aristotle, Jesus, King Charles I, William Penn, Benjamin Franklin, or Samuel Adams.

6. Write a radio script on "The Life of John Peter Zenger," following the general historical-type radio and television programs.

7. Draw a cartoon to illustrate our debt to the writers of the great documents of democratic ideas.

8. Invite a local judge or lawyer to class to discuss the importance of the great documents of liberty on our lives today.

9. Prepare a bulletin board, with the help of other students, to show the origins of our fundamental ideas of democracy.

10. Hold a panel discussion on the topic, "Improvements that need to be made in our community to live up to our democratic ideals."

FURTHER READINGS

Adams, Mildred, THE RIGHT TO BE PEOPLE. J. B. Lippincott Company, 1966.

Baker, Benjamin, and Friedelbaum, Stanley H., GOVERNMENT IN THE UNITED STATES. Houghton Mifflin Co., 1966. Chapters 1, 2.

Burns, James M., and Peltason, J. W., GOVERNMENT BY THE PEOPLE. Prentice-Hall, Inc., 1972. Chapter 2.

Fink, Sam, THE FIFTY-SIX WHO SIGNED. McCall Books, 1971.

McDonald, Forrest, E. PLURIBUS UNUM: THE FOUNDATIONS OF THE AMERICAN REPUBLIC. Houghton Mifflin Co., 1965.

Rossiter, Clinton, SEEDTIME OF THE REPUBLIC: THE ORIGIN OF THE AMERICAN TRADITION OF POLITICAL LIBERTY. Harcourt, Brace & World, 1953.

Saye, Albert B. and others, PRINCIPLES OF AMERICAN GOVERNMENT. Prentice-Hall, Inc., 1966. Chapter 2.

Shapiro, Martin (ed.), THE CONSTITUTION OF THE UNITED STATES AND RELATED DOCUMENTS. Appleton-Century-Crofts, Inc., 1966.

Whitton, Mary O., THESE WERE THE WOMEN, U.S.A. 1776-1860. Hastings House Publishers, 1954.

Young, William H., OGG AND RAY'S INTRODUCTION TO AMERICAN GOVERNMENT. Appleton-Century-Crofts, Inc., 1966. Chapter 2.

AMENDMENT—a change or alteration; a formal addition to a constitution, making a change in the structure or operation of government.

BILL OF ATTAINDER—a law passed to punish a person without giving him a judicial trial.

CHECK AND BALANCE—a system by which each branch of government has influence over other branches.

COMPROMISE—a settlement in which each side in a dispute makes concessions, each giving up some of its demands.

CONSTITUTION—the system of fundamental laws or principles under which a government operates.

CONSTITUTIONALITY—the quality or state of being in accord with or consistent with a constitution.

EXECUTIVE—the branch or part of the government which enforces the law and carries out or performs governmental activities.

EX POST FACTO—a law passed to punish a person for acts that were not illegal before the passage of the law.

HABEAS CORPUS—an order of the court requiring that an imprisoned person be brought before the court to determine whether his imprisonment is legal.

JUDICIAL—the branch or part of the government which interprets laws and administers justice.

LEGISLATIVE—the branch or part of the government which makes laws.

RATIFICATION—vote for approval; the act of approving a constitution.

VETO—the refusal of an executive (President, governor, mayor) to sign a bill passed by a legislature.

THE LANGUAGE OF GOVERNMENT

Familiarize students with the Constitution by referring to the annotated copy in the Appendix. These annotations, following many paragraphs of the Constitution, are designed by the authors to aid the students in understanding this basic document of American government and to visualize the manner in which this document pertains to our modern society.

3

The Constitution

About a hundred years after the founding of the government of the United States, a great British statesman, William E. Gladstone, stated ". . . the American Constitution is the most wonderful work ever struck off at a given time by the brain and purpose of man." This Constitution was unique in the development of governments at that time, because it was based on the

These young men and women being sworn into the Army will help to "provide for the common defense." The framers of the Constitution were aware of the necessity to provide security against attack. (Courtesy U.S. Army, Philadelphia RMS)

The U.S. Constitution is the oldest written constitution still in use in the world. Discuss how a basic structure of law written in the 18th century can still be fundamental for a society on the brink of interplanetary space travel.

idea that the power of government belongs to the people and that this power should be stated in writing.

It was the people who were setting up this government. It was the people who were to control the government of the nation. The delegates to the constitutional convention put their faith in the people rather than in one person or in a special ruling class. While they did not put complete trust in all the people (for not all adults were allowed to vote), they recognized that governments "derive their just powers from the consent of the governed." At that time, too, they felt there were some dangers in majority rule and wrote into the Constitution some limitations on rule by the people. For example, they did not give the people the right to elect the President or senators *directly.*

The Constitution of the United States is a brief and simple document. It can be read in a half hour, but some scholars spend their lives studying it. Its contents are organized in a clear, direct, logical way.

This "wonderful work" has stood the test of time. While it has been amended, interpreted, and modified in usage, it has been the basis of our government for nearly two centuries.

THE PREAMBLE The Constitution begins with a statement called the *Preamble* which reads:

The United States Constitution ranks above every other written constitution for the intrinsic excellence of its scheme, its adaptation to the circumstances of the people, the simplicity, brevity, and precision of its language, its judicious mixture of definiteness in principle with elasticity in details.

—JAMES BRYCE, British historian and statesman in *American Commonwealth*, 1888.

We the people of the United States, in order to form a more perfect union, establish justice, insure domestic tranquility, provide for the common defense, promote the general welfare, and secure the blessings of liberty to ourselves and our posterity, do ordain and establish this Constitution for the United States of America.

Thus it was the people of the United States who established the Constitution and the government which developed from it. They did so for a number of reasons which form the clauses in the Preamble. Let us briefly look at each of them.

"IN ORDER TO FORM A MORE PERFECT UNION." It was the year 1787 when this was written. The War for American Independence had been over for a number of years. The union of the thirteen states under the Articles of Confederation was beginning to break up, so a group of representatives had come together to remedy the defects in the Articles of Confederation. Instead they wrote a new Constitution which was intended "to form a more perfect union."

"ESTABLISH JUSTICE." This Constitution was to provide the basis for laws and courts which would assure everyone just treatment. The colonies had passed through a period in which they had experienced injustices. The government which they were establishing was to be one based on a Constitution insuring justice to all citizens.

"INSURE DOMESTIC TRANQUILITY." If the colonies, now freed from the rule of a European power, were to develop into a nation, they needed order in managing their affairs. The Constitution was to provide for such order and peace at home. This was a primary consideration if the United States was to take its place among the nations of the world.

Ask the students to find defects in the Articles of Confederation which made this form of government impractical (Appendix). Compare their discoveries with later text.

"PROVIDE FOR THE COMMON DE-FENSE." The Constitution was to provide for defending the states against any enemy from without. The colonies had joined forces in their struggle against England, and now they were establishing a Constitution to unite them in the event that any future threat would be made to their security.

"PROMOTE THE GENERAL WEL-FARE." This Constitution was to be the basis for building a nation in which the welfare of each person was to be the concern of all. The makers of the Constitution believed that whatever promoted the well-being of any individual helped the total group.

"AND SECURE THE BLESSINGS OF LIBERTY TO OURSELVES AND OUR POSTERITY." The blessings of liberty had been won through a long and bitter struggle which began at Lexington and ended at Yorktown. The Constitution was established to insure that these hard-won freedoms should be made secure for those who had won them and also for the millions of citizens who were to live under the Constitution in the years to come.

Those were the reasons why the framers of the Constitution believed it to be important that the people "ordain and establish this Constitution for the United States of America." They were men of vision, for the reasons stated by them have been important through the nearly two centuries that the government under this Constitution has been in operation. Wise they were too in developing a framework which has stood the test of time in welding the states together into a workable union.

Many times during the following years one or the other of these reasons became the basis for passing a new law or for giving a new interpretation of an existing one. Throughout the years, our Congresses have passed laws, our Presidents have acted, and our courts have interpreted laws so that the union might be strengthened and so that life, liberty, and the pursuit of happiness would be furthered. All of this has been an outgrowth of the original Constitution written by the framers in 1787.

THE ARTICLES OF THE CONSTITUTION   The Constitution which they wrote has seven articles following the Preamble. These seven articles provide the foundation for our government.

ARTICLE I deals with the *legislative* branch of the government. It contains ten sections which define the powers and duties of the Congress and the qualifications of congressmen. This article also sets forth the procedures for the election of members of the House of Representatives and the Senate. It describes in detail how laws are to be enacted and the limitations placed upon Congress and the states.

ARTICLE II deals with the *executive* branch of the government. It contains four sections which define the qualifications of the President, the method of his election, his powers and duties, and how he may be removed from office.

ARTICLE III deals with the *judicial* branch of the government. It contains three sections which provide for the setting up of a system of courts. This article defines the powers and limitations of the courts.

ARTICLE IV deals with certain *relationships among the states.* It tells how new states are to be admitted to the Union and guarantees to each state a republican form of government.

ARTICLE V gives the procedures for *amending* the Constitution.

ARTICLE VI contains *general provisions*

The signing of the Constitution climaxed four months of hard work, debate, and compromise. The delegates had fulfilled Washington's plea to "raise a standard to which the wise and honest may repair." (The National Archives, Washington, D.C.)

for the orderly change of the government under the Articles of the Confederation to government under the Constitution. It declares the Constitution—together with all laws and treaties of the United States—to be the supreme law of the land, and federal and state officials shall be bound by oath or affirmation to support it.

ARTICLE VII deals with the method of *ratification* of the Constitution. It states that the Constitution was to be in effect when ratified by nine states. Within a year after its writing, the Constitution had been ratified by eleven states. The new government was started in the spring of 1789 with the first Congress and with George Washington as the first President.

Amendments which have changed the original document in significant ways have been added to the Constitution over the years. Of the twenty-six amendments, the first ten, called the Bill of Rights, were added in 1791, two years after the adoption

of the Constitution. The Eleventh and Twelfth Amendments were added in the next thirteen years. Sixty years elapsed before the next three amendments were added—after the Civil War. The next two amendments, the Sixteenth and Seventeenth, were added in 1913. In the rest of this twentieth century, nine other amendments have been added. But one of these, the Twenty-first, repealed the Eighteenth, which had prohibited the manufacture, sale, or transportation of intoxicating liquors. This listing of amendments made over nearly two centuries indicates that the amending process has not been used very often. (The text of the Constitution and its amendments, together with explanations, are given in the Appendix.)

THE ARTICLES OF CONFEDERATION

How did the Constitution come into being? Why was it

"CHRIST · CHURCH · PATRIOTS · 1790"

TO·THE·GLORY·OF·GOD·AND IN·LOVING·MEMORY·OF JOHN·E·CRETH BORN·1839·DIED·1907 AND·TWELVE·YEARS FOR·NINETEEN·YEARS·A·VESTRYMAN RECTOR'S·WARDEN·OF·THIS·PARISH HEATON

The delegates to the Constitutional Convention were keenly aware of the seriousness of their undertaking. (Above) In this portion of a stained-glass window in Christ Church, Philadelphia, the delegates are shown seeking divine guidance for their deliberations. Many delegates, including Washington, worshiped in this church. An exterior view is shown at the right. (Courtesy of Christ Church, Philadelphia)

written? To learn the answers to these and other questions about the Constitution we need to examine the earlier document, the Articles of Confederation. During the War for American Independence the Second Continental Congress had taken on the powers necessary to wage war and to carry on domestic affairs. In 1777 this Congress developed a plan for a union of the states.

The Articles of Confederation gave the details of the plan. Since it was necessary

Explain the following: Under the Articles, Americans proclaimed that they were one nation, yet acted as though they were thirteen.

for all states to ratify the Articles before they could become effective, it was not until 1781 that the Confederation of the United States actually came into existence. In that year Maryland, the last of the thirteen states, ratified the Articles.

SHORTCOMINGS IN THE ARTICLES OF CONFEDERATION. Defects in the system of government established by the Articles of Confederation quickly became apparent. The government under the Articles of Confederation was unable to assure the rights proclaimed in the Declaration of Independence; it was weak and ineffective. We will perhaps best understand why this was so if we understand how that government differed from our present system of government.

There was no president with the responsibility to enforce national laws. There were no national courts. The Congress of the Confederation consisted of one house in which each state had one vote, even though a state might be represented by more than one delegate. Furthermore, the members of the Congress were responsible to the states, they received their salaries from the states, and the state legislatures could recall them at will.

The Congress of the Confederation did not make laws by a majority vote as our Congress does today. Nine votes were required instead of a majority of seven. The members came together to take care of affairs which were the concern of the several states. But they were not successful in handling these governmental affairs adequately.

The weaknesses of the government under the Articles of Confederation were due to a number of causes. First, as has already been mentioned, the men in the Congress were responsible, not to the people, but to the state legislatures by whom they were elected.

Second, the Confederation government had no power to tax; the Congress could only request money from the states, and these requests were often not heeded. Thus the Confederation government was frequently unable to carry on its business because of lack of money.

Third, the Congress had no power to regulate commerce with foreign countries and among the states. As a result various states had different tariff rates. They even began to charge duty on goods going from one state to another. This practice increased bad feelings among the states and made cooperation difficult.

Fourth, since there was no executive and there were no national courts, it was difficult to enforce laws passed by the Congress.

Fifth, since a vote of nine of the states was necessary to pass a law, it was even difficult to get any laws passed. Amendments to the Articles of Confederation were still more difficult to make, because the unanimous vote of all states was needed for amendments.

At least two other important factors were responsible for the gradual breakdown of the Confederation among the states and for the ridicule it was receiving from other nations.

The first of these was the argument among the states about the vote in the Congress. Under the Articles of Confederation each state had one vote in Congress regardless of its size. The states with the larger number of people wanted representation and voting in Congress to be based on population. But the smaller states continued to hold out for one vote for each state.

The second factor in the breakdown was the amount of paper money in circulation. Both the Confederation and the individual states had issued large amounts of paper money. Since it was well known that the paper money was almost worthless, trade and business suffered. Prices rose adding to the difficulties of the new nation.

Comparing the list of grievances in the Declaration of Independence and the provisions for governing in the Articles of Confederation, discuss the probable reasons the colonists were at first reluctant to have a stronger central government.

ATTEMPTS TO CORRECT THE WEAKNESSES. Such leaders as Washington, Hamilton, and Madison began to worry about this situation. Many people were convinced that something had to be done to strengthen the national government, to improve relations among the states, to establish prestige with other countries, and to get a good money system. These men felt that the Articles of Confederation needed revision.

A meeting was called by Maryland and Virginia to discuss disagreements regarding toll charges on vessels in Chesapeake Bay. This meeting was watched with interest throughout the states. The successful solution of this dispute prompted the calling of a general meeting of representatives of all the states at Annapolis in 1786. Although nine states had appointed delegates, only five of them were represented at the meeting. With only five of the thirteen states represented, little could be accomplished. However, the men present called upon all states to send delegates to another meeting to be held in a few months.

After some delay this meeting was approved by the Confederation. The states chose seventy-four delegates to meet in Philadelphia. They were appointed in response to the request "to take into consideration the situation of the United States, to devise such further provisions as shall appear to them necessary to render the constitution of the federal government adequate to the exigencies of the union."

All of the states except Rhode Island were represented at the meeting. Nineteen of the delegates of the other states did not attend for a variety of reasons. Most of the other delegates were late in arriving. In fact, it took almost two weeks to get enough delegates together to begin work. The meeting began near the end of May in 1787. A total of fifty-five delegates attended all or part of the convention. About three-fourths of them were regular in their attendance, while the other one-fourth either came late to Philadelphia, returned home for extended periods of time, or left the convention early.

WRITING THE CONSTITUTION

These fifty-five men who came together had been instructed to revise the Articles of Confederation. They soon realized, however, that revision was not enough. So they set to work to write an entirely new framework for the government of the United States.

By common agreement these men did their work in secret; that is, they agreed that their discussions and decisions were not to be made public until the task had been finished. This was done in order to give them sufficient time to attempt to solve the problems of the young and struggling nation without alarming the public and also to keep others from exerting undue pressure on the delegates.

The fifty-five men came from all walks of life. Among them were farmers, lawyers, merchants, doctors, soldiers, and educators. So they were representatives not only of the individual states, but they represented the various economic and social groups of the states. They were men of all ages, too. Many were yet in their early thirties and a few were in their twenties. On the other hand, there was the eighty-one-year-old Benjamin Franklin. All of them were very much concerned about the future of their country, and their patriotism and loyalty were unquestioned.

As a first order of business they selected George Washington as their chairman. This was a wise decision, because his position as commander-in-chief of the Continental armies had won him the respect of all. As

(Left) Many of these "continental" notes were issued during and after the Revolution. (Right) These are front and back views of the Fugio cent of 1787, the first official coin of the United States government. Why was paper money of little value during the Confederation period? (American Numismatic Society, both)

This was George Washington's chair when he presided over the Constitutional Convention. At the end of the Convention, Benjamin Franklin, referring to the painting on the back of the chair, observed that he was "happy to know that it is a rising and not a setting sun." (Independence National Historical Park Collection)

THE MEN OF THE CONVENTION

SOME WHO WERE THERE

Among the fifty-five men who attended the constitutional convention were some of the great men in our nation's history. They included:

GEORGE WASHINGTON of Virginia—surveyor, farmer, soldier, commander-in-chief of the Revolutionary army, first President of the United States

BENJAMIN FRANKLIN of Pennsylvania—inventor, statesman, signer of the Declaration of Independence, publisher, postmaster, philosopher

JAMES MADISON of Virginia—member of the Continental Congress, author of the Virginia Plan at the convention, Secretary of State, fourth President of the United States

ALEXANDER HAMILTON of New York—soldier, believer in strong central government, Secretary of the Treasury

ELBRIDGE GERRY of Massachusetts — wealthy landowner, signer of both the Declaration of Independence and the Articles of Confederation, Vice President under Madison

WILLIAM LIVINGSTON of New Jersey—state governor, lawyer, politician, poet, farmer

ROGER SHERMAN of Connecticut—member of the Continental Congress, signer of the Declaration of Independence, member of the drafting committee of the Articles of Confederation, U.S. Senator

These were some of the men who met, debated, discussed, compromised, and wrote the Constitution. All except Elbridge Gerry signed it.

SOME WHO WERE NOT THERE

But some of the great men of the period were not in Philadelphia for the convention for a variety of reasons. Among those not present were:

JOHN ADAMS—who was in London as minister to Great Britain

SAMUEL ADAMS—who wanted to stay in Boston

JOHN HANCOCK—who was carrying out his duties as governor of Massachusetts

THOMAS JEFFERSON—who was in Paris as minister to France

PATRICK HENRY—who declined the request to attend

In their study of the Constitution, political scientists study the men who wrote it. They look at the men to determine how their backgrounds, beliefs, and feelings influenced what they said and wrote. Would the presence of other men have brought about a different document? Would those who were not present have given our country a different constitution and perhaps other features in our form of government? So the political scientists study the lives of men to explain, at least in part, the happenings of great events in political life and government.

In one of his books describing the "Great Happening," as he calls the convention, one political scientist makes a thorough study of the delegates. He has this to say about them at the opening of the convention: ". . . we see the delegates . . . when the enduring reputations were still in the making, when the outcome of that summer could only be guessed at, when the victories and tragedies of later years could not even be imagined. We see them as men, as discrete individuals who had already demonstrated, each in his own way, the importance of will and nerve in history; and we see them as delegates, as instructed members of one or another of twelve separate teams that represented one or another of twelve 'sovereign, free and independent' states."[1]

[1]*1787—The Great Convention.* Copyright © Clinton Rossiter 1966. The Macmillan Company, New York, Collier-Macmillan, Canada Ltd. Toronto, Ontario.

chairman he could help to bring together those who held opposite points of view on many issues.

The convention met for four months, from May until September. No official minutes were kept of the many sessions. However, James Madison kept a careful and extensive diary of the proceedings, and it is from his record that we have gotten most of our information about the convention.

DISPUTES AND COMPROMISES. The twelve states (Rhode Island was not represented) were almost hopelessly divided on many issues. Early in the convention two plans for strengthening or changing the government were presented to the delegates. One was the *Virginia Plan,* which favored the large states. The other was the *New Jersey Plan,* which favored the small states.

There was a great deal of quarreling and bickering among the delegates on the items on which there were differences of opinion. How to bring the states closer together, how to weld one nation out of them and yet let them retain their sovereignty and independence—that was the almost impossible task of the convention. Of one thing the delegates were certain: if the nation was to be strong and united, the national government must have more power and authority than it had under the Articles of Confederation. They were determined to overcome the defects of that document. Yet they were constantly faced with the differences that existed among the states.

Gradually, as the weeks and months went by, the delegates compromised their differences and developed a new system for the government. They were in agreement that the new Constitution must give the national government the power to tax, to regulate commerce, and to compel obedience to its laws. Through a series of compromises they wrote a Constitution which each delegate could approve even though there might be sections with which he did not fully agree.

The feelings of the delegates at the close of the convention were expressed in a statement by Benjamin Franklin. On the back of the president's chair in the convention hall was painted a rising sun. Said Franklin on the last day, "I have often looked at that sun behind the president without being able to tell whether it was rising or setting. But now at length I have the happiness to know that it is a rising and not a setting sun." Little could he foretell how that sun of the new nation would rise in the next few centuries!

REPRESENTATION. The first great dispute among the delegates came over the *representation* in the new Congress. The small states, in the *New Jersey Plan,* maintained that the system of one vote to a state should be continued; they argued for equal representation for all states.

The large states, on the other hand, in the *Virginia Plan,* felt that representation should be on the basis of population. They believed that the states with more people should have more votes than those with smaller populations. They were afraid that the small states might pass laws which would be harmful to the large states.

Out of this debate came the *Connecticut Compromise,* the idea of a Congress consisting of two houses: the House of Representatives, in which states are represented according to population; and the Senate, in which each state, regardless of its population, has two representatives.

The idea behind this compromise was that the large states could control the House of Representatives and the small states could control the Senate. For a bill to become a law it must pass both houses, and thus either house could defeat a measure which the majority of its members did not approve.

COMMERCE. Under the Articles of Confederation much of the difficulty between states was caused by business rivalries. In order to eliminate these, the delegates agreed that the national government should *control commerce* among the states and with foreign countries.

But the delegates from the southern

THE VIRGINIA PLAN

1. The Articles of Confederation should be corrected or enlarged to accomplish the objectives of common defense, liberty, and general welfare.

2. Suffrage in the National Legislature should be proportioned on the basis of tax contributions or the number of free inhabitants of each state.

3. It should have two houses.

4. Members of the first branch should be elected by the people.

5. Members of the second branch should be elected by the first from persons nominated by state legislatures.

6. Each branch should be able to originate laws; the National Legislature should be given considerable authority in making laws for the Union.

7. A national executive should be chosen by the National Legislature.

8. The executive and a number of judges should form a council to review acts of the Legislature before they are put into operation.

9. Supreme and inferior courts should be established, with judges chosen by the National Legislature.

10. Provision should be made for admitting new states.

11. A republican form of government should be guaranteed each state.

12. The present Congress should continue in office until the reforms of the articles of union are adopted and until its work is completed.

13. There should be provision to amend the articles of union without the consent of the National Legislature.

14. The authorities of the several states should be required to support the articles of union by oath.

15. The amendments to the Articles of Confederation should be submitted to assemblies for consideration and decision.

THE NEW JERSEY PLAN

1. The Articles of Confederation should be so revised as to meet the needs of government and to preserve the Union.

2. Congress should be given certain additional powers, but suffrage should continue on the basis of one vote per state.

3. Congress should be given authority to request money from states on the basis of the whole number of free persons and three-fifths of all others and to enforce payment by all states.

4. Congress should be authorized to elect a federal executive of several persons, none of whom should be in charge of any troops.

5. A federal judiciary should be established, with judges appointed by the executive.

6. The acts of Congress made under the Articles of Confederation and the treaties of the United States should be the supreme law for all states and citizens to which they apply, and the executive should be given power to enforce them.

7. Provision should be made for the admission of new states.

8. Naturalization procedures should be the same for all states.

9. An offense committed in one state by a citizen of another should be punishable in the same manner as if he were a citizen of the first state.

SUMMARY OF IMPORTANT FEATURES

Note that although there are significant differences between these two plans, both of them aim at increasing the authority of the federal government.

states opposed complete control of commerce by the national government. They believed that this might eventually lead to regulation or even to elimination of the slave trade. They wanted some guarantee that the federal government would not interfere with this trade.

To satisfy them a compromise clause was put into the Constitution which forbade Congress to pass any laws which would restrict the slave trade until 1808, a period of about twenty years.

The South also feared that unlimited regulation of commerce by Congress might lead to a tax on exports. Since the South exported more goods than the North, it opposed such a tax and succeeded in having a clause inserted in the Constitution which prohibited a tax on exports.

SLAVES. Another controversy arose among the delegates over *counting slaves* in the population of a state. The northern delegates objected to counting the slaves, for this would give the southern states larger representation. The southern delegates, on the other hand, while wanting the slaves counted as people for representation purposes, did not want them counted as people in figuring direct taxes assessed on a population basis.

The controversy was settled by another compromise in which it was agreed that for purposes of both representation and direct taxation a slave was to be counted as three-fifths of a person. It should be noted, however, that the word "slave" was not used in the Constitution. (See Article I, Sections 2 and 9.)

THE PRESIDENT'S TERM. The *length of the presidential term* was the cause of another disagreement. Having just freed themselves from the rule of a king who ruled for life, many delegates were opposed to the lengthy rule of one person. They wanted a president elected for a very short term. Other delegates, however, liked the idea of a long term for the chief executive; some even stated that he should be elected for life. Their final decision was that the president should be elected for a term of four years but that he could be reelected.

These were the basic compromises which were written into the Constitution. The delegates disagreed on other issues also, but on none of them was the disagreement so great that it threatened the success of the meeting. With the settling of the basic questions on which there were violent differences of opinion, the delegates were able to complete the writing of the Constitution.

They defined the areas to be under the control of the national government and also those areas to be under the state governments. Ours was to be a federal government in which both state and national governments were given certain powers.

It was also to be a government in which power was not to be centered in one branch of government. It was to consist of three branches—legislative, executive, and judicial—with certain duties assigned to each. Each branch was to be a check on the other two branches. The delegates also recognized that in time changes might be necessary in the government under the Constitution, so they included the system of amending the Constitution.

In the next three sections each of these points will be taken up for further study: first, the division of powers between state and national governments; second, the division of duties among the three branches of the government; and third, the methods whereby the Constitution has been changed.

THE DIVISION OF POWERS BETWEEN STATE AND NATIONAL GOVERNMENTS

Since the Constitution provided for a dual system of government—

state and national—it was necessary to determine the areas in which each government was to operate.

POWERS GIVEN TO THE NATIONAL GOVERNMENT. Section 8 of Article I of the Constitution names the powers given to the Congress. The first paragraphs of this section gave the new national government those powers without which the Articles of Confederation had been unworkable. These include:

To lay and collect taxes, duties, imposts, and excises . . . but all duties, imposts, and excises shall be uniform throughout the United States.

Under the Articles of Confederation the Congress could only ask the states for money to carry on the national government; under the Constitution it could actually get money by levying taxes. In order to insure equal taxation, however, the Constitution provided that taxation should be uniform throughout the United States.

To regulate commerce with foreign nations, and among the several states, and with the Indian tribes.

This clause was also designed to correct a defect of the Articles of Confederation. Congress was given the authority to regulate foreign and interstate commerce. Section 10 of Article I of the Constitution further forbids a state to collect duties on foreign commerce passing through its borders.

To coin money, regulate the value thereof, and of foreign coin.

Under the Articles of Confederation the states issued their own money. The Constitution limited the coinage of money to the national government; in Section 10 the states were forbidden to issue money.

Section 8 lists many other powers given

The framers of the Constitution restricted the right to coin money to the federal government. Here a mint employee works on the design for the half dollar. (U.S. Treasury Department)

to the Congress of the United States. Among these are the powers to borrow money, to establish naturalization procedures, to provide for the punishment of counterfeiters, to establish post offices, to grant patents and copyrights, to establish courts, to declare war, to maintain an army and a navy, and to make the necessary laws to carry out the various provisions of the Constitution.

POWERS FORBIDDEN TO THE NATIONAL GOVERNMENT. The Constitution also names certain things which Congress cannot do. These are given in Section 9 of Article I. Congress was forbidden to make any laws regarding the importation of slaves until 1808—although again the word "slave" itself is not mentioned in the section! Further, Congress is not permitted to take away certain rights of the people. Congress cannot suspend the writ of *habeas corpus* except during rebellion or invasion, nor can it pass *bills of attainder* or *ex post facto* laws.

These guarantees were written into the Constitution as some of the basic rights which government cannot take away from the people. Under other forms of government, people do not always have these rights. In Hitler's Germany, for example, many people were imprisoned without knowing why; they were punished without a trial. The same condition exists in some countries today.

The national government was also forbidden to levy a direct tax except according to population, to levy taxes on exports, to pass commerce laws which would favor one state over another, to draw money from the treasury of the United States unless it was appropriated by law, and to grant titles of nobility.

Many of these restrictions were a direct result of the experiences that the delegates had had in foreign countries and as colonists under British rule. They were designed to avoid abuses which have arisen in many countries when an individual or a group of individuals gets too much power.

POWERS FORBIDDEN TO STATE GOVERNMENTS. Some of these same restrictions were placed upon the state governments. They, too, are not allowed to pass *bills of attainder* or *ex post facto* laws nor to grant titles of nobility. But they also are not permitted to do certain things which it was believed the national government could do better. Among these forbidden powers are the making of treaties with foreign countries and the coining of money. Also, no state is permitted to levy import or export duties or to keep troops or ships of war in time of peace without the consent of Congress.

POWERS GIVEN TO THE STATES AND TO THE PEOPLE. Ours is a government of the people. The Preamble of the Constitution begins with the words "We the people." In order to assure that the rights of the people would always be supreme, the Tenth Amendment to the Constitution states:

The powers not delegated to the United States by the Constitution, nor prohibited by it to the states, are reserved to the states respectively, or to the people.

This guarantee tried to make clear that the national government has only those powers which were specifically given to it. All others were reserved to the states or the people.

THE THREE BRANCHES AND THE SYSTEM OF CHECKS AND BALANCES

The Constitution also provides other precautions to prevent one person, a small group, or even the majority from getting too much power. It includes a system, commonly known as checks and balances, whereby individuals and groups in the three branches of the government have influence over the other branches.

THE THREE BRANCHES. The Constitution set up three branches of government: the legislative branch, which makes the laws; the executive branch, which enforces the laws and performs governmental activities; and the judicial branch, which interprets the laws.

The reason for such a system was that the delegates feared that if any individual or any group had sole power, the form of government might become too autocratic or dictatorial. Thus Congress makes the laws and the President enforces them, but he can enforce and administer only those laws which Congress passes. The interpretation of the laws is made by the courts.

Later chapters will present in detail the duties and powers of each of these branches. In this section, however, a number of illustrations of the system of checks and balances are given.

THE CHECKS AND BALANCES OF THE FEDERAL GOVERNMENT

BRANCH	CHECKS	IS CHECKED
LEGISLATIVE Makes the laws.	May pass laws over the President's veto.	President may veto bills passed by Congress.
	Senate may reject treaties and appointments made by the President.	Supreme Court may declare laws unconstitutional.
EXECUTIVE Enforces the laws.	May veto bills passed by Congress.	Senate may reject treaties and appointments made by the President.
	Appoints justices of the court.	Congress need not pass bills requested by the President.
JUDICIAL Interprets the laws.	May declare unconstitutional laws passed by Congress and signed by the President.	Congress may initiate a constitutional amendment to get a law which has been declared unconstitutional.

CHECKS ON THE PRESIDENT AND CONGRESS. In his messages to Congress, the President may request Congress to pass certain laws which he thinks are desirable. He also presents a budget in which he states the expenditures that he believes necessary. Congress studies these proposals of the President but passes only those laws that it believes necessary. It makes appropriations of money only for those items that it approves. It "checks" the President.

On the other hand, the President may *veto* any measure passed by Congress which he does not approve. In this way he "checks" Congress. Again, however, the Congress may pass a law over the President's veto through a two-thirds vote of both houses of Congress.

Another illustration of the system of checks and balances is in the making of treaties with foreign countries. The Constitution gives this power to the President, but it also states that any treaty must be ratified by a two-thirds vote of the Senate.

An example in which the Senate did not agree with the President was the question of whether the United States should join the League of Nations, which was set up following World War I. President Woodrow Wilson, together with leaders of other nations, started the League of Nations. President Wilson wanted the United States to join the League. The Senate, however, refused to consent to our joining, so the United States never became a member of the League of Nations.

Within the legislative branch itself each house acts as a check on the other. For a bill to become a law, it must be passed by both houses of Congress. Thus it sometimes happens that a bill which gets the approval of one house fails to become a law because the other house does not pass it by a majority vote.

THE COURTS CHECK AND ARE CHECKED. The third branch of the government, the judicial branch (the courts), acts as a check on the other two. Laws that are passed by the Congress and signed by the President must conform to the Constitution. When the constitutionality of a law is questioned or challenged, the courts de-

Point out that one check, judicial review, was a power created by the Supreme Court itself (Marbury v. Madison, 1803) during the period of Chief Justice John Marshall. (See Chapter 14, page 309.)

cide the issue. They have declared some laws unconstitutional; that is, the courts have said that these laws violate our Constitution. When this happens, the challenged law is no longer legal and cannot be enforced.

But also in such cases the Constitution has made a provision for checking the action of the courts. If enough members of Congress and enough states wish to put into effect a law which has been declared unconstitutional by the courts, they may amend the Constitution and thus make the law valid. This was done in the case of an income tax law which was declared unconstitutional by the Supreme Court in 1895. In 1913 an income tax was made legal by adoption of a Constitutional amendment. Today the income tax is the chief means of raising money for the national government, made possible by the Sixteenth Amendment.

CHANGING THE CONSTITUTION

The delegates to the Constitutional Convention realized that in the years to come some of the original ideas in the Constitution might need to be changed in order to fit the changing times. So they provided for an orderly method of amending, or changing, the Constitution. They believed, however, that the basic ideas in the Constitution were sound and that changes should be made slowly and not too easily.

CHANGING THE CONSTITUTION BY AMENDMENT. They provided that a proposed amendment may be *initiated* by a two-thirds vote of both houses of Congress or by a national convention called by Congress on application of the legislatures of two-thirds of the states. To become a part of the Constitution, the proposed amendment must then be *ratified* by a vote of three-fourths of the state legislatures or of state conventions called to consider it.

The procedure for amending the Constitution has been effective. While many ideas for amendments have been suggested, only thirty-one had been initiated by 1973, and of these only twenty-six have been ratified. Changes in the Constitution considered necessary as demonstrated by enough public support have been made. But they have been made only after thorough study and deliberation by many individuals and groups. The Constitution can be changed, but it cannot be shaken and altered by every whim.

Of the twenty-six amendments, the first ten, the Bill of Rights, deal with the freedoms which we enjoy under our form of

AMENDMENTS MAY BE INITIATED

by two-thirds vote of both houses of Congress

OR

by national conventions called by Congress on application of the legislatures of two-thirds of the states.

AMENDMENTS MAY BE RATIFIED

by vote of the legislatures of three-fourths of the states

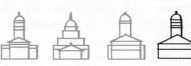

OR

by vote of conventions in three-fourths of the states.

government. The people wanted these written into the Constitution as a guarantee of their basic rights. Several states ratified the Constitution only after they were promised that these amendments would be made a part of the Constitution.

The Eleventh Amendment places a restriction on the judicial power of the United States. The Twelfth, Twentieth, and Twenty-second Amendments deal with the election and term of office of President and Vice President. The Thirteenth, Fourteenth, and Fifteenth Amendments were adopted soon after the Civil War and deal with the abolition of slavery and the extension of citizenship and suffrage.

The income tax was made possible by the Sixteenth Amendment. The procedure for electing senators was changed by the Seventeenth Amendment. The Eighteenth and Twenty-first Amendments deal with the manufacture, sale, and transportation of liquor.

Women were given the right to vote by the Nineteenth Amendment. Citizens of the District of Columbia were given the right to vote for President and Vice President by the Twenty-third Amendment. The Twenty-fourth Amendment prohibits the use of a poll tax as a requirement for voting in federal elections. The Twenty-fifth Amendment provides the means by which the Vice President can become acting President when the President is disabled. It also gives the procedure for filling a vacancy in the office of Vice President. The voting age was lowered to eighteen by the Twenty-sixth Amendment.

It should be noted that all amendments except the twenty-first[1] have been adopted by the Congress-state legislature procedure.

---

[1] Congress specified that this amendment, which repealed Prohibition, should be ratified by state conventions rather than state legislatures.

The system of a national convention called by Congress on the application of the legislatures of not fewer than two-thirds of the states has not been tried. At present this would require that thirty-four state legislatures make such a request. A great effort to use this procedure to amend the Constitution was made starting in 1962. This effort concerned an attempt to change the effects of the Supreme Court decision on the "one man-one vote" requirement for electing members of the state legislatures. (See Chapter 15.)

At one time nearly enough state legislatures had passed resolutions requesting Congress to call a convention. But so many legal questions were raised that scholars doubt that the plan will ever be used. Some of these questions are: Must the resolutions be passed in the same year? Must all of them have the same wording? Are the resolutions valid if copies have not been sent to the Congress?

CHANGING THE CONSTITUTION IN OTHER WAYS. The amendments are changes in our basic set of rules. They have been brought about by the prescribed procedure for amending the Constitution. Amendment, however, is only one of several ways our government has been changed and expanded. Other changes have been made through custom, by court interpretations, by the practices of political parties, through elaboration of the basic law by Congress, and through executive and administrative decisions. Many present-day governmental practices are not mentioned in the Constitution, but they are accepted as completely by the people as if they were part of the written Constitution.

Custom has added many accepted procedures. Here only a few will be mentioned, but attention will be called to others as the various branches of the government are studied more fully. The Constitution makes no mention of the President's Cabinet. Yet that body has been very important in the operation of the government; even George Washington called certain executives of the young government together for advice and for discussions of the affairs of the young and struggling republic.

Since then the Cabinet has been an accepted part of the governmental structure. Public interest in the members of the Cabinet is always great, and no one today seems concerned that this group is not mentioned in the Constitution.

Another example of custom is the address delivered by the President at the time of his inauguration. The Constitution says that he shall "give to the Congress information of the state of the union." Nowhere does it mention an inaugural address, but we have come to expect one, and custom dictates that the elected President give such an address at the time of his inauguration.

Court interpretations have added many practices to the operation of the government. Very early the United States Supreme Court established the practice of determining the constitutionality of laws passed by Congress when the constitutionality of a law was challenged and brought before the courts. In so doing, it broadly interpreted its duties and also, at the same time, established itself as a check on the other branches of the government. Today we accept judgments of the courts regarding the constitutionality of laws.

Many times the courts have added to the functions and powers of the federal government by interpreting the Constitution very broadly. The executive and legislative branches of the government derive some of their powers not from specific mention in the Constitution but from the decisions and interpretations made by the courts.

One example of this is the broad interpretation given to the power "to regulate commerce."

The practices of political parties have tended, also, to change the Constitution. Nominating conventions are not mentioned in the Constitution. We have, however, accepted them as a means for selecting presidential candidates. Political parties play a vital role in the selection and election of the chief executive. This was never mentioned by the framers of the Constitution. Thus the governmental practices have been extended or changed through the functioning of the political parties.

The elaboration of the basic law by the Congress itself has greatly changed the government under the Constitution. The Constitution gives the form and operation of the government in broad outline. It became the obligation of Congress to fill in the details. The first Congress was faced with the job of getting the government into operation. It established a system of courts and the first executive departments.

Other Congresses have enacted many laws extending the services of the government and providing for the necessary personnel to carry on the function of the government. They have set up many agencies which have become part of the "warp and woof" of the government, for example, the Atomic Energy Commission, the Civil Service Commission, the Federal Deposit Insurance Corporation, the Federal Communications Commission, and many more.

Many of the enactments of Congress have been made under the so-called "elastic clause" of the Constitution. This is the final clause in Article I, Section 8, which states that Congress shall have the power "to make all laws which shall be necessary and proper for carrying into execution the foregoing powers, and all other powers vested by this Constitution in the government of the United States, or in any department or officer thereof."

Under this clause Congress has passed many laws which it has considered "necessary and proper," so that the government could function as times have changed.

Executive or administrative decisions have brought about other changes in the government. As our country has grown and as the functions of the government have been expanded, many decisions not specifically delegated to the Presidents by the Constitution have been made by them. This has been especially true in recent years as the United States has become a world leader. Administrators of many governmental agencies must constantly make decisions within the general framework of powers set forth in the Constitution and of laws passed by the Congress.

The laws may be general in nature, but the specific details of applying the laws are often left in the hands of the administrators charged with carrying out the laws. The specific rules and regulations made by executive agencies thus become a means of expanding the government under the Constitution.

STUDY QUESTIONS

1. What are the six purposes of American government as stated in the Preamble to the Constitution?

2. With what phase of government does each of the seven articles of the Constitution deal?

3. What are five defects of the Articles of Confederation?

4. Why was the Annapolis Convention of 1786 held? The Philadelphia Convention of 1787?

5. Who attended the Philadelphia Constitutional Convention? Which state was not represented?

6. Who were the chief leaders of the convention?

CONCEPTS AND GENERALIZATIONS

1
The government of the United States is a government of law and not of men.

2
The government of the United States is a government of the people, not of an individual or of a ruling class.

3
The Constitution, laws, and treaties of the United States make up the supreme law of the nation.

4
The Constitution unites the states into one nation.

5
Power in the government of the United States is divided among its three branches: legislative, executive, and judicial.

6
The three branches of government balance and check one another.

7
Compromise is an important feature of the Constitution.

8
In our federal system of government certain powers belong to the national government and others to the states.

9
The Constitution guarantees the people certain basic rights.

10
The Constitution has been changed by the process of amendment; but custom, court interpretations, practices of political parties, and executive decisions have also changed our government.

7. How many states needed to ratify the Constitution to put it into effect?

8. How is your state affected by the compromise made on the method of representation in Congress?

9. Why was the slave question a part of the compromise over the control of commerce? Why was it also a part of the compromise over the question of representation?

10. What powers are denied to the states by the Constitution?

11. What powers are reserved to the states?

12. What powers are forbidden to the national government?

13. What are the basic checks and balances in our system of government?

14. How does each of the three branches of government check the other two branches?

15. What are the two ways in which an amendment to the United States Constitution can be initiated?

16. What are the two ways in which proposed amendments can be ratified?

17. Which methods have been used to initiate and ratify the amendments now in the Constitution?

18. How has the Constitution been changed by custom and usage?

19. Give an example of a law based on "the necessary and proper clause" of the Constitution.

20. What changes have been made in the Constitution (a) through the practices of political parties and (b) by the Congress?

IDEAS FOR DISCUSSION

1. Why were merchants especially concerned about the Articles of Confederation?

2. Might the government under the Articles of Confederation have survived if there had not been a period of rising prices?

3. The sessions of Congress, state legislatures, city councils, and the United Nations are conducted with reporters present. Would it have been wise to admit reporters to the Constitutional Convention instead of having secret sessions?

4. Why was the Twenty-second Amendment to the Constitution adopted? Does this amendment destroy the compromise made over the term of the President by the Constitutional Convention?

5. Would you favor or oppose an amendment to the Constitution that required an amendment to be ratified within five years after it had been initiated? Why?

6. Why were the famous "voices of the American Revolution," such as Patrick Henry and Thomas Paine, not heard during the Constitutional Convention?

7. What are the advantages and disadvantages of government by a written constitution?

8. How does the procedure for amending the United States Constitution compare with the procedure for amending the constitution of an organization of which you are a member? (For example, school government, school club, 4-H Club, Boy Scouts, or Girl Scouts)

9. Read again the Preamble on page 36. Discuss ways in which our country has met the purposes set forth in this statement. In what ways have we not yet fulfilled these purposes? Where have we fallen short?

10. The Preamble starts with the words "We the people. . . ." Charles Beard, a great historian, when challenged that it was not all the people but only the Anglo-Saxon members who really made our nation, replied: "During the early days of the Republic, peoples of many national origins worked together in our country, in peace and war. On battlefields, in council rooms, in civilian labors and sacrifices to support the armies of the war for independence, English, Scotch, Irish, Dutch, Germans, Jews, Welsh, French, Swedes, and Negroes—bond and free—took part, and forwarded the great cause which brought our nation into being." (See *The Republic*, pages 7-10.) Do you agree with Beard or his challenger? Why?

11. If the Twenty-fifth Amendment had been part of the Constitution in 1865, what effect might it have had on the government after Lincoln's assassination? In 1963, after the assassination of President Kennedy?

THINGS TO DO

1. Hamilton and Madison, with a little aid from John Jay, wrote a series of essays answering the objections to adopting the Constitution. They wrote without signing their real names but signing Publius, a Latin name. These essays were put together in a book called *The*

Federalist. Read one of the essays. Numbers 15, 16, and 41 are good examples.

2. Draw a large chart using overlapping circles as shown below. The sections represent:

    A. Restrictions on the national government

    B. Restrictions on the states

    C. Powers belonging only to the national government

    D. Powers belonging only to the states

    E. Powers that are shared by both the national government and the states

For each section list important powers or restrictions.

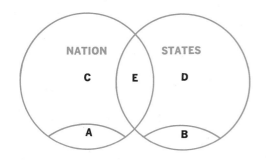

3. Prepare a report on the circumstances that brought about one of the amendments to the Constitution.

4. Prepare a miniature "Who's Who" booklet based on the lives of the members of the Constitutional Convention.

5. Prepare a chart showing the education, vocation, age, and political experience of the members of the Constitutional Convention. Consult books in the library.

6. Hold a panel discussion on the topic "Has the Constitution of the United States influenced the constitutions of other countries?"

7. Draw a chart to illustrate the theory of checks and balances.

8. Draw a cartoon to show that the Constitution is a "bundle of compromises."

9. Draw a cartoon to illustrate one of the ways in which the Constitution has been changed.

10. Imagine that you are a resident of New York or Virginia at the time of the ratification of the Constitution. Prepare an advertisement for a local paper in which you plead for ratification of the Constitution.

11. Prepare a report on an issue proposed as a Constitutional amendment. Has it passed the step of initiation? Consult past issues of the *Readers' Guide to Periodical Literature,* the *Congressional Quarterly,* and books on the Constitution. Some examples are the issues to limit the treaty powers of the President, to limit the income tax, to change the terms of office of federal judges, to prohibit child labor, to have a literacy test for voting, and to change the system of electing a President.

12. Draw a map of the original thirteen states, coloring the states to show their attitudes toward the method of representation in Congress.

13. Debate the strengths and weaknesses of the Virginia and New Jersey Plans.

14. Schedule for class showing one of the Encyclopaedia Britannica films in the OUR LIVING BILL OF RIGHTS series. Two good ones are *Justice under Law—The Gideon Case,* on the right to counsel, and *Liberty under Law—The Feiner Case,* on freedom of expression.

FURTHER READINGS

Bowen, Catherine Drinker, MIRACLE AT PHILADELPHIA: THE STORY OF THE CONSTITUTIONAL CONVENTION, MAY TO SEPTEMBER, 1787. Little, Brown and Co., 1966.

Chidsey, Donald Barr, THE BIRTH OF THE CONSTITUTION: AN INFORMAL HISTORY. Crown Publishers, Inc., 1964.

Donovan, Frank, MR. MADISON'S CONSTITUTION: THE STORY BEHIND THE CONSTITUTIONAL CONVENTION. Dodd, Mead, and Co., 1965.

Fribourg, Marjorie, BILL OF RIGHTS: ITS IMPACT ON THE AMERICAN PEOPLE. Macrae Smith Company, 1967.

Goldman, Peter, CIVIL RIGHTS: CHALLENGE OF THE FOURTEENTH AMENDMENT. Coward-McCann, 1965.

Hayman, LeRoy, WHAT YOU SHOULD KNOW ABOUT THE U.S. CONSTITUTION AND THE MEN WHO WROTE IT. Four Winds Press, 1967.

Locke, Raymond F., BIRTH OF AMERICA. Mankind Publishing Co., 1971.

Murphy, Paul L., THE CONSTITUTION IN CRISIS TIMES, 1918-1969. Harper & Row, Publishers, 1972.

Perloff, Harvey, ed., THE FUTURE OF THE UNITED STATES GOVERNMENT TOWARD THE YEAR 2000. George Braziller, 1971.

Ross, George E., KNOW YOUR DECLARATION OF INDEPENDENCE AND THE 56 SIGNERS. E. M. Hale & Company, 1966.

Rossiter, Clinton L., 1787: THE GRAND CONVENTION. Macmillan Co., 1966.

ACTIVIST—a person emphasizing vigorous political action.

ALL DELIBERATE SPEED—a phrase from a Supreme Court decision indicating that integration of schools should proceed without undue delay.

CLOTURE—a system by which debate in the United States Senate can be ended by vote of two-thirds of the senators present and voting.

DE FACTO SEGREGATION—actual separation of the races, as by residential patterns, in contrast to *de jure,* or legal separation.

GHETTO—a section of a city in which a minority racial or cultural group lives because of economic, legal, or social pressure.

GRANDFATHER CLAUSE—a voting eligibility provision requiring high standards of reading and ownership of considerable property except for descendants of men voting before 1867.

JIM CROW LAW—measure designed to prevent Negroes and whites from intermingling in public places.

LOBBYING—efforts to influence the members of a legislature.

NONVIOLENCE—refraining from the use of violence as a matter of principle.

SEPARATE-BUT-EQUAL—a phrase from an 1896 Supreme Court decision holding that segregation is acceptable if Negroes and whites have equal facilities.

THE LANGUAGE OF GOVERNMENT

4

The Struggle for Civil Rights

Vast differences sometimes exist between the theory of government as presented in the basic principles and the practice of government in day-to-day living. Although every citizen is guaranteed liberty, not every citizen has liberty. While free enterprise is our basic business system, sometimes competition is eliminated. In spite of the system of checks and balances, the relationships between executive, legislative, and judicial branches become strained. In practice government does not always operate in accord with our high ideals.

The first three chapters of this book have presented the basic principles of our governmental system. These fundamental ideas reflect the ideals or goals of our democratic society and the general framework by which our system operates. These chapters have presented the theory of our government. The remaining chapters of the book build on this theory and present many of the practical workings of government in action.

Nowhere in our nation is the discrepancy between theory and practice greater than in the treatment of minority groups: blacks, Indians, Spanish-speaking Americans, and Orientals. Presidents, editors, educators, and the courts have repeatedly pointed out that minorities have not been accorded the freedoms guaranteed all citizens. Often they are treated as "second-class citizens." Around the world the treatment of minorities in our country causes some people to distrust the ideals which we uphold.

Discussions of the gaps between our ideals and our practices are sometimes avoided. They are not easy to explain. Why do these gaps exist? In part they exist because men are a curious combination of good and evil. Ambition, greed, prejudice, ignorance get in the way of unselfishness, concern for one's fellow man, common decency.

Inability to achieve our highest ideals, however, cannot be explained entirely on the basis of the weaknesses of human nature. In part they arise because good men can differ. Two honest individuals may take the same facts and interpret them differently. These individuals can have similar experiences and react to them in different ways. So, governmental action often becomes a process of compromise, of moving as fast and as far as can be done at the time. In this sense government becomes "the art of the possible." The politician-statesman becomes the genius who is able to work out a solution which people live with for a time, until improvements can be made. When compromises are made, however, often those for and those against an issue are really not completely satisfied.

Another reason for the gaps between principles and practices arises because some people are more influential than others. In this sense the student of government needs to examine "who is trying to influ-

ence whom?" and how this is done. In this sense "politics" is the cause of differences between principles and practices. In the next unit these human political aspects of government will be dealt with in more detail.

In this chapter, however, the struggle for civil rights is presented for two reasons: First, elementary justice requires that minority groups be granted the rights which they have been denied for years, and second, the struggle for civil rights provides a case study which illuminates the nature and functioning of American government. Blacks are emphasized because they have received major attention in recent years.

SELMA   One starting place for describing the struggle for civil rights is Selma, Alabama.

Civil rights marchers in Selma in the spring of 1965 were attacked and stopped by some 200 state troopers using tear gas, nightsticks, and whips. The marchers were protesting the denial of Negro voting rights in Selma. Two weeks later, led by the Reverend Dr. Martin Luther King, Jr., a five-day, fifty-four-mile march from Selma to the state capitol at Montgomery was started, with over 4,000 federalized troops protecting the marchers.

Civil rights groups had selected Selma as the place to dramatize to the world the denial of voting rights faced by southern Negroes and the efforts being made to get more Negroes to register for elections.

The march was a success. The mistreatment of Negroes, witnessed by millions on television, horrified viewers. Although the daily number of·marchers was limited by court order to 300, on the final day there were some 25,000 non-marching demonstrators—Negro and white—from all parts of the country in front of the state capitol. The issue of unequal voting rights was

The 1965 civil rights march in Selma, Alabama, was completed with federal troops protecting the marchers. Representatives of many religious denominations joined the marchers. (UPI photo)

forcefully presented to the world. Selma became a landmark in the long struggle for civil rights.

THE ISSUE In the years since World War II the crucial social issue in our nation has been the effort to obtain full political and economic rights for Negroes. While in the early years of the civil rights struggle the focus was on the southern states, more recently the struggle has shifted to the problems of Negroes in the cities and suburbs of the North.

The issue confronting the nation is whether the basic ideals of democracy are to be available to all citizens. Specifically, the issue is whether liberty and other basic human rights are to be granted Afro-Americans and other groups. After waiting 100 years to obtain these fundamentals **for his race, the black is saying through his organizations and leaders that he has waited long enough.**

The late President John F. Kennedy stated the issue in this way:

> The Negro baby born in America today, regardless of the section of the nation in which he is born, has about one-half as much chance of completing high school as a white baby born in the same place on the same day, one-third as much chance of becoming a professional man—but twice as much chance of becoming unemployed, about one-seventh as much chance of earning $10,000 a year, a life expectancy which is seven years shorter and the prospect of earning only half as much.

On August 28, 1963, when nearly a

From "The Language of Government" vocabulary select those terms relevant to how the Negro's rights have been obstructed over the years.

quarter million people came to the Lincoln Memorial in Washington to urge Congress to pass civil rights legislation, the late Dr. Martin Luther King, the spiritual leader of the civil rights struggle, said:

. . . even though we face the difficulties of today and tomorrow, I still have a dream. . . . I have a dream that one day on the red hills of Georgia the sons of former slaves and the sons of former slave-owners will be able to sit down together at the table of brotherhood. . . . I have a dream that one day even the state of Mississippi, a state sweltering with the heat of injustice, sweltering with the heat of oppression, will be trans-

formed into an oasis of freedom and justice. . . . I have a dream that one day every valley shall be exalted, every hill and mountain shall be made low, the rough places will be made plain, and the crooked places will be made straight and the glory of the Lord shall be revealed and all flesh shall see it together.

As he finished speaking the people sang:

We shall overcome, we shall overcome,
We shall overcome, some day.
Oh, deep in my heart I do believe,
We shall overcome some day.

THE PAST HISTORY   The Constitution, especially the Bill of Rights, provided

In 1963 nearly a quarter million people poured into Washington for ceremonies in front of the Lincoln Memorial urging passage of civil rights legislation. (Wide World photo)

the foundation for civil rights in this country, but no provision specifically provided for *federal* protection of civil rights. Until after the Civil War the enforcement of civil rights was left to the individual states.

As the Civil War ended, however, the Thirteenth Amendment to the Constitution outlawing slavery was adopted and ratified in 1865. In 1866 Congress passed the Fourteenth Amendment, which was ratified by the states in 1868. This amendment guaranteed Negroes federal and state citizenship by providing:

> All persons born or naturalized in the United States, and subject to the jurisdiction thereof, are citizens of the United States and of the State wherein they reside. No State shall make or enforce any law which shall abridge the privileges and immunities of citizens of the United States; nor shall any State deprive any person of life, liberty, or property, without due process of law; nor deny to any person within its jurisdiction the equal protection of the laws.

In sections two and five of this amendment Congress was given the power to enforce, "by appropriate legislation," these guarantees, including the reducing of the basis of representation of the state in Congress if the vote was denied to citizens. This provision, however, has never been used.

The Fifteenth Amendment, passed in 1869 and ratified in 1870, provided that the right "to vote shall not be denied or abridged by the United States or by any State on account of race, color, or previous condition of servitude." Again Congress was given the power "to enforce this article by appropriate legislation."

Congress did enact five major civil rights and Reconstruction acts between 1866 and 1875, but by 1910 these acts had been so modified by state action and by Supreme Court decisions that they were without value. The United States Civil Rights Commission, after a thorough study, reported in 1963 that after 1875,

> The mood of the nation was no longer favorable to the vigorous enforcement of civil rights. . . . The next decades were to be the ebb tide in the Negro's struggle for equality under law.

In the South the Negro was systematically denied the vote through adoption of "grandfather voting" clauses, the exclusive white primary, literacy tests, and the poll tax.

The practice of segregation became legal also. In 1881 Tennessee passed a law requiring railroads to provide separate cars for Negroes. Within twenty-five years Jim Crow laws enforcing segregation were the rule. The Supreme Court accepted these conditions, with probably the most devastating decision being the *Plessy* v. *Ferguson* decision in 1896 which upheld the "separate-but-equal" doctrine.

Up to World War II minority group members were "second-class citizens" in much of the United States. During this period the federal government played a very limited role in the protection of civil rights.

NEGROES STRUGGLE
FOR IMPROVEMENT During the years from Reconstruction to World War II Negroes were trying to improve their condition. Although lack of public support for Negro education was general throughout the South, the development of Negro higher education resulted in the training of ministers, teachers, and tradesmen. Famous institutions such as Talladega College, Fisk University, and Tuskegee Institute developed during this period.

For thirty years, from 1865 to 1895, Frederick Douglass spoke for Afro-Amer-

The late Dr. Martin Luther King accepts congratulations from King Olav V of Norway after receiving the 1964 Nobel Peace Prize for his use of nonviolent methods in crusading for civil rights. (Wide World photo)

icans. He was born a slave in 1817, but at age twenty-one he escaped to the North where he became the orator of the rising abolitionist movement. He carried the tradition of democratic idealism into the Reconstruction period, when the goal was no longer the end of slavery but the enjoyment of political, civil, and social equality.

Booker T. Washington probably did more than any other person to publicize the doctrine of social rebirth of the Negro through industrial training. Washington was a skillful politician with a powerful personality. He believed the Negro should gain economic competence and then social and political gains would follow. While many Negroes applauded Washington's ideas and looked to him as their new leader, others followed the leadership of a New England Negro intellectual, W. E. B. DuBois, who openly opposed Washington and argued that Negroes should be educated as free men. DuBois stated that Negroes, "by every civilized and peaceful method, must strive for the rights which the world accords to men."

Negro leaders during this period were beginning organizations which were to become powerful. In 1905 a movement was started in Niagara Falls, Canada, by DuBois to obtain suffrage, civil rights, justice in the courts, and to end Jim Crow. In 1910, as a result of the so-called "Niagara movement," the National Association for the Advancement of Colored People was formally organized. It presently has more than 1700 chapters throughout the United States. The NAACP goal has been to obtain full citizenship for Negroes through pressure, lobbying, propaganda, and legal action. For nearly forty years the leading spokesman for this organization was Walter White. He investigated lynchings, race riots, and discriminations with vigor. His writings and speeches on behalf of civil rights provided a foundation for present struggles. The present director, Roy Wilkins, a University of Minnesota graduate, has been active in the civil rights movement for over thirty-five years.

In 1911 three other interracial agencies were merged into the National Urban League. The League has done important work in finding employment and improving living conditions especially for northern urban Negroes and southern Negroes who migrated to northern cities. For many years the astute political leader was Lester Granger, a Dartmouth graduate and social worker. The leader from 1961 to 1971 was the late Whitney Young, Jr., a former college dean of social work, noted for his urging of a "Marshall Plan" to rehabilitate lower-class Negroes. His successor is Vernon E. Jordan, Jr., a lawyer who led the struggle to get blacks elected to office in the South.

A third powerful organization which arose during this period was the Brotherhood of Sleeping Car Porters. Barred from white labor unions, Negroes were unsuccessful in their efforts to organize until 1925 when A. Philip Randolph organized the Pullman porters and maids. By 1937 this son of a minister, who studied labor economics in college, had obtained full recognition for the Brotherhood. He was the first Negro labor leader of national stature.

The migration of Negroes from the South to northern cities was accelerated during World War I and has continued at a high rate to the present. Changes in southern agriculture and the attraction of employment in northern industries provided a firm economic base for the movement. But the vision of the North as the great Promised Land of freedom and equality played an important part in this continuing migration. Some Negroes saw the freedom of the northern cities as an escape from the feudal South.

THE FRANKLIN D. ROOSEVELT YEARS. The vision of freedom, however, was in many cases a mirage. Even President Franklin D. Roosevelt, who was respected and supported by Negro leaders, recommended no civil rights legislation and none was passed by Congress during his Presidency. But his administration did take two executive actions of substantial importance:

(1) In 1939 the Attorney General established a Civil Liberties Unit in the Criminal Division of the Justice Department. This unit later became the Civil Rights Section.

(2) In 1941 a Committee on Fair Employment Practices was created to attack discrimination by unions and companies with government contracts or those engaged in war work.

During World War II most military units were segregated. Many Negroes left the military service at the end of the war convinced that since they had risked their lives for their country, they should now fight for full citizenship. Their actions gave momentum to the civil rights movement.

THE TRUMAN PROGRAM. The civil rights movement had received little serious attention from political leaders until 1947, when President Harry S. Truman established a President's Committee on Civil Rights. President Truman was the first president in our history to try to use the full power of the federal government to promote and pass comprehensive civil rights programs. Employing the recommendations of his Civil Rights Committee, the Truman program featured antilynching, antipoll tax, antisegregation in transportation, and fair employment laws.

In the 1948 presidential campaign Truman argued for a strong civil rights program. This position was at least partly responsible for the bolt from the Democratic party of the Dixiecrats and the loss of electoral votes by the Democrats in four southern states. After his election Truman tried to get his program through Congress, but he was blocked by southern Congressmen. Nevertheless, he did issue executive orders intended to end segregation in the armed forces and to prevent discrimination in federal employment and in work done under federal contracts.

BROWN V. BOARD OF EDUCATION. In the fifties a decision by the Supreme

Court changed the character of the civil rights struggle. Few decisions in the history of the Supreme Court have had the great impact that the case of *Brown* v. *Board of Education of Topeka, Kansas* has had. On May 17, 1954, Chief Justice Earl Warren, speaking for the unanimous decision of the Justices, said,

> In the field of public education the doctrine of 'separate but equal' has no place. Separate educational facilities are inherently unequal.

In this decision the Court also stated:

> In these days it is doubtful that any child may reasonably be expected to succeed in life if he is denied the opportunity of an education. Such an opportunity, where the state has undertaken to provide it, is a right which must be made available to all on equal terms.

In 1955 the Court ordered "that the defendants make a prompt and reasonable start toward full compliance" and proceed "with all deliberate speed" to admit children to schools on an integrated basis.

The Court cited the testimony of Dr. Kenneth B. Clark, a professor of psychology at City College, New York, on the harmful effects of prejudice on children as one reason for ending segregation. Clark has been called the scholar of the civil rights movement.

The Supreme Court decision encountered bitter protest in the South immediately. Anticourt bills were introduced in Congress, federal aid to education was opposed, and White Citizens' Councils spread throughout the South. Pupil placement plans, school closing laws, and private school plans were announced. Progress toward desegregation in the public schools was slow. Ten years after the historic decision, two of the four public school systems which had been defendants in the case had not admitted a single Negro. With the beginning of the fall 1964 school term the last of the southern states started to desegregate, although there are still school districts today in which only token integration has occurred.

The Supreme Court on November 15, 1965, held in two Virginia cases that "delays in desegregation of school systems are no longer tolerable." By unanimous decision the Court seems to have said that "the deliberate speed" policy is ended and that delays will not be tolerated. In the words of Justice Hugo L. Black from an earlier decision, "there has been entirely too much deliberation and not enough speed."

The conflicts over school desegregation have also moved to northern states where *de facto* segregation exists because of the pattern of housing. The central city tends to become Negro with some all-black schools while the suburbs tend to become white. Busing across district school boundaries to achieve integration has become an issue. The law on *de facto* segregation is not clear. The Supreme Court is expected to hear appropriate cases in the near future. Cases are presently in lower courts from Richmond, Detroit, and Denver.

THE EISENHOWER YEARS. The *Brown* v. *Board of Education* decision was given during President Eisenhower's administration. During his first years in office he had continued President Truman's efforts on civil rights with executive acts, but he recommended no special legislation. Following the 1954 Supreme Court decision he pointed to the need to comply with Court decisions, but he did not express a stand on the merits of the school desegregation decision.

Governor Orval Faubus of Arkansas in 1957 defied a federal court order to desegregate the Little Rock High School, setting a pattern for other southern politicians.

Political scientists are usually not lawyers, but Supreme Court decisions provide one of the important sources for their scholarly work. Indeed, within the field of political science, one of the specialties is constitutional law.

In the civil rights struggle, the student of political science has to be aware of the laws with respect to rights and the court decisions which apply to them. An example is the case of *Watson* v. *City of Memphis, Tennessee*. On May 27, 1963, the Supreme Court ruled that "slow and gradual" desegregation of municipally owned parks, museums, and recreational facilities in Memphis did not meet the constitutional obligations to integrate these public facilities.

The opinion of the Court was written by Justice Arthur J. Goldberg in a unanimous decision. In part, the decision stated, ". . . we cannot ignore the passage of a substantial period of time since the original manifest unconstitutionality of racial practices here challenged, the repeated and numerous decisions giving notice of such illegality, and the many intervening opportunities heretofore available to attain the equality of treatment which the Fourteenth Amendment commands the States to achieve. . . . Given the extended time which has elapsed, it is far from clear that the mandate of the second Brown decision requiring that desegregation proceed with 'all deliberate speed' would today be fully satisfied by types of plans or programs for desegregation of public educational facilities which eight years ago might have been deemed sufficient. Brown never contemplated that the concept of 'deliberate speed' would countenance indefinite delay in elimination of racial barriers in schools, let alone other public facilities not involving the same physical problems or comparable conditions."

As a result, President Eisenhower sent federal troops to Little Rock to control mobs who were trying to prevent nine Negro students from enrolling in the school.

In the area of civil rights legislation, Eisenhower recommended legislation in 1956, 1957, and 1959. The first Civil Rights Act of this century was passed in 1957; the second in 1960. The 1957 Act was mild. It created a permanent Civil Rights Commission, which made a major report recommending government action in the fields of voting, education, and housing. The act also provided that the Attorney General could intervene in cases where Negroes were discriminated against in voting. This procedure proved so slow that the 1960 Act tried another device to speed up the process. Federal courts were authorized to order a Negro registered if a pattern of discrimination was found after a lawsuit. This, too, proved to be a slow procedure.

THE KENNEDY-JOHNSON YEARS. In campaigning for the presidency John F. Kennedy promised "moral and persuasive leadership . . . to create the conditions" for compliance with court decisions and civil rights laws. Both he and President Johnson used the prestige and power of the White House to focus attention on the struggle for civil rights.

Until 1962 Kennedy did not seek any civil rights legislation, but, with his brother Robert Kennedy as Attorney General, he took executive action in civil rights areas. The most notable action was that of barring discrimination in federally-assisted housing.

Recognizing that many important House and Senate committees were chaired by southerners, Kennedy emphasized voting rights in the first civil rights legislation recommended to Congress. He thought that this type of legislation was the only kind

Leaders of the 1963 March in Washington meet with President John F. Kennedy. From the left: Whitney Young, Dr. Martin Luther King, Jr., John Lewis, Rabbi Joachim Prinz, Eugene C. Blake, A. Philip Randolph, President John F. Kennedy, Walter Reuther, Vice President Lyndon B. Johnson, and Roy Wilkins. (Wide World photo)

that could be forced through congressional committees.

The Kennedy position was strengthened in the spring of 1963 by a massive attack on discrimination in Birmingham, Alabama. The groundwork for this demonstration had been laid in earlier mass demonstrations from 1955–1962.

In 1955 and 1956 Negroes in Montgomery, Alabama, had successfully boycotted the segregated bus system. The idea spread, with public facilities in other southern cities becoming the targets of organized

Negro protests. They, too, were successful.

In 1960 four Negro college students walked into the local dime store at Greensboro, North Carolina, and sat down at the all-white lunch counter. When asked to leave, they refused. The manager closed the counter. As the word spread, dozens of other students from the all-Negro Agricultural and Technical College joined the demonstration. Shortly thereafter the sit-in technique was being used in restaurants, hotels, public beaches, and libraries over much of the Deep South.

This is a class to train typists at the Opportunities Industrialization Center (OIC) in Philadelphia, Pa. The OIC, founded and directed by Reverend Leon Sullivan, has served as a stimulating example to many groups endeavoring to give Afro-Americans a better opportunity in our society. (Photo by Truman Moore, from Opportunities Industrialization Center, Inc.)

In May, 1961, a biracial group of thirteen "freedom riders" left Washington, D. C. determined to abolish the pattern of segregation in public transportation. They used public waiting rooms, restaurants, and toilets without regard to segregation patterns. There were arrests, violence, and an outpouring of national support. The freedom rides, for there were a dozen of them, resulted in the almost complete elimination of discrimination in public transportation.

With the successful experience of these early demonstrations, the Birmingham demonstrations unfolded, leading to a highly successful march on Washington in 1963. Although the demonstrations were planned on the principles of nonviolence, throughout these years shocking violence against the Negroes took place, including the shooting to death of the Mississippi state leader of the NAACP and the killing of four Negro girls at Sunday school by a bomb. In 1964, the entire nation was outraged at the murder of three civil rights workers (two white and one Negro) near Philadelphia, Mississippi.

THIS PLACE ISN'T BIG ENOUGH FOR BOTH OF US, MAC

Engelhardt in the St. Louis Post-Dispatch.

President Kennedy was well aware of the complex issues involved. He responded to the mass pressures, as Martin Luther King said, ". . . because he thought it was right to do so." A broad civil rights program was submitted to Congress.

In his first message to Congress after the assassination of President Kennedy, President Johnson requested "the earliest possible passage of the civil rights bill for which he (President Kennedy) had fought so long." In 1964 Congress passed the third civil rights law, after employing cloture to end a three-months' filibuster in the Senate. Under this law federal examiners were authorized to register voters where discrimination existed.

In 1965, after the nation was shocked by the treatment of demonstrators in Selma, Alabama, President Johnson asked for another civil rights act, which was passed. The 1965 act suspended the use of literacy tests in much of the South and permitted the federal government to take over the registration of voters where less than 50 per cent of the voting age population was registered or had voted in 1964.

The principle behind the succession of civil rights acts was that if Negroes could vote, other problems of discrimination would yield to this political power.

In 1966 President Johnson called a White House Conference on Civil Rights with the theme "To Fulfill These Rights." Stirred by the riots in the Negro ghettos of northern cities, the Conference focused attention on the whole range of Negro problems—segregation, housing, education, employment, economic conditions, family life—in the North as well as the South.

The Johnson Administration submitted a new civil rights bill that, for the first time, aimed at ending discrimination against Negroes in the North. The bill attempted to deal with problems of discrimination in housing and selection of federal and state jurors. A so-called open housing provision was attacked, even though one-third of the states and over thirty large cities had such laws and ordinances. The bill was defeated in the Senate when two-thirds of the Senators refused to limit debate. The bill had previously passed the House. This was the first time since 1956 that a President's civil rights bill had been defeated.

President Johnson in a 1967 civil rights message to Congress called attention to the following advances made in the past few years, largely as a result of the civil rights acts and Supreme Court decisions:

- *Negro registration in the five southern states where voter discrimination was most severe has increased by 64 per cent, from 715,099 to 1,174,569.*

- *Twenty Negroes now serve in southern legislatures.*

- *In eleven southern states, 12.5 per cent of Negro students were enrolled in desegregated classes, in contrast to 1 per cent three years earlier.*
- *Negroes are admitted to hospitals that barred them in the past.*
- *Negroes traveling through most parts of the country do not need to suffer the inconvenience of searching for a place to rest or eat.*
- *Job opportunities and job training have provided self-sufficiency for millions.*

While progress was being made, the open housing provisions of a new civil rights bill prevented its passage in 1967. In a number of large cities throughout the nation—from New York's Harlem to Los Angeles' Watts, from Atlanta to Detroit to Newark—some Negroes were rioting as one means to express their frustrations and belligerence over their conditions. At the same time, other Negroes through their organizations were endeavoring to change conditions to conform to the basic ideals of America.

Following the 1967 riots President Johnson appointed a special commission headed by Governor Kerner of Illinois to study the causes of the riots. This commission reported in the spring of 1968 and stated, "Our nation is moving toward two societies, one black, one white—separate and unequal." The commission called for "national action on an unprecedented scale" to stave off domestic disaster and create "a true union" between black and white America. The report suggested more Negro policemen, better police protection for slum dwellers, the creation of two million jobs by government and private business, improved education, and better housing.

The report was criticized by some newspapers and commentators for not emphasizing the responsibilities of individuals and for urging more than could be undertaken.

As a presidential candidate Richard Nixon said the report blamed "everybody for the riots except the perpetrators of the riots."

As the civil rights struggle shifted from nonviolence to violence, a movement for Black Power developed. Poorly defined and never explicitly stated, the movement was variously interpreted to mean the use of political power through increasing the number of Negro voters, the use of economic power through the boycott, and in its most extreme form the use of a kind of guerrilla warfare.

To give prominence again to the nonviolent approach Dr. Martin Luther King, Jr. planned a march on Washington for the spring of 1968 to press for greater action. His murder in April 1968 did not stop his supporters from carrying out the plan. The march was held to dramatize the condition of the poor and to pay well-deserved tribute to Dr. King.

Confronted with these forces, and sensitive to the tributes by the masses, Congress passed the Civil Rights Act of 1968, an open housing bill, which, for the first time in history, made discrimination in the sale or rental of private housing a federal offense. Beginning in 1970 this prohibition against discrimination covered virtually all housing units with two exceptions: owner-occupied, single-family dwellings sold or rented without the aid of a real estate broker or agent, and boardinghouses or other dwellings with not more than four family units, one of which is occupied by the owner.

Included in the bill were federal penalties for interfering by force or threats with the right to vote, to serve on juries, to use public accommodations, to attend public schools, or to engage in other specifically protected activities.

The law made it a federal crime to cross a state line to incite a riot; to obstruct firemen and policemen engaged in suppress-

Discuss the possible impact that integration in the armed forces and the Vietnam and Cambodian conflicts have had or will have upon American society in general and Negroes in particular.

ing a riot; to transport in interstate commerce, or teach how to make and use, firearms, explosives, or incendiary devices in riots.

An unusual provision, reflecting the increased concern for all minorities, extended the protections of the Bill of Rights to American Indians.

Later in 1968, the Supreme Court in *Jones v. Mayer,* by a 7-2 decision, barred all racial discrimination, private and public, in the sale or rental of property.

THE CONTEMPORARY SCENE

For many years the NAACP, the Urban League, and the Brotherhood of Sleeping Car Porters were the Big Three of the Negro organizations. In recent years the NAACP under the executive leadership of Roy Wilkins has been considered to be the largest, most efficient, and best operated. But its top position is being challenged by more recent organizations.

SOUTHERN CHRISTIAN LEADERSHIP CONFERENCE. The bus boycotts in Montgomery, Alabama, moved Martin Luther King to the center of the national stage at the age of twenty-seven. Along with clergymen from other southern cities, he organized the Southern Christian Leadership Conference. King, the eloquent arouser of emotions, became the interpreter of the Negroes' plight. He preached the doctrine of nonviolence as practiced by the great Indian leader, Gandhi. He became a symbol for the masses of Negroes and also attracted many white followers.

Dr. King's untimely death on April 4, 1968, by an assassin's bullet, removed him from leadership of the Southern Christian Leadership Conference. King had gone to Memphis, Tennessee, to lead a nonviolent demonstration in support of a strike of sanitation workers, most of whom were Negroes. He was murdered while standing on the balcony of a motel. His successor was the Rev. Ralph Abernathy. Mrs. Coretta King, wife of the slain leader, has been active, too.

The Southern Christian Leadership Conference is a loose organization with branches in most southern cities. Voter registration, nonviolent marches, freedom rides, and leadership training programs featuring political techniques have been its chief activities. Since the summer of 1966 the Conference has pushed activities in northern cities, determined to modify the pattern of segregated housing.

CORE. For twenty years the Congress of Racial Equality (CORE) was a relatively unknown organization which had achieved success in desegregating restaurants and housing projects in northern cities. CORE had more experience than other organizations in nonviolent techniques. The sit-ins and freedom rides gave the organization a chance for leadership. James Farmer, a former program director of the NAACP and a clergyman, was national chairman of CORE. He was succeeded in 1966 by a North Carolina lawyer, Floyd B. McKissick, who was replaced in 1968 by Roy Innis, a more militant leader. The imaginative leadership attracted many students to the movement.

SNCC. College students were dedicated to the civil rights movement under the CORE programs and received financial support from the major organizations. But some were not satisfied with the results and decided to form an organization of their own with branches on college campuses. Thus was born the Student Non-Violent Coordinating Committee (SNCC). The organization's executive director was James Forman, a former Chicago teacher. Successors have included the more militant Harlem-bred Stokely Carmichael, H. "Rap" Brown, who openly preached violence, and equally militant Phil Hutchings. The existence of the organization indicates the dissatisfaction of some Negroes with the older organizations. In 1969 the name was changed to the Student National Coordinating Committee.

BLACK MUSLIMS. The leader of the Black Muslim movement, former Baptist minister, Elijah Muhammad, preached: "Whites are evil, Negroes are divine." Malcolm X, his chief lieutenant, formed a separate Black Nationalist movement but was assassinated in New York in 1965.

BLACK PANTHERS. A Marxist-oriented, militant group, the Black Panthers, has waged a class struggle under the leadership of Eldridge Cleaver, Minister of Information, and Bobby Seale, national chairman. Revolution through violence is advocated, but breakfasts for Negro children are promoted.

The Black Muslims and the Black Panthers have forced other civil rights groups to be more militant than they wish.

In the past, primarily middle-class

Believing that the white man is evil, the Black Muslims preach that black people should not try to integrate with whites but should form a separate state of their own. (UPI photo)

Negroes and some whites have been the members of these organizations, but increasingly the working class Negroes are joining. Although the majority of Negroes do not belong to any of these organizations, their leaders speak for them and express their dissatisfactions and frustrations. Financing the organizations has at times been a major problem.

In an analysis of the operations of the various civil rights organizations, a sociology professor points out that three types of protest strategies are employed:

1. *Legal*—an appeal to law through filing suits, carrying on court litigation, and encouraging favorable legislation;

2. *Educational*—an appeal to reason through researching, informing, consulting, persuading, and negotiating with political and economic leaders;

3. *Activist*—an appeal to morality through direct personal confrontation of the enforcers and tacit bystanders of the segregated system, usually through nonviolent, direct action in the area of public accommodations.[1] Violence, however, has been used when frustrations were high.

ASPIRATIONS. Nationwide, Negroes are a minority of 22 million out of a total population of over 200 million. As with all people there are great individual differences. Some are rich; some are poor. Some are athletic; some are not. Some are well-educated; some are illiterate. The fact is that whenever Negroes have been given opportunity, they have been successful. The great difficulty in the past has been that Negroes have been denied the chance to achieve. In spite of these difficulties, Negroes have achieved distinction in all of life's activities. To compile a list of Negroes

[1] James H. Laue, "The Changing Character of Negro Protest," *The Annals of the American Academy of Political and Social Science*, 357 (January, 1965), p. 122.

Mention why the Swedish Nobel authorities selected Ralph Bunche for the Peace Prize in 1950 and Martin Luther King for the same in 1964.

Carl Stokes is sworn in as mayor of Cleveland, Ohio, in 1967. He became the first Negro mayor of a major metropolitan city. (UPI photo)

who have added to the goodness of life in America would require many books the size of this one. A small sampling includes:

in government—Thurgood Marshall, Edward Brooke, Shirley Chisholm, Julian Bond, Charles Evers, Carl Stokes;

in literature—James Baldwin, Countee Cullen, Gwendolyn Brooks, Paul Lawrence Dunbar, Maya Angelou, Frank Yerby, Richard Wright;

in music—Marian Anderson, Louis Armstrong, Harry Belafonte, Duke Ellington, Leontyne Price, the Fifth Dimension;

in the dramatic arts—Bill Cosby, Sammy Davis, Jr., Katherine Dunham, Dick Gregory, Sidney Poitier, Pearl Bailey;

in athletics—Arthur Ashe, Jimmie Brown, Althea Gibson, Hayes Jones, Jesse Owens, Willie Mays, Jack Robinson;

in business—Samuel Fuller, John H. Johnson, Berry Gordy, Charles Spaulding;

in military service—General B. O. Davis, General Roscoe C. Cartwright, General Frederick E. Davison, General Oliver W. Dillard, General James F. Hamlet, Admiral Samuel L. Gravely, Jr.;

in religion—Bishop D. Ward Nichols, Rev. J. Oscar Lee, Bishop Joseph O. Bowers, Rev. Roy Nichols, Rev. Jesse Jackson;

in art—Richmond Barthé, Jacob Lawrence, Henry O. Tanner;

in medicine—Dr. U. S. Dailey, Dr. Charles Ford, Dr. Theodore R. M. Howard, Dr. Barbara Wright, Dr. T. K. Lawless;

in education — Kenneth Clark, Allison Davis, E. Franklin Frazier, Mordecai W. Johnson, Alain Locke, Carter G. Woodson, John Hope Franklin.

The Nobel Peace Prize has been granted to two Negroes: Dr. Ralph J. Bunche and Dr. Martin Luther King.

However, many Negroes are poor, unskilled people. They are trapped by life in the slums with little chance for improvement. Their aspirations are dulled.

Improving the economic condition of Negroes is one of the essentials if the civil rights struggle is to be successful. Former Vice President Hubert Humphrey, speaking to the White House Conference on Equal Employment Opportunity in 1966, pointed out that "in northern industrial centers one out of every three Negro workers has suffered unemployment in the past few years. In some neighborhoods the unemployment rate among Negroes is as high as 40 per cent."

The unemployment difficulties of Negroes are illustrated by the fact that in a predominantly Negro high school in one large northern city, not one Negro graduate of the June class had been able to locate a permanent job by the following October.

In New York in 1965 civil rights leaders summarized these conditions as follows:

The Negro community is still faced with the crushing burdens of disproportionate unemployment, low wages, inadequate and segregated education, police brutality, the miseries of slum living and continued stubborn resistance to the right to vote.

In its twentieth anniversary issue, *Ebony* magazine editorialized:

A Negro youth is instructed in welding. Instruction in a variety of trades provides opportunities for a career; however, more than vocational education is needed. (Courtesy of the Office of Economic Opportunity)

To deprive a man of his right to vote, his right to a decent public education, to restrict his freedom of travel and the right to live in the home of his choice, to take away any part of his right to gainful employment, is to punish him unjustly. . . .[1]

THE FUTURE The Nixon administration from 1968 to 1972 passed no major civil rights legislation. In 1970 the Voting Rights Act of 1965 was extended by Congress for an additional five years, but only after Congress defeated efforts by Nixon forces to modify the voting protections. President Nixon opposed the busing of pupils to achieve a racial balance.

The organizations of Negroes argued that President Nixon was doing as little as possible for them. Their position was that Nixon had been elected by a "Southern Strategy" of appealing to white southerners who wished to slow down or put a stop to the civil rights movement. Typical of this

viewpoint was a speech given at the 1970 convention of the NAACP in which the chairman charged that the Nixon administration had adopted "a calculated policy to work against the needs and aspirations of the largest minority of its citizens."

Nixon supporters challenged these attacks as misrepresenting the administration's record. They pointed to actions indicating concern for advancing the cause of civil rights such as: the development of the "Philadelphia Plan" to assist Negroes in obtaining employment in the construction industry, the expenditure of larger funds to aid school desegregation, and an increase in southern school integration.

What of the future? Three trends are appearing. First, the struggle for civil rights for blacks has moved into the North with demands for an end to segregated housing patterns, for equal employment opportunities, and for better education. Busing has become a central issue as a means to improved schooling.

Second, in the South and in the large cities of the North, blacks are using political power effectively. Voter registration has increased and the number of elected black officials has grown rapidly. The vision of political freedom is becoming a reality.

Third, other non-white minorities are on the move to share in the advances made by blacks. American Indians, Spanish-speaking Americans, and American Orientals have organized to demand fairer treatment and to enjoy the benefits of democracy.

There are nearly 800,000 American Indians. Over half this number live in five states: Arizona, California, New Mexico, North Carolina, and Oklahoma. But there are Indians living in every state. Most Indians wish to retain their rich cultural background and strive to maintain their tribal communities. Some 300,000 Indians live on reservations.

---

[1]"The Inevitable Questions" in November, 1965 issue. Reprinted by permission of *Ebony* magazine.

With respect to the future of the civil rights movement, discuss the means which each previously mentioned Negro group employs toward its ends.

Spanish-speaking Americans are divided into two major groups: Mexican Americans and Puerto Ricans. Mexican Americans, sometimes called Chicanos, include five million people while Puerto Ricans on the mainland number about a million and a half. In addition, there are more than a half million people of Cuban origin, a half million with origins in Central and South America, and about a million and a half that the census classifies as "other Spanish." Three-fifths of the Mexican Americans live in the Southwest while Puerto Ricans live mainly in the urban areas of the Northeast. Cubans tend to settle in the coastal South.

American Orientals consist of some 600,000 Japanese, 435,000 Chinese, and 345,000 Filipinos. Of the Japanese, more than 70 per cent are about equally divided between Hawaii and California. Of the Chinese, about 40 per cent live in California, about 20 per cent in New York, and about 12 per cent in Hawaii. Of the Filipinos, about 40 per cent live in California and about 30 per cent in Hawaii.

These groups intend to maintain their own cultural identities in American society. They are organizing to assert their rights and to end their second-class citizenship status. They hold that liberty, concern for the general welfare, majority rule, and minority rights, as described in Chapter 1, must be applied to them. They recognize and want others to recognize that America is a pluralistic, multi-ethnic society with many different life-styles. They want each individual to be respected as a person of worth. In this movement, many women too are insisting on equal rights regardless of sex.

The civil rights struggle thus has become a stage in the efforts to bring American ideals and practices into closer harmony.

CONCEPTS AND GENERALIZATIONS

1
The basic principles of American government are not always lived up to in actual practice.

2
The crucial social issue of our times within the United States is the effort to obtain full political, economic, and social rights for minority groups.

3
Until this decade, the mood of the majority was not favorable to the granting of full civil rights to Negroes.

4
The Supreme Court has reversed an earlier decision approving segregation and is now committed to the treatment of individuals as individuals without regard to race.

5
Because of past treatment, Negroes have a disproportionately large share of unemployment, unskilled workers, crime, poor housing, and nonvoting.

6
Negroes and whites have developed a variety of organizations to work for the improvement of life for Negroes.

7
When Negroes have been given the chance to succeed, they have achieved distinction in all walks of life.

1. Why did Selma, Alabama become a symbol for the civil rights struggle?

2. Why is the civil rights struggle the crucial issue of our times?

3. What aspects of the civil rights struggle are indicated by the quotations from President Kennedy and the Reverend King?

4. How does the distinction between federal protection of civil rights and state protection affect Negroes?

5. How did the 13th, 14th, and 15th amendments affect the federal-state power over civil rights?

6. Why, from 1875 to 1940, was "the mood of the nation no longer favorable to the vigorous enforcement of civil rights?"

7. How did the educational ideas of Booker T. Washington and W. E. B. DuBois differ?

8. What have been the unique contributions of the NAACP, the Urban League, the Brotherhood of Sleeping Car Porters, the Southern Christian Leadership Conference, CORE, SNCC, and the Black Muslims?

9. Who have been the leaders of these organizations?

10. What effects have the Negro migrations to the North had?

11. What contributions to civil rights has each of the recent Presidents made?

12. How has the Supreme Court changed its positions on civil rights?

13. Why have registration and voting been emphasized in the struggle for civil rights?

14. How effective have civil rights action programs been?

15. Have the summer riots helped or hurt the civil rights movement? Why?

16. Why have new Negro organizations been created in recent years?

17. What are the aspirations of Negroes?

18. What do you consider to be the future of the civil rights movement?

19. Which of the three types of protest activities do you consider to be most effective? Are all three types needed?

1. To what extent and in what ways is the civil rights struggle affecting your community? What are the hopes and aspirations and the fears and anxieties of individuals and groups in your community?

2. Urban League leader Whitney M. Young, speaking before the State Chamber of Commerce in Lansing, Michigan, in September, 1966 said, "Our problem is not good will or ill will but no will. If responsible people do not lead, irresponsible people will. Thus we have our Black Muslims and you have your John Birchers and Klans and these Nazi groups." Do you agree or disagree with this statement? Why?

3. Hold a panel discussion on the topic, "The Political Realities which Required Passing a Series of Civil Rights Acts in Successive Congresses."

4. "Black Power" and "White Backlash" were phrases used to describe aspects of the civil rights struggle. What do these phrases mean in your opinion? How have they helped or hindered the civil rights movement?

5. A newspaper correspondent, Bruce Biossat, began one of his columns with this paragraph:
"Rumblings among responsible Negro leaders suggest that they regard Stokely Carmichael, the young black segregationist, who heads the Student Non-Violent Coordinating Committee, as the worst drawback to their cause in years."
What is your opinion of this paragraph? On what evidence did you form your opinion?

6. James Farmer, speaking to a group of educators in 1966, said, "What progress has been wrought in the civil rights movement has not changed the life situation for the Negro. Negroes in the lower economic levels as yet have not been helped. In Watts and Harlem, Negroes believe that America has shut them out." Assuming that Mr. Farmer is correct, what could be done to change the situation? Assuming that Mr. Farmer is wrong, where is he in error?

7. In the civil rights struggle to what extent is social class rather than race the basic issue?

8. How are prejudices acquired? How can prejudices be removed? Can prejudiced people be prevented from harming others?

9. One Negro student reacted to the list of famous Negroes in this chapter by saying, "I don't like such a list. It seems to imply that

'These made it, why can't you?' " Another Negro student reacted, "I think the list is an inspiration. It shows that if we are given a chance we can succeed. And it's good for Whitey to know that we have famous people, too." How do you react?

THINGS
TO DO

1. Write a newspaper editorial stating your position on a civil rights issue.

2. Collect a series of pictures from newspapers and magazines showing scenes of violence in civil rights encounters. Analyze these pictures in terms of: the age of participants, the causes of the violence, the geographic location of the scene. What conclusions do you reach on these matters?

3. Prepare an oral report on a Negro who has achieved success. Include in your report some analysis of the ease or difficulty of obtaining information in standard references.

4. Conduct a public opinion survey of students in your school on a few important civil rights issues.

5. Compile the voting record of your congressman and senators on the civil rights acts, and draw generalizations about your district and state from this voting record.

6. Hold a sociodrama on a Negro-white conflict in your community. By shifting participants, try to develop alternative ways to react to the same situations. Discuss the implications of these dramas.

7. Prepare a chart showing the increase in Negro registration for voting in southern states.

8. Visit a meeting of a civil rights group or a civil rights government agency in your community. Report to the class on what happened and your reactions.

9. Compare the position on civil rights held by candidates running for an elective office.

10. Compare the handling of newspaper stories and editorials on a civil rights issue in newspapers from various parts of the country. What conclusions do you reach?

11. Divide the class into committees. Have each committee investigate and report on one of the following topics: progress on school integration in the South, the handling of *de facto* segregation in the North, economic opportunities for Negroes, Negro voting, housing patterns, education as the ultimate solution to racial prejudice.

12. Investigate and report to the class on the issues behind the complaints of "police brutality."

13. Have small committees interview the following types of leaders concerning their predictions on the future of the civil rights struggle: clergymen, teachers, elected officials, businessmen, labor leaders.

14. Invite a person active in the civil rights struggles to speak before your class.

15. Prepare a report on the civil rights struggles today of a minority group other than the Negroes.

FURTHER
READINGS

Abrams, Charles, FORBIDDEN NEIGHBORS: A STUDY OF PREJUDICE IN HOUSING. Harper and Row, Publishers, Inc., 1955.

Bruner, Richard W., BLACK POLITICIANS. David McKay Co., Inc., 1971.

Conrad, Earl, THE INVENTION OF THE NEGRO. Paul S. Eriksson, Inc., 1966.

Douglass, Frederick, LIFE AND TIMES OF FREDERICK DOUGLASS. Thomas Y. Crowell Co., 1966.

Farmer, James, FREEDOM — WHEN? Random House, Inc., 1965.

Franklin, John H., AN ILLUSTRATED HISTORY OF BLACK AMERICANS. Time-Life Books, 1970.

Friedman, Leon, THE CIVIL RIGHTS READER. Walker & Co., 1967.

Holt, Len, THE SUMMER THAT DIDN'T END. William Morrow and Co., 1965.

King, Coretta Scott, MY LIFE WITH MARTIN LUTHER KING, JR. Holt, Rinehart and Winston, Inc., 1969.

Klass, Morton and Hellman, Hal, THE KINDS OF MANKIND: AN INTRODUCTION TO RACE AND RACISM. J. B. Lippincott Company, 1971.

Lewis, David L., KING: A CRITICAL BIOGRAPHY. Praeger Publishers, Inc., 1970.

Little, Malcolm, THE AUTOBIOGRAPHY OF MALCOLM X. Grove Press. 1965.

Shapiro, Martin, THE COURT AND CONSTITUTIONAL RIGHTS. Scott, Foresman and Co., 1967.

Sterling, Dorothy, TEAR DOWN THE WALLS! Doubleday & Company, Inc., 1968.

Sterne, E. Gelders, HIS WAS THE VOICE: THE LIFE OF W. E. B. DUBOIS. The Macmillan Co., 1971.

Time Magazine, "Black America 1970" Special Issue, April 6, 1970.

Richard Brown—A Teacher

This is the life story of a teacher who is a Negro. In part the story is not true; names, locations, events have been changed to avoid any possibility of identification. In this sense this account is fiction. But, in a larger sense, this biography is true and similar to that of several other Negro teachers the authors have known.

Richard Brown was born in one of the states of the Deep South. His father was a Baptist preacher; his mother was an elementary school teacher. He was the middle child in a family of five children. As a preacher his father received little pay and was forced to supplement his income by working in a local store.

Richard was a fast learner. Although his elementary school was poorly equipped and classes were large, he learned to read well and to like books. His mother was able to help him with his school work, and he enjoyed competing with his older brother and sister. He lived in the Negro section of town, attended a segregated school, and was taught by Negro teachers. He had almost no contacts with white citizens, because his parents taught him to observe the mores of the South.

In high school Richard was a reasonably good athlete, but not good enough to attract the attention of any college. He was an excellent student and showed some leadership ability in student activities. Many of his friends dropped out of school, and he also wanted to do so—partly because the family needed money but mainly because he saw no real future ahead. But his parents insisted that he remain in school. During his last year in high school, one teacher whom he liked became especially interested in him and influenced Richard

to go to the college which he had attended.

The college was a state teachers college some forty miles from his home. His four years there were uneventful. He did not participate in athletics; he worked part time in the meager library; he studied a great deal. He graduated with honors and with a teaching certificate permitting him to teach science. Of most importance, he developed curiosity, a desire to learn more, and a determination to make something useful of his life.

He returned home and taught in his local high school. During his second year of teaching he married an English-speech teacher who was beginning her first year of teaching. They decided that he should get a master's degree. But the teachers colleges of his state did not give graduate degrees, and the larger universities did not admit Negroes. The state had, however, developed a system of tuition grants for Negro teachers by which payment would be made for attendance at northern schools. (Largely this was a device to avoid the pressure of admitting qualified Negroes to the universities.)

Richard Brown applied for a tuition grant and received one. For three summers he and his wife attended a large midwestern state university, where he earned his degree. The third summer the first of three children was born. Life in the North was not easy for the Browns. This was their first experience in a "nonsegregated" society. They found that the rooms which they rented, the barber and beauty shops, and some restaurants were really segregated. At the same time, they learned that fellow students and teachers, for the most part, treated them as equals. Mr. Brown recognized that he could hold his own in competition with white students. He learned too that segregated schools of his home state —in equipment, books, and general conditions of learning—were not the equal of those of the northern state. He began to form a resolution to try to improve the education of Negroes back home.

Then, he was offered a position in a fairly large city in the southern part of Ohio. The salary was good; the science laboratories were excellent; but the school was in a segregated Negro section. Most of the teachers were white, however, and there was a white principal. He accepted the position, reasoning that this type of experience would be good for him. It was; he became recognized as a very superior teacher, liked by his students and fellow teachers.

He taught in this school for three years and then was asked by the superintendent to transfer to a high school on the edge of the city where he would be the first Negro teacher in an otherwise all-white school. The challenge of this opportunity appealed to him and he accepted. Again he was successful, for he was well received by students, faculty members, and parents. During those years he lived on the border of the Negro ghetto in a home that had been built by the former white owners.

After five years in Ohio he received a grant from one of the larger foundations which was investing large sums of money in efforts to improve the quality of Negro education. He returned to the midwestern university for two years and graduated with a degree of Doctor of Philosophy. One of the professors on his doctoral committee said of him, "Dr. Brown is one of the ablest students in his field."

During those two years of advanced graduate work he had lived in a rented home on a street that was populated entirely by Negroes. But all the rest of this residential area contained homes of whites. His older child attended an excellent integrated elementary school which made a very favorable impression on the Browns.

At this point came the most important decision of Dr. Brown's life. He was offered a position as a professor in the college of his home state which had awarded him his A.B. degree. Almost at the same time he was offered a similar position at a state college in Pennsylvania. He and his wife debated the offers for days. One gave the opportunity to return home, to try to raise the level of Negro education in the South, and to be a leader among the Negroes there. The other meant that he would be a professor among other professors but with a good chance to rise in his profession. He decided to accept the position in Pennsylvania. When pressed as to why he made the decision, he said, "Much as I would like to help lead Negroes in the South to a better life, I cannot return my children to the segregated system under which I grew up."

Today Dr. Brown is a successful professor in Pennsylvania. He is honored by his fellow teachers and respected by his students. The family lives in an "open housing" area and the children attend integrated schools. Dr. Brown has become active in CORE and led the picketing around the city hall during an attempt to modify police treatment of Negro youth in the college community.

- How are the principles presented in this first unit illustrated by the life of Dr. Brown?
- For Dr. Brown and his family, are these principles myths or ideals?
- How typical was the Browns' decision not to live in the South?
- How would the experiences of Dr. Brown have been different if he had been: a Mexican-American, a Jew, an Irish-Catholic, an uneducated Negro, an uneducated white man from the South?

<u>2</u>
THE POLITICAL
PROCESSES

Andrew Sacks/Editorial Photocolor Archives

Intelligent decision-making is the goal of a democratic political system. Decisions have to be made, whether the problem is the obtaining of civil rights for Negroes, the passage of a disarmament bill in Congress, or the establishing of a one-way street in a local community.

The political processes are concerned with the activities by which these decisions are made, the persons who are chosen to make them, and the influences that operate on the decision makers. Normally one expects these political decisions to be made within the framework of government, but sometimes they are made outside governmental channels.

The activities of citizens are central to the process of making decisions. Citizens operate most often through elections, in political parties, through interest groups, and by their influence on public opinion.

Chapter 5 emphasizes the role of the people in these processes. Citizenship and immigration policies are highlighted.

Chapter 6 describes the election process—voting, election machinery, types of ballots, honest elections.

Chapter 7 discusses political parties and their activities in the political processes.

Chapter 8 stresses the efforts to influence citizens by changing public opinion and by the activities of interest groups.

ALIEN—a person who is not a citizen of the country in which he lives.

ANARCHIST—a person who believes in a society without government or laws and who sometimes tries to overthrow established governments.

CITIZEN—a person who is a member of a state or nation, owing it allegiance and entitled to full civil rights.

COALITION—a joining together into a combination or alliance.

IMMIGRANT—a person who leaves one nation to reside in another.

NATURALIZATION—a process by which an alien becomes a citizen.

QUOTA—the portion or share of a total number; the number of immigrants permitted to enter the United States from a particular country.

RURAL—relating to predominantly agricultural areas outside of cities and towns.

SOCIAL CLASS—a broad group of people with similar economic, cultural, or political behavior.

URBAN—relating to cities and towns.

THE LANGUAGE OF GOVERNMENT

All nations, free and nonfree, have regulations concerning nationality; but in a democratic society, citizenship is more than just nationality, more than just being a subject—with it go power and responsibility.

5

Citizens

A few years ago, a play was written about a young man who had come to this country from Ireland around 1900. He settled in New York and became active in politics. This politician-hero at one point in the play says,

> When I stood in the landing shed of this "promised land" . . . I made a vow:
> I'd fight my way to power if it killed me.
> Not only for myself but for our kind.[1]

The author of this play was telling the story of the masses of immigrants who came to this country at the end of the nineteenth century. To share in the equality of opportunity, the freedom, the free enterprise of this nation, many turned to politics. Here they could use their influence to get into the mainstream of American life. Through political power they could fight the preju-

[1]William Alfred, *Hogan's Goat*, Farrar, Straus & Giroux, Inc. Copyright © 1958, 1966 by William Alfred.

These people are embarking from a European port in the late nineteenth century to emigrate to America. Why did the United States cease welcoming so many to its shores? (Library of Congress)

dices which forced them to live in slums and work at menial jobs.

Oscar Handlin, historian of the immigrant movement, wrote of this period:

> The one association to which all Americans belonged was the Republic; the one activity in which all participated was politics.
>
> In a calendar meager with ceremonial moments, election day was one of the year's few memorable occasions. Now every man became a king, for he was the maker of his rules.[1]

At that period of our history there developed an Irish vote, a Polish vote, a German vote, a Scandinavian vote. These first gen-erations of immigrants found that the local political leader provided them with the chance to share in power. In return for their votes and their influence they received jobs, food, lodging, companionship, and eventually a better life. The immigrant dweller in the slums of yesterday lives in the suburbs today.

One of the most striking examples of this political process is the Kennedy family. President John Fitzgerald Kennedy's grand-fathers were Boston politicians, leaders of the Irish vote. On his mother's side, grand-father "Honey Fitz" Fitzgerald became mayor of Boston. In the next generation, the father, Joseph P. Kennedy, became a wealthy businessman, a backer of President Franklin Roosevelt, for which he was re-warded by being named ambassador to

[1]Oscar Handlin, *The Americans,* Atlantic—Little, Brown. Copyright © 1963 by Oscar Handlin.

Americans are diverse in ancestral background, in where they live and work, and in many other ways. (Clockwise, starting at top: USDA, National Film Board of Canada, American Airlines, Alan Cliburn, Bureau of Indian Affairs)

England. One son became President and two became senators. All had their base of political power in the masses of people seeking a share in the promises of America.

These immigrants and their leaders learned that the only guarantee that our democratic system will live up to its ideals and principles lies with the people. They used the political processes to gain power.

Our government works well when there is widespread citizen interest and participation and when citizens are alert and well informed. If citizens are ignorant, uninterested, too busy with other things, lacking in understanding of political processes, then our government declines in efficiency and we get poor government. When the people fail, then a constitution, a bill of rights, checks and balances, a court system, and all the other machinery of government cannot prevent the failure of government.

This is what is meant by that old saying 'Eternal vigilance is the price of liberty." Our form of government requires that citizens give constant attention to the affairs of government, for it is the citizens who rule. Any examination of the processes of government must include a study of people and their political activities as well as documents and principles.

WE THE PEOPLE There are more than 204 million people living in the United States. There are all kinds of people, for this is a nation of great diversity. We are first-generation Americans founding a new home in this great land. We are descendants of Pilgrims, who immigrated to our shores more than 350 years ago. We are white, Negro, Indian, Chinese, Japanese. We are Catholic, Jew, Protestant, Eastern Orthodox, Moslem, Buddhist, and others. We are rich and poor. We are businessmen, laborers, farmers, teachers, lawyers, nurses, truck drivers, schoolchildren, housewives. We are young, middle-aged, and old.

Here we have built a land with many types of people—for all kinds of people. We have said that we can be united although we are different. While we have had cases of intolerance and prejudice in our country, our great dream has been to learn to live together "with liberty and justice for all." This is one of man's great adventures. The success of the venture depends on citizen participation.

RURAL-URBAN. As our citizens participate, it is possible to classify them into various groupings according to the influences they have on the political process. One such classification is the rural-urban. The rural people, living in very small towns or on farms, have had great influence on American government. For over a century ours was predominantly an agricultural nation; the rural voters controlled the state legislatures and the Congress. They exerted great influence. As we became an industrial nation, the urban population in and around our larger cities grew rapidly and steadily and it continues to grow. A great struggle took place to shift power from the rural interests to the urban. At the same time, within the urban areas, power was being divided between the central city and the suburbs. (These matters will be discussed in greater detail in Chapters 9 and 15 and in Unit Five.)

SOCIAL CLASS. A second classification of people is by social class. While all persons are equal under the law, it is true that some have more money, some have better education, some live in larger houses. Scholars of society, the sociologists, have grouped people into broad classes: the upper class, the middle class, and the lower class. These classes are not fixed or permanent; people move up and down in the

With respect to the great diversity of the American people, introduce and discuss the term "cosmopolitan."

class system. In terms of influence on decisions, the upper class has always had more influence than its numbers would seem to justify. C. Wright Mills, in his book, *The Power Elite*, describes this position of influence in this way,

> In every town and small city of America an upper set of families stands above the middle classes and towers over the underlying population of clerks and wage workers. The members of this set possess more than do others of whatever there is locally to possess; they hold the keys to local decision; their names and faces are often printed in the local paper, in fact, they own the newspaper as well as the radio station; they also own the three important local plants and most of the commercial properties along the main street; they direct the banks.[1]

On a national scale, he says, ". . . they are in positions to make decisions having major consequences. . . . they rule the big corporations. They run the machinery of the state and claim its prerogatives. They direct the military establishment. . . ."

The middle class represents a powerful brake on this "power elite." In this country, with a large, strong, influential middle class, the upper class has lost some of its power. In some of the developing countries, for example, India, Egypt, and Brazil, one of the central problems is to develop a strong middle class which can curb the powerful upper classes in those nations.

The lower class has one great advantage —numbers. While in many day-to-day decisions the members of the lower class do not have the time, energy, or money to be active, still on great questions which affect their lives, because they are the largest class, they can exert powerful influence. The election of President Franklin Roose-

1 C. Wright Mills, *The Power Elite*, Oxford University Press. Copyright © Oxford University Press, 1956.

velt for four terms is explained, at least in part, by the fact that the masses of people felt it was time for them to exert influence and they responded to Roosevelt's appeals. As one political leader said, "The worker knows where the shoe pinches."

INTEREST GROUPS. A third way to classify the people is by interest groups. For most political scientists, the interest group is a more acceptable explanation of the political process than the social class or power elite explanations. They see people divided into a great many different groups. The same person may belong to a labor union, the American Legion, the Democratic party, the Baptist church, the NAACP, a bowling league, and the PTA. While not all these groups may try to influence political decisions directly, many do. When one group tries to get some action, it is likely to find another group opposing this action. A

Differing viewpoints in America are reflected through the variety of interest groups to which peo-ple belong. (Above) A group of hotel workers from New York demonstrate in favor of labor legis-lation. (Opposite page, left) Through his speeches Cesar Chavez, a union organizer among migrant workers, brings the plight of migrants to the attention of the public. (Above, AFL-CIO News photo; left, EPA Newsphoto/Editorial Photocolor Archives)

struggle then takes place between the com-peting groups. Political decisions are often the result of a bringing together of enough groups into a loose coalition to gain power.

The interest groups compete under the "rules of the game"—majority rule, minor-ity rights, checks and balances, and other legal aspects of government. The system is complicated by "overlapping memberships," by shifting of the coalitions, and by indi-viduals' changing group affiliations. Under this system of classification "the people" consists of a vast collection of competing groups engaged in political action. Public policy on any issue is the result of the bar-gaining or compromising that takes place among these groups.

Each of the above schemes for classify-ing people has been viewed in terms of its influence on political decisions. Each, in effect, attempts to explain why certain polit-ical action takes place. Running across each

of these systems of classification is a fourth, which describes those who may legally par-ticipate in certain types of political activi-ties. This system divides people into citi-zens and aliens.

THE CITIZENS   In the United States, as well as other countries, persons living within the boundaries of the country are either citizens or aliens. The citizens are those who are members of the nation which guarantees them protection, and in turn, to which they owe their allegiance. The aliens are those who are citizens of another nation, but may be temporarily or even sometimes permanently living away from their native land. Thus, a citizen of the United States is an alien when he is a tourist in France, and the French cook from Paris at a New York hotel is an alien in the United States because he has retained his French citizenship, even though he may have worked here for many years.

There are about four million aliens living in the United States. The rest of the people in our nation got to be citizens in one of two ways: (1) by right of birth or (2) by the process of naturalization. These ways of becoming a citizen are referred to in Section 1 of the Fourteenth Amendment to the Constitution: "All persons born or naturalized in the United States, and subject to the jurisdiction thereof, are citizens of the United States and of the state wherein they reside."

CITIZENSHIP BY BIRTH. About 90 per cent of the citizens of the United States became citizens by their birth. Birth determines citizenship in two ways. First, the place of birth determines citizenship. In general any person born in the United States or in any territory of the United States is a citizen of the United States. Hence, being born in any of the states, the District of Columbia, the territories of Guam or the Virgin Islands, or in the commonwealth of Puerto Rico makes a person a citizen of the United States.

Second, being born of parents who are citizens of the United States determines citizenship. In these days of widespread and speedy travel, with American citizens scattered all around the globe, many babies whose parents are United States citizens are born in foreign lands. In these cases an old practice, "the law of blood relationship," determines the citizenship. A high school teacher and his wife, formerly residents of the United States, went to Germany to teach in an American school. Their two children, born while they were in Germany, are citizens of the United States. The law of blood relationship applied, rather than the law of the place of birth.

There are, of course, many complications that can arise in applying these two rules. Suppose a child born in France has a father who is a United States citizen and a mother who is a French citizen. Would the child

MODELS

The word *model* is used in different ways. When a young lady works as a "model," she wears beautiful clothing to show customers, or she has her picture taken for an advertising agency, or she serves as a subject for an artist. Similarly, when a "model house" is advertised, a contractor has built a home to show his customers the type of house he can build and sell at a certain price.

The political scientist, along with other scientists, uses the word *model* in a slightly different way. The scientist employs this word to mean a theoretical description of a possible system of relationships, as, for example, in the sentence: The physicist builds a model of an atom. In the same way, some political scientists describe models which they think help to explain political phenomena. No one model perfectly explains such complex human behavior as is involved in political life, but these models do help in creating research plans and in simplifying ideas for teaching purposes.

Three models have been described to explain the political processes. One, called the *popular rule* model, describes the ideals of majority rule, one citizen-one vote, liberty, checks and balances, and similar ideas — somewhat as was done in the first three chapters of this book. A second model is called the *social class* model, which was described briefly in this chapter in the discussion of the power elite. The third model is the *pluralistic group* model, which was described previously in terms of interest groups.

No one of these models gives a completely accurate explanation of the political processes, but all offer helpful insights into the complexities of government and politics.

be a French or an American citizen? In general the law provides that, in such a case, if the father had resided in the United States ten years prior to the birth, of which five years must be after age fourteen, the child must live in the United States for at least five years between the ages of fourteen and twenty-eight or he loses United States citizenship.

Another complication concerns marriage. Historically, when a woman married she took the citizenship of her husband. Since 1922, however, a woman does not lose her United States citizenship when she marries a man of foreign citizenship. Actually she usually holds dual citizenship: in the United States and in the country of her husband. But if she should return to the United States, she would still be a United States citizen.

Similarly, an alien woman marrying a United States citizen does not automatically become a citizen. But she can become a citizen by a simplified naturalization process.

Another exception concerns those persons who were born in an outlying possession of the United States, or whose parents were born there. These persons are not full-fledged citizens, but legally are *nationals*. They owe allegiance to the United States; they are entitled to protection but do not have all the rights of citizens.

The details of citizenship are defined by laws passed by Congress. A Nationality Act was passed in 1940. Changes were made by the Immigration and Nationality Act of 1952. The law is interpreted by the courts, as is the case with all other laws. Amendments are made by Congress as changes are required. Both Congress and the courts have based the law on the two principles of the law of birthplace (*jus soli*) and the law of blood relationship (*jus sanguinis*).

CITIZENSHIP BY NATURALIZATION. Aliens may become citizens of the United States by a process called *naturalization*. Most aliens are permanent residents of our country. They have chosen to live and work here. Some aliens, however, are here only temporarily; they are guests visiting our country for a short time as students, tourists, or businessmen.

Aliens are not citizens, but they can enjoy most of the privileges of citizens as long as they are law-abiding, respectable persons. All aliens are entitled to the protection of our laws. They cannot, however, vote or hold public office. Naturalization provides the means by which an alien can become a citizen.

Naturalization is of two types: group naturalization and individual naturalization. Most aliens become citizens by individual naturalization, but group naturalization has been used often enough so that it ought to be better known than it is.

Group naturalization is the system by which an entire group of people are made citizens. This can be done either by an act of Congress or by a treaty. In 1924 all American Indians, in one group, were made citizens by an act of Congress. By similar acts, residents of Hawaii were made citizens in 1900, residents of Puerto Rico were made citizens in 1917, those of the Virgin Islands in 1927, and residents of Guam in 1950. Alaska was purchased from Russia in 1867. By the purchase treaty, the residents were made citizens of the United States.

Most aliens, however, become citizens by *individual action*. The first requirement is that the alien must have been "lawfully admitted for permanent residence." A person who was admitted for a brief pleasure trip, for example, would not be eligible for citizenship. Neither would a person who had entered illegally. Stowaways, deserters from ships' crews, and persons who have

At a court hearing a United States District Judge administers the oath to a group of seventeen aliens who have filed petitions to become naturalized American citizens. (U.S. Immigration and Naturalization Service)

sneaked across the border are not eligible for naturalization.

By law all aliens living in the United States are required to register and re-register each year in January. Presentation of the alien registration card by an applicant is usually sufficient proof that he entered the United States legally.

Until December 23, 1952, it was necessary to file a declaration of intention of becoming a citizen. Since that date, however, the declaration has not been required. The applicant may, if he wishes, still file the declaration, formerly called a *first paper*. Some aliens when seeking employment find it helpful to have filed the declaration. The declaration of intention is made at a naturalization court. There is a small charge.

THE PETITION. Today the applicant's first step toward naturalization is the filing of an application to petition for naturaliza-

tion. It is filed at the nearest office of the Immigration and Naturalization Service.

In addition to having been admitted legally, the applicant must:

1. Be at least eighteen years of age. If under eighteen, a parent who is a citizen may file for the child.

2. Be able to understand and use ordinary English. There is an exception for those physically unable to do so and for those who were over fifty on December 24, 1952, if they had lived in the United States for twenty years.

3. Have resided in the United States for five years and for the last six months of that period in the state where he petitions for naturalization. For husbands or wives of citizens the required residence is only three years after marriage. Special provisions make easier the naturalization of aliens who have served in the armed forces of the United States. There are no residence re-

quirements for veterans who served honorably in World War I or II. Veterans who served honorably at other than war times also are granted similar benefits through shortened residence requirements.

4. Be of good moral character, be loyal to the principles of the Constitution, and demonstrate a knowledge of the history and government of the United States. Some public school systems have special classes for applicants. The Immigration and Naturalization Service also has textbooks to help the applicants.

5. Not have belonged to an organization that advocated opposition to organized government or the overthrow of government by force or advocated these ideas for a period ten years before his application. An exception is allowed if the applicant can show that his membership was involuntary, without knowledge of the nature of the organization, or that he was under age sixteen. This requirement is aimed at anarchists, communists, or others who might be engaged in subversive activity.

THE EXAMINATION. The Immigration and Naturalization office notifies the applicant when and where to appear for an examination. The applicant must bring to the examination two witnesses of good character who have known the applicant at least six months. Sworn statements about the applicant are obtained from other witnesses who have known the applicant for the required period of his residence in the United States.

The witnesses are questioned by a naturalization examiner to be sure that the applicant meets the requirements for naturalization. If the petition seems proper to the examiner, the applicant pays a small fee covering the cost of the petition and the certificate of naturalization.

THE FINAL COURT HEARING. After the Immigration and Naturalization Service has made its investigation, the applicant is notified to appear in a federal or state court for a final hearing. Usually this hearing takes place thirty days or more after the filing of the petition. The judge, in most cases, does not examine the applicant but he can if he wishes. He usually follows the recommendation received from the Immigration and Naturalization Service. If the Service has recommended that the petition be denied, the applicant can ask the judge for a further examination.

When the judge grants the petition for citizenship, the applicant takes an oath giving up his allegiance to the foreign country and promising allegiance to the United States.

Of those persons in our country who were born in foreign lands, about three out of four have become naturalized citizens. About one in four of the foreign-born, living in our country, remains an alien today. Some of these aliens, through personal desire, lack of education, or just letting time pass, have not become naturalized citizens.

ALIENS. Aliens have the same civil rights as citizens. A glance at the Bill of Rights will show that references are to "people" or "persons." The word "citizen" is not used. The Supreme Court has held that aliens are entitled to these rights on the same basis as citizens.

Aliens may be deported if they entered the country illegally, if they engage in subversive activities, or if they are guilty of certain immoral and criminal acts. The alien is expected, in other words, to be law-abiding. Breaking the law may result in only the same penalties as for citizens, but in extreme cases deportation has taken place.

The alien does not have some of the privileges of citizens. He cannot hold public office. In some states he cannot practice law or medicine or teach in a public school.

He cannot vote, although in an earlier period this was possible in many states.

The alien has the same obligations as the citizen. He pays taxes; he must obey the law; he can be called for military service. It should be noted that, based on FBI records, the crime rate for aliens is lower than for natural-born citizens. The rigid standards for admission have weeded out the unfit, and with the chance for new opportunities aliens have contributed to the goodness of life in America.

LOSING CITIZENSHIP. A citizen of the United States can lose his citizenship. Citizens by birth lose their citizenship when they choose to be naturalized in some other country. Under a law suggested by President Eisenhower, native-born and naturalized citizens convicted of attempting to overthrow the government lose their citizenship and become aliens.

By federal law, citizenship may be lost also for such federal crimes as treason or bearing arms against the United States. Citizenship may also be lost by joining the army of a foreign government or by voting in an election in a foreign country.

Naturalized citizens can have their citizenship taken from them for several other reasons. If fraud or a falsehood was used in becoming naturalized, citizenship can be taken away. Falsely swearing that legal entry was made into this country is a typical example. If a naturalized citizen is disloyal to the United States, the courts can take away his citizenship. Residing abroad for three to five years after being naturalized was another cause for losing naturalized citizenship. But in 1964 the Supreme Court held this provision unconstitutional.[1]

IMMIGRATION   The greatest bar to becoming a citizen of the United States for many foreigners is that they cannot enter our country. Once the United States was the great land of opportunity, for historically we welcomed foreigners to our land. Millions came to make their homes here.

The Statue of Liberty is our symbol for this period when as a young nation with plenty of free land we welcomed the for-

---

[1] The Court reasoned that since the Constitution does not differentiate between native-born and naturalized citizens, Congress has no right to do so. This ruling casts doubt on some of the other bases on which naturalized citizens may be deprived of their citizenship but native-born citizens may not.

The Statue of Liberty is an early example of people-to-people friendship. The French people donated to pay for the statue, and the Americans contributed to pay for the pedestal. (New York State Dept. of Commerce)

Discuss the history of U.S. immigration, including the great influx of the 1840's and the so-called "new" immigration of the 1880-1914 era.

eign-born to our shores. On the pedestal of the Statue of Liberty are these lines by Emma Lazarus which remind us of that period.

Give me your tired, your poor,
Your huddled masses, yearning to
*   breathe free,*
The wretched refuse of your teeming
*   shore,*
Send these, the homeless, tempest-
*   tossed to me:*
I lift my lamp beside the golden door.

Gradually over the past seventy-five years this policy of welcome to all foreigners has changed. Restrictions have been placed on the number of people who are admitted. There have been various reasons for this. Our fertile land has been settled; sometimes there have not been jobs enough in our factories; some interest groups have claimed that certain immigrants would not make good citizens.

In 1882 Congress passed the Chinese Exclusion Act because some people, especially on the West Coast, claimed that the standard of living and the customs of the

Chinese prevented them from becoming a part of American life. Over the years other restrictions have been added. Criminals, paupers, the feebleminded, · the insane, anarchists, immoral people, polygamists, persons with contagious diseases, alcoholics, and adults who cannot read any language are now barred from entering the United States.

THE QUOTA SYSTEM. In the 1920's Congress gave special study to our immigration system and adopted a quota system. Each year a total of approximately 150,000 persons would be admitted to this country. From this total, various nations were allowed a certain number of persons, called a *quota*, who could come to the United States each year.

This quota was based on the number of people of each national origin who were in this country in 1920. The effect of this law was that England, Ireland, and Germany had large quotas. Russia, Italy, Greece, and some other countries had small quotas. Most persons from Asiatic countries were excluded.

Canada and the countries of Central and

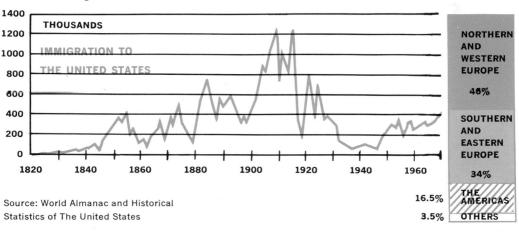

Source: World Almanac and Historical Statistics of The United States

The large graph shows the number of immigrants admitted to the United States annually since 1820. The graph on the right shows, by world regions, the per cent of immigrants living in the United States when the quota system ended in 1968.

South America were not affected by these quotas. There was no limit on the number of immigrants we accepted from these neighbors on the American continents.

The quota system and the depression years of the 1930's reduced the number of immigrants. During and after World War II, however, new attention was given to our immigration policy. In Europe thousands of persons had lost their homes in the war. These displaced persons longed to come to the United States, but the quota system closed the doors to them. In Asia enemy propagandists used our exclusion of the Asiatics as a powerful weapon against our democratic ideas. Congress decided it was time to examine again our immigration policy.

In 1943 Chinese were made eligible for citizenship and were given an annual quota of 105. People from India were made eligible in 1946 and given an annual quota of 100.

A Displaced Persons Act was passed in 1948. This act allowed an increase in im-migration by which war orphans and home-less persons could be admitted. In 1952 the restrictions on all Asiatics were re-moved, and quotas for Far Eastern nations were adopted.

In 1953 ways to admit special hardship cases were approved. These acts permitted increased immigration.

However, the 1950's brought new restric-tions. The threat of communism caused Congress to exclude applicants who are or have been "members of . . . a communist or other totalitarian party."

THE NEW PREFERENCE SYSTEM. The quota system was criticized because of its unfairness. Presidents Truman, Eisen-hower, and Kennedy in messages to Con-gress asked for a new system. Interest groups critical of the system pleaded that the system was based on prejudice against those who were different. The term WASP —white, Anglo-Saxon, Protestant—was used as a description of one who wanted to keep the old system. Over a period of years the political pressures from nationality groups,

Americans have often put pressure on Congress to pass special laws admitting refugees from calamity or oppression. Here refugees from Castro's Cuba are debarking at Key West, Florida. (UPI photo)

Negroes, labor unions, and churches finally resulted in 1965 in a new immigration law requested by President Johnson.

This law eliminated the national origins quota system on June 30, 1968. Under the new system 120,000 immigrants may be admitted each year from the nations of the Western Hemisphere (Canada, Central and South America). Previously there had been no limitation on immigration from these countries.

From other parts of the world, 170,000 persons may be admitted annually, but no more than 20,000 persons from one country. The law provides a series of *preferences* in the admission of immigrants. The highest preferences are given to those with close family relationships to U. S. citizens; to members of professions; to laborers with pecial, needed skills; and to refugees.

In the event that the limit of 170,000 immigrants is not reached in any year, the remainder will be distributed on a first-come, first-served basis without regard to preferences except for the limit of 20,000 for each country.

Congress, of course, without changing the basic policy still can, and does, pass emergency laws to admit special groups, such as refugees, when humanitarian conditions, reflected in overwhelming public opinion, warrant such action. Sometimes, too, laws affecting just one individual (private laws) are passed by Congress to admit a specific person—usually when hardship might otherwise result.

In addition to the permanent immigrants, increasing numbers of visitors come to the United States for temporary stays. Tourists, students, businessmen and their families, and relatives of citizens make up most of these persons.

Every temporary or permanent immigrant is expected to obtain permission from the United States consul in his country before departing for this country. In this way eligibility to enter is controlled. In the event an airline or steamship company brings an alien who cannot be admitted, the company is forced to return the person to the port from which he departed.

CIVIC RESPONSIBILITY Citizens and aliens, because they live in this country, receive

A jury listens to the cross-examination of a witness. One duty of a citizen is to serve on a jury if called. (UPI photo)

One of the most important of a citizen's civic responsibilities is to exercise his right to vote. Here workers at the polls are checking the registration list. (League of Women Voters)

certain rights. Teachers and preachers, however, for years have pointed out that "rights involve duties." The right to vote involves a duty to vote intelligently. The right to trial by jury involves a duty to serve on a jury. The right to free speech involves a duty to tell the truth. Rights and duties interact.

These civic responsibilities include also an understanding of political realities. Ideals are not always practiced, and it is a duty of another kind to be aware of practices which do not match principles and to work to correct them. The fact is that Negroes, in the past, have not been permitted to vote in some southern states. It is a fact that selection of juries has not always been done fairly. It is a fact that some newspapers slant stories to favor a particular point of view. It is a fact that earlier immigration policies reflected prejudice against certain groups. These are realities that influence the political processes.

The political ideal presumes that people will act rationally and have access to necessary information. Yet, poverty-stricken people do not have the time, energy, or money to acquire needed information. Too many persons think in terms of their prejudices

and not in terms of the available evidence. These, too, are realities.

Concern for the general welfare is an important part of the American dream, but the reality is that many people are motivated only by self-interest. There is no guarantee that the individual citizen will willingly sacrifice his personal interest for the greater good of others.

It is true that "for every right there is a duty," but civic responsibility requires recognition that "We the people" are very diverse. Our ideals do not as yet conform with our practices. Civic responsibility in a democracy, as will be noted in the next three chapters, means that the machinery and processes of political life must be understood and appraised. The good citizen understands the operation of these political processes and uses them to move us closer to our ideals.

STUDY QUESTIONS

1. How did the immigrants of the past generation use the political processes for establishing a place in our society?

CONCEPTS AND GENERALIZATIONS

1
The guarantee that our democratic system lives up to its ideals and principles depends to a great extent upon the effective use of the political processes by the people.

2
To gain political power, people organize themselves into a great variety of interest groups.

3
Public policy on any issue is the result of bargaining or compromise among these groups.

4
Citizenship in the United States is obtained by birth or by naturalization.

5
Citizenship by birth may be achieved in one of two ways: by place of birth or by being born of parents who are citizens.

6
Most aliens become citizens of the United States by individual naturalization, but group naturalization is done by act of Congress or by treaty.

7
Naturalized citizens and aliens have contributed to the gooodness of life in America.

8
The preference system of immigration used today has eliminated much of the prejudice against certain groups that existed under earlier immigration policies.

2. Which classification of people, the urban-rural, the social class, the power elite, or the interest group, seems most influential in your community?

3. Are you a citizen of the United States? If so, by what method did you become a citizen?

4. How can a person hold dual citizenship?

5. Give examples to illustrate "the law of birthplace" and the "law of blood relationship."

6. What is meant by the phrase "lawfully admitted for permanent residence"?

7. What people cannot become citizens of the United States?

8. What is the first step in the naturalization process?

9. What kind of examination is given?

10. How does the examination differ from the court hearing?

11. Why was the Chinese Exclusion Act adopted? Why was it changed?

12. How can a citizen of the United States lose citizenship?

13. Why was the quota system for immigration abandoned?

14. What are the major features of the present immigration law?

15. Why do some individuals not assume their civic responsibilities?

IDEAS FOR DISCUSSION

1. Aliens are sometimes treated differently in war periods than they are in periods of peace. Why? Is this fair? Could anything be done about it?

2. Is our present immigration policy satisfactory? Would you favor admitting more immigrants? Fewer immigrants?

3. Hold a panel discussion on the topic, "Differences in the problems of Puerto Ricans and Mexicans coming to the United States."

4. A writer has stated, "The success of our immigration policy depends on the persons administering the immigration laws." In what ways can immigration officials influence the workings of the immigration laws?

5. There are different ideas about the best way to blend immigrants into our population. One idea is called the *melting pot theory*—all immigrants would eventually lose their national traits and become like the native citizens. Another idea is called *cultural pluralism*—immigrants would be encouraged to keep desirable national traits but to adjust to American ways in other matters. Which idea should be our goal? Or would you prefer some other idea?

6. Senator J. William Fulbright, a former college president and since 1945 a U. S. Senator from Arkansas, said in a recent speech, "The case for government by elites is irrefutable insofar as it rests on the need for expert and specialized knowledge. The average citizen is no more qualified for the detailed administration of government than the average politician is qualified to practice medicine or to split the atom. But in the choice of basic goals, the fundamental moral judgments that shape the life of a society, the judgment of trained elites is no more valid than the judgment of an educated people."[1] What is the place of an elite in a democratic society?

7. Political scientists John C. Livingston and Robert G. Thompson, in *The Consent of the Governed* state, "Students of the politics of modern democracies find the categories of majority and minority rule inadequate to describe political realities. The key to a more adequate descriptive model created in recent years is the concept of minor*ities* rule. This term describes the situation in which public policies are the results of opinions and interests of neither a majority nor a minority, but rather arise through compromise of the interests of varied organized and vocal minorities. This model differs from the traditional descriptions of democratic politics."[2] Is the concept of minorities rule different from the interest group model?

THINGS TO DO

1. Prepare a report tracing the change in the citizenship policies affecting married women in the United States.

2. Report on the life of an immigrant and his contributions to the United States.

3. Draw a cartoon to illustrate the interest group concept.

4. A writer described a method of getting votes in one large city somewhat as follows: Men in various parts of the city helped persons get city jobs, supplied families with coal or milk when they were short of money, and held picnics and parties to which they invited people without charge. In return for these favors the men expected these people on election day to vote for their candidates. What are your reactions to this method of getting votes?

5. Prepare a bulletin board exhibit or an exhibit in a school hall to show other high school students what your class has learned about the citizen's role in government.

6. Hold a mock naturalization ceremony.

7. Prepare a chart showing effects of the changes that have occurred because of the shifts of population from a rural to an urban population.

8. Study the advertisements and writings during a recent election and report on the interest groups that supported certain candidates and issues.

9. Write an essay on the subject, "The Rights and Duties of the Adolescent Citizen."

10. Prepare a report on the citizenship requirements of another nation.

FURTHER READINGS

Burns, James M., and Peltason, J. W., GOVERNMENT BY THE PEOPLE. Prentice-Hall, Inc., 1972. Chapter 8.

Kresh, Paul, THE POWER OF THE UNKNOWN CITIZEN. J. B. Lippincott Company, 1969.

Livingston, John C., and Thompson, Robert S., THE CONSENT OF THE GOVERNED. The Macmillan Co., 1966.

Mills, C. Wright, THE POWER ELITE. Oxford University Press, 1956. (Paperback edition)

Rose, Arnold M., THE POWER STRUCTURE. Oxford University Press, 1967. (Paperback edition)

Severn, Bill, ELLIS ISLAND: THE IMMIGRANT YEARS. Julian Messner Publishers, 1971.

U.S. Immigration and Naturalization Service, THE IMMIGRATION AND NATIONALITY ACT. Superintendent of Documents, Washington, D.C., 1966. (Paperback edition)

---

[1] The Elite and the Electorate, Center for the Study of Democratic Institutions, 1963.
[2] John C. Livingston and Robert G. Thompson, *The Consent of the Governed*. The Macmillan Co. Copyright 1966.

ABSENTEE VOTING—a system by which a person who cannot be present at his regular voting place on election day may vote beforehand or by mail.

CAUCUS—a meeting of the members of a political party.

DIRECT PRIMARY—the first election to decide which of several persons will be chosen to run for an office.

NOMINATE—to select a person to be a candidate for a public office.

NONPARTISAN—not associated with political parties; no party affiliation.

OFFICE-COLUMN BALLOT—the arrangement of candidates on a ballot by the offices for which they are running.

PARTY-COLUMN BALLOT—the arrangement of candidates on a ballot by parties.

PRIMARY—same as direct primary; the first election to decide which of several persons will be chosen to run for office.

REGISTRATION—the act of getting one's name on the list of those eligible to vote.

SPLIT-TICKET VOTING—the voter votes for candidates of more than one party.

STRAIGHT-TICKET VOTING—the voter votes only for the members of one political party.

SUFFRAGE—the right to vote.

VOTING EXAMINERS—officials appointed by the United States Civil Service Commission to determine if eligible voters are denied the right to register and vote in a state and to make provisions for their registration.

THE LANGUAGE OF GOVERNMENT

Discuss with the students reasons for voter apathy in the U.S. Compare this to elections in foreign democratic nations. Consider possible remedies, such as fines for not voting, nationally declared holidays for elections, Sunday elections.

6

Elections— The Voters Decide

By the flip of levers on a voting machine or by making crosses on a paper ballot, citizens record their choices for public officials or their approval or disapproval of public issues. Alone, behind a curtain, so that no other person knows how they vote, this important citizenship task is performed.

In the voting booths the citizens decide whether those who represent them have acted in accord with their wishes or whether "it is time for a change." Since our society believes in majority rule, elections are the device by which the beliefs in democracy are put into practice. The voter's ⊠ is a symbol of our democracy.

The practice of choosing public officials and settling issues by voting, unfortunately, does not always measure up to the ideals of our democratic processes. Elections, while being decided by the majority of those who vote, sometimes do not attract a majority of those who are eligible to vote. Elections have not always been honest. In some elec-

Students need help in understanding charts, maps, tables, and diagrams. Take time to make sure these convey their full meaning. Emphasize that this information is part of the text and that it will aid them in understanding the material being studied.

97

Toward the close of World War I, suffragettes picketed outside the White House, demanding the right to vote. The center placard reads: "Mr. President, How long must women wait for liberty?" (Wide World photo)

tions there are so many officials to be selected and so many issues to be decided that voters are not able to vote intelligently.

These weaknesses in the election process get in the way of our basic principles. They have resulted in much research and investigation of the election procedures. To overcome the weaknesses, election rules and regulations, some of which are complicated, have been made. The goal has been to get honest elections with a high level of citizen participation.

VOTER
ELIGIBILITY
Who should be allowed to vote? All citizens? The rich? The poor? All races? People of all religions? Men? Women? The college graduate? The illiterate? The healthy? The sick? The law-abiding citizen? The criminal? At different times in our history we have answered these questions in different ways.

CITIZENSHIP VS. SUFFRAGE. Early in our history voting was strictly limited to white men who owned property. In some states there were religious qualifications too. Only a few could vote. One restriction after another was removed until today more people are eligible to vote than at any other time.

It is important to recognize that there is a difference between being a citizen and having the right to vote. Most high school students are citizens, but unless they are eighteen years old, they are not permitted to vote. Another way of saying this is that they have not been granted the suffrage. As citizens they are entitled to the protection of our laws; they are free to influence the opinions of others; they can perform many worthwhile civic acts. But suffrage is not granted until certain qualifications are met.

STANDARD QUALIFICATIONS
FOR VOTING
The qualifications for voting have in the past been decided almost entirely by the states. There are only a few national constitutional regulations on suffrage, which are stated in Article I of the United States Constitution and in the Fifteenth, Seventeenth, Nineteenth, Twenty-fourth, and Twenty-sixth Amendments. The constitutional regulations are (1) no citizen shall be denied the right to vote be-

Ask the student to consider how many people voted in the first presidential election in 1789. In this context discuss the growth of democracy.

cause of race, color, previous condition of servitude, sex, failure to pay a tax, or age—if eighteen years old or older, (2) those who vote for "the most numerous branch of the state legislature" must be allowed to vote in the election for United States senators and representatives.

These constitutional provisions have resulted in great political battles. A long, hard struggle was fought over the right of women to vote. In 1869 the territory of Wyoming was the first to permit women to vote. Prior to that two states, Kentucky and Kansas, allowed women to vote in school elections. By World War I eleven states had adopted women's suffrage. After that war, a period of determined agitation and pressure resulted in the adoption of the Nineteenth Amendment. The struggle to guarantee Negroes the right to vote was even longer and harder, as will be noted below.

AGE. A standard provision for voting for many years was that the voter must be twenty-one years old. Georgia in 1943 broke this long practice by changing the voting age to eighteen, and in 1955 Kentucky did the same. When Alaska became a state in 1958, the state constitution set the voting age at nineteen. This was lowered to eighteen in 1970. When Hawaii was admitted as a state in 1959, the state constitution provided for a voting age starting at twenty.

In 1970 Congress passed a law lowering the voting age to eighteen for all federal, state, and local elections. President Nixon opposed this action. He thought determining the age limit was a right of states and could be changed only by constitutional amendment, the process he favored. He did sign the bill, however, but asked for a swift court test of the constitutionality of the eighteen-year-old vote.

Shortly before Christmas 1970 the Supreme Court upheld the eighteen-year-old vote in *federal* elections but ruled that Congress acted unconstitutionally in lowering the voting age to eighteen for state and local elections.

Faced with the confusion of having a dual-system of voting, one for federal elections and one for state and local elections, Congress in March 1971 adopted the Twenty-sixth Amendment lowering the voting age to eighteen. The amendment was ratified by the states in the shortest period for any amendment—three months and seven days and became effective on June 30, 1971.

A group of suffragettes present their arguments to the Judiciary Committee of the House of Representatives in 1871. How long did it take before women were given the right to vote? (Library of Congress)

99

CITIZENSHIP. A second usual qualification is that of citizenship. All states now require that voters be citizens of the United States. This has not always been true. In the past some states have allowed aliens to vote, and states could do so again by changing their laws. It is doubtful, however, that this will happen in view of present world conditions and immigration policies.

RESIDENCE. The third general qualification is residence. For many years there was great variation in the residence requirements for voting. Most states required a residence period of one year in the state. Two had a three-month requirement. The rest required six months of residence.

In addition to the state residence requirements, there were county and precinct requirements in most states. The length of residence needed in the county varied from thirty days to one year. The length of residence needed in the precinct varied from ten days to six months.

Originally these residence requirements were intended to prevent dishonest politicians from bringing in voters to vote for their machine candidates. In local and state elections it was argued, too, that a voter should have lived long enough in the area to become acquainted with the candidates and issues. However, under modern transportation conditions people move easily and often from one place to another. Estimates are that one in five families moves each year. Residence requirements often prevented the adults in these families from voting.

In March 1963, President Kennedy appointed a Commission on Registration and Voting Participation to study the causes of the poor record of voter participation in the United States. In its report the Commission recognized the difficulties caused by citizens moving to new residences. In 1964,

for example, twenty-three million otherwise eligible voters moved. Of these, fifteen million were not able to qualify to vote for President in the November election because of state residence requirements for voting. The Commission recommended that state residence requirements should not exceed six months, and local residence requirements should not exceed thirty days.

Congress, in the 1970 Voting Rights Act, established a new residency requirement for voting in presidential elections. No state may deny the right to vote to a person who has lived in the state for thirty days immediately prior to the election of a President —providing other voter qualifications are met.

Finally, on March 21, 1972, the Supreme Court ruled that all lengthy state and local residency requirements are unconstitutional. The ruling struck down Tennessee's requirement of a year's residency for state elections and three months at the county level. The Court suggested that thirty days' residence should be enough but left to later decisions whether longer periods, say thirty-five to seventy-five days would be permitted. (See Table 1 in the Appendix.)

Until adoption of the Twenty-third Amendment, citizens of the District of Columbia were not permitted to vote for President. In effect, the people living in the capital city of Washington, D. C., the ninth largest city in the United States, could not vote for President because they were not residents of any state. The amendment was ratified by the necessary thirty-eight states in less than a year. Eligible citizens of Washington, D. C., voted for President and Vice President for the first time in history in 1964.

REGISTRATION. In addition to these three general qualifications of age, citizenship, and residence, there are several other

What is the residence requirement for a citizen to vote in your state?

A League of Women Voters mobile registration unit on the island of Oahu, Hawaii, aids in a voter registration drive by visiting beaches, shopping centers, and rural areas. (League of Women Voters)

important qualifications. One of these is *registration*, which is required in most states of some or all voters. Registration provides election officials with a list of those persons who are eligible to vote. Registration typically requires recording the name, address, length of residence, and perhaps other facts with a public official responsible for elections. The applicant signs his name in the presence of the official. Registration usually must be completed a required number of days before an election. At the time of voting, the signature and the other facts can be checked to determine if the person appearing to vote is the one registered.

In large cities, where even next-door neighbors are sometimes not known to each other, an efficient registration system is important to prevent dishonest voting. In a few states registration is required only in large cities.

PERMANENT REGISTRATION. There are two general systems of registration: permanent registration and periodic registration. During the past fifty years most states have adopted some form of permanent registration system. Under this system a voter who has registered keeps his name on the registration list until there is cause to remove it. The common causes for removing names are death and change of residence. In some states and cities failure to vote in a certain number of consecutive elections results in automatic removal of the nonvoter's name from the registration list.

A staff of persons constantly checks the list to keep names and addresses up to date. Death notices, telephone directories, and records of gas and electricity companies are among the sources that are checked to determine if voters may have died or moved. The disadvantage of permanent registration is the danger of dishonest practices. Sometimes people have voted in the place of dead persons or persons who have moved from the community.

PERIODIC REGISTRATION. Under periodic registration, the voter must appear at regular intervals and reregister. In some places this must be done each year. The disadvantage of this system is the inconvenience to the voter. Many voters fail to register at the proper time and then are not able to vote in the elections. Organized groups are more likely to get their supporters registered than are the citizens who do not belong to a group.

While there is no perfect system, the present trend seems to be to make registration convenient for the voters through a permanent system and then to check carefully to prevent dishonest voting. Without an accurate registration system it is possible for persons to vote falsely for others—the *ghost* system, or to vote more than once—the *repeater* system.

POLL TAX AND CIVIL RIGHTS.

Until recent years the poll tax was a special qualification for voting in many states. Usually the tax was one or two dollars for each adult and had to be paid each year. The effect of the tax was to deprive some poor people of the right to vote, and southern states employed it as one of the devices to keep Negroes from voting. Alabama, Arkansas, Mississippi, Texas, and Virginia had a poll tax requirement for voting until ratification of the Twenty-fourth Amendment, which forbids the use of a poll tax as a requirement for voting in federal elections. This amendment took effect in 1964.

In 1966 the Supreme Court ruled that the poll tax could not be used as a qualification for voting in any election—federal, state, or local. The case was *Harper* v. *Virginia State Board of Education,* and the Court stated:

> Voter qualifications have no relation to wealth nor to paying or not paying this or any other tax. Wealth like race, creed, or color, is not germane to one's ability to participate intelligently in the electoral process.

Discrimination against Negro voting has been persistent, effective, and abominably clever in some southern states. Although the Fifteenth Amendment, adopted in 1870, guarantees the vote to Negroes, there has been constant and long-continued harassment. Until the Supreme Court ruled the method unconstitutional in 1915, the "grandfather clause" was a favorite device. By this scheme those citizens whose fathers or grandfathers were eligible to vote before the Civil War did not have to meet certain requirements. This meant that Negroes had to meet requirements which were not required of white citizens. For example, in Mississippi, Negroes were required to interpret the state constitution in a "rea-

sonable" way. White officials opposed to Negroes' voting kept even well-educated Negroes from voting. The white primary was a similar scheme. Negroes were not allowed to vote in the primary election of the Democratic party. Since, at that time, the South was a one-party area, voting by whites in the primary really decided outcomes and elected the officials. The white primary was ruled unconstitutional by the Supreme Court in 1944.

When poll taxes, literacy tests, and the other schemes did not work or were declared illegal, fear and economic pressure were employed. In some communities even to express a desire to vote resulted in loss of jobs, reduced pay, or bodily harm. Great courage was required by determined Negroes to bring the facts of discrimination before the American public.

The seriousness of the problem and the complete injustice led to the passage of a series of civil rights laws beginning in 1957, as was described in Chapter 4. The voting rights aspects of these laws are summarized in the following paragraphs.

The Civil Rights Act of 1957 provided for a Civil Rights Commission with power to investigate attempts to deprive persons of the right to vote because of race, color, religion, or national origin. The act forbids any person, whether a private citizen or a public official, to use force or fear to interfere with the right of another citizen to participate in any aspect of the federal election process. The Attorney General was granted the power to obtain court orders, at public expense, to halt threatened violations of voting rights.

The Civil Rights Act of 1960 required state and local officials to keep records of federal elections, including primaries, for at least twenty-two months. The Attorney General was authorized to copy the state and local voting records. Stealing, tamper-

These citizens are lining up to register to vote at the Courthouse in Selma, Alabama, in 1965. They had been led by the Reverend Martin Luther King, Jr. (UPI photo)

ing with, or destroying voting records were made illegal. When a federal court finds that the right to vote is denied as a "pattern of practice" because of race or color, the court may appoint "voting referees" to determine the facts and report to the court. The court may then issue voting certificates to those it thinks qualified—which must be honored by local election officials or they may be held in contempt of court.

The 1964 Civil Rights Act was passed because the two previous acts had not eliminated discrimination. The procedures under these acts were slow and cumbersome; they had not appreciably increased Negro voting in the southern states. The four voting provisions of this new act were: (1) unequal voting registration requirements were prohibited, (2) the denial of the right to vote because of minor errors or omissions in applications was prohibited,

(3) all literacy tests were required to be conducted in writing, except in cases where the Attorney General agrees that the tests are administered fairly, and (4) any person with a sixth-grade education was exempted from taking a state literacy test.

The 1965 Voting Rights Act provided for the appointment of "voting examiners" by the United States Civil Service Commission. These examiners are to determine an individual's qualifications to vote and to require enrollment of qualified individuals by state and local officials in all elections, local and state as well as federal—including conventions of political parties. Two methods for appointing examiners are provided. One alternative is that a federal court could determine that examiners are needed to insure voting rights. A second alternative authorized the Attorney General to certify to the Civil Service Commission that

Most political scientists spend their lives in colleges and universities teaching, writing, doing research. Often these experts serve on governmental investigating commissions. Of the eleven members of the President's Commission on Registration and Voting Participation, appointed in 1963 by President Kennedy to study the causes of nonvoting, three were distinguished political scientists. To increase voter turnout, they made the following recommendations.

1. Each state should create a commission on registration and voting participation, or utilize some other existing state machinery to survey in detail its election law and practices.

2. Voter registration should be easily accessible to all citizens.

3. Residence requirements for voting for state officials should not exceed six months.*

4. Residence requirements for voting in county and city elections should not exceed thirty days.*

5. New state residents should be allowed to vote for President, regardless of their length of residence in the new state, if qualified to vote in the state from which they moved.*

6. Voter registration should extend as close to election day as possible, and should not end more than three or four weeks before election day.

7. Voter lists should be kept current.

8. No citizen's registration should be canceled for failure to vote in any period less than four years.

9. Voter registration lists should be used only for electoral purposes.

10. States should provide absentee registration for voters who cannot register in person.

11. Literacy tests should not be a requisite for voting.*

12. Election day should be proclaimed a national day of dedication to our American democracy. The commission suggested that "the states should consider declaring the day a half-day holiday."

13. Polling places should be so equipped as to eliminate long waiting periods.

14. Polling places should be open throughout the day and remain open until at least 9 P.M.

15. The states should provide every possible protection against election fraud.

16. Voting by persons eighteen years of age should be considered by the states.*

17. Candidacy should be open to all.

18. The right to vote should be extended to those living on Federal reservations.

19. Absentee voting by mail should be allowed for all who are absent from home on primary or general election day.

20. The poll tax as a qualification for voting should be eliminated.*

21. Each state should keep informed of other states' practices and innovations in election administration.

* The Twenty-fourth and Twenty-sixth Amendments, Voting Rights Acts, and Supreme Court decisions have achieved these recommendations.

voter discrimination existed based on: (1) valid complaints by twenty or more residents, (2) a literacy test or other device was used as a qualification for voting for the November 1964 election, and (3) the Director of the Census determined that less than 50 per cent of the persons of voting age in an area were registered to vote or actually voted in the 1964 presidential election.

After signing the 1965 Voting Rights Bill into law, President Lyndon B. Johnson hands one of the pens used to Dr. Martin Luther King, late head of the Southern Christian Leadership Conference. (UPI photo)

The law also has one unusual feature. Congress feared that states might invent new strategies of discrimination and, therefore, included a provision that a federal district court in the District of Columbia must approve new state voting rules. The Supreme Court in *South Carolina* v. *Katzenbach*, on March 7, 1967, unanimously upheld the constitutionality of the Voting Rights Act. In his opinion, Chief Justice Warren held that "rational and appropriate" methods had been used by Congress to end an "insidious and pervasive evil."

After passage of the 1965 law, examiners were appointed to register voters in forty-seven counties of five states. Since that time nearly one million Negro voters have been registered in the southern states, the majority being registered by local officials who voluntarily obeyed the law. There is an interesting by-product of the law: in some southern states, as Negro registration and voting have increased, so have the registration and voting of whites.

Why has it been necessary in order to obtain the fundamental democratic right to vote to pass so many laws over such a long period of time? A reasonable answer seems to be that the combination of longstanding prejudice and of the nature of political processes, involving compromises and group pressures, resulted in delay and partial solutions. The Civil Rights Act of 1957 was the best that could be obtained from a reluctant Congress. Political leaders took what they could get. Continued agitation and pressure led later to improved laws. Each new law built on the experience of the previous law. Such is the way of political processes.

LITERACY TESTS. The literacy test is at present illegal. But for many years about one-third of the states required some proof of minimum ability to read and write. The idea behind these tests was that the ability to read and write is the minimum requirement for intelligent voting. If all citizens are tested in the same objective way, there may be a good reason for such a test. Public issues are complex and difficult to understand. Perhaps the person who cannot read or write may not be able to vote intelligently. Testing for literacy, in this sense, is similar to having a minimum required voting age in order to have some assurance of intelligent voting.

Unfortunately the administration of literacy tests has not always been fair. In some places white people have been given very easy tests. Negroes and other minorities have been required to read and explain complicated parts of the United States Constitution.

When the President's Voting Commission made the twenty-one recommendations listed on page 104, they were unanimous on all the recommendations except Number 11 (on literacy tests). The majority report recognized the unfairness to Negroes and recognized, too, that "many media are available other than the printed word to supply information to potential voters." The minority report recognized the evils, but argued that there was a legitimate basis for fairly administered tests.

Under the provisions of the 1965 Voting Rights Act, the Attorney General decided that literacy tests were used to discriminate in six southern states. In addition he ruled that such tests were used to discriminate in forty counties in North Carolina and one county each in Arizona, Hawaii, and Idaho. In these last three states minority groups, other than Negroes, were being deprived of their votes.

New York state has been considered to have had one of the better literacy tests. New voters had to prove that they had at least an eighth-grade education or obtain a certificate of literacy. To insure unbiased administration of the tests, they were prepared by test experts in the state department of education under the control of the New York Board of Regents. Once each year the local school superintendent was responsible for giving the tests. While the New York system was administered fairly and honestly, Puerto Ricans living in New York who were literate in Spanish and not English were denied the vote. To correct this, the 1965 Voting Rights Act provided that no person may be denied the vote because he cannot read and write English, provided that he has completed the sixth grade in an American-taught school, even though a language other than English is used. The law recognizes Puerto Ricans are citizens and able to vote.

The 1970 Voting Rights Act settled the issue temporarily by suspending literacy tests in all states until August 1975.

OTHER QUALIFICATIONS. Citizenship, residence, and registration requirements are the framework of the individual states, but there are other limitations on voting that are almost self-explanatory. Conviction of a *crime* causes loss of the vote in some states, as does *dishonorable discharge* from military service. Either the governor, the official in charge of pardons, or the state legislature may restore the right to vote depending upon the state law.

The *mentally ill*, if declared mentally incompetent by a court, lose their suffrage in many states. The *pauper*, the one so poor he must live on public charity, is deprived of the vote in about a quarter of the states. As with the poll tax and the literacy test, not allowing the pauper to vote can lead to unfair political treatment—especially in times of widespread unemployment.

The history of suffrage in our country has had one central tendency: to allow more and more people to vote by removing the restrictions on voting. The great landmarks in this movement were the granting of the right to vote to Negroes by the adoption of the Fifteenth Amendment to the Constitution in 1870, the granting of voting rights to women by the adoption of the Nineteenth Amendment in 1920, the lowering of the voting age to eighteen by the Twenty-sixth Amendment, and the national voting laws passed since 1957 to eliminate discrimination against Negroes. But the trend started early in the nineteenth century and has continued. Has universal suffrage reached its limit? Or are there still citizens who are deprived of the right to vote?

THE VOTING
PROCESS   The interested eligible voter on election day goes to the neighborhood polling place. The polls in most places are open from early morning until early in the evening. The polls are in the charge of election officials. The selection of these officials is of great importance to insure the

Discuss the impact—if any—that pre-election opinion polls have upon the voter.

Several kinds of voting machines are used in elections throughout the country, but the general procedure is about the same.

To vote a straight ticket (top left), just pull the party lever to the right. This automatically gives the vote to all candidates on that row.

To split the ticket (top right), pull the party lever and move up the small handles above names of candidates not wanted. Then vote for candidates of other parties by moving the small handles over the candidates' names.

In a nonpartisan election (middle), all voting is done by moving the small handles over the names of the candidates.

To cast a write-in vote (bottom right), raise the slide over the name of an office and write the name of your choice on the paper.

When the polls are officially closed, the election officials remove the back of the machine and record the results (bottom left), which have been totaled automatically. (Bottom left, Automatic Voting Machine Corporation; all others, The Detroit Free Press)

honesty of the election. They are employed by the city or county in accordance with the various state laws. To insure that the officials do their duties properly, political parties or other citizens' groups may have authorized "watchers" at the polls to check on the election procedures.

Upon entering the polling place, the voter usually is asked to sign an application. This application is taken to an election clerk who checks the voter's signature and address against the official registration list.

The voter is then given the ballots and takes them into an enclosed voting booth or steps before the voting machine and pulls the lever which draws the curtain around him. In either case, voting is secret.

After the vote is completed, the ballots are folded, brought out, and deposited in the sealed ballot boxes. With the voting machine, after the small levers have been moved to cast the votes, the big lever is pulled which automatically records the vote and releases the curtain around the booth.

After all voters have had their chance to vote and the polls are closed, the votes are counted. With the voting machine this is a simple process of reading the tabulations on the back of the machine and recording them in the official election books. With ballots the count can be a long, slow, difficult process.

If democracy is to work, the counting of the ballots and the tabulation of results must be done accurately and honestly. Students of election procedures have developed many safeguards as a result of past efforts to steal elections. Most important, however, are honest election officials.

Your every voter, as surely as your chief magistrate, exercises a public trust.

—GROVER CLEVELAND, Inaugural Address, March 4, 1885.

TYPES OF BALLOTS. There are two general types of ballots: the *party-column,* or Indiana ballot, and the *office-column,* or Massachusetts ballot. On the *party-column* ballot the candidates are listed under the names of their parties. Thus on the ballot or voting machine the voter sees in bold letters the names DEMOCRATIC, REPUBLICAN, PROHIBITION, or SOCIALIST.

Under the party names, in parallel columns, the candidates are grouped in terms of the offices they are seeking. At the head of each column is a large circle or a lever. If a voter places his X in the circle or moves the lever, he has voted for all the candidates for that party.

Such voting is called *straight-ticket* voting. It is a simple way to vote for all the candidates of one party. A few states which use a party-column ballot have removed the circles or the levers at the head of the column to make it more difficult to vote a straight ticket.

The *office-column* ballot has the candidates arranged under the offices they are seeking. After the name of the candidate appears the name of the party.[1] Usually the names are arranged alphabetically. Sometimes the names are rotated so that each candidate's name appears at the top of the list an equal number of times. This is done because there seems to be a slight advantage for the first name on the list.

The office-column ballot makes voting a straight ticket more difficult. It encourages voters to vote a *split ticket,* that is, marking the ballot for some candidates of one party and some candidates of another party.

The ballot systems used in the United States today are adapted from the system which started in Australia about one hundred years ago. It is common to speak of

[1] In some elections there are no parties. In these *nonpartisan* elections the office-column ballot is used. See page 119.

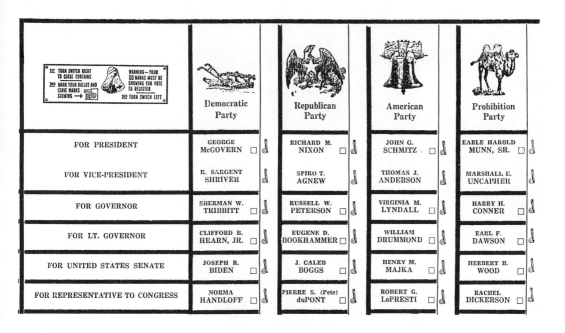

This is a portion of a party-column or "Indiana" ballot that was used in Delaware for the 1972 presidential elections. This ballot is to be used in a voting machine.

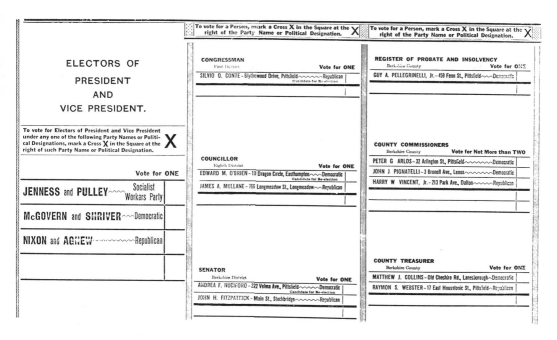

This is a portion of the office-block ballot used in 1972 in Massachusetts.

After the polls close, electric voting machines quickly tabulate results which are then removed on long sheets. (Automatic Voting Machine Corporation)

this system as the *Australian ballot system*. The chief features of this system are: (1) The vote is cast in secret. (2) The ballots are printed at public expense. (3) The ballot can be obtained only from an election official in the prescribed manner. (4) An official ballot cannot be taken from the voting place. (5) The names of all candidates and all parties for the offices to be voted on appear on the ballot.

VOTING REFORMS Election officials and political scientists have spent many hours studying the election process. They have tried to develop a system that will insure honest and fair elections. At the same time they have tried to get the greatest possible citizen participation. Some of the reforms or improvements they have developed are absentee voting; the use of

voting machines and electronic devices; the short ballot; and the timing of national, state, and local elections.

ABSENTEE VOTING. There are times when citizens are not able to get to the polls on election day. They may be in the hospital or away from home on business or vacation. Should these conditions deprive them of their votes? The states have answered this question by developing *absentee voting systems*.

By these systems the voter who knows he will be away applies for a ballot a certain number of days before the election. The application is usually made with a city or county election official. The ballot is sent to the voter by mail, is marked, and is mailed back in the special envelope provided. Sometimes a witness must certify that the voter marked his own ballot. On election day the unopened envelope is de-

LAFF - A - DAY

"Well, then, which candidate do you detest the most?"

livered to the voter's regular voting place. When the counting of ballots is to begin, the absentee envelope is opened and the ballot is counted the same as other ballots.

The absence from this country during World War II of many members of the armed forces called attention to the importance of absentee voting systems. A few states allow only those in military service to use the absentee voting system. In most states the ill or physically disabled may use this method, as well as those away on business or vacations.

VOTING MACHINES. The voting machine has long been advocated as a means of improving the voting process. The voting machine reduces the possibility of a dishonest count of the ballots, but it does not make it impossible. In some large cities voting machines have come into use as a part of governmental reforms.

These citizens are college students registering to vote for the first time after the eighteen-year-old vote was granted. The scene is in the lobby of a dormitory. (Andrew Sacks/Editorial Photocolor Archives)

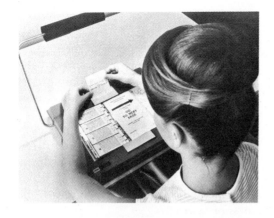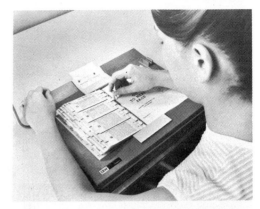

These photos illustrate how IBM's electronic voting system works. (Top left) The voter inserts the specially designed card in the vote recorder. (Top right) To cast the vote, a pen-like stylus is used to punch holes in the ballot card. (Bottom left) The card is placed in an envelope and inserted in the ballot box. (Bottom right) After the polls close, the cards are taken to a central headquarters where they are tabulated swiftly and accurately by an IBM machine. (IBM Corporation)

The chief disadvantage of the voting machine is the very high original cost. The original investment usually pays for itself over a period of years because of decreased printing costs plus the smaller payments to election officials, since the hours they spend in counting ballots are almost eliminated. In addition to the advantages of accuracy, the voting machine has much popular appeal because the results of an election can be known soon after the polls close.

Some persons object to the voting machine because they fear they may have difficulty operating it. Some do not like the voting machine because they lose their votes for some candidates and special issues by neglecting to pull levers. Actually, learning to operate a voting machine is as easy as learning to mark an office-column ballot.

ELECTRONIC VOTING. In an age of computers and space ships, the electronic technology experts are urging applications of their devices to the voting process. The president of the Columbia Broadcasting System says, "In the future, electronic scanners at polling places will very probably be able to identify voters, or prevent repeaters and unauthorized ballots, by a split-second survey of a voter's thumb."[1] Others have prophesied that some day the telephone or two-way TV will permit voting without leaving one's home.

Two new systems have been tried out in some voting districts. One, the Coleman Vote Tally System, makes use of the paper ballot, but the voter uses a special ink. After the voting period ends, the ballot boxes are taken to a central computing center where they are run through a machine which detects the ink marks, and the results are announced in a few moments. In one experiment it took clerks two and a half hours to count a set of ballots that were counted accurately by the Coleman system in ten seconds.

A second new system is the IBM Votomatic, invented by a retired political science professor. Each voter punches holes in an electronic punch card. The cards are then taken to the central headquarters to be tabulated by IBM machines. The machine is light, weighing only six pounds, and is easily transportable. The cost is one-tenth that of the regular voting machine.

These two new systems seem to have the virtues of simplicity, economy, and speed of counting. While political leaders agree that voting should be made easier, most are of the opinion that the difficulties are not mechanical but lie with the complexities of the election processes.

THE SHORT BALLOT. For some persons one of the discouraging things about voting is the great number of positions on which one must vote. The voter may know exactly whom he wants for President, governor, or mayor but finds on the ballot a dozen other offices. On these he may not be sure for whom to vote. Some ballots have so many offices and so many names that they are called "bed-sheet ballots." In addition there may be separate ballots with several special issues on which to vote.

In order to reduce the confusion of the

These are behind-the-scenes photos of election night in a television studio. (Top, left) A group of young women answer phones to determine statistics. (Above, right) These statistics are fed into computers. (Bottom, left) Finally the television camera is hooked up to the computer and the results are projected onto the screens of millions of television sets. (Photos courtesy of KYW TV-3, Philadelphia)

voter, there has been a movement to shorten the ballot. This is done by electing a few officials and having them appoint the lesser officials. For example, if the governor is elected and he appoints a secretary of state, a highway commissioner, an attorney general, a treasurer, and an auditor, the voter has to vote for only one person instead of six. The same procedure applied to cities and counties could reduce the difficult task of the voter in trying to learn to know all candidates.

The movement for the short ballot has made slow but steady progress. Voter interest might be increased and more intelligent voting result if the job of voting did not appear so complicated.

THE DATE AND TIME FOR ELECTIONS

In any one year the voter is usually asked to vote in two or more elections. In some states there are six different elections a year. The voter sometimes feels that he has just finished one election when he begins to be bombarded by the propaganda for a new election.

The frequency of elections is the result of having so many different governmental units. National, state, county, city, township, and school-district elections are held. If all these elections were combined and held at the same time, the task of the voter would be very difficult.

A kind of regular rhythm, therefore, has developed about our elections. National elections are held in November of the even-numbered years. Members of the United States House of Representatives and about one-third of the senators are chosen at this time. Presidents are elected at this November election every four years. Most states hold elections at the same time, although some states hold their elections in November of the odd-numbered years.

Local elections are usually held at some different time. November of the odd-numbered years is used for some city elections. School elections, judicial elections, and local elections are held in the spring in some communities.

Holding national, state, and local elections at different times gets strong support from students of government. When national, state, and local elections are held at the same time, the voters give most of their attention to the national campaign. When the elections are separated, the voters give greater attention to the specific issues of that election. To get more intelligent voting for local officials, it is usually recommended that the local election *not* be held at the same time as the national election.

States periodically need to examine the number and time of their elections. It may be possible to reduce the number of elections in some places. The task of the voter should be made as simple as possible, as long as the conduct of government can be kept at a high level. The elections should be held at times when the voters can give attention to a small number of positions and to a relatively few issues.

In addition to the dates when elections are held, the time of day when the polls should be open has received much discussion. Recommendation 14 of the President's Commission—that "polls should be open . . . until at least 9 P.M."—was intended to give voters ample opportunity to vote before or after their day's work. One serious objection has been raised in national elections because of the rapid reporting of election results on radio and TV. Because of the differences in time zones, the polls in the western states are still open when the first election results are reported in the East. By means of computers and statistical formulas, predictions of results are made based on key precincts in the East. Some

Evaluate the idea that elections—local, state, national—are too frequent and that there are too many candidates for too many offices.

political scientists think that knowledge of these predictions may influence voters in the West. Recommendations have been made, therefore, that the polls close at the same time throughout the nation. Polls in the East might remain open until 11 P.M. Eastern time while polls in the West would close at 8 P.M. Pacific time. Another suggestion is that no national election returns be given publicly until the polls in the West are closed.

GETTING THE CANDIDATES FOR OFFICE

When some citizens receive a ballot, they wonder, "How did *that* person get on the ballot?" They were aware of certain candidates running for the most important positions, but they did not know the candidates for the less well-known positions.

Their experience is not uncommon. For the prominent positions the way of choosing candidates is usually well known. For lesser offices the system may not be so well known. Regardless of the system used, there is one official word that means to select a person to be a candidate for office. This word is *nominate.*

The nomination process is very important. This first step in the election process often attracts less attention than the regular election. The power elite and the interest groups, however, have learned that to keep control they must get their candidates selected at this first stage. And in those sections of the country where one party regularly wins the elections, the nomination contest is the one place where citizens can exert influence because the candidate nominated is quite sure of winning the election. There are five different ways of nominating candidates. They are (1) self-announcement; (2) petition; (3) caucus; (4) convention; (5) direct primary.

SELF-ANNOUNCEMENT. In some local elections self-announcement is used for nominations. All that is required is for the interested candidate to inform the proper election official by a certain date that he wants his name on the ballot.

In a few places the self-announcement system requires that the candidate deposit a sum of money (usually $100) with the election official. If the candidate gets at least a small percentage of the votes in the election, the money is returned. If he falls below this percentage of votes, the government keeps the money. The effect of this requirement is to reduce the number of "self-starters."

PETITION. The petition system requires that to be nominated a certain number of voters sign a petition asking that the candidate's name appear on the ballot. Usually the number of signatures is a small percentage of the votes cast for the particular office at the last election.

The petition system is used mostly in local elections. Getting signatures on a petition is not too difficult, but persistence and time are required. Political parties and interest groups have the advantage in getting signatures because they have more workers who are willing to "push" petitions for signatures.

Requiring a large number of signatures helps the parties and interest groups. The independent may not be able to get enough signatures since he may have few helpers. Requiring a small number of signatures increases the number of candidates because more people will be able to get enough signatures.

CAUCUS. A meeting of the members of a political party or an interest group may be held to choose the candidates. For more than a hundred years the caucus or party meeting was the usual method for nominating candidates. Members of the party held

From time to time political observers have suggested that we have a national primary election. Discuss this idea.

At the Democratic convention in Miami Beach during July 1972, the Reverend Jesse Jackson was active as a delegate in the succesful fight not to seat Chicago's Mayor Richard Daley and his supporters. (UPI photo)

a meeting at a specified time and nominated candidates just as student councils, parent-teacher groups, and clubs of all kinds do in many places today. Typical of such caucuses are the following remarks from the floor: "I nominate Bob Smith." . . . "Are there any other nominations?" . . . "I move the nominations be closed." Formal and informal caucuses are still used every year in many places to name candidates for office.

But the caucus gained a bad reputation in this century. Some political leaders would call surprise meetings, or hold them at out-of-the-way places or at inconvenient times, or just let their own followers know when the meeting was to be held. Sometimes a "mob" would attend a caucus and defeat the wishes of the regular members.

The caucus was open to so much manipulation that it has been replaced by conventions and primaries. But when you read or hear about decisions being made "in a smoke-filled hotel room" you know that someone has held an informal caucus.

CONVENTION. The convention system is used for county, state, and national elections. The convention delegates are persons selected to represent other party members at the convention. Usually members of a party in a neighborhood precinct, either by caucus or by election, choose a member to be their delegate to a city convention.

When the delegates meet for the city convention, they choose delegates to attend the county convention. At the county convention, delegates are chosen to attend the state convention. The state convention in turn chooses delegates to attend the national convention.

This pyramid method of selecting delegates is an indirect way of giving control to the party members in the neighborhood. In theory the system seems to be democratic. The delegates to the state convention are selected by delegates who represent counties, cities, and finally precincts.

In practice the system has the same abuses as the caucus. If the neighborhood delegates are chosen by a few people through tricks that are common to caucuses, then the whole convention system is not really representative of the people. Actually delegates in many places are selected by a political boss or a member of the power elite. Interest groups gain control by quietly electing members of their group as neighborhood delegates. The delegates vote the way they are told to vote, and the conventions become "rubber stamps" carrying out the will of the leaders.

One way to defeat these practices is by alertness at the time of the selection of delegates. In addition, in most states, the convention system has been eliminated or modified by use of the direct primary election or by employing a combination of methods. One state, for example, uses the convention method for all offices except governor and members of the legislature. These top officials are selected in primaries. The argument is that the masses of voters will do well in selecting the candidates for these major offices, while political leaders and interest groups through a delegate system will choose better persons for the lesser offices.

In recent years, under the reformed selection procedures of the political parties, the quality of candidates chosen in conventions has been equal to that of those selected by other methods. Some political scientists, therefore, have felt that the convention system in itself is not bad. They feel that the evil was in the political conditions of the past seventy-five years and not necessarily with the convention system.

The convention is no longer the major way of selecting candidates in most places, except for the nomination of the President and Vice President. These national conventions which attract so much attention will be discussed in Chapter 11.

DIRECT PRIMARY. The direct primary election has replaced the convention as the major way of nominating candidates. The direct primary is really a preliminary election to decide who will be the candidates in the regular election.

It is direct because the people vote directly for the candidate they want nominated and not for a delegate or representative to act for them. It is primary because it comes first and is followed by the actual election. It is an election because the main features of the Australian ballot system are used: the state conducts the election; official polling places are used; ballots are printed by the government; and regular election officials are in charge of the primary.

The types of primaries are classified as (1) the open direct party primary, (2) the closed direct party primary, (3) the run-off primary, and (4) the nonpartisan primary.

OPEN PRIMARY. The open direct party primary is one in which the voter does not have to tell to which political party he belongs. It is open to all voters regardless of their party. Nine states use the open system. Under one plan the voter is given ballots for each of the parties. In the voting booth he votes the ballot of his choice. The ballots are folded separately. The marked ballot is given to the election official and placed in the box for marked ballots. The other ballots are placed in the box for unmarked ballots.

In another plan the candidates are arranged by party columns and the voter is instructed to vote for candidates in only one column. In the state of Washington, the voter is allowed to vote for candidates of different parties. One can vote in the primary for a Democratic governor, a Republican attorney general, and so on through the entire ballot.[1]

The chief advantages of the open primary

---

[1] California, at one time, achieved the same result by a system of cross-filing. A candidate could have his name on more than one party ballot.

Citizens are urged to vote in primary elections so that they may have a voice in choosing who will be candidates in the regular elections. (League of Women Voters)

are that the voter can keep secret his political party affiliation and can shift from one party to another at any time.

The chief objection to the open primary is that members of one party may "raid" another party by voting for a weak candidate of that party. If they succeed in nominating this poor candidate, the election of their own party candidate may be easier. For example, in an open primary in one state, only one candidate was running for governor on the Democratic ticket. Several candidates were competing for governor on the Republican ticket. The Republican candidate selected was one of the less able candidates, according to the newspaper reports.

The feeling was general that many Democrats had shifted parties in the primary to vote for the weakest Republican. In the final election the Democrat was elected governor. Many felt that it really was a contest between a strong Democrat and a weak Republican. Both major parties have occasionally used this procedure to win an election in states where there are open primaries.

CLOSED PRIMARY. The closed direct party primary is used in most states because of the desire to have candidates selected by the actual party members. In the closed primary the voter must state to which political party he belongs. Only the one ballot of the chosen party is given the voter.

The methods for determining the party to which the voter belongs vary from one state to another. At one extreme, when the citizen registers, he must state the party of his choice. He can change his party after that only at special times and under definite procedures. At the other extreme, all that is required is that the voter tell the election official at the time he votes which party ballot he wants. The voter's decision at that moment determines his party. It is important to note, however, that at either extreme the voter's party is no longer secret.

The chief argument for the closed primary is that since the primary is a party election only those willing to state they are party members should be permitted to vote. This argument has strong appeal to party leaders. The closed primary, they believe, makes the candidate more responsible to the party. Opponents of the closed primary think that a voter's party is his own business and that he should not be forced to reveal his choice of party. Just as the voting should be by secret ballot, one should be able to keep his party affiliation secret, they say. Voters who consider themselves independent voters find the closed primary especially unsatisfactory.

THE RUN-OFF PRIMARY. In some states, chiefly in the South, if a candidate does not receive a majority of the votes cast, a second election must be held between the two top candidates. This second election is called the "run-off" primary. It assures that the candidate has the majority of those voting in the primary. This is especially important in the South where the nominee of the Democratic party has for years won in the election.

NONPARTISAN PRIMARY. The nonpartisan primary is one in which there are no parties. It really is a preliminary election in which the "no-party" system has been adopted. Candidates get their names on the primary ballot by petition or by self-announcement. The primary election is then held and the two candidates with the highest number of votes are chosen to compete in the regular election which follows. There is no primary election for offices for which there are only two candidates.

School boards, city officials, and judges are commonly chosen by nonpartisan primaries. Two states, Nebraska and Minnesota, select legislators on nonpartisan ballots. The objection to the nonpartisan system is that it destroys party responsibility. The advantage is that national and state parties are not appropriate for all kinds of public offices, especially local and judicial offices.

THE EFFECTIVENESS OF PRIMARIES. How effective are the direct primaries? There are differences of opinion. The strengths seem to be that citizens can keep control of the party selections. The evil of the boss-controlled convention system is eliminated if the rank and file of party members will really vote. The boss, the machine, the elite control, or domination by one interest group can be eliminated by the primary system.

One weakness of the primary system is that citizens do not always vote, with the result that political bosses or special interest groups have kept control of some primaries. In addition, the primary has actually weakened the power of the political party in many places. The system is expensive to the taxpayers because the government, and not the parties, pays the cost. The number of elections is increased, and some people think this increases the burden on the voter. While these criticisms show that the primary is not perfect, it is so widely used today that changes are likely to come slowly.

The importance of the primaries as a way of choosing candidates to run for office is one indication of the prominent place political parties have in the election process. Political parties are so important that the next chapter will discuss their place and influence.

STUDY QUESTIONS

1. What are the ways in which the United States Constitution controls the qualifications of voters?

2. What are the standard voting qualifications of your state?

3. Why are registration laws necessary?

4. How is registration done in your community?

5. What are the special qualifications for voting in your community?

6. Where is the voting place for the adults in your neighborhood?

7. How have civil rights legislation and Supreme Court decisions changed voting regulations?

8. What are the two ways of arranging the names of candidates on ballots? Which method do you prefer?

9. Which type of ballot is used in your community? Are different types of ballots used in local, state, or national elections?

10. Why are each of the five chief features of the Australian ballot system important for honest elections?

11. Which of the voting reforms suggested in this chapter would you favor for your community? Which does the community already have?

12. Which of the ways of getting candidates to run for office is used in your local elections? In state elections? In national elections?

13. Why are criminals, the insane, and paupers not allowed to vote?

14. What is the difference between an open primary and a closed primary?

CONCEPTS AND GENERALIZATIONS

1
Suffrage is granted by the states within a framework established by federal policies.

2
The major federal policies are that the right to vote cannot be denied because of race, color, previous condition of servitude, sex, failure to pay a tax, or youth (age 18).

3
The major state policies that determine the suffrage are age, citizenship, residence, and registration qualifications.

4
Although the efforts to assure Negroes the right to vote resulted in compromises, delay, and partial solutions, there was continuous progress in the past decade.

5
Poll taxes and literacy tests as bars to Negro voting have gone the way of grandfather clauses and the white primary.

6
The history of suffrage in this country has been to allow more and more people to vote.

7
The arrangement of the ballot can aid or interfere with straight-ticket voting.

8
The ballots used in this country are modifications of the Australian ballot system.

9
Voting reforms—such as absentee voting, the use of voting machines, the short ballot, and changing the time of elections—are designed to get honest, fair elections with a maximum of intelligent voter participation.

10
The efforts to broaden participation in the selection of candidates have made the convention and the direct primary the most prominent nomination systems.

11
The closed primary is widely used among the states and is favored by most political leaders, but it is not approved by many independent voters.

IDEAS FOR DISCUSSION

1. Should the United States Constitution be amended to provide for uniform voting qualifications throughout the nation?

2. Should aliens be allowed to vote in your state?

3. Which is a better method to reduce dishonest voting: permanent or periodic registration?

4. Should voting on bond issues be limited to property owners?

5. A New York State literacy test used for many years had to be passed by any voter who could not present evidence of having passed at least the eighth grade in school. A sample test was about as follows:

READ THE FOLLOWING PARAGRAPH AND
WRITE YOUR ANSWERS TO THE QUESTIONS.

Indians lived on the western plains before white men came to our shores. The Indians hunted for buffaloes and used the meat and skins. The buffalo was a large animal with a dark-brown woolly coat. The buffaloes were usually found in large herds. They were easiest to hunt after heavy rains. The buffaloes liked to roll in mud. The mud kept the flies and other insects from bothering the buffaloes. As white men settled in America they moved west and killed thousands of buffaloes. By 1890 there were only 551 buffaloes left. Then efforts were made to protect them. Today there are about 5,000 buffaloes in the United States.

QUESTIONS

   a) Who lived in the West before the white man?

   b) What is the color of the buffaloes' coat?

   c) When was it easiest to hunt buffaloes?

   d) Why did the buffaloes like to roll in the mud?

   e) Who killed most of the buffaloes?

   f) How many buffaloes were left by 1890?

   g) How many buffaloes are there today?

   h) Did buffaloes usually travel in pairs?

Do you think a literacy test of this type is a good thing?

6. Are there any officials in your state or local government that you think should be appointed instead of elected? Are there any that you think should be elected instead of appointed? How would such changes affect the length of the ballots and the number of elections?

7. Groups of interested citizens are allowed to have "watchers" at elections. These "watchers" are there to check on the activities of the polling officials. Is the "watcher" necessary? Do "watchers" ever abuse their privileges?

THINGS TO DO

1. Conduct a neighborhood survey by means of committees to determine how many citizens were not able to vote at the last election because they had moved into your neighborhood too recently.

2. Hold a "get-registered" campaign before an election to dramatize the importance of registering in order not to lose one's vote.

3. Interview the persons in charge of registration and elections in your community to determine how the system works. How are names added to registration lists? How are names removed? Have there been any cases of fraud? How are voting-district officials selected? What improvements do the officials desire? How have civil rights laws changed the registration and election procedures?

4. Hold a mock election in school at the time of a regular election. Provide for registration, voting districts, counting the votes, and announcing the results.

5. Interview five adults to determine their attitudes toward the use of voting machines.

6. **Hold a panel discussion on the topic "Should eighteen year olds be given full legal rights along with the right to vote?"**

7. Prepare a calendar of elections showing the dates and types of elections that will be held in your community in the next four years.

8. Prepare a graph showing the numbers of persons voting in each election in your community for the past four years. Interview local election officials for the information, or consult files of past issues of local papers.

9. Interview a member of the League of Women Voters to find out what this group of women tries to do to improve voting in your community.

10. Visit a local polling place, and draw a diagram of the physical arrangements.

11. Some states hold a "run-off" primary. Investigate this type of primary, and report on it before the class.

12. Have a committee study the operation of voting machines in comparison with printed ballots. How is secrecy insured? How is a person kept from voting twice? Which system is more convenient? Which is less confusing?

13. Hold a mock convention of one of the political parties to nominate candidates for some of the major offices.

FURTHER READINGS

Bolton, Carole, NEVER JAM TODAY. Atheneum Publishers, 1971.

Burns, James M., and Peltason, J. W., GOVERNMENT BY THE PEOPLE. Prentice-Hall, Inc., 1972.

Chute, Marchette, THE GREEN TREE OF DEMOCRACY. E. P. Dutton & Co., Inc., 1971.

Connable, Alfred, and Silberfart, Edward, TIGERS OF TAMMANY. Holt, Rinehart and Winston, Inc., 1966.

Cooney, Timothy J., and Haughton, James, IT'S UP TO YOU: A GUIDE TO CHANGING THE SYSTEM. Ives Washburn, Inc., 1971.

Cotter, C. P., and Hennesy, B. C., POLITICS WITHOUT POWER. Atherton Press, 1964.

DeVries, Walter, and Tarrance, Lance, Jr., THE TICKET-SPLITTER. Eerdmans, 1972.

Fenton, John H., UNOFFICIAL MAKERS OF PUBLIC POLICY: PEOPLE AND PARTIES IN POLITICS. Scott, Foresman and Co., 1966.

Ferguson, John H., and McHenry, Dean E., THE AMERICAN SYSTEM OF GOVERNMENT. McGraw-Hill Book Co., 1967. Chapter 12.

Kosimar, Lucy, THE NEW FEMINISM. Franklin Watts, Inc., 1971.

Levy, Mark R., and Kramer, Michael S., THE ETHNIC FACTOR: HOW AMERICA'S MINORITIES DECIDE ELECTIONS. Simon & Schuster, Inc., 1972.

Michener, James A., REPORT OF A COUNTY CHAIRMAN. Bantam Books, 1961. (Paperback edition)

Noble, Iris, EMMELINE AND HER DAUGHTERS: THE PANKHURST SUFFRAGETTES. Julian Messner, Publishers, 1971.

O'Connor, Edwin, THE LAST HURRAH. Bantam Books, 1956. (Paperback edition)

Roosevelt, Eleanor, and Hickok, Lorena A., LADIES OF COURAGE. G. P. Putnam's Sons, 1954.

Rose, Richard, PEOPLE IN POLITICS. Basic Books, 1970.

Saye, Albert B., *et al.,* PRINCIPLES OF AMERICAN GOVERNMENT. Prentice-Hall, Inc., 1966.

Wallace, David, FIRST TUESDAY: A STUDY OF RATIONALITY IN VOTING. Doubleday and Co., Inc., 1964.

Young, William H., OGG AND RAY'S INTRODUCTION TO AMERICAN GOVERNMENT. Appleton-Century-Crofts, Inc., 1966. Chapter 5.

BIPARTISAN—representing two political parties.

BOSS—a leader of a political party who controls the organization of the party for personal gain.

BUREAUCRAT—an official, usually appointed, who administers an agency (a bureau) of the government.

COALITION—a union or alliance of differing persons or groups.

CORRUPT PRACTICE—a dishonest act; a morally weak act; an improper political or legal act.

HONEST GRAFT—taking money or accepting a favor, which is legally right but morally wrong, by a person in a political position.

PATRONAGE—the jobs or favors which are given by a person in politics.

PLANK—an idea or belief for which a political party stands, as stated in its official platform.

PRECINCT—a district or area containing one place to vote.

THE LANGUAGE
OF GOVERNMENT

In view of the extremely large role that parties play in political life today, emphasize the authors' statement that they were not even thought of when our Constitution was written, and that President Washington, as he saw them developing, was concerned they would split the country.

7
Political
Parties

A high school government class, during the first week of school one September, took a secret poll to determine how the class members would like to vote in the November presidential election that year. Some students had decided to vote Democratic; some had decided to vote Republican; one was going to vote the Socialist ticket; three students were undecided. During the remaining weeks that fall, before the election, the campaign was followed with care. The candidates and issues were discussed regularly in and out of class.

The day of the presidential election arrived. Another secret poll was taken. In addition students were asked to state whether they had changed their choices since the September poll.

The three undecided voters had made up their minds. The Socialist-inclined student continued to vote for the Socialist. Two votes had changed from Democratic to Republican; three votes had changed from Republican to Democratic. The rest had not changed their choices.

One class is not enough on which to make judgments, because other classes might react differently. In your school more students might shift from one party to another. Or loyalty to one of the parties might be greater.

The poll, however, does illustrate a few tendencies of political life in the United States. First, studies by political scientists have shown that most people continue to support the political party for which they first begin voting. For example, two-thirds of the people still are loyal to the same party for which they cast their first presidential ballot. Of these, 56 per cent have never voted for the presidential candidate of another party.

Second, the poll shows that there are two dominant parties, with a minority party not very strong. In the 1972 presidential election, for example, President Nixon, the Republican, defeated George McGovern, the Democrat, in a landslide. Nixon received an estimated 61% of the votes and McGovern received 38%.

Third, to win an election a political party usually must get the undecided voters to vote for its candidates. An exception is when a party fails to get its supporters to the polls. Undecided voters are most likely to be independent voters or those with weak allegiances to one of the parties. These voters make up about 15-20 per cent of the voters. As they shift from one party to another they control the balance of power and determine the winner. The shifts from one party to another may not be large, but they do much to determine the final result.

Party leaders are aware of these facts of political life and plan their strategies in accord with them. They know that power comes from winning elections. The major goal of Democrats and Republicans is to win. Control of the government goes to the political party that gets the most votes at the election.

THE NATURE OF A
POLITICAL PARTY   A political party is nothing more than a group of people with somewhat similar ideas who have joined together in a political organization to gain control of governmental policy. The political party wants its candidates in office because these persons can carry out the will of the party.

COALITIONS. The parties are loose organizations. A loyal, strong, hard core of faithful workers makes up the central, enduring strength of the party. But there is a fringe of the party support that is shifting, subject to the propaganda of another party, not easy to control. The votes of the fringe element of each party, together with the independent voters, must be struggled for at each election.

Party members do not all believe in the same things. There are some Democrats who believe many of the same things that Republicans do, and there are some Republicans who agree with ideas of Democrats. The range of opinion within a party is almost as great as the differences between parties. But people with many different opinions are held together in one party by their common desire to win at election time.

The two major parties today are made up of diverse groups who do not think alike. The Democrats are made up of a strong southern group who have tended to be conservative and have resisted efforts to grant the Negro full citizenship and a strong northern group which is liberal and active in support of Negro rights. Northern Negroes tend to belong to this wing of the Democratic party. The Republicans, in contrast, are divided not along sectional

Table 2 (Appendix) gives a breakdown of the presidential elections indicating the political party of each candidate. How many political parties are represented by the men who occupied the office of President?

Young Americans in great numbers worked for both Democratic and Republican candidates in the election of 1972. The volunteers rang doorbells, canvassed by telephone, stuffed envelopes, and passed out campaign literature on street corners. (UPI photo)

lines, but at the local level, between a strong conservative group and a powerful liberal group.

Within these rough divisions there are many shades of differing opinion, varying with different issues. These political parties are really grand *coalitions*, bringing together people who are united by one factor: the desire to gain power through winning elections. Each party knows that if it loses some big section of the public it will lose national elections. So each party struggles to hold in the party some proportion of farmers, labor union members, businessmen, Negroes, youth, older people, war veterans, Catholics, Protestants, Jews, and various other groups.

PARTY MEMBERSHIP. Neither the Republicans nor the Democrats have a definite membership. A voter becomes a "member" by registering and voting for the candidates of the party. Some go beyond this and contribute financially to the party. Others become volunteer party workers. Yet, party membership can be changed at the next election.

How do people decide which party to join? Studies of party affiliation show that the *family* is the most important factor. Typically, before an individual reaches

Compare the nature of American political parties with that of European political parties.

125

voting age, a party choice has been made. Growing up in the family is the chief influence. Voters tend to vote the same as their parents according to studies of voter behavior. When both parents support the same party, young adult voters tend to support that party. Approximately two-thirds of the families fall into this group. When parents are divided in party allegiance, the children tend to divide about equally between the two parties.

Economic circumstance is second in importance to family in the choice of party preference. While there are many individual exceptions, higher income groups tend to vote Republican and the lower income groups tend to vote Democratic. The biggest exception is, of course, in the South.

Political scientists make some other general observations but caution that family tradition probably is more powerful than these tendencies. They do note that descendants of northern Europeans tend to vote Republican, while descendants of southern Europeans tend to prefer the Democratic party. Again, the Republican party is more strongly Protestant than the Democratic. More older citizens are attracted to the Republicans; more younger ones to the Democrats. The inner cities in the large northern metropolitan areas tend to be Democratic while the suburbs tend to be Republican.

Getting large numbers of people to change these party allegiances seems to be very difficult. A different job, getting married, or moving to a new neighborhood does exert a social pressure that results in some shifts of party.

Great social forces cause shifts, too. The most skillful scholars of party membership have pointed out that "only an event of extraordinary intensity can arouse any significant part of the electorate to the point that its established political loyalties are shaken."[1] The Civil War and the economic depression of the 1930's did break the party affiliation of large numbers.

In spite of their importance in present-day government, political parties were not mentioned in the Constitution. Many men who wrote the Constitution feared that political parties might so split our young country that we could not endure as a nation. Even President Washington warned in his Farewell Address against the harmful effects of party spirit. Today, however, political parties are really the engines that keep our democracy moving. This great historical change in the importance of parties has come about because the parties provide essential services.

THE SERVICES OF POLITICAL PARTIES

The services of the political parties fall under five functions: (1) selecting candidates, (2) clarifying issues, (3) unifying government, (4) fixing responsibility, and (5) humanizing government.

SELECTING CANDIDATES. Political parties help select candidates by most of the methods described in the previous chapter. Petitions, caucuses, conventions, and primaries are used and made effective by the political parties. The values of these services are many. The candidates provide the leadership in our government. The winners become responsible for the conduct of the government, while the losers frequently become the major critics of governmental policy.

Some system is needed to attract good candidates to run for office and to discourage the unqualified but eager persons. While this is highly important for the well-known, highly publicized offices, it is equally important for the lesser offices.

[1] Angus Campbell *et al., The American Voter* (New York: John Wiley and Sons, 1960), p. 151.

As Republican candidate for the United States Senate from Illinois, Charles Percy appears on television to present his views to the voters. Television campaigning has become increasingly important in the modern-day political world. (Reprinted by permission of CBS News, a Division of Columbia Broadcasting System, Inc.)

Often it would not be possible to get good candidates if the party leaders did not encourage capable persons to run.

Without parties, voters would be faced with long primary ballots with so many candidates that it would become almost impossible to determine the qualifications of each candidate. With ten or more candidates for each of ten or more offices, the voter would become overwhelmed and the able, little-known candidate might lose out. Party selection and party support tend to avoid these difficulties. The political party has become an important device for getting good candidates for office. While parties sometimes reward second-rate persons by choosing them to run for an office, in the long run, under majority rule, with two strong parties, each party wants the best candidates available.

CLARIFYING ISSUES. The issues of the political campaigns are made clearer because of the political parties. The speeches of the candidates give voters a chance to hear different points of view.

The political parties buy radio and television time for their candidates. They purchase many types of advertising material. They hold meetings. The party workers talk with hundreds of people. In this campaigning the parties help to arouse and educate public opinion. The issues of public life are clearer because of the political parties.

The party platforms show the major principles for which the party stands. The individual items or "planks" in the platform show the central agreements of the party members.

Frequently there are great differences among the party members on the "hottest" issues. In these cases a very general wording for a plank is used in order not to offend too many people. Politicians speak of these planks as "the flowers to attract the bees."

When the platforms have generalized statements, the speeches of the rival candidates become tremendously important, since these remarks determine how the candidates interpret their platforms. Many thoughtful voters consider the speeches more important than the platforms. Certainly the extent to which the candidate supports the platform is of major importance to the intelligent voter. A digest of the 1972 platforms of the two major parties is given on the next two pages.

HIGHLIGHTS OF THE MAJOR PARTY PLATFORMS: 1972

DEMOCRATIC

The Democratic platform was adopted at Miami Beach on July 11, 1972, after an all-night session of debate. The complete platform contains some 24,000 words. Major excerpts are given below.

REPUBLICAN

The Republican platform was adopted at Miami Beach on August 22, 1972, after brief discussion. The complete platform contains some 23,000 words. Major excerpts are given below.

PREAMBLE

Skepticism and cynicism are widespread in America. The people are skeptical of platforms filled with political platitudes—of promises made by opportunistic politicians. The people are cynical about the idea that a rosy future is just around the corner. . . . They feel that the government is run for the privileged few rather than for the many—and they are right.

This year our Republican Party has greater reason than ever before for pride in its stewardship. . . . This political contest of 1972 is a singular one. No Americans before have had a clearer option. The choice is between going forward from dramatic achievements to predictable new achievements, or turning back toward a nightmarish time in which the torch of free America was virtually snuffed out in a storm of violence and protest.

VIETNAM

We pledge, as the first order of business, an immediate and complete withdrawal of all U.S. forces in Indochina. All U.S. military action in Southeast Asia will cease. After the end of U.S. direct combat participation, military aid to the Saigon Government, and elsewhere in Indochina, will be terminated. . . . We must insist that any resolution of the war will include the return of all prisoners held by North Vietnam. . . .

We will continue to seek a settlement of the Vietnam war which will permit the people of Southeast Asia to live in peace under political arrangements of their own choosing. . . . We believe that the President's proposal to withdraw American forces from Vietnam four months after an internationally supervised ceasefire has gone into effect throughout Indochina and all prisoners have been returned is as generous an offer as can be made by anyone.

AMNESTY

To those who for reasons of conscience refused to serve in this war and were prosecuted or sought refuge abroad, we state our firm intention to declare an amnesty, on an appropriate basis, when the fighting has ceased and our troops and prisoners of war have returned.

Here and now we reject all proposals to grant amnesty to those who have broken the law by evading military service. We reject the claim that those who fled are more deserving, or obeyed a higher morality, than those next in line who served in their places.

THE DRAFT

We urge the abolition of the draft.

We wholeheartedly support an all-volunteer armed force and are proud of our historic initiative to bring it to pass.

BUSING

We support the goal of desegregation as a means to achieve equal access to quality education for all our children. . . . Transportation of students is another tool to accomplish desegregation. It must continue to be available according to Supreme Court decisions. . . .

We are committed to guaranteeing equality of educational opportunity and to completing the process of ending de jure school segregation. . . . We are irrevocably opposed to busing for racial balance. Such busing fails its stated objective—improved learning opportunities—while it achieves results no one wants—division within communities and hostility between classes and races.

THE ECONOMY

The Nixon Administration has deliberately driven people out of work in a heartless and ineffective effort to deal with inflation. . . . Full employment—a guaranteed job for all—is the primary objective of the Democratic Party. . . . There must be an end to inflation. . . .

The goal of our Party is prosperity, widely-shared, sustainable in peace. We stand for full employment—a job for everyone willing and able to work in an economy freed of inflation. . . . we kept the inflation fight and defense employment cuts from triggering a recession.

TAX REFORM

The Democratic Party believes that all unfair corporate and individual tax preferences should be removed. . . . We, therefore, endorse as a minimum step . . . repeal [of] virtually all tax preferences in the existing law over the period of 1974-1976. . . . The cost of government must be distributed more fairly among income classes.

We pledge to spread the tax burden equitably. . . . we believe the Nation needs a rigid ceiling on Federal outlays each fiscal year. . . . We reject the deceitful tax "reform" cynically represented as one that would soak the rich, but in fact one that would sharply raise the taxes . . . of families in middle-income brackets as well.

DEFENSE

The Democratic Party pledges itself to maintain adequate military forces for deterrence and effective support of our international position. . . . the military budget can be reduced substantially with no weakening of our national security.

We believe that the first prerequisite of national security is a modern, well-equipped armed force. . . . We draw a sharp distinction between prudent reductions in defense spending and meat-ax slashes. . . . These slashes are worse than misguided; they are dangerous.

HEALTH CARE

America has a responsibility to offer to every American family the best in health care wherever they need it. . . . the next Democratic Administration should establish a system of universal National Health Insurance which covers all Americans with a comprehensive set of benefits. . . . The program should be federally-financed and federally-administered.

Our goal is to enable every American to secure quality health care at reasonable cost. . . . To assure access to basic medical care for all our people, we support a program financed by employers, employees and the Federal Government to provide comprehensive health insurance coverage. . . . We oppose nationalized compulsory health insurance.

CRIME

The Nixon Administration campaigned on a pledge to reduce crime. . . . that pledge has been broken. . . .

We have solid evidence that our unrelenting war on crime is being won. . . . we have established a renewed climate of respect for law. . . .

WOMEN

The Party pledges: A priority effort to ratify the Equal Rights Amendment; elimination of discrimination against women in public accommodations and public facilities, public education and in all federally-assisted programs and federally contracted employment . . . enforcement of all federal statutes and executive laws barring job discrimination on the basis of sex. . . .

We will work toward: Ratification of the Equal Rights Amendment; equal pay for equal work; appointment of women to highest level positions in the Federal Government. We pledge vigorous enforcement of all Federal statutes and executive orders barring job discrimination on the basis of sex.

URBAN ILLS

The Nixon Administration has neither developed an effective urban growth policy. . . . nor concerned itself with the needed recreation of life in our cities. . . .

Our Party stands for major reform of Federal community development programs and the development of a new philosophy to cope with urban ills.

Without party labels, in national or state elections, it might be difficult to vote wisely because few of the candidates are known personally to many voters. The parties also render important service by their efforts to get people to register, to study campaign issues, and to vote intelligently.

UNIFYING GOVERNMENT. Government is unified because of the parties. Since our government is divided into local, state, and national levels, and then at each level is separated into executive, legislative, and judicial branches, it would be easy for the government to become disorganized. The political party provides one of the unifying forces. When the executive and legislative branches are in control of persons from the same party, our government usually works at peak efficiency. The party leaders in the legislature provide the avenue by which the executive can exert party leadership.

When a President or a governor is confronted with a legislature in which one or more of the houses is controlled by the opposite party, he finds it very difficult to get his desired legislation passed. Divided party responsibility then tends to give disunity.

The party also provides unity through the appointments to executive positions. The party in power tends to select for those offices persons who hold the views of the party. These appointed persons support the views of the chief executive and often can be dismissed if they don't. Unity of administration is thus achieved. To get this unity, party leaders often object to putting key positions under civil service. They hold that these *bureaucrats* prevent a new administration from performing its function of putting new policies into effect, and, as a result, government policy is not unified.

FIXING RESPONSIBILITY. When a party gets the power to govern, the public holds that party responsible for action or inaction while it is in control. The majority party is accountable for its deeds and misdeeds. This means that usually the public holds the chief executive responsible—whether he controls the legislature or not. The party has to stand behind those elected and assume responsibility for their activities.

The party that is not in power has a related responsibility—to be critical. The party out of power performs a public service, with great joy at times, by pointing out the defects in the actions of the majority party. The "loyal opposition" keeps issues before the public, forces the party in power to operate at a higher level than it might otherwise do, and exposes the weaknesses of its opponents.

HUMANIZING GOVERNMENT. A lesser recognized, but important function of the political parties, lies in their social and human activities. A social life for many people is provided by party dances, picnics, conventions, and work at campaign headquarters. These activities frequently become hobbies and recreation for party workers.

The activities of party workers provide a link between a sometimes impersonal government and the voters. The local district leader of the party becomes aware of the needs of the people in his precinct and communicates this information to public officials. He has easier access to these officials than does the ordinary citizen. At the same time the neighborhood political leader is able to assist citizens with their problems. He can help with complaints; he can dispense some favors; he can provide some services. Some of this may be classed as political favoritism, but some is legitimate help which should be available to any citizen. The party leader is successful because he knows his way around government

This campaign advertisement was one of many that appeared in newspapers and magazines and on radio and television in 1972 asking for contributions. Most campaign contributions come from corporate business executives rather than from ordinary citizens. Does this affect the kind of legislation that is written? If so, how?

offices better than most citizens. Political parties help make government less remote from the people.

EFFECTIVENESS OF THESE SERVICES. The parties do not perform these services of selecting candidates, clarifying issues, unifying government, fixing responsibility, and humanizing government equally well. In actual practice they serve best in the process of selecting candidates. The parties are weakest in their unifying of government. They do reasonably well in fixing responsibility and humanizing government—depending upon the ability of the leaders.

The record on the clarification of issues is muddled. On some issues, such as unemployment, the position of political parties has been made very clear. On other issues —foreign policy, race relations, and labor-management relations, for example—there have sometimes been uncertainty and misunderstanding.

THE TWO-PARTY SYSTEM

There have always been two major political parties in the United States. The names of the parties have changed over the years, but the two-party system has been an important central feature of our political life. England is the only other great nation with a similar experience with the two-party system.

Most European nations have numerous parties—a *splinter-party* system. The results of having so many parties have not been entirely satisfactory. Governments change rapidly; stable government is hard to achieve; responsibility is hard to fix. In a crisis a dictator has an easy road to power, and a tyrannical one-party system may result. Most observers believe that a two-party system works better. Our present two major parties have dominated our politics for more than a hundred years.

THE DEMOCRATIC PARTY. The *Democratic party* traces its history back to the beginnings of our government. During Washington's administration, opposition developed to Hamilton's *Federalist* ideas for a strong, central government.

Under the leadership of Thomas Jefferson, the opposition became known as the *Anti-Federalists* and shortly as the Republicans. This party is also referred to by

With respect to countries having a splinter-party system, introduce and describe the term "coalition government."

Rarely does the title of a book greatly influence the public, and even more rare is it for the title of a book to change the direction of a scholarly field of inquiry. Yet, this was the effect of a book written by Professor Harold D. Lasswell. In 1936 he published a small book of 250 pages giving his interpretation of the efforts of the politician to calculate "probable changes in influence and the influential." He gave the book the title *Politics: Who Gets What, When, How.*

In the forty years since Lasswell wrote this book political science has given more attention to practical, actual, living forms of governmental practice. Lasswell conceived of political science as "the study of influence and the influential." His book began with the "methods *of* the influential and concluded with the consequences *for* the influential."

Harold D. Lasswell was born in a small town in Illinois, the son of a minister. After finishing high school, he attended the University of Chicago, from which he graduated in 1922. He studied in Europe for three years and returned to Chicago, where he received the degree of Doctor of Philosophy in 1926. He taught political science at the University of Chicago until 1938. Then, because of his interest in personality and mental health as related to politics, he taught for a year in Washington, D.C. at the Washington School of Psychiatry. From 1939 until 1945 he served as director of War Communication Research of the Library of Congress. Here his studies of propaganda were important during World War II. Since the war, he has been a professor in the Department of Law and Political Science at Yale University. In 1956 he was president of the American Political Science Association. He has written more than a dozen political science books.

historians as the Democratic-Republicans, in order to avoid confusion with the later Republican party.

This earlier Republican party kept control of the government for twenty-four years, and finally the Federalist party disappeared. The "Era of Good Feeling" lasted for the two terms of James Monroe. Then the Republicans divided into Democratic-Republicans and National Republicans. During Jackson's administration (1829-1837) the Democratic-Republicans became known as the Democrats. The party has continued under that name to this day.

THE REPUBLICAN PARTY. The *Republican party* was born in 1854. A Whig party had developed from the National Republican opposition to Jackson. But many people who opposed slavery were not satisfied with either the Democrats or the Whigs. They wanted an antislavery party. The new Republican party gave them this chance. In 1860 Lincoln was elected as the first Republican President. From then until 1932 the Republicans dominated national politics. The only Democratic Presidents elected during those years were Cleveland and Wilson.

Since 1932 the Democrats, through the elections of Roosevelt, Truman, Kennedy, and Johnson, have dominated nationally, although the Republicans elected Eisenhower in 1952 and in 1956 and Nixon in 1968 and in 1972.

MINOR PARTIES. In nearly every election there are some minor parties. Originally the Republican party was a minor party. With this exception, none of the minor parties has replaced a major party. But the minor parties have played an important part in our government.

The minor party is free to advocate special issues that may not have wide popular appeal. If an issue becomes popular, one or both of the major parties will undoubtedly adopt the issue and win over many of

Sargent Shriver shares the platform with Presidential Candidate George McGovern after the Democratic National Committee nominated him for the Vice Presidency. (UPI photo)

the followers of the minor party. Freedom for slaves, free coinage of silver, direct election of senators, the income tax, and old-age pensions have followed this pattern. In these cases the minor party lived and died because of the special issue.

Today the public opinion poll does what the protest ballot cast for a minor party once did. Political leaders through continuous use of political polls are able to determine even small shifts in the public's reaction to special issues.

A minor party, however, may become strong enough to influence the election of the President. In our history this has happened when the party has developed around a powerful leader. In 1912 one wing of the Republican party left that party to form the Progressive party. Theodore Roosevelt was the Progressive candidate. His vote-getting power was so great that he pulled enough votes away from Taft, the regular

Republican candidate, so that Wilson, the Democrat, was elected.

In 1924, 1948, and 1968 similar attempts were made to pull voters away from the major parties. Neither La Follette, Henry Wallace, nor George Wallace were as successful as Teddy Roosevelt and did not influence the presidential elections sufficiently to change the results. La Follette received nearly five million votes in 1924; Henry Wallace, slightly over a million votes in 1948; George Wallace, over nine million votes in 1968. Yet, Nixon, the winner in 1968, got over thirty million votes.

Southern opposition to the civil rights program of Democrat Harry Truman also led in 1948 to the formation of the States' Rights party, with Senator Thurmond of South Carolina as the presidential candidate. Although Thurmond received slightly more than a million votes, he did get more votes than Henry Wallace and won the

President Richard Nixon and Vice President Spiro Agnew were renominated by the Republican Party at its convention in 1972. Here they appear before the enthusiastic delegates. (UPI photo)

election in Alabama, Louisiana, Mississippi, and South Carolina. This threat of a third party based in the South has been used in each election since 1948 to keep a brake on the civil rights movement. George Wallace of Alabama used this tactic in 1968 with his American Independent Party and won the states of Alabama, Arkansas, Georgia, Louisiana, and Mississippi.

In addition to losing their chief issues to the major parties, the minor parties have other disadvantages. In some states it is difficult to get on the ballot. In these states, in order to reduce the size of the ballot, laws have been passed that a party cannot reappear automatically on the ballot if a specified percentage of voters did not vote for the party at the previous election.

The financial problems of the minor parties are many. Minority groups have little financial support.

Organization is difficult too. People who advocate unpopular causes, frequently, are not good at getting along with other people. They do not fit into party organization too well. Finally, the American people seem to like a winner. Voters do not like to throw away their votes on a party that cannot win. As a result, in the eight presidential elections before 1968 minor parties received only an average of 2 per cent of the total vote.

In spite of these difficulties the Socialist and Prohibition parties have existed for many years. In Wisconsin the Progressive party has had a powerful influence on state elections. In New York City in past years the American Labor party, the Conservative party, and the Liberal party have competed successfully with the major parties in races for mayor and city council.

In recent years the presidential candidates of several minor parties have been on the ballots of one or more states. Among these parties were: American, American

Independent, Communist, Human Rights, National Peoples, New Politics, Prohibition, Socialist-Labor, Socialist-Worker, States' Rights, Progressive, and Peace and Freedom.

PARTY ORGANIZATION

Much of the success of the major parties results from their strong party organizations. Between elections both Democrats and Republicans maintain organizations that extend from the national level directly down to the local neighborhood. But these organizations are not highly organized like an army or a police department. They are loose organizations with little real discipline of members and with a small paid staff that depends greatly on volunteer help. Both parties are organized in the same manner.

THE NATIONAL CHAIRMAN. At the top of each organization is the national chairman with a central staff of clerks, secretaries, and public relations employees. He is officially selected by the national committee but is really nominated by the presidential candidate of the party. The national chairman is the executive head of the party.

He is a combination of campaign manager, party spokesman, and skilled administrator. He travels all over the country keeping in touch with party leaders and

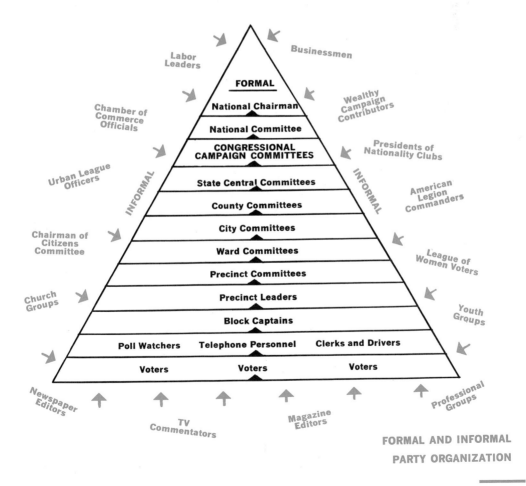

FORMAL AND INFORMAL

PARTY ORGANIZATION

The chairman of the national committee is the executive head of the party. Left, Senator Robert Dole, Chairman of the Republican National Committee, addresses a party gathering. At right is the Democrat's top executive, Jean Westwood, the first woman to head either of the major US political parties. (Right, UPI photo)

making speeches, but he bases his operations from a central headquarters. Presently both the Democrats and the Republicans are headquartered in Washington, D.C.

THE NATIONAL COMMITTEES. The Republican National Committee consists of one man and one woman from each state, territory, and the District of Columbia. In addition, the Republicans include on their National Committee the state chairmen of those states carried by the party in the last presidential election and of those states that have a Republican majority in their delegations to Congress.

The Democratic National Committee also has one man and one woman from each state, territory, and the District of Columbia. In addition, there are 161 members selected on the basis of the Democratic strength in the electoral college for the past three elections plus three representatives of Democratic governors and four of members of Congress. The effect is to give power to states where the party wins elections.

While the national committee on paper appears to have great influence, in fact it is primarily concerned with the problems of presidential elections. The members of the committee, however, are quite powerful individuals in their own states and have

considerable political power. The national committee determines party policy between national conventions, leaving the administrative work to the chairman and his staff.

CONGRESSIONAL CAMPAIGN COMMITTEES. A congressional campaign committee is organized for the House and a senatorial campaign committee for the Senate. Members of these committees are elected from the membership of each house, but provisions are made for representation from congressional districts where the party does not have a member in Congress.

The committees are very active, with full-time paid staffs. In the "off-year" congressional elections (when a President is not being elected) they have great influence in party circles.

THE STATE CENTRAL COMMITTEE. Every state has a central committee for each of the major parties. Some committees are small, with a dozen members; some committees are large, with several hundred members. Members are usually selected either by direct primary or by conventions. The committee activities at the state level are similar to those of the national committee.

The state chairman is the operating head of the state committee. Within a state, the chairman is sometimes a very powerful political figure, and some state chairmen have certainly been more influential than the governors. Often, however, the chairman is the spokesman for the governor, a senator, or some other strong political leader or group.

LOCAL COMMITTEES. The *county committee* is very important in rural areas and in many urban areas such as Cook County, Illinois, which includes Chicago. Nearly every county has a committee, although some counties in the South do not have Republican committees.

The committees are usually selected either by direct primary or by party caucus. The chairman of the county committee is a powerful political figure. Because citizen attention is often focused on state and national affairs, many county chairmen can do about as they please. The county chairman has many political jobs to distribute. He quietly but directly influences the delegates to state and national conventions.

The *city organization* is sometimes a part of the county organization and is sometimes separate but closely related. The mayor, the chairman of a city committee, or the county chairman may serve as head of the city organization. Usually this head is elected to the position through the party machinery, but sometimes he becomes the head because of his great influence.

Ward, *district*, or *precinct* organizations are a part of the county or city organization. The variations at this level are very great. Chicago has a well-organized precinct system at work the year round on the neighborhood level. In contrast, Los Angeles has a loose precinct organization, which differs for the two major parties. In the South there is practically no organization at the precinct level.

The *precinct captain* or *committeeman* is the worker for the party who has the most direct contact with the voter. He is the vote-getter and in many places the money-raiser. His job is to know the people in his neighborhood. He knows which party they prefer, whether they have voted, and whether they need transportation to the polls. He knows whether he can count on them for getting signatures on petitions, for distributing hand bills, for serving as watchers at the polls. He must know and like people. If he is successful, the party is successful. It is at this level that most young people begin their careers in politics.

The ambitious precinct worker may become the ward committeeman. This job requires less direct contact with the voters, but it does require considerable executive ability. The ward committeeman is a kind of middleman between the precinct captains and the city or county chairman.

INFORMAL ORGANIZATION. The formal structure of the party organization does not tell the complete story. Persons of influence as well as interest groups exert power through the various committees. A friend who can speak directly to a precinct leader can often change an action. A labor union leader or a businessman who "has the ear" of a county chairman can defeat the wishes of party members. The NAACP, a White Citizens' Council, an American Legion post, or a teachers' group may have power because one of its members has come to occupy a key post in the party structure.

Some political scientists have called party organization, with its many ramifications, the "hidden government." By this they mean that power is gained by those who are not necessarily a part of the formal elected or appointed group of public officials. Outside the formal party structure, too, there exists a wide range of clubs and associations that are encouraged by the political parties and support one of the parties.

Young adults attend Leadership Training School sponsored by the Young Republican National Federation. Out of these sessions come young men and women prepared to help their party campaign. (Republican National Committee)

At the national level are the *citizens groups,* typified by the "Citizens for———" committees. These groups raise money, set up headquarters, distribute campaign literature, and engage in other campaign activities. To their membership are attracted persons such as independent voters who would not normally participate in party activities. Persons leaving one party and joining the other often make this transition through membership in these citizen committees.

Political clubs operate loosely alongside the formal party structure. The Young Democrats, the Young Republicans, the Republican Women, and the Democratic Women have a semi-independent status but provide a training ground for political activity as well as personnel for carrying on campaign activities.

The most famous of these clubs is Tam-

many Hall in New York City—the group that exerted control over Democratic politics for many years. The group began as a social-political club in the early history of our country and remnants of its influence still exist in New York. Similar clubs have grown up around nationality groups. German, Irish, Polish, Italian, and other ethnic groups provided a social base in the large city and came to realize the power that could be exerted politically.

BOSSES AND MACHINES. From the national committee to the precinct worker there seems to be a direct chain of command. To the uninformed citizen it might seem that all the national chairman needs to do is give an order and the doorbells of voters will begin to ring at the neighborhood level. Actually this is not true. The national committee is powerful, but its power is weakened as ideas or suggestions drip down through the committee organization.

Now and then master organizers like Herbert Brownell, James Farley, Mark Hanna, or the Kennedys will tie all of these committees together into an effective organization. But most of the time the organization is loose. Local and state leaders are jealous of their powers and frequently are more concerned about politics at their level than on the national level. As a result there never has been a real national political boss or a national political machine.

This condition is not true at the state or local level. The following are famous examples, both past and present, of control of the party organization at these levels: Hague of New Jersey, Crump of Tennessee, Pendergast of Kansas City, De Sapio of New York, Lawrence of Pittsburgh, and Kelly, Nash, and Daley of Chicago.

When a party leader gains control of the party organization and uses it for his personal, selfish purposes, he is called a "boss." The organization he controls is called a "political machine." Most bosses have never extended control beyond the city or county level, and no boss has been able to control a machine beyond the state level.

The boss profits from placing judges, aldermen, and mayors in power. In return for getting them elected he demands special favors. Sometimes this may be the right to name persons to public jobs. This ability to give jobs to people is called "patronage."

"Honest graft" is another means of profit for the boss. He is able to get advance information about a new bus line, park, or housing project. By buying property at a low price, he can sell it later at a high price when the public improvement has raised property values. He may profit by getting government contracts for construction of streets, highways, and public buildings or by selling supplies to public insti-

tutions. In all these cases he tries to be legal. He profits only because of his special position and knowledge.

The boss sometimes profits, too, by real graft. Here he disobeys the law. National and local investigations have revealed many cases of protection being given to gamblers and to people in other rackets by public officials. A reform mayor of New York City uncovered cases of money being pocketed from fees that were to be paid the city and from money that should have been spent for food and medical care for the poor. These forms of dishonesty are approved by some bosses and are considered a way to keep the machine "oiled."

Boss rule seems to be breaking down. As citizens have learned more about the operation of government, they have taken a more active interest. With interest have come reform movements that have wiped out bosses and machines in many communities. The big city bosses thrived on the uninformed immigrant, the ignorant Negro who had been deprived of an education in the rural South, and the poor worker attracted to the city by the chance for a job. The children of these people have received better educations. They learned the lessons of politics and have not been willing to put up with boss control.

Politics is still a long way from perfection, but compared to the early years of this century great strides have been made.

PARTY FINANCE   To win elections the political parties require much money. Financing

---

Politics is still the greatest and most honorable adventure.

—PRESIDENT JOHN F. KENNEDY

a party is a big business. Money is required to pay the staffs of the various committees; to pay travel expenses; to buy radio and television time; to pay for advertising in newspapers and magazines and on billboards; and to prepare campaign literature. Television has become a very expensive item. It is estimated that twenty million dollars were spent for television time in the 1968 presidential campaign.

Money for these purposes does not ordinarily come from graft of either the honest or dishonest type. The money comes from contributions or gifts of many different types.

SOCIAL FUNCTIONS. Have you ever paid one hundred dollars for a dinner? Hundreds of faithful party workers do this each year at the Jefferson, Jackson, or Lincoln dinners that are held. These dinners are devices to raise funds and to rally the party workers. They serve the same function as the football pep rally in your school—only they cost one hundred dollars to attend. Such social functions are attended by candidates, officeholders, party workers, and their friends.

GIFTS. Another way in which funds are raised is by gifts. Attempts are made to get small gifts from thousands of persons who are sympathetic to the party. Except for a few minor parties, in this country parties do not collect dues from their members. The parties rely on contributions from many individuals.

Neither gifts from the rank and file nor money paid to attend social functions, however, are enough to finance the parties. As a result large gifts are obtained from wealthy individuals, from business, labor, and farm groups, and from other organizations with a special economic stake in government decisions. Some of these "gifts" are in the form of advertising space purchased in a variety of party publications.

Some of these individuals and groups sometimes give money to both major parties—to be sure that they have backed the winning party.

ASSESSMENTS. A third way in which funds are raised is by assessments of some governmental employees and officeholders. There was a time when it was a fairly common practice in some states and cities to require from 2 to 10 per cent of salaries from those persons who got jobs through party influence. Money from these assessments went into the party treasury.

The federal government and many states have made such assessments illegal. If contributions are made to the party by governmental employees, however, who is to say that they are or are not "voluntary"? Contributions from government workers who are loyal to the party are still an important source of funds.

CONTRIBUTIONS BY CANDIDATES. The candidates' contributions are a fourth way in which money is obtained. Each candidate is expected to finance a good share of his own campaign and to give something extra for the party. The candidate is expected to receive contributions from his friends. Wealthy men have been nominated for office with the hope that they would become large givers to the party.

CONTRIBUTIONS BY INTEREST GROUPS. Political campaigns have become so expensive that neither party can raise sufficient funds through regular party channels. One of the chief devices to increase funds has been to create the "Citizens for————" committees referred to earlier. These committees, led by interested amateurs but encouraged by party regulars, raise substantial amounts of money from gifts. They also do active campaigning. The political arm of labor, COPE (the Committee on Public Education of the AFL-CIO), raises considerable sums from voluntary contributions as well as paying part of its expenses from regular union dues. Trade associations and other interest groups, seeking a reduction in a tariff or a modification of a federal regulation, make contributions and pay for political activities for candidates they support. Business and industry buy full-page, tax-deductible advertisements in convention programs and in party yearbooks and almanacs. With prices ranging from $5,000 to $15,000 a page, substantial sums are raised.

In summary, these contributors can be classified roughly into two groups: (1) those friends of the party and of candidates who are truly interested in their future, and (2) those who want or hope to get something in return.

CORRUPT PRACTICES
ACTS   Raising these large sums of money involves dangers of corruption and dishonesty. The outright buying of votes is rare. But some people who give money for political purposes expect a return in the form of a favorable law, a friendly judge, or an administrative decision that will be helpful. Such special favors are a constant threat to the democratic election process.

To protect us against the dangers from improper collection and use of party funds, the states and the federal government have passed *corrupt practices acts.*

STATE ACTS. The state laws usually place a limit on the size of the contribution from any one person and the amount of money that can be spent by a candidate in the campaign. Some states do not permit solicitation of money from governmental employees. Corporations and labor unions are not allowed to make contributions in some states.

Most states require candidates to file a statement of their campaign receipts and expenses. Such statements are then available for public examination.

NATIONAL ACTS. Congress for more than fifty years has been writing similar laws. Four of these laws are best known. First, the *Federal Corrupt Practices Act of 1925* limited the amount of money that a candidate for Congress could spend to get elected. The law permitted a candidate for the Senate to spend up to $10,000 and a candidate for the House of Representatives to spend up to $2,500 to be elected. Or, an amount could be spent equal to three cents per vote in the last election, not to exceed $25,000 for senatorial candidates and $5,000 for candidates for the House of Representatives. This law was repealed in 1972 by the Election Campaign Act described later.

Second, the *Hatch Acts of 1939 and 1940* placed limitations on the size of contributions and on total expenditures. No national political committee may receive or spend more than $3,000,000 in one year. No individual contribution of more than $5,000 per person can be received in any one year. (This provision was repealed by the 1972 Act.) Federal employees are not permitted to take part in political campaigns. Bribery is illegal. The laws do not allow corporations, national banks, or labor unions to contribute.

Other national laws required candidates for federal office to make financial reports. These laws contained loopholes that made them of slight effect. President Johnson described them as "more holes than loops." The corporation may not give money, but a company official as an individual may. His wife, brothers, sisters, and every other member of the family each can give. Political advertising can be purchased and gifts can be made to "citizens' committees."

The labor union cannot contribute, but the political action committee of that union can carry on political activities from money given by the union. The weaknesses were demonstrated by the fact that the Justice Department never prosecuted anyone for violation of the law.

The *Federal Election Campaign Act,* the third of the great efforts to control campaign financing, was passed because of growing concern over the increased cost of political campaigns. The law took effect April 7, 1972. Its key provisions are:

• Candidates for Congress and the Presidency are limited to spending 10 cents per eligible voter or $50,000, whichever is greater, for advertising on television, radio, newspapers, billboards, and automatic telephone equipment. Of the total amount spent, 60 per cent could be used for broadcast advertising time. This spending limitation will be increased annually in proportion to increases in the Consumer Price Index. The base year is 1970. Candidates for nomination to the presidency are limited by the same formula as computed for each state in which they compete.

• Promises of employment or other political rewards in exchange for political support are prohibited.

• Candidates and political committees must report names and addresses of all persons making contributions or loans of more than $100. Expenditures of more than $100 must be reported, too.

• Reports of contributions and expenditures must be reported quarterly.

• The officials authorized to oversee the law are: the Clerk of the House for House candidates, the Secretary of the Senate for Senate candidates, and the Comptroller General for presidential candidates.

Critics were disappointed in this last provision thinking that political appointees would not enforce the provisions. A new organization, *Common Cause,* a nonpartisan, independent citizens' lobby enlisted

Campaign costs seem to rise at every election. Why is this considered an evil? (Fitzpatrick in the St. Louis Post-Dispatch)

volunteers across the country to try to see that all candidates made accurate and prompt reports. Reformers had desired the appointment of an independent elections commission to supervise the collection of reports and inform law enforcement officials of violations. The Senate passed such a provision but the House refused to accept it.

These efforts to regulate campaign finances rely mainly on publicity. There is a widespread belief that the American people will not stand for one party or candidate spending much more money than the other. The poor man should have as much chance for office as the wealthy. Citizens are entitled to know who are backing candidates and how much money they are contributing.

To use publicity to control political spending requires each party and each candidate to tell where all the campaign money was obtained and how it was spent. All other groups engaged in political activity must do the same thing. If these facts were available, the public through newspapers and television publicity could find out where the money came from and how it was spent.

The fourth law on campaign financing reform, adopted by Congress in 1971, was an effort to increase greatly the number of small contributors. A federal tax benefit was established making it possible for political contributions to be deducted from the personal income tax. For an individual $12.50 and for a married couple $25 could be used as a tax credit, or alternatively, $50 for an individual and $100 for a couple could be deducted from taxable income. Contributions to candidates or political committees for federal, state, or local elections of any type—general, primary, or special—were eligible.

By another provision, taxpayers were authorized to direct on their income tax returns that one dollar, in the case of an individual, or two dollars, in the case of a couple, could be paid into a public campaign fund. The money could be designated for use by the candidate of a chosen party or for a general campaign fund. But the provisions were not to go into effect until after the 1972 presidential election. When this provision becomes effective, it is estimated that more than twenty million dollars will be available for each of the major parties.

STUDY QUESTIONS

1. Why have political parties developed in the United States?

2. What are the chief functions of political parties?

3. How do the platforms of the Democrats and the Republicans differ?

4. What is a plank in a political platform?

5. How do political parties unify government?

CONCEPTS AND GENERALIZATIONS

1
Allegiance to a political party is fairly permanent and not easy to change.

2
Family tradition and economic conditions are the chief factors in determining party affiliation.

3
Political parties are loose organizations, like coalitions, with their diverse elements united to gain power through winning elections.

4
Political parties provide necessary and useful services in a democratic government.

5
Parties are most effective in selecting candidates and weakest in unifying government.

6
Our system of government works best with two strong political parties.

7
Minor parties have had some success as the initiators of new ideas.

8
The function of the minor party in advocating new ideas is being replaced by the public opinion poll.

9
The formal organization of political parties by committees is not as efficient as it appears to be in theory.

10
The informal organization of interest groups has great influence on the party organization.

11
The political boss is disappearing as voters have received better political education.

12
Political parties require enormous financial support for their activities.

13
Present laws regulating the raising and spending of money for political campaigns are ineffective, but Congress and state legislatures have not been able to pass adequate reform measures.

How do they clarify issues? fix responsibility? humanize government?

6. What interest groups provide the chief support for the Democrats? for the Republicans?

7. What minor parties exist in American politics today?

8. Why have minor parties had a difficult time gaining followers in the United States?

9. What is the committee structure of a political party?

10. Who are the present national chairmen of the major political parties?

11. What are the differences between a political boss and a national chairman?

12. Why are the congressional and senatorial campaign committees of great importance?

13. How does a political boss get his power?

14. How are political parties financed?

15. What are the corrupt practices acts?

16. What are the chief restrictions on political expenditures?

17. How do citizens decide to which party they will belong?

IDEAS FOR DISCUSSION

1. Do you think you should become an active member of a political party? Why or why not?

2. Why are some party planks very general rather than specific? Defend your answer by showing examples from a recent election.

3. One writer has said that the differences *within* the Democratic and Republican parties are greater than the differences *between* them. Do you agree or disagree?

4. Another writer has said that the difference between the present political parties is the difference between "tweedle-dee" and "tweedle-dum." Do you agree or disagree?

5. What public issues do you think have been clarified by the present political parties?

6. Who do you think might be the groups of people who would form the hard core if a strong third party were to arise in America?

7. Compare the organization of one of the major political parties with the sales organization of one of the major business corporations. How are they alike? How do they differ?

8. Morally, are there any real differences between "honest graft" and graft?

9. It is sometimes said that a poor man cannot afford to be a candidate for public office. Do you agree or disagree?

10. Do you think the present actions of political leaders and political parties in the United States are increasing or decreasing "faith in one's fellowman"?

11. A study of high school students in one city showed that 60 per cent would *not* care to be candidates for public office, 25 per cent were in doubt, and 15 per cent thought that some day they would like to be candidates for public office. What are your reactions to these percentages? Why do you think the students felt as they did?

12. Is there a place for the independent voter in American politics?

13. Discuss this situation: A dentist, after establishing a good practice in a medium-sized town, joined a political party and devoted much of his time in the evenings to attending political meetings, making speeches, and handing out political pamphlets. How do you react to these political activities of the dentist?

14. David Lawrence, a Washington columnist, stated that "the political party which can get to the polls the largest number of stay-at-home voters with a liking for that party can win any election." In other words, he believes that the nonvoter who votes decides the elections. What does this mean for the party worker?

THINGS TO DO

1. Organize class committees to attend meetings of different political parties and report on their experiences.

2. Collect advertising material of various types from a political campaign. Arrange these materials for a special bulletin board display.

3. Prepare a report on the beliefs and activities of one of the minor parties that appeared on the last presidential ballot.

4. Study the election laws of your state to determine how a minor party may get on the ballot.

5. Prepare a report on the activities of one of the national chairmen.

6. Find out who the members of the national

committees are from your state. What have been their state political activities? How were they chosen?

7. Organize a small committee of class members to interview precinct committeemen in your neighborhood. What duties are performed? What relationship is there between the precinct committee and other committees, including state and national? Report to the class.

8. Hold a "one-sentence" debate on this topic: "*Resolved*, That high school students should join the Democratic party." (In a one-sentence debate each student states an argument in one sentence. The class is divided into sides, and statements are heard first from one side and then from the other.)

9. Hold a panel discussion on this topic: "Local officials should be chosen by a non-partisan system."

10. Prepare an oral report on one of the following topics: the presidential preference primary, patronage, political, clubs, party social functions.

11. Write a radio script dramatizing the episodes in the life of a man who is seeking political office.

12. Draw a cartoon to show the beliefs of one party on a specific political issue.

13. Interview a public official who has recently been elected to office to ascertain the sources of his campaign funds and how the money was spent.

14. Prepare a report on the state laws concerning the financing of a political candidate for state office.

FURTHER READINGS

Bone, Hugh A., AMERICAN POLITICS AND THE PARTY SYSTEM. McGraw-Hill Book Co., Inc., 1965.

Brooke, Edward W., THE CHALLENGE OF CHANGE: CRISIS IN OUR TWO-PARTY SYSTEM. Little, Brown and Co., 1966.

Burns, James M., and Peltason, J. W., GOVERNMENT BY THE PEOPLE. Prentice-Hall, Inc., 1972. Chapter 12.

Crick, Bernard, IN DEFENSE OF POLITICS. University of Chicago Press, 1962.

Felknor, Bruce, DIRTY POLITICS. W. W. Norton & Co., Inc., 1966.

Fenton, John H., UNOFFICIAL MAKERS OF PUBLIC POLICY: PEOPLE AND PARTIES IN POLITICS. Scott, Foresman and Co., 1966.

Ferguson, John H., and McHenry, Dean E., THE AMERICAN SYSTEM OF GOVERNMENT. McGraw-Hill Book Co., Inc., 1967. Chapter 11.

Goldman, Ralph M., THE DEMOCRATIC PARTY IN AMERICAN POLITICS. The Macmillan Co., 1966.

Hart, Jeffrey, THE AMERICAN DISSENT: A DECADE OF MODERN CONSERVATISM. Doubleday and Co., Inc., 1966.

Hinderaker, Ivan, PARTY POLITICS. Holt, Rinehart and Winston, Inc., 1956.

Jones, Charles O., THE REPUBLICAN PARTY IN AMERICAN POLITICS. The Macmillan Co., 1965.

Ladd, Everett C., Jr., AMERICAN POLITICAL PARTIES. W. W. Norton & Co., Inc., 1971.

Lasswell, Harold D., POLITICS: WHO GETS WHAT, WHEN AND HOW. Peter Smith, Publisher, 1936.

McKone, Jim, TO WIN IN NOVEMBER. Vanguard Press, Inc., 1970.

Moscow, Warren, THE LAST OF THE BIG-TIME BOSSES. Stein and Day, 1971.

Porter, Kirk H., and Johnson, Donald B., NATIONAL PARTY PLATFORMS, 1840-1964. University of Illinois Press, 1966.

Ribicoff, Abraham, and Newman, Jon O., POLITICS: THE AMERICAN WAY. Allyn and Bacon, 1967.

Rossiter, Clinton, PARTIES AND POLITICS IN AMERICA. Cornell University Press, 1960. (Paperback edition)

Saye, Albert B., *et al.*, PRINCIPLES OF AMERICAN GOVERNMENT. Prentice-Hall, Inc., 1966. Chapter 7.

Sindler, Allen P., POLITICAL PARTIES IN THE UNITED STATES. St. Martin's Press, Inc., 1966.

Stave, Bruce M., ed., URBAN BOSSES, MACHINES, AND PROGRESSIVE REFORMERS. D. C. Heath & Co., 1972. (Paperback edition)

Young, William H., OGG AND RAY'S INTRODUCTION TO AMERICAN GOVERNMENT. Appleton-Century-Crofts, Inc., 1966. Chapter 7.

INTEREST GROUP—an organization of persons who have some common interest; a pressure group.

LOBBYING—the process of influencing the conduct of government.

LOBBYIST—the paid agent of an interest group.

PRESSURE GROUP—an interest group that tries to influence governmental processes.

PROPAGANDA—efforts to influence public opinion.

PUBLIC OPINION—the attitude of a particular group of people at a given time on a socially significant issue; majority opinion.

SAMPLE—the cross-section of people to be interviewed in a public opinion poll or survey.

8
Influencing the Citizens

Intelligent, informed citizens are essential to a system of democratic government. In theory, thoughtful citizens will study and discuss controversial public issues, deliberate over alternative solutions to public problems, and, finally, determine governmental policy through their best judgment. It is in this sense that democratic government is sometimes called government by public opinion.

In practice, democratic government does not measure up to these ideals. Citizens are not always informed. Some citizens do not have the ability to understand complex issues. Sometimes essential information is not available to citizens. There are citizens with such deep-seated prejudices that they cannot recognize and accept facts which they hear and read; emotion prevails over their intelligence. Selfishness or individual concerns may also win out over the common good.

Even though theory and practice differ, the ideal of the thoughtful, well-informed citizen is a desirable goal. While the goal

THE LANGUAGE OF GOVERNMENT

is not reached in the solution of all social problems nor in the selection of all public officials, the goal is still justified. On many issues public policy is in accord with the wishes of most people. And the acts of public officials tend to be those supported by public opinion—although through courage, wisdom, and ideals (or their opposites), the official may not act according to the opinion of the majority.

The ways in which citizens are influenced, then, become very important in a system of democratic government. What citizens believe, how they get their beliefs, and how they act on these beliefs are important aspects of the political processes. In this chapter these matters are discussed under three headings: (1) Public opinion, (2) Interest groups, and (3) Voting behavior.

PUBLIC OPINION

Public opinion is the sum of the opinions of all individuals. In this sense public opinion is a collection of individual opinions. These individual opinions on any one specific issue are not alike; they differ. So the opinion of one person may cancel out the opinion of another person.

Individuals have had different experiences. They have read different papers. They have seen different movies and different television shows. They have listened to different radio programs. They have heard different family discussions. They have been to different schools. As a result they have developed different ideas and acquired certain prejudices.

Some have more and deeper prejudices than others. Some express their ideas more clearly or with louder voices than others.

Every citizen contributes to public opinion, for the attitudes, beliefs, and thoughts of each person are important. Yet, public opinion is finally the mixture or composite of all these differing opinions. In this sense, "public opinion" is nothing more than majority opinion; it is the opinion held by most of the people.

Two other characteristics of public opinion are worthy of note. First, public opinion is related to a *specific issue*. Public opinion is not generalized; it is precise. How does the public react to riots? What are the beliefs about space flights? the United Nations? the income tax? What actions should be taken to help the poverty-stricken? the aged? the ill? Where should a new highway be placed? Specific issues on these opinions can be formed.

Second, the public is not one, big, general public. Rather, the "public" is *a great many publics*. Consider the example of the United Automobile Workers (UAW) wanting an increase in hourly wages when a new contract is written. The members of the UAW make up one public hoping for the raise, but even this public has several sub-publics: those union members who want the increase even if it means a strike, those who want the wage only if it can be gotten without a strike, those who think their leaders have gone too far, those who think their leaders haven't gone far enough. In addition there are many other publics involved. The automobile executives who doubt the wisdom of an increased wage in terms of productivity are a different public. So are the stockholders who fear a decreased dividend. There are others, too: government officials who fear inflation; government officials who want the votes of the union members; consumers who question what will happen to the price of autos; leaders and members of unions in other industries who are watching the effects on their unions. Each of these publics has an interest in the collective bargaining of the automobile industry.

Ask the students to evaluate the following question: Is it possible for even a democratic government to influence, if not control, public opinion in some areas?

Each "public," then, is a group which holds similar views on a particular issue. Some individuals belong to one public; some to another. Membership in these publics is shifting and does not remain constant. The "opinion" may be deep-seated and have been held for a long time, or it may be superficial and scarcely more than a passing whim.

People change their opinions and shift from one public to another. Ideally they change because they have discovered a new fact or have made more careful study. In practice changes are made for less logical reasons: a spokesman for an idea makes a better impression on television; a good friend is in favor of something; an easy dollar can be made.

What is public opinion? It is the attitude of a particular group of people at a given time on an issue that is of social significance.

MEASURING PUBLIC OPINION. While no exact yardstick or thermometer or speedometer has been developed to mea-

The in-person interview is one way to conduct a public opinion poll. Pollsters also pick names at random from telephone books and ask their questions over the phone. Do you think the publicity given to the results of public opinion polls affects the way people vote?

sure public opinion, there are three usual devices used. These devices are elections, public opinion polls, and "grass-roots" expressions.

ELECTIONS. The first important way by which public opinion is measured is by elections. While in any election there may be a conflict of opinion, the ballot box is the method by which democracy makes decisions. Sometimes it is hard to decide why a candidate won. Did he win because of his stand on an issue? Or did he win because of his smile, his speech-making ability, or the weakness of his opponent?

It is unusual for an election to provide a clear-cut decision on an issue, although the officials elected interpret the results to mean approval of their policies. Was Nixon's defeat of McGovern an expression of approval for the President's policies? for a weaker civil rights program? for reduction of tensions with Russia? Or was his victory a result not of voting for Nixon, but of voting against McGovern? One cannot be sure from election results exactly what the public said.

Elections are not perfect measures of public opinion, but in spite of imperfections and weaknesses, they are the best method yet devised to arrive at public decisions.

PUBLIC OPINION POLLS. Public opinion polls, a second method for measuring public opinion, are scientific devices for measuring the way all the people feel about specific issues. A *few* people are asked questions, and on the basis of their answers a prediction is made of how *all* people feel. The accuracy of the opinion polls depends on (1) the nature of the questions asked and (2) the extent to which a true cross-section of the people is interviewed.

The questions. In a good opinion poll the questions to be asked are first tested to make sure there is no misunderstanding of them. This pretesting insures that each

In recent years public opinion pollsters have made increasing use of computers. Information derived from polling a cross-section of the population is fed into the computer in order to predict the majority opinion about an issue. (U.S. Dept. of Commerce)

person will know the exact meaning of the questions being asked. For example, the question "Should the electors approve the proposed school bond issue?" is not a good question because not all people will understand the word *electors*.

Another weakness is that some people will answer the question in terms of what they think *other* people should do, but some will answer in terms of what *they* themselves would do. A better question would be "Do you favor the proposed school bond issue?" This is a direct question, and the person knows that he is to tell what he thinks.

Once the wording of the question has been agreed upon, each person must be asked the question with exactly this wording. Since most opinion polls are taken by oral interviews, this use of the exact wording becomes very important.

The sample. The cross-section of people to be questioned is called the sample. The sample must be chosen with great care. In the early history of polling, before scientific methods were developed, efforts were made either to poll all the people or to poll certain types of people. Polling *all* the people is usually impossible. The results are not accurate because nothing is known about

TRUDY

"Just a simple 'yes' or 'no' will do, Madam."

© 1967, King Features Syndicate, Inc.

the people missed. Today national polls use samples that vary in size from 2,000 to 60,000 persons.

Polling only certain types of people causes inaccuracy. A generation ago, the *Literary Digest* was a well-known magazine that was famous for its presidential polls. But the sample was selected chiefly from subscribers to the magazine, automobile registration lists, and telephone directories. What kinds of persons would such a sample neglect? All the poor people who could not afford the magazine, an auto, or a telephone!

In 1936 the magazine predicted that Landon would defeat President Franklin Roosevelt, but Roosevelt won by a landslide. The poll was wrong because the sample had not included low-income groups.

No public opinion poll is completely reliable. A classic example of failure to gauge accurately public opinion was the 1948 presidential election when it was wrongly predicted that Thomas Dewey would defeat President Harry S. Truman. (Wide World photo)

In more recent years Gallup, Roper, Harris, Crossley, universities, and industries have developed improved polling techniques. The polls were wrong in predicting the 1948 presidential election because they did not measure the shift in votes toward Truman in the last few weeks before the presidential election. The polls have been correct in predicting the presidential winners since then, but did not predict the size of Eisenhower's vote or the closeness of the Kennedy victory. In 1972 the polls were correct in predicting an overwhelming victory for President Nixon.

Opinion polls have come to be an important device for measuring public opinion. Business uses polls today to measure customers' preferences. In government, polls are used to determine what the public thinks on specific issues. In politics, some candidates try to get some measure of their chances of being elected before they decide to run for office. They test opinion during their campaigns to determine what issues appeal to voters and how they react to speeches. President Kennedy was one of the first to use public opinion polls on a grand scale. He employed a national polling organization to measure many effects of his campaigning. Mayors, governors, congressmen, as well as presidential candidates, have followed his example.

As a result of the great use of the opinion poll, the poll has become not only a device for measuring opinion but a device that also influences opinion. What the public thinks, wants, or feels is no longer a matter of guesswork. Pollsters can determine reasonably well how people will react to any public issue. While polling is not perfect, it is a valuable, effective, and helpful device for measuring public opinion.

"GRASS-ROOTS" EXPRESSIONS. A third way that public opinion is measured is by studying the things that ordinary citizens are writing or saying. The barber, the elevator operator, the gasoline station attendant listen to many people each day. Sometimes persons in these occupations get a rather good idea of what citizens are thinking. They get a rough idea of what public opinion is. They know what Mr. Average Citizen is saying about issues. They are close to the people. We say that these people know what is going on at the "grass roots."

Persons in public life have found it valuable to study the conversations and the writings of these typical citizens. Congressmen, after spending months in Washington, are eager to get back home to find out what the people are thinking. They have learned to "keep an ear to the ground." Many times, however, public officials cannot get out and talk with dozens of people. So they have come to rely on the letters, telegrams, and telephone calls they receive.

A newspaper editor in a large city once said that if ten letters on one subject were written to the letter box of his paper, he knew that he was dealing with an important public issue. Similarly, public officials are alert to the messages they receive from the grass roots.

When an important issue is before Congress, senators and congressmen will sometimes be deluged with letters, telegrams, and phone calls. One farm organization has stated that on any issue 150,000 telegrams could be wired to Congress from its members in less than two days. Other organizations can do as well. Men in public life know that some of these outbursts are not spontaneous but are part of a well-planned campaign. Yet they must try to judge whether the expression is a good measure of the real desires of the citizens.

One way of finding out is to study the messages to see whether they are alike or different. One thousand letters, each written by hand, telling in the words of the

For years political science as a field of study was dominated by historical, legal, and descriptive approaches. Each of these approaches makes important contributions to our understanding of government and politics. Since World War II a new emphasis has appeared among some political scientists based on the use of polling techniques or survey methods.

These survey methods make use of interviews with a very carefully selected sample of citizens. In the nationwide samples used by the Institute of Social Research at the University of Michigan for their famous voter studies, some 2,000 voters are interviewed. From these one- to two-hour interviews conclusions are drawn for the entire voting population with a very small margin of error. Developments in mathematics, particularly in computers, have enabled these research scientists to be remarkably accurate in drawing conclusions from their surveys.

The branch of political science that emphasizes the use of survey methods has come to be called the *behavioral* approach, because the primary interest is in how human beings behave. This approach has been aided by large grants from foundations, such as the Ford Foundation, as well as by government grants. The behavioral approach has brought about, too, a union of social psychologists and sociologists with political scientists in these endeavors.

Because of the invention of the survey method and the caution, modesty, and thoroughness of the leading experts in the field much more is known, and is being learned, about voter behavior and the process by which decisions are made in government.

writer why he is for or against a law, are more influential than 10,000 mimeographed letters all saying the same thing. The public official learns to pay great attention to the messages from individuals. He also learns to balance the push of one organization against the opposite push of another organization.

CHANGING PUBLIC OPINION. At any given moment public opinion can be measured by some device, but public opinion does not stay fixed for long. Opinion is constantly changing. The losers in an election reorganize and try to convince people to vote differently at the next election. If a public opinion poll shows that citizens are thinking one way, the opposition group will try to find ways to change the opinion. This is the nature of life in the United States. Individuals and groups are constantly at work trying to convince people to change their opinions. The communications industries—newspapers, magazines, radio, television, and movies—are the chief agencies in the changing of opinion, while interest groups provide the major forces for change.

NEWSPAPERS AND MAGAZINES. The newspapers and magazines are influential forces in changing opinion. While all of us get opinions from friends, families, school experiences, church activities, and other associations, newspapers and magazines are certainly powerful molders of opinion. There are about 1,700 daily newspapers in the United States with a combined circulation of about sixty million. A single issue of a popular magazine will be read by several million people.

Since these publications influence public opinion, their policies are of great importance to our democratic way of life. The policies of a newspaper or magazine are determined by the owner. The publication is a business enterprise and is operated for profit. Profit depends on having readers. If there are many readers, the publications will be able to sell more advertising. They will not be able to stay in business without considerable advertising. So an owner has to satisfy the readers and the advertisers and himself.

As a result, most newspapers and magazines try to do an honest job of reporting. They try to give the facts, to keep headlines in harmony with the news story, and to state their own opinions on the editorial page and not in the news stories. But not all publications follow these high standards.

Some reporting is deliberately biased. Some headlines distort the facts of a story. Some points of view are featured while differing views are played down. One of the biographers of President Kennedy wrote that a well-known weekly magazine in the President's opinion was "consistently slanted, unfair and inaccurate. . . . highly readable, but highly misleading" in the treatment of his administration.

Two criticisms of modern newspapers have been made frequently. One is that the newspaper is prepared more for the unintelligent citizen than for the thoughtful one. Crime stories, comics, sports news are used to attract readers. In the process, critics say, the important stories of public issues may get played down and not receive the attention they deserve. But is this the fault of the newspaper? The really good citizen is interested in all aspects of life. He finds time for comics, sports, and crime news as well as time to keep up with the affairs of public life.

The second criticism of newspapers is the growth of a monopoly of news. More and more communities are becoming one-newspaper towns. There is, at the same time, an increase in the newspapers published in different cities but owned by the same person or group. The best known of these newspaper chains are the Hearst papers and the Scripps-Howard papers, but there are a number of other chains.

The fear is that readers will be limited to one set of ideas which represent the opinions of the owners of the papers.

Newspaper editors and publishers have adopted a code for the conduct of their papers. By self-discipline they hope to avoid government interference which destroys a free press in nondemocratic countries and at the same time to protect their readers.

The opinions of millions of people are strongly influenced by the newspapers and magazines that come into their homes or that are available to them in public libraries throughout the nation. (Houston Public Library)

Readers' service departments of newspapers and magazines receive hundreds of letters from subscribers. Opinions on specific articles are a reflection of public opinion. (TV Guide)

The Supreme Court has held that prior censorship of the press violates the Bill of Rights. In a Minnesota case, *Near* v. *Minnesota, 1931,* a state law had been passed by which, "a malicious, scandalous and defamatory newspaper, magazine, or other periodical" could, in effect, be prevented from publishing. A publisher, Near, was not able to publish his paper because of statements made about public officials. He appealed to the Supreme Court. The Court held the law was "an infringement of the liberty of the press guaranteed by the Fourteenth Amendment."

Even in one-newspaper cities, readers are not helpless if their local paper distorts the news. They can check up on the newspaper by reading magazines which present different points of view. Television and radio also provide citizens with information that counteracts newspaper monopoly.

TELEVISION AND RADIO. Television has become a powerful instrument to change public opinion. Without a good television personality it is becoming increasingly difficult to be elected to public office. Advertisers have found TV to be effective in changing buying habits. While much programming on television has been described as a "vast wasteland," there is no doubt of the tremendous power of the "tube."

Radio broadcasting is not as influential

as in the days when former President Franklin Roosevelt with his "fireside" radio talks was elected four times in spite of the fact that a majority of the newspapers opposed him. But radio is still a powerful voice.

Television and radio differ from newspapers because there are a limited number of stations that can be accommodated by the available broadcasting bands. The airwaves cannot be cluttered up with an unlimited number of stations; so government has to regulate broadcasting. The Federal Communications Commission has this responsibility. It has had to decide how many stations there will be and who can own these stations, and has set up rules to be sure that different sides of public issues are presented over the air. In general the policy has been to insure that all candidates and parties have opportunity for equal time.

In addition to giving us the chance to hear and see leaders in public life, the airways bring us news commentators and special documentaries whose influence is very great. Some of these news commentators strive to be solely reporters of news. Others, however, are accused of trying to slant the news to favor certain groups or interests.

There has been some criticism that newspaper owners control too many broadcasting stations. There has been criticism that advertisers have too much influence on the type and quality of programs. There are critics who fear the national networks are too powerful. The danger of monopolizing the airways has been a subject of much study and discussion. The FCC has established general policies for broadcasters and requires that a certain amount of time be devoted to news and public affairs. The broadcasting industry has its code of conduct, which sets ideals for programming.

THE MOVIES. While movies are primarily for entertainment, their influence on public opinion is very great. The ideas of many people toward wealth, recreation, sex, home life, and different jobs were probably formed at movies. Visitors to our country from foreign lands are amazed to find that life in the United States is not the way the movies have pictured it to them. If these visitors are right, perhaps those of us who see movies here should be more alert to what the movies are teaching us. Is the movie giving us a true picture? Or in telling a dramatic story is the movie giving us a false picture?

The movies have been so influential that some states and cities have set up censor boards. Parent groups and church groups, too, have tried to review and rate films. The film industry itself has its own board of censorship and its production code. These activities are a recognition that movies are very powerful in forming opinions.

The ownership of the motion picture business has been investigated by the federal government. As with other molders of public opinion the fear of monopoly has been great. Some years ago the producers of films were compelled by government action to sell their movie houses. The purpose was to separate the production from the distribution of films. The increasing use of movies on television increases their power over public opinion. A movie that might have been seen by ten million people in movie houses over several months may be seen by several times that number in one evening on television.

INTEREST GROUPS   Public opinion is influenced by the groups or organizations to which so many people belong. Americans are great "joiners." We belong to all kinds of organizations: parent-teacher groups, church

Discuss the pros and cons of lobbyists and pressure groups. Are they in the best interests of the country? Do they somehow all cancel each other out? Do they somehow collectively represent the peoples' interest?

organizations, labor organizations, clubs, bowling leagues, fraternal associations, luncheon clubs, discussion groups, alumni associations. Name almost any activity in American life, and you will find some type of organization has developed around that interest.

These organizations play a tremendous part in changing public opinion. The friends we know in these groups give us ideas. They tell us what they heard someone say about the mayor. We tell them about our experience with a member of the city council. These conversations are important sources of our opinions.

In addition, the experiences of members of these organizations are for them an important training school for democracy. Political scientists have come to believe that these organizations are of far greater importance in the success of democratic government than is generally recognized.

NATURE OF INTEREST GROUPS. An interest group is exactly what its name implies. It is an organization of persons who have some common interest. Often to promote this interest it is necessary to influence public policy. This is done by helping elect candidates to office, working in political parties, or trying to get help from legislators or administrators. Frequently, when interest groups exert these efforts they are called *pressure* groups. For practical political purposes, interest groups and pressure groups are synonymous.

Interest groups differ from *political parties* in one very important respect. Interest groups are attempting to influence specific policies, while political parties are striving primarily to control the government by electing officials. Interest groups are active in political campaigns. They make financial contributions to the parties; they get their members to campaign for certain candidates; they influence nominations. But

their purpose is to gain support for their special interests. Their interest in public issues is usually narrow and confined to the question: How will this affect our group?

Political parties are coalitions of interest groups which aim to gain control of the machinery of government. The political parties control the nomination process; they want to win elections. The political party is concerned with the total range of public issues. The interest group is concerned with its specific interest.

THE RANGE OF INTEREST GROUPS. Pressure groups are of many kinds and many varieties. They are huge, with millions of members; and they are small, with a few dozen highly dedicated members. They cut across all human activities: economic, social, political, professional, recreational, religious, educational. They can be classified in many ways. One of the easiest systems of classification is in terms of what they are trying to do for their members. Are they trying to get special economic or other advantages for their members? If so, they are *private* interest groups. Are they trying to promote some special public policy? If so, they are *public* interest groups.

PRIVATE INTEREST GROUPS. Private interest groups tend to be concerned with economic conditions. *Business groups* are one example. They may operate at local, state, or national levels or at all three. The chambers of commerce are typical—with local, state, and national organizations which speak out for thousands of businesses. The National Association of Manufacturers (NAM) is a similar organization of the larger manufacturing industries in the country.

In addition there are *trade associations* which support the interests of a particular industry. Included in this group would be the American Trucking Association, the

American Bankers Association, the Association of American Railroads, the Automobile Manufacturers Association, the National Association of Real Estate Boards, the National Association of Electric Companies, the Retail Merchants Association, the Toy Manufacturers of the U. S. A., and many others. Clearly these and similar organizations have a primary concern in protecting and promoting their business interests.

Labor organizations represent another type of private interest group which is mainly concerned with economic matters. The most powerful organization is the American Federation of Labor—Congress of Industrial Organizations (AFL-CIO), a unifying group for some 13,500,000 members in 130 separate unions. In this federation are barbers, bricklayers, carpenters, garment workers, restaurant employees, printers, postal clerks, railroad trainmen, steel workers, teachers, upholsterers, and others. Each of these unions is organized at local, state, and national levels.

In addition there are powerful independent unions which are not part of the AFL-CIO. These include, among others, the United Electrical, Radio and Machine Workers of America, the National Federation of Federal Employees, the Brotherhood of Locomotive Engineers, and the United Mine Workers. In 1969 the unions of auto workers, teamsters, and chemical workers joined in the Alliance for Labor Action.

Farm groups have three powerful general organizations and many organizations serving the interests of those concerned with only one commodity. The general organizations are the American Farm Bureau Federation, the National Grange, and the National Farmers Union. As with other interest groups, each has a staff of well-paid, qualified employees. The Grange is the oldest organization, dating from 1867,

Farmers have a number of organizations to express their views. Delegates to this national meeting of the National Grange come from all parts of the country. (The National Grange)

and is second in size with 800,000 members. The Farm Bureau has become twice that size, although it did not begin national activities until 1920. The National Farmers Union was founded in 1902 and is most active in the farm areas west of the Mississippi River. Third in size, it represents some 250,000 farm families.

The special commodity organizations include: the National Cotton Council, the National Dairy Council, the National Milk Producers Federation, and the Vegetable Growers Association of America. Producers of corn, fruit, cattle, peanuts, soybeans, tobacco, wool, and other commodities have their special organizations caring for their special interests.

Another group of private interest groups consists of those in the *professions*. Perhaps, best known are the American Medical Association, the American Dental Association, and the American Bar Association representing the medical doctors, the dentists, and the lawyers. Osteopaths, nurses, librarians, engineers, architects, insurance agents, barbers, and social workers are similarly organized. Teachers have two powerful organizations: the American Federation of Teachers, a member of the AFL-CIO, and the National Education Association. Each of these professional organizations carries on activities to raise the professional competence of its members, but each, also, is promoting the interests of its members in the political arena.

PUBLIC INTEREST GROUPS. Some groups are not primarily concerned with the interests of their own members but are interested in some public policy. The American Cancer Society is a good example. Ending cancer as a disease is its major goal. To this end it carries on research and tries to educate citizens to symptoms of cancer. But the Society also has a stake in public policies which might lead to cancer. So, it supported the efforts to put a "health danger" warning on cigarette packages and to curtail cigarette advertising on television.

The American Civil Liberties Union is concerned with protecting the freedoms guaranteed under the Bill of Rights. The United Nations Association educates people about the work of and the necessity for the UN. The Planned Parenthood Federation carries on a program of family planning. The League of Women Voters is dedicated to improving intelligent participation in public affairs. The Daughters of the American Revolution wish to perpetuate patriotic ideals. The National Conference of Christians and Jews is attempting to improve the quality of human relations among religious, ethnic, and racial groups. Common Cause tries to make government more responsive to the people.

Reform movements of all types have interest group organizations. Air pollution, auto safety, conservation, recreation, use of alcohol, and crime prevention are some of the rallying points which have attracted persons into groups to effect changes.

Some groups are difficult to classify into public or private, although they tend to think of themselves as public groups. The American Legion and the National Association for the Advancement of Colored People (NAACP) are good examples. The former is concerned with the war veteran; the latter with the Negro. These and similar organizations provide many activities and services for their members, but they also have a primary concern in the laws and acts of public officials which affect their groups.

Religious groups are also difficult to classify. They have many private interests, but they also have a real public interest. The National Catholic Welfare Conference unifies the activities of the

Roman Catholic Church in the United States. The National Council of Churches coordinates activities for some thirty Protestant churches. The American Jewish Congress serves in a similar capacity for those of the Jewish faith.

Interest groups are growing in numbers and influence. The number of private interest groups has increased more rapidly than the public interest groups. The reasons for this growth are found in the condition of American life. Freedom of speech and assembly are guaranteed, so interest groups are easy to form. As citizens have seen the success of pressure group activities, they have been willing to form new organizations and to join existing ones. Specialization as a part of modern living has caused individuals with similar special interests to form pressure groups. Finally, governmental activities have grown as life has become less simple. With the complicated, interrelated aspects of life today, citizens increasingly look to government for assistance and find the interest group a good vehicle for satisfying their needs.

STRATEGIES OF INTEREST GROUPS Interest groups try to change public policy in directions that will be favorable to their members. Three general approaches are used: (1) lobbying, (2) changing public opinion, and (3) winning elections.

LOBBYING. Lobbying is the process of influencing the conduct of government. Much lobbying is done with members of legislatures, as will be discussed in Chapters 10 and 15, but the process is not limited to legislatures. Lobbying is done with elected officials and with governmental bureaucrats. Influence is used at any point in the process of government where it will be effective.

Why does pressure work? The answer is to be found in the way we choose our elected officials. Members of state legislatures and Congress, and some members of city councils are chosen from geographic districts containing a diversity of citizens. Elected administrative officials have a similar diverse backing, since to be elected they must have widespread support. So legisla-

These dairy farmers used a direct method of influencing public opinion. Members of the National Farmers Organization bought all the milk in three stores and fed it to hogs in their efforts to get a higher price for their milk. (UPI photo)

BIG SPENDERS

Listed below are the fifteen interest groups which spent the most money among the 296 lobbying organizations registered with Congress during a recent year.

United Federation of Postal Clerks (AFL-CIO)	$286,972.
Brotherhood of Locomotive Firemen and Enginemen, Grand Lodge (AFL-CIO)	199,261.
AFL-CIO (national headquarters)	169,705.
American Legion	137,193.
American Farm Bureau Federation	133,944.
U. S. Savings and Loan League	120,899.
National Association of Real Estate Boards	118,289.
Central Arizona Project Association	117,300.
International Brotherhood of Teamsters	100,525.
National Housing Conference, Inc.	94,444.
Council for a Livable World	90,597.
National Federation of Independent Business	90,244.
National Farmers Union	87,679.
National Association of Home Builders of the United States	73,577.
National Education Association, Division of Federal and State Relations	73,055.

Reprinted with permission of Congressional Quarterly, Inc.

---

tors and administrators often listen to the majority, which is made up of a coalition of different groups. The minority sometimes has difficulty being heard and getting action.

Under these conditions the public official becomes a "broker" trying to resolve the conflicts of interests among those who put him in office. Bargaining and compromise have to be employed. Democratic leadership becomes the ability to work out schemes between competing groups. In this sense democracy is defined as the process of compromise.

To operate effectively under this system, many interest groups employ paid agents, their lobbyists, to watch out for their interests at the city hall, the state capitol, and in Washingon, D. C. These lobbyists know the inner workings of government, the strengths and weaknesses of government officials, and the trends in politics. Their backgrounds have been as lawyers, reporters, public relations experts, special training in the interest they represent, and/or previous experience as a public official. Defeated congressmen often remain in Washington as lobbyists for interest groups.

The lobbyist exerts pressure in many ways. He is a supplier of information of many kinds. The public official cannot be well informed on all matters. The lobbyist with his special attention to his interest becomes an expert in his field and has access to, and can supply, needed information. Public officials come to depend on capable lobbyists for essential information which may be supplied individually, or often lobbyists testify before legislative committees.

The lobbyist cultivates social contacts with public officials. He entertains at dinners; he provides trips at his expense; he goes to the important parties. He hopes, at the least, to know the official well enough to get him to listen at the right time, and, at best, to know that he will vote for the lobbyist's interests at the proper time. It is well to recognize that the lobbyist is just as interested in the defeat of some measures as he is in getting new measures into law.

The lobbyist applies "heat." In politics, "heat" consists of threats and actions. Withdrawal of contributions to campaign funds, getting members of the interest group to write letters and send telegrams of support or opposition, placing an editorial in the local paper, getting a commentator to say something good or bad about an official are all ways of putting pressure on an official.

In general lobbyists are skilled professionals doing an effective job for the groups they represent. They are persistent. If they lose in one house, they try to win in the other. If they lose there, they try to get the support of the chief executive. If they lose with him, they try to influence the bureaucrat who must carry out the activity. They are intelligent, resourceful, and usually honest. Most lobbyists are trusted men. But the chances for dishonesty and corruption are great, so laws regulate the conduct of lobbyists. These regulations will be discussed later in connection with the legislative process in Congress and state legislatures.

PROPAGANDA. Interest groups are concerned that more and more citizens think the way they do. Their activities are not limited to pressure on public officials. They try to influence public opinion. These efforts to convince or persuade citizens are quite generally labelled as *propaganda*.

Propaganda can be good or it can be bad. The advertiser, the salesman, the preacher are propagandists because they are trying to persuade us to do or to believe certain things. For the most part their efforts are considered to be honest and sincere, although there has been criticism of unfair advertising.

On political issues, however, there is some tendency to think that propaganda is tricky, deceitful, or evil. Politicians are pictured as trying to fool the people through clever propaganda devices. Actually, however, people in political life are so constantly in the news that most of them have found that the only way to survive is to tell the truth.

But not all men are truthful. Some people do try to change our opinions by unfair methods. So it is important to be aware of how people try to change our opinions. But in learning to protect ourselves from the person who tries to be too clever, it is not necessary to distrust all mankind. Democracy places great faith in people. Democracy will be destroyed when citizens no longer trust one another.

This point can be illustrated by a Gallup Poll which was taken after World War II in both Germany and the United States. This question was asked: "Do you think most people can be trusted?" In Germany only 6 per cent of the people answered "Yes." In the United States 66 per cent of the people answered "Yes." One difference between life in a democracy and in a dictatorship seems to be the trust we place in other people.

Because we trust people, however, does not mean that we close our jails, dismiss our policemen, and stop locking the front door when we leave home. Neither does it mean that we should not be aware of the ways in which people try to change our minds. Most of us know that speakers learn clever ways to get us to agree with their speeches. Writers, too, become skilled in stating things in ways that appeal to us. We do not complain at the clever use of a gesture or an exclamation point. We like things presented to us in attractive ways. But we do need to develop the ability to detect and analyze propaganda.

PROPAGANDA DEVICES. Much study has been given to the detection and analysis of propaganda. In the years before World War II, the Institute for Propaganda Analysis was created to study propaganda. In its efforts to learn more about "the fine art of propaganda" the conclusion was reached that there are seven propaganda devices quite generally used. These are:

1. Name-calling. "Bad" names are applied to individuals or groups in order to get us to dislike them. *Examples:* Jim S. is a tool of the "international bankers." . . . Joe H. is a "right-winger, a Bircher." . . .

Harry H. is a "labor racketeer." . . . Bill W. is an "Uncle Tom." . . . "He's a whitey . . . a honky."

2. Glittering generalities. An approved word like home, love, democracy, justice, church, or patriotism is used to get us to accept an idea without any other evidence. *Examples:* "Sincere believers in democracy, patriotic citizens of all faiths will rally to the support of this man who has been so falsely accused." . . . "This is an American policy, a democratic policy." . . . "Vote for the Great Society."

3. Transfer. The respect and admiration we have for church, motherhood, or science is used to gain our sympathy for something else. *Examples:* "In a scientific spirit let us inquire into the evidence which shows that this public official has abused his power." An advertisement for a toothpaste begins with the words "Years of research have proven. . . ."

4. Testimonial. The propagandist uses the names and statements of well-known, highly regarded persons to gain support for his position. *Examples:* "The President said . . . ," "Our preacher said . . . ," "Johnny Carson said . . . ," "Have you heard that the Mets are using . . . ?"

5. Plain-folks appeal. A person or an idea is associated with the common, the very ordinary. Support is sought because "the people" want it. *Examples:* A picture of a politician kissing a baby or catching a fish. . . . The mayor is introduced, "Our Honorable Mayor began his life in a simple three-room cottage. He was one of ten children. He helped support the family by selling newspapers. . . ."

6. Card-stacking. The propagandist deliberately selects certain facts, distorts other facts, or omits facts to present a false picture. Half-truths, omission of key facts, exaggerations, and false testimony are used to "stack the cards" for or against a cause.

Examples: The German dictator Hitler deliberately used the "Big Lie" to gain support for his ideas. . . . A speaker says, "In yesterday's New York *Times,* on page 4, you will find the statement that. . . ." (Since the New York *Times* reports news with thoroughness, one can usually find something in the *Times* to support a point, but this does not mean the paper approves it; it may be only reporting the news.)

7. Getting on the band wagon. This device makes use of the desire of most people to be on the winning or popular side. It gets people to do things because it is the popular thing to do. *Examples:* "Don't throw away your vote. Vote for Kelley for governor. The latest public opinion poll shows that he is going to win by a huge majority.". . ."Buy a——— car. Watch your neighbors look at you with new respect. Notice the admiring glances you get when you pull up to a stoplight."

THE CITIZEN AND PROPAGANDA. When attention was first directed to these devices, propaganda analysis had great influence. The search for the seven devices in writings, speeches, and movies helped draw attention to the nature of propaganda. Citizens became more alert to the ways in which some people were trying to influence them.

As the years have gone by, however, students of propaganda have come to believe that the analysis of propaganda is more complex. Detecting one or more of the seven devices is only one step in protection against misleading propaganda, because the skilled propagandist has learned to be very clever in the use of modern methods of communication.

Music, color, beautiful girls, lighting are employed skillfully in advertising as well as in political rallies. Repetition is used powerfully; the same simple message is repeated again and again. Good things about the opposition are rarely mentioned.

The best defense against the antisocial, selfish propagandist is a well-informed, well-educated people. Citizens who have learned to look for evidence, to ask questions, to weigh one statement against another will not be misled. Neither will they lose their faith in their fellow men. In a democracy citizens have to learn to sift the true from the false. They have to learn not to be blinded by prejudice, tricked by the clever, or overwhelmed by the repetition of ideas. Democracy survives because of the truth of the old saying, "You can't fool all the people all the time."

PROPAGANDA TESTS. In this process of reaching an opinion some citizens have been helped by answering the following questions:

1. What is the person trying to prove?

2. What is the person's reputation for telling the truth?

3. Has the person presented any evidence, or has he used only the propaganda devices?

4. Has the person presented evidence for his own case, or has he limited himself to attacking his opponent?

5. Are the arguments emotional, logical, or a combination of both?

6. Are the conclusions based on the evidence?

As interest groups and their lobbyists recognize that public officials and interested citizens want objective, factual information, they may rely less and less on tricks of propaganda in their efforts to persuade.

WINNING ELECTIONS. A third strategy of interest groups is to win elections. Interest groups work very hard to get public officials elected who are sympathetic to their causes and to defeat those who are not in their favor. Candidates want support during the election campaign. Interest groups may help by supplying money, by publicly endorsing the candidate, by working for him on election day. They try to get a promise from the candidate before he is elected. Sometimes they support more than one candidate to be sure to back a winner.

Many interest groups claim to be *nonpolitical.* What they seem to mean is that they are bipartisan—in the sense that they will support either party which will champion their cause. In extreme cases they have organized into a third party. Their goals are those of the interest group, not of the party, as was discussed earlier. They are willing to keep a foot in both parties. The policy is one of helping friends and defeating enemies—regardless of party. The lobbyist knows the procedures of political parties as well as the party leaders. He uses these procedures for his ends when he can.

In recent years some interest groups, especially business and labor, have encouraged their members to be more active in party politics. Books and pamphlets are published to show members how to participate at the local level. Lectures and seminars are held to teach effective political practices.

One group, the League of Women Voters, has deliberately avoided an active partisan political role but has been very effective at supplying unbiased information about candidates and election issues.

VOTING BEHAVIOR

The ballot box under a democratic system is the place at which, ideally, decisions are made based on the opinion of the public. The voter casts his ballot, officials are elected, issues are decided, and some interest groups achieve their goals. This traditional view of democracy requires that citizens be (1) interested in governmental affairs, (2) informed and willing to spend time studying issues, and (3) well enough educated to be able to

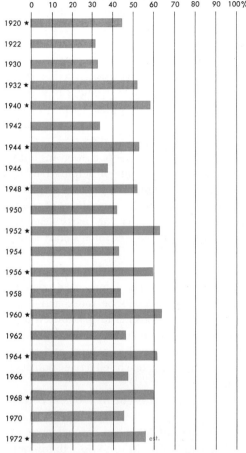

1920 ★

1922

1930

1932 ★

1940 ★

1942

1944 ★

1946

1948 ★

1950

1952 ★

1954

1956 ★

1958

1960 ★

1962

1964 ★

1966

1968 ★

1970

1972 ★   est.

★ Presidential election

Source: Bureau of the Census

The graph shows the percentage of eligible voters who voted in national elections in selected years. Why was the percentage larger in presidential election years?

make intelligent decisions. How close to this ideal are voters in our country?

For a quarter of a century, some political scientists have been studying voter behavior by thorough research methods. The information they have uncovered shows two general conditions about the behavior of voters: (1) Nonvoting is very high in the United States. (2) Voters are greatly in-

fluenced by some factors that seem *not* to be a logical part of careful thought or good education.

NONVOTING. The failure of many citizens to vote is a major weakness in the election process. The voting record of the American people is not good. On a national basis the largest percentage of voters cast ballots in 1900, 1952, 1960, 1964, and 1968. In those hotly contested presidential elections about two-thirds of the eligible voters went to the polls. In other years, when the candidates and the issues were less dramatic, Presidents have been elected with less than half the eligible voters voting.

Presidential elections usually attract many more voters than do other elections. In congressional, state, and local elections the percentage of those voting is sometimes very small. In one large city only 7 per cent of the voters went to the polls to elect members of the board of education. A governor of one state was elected with only 25 per cent participation by voters. In another case a congressman was chosen with only 15 per cent of the adults bothering to go to the polls.

Why do people fail to vote? There are many reasons given. Among the most important are:

- *Citizens not having resided long enough in the state, city, or precinct*
- *Lack of any real contest between candidates or parties*
- *Discouragement because of the length of the ballot, the difficulty of getting information about candidates, and the frequency of elections*
- *Bad weather, illness, working hours, family cares, or other personal reasons*
- *Disgust with politics and politicians*
- *Indifference*

Many studies have been made of voters

In regard to increasing voter turnout, ask the students to consider the effects of lengthening the terms for some offices, such as U.S. Representative, and of making more offices, such as judges, appointive rather than elective.

and nonvoters. These studies have shown that those with more schooling vote more than those with less education. The college graduate is more likely to vote than the high school graduate; the high school graduate is more likely to vote than the person who has finished only elementary school.

Persons with higher incomes vote more regularly than persons with low incomes. People in the northern states vote more than people in the southern states. Men have better voting records than women. Church members participate more than nonchurch members. Residents of cities have better voting records that those who live on farms. Those who are active in politics vote more than those who are inactive. Those who have a high sense of civic duty vote regularly, while those who have a low sense of citizenship obligations vote very rarely. Indeed, it appears that as many as 6 per cent of those eligible to vote are so separated or alienated from society that they practically never participate in elections under any circumstances.

An important aspect of the nonvoting problem which is beginning to receive more attention is that of the *nonvoting voter*. There are many citizens who go to the polls and do vote, but who do not vote for all candidates and all issues. More voters vote for President than for any other office. Of those voting, fewer vote for governor, still fewer for mayor, or congressman, or sheriff. On a voting machine, issues in the lower corners are voted less than those higher on the machine. On paper ballots, the offices that are at the top of the ballot receive more votes than those at the bottom of the ballot. The nonvoting voter does not participate regularly in all elections but participates more in presidential elections than in other elections. He tends to participate least in local school district elections.

INTELLIGENT VOTING. The ideal

Do citizens really vote intelligently when they go to the polls, or are they influenced by emotions and prejudice? (Fischetti; reprinted by permission of NEA)

of the good citizen holds that each person will vote after thoughtful consideration of available facts. Do studies of voting behavior support this theory?

In the previous chapter, on political parties, it was pointed out that voters tend to continue to vote for the party for which they first started voting and that they make this choice largely in terms of family background. *Habit* seems to be a great influence in voting. Regardless of the candidates, regardless of wars, depressions, riots, or other social trends, millions of voters will vote for the party of their habitual choice. This loyalty may not be unintelligent, however. It may represent the voter's reasoned judgment.

Voters tend, too, to vote in terms of their *group* interests. Since the family is the strongest group influence, husbands and wives tend to vote alike and their children vote in ways similar to their parents.

Membership in Rotary Club, the American Legion, the NAACP, or other interest groups tends to influence voters, too.

Voters are influenced by *economic* and *geographic* factors. Members of labor unions tend to vote Democratic while businessmen tend to vote Republican. Those of lower income tend to be Democrats while those of higher incomes tend to be Republican. Lower income groups in the inner city tend to support Democrats; those in suburbia tend toward the Republicans. The South has been the geographic stronghold of the Democratic party.

The foremost students of voter behavior have summarized their years of study in these four conclusions:

1. There is low emotional involvement of the voters in politics.
2. There is slight awareness of public affairs.
3. There is a failure to think in rational, idealistic terms.
4. There is a continuing sense of attachment to one or the other of the two major political parties.[1]

---

[1] Adapted from Campbell, Angus and others, *The American Voter* (New York: John Wiley and Sons, 1960), page 541.

STUDY QUESTIONS

1: Why does democratic government not measure up to its ideals?

2. How do "public opinion" and "majority opinion" differ?

3. Give an example of public opinion being a "specific opinion."

4. Give an example of public opinion being made up of a great many publics.

5. How is a public opinion poll taken?

CONCEPTS AND GENERALIZATIONS

1
The ideal of the thoughtful, well-informed citizen is a justifiable goal for a democratic society, even though it is not achieved.

2
Public opinion is majority opinion.

3
Public opinion is related to a specific issue.

4
The public is really a number of sub-publics.

5
Public opinion is measured by elections, polls, and "grass roots" expressions.

6
Newspapers, magazines, radio, and television are the chief agencies for changing public opinion.

7
Interest groups provide the major driving forces for influencing public opinion.

8
Interest groups are of two types: private and public. Private interest groups tend to be concerned chiefly with economic matters. Public interest groups tend to be concerned with some public policy.

9
Interest groups influence public policy by lobbying, employing propaganda, and winning elections.

10
Lobbying can be either good or evil, depending on the activities of the lobbyist.

11
The detection of propaganda is aided by being aware of the seven common devices used by the propagandists.

12
Nonvoters are of two types: those who fail to vote regularly; and those who vote in some elections for some candidates and some issues, but not in all elections for all candidates and issues.

13
Habit, loyalty to party, economic circumstance, and geography appear to be more influential than rational thought processes in voting.

6. How can a public official know what the opinions of citizens are at the grass roots level?

7. How can public opinion be changed?

8. How has public opinion in your community been changed on some public issue?

9. Why were codes of ethics adopted?

10. How do interest groups and pressure groups differ?

11. How do private interest groups and public interest groups differ?

12. What strategies do pressure groups employ?

13. Give an example of each of the propaganda devices. Which of your examples are "good" propaganda and which are "bad" propaganda?

14. How can propaganda be tested?

15. Why are some interest groups bipartisan rather than nonpartisan?

16. Why do some citizens fail to vote?

17. What do you consider intelligent voting to be?

IDEAS FOR DISCUSSION

1. How is the independent voter influenced by political propaganda?

2. Some people think that teaching the propaganda devices to high school students will cause them to be less idealistic and to become cynical. Do you agree or disagree? What per cent of people do you think try to "deceive" you?

3. How is public opinion changed in your school?

4. Is it proper in a democracy to regulate agencies that influence public opinion? Is this done in the United States? Is it done in countries ruled by dictators?

5. Which of the interest groups named in this chapter exist in your community? Which are most influential in changing opinion?

6. How influential are cartoons in changing public opinion?

7. After the death of the distinguished Harvard political scientist, V. O. Key, Jr., a book which he was writing was completed by one of his students. In this book, *The Responsible Electorate*, Key argued that "voters are not fools . . . (they are) moved by concern about central and relevant questions of public policy, of governmental performance, and of executive personality." How does this view of the voter differ from other studies of voting behavior?

8. Professor Key argued that elections are won by three types of voters, "standpatters . . . those who cast their ballots for candidates of the same political party at two successive elections . . . the switchers . . . (those) who move across party lines . . . new voters . . . who were too young to vote at the preceding election. . . ."[1] What hunches do you have about the influence of each of these types of voters in your community?

9. Do interest groups give more power to the aggressive-emotional type of personality versus the thoughtful-rational type? Why?

10. How accurate are public opinion polls?

11. When is lobbying good? When is it evil?

THINGS TO DO

1. Analyze the propaganda devices used in a political campaign in your school. Does your school need a code to regulate these campaigns? How do the appeals for votes rate when checked by the propaganda tests given on page 163?

2. Have committees compare the way in which a controversial public issue was handled in your local newspaper with the way it was handled in two other newspapers and in two weekly news magazines. Was the local paper story more or less objective than the Associated Press or the United Press International stories?

3. Prepare a list of the major organizations or associations which try to influence public opinion in your community. Check with adults in your family or in your neighborhood to find out which of these organizations they support by giving time or money.

4. Analyze the predictions of public opinion polls in the last presidential election.

5. Compare the treatment of the same controversial issue as reported by different television or radio commentators.

6. Make a bulletin board display of public opinion devices. A student committee should list radio and television programs that are recommended for student listening or viewing.

---

[1] V. O. Key, Jr., and M. C. Cummings, Jr., *The Responsible Electorate*, The Belknap Press of Harvard University Press, 1966.

7. Prepare a notebook with examples illustrating types of propaganda techniques.

8. What are the attitudes of members of your class toward politics? Do they tend to agree or disagree with the following statements?

a) It doesn't matter which way you vote, because the politicians will do things the way they want anyhow.

b) Well-qualified men of good character remain in public office a long time.

c) Most public officials remain in politics because of a sincere desire to serve the people.

d) Politics is a messy business.

e) Candidates are usually elected to public office because of political pull.

f) Laws passed as a result of the work of lobbyists usually are *not* for the public good.

g) Rich folks are in control of everything, and it doesn't make any difference whether poor people vote or not.

h) News about sports, fashions, or movies is less interesting to most people than news of election contests.

9. Write to one of the opinion-forming agencies for its code of ethics and report to the class on its major provisions.

10. Voting behavior studies are influencing the study of political science. Prepare a report on these studies.

11. Analyze the extent of nonvoting in your community in the last three elections.

12. By use of the index in President Harry S. Truman's two-volume memoirs, YEARS OF DECISIONS and YEARS OF TRIAL AND HOPE, prepare a list of his comments on lobbyists.

FURTHER READINGS

Allen, Robert W., and Greene, Lorne, THE PROPAGANDA GAME. Wff'n Poof, 1966.

Baker, Benjamin, and Friedelbaum, Stanley H., GOVERNMENT IN THE UNITED STATES. Houghton Mifflin Co., 1966. Chapter 10.

Barber, James A., Jr., SOCIAL MOBILITY AND VOTING BEHAVIOR. Rand McNally & Co., 1971.

Barber, James D., CITIZEN POLITICS: AN INTRODUCTION TO POLITICAL BEHAVIOR. Markham, 1972.

Bullitt, Stimson, TO BE A POLITICIAN. Anchor Books, 1959. (Paperback edition)

Campbell, Angus, *et al.,* ELECTIONS AND THE POLITICAL ORDER. John Wiley & Sons, Inc., 1966.

———, THE AMERICAN VOTER. John Wiley & Sons, Inc., 1964.

Ferguson, John H., and McHenry, Dean E., THE AMERICAN SYSTEM OF GOVERNMENT. McGraw-Hill Book Co., 1967. Chapter 10.

Hennessey, Bernard C., PUBLIC OPINION. Wadsworth Publishing Co., 1965.

Holtzman, Abraham, INTEREST GROUPS AND LOBBYING. The Macmillan Co., 1966.

Lubell, Samuel, THE HIDDEN CRISIS IN AMERICAN POLITICS. W. W. Norton & Co., Inc., 1970.

Patterson, Franklin, ed., PRACTICAL POLITICAL ACTION: A GUIDE FOR YOUNG CITIZENS. Houghton Mifflin Co., 1963.

Safire, William, THE NEW LANGUAGE OF POLITICS. Random House, Inc., 1968.

Scammon, Richard M., and Wattenberg, Ben J., THE REAL MAJORITY. Coward, McCann & Geoghegan, Inc., 1970.

Schwartz, Alvin, WHAT DO YOU THINK? AN INTRODUCTION TO PUBLIC OPINION. E. P. Dutton & Co., 1966.

Seasholes, Bradbury, PARTIES, PRESSURE GROUPS, AND VOTING BEHAVIOR. Scott, Foresman and Co., 1966.

Key, V. O., Jr., and Cummings, M. C., Jr., THE RESPONSIBLE ELECTORATE. The Belknap Press of Harvard University Press, 1966.

———, PUBLIC OPINION AND AMERICAN DEMOCRACY. Alfred A. Knopf, Inc., 1961.

Warren, Robert Penn, ALL THE KING'S MEN. Harcourt Brace Jovanovich, Inc., 1946.

The Passage of the Civil Rights Act of 1964

In this unit the major political processes of American government have been described. Citizenship, elections, political parties, and interest groups have received special attention. In the next few pages, some materials about the passage of the Civil Rights Act of 1964 are presented.

*　*　*

THE VOTE. The 1964 Civil Rights bill passed the House of Representatives on February 10, 1964 by a vote of 290 to 130. The bill passed the Senate, 73 to 27, on June 19, exactly a year from the day that President Kennedy had proposed the legislation. The Senate debate lasted eighty-three days. How the Senate voted on the final passage of the bill is shown in the table on page 172.

SORENSEN. The following excerpts from Kennedy, by Theodore C. Sorensen, pages 496-506, describe part of the struggle for passage.[1]

On June 19 President Kennedy sent to the Eighty-eighth Congress the most comprehensive and far-reaching civil rights bill ever proposed. It codified and expanded the pattern his executive actions had already started. It was accompanied by a message as forceful as his June 11 manifesto. It was to differ only slightly from the Civil Rights Act enacted by that Congress the following year. But it was different in several respects from the

---

[1] Abridgement of pp. 496-506 KENNEDY by Theodore C. Sorensen. Copyright © 1965 by Theodore C. Sorensen. Reprinted by permission of Harper & Row, Publishers.

bill we had first discussed with Justice the previous month.

With the backing of the Vice President, a Community Relations Service had been added to work quietly with local communities in search of progress. (Negro Congressmen had urged that the words "mediation" and "conciliation" had an "Uncle Tom" air about them and should be stricken from the title.) . . .

The President, aware of the emotions surrounding the initials FEPC, decided finally to omit it from the bill but to endorse a pending FEPC measure in his message. . . .

A host of other proposals had been suggested to the President, but he was looking for a law, not an issue. This Congress and future Congresses could amend and improve his effort. He wanted a package unencumbered by any provisions that went beyond the clearly legal, reasonable and necessary—because he wanted it to pass.

He [the President] was asking Congress to swallow a pill many times larger than those it had previously refused to swallow. This was no grandstand play for a lost cause or a political effort. He was not interested in a "moral victory" on a legislative issue—he wanted a legislative victory on a moral issue. . . .

Bipartisan sponsorship would be sought to the extent possible—resulting in Democrat Mansfield's introducing the whole bill and simultaneously cosponsoring with Republican Dirksen the same bill minus the public accommodations sections (to which the Republican leader was opposed). . . .

The one tactical paragraph of his message which received as much careful attention as the portions dealing with legislation concerned the problem of continued Negro demonstrations. Southerners and Republicans warned that further pressures would surely defeat the bill. Negroes warned that they would not give up their chief weapon . . . In the message [he stated]. . . .

"But *as feelings have risen in recent days,* these demonstrations have increasingly endangered lives and property, inflamed emotions and unnecessarily divided communities. They are not the way in which this country should rid itself of racial discrimination. *Violence is never justified; and, while peaceful communication, deliberation and petitions of protest continue, I want to caution against demonstrations which can lead to violence.*

This problem is now before the Congress. . . . *The Congress should have an opportunity to freely work its will."* [The italicized portions were personally added by the President to the final draft]. . . .

The President did not rely on eloquence alone. . . . He kept Eisenhower—who was sympathetic but not enthusiastic about the legislative approach—fully informed. Along with the Vice President, he consulted frequently with the leaders of both parties, once with Republican leaders Dirksen and McCulloch alone to brief them on the need for the bill and its details. Bob Kennedy and Burke Marshall held a series of Capitol Hill briefings to which all Democratic Senators, and all but the Deep South Congressmen, were invited. The decision to send a bill, the President stressed to each group, was final, but their comments and suggestions for its contents were welcome. . . .

Special attention in the House focused on William McCulloch of Ohio, the key Republican on the House Judiciary Committee and a respected conservative. McCulloch's constituency might normally have been considered too rural and Republican to have made him a champion of Negro rights, but his conscience responded to the reason of the administration and to the realities of the situation. . . .

A subcommittee considering the bill under the chairmanship of Congressman Celler, split along bipartisan lines, reported out an expanded bill which appeared to be stronger and had the unyielding support of the civil rights groups, but which in fact included provisions that were of doubtful constitutionality and contained the seeds of more turmoil than solutions. Southern Democrats gleefully joined Northern liberal Democrats in giving the bill more weight than the House Rules Committee and full House membership were capable of carrying. The President had the choice of either making this new version the official Democratic bill, which would have increased enormously his prestige and influence with liberal and civil rights groups, or risking an all-out effort to re-create the badly damaged bipartisan consensus. He chose the latter course. . . .

The President, accompanied by the Vice President and Attorney General, embarked on an unprecedented series of private meetings in the White House—seeking to enlist the cooperation and understanding of more than sixteen hundred national leaders: educators, lawyers, Negro leaders, Southern leaders, women's organizations, business groups, governors, mayors, editors and others, Republicans as well as Democrats, segregationists as well as integrationists. . . .

The over-all response made Kennedy proud of his country. The citizen "lobby" on behalf of the bill—led particularly by religious groups and supported by editorial writers usually poles apart—was massive and effective. Even more striking was the voluntary removal of segregation signs and practices in chain stores, theaters and restaurants. Southern mayors and chambers of commerce began talking with Negro leaders. Employers and unions, North and South, began lowering racial bars. The nation's clergy were goaded into effective action on a major moral issue which had long preceded Kennedy's leadership. Progress was slow and insufficient, but, compared to the previous hundred years, rapid and gratifying. . . .

Polls showed a majority in white America in favor of the Kennedy bill, but they also showed a majority feeling that Kennedy was pushing too fast. Signs of a white "backlash" in Northern suburbs were widely discussed. . . .

At times he [the President] found it hard to believe that otherwise rational men could be so irrational on this subject. (He was even surprised to find deep feelings against Negroes' sitting beside whites at a lunch counter. To him that seemed the least controversial part of his bill.) Those who thought he was pushing too fast seemed to think he was taking something away from whites and giving it to Negroes, he said; and he explained over and over that he sought for the Negroes not preference but equality, not special privilege but opportunity; he sought not to drag down white standards but to raise Negro standards.

Privately he confided to a Negro leader that "this issue could cost me the election, but we're not turning back." Publicly he remained cautiously optimistic. . . .

SCHLESINGER. The following excerpts from *A Thousand Days*, by Arthur M. Schlesinger, Jr., pages 973-977, describe another author's view of the Civil Rights Act.

Liberal Democrats in the House, backed by the civil rights leadership, continued to think the administration bill inadequate; for its part, the administration feared a stronger bill would face trouble in the House Rules Committee and later in the Senate. Then the civil rights forces, arguing that the House had to send the Senate the strongest possible bill to give the Senate leaders room for maneuver in face of a filibuster, attracted the support of southerners, who felt that,

the stronger the bill was, the less the chance of passage. After long weeks of discussion and infighting, the President called in the House leaders in late October and, with the help of Charles Halleck, the Republican leader, personally worked out a compromise—FEPC was retained with enforcement in the courts; the Attorney General, while not given all the authority the civil rights people had proposed, received power to enter any civil rights case in federal courts and to initiate suits to desegregate public facilities; and the bill was strengthened in other ways. Robert Kennedy called the result a "better bill than the administration's." The Judiciary Committee approved it on October 29 and reported it to the House on November 20. The best civil rights bill in American history thus passed the first obstacles on its road to enactment. The House vote in January 1964 was the fulfillment of the agreement the Democratic and Republican leaders had made with Kennedy in the October White House meetings.

Yet, even when enacted, the new program would meet only part of the causes of the growing unrest. Its provisions were designed for the Negroes of the South. To the Negroes of the North the rights it offered were those they nominally possessed already. And to the heart of the now boiling northern unrest—to the frustrations in the black ghettos of the cities—it offered nothing. . . .

The fulfillment of the Negro revolution plainly demanded much more than the achievement of the Negroes' legal rights. . . . As A. Philip Randolph told the AFL-CIO convention in November 1963, "The Negro's protest today is but the first rumbling of the 'under-class.' As the Negro has taken to the streets, so will the unemployed of all races take to the streets. . . . To discuss the civil rights revolution is therefore to write the agenda of labor's unfinished revolution.". . .

The President was keenly aware of the

THE SENATE VOTE
June 19, 1964

ALABAMA		INDIANA		NEBRASKA		SOUTH CAROLINA	
Hill	N	Bayh	Y	*Curtis*	Y	Johnston	N
Sparkman	N	Hartke	Y	*Hruska*	Y	Thurmond	N
ALASKA		**IOWA**		**NEVADA**		**SOUTH DAKOTA**	
Bartlett	Y	*Hickenlooper*	N	Bible	Y	McGovern	Y
Gruening	Y	*Miller*	Y	Cannon	Y	*Mundt*	Y
ARIZONA		**KANSAS**		**NEW HAMPSHIRE**		**TENNESSEE**	
Hayden	Y	*Carlson*	Y	McIntyre	Y	Gore	N
Goldwater	N	*Pearson*	Y	*Cotton*	N	Walters	N
ARKANSAS		**KENTUCKY**		**NEW JERSEY**		**TEXAS**	
Fulbright	N	*Cooper*	Y	Williams	Y	Yarborough	Y
McClellan	N	*Morton*	Y	*Case*	Y	*Tower*	N
CALIFORNIA		**LOUISIANA**		**NEW MEXICO**		**UTAH**	
Engle	Y	Ellender	N	Anderson	Y	Moss	Y
Kuchel	Y	Long	N	*Mechem*	N	*Bennett*	Y
COLORADO		**MAINE**		**NEW YORK**		**VERMONT**	
Allott	Y	Muskie	Y	*Javits*	Y	*Aiken*	Y
Dominick	Y	*Smith*	Y	*Keating*	Y	*Prouty*	Y
CONNECTICUT		**MARYLAND**		**NORTH CAROLINA**		**VIRGINIA**	
Dodd	Y	Brewster	Y	Ervin	N	Byrd	N
Ribicoff	Y	*Beall*	Y	Jordan	N	Robertson	N
DELAWARE		**MASSACHUSETTS**		**NORTH DAKOTA**		**WASHINGTON**	
Boggs	Y	Kennedy	Y	Burdick	Y	Jackson	Y
Williams	Y	*Saltonstall*	Y	*Young*	Y	Magnuson	Y
FLORIDA		**MICHIGAN**		**OHIO**		**WEST VIRGINIA**	
Holland	N	Hart	Y	Lausche	Y	Byrd	N
Smathers	N	McNamara	Y	Young	Y	Randolph	Y
GEORGIA		**MINNESOTA**		**OKLAHOMA**		**WISCONSIN**	
Russell	N	Humphrey	Y	Edmondson	Y	Nelson	Y
Talmadge	N	McCarthy	Y	Monroney	Y	Proxmire	Y
HAWAII		**MISSISSIPPI**		**OREGON**		**WYOMING**	
Inouye	Y	Eastland	N	Morse	Y	McGee	Y
Fong	Y	Stennis	N	Neuberger	Y	*Simpson*	N
IDAHO		**MISSOURI**		**PENNSYLVANIA**			
Church	Y	Long	Y	Clark	Y		
Jordan	Y	Symington	Y	*Scott*	Y		
ILLINOIS		**MONTANA**		**RHODE ISLAND**			
Douglas	Y	Mansfield	Y	Pastore	Y		
Dirksen	Y	Metcalf	Y	Pell	Y		

N—No
Y—Yes

Democrats are in regular type; Republicans are in *italics*.
Reprinted with permission of Congressional Quarterly, Inc.

---

larger contexts. When civil rights leaders had reproached him in 1961 for not seeking legislation, he told them that an increased minimum wage, federal aid to education and other social and economic measures were also civil rights bills. He knew that a slow rate of economic growth made every problem of equal rights more intractable, as a faster rate would make every such problem easier of solution.

In 1963 he counted on his tax cut to reduce Negro unemployment; he reviewed and enlarged his educational program—vocational education, adult basic education, manpower development, youth employment—to help equip Negroes for jobs; and his concern for the plight of the Negro strengthened his campaigns against juvenile delinquency, urban decay and poverty. . . .

By 1963 the revolution was enlisting the idealism not only of the Negroes but of the universities and churches, of labor and the law. It was also attracting some who, as one put it, if they could not get their places around the table, threatened to knock its legs off. A generation ago Roosevelt had absorbed the energy and hope of the labor revolution into the New Deal. So in 1963 Kennedy moved to incorporate the Negro revolution into the democratic coalition and thereby help it serve the future of American freedom.[1]

THE FILIBUSTER. The Senate debated eighty-three days before passing the 1964 Civil Rights Act. A brief sample from one day of the filibuster is given below from the *Congressional Record*.

Before the distinguished Senator from Mississippi starts his address, the Senator from Virginia would like to know whether or not the Senator agrees with our colleague, the Senator from Georgia [Mr. TALMADGE], who in an excellent speech yesterday on the same issue indicated some of the people who would be affected if a genuine and bona fide jury trial provision is not inserted in the bill. He said:

"In the 55-page, 11-title bill, the Senate is now considering, 5 of those titles would authorize the Attorney General of the United States to file suits, at the expense of the taxpayers of the United States, and with the assistance of a myriad of Federal attorneys, against any one of the 190 million citizens of the United States of America, and to have them jailed without any right of trial by jury."

Does the Senator agree with that statement?

Mr. EASTLAND. Yes. I think that is a fine statement.

Mr. ROBERTSON. The Senator from

[1] Arthur M. Schlesinger, Jr., *A Thousand Days: John F. Kennedy in the White House.* Houghton Mifflin Co., 1965.

Georgia [Mr. TALMADGE] then said:

"The Attorney General could jail a barber for not shaving the face of someone that he thought the barber should shave. The Attorney General could jail the owner of a hamburger stand or the owner of a hotdog stand, at will, for not serving a hamburger or a hotdog to someone whom the Attorney General thought he should serve."

Does the Senator agree with that statement?

Mr. EASTLAND. Yes, I agree with that statement. In the case of a barber, a personal service is involved. So it would involve involuntary servitude. It would be a form of slavery.

Mr. ROBERTSON. Prohibited by the 13th amendment.

Mr. EASTLAND. Prohibited by the 13th amendment to the Constitution.

Mr. ROBERTSON. The Senator will agree that in 1883 the Supreme Court overruled the accommodation bill that was passed then. Is not that decision still the law of the land?

Mr. EASTLAND. Yes.

Mr. ROBERTSON. Only 10 years ago the Supreme Court held that separate but equal schools were illegal and would have to be desegregated. We are told that is the law of the land. If that is the law of the land, why is not the decision that was handed down back in 1883 still the law of the land?

Mr. EASTLAND. It is. This bill is unconstitutional.

Mr. ROBERTSON. We are asked to enact title II, the counterpart of what the Court said in 1883 was illegal. Is that not correct?

Mr. EASTLAND. Yes. It involves the same principle, and it is unconstitutional for the same reason.

Mr. ROBERTSON. The Senator from Georgia [Mr. TALMADGE] said yesterday that under this bill the Attorney General "could jail all the voting registrars of the United States of America, without regard to the area in which they reside and without any right whatsoever to trial by jury."

Does the Senator agree with that statement?

Mr. EASTLAND. I agree.

Mr. ROBERTSON. The Senator from Georgia [Mr. TALMADGE] continued:

"The bill would give the Attorney General of the United States power to file suits in the name of the Government of the United

States against all of the school board members in America, and jail them without trial by jury."

Does the Senator agree with that statement?

Mr. EASTLAND. Yes; I agree with that statement.

Mr. ROBERTSON. In that excellent address of yesterday, the Senator from Georgia quoted from the speech of a very able and beloved former Member, Andy Schoeppel.

Mr. EASTLAND. Senator Schoeppel was one of the most able Senators who ever sat in the Senate.

Mr. ROBERTSON. Is it not correct that in 1957, when a Republican Attorney General had framed a civil rights bill that did not provide for jury trial, Andy Schoeppel stood on the floor of the Senate and, in an eloquent speech, demanded that a jury trial provision be put in the bill?

Mr. EASTLAND. That is correct. He was one of the great men and one of the great Senators in the history of this body. He was a great lawyer. He was independent of all outside influence.

Mr. ROBERTSON. The point I am making is that he had the courage of his convictions. Did not the Senate go along with him in 1957?

Mr. EASTLAND. Yes.

Mr. ROBERTSON. Did not that 1957 bill also provide for title III, which would have allowed the Attorney General to inject the Government as a party in any number of operations? And did not the Senate take that provision out of the bill?

Mr. EASTLAND. What my friend says is correct.

Mr. ROBERTSON. Is it not true that we are asked to put into the bill an FEPC provision which was not in the 1957 bill?

Mr. EASTLAND. That is correct.

Mr. ROBERTSON. Is it not correct that we are asked to put in the bill title III, which the Senate took out in 1957?

Mr. EASTLAND. That is correct.

Mr. ROBERTSON. Is it not true that we are asked to put in title II, which was not even suggested in 1957, and which the Supreme Court since 1883 has declared to be unconstitutional? Are we not asked to put that back?

Mr. EASTLAND. That is correct. We are being asked to change our minds.

Mr. ROBERTSON. We are being asked to change our minds. What does the Senator propose to say about that?

Mr. EASTLAND. I shall discuss it today, and on other days.

Mr. ROBERTSON. Has the Senator from Mississippi changed his mind?

Mr. EASTLAND. No; I have not changed my mind. I am staying with the Constitution.

Mr. ROBERTSON. The position of the Senator from Virginia and that of the Senator from Mississippi will be very close together.

I thank the Senator for yielding.

Mr. RUSSELL. Mr. President, will the Senator from Mississippi yield to me, to permit me to submit a unanimous-consent request?

The PRESIDING OFFICER (Mr. INOUYE in the chair). Does the Senator from Mississippi yield to the Senator from Georgia?

Mr. EASTLAND. I yield.

Mr. RUSSELL. Mr. President, I ask unanimous consent that the Senator from Mississippi may yield to me, to permit me to make a brief statement in the nature of a statement of privilege, with the understanding that that will not in anywise affect his rights to the floor.

Mr. EASTLAND. And also with the understanding that my subsequent remarks will not count as a second speech on the pending amendment.

The PRESIDING OFFICER. Without objection, it is so ordered.

Mr. RUSSELL. Mr. President, I regret very much that in the course of this debate there has arisen what I am sure it will be agreed is a misunderstanding as to a commitment that it is claimed or implied I made with respect to a vote on the so-called jury-trial amendment. I have particular reference to the amendment proposed by the Senator from Illinois [Mr. DIRKSEN], the minority leader, and the Senator from Montana [Mr. MANSFIELD] the majority leader.

I am glad the distinguished majority leader is in the Chamber. I tried to contact the minority leader this morning, but was informed that he was not in the Capitol today; and therefore it was impossible for me to get him to the floor.

However, earlier in the week, I did tell the minority leader that I intended to make a statement on this situation, as soon as it was possible for me to do so. I would have made it yesterday, but for the fact that I was compelled to be away from the Capital.

Mr. President, I refer, first, to an article published on May 13, 1964, in the New York Times. The article is entitled "Rights Backers Seeking Cloture Within 2 Weeks." The article, which was written by E. W. Kenworthy, is rather long. I shall read excerpts from it, and ask unanimous consent that the entire article be printed in the RECORD at the conclusion of my remarks.

● What political processes are illustrated by the passage of the Civil Rights Act?

● How was passage of the act accomplished?

● Why did it take so long to get the bill passed?

● How would you have reacted to the bill if you were: a Georgia senator, a Negro representative from the inner city of Chicago, the Attorney General, a representative from a suburban area in New York?

● What generalizations about the political processes do you conclude from these materials?

3
NATIONAL GOVERNMENT

VOTE 1972
CHISHOLM

Discuss the federal concept of government. Compare our federal concept to that of others such as Canada or the Federal Republic of Germany. Contrast federalism to more traditionally centralized nations such as France.

There are three levels of government in the United States: national, state, and local. In this unit and the following two units these three levels will be treated. This unit deals with the national government—the government of the United States of America. Often this national government is called *federal government* because the states and the nation are joined in a federal system.

Ours is a government of law based on the Constitution. So the unit begins with a description of the work of Congress including the ways in which laws are passed.

The President is the central figure in government. He has great influence on the passage of laws and is responsible for the administration of the laws and the conduct of the government. He is aided by the executive departments in the cabinet and by numerous independent agencies.

The federal court system interprets the laws. The courts are the guardians of the personal liberties of individuals. The courts also provide a check on the work of Congress and the President. The Supreme Court is the final authority in the interpretation of laws and on the acts of public officials.

Chapter 9 describes the structure of Congress, including the qualifications and duties of the members of Congress.

Chapter 10 tells how Congress carries on its work and the manner in which laws are passed.

Chapter 11 deals with the President and the executive office. The qualifications, nomination, election, and duties of the President are treated.

Chapter 12 discusses the President's Cabinet and the eleven executive departments.

Chapter 13 concludes the study of the executive branch with a description of the more important independent agencies.

Chapter 14 describes the operation of the federal courts, emphasizing the importance of the judges as human beings and the place of the Supreme Court.

APPORTION—to divide into proportional shares; to distribute the 435 memberships in the House of Representatives among the states.

BICAMERAL—a legislature with two branches, or houses.

CENSUS—an official counting of the number of people in a country.

CONTIGUOUS—in close contact; touching; near.

ELASTIC CLAUSE—the "necessary and proper" clause of the Constitution.

EXPRESSED POWER—a specific power given to Congress by the Constitution; an enumerated power.

FRANKING—the privilege of sending mail without cost.

GERRYMANDER—an unfair division of legislative districts to give one political party greater power.

IMPEACH—to make an official accusation against a public official for improper conduct.

IMPLIED POWER—a power that is not directly specified; a power derived from the "necessary and proper" clause.

LAME DUCK—a person defeated for public office or not a candidate for re-election but completing the balance of his term.

REAPPORTIONMENT—to apportion again; to redivide the 435 memberships in the House of Representatives among the states.

SENATORIAL COURTESY—a custom under which senators have agreed that they will not approve an appointment by the President to a position in a particular state, if it is opposed by a senator from that state who is a member of the same party as the President.

SESSION—a yearly meeting of Congress.

TERM—the time or period during which something lasts; the two sessions of Congress from one election to the next.

THE LANGUAGE OF GOVERNMENT

Many political viewers believe that Congress has lost power over the years vis-à-vis the Executive branch of government. Analyze the pros and cons of this belief.

9

The Congress

Washington, D. C., has thousands of visitors each year. Many are tourists wanting to see their capital city. They visit the White House, the Capitol building, the Library of Congress, the Supreme Court. They watch the printing of money. They show their respect and appreciation for our past leaders by visiting the Washington Monument, the Jefferson Memorial, the Lincoln Memorial, the grave of President Kennedy. They drive down the beautiful highway along the Potomac River to see Mount Vernon, George Washington's home.

Most visitors leave Washington, D. C., with greatly increased respect and admiration for the government of the United States. They realize the power and the importance of our government. They are impressed by the beauty of our capital city.

Sometimes, however, visitors are disappointed. They have dreamed such wonderful dreams. Their expectations have been so great. They have anticipated supermen and have seen ordinary people. While they have seen beautiful buildings, away from main streets they have seen slum areas, as in other big cities.

This panoramic view of Washington, D. C., shows the white-domed Capitol in the center. Looking directly down the Mall behind the Capitol is the Washington Monument, and beyond it the columned facade of the Lincoln Memorial. In front of the Capitol to the left is the National Art Gallery. (Courtesy of Washington Convention and Visitors Bureau)

REACTIONS TO CONGRESS

The disappointments frequently arise from a visit to Congress. Citizens have read about the great speeches and the heated debates. They are not prepared for the hours when activity in Congress seems dull and uninteresting. They do not understand the confusion of some parliamentary procedures. They are bewildered.

One high school student after a visit to Congress said, "That was a complete waste of time. Only a handful of congressmen were present. No one paid any attention to the man who was speaking. One congressman was reading a newspaper; others were talking to each other. Congressmen were getting up and leaving the room. Others were drifting in. There didn't seem to be any order. If that's the way our government is operated, no wonder we are in such a mess."

But another high school student, visiting Congress on a different occasion, said, "That really was exciting. A Republican leader was trying to defend his vote on a

Point out the many duties that a congressman has other than simply appearing on the Senate or House floor every day. Include office work, and committee meetings and hearings.

foreign policy bill. Some other Republicans who didn't agree with him would interrupt him to ask questions. One of the ladies kept after him with her questions. Now and then Democrats from their side of the hall would join in the questioning. Most of the time, though, this Republican leader stood before his microphone and really told them what he thought. It was better than a movie."

How could two students get such different impressions? Chiefly because they visited at different times. One visited when nothing of national importance seemed to be taking place. The other visited when a major policy speech was being made. One was lucky; the other was unlucky. Yet, if the first visitor had known more about the workings of Congress, he would not have jumped to the conclusion that things were in a "mess."

THE MEMBERS OF CONGRESS

Article I of the Constitution states, "All legislative powers herein granted shall be vested in a Congress of the United States, which shall consist of a Senate and House of Representatives." The Senate has 100 members, two senators for each state. The House has 435 members divided among the states in proportion to population. This system of two houses, a *bicameral* legislature, was one of the compromises between large and small states in the writing of the Constitution. The Articles of Confederation had provided for a one-house legislature.

While a few members of Congress would be included among the great men and women of this generation, most members of Congress are ordinary, perhaps slightly above-average, people. Now and then a rascal is elected. Once in a while congress-

CONGRESS IN BRIEF

	HOUSE OF REPRESENTATIVES	*SENATE*
MEMBERSHIP	435	100
SELECTED BY	Voters in congressional districts	Voters of the state
QUALIFICATIONS	Twenty-five years of age Seven years citizen of United States Inhabitant of state represented	Thirty years of age Nine years citizen of United States Inhabitant of state represented
TERM	Two years	Six years
SALARY	$42,500	$42,500
SPECIAL POWERS	Impeach officials Start revenue bills Select a President when there is not an electoral majority	Try impeachment cases Select a Vice President when there is not an electoral majority Approve treaties Approve appointments
PRESIDING OFFICER	Speaker. Elected by members of House Receives $62,500 and $10,000 for expenses	Vice President Receives $62,500 and $10,000 for expenses
MEETINGS	Capitol Building, Washington, D.C., January 3, each year until adjournment	Capitol Building, Washington, D.C., January 3, each year until adjournment

Edward W. Brooke is the first Negro to serve in the United States Senate since Reconstruction. A lawyer, Brooke was elected to the Senate from Massachusetts in 1966, where he had held the post of Attorney General. (Brooke for U.S. Senator Committee)

men recognize that one of their members is not as intelligent as he should be, but at the other extreme they know that some members have brilliant minds. On the whole, most of the members have good ability and try to represent well the people who elected them.

PREVIOUS EXPERIENCE. In a typical Congress, the previous experience of the largest group has been as lawyers. Thus, in a recent Congress, there were 246 lawyers in the House of Representatives and 68 lawyers in the Senate. In this Congress there were 57 farmers, 49 newspaper men, 72 educators, 184 businessmen and bankers,

5 doctors, 2 ministers, and 2 engineers. (Some members list more than one occupation so that the total of the occupations is more than the membership of Congress.) In the House 2 members were serving their first term, and in the Senate there were 9 first-termers. For all the members of Congress, slightly over 90 per cent had had previous experience in politics or government service and over two-thirds had been in military service.

In the 1972 Congress there were 13 women, 12 in the House and 1 in the Senate—Margaret Chase Smith of Maine, who was first elected to the Senate in 1948. Thirteen Negroes represented congressional districts in large northern cities. The first Negro to be elected to the Senate by popular election was Edward W. Brooke of Massachusetts in 1966.

THE NEW CONGRESSMAN. A new member of Congress faces many problems. His life is not easy. He has to find a place to live in a strange city where there is a great shortage of housing. He is given an office in one of the Senate or House Office buildings, depending on which branch of Congress he serves.

He has to find and train an office staff. Much of his success will depend on the courtesy and efficiency of this staff. The folks back home expect their letters to be answered promptly and accurately. If they visit Washington on business, they may want help in seeking the proper government officials. A congressman's secretaries can help or injure his career.

Unless he has served in a state legislature or a city council, he may need to spend many hours studying in order to learn enough parliamentary procedure to understand what is going on. Most important of all, he will be assigned to a committee. This committee appointment is his most important opportunity while he is in Washing-

A DAY IN THE LIFE OF A MEMBER OF CONGRESS. Top left, Senator Hiram Fong listens to a witness during a hearing of the Senate's Special Committee on Aging. Representative Martha Griffiths reads one of the many papers that comes across her desk. Lower left, Senator Harry F. Byrd talks with a constituent. Representative Louis Stokes addresses a meeting. (Lower left photo, Dev O'Neill, House Democratic photographer)

ton. His success as a member of Congress will be measured chiefly by the work he does on a committee.

CHOOSING CONGRESSMEN

The 435 members of the House of Representatives are elected for two-year terms. The Constitution provides that the number of representatives for each state shall be determined by the population based on the last census. Each state, however, has at least one representative.

THE CONGRESSIONAL DISTRICT. By the 1970 census, Alaska, Delaware, Nevada, North Dakota, Vermont, and Wyoming have one representative each. All the other states are divided into congressional districts. A congressional district should contain approximately 467,091 people based on the 1970 census. Thus, California has 43 representatives; New York, 39; Pennsylvania, 25; Illinois, 24; Texas, 24; Ohio, 23; and Michigan, 19.

When the Constitution was adopted, the House of Representatives had 65 members. As the population of the country grew, the number of representatives was increased until the total of 435 was reached in 1910. Adding the new states, Alaska and Hawaii, increased the size to 437 temporarily. In 1963, the House returned to the 435 size.

The large number of representatives makes it very difficult to produce laws efficiently. The length of speeches has to be limited. Attendance during speeches tends to be poor. Many rules are necessary. Committee assignments are harder to give out fairly. As a result, our congressmen have felt that the House should not be increased in size—even though the population of the nation continues to grow. Efforts to reduce the size of the House have failed in the past because congressmen feared that it might be their districts that would be eliminated

in the reduction. Since 1929 the intent has been to keep the House at 435 members, although those interested in congressional reform have urged a gradual reduction to 300 members.

REAPPORTIONMENT. The writers of the Constitution recognized that the population would increase and that people would move about, although they would undoubtedly be shocked at our present size and the mobility of the population. To maintain equal representation in the House, the Constitution provides, "Representatives . . . shall be apportioned among the several states . . . according to their respective numbers . . . every . . . ten years." (Article I, Section 2, Clause 3).

After each census Congress determines the number of House seats in relation to the total population. From 1790 to 1910 this presented no great problem, because the size of the House was merely increased —except after the 1840 census, when the number was *decreased* from 242 to 232 seats.

After the census of 1920 Congress could not agree on a system for dividing the seats. There were objections to increasing the size of the House, but eleven states would lose representatives if the number was kept at 435. Congress could not reach a solution so no reapportionment was made after the 1920 census. Finally, with the 1930 census about to be made, Congress passed the 1929 Reapportionment Act which provided for an automatic reapportionment feature if Congress failed to act. Under this plan, the President, using material from the Census Bureau, reports to Congress on the number of seats for each state. If neither house *rejects* the plan, it becomes effective within sixty days. The presidential plan has been used since then with one exception. Following the 1940 census, the plan was used but the formula for dividing seats was altered.

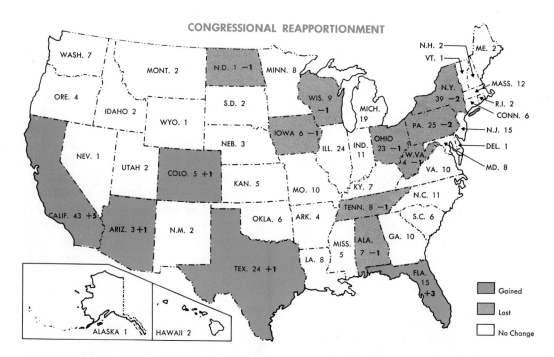

Based on the 1970 census, congressional districts were reapportioned to take effect with the 1972 elections. The map shows which states gained representatives, which lost representatives, and which stayed the same. The figure after the state name is the present number of representatives followed by the gain or loss, if one occurred.

Based on the 1970 census, five states gained representatives and nine states lost representatives.

Once the decision on the number of representatives has been made, some bitter political fights are waged in the attempts to set new boundaries for congressional districts. Until recent court decisions, states did not always create new boundaries because state legislatures could not agree on a system. In these cases the additional representatives were elected by a state-wide election. These representatives were called *representatives-at-large.* Similarly, if a state lost representatives and did not reapportion, all members were elected by statewide elections. If the state's number remained the same, boundaries were not always changed even though shifts in population

had taken place within the state. Before the 1970 census the courts had changed these conditions.

GERRYMANDERING. In most states attempts are made to divide the state in such a manner that the political party in control will get the most representatives. This is done by drawing the boundary lines so that either (1) most of the opposition party is in a few districts—to keep down the number of representatives elected from that party—or (2) the opposition party is scattered among several districts and cannot get a majority vote in any.

Figures 1, 2, and 3 on the next page show how this might be done. The shaded part of Figure 1 shows a voting area that is almost entirely Republican. The rest of the district is chiefly Democratic.

Figure 2 shows how the districts could be

divided so that the Republicans would be kept in one district. Figure 3 shows how the Republican votes might be split between two districts.

If the Democrats were in control of the reapportionment, they would probably use the system in Figure 3 and get three representatives. If the Republicans were in control, they would probably use the system of Figure 2 and be sure to elect one representative.

This political device for drawing district boundaries to favor one party is called *gerrymandering*. The name has been used since 1812 when Governor Elbridge Gerry of Massachusetts got his legislature to draw district boundaries in a strange manner. The map of one district looked like a type of lizard sometimes called a salamander. A newspaperman looked at the map and coined the term *gerrymander*. Both the name and the practice have stayed with us, because in practical politics no party wishes to lose a district if this can be avoided.

The chief protection the public has against the unfair use of this power to draw boundaries depends on the voters understanding the issues involved. State legislatures are responsible for reapportionment. If there is a strong public belief in fair and honest drawing of boundaries, legislatures will be less likely to try for unfair political advantage. Backed by such public sentiment, some legislatures might give up their right to draw the boundaries and have this task assigned to commissions on a nonpartisan basis.

Reapportionment has become increasingly important in this century as the shift from chiefly an agricultural to an industrial nation has taken place. With this change came the movement of people to the large cities and later the movement to suburban areas around them.

If the people of these large cities are to be represented adequately in Congress, changes in the congressional districts must take place. For example, based on the 1970 census, one congressional district in the Chicago metropolitan area had a population of 662,145 while another congressional district in western Illinois had a popula-

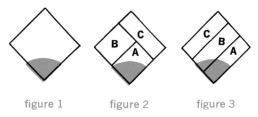

figure 1   figure 2   figure 3

GERRYMANDERING

At the left is a drawing of the original gerrymander which appeared in the Boston Gazette, March 26, 1812. *The drawings at right show how gerrymandering can be accomplished. (See the explanation on this page.) Source: Library of Congress.*

tion of only 423,070. These inequalities exist, too, in state legislatures and will be discussed in Chapter 15.

For many years the chief protection the public had against the unfair drawing of congressional boundaries was public interest and the watchfulness of pressure groups. Then, in 1964, the Supreme Court made one of its historic decisions in the case of *Wesberry* v. *Sanders,* challenging the congressional districts of Georgia. By a 6-3 decision the court held that "as nearly as is practicable one man's vote in a congressional election is to be worth as much as another's."

The majority opinion said, ". . . there is no excuse for ignoring our Constitution's plain objective of making equal representation for equal numbers of people the fundamental goal for the House of Representatives."

The effect of this decision was momentous. Within two years, thirty-one states had been redistricted to meet the Court's "one-man, one-vote" rule. All states, following the 1970 census, struggled to reapportion congressional districts on a basis that was fair and that would stand up in the courts.

To get ready for this reapportionment Congress debated for over two years on an equitable basis for dividing the population into districts. The major issue became: By what percentage could the district with the largest population in a state differ from the district with the smallest population? Some argued for allowing only a 10 per cent difference. Others argued for as much as a 30 per cent difference.

The House and Senate were unable to agree on a bill and finally only passed a ban on at-large elections in states with more than one representative.

Then, in April 1969, the Supreme Court in *Kirkpatrick* v. *Preisler,* by a 6-3 decision, ruled that states must strive for districts with absolutely equal populations. Any variation, "no matter how small," must be justified or shown to be unavoidable. By this case a Missouri redistricting with a 3.1 variation was overruled. At the time, thirty-three other states had a variation of more than 3.0 per cent. Clearly the Supreme Court intended that, following the 1970 census, congressional districts would be equal.

After the 1970 census, these states gained representatives: California - 5, Florida - 3, Arizona - 1, Texas - 1. States that lost representatives were: Pennsylvania and New York - 2 each; Alabama, Iowa, North Dakota, Ohio, Tennessee, West Virginia, and Wisconsin - 1 each.

The long-range effect of the 1970 reapportionments will be to decrease the power of rural areas and increase the power of suburban areas in the House.

CHOOSING SENATORS. In the choice of senators these problems of reapportionment do not exist, because senators represent entire states. Each state has two senators. Although Nevada, according to the 1970 census, has a population of 488,738 and New York has 18,190,740 population, the Constitution provides that each state shall have two senators. This provision of the Constitution is one of the great compromises that has helped make our Constitution a successful document. Our forefathers agreed that the House of Representatives should represent people and the Senate should represent states.

The Senate's 100 members are elected for six-year terms, but only about one-third of the senators are elected at any one election. It thus takes six years to change completely the membership of the Senate. This longer term and the more permanent membership means that the Senate usually does not change its position on public questions as quickly as the House.

The smaller size of the Senate in some

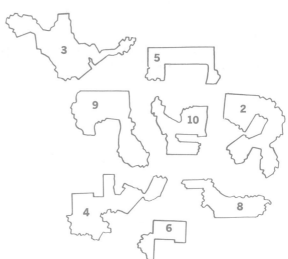

NORTH CAROLINA CONGRESSIONAL
DISTRICT MAPS, 1966

ways makes for greater efficiency. This advantage of size, however, is offset on some occasions by the great freedom of debate which is allowed in the Senate. In the House, speeches are strictly limited in length of time, but speeches in the Senate can, and do, go on and on.

Until 1913 senators were elected by state legislatures, but in that year the Seventeenth Amendment to the Constitution was adopted. It provided for direct election of senators by the people of the state. The purpose of the amendment was to make the Senate more representative of the people.

OTHER REPRESENTATION. Guam and the Virgin Islands each elect a delegate and Puerto Rico elects a commissioner to Congress. They can debate and can serve on committees of the House of Representatives, but they have no vote. Alaska, Hawaii, and twenty-nine other territories, before becoming states, elected 169 territorial delegates to the House. These delegates did not vote, but represented the territories until they became states.

The citizens who live in Washington, D.C. are represented in Congress by a non-

In 1966 the state legislature of North Carolina adopted a new plan for Congressional districts, resulting in some of the strange shapes shown here. The federal court rejected the plan stating, "a motive to retain incumbent Congressmen. . . . may not predominate over the requirement of practical equality, and we think that compactness and contiguity are aspects of practicable equality." The court called the boundaries of these districts "tortuous lines." In 1967 the state legislature approved new boundaries.

—Source: *Congressional Quarterly,* September 16, 1966.

voting delegate. The District of Columbia is governed by Congress, but Congress does not give the eligible citizens the right to vote for congressmen. Residents of the District of Columbia can, however, now vote in the presidential elections.

VACANCIES. In the case of death or resignation of a member of the House, the vacancy is filled by a special election. The governor of most states must call this special election within thirty days after the vacancy occurs.

A Senate vacancy is also filled by election,

but the governor may appoint a temporary successor if the state law permits. The new senator serves for the unexpired term or until the next regular election, depending upon the state law.

QUALIFICATIONS AND RIGHTS OF CONGRESSMEN

Some of these qualifications and rights are specified in the Constitution. Others have been established over the years by rules laid down by the House and Senate.

CONSTITUTIONAL QUALIFICATIONS. A member of the House of Representatives must be at least twenty-five years old and a senator must be at least thirty years old, according to the Constitution (Article I, Sections 2 and 3). The youngest senator in a recent Congress was thirty-four years of age; the youngest representative was twenty-eight years old. The oldest senator was eighty-nine years old; the oldest representative was eighty-four. The average age of senators was fifty-eight and of representatives, fifty-one.

An interesting comparison is that the youngest signer of the Constitution in 1789 was twenty-seven years old, the oldest was eighty-one, and the average of all the signers was forty-three.

Members of the House must have been citizens of the United States for at least seven years. In a test case in 1930, based on the election of Mrs. Ruth Bryan Owen from a Florida district, the House decided that the seven years could be any seven years and need not be the seven years immediately before the election. Senators must have been citizens for at least nine years.

Representatives and senators must be inhabitants of the state when they are elected (Article I, Sections 2 and 3). In the case of representatives, by custom, but not by law, representatives are residents of the districts which elect them. The most notable exception to this practice was President Roosevelt's son, Franklin D. Jr., who lived in a different New York district than the one from which he was elected. He served in the House from 1949-55.

In England members of the House of Commons quite frequently are elected from districts in which they do not live. The British follow this practice to enable young men of ability to get early training in Parliament and sometimes to elect important party leaders from "safe" districts— those in which one party normally wins. Some political scientists think our Congress would be less subject to local pressures if we adopted the British practice on a more widespread basis.

In the case of the Senate, the 1964 election brought the "inhabitant" issue to national attention. Robert F. Kennedy, the Attorney General, and Pierre Salinger, the press secretary of the President, decided to be candidates for the Senate in states where they were not living. Kennedy chose to run in New York, although he was a registered voter in Massachusetts, lived in Virginia, and worked in Washington, D. C. He leased a house in New York shortly before being nominated for the Senate. Salinger was denied a place on the California ballot by the California Secretary of State because he lived in Virginia, but on appeal to the California Supreme Court he was placed on the ballot. In both states the issue was raised of being a "carpetbagger"—a term of scorn carried over from the Reconstruction period when northerners moved to the

---

The law must be stable, but it must not stand still.

—ROSCOE POUND, Dean Harvard Law School (1916-1936), *Introduction to the Philosophy of Law,* Yale University Press.

Congressional Record

United States of America

PROCEEDINGS AND DEBATES OF THE 90ᵗʰ CONGRESS, SECOND SESSION

| *Vol. 114* | WASHINGTON, WEDNESDAY, OCTOBER 2, 1968 | *No. 162* |

Senate

(Legislative day of Tuesday, September 24, 1968)

The Senate met at 10 a.m., on the expiration of the recess, and was called to order by the President pro tempore.

The Chaplain, Rev. Frederick Brown Harris, D.D., offered the following prayer:

God and Father of mankind, we would bring to this, our daily altar of prayer, our inner selves, cluttered and confused where the good and the evil, the petty and the great, the wheat and the tares, are so entwined.

As heralds of good will, send us forth across all the barriers of race and creed, to make our contribution to the glad day when justice and understanding shall engirdle this worn and weary earth.

As today's discords bombard our ears, we are grateful for friendships which stand all tests, for music which gives wings to our spirits, for truth which breaks the shackles of error, and for human beacons of righteousness where Thou dost show sufficient of Thy light for us in the dark to rise by.

Undergird us with Thy might to exercise the potent ministry to all the world to which, in Thy providence, we believe Thou hast called us in this age on ages telling.

We ask it in that Name which is above every name. Amen.

THE JOURNAL

Mr. MANSFIELD. Mr. President, I ask unanimous consent that the Journal of the proceedings of the legislative day of Tuesday, September 24, 1968—embracing the calendar days of Tuesday, September 24, through Tuesday, October 1, 1968—be approved.

The PRESIDENT pro tempore. Without objection, it is so ordered.

COMMITTEE MEETINGS DURING SENATE SESSION

Mr. MANSFIELD. Mr. President, I ask unanimous consent that the Committee on the District of Columbia and the Committee on Rules and Administration be authorized to meet during the session of the Senate today.

The PRESIDENT pro tempore. Without objection, it is so ordered.

THE CALENDAR

Mr. MANSFIELD. Mr. Presider I ask unanimous consent that the Senate proceed to the consideration of measures on the calendar, beginning with Calendar No. 1563.

The PRESIDENT pro tempore. Without objection, it is so ordered.

WILLIAM W. HIEBERT

The bill (H.R. 13160) for the relief of William W. Hiebert was considered, ordered to a third reading, read the third time, and passed.

Mr. MANSFIELD. Mr. President, I ask unanimous consent to have printed in the RECORD an excerpt from the report (No. 1578), explaining the purposes of the bill.

There being no objection, the excerpt was ordered to be printed in the RECORD, as follows:

PURPOSE

The purpose of the proposed legislation is to relieve William W. Hiebert, of Alexandria, Va., of all liability for repayments to the United States of the sum of $149.04 representing overpayments of salary which he received as an employee of the General Services Administration for the period from February 12 through June 6, 1967, as the result of administrative error. The bill would authorize the refund of any amounts repaid or withheld by reason of the liability.

STATEMENT

The General Services Administration, in its report, states that it has no objection to enactment of the bill. The General Accounting Office states that it has concluded that the question of whether the facts and circumstances of this case warrant relief legislation is a matter of policy for determination by the Congress.

As is authorized in the General Services Administration, Mr. Hiebert received a TAPER appointment in the Defense Materials Services, GSA, as storage specialist, GS-9, $7,479, on June 6, 1966. That salary was increased to $7,696 on July 3, 1966, in accordance with the Federal Employees' Salary Act of 1966. On August 14, 1966, Mr. Hiebert was converted to a career-conditional appointment as storage specialist, GS-7, $7,729 (seventh step), as a result of his passing the Federal service entrance examination.

Mr. Hiebert was promoted back to storage specialist, GS-9, $8,218 (third step) on February 12, 1967. This promotion was un-

authorized in that he had not served a total of 1 year at GS-7 or GS-9, and was not eligible for promotion back to GS-9 until June 6, 1967, in accordance with the so-called Whitten amendment, 65 Stat. 757, as amended, as implemented by Civil Service Commission regulations (Federal Personnel Manual, ch. 300, pp. 300-311 and 312). A personnel action was subsequently taken correcting this erroneous promotion so that the effective date became June 1967 instead of February 1967, and he was obliged to repay $149 to the Government.

In indicating that it had no objection, the General Services Administration stated:

"Since the overpayment resulted from an administrative error and not through the fault of Mr. Hiebert, GSA does not object to the enactment of H.R. 13160."

In view of the foregoing circumstances, the committee recommends that the bill H.R. 13160 be considered favorably.

LT. HERBERT F. SWANSON

The bill (H.R. 14079) for the relief of Lt. (j.g.) Herbert F. Swanson, and others, was considered, ordered to a third reading, read the third time, and passed.

Mr. MANSFIELD. Mr. President, I ask unanimous consent to have printed in the RECORD an excerpt from the report (No. 1564), explaining the purposes of the bill.

There being no objection, the excerpt was ordered to be printed in the RECORD, as follows:

PURPOSE

The purpose of the proposed legislation is to relieve nine named naval officers of the liability to refund amounts paid them as submarine pay in the period from July 3 through October 2, 1967, while attached to one of two submarines during builder's trial but prior to commissioning of the ships.

STATEMENT

The Department of the Navy in its report to the House Committee on the bill states that it has no objection to the enactment of the legislation, as amended by the committee. The Comptroller General in a report in behalf of the General Accounting Office stated the question of whether these officers should be relieved under these circumstances is a matter of policy for the Congress to decide.

The bill H.R. 14079 was the subject of a House judiciary subcommittee hearing on May 8, 1968. The testimony at that hearing

S 11825

189

South to take advantage of the disorganized conditions after the Civil War. In New York, Kennedy won and became a senator. In California, Salinger was defeated by George Murphy, who had achieved prominence as a dancer, singer, and movie executive. The long-run effects of these two efforts could be to encourage other persons of prominence to seek election in states where they do not reside at that particular time.

OTHER QUALIFICATIONS. Both the House and the Senate have the Constitutional right to decide whether a member has been properly elected and whether he is qualified to serve. The House decides these cases for its own members and the Senate for its members. By a majority vote either house may decide not to allow a person to serve who has been elected. By a two-thirds vote either house may expel one of its own members. Each house, therefore, can decide whether the Constitutional qualifications have been met and, in addition, set up its own special qualifications.

These powers are rarely used. A member of the House was expelled during World War I because he was accused of disloyalty. In 1967, Adam Clayton Powell, a black congressman elected from Harlem for his twelfth term, was denied his seat by vote of the House, 307 to 116. His defeat, according to his opponents, was the result of his misuse of public funds, absenteeism, and his irritating tactics as chairman of the House Committee on Education and Labor. His defenders claimed that he would have been seated if he had not been black. Powell and his constituents demanded he be seated. Powell was seated later after the House fined him $25,000. He was not re-elected in 1970 and died in 1972.

Three times in this century men who seemingly have been duly elected to serve in the Senate have not been allowed to serve: one man was not admitted because he was accused of buying votes; another man was not admitted because he had accepted large campaign contributions from public utility companies even though he was a member of a commission which had to regulate their rates; the third man was expelled because of improper statements made about Negroes and for accepting improper gifts. The *threat* to expel members or to deny admittance to Congress has been used on other occasions and serves as a guard against notoriously improper conduct.

SALARIES. Congress determines the rate of pay for its members. Representatives and senators receive the same salaries. In 1968 the yearly congressional salary was increased from $30,000 to $42,500. The Speaker of the House receives the same salary as the Vice President: $62,500 plus a $10,000 taxable expense allowance. Congressmen pay income tax on their salaries but are given a special $3,000 tax exemption for "living expenses" while away from home. This helps pay rent and grocery bills in Washington, D. C.

There is also an allowance to senators and representatives for hiring administrative assistants and office help. Free office space is provided in the House and Senate Office Buildings in Washington, and funds are provided to rent office space in the home district.

Congressmen are allowed free postage on all official business. They do not have to use stamps but are allowed to write their names on the envelope where the stamp would normally go. This system is called *franking.* There is an allowance for long-distance telephone calls, telegrams, and stationery. For travel to and from Washington for each session of Congress, the member is allowed twenty cents a mile plus limited funds for in-session trips home.

The congressman qualifies for a pension,

after age sixty-two, if he has served in Congress for six years and if he has contributed 6 per cent of his salary to the pension fund. The size of the pension depends on the length of service. He is also eligible to purchase group life and health insurance.

Unless members of Congress are wealthy, they have financial problems. The high costs of campaigning, keeping two homes, travel to and from Washington, the many charitable requests, plus the need to entertain many visitors means that even the congressman of average means has difficulty living on his salary. Although congressmen determine their own salaries, there is reluctance to increase salaries because of the public protests that arise. To avoid this, a provision was included in a law that salaries for congressional, executive, and judicial positions will be reviewed every four years by a special commission whose recommendations will be put into effect unless defeated by Congress.

THE CONGRESSIONAL RECORD. Speeches, debates, and the record of the motions and votes on bills are published in the *Congressional Record.* Originally this *Record* provided the official minutes of all the things said in Congress. Today the *Record* also contains some speeches and other materials which actually have not been presented completely on the floor of either house. If a congressman asks to have his remarks "extended in the *Record*," the request will be granted—unless a member objects. This saves the members from listening to many lengthy speeches and yet a member can have his remarks recorded in the *Record.*

Each congressman receives sixty copies of the *Congressional Record.* In addition he can get as many reprints of his speeches as he wishes by paying the Government Printing Office the cost of the printing.

SPECIAL PRIVILEGES. Certain special privileges are given to senators and representatives by the Constitution. Article I, Section 6 states: "The senators and representatives . . . shall in all cases, except treason, felony, and breach of the peace, be privileged from arrest during their attendance at the session of their respective houses, and in going to and returning from the same; and for any speech or debate in either house, they shall not be questioned in any other place."

This provision is an encouragement to complete freedom of speech. Congressmen cannot be sued for libel or slander for things they say in Congress. The provisions on arrest are designed to prevent arrest for political reasons, a type of arrest which is almost unknown in this country but which happens today in other parts of the world where tyrants or dictators rule. In actual practice senators and representatives must obey laws just as any other citizen. The provision is only effective when arrest might prevent a member from voting.

THE SESSIONS OF CONGRESS

In discussing the working of Congress, two words are often used—*session* and *term.*

THE SESSION. Congress meets every year. Each yearly meeting is called a *session.* The first session begins on January 3 of each odd-numbered year—approximately two months after new members are elected in November. The second session begins the following January 3.

THE TERM. The two sessions together are called a *term.* Starting with the first Congress, which met in 1789, each Congress has been numbered by these terms. The Congress that began a new term on January 3, 1973, is the Ninety-third Congress.

Congress adjourns when it wants to, but one house cannot end a session without the consent of the other. Sometimes Congress meets for four or five months; sometimes it has met for almost all the year. Because of the complicated problems of recent years the trend has been to meet longer. But congressmen seeking re-election need time to campaign, so that by summer of even-numbered years there is great pressure to adjourn. A congressional reorganization act of 1946 requires Congress to adjourn not later than July 31, unless Congress decides on a later date; but this fixed date has been met only in two presidential election years.

One device that is used now and then is to recess rather than to adjourn. By this system, if a matter of great importance arises, the members can be called back to Washington by the leaders of Congress without calling a special session.

SPECIAL SESSIONS. The President has the sole power to call special sessions of Congress. Thus if Congress has adjourned, but the President thinks a matter should be considered by the Congress, he can call a special session. The chief matters which are considered are normally those which the President names in his call for the session, but the Congress is free to deal with other matters also. The Senate may be called into special session alone if a treaty or presidential appointment requires Senate action. No special session has been called since 1948 chiefly because of the long regular sessions held by the Congresses.

THE DATE OF OPENING. The January 3 date for the opening of Congress was fixed by the Twentieth Amendment to the Constitution, adopted in 1933. This Amendment moved forward—from March 4 to January 3—the time that federal officials take office.

It took twenty years to get this simple amendment passed. The amendment was a recognition that with modern transpor-

tation and communication it no longer took four months to notify a candidate that he had been elected and to allow him time to get to Washington. While these conditions were true at the time of the adoption of the Constitution, they had no longer been true for many, many years.

Before the adoption of this amendment, senators and representatives who had been defeated in the November election would return to Washington for the second session of their term which met from December to March. These defeated members were called *lame ducks*—a nickname that showed they had been "shot" but weren't quite dead. The phrase has become part of the American language and now is used to describe any person who has been defeated for an office but is finishing his term of office.

THE POWERS OF CONGRESS

Congress is one of the most important legislative bodies in the world; it has great powers. But Congress does not have unlimited power.

De Tocqueville (Library of Congress)

Include the concept of concurrent congressional powers, and a discussion of the intricacies of presidential disability.

CONSTITUTIONAL PROVISIONS. The Constitution (Article 1, Section 8) lists the specific powers which Congress has. Then, in the Tenth Amendment, the Constitution states that powers not given to the United States and not taken away from a state are "reserved to the States respectively, or to the people."

The intent of the Constitution is clear. Congress is to have those powers which are *named* in the Constitution. The states and the people are to have *all other powers.*

As the years have gone by since the writing of the Constitution, life in America has changed very greatly. Automobiles, airplanes, television were not even dreams in the days of Washington, Hamilton, and Madison. These great leaders could not foresee the difficult problems that would arise in a modern, industrial, high-speed society.

As a result of these social and economic changes, the powers of Congress have been greatly increased over the years. Matters that were once the exclusive concern of the states are now dealt with by Congress. This growth in the power of the federal government, through laws passed by Congress, has changed the relationships between the states and the national government. The influence of the states has decreased while the impact of the national government has greatly increased. As will be discussed in Chapter 18, these state-federal relationships have become of great importance—especially if states are to be effective.

These changes came about because of a distinction which developed between *ex-*

ALEXIS DE TOCQUEVILLE

At age twenty-six, Alexis de Tocqueville, a young lawyer, was sent by the French government to the United States to investigate and report on the penitentiary system of the United States. He arrived in 1831 and his report was published two years later.

He was so enthusiastic about what he had seen in the United States that in 1835 he published a book that has become a classic in political science. The title of the book is *Democracy in America.* The French Academy gave him a prize for writing this book; it was soon translated into the major European languages.

Because of his profound insights into the operation of our democratic government, the book is still studied with care by students of government. Tocqueville served in the French legislature and as a member of the French Cabinet in his later years, but he is still best known for his famous book.

In one chapter he wrote about the dangers of tyranny in the United States in these words:

"In my opinion the main evil of the present democratic institutions of the United States does not arise, as is often asserted in Europe, from their weakness, but from their overpowering strength; and I am not so much alarmed at the excessive liberty which reigns in that country as at the very inadequate securities which exist against tyranny.

"When an individual or a party is wronged in the United States, to whom can he apply for redress? If to public opinion, public opinion constitutes the majority; if to the legislature, it represents the majority and implicitly obeys its injunctions; if to the executive power, it is appointed by the majority, and remains a passive tool in its hands; the public troops consist of the majority under arms; the jury is the majority invested with the right of hearing judicial cases; and in certain States even the judges are elected by the majority. However iniquitous or absurd the evil of which you complain may be, you must submit to it as well as you can. . . .

"I do not say that tyrannical abuses frequently occur in America at the present day, but I maintain that no sure barrier is established against them. . . ."

Congress, according to the Constitution, has the power to "establish post offices" and in 1970 created a government corporation to operate post offices like this one in Washington, D.C. (Post Office Department photo)

pressed powers and *implied* powers. Expressed powers are those which are specifically stated in the Constitution. Implied powers are those which are "read into" the Constitution without being stated exactly.

The right of Congress to use implied powers was settled early in our history by the Supreme Court in the case of *McCulloch v. Maryland.* The state of Maryland was challenging the right of Congress to establish the Second Bank of the United States. Chief Justice Marshall wrote ". . . there is no phrase in the (Constitution) . . . which requires that everything granted shall be expressly and minutely described. . . . Let the end be legitimate, let it be within the scope of the Constitution, and all means which are appropriate, which are plainly adapted to that end, which are not prohibited, . . . are Constitutional." Because Congress has the right to borrow money, to regulate commerce, to lay and collect taxes, the Supreme Court implied that Congress had the power to create a bank. This liberal interpretation of the Constitution has been continued to the present—giving Congress adequate power to deal with the issues of our time.

THE EXPRESSED POWERS. The powers expressly stated in the Constitution

can, for convenience, be grouped into nine general powers.

1. FINANCIAL. Congress may tax, borrow money, pay debts, and coin money.

2. COMMERCE. Congress may regulate

High on a hill in St. Thomas, Government House is the center of administrative activity on the American-owned territory of the Virgin Islands. The United States Congress has constitutional power to regulate American territories. (Photo courtesy of U.S. Virgin Islands)

commerce between states and with foreign nations. Bankruptcy, weights and measures, patents, and copyrights may be regulated.

3. NATURALIZATION. Congress may make rules by which foreigners may become citizens.

4. POSTAL. Congress may establish post offices and post roads.

5. LAW ENFORCEMENT. Congress has power over many crimes. Among these are counterfeiting, treason, and piracy.

6. JUDICIAL. Congress has power to establish all federal courts below the Supreme Court.

7. NATIONAL DEFENSE. Congress may declare war and provide an army, a navy, and a militia.

8. TERRITORIES AND THE DISTRICT OF COLUMBIA. Congress has power over the admission of new states, the regulation of territories, and the government of the District of Columbia.

These eight powers are specifically stated in the Constitution, Article I, Section 8, Clauses 1-17. These powers are discussed in greater detail in other parts of this book, especially in Units Seven and Eight. Here it is important to note only that these powers are specifically stated in the Constitution and no one can question the right of Congress to deal with these matters.

9. VICE PRESIDENTIAL VACANCY AND PRESIDENTIAL DISABILITY. In 1967, two new expressed powers were given to Congress with the ratification of the Twenty-fifth Amendment to the Constitution. Whenever there is a vacancy in the office of Vice President, the President nominates a new Vice President who takes office when approved by a majority vote in each house of Congress. Furthermore, if the President has been disabled and has not been able to discharge his duties, but states that he is now able to perform those duties, yet the Vice Presi-

Vice President Hubert Humphrey (right) confers with the White House Press Secretary while President Johnson was recuperating from surgery in 1965. During periods of presidential disability, the Vice President carries on his duties. (UPI photo)

dent and the principal officers of the executive departments state that he is not able to perform the duties, Congress by two-thirds vote can decide that he is disabled. These provisions were the result of anxiety over illnesses of Presidents Wilson and Eisenhower and provide for an orderly system for deciding how serious the illness of a President may be.

THE IMPLIED POWERS. The last item in Article I, Section 8, reads:

The Congress shall have the power to make all laws which shall be necessary and proper for carrying into execution the foregoing powers, and all other powers vested by this Constitution in the government of the United States, or in any department or officer thereof.

This is the famous *elastic* clause of the Constitution. This clause has been *stretched* so that Congress seems at times to have power to do anything that the majority wants done except for the specific things which Congress is told it cannot do in Article I, Section 9.

The writers of the Constitution expected that Congress would surely need to use the powers which they were specifically given if we were to have a strong national government. There were certain powers which they knew that the national government should never be allowed to use. They expected that most of the other powers would be used by the states. But the addition of new states, inventions, urbanization, and other changes have made it "necessary and proper" for Congress to use many powers which were not listed in the Constitution.

An example will illustrate this point. The Constitution states that Congress has the power "to raise and support armies; . . . to provide and maintain a navy." What about the air force? The Wright Brothers did not fly their first airplane until 1903. For more than a hundred years after the adoption of the Constitution, no one could have guessed the importance of air power in modern war. Because airplanes were not mentioned in the Constitution, should Congress not be allowed to provide an air force? Most people would think this was silly.

How can Congress legally provide an air force? Two possibilities seem reasonable.

First, it could be argued that an air force is an important part of an army and a navy, and therefore Congress has the power ʄo establish an air force as part of the army or the navy. In recent years, though, it has seemed wise to have an air force that is an equally important branch of our military defense.

Second, it could be argued that an air force is "necessary and proper," and Congress could pass any laws to establish an air force under the elastic clause.

Can Congress pass laws about television, atomic energy, streamlined trains, space flights, rainmaking? It does.

Congress today uses many powers that come from its right to do things that are "necessary and proper." These are *implied* powers. They are not stated directly in the Constitution, but they are believed to be stated indirectly.

Does this mean that Congress can do anything it pleases? Are there no limitations on Congress? Is the federal government to grow bigger and bigger? What has happened to "states' rights"? These are important questions to which we as a people have not yet found an entirely satisfactory answer.

Through the Supreme Court, political parties, Congress, the President, the executive departments, the state governments, and elections, we are working out an answer by trial and error, by discussion, by approving or disapproving specific actions. These relationships between the federal government and the states evolve within the general framework of the Constitution.

SPECIAL POWERS OF THE HOUSE. In addition to the general powers of Congress, each house of Congress has a few special powers which the other does not have. The House of Representatives has three of these special powers:

1. TO IMPEACH OFFICIALS. The House has the power to start ouster proceedings of an official by bringing an accusation, called an *impeachment*, against him. A majority vote is needed to impeach.

2. TO START REVENUE BILLS. All laws dealing with revenue—the raising of money —must *start* in the House. Tax laws, for example, must begin in the House. But since the Senate can amend the laws passed

by the House, this special power of the House is not of great public importance. It has only parliamentary significance. In actual practice the budget and tax laws are the result of much joint effort by both House and Senate.

3. To SELECT A PRESIDENT WHEN THERE IS NOT AN ELECTORAL MAJORITY. If no candidate for President receives a majority of the votes in the electoral college, the House elects a President from the three candidates with the highest votes (Amendment Twelve of the Constitution). In 1801 the House chose Jefferson as President, and in 1825 it selected John Quincy Adams as President. In this century, the possibility of having a President selected by the House has developed because of third parties. In 1948 if Dewey had defeated Truman in Ohio and Illinois, where Truman won by a combined margin of less than 50,000 votes, the election of the President would have been by the House, since the Dixiecrat, Thurmond, had carried four southern states.

SPECIAL POWERS OF THE SENATE. The Senate has four special powers:

1. To TRY IMPEACHMENT CASES. After the House has started ouster proceedings

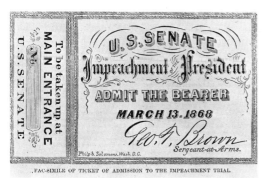

.FAC-SIMILE OF TICKET OF ADMISSION TO THE IMPEACHMENT TRIAL.

The House of Representatives has the sole power to impeach; the Senate has the sole power to try impeachments. Andrew Johnson, the only President to be impeached, was acquitted when the vote for conviction fell one short of the necessary two-thirds. (Library of Congress)

of an official by impeaching him by a majority vote, the Senate must conduct the trial. A two-thirds vote of the senators present is necessary for convicting an impeached official.

The Chief Justice of the Supreme Court presides over the Senate during the trial. The penalty is removal from office and, if the Senate desires, the official can be forbidden ever again to hold an office in the national government. In our entire history only four officials—all judges—have been removed from office by the impeachment process.

2. To SELECT A VICE PRESIDENT WHEN THERE IS NOT AN ELECTORAL MAJORITY. If no candidate for Vice President receives a majority of the votes in the electoral college, the Senate selects a Vice President from the two candidates with the highest votes. The Senate selected Vice President Richard M. Johnson in 1837.

3. To APPROVE TREATIES. Treaties are made by the President with the "advice and consent of the Senate." A two-thirds vote of the senators present at the final vote is necessary to approve the treaty.

This constitutional provision for a two-thirds vote has made it very difficult for the United States to make treaties when there is much difference of opinion about a treaty. At the end of World War I, President Woodrow Wilson had helped design the League of Nations. The Senate, however, on three different occasions did not give the two-thirds vote necessary for ratification of the League of Nations.

Some people blame our failure to join the League on party politics. Others say the fault was President Wilson's failure to get advice from the senators before the League of Nations was fully planned.

In the years since the refusal to join the League, Presidents have been more careful to consult with senators on important international affairs. Presidents have usually gotten advice from the members of the Senate Foreign Relations Committee. However, even with the best cooperation between the President and the Senate, the making of a treaty is very difficult. A small minority can prevent a treaty which most of the people may want.

In recent years there has been public discussion on the subject that the Constitution should be amended to change the treaty-making process. One proposal provides that treaties should be approved by a majority vote of the House and Senate. Such a proposal has not gotten very far, though, because the senators consider ratifying treaties as one of their great powers, and they guard it jealously.

A second proposal would merely reduce the size of the majority required in the Senate and require ratification by only a majority of those present.

A third proposal is that the Constitution be amended to provide that no provision of a treaty or other international agreement which conflicts with the Constitution shall have any force or effect. Those favoring this amendment fear that, through the United Nations or international conferences, agreements would be made that might have the effect of changing the Constitution. Those opposed fear that such an amendment would make it impossible for the executive branch to carry on international affairs. This amendment failed in 1954 by one vote to get the necessary two-thirds majority in Congress.

4. TO APPROVE APPOINTMENTS. Under the Constitution the President makes appointments to the more important governmental positions. But a majority vote of the Senate is required to approve these appointments. The effect of this procedure is to give the senators great control over political appointments.

In practice the President consults with a senator of his own party before an appointment is made in that senator's state. If the President does not appoint someone the senator wants, the other senators have adopted a neat little custom of refusing to approve the appointment. This custom, called *senatorial courtesy*, actually gives senators control over appointments in their states if they are members of the same political party as the President.

In those states where the senators are of a different party from that of the President, the President may consult with the state political leaders of his party on appointments. He is much freer to appoint a person of his own choice in these states than he is where he has to be careful of senatorial courtesy.

STUDY
QUESTIONS

1. If you visited Congress what would you expect to see and hear?

2. What problems does a new congressman face?

3. How is the number of members in the House of Representatives determined? Why, after 1910, was the number kept at 435? What is the term of office of a representative?

4. Did your state gain, lose, or keep the same number of representatives after the last census? How is the size of a congressional district determined?

5. What effects has the "one-man, one-vote" decision had on congressional districts in your state?

6. How many senators are there? What is their term of office? How many members are elected at any one election?

7. Why was the method of selecting senators changed in 1913?

8. How is Puerto Rico represented in Congress?

9. How are vacancies in the House of Representatives filled? In the Senate?

CONCEPTS AND GENERALIZATIONS

1
Congress is a bicameral legislature with a large House of Representatives and a smaller Senate.

2
While lawyers are the predominate occupational group in Congress, members come from a great variety of occupations. Most members have had previous public and military service.

3
A new congressman faces many social, political, and economic problems in order to become effective.

4
The reapportionment of the House of Representatives was an undemocratic political football until the Supreme Court made the "one-man, one-vote" rule.

5
The constitutional qualifications for Congress are minimal; the political qualifications are great.

6
In view of the importance of their positions and the personal economic problems in connection with their official positions, congressmen are not very well paid.

7
Congress has the power to discipline its members but has been reluctant to do so.

8
A Congress begins a new term on January 3 of odd-numbered years following the November elections.

9
The implied powers of Congress have become as important as the expressed powers.

10
The House of Representatives and the Senate have special powers. Those powers dealing with impeachment, selection of a President, and approval of treaties and appointments are of great importance in the conduct of government.

10. What are the constitutional qualifications for a representative? a senator?

11. How have the residence requirements for members of Congress been affected in recent years?

12. What is the *Congressional Record?*

13. Give an example of each of the eight general powers of Congress.

14. Why is the "necessary and proper" clause in the Constitution so important?

15. What are the three special powers of the House of Representatives?

16. What are the four special powers of the Senate?

17. Why does the Constitution give special privileges to congressmen?

18. Which states have more senators than representatives?

IDEAS FOR DISCUSSION

1. There have been proposals that sessions of Congress should be televised. Do you favor or oppose the televising of congressional sessions? Why? What effects would televised programs have on citizens' attitudes toward Congress?

2. Is the distribution of occupations among members of Congress satisfactory to you? Are there too many lawyers? Are there any occupations not represented in Congress that should be?

3. Congressmen are called upon to do a great many things for citizens from their districts. One congressman said, "I was elected to legislate, but I'm lucky to spend 10 per cent of my time at it. I spend the other 90 per cent giving services to my constituents." Is it wise for citizens to make so many requests of the members of Congress?

4. Are the salaries of congressmen large enough?

5. A total of 28 million words was printed in the *Congressional Record* during a recent Congress. The speeches, reports, and special articles published equaled 280 ordinary-sized books. Do you think it is desirable to have this complete record of congressional activity?

6. When a speaker says, "I now quote to you from the *Congressional Record*," to what extent should you consider such a quotation as good evidence on the subject under discussion?

7. Should more women be elected to Congress? How many members of the present Congress are women? How many members are Negroes? Should more Negroes be elected?

8. One midwestern senator reports that he receives 1,500 to 2,500 letters at his Washington office each week. To answer these letters and to help him with all his other duties, he has a staff of nine persons. Would it be wise for citizens to write him fewer letters? Should they write more letters?

9. Divide the class into groups of six or seven students each. Have each group discuss the question "Should a congressman represent his local district or the nation as a whole?" Have a spokesman for each group report the reactions to the class. Were the groups in common agreement?

10. The Senate is called a "continuing body." Why? How does this differ from the House of Representatives?

11. Should the Constitution be amended to require a representative to reside in the district which elects him?

12. The Houses of Congress have the right to decide whether a person elected to Congress shall be permitted to take office. This makes it appear that Congress can say to the people of a state, "You had no right to elect this person," and so take away their right of free choice in an election. What do you think?

THINGS TO DO

1. Plan a trip to Washington, D. C. Decide the places you would like to see, the method of transportation, the approximate cost.

2. On an outline map of the United States show the party affiliations of members of the Senate from each state. Use a different color for each party. Do the same for the House of Representatives.

3. Draw a diagram showing how congressional districts in your state might be gerrymandered.

4. Prepare a biography of your representative or of one of your two senators.

5. Have a committee examine several issues of the *Congressional Record*. Make a study of the contents, and report on the work of Congress as it is given in the *Record*.

6. Examine an issue of the *Congressional Directory* at a library, and report your findings and reactions to the class.

7. Prepare a list of the personal and political qualifications needed by a member of Congress that go beyond the constitutional qualifications.

8. Appoint a bulletin board committee to keep a "Congress" bulletin board up to date. Include pictures of important leaders, clippings from local papers, and the original work of students.

9. Investigate and report to the class on the treatment of Senator Thomas J. Dodd of Connecticut and Representative Adam Clayton Powell by the Ninetieth Congress.

10. Investigate and report on the Congressional reapportionment issue as it affects your state.

FURTHER READINGS

Bailey, Stephen K., THE NEW CONGRESS. St. Martin's Press, Inc., 1966.

Baker, Benjamin, and Friedelbaum, Stanley H., GOVERNMENT IN THE UNITED STATES. Houghton Mifflin Co., 1966. Chapter 11.

Baker, Gordon, THE REAPPORTIONMENT REVOLUTION. Random House, Inc., 1965.

Burns, James M., and Peltason, J. W., GOVERNMENT BY THE PEOPLE. Prentice-Hall, Inc., 1972. Chapter 16.

Drury, Allen, A SENATE JOURNAL 1943-45. McGraw-Hill Book Co., Inc., 1963.

Ferguson, John H., and McHenry, Dean E., THE AMERICAN SYSTEM OF GOVERNMENT. McGraw-Hill Book Co., Inc., 1967. Chapter 13.

Griffith, Ernest S., CONGRESS: ITS CONTEMPORARY ROLE. New York University Press, 1962.

Jewell, Malcom E., and Patterson, Samuel C., THE LEGISLATIVE PROCESS IN THE UNITED STATES. Random House, Inc., 1966.

Kennedy, John F., PROFILES IN COURAGE. Pocket Books, Inc., 1964. (Paperback edition)

Miller, Clem, MEMBER OF THE HOUSE: LETTERS OF A CONGRESSMAN. Charles Scribner's Sons, 1962. (Paperback edition)

National Council for the Social Studies, JUDGMENT-CASE STUDY NO. 2, CONGRESSIONAL REAPPORTIONMENT. The Council, 1965. (Paperback edition)

Riegle, Donald, and Armbrister, Traver, O., CONGRESS. Doubleday & Co., Inc., 1972.

White, William S., CITADEL: THE STORY OF THE U.S. SENATE. Harper & Row, Publishers, Inc., 1957.

Wilcox, Francis O., CONGRESS AND FOREIGN POLICY. Harper & Row, Publishers, Inc., 1971.

CLOTURE—a procedure by which debate can be ended in the United States Senate.

CONFERENCE COMMITTEE—a special joint committee from both houses of a legislature that attempts to make bills alike.

CONGRESSIONAL RECORD—the official publication containing a complete daily account of all the business conducted by Congress.

FILIBUSTER—a scheme whereby one senator, or a small group of senators, may talk against a bill for so long that all business of the Senate is stopped.

IMMUNITY—freedom; to be free from arrest for a crime.

JUNKETS—pleasure trips; disguised vacations.

LOGROLLING—a legislative practice of trading votes; an informal agreement between two legislators to vote for each other's bills.

PARLIAMENTARIAN—an expert in the rules and customs of a legislative body.

PIGEONHOLING—a method of defeating a bill by keeping it in a committee.

POCKET VETO—the defeating of a bill by the executive refusing to sign it at the end of a legislative session.

PRO TEMPORE—temporary; for the time being.

REFERRAL—the passing along or forwarding of something; the sending of a bill by the presiding officer to a committee.

RIDER—a bill which might not pass by itself attached as an amendment to a bill which is sure to pass.

SENIORITY—a system of choosing committee chairmen and members on the basis of length of service.

SPEAKER—the presiding officer of the House of Representatives.

VETO—the refusal of an executive to sign a bill; the action of the President, governor, or mayor in not approving an act passed by Congress, a state legislature, or a city council.

WHIP—a leader of the party in Congress or other legislature who has responsibility for getting members to vote.

THE LANGUAGE OF GOVERNMENT

Point out how a filibuster can be defeated in the Senate by cloture if sixteen members sign a petition and two days later two-thirds of the Senators vote for it. (Refer to pages 210-211.)

10

The Work of Congress

One lone United States senator had been speaking for a long time. He was very tired. His doctor urged his wife to beg him to stop speaking for the sake of his health, but he spoke on hour after hour. He was determined that a civil rights bill would not pass until he had demonstrated his opposition to the bill. Other senators favoring the bill had the votes to pass it when he stopped speaking.

After twenty-four hours and eighteen minutes he did stop and the 1957 civil rights bill was passed. During those long hours, he twice yielded the floor to another senator who had agreed to give it back to him after he returned from the restroom.

A few times he had a quick chance to get his breath when he would permit another senator to ask a question. Now and then he sipped a little orange juice. Sometimes while speaking he would gulp tiny pieces of bread. A few times he took bites of cooked hamburger. But hour after hour he talked. Sometimes he would pace up and down to try to rest his tired, aching legs. He could not sit down because Senate rules require that the speaker remain on his feet. During the night only three persons were in the Senate gallery: his wife, an unknown man who snored softly, and the official representative of the NAACP.

What did he talk about? Things that had interested him as a public servant for many years. At one stage he read the election laws of each of the then forty-eight states. Finally, at nine o'clock in the morning, the senator while not yet exhausted stopped speaking.

He had dramatized southern opposition to a civil rights bill. He had set a new record for the longest *filibuster* by one senator, exceeding the old record by one hour and fifty-two minutes. The new champion was Senator Strom Thurmond, then a Democrat, of South Carolina.

The privilege of unlimited freedom of debate is almost sacred to senators. They look upon the Senate as the only place left in the world where there is complete freedom of speech. Here one senator or a small group can "talk a bill to death." In one civil rights battle, southern senators organized into three platoons, each platoon holding the floor of the Senate for eight hours.

By means of the filibuster a minority can defeat the will of the majority. Talking is only one of the weapons of the filibuster; roll calls, points of order, quorum calls, and useless amendments are also tools employed by those engaged in a filibuster.

The filibuster has been used against a communications satellite bill, an off-shore oil well bill, a treaty-making amendment, a right-to-work amendment to the Taft-Hartley Act, home rule for Washington, D. C., and several appropriation bills. For the past quarter of a century, however, the filibuster has been the final weapon of

southern senators opposed to civil rights and voting rights bills which would give Negroes their guaranteed rights as citizens. In simple form the history of this period has been that the President would request a civil rights bill, the House of Representatives would pass it, and if the bill came close to passage in the Senate the bill would be defeated by the filibuster. Not until 1964 and 1965 did the Senate end the filibusters and get these laws passed without damaging compromises. Previously filibusters or the threat of a filibuster had resulted in weakening the bills.

In the workings of Congress the issue of unlimited debate in the Senate has come in direct conflict with the rights guaranteed minorities in the Bill of Rights.

PROBLEMS OF CONGRESS

Freedom of debate is only one of the problems encountered in getting

Senator Strom Thurmond points to a clock in the Capitol early in the morning during his record-breaking filibuster against the 1957 civil rights bill. He had yielded to a colleague to get a short break. (UPI photo)

the congressional work done. Another problem is which of the thousands of proposed laws, presented at every session of Congress, should receive the most careful consideration. How can so many laws receive adequate attention?

Who will take the time and have the knowledge and experience to study each law with great care? In one session, Congress passed laws which resulted in the spending of more than 100 billion dollars. Other laws that were passed concerned very complex industrial problems. Can a congressman learn enough about each law to vote wisely?

Still another problem is: How can a large legislative body be divided into small groups to get work done? The Senate has 100 members; the House, 435 members. It is harder for a large group to get things done than it is for a small group. Can a

fair method be used to divide up the work of Congress? One of the difficult problems is that of getting information. Should congressmen rely on lobbyists? How can they get more information from the executive branch? Should congressional committees do more of their own investigating? Can these investigations be carried on without destroying rights of individual citizens?

The problem of the ethics of congressmen arises from time to time. Should congressman be required to reveal publicly their sources of income? Should Congress be stricter in its discipline? Can the public be assured of a high level of honesty among the members of Congress?

To solve these and other lawmaking problems, Congress has employed five general procedures: (1) selecting capable leaders, (2) organizing through political parties, (3) establishing rules, (4) using committees, and (5) providing expert help and services.

Women are taking an increasingly important part in Congress. Shown are congresswomen in the Congressional Ladies' Reading Room. (National Geographic Society Photographer. Courtesy U.S. Capitol Historical Society)

SELECTING LEADERS   Groups as large as the House of Representatives and the Senate must rely upon persons in leadership positions for efficiency of operation. The presiding officers, the floor leaders, the party whips, and the committee chairmen are mainly responsible for the quality and quantity of legislation.

Between the November election and the January 3 opening of a new Congress, politicians, commentators, and many other citizens are very much interested in who will be the new leaders of the Congress. Under the Constitution, the Vice President will be the presiding officer of the Senate. But who will be the Speaker of the House? Who will be the floor leader for the Democrats? For the Republicans? Who will be their chief assistants? These leaders will

Emphasize the impossible job that congressmen have with respect to knowledge about every piece of proposed legislation.

A convenience for members of Congress and their visitors is this subway, which runs from the Senate and new House offices to the Capitol. (George F. Mobley, National Geographic. Courtesy U.S. Capitol Historical Society)

determine much of the success of the Congress. They will get national recognition.

Before Congress starts, each political party holds separate meetings, called *caucuses,* of its members in the House and in the Senate to decide who shall be named for these leadership jobs. A member is expected to vote in Congress according to the decision made in the caucus.

THE SPEAKER. Later, when the House of Representatives holds its first meeting, the Speaker is formally elected. Each party names the candidate selected in its caucus. The party with the majority, of course, gets its man elected.

The Speaker is a very powerful person. Years ago the Speaker of the House was almost a dictator of legislation. Under strong-willed Speakers the wishes even of the majority of the House could be defeated. In recent years the power of the Speaker has been reduced, but he still has

great power. Three features of his power are: (1) his role as the presiding officer, (2) his power of referral to committees, and (3) his parliamentary decisions. Intertwined with and supporting these, of course, is the strength he gets as the leader of the majority party in the House.

PRESIDING OFFICER. As with all presiding officers, he has the duty to keep order and to decide which member shall be granted the right to speak. Because he is a political party leader, the members expect the Speaker to give key members of his own party the chance to be heard in any crucial situation. He does not have to give all persons who wish to speak this opportunity, as is the case with most chairmen of discussion groups in school or adult life; but he tries to be reasonable and fair to all members regardless of their party.

REFERRAL. A second important power of the Speaker is the power to send proposed laws to a proper committee. This power of referral gives him much control over the final outcome of a bill. He knows the membership of each committee and how the committee members are likely to vote.

A bill on workmen's compensation, for example, might seem logically to be a proper one to send to the House Committee on Education and Labor. But, if this bill calls for spending money, it might be sent to the Committee on Appropriations. If taxes will be required to pay the costs, the bill might instead be sent to the Ways and Means Committee which considers the ways and means of financing government. Where will the Speaker send the bill? Usually to the committee which he thinks would treat the bill the way he wants it treated.

PARLIAMENTARY DECISIONS. A third power of the Speaker comes from the many parliamentary decisions which he has to make. Each Speaker is aided by an expert *parlia-*

The Speaker of the House of Representatives Carl Albert is being sworn in. Seated in front of him are official reporters for Congress. The Sergeant at Arms is standing at the right of the Speaker. (UPI photo)

mentarian whom he asks for advice. In the usual routine of deciding whether there were more ayes than noes, whether a member of Congress is out of order, and what is the proper order of business, the Speaker's decisions tend to be final. These decisions help to move a bill closer to becoming a law, or they prevent further action.

A Speaker does not abuse these powers. He could not for long periods keep members of the minority from speaking. The members of his own party would object to such unfairness. So he strives to be fair. He is rightfully proud of his position. He wants Congress to be efficient. Yet the Speaker is a party leader and knows that party success depends upon getting the party ideas written into the nation's laws. Sometimes, therefore, the Speaker feels he must use his powers in ways that will help get important laws passed. The powerful Speakers have been men greatly honored

for their distinguished service to their country. Among these would be Henry Clay, James K. Polk, Thomas B. Reed, Joseph G. (Uncle Joe) Cannon, Champ Clark, Nicholas Longworth, Joseph W. Martin, and Sam Rayburn. For twenty-one years, from 1940 to 1961, Democrat Rayburn of Texas and Republican Martin of Massachusetts alternated as Speaker, as their respective parties had a majority in the House. During that period Martin was Speaker from 1947 to 1949 and from 1953 to 1955. In the other seventeen years Rayburn was Speaker. After his death, Democrat John McCormack of Massachusetts was selected Speaker and served from 1962 to his retirement in 1971.

THE VICE PRESIDENT. In the Senate the Vice President is the presiding officer, but he does not have as great power as the Speaker. Sometimes his party is not the majority party in the Senate. Sometimes he is not an important political person

The presiding officer of the Senate is the Vice President. This is a rare photograph because Senate rules ordinarily forbid taking pictures in the Senate Chamber. (George F. Mobley, National Geographic. Courtesy U.S. Capitol Historical Society)

even in his own party. He is usually, therefore, a fair and just chairman who tries to help the Senate be "the greatest deliberative body in the world." In the Senate, he has the title of President of the Senate.

The Vice President does have one power that at times is very important. He has a vote in case of a tie. Several times in the history of the Senate this vote has been crucial. One Vice President was not in the Senate to vote on one tied measure with the result that his party did not get the law passed.

Some Vice Presidents have had great influence on the Senate. This influence came about because the person had great political experience and power rather than because he was the presiding officer.

Recent Presidents have tended to assign their Vice Presidents important executive responsibilities, which has increased their influence but keeps them away from the Senate more often. Vice Presidents who have previously been senators have considerable influence because of their knowledge of other senators and the traditions of the institution. Vice President Alben W. Barkley of Kentucky served in the House of Representatives from 1913 to 1927 and then was a senator from 1927 until his election to the vice presidency in 1949. He was very influential and exceedingly popular. He was nicknamed the "Veep"—a term which his grandchildren were supposed to have called him—a word that has become part of our language as a substitute for Vice President.

The *President pro tempore* is elected by the Senate to preside during the frequent absences of the Vice President or when there is a vacancy in the office. The President "pro tem" is always chosen from the majority party of the Senate.

These engravings of (above) the House of Representatives and (below) the Senate Chamber were made about 1850. Although some modifications have been made, the basic rules of Congress are the same now as they were then. (Library of Congress)

FLOOR LEADERS. Each party in each house, through the party caucuses, selects floor leaders. These majority and minority floor leaders are the managers of the legislative programs of their parties. Each has a special desk near the front of the legislative chamber. The job of the floor leader is to get the party's laws passed and to keep the other party's laws from being passed. The majority leader, when the party in control is the party of the President, is really a kind of legislative campaign manager for the President. He tries very hard to get the laws passed that the President wants to have passed.

The two floor leaders try to reach agreements on the amount of time to be given to debate on a proposed law. They decide which members of their party are to speak on the law and the amount of time a speaker is to have. They manage the parliamentary moves by which one party tries to win over the other in the legislative strategy.

PARTY WHIPS. Assisting the floor leaders are "four men with strong legs," as one journalist described the party whips. Each party in each house has one member whose job is to keep track of all the members of the party and to get those members to the floor whenever their vote is needed. The whip has to know where the members are every day and almost every hour. If an important vote is to be called, the whip tells the members when the vote is likely to be held. Each whip is helped by about a dozen members who aid in the job of keeping in close touch with the other members.

The usual procedure at the end of each week is for the whip to send a *whip notice* to all members of his party. This notice tells what the day-to-day legislative business will be for the coming week. He may inform them in the notice that on Wednesday a vote will be held on a bill which the party leaders think must be passed. His assistants with checking sheets make a *whip check* by which they find out who is voting for the bill, who is voting against the bill, and who remains uncertain.

Within three or four hours the whip knows what the chances are for the bill to pass. Then, he has the weekend, Monday, and Tuesday to try to convince those who are uncertain to vote for the bill and to change the "no" votes to "yes" votes. On Wednesday his job is to get all of his members on the floor for the actual vote.

Because of debates and amendments he cannot be sure of the exact time when the vote will take place, but a roll call takes about forty-five minutes, and after the roll call absent members are called again. While the roll is being taken, the whip and his assistants "use their legs" and get members to the floor to vote.

To get the one vote that may mean victory for a bill, men have been called away from conferences with the President, roused at night from sleep, and have been carried in on stretchers from hospitals.

COMMITTEE CHAIRMEN. The other important leaders in the Congress are the chairmen of the committees which will be discussed below. At this point it is only important to note that these chairmen have leadership and power. A chairman can under most conditions decide which bills will be discussed in the committee. He schedules the times for discussing the bills. When the bill is taken before the House or Senate, he is responsible for leading the debate on the bill. He appoints the subcommittees that carry on investigations as well as study of special features of bills. A good idea of the importance of committee chairmen can be gained from the fact that when the President invites party leaders to the White House he includes key committee chairmen.

ORGANIZING THROUGH POLITICAL PARTIES

Since congressional leaders are chosen by party members in party caucuses, the major control of Congress is through political parties. The majority party really determines the quality and the output of the Congress. This party because it has the most votes holds the key positions. The leaders can determine which bills will come to a vote and when the vote will be held. If the members of the majority party vote together, based on the decisions reached in the party caucus, they can always get their bills passed.

MINORITY CRITICISM. The minority party, never having enough votes to pass a law, can argue, criticize, and suggest amendments, but the laws ordinarily get passed because the majority party wants them. This power to criticize is, however, a very important power. Much of the effectiveness of our form of government depends upon the minority party's constantly searching for flaws in the work of the party in power.

The searchlight of criticism reveals weaknesses that might be harmful to the nation. A representative government gains much of its strength from sincere, patriotic accusations and judgments of the minority party.

A visitor to Congress can recognize the organization by political parties in the seating arrangements of the House and Senate. As one looks down from the visitors' gallery in either house the Democrats are seated on the left. On the right are the Republicans. An aisle divides the two parties, with the floor leaders and the whips having desks to the left and right.

CROSSING PARTY LINES. In spite of the power of the party caucus and the pleadings of the floor leaders and whips, party members do not always vote together. In addition to being party members, senators and representatives are first of all representatives of the people "back home." They vote the way those people or interest groups, which support them, desire as often as they honestly can. The social and economic conditions in their section of the country may be of more importance on a particular issue than party loyalty.

Always, too, there are some members of Congress who have sincere convictions about special issues. These men will not violate these convictions by voting against their own honest beliefs, in spite of their loyalty to their party, to the people, or to the interest groups. Thus on nearly every bill before Congress some Democrats vote with Republicans and some Republicans with Democrats.

It is this independence of the legislators which requires the whips to have "strong legs." In spite of all their running around, tracking down members, and arguing for votes, they cannot be sure of the way each party member will vote until the vote has been cast.

ESTABLISHING RULES

The Constitution (Article I, Section 5) gives each house the right to:

- *judge the elections, returns, and qualifications of its members.*
- *determine the rules of its proceedings.*
- *punish its members for disorderly conduct.*
- *expel a member by a two-thirds vote.*
- *keep a journal of its proceedings.*
- *record the votes of each member if one-fifth of the members present desire it.*

Based on these provisions, each House has created a set of rules for the conduct of business.

THE HOUSE RULES. The rules of the House of Representatives, because it is larger, are more complicated and stricter than those of the Senate. Otherwise this large group could get little work done. House rules provide for a regular order of business for each day, but allow exceptions to the regular order by unanimous consent or by a special order from the Rules Committee. No member of the House may speak for more than one hour without unanimous consent. By majority vote the time allowed for debate can be limited. Visitors to the House notice that it is common practice to allow "the Honorable Congressman from Pennsylvania two minutes to be followed by the Honorable Congressman from New Mexico for three minutes."

The original rules of the House were written by Thomas Jefferson in a *Manual of Parliamentary Practice*. Today there are more rules and they are more complicated. Each new House of Representatives may adopt its own rules, but customarily the rules of the previous House are approved with few if any changes.

To the average citizen these rules seem complicated. For the new member of the House they require study, just as the rules of football or basketball require study by players. As in athletic contests, the rules are important because they keep the game orderly. Under these rules, members of Congress have been declared ineligible; they have been expelled—just as happens now and then to school athletes.

THE SENATE RULES. The Senate rules are simpler than those of the House because there are fewer members and there is less regulation of speech-making. Since the Senate is a continuing body, unlike the House, the rules continue from one Congress to another unless amended. Senators believe that courtesy and mutual respect are more important than complicated rules. The most discussed rule of the Senate is a rule which provides a way to end filibus-

BERRY'S WORLD

"I'll have to hang up now—daddy is invoking the 'cloture rule.'"

Jim Berry; reprinted by permission of NEA.

ters, such as the lengthy one of Senator Thurmond.

CLOTURE. Senate Rule 22 can be used to prevent endless talking as a way of defeating a bill. It provides that if at least sixteen senators sign a petition asking that no senator be allowed to speak more than one hour, then two days later the issue of limiting speeches to one hour must be voted on in the Senate. If two-thirds of the senators *present and voting* favor the rule, further debate on the bill before the Senate is limited to one hour per senator. This *cloture* rule was adopted in 1917 and was last amended in 1959. It has been used successfully twelve times. In 1964, it was used to end a filibuster on civil rights for the first time in history. From 1938 to 1964, cloture on civil rights was defeated eleven times. It was used in 1965 on the

Describe what is meant by the statement that the Senate is a continuing body.

Voting Rights Act, in 1968 on the Open Housing—Civil Rights Act, and in 1972 to give enforcement power on employment discrimination. The other eight cases in which the Senate ended debate by cloture were: 1919—the Versailles Treaty; 1926—joining the World Court; 1927—a branch banking bill; 1927—a prohibition bill; 1962—the Communications Satellite bill; twice in 1971 to extend the military draft; and 1972 on the arms treaty with Russia.

USING COMMITTEES

The work of Congress is done largely through committees. No one can understand Congress or members of Congress without knowing the fundamental importance of the committees. The fate of any idea is decided in committee. The reputations of members of Congress are determined primarily by the committees to which they are appointed and the kind of work they do on the committees.

Speeches made in Congress look nice when printed in the *Congressional Record*. Congressional debates and parliamentary strategy are exciting, but the important work of Congress is done by a committee's careful study of bills plus the give and take in the necessary compromises that are made by committee members.

THE IMPORTANCE OF COMMITTEES. The importance of committees is illustrated by noting that a member of Congress' legislative day is divided roughly into two parts. Mornings are used for committee work. Afternoons are the time for meetings of the House and Senate.

The reason for committees is easily understood. With thousands of proposed laws presented to Congress each year, it is impossible for the entire membership of each house to study and discuss the bills. As our country grew, the work of Congress

and the size of Congress increased. It was natural, therefore, to create committees as a way of dividing up the work.

THE NUMBER OF COMMITTEES. By the end of World War II critics of Congress were saying that there were too many committees. The system had grown to the point where there were too many separate working groups. There were too many pieces; no one was looking at the total product.

In 1946, after careful study by some of the ablest men in and out of Congress, the Legislative Reorganization Act was passed. Among other things this act reduced the number of congressional committees from eighty-one to thirty-four. Today the House has twenty-one regular committees and the Senate has seventeen. The size of these committees varies from seven to fifty-five members.

THE REGULAR COMMITTEES. The regular committees of Congress are:

HOUSE COMMITTEES
Agriculture
Appropriations
Armed Services
Banking and Currency
District of Columbia
Education and Labor
Foreign Affairs
Government Operations
House Administration
Interior and Insular Affairs
Internal Security
Interstate and Foreign Commerce
Judiciary
Merchant Marine and Fisheries
Post Office and Civil Service
Public Works
Rules
Science and Astronautics
Standards of Official Conduct
Veterans Affairs
Ways and Means

COMMITTEE MEMBERSHIPS. Memberships on some committees are more highly prized by members of Congress than memberships on other committees. How are these valuable positions distributed? Who decides to which committees a member of Congress shall be appointed? These decisions are made by the party caucus. The parties are free to decide in their own ways how their committee members shall be named.

The present system is that each party in each house uses a kind of nominating committee to suggest names to the caucus. The caucus usually approves these nominations, and when the names are submitted to the houses the names are almost automatically approved.

The Republicans in the House of Representatives use a Committee on Committees

A Joint Senate-House Economic Committee hearing is chaired by Senator William Proxmire of Wisconsin. The witness and his consultants are at the table facing the Congressmen. Spectators are seated behind them. (EPA Newsphoto/Editorial Photocolor Archives)

as the nominating group. There is one committee member from each state having a Republican representative. A committee member has as many votes for nominations as there are Republican representatives from his state.

The Democratic representatives use the Democratic members of the powerful Ways and Means Committee as their nominating committee.

In the Senate the Republicans name a special Committee on Committees to nominate the slate of committee members. The Democrats use a Steering Committee headed by the majority leader.

SENIORITY. One might imagine that the party leaders give the most careful thought to the qualifications of those nominated for the various committees. For the assignment of a new member this is true. The future of the party, and certainly the destiny of the new members, may be determined by these first committee assignments.

In the House a representative is limited to service on one committee, while in the Senate members may serve on two committees. Exceptions to these general rules are not uncommon.

After the initial placement on a committee, the most important factor in the operation of committees is *seniority*. By this practice the committee member of the majority party who has served longest on a committee is made the chairman. If a member has the highest seniority on two committees, the tradition is that he shall be allowed to decide which chairmanship he wants. He cannot be chairman of more than one committee.

When a vacancy occurs on a committee, because of death, failure to be re-elected, or a resignation from the committee, the nominating committees for each party get requests for assignment to the more powerful committees from members with greater seniority in Congress. Based on ability, length of service, and party loyalty, these requests are honored; but the member who changes to a new committee starts as a *new* member of that committee. His seniority does not carry over from the previous committee.

In actual practice, then, the nominations for committee assignments determine who among the *new* members will be selected for those committees which are least popular among the members with previous service. For these new persons the first step up the ladder to power and greatness may be started by membership on such a committee.

CRITICISMS OF SENIORITY. Is this seniority method wise? Some critics of Congress think it is not. The 1946 *Reorganization of Congress Report* recommended elimination of the seniority rule and substitution of choice by qualification and merit. Since each congressman thinks he has good general qualifications and considerable merit, such a procedure might be difficult to work out. Most important of all, the members who have been in Congress the longest time and have the most power have not been friendly towards giving up a system by which they get rewards.

The chief advantage of the seniority rule is that committee members who remain in Congress do become thoroughly familiar with the subjects that come before their committees. By remaining on one committee for many years, the chairman usually is exceedingly well informed about the work of the committee.

Some results of the seniority system, however, do seem absurd. President Johnson with the apparent approval of the majority party, for example, was pressing forward with the war in Vietnam. Yet the chairman of the Foreign Relations Committee, Senator Fulbright, was opposed to the conduct of

ON ELECTING A CONGRESSMAN

A man must learn to be a Representative or Senator, just as he must learn to be a farmer, carpenter, blacksmith, merchant, engineer, lawyer, doctor, preacher, teacher or anything else. The best plan for a constituency to pursue is to select a man of good sense, good habits, and perfect integrity, young enough to learn, and re-elect him so long as he retains his faculties and is faithful to his trust.

—CHAMP CLARK, Speaker of the House (1911-1919).

the war. He really was chairman because in election after election he had been returned to Congress by people who favored him. Yet he was in disagreement with the President and leaders of his party.

Similarly, it seems unwise for a well-educated farmer not to be placed on the Agriculture Committee because he has less seniority than a member who cares little about farming. And should any member get seniority benefits if he has been a poor committee member?

One of the worst effects of the seniority system has been in the area of civil rights. Southern Democratic congressmen, with a segregationist tradition, have been re-elected from their one-party districts again and again. Under the seniority system, whenever there is a Democratic majority, they control the chairmanships of key committees. In the Ninety-second Congress (1972), for example, twelve of the seventeen Senate committees were headed by Senators from the South or border states. In the House, twelve of the twenty-one committees had chairmen from these southern-oriented states. In 1967 eleven senators, all from the South, voted against the appointment of a Negro, Thurgood Marshall, to the Supreme Court. Five of these senators were chairmen of committees. Because of the control over key positions in Congress, the

importance of registration and vote of Negroes and other minority groups is crucial if this dominance by the South is to be ended.

PARTY MEMBERSHIP. By a kind of gentlemen's agreement, both parties are represented on all committees roughly in proportion to their memberships in Congress. For example, if two-thirds of the members of the House are Republicans, the Republicans will take two-thirds of the memberships on the committees and leave one-third of the memberships for the Democrats.

PROVIDING EXPERT HELP AND SERVICES   A member of Congress is a very busy person, with difficult work to do and not enough hours in the day to get

The main reading room of the Library of Congress in Washington, D.C., with its extensive card catalogs, is a vast storehouse of information where members of Congress and other citizens may do research. (Library of Congress)

his work done. Sometimes it seems he needs to know more than one person can possibly know. This means that the member must be given expert help. This help comes in two forms: (1) Help given by the government. (2) Help given by those outside the government.

AID BY THE GOVERNMENT. The help given to Congress is very small in terms of the volume of work and the great responsibilities of congressmen. Business, labor, and farm leaders as far back as 1945 signed a plea that Congress spend more money to provide necessary help. While it is true that each member of Congress has an office staff, as does each committee, more help is needed.

At present there are *Legislative Counsels* (lawyers) for the House and the Senate to help members or committees write proposed laws in the proper legal language. There is a *Congressional Research Service* which gathers information and makes it available to the members and their staffs. Attached to this service are well-informed specialists in many fields. The Congressional Research Service is a department of the Library of Congress.

In addition to the administrative assistants and other help given each member of Congress to operate his office, committees are staffed with experts and provided with secretarial and clerical help. The original intention was that a permanent professional staff be built up to do the expert research required by the committees. Shifts in party control of Congress, however, have resulted in some political changes in these professional staffs. In recent Congresses there have been struggles to give the minority party a chance to select some members among these professionals. More than one thousand persons are employed to aid the committees.

Clerks, messengers, page boys, guards,

Senator Mike Mansfield confers with a member of his secretarial staff in his office. Because of the great volume of work, each senator must have a staff of assistants to provide expert help. (George F. Mobley, National Geographic. Courtesy U.S. Capitol Historical Society)

shorthand reporters, janitors, guides, and a host of other employees are needed to serve the Congress. The annual budget for Congress is growing and in recent years has been over 200 million dollars.

Some experts feel there is need for more special research work and insist that Congress should have more independent staff investigators. These political scientists believe that congressmen should not rely so greatly upon reports received either from executive departments or from nongovernmental sources. In Congress knowledge is powerful. The better the information and the better the understanding of the members of Congress, the more effective will their work be.

AID FROM NONGOVERNMENTAL SOURCES. Congressmen get help from

The term "lobby" comes from the fact that in the past people who wished to influence a legislator waited in a lobby, or anteroom, outside the legislative chamber. Shown here is the lobby outside the Senate Chamber. (George F. Mobley, National Geographic. Courtesy U.S. Capitol Historical Society)

many people outside the government. Washington is the headquarters for many of the interest groups in American life which are trying to influence laws that Congress might pass. These *lobbyists* do their work so well that some writers have called them "the third house" of Congress.

There are good lobbies and bad lobbies. There are proper methods of lobbying and there are improper methods of lobbying. The lobbyist who offers a lawmaker a bribe is committing a crime and deserves severe punishment. But the lobbyist who spends many hours digging out some important facts on how a law will affect the interest group that he represents is giving a useful service.

Under our representative form of government, citizens have the right to express their points of view. Lobbyists help in this process by getting points of view before the members of Congress.

THE CONTROL OF LOBBYISTS. Because the activities of lobbyists are sometimes helpful but sometimes harmful and because sometimes they are secret while other times they are open for public exami-

nation, Congress has tried to control lobbying. In 1946, as part of the Legislative Reorganization Act, a Regulation of Lobbying section was included. Under this law all lobbyists must register with the clerk of the House of Representatives. They must furnish the following information: name of employer; length of employment; amount of salary, including any expense accounts; the way funds are received and spent; and the proposed legislation they are employed to support or oppose.

When these measures were adopted some lobbyists were reluctant to register, although most did. The law has been tested several times in the Supreme Court. In 1954, in the case of *United States* v. *Harriss,* the Supreme Court rejected the plea that the law violated freedom of speech, freedom of the press, and freedom of petition. Chief Justice Warren in his written opinion stated that Congress merely wanted to know "who is being hired, who is putting up the money, and how much."

Although the law is vaguely worded and has some loopholes, many organizations report each year. At present more than 4,000

Have a committee summarize the lobby reports based on the *Congressional Quarterly* findings.

lobbyists have registered in Washington. However, no federal officer or agency is responsible for checking the accuracy or completeness of the reports filed. The reports of those filing are given in the *Congressional Record* and summarized in the magazine *Congressional Quarterly*. In a 1966 congressional committee report it was recommended that the present Lobbying Act be strengthened in four ways:

1. To require registration of individuals and organizations who influence legislation as a "substantial purpose" instead of limiting registration to those with *direct* contact with Congress.

2. To require more complete reporting of expenditures for influencing legislation.

3. To transfer to the General Accounting Office the responsibility for receiving reports and keeping records.

4. To require listing of special fees used for purposes of influencing legislation.

Congress has not acted favorably on any of these recommendations. The intensity and efficiency of lobbying has not been diminished by the present regulations, but the public is somewhat better informed than before the passage of the 1946 act.

A LAW IS PASSED

The leaders, the parties, the rules, the committees, and the expert help, which have been discussed, are all finally concerned with the passage of laws. Lawmaking is the main job of Congress. How are laws made? This question can be answered in highly complicated ways. A fairly simple ten-step process containing the essentials is as follows:

1. INTRODUCING A BILL. A member of the House introduces a proposed law by dropping it into a box on the desk of the clerk in the House. A senator introduces a proposed law by announcing orally

What is the cartoonist implying about the motives of lobbyists? (Fitzpatrick in the St. Louis Post-Dispatch)

to the Senate that he wishes to do so. From the time the document is introduced until it becomes a law, it is called a *bill.*

The bill can be introduced by one or by several members. The bill may have been written by a legislator with the help of the Legislative Counsel, it may have been prepared by lobbyists, or it may have been prepared by someone in the executive branch of the government. Regardless of who actually wrote the bill, a member of

Since 1971 girls can be appointed Congressional pages. Shown here are four Senate pages. (UPI photo)

Discuss the points at which individual citizens, lobbyists, and interest groups can influence the law making process.

Congress must introduce it. Some 20,000 bills are introduced in each Congress. On the opening day of a recent Congress 2,468 bills were introduced.

2. *SENDING THE BILL TO A COMMITTEE.* The presiding officer (Speaker or Vice President) refers the bill to a committee after giving the bill a number. In most cases, of course, the clerk with the advice of the parliamentarian takes care of routine referrals, but in borderline cases or with bills of great importance the presiding officer will make the final decision. In other cases the clerk is only acting for the presiding officer, who really has the authority.

In the House the number of the bill is preceded by the letters *H.R.* In the Senate the letter *S.* precedes the number. The title of the bill is printed in the *Journal*[1] and in the *Congressional Record*, which becomes the "first reading."

3. *THE COMMITTEE HEARING.* Since only 10-15 per cent of the bills introduced will ever become laws, the committee must begin the process of deciding whether the bill is worthy of becoming a law. The chairman and the committee may quickly decide that the bill is not a good one. Without spending much time they may let the bill *die in committee.* In this case the bill is usually never heard of again.

If the committee decides to study the bill, the bill will usually be assigned to a subcommittee. The subcommittee may let the bill die, or it may after careful study give a favorable report to the whole committee. The subcommittee and the whole committee may hold hearings on the bill. Witnesses may be invited to express opinions about the bill. It is at this point that interest groups and lobbyists formally present their views. Both those in favor and those opposed to the bill are heard. The committee strives to get expert information. Public meetings may be held, but the committee can hold secret meetings.

As a result of this study and discussion, the committee may decide to report the bill back to the House or Senate, or it may decide to keep the bill in committee until the session of Congress is over, which of course defeats the bill for that session.

This delaying device is called *pigeonholing*—a term borrowed from the small compartments used for filing papers in an old-fashioned desk. The bill is pigeonholed usually because it has some powerful political supporters. Committee members do not want to give a favorable report on the bill, but they keep the bill for *additional study.* Studying can take a long time! The supporters of the bill can be assured that the bill is getting attention, but nothing ever happens. Thus the bill does not become a law, but the displeasure of some interest group may be avoided.

Could pigeonholing be used to prevent the passage of a very good law? This has happened, for the power of a committee is almost autocratic. Especially in the case of bills affecting Negroes or other minority groups, some method of getting a bill from a committee dominated by a southern segregationist chairman is essential. So each house has a *discharge rule* by which a majority may vote to have a bill returned from a committee for action by the entire body. But this discharge action is used very rarely; very few bills are ever taken from a committee.

4. *THE COMMITTEE REPORT.* After the committee has held its hearings and has studied the bill, it reports its findings to Congress. The report of the committee may take several forms. The report could be an unfavorable one—the committee may not

---

[1] Each house keeps a *Journal* which contains a brief and accurate report of the daily proceedings.

like the bill but for some reason feels that Congress should have a chance to consider the bill. This happens rarely, but once in a while a committee returns a bill with the report that it does not favor its passage.

The committee can report the bill back with a favorable report. This happens more frequently than an unfavorable report, but it also is not too frequent an occurrence.

Usually the bill is reported back with amendments, or a new bill is substituted. As the committee studies the bill and collects information about it, parts are found that need changing. In such cases the committee will make the necessary amendments and report the bill as amended.

Substituting a new bill takes place when the committee feels that the original bill really needs to be completely rewritten. In such cases the ideas of the original bill were probably good, but the committee feels that the wording should have been worked out more carefully.

Since bills are considered in both the Senate and the House, it may happen that, at about the same time, one house may have passed a bill more quickly than the other house. When this happens, it may be that the house which has not yet passed the bill will find it more efficient to substitute the other house's bill for the one being considered.

5. THE CALENDARS AND THE DEBATE. When the committee has reported on the bill, it is placed on a calendar of the House or the Senate, whichever house of Congress is considering the bill. A calendar is merely a schedule showing the order in which bills have been reported from the committees.

As bills are reported by committees they actually are sorted and placed on different calendars. In the House the *Union Calendar* receives bills on revenue, appropriations, and public property. The *House Calendar* receives all other "public" bills, that is, general laws relating to the country as a whole. The *Private Calendar* receives all bills that are personal or local—a pension to a person, damages caused by governmental operations, the building of a public works project in a city. The *Consent Calendar* is a special calendar for noncontroversial bills which are taken out of their order by unanimous consent of the House of Representatives. These are usually minor bills. These calendars help to separate the more important from the less important bills. Certain days of the month are assigned for debating the bills from each of the calendars.

In the Senate there is only one calendar. All Bills are placed on the *Calendar of Bills,* except for bills that are passed by unanimous consent at the time they are reported. These are usually noncontroversial bills. All other bills are placed on the one calendar.

Getting a bill on the calendar is no guarantee that the bill will be considered by the entire body. There are so many bills reported favorably by the committees that special provisions are made to be sure that important bills will be considered. The value of these provisions is that a very important bill may have had very long committee hearings and have been returned by the committee late in a session.

Less important bills receive little attention in the committees and are reported early in a session. Thus many of the minor bills may be ahead of the major bills on the calendar, so some system is necessary to be sure that the most important bills are handled promptly.

In the Senate, bills are considered out of their regular order by unanimous consent or by a motion requiring a majority vote. Actually the leaders of the majority party control the order of considering bills.

In the House, the Rules Committee has authority to decide which of the bills on a calendar will be debated. What happens if the Rules Committee does not pass a "rule" to consider a bill? The bill is then defeated just as though it had been pigeonholed by one of the other committees at a hearing. Thus a bill can be buried at two places: in committee by not reporting it or in the Rules Committee by keeping it on the calendar.

But, just as by a majority vote of the House a bill can be brought from committee, so by a two-thirds vote the House may order the Rules Committee to place a bill before it. This provides a device by which the powerful Rules Committee can be defeated if two-thirds of the members of the House agree.

When the time for the debate on the bill arrives, a clerk reads the bill in full (the second reading). A member of the committee then explains the bill and gives the reasons for the committee action. Debate is then held and amendments are offered.

The debates on bills before Congress receive wide publicity. Newspapers, radio, and television give them great attention. On important bills there is much debate. But many bills are passed with little discussion. They are dealt with in a routine fashion. To assist in having time for debate on the important bills, the previously discussed calendar system is used. Much of the debating is done in an informal session called the Committee of the Whole. By this device, the House or the Senate shifts from formal procedures to ones that require fewer rules. The official presiding officer does not preside, but some other member takes his place. No record of a member's vote can be demanded. In effect the legislative body forms itself into a large committee. In the House, in contrast to the Senate, the length of speeches is strictly limited. There is a one-hour limitation on a single speech by any member, and the party floor leaders usually agree in advance on the total time to be allowed for debate on a bill.

The House uses the Committee of the Whole on most bills; the Senate seldom uses it because of its smaller size. The Senate will become the Committee of the Whole usually in considering treaties and sometimes in the discussion of an appointment made by the President.

6. *THE VOTE.* After the debate is ended, the vote may be taken in any one of four ways: First, by "sound of voices." Those for the bill say "aye"; those against say "no." The presiding officer decides the result. Any member not satisfied with the decision may call for a second method—a division. In this method all those in favor of the bill stand; all those opposed are then asked to do the same. A clerk counts the members each time.

A third method may be used in the House of Representatives when requested by one-fifth of the members. This is a vote "by tellers." By this system the representatives pass down the center aisle and are counted by tellers. Those in favor of the bill turn one way; those opposed to the bill turn the other way. If a record of the vote is required, a member hands the teller his name written on a slip of paper. This procedure must be requested by at least twenty members.

A fourth method also provides a record of the vote. For many years under the roll call system, the roll of members was called and every member answered to his name and gave his vote. This was a time-consuming operation, often taking forty-five minutes or more in the House and thirty minutes in the Senate. To speed up the process, the House began using an electronic voting machine in 1973. To obtain a roll call vote the approval of one-fifth of the membership is required. The entire voting record is published in the *Journal* and in the *Congressional Record*.

Before the final vote is taken by any of these methods, the title of the bill is read. This is the "third reading." Although the second reading is the only full reading, there are provisions by which the bill could be read in full at the first and third readings if this seems desirable. Since each member of Congress has a complete printed copy of each bill, the one complete reading is usually enough.

7. THE BILL IS SENT TO THE OTHER HOUSE. When a bill has passed one house, it must be sent to the other house. House bills go to the Senate; Senate bills go to the House. It does not matter in which house a bill starts, with the exception of revenue bills, which must start in the House of Representatives.

When the bill is received by the second house, the six steps described above are repeated. Again the danger spots for the bill are not getting reported by the committee and not getting off the calendar.

8. THE CONFERENCE COMMITTEE. When the bill has passed both houses, there is always the possibility that the bills are not exactly the same. One house may have added an amendment or changed a sentence so that the bills are not identical. In this case the bill has to be returned from the one house to the other. If the first house agrees with the changes, it again passes the bill and there is no difficulty.

What happens if the first house refuses to agree with the changes made by the second house? In this case each house appoints three or more members to meet together as a temporary joint committee to see if agreement can be reached on the differences. This joint committee is called the *conference committee*. The conference

The Clerk of the House must sign a certificate that a bill has passed the House before it can be sent to the Senate. (National Geographic Society Photographer. Courtesy U.S. Capitol Historical Society)

committee makes the necessary compromises and reports back to the houses.

9. THE HOUSES VOTE ON THE CONFERENCE REPORT. The bill reported back by the conference committee is considered at the same time by both houses. No changes in the bill can now be made. Usually the bill is passed almost automatically, but sometimes one house refuses to accept the action of the committee. The bill must then be placed before a new conference committee. Once in a great while several conference committees are necessary before the bill is finally approved by both houses.

10. THE PRESIDENT GETS THE BILL. When the identical bill has received a majority vote in each house, it goes to the President. The President has three choices: (1) He may sign the bill. If he does, the bill becomes a law. (2) He may *veto* the bill. If he uses his veto, the bill can become a law only by a two-thirds vote of each house. (3) He may neither sign nor veto the bill. If Congress is in session and the President does not sign the bill within ten days (not counting Sundays), the bill becomes law without his signature. But if Congress has adjourned during this period and the President has not signed the bill, it does not become a law. This method of defeating bills after the end of the legislative session is called the *pocket veto*.

Presidents sign most of the bills that are passed by Congress. In this century about 1,400 bills have been defeated by pocket veto or by direct veto. Presidents usually prefer to veto only those bills which they oppose as a matter of national political policy.

THE STRATEGY OF MAKING LAWS

The period from the introduction of a bill until it is finally made a law is usually a fairly long one. The bill can be defeated in many ways. Final success depends on timing, on mobilizing support, on being alert to the devices of the opposition.

Getting a law passed in many respects is like winning a football game. Fumbles, school spirit, trick plays, scouting the opponents, natural ability, team play—all are important even for two evenly matched football teams. Sometimes games are won or lost by the play that the quarterback calls in a critical situation. Just as there is strategy in winning athletic games, there is strategy in getting laws passed.

The floor leaders and whips are much like captains and quarterbacks. They become experts in knowing just what to do in certain situations. For example, in the midst of a debate a floor leader may discover that some of the opponents are absent; and he will hurriedly call for a vote, hoping to take the other side by surprise and get the vote over before the opposition whips can round up enough of their members.

LOGROLLING. One of the standard "plays" used in lawmaking is the one called *logrolling*. By this device one congressman agrees that he will vote for a certain bill if the other congressman will vote for his bill. This type of vote trading gets its name from the early pioneer days when neighbors would help each other roll logs to put up their log cabins.

THE PORK BARREL. Logrolling is most common with *pork-barrel* legislation. This name is applied to those laws that provide special projects in a congressman's district, such as post offices, harbor construction, dredging of rivers, or defense contracts for local industries.

These laws usually contain many items calling for spending money in different districts. Since a congressman likes to get some federal money spent in his district, he may trade votes with another congressman, thinking he will get his share of the "pork." Of course, the pork is really money, and the pork barrel is really the United States Treasury. Many citizens, therefore, and many congressmen are critical of logrolling and pork-barrel legislation and are wondering if as a nation we can afford this type of legislation.

THE RIDER. Another trick play sometimes employed in Congress is to fasten one bill that does not have much chance of being passed to another bill that is very important and will be passed. Such an attached bill is called a *rider*. Usually the rider is added as an amendment, and sometimes some congressmen do not realize that they are voting for an amendment which they really would not want.

Mention that a rider is sometimes used by Congress to get something past a possible Presidential veto.

Include in your discussion the famous Army-McCarthy Hearings of the early 1950's conducted by the highly controversial Senator Joseph McCarthy of Wisconsin. (See Chapter 26, page 567.)

CONGRESSIONAL INVESTIGATIONS

There is an old saying, "A woman's work is never done." In many ways this saying is true of Congress too. A law gets passed, but does the law work the way it was intended? Does the President administer the law effectively? Is there need for a new law or for an amendment to an old one?

Because answers are needed to these questions, the work of Congress does not stop with the passage of a law. Most congressmen are very busy during and after the sessions of Congress trying to find out how effective their work has been. Much of this searching is done on an individual basis, but some of the work is so important that Congress provides funds for special investigations by certain committees.

The congressional investigation is an American political phenomenon of this century. Although committees of Congress have made investigations since the first Congress, in the past fifty years the investigating committee has become an important feature of our government. Congressional committees have probed into many aspects of American life.

TYPES OF INVESTIGATIONS. Investigations are generally of three types: (1) those designed to seek information to help Congress pass laws, (2) those which try to determine if laws passed are accomplishing what was intended, (3) those which examine the administration of the laws.

Before World War I a House committee studied banks and the system of borrowing money in this country. This investigation led finally to the adoption of the Federal Reserve Banking System.

Since then legislative investigations have been made of the air service, un-American activities, the Teapot Dome oil scandal, public utility companies, munitions makers, the Veterans Administration, the Pearl Harbor disaster, campaign expenditures, crime conditions, the Teamsters Union, insurance companies, the drug industry, and many other matters. These investigations have been made by House committees, by Senate committees, and sometimes by joint committees of both houses.

BENEFITS. The investigating committee is able to mobilize the forces of public opinion and fix the attention of the American people on weaknesses in our life. The crime investigation under the chairmanship of Senator Estes Kefauver in 1950–51 was the first investigation to make use of television. The questioning of witnesses before TV cameras created a nationwide audience. Day after day thousands of people followed the work of this committee. Some people believe that this one investigation did more than any other single event to interest American women in politics.

The congressional committee has the right to compel a witness to appear before it. Failure to do so can result in a fine or a jail sentence. This right of *subpoena* has helped congressional committees uncover corruption, fraud, inefficiency, and disloyalty. The investigations have helped keep governmental officials honest and efficient. They have obtained essential information to help Congress make better laws.

CRITICISMS. The investigating committees are, however, criticized a great deal. Some committees have been accused of not respecting the basic freedoms of the individual. Is it right to have to testify before a television camera? Some methods used have seemed unfair to those who fear we may lose our civil liberties. Others point out that these investigations are too hit or miss—an investigation is held one year and then nothing is done for years after. These critics prefer the methods of the British Royal Commissions to the methods of our investigating committees. These commissions, composed of an expert staff plus members of Parliament, regularly study major problems with thoroughness.

Another serious criticism of congressional investigations is that they are sometimes not investigations but "political fishing trips." The investigators, it is said, are seeking to get personal political publicity and fame. Or they are accused of trying to uncover activities that will embarrass their political enemies. When the Congress is of one party and the President is of another, the congressional investigation can easily become a device for fixing attention on the President's weaknesses or mistakes.

Some investigations, too, are criticized as paid "vacations" for travel. While most investigations are held in Washington, congressmen have carried on investigations in all parts of the world. Frequently these trips are called *junkets* in the public press, implying that the congressmen are really more concerned with free travel, food, lodging, and entertainment than they are with seeking out facts.

These criticisms, however, are chiefly of abuses of the investigation system as used by Congress. The investigating committee has been too important in American life to be abandoned.

IMPROVEMENTS. Congress, therefore, has tried to establish some general rules for the conduct of investigations. Adopted in 1955, the House rules include: informing witnesses in advance of the subject of the investigation, permitting a witness to have a lawyer present to assist him, permitting a person whose reputation may have been damaged by others to come and testify before the committee or to submit a written statement, requiring that testimony that might harm a person's reputation be given in a closed (non-public) session, prohibiting the release of any testimony given in closed session without the authorization of

the committee, and allowing a witness to request that no television camera or lights be directed at him while testifying. Since 1971, a majority vote of the committee is required to permit broadcasting by radio or television and the consent of the witness is required for a photograph or a broadcast. These "fair play" rules have helped protect the rights of individuals.

The Senate has not adopted such a set of rules but permits each committee to establish its own procedures. For example, the Government Operations Committee requires that two senators be present when testimony is taken, allows a person who has been criticized in testimony to answer the charges in person or in writing, and permits a person being investigated to submit questions for cross-examination. Other Senate committees have not been equally careful of individual rights.

The Supreme Court has heard a variety of cases involving Congressional investigations. Several have centered on the issue of the Fifth Amendment, which provides that a person shall not "be compelled in any criminal case to be a witness against himself." This protection against self-incrimination has been used, for example, by gamblers who held that testifying might cause them to be found guilty of violating a law. Persons accused of being communists and engaging in subversive activities have employed the Fifth Amendment, as have members of the Ku Klux Klan.

To get around this refusal to testify Congress passed a law by which committees can grant *immunity* from prosecution to witnesses. If the witness still refuses to testify, the person can be accused of contempt of Congress and placed in jail. In reviewing these sentences for contempt, the Supreme Court has upheld the sentences when the questions asked were pertinent to the investigation and the witness was informed of this (*Barenblatt* v. *United States*, 1959). It has denied the contempt sentence in a case where the committee failed to hear the witness in a closed session (*Yellin* v. *United States*, 1963).

Although the conduct of investigations is still hazardous for individual rights, there has been great improvement since the days when Senator Joseph McCarthy was free to destroy the reputations of citizens—before he was censured by the Senate in 1954.

CONGRESSIONAL REFORMS

The Congress of the United States is one of the great legislative bodies of the world. On most great national issues it eventually serves the people well. But the spotlight of public opinion is constantly on it so that flaws are discussed and criticized continuously. In the preceding pages some of the defects have been noted: filibustering, seniority, control by southern committee chairmen, regulation of lobbyists, abuse of investigative powers. Numerous suggestions are made to improve the national legislature.

ETHICAL CONDUCT. Congress is very vigilant in seeking to locate dishonesty in the administrative and judicial branches of government, but critics point out that it is very loose in similar controls over its own members and staff activities. In 1967 Senator Dodd of Connecticut was censured by his colleagues for using campaign funds for personal use. The same year Congressman Adam Clayton Powell of New York was removed as chairman of the House Committee on Education and Labor and, as previously noted, later rejected as a member. The secretary of the Senate Democratic majority, Bobby Baker, was in the headlines for months until his conviction in 1966 of income tax evasion, theft, and conspiracy to defraud the government.

These and similar situations resulted in a public demand for higher ethical conduct by employees and members of Congress. There were suggestions that congressmen should report annually the sources and total amounts of their incomes. Individual senators and representatives did so, but no law requiring them to do so was passed. Both the Senate and House had committees investigate and report on "standards of official conduct," with the hope of establishing a code of ethical conduct.

In 1968 both the House and the Senate adopted codes to guide the ethical conduct of members and employees. The Senate restricted outside employment and fund-raising by its employees, limited the acceptance and use of political contributions and required public reports of them, and required Senators to file a copy of their income tax report and other financial matters in a sealed envelope which could be opened in the event of an investigation. House rules were similar but required members to list publicly major sources of income. Totals would not be reported but could be examined in case of an investigation. Critics thought the new codes were some improvement but insisted that they did not go far enough.

ERRAND-BOY FUNCTIONS. There is much criticism of congressmen for being too concerned with taking care of individual and local concerns. Much of the time of a member of Congress is taken up with getting information, doing favors, and otherwise helping some voter back home. Concerns of the local district or state seem on occasion to receive more attention than matters of national importance. Some congressmen have reported that three-fourths of their time is spent in these "errand-boy" functions. Much of this seems necessary to be re-elected.

President Johnson in his 1966 State of the Union message supported the idea of

Elaborate on the authors' reference to the British parliamentary system of a question period for members of the Cabinet. Do we have anything similar to this?

a constitutional amendment to increase the term of House members to four years. This idea had been advocated by the American Political Science Association several years earlier—based on the argument that if a member did not have to seek election so often he could devote more time to legislative matters. The amendment idea has made little progress—partly because senators are reluctant to give up the advantages they have with a longer term.

EXECUTIVE RELATIONSHIPS. When Congress functions at greatest efficiency, the President usually provides the leadership. He becomes the chief legislator through party leadership and through his ability to mobilize public opinion in support of laws that he wants. Critics point out, however, that Congress should not become a rubber stamp, automatically approving the President's requests. Congress needs to examine, criticize, amend, and study proposals that come from the executive branch.

LEGISLATIVE COUNCIL. A legislative council, a planning group, has been proposed to increase planning on national policies. This council might consist of the Vice President, the Speaker, the majority leaders, and chairmen of regular committees. They would meet together regularly to plan ways of improving the legislative process and to develop more effective ways of working with the President.

Although this idea has been recommended in several studies of Congress, it has never been put into effect. The nearest thing to it has been the practice of some Presidents to hold regular meetings with the leaders of the legislature. This practice works well when all are members of the same party. Presidents Franklin D. Roosevelt, Dwight D. Eisenhower, and Lyndon Johnson held regular Monday morning meetings of this type.

But the practice cannot work well when Congress is controlled by a political party different from the President's. Presidents Hoover, Truman, Eisenhower, and Nixon, for example, were faced with this condition during parts of their administrations.

QUESTION PERIOD. Relations with the executive branch would be improved in the opinion of several reformers if members of the Cabinet could speak and be questioned before either house, in addition to their appearances before committees. Great Britain and other countries use a question period regularly to obtain information and to educate public opinion. Senator Kefauver proposed that two hours each week be devoted to such a question period. Little movement toward this device can be noted.

ITEM VETO. Some political scientists think the President should have the power to veto an item of a bill without having to veto the whole bill. Now, when a bill comes to the President, he has to accept the whole bill or veto the whole bill. An *item veto* would permit checks on riders, logrolling, and much of the pork-barrel legislation; for then the President could veto those items which he thought were undesirable. The interest of congressmen in local matters could thus be decreased. Some states and cities have given their executives this power of item veto.

Opponents of the item veto argue that the President has too much power now, that it is the right of Congress to legislate and Congress should keep it. They think the President should not have more power over the making of laws. They point out that Congress in the Legislative Reorganization Act of 1946 tried to eliminate riders from all appropriation bills. They want Congress to reform itself without increasing the power of the President.

JOINT COMMITTEES. Another reform proposal is that the two houses of Congress should have more joint committees. You may have noticed in reading the list of committees on pages 211-212 that both houses have committees dealing with the same subjects. Why not have the committees meet together to hear bills? Why have separate hearings? Some critics say that the time of congressmen could be saved, that witnesses before the committees would only have to appear once, that joint committees would be less costly.

Opponents of this idea argue that joint committees would destroy the very fundamentals of the two-house legislature. In practice some regular committees do hold joint committee meetings once in a while, and there are some special joint committees such as the one on atomic energy.

THE LEGISLATIVE REORGANIZATION ACT. A beginning of the streamlining of Congress was made with the passage of the 1946 Legislative Reorganization Act. Some of the results of this act have been described in this chapter. In summary, the act decreased the number of standing committees in each house, provided additional expert help for Congress, and enlarged the Legislative Reference Service, now the Congressional Research Service. It also provided that on appropriation bills time must be allowed for members to study the committee hearings and reports before the bills are taken to the floor. Lobbyists are required to register and make financial reports.

During the next twenty-five years there were great efforts to continue Congressional reforms. Finally the Legislative Reorganization Act of 1970 was passed. The goals of this act were threefold: to streamline the legislative processes, to open the operations of Congress to public examination, and to make the system more democratic for better protection of minority rights.

The provision providing for recorded teller votes produced dramatic results. The number of House members actually voting was twice as large as in previous sessions. Moreover, on crucial amendments, record votes are now taken. These important votes that were formerly hidden from the public are now visible.

Committee procedures were refined. One provision required that votes taken in the committee be made public. Other reforms included: prohibiting proxy voting except under specified conditions;

allowing committee members three days to file supplemental and minority views; opening committees to the public in general; and announcing hearings of committees one week in advance.

All together there were some forty specific provisions in the 1970 Act. But reformers were not entirely satisfied. They thought that additional reforms were still needed. One focus of attack was the seniority system by which chairmen have been appointed. The 1970 reforms are successful only with a cooperative chairman. Once chairman achieves his position, only his departure from Congress removes him from the chairmanship. Sometimes a chairman operates democratically, sometimes despotically. Committee members are sometimes reluctant to force the chairman to abide by the rules. The method of appointment of the chairman is therefore crucial to continued reform.

Another point of attack is a procedure of the House Rules Committee by which a bill can be brought to the floor under a closed rule. The closed rule prohibits any amendments. Most bills are reported under open rules, but substantial numbers, especially appropriation bills, receive a closed rule. Reformers want the closed rule eliminated.

STUDY QUESTIONS

1. How is the work of Congress carried on?

2. Why are the committees so important? How influential are the chairmen?

3. Why is the Speaker of the House of Representatives a powerful person? What are his powers?

CONCEPTS AND GENERALIZATIONS

1
The leadership in Congress, chosen along party lines, is crucial in getting laws passed.

2
The traditions and practices of Congress have handicapped Negroes in their efforts to obtain full civil rights.

3
The work of Congress is done largely through committees.

4
Seniority is a powerful influence on the career of an individual congressman and on the quality of legislation.

5
The government supplies some assistance to congressmen in studying bills.

6
Interest groups through lobbyists are very influential in their effects on legislation.

7
Regulation of the conduct of congressmen and of lobbyists is quite loose.

8
Most congressmen are honest and sincere, and desire to render effective service.

9
The procedures for passing a law through the Senate are simpler than in the House.

10
The major points at which the public can influence legislation are at hearings and by exerting pressure on congressmen before the vote.

11
Strategy is an important part of getting laws passed.

12
Congressional investigations are important and often useful, but this power has sometimes been abused, particularly in the area of individual rights.

13
The reform of Congress is important unfinished business. Possible areas of reform include: the seniority rule, ethical conduct, better relationships with the executive branch, and more use of joint committees.

4. Under what conditions does the Vice President have a vote in the Senate?

5. Why is the work of floor leaders and whips so important?

6. How does the majority party control legislation?

7. Why is the minority party important in Congress?

8. How do Senate and House rules differ? Why does the House limit the length of speeches?

9. How do Senate and House committees differ?

10. On what committees do your Senators and Representative serve?

11. How are the members of congressional committees selected?

12. What help does Congress supply its members?

13. How do lobbyists help members of Congress? How are lobbyists controlled?

14. Outline the steps from the introduction of a bill until it becomes a law.

15. Why is the Rules Committee so important in the passage of a law?

16. How important is the veto power of the President? Do you favor an item veto? Why?

17. Why is parliamentary procedure to some extent a matter of strategy and thus somewhat like playing a game?

18. How are congressional investigations conducted?

19. Why are congressional reforms recommended? Which reforms do you favor or oppose and why?

IDEAS FOR DISCUSSION

1. Do you think the Senate should adopt rules to prevent filibustering? Why?

2. Should a member of Congress ever vote against the wishes of the party? Should the member ever vote against his own beliefs? Why?

3. On the opening day of a recent session of Congress, 329 measures were introduced. The two most popular subjects of these bills were aid to veterans and tax reduction. One representative introduced forty-two proposals, and another introduced thirty-four. Why are so many bills introduced on opening day?

4. The late Senator George W. Norris is generally considered by historians to have been one of the great liberals of this century. Speaking about parliamentary procedures, he once said, "I am one of the best compromisers in Congress. When I can't get what I want I take what I can get. But compromises should be arrived at honestly, in sincere effort to do what is best, and not to be used as mere devices in the game of practical politics." What do you think of this point of view?

5. Private bills are distinguished from public bills because they apply to specifically named individuals and are not for general application. In a recent Congress 2,463 private immigration bills were introduced, of which 406 passed. One congressman in commenting on this situation said, "I believe that the practice of introducing private bills has been abused; that the Congress should not divert its attention from national problems to consume its energies in passing legislation for just one person; that laws should apply equally to all persons under established standards, and that exceptions should be held to the minimum." Do you agree or disagree? Why?

6. When Lyndon B. Johnson was the Senate minority leader in the Eighty-third Congress, *Time* magazine reported that in making committee assignments "he dared to violate the traditions of seniority. To get all his men working where they would do the most good, he cajoled, horse-traded, and argued some old-timers into giving up some of their key committee seats. By that method he found an Armed Service Committee seat for Missouri's freshman Senator Stuart Symington, onetime (1947–1950) Secretary of the Air Force, and placed Montana's freshman Mike Mansfield on Foreign Relations." Why was this item newsworthy? What were the longtime effects?

7. Should ex-Presidents be given a permanent seat in the United States Senate? With or without vote?

8. Do you believe that joint congressional committees would make Congress more effective? Would such a system tend to do away with our bicameral Congress?

9. Much criticism has been made of congressional investigations. What is the nature of these criticisms? Do you favor putting some controls on the investigations?

10. Sometimes the Vice President is not a member of the same party as the majority in the Senate. Would you favor changing the Constitution to have the Senate elect its own chairman as is done by the House of Representatives? Why?

11. Make a chart listing the floor leaders, party whips, and chairmen of all committees of the House of Representatives or the Senate. Give the following information about each chairman: party affiliation, number of years in Congress, home state.

THINGS TO DO

1. Prepare a chart showing the way your senators or representative voted on important legislation in the last Congress. Consult issues of the *Congressional Quarterly.*

2. Hold a mock session of the Senate.

3. Prepare a report on a leader in the present Congress.

4. Investigate the frequency with which Presidents have used their veto power. What conclusions do you draw from the veto records of past Presidents?

5. Prepare a report on a well-known Speaker of the House.

6. Hold a panel discussion on one of the following topics:

The seniority system for assignments to committees in Congress should be abolished.

The President should be given the power of item veto.

The investigations by congressional committees should be under stricter congressional rules.

The lobbyist system helps to improve the laws passed by Congress.

7. Prepare a short broadcast describing the opening session of Congress.

8. Investigate the work of the Congressional pages.

9. Write an editorial urging a specific congressional reform.

10. Color a map of the United States by states to show the political make-up of the present Congress.

FURTHER READINGS

Bailey, Stephen K., THE NEW CONGRESS. St. Martin's Press, Inc., 1966.

———, CONGRESS AT WORK. Holt, Rinehart and Winston, Inc., 1952.

Berman, Daniel M., A BILL BECOMES A LAW. The Macmillan Co., 1962. (Paperback edition)

Brinkley, D., and others, CONGRESS NEEDS HELP. Random House, Inc., 1966.

Clapp, Charles L., THE CONGRESSMAN: HIS WORK AS HE SEES IT. The Brookings Institution, 1963.

Clark, Joseph S., CONGRESSIONAL REFORM: PROBLEMS AND PROSPECTS. Thomas Y. Crowell Co., 1965.

Ferguson, John H., and McHenry, Dean E., THE AMERICAN SYSTEM OF GOVERNMENT. McGraw-Hill Book Co., Inc., 1967. Chapter 14.

Froman, Lewis, CONGRESSMEN AND THEIR CONSTITUENCIES. Rand McNally & Co., 1963.

Jewell, Malcom E., and Patterson, Samuel C., THE LEGISLATIVE PROCESS IN THE UNITED STATES. Random House, Inc., 1966.

Lowi, Theodore J., ed., LEGISLATIVE POLITICS U.S.A. Little, Brown and Co., 1965.

Morrow, William L., CONGRESSIONAL COMMITTEES. Charles Scribner's Sons, 1969.

Pearson, Drew, and Anderson, Jack, THE CASE AGAINST CONGRESS. Simon and Schuster, 1968.

Travis, Walter E., ed., CONGRESS AND THE PRESIDENT. Teachers College Press, 1971.

Young, Roland, THE AMERICAN CONGRESS. Harper & Row, Publishers, Inc., 1958.

BUREAU—an office; a division of a governmental agency.

DARK HORSE — a person unexpectedly nominated for a public office; one who has had only a slight chance of being nominated to public office.

ELECTORAL COLLEGE—group of electors from each state who choose the President and Vice President in December after the popular election.

EXECUTIVE AGREEMENT—a formal agreement between the President and the heads of one or more nations which does not require approval by the Senate.

INAUGURATION—a formal ceremony at which an elected official takes office.

KEYNOTE ADDRESS—the first major speech at a national political convention stating the policies of the party.

NOMINATION—naming of candidates for political office.

PARDON—release from punishment for a crime; forgiveness.

PRESIDENTIAL PREFERENCE PRIMARY—a primary election held in some states to determine who shall be the state's preferred presidential nominee of a political party at a national convention.

QUALIFICATION—quality or characteristic needed to be eligible for an elective or appointive office.

REPRIEVE—power of the executive to postpone punishment for a crime.

THE LANGUAGE OF GOVERNMENT

Mention that a President of the United States is both a head of state and a head of government, a position which is split in many countries between a prime minister or premier and a president or monarch.

11

The Presidency

"I do solemnly swear (or affirm) that I will faithfully execute the office of President of the United States, and will to the best of my ability, preserve, protect, and defend the Constitution of the United States." With these words from Article II of the Constitution a new or reelected President takes over the duties and responsibilities of his office.

George Washington, as the nations' first President, took this oath in a Wall Street building in New York City on April 30, 1789. Most Presidents now take the oath at inauguration ceremonies on the steps of the Capitol Building in Washington, D. C.

But the oath of office has been taken at unusual times and in unusual places. President Calvin Coolidge took the oath of office by the light of an oil lamp during the middle of the night in the Vermont home of his father after the death of President Harding. The oath was administered by Coolidge's father, a notary public. For President Lyndon B. Johnson the setting was the presidential plane at a Dallas airport soon after the assassination of President John F. Kennedy.

The office of the Presidency is one of the most powerful positions in the history of the world. President Harry S. Truman described the office as follows:

> The Presidency of the United States is a terrible responsibility for one man. . . . He has an executive job that is almost fantastic. There has never been one like it. . . . Every final important decision has to be made right here on the President's desk, and only the President can make it. . . . His decisions affect millions not only in his own country but around the world.[1]

The writers of the Constitution did not foresee the kind of office they were creating when they wrote into the Constitution this simple statement: "The executive power shall be vested in a President of the United States of America." The Constitution describes the qualifications which a person seeking to be President must meet, a method for electing the President, a way of removing him from office, and names his powers and duties. Most of these constitutional provisions for the Presidency, written in 1787, are still in effect, but the office is considerably different from what originally had been planned. It has been expanded and changed through laws, custom and usage, court decisions, public opinion, and executive orders until today it is truly one of the world's most difficult and important jobs.

QUALIFICATIONS OF
THE PRESIDENT
The fulfillment of the American dream of living in the White House is a possibility for most American citizens. The probability that this dream will come true, however, is very small.

1 From MR. PRESIDENT. Copyright 1952 by William Hillman and Alfred Wagg. Published by Farrar, Straus and Cudahy, Inc.

Fewer than forty men have been President of our country. How did they happen to be selected? What are their special qualifications?

A person chosen for this high office must meet the constitutional qualifications. But beyond meeting some minimum requirements Presidents have actually had little in common. They have brought to the office a wide range of experience and background based on certain political as well as personal qualifications.

CONSTITUTIONAL QUALIFICATIONS. The Constitution requires only these three qualifications for a President:

1. He must be a natural-born citizen of the United States.
2. He must be at least thirty-five years of age.
3. He must have been a resident of the United States for a period of fourteen years.

These qualifications are similar to those required of senators and representatives. They are, however, more exacting with regard to age and length of citizenship. The minimum age of a President is higher than that of congressmen. In practice most Presidents have been much older than thirty-five. President Theodore Roosevelt was the youngest man ever to hold this office. He was forty-two years old at the time of his inauguration. President John F. Kennedy was forty-three. Most of the others were in their fifties or sixties. President William Harrison was the oldest, having

> *When I ran for the Presidency of the United States, I knew that this country faced serious challenges, but I could not realize—nor could any man realize who does not bear the burden of this office—how heavy and constant would be those burdens.*
>
> —PRESIDENT JOHN F. KENNEDY, broadcast address, July 25, 1961. *Public Papers of the Presidents of the United States—John F. Kennedy, 1961,* p. 539.

Many have aspired to the great honor of occupying the White House despite the heavy responsibilities that accompany the Presidency.
(Top) The South Portico is also called the Diplomatic Entrance. (Washington Convention and
Visitors Bureau)
(Bottom left) The Yellow Oval Room serves as
a reception room for distinguished visitors.
(White House Historical Association)
(Bottom right) The Red Room, one of three
parlors on the ground floor, is furnished in the
Empire style, which was popular from 1810 to
1830. (White House Historical Association)

been sixty-eight when he was inaugurated.

Only a person who is a natural-born citizen of the United States can become President. It is generally believed that a citizen born abroad of American parents could become President, but this issue has never been officially settled.

The Constitution places another special qualification upon the President. To become President, a person must have lived in the United States for a period of fourteen years. These years need not be continuous, nor need they be fourteen years immediately before becoming President. The reason for including this qualification, however, is to make sure that the President would be familiar with American customs and ways by having lived in the United States.

Herbert Hoover is an example of a President who spent much of his life outside the United States. Nevertheless he was eligible for the Presidency because he had lived here more than fourteen years.

According to the Twelfth Amendment to the Constitution, the qualifications for the Vice President are the same as those for the President.

POLITICAL AND PERSONAL QUALIFICATIONS. While any person who meets the constitutional qualifications can become President, a study of the men who have been President shows that there are certain other factors which operate in the selection of Presidents. The Constitution places no restrictions on sex or race. Women are eligible; so are people of all races. However, until now all of our Presidents have been men of the white race.

Place of birth or residence is important in the selection of a President. Only five Presidents—Hoover, Truman, Eisenhower, Lyndon B. Johnson, and Nixon—were born west of the Mississippi River. Certain states have produced more than their proportional share of Presidents. Virginia was the birthplace of seven of the first twelve Presidents, and also of Woodrow Wilson. Seven were born in Ohio, four in New York, and three in Massachusetts.

Two were born in North Carolina, Texas, and Vermont. One was born in each of these: Iowa, Kentucky, Missouri, New Hampshire, New Jersey, Pennsylvania, South Carolina, and California.

A number of other states were the home

President Dwight D. Eisenhower was born in Texas, but he lived in this home in Abilene, Kansas, from the age of two until he entered West Point. (Courtesy Kansas Dept. of Economic Development)

In case of the death of a President, succession to the office must be speedy and orderly. Here Harry S. Truman is sworn in after the death of President Roosevelt in 1945. (Wide World photo)

states of the Presidents at the time of their election. For example, Lincoln was born in Kentucky, but he was a resident of Illinois at the time of his election; and Hoover, born in Iowa, was living in California when he was elected President.

Twelve men were Vice President before they became President. Eight of these succeeded to the Presidency through the death of the President. Most of our Presidents have also held other governmental positions before being nominated to the Presidency.

A person wanting to be President must meet the qualifications set forth in the Constitution. However, the facts given above indicate that politically it would be well for him to be living in either the north central or eastern states and to be engaged in political activity. With the westward movement of the population, however, more of our Presidents will undoubtedly be elected from the West.

Nominations for the Presidency have usually gone to persons living in large states or in states in which there is no clear-cut majority for one political party

and in which a nomination might sway the vote to a particular party. To get votes parties usually nominate a President from one section of the country and a Vice President from another.

SUCCESSION TO THE PRESIDENCY

In the event that the President cannot serve, according to the Constitution his duties and powers shall devolve on the Vice President. The Constitution states further that if neither the President nor the Vice President is able to serve, the Congress shall decide what officer shall act as President.

Until 1947, the succession was determined by a law passed in 1886, which said that in such a case the Secretary of State should succeed to the Presidency and after him the other members of the President's Cabinet in the order that their departments were established. These Cabinet members are appointed by the President with the approval of the Senate.

At the time of the death of President

Franklin D. Roosevelt in 1945, many people became concerned about the possibility of the succession to the Presidency of an appointed person rather than an elected one. This was a real possibility. If, for some reason President Truman had been unable to complete the unexpired term of President Roosevelt, the Secretary of State —an appointed person—would have become President.

As a result of this concern Congress passed a law in 1947 which says that the succession to the Presidency should be in this order: Vice President, Speaker of the House of Representatives, President pro tempore of the Senate. All of them are officials elected by the people. If none of these can serve, then Cabinet officers shall succeed to the Presidency in the order the departments were established. The law is important in the event some great catastrophe should kill many of the officials at the same time.

The Twenty-fifth Amendment to the Constitution, adopted in 1967, set up a procedure for filling the office of Vice President if it becomes vacant. The President nominates a person to become Vice President who takes office after confirmation by a majority vote of both houses of Congress. So, except for the period of time necessary to fill a vacancy, the Constitution now provides for always having a Vice President to succeed to the Presidency.

The Twenty-fifth Amendment also set up a procedure for carrying on the Presidency if the President is disabled. Several times in our history Presidents have been seriously ill. Two of them were Wilson and Eisenhower. At those times there was great concern about the fact that the nation was without the full services of a constitutional chief executive. By the Twenty-fifth Amendment the Vice President can now become Acting President through procedures initiated either by the President or by others if in their judgment the President is unable to discharge his duties.

ELECTION OF THE PRESIDENT

Every four years a President and a Vice President are elected. The election is held on the first Tuesday after the first Monday in November in years divisible by four, for example, 1972, 1976, and 1980.

Actually, however, the voters do not directly elect a President. They vote for electors who choose the President. The reason for this is that the writers of the Constitution thought that the election of the President was too important to trust it to a direct vote of the people. They therefore created a system for election of a President by means of electors.

Each state has as many electors as it has senators and representatives in Congress. Thus New York with two senators and thirty-nine representatives has forty-one electors, while Nevada has only three. The District of Columbia also has three.

The Constitution gives the state legislature the power to decide how the electors are to be chosen. Originally the state legislatures chose the electors, but today they are chosen by a vote of the people from nominations made by the political parties.

The original plan for the election of the President and the Vice President has been changed considerably by Constitutional amendment and by custom. In order to understand the election of the President we will describe: (1) the original plan; (2) the changes made by Constitutional amendments; (3) the changes made by custom and usage; (4) the present plan of election; and (5) proposed changes.

THE ORIGINAL PLAN. The winning electors were required to meet in their re-

Make sure that the student understands why the Electoral College was originally created, the operation of it today, and its major contemporary criticisms.

spective states and vote by ballot for two persons. At least one of the two had to be a resident of another state. There was good reason for this. If all electors voted for residents of their own states, no person could receive a majority of the votes.

The list of the persons voted for and the number of votes for each were to be sent to the President of the Senate. It became his job to count the votes in the presence of the members of both houses of Congress. The person with the highest number of votes was declared President if he had a majority of the votes of all the electors.

If the vote resulted in a tie or if no person had a majority, then the President was to be chosen by the House of Representatives. (See Article II, Section 1, Clause 2.) In the case of a tie vote, the members of the House were to choose the President from those with the tie votes. If no one had a majority, they were to choose one from among the five highest on the list. In choosing the President in the House of Representatives each state had only one vote regardless of the number of representatives it had. To be elected it was necessary to have a majority of all the states.

After the election of the President, the person with the next highest number of electoral votes was made Vice President. In the case of a tie vote for this position, a choice was to be made by the Senate from among those having an equal number of electoral votes.

THE CHANGES MADE BY CONSTITUTIONAL AMENDMENTS. The original plan of electing a President and a Vice President by the Electoral College—as it is called—worked well in the election of George Washington. But experience soon showed that it needed to be changed. In the election of 1800 Thomas Jefferson and Aaron Burr had an equal number of electoral votes. The electors had wanted Jefferson to become President and Burr Vice President; but since the two men had the same number of votes, the choice according to the Constitution had to be made by the House of Representatives. The latter chose Jefferson, but they could have made Burr President.

This event led to the passage of the Twelfth Amendment to the Constitution. This amendment provides that the electors should specify which person they want to be President and which one they want to be Vice President. Over the years other changes in the election of the President have been made. Amendment Twenty deals with the terms of office of President and Vice President, setting noon of January 20 for the beginning of a new term. Amendment Twenty-two limits a President to two elected terms.

THE CHANGES MADE BY CUSTOM AND ·USAGE. Many of the procedures used in connection with the election of a President are not mentioned in the Constitution. *Nominating the presidential candidates* is a sample of accepted practices under our "Unwritten Constitution."

In November 1972 Richard M. Nixon was re-elected President of the United States.[1] He defeated Democratic candidate George McGovern. In President Nixon's case, it was generally accepted that he would be the 1972 candidate of the Republican party. There was no such agreement on a Democratic candidate. Several people competed for the honor until the Democratic Convention in Miami Beach chose McGovern. Later, at the same place Republicans confirmed the nomination of Nixon.

---

[1] On January 20, 1969, President Richard M. Nixon became our thirty-seventh President. Only thirty-six men have held the office of President, but Grover Cleveland is counted twice because his two terms were not consecutive. Other Presidents who had more than one term are counted once.

Heated debate over delegate representation at the 1976 nominating conventions raged at both the Democratic and Republican conventions in 1972. Here members of the Republican Rules Committee hear testimony on the proposal to give bonus votes to states electing Republican governors and members of Congress. (David Tenenbaum /College Newsphoto Alliance)

In the years before any election many names are in the news as possible candidates. What are the steps that get one of them into the White House?

Many names are proposed as possible presidential candidates. Newspapers, radio, and television constantly discuss possible candidates. Political leaders get together and assess possibilities. Finally, the *announcement of candidacy* is the first big step on the road to the White House. The next is to be nominated by a political party. Several parties nominate candidates, but only Democrats or Republicans have been able to elect a President since 1852.

NATIONAL CONVENTIONS. In order to be nominated a person must secure more than half of the votes cast by delegates at a *party nominating convention* held during the summer before the November election.

To win these delegates, between the announcement and the convention, the can-didates spend their time trying to woo delegates. They may compete in the presidential preference primaries from New Hampshire to Oregon. A number of states and the District of Columbia hold primaries, but a candidate need not compete in all of them. Some who lose in an early primary withdraw from the race, since the primaries are held on different dates from March through June.

The number of delegates each state has at the conventions is decided by the parties, although a few states have laws on the method of selection. The number is based on membership in Congress and is generally two or three for each senator and representative.

In addition, states are allotted bonus delegates on the basis of votes for the party's candidates in the previous election. The territories, too, are permitted a few delegates.

In 1972 the Republican party had 1,347 votes at its convention. At least 674 votes were necessary for nomination. For the Democratic party these numbers were 3,016 and 1,509, respectively. Some Democratic delegates had half or smaller votes.

The procedure for selecting delegates varies with states. In general there are three methods. In more than half of the states political party conventions on the state level are held at which the delegates to the national convention are elected. In about one-third of the states the presidential primary elections are held to choose delegates. In a few states the state central committee of the party appoints the delegates.

In every case persons favoring a particular candidate try to have themselves elected or appointed so that they may cast their votes for their preferred candidate at the national nominating convention.

The national conventions are among the most exciting events in American politics. They are attended by thousands of people in addition to the delegates. By means of television, radio, and newspapers citizens throughout the country become spectators at these conventions.

The conventions open with the call to order by the national chairman. A temporary chairman presides until the permanent chairman is chosen by the convention. The temporary chairman or another prominent person gives a rousing speech, the *keynote address,* which is designed as a "pep talk" for the party followers.

The background work of the convention is carried on by four committees, with each state having one representative on each committee. Committee 4 has one man and one woman from each state.

1. *The Committee on Rules and Order of Business* determines the general order of business of the convention and ordinarily recommends that the rules of the preceding convention be adopted. The major rule change in recent years has been in the Democratic conventions where nominations for President are now by a majority vote instead of the old two-thirds rule.

2. *The Committee on Permanent Organization* nominates a permanent chairman and other officials. When the permanent chairman is elected by the convention, at an early session, he delivers one of the major speeches.

3. *The Committee on Credentials* decides which delegates shall be seated in those cases where there is a dispute over the proper delegates from a state. Because these decisions, in a close contest, may determine the party's choice for President, the struggles are heated, sometimes prolonged, and usually important. A delegation may challenge the ruling and take its case to the convention for a decision.

4. *The Committee on Platform and Resolutions* prepares the party *platform.* This is a statement of the things the party proposes to do if its candidates are elected. In a way the platform is a party's promise of the program it will carry out if elected. Since under convention procedure the platform is adopted before the presidential candidate is named, the speeches of the person nominated are frequently as important as the platform.

Once the platform has been adopted, the convention begins the big job of choosing the presidential candidate. For many years both the Democrats and the Republicans nominated candidates by calling the roll alphabetically starting with Alabama. A state could place a name in nomination by a speech of praise, "yield" to another state to nominate "the next President of the United States," or "pass." In 1972 the Democrats chose the order of nominating candidates by having them draw lots.

Speeches seconding the nomination are made. For years there were demonstrations for favorite candidates. Marching, noise, bands, banners, organ music added to the excitement. Because of television coverage these time-consuming and distracting matters were curtailed in 1972. When all nominations have been made, the voting begins. Voting is done orally by calling the roll of states with the state chairman reporting the vote of the state. Some delegates come to the convention free to vote for any person they wish. Others come pledged or instructed to vote for a particular person. Usually, however, such pledged delegates are free to change their choice after the first ballot. Voting continues at the nominating conventions until some person receives the required number of votes for nomination.

Sometimes this leads to "horse trading" or bargaining whereby delegates trade with one another. A group of delegates may, for example, agree to support a particular candidate for the Presidency if their own special choice is guaranteed the vice-presidential nomination. At other times a deadlock may lead to the nomination of a dark horse, a candidate on whom the delegates agree as a compromise. President Warren G. Harding is an example.

After the delegates agree on a presidential candidate, they nominate in the same way a person as the candidate for Vice President. Usually the presidential candidate has much to say in the choice of his running mate. In 1972 the Democratic National Committee nominated Sargent Shriver for the vice presidency after Thomas Eagleton, the nominee of the convention, withdrew because of publicity concerning his health.

The practice of having nominating conventions is an example of constitutional change through usage. The Constitution says nothing about political parties or nominating conventions.

There is some dissatisfaction, however, with the nominating conventions. Some people think that a national primary election for President should be held, as is done in many states to nominate state officials. In such an election all voters could share in the naming of the party presidential candidates.

THE PRESENT PLAN OF ELECTION. Between the time of the national conventions and the election a great deal of campaigning is done by all parties trying to convince the people to vote for their candidates. But actually the people do not vote directly for a President. They vote for the presidential electors, as the framers of the Constitution directed. A change through custom has been made here too, however. In many states the names of the electors no longer appear on the ballot, but instead the names of the presidential and vice-presidential candidates themselves are given.

The electors in each state almost without exception vote for the nominees of the party which elected them. While the people actually vote for electors, they are in effect voting directly for President and Vice President by electing electors who are pledged to vote for the candidates of the people's choice. So the electoral college has become nothing more than an awkward adding machine.

On a designated day in December following the November election, the electors meet in their respective state capitals and cast their votes for President and Vice President. The results of their voting are sent sealed to the President of the Senate. He opens and counts them in January before a joint session of Congress.

The election does not become official until the votes are counted before Congress. However, the actual result is usually known immediately after the November election because, in practice, each state's electoral votes go to the presidential and vice-presidential candidates getting the highest popular vote in the state. To be elected, candidates must receive a majority of the electoral votes. In 1972 that meant 270 of the 538 votes (100 for the number in the Senate, 435 for the number in the House of Representatives, and 3 for the District of Columbia).

If no candidate receives the necessary majority, the House of Representatives must choose the President from among the three (changed from five to three by the Twelfth Amendment) persons having the highest number of votes. In this voting, however, each state has only one vote. The House members from each state meet to decide for whom they will cast their vote. To be elected, a candidate must receive more than half of the votes of all the states (twenty-six at the present time).

Similarly, if none of the vice-presidential candidates has a majority, the Senate chooses a Vice President from the two highest for that position. In this case a majority vote of all the senators is necessary (51 of the 100 at the present time).

PROPOSED CHANGES. The electoral college system, as written into the Constitution, was essentially a compromise between those delegates who wanted the President elected directly by the people and those who wanted him elected by Congress. The delegates were not exactly sure how the plan would function. It is very likely that they had different opinions regarding the operation of the electoral college system.

From the very beginning the system was criticized, and proposals for its elimination or change have been made in every Congress since 1797. But until the present time it has not been changed because no proposal has had enough support in Congress.

"We're Almost Ready To Take Off Again"

from Straight Herblock *(Simon & Schuster, 1964)*

However, because of the growing criticism of the electoral college and the increasing interest in its reform, it is possible that a change may be approved by Congress and the states in the next few years. There are four types of proposed changes being given some consideration.

One suggestion is that the President be elected on the basis of the popular vote, so that the candidate who receives the highest number of votes of the people would be elected. In several elections the person chosen has not had the most popular votes. For example, Harrison, in 1888, won the election because he had a majority of the electoral votes; but Cleveland, his opponent, had a greater popular vote.

Some states with a small population, however, oppose the election of the President by a direct vote of the people. Their small number of votes might be very insignificant in a popular vote of 65 to 75 million. But even a state with only three electoral votes may be very important in the electoral college.

Another suggestion is to divide each state's electoral vote in the same proportion as its popular vote. At the present time the candidate who receives the highest number of popular votes in a state receives *all* of the state's electoral votes.

According to this suggestion for proportional voting, each candidate receiving votes in a state would receive a portion of the state's electoral votes. Thus, if a candidate received 55 per cent of the popular votes, he would receive only 55 per cent of the electoral votes. His opponents would receive the remaining 45 per cent.

A third type of proposal would require each state to give its electoral votes automatically to the candidate who receives the greatest number of popular votes in the state. This is generally the present practice. But under this proposal the electors would be abolished; there would be no opportunity to give electoral votes to a candidate who was not the people's choice, as was done by one Oklahoma elector in 1960. He voted for Democratic Senator Harry F. Byrd although the Republican candidate, Richard M. Nixon, received the other seven state electoral votes.

Finally, a fourth type of proposed change would divide the states into districts similar to the congressional districts. Each district would have one vote, with the vote going to the candidate receiving the highest number of popular votes in the district. In addition each state would receive two additional votes for the candidate receiving the highest number of votes in the state.

Each of these proposals has supporters and also opponents. But the current dissatisfaction with the electoral college system indicates that some reform may be made. Recent suggestions for a change in the method of electing the President have been made to Congress by Presidents, by political parties, and by a commission of the American Bar Association.

INAUGURATION OF THE PRESIDENT

After their election the President and the Vice President are inaugurated on January 20. This date is the result of a change in the Constitution and came about with the adoption of the Twentieth Amendment in 1933. Until that time the President took office on March 4 following his election. This length of time (from November to March) was necessary when the Constitution was written because transportation and communication were slow.

With improved means of transportation and communication this long period of time is no longer needed, and the date of taking office was changed to January 20 so that the President-elect could begin sooner to carry out the policies for which he had been elected.

Both the President and the Vice President take the oath of office at the inauguration. Also, traditionally the President makes an address in which he indicates plans for his administration. This address is listened to carefully by both citizens of the United States and people of other nations for clues regarding possible new policies and programs of a new administration.

REMOVAL FROM OFFICE

The President and other government officials may be removed from office for treason, bribery, or other high crimes and misdemeanors. The House of Representatives alone has the power to *impeach* a person, that is, to make the

Many First Ladies in the twentieth century have participated actively in public affairs. Eleanor Roosevelt toured the nation both on her own and as the eyes and ears of her husband. Jacqueline Kennedy undertook a project to restore early nineteenth century furnishings to the White House. The "Keep America Beautiful" campaign was the special concern of Lady Bird Johnson. Pat Nixon made several goodwill tours including a trip to Africa in 1972. (UPI photo)

accusation. Only once has a President of the United States been impeached. That was President Andrew Johnson, who had succeeded to the Presidency on the death of President Lincoln. Most congressmen violently disagreed with President Johnson's policies.

Impeachment cases are tried by the Senate. In impeachment proceedings against a President, the Chief Justice of the Supreme Court presides. To convict the person being tried, a two-thirds vote of the senators present is necessary. It was this two-thirds provision which kept Andrew Johnson from being removed from office in 1868. More than a majority of the Senate voted to find him guilty, but they failed by one vote to get the necessary two-thirds vote.

DUTIES OF THE PRESIDENT

With his inauguration the President takes over the duties of the office to which he has been elected.

The Constitution devotes only a few paragraphs—altogether a little more than 300 words—to the duties and powers of the President. Yet from those few statements has grown one of the most important and powerful positions in the history of the world. His duties are many and varied—executive, judicial, and legislative.

EXECUTIVE DUTIES. The section of the Constitution which deals with the duties of the President begins with this simple statement: "The President shall be commander in chief of the army and navy of the United States, and of the militia of the several States, when called into the

Include the fact that although the President is commander-in-chief of the armed forces, only Congress can appropriate the funds needed to implement Presidential orders.

actual service of the United States." In peace and in war the President is head of the armed forces.

The control of the military is always in the hands of an elected official who can be voted out of office by the people at the next election or removed from office by the people's representatives.

Under the provisions of this section of the Constitution Presidents have appointed and removed generals, they have sent the army and navy to protect American interests, they have dispatched marines and others to trouble spots. For example, President Truman appointed General Eisenhower to be Chief of Staff of the United States Army in 1945; President Theodore Roosevelt sent the marines to Nicaragua and other Latin-American countries soon after 1900; Presidents Eisenhower, Kennedy, and Johnson sent troops to Vietnam in the last decade; and President Johnson sent marines to the Dominican Republic in 1965.

The President has the power to make treaties with foreign countries. But the Constitution provides a rigid safeguard. All treaties must be approved by a two-thirds vote of the Senate.

However, the President can make executive agreements without Senate approval. These are agreements between the executives of two nations and are usually made when there is not time or the desire to wait for Senate action. An example was an agreement made by President Franklin D. Roosevelt with Prime Minister Winston Churchill before the United States entered World War II to exchange fifty United States destroyers for leases of British naval bases.

Over the years there have been various attempts to take away some of the presidential power for making such agreements.

THE MEN BEHIND THE PRESIDENT

In making a study of the Presidency, political scientists often study the men behind the President to get a fuller explanation of presidential actions and decisions. In a book published in 1960, Louis W. Koenig writes about seven of these men. He called his book *The Invisible Presidency*.

The Prologue to the volume begins with this paragraph,

"American history is customarily written as a saga of great men, especially great Presidents. It needs also to be written—or rewritten—in terms of 'second men,' the spectral figures who toil influentially in the shadows around the presidential throne. These little-hailed heroes are the President's favorite all-around advisers and assistants. Their invention, zest and talent for achievement have won fame for many a presidential administration and saved others from terrible failure."[1]

The seven men discussed in the book and the Presidents they served are:

Alexander Hamilton—George Washington

Martin Van Buren—Andrew Jackson

William Loeb, Jr.—Theodore Roosevelt

Colonel Edward M. House—Woodrow Wilson

Thomas G. Corcoran—Franklin D. Roosevelt

Harry Hopkins—Franklin D. Roosevelt

Sherman Adams—Dwight D. Eisenhower

Dr. Koenig tells about the work of each of them and the part each played in the administration of the President under whom he worked. Each of these men had a tremendous influence on the actions of Presidents and through them on the people and times of their day. Dr. Koenig consulted numerous sources in bringing together pertinent information about each of them.

[1]Louis W. Koenig, *The Invisible Presidency*. Holt, Rinehart and Winston, Inc., 1960, p. 3.

The President frequently uses radio and television to report to the people. Here President Nixon announces his wage and price control program in August, 1971. (Official Photograph, The White House)

Senator John W. Bricker of Ohio in 1954, for example, proposed a constitutional amendment. Under the Bricker amendment Congress would be given the power to regulate executive agreements. They could be enforced only after necessary legislation, and no agreement would be valid which violated the Constitution. The proposal failed to pass the Senate by one vote. Presidents have continued to make many executive agreements.

The President receives the representatives of other governments, and either he or an assistant acts as the United States representative in dealing with other countries.

The President has the duty of appointing many government officials, such as ambassadors, ministers, consuls, judges of the Supreme Court and other federal courts, certain postmasters, and the heads of various departments and agencies. These appointments must be approved by the Senate. He usually confers with congressional leaders before making major appointments.

When appointments are made to federal positions in a state, the President will ordinarily discuss the appointment with senators of that state who are members of his party, in accord with the custom of *senatorial courtesy*. Sometimes the Senate investigates an appointee thoroughly before approving his appointment.

Occasionally a person appointed by the President does not get approval of the Senate. This may happen if members of the Senate feel that the person was appointed for purely political reasons, if they believe his past record shows him to be unfit for the office, if they believe he has not always acted in the best interests of the

Making treaties is an important executive duty. Here, the late President John F. Kennedy signs the Nuclear Test Ban Treaty in 1963. What limitation does the Constitution place on the President's treaty-making power? (Wide World photo)

United States, or if they merely wish to block an appointment because of personal or political differences with the President. Without Senate approval the person does not get the position. Some noted appointments that did not get Senate approval are Justice Fortas as Chief Justice of the Supreme Court by President Johnson, and Judges Haynesworth and Carswell as Associate Justices by President Nixon.

If a vacancy occurs while the Senate is not in session, the President may make a temporary appointment, called an *interim* appointment. The appointee must be approved at the next session of the Senate. Many minor officials are appointed by the President or by the heads of the various departments without the consent of the Senate. Most government workers, however, are not appointed but hold their jobs under civil service.

The President must see to it that the laws of the United States are "faithfully executed." From this we get the name *executive branch.* He has the duty to enforce all laws of the country even though he may not approve a particular law.

According to the Constitution, the President may ask for written reports from the heads of the various executive departments. He is in constant communication with the many activities of the government. Personal and written reports keep him informed about all phases of the work of the government and help him to make decisions. He coordinates all executive activities of the government and has the final responsibility for having each department carry out its duties according to the Constitution and the laws passed by Congress.

JUDICIAL DUTIES. Many special powers and duties are given the President.

He has the power to grant reprieves and pardons to persons who have committed offenses against the United States.

A *reprieve* delays the execution of a penalty. When the President grants a reprieve, he postpones the time when the punishment is to be given. This is sometimes done in the case of a severe penalty when the President feels that postponement may allow time for new evidence to be presented.

A *pardon* expunges the sentence of a convicted person. When the President grants a pardon, he is really saying that the person pardoned is to be completely free and not considered a criminal. No pardons may be granted in impeachment cases. The power of the President to grant reprieves and pardons is a judicial one, for it deals with punishment for violation of laws.

LEGISLATIVE DUTIES. Congress has the power and the duty to make the laws for the nation. But the President has many legislative responsibilities. He suggests ideas to Congress which he believes should be made into laws. In addition, all laws passed by Congress must be submitted to him for his signature. Without his signature a bill does not become a law except under certain conditions.

After a bill is passed by both houses of Congress the President has a period of ten days (Sundays are not counted) in which to decide whether to sign it or not. If he signs it, it becomes a law. If he does not approve the bill, he may *veto* it. In that case he returns it with the reasons for his veto to the house where it was started. If both houses of Congress pass it again by a two-thirds vote, it becomes a law without his signature.

A bill also becomes a law without his signature if he does not return it within ten days. An exception, however, occurs if Congress passes bills within ten days of adjournment. These bills must be signed by the President to become laws. Any that he does not sign are automatically killed— the *pocket veto.*

The President must from time to time give Congress information about the state of the union. He does this soon after the opening of a session of Congress in his State of the Union address. At that time he reports to Congress about the affairs of the nation. He may at the same time suggest to Congress ideas which he believes should be made into laws.

The first Presidents delivered their messages in person, but after that it became customary for the President to send his message to Congress to have it read. President Wilson revived the old method of reading his own message, and since then messages have again been delivered in person. Today by means of radio and television the message is heard by millions of people, both in our country and in foreign lands.

The President also has the authority to call a special session of Congress or of either house. He may also adjourn a session of Congress if there is disagreement between the two houses about the time of adjournment.

The powers and duties of the President fall, then, into three general classifications: executive, judicial, and legislative. Most of them are executive powers by which he administers the affairs of the nation. These include his duties to carry out the federal laws, to make necessary appointments, to make treaties, and to act as commander in chief of the armed forces.

When he grants pardons and reprieves, he is sharing in the judicial powers of the government. His legislative duties include the making of suggestions to Congress about laws he believes necessary, the calling of special sessions of Congress, and the important power of signing or vetoing laws passed by Congress.

EXECUTIVE OFFICE OF THE PRESIDENT

Most people think of the White House as the home of the President and his family. It is that, but it is also the executive office of the President and his close administrative advisers. Chief among these advisers are various special assistants to the President, presidential secretaries, an armed forces aide, the presidential physician, a press secretary, administrative assistants, a social secretary, an executive clerk, a chief usher, and a press secretary and staff director for the first lady. Together they comprise the staff of the *White House Office.*

This staff assists the President in carrying out the many details of his immediate duties and responsibilities. They maintain communication with Congress and individual congressmen, with the heads of executive departments and agencies, with the news media, and with the general public. They handle official documents, write speeches, make arrangements for state dinners and receptions, and carry out other duties at the direction of the President.

Directly under the control of the President are also a number of other offices, bureaus, and councils. The *Office of Management and Budget* prepares the budget of the government and supervises its administration. It is also a watchdog agency to improve the efficient and economical operation of government agencies and services.

The *Council of Economic Advisers* helps the President in the preparation of his annual economic report to the Congress, advises him on economic conditions, helps him decide whether to raise or lower taxes, and tries generally to improve the economic life of the nation.

The purpose of the *Office of Economic Opportunity* (OEO) is to eliminate or reduce poverty through a variety of activities and services. These are generally designed to help unemployed individuals and out-of-school youth acquire basic skills and education and vocational training necessary for getting and keeping a job. The OEO program includes, among others: Job Corps, Work Experience Programs, Urban and Rural Community Action Programs, and Volunteers in Service to America (VISTA). Individuals in the VISTA program volunteer to provide their services to help communities throughout the United States solve economic and social problems. In July 1971 VISTA was transferred to a new agency, Action.

The National Security Council, the Office of Emergency Preparedness, and the Office of Science and Technology aid the President in promoting the national security. The members of the *National Security Council* are the President, the Vice President, the Secretary of State, the Secretary of Defense, and the Director of the Office of Emergency Preparedness. Its purpose is to consider policies on matters affecting national security and to make recommendations to the President.

The *Office of Emergency Preparedness* advises the President in coordinating and determining policy for all *emergency* preparedness activities of the government. These include developing and planning the emergency use of manpower, materials, industrial capacity, transportation, and communication; the civil defense program; preparing for stabilizing the civilian economy in an emergency; and planning for rehabilitation after an enemy attack. The office also develops plans for carrying on federal, state, and local governments under emergency conditions.

The *Office of Science and Technology*

THE EXECUTIVE BRANCH OF THE FEDERAL GOVERNMENT

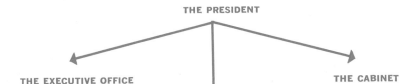

THE PRESIDENT

THE EXECUTIVE OFFICE

The White House Office
Office of Management and Budget
Council of Economic Advisers
Domestic Council
National Security Council
Central Intelligence Agency
Council on Environmental Quality
Office of Emergency Preparedness
Office of Telecommunications Policy
National Aeronautics and Space Council
Office of Science and Technology
Office of Economic Opportunity
Office of Special Representative for Trade Negotiations
Office of Intergovernmental Relations
Council on International Economic Policy
Office of Consumer Affairs
Special Action Office for Drug Abuse Prevention

THE CABINET

Secretary of State
Secretary of the Treasury
Secretary of Defense
Attorney General
Secretary of the Interior
Secretary of Agriculture
Secretary of Commerce
Secretary of Labor
Secretary of Health, Education, and Welfare
Secretary of Housing and Urban Development
Secretary of Transportation
United States Representative to the United Nations

THE INDEPENDENT AGENCIES (a partial listing)

AGENCIES FOR SPECIAL SERVICES

United States Civil Service Commission

General Services Administration

Administrative Conference of the United States

AGENCIES FOR SPECIAL PROJECTS

Veterans Administration

United States Information Agency

Environmental Protection Agency

Selective Service System

National Aeronautics and Space Administration

National Foundation on the Arts and the Humanities

National Science Foundation

Atomic Energy Commission

THE REGULATORY AGENCIES

Interstate Commerce Commission

Civil Aeronautics Board

Federal Reserve System

Federal Trade Commission

Federal Power Commission

Federal Communications Commission

Securities and Exchange Commission

Federal Maritime Commission

National Labor Relations Board

Federal Mediation and Conciliation Service

National Mediation Board

Equal Employment Opportunity Commission

GOVERNMENT CORPORATIONS

Federal Deposit Insurance Corporation
Tennessee Valley Authority
Panama Canal Company
Postal Service

gives advice to the President about develop-ing policies and coordinating programs dealing with science and technology. The purpose is to assure that these are used most effectively in the interests of national security and general welfare.

The *Central Intelligence Agency* advises and makes recommendations to the National Security Council on intelligence activities of the government. It provides for the appropriate dissemination of intelligence information within the government.

The *National Aeronautics and Space Council* advises the President about aeronautics and space activities. It fixes responsibilities of federal agencies engaged in space work.

The *Office of the Special Representative for Trade Negotiations* advises the President on the trade agreements program and helps in its administration.

The *Office of Intergovernmental Relations* works to strengthen relations among the levels of government: state, national, local.

The *Domestic Council* makes domestic policy recommendations to the President.

The *Council on Environmental Quality* formulates and recommends national policies to improve the environment.

The *Office of Telecommunications Policy* coordinates the telecommunications activities of the government.

Recent additions are: *Council on International Economic Policy, Office of Consumer Affairs,* and *Special Action Office for Drug Abuse Prevention.*

REWARDS OF THE
PRESIDENT   The President has a strenuous job. Often it must seem thankless. He must make many decisions. Some people will like a decision he makes; others

will not. There are always those who are opposed to his decisions. There are usually at least two sides to every issue, and in taking a stand the President often makes enemies of those who think differently than he does.

There are also many rewards. First, there is the satisfaction of serving one's country and of doing a good job. It is the satisfaction that comes to all of us when we do a good piece of work.

Second, there are the esteem and distinction that go with the job. To be the leader of this great country brings with it prestige and honor both from within and without the nation. The Presidency of the United States is one of the world's most honored positions, and the person who holds the office receives the honor. Even citizens who are opposed to a President's program and policies respect him as President of the nation.

Third, there is the opportunity to be reelected to office. Many Presidents have served more than one term. When Washington refused to run for a third term, he set a precedent which was not broken until Franklin D. Roosevelt was elected to third and fourth terms in 1940 and 1944. By the Twenty-second Amendment to the Constitution, however, no President can now be elected more than twice.

Fourth, there is the salary and other financial benefits which go with the office. The Constitution says: "The President shall, at stated times, receive for his services a compensation, which shall neither be increased or diminished during the period for which he shall have been elected, and he shall not receive within that period any other emolument from the United States, or any of them."

The President's yearly salary is now $200,000. He also receives an allowance of $40,000 for travel and entertainment, a tax-

Mention that once broken the two-term tradition, like other traditions, was then written into law.

On November 7, 1972, President Richard M. Nixon was returned to office by the electoral votes of 49 states and with a wide margin in popular votes. (Courtesy, The White House)

able expense fund of $50,000, and free medical and dental care. Besides this, Congress appropriates money for the operation of the presidential offices and the White House. Ex-Presidents receive a pension of $25,000 a year. Office space and help are also made available to them. Widows of former Presidents are given pensions of $10,000 yearly.

The Vice President receives a $62,500 salary, plus a $10,000 taxable expense allowance.

While these salaries may seem high to some people, they are lower than many salaries paid to individuals in large corporations or in the entertainment field.

The salary of the President cannot be changed during his term of office. Neither can he receive a special salary from a state. The reason for these provisions is to keep him from being influenced by either Congress or the states in the exercise of his duties.

CONCEPTS AND GENERALIZATIONS

1
The Presidency is one of the most powerful positions in the history of the world.

2
The office of the Presidency has been greatly expanded from the position originally established by the Constitution.

3
The qualifications for the Presidency make most people eligible for the office, but only a very few people have become President.

4
A presidential candidate may have fewer popular votes than an opponent and still win the election.

5
Actual and proposed changes in the procedure for electing the President are designed to make the election more democratic.

6
The President is the head of the executive department, but he also has legislative and judicial responsibilities.

7
A presidential veto may be overridden by a two-thirds vote of Congress.

8
The staff of the White House Office is assigned important responsibilities for the welfare and security of the nation.

9
The President's salary is only one, and for many Presidents the least important, of the rewards of office.

1. What are the Constitutional qualifications for the Presidency?

2. What are some important practical qualifications for the Presidency?

3. What are some political considerations in nominating a person as a candidate for President?

4. What is the present system of succession to the Presidency?

5. What two important omissions in the Constitution were corrected by the Twenty-fifth Amendment?

6. Why did the writers of the Constitution provide for the electoral college system of electing the President?

7. What changes have been made in the electing of the President since 1789 by (a) Constitutional amendment and (b) custom and usage?

8. How are the delegates to the national conventions chosen?

9. How does your state choose its delegates?

10. Name the convention committees and give their responsibilities.

11. What are the steps in the election process after the candidates are nominated?

12. How is the President chosen if no candidate receives a majority of the electoral vote?

13. What suggestions have been made to change the presidential election system?

14. What are the steps that must be taken to remove a President from office?

15. Give the duties of the President under each of these areas: (a) executive; (b) judicial; (c) legislative.

16. Why is the White House also called the Executive Mansion?

17. Who are the members of the staff of the White House Office?

18. What are the duties and responsibilities of the offices and bureaus under the direct control of the President?

IDEAS FOR DISCUSSION

1. Many people are not satisfied with the party convention system of nominating presidential candidates. Some of them have suggested that presidential candidates be nominated by means of a direct primary. Discuss the advantages and disadvantages of using a direct primary for making nominations.

2. The Constitution gives Congress the responsibility of deciding elections which are not determined by the electoral college. Why does the House of Representatives choose the President and the Senate the Vice President? Do you have any suggestions for changing this procedure?

3. Various proposals have been made for changing the system of electing the President. Two proposals are (a) direct popular vote of all people; and (b) retain the electoral college system, but give each candidate a part of each state's electoral votes in proportion to the popular vote cast for each. Do you prefer either of these to the present system? Could a candidate be elected according to *a* and lose that same election under *b*?

4. Sometimes the President has been a member of one party while the majority in Congress was of another party. There are people who believe that our government accomplishes little during those times. What are the disadvantages of such situations? May there be any advantages? If you think the disadvantages are greater than the advantages, what changes would you suggest?

5. Radio, television, newspapers, and magazines have helped to give citizens more information about presidential candidates than was possible years ago. Has this resulted in electing better Presidents?

6. The Constitution includes a method for removing a President from office. Why did the writers (a) provide a method for removing a President from office; (b) make it difficult to remove a President?

THINGS TO DO

1. Make a chart of the presidential candidates of the principal political parties since 1900. What were their home states? What were their personal and political qualifications for office?

2. Make a study of one of the following presidential campaigns and elections and report to the class on some of its interesting and unusual features:

a) Thomas Jefferson, 1800

b) John Quincy Adams, 1824

c) Abraham Lincoln, 1860

d) Rutherford B. Hayes, 1876

e) Woodrow Wilson, 1912

f) Franklin D. Roosevelt, 1940

g) Harry S. Truman, 1948

h) Dwight D. Eisenhower, 1952

i) John F. Kennedy, 1960

j) Lyndon B. Johnson, 1964

k) Richard M. Nixon, 1968

3. In your reading and study of the current news keep a record of the instances in which the President is mentioned. Use this information to make a chart of his many day-to-day activities.

4. Use an outline map of the United States to show (a) the states in which the Presidents were born; (b) their home states at time of election. What conclusions can you make from the map you have made?

5. Many interesting biographies of our Presidents are in your school and public libraries. Read one of them to learn more about the making of a President and of his life as President. Following are some suggestions:

Armbruster, Maxim, *The Presidents of the United States: A New Appraisal.* Horizon Press, 1963.

Burns, James, *John Kennedy: A Political Profile.* Harcourt, Brace & World, 1959.

Lorant, Stefan, *Lincoln—a Picture Story of His Life.* Harper & Row, 1957.

6. The home of the President, 1600 Pennsylvania Avenue, is a famous address. Prepare a list of other world-famous addresses. Include a statement for each telling why it is famous.

7. Make arrangements for showing a film on the Presidency. *The President* is a 16mm. Encyclopaedia Britannica film which you will find both interesting and instructive.

8. The story of the election of a President is well told by Theodore H. White in his books listed in the bibliography. Report to the class on some of the unusual features of one of the elections.

FURTHER READINGS

American Heritage, THE PRESIDENCY. American Heritage Publishing Co., 1964.

Barclay, Barbara, LAMPS TO LIGHT THE WAY: OUR PRESIDENTS. Bowmar, 1971.

Bell, Jack, THE PRESIDENCY: OFFICE OF POWER. Allyn and Bacon, 1967.

Burns, James MacGregor, PRESIDENTIAL GOVERNMENT: THE CRUCIBLE OF LEADERSHIP. Houghton Mifflin Co., 1965.

Harwood, Michael, IN THE SHADOW OF PRESIDENTS: THE AMERICAN VICE-PRESIDENCY AND THE SUCCESSION SYSTEM. J. B. Lippincott Company, 1966.

Johnson, Lyndon Baines, THE VANTAGE POINT: PERSPECTIVES OF THE PRESIDENCY, 1963-1969. Holt, Rinehart and Winston, Inc., 1971.

Kittler, Glenn D., HAIL TO THE CHIEF! THE INAUGURATION DAYS OF OUR PRESIDENTS. Chilton Co., 1965.

Liston, Robert A., PRESIDENTIAL POWER: HOW MUCH IS TOO MUCH. McGraw-Hill Book Co., Inc., 1971.

Lomask, Milton, I DO SOLEMNLY SWEAR: THE STORY OF THE PRESIDENTIAL INAUGURATION. Farrar, Straus & Giroux, Inc., 1966.

Lorant, Stefan, THE GLORIOUS BURDEN; THE AMERICAN PRESIDENCY. Harper & Row, Publishers, 1968.

Michener, James A., PRESIDENTIAL LOTTERY: THE RECKLESS GAMBLE IN OUR ELECTORAL SYSTEM. Random House, 1969.

Morris, Richard B., GREAT PRESIDENTIAL DECISIONS; STATE PAPERS THAT CHANGED THE COURSE OF HISTORY. J. B. Lippincott Company, 1965.

Neustadt, Richard E., PRESIDENTIAL POWER. New American Library, Inc., 1964. (Paperback)

New York Times, THE KENNEDY YEARS. Viking Press, 1966.

New York Times, THE ROAD TO THE WHITE HOUSE: THE STORY OF THE 1964 ELECTION. McGraw-Hill Book Co., Inc., 1965.

Robinson, Lloyd, THE HOPEFULS: TEN PRESIDENTIAL CAMPAIGNS. Doubleday & Co., Inc., 1966.

Rossiter, Clinton, THE AMERICAN PRESIDENCY. Harcourt, Brace Jovanovich, 1966. (Paperback)

Sayre, Wallace S., and Parris, Judith H., VOTING FOR PRESIDENT: THE ELECTORAL COLLEGE AND THE AMERICAN POLITICAL SYSTEM. The Brookings Institution, 1970.

Warren, Sidney, THE PRESIDENT AS WORLD LEADER. J. B. Lippincott Company, 1964.

White, Theodore H., THE MAKING OF THE PRESIDENT, 1960. New American Library, Inc., 1967. (Paperback)

———, THE MAKING OF THE PRESIDENT, 1968. Atheneum Publishers, 1969.

AMBASSADOR—the highest official representative of one country to another country.

ANNUITY — regular monthly or yearly payments to an individual from a fund to which the individual has made prior payments.

CENSUS—an official counting of the people, farms, business places, children of school age, or other groupings of a nation, state, or community.

CONSUL—a member of the Foreign Service who assists American citizens and businesses in foreign countries in matters affecting their business and commercial interests.

EMBASSY—the official office or residence of an ambassador in a foreign country.

INTERNAL REVENUE—income of the government from domestic, as distinguished from foreign, sources.

PASSPORT — a document issued by the government giving a citizen permission to travel in foreign countries.

PERSONA GRATA—a person who is welcome in a foreign country; an official representative of his country.

PERSONA NON GRATA—a person who is unwelcome in a foreign country; an official representative of a country who is to be recalled by his government at the request of the foreign government.

REVENUE—the income of government.

TARIFF—a tax on imported goods; also called duty.

VISA—a special document or an endorsement on a passport giving a person permission to enter a foreign country.

THE LANGUAGE
OF GOVERNMENT

12

The President's Cabinet and the Executive Departments

"There is hereby established at the seat of government an executive department to be known as the Department of Transportation. There shall be at the head of the Department a Secretary of Transportation, who shall be appointed by the President, by and with the advice and consent of the Senate."

Thus was established the latest in a series of departments designed to help the President carry out the duties of his office. The paragraph is only a small part of a total act passed by Congress on October 15, 1966. The act spells out in detail the organization and function of the Department of Transportation. Over the years similar acts of Congress established other departments, so that there are now eleven in all. The heads of these departments, together with the United States Representative to the

United Nations, form the President's Cabinet.

The Constitution does not mention the President's Cabinet, but the basis for it is in the Constitution. The document states that one of the duties of the President is to see that the laws of the land are "faithfully executed." This is a huge task. Thousands of laws have been passed by Congress. To enforce these laws and to carry out the directions of the Congresses, many executive and administrative agencies have been established to assist the President.

The writers of the Constitution recognized that the Presidency was not a one-man job. They stated that the President could ask for written opinions of the principal officers of the executive departments. They thus implied that there would be executives to help the President. But they made no provisions for the establishment of executive departments. These were started by Congress.

THE EXECUTIVE DEPARTMENTS

The first Congress after the adoption of the Constitution provided for three departments: State, Treasury, and War. It also established the office of Attorney General, although the Department of Justice with the Attorney General as head was not created until 1870.

These departments in Washington's day employed only a few people to carry on the work of the national government. Today there are eleven departments and more than fifty additional independent agencies and commissions, employing more than two million persons. Carrying on the government of the United States is the biggest business in our country. The many laws passed by Congress, the growth of the nation, the spread of industry, and the great demand of the people for more and more services from the national government have accounted for this large increase.

The eleven executive departments are listed on the next page. The Department of Defense combined the earlier Department of War and Department of the Navy in order to bring our armed forces under one head. At the time of this unification of the armed services, a separate post for the air force was also created. There are now three divisions—army, navy, and air force—under the Secretary of Defense.

The Department of Health, Education, and Welfare (HEW) replaced the former Federal Security Agency and gave Cabinet status to the health, welfare, and educational programs of the government. The Department of Housing and Urban Development (HUD) is responsible for the housing and urban development activities of the federal government. The most recent department, Transportation, has responsibility for providing leadership in the development of national transportation policies and programs.

THE PRESIDENT'S CABINET

President Washington developed the custom of calling together the heads of the executive departments for regular meetings. At these meetings he would discuss with them various problems confronting the new nation. Other Presidents have continued this practice.

These meetings are closed to the public and to the press. They are unofficial and no official records are kept. Only the President gives out information about the topics discussed. He decides whether to accept the advice given him by the *Secretaries*, as the heads of the various departments are called. He alone has the responsibility to make decisions. But he frequently bases them on the opinions of these close advisers,

Point out that it was the original intention of the framers of the Constitution to have the Senate be the advisory body of the President.

255

THE ELEVEN DEPARTMENTS OF THE EXECUTIVE BRANCH[1]

NAME	YEAR ESTABLISHED
State	1789
Treasury	1789
Defense	1947[2]
Interior	1849
Justice	1870[3]
Agriculture	1889[4]
Commerce	1913[5]
Labor	1913[5]
Health, Education, and Welfare	1953
Housing and Urban Development	1965
Transportation	1966

[1]The Postal Service was created by the Continental Congress in 1775 and established by the U.S. Congress in 1789. The Postmaster General became a member of the Cabinet in 1829, and the Post Office Department was established as a department in 1872. It was terminated as a department in 1970.
[2]The Department of Defense combined into one the Department of War, established in 1789; the Department of the Navy, established in 1798; and the Department of the Air Force, established in 1947.
[3]The post of Attorney General was created in 1789, but the Department of Justice was not established until 1870.
[4]The Department of Agriculture was created in 1862, but was not established as an executive department until 1889.
[5]In 1913 the Department of Commerce and Labor, which had been created in 1903, was divided into two separate departments.

a group that has come to be known as the *Cabinet.* Their salary is $60,000 a year.

The Vice President attends Cabinet meetings. The United States Representative to the United Nations also holds Cabinet rank and attends some meetings. Others are invited for discussion of particular subjects.

The members of the Cabinet are selected by the President and approved by the Senate. This is one of the President's first jobs after his election. He makes his selections with a great deal of thought.

In choosing these people he pays attention to many factors. During his campaign for the Presidency he may have promised some individuals important government posts in return for their support. These promises must now be considered, and some of the individuals may be offered Cabinet posts. For example, the Postmaster General in some Cabinets has been the chairman of the National Committee of the President's political party.

In general, the President will offer Cabinet positions to prominent members of his own party in order to keep the continued support of his political party and also to have executives who will carry out party policies. This rule is sometimes broken if a President feels it wise to gain the favor of members of the opposition party. For example, President Franklin Roosevelt, a Democrat, had two members of the Republican Party in his Cabinet in order to present a unified, bipartisan front to the world during World War II.

Ordinarily a President will try to have various sections of the country represented in his Cabinet. This helps him keep in touch with many people, and it gives the people of the regions represented the feeling that their problems can be brought to the attention of the President.

Each Cabinet member except the United States Representative to the United Nations is the head of an executive department. Therefore, in making his selections, the President tries to choose individuals who

He [the Secretary of State] must be strong enough to resist demands from factions within the country having at heart some particular or local grievance. It is proper that such particularized views and pressures be expressed. That is the way our democracy works. There is no way of preventing this; nor should there be. But, at the same time, the secretary of state must be strong enough to say no. And this will make him unpopular.

—Former Secretary of State JAMES F. BYRNES (1945-1947). From *An Uncertain Tradition: American Secretaries of State in the Twentieth Century* by Norman A. Graebner copyright © 1961 by McGraw-Hill Book Company, Inc. Used by permission of McGraw-Hill Book Company.

As Administrator of the Bureau of Security and Consular Affairs of the Department of State, Barbara Watson is responsible for the passport office, the visa office, and the office of special consular services with 280 consulates. Miss Watson is shown conferring with representatives of Congress. (photo courtesy of Ebony magazine)

have the administrative ability to operate a department. If possible, each person should also have the technical knowledge for his special area. This is, however, not a primary consideration, for the technical knowledge needed to operate a department can be supplied by its permanent civil service employees.

THE DEPARTMENT
OF STATE
When the President holds a Cabinet meeting, the Secretary of State sits at his right side. This is because the Department of State is the first and most important of the departments. Many outstanding statesmen have held the post of Secretary of State. The first was Thomas Jefferson, who later became President. The list of Secretaries of State includes such famous people as John Marshall, Henry Clay, Daniel Webster, Elihu Root, William J. Bryan, Charles E. Hughes, Cordell Hull, George C. Marshall, John Foster Dulles, and Dean Rusk.

The Secretary of State has a large staff to help him. A recent manual of the United States government lists the names of more than one hundred people who head various agencies under the supervision of the Sec-

retary of State. These people have thousands of other employees under them who carry on the work of the department both at home and abroad.

Most of these people have made government service a lifetime career, and most of them hold their positions under civil service. Ordinarily only the Secretary of State, the under secretaries, the assistant secretaries, and our chief representatives in foreign capitals hold their positions by appointment of the President; the rest are civil service employees and cannot be removed from office by him. As in other departments they form the *bureaucracy*, the permanent employees who have continuing influence over governmental policies.

DOMESTIC DUTIES. The Department of State has two kinds of duties, domestic and foreign. The domestic duties are of minor importance, such as keeping the seal of the United States and writing to governors.

The Secretary of State once had responsibility for keeping the file of laws and treaties. This work was transferred to the Archivist of the General Services Administration. The Great Seal of the United States is still in his care. He has responsibility for affixing it to official documents.

According to government protocol, Cabinet members are ranked according to the date of origin of the Department which they head.

257

He also carries on official correspondence for the President with state governors.

FOREIGN DUTIES. The foreign duties of the Department of State are of major importance. They had their beginnings in Revolutionary days. The department replaced some earlier committees and departments which had handled foreign affairs since our break with England in 1775.

The duties now include the supervision of all our representatives to other governments, the negotiation of treaties, and the carrying on of communications and correspondence with representatives of foreign governments. Sometimes a President may deal directly with another government. A dramatic example of this is the "hot line", the telephone between the White House and the Kremlin. However, by far most of our dealings with other governments are handled by the Department of State. This places a great responsibility upon the Secretary of State, and for this reason Presidents have been very careful in filling this position with capable men. They have usually tried to get an outstanding statesman to accept this position.

The representatives of foreign governments to our own country are received by this department. The department also has supervision of the foreign travel of United States citizens and regulates the travel of foreigners in the United States. It issues passports to Americans wishing to travel in foreign countries and visas to foreigners wanting to enter the United States.

THE GREAT SEAL OF THE UNITED STATES

The Great Seal is the coat of arms of the United States, an official emblem, mark of identification, and symbol of authority of the United States government. It is used to certify certain papers after the President has signed them and they have been countersigned by the Secretary of State. Both sides of the seal are on one-dollar bills.

The story of the Great Seal begins July 4, 1776. Immediately after adopting the Declaration of Independence, the Continental Congress appointed Franklin, Adams, and Jefferson as a committee to make a design for the new nation. Congress approved the design in 1782 and by law adopted it on September 15, 1789 as the seal of the United States and placed it in the custody of the Secretary of State.

The thirteen stars and stripes represent the thirteen original states. On one side, the motto "E Pluribus Unum" (One out of many), signifies the union of one nation from separate states. The olive branch symbolizes peace and the arrows, military readiness.

On the other side, not shown, the symbols mean:

Pyramid—Strength

"Novus Ordo Seclorum"—A new order of the ages

MDCCLXXVI—1776

Eye—Watchfulness of Providence

"Annuit Coeptis"—He has favored our undertakings

For example, if you should be planning a trip to another country, you would need to apply to the State Department for a *passport*. This is an identification certificate showing that you are a citizen of the United States. Application forms for passports may be obtained from the Secretary of State or from clerks of federal courts and certain state courts.

THE FOREIGN SERVICE. All ambassadors, consuls, and other representatives to foreign countries are in the Foreign Service of the Department of State. There are many reasons for maintaining representatives abroad. They look after the interests of the United States and its citizens. They represent the President and keep him informed of developments which may affect the United States. They help Americans doing business or traveling in foreign countries.

The chief officers in the Foreign Service are ambassadors. They are appointed by the President and approved by the Senate. The position of ambassador is one of honor. For that reason ambassadorships are often highly desired by some individuals. However, because an *embassy*, the official residence of an ambassador, is costly to maintain, until recently only wealthy people could accept the position. Their salaries and allowances did not cover their actual expenses.

As the official representatives of the United States, they hold many receptions and official functions which are very costly. The Foreign Service Act of 1946 increased their salaries and allowances considerably, so that now they can ordinarily meet the expenses of their office. Under this act our Ambassador to London, for example, now receives more than $65,000 a year in salary and allowances.

Before a person is appointed as an ambassador, our government finds out whether the person is acceptable to the government of the country to which he is to be sent. An acceptable person is said to be *persona grata*. As long as he remains so, he lives in the foreign country as our representative. As such, he cannot be arrested, his home is regarded as American property, and he is not subject to the laws and regulations of the country.

The United States maintains representatives in nearly every country in the world. Shown here is the official residence, or embassy, of our ambassador to India. (U.S. Dept. of State)

Should he, however, commit acts which make him unacceptable to the foreign government, he becomes *persona non grata*, and our government is asked to recall him from the foreign country.

The duties of ambassadors are largely political. But they carry on a wide variety of activities, from helping a stranded American tourist to making treaties with other nations. Lesser officials who also look after our political interests in foreign countries are ministers, envoys, and diplomatic agents. Our commercial and business interests are given assistance, when needed, by *consuls* in the Foreign Service.

All of these people aid the President in developing our program of foreign relations. Their speeches and actions often determine the opinions that people in other countries have of the United States.

As the nations of the world are brought closer and closer together through more rapid means of communication and trans-portation, the work of the Foreign Service becomes ever more important. In the interest of world peace and harmony its work is truly important.

OTHER BUREAUS. Among the many bureaus of the State Department are these: Public Affairs, Economic Affairs, East Asian and Pacific Affairs, Inter-American Affairs, African Affairs, European Affairs, Near Eastern and South Asian Affairs, Educational and Cultural Affairs, and Security and Consular Affairs.

The Peace Corps was part of the State Department from 1961 to 1971 when it was transferred to a new agency, *Action*. Volunteers provide needed skilled manpower for the developing nations of the world. Its purpose, as stated in the Peace Corps Act, is

to promote world peace and friendship through a Peace Corps, which shall make available to interested countries and areas men and women of the United States qualified for service abroad and

The Peace Corps has proved to be one of our most effective vehicles for promoting friendship and better understanding between us and other peoples of the world. This volunteer is teaching a class in English in Afghanistan. (Peace Corps)

willing to serve, under conditions of hardship if necessary, to help the peoples of such countries and areas in meeting their needs for trained manpower, and to help promote a better understanding of the American people on the part of the peoples served and a better understanding of other peoples on the part of the American people.

An important addition to the State Department is the Agency for International Development (AID). This agency has the responsibility for carrying out nonmilitary foreign assistance programs of the United States. It provides supervision and general direction for all assistance programs under the Foreign Assistance Act of 1961. It also has certain functions under earlier acts; one of these is the development of Latin America. The major areas through which it provides this assistance are: development loans and grants, investment guaranties, investment surveys, development research, international organizations, contingency fund, and Alliance for Progress.

THE DEPARTMENT OF THE TREASURY

If you examine some United States paper money, you will find two signatures on it. One is that of the Secretary of the Treasury and the other is that of the Treasurer of the United States. These are the people who take care of the financial matters of the nation. The Department of the Treasury handles all the national financial and monetary problems, besides being in charge of a number of miscellaneous bureaus.

This department was one of the original ones established by the first Congress. Alexander Hamilton was its first Secretary in President Washington's Cabinet. He had the difficult task of putting the new nation on a sound financial basis. Congress had given him rather broad powers to manage finances and to establish public credit.

He had the duty to issue warrants for the payment of the public money according to the appropriations voted by Congress. He was required to furnish Congress with financial information whenever requested to do so.

The present Secretary of the Treasury still has the same powers and duties. The scope of his position, however, has been greatly enlarged through the growth of the nation. At the present time more than 200 billion dollars are expended every year under his supervision.

The Office of the Treasurer of the United States is a bureau in the Treasury Department. It is the job of the Treasurer to take care of the *revenue* (money) of the nation and to spend it only upon the written notice of the Secretary of the Treasury.

REVENUE. The revenue of the United States is obtained from several sources. One of the defects of the Articles of Confederation was that the federal government had no power to levy and collect taxes. Under the Constitution the government has that power. With the passage of the Sixteenth Amendment, the federal government was given the power to levy a tax on incomes of individuals and corporations. Today most of the federal revenue is obtained through the income tax. About 125 billion dollars are received from this source annually. Most wage earners pay income taxes either through direct payment to the government or through a withholding tax whereby the employer deducts a certain amount of money each pay period and sends it to the government at regular intervals. (See Chapter 24.)

The income tax is known as *internal revenue*, because it is collected from within the country. Additional internal revenue is collected through taxes on airline tickets;

Relate how the first Secretary of the Treasury, Alexander Hamilton, fought for the establishment of a national bank.

on gasoline and lubricating oil; on telephone and telegraph charges; on stamp taxes for cards, deeds, bonds, stocks, liquors, and wines; on cigarettes, cigars, and tobacco; and on a number of other items.

The Internal Revenue Service is the agency within the Treasury Department which is charged with the collection of these taxes. It has thousands of workers in offices throughout the country. Besides the collection of taxes, it has the duty to prepare and to distribute the necessary tax forms and to give instructions for filing tax returns.

One of its divisions is charged with the investigation of alleged tax evasions and frauds. For example, it prosecutes individuals and corporations who are accused of making false reports on their income tax returns. false reports on income tax returns.

Some federal revenue is obtained through the operation of the Bureau of Customs. Duties, or *tariffs*, which are taxes on imports, are levied on some goods coming into the country; and it is the duty of the Bureau of Customs to collect these taxes.

Tariffs were at one time a chief source of federal revenue. At the present time, however, they supply only a small part of the federal income. The Bureau of Customs helps in the prevention of smuggling, it enforces laws regarding imports, and it checks exports to other countries.

COINAGE AND PRINTING OF MONEY. The Treasury Department has two bureaus which issue United States money. The Bureau of Engraving and Printing issues all of our paper money, and the Bureau of the Mint issues the metal coins we use. Paper money is printed in Washington, and the coins are stamped in mints located in Philadelphia and Denver. The Bureau of Engraving and Printing also produces postage stamps, Treasury bonds, and food coupons.

BANKING AND BONDS. Some of the money of the United States is held in the treasury at Washington, and some of it is deposited in Federal Reserve, national, and state banks throughout the country. The supervision of the national banks is an important function of the Treasury Depart-

Bills of United States currency roll off a new high-speed press. Printing currency and coining money is one of the important functions of the Treasury Department. (Bureau of Engraving and Printing)

Congress chartered the first Bank of the United States in 1791. Here is the Philadelphia branch of that bank, founded in 1795. Supervising the national banks is another duty of the Treasury Department. (Library of Congress)

Some currency is deposited in Federal Reserve, national and state banks. These men are assembling money in a Federal Reserve bank for distribution to member banks. (Federal Reserve Bank of Philadelphia)

ment. The person directly in charge of this work is the Comptroller of the Currency.

To finance the many governmental activities, the national government through the Treasury Department has borrowed many billions of dollars since 1929. The national debt is now more than 400 billion dollars. Most of the money is owed to banks and insurance companies. But some of it is owed to individuals who hold government bonds. Some of this money is owed to you if you own government savings bonds. The United States Savings Bond Division in the Department of the Treasury promotes the sale of savings bonds.

Thus the Department of the Treasury collects the money for the federal government and spends it as Congress directs. If necessary, it borrows money, up to limits set by Congress, to carry on government business. The Treasury deals with financial matters, but it also has other duties.

SECRET SERVICE. The United States Secret Service is a branch of the Treasury Department. It is charged with the protection of the President and Vice President and their families, the President-elect, presidential candidates, and past presidents. It deals with counterfeiting and other crimes involving tampering with money.

THE DEPARTMENT OF DEFENSE

Late in 1951 President Truman started a nation-wide argument when he ordered General Douglas MacArthur to come home from Korea and replaced him with General Matthew Ridgway as Far Eastern Commander. Some people agreed with the President's action; others said General MacArthur should have been kept in his command; some congressmen even started talking about impeaching the President. This use of presidential power was unusual. But MacArthur came home; the President had acted within his constitutional powers as commander in chief.

The Secretary of Defense heads the executive department that helps the President carry out his duties as commander in chief. This department was created in 1947, and grew out of the experience of World War II that showed the need for closer cooperation among our armed services. The National Security Act combined into the Department of Defense the earlier Departments of the Army and the Navy and a new Department of the Air Force. Each of these departments is headed by a secretary who operates under the Secretary of Defense. (See Table, page 256.)

These four secretaries are nonmilitary persons, but much of the work of the Defense Department is carried out by military officers who head the army, the navy, and the air force. These military leaders comprise the Joint Chiefs of Staff.

Emphasize the fact that our military forces historically have been under civilian governmental control.

Their work includes military planning, and they are the principal military advisers to the President. The Commandant of the Marine Corps attends meetings of the Joint Chiefs of Staff.

The offices of the Department of Defense are located in the largest office building in the world, the Pentagon. The activities of this department have become increasingly important since the beginning of World War II. These activities include (1) providing adequate defense for the nation; (2) arranging for the manufacture and improvement of weapons, planes, tanks, ships, and other equipment; and (3) recruiting men and women for our army, navy, and air force, through an Assistant Secretary of Defense who is in charge of manpower and reserve affairs. The Defense Department has a variety of agencies and boards which help in the development of an organized defense program. But the three military departments—the army, the navy, and the air force—are in direct charge of the defense of the nation.

THE ARMY. The army has responsibility for the operation of all our land forces. Its main wartime job is to conduct land campaigns and to defeat the armies of our enemies. It protects various installations in the United States and in the territories which are considered important for the nation's security. For example, it safeguards the Panama Canal and the locks at Sault Ste. Marie.

The Secretary of the Army also has certain nonmilitary responsibilities. He has responsibilities for maintaining and operating the Panama Canal. An extensive civil works program is carried on under the Corps of Engineers. This program includes such activities as the approval of plans for bridges, the improvement of waterways, and the control of floodwaters.

While the head of the Department of the Army is a civilian, the actual military operation is carried on by the army chief of staff, who is charged with planning, developing, and carrying out the army program. He has a large number of assistants, commissions, and boards who aid him in this big job.

THE NAVY. The navy has the responsibility for the operation of all our naval forces and the marine corps. In time of war or at other times of emergency the President may also place the coast guard under its rule. The navy has supervision of our fleets and seagoing forces and of certain shore establishments.

As in the case of the army, the Secretary of the Navy is a civilian, and his principal military adviser is the chief of naval operations. This person has responsibility for the use of our naval forces in wartime and for maintaining them and keeping them ready for war during peacetime. He carries out his duties with the help of many bureaus and boards.

THE AIR FORCE. The air force has primary responsibility for defending the United States against air attack. It has the job of developing and maintaining an adequate air force to make our nation supreme in the air. These responsibilities are in the hands of a civilian, the Secretary of the Air Force.

The chief of staff of the air force is his chief adviser and is charged with carrying out all operations of the air force in times of war and peace. The extensive duties of the Department of the Air Force are carried out by a great variety of boards and specialized individuals.

THE DEPARTMENT OF JUSTICE Late in the afternoon on a hot summer day in 1935 a man was shot by agents of the Federal Bureau of Investigation as he left a theater in Chicago's North Side. This man, John Dillinger, had been hunted for years by local, state, and federal officers. Finally the Federal Bureau of Investigation had learned of his whereabouts, and he died trying to escape the trap FBI agents had set for him. He had committed crimes involving federal laws, and so the FBI had been brought into the search for him.

The Federal Bureau of Investigation is perhaps the best-known agency of the Department of Justice. The duties of this department are to enforce federal laws, to represent the United States government in legal matters, to supervise the federal prisons, and to furnish legal advice and opinions to the President and the executive agencies.

The head of the department is the Attorney General. He is the chief law officer of the United States government. In very important cases he appears personally before the Supreme Court.

To carry out the work of federal law enforcement, the United States and its territories are divided into nearly 100 districts. Each of these districts has a marshal and an attorney assigned to it. The marshal makes arrests and sees that the court orders are carried out. The attorney prepares and pleads the federal cases in the district courts.

The Department of Justice has a number of divisions with specialized duties. The Antitrust Division deals with violations of federal antitrust laws. The Tax Division deals with violations of the federal tax laws. With the growth in recent years of the number of persons paying income taxes, the work of this division has been greatly increased.

Other divisions are the Civil Division, which deals with claims for and against the federal government; the Land and Natural Resources Division, which deals with all matters relating to real property, including lands, water, and related natural resources; the Internal Security Division, which handles cases of subversive activities directed against internal security; the Civil Rights Division, which handles cases dealing with civil rights issues; and the Criminal Division, which represents the United States in all cases involving violations of federal laws, such as counterfeiting, forgery, kidnapping, treason, traffic in narcotics, extortion, and espionage.

Four important bureaus of the Justice Department are the Federal Bureau of Investigation, the Bureau of Prisons, the Immigration and Naturalization Service, and the Bureau of Narcotics and Dangerous Drugs. The first, as was just noted, has become famous because of the skill and thoroughness with which it tracks down criminals. It has developed a reputation similar to that of the Royal Canadian Mounted Police in "getting their man." They investigate reported violations of more than 170 matters that are under their authority.

The Bureau of Prisons supervises the prisons and correctional institutions of the federal government. There are more than twenty of various types. Some famous prisons are at Leavenworth in Kansas and Atlanta in Georgia.

An important service of the Justice Department is the Immigration and Naturalization Service. The duties of this service include (1) supervising the admission of immigrants and the naturalization of aliens; (2) patrolling the borders of the United States to prevent illegal entry into the country; (3) investigating reported cases of violation of immigration laws and recommending prosecution of persons who violate the immigration laws; and (4) aiding aliens who wish to become citizens and cooperating with public schools in preparing these aliens for citizenship. District offices of the Immigration and Naturalization Service are located throughout the country. It also has offices in several foreign countries.

In 1968 the Bureau of Narcotics and Dangerous Drugs was added to the Department of Justice. It was formed by combining two earlier existing bureaus, Narcotics, in the Treasury Department, and Drug Abuse Control, in the Department of Health, Education, and Welfare. The primary responsibility of this bureau is to enforce laws relating to narcotics and dangerous drugs. The bureau also carries on an educational program to prevent drug abuse.

Since 1966 the Department of Justice has had new duties under the Civil Rights Act of 1964, enforcing desegregation in public facilities and the ending of discrimination by employers and unions. New duties have been added also by the Civil Rights Act of 1968, which was aimed chiefly at ending discrimination in the sale or rental of housing. The Voting Rights Acts of 1965 and 1970 gave the department responsibilities with regard to election laws and practices. (See pages 103-106.)

Through its Community Relations Service the Department of Justice provides assistance to communities and individuals in resolving difficulties and conflicts relating to discriminatory practices. The Service has encouraged groups of citizens to foster understanding at the local level. However, the principal activity of this agency, in addition to resolving racial difficulties, consists of developing programs and activities to preclude such difficulties by eliminating the disadvantages and discrimination suffered by all minorities.

THE POLITICAL SCIENTIST AND GOVERNMENT

Political scientists are frequently called on to render services of various kinds to the government either as consultants or as full-time employees. One far-reaching activity in which a number of political scientists were engaged was a study of the operation of the executive branch of the federal government, "The Commission on Organization of the Executive Branch of the Government." Political scientists were among the members of both the commission and the several task forces.

Popularly, this commission was known as the "Hoover Commission," because it was chaired by former President Herbert Hoover. It was a congressional commission, created by unanimous vote of Congress in 1947. Its twelve members were assisted in their assignment of developing a blueprint of good government by twenty-four task forces. The membership of these groups included, besides political scientists, economists, college presidents, public accountants, government career employees, medical doctors, professors, business executives, bankers, lawyers, and many other specialists. In small committees they examined and evaluated many aspects of the executive branch and made recommendations for changes.

The publisher's preface to one of the volumes reporting the work of the commission states its task and results in these words:

"The task forces were given time, opportunity, and staffs with which to pursue their inquiries until they got to the heart of each problem. Then, after periods of 10 to 14 months, they returned to the Commission with their findings in each field.

"The result was the most imposing collection of facts, figures, and opinions on Government that has ever been assembled. It amounted, in fact, to some 2,500,000 words of basic data of the most valuable sort.

"From this massive bulk the Commission then prepared to carve out the model of a streamlined, modern Government."[1]

[1]The Hoover Commission Report on Organization of the Executive Branch of the Government, McGraw-Hill Book Co., 1949, pp. vi-vii. Used by permission of McGraw-Hill Book Company.

THE DEPARTMENT OF
THE INTERIOR

Near the city of Las Vegas in southeastern Nevada is Hoover Dam, one of the highest dams in the United States, that holds back the waters of the Colorado River. The 726-foot-high dam is used for flood control, furnishes water for irrigation, and produces much electric power. Lake Mead, formed by the dam, 115 miles long with an area of nearly 229 square miles, is one of the world's largest artificial lakes. The lake provides recreational facilities for thousands of people each year.

Hoover Dam is an excellent example of the type of work carried on by the Department of the Interior. The work of this department concerns mainly the management, the conservation, and the development of the natural resources of the United States and

United States territories. Several bureaus also have (1) supervision of the territories and island possessions of the United States and (2) the responsibility of watching over the interests of the American Indians and the natives of Alaska.

The Bureau of Indian Affairs tries to improve life for about 400,000 Indians and 40,000 Alaskan natives. Its responsibilities include better use of their land and other resources, the improvement of schools and health services, and the provision of welfare aid. The Bureau of Land Management has responsibility for the wise use of public lands. The Bureau of Mines has responsibility for improving safety in mining and for conserving mineral resources.

The National Park Service regulates the use of our national parks. For example, Yellowstone National Park and Rocky

Mt. Rainier National Park, with its spectacular scenery, attracts many visitors. The National Park Service preserves and protects the natural beauty of this and other parks. (Rainier National Park Company, Tacoma, Washington)

Hoover Dam, 726 feet high, is one of the highest dams in the world. It is operated by the Bureau of Reclamation of the Department of the Interior. (Bureau of Reclamation, Dept. of the Interior)

Mountain National Park are supervised by it. The Bureau of Reclamation has responsibility for conservation, development, and wise use of the land and water resources of the West. Much of our irrigation work is supervised by this bureau; for example, Hoover Dam is one of its projects.

Pollution of the nation's lakes and rivers is a growing problem. Congress has passed several acts to deal with this problem. The result was the establishment of the Federal Water Pollution Control Administration in the Department of the Interior to prevent and control water pollution. The agency was abolished in 1970 and its functions were transferred to the Environmental Protection Agency. (See page 573.)

A related activity is carried on by the Office of Saline Water. It carries on a research and development program looking for practical and economical means for desalting sea water for agricultural and other uses.

Other agencies of the department have responsibility for the administration of Pacific Islands and for the development of programs of outdoor recreation. Several bureaus have supervision of various power projects and of the use of natural resources for defense purposes.

THE DEPARTMENT OF AGRICULTURE

Along a lonely road in Oregon a crew of men are stringing an electric light-and-power line to a remote farming region. They may be doing this under the Rural Electrification Administration. Assistance for farmers in obtaining electricity is furnished by this agency of the Department of Agriculture.

The aim of this department is to furnish agricultural information to improve the work and life of the farmers of the nation. Rural electrification is only one of its many services. The department has extensive research, marketing, and educational programs.

The research deals with many phases of farming and the findings are made available to farmers throughout the country. For example, studies carried on by the department on such items as soil chemistry, crop and livestock production, farming techniques, and marketing procedures help farmers with their production and marketing problems. A continuous educational program assists the farmers of the United States in making the most effective use of the soil.

To carry on its big program of agricultural assistance, the Department of Agriculture maintains many bureaus and regional offices. One is the Federal Crop Insurance Corporation whose purpose is to develop a system whereby farmers can insure crops against hazards over which they have no control. Another is the Commodity Credit Corporation which has the responsibility of maintaining price support for certain products.

These and similar services of the Department of Agriculture have helped to improve greatly the working and living conditions of the farmer during the past fifty years. These activities are discussed more fully in Chapter 29. A former department agency which is now independent, the Farm Credit Administration, provides a credit system to help farmers in making loans.

THE DEPARTMENT OF COMMERCE

Every ten years the federal government makes a complete count of all people in the United States. This is known as a *census* and is made by the Bureau of the Census of the Department of Commerce. The Constitution provides for a census of the people in order to determine

Point out that the U.S. Government first conducted a census in 1790.

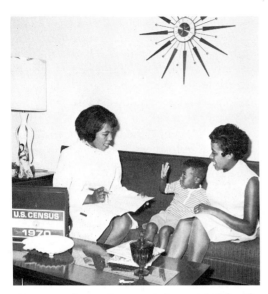

A census-taker gathers statistics needed by the Bureau of the Census. Much valuable information is secured by the various kinds of censuses taken by the Bureau. (Bureau of the Census)

the number of representatives in Congress from each state. But counting people is only part of the work of the Census Bureau. Censuses are also made of housing, agriculture, manufacturing and mineral industries, retail and wholesale businesses, service trades, and governmental units.

These censuses are made by the Department of Commerce to help carry out its purpose to promote and develop the foreign and domestic commerce of the United States. Information gained from the censuses helps industries to make plans for the future. For example, a census may show how many families are in need of housing or the number of persons interested in buying a new refrigerator.

Another agency of the department is the Bureau of Domestic Commerce. It promotes the growth of the industry and commerce of the nation. It also has the duty to develop readiness plans for the mobilization of industry. A related agency is the Bureau of International Commerce.

Additional agencies help the businessman by giving him information about business conditions both at home and abroad. The Patent Office issues patents to inventors to safeguard their rights to their products.

The Department of Commerce has an agency, National Bureau of Standards, which has charge of setting up standards for weights and measures and for various machines and products. For example, it has the standard measures for the length of a yard, the weight of a pound, the amount of steel in certain gauge metal, and the length and width of a size 7C shoe.

One way in which the Department of Commerce influences each of us frequently is through the National Weather Service which reports and forecasts the weather. Over 300 local offices of the Weather Service keep us continually informed about weather conditions throughout the country. We can know for several days ahead what our weather will be.

The National Weather Service is an office of the National Oceanic and Atmospheric Administration. Other offices of this Administration are the National Marine Fisheries Service, the National Ocean Survey, and the National Environmental Satellite Service. Their duties include making ocean surveys and carrying on sea research.

Special functions dealing with unemployment have been assigned to the Economic Development Administration. It develops long-range programs for areas having a high rate of unemployment and low family incomes. It seeks to develop new employment opportunities and to expand existing facilities in these areas.

THE DEPARTMENT OF LABOR

We often hear people talking about the cost of living. They may make comments comparing the cost of food today with the cost a few years ago. They talk about the costs in one city being higher than the costs in another.

The Bureau of Labor Statistics in the Department of Labor has taken the guesswork out of such comparisons. This bureau publishes an index which tells whether the cost of living has gone up or down. The index is based on information collected regularly by the bureau in fifty-six cities. It is used by business and labor in many ways, one of which is to regulate wage rates in some industries.

The cost-of-living index is one of the many services of the Department of Labor. The purpose of the department is to administer and enforce laws designed to improve the working conditions of the worker in the United States. Just as the farmer has the Department of Agriculture and the businessman the Department of Commerce, so the worker has the Department of Labor to help him.

The Department of Labor maintains regional offices throughout the country for the purpose of administering various labor laws. One of these laws is the Fair Labor Standards Act. This law regulates wages and hours of workers engaged in interstate commerce or in producing goods which cross state lines. The law provides for a minimum wage and maximum hours for such workers. It also regulates child labor in those industries.

Through the Occupational Safety and Health Administration the department develops programs of safety in industry. The Office of Wage and Compensation Programs, established in 1972, administers programs dealing with various laws affecting low incomes, wage rates, federal employee compensation, and employment discrimination.

A special Women's Bureau has charge of improving the working conditions of women. It collects data and compiles reports dealing with their welfare.

The Manpower Administration deals with various programs related to manpower. Its bureaus and agencies are responsible for the welfare and training of apprentices, for employment security, and the improvement of employment conditions. One agency, the United States Training and Employment Service, administers a nationwide system of public employment service, promoting maximum use of the nation's manpower.

THE DEPARTMENT OF HEALTH, EDUCATION, AND WELFARE

Almost every shopping trip to a grocery or a drugstore brings you into contact with the services of the Food and Drug Administration. This agency of the Department of Health, Education, and Welfare (HEW) has responsibility for checking foods, drugs, and cosmetics to determine their contents. These items must meet certain standards of purity, must be safe, and must conform to the label on the package. For example, before new drugs can be offered for sale, they must be safe. If a drug company cannot show that the product is not harmful when used as directed, the Food and Drug Administration may not allow it to be marketed.

Newly filled capsules await analysis by the Quality Control section of Smith Kline & French Laboratories. Regular analysis ensures purity. (Smith Kline & French Laboratories)

Point out that the first Secretary of HEW was a woman appointed by President Eisenhower.

The work of the Food and Drug Administration has been carried on since 1907, even though the Department of Health, Education, and Welfare, of which it is currently a part, has been in operation only since 1953.

If you are now working or have worked, your employer asked you to get a social security card from the Social Security Administration. Most jobs in the United States are today covered by social security. So are most self-employed persons. Your social security card has on it a number against which are credited all of your earnings covered by social security. These credits may entitle you to benefits of several kinds: old-age retirement benefits, permanent and total disability benefits, survivor benefits, and Medicare.

The contribution for these benefits is a deduction from the employee's wages. In the closing days of its 1972 session Congress set the rate for 1973 at 5.85 per cent on earnings up to $10,800 for a maximum of $631.80. In 1974 the maximum will be $702 on earnings up to $12,000. In 1978 the rate will be raised to 6.05 and to 7.3 by 2011. The employer pays a like amount for each employee. The rate for self-employed persons is about 50 per cent more than for employees.

Upon reaching age sixty-five, the employee, male or female, may retire and receive a monthly retirement payment, called an *annuity*, for the rest of his or her life from the Social Security Administration. A worker may retire as early as age sixty-two, but then the benefits are reduced. The amount received depends upon the amount of earnings and the number of dependents.

If the worker should die before or after retirement, the survivors—the widow or widower and any minor children—will receive specified annuity payments. If a widow does not have children, she receives benefits only when she reaches age sixty-two.

If the worker should become permanently and totally disabled before age sixty-five, the worker can receive monthly benefits if he or she has worked for at least five years in occupations covered by social security. Additional payments may also be made to dependents. These parts of the social security program are known as Old-Age, Survivors, and Disability Insurance (OASDI).

A reorganization of the Department of Health, Education, and Welfare in 1967 created the Social and Rehabilitation Service. A number of important agencies were assigned to it. One is the Administration on Aging. A further reorganization was made in 1969 establishing the Office of Child Development. This office provides services of various kinds related to children and youth.

The Public Health Service of the federal government dates back to 1798, when Congress authorized marine hospitals to care for merchant seamen. Today the Public Health Service is under the direction of the Surgeon General and is responsible for protecting and improving the nation's health.

The Public Health Service carries on an extensive program of research and education, and it cooperates with state agencies to reduce sickness and disease.

The Office of Education is another major division of the Department of Health, Education, and Welfare. Historically, education has been a local and state function in which the Office of Education has not interfered. Its services have been mainly of four kinds:

1. Collection of many kinds of information about schools and colleges.

2. Studies of educational problems.

3. Advisory and consultant help to states and interested groups and individuals.

4. Administration of educational programs supported by federal funds.

In recent years this office has been greatly expanded to handle the many educational programs of the federal government. Many of these programs have been set up as a result of far-reaching acts of Congress, such as the National Defense Education Act and the Elementary and Secondary Education Act. One branch of the Office of Education has the responsibility to assure that funds provided under these and other acts are used without discrimination in regard to race, color, or national origin.

Until 1970 the Bureau of Federal Credit Unions was a part of HEW. In that year it was set up as an independent agency and its title was changed to National Credit Union Administration. It charters, examines, and supervises federal credit unions. These are cooperative associations that receive savings from, and make loans to, members. Most credit unions make loans at nominal interest rates.

THE DEPARTMENT OF HOUSING AND URBAN DEVELOPMENT

This department was established by Congress in 1965. Its first secretary was Robert C. Weaver, the first Negro member of the Cabinet.

The act establishing the department brought together various agencies of the federal government dealing with housing. But the Department of Housing and Urban Development (HUD) is to deal with more than housing. The act declares that "the general welfare and security of the nation and the health and living standards of our people require, as a matter of national purpose, sound development of the nation's communities and metropolitan areas in which the vast majority of its people live and work."

In keeping with its purpose it carries on urban development work. Its many activities in this area include land-use planning, urban renewal, and urban mass transportation systems. Its work for improved living includes assistance in providing such facilities as sewage treatment plants and water purification systems.

Its best known agency is the Federal Housing Administration (FHA). If your family has built or bought a home during the past thirty-five years, it is very probable that the FHA insured the mortgage loan.

The FHA does not provide the money for building homes, but it guarantees that the loan will be repaid. Any responsible person whose income is large enough to make it reasonably sure that he will repay a loan can apply for an FHA insured mortgage at a bank or other lending institution. If the application is approved, the money is lent by the private lending institution and insured by the government.

The borrower receives the money and repays it in regular monthly payments over a period of years. The time of repayment varies with the type of loan, but it may be as long as thirty-five years. The FHA provides additional service by checking the location and the plans of the house and by inspecting it during construction.

A chief purpose of the department is the improvement of housing conditions throughout the nation. The work with individuals under the FHA program is only one of many activities it carries on to improve housing. Some others are cooperative housing, nursing homes, housing for the elderly, condominium housing, armed services housing, and group medical practice facilities.

THE DEPARTMENT OF TRANSPORTATION

In 1966 President Johnson signed a bill creating the

Discuss the background of Dr. Robert Weaver and his great experience in housing administration at the local, state, and national levels.

latest cabinet-level department, the Department of Transportation. The department has responsibility for transportation operations of the federal government.

The Federal Highway Administration maintains and carries forward the vast system of federal roads. It is promoting uniform standards for developing state highway safety programs designed to reduce traffic accidents.

The Federal Aviation Agency was transferred to this new department, and its name was changed to the Federal Aviation Administration. It has responsibility for air safety, for prescribing aircraft and airline regulations, and for operating aviation facilities. It has an extensive research and development program whose aim is to provide the best and safest air transportation.

The Federal Railroad Administration carries out safety functions pertaining to the nation's railroads. It has responsibility for regulating rail carriers and pipelines and the hours of service of railroad employees. It investigates railroad accidents and has authority to prescribe the installation of safety devices.

The coast guard was transferred to this department from the Department of the Treasury. In time of war it will be assigned to the navy. Its peacetime activities deal mainly with search and rescue operations on water. The Maritime Administration remains a part of the Department of Commerce.

The Urban Mass Transportation Administration carries on research and development programs to improve the mass transportation systems of urban areas. It makes grants and loans to state and local governmental bodies to assist them in providing better transportation services.

The Saint Lawrence Seaway Development Corporation maintains the seaway in cooperation with the Saint Lawrence Seaway Authority of Canada.

The National Highway Traffic Safety Administration was established by Congress to reduce the mounting number of deaths and injuries due to highway traffic accidents. The National Transportation Safety Board is charged with the investigation of accident conditions in civil aviation and surface transportation. The board is independent and reports annually directly to Congress on its work and on recommendations for suggested safety legislation.

THE PEOPLE IN GOVERNMENT   This chapter has presented the chief services of the eleven departments of the executive branch. The next one will discuss the services of additional agencies of the federal government. All of these are performed by people—more than two million of them, none of whom hold elective office. As a matter of fact the whole operation of the executive branch revolves around the person elected as President, emphasizing again the power and influence of the Presidency.

All other persons in the executive branch receive their positions either by appointment or through the civil service selection process. Several hundred individuals are appointed to top level positions. These are the persons who set policies for departments and bureaus; they may be considered the managers of government operations. Many of them are political appointees who carry out the philosophy of the administration. Their term of government service is usually relatively short, averaging three to four years. Among them are the secretaries of the departments and members of the White House staff.

Some of these individuals are close associates of the President. Their appointment

With respect to people in government, explain the functions of the Civil Service Commission established in the Pendleton Act of 1883. (See Chapter 13, pages 279-280.)

An Amtrak train travels through some beautiful scenery on its route through the West. The Federal Railroad Administration in the Department of Transportation sets and enforces safety standards to make the journey a safe one. (Santa Fe Railway photo)

to a high level government post is taken for granted because of their support of the President, their influence in his political party, and their efforts in his campaign. Some of them want and seek political appointment. Often, however, certain individuals are secured for these policy and managerial positions only after repeated urging by the President or his associates. Sometimes accepting the appointment means personal and financial sacrifice. They do so because of loyalty to the President, a sense of duty to serve their country, or a feeling of party responsibility.

Also included among the top appointments are individuals who fill the next level positions. These are people who help to establish effective control within departments and agencies. Included here are assistant secretaries, deputies, and others of similar status.

The vast majority of the federal employees, however, are career employees. They spend a lifetime of employment in the federal service. These are the employees who carry on the actual day-to-day work of the eleven departments and the many other federal agencies. Because of their long service they come to think of their agency or bureau as their particular domain. Their quality and ability is comparable to that of persons occupying similar positions in large corporations and labor unions. They are the *bureaucrats* who because of their familiarity with the operation and their long service tend to set policies and efficiency standards. They frequently determine what is the correct procedure and how much and what service their bureau should give.

This condition has both good and bad features: good, because long service gives them the needed insights and experience for doing effective work; bad, because they tend to determine policies which might better be set by the policy-making individuals elected or appointed to do so and who more directly represent the will of the citizens.

STUDY QUESTIONS

1. How are the departments of the national government established?

2. Who are the people who compose the President's Cabinet?

3. What are the factors which determine the selection of Cabinet members by the President?

4. Which duties of the Department of State are more important: domestic or foreign? Give reasons for your answer.

5. Why does our nation have representatives in foreign countries?

6. What is the difference between the Treasurer of the United States and the Secretary of the Treasury?

7. Why were the former Departments of the Army and Navy combined into the Department of Defense?

8. What are some of the chief duties assigned to the Department of Justice?

9. In what ways is the Department of the Interior involved in the conservation of our natural resources?

10. How does the research program of the Department of Agriculture help farmers?

11. What is the purpose of the various censuses made by the Department of Commerce?

CONCEPTS AND GENERALIZATIONS

1
The President's Cabinet developed to its present position of importance from a simple statement about executive departments in the Constitution and the need of Presidents for a group of advisers.

2
Executive departments were created as social and economic changes demonstrated they were needed.

3
The administration of the government of the United States is the largest business in the nation.

4
Many factors are considered by a President in selecting Cabinet members, including personal and political considerations as well as administrative and technical abilities.

5
Generally, the Secretary of State occupies the position of highest honor and prestige in the President's Cabinet.

6
Our relations with other nations are influenced greatly by the policies and practices of the Foreign Service in the Department of State.

7
Each of the executive departments has responsibility for performing special functions for the welfare of the people and/or for providing services for improvements in some aspects of living.

8
The most recent departments—HEW, HUD, and Transportation—reflect relatively new emphases in the services of the federal government.

9
The executive departments employ under civil service a vast number of minor executives and other employees who have great influence on the operation of government.

12. Mention some of the labor laws administered by the Department of Labor.

13. What are the four chief educational services of the Department of Health, Education, and Welfare?

14. What are the housing activities of the Department of Housing and Urban Development?

15. What are the chief duties of each of the main divisions of the Department of Transportation?

16. Here is a list of some of the duties of the executive departments. To which department does each one belong?

  a) Protects the President and his family
  b) Carries on dealings with foreign governments
  c) Supervises federal prisons
  d) Has charge of Indian affairs
  e) Collects information about schools and colleges
  f) Issues passports
  g) Manages financial matters
  h) Carries on research about soil conditions
  i) Safeguards the Panama Canal
  j) Prosecutes persons accused of crimes against the federal government
  k) Prescribes regulations for airlines
  l) Supervises the island possessions of the United States
  m) Issues the cost-of-living index
  n) Conducts the United States census
  o) Issues social security cards
  p) Provides services for businesses
  q) Operates the National Weather Service
  r) Checks the content of foods and drugs
  s) Supervises national parks
  t) Insures home mortgages
  u) Carries on water rescue operations

IDEAS FOR DISCUSSION

1. The members of the President's Cabinet are his confidential advisers. There is some feeling that he should be permitted to choose whomever he wishes without getting approval of the Senate. What do you think of such a proposal?

2. "The Secretary of State is really our Foreign Minister." If you agree that this is true, what are the qualifications you would want in a person if you were selecting the Secretary of State?

3. If you were planning a reorganization of the federal government, would you keep the Secret Service in the Treasury Department? Would you suggest placing it in another department or agency? Would you move any other activities discussed in this chapter to other departments or agencies?

4. Should the Secretaries of Defense, Army, Navy, and Air Force be members of the military forces? Discuss reasons for your answer.

5. The meetings of the President's Cabinet are executive sessions, not open to the public and the news media. Should press reporters be permitted to attend to report on discussions held and decisions reached? Give reasons for your opinion.

6. While coming in for a landing a military airplane developed engine trouble and made a crash landing on a picnic area after missing several houses in a neighboring residential area. Several people were killed and others were hurt seriously. Some residents, fearful of further incidents of this kind, demanded that the airport be closed. What information will the Department of Defense need to reach a decision?

7. The Department of Health, Education, and Welfare was created in 1953. In recent years there has been some discussion about the establishment of a separate Department of Education. Would you favor such a move? Why?

THINGS TO DO

1. Make a chart giving information about the present Cabinet members. Include such items as name, residence, occupation, and party affiliation.

2. Appoint a committee to watch the daily papers for reports of Cabinet meetings and also for statements from Cabinet members. Clip these articles for a bulletin board display on "The Cabinet at Work."

3. Make a study of the location of the embassies of the United States government. Chart them on an outline map of the world. You may also wish to add our consulates.

4. Make a study of the programs under the supervision of the Department of Interior. On an outline map of the United States show the location of national parks, dams, and reclamation and irrigation projects.

5. If you live in an agricultural area, interview your county agent to learn what activities of the Department of Agriculture are carried on in your county and state. How has this department helped the farmers in your area?

6. On an outline map of the United States show the extensive limited-access highway system being developed throughout the nation through the cooperation of all levels of local and national government.

7. President Nixon recommended to Congress the reorganization and consolidation of several departments. Report to the class on his recommended plan and discuss its strengths and weaknesses.

FURTHER READINGS

Borklund, Carl W., MEN OF THE PENTAGON: FROM FORRESTAL TO MC NAMARA. Frederick A. Praeger, Publishers, 1966.

Flak, Eugene H., and O'Hara, M., SUMMER JOBS IN NATIONAL PARKS. Taplinger Publishing Co., Inc., 1967.

Heller, Deane and David, PATHS OF DIPLOMACY: AMERICA'S SECRETARIES OF STATE. J. B. Lippincott Company, 1966.

Johnson, G. W., CABINET. William Morrow and Co., 1966.

Lavine, David, OUTPOSTS OF ADVENTURE: THE STORY OF THE FOREIGN SERVICE. Doubleday & Co., Inc., 1966.

Neal, Harry Edward, PATHFINDERS, USA: YOUR CAREER ON LAND, SEA AND AIR. Julian Messner, Inc., 1957.

———, YOUR CAREER IN FOREIGN SERVICE. Julian Messner, Inc., 1965.

Panetta, Leon E., and Gall, Peter, BRING US TOGETHER. J. B. Lippincott Company, 1971.

Paxton, Glenn, COAST GUARD: FROM CIVILIAN TO COAST GUARDSMAN. Viking Press, Inc., 1962.

Sparks, Will, WHO TALKED TO THE PRESIDENT LAST? W. W. Norton & Co., Inc., 1971.

Terrell, John Upton, THE UNITED STATES DEPARTMENT OF JUSTICE: A STORY OF CRIME, COURTS, AND COUNTERSPIES. Meredith Press, 1965.

———, UNITED STATES DEPARTMENT OF COMMERCE: A STORY OF INDUSTRY, SCIENCE, AND TRADE. Meredith Press, 1966.

Wattenberg, Ben J., and Scammon, Richard M., THIS U.S.A.: AN UNEXPECTED FAMILY PORTRAIT OF 194,067,296 AMERICANS DRAWN FROM THE CENSUS. Doubleday & Co., Inc., 1965.

BOYCOTT—to join together with others to stop buying the products of a certain business; an attempt by a labor or other group to force an employer to meet its requests by joint agreement not to buy the company's products.

CORPORATION—a group of individuals who have a charter granting them permission to operate a business with privileges and liabilities as a group and not as individuals.

INDEPENDENT — free from control; agencies having a large measure of freedom—the degree varies with the agency.

LOCKOUT—refusal of an industry to permit employees to come into its buildings to work until they agree to its terms.

MONOPOLY—complete control of a service or the production of a commodity.

QUASI-JUDICIAL — judicial to some extent; an agency having powers which are somewhat judicial.

QUASI-LEGISLATIVE — legislative to some extent; an agency having powers which are somewhat legislative.

REGISTER—the list of eligible candidates for a civil service position.

SECONDARY BOYCOTT—the boycott of a second company which is doing business with a company involved in a labor dispute.

SECURITY — a legal document showing ownership of a company; stock or bond certificate.

STRIKE — the refusal of employees to work, usually because of wages, other benefits, or working conditions.

THE LANGUAGE OF GOVERNMENT

Make it clear to the students that the so-called independent agencies do not fall under an executive department as such.

13

The Independent Agencies

The *United States Government Organization Manual* is published annually by the National Archives and Records Service of the General Services Administration. The manual describes the organization and duties of the many divisions of the three branches of the federal government. It lists the chief officers and describes briefly the duties and responsibilities of the many departments, boards, agencies, bureaus, and commissions of the government.

The manual is a book of some 700 pages. Only a small portion is devoted to the legislative and judicial branches; most of it deals with the executive branch. About half of the book describes the work of the executive departments; while approximately 200 pages give information about government agencies, boards, bureaus, and commissions outside the executive departments. These administrative units are classified as the *Independent Agencies,* to distinguish them from the regular departments. (See the chart on page 249.)

FUNCTIONS OF
THE AGENCIES

These independent agencies are generally described as *executive* agencies since most of their powers are administrative or executive. But their duties frequently go beyond executive powers. Sometimes they have the power to make rules and regulations; in such cases their work is *legislative* in nature. At other times their duties include making judgments and handing out penalties; in these cases their work is *judicial* in nature. Because of these powers, some of these agencies are often called *quasi-legislative* or *quasi-judicial* agencies, which means that to a degree, or in part, they are legislative or judicial and not merely executive.

Some of the independent agencies have one person as the executive head, similar to each of the eleven departments in the Cabinet. But some are headed by boards and commissions of several members, and some are really corporations publicly owned but controlled by a board of directors just as any business corporation.

In theory all of these agencies are directly responsible to the President. In actual practice it is impossible for the President to be the "chief" executive for the many unrelated agencies. As a result the President keeps in close touch with some of these agencies while others are quite free from presidential control.

Actually, one of the reasons for the creation of some of the independent agencies is to keep them free of presidential control. The boards and commissions under which many of them operate help to reduce presidential control. While members are appointed by the President, their terms of office are usually longer than that of a single presidential term, and the terms of members of some agencies are staggered. So the President can ordinarily not control an entire board through his appointment power.

There are several other reasons for establishing independent agencies and for not including their duties in Cabinet departments. The services of some agencies are really business operations and are generally more effectively performed by independent boards or commissions. Further, highly specialized services, such as those related to science and aeronautics, could perhaps best be handled by a separate agency with specific responsibility. Finally, as has already been mentioned, some services of the government are legislative and/or judicial in nature and should not be directly included in the purely executive departments.

Over the years, however, there has been some concern that the *administrative* duties of the independent agencies should be more clearly fixed and that these should be under greater presidential control. This concern has brought about two results. One is the creation of more executive departments and the placement of some independent agencies into executive departments. The other is greater administrative authority for the chairmen of some agencies.

Although these independent agencies are

Responsibility for their [national policies] execution has been lodged in nearly seventy departments and agencies and over two thousand component units—some old, some new; some big, some small; some single-purposed, some multi-purposed; some concentrated geographically, some widely scattered; some highly responsive to Presidential influence and control, some almost totally immune to Presidential influence and control.

—Stephen K. Bailey, "The President and His Political Executives," *The Annals of the American Academy of Political and Social Science,* September, 1956, p. 24.

entirely unrelated, to help describe them in this chapter they have been grouped under four headings: (1) agencies for special services; (2) agencies for special projects; (3) regulatory agencies; and (4) government corporations.

AGENCIES FOR SPECIAL SERVICES

Some agencies of the federal government are necessary to give special services to the eleven departments and the other independent agencies. The two most important agencies of this type are the United States Civil Service Commission and the General Services Administration.

The United States Civil Service Commission is similar to the employment office or personnel department of a business. The General Services Administration is somewhat like the purchasing department of a big business plus the custodial department plus the record-keeping department.

THE UNITED STATES CIVIL SERVICE COMMISSION. The number of civilian employees of the federal government was 2,984,000 in October of a recent year. The following January another

political party took control of the government after being out of power. But only a small percentage of the government workers were replaced by members of the incoming party because most of the employees were under civil service.

It was not always this way. For decades a government job was a reward given to a faithful party worker. The famous slogan of President Andrew Jackson's administration was "To the victors belong the spoils." So he proceeded to replace the government workers with others of his own choosing and party. Other Presidents did the same. The inefficiency and disruption of government service became so bad because of this practice that in this century more and more government workers have been placed under civil service. Today only persons in major positions, generally policy-making, are changed when a new President takes office.

Department heads and persons in the chief diplomatic positions receive their positions through appointment. These officials serve at the pleasure of the President. They may be removed from office by him. But most employees are hired from civil service

Civil service applicants type during a competitive examination given by the Civil Service Commission. There are many civil service positions available to those who qualify. (U.S. Civil Service Commission)

lists. Persons get their places on these lists by passing competitive examinations. After a short probationary period, such persons are given permanent employment and may not be removed except for cause.

The federal government employs more persons than any one business in the nation. Most of these employees get their jobs through the United States Civil Service Commission, the personnel agency of the federal government. The commission has three members, one of whom is designated as chairman by the President.

The work of this commission is important in recruiting the many persons needed each year to fill the civil service positions and to provide for the orderly promotion and dismissal of persons in the service. The purpose of the civil service is to assure the government an adequate supply of efficient, qualified employees. Civil service provides for an examination system whereby only the most qualified persons applying for particular positions are hired. It guarantees these persons permanent employment and a chance for promotion based on merit if their work is satisfactory.

Announcements about examinations for civil service positions are placed in post offices, in the regional offices of the Civil Service Commission, and in other governmental buildings. Persons interested in governmental employment watch for these announcements. They may also request the Civil Service Commission to send them information about examinations and to notify them of future examinations for particular positions.

After your graduation from high school or college, you may become interested in securing employment in an agency of the federal government. If you wish to secure such a civil service position, you should:

1. Study the announcement to determine whether you meet the minimum qualifica-tions with reference to education, training, experience, age, residence, and any specialized abilities.

2. Fill out the necessary application forms.

3. Take the examination at the appointed time and place.

4. Present yourself for an interview if requested.

The names of persons who make passing grades on the examination and interview are placed on the eligible list, or *register*, for the position covered by the examination. As vacancies occur the positions are filled from the names at the top of the register. According to law the personnel directors of government agencies may choose one from among the three top names furnished them by the United States Civil Service Commission.

THE GENERAL SERVICES ADMINIS-TRATION. To carry on the many services of government, the United States buys many items and large amounts of property, constructs and maintains hundreds of buildings, and keeps huge files of important papers and documents. The business of the federal government has become so large that buying, selling, and storing the many items for carrying on its work has become a huge undertaking. In 1949 these tasks were assigned to one agency, the General Services Administration. It is directed by an administrator, appointed by the President with the advice and consent of the Senate.

This agency maintains five chief services: (1) The Federal Supply Service purchases supplies of all kinds for all federal agencies. (2) The Property Management and Disposal Service deals with military and industrial materials which are critical in emergencies, procures and stores them and also disposes of them when they are no longer needed; the service also develops policies and regu-

Many valuable records—some dating back to 1774—are stored in the National Archives Building in Washington, D.C. The proper storage and preservation of these materials is one of the responsibilities of the General Services Administration. (Washington Convention and Visitors Bureau)

lations to promote maximum use of excess properties by the executive agencies. (3) The Public Buildings Service constructs, alters, repairs, maintains, operates, and controls federal buildings. (4) The Automated Data and Telecommunications Service is responsible for developing policies and procedures for procuring and utilizing automatic data processing and communication services. (5) The National Archives and Records Service preserves or disposes of government records. It has responsibility for administering presidential libraries and for publishing laws, constitutional amendments, presidential documents, and administrative regulations. One of its offices publishes the *United States Government Organization Manual,* which was mentioned at the beginning of this chapter.

The growth of the government has made each of these a big job. For example, the National Archives and Records Service must determine which records shall be kept and which shall be destroyed. Those that are kept must be properly stored, filed, and catalogued so that they can be found when needed. Since one billion letters are written each year by governmental officials and 25,000 employees are required to handle incoming mail, the task is not a simple one. To file government documents the government uses the equivalent of seven Pentagons.

AGENCIES FOR SPECIAL PROJECTS

As American life changes under the stress of war or new inventions or changed economic conditions, the government is called upon to solve some special problems. Sometimes this is done by establishing a new bureau in one of the Cabinet departments. More frequently, however, an agency is created to deal with a special problem.

Six important independent agencies of this type are the Veterans Administration, the United States Information Agency, the Selective Service System, the National Aeronautics and Space Administration, the National Science Foundation, and the Atomic Energy Commission. Each of these agencies has evolved to deal with a specific governmental problem.

THE VETERANS ADMINISTRA- TION. One of the largest agencies of the

Point out that the head of the Veterans Administration, although not represented in the Cabinet, is directly responsible to the President.

federal government is the Veterans Administration (VA). This agency administers the laws which provide benefits for former members of the armed forces and their dependents. The vast program includes such services as taking care of the disabled veterans, making payments to veterans and their dependents, providing education and training programs for veterans, offering home loans and insurance of loans, servicing veterans' life insurance, and maintaining veterans' hospitals.

Large numbers of persons have served and are continuing to serve in the armed forces. All of these—about one of every seven people in the nation—and some of their dependents are eligible under our laws for some of the benefits for veterans.

Veterans' hospitals and district or regional offices are located in every state and in the territories. This makes it possible for the veteran to apply near home for medical care or for other services. The huge

VA program is one of the costs of our past wars; more than eight billion dollars are spent each year to maintain it.

The Veterans Administration is headed by a single executive, the Administrator of Veterans Affairs, who is appointed by the President.

THE UNITED STATES INFORMATION AGENCY. The United States Information Agency (USIA) was established in 1953. It came about as the result of a need to have the people of other nations get a clearer understanding of the United States and its people. Too many were receiving a distorted picture of our people and of our objectives. Through this agency we deliberately set out to tell the world about us and our government.

The purpose of the agency is to bring evidence to the people of other nations to show them that the United States is concerned with advancing their hopes for freedom, progress, and peace. Its aim is to

The United States Information Agency uses a variety of means of communication to tell the world about our nation and its policies. The Voice of America; shown here broadcasting in Burmese, transmits by radio to many nations and in many languages.

The National Aeronautics and Space Administration is responsible for developing our knowledge of space and the techniques of space exploration. This is a view of the earth taken by a satellite from an altitude of over 22,000 miles. (NASA photo)

AMTRAK

AMTRAK is a government corporation established by Congress in 1970 in an attempt to restore railroad passenger service as an important part of the transportation system of our country. AMTRAK is a new word in the American language. The term is a substitute for the official name: The National Railroad Passenger Corporation.

Railroads in the United States for years had been losing money on passenger service. Accusations were made that service was deliberately being allowed to deteriorate to hasten the time when railroads could get out of the passenger business. People who preferred the railroads to airline or bus travel protested. They pointed out that trains in Europe are clean and efficient. Ecologists argued that the environment would be cleaner if more people were transported by rail.

Congress set up AMTRAK to determine if rail passenger service could be revitalized. The corporation is governed by a board of directors of fifteen members, one of whom must be the Secretary of Transportation. The private railroads were allowed either to continue to operate their own passenger services or to transfer their intercity passenger operations to the new corporation. Nineteen of the twenty-two passenger-carrying railroads turned over their operations to AMTRAK. In return they were given stock in the new corporation or, as an alternative, could claim a tax deduction.

A new image of travel by rail is being built by AMTRAK. New outfits were designed for ticket agents, conductors, and attendants. Terminals in large cities were consolidated. On-time performance was improved and trains were cleaner.

Passenger volume has, however, remained light. Congress gave a federal grant to get operations started on May 1, 1971, and has made subsequent grants. When the law was passed Congress stated the corporation was to be run at a profit. Whether this will be possible is one of the unknowns.

AMTRAK does not operate its own trains but contracts with the railroads for services. Some members of Congress insist that AMTRAK should have its own employees and equipment for proper service and efficiency.

AMTRAK is an experiment to determine whether rail passenger service can be saved to the advantage of the American people.

show that our policies and objectives are in harmony with their hopes.

This purpose is carried out through four kinds of activities. First, the agency explains and interprets the objectives and policies of our government. Second, it shows. how these policies agree with the hopes and wishes of people of other nations. Third, it exposes attempts to distort and discredit the policies of our government. Fourth, it explains the important features of the life and culture of the people of the United States.

The agency maintains field offices in more than 100 countries throughout the world. These offices attempt to see that the United States receives good publicity in the countries in which they are located. They have the task of bringing to these people a true picture of the United States and its people.

An Office of Policy and Plans is responsible for formulating the overall policies of the agency. This office gets information about our national and foreign policies from the Department of State, the National Security Council, and other government agencies. It selects ideas and events which should be given special emphasis and develops a program of information to be spread to other people.

The agency has a number of services which concern themselves with the various media of communication. The Broadcasting Service (Voice of America) beams English and foreign language radio programs to the communist bloc countries and to other selected countries.

Another service supplies English and foreign language books to libraries and information centers. Other services provide motion pictures, television tapes and films, press materials, pamphlets, and pictures for overseas use.

THE SELECTIVE SERVICE SYSTEM. The Selective Service System has the responsibility of registering all men between the ages of eighteen and twenty-six and of providing the armed forces with men as needed. The local boards of the system register, examine, classify, and select men according to laws passed by Congress. (See Chapter 26.)

The number of men inducted by each board each month is determined by the needs of the armed forces. The system is headed by the Director of Selective Service, who is appointed by the President with Senate approval.

THE NATIONAL AERONAUTICS AND SPACE ADMINISTRATION. The National Aeronautics and Space Administration (NASA) is charged with carrying out the policy of Congress that activities in space should be devoted to peaceful purposes for all mankind. With this goal in mind NASA has four chief functions: (1) To carry on research to solve the problems of flight in and out of the earth's atmosphere, and to develop, construct, test, and operate aeronautical and space vehicles; (2) to experiment with manned and unmanned vehicles for the exploration of space; (3) to arrange for effective utilization of the scientific and engineering resources of the nation and for cooperation with other nations carrying on space activities for peaceful purposes; and (4) to provide for dissemination of information about NASA's activities.

Much of NASA's activity is in the field of space and aeronautical research. This is carried on in NASA's field centers and by private organizations having contracts with NASA. The result has been the many successful space flights of the United States, both manned and unmanned. One of the goals, to land men on the moon, has been reached. Further moon landings and the exploration of planets other than our own are being planned.

THE NATIONAL SCIENCE FOUN-DATION. A national concern about the need for strengthening science education and scientific research led to the establishment of the National Science Foundation in 1950. Its present activities may be grouped in ten categories: (1) Directing research efforts to improve the quality of the environment; (2) developing and providing information about the nation's scientific resources; (3) awarding grants and contracts to universities and other non-profit institutions to carry on basic research; (4) making large facilities, such as observatories, available to scientists by means of financial support; (5) maintaining a register of scientific and technical personnel and acting as a clearinghouse on scientific needs and resources; (6) awarding graduate fellowships to qualified students in mathematics, engineering, physics, biology, and in medical and social sciences; (7) carrying on programs to improve science education by providing financial support for institutes for teachers in various fields, for projects to develop improved materials of instruction, and for more experiences in the field of science for high ability high school and college students; (8) strengthening programs related to marine life; (9) supporting the development and use of scientific knowledge; and, (10) providing opportunities for greater dissemination of scientific information, both within and outside of the federal government and also with foreign countries.

THE ATOMIC ENERGY COMMIS-SION. In the cool desert dawn of Nevada a group of tense men stood waiting. Suddenly a terrific explosion shook the earth, and a towering mushroom of smoke rose in the sky. Another atom bomb had been exploded by our armed forces and scientists. This was one more step in our research about the atom and atomic power.

That was before 1963 when such tests were outlawed by the Nuclear Test Ban Treaty. Underground testing is still performed.

Soon after World War II and the dropping of the atom bombs on Nagasaki and Hiroshima, Congress created the Atomic Energy Commission. The world recognized that the atom bomb was the most powerful force that had yet been devised by man. In the United States the Atomic Energy Commission is charged with developing the power of the atom, not only for the common defense and security, but also for "improving the public welfare, increasing the standard of living, strengthening free competition in private enterprise, and promoting world peace."

The Atomic Energy Commission promotes many research and study programs to carry out these purposes. Atom bombs—and hydrogen bombs—are now vastly more destructive than at the end of World War II. But atomic power is also being used constructively for peacetime activities. Much research by both the federal government and by private enterprise is being done on this use of atomic power.

Just as the atom bomb changed warfare and made it more destructive and horrible, atomic power is changing our peacetime living and may bring further results that we can not even imagine today. The Atomic Energy Commission consists of five members, all appointed by the President with the advice and consent of the Senate. One member is named chairman by the President.

THE REGULATORY AGENCIES

Some of the independent agencies have been established to provide effective regulation of certain aspects of our economic life. Railroads, television and radio, banks, public utilities, labor unions,

Include the fact that there are well over 100 agencies that have the power to issue rules and regulations affecting the public. Most are regulatory agencies.

The merger of the Pennsylvania and the New York Central into the Penn Central Railroad made this the largest rail line in the nation. Such mergers must be approved by the Interstate Commerce Commission. (Penn Central Photo)

and business corporations are among the groups that have come under the guidance of these agencies. Most of these agencies have legislative and judicial power as well as executive power, as was described earlier in the chapter. Some of the agencies are quite old, and some are relatively new.

The President is not able to exert complete control over these commissions because some terms of commissioners are longer than those of the President. Congress has felt that this type of political independence was important because these agencies have such great power over our economic system. One effect of this independence is to prevent the President from having full executive control over their administration. Also, Congress feels that these agencies are responsible to it. Congress has created them, has defined their purposes in congressional acts, and controls them by providing or withholding funds in appropriation acts.

Ten of these agencies are described in the following pages.

THE INTERSTATE COMMERCE COMMISSION. This commission was set up in 1887 to regulate the freight and passenger rates of railroads, some of which were engaging in unfair practices. In cer-

tain cases refunds or rebates were made to large shippers but were not allowed to the smaller companies. For example, the rate per ton of freight was the same whether the shipment was one ton or a hundred tons. But the railroad might give the large shipper a rebate in order to get his business. This was unfair to the small shipper and gave an advantage to the large shipper, who could then sell his goods at a lower price.

In other cases long-haul rates were lower than short-haul rates. There was little or no uniformity in the rates of different railroads. To correct these and similar abuses, Congress created the Interstate Commerce Commission (ICC).

The power of the commission has been gradually increased over the years through additional laws passed by Congress. The work of this commission enters into the cost of much of the food and other goods we buy and of trips that we take by bus, boat, or train. Its duties are varied, but all are related to freight and passenger service.

However, with the creation of the Department of Transportation in 1966 some of the duties of the Interstate Commerce Commission were transferred to the new department. Safety measures affecting common carriers are now the responsibility of that department. Rate-setting functions remain the duty of the Interstate Commerce Commission. It regulates the rates of all interstate common carriers: railroads, motor vehicles, boats, express companies, sleeping- and chair-car companies, and certain pipe lines.

The commission tries to do its work in such a way that the interests of both the public and the carriers are served and protected. It consists of eleven members appointed by the President who designates one of them as chairman.

THE FEDERAL RESERVE SYSTEM.
Another older agency, begun in 1913, is the Federal Reserve System. The act which established this system stated that it was "to provide for the establishment of Federal Reserve Banks, to furnish an elastic currency, to afford means of rediscounting commercial paper, to establish a more effective supervision of banking in the United States, and for other purposes."

There is a Federal Reserve Bank in each of the twelve Federal Reserve Districts into which the country is divided. Each one is privately owned but is under federal supervision. These banks are really "bankers' banks." All national banks must become members of a Federal Reserve Bank by buying some of its stock. State banks may join if they meet the Federal Reserve requirements.

The Federal Reserve System is operated by a Board of Governors composed of seven members appointed by the President and approved by the Senate. In making the appointments the President must give fair representation to various interests: financial, agricultural, industrial, commercial, and geographical. The members serve staggered terms of fourteen years and cannot be reappointed. One member retires every second year.

Shown are (top) trailer freight cars and (bottom) an airfreighter being unloaded. Both are common carriers, regulated by the Interstate Commerce Commission. (top, Union Pacific Railroad Photo; bottom, American Airlines)

The Board of Governors has certain controls over the money of the nation. These are (1) to determine the amount of reserve funds which member banks must have on deposit in their Federal Reserve Bank; (2) to issue Federal Reserve notes and thus increase the amount of money in circulation; and (3) to control the interest rate charged to banks on their loans from Federal Reserve Banks and the interest rate paid by member banks to their depositors.

These responsibilities have been given to the board to help regulate the banking services of the nation. The effect of these powers has been to make the Federal Reserve System a chief regulator of our entire economic system. Raising the interest rate is like "putting on the brakes"; our economy is slowed down. Lowering the interest rate is like "stepping on the gas"; our economy is speeded up.

THE FEDERAL TRADE COMMISSION. A few years ago sweaters which were highly flammable were being sold in various parts of the country. These sales were a violation of local ordinances in many places, but they also came under the control of the Federal Trade Commission if interstate marketing was involved. This commission is charged with keeping business competition in the United States free and fair. One of its purposes is to protect the purchaser in connection with such items as flammable materials and the labeling of wool and fur fabrics.

Another important responsibility of this commission is to prevent *monopolies*. A monopoly exists when one company or a group of companies has control of one kind of business. The purpose of the commission is to maintain a free competitive economic system in which everyone may do business. It aims to prevent the free-enterprise system from being stifled by monopoly or from being corrupted by unfair or deceptive trade practices.

The commission was created in 1914. The five members of the commission are appointed by the President with Senate approval for seven-year terms.

THE FEDERAL POWER COMMISSION. The industrial United States is dependent upon power—the power of its waterfalls, the power of its hydroelectric plants, the power of its natural gas, the power created in various other ways and made available by many public utilities. Some regulation of that power is needed

for the welfare of the people and the nation.

States have agencies which regulate within their borders, but regulation of power facilities which cross state lines is in the hands of the Federal Power Commission. This commission, created in 1920 and reorganized in 1930, has a variety of duties regarding navigation and development of power on federal streams, licensing and regulating public utilities engaged in interstate commerce, developing hydroelectric power in flood-control projects, and transporting natural gas from one state to others. The commission also has certain emergency powers whereby it may take over and operate electric projects when the safety of the nation is involved.

The commission has five members appointed by the President for five-year terms. The President names the chairman.

THE FEDERAL COMMUNICATIONS COMMISSION. A turn of the dial on your radio or television set tunes out one station and brings in another. It is not by chance that there are not two stations on the same spot on your dial. The Federal Communications Commission (FCC), which licenses all radio and television stations, determines the wavelength at which a station may broadcast. This commission was established in 1934 to regulate and control the interstate and foreign communications by radio, television, telephone, and telegraph.

The commission receives requests for the establishment of radio and television stations. In recent years it has had the task of assigning the limited number of channels for television broadcasting to the many applicants in cities across the country. In designating the location of stations, it tries to do it in such a manner that there will be no interference among stations.

The rates of telephone and telegraph companies engaged in interstate service are

Ralph Nader, outspoken consumer advocate, came into prominence as the author of the book *Unsafe at Any Speed*. Since his efforts to make automobiles safer, Nader has conducted a series of investigations designed to benefit consumers in other areas. One of his basic charges is that federal regulatory agencies are not responsive to the complaints of citizens.

He claims that bureaucrats in agencies which were originally created to protect consumers tend to show favoritism toward private industry. Nader wants these agencies to be more sensitive to the interests of the general public.

One procedure used by Nader is the setting up of a specific project to investigate an agency. Young lawyers and students who often devote a summer to the project make investigations that culminate in a report released to the public. Typical of these is the *Nader Report on the Federal Trade Commission* by Edward F. Cox and others. These crusading staff members have become known as Nader's Raiders.

Nader has also created the Center for the Study of Responsive Law, an organization that devotes continuing study to all types of consumer problems as related to government and law.

---

also under the control of this commission. It is composed of seven members appointed by the President with Senate approval. The President names the chairman.

THE SECURITIES AND EXCHANGE COMMISSION. One of the principal causes of the depression in the 1930's was the stock market crash of October, 1929. This crash led to the demand for federal regulation of the stock market and the sale of stocks and bonds. Most companies selling stocks and bonds have excellent reputations and give the investor honest information about investments. Some groups and individuals, however, make use of the average person's ignorance about stocks and bonds to carry out frauds and swindles. Some states have tried to protect individuals against such frauds. But they have not been effective on a national scale.

In 1933-1934 Congress passed several laws establishing the Securities and Exchange Commission (SEC). This commission was assigned the duty of protecting the citizens of the nation against willful fraud in the sale of stocks and bonds. The commission consists of five members appointed by the President with the consent of the Senate. Each member serves for five years, but only

one member's term expires each year. The President names the chairman.

One of the commission's duties is to make provisions for the registration of stocks and bonds. Companies offering stocks and bonds for sale are required to give the commission complete financial and other information needed by investors. This information is made available to the public.

These reports are helpful to investors in determining the relative worth of the various *securities*—stocks and bonds. The commission also tries to eliminate dishonest practices in the sale of securities. Another of its chief duties is to prevent the use of interstate commerce facilities or the mails for the sale of securities not properly registered with the commission.

The SEC also has certain duties with regard to the regulation of holding companies in the field of gas and electric public utilities. Investment companies and advisers must be registered by the commission as a protection to the public and the investors. The law gives the commission further controls of the stock market by authorizing regulations regarding down payments and time payments in buying stocks and bonds.

THE NATIONAL LABOR RELATIONS BOARD AND OTHER RELATED AGENCIES. Many Americans are affected by labor-management troubles in large and important industries. A strike or a lockout affects not only the employers and employees but much of the public as well through a reduction in goods or services supplied by the company.

Many people feel that the government has an obligation to protect the interest of the general public through an orderly process of dealing with possible disputes between management and labor. Three agencies have been created to assist in handling these employer-employee problems: the National Labor Relations Board, the Federal Mediation and Conciliation Service, and the National Mediation Board.

The *National Labor Relations Board* (NLRB) was set up as the result primarily of two laws of Congress, the Wagner Act of 1935 and the Taft-Hartley Act of 1947. The board consists of five members appointed for five-year terms by the President with the consent of the Senate.

Employers are required under these laws to bargain with union representatives. They are forbidden to discriminate against an employee because of union activities. They may not give a union financial help or make union membership or nonmembership a condition of employment.

Unions or their agents are forbidden to interfere with employees in the exercise of their rights to form an organization for collective bargaining. They may not force or attempt to force an employer to discriminate against an employee because of membership or nonmembership in a union. They may not try to force an employer to bargain with a particular labor organization when another one has been certified by the board as the representative of the employees.

The NLRB has the right to issue orders requiring employers and labor organizations to stop unfair labor practices, to designate the appropriate units for collective bargaining, to conduct hearings and investigations, to conduct elections to determine employees' choices for their representatives in collective bargaining, and to petition the federal courts for the enforcement of its orders.

The Landrum-Griffin Act, passed in 1959, requires labor unions and management to make certain financial and other reports to the federal government. It regulates picketing and prohibits secondary boycotts. The latter involve union pressure against a neutral employer to force him to stop doing business with an employer having labor trouble.

If there is a dispute between unions, the NLRB is directed by law to conduct secret elections to determine which union shall be the bargaining agent for a group of employees.

At the time of passing the Taft-Hartley Act Congress also set up the *Federal Mediation and Conciliation Service*. Its purpose is to prevent or to settle major disputes between management and labor. It differs from the NLRB in that it has no law-enforcement authority. The director is appointed by the President with the advice and consent of the Senate.

The federal mediator has conferences with the representatives of both sides in an attempt to settle the differences. He acts in the interest of the general public in trying to reach an agreement.

The *National Mediation Board* is charged with helping to adjust any differences between the managements and their employees of railroads, express and Pullman companies, and airlines. The Railway Labor Act, which established the board in 1934, requires it to avoid any interruption of service, to allow employees free choice in joining a labor organization, and to provide for settlement of disputes concerning rates of pay or working conditions. The board consists of three members appointed by the President with Senate approval. The board selects its own chairman.

THE EQUAL EMPLOYMENT OPPORTUNITY COMMISSION. The Civil Rights Act of 1964 created the Equal Employment Opportunity Commission. The work of the commission is of two kinds. One is to end discrimination based on race, color, religion, sex, or national origin in all matters affecting employment. The other is to initiate and promote action programs designed to provide new job opportunities for members of minority groups and for women.

In carrying on its work the commission investigates charges of discrimination, which must be in writing. If its investigation leads it to believe that a charge is true, it tries to get the situation corrected by having the employer, labor organization, or employment agency stop its discriminatory practices. If it is unsuccessful, the case may be taken to court to force a remedy of the situation.

The commission consists of five members appointed by the President with the consent of the Senate. Their term of office is five years, with one member's term ending each year. The President names the chairman and vice chairman.

GOVERNMENT CORPORATIONS

Establishing a government corporation to perform an important public service is a legal device that has been used many times in the history of our country. Hamilton used it to create the Bank of the United States. A government corporation was established for the building of the Panama Canal. However, more of these corporations were created during the depression and World War II than in any previous period.

Most of these corporations were engaged in making loans to farmers or homeowners, but some were gigantic business operations. All had the common features of being owned by the government and controlled by boards of directors appointed by the President.

One of the most famous and powerful of these corporations was the Reconstruction Finance Corporation (RFC). Although abolished by Congress in 1953, the RFC is mentioned here, because it had an important influence on our economic life from the time of its creation in 1932 until after World War II. The RFC made loans to banks, railroads, defense industries, and state and local governmental agencies. These loans totaled billions of dollars and helped to maintain and expand the industrial life of the nation through years of depression, war, and the post-war period.

Of the present government corporations, three are of major importance: the Federal Deposit Insurance Corporation, the Tennessee Valley Authority, and the Postal Service.

FEDERAL DEPOSIT INSURANCE CORPORATION. In 1933 many banks in

Each depositor insured to $20,000

FEDERAL DEPOSIT INSURANCE CORPORATION

This emblem is displayed by every bank that is insured by the Federal Deposit Insurance Corporation. How does the FDIC determine whether a particular bank may be insured? (Federal Deposit Insurance Corporation)

the nation closed because they could not give the depositors their money when they wanted it. To safeguard the deposits in other banks, the government closed all the banks for a time. Many depositors lost part of their savings in the banks. To prevent such a condition from happening again, the government established the Federal Deposit Insurance Corporation (FDIC).

This government agency insures the accounts of depositors in member banks. Banks which are members of the FDIC display an emblem of membership. Each account in these banks is now insured up to $20,000 by the FDIC. This means that if the bank were to fail, the FDIC would pay each depositor the full amount of his account up to $20,000.

The insurance funds are raised by the FDIC through an annual fee paid by member banks. These fees are paid in much the same way that premiums are paid on other insurance policies. All national banks belong to the FDIC, and others may join by applying to the governing board.

About 97 per cent of all banks now have federal deposit insurance. To assure that banks are safe institutions for the deposit of money, the FDIC carries on a program of examination of banks and requires certain prescribed practices, such as insurance against burglary.

The FDIC board consists of three members: the Comptroller of the Currency and two other persons appointed by the President and approved by the Senate for terms of six years. The board selects one of its members as chairman.

A similar organization, the Federal Savings and Loan Insurance Corporation, insures the deposits in savings and loan associations up to $20,000.

TENNESSEE VALLEY AUTHORITY. One of the big power projects of the federal government is the Tennessee Valley Author-

ity (TVA). It had its beginning during World War I, when a dam and two nitrate plants were built at Muscle Shoals in Alabama for the production of explosives. This was a war measure. It was stopped at the end of the war because many people were opposed to the operation of a business by the government. They wanted the government to sell the Muscle Shoals operation to private industry. However, there were other people who wanted the government to expand the operation and to develop a large conservation program and an extensive hydroelectric power system in the area.

The latter group won its point. The operation was started again under government control. Under the leadership of Senator George W. Norris of Nebraska, Congress passed an act setting up the Tennessee Valley Authority. The act authorized the TVA: (1) to improve the Tennessee River for navigation; (2) to operate the dam and plants at Muscle Shoals; (3) to develop new types of fertilizers for use in agricultural programs; (4) to develop a flood-control program; and (5) to develop a hydroelectric power program. The TVA also makes investigations for the proper conservation, development, and use of the resources of the region.

The TVA is operated as a corporation by a board of directors of three members appointed by the President with Senate approval. Since 1933 it has become a huge enterprise with more than forty dams and an extensive flood-control and soil-conservation program. The lakes created by the dams have helped to make the TVA land a fine recreational area. The dams provide power for many hydroelectric plants and the TVA has been able to distribute electric power at low cost.

The TVA and similar projects have provoked much controversy about "government in business." The right of the government to operate the TVA has been challenged in the courts, all the way to the United States Supreme Court. The court has decided that the TVA has the right to generate and sell electric power. That did not completely end the arguments; some people still maintain that the government should get out of the power business. But the idea that the government has the right to develop and operate projects such as TVA for the benefit of the nation has now been widely accepted.

POSTAL SERVICE. In August of 1970 President Nixon signed a history-making document dealing with the Postal Service. Present were six men who at one time had held the position of Postmaster General. Thus ended several years of work to change the postal system from a cabinet-level department to a government-owned corporation. (See Table, page 256.)

National concern about needed improvements prompted President Lyndon Johnson to appoint a commission to investigate postal organization. The commission issued a report in 1968 recommending the creation of an independent, government-owned corporation. In 1969 President Nixon asked Congress to establish such a corporation.

During the 1970 session, Congress discussed postal reorganization plans in connection with postal rates and federal employee pay raises. Strikes of postal employees in several cities during the spring of 1970 emphasized the need for attention to the pay scales of postal workers and for changes in the postal service. The result was the Postal Reorganization Act of 1970.

Some major provisions of the act are:

- *The Post Office Department was replaced by a government-owned corporation, the Postal Service.*

- *The act established an eleven-member Board of Governors to head the Postal Service; nine appointed by the President (no more than five from one political party, one member's term expiring each year) and confirmed by the Senate and the Postmaster General and his deputy.*

- *A Postal Rate Commission with powers over postal rates and services.*

- *Collective bargaining to determine compensation and working conditions.*

- *Freedom from political considerations and influence.*

- *The Board of Governors can borrow heavily to mechanize mail handling and improve service.*

After a few years Congress will evaluate the Postal Service to determine the need for further changes.

REORGANIZATION OF GOVERNMENT ADMINISTRATION
The discussion of these independent agencies gives a brief overall view of the major activities of our government. Agencies are listed in the *United States Government Organization Manual* in alphabetical order.

All were created by acts of Congress or set up by the President under powers given him by the Constitution or by Congress. Their purpose is to serve the nation and its people at home and abroad.

Good administration requires that the operation of government should be under continuous study to make it more effective and efficient in carrying out its duties and in giving service. Sometimes agencies do not carry out their duties as efficiently as possible. Sometimes the same or similar services are given by two or more agencies.

Sometimes an agency continues to exist when its service is no longer needed. Such conditions are likely to happen in an opera-

Ask the student to compare in his mind the efficiency of big government to that of big business.

293

tion as large and complex as our federal government, which carries on many services and employs so many people.

For more than sixty years Presidents have called attention to the need for some reorganization of the administration of government. Some changes have been made, but not enough. There is still too much duplication of services and continuation of agencies no longer needed. This fact has become especially important during the very rapid growth of government in the past forty years. Some progress in reorganization was made under President Franklin D. Roosevelt.

Congress, however, took a big step toward making the government more workable and efficient when it established the *Commission on Organization of the Executive Branch of the Government* in 1947 and created a second commission in 1953. Known as the "Hoover Commission" and the "Second Hoover Commission," because former President Herbert Hoover was chairman, these commissions made various reports for streamlining government. The commissions were not agencies of the executive; they were commissions of the legislative branch and presented their reports directly to the Congress.

The commissions reported, for example, that fourteen different agencies were performing the same services without any of them knowing what the others were doing. In another case twenty-six different departments or agencies were carrying on parts of a program without any coordination. In a third instance ninety-three different groups were performing services which were somewhat alike. These are samples of situations which needed correction.

Many of the recommendations of the commissions have been put into effect. A good start has been made. But more needs to be done.

What of the future? Changes in organization usually come slowly. There are often interest groups which want to see a particular agency or bureau continued for one reason or another. In reorganization a person may lose his position or his authority, or a community may lose a particular government agency. Most people are willing to have changes made in some areas or departments but not in the ones in which they have a special interest.

To speed up reorganization, following the reports of the Hoover Commissions, Congress has given the President the authority to reorganize agencies of the executive branch. Reorganization plans submitted by the President go into effect automatically sixty days after being submitted to Congress, unless *either* the House or the Senate during that period defeats the plan by majority vote. The plan as submitted cannot be amended; it can only be rejected. Between 1949 and 1967, seventy-eight reorganization plans were submitted by Presidents, of which eighteen were rejected by the Congress. It is generally recognized that other plans were not submitted because they might have been defeated. One of the most important recent reorganization plans provided a new system of city government for Washington, D. C., as will be discussed in Chapter 19.

STUDY QUESTIONS

1. Why are some of the independent executive agencies often called quasi-legislative or quasi-judicial agencies?

2. What are some reasons for establishing independent agencies?

3. What is meant by the statement, "serve at the pleasure of the President"?

4. What are the steps a person must take to get a civil service position?

5. What is the work of each of the chief services of the General Services Administration?

CONCEPTS AND GENERALIZATIONS

1
The independent agencies are administrative units outside of the eleven departments.

2
Since some of the duties of the independent agencies are legislative and judicial in nature, they are also known as quasi-legislative and quasi-judicial agencies.

3
The United States Civil Service Commission is the employment agency of the federal government.

4
The General Services Administration is the housekeeping agency of the federal government.

5
Laws and regulations affecting veterans and their dependents are administered by the Veterans Administration.

6
The United States Information Agency provides information about the United States to people of other nations.

7
Manpower for the armed forces is provided through the Selective Service System.

8
United States activities in outer space are under the control of the National Aeronautics and Space Administration.

9
The National Science Foundation is charged with upgrading science and research.

10
Atomic power is being developed for peacetime uses.

11
The regulatory agencies are concerned with the improvement of all aspects of the nation's economic life.

12
Governmental corporations are similar to private corporations in their operation.

13
Reorganization plans for executive agencies are directed toward greater effectiveness and efficiency.

6. Why is the work of the United States Information Agency important?

7. What is the chief purpose of our space program?

8. Why was the National Science Foundation established?

9. What duty has been given to the Atomic Energy Commission?

10. Why is it wise to have a government agency regulate rates of common carriers?

11. What controls does the Federal Reserve System have over the nation's money?

12. What are the duties of the Federal Trade Commission?

13. Why is the work of the Federal Trade Commission important?

14. Which power facilities are regulated by the Federal Power Commission?

15. What communications facilities are controlled by the Federal Communications Commission?

16. How does the Securities and Exchange Commission protect investors?

17. Which federal agencies deal with labor-management troubles?

18. Why is the work of the Equal Employment Opportunity Commission important as a civil rights agency?

19. Why is it unlikely that we would have a repetition of the bank closings of 1933?

20. What are some of the many parts of the program of the Tennessee Valley Authority?

21. What has been the effect of the reports of the "Hoover Commissions"?

IDEAS FOR DISCUSSION

1. War veterans who pass civil service examinations are given an additional five points on their ratings, and those who have been disabled in military service are given ten extra points. Some people think that these so-called preferential ratings should be abolished. Do you think war veterans should receive these preferences? Why?

2. At one time most people believed that disputes between the workers and the owners of a factory or business were the concern of those people only. What factors can you suggest which have helped to change this opinion on the part of many people?

3. X College applies to the Federal Communications Commission for a license to operate a television station. At the same time Y Corporation also applies for a license. What factors will help the Commission decide whether one, both, or neither get licenses?

4. The Federal Reserve System, the Federal Deposit Insurance Corporation, and the Securities and Exchange Commission are agencies of the national government which exercise some control over money, banking, and business. Some people object to government control, others want more of it. What do you think are the advantages and disadvantages?

5. The reports of the Hoover Commissions on Organization of the Executive Branch of the Government propose that the President's authority over executive agencies be more clearly defined. Do you think this is wise? Why?

6. A railroad wishes to discontinue its passenger service and applies to the Interstate Commerce Commission for permission to do so. What kinds of information will the Commission need in order to reach a decision?

7. A Negro is fired from his position as inspector in a manufacturing plant. He appeals to the Equal Employment Opportunity Commission, charging discrimination and stating that he was fired because of his color. As a member of the Commission, what information and evidence will you want in order to decide the validity of his charge?

THINGS TO DO

1. Get a copy of the current issue of the *United States Government Organization Manual*. Report to the class on the activities of an agency not discussed in this chapter.

2. Select one of the independent agencies for study. Classify its duties as (a) executive, (b) legislative, or (c) judicial.

3. Go to the local office of the Civil Service Commission or to the post office and get information about civil service job opportunities now open. Report to the class about qualifications and salaries for these positions.

4. Use a bulletin board on which committees may post newspaper clippings about current activities of governmental agencies.

5. Make a study of recent labor-management difficulties. What agencies of the federal government were or are involved in settling these difficulties?

6. Check newspapers and periodicals for a report on an activity of the Interstate Commerce Commission. What was the point at issue? Prepare a report giving the decision of the Commission and your opinion.

7. Find out if there is a Federal Reserve Bank or a branch in your city. If there is, visit it and report on its activities. If not, discuss with your local banker the relationship of the local bank to the Federal Reserve System.

8. Check the financial page of your daily paper for references to the Securities and Exchange Commission. Report to the class on the references for one week.

9. Report to the class on any recent developments in the use of atomic power.

10. What facilities of the Veterans Administration are located in your city, community, and state? Find out about the services they offer and the extent to which they are used.

11. Debate the issue of government ownership and operation of the Tennessee Valley Authority versus the advisability of turning over the facility to private ownership.

FURTHER READINGS

Cox, Edward F., *et al*, THE NADER REPORT ON THE FEDERAL TRADE COMMISSION. Richard W. Baron Publishing Co., Inc., 1969.

Fleming, Alice, IDA TARBELL: FIRST OF THE MUCKRAKERS. Thomas Y. Crowell Co., 1971.

Lent, Henry B., PEACE CORPS. Westminster Press, 1966.

MacCloskey, Monro, OUR NATIONAL ATTIC: THE LIBRARY OF CONGRESS; THE SMITHSONIAN INSTITUTION; THE NATIONAL ARCHIVES. Richard Rosen Associates, 1968.

Scott, Ann Herbert, CENSUS, U.S.A.: FACT FINDING FOR THE AMERICAN PEOPLE, 1790-1970. Seabury Press, 1968.

Spencer, Sharon, BREAKING THE BONDS. Grosset & Dunlap, Inc., 1963.

Sutton, Ann and Myron, GUARDING THE TREASURED LANDS: STORY OF THE NATIONAL PARK SERVICE. J. B. Lippincott Company, 1965.

Weaver, John D., THE GREAT EXPERIMENT: AN INTIMATE VIEW OF THE EVERYDAY WORKINGS OF THE FEDERAL GOVERNMENT. Little, Brown and Co., 1965.

ADMIRALTY—dealing with affairs of the sea and ships; referring to the law of the sea and ships.

APPEAL — a request to have a law case taken to a higher court to be heard again.

APPELLATE JURISDICTION—the right of a court to hear cases that have been appealed.

BANKRUPTCY—the condition of being unable to pay one's debts.

CIVIL CASE — a legal dispute involving two or more citizens.

CONCURRENT JURISDICTION — the right of two or more courts to hear a legal case.

COURTS-MARTIAL—courts made up of military officers to try those accused of violating military law.

CRIMINAL CASE — a court action in which a person is accused of breaking the law.

DEFENDANT — an accused person; the person in a legal action against whom the claim or accusation is made.

DISSENTING OPINION — a statement written by a judge or justice who disagrees with the opinion of the majority.

EN BANC—all judges of a court are present to hear a case. (A word from the French meaning "on the bench.")

JUDICIAL REVIEW—the right of a court to determine whether a law or an act is constitutional.

MAJORITY OPINION—a statement written by a judge or justice expressing the opinion of the majority.

MANDAMUS—a court order compelling a person to do something.

ORIGINAL JURISDICTION—the court which has the right to hear a legal case for the first time.

PRECEDENT—an act that serves as an example for later action.

As the authors note, judicial powers are described in less than a page, but it is interesting to point out that the greatest power the Supreme Court has, namely judicial review, was not specifically mentioned in the Constitution.

14

The Federal Courts

The separation of powers into executive, legislative, and judicial branches which check and balance each other is one of the basic principles of American government. The Constitution requires several pages to describe the legislative powers. The executive powers are described in fewer pages. The judicial powers are described in less than a page. But the space devoted to each branch is not an accurate measure of its powers.

In some respects the judicial branch is most powerful because it can and does overrule Congress and it can and does overrule the President. As was described earlier, when the Congress and the President were unable or unwilling to act, the Supreme Court forced the integration of schools in the case of *Brown* v. *Board of Education* in 1954. When Congressional and legislative districts were not equal with respect to population, the Supreme Court compelled reapportionment in several decisions starting with *Baker* v. *Carr* in 1962. Thus, al-

Discuss the famous Dred Scott case, 1846-1857, which started in the Missouri state courts and ended up in the U.S. Supreme Court. (See page 309.)

though the judicial branch is described only briefly in Article III of the Constitution, the judicial branch is of great importance.

The opening sentence of Article III states, "The judicial power of the United States shall be vested in one Supreme Court and in such inferior courts as the Congress may from time to time ordain and establish." Based on this authority Congress has created a federal court system with the United States Supreme Court at the top, courts of appeal in an intermediate position, and federal district courts at the bottom level. To deal with specialized cases, special courts have been established by Congress.

Each state also has a court system, but the state courts are separate and independent of the federal courts. Citizens are sometimes confused about these various courts. They are not always sure which is the federal court and which is the state court. They wonder why one case is tried in a federal court and another case is tried in a state court. They ask whether a case can be moved from a state to a federal court or from a federal to a state court.

THE RELATIONSHIP OF THE FEDERAL AND THE STATE COURT SYSTEMS

To clear up these confusions, the average citizen needs to know that there are *two* court systems, the federal and the state. The relationship of the federal and state court systems can be difficult to understand if one gets lost in details. But the relationship is simple to understand if some of the details are omitted. For most citizens the general ideas are sufficient.

CASES START IN ONE SYSTEM. A first principle is that a law case must go either to one of the federal courts discussed in this chapter or to one of the state courts discussed in Chapter 17. The people or parties involved in the case and the kind of legal question will decide whether the case is one for the state or for the federal courts.

Cases do not go to both state and federal courts. They must go to one or the other. Having been started in one system, they cannot be changed to the other system except under very special circumstances. State and federal court systems are *separate systems.*

CASES USUALLY START IN A LOWER COURT. A second principle of the relationship of courts is that cases are usually started in a lower court and are appealed to a higher court. If one party is not satisfied with the decision in the lower court, the case may be taken to a higher court—if the higher court agrees that there is cause for the appeal.

The diagram of the courts on page 299 helps to show the separation of the court systems and the movement upward through the courts. The right to appeal from a state supreme court to the United States Supreme Court depends on specific facts, such as whether the Constitution of the United States is involved in the dispute.

FEDERAL CASES

The Constitution (Article III, Section 1, Clause 1) describes two types of cases that may go to federal courts: (1) those involving certain *people or parties,* and (2) those involving certain kinds of *legal questions.* Based on these constitutional provisions, the kinds of cases that may be tried in federal courts are:

1. Cases brought to federal courts because they involve these people or parties:

● *The United States*
● *Ambassadors, public ministers, or consuls*

- *Two or more states (Although by the Eleventh Amendment to the Constitution a state cannot be sued by a citizen of another state or of a foreign country without its consent.)*
- *Citizens of different states (Under the law a corporation is considered to be an individual and, hence, a citizen of the state from which it gets its charter.)*
- *Citizens of the same state claiming lands under grants of different states*
- *A state (or its citizens) and a foreign country (or its citizens).*

2. Cases brought to federal courts because they involve these legal questions:

- *Cases arising under the Constitution, laws, and treaties of the United States*
- *All admiralty and maritime cases (roughly, those cases dealing with the sea or with ships).*

FEDERAL OR STATE COURT? Under these provisions cases *may* come before federal courts, but they do not have to. In most legal matters a case can come before either a federal or a state court. The wish of the person starting the lawsuit determines which court system will consider the case, unless Congress has specifically stated to which kind of court the case should go.

Congress has been very careful to describe the kinds of cases that are to go to federal courts in order not to take away rights of the state courts. For example, crimes committed against laws of the United States go to federal courts. Crimes committed against state laws are tried in the state courts, unless an official of the United States is involved.

In disputes between individuals, the same general rule applies. If United States law is involved, the case would go to a federal court. If state law is involved, the case would go to a state court. But there are many exceptions. For example, public housing is under United States law, but most public housing cases are tried in state courts.

If persons living in two different states are involved in a lawsuit, the general rule is that the case would be tried in a federal court, because a state court might tend to favor the person from that state. But there is an exception: the rule only applies if more than $10,000 is in dispute. If less than $10,000 is involved, the case would remain in the state court.

Perhaps enough has been said about where cases go to show that it is not easy to determine exactly in which court system a case is heard. In practice, the person starting the case decides whether to go to a state or federal court. The other party (the defendant) can then plead with the court as to whether the case is being tried in the proper court.

TYPICAL FEDERAL CASES. What are some disputes that are tried before federal courts? An answer to this question can be found by looking at a book that is published about every two months. In this book, called the *Federal Digest*, every case coming before a federal court is listed with a brief two-or-three-sentence digest of the case. Issues of this digest are larger than this textbook, and the print is much smaller than the print on this page. Thousands of cases are listed. Each case is under a special

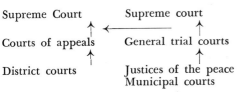

THE RELATIONSHIP OF
FEDERAL AND STATE COURTS

FEDERAL COURTS	STATE COURTS
Supreme Court	Supreme court
Courts of appeals	General trial courts
District courts	Justices of the peace Municipal courts

These young men are destroying their draft cards despite a federal law prohibiting it. What did the Supreme Court decide about such cases? (UPI photo)

heading. Here are some sample headings from the digest with an example of a case for each:

ADMIRALTY. One tugboat collided with another tugboat in a harbor. Which of the owners should pay the damages?

ALIENS. A native of China entered this country illegally. He returned to Formosa on a passport obtained dishonestly. Can he reenter the United States?

BANKRUPTCY. A bank is suing to recover the money for a loan made to a farmer.

CONSTITUTIONAL LAW. Was an employee of a Maryland corporation working in New York able to bring suit in New York for alleged failures of the corporation to pay him during an illness?

CRIMINAL LAW. Should a confession obtained in an assault case be accepted as evidence?

INTERNAL REVENUE. A man claims that the money the court orders him to pay his divorced wife should be deductible from his income tax.

LABOR RELATIONS. Was a chauffeurs' union within the law in trying to get employees of one taxicab company to join their union?

LANDLORD AND TENANT. Could the tenants collect money for painting and repairing they had done?

MONOPOLIES. An ice cream company is suing a dairy claiming that the dairy is trying to prevent competition.

PATENTS. A manufacturer of electrical equipment is suing a maker of radio and television sets about the ownership of a patent on a latch for cabinets.

SELECTIVE SERVICE. The world heavyweight boxing champion, Muhammad Ali (Cassius Clay), is tried for refusing to submit to induction into military service—claiming that he is a minister of the Black Muslim faith.

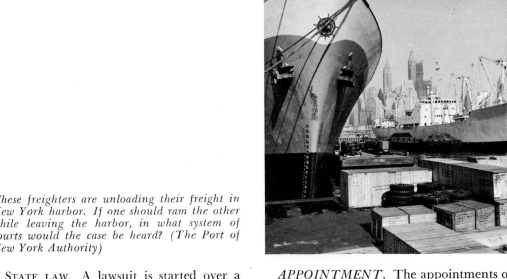

These freighters are unloading their freight in New York harbor. If one should ram the other while leaving the harbor, in what system of courts would the case be heard? (The Port of New York Authority)

STATE LAW. A lawsuit is started over a conflict in the state and federal laws governing savings and loan associations.

TRADEMARKS. A mail-order house sues an art company over the use of a name on a label.

WORKMEN'S COMPENSATION. Can a workman be paid, under the Workmen's Compensation Act, for an illness caused by too-long exposure to the sun while he was working?

These cases are typical of the thousands coming before the federal courts each year. They illustrate the basic principle that some cases come to federal courts because of (1) the people involved and (2) the kinds of legal questions.

THE FEDERAL JUDGES

The judges of the federal courts who hear these cases are appointed by the President of the United States, with the approval of the Senate.

APPOINTMENT. The appointments of the President are usually accepted, but there have been times when the Senate did not give approval. The Senate holds to the traditional "senatorial courtesy" rule of supporting a senator rather than the President. By this policy the Senate will not approve a person if a senator of the same political party as the President does not want the person as a federal judge in his state.

By this practice, southern Democrats have been able to appoint segregationists to the courts in the South. Senator Eastland of Mississippi, chairman of the Judiciary Committee since 1956, has been the enforcer of the "senatorial courtesy" practice. Although President Eisenhower with no southern Republican senators to appease was able to appoint able judges, Democratic Presidents have not been able to get around the opposition of southern senators. One southern judge appointed by President Kennedy stated that the Supreme Court's

Point out that a President who has the opportunity to appoint several judges during his years in office may, by appointing those of a certain known political philosophy, create a lasting impact on judicial history.

In his term as Chief Justice, John Marshall established firmly that the federal judiciary, and the Supreme Court in particular, was an equal branch of the federal government. He is also responsible for the idea, now generally accepted, that the Supreme Court could decide on the constitutionality of a law. (Library of Congress)

integration ruling was "one of the truly regrettable decisions of all times." Fortunately some of these judges have in recent years been willing to place the Constitution ahead of their prejudices and practice "equal justice under law" for Negroes.

The senators, therefore, have much to say about the appointments of federal judges. In most cases the appointed judge has been selected by the President after consultation with the Attorney General and with the senator of his party from the state where the vacancy existed. Once a judge is approved by the Senate he holds office "during good behavior." In practice this normally means an appointment for life.

IMPEACHMENT. The only way to re-

move a judge is by impeachment and conviction. Getting the necessary votes in the House and Senate for impeachment and conviction is very difficult and has happened only twice in this century. A judge was removed in 1913 for carrying on business relations with persons coming before his court. Another judge was removed in 1936 because of scandals involving his court.

Fortunately federal judges have, for the most part, been persons of honesty and ability. They have earned the respect of the people and have conducted the federal courts so that people have confidence in them.

SALARIES AND BENEFITS. The salaries of federal court judges vary from $40,000 a year for judges of district courts up to $62,500 for the Chief Justice of the Supreme Court. Associate Justices of the Supreme Court receive $60,000 a year. The salaries cannot be decreased while they hold office.

Judges cannot be removed because of their age or because of sickness. Judges who are physically or mentally unable to do the court work may retire on half salary. A judge who has served for at least fifteen years may retire at sixty-five. A judge, at seventy, who has served for ten years, may retire with full salary for the rest of his life. A retired judge may be called back to service at any time by the Chief Justice of the Supreme Court.

Congress has the right to abolish any federal court except the Supreme Court.

> *Judges are apt to be naive, simpleminded men. . . . We too need education in the obvious—to learn to transcend our own convictions and to leave room for much that we hold dear to be done away with short of revolution by the orderly change of law.*
>
> —OLIVER WENDELL HOLMES, JR. (Justice of the Supreme Court, 1902-1932), *Law and the Court*, 1913.

But if a court is abolished, the judge must be transferred to another court. His job cannot be taken away by abolishing his court. When a person accepts a position as a federal judge, he realizes that he probably will keep his position for life and be financially independent.

THE KINDS OF FEDERAL COURTS

Since the Constitution mentions only the Supreme Court, all other federal courts are established by laws of Congress. In 1789 Congress created a system of federal courts which still provides the basic structure of our court system.

THE DISTRICT COURTS. The district court is the starting place for most federal cases. There is at least one district court in each state and at least one judge for each district. As our population has grown and the business of courts has been increased, extra districts have been created and extra judges have been added.

Today there are ninety districts and some 390 judges. California, New York, and Texas are divided into four districts; Alabama, Florida, Georgia, Illinois, North Carolina, Oklahoma, Pennsylvania, and Tennessee have three. Thirteen states have two districts. The southern district of New York in New York City has twenty-four judges. Chicago has twelve; Detroit, nine; Los Angeles, fourteen; Philadelphia, eighteen; Pittsburgh, ten. Thus, in our heavily populated areas many cases can be heard at the same time.

The district court is the court where cases start, except for a very few cases which may be started in the Supreme Court. The district court thus has *original jurisdiction;* it is the first to hear and decide the case. Cases in which ambassadors, public ministers, consuls, or states are parties may be started in the Supreme Court—but they do not have to start there. The Supreme Court has original jurisdiction in these cases, but it has been held that the Supreme Court can share this jurisdiction with the district courts.

The district court is the principal federal court and does the most business. Both criminal and civil cases are tried before the district court. Usually cases are tried before one judge, but in certain types of cases three judges are used. The procedure in these trials is quite similar to that used in the state courts, which will be discussed in Chapter 17. If a party is not satisfied with the decision of the district court, this dissatisfied party may appeal to the court of appeals. In a few instances appeals can be made directly to the Supreme Court.

In each district court, in addition to the judges, there are certain other officials. The chief ones are (1) a district attorney, representing the Department of Justice, who prosecutes persons violating federal laws and represents the United States government in any case arising in the district in which the government is a party; (2) a marshal, who makes arrests and carries out the orders of the court; (3) commissioners, who conduct preliminary hearings in criminal cases to decide whether the accused person shall be held for trial; and (4) a chief clerk, who keeps the seal of the court and the records of the court orders and activities. The attorneys, marshals, and commissioners are political appointments for four-year terms made by the President with the consent of the Senate.

THE COURTS OF APPEALS. While the Supreme Court is the highest court of appeal, intermediate courts called courts of appeals have been established by Congress. (Until 1948 these courts were named circuit courts of appeals.)

These courts were created to relieve the Supreme Court of a great deal of the appeal

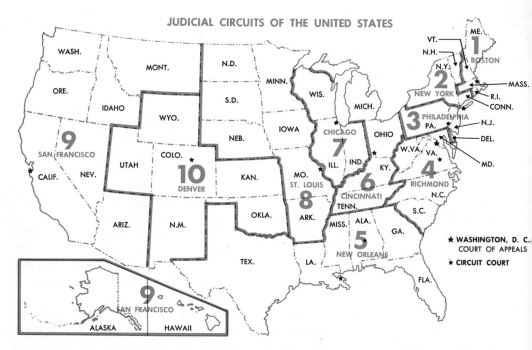

JUDICIAL CIRCUITS OF THE UNITED STATES

On this map are shown the judicial circuits of the United States. There is also a court of appeals in Washington, D. C. The cities where the court for each circuit is located are listed below (the court does sit in other cities, however):

Circuit 1	Boston, Mass.	Circuit 5	New Orleans, La.
Circuit 2	New York, N. Y.	Circuit 6	Cincinnati, Ohio
Circuit 3	Philadelphia, Pa	Circuit 7	Chicago, Ill.
Circuit 4	Richmond, Va.		

Circuit 8	St. Louis, Mo.
Circuit 9	San Francisco, Calif.
Circuit 10	Denver, Colo.

work. In 1891, when these courts were established, the Supreme Court was about three years behind in its work. Today there are eleven judicial circuits in the United States, including the one for the District of Columbia.

The judges of these appeal courts consist of a Justice of the Supreme Court assigned to the circuit (but who rarely has time to serve) and three to fifteen permanent appeal judges for each circuit. A district judge may also be assigned to assist the court of appeals, but of course he could not serve if an appeal was being made from his own decision. At least three judges must be present to hold court.

In the court of appeals, cases are not being heard for the first time. A court which hears appeals only is called an *appellate* court. In some cases appeals can be made from the court of appeals to the Supreme Court; for example, if a state law is declared unconstitutional. But for most cases the court is the court of last appeal—in order to ease the burden on the Supreme Court and to leave this highest court to deal with the most important cases.

One interesting feature about the courts of appeals is that under the leadership of the chief judge of each judicial circuit the federal judges of the district meet regularly to discuss the conditions of the federal

The white marble Supreme Court Building was completed in 1935. The inscription over the entrance reads "Equal Justice under Law." (Washington Convention and Visitors Bureau)

courts and to recommend ways of improving the courts.

In 1968 a Federal Judicial Center was created to study ways to correct weaknesses in the federal courts.

THE SUPREME COURT. The highest court is the United States Supreme Court, which meets in Washington, D. C., in a beautiful building a short distance from the Capitol Building. By law the Court must meet each year on the first Monday in October and continue until its work is done. Normally, to hear the approximately 1,000 cases that come before the Court, a session will last from October until June.

The Supreme Court has both *original* and *appellate* jurisdiction.

A Chief Justice and eight associate justices make up the membership of the Supreme Court. The size is determined by Congress. The nine-member court has been used since 1869, but prior to that time the size had varied from five to ten justices. The last serious attempt to change the size of the Court was in 1937, when President Franklin Roosevelt tried to enlarge the Court to fifteen members. After one of the most exciting and lengthy debates in congressional history the bill to "pack" the Supreme Court was defeated.

In the early years of our history, membership on the Supreme Court was not considered much of an honor. Today, to be a member of the Supreme Court is one of the highest distinctions any lawyer could ever achieve.

Less than one hundred persons have served as justices during the entire history of our country; yet among these are some of the most famous people who have served our nation. The names of Justices Marshall, Taney, Taft, Hughes, Holmes, Warren, and others will always be listed among the great of our nation.

PROCEDURE. The Court meets daily from Monday through Friday. The work of the Court is done largely by a review of the printed record of the case as it was tried in a lower court. Two-week periods for hearing the arguments of the lawyers alternate with two-week periods for study of cases. Only about 5 per cent of the cases appealed to the Supreme Court are accepted for this decision-making process.

Many times, until late in the evenings, the individual justices study the records of the cases that are before the Court. On Fridays the justices usually confer on cases and decide cases by a majority vote. One justice is assigned to write the decision for the majority. Other justices who agree with the decision sometimes write opinions, too, in order to show why they voted with the majority.

Each justice who does not agree may write an opinion showing why he disagrees with the decision. These *dissenting opinions* of the minority are read with almost as great care as the majority opinions. Why? Because in the past the dissenting opinion on some matters became the majority opinion years later when new justices were appointed and changes in social and economic conditions had occurred.

Justice Holmes, who served on the Court from the age of sixty-one until his retirement at age ninety-one, was known as the "great dissenter" because he sometimes disagreed with the majority. Yet many of his dissenting opinions are accepted by the Supreme Court today. His dissents were not frequent, but when he did differ from the majority his arguments were so powerful and were written so clearly that they have influenced later justices.

SUPREME COURT MEMBERS. Justices are human beings. They are influenced by their past experiences. They are influenced by their knowledge and study of law. They are careful students of legal precedents. They look at today's problems, in part at least, from their early training. Their home backgrounds, their schooling, their early work, the kinds of newspapers they read, their legal experiences—these factors and others influence them when they come to make a final decision.

It is fortunate that among our Supreme Court justices have been some of our ablest statesmen. It is fortunate, too, that justices have come from different walks of life. Some have been very wealthy lawyers. Others have been lawyers of moderate means. Some have been able professors of law at great universities. Some have been active in political life—as members of Congress, as judges, or as administrators appointed by the President. Nearly all have been active members of a political party.

Of the 1972 Supreme Court members, Justice Douglas had been a law professor. Justice White had been a Deputy Attorney General in the Department of Justice. Justice Brennan had been a judge of the New Jersey Supreme Court. Justice Marshall, the first Negro appointed to the Court, had been the chief attorney for the NAACP, a federal circuit judge, and Solicitor General. Justice Stewart had been a judge of the Sixth Court of Appeals. Jus-

The Justices of the Supreme Court. From left to right, front row: Associate Justices Potter Stewart, William O. Douglas; Chief Justice Warren E. Burger; Associate Justices, William J. Brennan, Jr., Byron R. White; back row: Associate Justices, Lewis F. Powell, Jr., Thurgood Marshall, Harry A. Blackmun, and William H. Rehnquist. (UPI photo)

tice Blackmun had been a judge of the Eighth Court of Appeals. Justice Powell, a prominent Virginia attorney, had been a president of the American Bar Association. Justice Rehnquist had been an Assistant U.S. Attorney General. Chief Justice Warren E. Burger practiced law in Minnesota for twenty years, served in the Justice Department for four years, and was a judge of the District of Columbia Court of Appeals for thirteen years.

Why are the training and background of the justices so important? Why is appoint-

ment to the Supreme Court today honored so much more than it was in our early history? To answer these questions requires understanding of a simple but very important practice in American government—the practice of *judicial review.*

JUDICIAL REVIEW

Judicial review is the right of a court to determine whether a law or an act is constitutional. By this power a court can say to the President of the United

"You Mean These Apply To The Riff-Raff Too?"

Copyright 1966 Herblock in the Washington Post.

States, "You cannot do that specific thing." A court can say to a state, "You cannot have that law." A court can tell Congress, "You were wrong in passing that law; the Constitution does not allow you to make such a law."

Any court may use judicial review, but in every important case the United States Supreme Court will finally have to decide whether the act or law is constitutional.

REVIEW OF AN EXECUTIVE ACT. An example will show how judicial review works. Near the end of President Truman's term of office the steel companies and the steelworkers could not agree on the wages to be paid. After months of dispute the workers decided to strike. At this time American soldiers were fighting in Korea. President Truman felt that a steel strike would mean that tanks, airplanes, and bullets would not be made and delivered to the soldiers. He believed that getting war materials to our soldiers was necessary for the conduct of the war. A strike would weaken our military position. He therefore ordered the government to take over the steel companies and to operate the companies in order to maintain the supply of steel for our fighting men.

With the government operating the steel mills, the workers went back to work. The owners, however, objected to the government taking their property. They argued that under our Constitution no one can take private property except by proper legal procedures. The lawyers for the steel companies went to a federal district court and asked that the companies be returned to the owners. The judge decided that the President did not have the power to take the companies from the owners. He ordered the property returned to the owners.

The government lawyers did not agree with the decision of the judge. They appealed to the United States Supreme Court. They and the lawyers for the steel companies presented their arguments before the Supreme Court. The justices studied the case. They decided by a majority of six to three that the government did *not* have the power under our Constitution to take the property from the owners.

After the Supreme Court announced this historic decision, the President returned the companies to the owners. He recognized that the Constitution as interpreted by the Supreme Court is the supreme law of the land and that even the President must abide by the Court's decisions.

REVIEW OF A CONGRESSIONAL LAW. In the steel company case the Court was reviewing an act of the executive branch of government. This use of judicial review has been fairly rare. More common has been the review of laws passed by Congress. The procedure is the same. Some person must go before a court and plead that a law passed by Congress is not proper under our Constitution. The court hears the arguments and decides whether or not the law is constitutional. The Supreme Court does not tell Congress, before a law is passed, whether the Constitution allows such a law. The Supreme Court only considers the constitutional question when a case is brought before it.

The first time a law passed by Congress was declared unconstitutional was in 1803 in the case of *Marbury* v. *Madison*. Marbury had been appointed a federal judge by President John Adams at the very end of his presidential term. In the last hours of his Presidency Adams was busy signing documents. One of these documents made Marbury a judge.

The document was not delivered to Marbury that night but remained on the President's desk and was still there when Jefferson took over the Presidency the next day. Marbury went to Jefferson's new Secretary of State, Madison, and asked for the signed document making him a judge. Madison would not give it to him because he believed Jefferson now had the power to appoint another person to the position.

Marbury appealed to the Supreme Court under a law passed by Congress in 1795 which gave a court the right to compel (*mandamus*) a public official to do something. Chief Justice John Marshall wrote an opinion for the Supreme Court which held that Congress had no power under the Constitution to pass such a law. Because the law was unconstitutional Mr. Marbury did not get to be a judge, and, more important, the Supreme Court demonstrated its authority to decide constitutional questions.

Fifty-four years passed before the Su-

In the "Dred Scott Decision" the Supreme Court declared the Missouri Compromise unconstitutional. The Court also declared that a slave was not a citizen. Which amendments made this decision obsolete? (Library of Congress)

preme Court again declared unconstitutional a law passed by Congress. Then, in the famous Dred Scott decision of 1857, the Missouri Compromise regulating slave territory was declared unconstitutional. Dred Scott, a slave, asked the Court for his freedom because he had once lived as a free man in Illinois. The Supreme Court did *not* give Scott his freedom, and, in addition, ruled that Congress had no right to try to control slavery in the territories as was attempted in the Missouri Compromise legislation. This decision helped to bring on the Civil War.

In the past 100 years judicial review has been used approximately eighty times to declare unconstitutional laws passed by Congress. Other famous decisions were those on an income tax, a child labor regulation, minimum wage payments to women, and some of the acts under the

New Deal program of President Franklin D. Roosevelt.

REVIEW OF STATE LAWS. The Supreme Court has used its power of judicial review more frequently on laws passed by state legislatures. This power to review the laws of state legislatures was first used in 1810 (*Fletcher* v. *Peck*) when a Georgia law on land grants was declared improper because it violated a contract. In 1819 in the Dartmouth College case the Supreme Court stated for a second time that a state law could not change a contract. In this case a New Hampshire legislature had changed Dartmouth's charter without the consent of the college.

The great Justice Holmes once commented on this right of the Supreme Court to decide whether state laws conformed to the Constitution. He said that he did not believe the Constitution would come to an end if the Supreme Court lost the power to declare an act of Congress unconstitutional, but that the Union would be in great danger if the Supreme Court "could not make that declaration as to the laws of the several states."

In addition to declaring state laws unconstitutional, the Supreme Court can decide whether the acts of state administrators and of state judges in enforcing laws conform to the Constitution of the United States.

The power of judicial review makes the Supreme Court the most important court in the world. The Court has a kind of "judicial veto" over all laws passed by Congress and by the state legislatures, as well as the power to review the acts of all executives and all courts on any matters involving the Constitution.

THE SOURCE OF JUDICIAL REVIEW. How has the Supreme Court gotten this power? Where in the Constitution is the Supreme Court given the right of judi-

"Well, it's sort of like the authority your mother has at home."

Hollett in the Detroit Free Press. © *1957 United Features Syndicate.*

cial review? The answers to these questions are simple ones. The Supreme Court has gotten the power of judicial review by using the power. The Constitution does not directly give the power to the courts.

There have been strong arguments as to whether the writers of the Constitution intended the courts to have the power of judicial review. But the fact is that throughout our history the courts have used the power until today judicial review is generally accepted as a basic part of American government. This is an example of the expansion of the Constitution through usage.

From time to time proposals have been made to take away or to control this power, but none of these proposals has been successful. Judicial review seems now to be a permanent, fundamental principle of American government.

THE BELIEFS OF SUPREME COURT MEMBERS. Because of the great power of the Supreme Court, it is easy to understand that the life of each new justice is studied with great care to determine how he will interpret the Constitution. Dred Scott, the slave, lost his freedom because of the Supreme Court decision. Five of the justices at that time had been owners of slaves. Did this fact influence their decision?

The justices who declared New Deal laws unconstitutional were called "the Nine Old Men." This nickname was more than a reference to their ages. Their critics were saying that the majority of the justices were very conservative men who had fallen behind the times. Were these critics correct? Or were their supporters right who said these justices provided a needed balance in a period of social upheaval?

There is no question but that the social, economic, and political beliefs of the justices influence their decisions as they explain the meaning of the Constitution. These beliefs may be different from those of the President, the Congress, or the majority of the people. But the Constitution is what the justices say that it is at any particular moment.

SPECIAL COURTS   The district courts, the courts of appeals, and the Supreme Court are the regular federal courts. In addition to these

THE WARREN COURT

Earl Warren was appointed Chief Justice of the United States Supreme Court by President Eisenhower. He served from 1953 to 1969. Prior to service on the Court he had been governor of California, state attorney general, Alameda County district attorney, and deputy city attorney in Oakland, California. In 1948 he was the Republican candidate for Vice President.

During his years of service as Chief Justice, the Supreme Court moved in new directions in the protection of the rights of the individual. Future historians will probably look upon the Warren Court as one of the most important in all our history.

The following are some of its major actions:

Reversed the "separate-but-equal" definition so that the law of the land required school integration and stated that racial discrimination in other areas was no longer legal.

Compelled the reapportionment of state legislatures and Congressional districts.

Changed the standards in treatment of those accused of crimes by insisting on legal counsel, limiting "unreasonable search and seizure" by police, and modifying the administration of courts for juveniles.

Declared official school prayers and required Bible reading illegal in public schools.

Redefined the punishment of communists by requiring that the accused have knowledge that the party advocated the overthrow of government by force.

Redefined the conditions under which United States citizenship can be taken away.

Tried to find a path between censorship and freedom in areas of obscenity.

Established a new principle for antitrust legislation by ruling that one company could not eliminate competition by purchasing its chief competitor.

courts there are some special courts which Congress has created.

THE COURT OF CLAIMS. This is the oldest of these special courts. It was established in 1855 to deal with claims that citizens might have against the government. From the times of the early kings there has been a tradition that a government cannot be sued without the consent of the government. This tradition grows from the old idea that "a king can do no wrong."

When a citizen had a just claim against the United States government, therefore, he had to get Congress to pass a law paying his claim. This system was awkward and not satisfactory. So Congress set up a special court to hear these claims. Congress grants this court funds to pay the claims which the court considers justified. The court is located in Washington, D. C., and has a chief judge and six associate judges. The judges hear cases as a group (*en banc*), with all being present.

THE CUSTOMS COURT. This court deals with cases arising from the importa-

A customs inspector boards a ship to check and evaluate its cargo. If an importer should contest the inspector's ruling, to what court would he take his case? (Bureau of Customs)

tion of goods into this country. By law most imports are taxed when they enter the country. The total amount of the tax is determined by customs officials according to the values they put on the imports.

Since the profit of the importer depends in part on the amount of the tax, disputes arise over interpretations of the law. From 1890 to 1926 these disputes were handled by a special Board of Appraisers. In 1926 Congress changed the name of this board to the United States Customs Court. The court normally meets in New York City, but it meets also in most large cities and in any place where there is a port of entry into the United States. The court has nine judges, one of whom serves as chief judge. Some cases are heard by individual judges, others by teams of three judges.

THE COURT OF CUSTOMS AND PATENT APPEALS. This court is the appeal court for cases originally heard by the Customs Court. The court also hears appeals from the decisions of the Patent Office on disputes over patents and trademarks. The court is located in Washington, but it also hears cases in New York. The court has a chief judge and four other judges. Cases are heard by the judges as a group.

TERRITORIAL COURTS AND COURTS OF THE DISTRICT OF COLUMBIA. These courts are provided to give territories and the District of Columbia courts which are similar to the federal district courts. The Panama Canal Zone, Puerto Rico, Guam, and the Virgin Islands are the territories having such courts.

These territorial courts, except in Puerto Rico, handle cases that are local as well as federal in character. Thus they combine the practices of both state and federal courts as we know them. In the District of Columbia in addition to the district court there is a United States Court of Appeals for the District, as was mentioned in the discussion of the courts of appeals, and special local courts.

THE UNITED STATES COURT OF MILITARY APPEALS. This court was established in 1950. The court reviews cases involving courts-martial and other questions referred to it by the Judge Advocates General of the armed services. The court has three judges.

THE TAX COURT OF THE UNITED STATES. This court is not strictly speaking a part of the federal court system. It is an independent executive agency created to decide disputes over income taxes, excess profits taxes, or estate and gift taxes. Because it is an extremely busy and important court, it is mentioned here.

The court has sixteen judges, one of whom is chosen as chief judge. The main office is in Washington, but cases are heard at various locations within the United States for convenience to taxpayers. Decisions can be appealed to a United States court of appeals.

THE HUMAN SIDE
OF JUSTICE
The lives of many people are changed because of court decisions. Basic governmental policies that have altered our nation's history have been determined by our courts. Naming the courts, telling the kinds of cases that appear before the courts, learning the meaning of such words as *judicial review* or *original jurisdiction* may fail to convey this human side of the courts. Men are richer or poorer, happier or unhappier because of the courts. Yet the judges are human beings just like parents, teachers, labor leaders, or businessmen. They do the best they know how in the light of their experiences and their training. They sometimes make mistakes. Now and then they seem to be very ordinary people. Sometimes they seem to have the genius of very great statesmen.

The human being is the most important factor in government. Whether it be a President, a cabinet member, a congressman, a diplomat, a party politician, or a judge, our nation needs the best ability we can develop. The homes, the churches, and the schools must continue to produce fine, upright, well-educated people if our governmental system is to be effective.

Because of the power of our courts we need judges of great ability and great honesty. In our federal courts we have been fortunate in getting a high level of ability. The great strength of our courts has been in the human qualities of the judges.

STUDY
QUESTIONS

1. How many court systems are there in the United States?

2. What does the Constitution say about courts? Was it wise that Congress was given the power to establish courts? Why?

3. What kinds of cases may be tried in federal courts?

4. What factors decide whether a case shall be tried in a federal or a state court?

5. How are federal judges appointed? Why does the President usually consult with a senator before appointing a judge? What effects has this had on the judiciary in southern states?

6. How can a federal judge be removed from office? What is meant by holding office "during good behavior"?

7. Why are cases involving residents of two different states brought before a federal judge?

8. What courts are in the federal court system? What are the special responsibilities of each?

9. How does the procedure in the Supreme Court differ from that in a district court?

10. How many members are there on the Supreme Court? Who is the most recently appointed member?

CONCEPTS AND GENERALIZATIONS

1

There are two court systems in the United States: federal and state.

2

Law cases are usually started in a lower court and appealed to a higher court.

3

The Constitution describes the types of cases that may go to federal courts: those involving certain people or parties and those involving certain kinds of legal questions.

4

Federal judges are appointed by the President with the advice and consent of the Senate.

5

A federal judge normally holds his office for life or until his retirement.

6

There are three regular federal courts: district courts, courts of appeals, and the Supreme Court.

7

Special federal courts have been created to deal with special problems.

8

Judicial review enables the Supreme Court to forbid acts of the executive, to declare laws passed by Congress unconstitutional, and to declare laws passed by state legislatures unconstitutional.

9

The social, economic, and political beliefs of judges influence their decisions.

11. Why is judicial review of such great importance under our system of government? How did the federal courts get the power of judicial review?

12. What was the *Marbury* v. *Madison* case? The Dartmouth College case? The steel seizure case? Why is each case important?

13. How does the Supreme Court act as a check on Congress and the President?

14. What is the function of each special court?

15. Why is the human side of the judges so important?

IDEAS FOR DISCUSSION

1. It has been said that the Supreme Court is "a third house of Congress." Do you agree or disagree with this idea? Why?

2. The Constitution does not provide for judicial review and did not provide for the specific federal courts other than the Supreme Court. Do you think these omissions are strengths or weaknesses in the Constitution? Why?

3. Is the salary of a federal judge high enough?

4. In 1968 *The Washington Post* used this example to describe the inequality of the witness fee: "Sam is a $40-a-day truck driver. Last year he appeared 16 times in District Court as a witness in a murder case. Each time he was paid a $4 witness fee by the court. His boss refused to pay him his usual $40 a day during the appearances. Result: Sam, who has six children, is $574 out of pocket."[1]
By 1973 the witness fee in a district court was $20 a day. What conclusions do you reach?

5. A newspaper headline read: "Senate, House OK Bill Adding 73 U. S. Judges." What do you think would have been the chief arguments of those supporting this bill?

6. Should judges be automatically retired when they reach age seventy? Why?

7. The federal courts have ruled that baseball is not subject to regulation under the commerce clause. Although players go from state to state, the courts held that baseball is a sport and not commerce. Why did this case get before a federal court?

8. Some citizens are dissatisfied with court decisions in judicial review cases. Should this power be taken away from the courts—by a constitutional amendment if necessary?

---

[1] *The Washington Post.* February 28, 1968.

9. Federal judges are appointed by the President. Some people think that this places too much power in the hands of the President and that citizens should have a voice in the selection of judges. Would you favor the popular election of Supreme Court justices and other federal judges? Why?

10. A majority vote of the Supreme Court is needed to declare a state or federal law unconstitutional. Would you favor increasing this to a two-thirds vote? Why?

11. An example of our democratic form of government is the power of the Supreme Court to make decisions against the President, stating that a particular action was not constitutional or legal. How does this power differ from what might happen in a country under authoritarian government?

12. How do the expression "The king can do no wrong" and the establishment of the United States Court of Claims arise from two different points of view of government?

THINGS TO DO

1. Prepare a "Who's Who" booklet giving brief biographies of the present members of the United States Supreme Court.

2. Prepare a scrapbook to illustrate law cases that are being heard by federal courts and state courts.

3. Consult the most recent *Statistical Abstract of the United States* to determine the number of cases that were handled by each of the regular United States courts and how they were decided. For example, how many written opinions were given by the United States Supreme Court?

4. Prepare an oral report on the life of Justice Holmes, Justice Benjamin N. Cardoza, Justice John Marshall, or another judge in whom you are interested.

5. Locate information on the federal courts that serve you. What is your nearest federal district court? How many judges serve in this court? In what federal appellate court district are you? Where is the court of appeals for the district located?

6. Prepare a chart of the federal court system.

7. Write an imaginary account of a visit to the Supreme Court on the day that an opinion is given.

8. Write an imaginary diary in which you pretend that you are a lawyer trying to prove that a certain law is unconstitutional. In the diary show the main events in the process.

9. Locate newspaper or magazine articles about one of these occasions when the Supreme Court was in the news and report your findings to class.

a) 1935–36. Decisions on "New Deal" legislation.

b) 1937. President Roosevelt's plan to reorganize the Supreme Court.

c) 1954. Decisions on segregation in public schools.

d) 1962. Decisions on reapportionment of legislatures.

10. Investigate and report to the class on the Administrative Office of the United States Courts.

FURTHER READINGS

Acheson, Patricia C., THE SUPREME COURT: AMERICA'S JUDICIAL HERITAGE. Dodd, Mead, and Co., 1961.

Baker, Benjamin, and Friedelbaum, Stanley H., GOVERNMENT IN THE UNITED STATES. Houghton Mifflin Co., 1966. Chapters 5, 6.

Burns, James M., and Peltason, J. W., GOVERNMENT BY THE PEOPLE. Prentice-Hall Inc., 1972. Chapter 19.

Cushman, Robert E., ed., LEADING CONSTITUTIONAL DECISIONS. Appleton-Century-Crofts, Inc., 1963.

Ferguson, John H., and McHenry, Dean E., THE AMERICAN SYSTEM OF GOVERNMENT. McGraw-Hill Book Co., 1967. Chapter 17.

Foundation of the Federal Bar Association, EQUAL JUSTICE UNDER LAW: THE SUPREME COURT IN AMERICAN LIFE. Grosset & Dunlap, Inc., 1965.

Habenstreit, Barbara, CHANGING AMERICA AND THE SUPREME COURT. Julian Messner, Inc., 1970.

Harris, Richard, DECISION. E. P. Dutton & Co., Inc., 1971.

McCloskey, Robert G., THE MODERN SUPREME COURT. Harvard University Press, 1972.

Roche, John P., COURTS AND RIGHTS: THE AMERICAN JUDICIARY IN ACTION. Random House, Inc., 1966.

Young, William H., OGG AND RAY'S INTRODUCTION TO AMERICAN GOVERNMENT. Appleton-Century-Crofts, Inc., 1966. Chapter 16.

The Story of a Presidential Hopeful: George Romney

Being President of the United States is an arduous, almost impossible, task. But running for office is, too. Nevertheless, there are always individuals who try to get there. Although only one person reaches the goal every four years, a few make it to the final round, and get their names on the ballot. Others drop out along the way, by their own choice or because their party eliminates them at the conventions.

Some who seek the office start early in the campaign race. Others "toss their hat in the ring" only a relatively short time before the conventions. Some early starters also drop out early, as did Governor George Romney in his bid for the 1968 Republican presidential nomination.

* * *

Headlines and news items tell the campaign story. (CSM-*Christian Science Monitor;* DFP-*Detroit Free Press;* DN-*Detroit News;* NYT-*New York Times.*)

AN UNOFFICIAL CANDIDATE

ROMNEY PUTS '68 LOW ON HIS LIST (DN 1-1-67) [1]

ROMNEY WON'T ENTER RACE UNTIL HE'S SURE HE'LL WIN (DFP 2-23-67) [2]

GRASS ROOTS DRIVE BOOSTS ROMNEY (CSM 2-24-67) [3]

---

[1] Excerpts reprinted by permission of *The Detroit News.*

[2] Excerpts reprinted by permission of *Detroit Free Press.*

[3] Excerpt Reprinted by permission from The Christian Science Monitor © 1967 The Christian Science Publishing Society. All rights reserved.

ROMNEY TOPS ALL RIVALS IN CALIFORNIA SURVEY (DN 4-2-67)

If the contest for President of the United States were between these men, for which one would you vote?

Johnson	38%
Romney	48%
Don't know	14%

Romney	51%
Kennedy	37%
Don't know	12%

If the contest for the Republican nomination for President of the United States were between these men, for which one would you vote?

Romney	35%
Nixon	32%
Percy	10%
Reagan	9%
Don't know	14%

Which of these men do you think can win next year?

Romney	46%
Nixon	16%
Reagan	11%
Percy	8%
Don't know	19%

ROMNEY TO STEP UP POLITICKING (DFP 6-8-67)

HIS RELIGION

ROMNEY DENIES MORMON POLICY CURBS HIS CIVIL RIGHTS EFFORTS (NYT 2-21-67) [4]

Gov. George Romney asked the American people today to judge him as a citizen with individual views rather than as a member of his church.

The Republican leader declined to discuss the doctrines of the Church of Jesus Christ of Latter-day Saints, to which he belongs, on the ground that it would "inject the church into public affairs."

---

[4] © 1967/68 by The New York Times Company. Reprinted by permission.

He denied, however, that Mormon restrictions on the participation and advancement of Negroes in the church prevented him from working as a public official to eliminate racial discrimination.

NEGROES ASK ROMNEY TO QUIT CHURCH (DFP 2-23-67)

The head of a group of Negro Democrats called on Gov. Romney Wednesday to prove his belief in racial equality by resigning from the Mormon Church.

ROMNEY CHALLENGED ON MORMON BELIEF (DFP 5-2-67)

RELIGION ATTACKS HIT BY ROMNEY (DN 5-3-67)

ROMNEY GETS A BOOST BY ONE OF HIS ELDERS (DFP 10-16-67)

HIS BIRTH

DOUBTS CAST ON ELIGIBILITY OF ROMNEY (DFP 5-15-67)

Chairman Emanuel Celler of the House Judiciary Committee said Sunday he had "serious doubts" about whether Mexican-born Michigan Gov. Romney is eligible for the presidency. . . .

After considerable research, Celler said in a television interview, he still had "serious doubts that Romney is eligible. It is a wide open question."

Romney . . . was born in a Mormon community in Mexico. Celler said he understood Romney did not enter this country until he was 6.

ELIGIBILITY CRITICS IRK ROMNEY (DFP 10-15-67)

Gov. Romney replied with some irritation Saturday to suggestions that he is not eligible to be president because he was not born on United States soil.

"I didn't do anything to be an American citizen except to be born," he said. "I am a citizen, naturally born."

SUPPORT

GOVERNORS DELAY ON ROMNEY SUPPORT (DFP 6-30-67)

Despite a couple of boosts for Gov. Romney, Republican governors . . . are about to put off at least until December any attempts to get behind a candidate for the 1968 presidential nomination.

GOP GOVERNORS WILL BACK ROMNEY (DFP 7-2-67)

A survey of Republican governors who assembled here for politics, fun and games . . . shows that when the chips are down the majority will side with Gov. Romney.

Though Romney did not get the public support he had hoped for from the governors . . . it was clear he was the most popular candidate for the 1968 Republican presidential nomination.

Conversations . . . indicate that 16 of Romney's 24 gubernatorial colleagues will end up in his camp.

GOP GOVERNORS COOL TO ROMNEY'S BID (DFP 10-22-67)

George Romney still must show his fellow governors he has what it takes to be President.

A year ago when the governors assembled in Los Angeles for their annual convention, most of the GOP delegation was talking about the need to rally behind a party moderate in the presidential maneuvering.

Romney was considered the most likely choice. If he could win reelection [as governor] by a goodly margin, he would be the logical rallying point for the 1968 presidential campaign.

Romney won big last November and has been acting like a would-be President ever since. With two exceptions, however, the other 24 Republican governors are dodging any commitment to Romney.

Detroit News BIDS ROMNEY YIELD AND BACK ROCKEFELLER (NYT 9-9-67)

The *Detroit News* . . . will urge him [Romney] to get out of the Republican presidential race in favor of Governor Rockefeller of New York.

In an editorial . . . [The *Detroit News*] has abandoned hope that the Michigan Governor will "finally organize and coordinate a purposeful campaign and articulate specific goals."

. . . Governor [Rockefeller] issued this statement: "I have supported George Romney in the past, and I will continue to support him in the future, and I repeat what I have previously said, that under no circumstances will I be a candidate."

VIETNAM

ROMNEY PINPOINTS HIS CRITICISM OF VIETNAM WAR (DFP 2-26-67)

ROMNEY PLEDGES SILENCE ON WAR (NYT 3-2-67)

ROMNEY BACKERS SPLIT ON WAR (NYT 3-27-67)

A major political struggle is under way among advisers of Gov. George Romney over whether the Michigan Republican should emerge as a hawk or a dove on the critical issue of Vietnam.

ROMNEY BACKS LBJ ON WAR; WARNS OF ESCALATION PERILS (DFP 4-8-67)

ROMNEY RAPS ESCALATION IN VIETNAM (DFP 4-29-67)

ROMNEY RENEWS VIETNAM CHARGE (NYT 9-10-67)

Gov. George Romney declared today that "the American people need a Government and a President we can believe." However, he still refused to offer himself as a Presidential candidate.

The Michigan Governor renewed his charge that the Johnson Administration had not told the truth about Vietnam, and he refused to back away from his statement earlier this week that he had been "brainwashed" during a Southeast Asian tour in 1965.

. . . By brainwashing, he told reporters, he meant "the same thing you mean when you write about the credibility gap, snow jobs and manipulation of the news."

CHINA

ROMNEY: EASE STAND ON CHINA (DFP 8-19-67)

Romney said Friday the United States should abandon its "rigid" opposition to admission of Red China to the United Nations.

CIVIL RIGHTS AND TOUR OF CITIES

GEORGIA HEARS RIGHTS PLEA BY ROMNEY (DN 5-1-67)

ROMNEY PRAISED BY ROCKEFELLER (DFP 8-2-67)

Gov. Nelson Rockefeller has told Gov. Romney that his charge that President Johnson played politics during the Detroit riots was "forthright, courageous and effective."

ROMNEY VISITS SLUMS—GETS FRIENDLY RECEPTION AT START OF 17-CITY TOUR (NYT 9-12-67)

MILITANT NEGROES APPLAUD ROMNEY (DN 9-14-67)

Gov. Romney is selling an unorthodox approach to the nation's racial problems in his tour of the country's urban areas. But it brought shouts of agreement from militant Negroes in this troubled city [Rochester, N.Y.].

Romney is saying that the biggest civil rights effort is needed not by the federal, state or local governments but in the private sector of society.

Speaking to a militant group named FIGHT last night, Romney said, "The place where the action has to occur is at the local level. I happen to believe personally that most of the action is going to have to come from the private area."

His comments brought shouts and clapping from a crowd jammed into the store-front headquarters of FIGHT. . . .

ROMNEY TOURS BROOKLYN (NYT 9-16-67)

ROMNEY IN TOUR OF HARLEM AREA— HE CALLS CONDITIONS WORSE THAN THOSE IN DETROIT (NYT 9-17-67)

ROMNEY WARNS, SEEDS OF REVOLUTION HAVE BEEN SOWN IN GHETTOS (NYT 10-1-67)

CONCLUDING EVENTS

These excerpts from *Newsweek* tell the Romney story for the four-month period, November 6, 1967 to March 11, 1968.[1]

11-6-67, p. 28

Of all the not-quite candidates, George Romney had the roughest week. Deep in Goldwater country . . . he was asked the inevitable question: "Why didn't you support Barry Goldwater during the 1964 election?" Romney tried to quip: "Like these news fellows over here say, a foreign correspondent has to live if he wants to write his story. I wanted to live to write the Michigan story." That brought angry mutters and a few boos from the 1,000 assembled faithful. Perspiring, Romney made another stab—a few claps, but even more boos.

11-27-67, p. 29

It's official!

After nearly a year of coast-to-coast campaigning, Michigan's moderate GOP Gov. George Romney took time out last week for a formality: he declared himself a Presidential candidate. In a preachy ten-minute statement, Romney decried

expanding government "control over our lives," a succession of "unfilled promises" to the slum poor, an Asian land war with "no end in sight," and the "growing aimlessness and flabbiness" of the American nation. "But I am confident that the American people can reverse this trend," he said—adding that what the Americans need is "leadership . . . worthy of God's blessing."

Romney thus became the first of leading GOP contenders to make it official. . . .

1-8-68, p. 19

. . . Just five months ago, the Michigan governor was on top of the world—or, at least, on top of the polls. Then he began to open his mouth. The result has been one of the most startling political vanishing acts. . . .

Although Romney announced his candidacy back in November and has been busily campaigning since, his positions on major issues remain befogged and befuddled. Only his complaint that he was "brainwashed" by U.S. officials in Vietnam two years ago has caused any stir—and so unfortunate was that gaffe that Romney is unlikely to live it down soon. . . .

1-15-68, p. 17

Romney will start dealing with Vietnam and other issues in New Hampshire late this week, when he opens a five-day stumping tour. Once he hits his campaign stride, his chances are all but certain to begin looking up. Thus far, Romney's press has been horrendous, but New Hampshire Republicans and independents may find his earnest enthusiasm appealing. In Wisconsin, too, Romney has built a well-financed campaign apparatus, is standing well against Dick Nixon in the polls and could wind up collecting some delegates in the April 2 primary.

But whether Romney can engineer a real upset is problematic. . . .

[1] Copyright: Newsweek, Inc. November 1967, January, February, March 1968.

1-22-68, pp. 20-21

. . . for nearly two hours last week he [Romney] stood smiling and shaking hands outside a factory gate in Nashua, N. H., as dawn broke over the snow-blanketed city and the temperature edged slowly upward from 15 degrees below zero. . . .

Clutching voters at the shoulder, grasping them with a firm hand, fixing them with an earnest eye, Romney captured one New Hampshireman after another . . . "We've got to get this country back on the track," he told them. "We've got to restore purpose and integrity.". . .

By and large, the citizens seemed to take kindly to the man from Michigan, listening politely to what he had to say. Hardly ever was he treated to an outright rebuff. But at some of his encounters Romney struck a deep vein of New England granite. . . .

"I'm an underdog," Romney admitted with relish. "I love being an underdog. I've been an underdog all my life.". . .

1-29-68, p. 25

. . ."We're going to win here, buddy— I can feel it in my bones," boomed his Manchester campaign chairman. George Romney's handsome face broke into a broad grin. "I think we've got some momentum going," he beamed. "I'm going to win."

Perhaps he will not win, but no one can doubt his momentum. For in his brief initial sortie into New Hampshire, Romney had managed to disengage foot from mouth and begin the long hike back into credibility as a Presidential candidate. . . .

. . . most of the reporters guessed he'd get about 45 per cent of the vote in a straight race with Nixon, which would very nearly deprive Richard Nixon of the convincing New Hampshire victory he says he needs.

2-19-68, p. 27

It was in Wisconsin that Romney came out vigorously against Nixon on Vietnam, and probably set the pattern for the rest of his primary campaign. In Kenosha, he again dared Nixon to a debate on Vietnam. "I don't know why either of us should be shy about a debate," he said. "If it would help, I'd gladly lend him my make-up man."

3-4-68, p. 22

. . . a write-in drive for New York Gov. Nelson Rockefeller bubbled to the surface—causing concern in George Romney's moderate camp. . . .

3-11-68, pp. 27-28

With startling suddenness last week, the Republican Presidential picture took on a tantalizing new look. . . . Michigan's George Romney abruptly took himself out of the running. . . .

Romney's withdrawal was one of the most astonishing turnabouts in the annals of American politics, but it had a certain logic to it. It was, after all, reasonable to expect that the Michigan governor would have had to drop out after losing to Nixon in New Hampshire and in the Wisconsin primary on April 2. Still, by anticipating the inevitable by five weeks, Romney upset all the timetables so carefully plotted by Nixon and Rockefeller's boosters. . . .

A special Harris survey for *Newsweek*, completed just before Romney pulled out, explains the collapse of the Romney crusade in New Hampshire. . . . No matter how hard Romney tried, Harris found, he never convinced New Hampshire Republicans that he was of Presidential caliber. . . .

Soundings by Romney's own staff matched the Harris findings. And the tidings from around the rest of the country were as grim as the New Hampshire readings. Finally, top Romney strategist Leonard Hall decided it was time to bring the matter to a head. At a meeting of the Romney high command . . . , the governor and his advisers surveyed the situation and concluded that it was time to pull out. Next morning, Romney honored a date for a television interview—during which he kept his secret and acted for all the world as if he were still a candidate—then flew down to the National Governors' Conference in Washington to drop the bombshell.

. . . Romney handled his farewell like a pro. His jutting jawline wreathed in a winner's smile, he faced the network TV cameras and an SRO crowd of newsmen and delivered a graceful five-minute valediction. "It's clear to me," he admitted frankly, "that my candidacy has not won the wide acceptance with rank-and-file Republicans that I had hoped to achieve."

In its March 8, 1968 issue, *Time* (pp. 20-22) put it this way:[1]

For George Romney it was the final indignity: never in his lurching pursuit of the presidential nomination had he created the impact wrought in the five minutes he took to end the quest. . . .

By the beginning of last week, the Michigander's own opinion sampling and other polls showed Romney trailing by 6 and 7 to 1. . . . Romney advisers decided that withdrawal was the only feasible course; . . . They relayed their prognosis to the candidate in a late-night meeting. . . . Romney slept on it, and by the time he finished breakfast next morning his mind was made up to quit. . . .

Romney made it official by reading a 387-word statement to reporters. . . . Perhaps because of the relief he felt after a long ordeal, he performed more gracefully than he had on most occasions during his 102 days of declared candidacy and during the earlier buildup. He candidly admitted failure to attract the support he needed, blamed no one for his troubles. . . .

The reasons for George Romney's abrupt exit from the New Hampshire primary last week are abundantly clear in a Roper poll commissioned by *Time*. Like Romney's own samplings, the Roper survey . . . presaged humiliating defeat for the Michigander. . . .

Richard Nixon	65%
Nelson Rockefeller	13%
George Romney	9%
Ronald Reagan	1%
Other Candidates	4%
Undecided or not answering	8%

The campaign of 1968 was not the end of Romney's political life. Richard Nixon won the nomination and the election in 1968. He offered Romney the post of Secretary of Housing and Urban Development in his Cabinet. Romney accepted. He became a Nixon supporter and campaigned for him in 1972. In August of 1972 Romney said he would resign from the Cabinet after the elections to return to private life.

Investigate and discuss these questions.
- How has religion influenced the choice of President?
- Has the issue of natural-born citizenship been settled?
- How do stands on foreign policy and civil rights affect a candidate's chances?
- Was the press fair to Romney?
- How does a candidate try to qualify himself for the Presidency?
- Can a candidate talk too much?
- What are the crucial issues?
- Is this the typical story of presidential hopefuls and losers?
- Review the story of Democrats like Hubert Humphrey or Edmund Muskie who, in the 1972 campaign, had a rise and a fall similar to Romney in 1968.

[1] By permission from TIME, The Weekly Newsmagazine; Copyright Time, Inc. 1968.

4

STATE
GOVERNMENT

Virginia State Travel Service

Discuss the general state of state government and power vis-à-vis the federal government in this age of national centralization.

Role-playing adds zest to a class and is sometimes effective in changing attitudes. Ask one student to portray a Democratic governor and another student to play a Republican Speaker of the House. Invite other students to interview each official on issues discussed in this unit.

The picture on the opposite page is of the Virginia State Capitol at Richmond.

State governments have never been more important and powerful than they are today. Great governmental power has been centralized in the federal government, but much governmental power remains with the states. The state governments are powerful and busy. Making them more effective is essential if states are to keep their proper positions in the federal system.

Urgent demands are made upon the states to solve difficult and complex problems. Urbanization, race relations, poverty, traffic conditions, air and water pollution, and other severe problems require the attention of state officials. Yet, some states are poorly organized to solve these complicated problems.

While the government of states is similar there are important differences. Each state has a governor, a legislature, and a system of courts. But states differ in these matters too. Some states give the governor great authority; other states divide up his author-

ity so that he has difficulty governing. All state legislatures, except Nebraska, have two houses. But these legislatures differ in their efficiency. In some states judges are elected; in others they are appointed. Some states have eliminated justices of the peace; others retain them. This unit deals with these likenesses and differences.

Chapter 15 describes the state constitutions, the legislatures, and suggestions for their improvement.

Chapter 16 treats the governor and the administration of state government including the reorganization of state administration.

Chapter 17 deals with the state courts and their procedures in civil and criminal cases. Ways of improving these judicial procedures are discussed.

Chapter 18 considers three great problems of state governments: services and activities, relations among the states, and relations with the federal government.

BALANCED LEGISLATURE – a law-making body in which members of the lower house are selected by population apportionment, but those in the upper house are selected from geographic areas.

BICAMERAL – a legislature with two branches or houses.

INITIATIVE–the method by which citizens, outside the legislature, can propose a law or amendment.

LEGISLATIVE COUNCIL–a permanent research committee of a legislature which meets continuously even when the legislature is not in session.

LEGISLATOR–a member of a lawmaking body.

RATIFICATION – a vote for approval; the act of approving a constitution or a constitutional amendment.

REAPPORTIONMENT – the act of apportioning again; the process of dividing the legislature on the basis of population changes after each census.

REFERENDUM–the submitting of a bill, a constitution, or a constitutional amendment to the direct vote of the citizens.

TERRITORY–a part of the nation that does not have the status of a state: it has its own legislature but an appointed governor.

UNICAMERAL – a legislature with one branch or house.

THE LANGUAGE
OF GOVERNMENT

Ask a student to report on the electric voting system in the federal House of Representatives.

15

State Constitutions and Laws

For generations legislatures recorded their votes by the slow process of a roll call. Then someone invented an electric machine that could speed up the vote. About half a century ago the Wisconsin legislative assembly began to use a voting machine of this type. Today three-fourths of the states use such a machine in one or both houses of the legislature.

The legislative voting machine is very simple. On the wall near the speaker's desk is a large board listing in alphabetical order the names of the members in large white letters. On the desk of each member are buttons that look much like those of the ordinary electric doorbell. When the speaker calls for the vote, members voting "yes" press one button, members voting "no" press another button.

On the board, lights go on showing how the members voted. Lights of one color, in one column, show the "yes" votes; lights of another color, in a second column, show the "no" votes.

A record is made of the vote instantly by means of special photographic equipment. The whole voting procedure takes less than a minute. In contrast, the older methods of roll call took forty-five minutes or more. State legislatures using electric voting machines save more than a hundred hours each session. Slowly one state after another has adopted them. Between 1917 and 1943 only eleven states installed these machines. Since that time twice that number have done so. At present still more states are studying the use of the electric voting machine for their legislatures.

STATES TRY NEW IDEAS

The experience with the voting machine illustrates an important feature of our federal system. One state can try an idea. If it works after thorough trial, other states and the federal government can adopt the idea. Individual states under our system can experiment with new ideas.

Wisconsin was the first state to try the electric voting machine. Nebraska has tried a legislature of one house. Georgia and Kentucky first lowered the voting age to eighteen, Alaska to nineteen, and Hawaii to twenty. New York and Michigan are examples of states that have reorganized the administrative side of state government by combining departments to give the governor greater power.

These states, and many others, too, have been willing to experiment. They have shown that state governments are important laboratories for improving government. While most features of state governments are similar from one state to another and in fact are much like those of the federal

Voting on bills in the Wisconsin State Assembly in Madison is speeded by an electric vote counter and tabulator. The results are revealed instantly on the electric signboard shown here. (State Historical Society of Wisconsin)

government, still, differences among the states are important in American life. In the study of state government it is valuable to examine the differences as well as the likenesses. A different idea, like the voting machine in the Wisconsin legislature, may be the new idea that will spread from one state to another.

STATE CONSTITUTIONS

The basis of all state government is the state constitution. Each state has a written constitution—a practice that began with the thirteen original states and has continued to our time.

As part of the process of admitting a new state into the Union, a territory desiring to become a state must write a constitution which has to be approved by Congress. Thus, from the successful attempts of

Stress the idea that each state coming into the Union has automatically been equal to those previously admitted.

325

This is Hawaii's new state capitol building, located in downtown Honolulu. The building was designed to harmonize with Hawaii's sunny environment. (Hawaii Visitors Bureau)

Alaska and Hawaii to become states back to the first states, the writing of a constitution has been the foundation of all state governments.

TERRITORIES BECOME STATES. The Constitution provides that "new states may be admitted by the Congress into this union . . ." (Article IV, Section 3, Clause 1) and that "the Congress shall have the power to dispose of and make all needful rules and regulations respecting the territory or other property belonging to the United States . . ." (Article IV, Section 3, Clause 2).

The writers of the Constitution probably did not dream that under this provision the thirteen original states would grow to the present number. They were thinking of the western lands beyond the Appalachian Mountains, such as those regulated by the Northwest Ordinance of 1787.

But the pattern that developed for those areas proved to be satisfactory later for the rest of the territories under the control of the United States. The pattern provided a simple transitional system from territorial government to statehood.

The steps in this system are:

1. TERRITORIAL GOVERNMENT IS ESTABLISHED. A governor, secretary, and judges are appointed by the President. As the population grows, the territory is permitted to elect a territorial legislature and to send a delegate to Congress. At present Puerto Rico elects a Commissioner who serves as its delegate to Congress. Guam and the Virgin Islands similarly elect delegates.

2. THE TERRITORY MAKES AN APPLICATION TO CONGRESS TO BECOME A STATE. The application is usually made when the territory has shown ability in self-government and the population of the territory has increased, although no special size is required.

3. AN ENABLING ACT IS PASSED IF CONGRESS AGREES. This act permits the territory to write a constitution. The people of the territory must approve the constitution by majority vote.

4. THE CONSTITUTION IS PRESENTED TO CONGRESS. Congress discusses the proposed constitution and the desirability of the territory's becoming a state. Congress may suggest changes in the constitution.

5. CONGRESS APPROVES THE CONSTITUTION. The Senate and House must approve the constitution in a joint resolution admitting

the territory as a state. The President must approve this bill and execute necessary steps for admission.

The differences in the time spent as territories have been very great. Alabama was a territory for only two years; New Mexico and Hawaii were territories for sixty-two years and fifty-nine years respectively. Alaska was a territory for forty-seven years. The average time has been about twenty-eight years.

In this process the key to becoming a state is the writing of an acceptable state constitution.

METHODS OF WRITING. The state constitutions of the thirteen original states were prepared by the state legislatures. They tended to make the legislature supreme and to keep the governor and the courts inferior. Then the people of Massachusetts had a new idea. Through their town meetings the idea spread that constitutions should come from the people and not from the state legislature.

In 1778 the people of Massachusetts, in town meetings, rejected a constitution that had been prepared by the legislature. A special constitutional convention was then called to write a new constitution. When this constitution was completed, it was submitted to the people through town meetings for acceptance. New Hampshire about the same time was trying a similar procedure.

Based on the practice of these two states, state constitutions since that time have been developed by constitutional conventions and have been submitted to the people for approval. The usual procedure requires three votes at different times: (1) the people vote to hold a constitutional convention; (2) the people choose delegates to participate in the writing of the constitution; (3) the people vote to accept or reject the constitution as submitted by the convention.

The models established by Massachusetts and New Hampshire have had the effect of placing the fundamental law of the state under the direct control of the people. This has made the state constitution the supreme state law which governs the acts of the legislature, the governor, and the courts.

THE PARTS OF THE STATE CONSTITUTIONS. State constitutions, of course, vary from one state to another because of differences in geography, population, political conditions, and willingness to try new ideas. In general, though, the constitutions have these main parts:

1. *The preamble:* a brief statement of the chief purposes of the state government

2. *The bill of rights:* a list of the basic freedoms which government cannot take from the people

3. *The plan of organization:* a description of the powers and duties of the legislative, executive, and judicial branches

4. *Special provisions:* provisions for special subjects such as state finance and taxation, local government, public education, highways, elections, and public utilities

5. *Amendment and revision:* a description of the ways by which the constitution can be changed.

CHARACTERISTICS OF STATE CONSTITUTIONS   Three special characteristics of state constitutions are worthy of note.

LENGTH. First is their length. Compared to the United States Constitution, most state constitutions are long and deal with a great many subjects. The average length of a state constitution is 25,000 words, more than three times the length of the United States Constitution. The longest constitution is that of Georgia, which contains about 500,000 words. The shortest constitution is that of Vermont, which has approximately 7,600 words.

Discuss why it is that there are movements to rewrite state constitutions which are more or less a century old; whereas, few people suggest rewriting the U.S. Constitution of 1789.

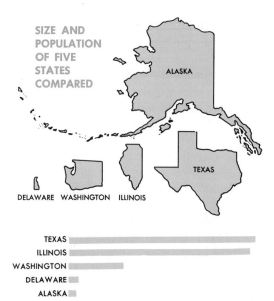

SIZE AND
POPULATION
OF FIVE
STATES
COMPARED

ALASKA

TEXAS

DELAWARE WASHINGTON ILLINOIS

TEXAS
ILLINOIS
WASHINGTON
DELAWARE
ALASKA

The top graph shows the comparative size of five states. The lower graph shows their populations as percentages of Texas' population.

Ideally, a state constitution should be brief and contain only basic principles.

The great length of state constitutions seems to be the result of two factors. State constitutions tend to deal with matters in great detail rather than follow the practice of the United States Constitution, which is a document of general policy. Thus the state constitutions sometimes get to be more like complicated laws than brief descriptions of fundamental policy. State constitutions are long, too, because states include material on many different subjects. States regulate labor, business, schools and colleges, charities, health practices, insurance, marriage, divorce, crime, local governments, highways, banks, and many of the other phases of modern life. These matters tend to be included in state constitutions.

AGE. Age is a second feature of state constitutions. While Alaska, Connecticut, Florida, Georgia, Hawaii, Michigan, Missouri, New Jersey, and Pennsylvania have fairly new constitutions, the average age of

the state constitutions is more than seventy years. The constitutions of most New England states are more than 100 years old.

The age of a constitution is computed from the time of its original adoption. Many of the constitutions have been amended, but the basic documents were written in the nineteenth century. While it is true that the United States Constitution is more than 175 years old, it is a statement of general policies.

The combination of length and age plus the inclusion of specific details has raised this question about many state constitutions: Are these constitutions adequate for the last quarter of the twentieth century? This is a crucial question for the future of state government and leads to a third feature of the state constitutions, the method of amendment and revision.

AMENDMENT AND REVISION. State constitutions can be amended or revised by constitutional conventions, by proposals from the legislature, and by direct popular initiative.

The *constitutional convention* method for revising a state constitution is much like the system described for developing the original constitutions. The constitutions of some states provide that every twenty years the people must vote as to whether a constitutional convention shall be held to revise the constitution. In other states the required number of years varies from seven to sixteen. In still other states there is no requirement of this type, but conventions may be called at any time by a vote of the legislature.

Legislative proposals for amendments to constitutions are used when the entire constitution is not to be revised. All states provide a method for amending their constitutions by proposals from the legislature.

The amendment must first be approved by the legislature. The size of the required

A constitutional convention may be called, and in some states must be called, to revise a state constitution. Here is a session of a recent constitutional convention in New York. (Wide World photo)

majority differs among the states, and, in addition, some states require that the proposed amendment be passed in two sessions.

In some states this process is fairly simple; in other states it is very difficult. Tennessee, for many years, had the most difficult system. The Tennessee constitution adopted in 1870 was amended for the first time in 1953. Amendments had to be proposed by a majority vote of both houses at one session, approved by a two-thirds vote of both houses at the next session, and ratified by a majority of the voters voting for governor at the next election. In addition, the legislature could not propose amendments oftener than once in six years.

The 1953 constitutional revision eliminated the six-year limitation and provided that the legislature at any general election could submit the question of calling a constitutional convention to the voters. However, the rest of the slow amending process was retained.

Most states, fortunately, have simpler methods for amending their constitutions. Estimates are that state constitutions get amended on the average about two times every three years. Since 1921 Louisiana has amended its constitution nearly 500 times. California has amended its constitution more than 350 times since 1879. In contrast, New Jersey has amended its constitution only sixteen times since 1947.

Based on the number of amendments approved, the most popular and effective way to change state constitutions is by having the legislature make proposals which the voters may approve.

Another way to make amendments is by *direct popular initiative,* which is used in fifteen states.[1] Under this system a certain per cent or number of voters in the state must sign a petition asking that an amendment be submitted to the voters for approval. When the necessary signatures have been obtained, the proposed amendment is submitted to the voters in an *initiative* election.

This system for initiating constitutional amendments varies from state to state. In most states 8 or 10 per cent of the voters must sign the petitions, but Arizona and Oklahoma require 15 per cent, and Massachusetts requires only 3 per cent. In North Dakota 20,000 voters must sign the petition.

Oregon in 1902 was the first state to adopt this method of amending the constitution. Massachusetts in 1918 was the last state to add this feature until Florida in 1968 and Illinois in 1970 adopted the direct initiative as a means of amending their constitutions. In the early part of this century some people wanted to change their state constitutions but were finding it difficult to do so. Liberal leaders in these states, however, succeeded in developing the initiative system as a way by which the people could make amendments.

This movement had not spread to other states in fifty years, partly because legislatures became more willing to submit amendments to the people. Direct popular initiative of amendments has never been a rival to the method of legislative proposals, but it is always a threat. In states using the initiative method an average of ten amendments has been added to each constitution by this procedure.

RATIFICATION. A new constitution or constitutional amendment must in all states except Delaware be submitted to the voters for final approval. If the majority approve, the amendment or revision is considered to be *ratified.* The election at which ratification is voted on is called a *referendum* election.

---

[1] Arizona, Arkansas, California, Colorado, Florida, Illinois, Massachusetts, Michigan, Missouri, Nebraska, Nevada, North Dakota, Ohio, Oklahoma, Oregon.

Explain the increasing use of constitutional commissions in the revision process. See the *Book of the States, 1972-73,* pages 7-10.

Many organizations are interested in the improvement of government. Some special-interest groups and political parties represent types of organizations that strive for certain improvements because of self-interest. There are, however, organizations that are concerned with improvement primarily because they believe in good, effective government. The American Political Science Association and the League of Women Voters are such organizations.

An organization that is not so well known by the public is the Committee for Economic Development (CED), which tries through objective research and discussion to bring about public understanding of important issues. The CED is made up of 200 leading businessmen and educators. From time to time a special committee or task force is appointed to prepare a statement on a national policy.

In 1967 the CED's Special Committee for Improvement in Government issued a report, *Modernizing State Government*. Of the fifteen members responsible for preparing this report, nine members were political scientists from universities; four members were actively engaged in government work; two others were staff members from the famous Brookings Institution—a nonpartisan research organization in Washington, D. C. The recommendations of this committee are still recognized as being the most up-to-date and authoritative available on state government. In this and other chapters, specific recommendations from *Modernizing State Government* will be given.

The constitution of Michigan is an example of this ratification procedure. In 1961 the people voted to hold a constitutional convention. Later that year they elected delegates to the convention. For months the delegates worked on the writing of a new constitution. In 1963 the new constitution was submitted to the people for their approval. They voted to accept the new constitution.

In Delaware constitutional amendments are ratified by legislative process. Two successive sessions of the legislature must vote approval for ratification.

THE FUTURE. The future for constitutional revision is not clear. Since World War II more than one-half of the states have started movements for changing state constitutions. There is growing awareness that many constitutions are old. There is criticism that the constitutions do not reflect the conditions of modern times. Groups of lawyers, businessmen, labor leaders, taxpayers' organizations, and leagues of voters have taken leadership to get changes.

If these movements continue, many state constitutions may be changed. On the other hand, it is well to recognize that the forces that have prevented change in the past continue to operate and may continue to delay the writing of new constitutions.

With respect to state constitutions the Committee for Economic Development (CED) in *Modernizing State Government* recommended:

State constitutional revision should have the highest priority in restructuring state governments to meet modern needs. Stress should be on repealing limitations that prevent constructive legislative and executive action, on clarifying the roles and relationships of the three branches of government, on permitting thorough modernization of local government in both rural and urban areas, and on eliminating matters more appropriate for legislative and executive action.

Ideally, a constitution is a statement of basic principles, outlining powers, relationships, and responsibilities. It

Nebraska's unicameral legislature meets in the state capitol building at Lincoln. What advantages do some political scientists see in a unicameral legislature? (Nebraska Game, Forestation and Parks Commission)

should not be encumbered with a vast bulk of ordinary statute law as so many state constitutions now are.[1]

STATE LAWS

The state constitution is the supreme law of the state. It is superior to any law passed by a state legislature. The state constitutions are outranked only by the United States Constitution and the laws,

---

[1] Committee for Economic Development, *Modernizing State Government,* pages 19-20.

treaties, and Supreme Court decisions of the United States government.

Of course, the relationship of all these important documents must finally be decided by the courts in terms of specific cases. But granting the superiority of the United States Constitution, the laws passed by Congress, and the state constitutions, it is still probably true that most citizens are more directly influenced by state laws than by any other single source of laws.

THE ORGANIZATION OF STATE LEGISLATURES. State laws are passed by

Ask students to examine their own state with respect to the organization of the legislature, reapportionment, the election of legislators, their pay, and qualifications. (Table 3 Appendix)

state legislatures. With the exception of Nebraska, these legislatures are bicameral, like Congress. The organization and the procedures are similar to those of the national government. The smaller upper house is called the senate. The larger lower house is called the house of representatives except in the following cases: California, Nevada, New York, and Wisconsin use the name "assembly"; New Jersey uses the name "general assembly"; Maryland, Virginia, and West Virginia use the name "house of delegates."

Nebraska is the only state that has abandoned the bicameral legislature. In 1937 Nebraska adopted a one-house (*unicameral*) legislature of forty-three members (recently increased to forty-nine). Before this time the bicameral legislature of Nebraska had 133 members. This trial of the one-house legislature has been watched by many other states. Some political scientists are enthusiastic about it.

The chief argument for the two-house legislature is the traditional one of one house checking on the other. The check-and-balance system is a deep-seated part of our historical past. Many citizens believe that it is wise to have bills considered by two different groups. They point to the number of bills that are rejected by one house after they have been passed by the other house. These citizens also mention the times that amendments are made by one house to the bills passed by the other house.

Against these arguments the supporters of a one-house legislature point out that the governor's veto and general public opinion are more effective checks on any legislative act than is the two-house system.

They favor the unicameral system because (1) the one-house legislature has improved and simplified legislative procedure; (2) the expense and slowness of two-house legislatures have been reduced; and (3) laws are made in the open with less secrecy and fewer deadlocks—responsibility for passing or not passing laws can more easily be fixed.

The future of the unicameral legislature is not clear. Whenever efforts are made to improve the legislative process, the Nebraska experiment is sure to be discussed, but in over thirty years no other state has changed to a one-house legislature.

The CED committee which prepared the policy statement on *Modernizing State Government,* while not giving an outright recommendation to the unicameral legislature, looked upon it with favor and noted that "The citizens of Nebraska seem well satisfied with their unicameral legislature. . . . Most Canadian provinces and American municipalities use the unicameral system. Several great cities with unicameral councils have larger budgets and more employees than the average state."[1]

THE SIZE OF STATE LEGISLATURES. The decrease in size of the Nebraska legislature has centered attention, also, on the relation of size to the efficiency of legislatures. In general as legislatures increase in size, committees become more important, party discipline becomes greater, there are more inexperienced members, and there is less freedom for the individual legislator to speak.

The legislatures vary greatly in size. The senates average about forty members, and the houses of representatives average about 120. The extremes for the senates are Alaska and Nevada with twenty members and Minnesota with sixty-seven. Among the houses of representatives, Alaska and Nevada with forty each have the smallest membership, and New Hampshire has the largest with

[1] Committee for Economic Development, *Modernizing State Government,* page 36.

Serving as a page can be an interesting and instructive experience. This high school student is a page in the Wisconsin State Assembly and assists the assemblyman for whom he works in many ways. (Milwaukee Journal photo)

about 400 members. (The New Hampshire membership varies because of a system of representation by small towns.)

Modernizing State Government recommended that "no state legislature should have more than 100 members in total; smaller states would be better served by still fewer members."[1]

REAPPORTIONMENT. For many decades state legislatures were dominated by

[1] Committee for Economic Development, *Modernizing State Government,* page 20.

rural legislators. While citizens were moving off the farms to urban areas state legislatures were not reapportioned. As a result the vote of the city person often did not count for as much as the vote of the person in the rural area in the election of members of the state legislature, and there was a long struggle to change the representation in state legislatures.

An example from one state will show how the conflict arose. The state of Tennessee had ninety-nine representatives in the lower house of the legislature. In the 1960 census it had a population of 3,567,089 people. How many people should each representative serve? As a simple arithmetic problem, the answer was:

$$\frac{3,567,089}{99} = 36,031$$

Each representative, thus, should be serving about 36,000 people.

In Tennessee, however, the representative from Moore County represented 3,454 persons. But the seven representatives from Davidson County represented 399,743 people, or one representative for 57,106 people. The vote of the farmer from Moore County was about sixteen times more valuable than the vote of a citizen from Nashville, in Davidson County.

For years after each census similar conditions existed in every state with a large city. The vote of a Detroiter was not worth as much as that of a person who lived in the Upper Peninsula of Michigan. The vote of a citizen of Chicago was not as valuable as that of the downstate Illinois citizen. The upstate New Yorker was better represented than was the citizen of New York City. Throughout the other states the same conditions were true.

Around each of the large cities were growing metropolitan areas where thousands and thousands of other persons live.

The suburban areas were the most poorly represented areas in the state legislatures.

All state constitutions, except those of Delaware and Maryland, provided that after every census the state legislature should be reapportioned. Usually this power was given to the state legislature. But legislatures often had not been reapportioned every ten years.

Some examples after the 1960 census were: Alabama had not reapportioned since 1906. The last reapportionment for Indiana was 1921. Delaware had not reapportioned since 1897.

The combination of a growing urban population and the failure to reapportion legislatures brought about a condition which has troubled free men several times in past history. England in the nineteenth century had some bitter political battles before industrial areas were given proper representation. This story of the elimination of the "rotten borough" from England was a famous landmark in the struggle to give the ordinary man the right to vote.

In our own country the cry "No taxation without representation" was used by our colonial forefathers to express their resentment of a system in which the colonies were not properly represented.

Political leaders in large cities used the same arguments that had been used in those earlier struggles. They said, "Urban people pay most of the taxes. Why shouldn't they be properly represented. . . . Look at our legislature. You'd think the fewer people an area has, the more it counts in the legislature."

For years courts refused to hear cases on legislative reapportionments. The courts held that reapportionment was purely a political matter. But, in a series of cases, the United States Supreme Court reversed this policy. Tennessee had not reapportioned her legislature since 1901, and the court decided, in *Baker* v. *Carr* (1962), that citizens could challenge the apportionment in the federal courts. In a 1964 case (*Reynolds* v. *Sims*), the Court made it clear that not just one but both houses of the legislature must meet the standard of "one man, one vote."

Prior to this case there had been pleas that the lower house of a state legislature should be apportioned by population, but the upper house should be divided by geographical areas. The example was, of course, the method of representation in the Congress of the United States. This system became known as the *balanced legislature*. It was this system which the Supreme Court denied in *Reynolds* v. *Sims*. The Court said,

> Legislators represent people, not trees or acres. Legislators are elected by voters, not farms or cities, or economic interests. As long as ours is a representative form of government, and our legislatures are those instruments of government elected directly by and directly representative of the people, the right to elect legislators in a free and unimpaired fashion is a bedrock of our political system. . . . The fact that an individual lives here or there is not a legitimate reason for overweighting or diluting the efficacy of his vote . . . the weight of a citizen's vote cannot be made to depend on where he lives.

Based on these decisions, state and federal courts have forced the legislatures to be reapportioned to make a vote in the metropolitan area equal to one in the rural area. After the 1970 census the states took major action to eliminate population inequalities in legislative districts.

Although efforts were made to amend the United States Constitution to permit states to have balanced legislatures, these efforts seem to have failed. For the present the

Legislators find it difficult to keep track of all the information they need. This combination computer-printer device, used by Pennsylvania legislators, can give in seconds the history and status of any bill under consideration, either on the screen or in printed form. (IBM photo)

Supreme Court decisions have settled the rural-urban conflict by forcing the states to reapportion.

THE ELECTION OF STATE LEGIS-LATORS. In most states members are elected to state legislatures from single-member districts for two- or four-year terms. Senators usually have a longer term than representatives. The elections are usually held in November of the even-numbered years at the same time that other national and state officials are chosen. A few states hold state elections in the odd-numbered years so that the attention of the voters will not be fixed on national issues.

The candidates are nominated by political parties and elected from partisan ballots, except in Minnesota and Nebraska.

QUALIFICATIONS. While the average age of members of state legislatures tends to be around fifty years, it is worthy of note that the most common minimum required age for house membership is twenty-one and for the senate only twenty-five. As a result, many young people get their start in political life as members of state legislatures. From there they may go to a higher governmental position. Examples are former

President Franklin D. Roosevelt and former Attorney General Herbert Brownell, who were members of the New York legislature at the age of twenty-eight.

The state constitutions describe the legal qualifications for members of the legislatures. Besides minimum age, United States citizenship and residence in the state and in the district are usual requirements. More important, of course, are the political qualifications: public service, party activities, speaking ability, education, appearance, and ability to win over the voters.

Most members of state legislatures are not very well known. Public opinion polls have shown that fewer citizens can name their state representatives than their Congressmen or members of the city council. Considering the importance of their positions this lack of prestige and public recognition is unfortunate. Too often legislators are best known to lobbyists.

SESSIONS. Regularly scheduled annual sessions are now the rule in most states. (See Table 3 in the Appendix.) The trend toward the annual session gained momentum after 1960 as the work load of the legislatures greatly increased. Voters in a few states, however, have refused to permit annual sessions. In these states the legislatures meet only in odd or even numbered years.

The governor can call a special session in every state. In several states the legislature itself can also call a special session. Annual sessions tend to eliminate the special sessions which are called when legislatures meet on the biennial basis.

About half the states place a limit on the length of time the legislature can meet. The usual limitation is sixty days, but Georgia and Wyoming allow only forty days, and a few states permit 120 days or more. The time limits tend to increase the difficulties that arise at the ends of sessions.

Legislatures get into a crowded period of hurried activity near the ends of sessions. More bills come from committees than can be carefully studied. The legislative day has to be lengthened. Sometimes the clock has to be stopped to permit the legislature to finish its business if there is a legal time limit. This legislative "traffic jam" is worse in states with time limits than it is in other states, but it is bad in most states. One observer in the last day of one legislative session noted that the average time devoted to dozens of bills was ninety seconds each.

Michigan has tried to correct this condition by setting final dates when bills must be introduced and when bills must be reported from committee. As a result, instead of having about 200 bills to deal with at the end of the session, only a few have to be considered.

California from 1911 to 1959 tried a scheme of split sessions for the same purpose. After a first session of thirty days when bills were introduced, the houses adjourned for thirty days, giving the members time to study the bills and to discuss them with voters in their districts. The second part of the session then lasted ninety

> *Your representative owes you, not his industry only, but his judgment; and he betrays instead of serving you if he sacrifices it to your opinion.*
>
> —EDMUND BURKE, British Statesman, Member of Parliament, in Speech to Electors of Bristol, 1774.

days. During this part, new bills could be introduced only under special conditions. A few other states have used split sessions.

The CED committee in *Modernizing State Government* recommended that sessions should be held annually and that there should be no time limits for adjournment. Annual sessions of unrestricted duration, it was argued, "afford more days and weeks for deliberations . . . reduce the flood of hasty and ill-considered legislation in the waning hours of a session . . . allow more continuity and more effective use of research and secretarial staffs."[1]

THE PAY OF LEGISLATORS. A glance at the table of the state legislatures (see Table 3 in the Appendix) will show that the pay of members is low. California pays the most, $19,200 per year, but the salaries of $5.00 to $20.00 a day or a few hundred dollars a year paid by other states are exceedingly low. In these cases legislators are receiving less than the janitors who clean the capitol building or the guards at the spectators' galleries. The salaries remain low for two reasons: (1) in some states the salaries are fixed by the state constitutions, which makes it very difficult to increase them; (2) in other states the legislatures determine salaries and members do not increase the salaries for fear of criticism.

In addition to the salaries, small amounts are paid to legislators for office expenses and transportation costs. There are a few

---

[1] Committee for Economic Development, *Modernizing State Government*, page 37.

In November 1972, New Jersey became the first state to extend benefits to Vietnam veterans. Governor William Cahill signed the bill while William J. Keenan, Director of Community and Professional Services for New Jersey, looked on. (Courtesy, N. J. Public Information Officer, Al Fulling)

special privileges, such as freedom from arrest during a session and freedom from being questioned in any other place about what one has said on the floor of the legislature. But most members of legislatures find that for their hard work they get only honor and a feeling of service. Most members are poorer financially because they serve in the legislature.

Such conditions are ideal for the dishonest person who wants to corrupt legislators. Buying a dinner now and then, turning a piece of business to a lawyer member, putting the member on the payroll of your business become the devices by which members of legislatures no longer represent the people. In view of the low salaries and the general lack of public interest in the work of state legislators, the miracle is that

most remain honest and do not give in to the pressures of special interest groups. Fortunately, most legislators are honest.

In *Modernizing State Government* it was recommended that "$15,000 should be the current minimum legislative salary. Salaries in the larger states should be at least $25,000 annually."[1]

THE LEGISLATURE
AT WORK
The making of a state law is very similar to the passage of a law by Congress. The steps described on pages 217-222 are followed very closely and need not be repeated here in detail.

---

[1] Committee for Economic Development, *Modernizing State Government*, page 20.

Point out that the state legislature is, under our federalism, the ultimate repository of all government powers which are not delegated to another agency.

INTRODUCING A BILL. Bills are introduced by members, but these bills come from a variety of sources. A corporation, a labor union, a farmers' organization may actually have prepared the bill. The idea for a bill may have come from a voter "back home."

Since legislators are not trained in all the subjects that come to the legislature, most states now provide *Legislative Reference Bureaus* to assist legislators in the study and drafting of bills. These bureaus are like special libraries and are departments of the state library in some states. They help the legislator to locate important information as he studies a new bill and also help him to write the bill if he plans to introduce a bill of his own.

PRESIDING OFFICERS. After a bill is introduced it is assigned to a committee by the presiding officer. The presiding officer in the lower house is called the *speaker* in all states. He is the most important member. In addition to assigning bills to committees, he appoints members to committees, interprets the rules, and grants permission to speak during debates.

The speaker is also usually the leader of the majority party and thus has great political influence. In contrast to Congress, where the power of the Speaker has been reduced, as described in Chapter 9, little has been done in the state legislatures to reduce the power of the speaker.

Three-fourths of the states elect a lieutenant governor who presides over the upper house, or senate. In the other states the senates choose their own presidents. The presiding officer of the senate is usually not as powerful as the speaker. He usually has to share his power of committee appointments with the whole senate or with a special committee.

COMMITTEES. The committees to which the bills are assigned do the most important work of the legislature. Here is where hearings are held, issues are studied, and rewriting is done. Here is where bills may be pigeonholed.

Most states appear to have too many committees. Although several states have less than ten committees in the lower house, the average number of committees is nineteen for the lower houses and eighteen for the senates. The trend in most of the states in recent years has been to reduce the number of committees.

A large number of committees tends to reduce the time spent in careful study of bills and to decrease the efficiency of the individual legislator because he belongs to too many committees. Also, it becomes almost impossible for the general public to know when hearings are to be held.

Connecticut, Maine, and Massachusetts use joint committees of upper and lower houses almost entirely. The joint committee practice eliminates duplication of effort, saves time of legislators and witnesses, and the public can follow the hearings better. There is a trend for committee hearings to be open to the public, but less than half the states require open hearings.

PASSAGE. When a bill has been reported on favorably by a committee, it is returned to the legislature for debate, possible amendment, and passage or rejection. If passed it goes to the other house and, after final passage, to the governor. In all states except North Carolina the governor has veto power which is similar to the veto and pocket veto of the President.

SAFEGUARDS ON LEGISLATION. At every stage of the legislative process, persons or groups with special interests are active to advance or protect these interests. Much of this activity is entirely proper and frequently helpful to the legislatures. Some of it is dishonest, or, if it is not actually dishonest, it is certainly not for the general

At committee hearings, legislators hear opinions and information both for and against a pending bill. Here an interested crowd in the visitors' gallery listens intently to a hearing in New York's Assembly chamber. (Wide World photo)

welfare. Clever men have learned to play tricks on the public. The title of a bill might say one thing; the body of the bill might be quite different. Appropriations for undesirable purposes might be attached as riders to highly valuable bills. Bills that would never receive public support might be hurried through legislatures in the last hectic days of the session.

Protection against these evils requires constant watchfulness. Safeguards have been developed by some legislatures: titles must express the contents of the bill; a bill cannot be introduced in the latter part of the session without special approval; bills must be printed before final passage; a record of the voting must be kept. Such rules have helped to keep the legislative process honest.

THE LOBBYISTS. Lobbying has been regulated too. Just as the Congress has felt it necessary to keep some control over those who work for special-interest groups, so too some state legislatures have tried to regulate the lobbyists. The usual requirement is that they must register, show who employs them, and report their expenditures. A few states forbid lobbyists to appear on the floor of the senate or house. In some states, however, the lobbyists are free to be anywhere and are usually on hand when important decisions are made.

The only real safeguard against improper lobbying is the integrity of the members of the legislature. It is sometimes difficult to detect good lobbying from bad. The good is helpful to the legislature; the bad is harmful. Farmers, teachers, war veterans,

GRASS ROOT ROUTE

The Flint Journal, *Booth Newspapers, Inc.*

labor leaders, and business groups help legislatures when they supply information and criticize proposed laws honestly. Because gamblers, racketeers, and other antipublic groups do improper things is no reason to think ill of all lobbying.

LEGISLATIVE COUNCILS. In most of the states, legislative councils have been created. These councils are permanent legislative research committees. Made up of leading legislators appointed by the houses, these councils study important state problems continuously, not only when the legislature is in session. The councils have paid staffs, carry on research, and finally draft bills.

Kansas created the first council of this type in 1933. As the council idea develops, it could do much to help solve major state problems. The council is an important step in improving the work of the state legislatures.

INITIATIVE AND REFERENDUM. There is one great difference between lawmaking on the state level and lawmaking on the national level. Some states permit direct participation by the people in the making of laws. National laws are made only by Congress through the representative system with no direct vote by the people.

When the people are allowed to vote directly for laws, they are using either the *initiative* or the *referendum.* South Dakota, in 1898, was the first state to adopt these practices for lawmaking. Since then over one-half of the states have adopted some form of the initiative or referendum. About two-thirds of these states are west of the Mississippi River. The greatest use of these direct devices has been by the three West Coast states. The states using the initiative and referendum, with the chief features, are shown in Table 4 in the Statistical Appendix.

The initiative gives the voters a way of making laws by getting a required number of signatures on a petition. The process is much the same as the initiative method of amending state constitutions.

First, some person or group must write the proposed law in the form of a bill. Second, people are asked to sign petitions requesting the law to be enacted. Third, when enough signatures have been obtained (usually 5 to 10 per cent of the registered voters), the petitions are filed with the secretary of state. Fourth, under *direct initiative* the proposal is placed on the ballot at the next regular election. With a majority approval, the bill becomes a law.

Under *indirect initiative* after the petitions have been filed, the proposal is sent to the legislature. If the legislature approves the bill, it becomes a law. If the legislature does not approve, the bill must then be placed on the ballot, giving the voters the final decision. Of the states using the initiative, over two-thirds have the direct type.

The *referendum* in some respects is like the indirect initiative, because the vote of the people comes after the action of the legislature. By the referendum a bill passed by the legislature does not become a law until the voters have approved it. The referendum is used in two ways: optional and mandatory.

Under the *optional system* the legislature may decide that a bill which it has passed shall not become a law until the voters have approved it at the next regular election. By the optional system the voters are usually asked to decide controversial matters.

Under the *mandatory system* after the legislature has passed the bill, petitions must be signed in the same manner as with the initiative. Petitions are circulated by persons and groups opposed to the law. If enough signatures are obtained, the bill must be voted on at the next election.

The initiative and referendum came into existence as a protest against control of legislatures by special-interest groups. Both the initiative and the referendum represent dissatisfaction with state legislatures. These procedures give final lawmaking power to the people.

Not all agree with the value of these devices. Some argue that the ballot gets too crowded with so many measures. Others say that only the highly organized groups can get enough signatures on the petitions. Still others think that voters are not good lawmakers because they cannot spend the time in careful study of bills.

With the initiative and referendum, all the voters can do is say "yes" or "no." Some political scientists say this is not good lawmaking because good laws are the result of compromise, of amendment, of give and take between interested groups.

Regardless of the merits or weaknesses of these arguments, the fact is that in those states having initiative and referendum important laws have been submitted to the voters. Here are a few examples: Michigan voters approved the sale of colored oleomargarine. Oregon voters accepted a sales tax. North Dakota voters created a scholarship system. California voters defeated a bill to make gambling legal. California approved an old-age pension plan in an election one year and defeated the same plan the following year. Kansas repealed a state prohibition act. Bonus and pension plans for veterans of World War II have been voted on in several states.

It is worthy of note that most states using the initiative and referendum adopted these practices in the first two decades of this century, and none of these states has repealed them. Yet in the last quarter of a century only Alaska has been added to the states using these forms of direct legislation by the people.

THE · IMPROVEMENT OF STATE LAWMAKING. In early American history, state legislatures were held in high regard. Having thrown off the tyranny of a king, people looked to their legislatures for protection of individual rights and the general welfare. Gradually during the nineteenth century this faith in legislatures came to an end. By 1900, state legislatures were distrusted. The rise of the initiative and referendum is one symptom of this changed attitude. The length of constitutions is another symptom.

Gradually during our twentieth century there has been a rebuilding of the faith in the state legislature. That process is still going on and has been strengthened by the nationwide attention which has been given to the reapportioning of the state legislatures.

An organization called the Council of State Governments, created in 1933, has helped strengthen state government. Each state is represented in this organization. The Council has achieved national recognition for its work in improving the government of states. Several years ago a committee of the Council in a report on "Our State Legislatures" made these major recommendations for improving state lawmaking which are much like those of *Modernizing State Government:*

1. The position of the legislator should be made more attractive by paying better salaries and lengthening the term of office. Salaries should be fixed by law rather than by the constitution. With longer terms of office, continuity in office could be achieved by not having all legislators elected the same year. These recommendations it is hoped will attract more competent persons to serve as legislators.

2. Restrictions on the length of sessions should be removed. Legislatures should be free to meet as often as necessary.

3. Committees should be reduced in number wherever practicable. The work of committees should be organized so that individual committees deal only with related subjects. The work of one committee should about equal that of another. The committees of the two houses should cooperate. Permanent, public records of committee action should be kept. All committee meetings should be scheduled in advance with the time and place of meetings clearly stated. Public hearings should be held on all major bills.

4. Special assistance should be provided the legislatures. Skilled, full-time legislative employees should be appointed on the basis of merit and competence. They should retain their positions regardless of changes in legislative party control. Legislative reference services should be strengthened. Legislative councils or between-session committees with adequate provisions for research should be provided.

5. The rules of the legislatures should provide a deadline after which new bills could not be introduced in order to end the congestion at the end of the session. The rules should be revised to speed up procedure with due caution for careful deliberation and the protection of minority rights. The legislature should provide a budget for paying for the legislative expenses. The rules should prevent undue special legislation.

STUDY QUESTIONS

1. Why are state governments called laboratories for improving government?

2. How do territories become states?

3. How are state constitutions adopted?

4. What are the typical parts of a state constitution?

5. Why are so many state constitutions lengthy documents?

6. In what three ways can state constitutions be amended?

7. When was your state constitution adopted? When was the last amendment made?

8. Does your state have a bicameral or a unicameral legislature? What are the official names of the houses?

9. Why has the bicameral legislature been kept in most states?

10. What are the arguments for and against the one-house legislature?

11. What is the size of the legislature in your state? What is the term of office of legislators? How often are sessions held? What are the salaries of legislators?

12. Why is the process of reapportionment so important?

13. What were the effects of *Baker* v. *Carr? Reynolds* v. *Sims?*

14. What are the steps in passing a law in your state legislature?

15. How do committees of the legislature carry on their work?

CONCEPTS AND GENERALIZATIONS

1
Individual states under our federal system can be laboratories for trying new ideas in government.

2
To become a state, a territory must develop a constitution which is satisfactory to Congress.

3
State constitutions must be approved by the people of the state.

4
State constitutions tend to be too long and detailed, rather than statements of general principles.

5
State constitutions need to be revised systematically to keep up with changing social and economic conditions.

6
Only Nebraska has a unicameral legislature.

7
State legislatures tend to have too many members.

8
The Supreme Court forced the reapportionment of legislatures—ending their domination by rural interests.

9
Most state legislators are not well known, and their salaries tend to be too low.

10
Annual sessions of state legislatures with no time limits are desirable.

11
The process of passing a law in a state legislature is similar to that used by Congress.

12
The great difference between lawmaking in the nation and in the states is that some states provide for direct legislation by the people through the use of the initiative and referendum.

13
The improvement of state lawmaking is necessary if the people are to look again upon their legislature with the respect in which it was held in our early history.

16. How can a member of a legislature know a good lobbyist from an evil one?

17. Does your state hold state elections at a time which avoids conflict with national elections?

18. What can be done to improve the process of making state laws?

IDEAS FOR DISCUSSION

1. The Constitution of the United States is older than most state constitutions, but there is much more pressure to revise state constitutions than to revise the United States Constitution. Why?

2. Why did the United States acquire territories and dependencies beyond the boundaries of the forty-eight adjoining states?

3. Have the admissions of Alaska and Hawaii as states been beneficial? What effects have their admissions had on national politics? What effects have the admissions had within the states of Alaska and Hawaii?

4. Is a small or a large legislature more desirable? Why?

5. A magazine writer says, "The state legislature is the neglected stepchild of our democracy." He found that only one citizen in thirty knew the name of the person or persons representing him in the state legislature. What conclusions do you make from these statements?

6. In one midwestern state there are 350 registered lobbyists—about three lobbyists for each member of the legislature. Is this condition desirable?

7. Should a member of a state legislature be required to be a high school graduate? If you desired this requirement for your state, would the constitution have to be amended or would a law have to be passed?

8. What are the advantages and disadvantages of the initiative and referendum? Do you agree with the policy of your state on these matters?

9. Do you agree or disagree with the recommendations at the end of this chapter for improving state legislatures?

10. An experienced member of a state legislature was quoted as saying, "Most of the lobbyists are mighty good fellows and are helpful. I am just a businessman with a small retail business. There are lots of things I don't know, so I go to these fellows to find out. They are experts in their line, and good men. A lot of them tell me what's what even when it's against their own interests. They know they have to be on the level with me and they are. They are among the most able and honest men around the Capitol and I am not ashamed to go to them for advice." Based on this quotation, would you vote for this legislator if you had the chance?

11. Has reapportionment in your state reduced the inequalities between urban and rural districts?

THINGS TO DO

1. Outline the chief parts of your state constitution. Are any of the usual parts of state constitutions missing? Does your constitution have any features that are different from the usual ones?

2. Prepare a chart showing the method by which your state constitution can be amended.

3. Prepare a calendar showing the times when elections are held in your state.

4. Have small committees or individuals find the answers to these questions: What is the average age of the legislators in your state? How many women are members of the state legislature? What are the occupations of the legislators? How many terms have members served? How many committees are there? On the average, on how many committees does a legislator serve? (Consult the Blue Book, the legislative handbook, or the state manual of your state.) Present this information to the class by means of graphs.

5. Invite a member of the state legislature to speak to your high school assembly on the work of your state legislature.

6. Have a committee of students interview a cross-section of adults to determine (a) whether they know the names of their state legislators; (b) how efficient they think their legislature is; and (c) whether they are friendly or unfriendly to lobbying.

7. Hold a mock session of your state legislature, and demonstrate how a law is passed.

8. Write an editorial defending a change which you think should be made in your state government.

9. Draw a cartoon showing your position on an issue before the state legislature.

10. Visit your state legislature.

11. Study maps of the legislative districts for your state and report to the class on the manner in which the boundaries were drawn. Is there any evidence of gerrymandering?

12. Prepare a special report on proportional representation.

FURTHER READINGS

Adrian, Charles R., GOVERNING OUR FIFTY STATES. McGraw-Hill Book Co., 1967. Chapters 1, 2, 14.

Baker, Gordon, THE REAPPORTIONMENT REVOLUTION. Random House, Inc., 1966.

THE BOOK OF THE STATES, 1972-1973. Council of State Governments, 1972.

Citizens Conference on State Legislatures, THE SOMETIME GOVERNMENTS. Bantam Books, 1971.

Committee for Economic Development, MODERNIZING STATE GOVERNMENT. The Committee, 1967.

Elazar, Daniel J., AMERICAN FEDERALISM: A VIEW FROM THE STATES. Thomas Y. Crowell Co., 1966.

Ferguson, John H., and McHenry, Dean E., THE AMERICAN SYSTEM OF GOVERNMENT. McGraw-Hill Book Co., Inc., 1967. Chapters 26, 27.

Heard, Alexander, ed., STATE LEGISLATURES IN AMERICAN POLITICS. Prentice-Hall, Inc., 1966.

Jewell, Malcolm E., and Patterson, Samuel C., THE LEGISLATIVE PROCESSES IN THE UNITED STATES. Random House, Inc., 1966.

Maddox, Russell W., and Fuquay, Robert F., STATE AND LOCAL GOVERNMENT. D. Van Nostrand Co., Inc., 1966. Chapters 3, 6, 7.

Mitau, G. Theodore, STATE AND LOCAL GOVERNMENT: POLITICS AND PROCESS. Charles Scribner's Sons, 1966. Chapters 3, 4.

THE MODEL STATE CONSTITUTION. National Municipal League, 1963.

Munger, Frank, ed., AMERICAN STATE POLITICS. Thomas Y. Crowell Co., 1966. Nos. 4, 10, 16, 22, 28.

Polsby, Nelson W., ed., REAPPORTIONMENT IN THE 1970s. University of California Press, 1971.

Ross, Russell M., and Millsap, Kenneth F., STATE AND LOCAL GOVERNMENT AND ADMINISTRATION. Ronald Press Co., 1966. Chapters 7, 10, 11, 26.

Snider, Clyde F., and Gove, S. K., AMERICAN STATE AND LOCAL GOVERNMENT. Appleton-Century-Crofts, Inc., 1966. Chapter 1.

AUDITOR—officer who authorizes the ex
penditure of state funds according to law
and audits state accounts.

BUDGET—a plan showing the expected
income and the proposed expenditures of
government.

COMMUTATION—a change of a court
sentence to one that is less severe, usually
from a death sentence to life imprisonment.

EXTRADITION—the process of turning
over a criminal or a person accused of a
crime from one state to another.

GUBERNATORIAL—relating to the governor or his office.

ITEM VETO—the power of an executive
to refuse to approve parts of a bill.

PARDON—release from punishment for a
crime; forgiveness.

QUASI-JUDICIAL—to some extent like a
court; an agency having powers to interpret laws or settle disputes in a way similar
to a court.

QUASI-LEGISLATIVE — to some extent
like a legislature; an agency having powers to make rules and regulations that are
like laws.

REPRIEVE — postponement of punishment for a crime.

RIDER—an amendment which might not
pass by itself attached to a bill which is
sure to pass.

VETO—the refusal of an executive to sign
a bill passed by a legislature.

THE LANGUAGE
OF GOVERNMENT

—

Emphasize that since our establishment as a nation, there
has been a tendency to impose restrictions upon legislative authority while increasing the powers of the governor.

16

The Governor
and Other State
Executives

Governors should become chief executives in fact as well as name. Except for
a jointly elected lieutenant governor, the
governor should be the state's only elective executive official. He should have a
four-year term, and freedom to seek re-
election without restriction as to number
of terms. . . . The governor should have
appointive and removal powers over all
major executive department heads. The
governor's salary should be at least that
of a member of Congress (now $42,500
annually); chief executives of larger
states should receive substantially more.[1]

This recommendation was made by a
special committee of the Committee for
Economic Development after an extensive
study of state government. It was the opinion of this committee that if state govern-

—

1 Committee for Economic Development, *Modernizing State Government*, pages 20-21.

ments are to meet the problems of our times, the position of governor should be strengthened; he should be given greater authority in the administration of state government.

The power of the governor has gradually been increased throughout our nation's history. While he does not have as much authority as the national committee recommends, his position even now is an important and powerful one. This was not always so. The first state governors inherited the dislike that citizens had for the colonial governors. These colonial governors were the symbol of the British crown, and as such they were subject to the ill feelings that many colonists had toward the British king.

When the states established their own independent governments, they wanted to reduce the power and authority of the governors and looked to the legislatures as the guardians of the people's rights. The legislature was made the important branch of state government.

THE POSITION OF THE
GOVERNOR   Some results of these early efforts to keep down the power of state governors still exist. In a few states the governor is limited to one term; in others he is limited to two terms. Length of the governor's term is another restricting factor—several states limit the term to two years. (See Table 5 in the Appendix.) States with these limitations keep their governors from becoming the kind of powerful chief executives which the national committee thought is necessary today.

Another factor which weakens the power of the governor is the direct election by the people of heads of administrative departments. In only four states is the governor the only elected executive official. In the other states from a few to many administrative heads are elected by the people or by the state legislature. This gives these administrators a high degree of independence from the governor, and sometimes their political ambitions make them his rivals. If the elected attorney general or the secretary of state is of a different political party, he not only can refuse to assist the governor, but actually can use his office to defeat the governor's programs.

But these restrictions should not detract from the present important position of the governor, and this importance is growing. Over the years a number of factors have combined to increase the power and influence of the governor. State legislators have too often been mediocre persons. Because of the low pay attached to their positions, not enough strong and highly capable people have been attracted to the legislature. Strife, inefficiency, rural domination, and sometimes corruption caused people to lose confidence in their legislatures. As the legislature declined in importance, the governor became stronger.

Another factor has been the great number of elected officials. Voters could not concentrate full attention on all of them. They began to look to the governor as the responsible official, and he assumed greater authority in line with this responsibility. Also depressions, riots, floods, and other catastrophes caused people to look more and more to the state for help in the solution of problems. The state government thus became stronger, and as this happened the people looked to the governor for leadership. Statewide problems, such as adequate highways and financial support for the schools, have frequently been made the concern of the governor.

In recent years, too, many state governors have been outstanding individuals. This has increased the importance of the position they held. For some, the governorship has been a stepping-stone to the White House. Examples are Franklin D. Roosevelt and Woodrow Wilson. Some others did not get to the White House but were presidential candidates, for example, Thomas E. Dewey, Alfred E. Smith, and Adlai Stevenson. Many governors have become United States senators. A former California governor, Earl Warren, was appointed Chief Justice of the Supreme Court. The elevation of governors to positions of national prominence has increased the prestige of the position of governor. The governorship is not only an important position but it leads to other important positions.

As was noted earlier, however, our state constitutions have not given the governor powers to the same degree that our federal Constitution grants great powers to the President. The governor in most states is only one of several elected officers.

The President appoints the members of his Cabinet. He alone has the sole executive responsibility and authority. On the state level, most constitutions provide for the election of such other officials as lieutenant governor, secretary of state, treasurer, superintendent of public instruction, auditor, and attorney general.

If these officials are members of the same political party as the governor and if they share his political views, there is usually harmony in the executive branch. However, if they differ with the governor on policy matters, there is often quarreling and bitter disagreement and the program of the state suffers.

QUALIFICATIONS. The Constitution of the United States sets up some qualifications for the person who wishes to become President. State constitutions have similar qualifications for the governorship. Ordinarily the governor must be a citizen and a resident of the state for a certain number of years. Most states set a minimum age, usually about thirty years.

Political parties also are concerned about getting a qualified and acceptable candidate. They want him to be a good speaker and to have a pleasant personality. He should be well known and preferably have held other important positions in the state. He must also be a vote-getter. A strong candidate for governor will frequently help to elect other officials of his party.

Candidates for governor are nominated in two ways. Many states hold primary elections at which the several parties select their candidates from among all of the people seeking the office. Other states hold nominating conventions and select candidates in much the same manner that presidential candidates are selected by the national conventions.

REWARDS OF OFFICE. There is a wide variation among states in the amount of salary paid to governors. Salaries range from $10,000 to $85,000, with most of them between $25,000 and $40,000. Nearly all states provide the governor with some type of expense account.

Most states have an official residence for the governor. This is usually a stately mansion. However, five states do not yet have a "governor's mansion." Current information about the term of office, salary, and official residence of governors is summarized in Table 5 in the Appendix.

THE WORK OF THE GOVERNOR The governor has a highly honored position, but there is much more to his position than honor. His job is a difficult one, especially in our large and populous states. He is a very busy person and often has little time for himself and his family.

Using Table 5 in the Appendix, have the students discuss the rewards of being governor in their state in comparison with other states.

The official residence of the governor of New Jersey, called "Morven," is located in Princeton and was built in 1701. (Courtesy of New Jersey Dept. of Conservation and Economic Development)

In general the governor has three kinds of duties: executive, legislative, and judicial. Since he is the chief executive officer of the state, most of his duties and responsibilities are executive in nature. However, he does have responsibilities in the other two areas. His duties on the state level are similar to those of the President on the national level.

EXECUTIVE

POWER As the chief executive officer of the state, the governor has the responsibility for administering the affairs of the state and for carrying out its laws. His legal authority is not nearly so great, however, as many people think it is. His powers on the state level are much more limited than the national powers of the President. It has already been noted that the governor in many states does not appoint all the people who share executive power with him. Some very important officials, such as the secretary of state, the attorney general, and the treasurer, are elected by the people in these states.

These officials often may feel no responsibility to the governor and occasionally try to block his program. This is recognized as a serious handicap for good administration. Many political scientists feel that the governor should be given the opportunity to appoint people to these positions and then be held responsible for developing a good program for the state.

APPOINTMENT. Aside from these elected officials, however, the governor has rather broad powers to appoint people to important state positions, boards, and commissions. But also in these appointments he is limited in two ways.

HOW THEY BECAME GOVERNOR

Political scientists carry on research about politics, political life, and all phases of governmental activities. They try to determine causes and reasons for political happenings. On the basis of data gathered they try to predict the outcomes of elections, the effects of certain laws, the results of political circumstances, the consequences of administrative practices and judicial decisions. They make studies of the operation of government. They search for answers to political questions.

Research supplies information about trends and changes in government. When published, it is available to people in and out of government to help them make decisions.

An example of research about the office of governor is a study made by Professor Joseph A. Schlesinger of Michigan State University. He reports his study in a monograph, *How They Became Governor*. In this study Professor Schlesinger analyzed the pre-governor careers of the 995 governors elected by the forty-eight states between 1870 and 1950.

Some significant and interesting findings are summarized in Table 1 on page 351, which gives the pattern of office experience of all of these governors.

This means that 521 of the 995 had served in the state legislature, 200 had this as their last office before becoming governor, 312 had it as their first office, and 130 as their only office—all before being elected governor. The other data are to be interpreted in the same way.

Professor Schlesinger then analyzes these data and gives case studies to illustrate the operation of the various office types in a number of states. Table 2 gives an example of this analysis, showing the decline in the importance of the legislature.

Note the following:

1. The number of governors elected is about the same in the first and last decades.

2. In the first decade about two-thirds of them had legislative experience, but in the last decade only two-fifths had this experience.

3. In the first decade one-third of the governors came directly from the legislature; in the last decade only about one out of eight did.

First, his appointments must often be approved by the state senate, so that appointments are sometimes made with a view toward getting senate approval rather than toward securing the best possible and most highly qualified person of those available for the position.

Second, appointments to boards and commissions are often made for staggered terms and for periods longer than the governor's term of office. Thus, many members of

boards and commissions may have been appointed by previous governors, and these members may feel little or no responsibility to the present governor since he did not appoint them.

Beyond these limitations, however, the governor has the responsibility for administering the government of the state. He enforces the laws of the state, he is in charge of the national guard in the state, he controls the operation of many state institutions, he is in charge of the state police, and he finally represents the state as its executive head whenever the occasion requires.

LAW ENFORCEMENT. Attention should be called to one other limitation in carrying out the state laws. To a large extent the state laws are enforced by city

TABLE 1   PREVIOUS POLITICAL EXPERIENCE OF 995 GOVERNORS[1]

Office Types	No. with This as Experience	No. with This as Office Before Governorship	No. with This as First Office	No. with This as Only Office
State Legislature	521	200	312	130
Law Enforcement	319	162	200	85
Administrative	292	136	167	58
Local Elective	197	74	118	35
Statewide Elective	188	157	21	21
Federal Elective	138	112	26	25
No Office	88	88	88	88
Other		66	63	

TABLE 2   CHANGES IN LEGISLATIVE EXPERIENCE

Decade	No. of Governors Elected	Percent with Legislative Experience	Percent with Legislature as Last Office
1870-79	122	65	33
1940-50	123	41	13

[1] Joseph Schlesinger, *How They Became Governor.* Published by the Governmental Research Bureau, Michigan State University, copyright 1957 by the State Board of Agriculture, State of Michigan. Reprinted with the permission of the Social Science Research Bureau, Michigan State University, East Lansing.

State police often render help, as well as enforce the laws. This Pennsylvania State Trooper is assisting a confused motorist to read his map and find his way. (Pennsylvania State Police)

police and county sheriffs. These are local officers responsible to the people of their local areas. They are not under the control of the governor and are not responsible to him. Sometimes he can do very little to make them work as efficiently and honestly as he would like.

If these local officers do their work well, enforcement of state law is good. If they do not, state law enforcement often breaks down. States, however, recognize this problem, and under certain conditions some governors have the right to remove local officials who neglect their duty, or the governors may enforce laws by using the state organizations.

The governor has control of two groups which help him to enforce state laws and to maintain order. These are the national

guard unit, or state militia, and the state police. The governor is the commander-in-chief of the national guard. He has power to call out the guard to help in various emergencies.

National guard units have aided in times of disaster, such as floods and epidemics; they have put down riots; they have maintained order in labor disputes; they have helped local officers in various police functions. Members of the national guard are volunteers who serve on a part-time basis in peacetime. During a war or other emergency the national guard becomes a part of the United States armed forces when called into national service by the President.

The state police force differs from the state militia in that the members are full-time law enforcement officers. State police are important in crime and traffic control. They have achieved an excellent reputation in preventing crime and in apprehending criminals.

State police in many states are developing a reputation similar to that of the FBI and the Canadian Mounties, who always "get their man." Some of the duties of the state police are maintaining order, putting down riots, investigating fires, enforcing game laws, inspecting factories and amusement places, and rendering services to people in distress. An important duty is traffic control and the enforcement of traffic laws, and in a few states this is their only duty.

Some groups have objected to the establishment of a state police force on the basis that it gives too much power to the governor and takes away some control from local law enforcement persons. These objections must be weighed, however, against the excellent work that has been done by state police. While it is true that the state police organization is under the governor's control and is a powerful weapon in his hands, it is also true that in our system of government there are checks and balances even on a governor who assumes too much power. State police can be and are a valuable supplement to local law officials. However, state police ordinarily do not operate in incorporated local communities unless invited to do so.

The members of the state police force are carefully selected. They must pass a rigid examination before being accepted for the force. After selection they are given a period of intensive training in modern police methods and crime prevention and detection. Because of these factors it is very likely that the importance of state police forces will continue to increase.

THE BUDGET. The governor has an important executive power in setting up the state budget, as the plan for the expenditure of state money is called. As we shall see later in this chapter, the state budget is determined cooperatively with the legislature. But state administration depends in large measure on the budget, and the governor with his department heads is responsible for making it. He then has financial responsibility to operate state functions and agencies in keeping with budget allocations.

The governor may call out the National Guard in times of disaster, such as severe storms. While Governor of Texas, John Connally inspected an area badly hit by a hurricane. (UPI photo)

LEGISLATIVE POWER

We usually think of the governor as the executive of the state and of the legislature as the lawmaking body. This is true, but in practice the governor has a good deal of control over legislative matters. Many governors of recent years have taken over more and more leadership in the legislative program of their states.

In many cases the public has come to rely on the governor for direction of the state's program of action. Voters expect the governor to present a program to the legislature, to work for its approval, and to put it into action.

The governor, like the President, usually has three kinds of legislative powers: (1) to send messages to the legislature; (2) to call a special session of the legislature; (3) to sign or veto bills passed by the legislature.

MESSAGES. The governor may send messages on various legislative proposals to the legislature. The state constitution requires him to report to the legislature on state conditions. Sometimes his message concerns the recommendations from various state departments. At other times the message may be a proposal to initiate a particular program in the state; for example, it may suggest a new form of state tax or it may suggest a system of state toll roads.

The degree to which the legislators pay attention to his message depends upon a number of factors: the party to which he belongs, the respect the legislature and the public have for him, the amount of public support he can get for his proposals, his strength in the state and in the party. A strong governor concerned about his proposals will work cooperatively with legislators to gain support for his program. He will work vigorously to get his measures approved.

SPECIAL SESSIONS. The state constitutions set the time for the regular sessions of the legislature. The governor, however, has the power to call a special session if he feels that there is sufficient reason for doing so.

Many states have had such special sessions in recent years, and governors have found them a good device for forcing the legislatures to study problems which the governors have considered urgent. Special sessions are especially effective when, as in about one-half the states, the legislature can deal only with the topics mentioned by the governor in his call for the special session.

VETO. Perhaps the greatest influence of the governor on legislation lies in his power to veto bills passed by the legislature. Only the governor of North Carolina does not have this power. The veto power of a governor is similar to that of the President. Bills passed by the legislature must be submitted to the governor for his signature before they become laws. He has from three to fifteen days, depending on the state, to study the bills while the legislature is in session. Usually he has a longer period of time for bills which are presented to him after the adjournment of the legislature.

In some states after the legislature has adjourned, bills which he does not sign do not become laws; they are pocket-vetoed.

If the governor vetoes a bill, it may become a law if it is passed over his veto. The number of votes needed to override a veto varies with different states. While most states require a two-thirds vote of each house, several of them require a three-fifths majority, and others only a simple majority.

In order to help in the efficient operation of the state's business, most states allow the governor to veto parts of appropriation bills. The governor, of course, may veto the whole bill. However, if he believes that in general the bill is a good one but that certain items are undesirable, he may veto those items while approving the rest of the bill. This *item veto* is a power that the President does not have.

Sometimes legislatures will attach an unacceptable *rider* to an otherwise good bill in the hope of having it ride in on the strength of the good bill and thus become a law. The item veto gives the governor the power to strike out such a rider.

Governors have made extensive use of the veto. The threat of the veto and its use have helped to improve the bills passed by state legislatures, and the influence of the governor upon state legislation through the use of the veto has been an important one.

FINANCES. These legislative powers give the governor additional financial control in the suggestions he makes regarding state taxes and in the preparation of the state budget. With his advisers and department heads he makes a plan of the amount of money the state will need to carry out its program. This budget is presented to the legislature for approval, revision, additions, or changes.

After the budget is approved by the legislature, the governor and other administrative officers have the duty to spend the state's money according to this budget. Actually, they carry out the state's financial program according to the appropriation acts and tax-borrowing measures which give effect to the budget.

LEGISLATIVE HARMONY. To get the state legislature to work in harmony with him is the goal of every governor. He tries to get the cooperation of the legislature to put his program into operation. If the governor and the state legislature are at odds with each other, the state governmental program may suffer serious consequences.

Such differences may come about if there is personal antagonism, that is, if the legislators do not like the governor or vice versa.

Differences may also result if the governor and the majority of the legislators belong to opposing political parties. Again, the governor and the members of the legislature may have conflicting ideas regarding policies and appropriate functions of state government.

To keep such differences from hurting the state's program and his own political career, the governor usually tries to avoid open conflicts with the legislature and strives for harmony. There have, however, been occasions when governors have welcomed open differences with the legislature in order to bring their ideas before the people. In such cases the voters will decide at the next election whether they agree with the governor, provided he is eligible and seeks reelection. Usually if they keep him in office, it is a sign that the majority of the voters favor his program.

JUDICIAL POWER

As part of the system of checks and balances in our form of government, the governor also has some judicial power.

PUNISHMENTS. He may grant reprieves, pardons, and commutations. A *reprieve* is a postponement of punishment for a crime; a *pardon* is a warrant setting a person free; and a *commutation* is an order changing a sentence to a lighter one, for example, from death to life imprisonment.

The governor has been given these powers in order to make certain that innocent persons are not punished and to protect convicted persons when some doubt arises about their having actually committed the crime of which they have been found guilty. New evidence brought to the attention of a governor has often led to a reprieve or a pardon.

American justice is based on the ideas

Point out that the responsibility of this judicial power has weighed so heavily on some governors of states with capital punishment that wardens have been ordered to telephone the governor as close as fifteen minutes before an execution.

A strong governor can secure a great deal of cooperation from the state legislature. Here Governor Nelson A. Rockefeller of New York addresses an opening session of the New York State Legislature in Albany. (UPI photo)

that a person is innocent until proved guilty and that no one should be punished unjustly. The judicial powers of the governor are granted him by the state constitution to aid in seeing that justice is done.

The governor does not have unlimited power in these judicial matters, however. Some state constitutions require the governor to report to the legislature on the pardons, reprieves, and commutations granted and to present his reasons for doing so. Also some states have established pardon and parole boards to advise the governor about cases which should be considered for possible action. In some instances the boards determine which individuals should be given lighter sentences or full pardons.

EXTRADITION. The governor also has quasi-judicial powers in asking for the return of a person who is accused of having committed a crime and has fled to another state. This process of returning an accused person is usually known as *extradition*, though the technical term is *interstate rendition*. The governors of both states participate in extradition, which works in this way:

An individual is accused of committing a crime in state A and has fled to state B. The governor of A asks the governor of B to return the accused person. Before asking for extradition, however, governor A studies the evidence against the accused. Governor B also assumes judicial functions because he, too, studies the case to determine whether or not to return the fugitive to state A.

Under certain circumstances some governors have refused to extradite persons for various reasons, as, for example, if a governor felt the accused person would not be given a fair trial in the other state, if the crime was committed many years ago, or if the accused was now living as a respectable citizen in the state to which he had fled.

OTHER STATE EXECUTIVE OFFICERS

It has already been mentioned that nearly all states elect executive officers besides the governor. These officers are usually elected at the same time as the governor and for terms of the same number of years. It has also been noted that this division of executive authority is often not in the best interest of the state, especially if there is political rivalry between the governor and other officials. Effective administration of state government becomes really difficult if the governor and the other executives are members of opposing political parties.

More and more people are accepting the point of view that these other executive officials, except the lieutenant governor, should be appointed by the governor and should be responsible to him. Responsibility for the administration of the state government could then be fixed in one person.

Under the present operation of state governments, the governor has control of only a portion of the administration of the state's business. Other elected officials share the administration with him. While the number and kind of elected officials vary somewhat from state to state, the following are common in most states: lieutenant governor, secretary of state, auditor, treasurer, attorney general, and superintendent of public instruction.

THE LIEUTENANT GOVERNOR holds a position in the state similar to that of the Vice President in the United States. He takes over the duties of the governor in the event of the governor's death, disability, resignation, removal from office, or when the governor is out of the state.

Aside from that, the lieutenant governor has no special duties except to serve as president of the state senate in most states. He usually cannot vote on issues decided by the senate except in the case of a tie vote.

A significant undesirable fact about the lieutenant governor is that in some states he need not be a member of the same political party as the governor. Although both are elected at the same time, they are elected independently and not as a team.

THE SECRETARY OF STATE performs many important duties. He is the keeper of the state records. He has charge of the state seal, which is used for making documents official. He compiles records of state election returns and issues certificates of election.

Corporations chartered in a state usually receive their incorporation papers from the secretary of state. Drivers' licenses, motor vehicle titles, and similar documents are often under the control of his office and are issued by the secretary of state. He is in charge of elections and carries on official correspondence with the national government and with other states.

THE AUDITOR is the supervisor of the state's finances and the guardian of the state's money. He checks to see that money is spent according to law. He issues written orders authorizing the treasurer to pay state bills. But he does so only after he has checked expenditures to make sure that money is being spent legally and in keeping with the state budget. In some states, however, expenditures are checked *after* the money is spent.

The auditor audits all state accounts. In recent years this has become a highly important and complex job, since state expenditures have risen sharply, reaching several billion dollars yearly in an increasing number of states.

THE TREASURER is the custodian of

the state's money. He is in charge of all state money and bank accounts. The auditor checks to make sure that money is spent legally, but the treasurer spends the money. He is responsible for receiving and keeping all state money, and he pays it out only on written orders from the auditor or other official with power to issue such orders.

Some state constitutions have placed special restrictions on the office of treasurer. In some states he may not be elected to succeed himself; in others his term of office is shorter than that of other elected officials.

THE ATTORNEY GENERAL is the chief legal officer of the state. He gives legal advice to the governor, to the mem-

bers of the legislature, and to state boards and commissions. The attorney general and members of his staff represent the state in any lawsuits or court proceedings which involve the state. Often he has special duties as the enforcement officer of tax laws.

THE SUPERINTENDENT OF PUBLIC INSTRUCTION has charge of state laws regulating the educational system of the state. Together with the state board of education, he supervises teacher training and issues teaching certificates to persons qualified to teach according to state law. He has charge of allocating state money to school districts of the state.

In many states he and his staff are

State agencies perform a variety of functions. These men from the Colorado Game, Fish and Parks Department are stocking a stream with game fish. (Colorado Game, Fish and Parks Department)

A state health department or board of health has many responsibilities. For example, it may set the requirements that nurses, such as those shown, must meet in order to be licensed. (City of Philadelphia, Office of the City Representative)

charged with the responsibility of helping local schools improve their instructional programs. Members of the department of public instruction sometimes aid in the selection of textbooks, the preparation of courses of study, and the planning of state educational conferences.

STATE AGENCIES

State administration can become very complex with so many individuals sharing the administration of the state. But even that is not the whole story. Each state has many agencies with elected or appointed boards and commissions who further add to the complicated machinery that is state government.

Some of these are established by the state constitution and others by the state legislature. Some are under the control of the governor; others are independent agencies not responsible to him. While sometimes the governor may appoint the members of a commission, he may have no further control of them after appointments are made.

TERMS. Usually the members of a state board are elected or appointed for staggered terms; for example, the members of a particular board may serve for six years, with one or two of them being elected or appointed every two years. This is done so that the board will always have some continuing members who know and understand the board's work. Also, in the case of appointed boards, a new governor may not unduly influence a board, for it will take several years to fill the board with his appointees.

Sometimes the law may specify that a board should include members from two or more political parties. The purpose is to prevent one political party from having too much influence. In such cases the law usually states that no more than half of the members of a board may be from one party, for example, four out of eight members.

QUASI-LEGISLATIVE AND JUDICIAL ACTIVITIES. In the chapter on independent agencies of the federal government it was noted that their duties were largely administrative but that certain

Most of these agencies were created by state legislation and thus are usually referred to as statutory agencies.

359

boards and commissions had some legislative and judicial duties. This is also true of state agencies.

Many are mainly administrative since they carry out the laws or the provisions of the constitution related to them. For example, in some states, a board of regents administers the affairs of the state university, a board of health enforces state health laws, and a highway commission supervises the state roads. In actual practice, of course, the board determines policies and hires an administrator to carry out the policies.

But many state boards and commissions are quasi-legislative and quasi-judicial in that they are required to make regulations and judgments. For example, a public utility commission makes decisions regarding rate increases, and a workmen's compensation commission judges workers' claims for compensation. Some agencies have the special duty of granting licenses. For example, boards of examiners have the responsibility of licensing doctors, nurses, lawyers, barbers, veterinarians, and the like.

In the table on this page, the administrative departments of one state give an idea of the number and kinds of agencies in operation today. Some of these departments are controlled by a board or commission. Others are administered by one person, usually called a director.

The table shows how involved and complex state government is. Each of these departments has many workers. To select, train, and supervise the workers takes much time and effort. To house and operate these agencies takes large sums of money and many buildings. By actual count, one state, for example, owns or rents 1,200 separate state buildings. These include office buildings, institutions, homes, barns, workshops, and special buildings of all kinds. It has been estimated that the amount of floor space they contain would be equal to the floor space of a one-story building 100 feet wide and 65 miles long. This is truly big business.

ADMINISTRATIVE DEPARTMENTS OF THE STATE OF NEW YORK[1]

Agriculture and Markets	Labor
	Workmen's
Audit and Control	Compensation
Banking	Board
Civil Service	Law
Commerce	Mental Hygiene
Conservation	Motor Vehicles
Correction	Public Service
Education	Social Services
State University	State
Executive	Taxation and
Health	Finance
Insurance	Transportation

Other Offices, Agencies and Divisions

Athletic Commission	Lands and Forests
Atomic and Space Development	Licensing Services
	Liquor Authority
Budget	Lottery Control
Civil Defense	Military and Naval
Counsel to the Governor	Affairs
	Oil and Gas
Fish and Game	Parks
Housing and Community Renewal	Port of New York Authority
	Power Authority
Human Rights	Probation
Judicial Conference	Racing
Labor and Management Practices	State Police
	Thruway Authority
	Veterans' Affairs

[1]Article 5 of the Constitution of the State of New York states: "There shall be no more than twenty civil departments in the State government, including those referred to in this Constitution...."

ADMINISTRATIVE REORGANIZATION

Each state has added to the number of its specialized agencies until the proper functioning of state government has become almost impossible to control. The number of state employees has grown to nearly three million. The number for the states varies. Nevada, for example, has about 8,000 employees

In reference to the Hoover Commission at the national level, point out that these state survey agencies of reorganization were popularly called "Little Hoover Commissions."

while California has about 250,000. But, Nevada's rate is about 130 employees for each 10,000 people and California's is about 100.

During the past fifty years most states have discussed some form of state reorganization in order to avoid duplication of duties, to give administrators greater control over the many state agencies, and to deal with the growing complexity of state government. One way this can be accomplished is to combine departments and agencies into a small number of major departments. Illinois was the first to do so in 1917. It combined its more than seventy-five agencies into nine departments. A few other states have taken similar steps. Recently, for example, Michigan combined related departments into single super-departments and organized more than 130 boards, commissions, and agencies into nineteen departments.

A forward step in the reorganization of state governments came with the establishment of state departments of administration. Nearly three-fourths of the states now have such a department. Usually the department of administration is responsible to the governor and has control of state business and finance. It prepares the budget, controls purchasing, lets contracts for buildings, inspects state property, and is, in general, the business side of state government. A few states have gone further and have given this department duties related to state planning and personnel. To become particularly effective, the department needs to be directly responsible to the governor.

These steps toward effective reorganization of state government are good, but much still needs to be done to achieve central control and responsibility. Many state agencies need to be placed under administrative heads who are directly responsible to the governor. States need to give their

In order to make government more efficient, a number of political scientists have argued that there should be only two or three elected state officials. Some of my observations support their case. Our present Michigan political-governmental system, however, presents us with a reasonable alternative. The members of the Administrative Board are nominated in convention, except for the Governor and the Lieutenant Governor who are elected by the people. The convention is a party organism and that organism is, or should be, led by the Governor. Thus, if the Governor is a leader he should be able to influence the selection of his colleagues on the Administrative Board. In a sense, they are independent because the people elect them; in another sense, they are bound to the Governor because of his influence in their selection, his help in their election, and his heading the ticket. I would not favor primary selection of these Advisory Board members.

—G. MENNEN WILLIAMS (Six-term governor of Michigan), *A Governor's Notes*, p. 21. Published by the Institute of Public Administration, the University of Michigan, 1961.

governors authority to initiate reorganization similar to that given to the President by Congress after the Hoover Commission report, as described in Chapter 13. Several states have already done so. For some changes only an act of the state legislature is necessary; others need constitutional revisions.

This chapter began with a recommendation of the national committee which had carefully studied state government. It ends with the committee's recommendation on reorganization:

State administrative operations should be organized along broad functional lines, with the governor empowered to appoint and control department heads. Most boards and commissions, except for higher education and regulatory functions, should be limited to an advisory role. We recommend that every governor have power to initiate administrative reorganizations and put them into operation through executive order, subject only to legislative veto within a specified time.[1]

_____
[1] Committee for Economic Development, *Modernizing State Government,* page 56.

STUDY QUESTIONS

1. Why did the Committee for Economic Development recommend strengthening the position of the governor?

2. Why were governors given only limited powers by the early states?

3. What are some present-day results of the attempts to keep down the power of governors?

4. What factors have combined to make the position of governor important?

5. How do the state powers of the governor differ from the federal powers of the President?

6. What are the usual qualifications for governor?

7. In what ways is the executive power of the governor limited?

8. Which groups having some responsibility for enforcing state laws are largely independent of the governor?

9. What are the legislative powers of the governor?

10. What factors influence the legislature in its considerations of the governor's request for legislation?

11. Why does the governor usually try to work in harmony with the state legislature?

12. What are the judicial powers of the governor?

13. Give the common duties of each of the following state officers: lieutenant governor, secretary of state, auditor, treasurer, attorney general, and superintendent of public instruction.

14. What provisions limit the powers of governors and political parties over state boards and commissions?

15. Why are state boards and commissions known as quasi-legislative and quasi-judicial agencies?

16. Why is the reorganization of state government important and necessary for most states?

17. What steps toward reorganization have been taken by some states?

1
The colonial governments and the first state governments kept the power of the governor at a minimum.

2
This early concern for limiting the power of governors is today reflected in such factors as limits on the number of terms, length of terms, and sharing administrative authority with other elected officials.

3
The authority of governors has grown throughout the nation's history.

4
The duties of the governor are executive, legislative, and judicial. His success in performing these duties depends on his political and legal powers.

5
The chief executive duties of the governor are related to appointments, law enforcement, and state finances.

6
The governor's legislative powers consist mainly in sending messages to the legislature, calling special legislative sessions, and approving or vetoing bills.

7
The judicial powers of the governor concern pardon, reprieve, commutation, and extradition.

8
Other elected administrative officials common to most states are: lieutenant governor, secretary of state, auditor, treasurer, attorney general, and superintendent of public instruction.

9
States have many independent agencies, boards, and commissions which have executive, quasi-legislative, and quasi-judicial responsibilities.

10
State administrative reorganization is providing greater authority for the governor and more efficient state administration.

11
Each state needs to examine the governor's legal position to determine if he has sufficient authority to be a real leader.

IDEAS FOR DISCUSSION

1. Discuss the following issue: "The primary election is a more democratic method of nominating candidates for governor than is the nominating convention."

2. Some political scientists think that the governor should have the power to appoint other members of the state administrative staff just as the President appoints the members of the Cabinet. They say this will lead to improved state government. Other people think that increasing the governor's appointive power decreases democratic government. What is your opinion?

3. Should the governor be given the right of item veto for all bills passed by the legislature?

4. The fact that "the governorship leads to other governmental offices" shows that many governors are outstanding people. Discuss this statement.

5. Do you agree that a two-year term of office for governor is too short for good government? Why?

6. A conference of the state governors is held annually. What issues are discussed at such meetings? What, in your opinion, are the values of these conferences?

7. It is generally believed that state government is most effective when the majority of the state legislators and the governor are members of the same political party. What is the situation in your state with regard to party membership of governor and state legislators? How, in your opinion, has it affected state legislation and administration?

8. Are any state issues and problems, considered important by your governor, being avoided by your state legislature? If so, why? How do you suggest that these issues be brought out for full discussion and action?

THINGS TO DO

1. Read your state constitution to learn the qualifications and duties of your governor. Report to the class on your study.

2. Get a copy of a recent message by a governor to a state legislature. Make an outline showing (a) the legislation requested by the governor, (b) action taken by the legislature on these requests, and (c) requests still being considered by the legislature.

3. Report to the class on some recent use of judicial power by the governor of your state. Tell the story of a recent pardon, reprieve, or commutation of sentence, or of extradition proceedings involving a person from your state.

4. Clip articles about the governor's activities from recent issues of your newspapers. Use these for a bulletin board display to show the work of the governor.

5. From your state administrative manual or the *Book of the States* get the information to make a chart of the boards and commissions of your state. On the chart include such items as membership, term of office, and duties.

6. Visit your state capital and report to the class your observations of the state executive offices and agencies.

7. Draw a cartoon to show the busy life of the governor.

8. Make a study of your governor's actions on bills passed by the legislature. How many bills did he sign into law? How many did he veto? What types of legislation were vetoed?

FURTHER READINGS

Adrian, Charles R., GOVERNING OUR FIFTY STATES AND THEIR COMMUNITIES. McGraw-Hill Book Co., Inc., 1967.

Anderson, William, and others, GOVERNMENT IN THE FIFTY STATES. Holt, Rinehart and Winston, 1967.

THE BOOK OF THE STATES, 1972-1973. Council of State Governments, 1972.

Graves, W. Brooke, AMERICAN STATE GOVERNMENT. D. C. Heath & Co., 1953. Chapters 9 and 10.

Lockard, Duane, THE POLITICS OF STATE AND LOCAL GOVERNMENT. Macmillan Co., 1963. Chapter 13.

Macdonald, A. F., AMERICAN STATE GOVERNMENT AND ADMINISTRATION. Thomas Y. Crowell Co., 1960. Chapter 10.

Ross, Russell M., and Millsap, Kenneth F., STATE AND LOCAL GOVERNMENT AND ADMINISTRATION. Ronald Press Co., 1966. Chapters 13-15.

Sanford, Terry, STORM OVER THE STATES. McGraw-Hill Book Co., 1967.

ACQUITTAL—the act of setting free by declaring a person not guilty.

APPELLATE JURISDICTION—the right of a court to hear cases that have been appealed.

CHALLENGE—the right of a lawyer to object to the qualifications of a prospective juror.

CHARGE—the instructions the judge gives to a jury.

CIVIL CASE—a legal dispute involving two or more citizens.

CRIMINAL CASE—a legal action in which a person is accused of breaking a law; one in which a wrong has been done against the whole community.

CROSS-EXAMINATION—the process of questioning a witness of the opposite side in a lawsuit.

DOCKET—a list of court cases.

FELONY—a serious crime such as murder, kidnapping, or theft.

GRAND JURY—a jury that decides whether or not there is enough evidence to think that an accused person might be guilty.

HUNG JURY—one in which the jurors cannot agree upon a decision.

INDICTMENT—a statement formally accusing a person of a crime.

KANGAROO COURT—an irregularly conducted court which disregards legal procedures.

MISDEMEANOR—a minor crime.

PANEL—the group of persons who have been called for jury service.

PETIT JURY—a jury that determines the guilt or innocence in a criminal case or the right or wrong in a civil case; a petty jury.

PLAINTIFF—the party making the complaint in a civil case; the opposite of the defendant.

SUBPOENA—an order to appear in court.

TRIAL COURT—a lower court in which a jury may be used.

WARRANT—a written order authorizing an act; a court order permitting an arrest, the taking of property, or a search.

THE LANGUAGE OF GOVERNMENT

Mention that in many states the trial of misdemeanors is by juries of less than twelve, whereas twelve is still almost universally required in the trial of major crimes.

17

The State Court System

Twelve men and women had sat for three months in a jury box listening to testimony. Their newspapers, their television programs, their contacts with other people had been strictly limited to avoid any influences that might prejudice their thinking. They were not permitted to go home; nights they had to stay in a hotel. They had listened to dozens of witnesses. They had heard hours of testimony. They had listened to the pleas of the lawyers and the charge and final words of advice from the judge.

Now they were alone in a room in the courthouse. They had to decide whether a man was guilty of murder. If guilty, he could be sentenced to prison for life. If not guilty, he would be free to return to as normal a life as possible. Twelve citizens carried the responsibility for the fate of one man. Why?

Inherited from the English system of justice was the right to trial by jury. Our forefathers before approving the Constitution insisted that a Bill of Rights be added. Included in these ten amendments is the Sixth Amendment which states:

> In all criminal prosecutions, the accused shall enjoy the right to a speedy and public trial, by an impartial jury of the State and district wherein the crime shall have been committed, which district shall have been previously ascertained by Law, and to be informed of the nature and cause of the accusation; to be confronted with the witnesses against him; to have compulsory process for obtaining witnesses in his favor, and to have the assistance of counsel for his defense.

Amendment Seven of the Constitution grants the same right of jury trial to civil cases involving controversies of more than twenty dollars.

Jury trial is one of the rights guaranteed all citizens. It is one important element of equal justice under law.

Mayor John Lindsay of New York City listens in on hearings in Bronx Traffic Court. Traffic courts are one of a number of lower courts that states have to try minor offenses. (UPI photo)

THE SYSTEM OF STATE COURTS

To make justice possible in the United States there are two systems of courts, as was discussed in Chapter 14. One is the federal system; the other is the state system. In each court system a jury trial is guaranteed.

Each state has its own court system. While the names for the courts differ among the states, the court *system* is much the same. This system is established in the constitution of each state. Each state has lower courts. Each state has some type of general trial court. Each state has one high court and some special courts.

THE LOWER COURTS. A farmer has a dispute with a neighbor over the location of a fence. A man gets arrested for speeding. Another man is arrested for fighting.

A landlord cannot get a roomer to pay $25 for rent due. Where are these small disputes and law violations decided? In some rural areas they are tried in *justice of the peace* courts. In most cities they are tried in *municipal* courts. In other places they are tried by magistrates attached to the general trial courts.

The justice of the peace need not be a lawyer. Farmers and factory workers, for example, have been justices of the peace. Married women, in addition to their household duties, have also held the office. Many of these people have had no special training. This lack of training is a great weakness of justice of the peace courts, because if the person in charge of the court is ignorant of the law, justice may not be done. Even though these courts handle cases where less than a few hundred dollars are in dispute and deal with minor law violations, the citizen before the court has a right to justice.

Many justices of the peace have other jobs. Holding court is only a part-time job for them. Usually these justices are not paid a salary. Instead they get a fee from each case they hear. Once in a while, a "J. P." will try to earn more fees by getting extra business. For example, the justice may be willing to "hold court" at odd hours in the night to reach a decision on a traffic case or to marry a couple.

Because of these conditions, two important study commissions in 1967 (the Committee on Economic Development, in *Modernizing State Government*, and the President's Commission on Law Enforcement and Administration of Justice) recommended that these courts be abolished. It is worthy of note that, as far back as 1931, the Wickersham Commission, appointed by President Hoover to study law enforcement and crime, made the same recommendation. But justice of the peace courts have been hard to eliminate because they do give quick decisions and the justices are close to the people who elect them. Most justices are honest, sincere people even though they may not know much about legal matters.

Gradually justice of the peace courts are being eliminated or modified. Some states have abolished these courts. Other states have set up minimum qualifications for holding the office and have abandoned the fee system in favor of a regular annual salary.

As cities grew in America, the small disputes and law violations became a great problem. The justices of the peace were not capable of handling most of the cases, and there were too many cases for their courts. In small towns and medium-sized cities *police* or *magistrate* courts developed.

Since 1958 Judge Mildred L. Lillie has served on the California Court of Appeals. Here she administers the oath of office to Sam Yorty, Mayor of Los Angeles. Judges occasionally participate in such ceremonial functions. (UPI photo)

Judges of these courts are usually elected and receive low salaries. They are criticized as much as the justice of the peace courts and their abolition is urged by the expert commissions.

In the larger cities, the *municipal* or city court developed. Chicago was the first to try such a court in 1906. Today Baltimore, Cleveland, Detroit, Los Angeles, and other large cities have municipal courts. The judges of these courts are lawyers. They are elected, usually for a term of four to six years. They receive a fixed salary. Most experts feel that these city courts are better than the justice of the peace or magistrate courts, but are critical of the election of the judges and their failure to keep up to date with their work. Justice tends not to be speedy, but to be slow.

GENERAL TRIAL COURTS. When serious law violations, such as murder, robbery, or shooting, take place, the person is brought to trial in some court higher than the justice of peace, the magistrate, or the municipal court. This general trial court is used also when there are disputes over large sums of money. These courts are usually known as *district* or *county* courts, but some states have different names for them. Some call them circuit courts; others call them superior courts; the state of New York calls them supreme courts.

In some states there are both county courts and district courts. In other states the county court has been replaced by the district court. But regardless of the name these general trial courts are the basic courts of the land. They handle most of the cases. They influence the lives of many people.

The judges of these courts are usually elected, but in some states they are appointed by the governor. They are paid salaries. The usual term of office is four to six years. These courts are *trial courts*—

ILLINOIS COURT SYSTEM

SUPREME COURT
CHIEF JUSTICE
6 ASSOCIATE JUSTICES

Justices are elected for ten-year terms. The Supreme Court administers all state courts. It hears some original cases and appeals from the appellate courts.

APPELLATE COURTS
5 COURTS

Judges are elected for ten-year terms. They hear appeals from circuit courts.

CIRCUIT COURTS
21 COURTS

Judges are elected for six-year terms. They have jurisdiction over all lower-court cases, both civil and criminal. They appoint magistrates to hear minor cases.

METHOD OF ELECTION
All judges are elected for first term on partisan ballot. They run for re-election unopposed and serve second term if approved by majority of voters.

for a jury may be used to decide guilt or innocence. Some cases are brought from the lower courts to the district courts when the person is not satisfied with the decision in the justice of the peace, magistrate, or municipal court.

These *appeals* are not frequent, however. Most of the work of these courts is the original trial of cases. In legal language this means that the general trial court has *original jurisdiction;* it is the first to hear and decide the case. When the trial court is hearing a case that has been appealed from a lower court, the court has *appellate jurisdiction.* These ideas will be made clearer by reading about some actual cases.

THE CIRCUIT COURT. Yorkville, Illinois, is a small town in northern Illinois. Yorkville is the location of the county government of Kendall County—a rural county about forty miles from the great commercial and industrial city of Chicago.

In the county courthouse is the circuit court—the trial court in Illinois. This court is on the main floor. Some examples of cases tried in that court during a period of three months are: an adoption, a mortgage foreclosure, a person accused of carrying a loaded gun in a car, a burglary, a case in which a man was accused of not having a valid fishing license, a charge of disorderly conduct, a delinquent child case, a case involving illegal transportation of liquor, a case in which offensive material had been deposited on the highway. There were cases of drunkenness, and others of assault and battery. One case involved a young man who had not stopped at a stop sign and when arrested did not have a legal driver's license. This was the first trial of these cases. The court had original jurisdiction.

This circuit court of the Illinois Sixteenth Judicial District was part of a new court system adopted in Illinois in 1962 by constitutional amendment. This new, modern court system eliminated justice of the peace courts and unified all the courts into one system. As the court opened one March, there were many cases scheduled to be heard. The judge, the clerks, the lawyers for the first case, the witnesses, and the citizens who might be called to serve on the jury were ready. Reporters and spectators were present. The court session was about to begin.

Here was the case of an architect suing to get some money he claimed was due for designing a house. Another case on the *docket* was that of some homeowners who were asking the court to forbid a man to start a slaughterhouse in their neighborhood.

The case involving the most money was a case where a man had died and had left money and property valued at one and a half million dollars. The children of the man did not agree on how this money was to be divided.

There was one case of an attempt to commit murder, another case where an automobile accident had caused the death of a man, three cases where someone had stolen property, one case of a driver leaving the scene of an accident. Fourteen of the cases were for divorces.

Most of the cases were *civil cases*—disputes between two parties—in which the court would have to decide who was right. The rest of the cases were *criminal cases*, in which the court would have to decide whether the accused was innocent or guilty.

These were all cases that are typical of the general trial courts throughout our country. Counties with a larger population would have many more cases, but the kinds of cases would be much like those of the Kendall County Circuit Court.

THE APPELLATE COURTS. In about one-third of the states, chiefly those with large populations, there are appeal courts between the general trial courts and the highest court. These courts have been established to decrease the number of cases going to the state's highest court. The courts have a variety of names: court of appeals, circuit court of appeals, and appellate court. These courts have only appellate jurisdiction; they do not have any original jurisdiction. Illinois has five of these appellate courts. In the examples given above on this page, a dissatisfied party could appeal from the Kendall County Circuit Court to the appellate court.

THE STATE SUPREME COURT. The highest court of the state is the state su-

Man's capacity for justice makes democracy possible, but man's inclination to injustice makes democracy necessary.

—REINHOLD NIEBUHR, *The Children of Light and the Children of Darkness*, Charles Scribner's Sons.

Mention that although state supreme court decisions stand for only the courts of that state, frequently they are cited in other jurisdictions as persuasive precedents.

This county courthouse at Santa Barbara, California, was completed in 1929. It is considered one of the outstanding examples of Spanish-Moorish architecture in America. (Santa Barbara Chamber of Commerce)

preme court. A few states use a different name. A state supreme court usually has several judges who sit as a group to decide cases that are appealed from the general trial courts or appellate courts. Five or seven judges are most common in these highest state courts, but anywhere from three to nine judges are used in one or more states.

In most states the judges are elected, but in several states they are appointed by the governor or selected by other methods. Terms of state supreme court judges vary from two years to life, with six to twelve years being most common.

Nearly every case that comes before a state supreme court is an appeal from one of the other state courts. A state supreme court rarely hears a case for the first time. The court procedure is much like that of the United States Supreme Court, described in Chapter 14.

PROCEDURE IN A STATE SUPREME COURT. Many high school students get their vivid impressions of courts from television, movies, or radio. They are familiar with the judge, jury, witnesses, and the lawyers. In contrast, a state supreme court rarely hears witnesses, and there is no jury. There are only judges and lawyers.

Point out that a dissenting opinion can affect judicial history later. Use Oliver Wendell Holmes, Jr., as an example.

A lawyer reviews a case before the Wisconsin State Supreme Court. Notice that each justice is provided with a printed record of the case. (State Historical Society of Wisconsin)

The supreme court judges get their information from the printed record of the case. Every statement made by the witnesses and lawyers in the trial court was recorded by a court reporter. If the case is appealed, these records must be printed, the expense being paid by the party that lost the case. The supreme court judges, instead of hearing witnesses, hear the arguments of the lawyers and read the records of the things the witnesses have said in the earlier trial in the lower court. These judges read and study the record; ordinarily they do not listen to hours and hours of testimony.

In a typical supreme court case, the day before the judges are to consider the case, the case is assigned to one of them. He studies the case the night before it comes before the court. Early the next morning the judges meet, and each judge reviews the main facts and questions of law for the

case assigned to him for that day. This preliminary review takes about an hour, sometimes longer.

At ten o'clock the judges will put on their robes and go into the courtroom. Here the cases are called in order. Each judge has his printed record of the case before him. In some cases there is no oral argument by the lawyers; in other cases each side may have up to one hour to argue the case. The moment the hearing of one case is completed, the next is called. On a typical day about fourteen cases are heard in this manner.

Late in the afternoon the justices meet to discuss the cases they have heard that day and to assign cases for the next day. About three weeks of each three months are spent in this manner. As a result of the daily conferences, each judge has a good idea of the points in dispute. Following the hearings of the cases, each judge studies the cases with great care. This period of study requires many weeks.

When he has completed his study, the judge writes his decision on each case assigned to him. If the other judges agree with his opinion, they sign it. If they do not agree, they write an opinion of their own. The opinion which receives the most votes is the winning opinion.

OTHER STATE COURTS. In some states certain types of cases are so common that special courts have been established to deal with these cases. In these courts the judges become unusually expert in dealing with these special types of cases. The special courts, too, have helped relieve the overcrowding in the regular courts.

One special type of state court is the *probate court*. This court deals with the estates of people who have died. Upon the death of a person, the judge reviews the will and appoints someone to carry out the provisions of the will. If there is no will, the judge determines to whom the property of the dead person should go in accordance with the state law. In some states the probate judges also appoint guardians, supervise juveniles, and try cases of mentally incompetent persons.

In some states there are special *juvenile courts* to deal with all cases of badly behaved, dependent, or neglected boys or girls —usually under sixteen or seventeen years of age. The juvenile court is not conducted in the same manner as other courts. Names of juvenile offenders are not ordinarily given to newspapers. Publicity is avoided because it might harm a young person for the rest of his life. At the same time it is well to note that even juveniles have a court record if they are found guilty in a juvenile court.

The informal methods used by juvenile courts, and probate courts in their dealings with juveniles, were adopted because the intent was not to punish children and youth but to help them. Although the first juvenile court was established in 1899, the United States Supreme Court had never reviewed a state juvenile court case until 1967. Then, a case of a boy of fifteen who had been sent to a state school until he reached the age of twenty-one was reviewed.

By an eight-to-one majority the Supreme Court ruled *In the Matter of Gault* that "Neither the Fourteenth Amendment nor the Bill of Rights is for adults alone. Under our Constitution, the condition of being a boy does not justify a kangaroo court." The court ruled that an accused juvenile is entitled to timely notice of charges. He must be told of his right to a lawyer and of his right to remain silent. He must be given the right to confront and cross-examine witnesses.

In the past the juvenile judge had tried to be a friend and helper. He attempted to locate the cause of the difficulty and to get proper treatment. He was not interested in punishment; he was attempting to save a young person from future difficulty if he could. Great judges of juvenile courts were rare combinations of the best of parents, teachers, psychologists, ministers, and priests. They helped many young people to become fine citizens. But with the fifteen to seventeen age group having the highest crime rate in the nation, it is expected that reforms in juvenile justice will take place in the years ahead.

The *small claims court* is a special court which has been developed in many cities to assist the poor. Here people who could not afford to hire a lawyer and sue for a few dollars can get help in collecting their money. A landlady, for example, cannot collect $5.00 from a roomer. She appeals to the small claims court. The judge calls in the roomer, hears both sides of the story, and decides whether the money should be paid. No lawyer is required; usually there are no court costs. The court exists to help poor people get the money that is due them. Newsboys, owners of very small businesses, clerks in stores have found the small claims court to be helpful.

The *domestic relations court* has been developed to deal with the difficult problems of family life. Quarrels that might lead to divorce or separation provide the usual type of case for these courts. These problems between husbands and wives often cannot be solved by regular legal procedures. Expert understanding of human behavior is needed. Judges of these courts must have sympathy, willingness to listen, and understanding of family problems.

Sometimes they are able to help people overcome their differences and lead happy lives. Other times divorce may be necessary, but the judge attempts to be fair to husband, wife, and children. Special training in social work and psychology is useful to these judges. Some of the ablest of these judges are women, although women have become famous as judges of other courts too.

The *traffic court* is another type of special court. Violations of traffic laws are handled in this court. Each year some thirty million drivers are charged with some type of traffic offense. For some the appearance before a traffic court may be their only direct contact with our court system. In some communities this is a valuable experience because the courts are conducted with efficiency, with proper safeguards for the accused, and in ways that improve safety. In other communities traffic courts are slow, time-consuming, and accused persons are treated as though they were guilty and must prove their innocence. Sometimes pressures to convict are present because the fines are either an important way to get local revenue or the judge is paid by a fee system.

The American Bar Association, the professional organization of lawyers, has pleaded for improvements in these traffic courts.

All of these special courts have taken over certain specific duties of the regular state courts. Appeals from the special courts can be made to the regular courts.

COURT PROCEDURE

Cases which come before the state courts are of two general types: civil and criminal. The architect suing for his fee, the wife seeking a divorce, the automobile owner seeking payments because of a collision are examples of civil cases. In all civil cases damages are sought.

In these cases the individuals have a disagreement. The court lists such a case as *John Doe* v. *Mary Roe*. The duty of the government is to supply the court machinery by which some reasonable settlement of the dispute can be reached. Most of the settlements in civil cases require the payment of money.

Stealing, killing, and kidnapping are examples of criminal cases. In these cases some law has been violated so that all people of the community are concerned. The court lists such a case as *People of the State* v. *John Doe*. The duty of the government is to determine whether the person is innocent or guilty. The criminal case ends with *acquittal* or with a *conviction* which results in either a fine or imprisonment or both.

The procedure in civil and criminal cases is somewhat alike. In each case there are (1) an accusation, (2) a trial, and (3) a decision. But the differences between civil and criminal cases are important enough to treat them separately. For example, in a civil case a person who has been wronged might forgive the wrongdoer and stop the court proceedings. In a criminal case, the

Court procedure involves three steps: review of the facts, determination of the law, and application of the law.

If a court action results from this accident, it would probably be a civil case. Could there also be a criminal case? (Photo by De Lange)

person who has been wronged has no power to stop the case by forgiving the offender.

CIVIL CASES. The *accusation* in a civil case is made by the person who thinks a wrong has been done. This person (the *plaintiff*) usually hires a lawyer, who prepares a complaint telling the injury or damage that some person has done against his client. The person who is accused (the *defendant*) also usually hires a lawyer. The defendant's lawyer then answers the complaint. He may admit the facts of the accusation but argue that nothing illegal has been done. The judge will determine this matter.

Or the defendant may deny the facts, or he may admit the facts but offer a reasonable basis for his actions. Several exchanges of legal papers may take place. If no agreement is reached, the case is listed for trial by the clerk of the court.

The *trial* may take place before either a judge or a judge and jury. The right of trial by jury is guaranteed, but some civil cases today are tried without juries by mutual agreement of the judge and the lawyers for the two sides. The cost of having a jury, the delay in getting a decision, and the difficulty of explaining some complex problems to juries have caused a decline in the use of juries in civil cases. When a jury is used, it will ordinarily have twelve members, although some states permit juries of six to eight persons.

The trial begins with the lawyer for the plaintiff telling the court what he intends

The really poor person has a difficult time in courts. If arrested or faced with a civil suit, the cost of defending oneself without help is impossible; the lawyer's fees and court costs are too great for one who lives in poverty.

For many years thoughtful persons concerned about equal justice for all have been attacking this problem. For example, the *small claims court* described in this chapter was created to make court action possible for the poor.

Beginning in 1963, the United States Supreme Court, in the case of *Gideon* v. *Wainright,* ruled on a series of cases which, in effect, compelled state and federal courts to live up to the promises of the last phrase of the Sixth Amendment, which states that the accused shall have the right ". . . to have the assistance of counsel for his defense." The court has ruled that from the time of arrest through the court trial on through appeals the poor person is entitled to a lawyer.

Four types of help are available at present to the poor:

(1) If no other assistance is available, the judge can appoint a lawyer who will be paid at public expense or serve without a fee.

(2) Some states have created an office of *public defender*—a lawyer is paid by the state to defend poor people in the same manner that the prosecuting attorney is paid to try to prove guilt.

(3) Legal aid bureaus, financed by gifts to community funds and united foundation drives, are staffed by full-time lawyers with offices in social agencies. Their services are available to the poor in all types of cases.

(4) Under the federal poverty programs, money has been made available to provide neighborhood legal centers for poverty-stricken people in slum areas.

to prove. After this explanation he calls the witnesses and questions them. When he has asked a witness all the questions he wishes, the attorney for the defendant may *cross-examine* the witness.

The cross-examination of witnesses is one of the great heritages of English-speaking countries. It is an important device to discover the truth or falsity of the testimony, even though clever lawyers may sometimes appear to make an honest witness seem to say false things.

After the plaintiff's case has been presented, the defendant's case is presented in the same way. After all the witnesses have been examined, the lawyers again speak to the court, summarizing the proof of the case as they see it. The judge then instructs the jury (if one is used) on the points of law important in the case. Finally, he asks the jury to retire to reach a decision. If no jury is used, the judge considers the case after adjourning the court.

The *decision* is reached by the judge or the jury. This decision is called a *verdict.* If the verdict is for the plaintiff, the decision must tell the amount of damages to be paid by the defendant. If no appeal to a higher court is made, the sheriff or other court officer is authorized to make the defendant pay.

CRIMINAL CASES. The *accusation* in a criminal case is usually started by the arrest of the suspected wrongdoer. The arrest is made by a sheriff or policeman— without a court order (*a warrant*) if a serious crime has been committed. In other cases a warrant is necessary before an individual can be arrested. The accused person is usually brought before the lowest court in the state system. If the offense is a *misdemeanor* (a minor offense such as speeding, drunken driving, illegal parking, or violation of some health ordinance), the case is settled at once.

If the arrest is because of a *felony* (a seri-

This was the first all-Negro jury in the history of Houston County, Alabama. Federal courts have ruled that Negroes may not be excluded from jury panels. (Wide World photo)

ous crime such as murder, kidnapping, or burglary), the court will hold the suspected person for a formal accusation of the crime. This accusation is usually made by a grand jury, but in some states it may be made by the prosecuting attorney. During this period the person may be held in jail or may be released on bail, depending on the seriousness of the crime.

The *grand jury* is usually a group of from six to twenty-three persons, although Michigan and a few other states permit a "one-man" grand jury. In these cases, one judge is appointed to serve as the single juror. A grand jury, regardless of size, has one job to do: to determine whether enough evidence exists to bring the suspected person to trial. The grand jury considers matters presented to it by the prosecuting attorney. The sessions of the grand jury are secret. Only the prosecuting attorney and witnesses appear at these sessions. The grand jury protects an innocent person from the expense and the bad publicity of a criminal trial.

Grand juries have the right to call witnesses. The writ to compel a witness to appear is called a *subpoena*. Grand juries investigate graft or corrupt alliances of public officials with criminals, as well as other possible crimes. If a grand jury thinks there is enough evidence of guilt, an *indictment* is made.

It is always important to realize that grand juries do not hear the defense of the suspected persons. They only seek evidence that the persons may be guilty.

The accused person, after indictment, is brought before the court. He may plead guilty or not guilty. If the plea is guilty, the judge sentences the person. If the plea is not guilty, a trial is held.

The *trial* in a criminal case is held before a jury, usually of twelve men or women, called a *petit* jury. The members of these juries are selected from a group of about forty persons who have been called for jury service by the court. This *panel* has been chosen by lot from the citizens of the community. The honest selection of jury panels is of great importance, since justice will depend on the ability and fairness of the jurors.

In the selection of the persons from the panel to serve on the jury, the lawyers for both the prosecution and the defense are allowed to question each possible juror. They try to decide whether the person could have any possible prejudice for or against the defendant. Each attorney is allowed a number of *challenges* by which he may say he does not want a certain person on the jury—without giving any reason for his dismissal of the prospective juror.

The selecting of a jury may take a very long time; sometimes several panels may have to be called. The lawyers try to get jurors who have not heard about the case, do not have opinions about the type of case, or who seem to have the ability to withhold judgment until all the evidence is presented.

Once the jury is selected, the trial proceeds much as in a civil case. The prosecuting attorney speaks and calls witnesses. So does the lawyer for the defense. Cross-examination can be intense and dramatic. Finally, summaries are made by each side, the judge *charges* the jury, and the jury *retires* to reach a decision.

The *decision* of the jury is reached in secret session. Only the jurors are present. If agreement becomes impossible, a *hung* jury is declared and a new trial will have to be held or the case is dismissed. After the jury has decided if the person is guilty or not, the verdict is reported to the court.

In most states the jury determines only the guilt or innocence of the person. The judge then determines the amount of punishment within the limits set up by the law. If the person is found guilty, he must begin to serve his sentence, or pay his fine, unless an appeal to a higher court is made and allowed.

THE IMPROVEMENT OF COURTS

Courts and court procedures exist to get justice. Are our courts as good as they can be? Do our court procedures give justice? Do they get in the way of justice? For the past quarter of a century these questions have been discussed by all types of citizens. The American Bar Association, the Committee on Economic Development, the President's Commission on Law Enforcement and the Administration of Justice, judges, attorneys general, and political scientists have debated these matters.

Their suggestions for improvement can be grouped under four headings: (1) getting better judges; (2) getting better juries; (3) making courts speedier and more efficient; (4) developing unified, centralized court organizations.

BETTER JUDGES. Most state courts, except for some justices of the peace, have judges who are well qualified by legal training. They are graduates of law schools and have practiced law. But judges need more than legal training. They need to be honest, fearless, and free from any type of social or political pressure. They need to have a broad understanding of human nature and of social problems if they are to give justice and not merely be legal mechanics. Not all judges measure up to these qualifications.

Investigations of crime and corruption in political life have shown that criminals have helped elect some judges. These criminals wanted the help of a judge if they got arrested. If a judge owes his job to some political machine, to undue support from industrialists or labor leaders, or to the help of some legislator or governor, then he may not feel free to deal honestly with some cases that come before him. These dangers of dishonesty or political pressure have brought forth many suggestions for improving the quality of judges.

A life term of office for state judges has been recommended as one way to get better judges. The judges in Massachusetts and a few other states and all federal judges hold office during "good behavior." In effect, they have appointments for life.

Those believing in life terms argue that better lawyers will be interested in becoming judges if they know the job is to be permanent. Since the qualities that make a good judge do not always make a good political candidate, some lawyers do not wish to become judges under an elective system. Some excellent lawyers, knowing they will have to run for office every few years, hesitate to give up their well-developed legal practices for a political career as a judge. A judge with a life position does not have to submit to pressure from anyone. He can be truly independent.

Opponents of life terms argue that the best defense against getting poor judges is to give the people a chance to defeat them in an election every few years. They contend that good judges win elections and poor ones lose elections. They say if the voters will watch "the kind of company the judge keeps," the voters will be able to spot the judge who is obeying the orders of some boss and defeat him at an election.

The method of selecting judges is, therefore, one key to getting better judges. The states have experimented with various ways to get judges. In some states the governor appoints the judges. In other states judges are elected. Combinations of these two plans are common.

In some states judges are elected on nonpartisan ballots and at different times from other state officials. In other states the lawyers of the state through the state bar association nominate certain lawyers, and the governor appoints judges from this recommended list.

In Missouri the governor appoints a judge for his first term from a list of three persons submitted to him by a nonpartisan commission. The commission consists of the chief justice of the state supreme court, three attorneys selected by the state bar association, and three laymen appointed by the governor. After the judge has been in office for one year, his name must be submitted to the voters for approval at the next general election. If approved, he serves out the balance of his term (twelve years for higher courts; six years for lower). Near the end of each term the judge decides whether he wishes to continue in office. If he does, his name goes on the ballot unopposed. The citizens then vote on whether they are willing to have him serve another term. The effect is to give the voters a regular chance to recall a judge whom they may not want. Commonly called the *Missouri Plan*, it has been recommended by the American Bar Association.

In *Modernizing State Government*, the committee held that popular election is not a satisfactory way to select judges and recommended that:

> Each judge be appointed by the governor from a list of nominees submitted by an independent selection committee. Judges should have a tenure of no less than ten years—with the right to be reappointed or to stand for noncompetitive re-election.

A further recommendation was that:

> Each state pay the justices of its highest court salaries no less than those of federal district court judges (currently $40,000), and that larger states set proportionately higher salaries. Corresponding pay scales should be established for all lesser judicial positions.[1]

1 Committee for Economic Development, *Modernizing State Government*, page 66.

BETTER JURIES. Trial by jury is one of the oldest democratic rights. It was listed in the English Magna Carta in 1215. It is a foundation stone of freedom. Nevertheless, there are many critics of the jury system. The major criticisms are these:

- *Getting a good jury is a very slow, expensive process. The cost is so great that the jury system should be abandoned for most cases.*

- *Juries too often have people who are not competent to decide the complicated questions that come before them. The lawyers eliminate so many of the prospective jurors by challenges that some juries consist of uneducated people who do not read or discuss public affairs.*

- *Juries are not selected fairly. Although juries are supposed to be selected by chance, some people never get called for jury service, while other people are called with surprising regularity, particularly those who are poor or out of work.*

- *Juries are sometimes influenced by tricks of lawyers rather than by the logic of the case. Some lawyers are better actors than others, and in a jury trial the side with the best lawyer-actor often wins the case.*

Defenders of the jury system admit that there are defects in the operation of the jury system, but they think the jury is a necessity to prevent injustice. So against these criticisms they present the following defense:

- *Getting a good jury can be speeded up and made less costly if the judge will be alert to his responsibilities. A good judge can prevent lawyers from making a comedy of their right to challenge jurors.*

- *While some jurors may not be able to understand the facts of a technical case, judges too are not experts in all areas of life. Justice is safer in the hands of a jury of ordinary citizens than in the hands of one person. If incompetent persons are serving on juries, something is wrong with the lawyer who allowed such persons to get on the jury without a challenge.*

- *Jurors in many places are selected with absolute fairness and completely by chance. If a state is not operating under such a system, it could easily adopt a fair, honest system.*

- *Legal tricks and acting do not work as well with juries as the movies, newspapers, or TV shows lead one to believe. Most lawyers win cases before juries because they have a good case which they have studied with care and which they present so that an ordinary person can understand the issues.*

With so many criticisms, efforts to improve the operation of the jury system have been tried in several states. Some states now use a smaller number of jurors instead of the usual number of twelve on the basis that they can agree more readily with little danger of injustice. In 1970 the U.S. Supreme Court approved the small jury.

Another proposal is not to require a unanimous verdict. A three-fourths majority is used in some states and was approved by the Supreme Court in 1972. This plan greatly reduces the number of hung juries. It is worthy of note that the constitutional guarantee of trial by jury (Amendment Seven) says nothing about the size of the jury or the size of the majority needed for conviction.

The plan of permitting the waiver of a jury trial in civil cases is operating in most states. About one-third of the states have

Cite the 1970 decision of the United States Supreme Court in *Williams v. Florida* declaring six-member juries constitutional.

extended this plan to criminal cases, too.

Alert newspapers have provided useful services by publicizing the system for selecting the jury panels, the kinds of excuses that judges accept in excusing persons from jury service, the pay for jury service, and the efficiency with which members of jury panels are handled in the courts. Publicity of this type has helped raise the level of jury service.

SPEED AND EFFICIENCY. Delay is an enemy of justice. Sometimes years pass before a case is brought to trial. In one city the courts were so far behind with their work that it took from two to four years to bring a case to trial. In contrast, another large city was bringing cases to court three weeks after the case happened.

When years go by before a case is brought to trial, witnesses may move away or die. Memories of the remaining witnesses may not be clear. It is very hard to recall vividly events that took place several years earlier. Time destroys the accuracy of the testimony of the witnesses.

Some people believe that quick justice is better than slow justice because of its effect on citizens. Poor people cannot afford long-drawn-out legal battles. They lose faith in courts if they feel that the rich have defeated them by delaying tactics. Similarly, criminals seem to be more fearful of quick, speedy justice than they are of some penalty which seems far off and uncertain.

To speed up court procedure several things have been done. In communities where the population has been increasing, additional judges have been added. In other places plans have been worked out to move judges from one part of the state to another on a temporary basis. Where courts do not have many cases, a judge will be assigned to a court that is behind schedule.

Allowing juries to decide cases by a

A. C. Kaufman and the McNaught Syndicate.

three-fourths majority instead of by unanimous vote has eliminated many hours of court work. Eliminating appeals to higher courts on minor technicalities has helped to speed up court work too.

Using thirteen or fourteen jurors prevents sickness or death of a juror from stopping a case. If all jurors remain healthy, the extra jurors are dismissed by the judge before the twelve jurors retire to reach a decision.

A great aid to improved court efficiency is the *pretrial conference.* Under this system the lawyers meet with the judge about two weeks before the case is to come before the court. The lawyers describe the case. They agree on certain facts and disagree on others.

In an automobile accident case, for example, they might agree on weather conditions, time of the accident, the statements of extent of injuries, and the existence of a stop sign. The only disagreement might be over the speed of the two cars.

With these agreements the only argument before the court would be over the speed of the cars. The time of witnesses, lawyers, judge, and jury is saved. In about three out of five cases, settlements are reached during the pretrial conference and the cases never come to trial.

UNIFIED, CENTRALIZED COURT ORGANIZATION. The courts have been described in this chapter as parts of a regular system. But there are many problems in the organization of courts. In some states higher courts have no control over lower courts. Special courts sometimes do not have a good relationship with the regular courts. Judges with little work often cannot be transferred to courts with heavy work loads. These are the effects of decentralization.

One unified, centralized court system has consistently been urged for each state. The Model State Constitution of the National Municipal League provides for such a system. So does the Model State Judicial Article of the American Bar. The *Modernizing State Government* report made a similar recommendation that:

> Each state create a unified judicial system embracing all nonfederal courts, judges, and other court personnel. Administration of this system should be centralized to insure the best use of manpower and facilities.[1]

Under a unified, centralized court system the state supreme court has authority over all the courts in the system. The court has authority to set up rules, transfer judges, and supervise the administration of the courts. Alaska, Hawaii, Illinois, and New Jersey are among the states with unified, centralized systems. Centralizing the administration of the courts seems to help in get-

ting justice. Because the state supreme court has many duties and may find it difficult to administer the entire court system, some states have created an administrative officer to carry out these duties under the direction of the supreme court justices.

In about two-thirds of the states *judicial councils* have been created. These councils consist of one or more supreme court justices, judges from trial and appellate courts, the attorney general, a few legislators, and sometimes professors of law. These councils continuously study the operation of the courts, compile statistics, do research, and make recommendations to the supreme court or the state legislature. These councils provide a careful and thoughtful review leading to needed reforms. They are most effective when the entire court system is unified and centralized.

STUDY QUESTIONS

1. What are the names of the courts in the court system of your state?

2. Why are justice of the peace courts sometimes good courts? Why are they sometimes poor courts?

3. What kinds of cases are tried in lower courts?

4. What kinds of cases are tried in general trial courts?

5. What kinds of cases are tried in a state supreme court?

6. How many members are there on the highest court of your state? What is their official title? Are they appointed or elected?

7. How does the procedure differ in a case before the state supreme court compared to a case before a lower court?

---

[1] Committee for Economic Development, *Modernizing State Government*, page 64.

CONCEPTS AND GENERALIZATIONS

1
In state and federal courts a jury trial is guaranteed.

2
Justice of the peace courts are considered to be inferior and should be abolished.

3
Judges should be paid a fixed salary and should not be paid by fees.

4
The general trial courts are the basic courts of the state, and the supreme court is the highest court of the state.

5
Special courts, such as probate courts, juvenile courts, and traffic courts, have been created to relieve the workload of the general trial courts.

6
The procedures in civil and criminal cases are based on accusation, trial, and decision.

7
Cross-examination is an important method of determining the truth or falsity of the testimony of a witness.

8
The method of selecting judges recommended by the American Bar Association is to have judges appointed by the governor from a list submitted by an independent commission and to have the judge at the end of his term run for reelection without competition.

9
The jury system may be improved by having a smaller number of jurors, not requiring a unanimous decision, permitting waiver of jury trial by mutual agreement, and by bettering the selection and treatment of jurors.

10
Unified, centralized court systems with the state supreme court having authority over lower courts assist in speeding up court procedures and in obtaining equal justice for all.

11
Judicial councils are needed to study continuously the operation of the state courts.

8. What is the special work of the probate court? The juvenile court? The small claims court? The domestic relations court? The traffic court? The police court?

9. How do civil and criminal cases differ?

10. What is the procedure in a civil case?

11. What is the procedure in a criminal case?

12. Why are the proceedings secret before grand juries?

13. How could the courts of your state be improved?

IDEAS FOR DISCUSSION

1. Should a judge be paid a salary, or should he be paid by fees? Why?

2. Should judges be selected on a nonpartisan ballot?

3. If you were falsely accused of a crime, would you prefer to have your case tried by a judge without a jury?

4. Chief Justice Charles Evans Hughes once said, "The Supreme Court of the United States and the courts of appeal will take care of themselves. Look after the courts of the poor, who stand most in need of justice. The security of the Republic will be found in the treatment of the poor and ignorant; in indifference to their misery and helplessness lies disaster." What conclusions do you make from this statement?

5. Justice Lummus of the Massachusetts State Supreme Court once said, "There is no certain harm in turning a politician into a judge. He may be or become a good judge. The curse of the elective system is the converse: that it turns every judge into a politician." What conclusions do you make from this statement on the selecting of state judges?

6. Should the state supreme court supervise the work of all the courts in a state?

7. A recent president of the American Bar Association said, "What the country needs is more courts and a streamlining of court procedure. Bar associations are continually recommending reforms, but legislatures, and sometimes the press, are likely to oppose them. People are reluctant to take on something new." Who are the persons or groups that should take leadership in judicial reforms?

8. A few years ago in one large city 10,869 cases were awaiting jury trial. The judges called attorneys together in a series of pretrial conferences. In one month 5,800 cases were settled without a court trial. What conclusions do you make from these facts?

9. A person may be tried under criminal law and sued in civil law for the same act. Tell about such a case. Is justice being done?

THINGS TO DO

1. Interview a court official to determine the system by which jurors are selected in your community.

2. Arrange with a judge to visit a court while a trial is in session. If possible arrange for students to be selected from your class as a mock jury.

3. See the classroom movie *Justice Under Law,* adapted from the 20th Century-Fox film *Boomerang.* Before viewing the film hold a brief discussion on the question "Should a prosecuting attorney try as hard to prove the innocence of a person accused of a crime as he does to prove his guilt?"

4. Prepare a report on the alliance of criminals with some judges.

5. Make a survey of the adult members of the families in the class. How many have served on juries? How many have been witnesses in court cases? How many have been parties in a court case? What opinions do these persons hold about courts? What conclusions do you draw from your survey?

6. Hold a mock trial of a fictitious case. For example, pretend that a class member has been kidnapped near an entrance to the school. Select a judge and lawyers. Locate witnesses. Select a jury. Conduct the trial.

7. Interview the clerk of a court to determine how speedily cases are being brought to trial.

8. Consult the classified section of your local telephone directory. Count the number of attorneys listed. Count the number of physicians. Which is greater? A psychologist once studied the "goodness of life" in communities and stated that communities were better where the physicians outnumbered the attorneys. How does your community rate in this regard according to your directory count? Do you agree with the psychologist?

9. Hold panel discussions on the following issues:

Jury trials should not be used in civil cases.
State judges should be appointed by the governor from nominations prepared by the state bar association.

A poor person cannot afford to go to court in our community.

10. Prepare a chart showing the names of judges, methods of selection, terms of office, and salaries for each of the major courts in your state to which you might bring a legal case.

11. Invite a lawyer to come to your class to answer your questions about courts.

12. Prepare a report on the court procedures for juveniles in your community.

FURTHER READINGS

Adrian, Charles R., STATE AND LOCAL GOVERN-MENTS. McGraw-Hill Book Co., Inc., 1967. Chapter 17.

Ferguson, John H., and McHenry, Dean E., THE AMERICAN SYSTEM OF GOVERNMENT. McGraw-Hill Book Co., Inc., 1967. Chapter 29.

Glick, Henry R., SUPREME COURTS IN STATE POLITICS. Basic Books, 1970.

Hanna, John P., TEENAGERS AND THE LAW. Ginn and Co., 1967. (Paperback edition)

Maddox, Russell W. (ed.), ISSUES IN STATE AND LOCAL GOVERNMENTS. D. Van Nostrand Co., Inc., 1966. Chapters 8, 9.

Mitau, G. Theodore, STATE AND LOCAL GOVERNMENT: POLITICS AND PROCESSES. Charles Scribner's Sons, 1966. Chapter 7.

Munger, Frank (ed.), AMERICAN STATE POLITICS. Thomas Y. Crowell Co., 1966. Nos. 6, 12, 18, 20, 24.

National Council for the Social Studies, JUDGMENT-CASE STUDY NO. 3, THE RIGHT TO LEGAL COUNSEL. The Council, 1966. (Paperback edition)

Paulsen, Monrad G., EQUAL JUSTICE FOR THE POOR MAN. Public Affairs Pamphlets, 1967.

Ross, Russell M., and Millsap, Kenneth F., STATE AND LOCAL GOVERNMENT AND ADMINISTRATION. Ronald Press Co., 1966. Chapter 12.

Sagarin, Mary, EQUAL JUSTICE UNDER LAW. Lothrop, Lee & Shepard Co., Inc., 1966.

Schmidt, Karl M. (ed.), AMERICAN STATE AND LOCAL GOVERNMENT IN ACTION. (Dickenson), Wadsworth Publishing Co., 1966. Chapter 6.

Snider, Clyde F., and Gove, S. K., AMERICAN STATE AND LOCAL GOVERNMENT. Appleton-Century-Crofts, Inc., 1966. Chapter 11.

Tolchin, Martin, and Tolchin, Susan, TO THE VICTOR. Random House, Inc., 1971.

ARSON—the crime of purposely setting fire to property.

CLEARING HOUSE—an agency for collecting, classifying, and distributing information.

COMPACT—an agreement.

CREATIVE FEDERALISM—a working partnership among federal, state, and local governments.

FULL FAITH AND CREDIT—the principle that the acts, records, and judicial proceedings of one state shall be honored in another state.

GRANT-IN-AID—money provided by one unit of government to help another unit to carry on some service.

INTERSTATE COMPACT—a written agreement between two or more states that has been approved by Congress.

MATCHING FUND—a grant which requires the receiver to pay a certain percentage of the total amount.

MEDIATION—the process by which one or more persons, selected to assist in settling a dispute, make suggestions or offer compromises, as for example, in a labor dispute.

REGIONALISM—the administration of a governmental unit by the federal government and the states without regard to state boundaries.

SHARED REVENUE—monies collected by one unit of government which are returned to another unit of government.

UNIFORM STATE LAW—a model law prepared by an organization for possible adoption by all states.

THE LANGUAGE
OF GOVERNMENT

18
Problems of
State
Government

State governments are on trial today. At a period in history when great social changes are underway, state governments are accused of not coming to grips with fundamental issues of our times. Improvements are necessary; if these improvements are not made, then the federal government will undoubtedly take on more and more responsibilities.

In the previous three chapters, which have described the general structure of state government, attention has been called to a few major problems which face the state. One of these, legislative reapportionment, seems to be on the way to solution. The concept of "one man, one vote," enforced by the federal courts, appears to make possible legislatures which are in better tune with the needs of all the people.

Another problem, the reorganization of state government to enable the governor to

Many students profit from a change in the type of homework. Suggest that some students write to someone in another state on the ideas expressed in this unit.

383

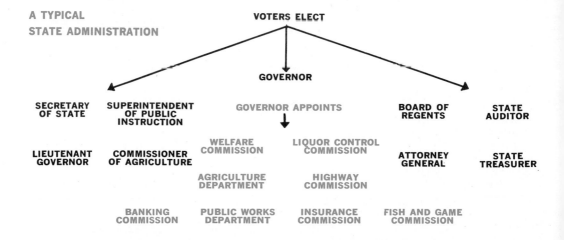

A TYPICAL STATE ADMINISTRATION

VOTERS ELECT

GOVERNOR

SECRETARY OF STATE

SUPERINTENDENT OF PUBLIC INSTRUCTION

GOVERNOR APPOINTS

BOARD OF REGENTS

STATE AUDITOR

LIEUTENANT GOVERNOR

COMMISSIONER OF AGRICULTURE

WELFARE COMMISSION

LIQUOR CONTROL COMMISSION

ATTORNEY GENERAL

STATE TREASURER

AGRICULTURE DEPARTMENT

HIGHWAY COMMISSION

BANKING COMMISSION

PUBLIC WORKS DEPARTMENT

INSURANCE COMMISSION

FISH AND GAME COMMISSION

govern, is progressing more slowly, but the pattern of good administrative organization now exists in some states and could be made effective in others.

The problem of inequities and injustices to Negro citizens and other minorities in an integrated society which respects persons as individuals, is far from solved. But the Supreme Court decisions and the civil rights struggles have aroused public interest and deepened the determination to bring our actions into closer harmony with our ideals.

Less glamorous and lacking the dramatic appeal of these problems are three issues of great concern to experts on government. These are: (1) What services should states perform? (2) How can relations among the states be improved? and (3) How can relations between the federal government and the states be improved? This chapter deals with these important questions.

SERVICES AND ACTIVITIES
OF STATES   While the glamour, the drama, and the publicity are centered on the national government in Washington,

D. C., the states affect our lives constantly. When you are born, the state records your birth. The state is responsible for your education. The state grants you a driver's license. Your marriage and even—if unhappily it becomes necessary—your divorce are made legal by the state. The age at which you can go to work, the conditions of your employment, the pay for any accident on the job are determined by the state.

When the undertaker buries you, he will do so according to state law. If you leave any money or property for your heirs, a state judge will decide how these possessions are to be divided. The state influences your life from birth to death and after.

Local communities are increasingly dependent on states for help with schools, highways, welfare, and police activities. Citizens look to the state capital for help on their problems.

In the years after the American Revolution the activities of state governments were rather meager. In this twentieth century these activities have multiplied many times. State legislatures, governors, and state courts face problems that are complex and that

Emphasize how many state activities are supplemented by federal funds and direction.

VOTERS ELECT

GOVERNOR

GOVERNOR APPOINTS

DEPT. OF EDUCATION (Commissioner)	STATE HIGHWAY DEPT. (Commissioner)	DEPT. OF TREASURY (StateTreasurer)	DEPT. OF STATE (Secretary)	CIVIL SERVICE COMMISSION (Commissioner)	DEPT. OF AGRICULTURE (Secretary)
DEPT. OF LAW AND PUBLIC SAFETY (Attorney General)	DEPT. OF BANKING AND INSURANCE (Commissioner)	DEPT. OF INSTITUTIONS AND AGENCIES (Commissioner)	DEPT. OF LABOR AND INDUSTRY (Commissioner)	PUBLIC UTILITIES COMMISSION (Board)	DEPT. OF CONSERVATION AND ECONOMIC DEVELOPMENT (Commissioner)
		DEPT. OF DEFENSE (Adjutant General)	HEALTH DEPT. (Commissioner)		

are important to many citizens. To meet these problems, and their obligations to citizens, state governments are involved in many activities and the number is increasing. Which activities are necessary? Which can the state afford?

It is not easy to classify or describe these activities and services. Some are so important that they are treated more fully in Unit Eight of this book. Here brief descriptions are made of the major state services according to a classification system adapted from one prepared by the Council of State Governments, an organization representing the fifty states.

EDUCATION. States are responsible for their public school systems. Continued large enrollments require the training and certification of qualified teachers and the providing of more classrooms. Consolidation of small, inefficient school systems is necessary.

School systems must not only be financed, but ways must be found by which the inequalities between rich suburban schools and poorer rural and city districts can be equalized. Funds from the federal government, for example for poverty areas, must be distributed. Desegregation plans must be put into effect.

State universities, professional schools, and community or junior colleges must be operated to provide for the education of youth beyond the high school.

Support of libraries is receiving greater attention. Statewide systems of libraries are necessary to make library resources available to citizens throughout the state.

HIGHWAYS AND TRAFFIC. States provide the major highway systems which carry a large part of today's traffic. States also channel funds to local governments to aid them in paying for rural roads and for certain streets and highways in cities.

A national interstate highway system is now financed mainly by grants from the federal government, but state highway departments have responsibility for planning, building, and maintaining these highways. Relocation of families when highways are built is a matter of growing concern for state and local governments.

The states issue auto licenses and drivers' licenses. They conduct safety campaigns and highway beautification programs. Increasingly the states are studying mass transportation problems.

HEALTH AND WELFARE. Originally state health departments were gatherers of

Each state is responsible for its educational system. What are some of the problems that states face in their efforts to provide equal educational opportunity for all citizens? (National Education Association)

statistics, but under modern medical conditions their activities are many-sided. They are concerned about prevention of accidents, air and water pollution, control of communicable diseases, and food and milk sanitation.

Research into cancer, diabetes, arthritis, and heart conditions is undertaken by state agencies. Doctors and nurses are licensed.

State hospitals—especially for the mentally ill and the disabled—are operated. Special programs are developed for the older citizens as well as for children and youth.

Aid to dependent children, the blind, the crippled, and the aged are provided by states with large amounts of federal aid.

CORRECTIONS AND PUBLIC PROTECTION. The state has major responsibility for the prevention of crime and for the confinement and retraining of criminals. Systems of state prisons and reformatories are operated. Parole and probation systems are administered.

State police, highway patrols, the state militia, and civil defense activities are important aspects of control over crime, traffic, and civil disorders. State fire marshals investigate cases when arson is suspected and in many states have responsibility for making building inspections for fire safety.

NATURAL RESOURCES. The many years of control of state legislatures by rural interests resulted in various state aids to agriculture, such as control of pests, soil testing and information, crop rotation, seed improvement, and marketing information. The United States Department of Agriculture has actively cooperated in these undertakings.

With urbanization has come great attention to water and air pollution and to conservation of natural resources. The use of natural resources of the state for recreation, not only for the citizens of the state but as an attraction for tourists, continues to grow. For these purposes, state parks are operated and maintained.

Protection of forests, oil, gas, and other natural resources from damaging exploitation is now recognized as a state responsibility.

LABOR REGULATION. The states, in cooperation with the federal government, provide unemployment compensation and operate employment offices. State regulations are established for occupational safety and health. With the emphasis on civil rights, prohibitions against discrimination in employment are being written into law and are being enforced.

State mediation services to aid in settling

Notice the striking view along this highway in Alaska. The construction and maintenance of highways has become a constantly increasing problem for the states. (Alaska Dept. of Highways)

disputes between labor unions and management are available. Regulations concerning working conditions for children and women are established and enforced. Minimum wage laws exist in some states.

BUSINESS AND INDUSTRY REGULATION. Public utility commissions regulate the industries supplying electricity, gas, and telephone service. Rates and conditions of operation of these industries are determined by these state agencies. In some states there is public ownership of these utilities.

State banks are chartered and regulated. Corporations must also be chartered by states. Insurance companies selling policies in the state must comply with state regulations.

The sale and manufacture of alcoholic beverages are under state control. In some states the state operates the liquor business.

States have created business development commissions which try to attract new businesses to the state.

OTHER SERVICES AND ACTIVITIES. In addition to these varied activities there are many others that are difficult to classify. State *licenses* are needed for many occupations and professions, such as barbers, beauticians, accountants, doctors, nurses, airplane pilots, teachers, lawyers, and commercial fishermen. War *veterans* are assisted in many ways. *Elections* are conducted under state regulations. *Marriages and divorces* are legalized according to state laws.

The decisions that are made on the financing and operation of these many activities determine the major functions of state government. The degree to which state regulations are enforced affects the quality of state activities and services.

RELATIONS AMONG THE STATES   The relationships among the fifty states create many problems. Each state has its own laws and each state is independent of other states. The writers of the United States Constitution, however, recognized that the states had been so independent under the Articles of Confederation that the federal system was necessary. Yet, while providing a strong central government, the Constitution in Article IV

Concerning the cooperation of two or more governmental units in the performance of a particular function, discuss what is called functional consolidation or functionalism.

The states are concerned with the health and welfare of their citizens. This is an area in Minneapolis, Minnesota, before and after redevelopment. What happened to the people who originally lived here? (Minneapolis Housing and Redevelopment Authority)

described the general basis for relations among the states.

Problems of relationships among the states arise because state boundaries are not walls; they are only political lines. Across these boundaries move people, trade, crime, water, disease. The states have had to learn to cooperate to solve the problems created by movements across state boundaries.

A few illustrations show the importance of getting interstate cooperation.

EXAMPLE 1: WATER. Not many years ago New York City was so short of water that for many months strict regulations of the use of water had to be enforced. To prevent water shortages in the future, New York decided to build dams across mountain streams to store the water in the spring months. This water would be released gradually during the summer and fall.

Pennsylvania and New Jersey objected to this plan. Why? Because the dams would slow up the flow of water into the Delaware River—water needed for drinking, sanitation, and industrial uses in their states. How could the three states work out some agreement on the use of the water?

EXAMPLE 2: DIVORCE. A man and wife live in one state for several years. But they are not happy living together. In their state, however, obtaining a divorce is a slow process, and the causes recognized for divorces are few.

The wife decides to move to another state where she can live for a few months and then obtain a divorce very easily. Does the state of her original residence recognize the divorce she gets in the other state?

EXAMPLE 3: PROBATION. A man committed a crime in State A. He was tried, convicted, and served ten years of a twenty-year prison sentence. The parole board decided to release him on probation for good behavior.

The prisoner was glad to get out of prison. He and his family felt that if he was to become an honest, useful citizen, he should move to State B where he would not be known. They wanted to get away from the friends in his old gang. Should he be allowed to leave the state? Should the state where he made his new home know that he is an ex-convict on probation?

EXAMPLE 4: SPITE LEGISLATION. State A passed a law that all public build-ings in the state must be built with stone produced in the state. State B felt that this law prevented owners of quarries in their state from selling stone to State A. So State B's legislature passed a law that its state institutions could not buy dairy prod-ucts from State A. Should the farmers in State A be hurt because of the harm to the stone producers in State B? Is this type of "spite" legislation good for trade among the states?

These examples and the questions they raise could be multiplied. Irrigation proj-ects, flood-control projects, regulations of trucks on highways, fishing rights, and dis-

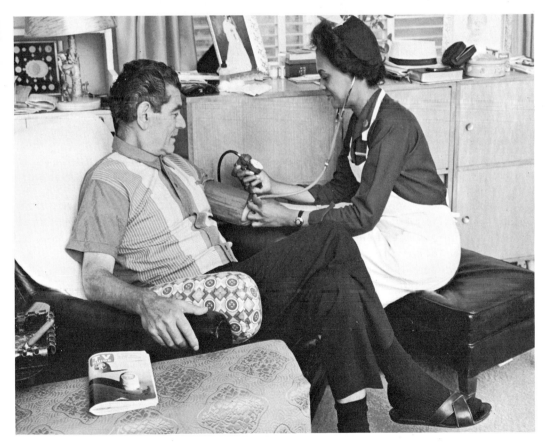

The provision of health services to those who need it has become an increasingly important func-tion of government. Here a visiting nurse checks a patient's blood pressure. (Visiting Nurse Service of New York)

This is an aerial view of the state penitentiary near Joliet, Illinois. Should the states be concerned with the rehabilitation as well as the confinement of criminals? (Illinois Dept. of Public Safety)

tribution of oil create similar problems that require cooperation among states.

The solutions to the problems of this type have taken different patterns over the years. The problems have had to be attacked in many different ways. In general, four chief methods have been employed: (1) judicial settlement, (2) "full faith and credit," (3) interstate compacts, and (4) voluntary cooperative efforts.

JUDICIAL SETTLEMENT. Under the United States Constitution the system of federal courts handles disputes "between two or more states;—between a state and citizens of another state;[1]—between citizens of different states. . . ."

[1] The Eleventh Amendment limits this clause to suits by a state against citizens of another state.

"In all cases . . . in which a state shall be a party, the Supreme Court shall have original jurisdiction." (Article III, Section 2, Clauses 2 and 3.)

Over the years, therefore, controversies between states have been brought before the federal courts for judicial settlement. The Supreme Court has handed down more than 100 decisions in disputes between states. Many of these cases have been over boundary lines. But water pollution, irrigation, floods, and bond issues have been before the court, too. The right of the Supreme Court to settle interstate conflicts is so taken for granted by this time that often this important function of the courts is neglected.

FULL FAITH AND CREDIT. The Constitution, in Article IV, Section 1, establishes the basic policy which governs the relations among the states. This section states, "Full faith and credit shall be given in each state to the public acts, records, and judicial proceedings of every other state. And the Congress may by general laws prescribe the manner in which such acts, records, and proceedings shall be proved, and the effect thereof."

Because of this "full faith and credit" clause the laws and court decisions of one state are accepted in another state. Thus a will made in Kansas is legal even when the person dies as a resident of Oregon.

Birth records, marriage certificates, and titles to land are recognized in all states. If a court in Rhode Island decides that Mr. X must pay damages of $1,500 to Mr. Y, Mr. Y can collect even if Mr. X moves to Pennsylvania. The Pennsylvania courts will uphold the Rhode Island decision in the case.

There are two important exceptions to the "full faith and credit" clause. The clause applies only to civil cases, not to criminal cases. Criminal cases are handled by the process of extradition, as described in Chapter 16.

A second exception concerns divorce. At the time of the writing of the Constitution,

State parks attract out-of-state tourists as well as state residents to enjoy their recreational facilities. Shown here is a view of the unspoiled wilderness of a state park in the Davis Mountains, Texas. (Courtesy of Texas Parks and Wildlife Dept.)

This is a section of the Friant-Kern irrigation canal, part of California's Central Valley Project. Water from a part of the state that has heavy rainfall is shared with a part of the state that has little rain, and a large area of fertile farmland is created. (Bureau of Reclamation, Department of the Interior)

courts did not grant divorces. Today some of the most difficult cases involving "full faith and credit" center in divorce.

In Example 2 on page 388 recent Supreme Court decisions indicate that the wife's divorce would be legal in the state of her original residence. But there are exceptions. These exceptions result in interstate conflict and difficult personal problems. To avoid these difficulties a few states have adopted a uniform divorce recognition act.

While "full faith and credit" provides a workable system for smoothing conflicts among the states, the system is far from perfect. The conflict between laws of different states provides much of the work of the Supreme Court. Many law students will testify, too, that some of their most

difficult study in law school is in this area of "conflict of law."

INTERSTATE COMPACTS. A little noticed provision of the Constitution provides a third way in which states can solve interstate problems. Article I, Section 10, Clause 3, states, "No State shall, without the consent of the Congress, . . . enter into any agreement or compact with another state, or with a foreign power. . . ."

Under this provision states have reached formal agreements, have had them approved by Congress, and have thus been able to cooperate with each other. These agreements have come to be known as *interstate compacts*. Before World War I compacts were used mainly to settle boundary disputes, but since that time compacts have been used in an increasing variety of ways.

The Supreme Court has ruled that a state may delegate powers to an interstate agency of which it is a member and may assume long-time financial obligations under compacts. The evidence indicates that great achievements can be brought about by interstate agreements.

The dispute over water described in Example 1 on page 388 was settled by the Supreme Court based on the 1936 *Delaware River Basin Compact*, which provides for an interstate commission on problems created by the Delaware River. This commission has representatives from each of the cooperating states: Delaware, New Jersey, New York, and Pennsylvania. In 1961 the compact was enlarged to include the federal government—making it an interstate–federal compact. Before this compact the states had fought several years before the Supreme Court to get control of the water.

During those years writers were describing the Delaware River in these terms:

"God made the Delaware River a beautiful river, but man made it a dirty sewer."

"The river is a suffering, diseased mess, its life stream clogged with every sort of filth, from coal dust to industrial poisons to human refuse."

The compact was organized to get the states and federal government to work together. Dams, reservoirs, sewage-treatment plants were built. Drinking water for cities was made available, floods were controlled, pollution was decreased, recreational facilities were improved, and the salt water flow into the Delaware tidal area was controlled.

The Delaware River Basin Compact is only one of many such compacts. Here are other noteworthy examples:

THE PORT OF NEW YORK AUTHORITY. New York and New Jersey since 1921 have cooperated to develop the great port facilities. Bridges, tunnels, and airfields were also built and operated by the Authority.

THE YELLOWSTONE RIVER COMPACT. Montana, North Dakota, and Wyoming entered into an agreement to plan for the use of the waters of the Yellowstone.

THE OHIO RIVER VALLEY WATER SANITATION COMPACT. To change the "Beautiful Ohio" from what was rapidly becoming an open sewer and a menace during floods, eight states have signed an agreement to cooperate in plans for the Ohio River Valley.

These compacts illustrate the principle that many compacts are written to solve problems of *water resources*. But compacts are also concerned with other issues, some with *economic factors*. Examples include:

The *St. Louis Bi-State Agency*, by which Missouri and Illinois reached an agreement to develop the area around St. Louis as one economic unit.

The *Interstate Oil Compact*, by which thirty-three states cooperate to conserve oil and gas to prevent physical waste of these natural resources.

Three compacts have been developed by regions to provide for better utilization of the fisheries of their regions. They are the *Atlantic States Marine Fisheries Compact*, the *Pacific Marine Fisheries Compact*, and the *Gulf States Marine Fisheries Compact*.

Still other compacts are concerned with *general welfare provisions*. Example 9, on page 388, concerning the man on probation would come under the provisions of the *Interstate Compact for the Supervision of Parolees and Probationers*. This agreement provides for the interstate supervision of persons released from prison. Those on probation are permitted to move to new states and their probation is supervised by the new states. All fifty states are members of this compact.

Other compacts of this type include the

New England Welfare Compact by which Maine, Vermont, Rhode Island, and Connecticut agreed that any resident of the region can receive welfare assistance regardless of normal residence requirements.

The *Interstate Compact on Mental Health* provides, for those states that are members, for treatment and institutionalization of mental patients on the basis of need rather than residence.

One of the newer compacts is the *Compact on Education* establishing a commission to study and make recommendations about education problems. It is expected that this compact will make possible a forum for sharing experiences, raising standards, and discussing educational policies.

The Committee for Economic Development report on *Modernizing State Government* expressed the opinion that the states have been too slow to make use of interstate compacts and were leaving too much of the responsibility for solving interstate problems to the national government. The report recommended that

> . . . every state actively explore opportunities for cooperation through use of interstate compacts . . . (and) called on Congress to enact general permissive legislation authorizing the states to create joint authorities for handling interstate metropolitan problems.[1]

VOLUNTARY EFFORTS. The American people have a genius for getting things done by voluntary agreement. In all walks of life people get together and reach decisions on important matters. We are organized into hundreds of groups of all kinds and all types from Rotary Clubs to the Society for the Preservation and Encouragement of Barber Shop Quartet Singing in America. In these countless organizations

we learn to understand each other better. Somehow many important things are done by the simple process of getting together and learning what needs to be done.

This process is at work on the problems of interstate relations. Since 1908 the governors of the states have met each year at the Governors' Conference. Similar meetings of attorneys general, secretaries of state, legislators, purchasing agents, and other state officers are held. At these meetings understandings about many problems are reached. The exchange of information on mutual problems, including the learning of ways in which other states deal with issues, has been helpful. Conflicts between states that might become difficult are resolved in friendly interchange of ideas.

Since 1935 the Council of State Governments has provided a *clearing house* of information, research, and encouragement for cooperation among the states. This council was established by the states to serve the states. It is supported by the states. Although it has no official power, it has become very important in calling attention to matters that may help or harm states.

It has done much to eliminate the barriers to trade between states by giving publicity to the evils of "spite" legislation. Example 4 on page 389 was solved by this type of voluntary understanding of the evils which might develop if all states adopted "buy at home" laws.

Each state is a member of the Council. Administrative officials and members of the legislature make up a Commission on Interstate Cooperation in each state. These commissions have responsibility for carrying on the activities of the Council. A major publication of the Council is *The Book of the States*, which is published every two years. This book is the most accepted authority on trends in state government. The Council also publishes a

---

[1] Committee for Economic Development, *Modernizing State Government,* Page 73.

The governors of all the states and the governors of the Virgin Islands, Guam, American Samoa, and the Commonwealth of Puerto Rico meet at least once each year at the National Governors' Conference. The meetings, which have been held since 1908, give opportunity to exchange points of view, to foster interstate cooperation, to promote greater uniformity of state laws, to work for greater efficiency, to improve state-local and state-federal relations, and to engage in some active political exchanges.

The conferences are held in various parts of the country. Recent conferences have been held in Minneapolis, Minnesota; Beverly Hills, California; Palm Beach, Florida; White Sulphur Springs, West Virginia. The 1967 conference was held aboard the steamship *Independence* on a cruise from New York to the Virgin Islands and back to New York.

At these conferences stands are taken on important issues. The Interstate Compact on Education was first agreed on at the 1965 conference. Positions have been taken on air pollution, conservation, the federal government's sharing taxes with the states, highway construction, urban renewal, and other matters vital to the states. Following one conference, President Johnson had all the governors flown to the White House to brief them about the Vietnam War.

Politics is an important occupation at these meetings. The governors try to get resolutions passed favorable to their party's national policies. Press conferences are held that receive national attention—especially those of governors with presidential possibilities. Governors appear on national television programs like "Face the Nation," "Issues and Answers," and "Meet the Press." During the conference the attention of the nation is on the problems of states.

For half a century these conferences have been a strong, constructive force. State governments have been improved, relations among the states have been bettered, and the federal system has been improved.

quarterly journal, *State Government,* from its central office in Lexington, Kentucky.

Another influential group is the National Conference of Commissioners on Uniform State Laws. Organized in 1892, the Conference has been in continuous existence. This organization meets annually. It has written nearly 200 model laws and encourages the states to adopt these laws. The Council of State Governments has worked actively in this field, too.

As a result of these efforts, the laws of many states are similar on business records, checks, notes, sales, aviation, public health, and transportation of agricultural products. When state laws are alike or similar on these matters, cooperation among the states becomes easier.

As states improve in solving their interstate conflicts, the tendency for the national government to take over state functions diminishes. But the national government is so strong that its relations with the states present special problems, too.

FEDERAL-STATE RELATIONS

The federal system, with a strong national government and fifty independent states, means that on many occasions and on many matters the national government in Washington and one or more of the states must cooperate. Social conditions, such as discrimination against Negroes, do not respect state boundaries. Even when the federal government takes leadership, as in the integration of schools, the granting of full rights to the Negro is dependent on the cooperation of the states.

In a similar manner, floods do not confine themselves to the territory of one state. Great river systems—such as those of the

Mention the fact that a great deal of legislation passed by Congress and the state legislatures has supplemented and strengthened laws passed by the other.

Federal troops enforced a court order to desegregate Central High School in Little Rock, Arkansas, in 1957. Since then the states and the federal government have increasingly cooperated to give full rights to Negroes. (Arkansas Gazette)

Tennessee River, the Missouri River, or the Columbia River—which flow through or between several states have required federal-state cooperation for their control.

Other national disasters, such as unemployment, droughts, or war have required the combined efforts of the federal government and the states. Some governmental functions are so important—highways, housing, and education, for example—that both levels of government have had to cooperate. As new or better services have been required by the people, attempts have been made to adjust the federal system to meet these modern conditions.

This partnership of the federal and state governments occurs in many phases of government. Elections are state functions. Yet during war periods the federal government and the states have cooperated to let those in military service vote even when they were in foreign lands. The draft boards under the Selective Service System are ex-

amples of states and local units working with the federal government.

The federal government provides services and special funds to schools, although education is under state and local control. The Public Health Service works cooperatively with state and local health boards.

It is clear that the federal government and the states are frequently concerned with the same public matters. There is an interlocking relationship on many of these matters. Moreover, powerful political leaders, whether they are in the White House or in state capitols, wish to gain power and fame by satisfying the demands of citizens on these matters.

Sometimes there is conflict over these matters. There are claims that too much power is centralized in Washington or that "states' rights" are violated. But there are equally strong voices that maintain that states have become ineffective and the federal government must act if problems are to

This scene of desolation is the result of a severe and prolonged drought. States and the federal government combine their efforts in order to ease the results of such natural disasters. (USDA photo)

be solved. In these cases of conflict, the state and federal governments are viewed as rivals.

COOPERATION. In practice, over the years, in spite of conflicts and rivalries the states and the nation have developed ways of working together. A few of the many types of cooperation will illustrate the process.

Both the states and the federal government collect taxes. In administering several of these taxes—gasoline tax, income tax, and cigarette tax—the states receive assistance from the United States Internal Revenue Service. Auditing information is exchanged between state tax agencies and the national government.

Both states and the federal government are concerned about the preservation of the natural beauty of our nation. "America, the Beautiful" is a goal of both levels of government. So the federal government helps the states pay the costs of screening junkyards, eliminating unsightly billboards, and developing scenic areas along roads and highways.

In efforts to improve the health of our people, the federal government and the states cooperate in establishing mental health centers, in building hospitals, in developing facilities for retarded children, and in research on many types of programs including those for crippled children, child health, maternal welfare, and medical care for the aged.

Another type of cooperation involves the cooperation of certain types of officials. Agents of the Federal Bureau of Investigation, for example, in some cases assist state and local police officials in the arrest of persons accused of crimes. The county agriculture agent helps farmers under both state and federal programs. Officials in public health services, forestry, and other services cooperate, too.

GRANTS-IN-AID. The method of federal-state cooperation which has grown very rapidly and has been unusually effective is the *grant-in-aid.* These grants are given by the national government to states, usually for a specific purpose. When the federal government gives money to a state to build highways, the money is a grant-in-aid. Similarly, when a state gives money to a school district, the grant-in-aid device is being used.

Granting of funds to another unit of government has become widely used in recent years. The working of this system with counties and cities will be discussed in the next unit. On the federal-state level the system has been growing until at present 20 to 25 per cent of the money spent by states comes from federal grants.

Outright grants by the federal government were made to the states in the early years of our government. In this century, however, most grants have been on a *matching fund* basis. The federal government normally gives the money only if the state pays a certain percentage of the total. Usually the federal government sets up certain conditions which must be met if the money is to be given to the state. These minimum standards have helped to improve the services in some states, but they have been viewed as "dictation by federal bureaucrats" in some cases. While states are not compelled to accept these grants, failure to do so means that benefits are not received.

Federal grants for highways have been made for three general purposes: (1) to build national highways; (2) to develop secondary highways from farms to markets; and (3) to help build extensions of highways in urban areas. The minimum standards of construction are strictly enforced. Moreover, if the highways are not maintained in good condition, future federal grants will be withheld.

States have received grants from the federal government to help schools, as will be discussed more fully in Chapter 31. Help has been given to elementary, secondary, and vocational education and to higher education programs. Assistance has also been given to areas where huge federal projects have placed an unfair burden on school districts. Schools near military bases, defense production areas, and places where atomic plants have been built usually are eligible for grants.

State services to help the old, the needy, and the unemployed receive large federal grants. The Social Security Program is financed in part by the grant-in-aid system. Unemployment compensation, old-age support, aid to dependent children, and aid to the permanently and totally disabled needy persons come under these provisions. (See Chapter 31.)

Natural resources, transportation, communication, housing, state militia, and veterans have been aided by grants-in-aid. Over the years there has been an upward spiral in the amount of money given to the states. At the present time, more than twenty billion dollars is spent each year for these federal grants.

Most people seem to favor the grant-in-aid system because standards are upheld,

state administration is improved, and poor states get help that is badly needed. The U. S. Commission on Intergovernmental Relations, reporting back in 1955, stated that the federal grants-in-aid are a "fully matured device of cooperative government."

There are objections to the system, however. Some object to the extent of the federal supervision over state activities. Others argue that rich states are really forced to help poor states. There is some feeling that states neglect some important state activities by reducing their appropriations and using this money to match federal funds for other activities.

REGIONALISM. A second form of federal-state relations which has received great attention is known as *regionalism*. Regionalism is the administration of a governmental unit by the federal government and the states without regard to state boundaries. Some years ago an extreme form of regionalism was advocated. There were people who wanted metropolitan areas in neighboring states to divorce themselves from the states and to unite into new regional governments.

These "city-states" would be independent governmental units between the United States government and the states. Thus a new "Chicago" might include much of northern Illinois and Indiana. A new "New York" would include parts of Connecticut, New York State, and New Jersey.

It is doubtful that either the national government or the states would give up powers to such "regions." This extreme form of regional government might have value in solving problems that cross state boundaries, but it has not been practical from a political point of view. A regional government of this "city-state" type has never been established in this country.

Instead, regionalism of a different type developed from experience with the Tennessee Valley Authority. The Norris Act, establishing the TVA in 1933, created a new type of governmental unit. This unit is essentially a government-owned corporation. The corporation is headed by a board of directors appointed by the President with the consent of the Senate. The TVA has had power to *plan* and to *finance* its work. As a result twenty-one dams and a multi-million-dollar power development have been built and floods of the Tennessee River controlled. (See Chapters 18 and 29.)

This corporation owned by the federal government affects the lives and property of persons in parts of seven states: Tennessee, Alabama, Georgia, Mississippi, Kentucky, North Carolina, and Virginia. These states have been encouraged to *administer* the TVA programs. The TVA formula for regionalism has been: limit the regional authority to finance and planning; encourage states, counties, and other local governments to do the actual administration.

Although the TVA was criticized by some people as a threat to private business, there is general agreement that this form of governmental unit has worked effectively at a level between national government and state governments.

The Columbia River projects in the Pacific Northwest and the development of the Appalachian area have followed the regional formula. The Columbia River Basin with federal power projects affects five northwest states.

The Appalachian Regional Development Act plans for the economic redevelopment of an entire region consisting of one whole state and parts of eleven others. Planning under the law must be done cooperatively by federal, state, and local officials.

SHARED REVENUES. Several plans have been proposed to change the traditional use of grants-in-aid by giving back to the states tax money that has been collected by the federal government. Under these proposals a certain percentage of federal tax revenues would be returned to the states with few or no restrictions on how the money could be spent.

One effect of these proposals would be that the federal government would be a tax collecting agency for the states. To accomplish the same purpose, some economists and political scientists have urged that individuals be permitted to reduce their federal income tax, to a greater extent than under present deduction provisions in order to increase payments of state income taxes.

Discussions of sharing federal revenue by these schemes assume that the federal government raises more money than it needs and that states could spend this money more wisely than under the present system of grants-in-aid.

CREATIVE FEDERALISM. The necessity of federal-state cooperation is generally recognized. In the process of this cooperation, however, states need to be strengthened. There is a partnership, but each partner needs to have the strength to be a good partner.

President Johnson coined a phrase to express what he thought was needed. He called this *creative federalism.* He was concerned that the federal government should not contribute to state and local fragmentation. In his State of the Union message in 1967 he stated, "Federal energy is essential. But it is not enough. Only a total working relationship among federal, state and local governments can succeed."

President Nixon in a message to Congress supported these views on strengthening the states through shared revenues and decentralization. He stated, "It is time for a New Federalism in which power, funds, and responsibility will flow from Washington to the states and to the people."

The evolution of future relationships of

the federal government and the states is unclear, but Congress in September 1972 passed a law providing for sharing 30.1 billion dollars of federal revenue with the states. (See Chapter 33.)

(See Chapter 33.)

STUDY QUESTIONS

1. What are the major problems faced by state governments at present?

2. What are the major activities and services provided by state governments?

3. What types of activities are regulated by state governments?

4. How are relationships among the states controlled by judicial settlement?

5. What is the significance of the "full faith and credit" clause?

6. Is your state a member of any interstate compact?

7. How do states cooperate through voluntary efforts?

8. Give an example to illustrate the "marble cake" comparison.

9. Give an example to illustrate "federal-state" cooperation.

10. What grants-in-aid does your state receive?

11. Distinguish between a matching fund and an outright grant.

12. How has regionalism developed in our country?

13. Is the idea of "shared revenues" acceptable to you? Why?

14. Are states dependent on the federal government? Should they be?

IDEAS FOR DISCUSSION

1. During the past fifty years what important economic and social changes have taken place in your state? Has the state government been able to adjust to these changed conditions?

2. Consult your local telephone directory to determine if any state offices are located in your local community. Were those offices in your community in 1940?

CONCEPTS AND GENERALIZATIONS

1
If state governments are unable to provide the services required by citizens, the federal government will take on more responsibilities.

2
The services and activities of states have increased greatly in this century.

3
Education, highways, health, welfare, crime control and prevention, wise use of natural resources, and regulation of labor and business are included in the major state activities.

4
The United States Supreme Court has the final authority to settle disputes between states.

5
The basic policy governing the relations among the states is that each state shall give full faith and credit to the acts, records, and judicial proceedings of every other state.

6
The interstate compact is an increasingly used device to solve problems of interstate relations.

7
The exchange of ideas and information which takes place at voluntary meetings and conferences of state officials helps solve some problems of interstate relations.

8
The Council of State Governments is the major organization for promoting cooperation among the states.

9
The states and the federal government are frequently concerned with the same public matters.

10
The grant-in-aid, whose use has increased rapidly, is one of the most effective devices for cooperation between states and the federal government.

11
The use of government-owned corporations to develop large regions has been another effective device for federal-state cooperation.

3. Is the historic "states' rights" argument relevant to the issues raised in this chapter?

4. Will your state need to revise its constitution to solve the problems discussed in this chapter?

5. A professor of political science in a newspaper interview said, "State constitutions are antiquated, yet the people are content with them in most cases. The state legislatures are in many cases nonrepresentative, and state administration is often disorganized. State governors normally don't have powers commensurate with their responsibilities." Do you agree or disagree with the professor? Why?

6. A famous Justice of the United States Supreme Court once wrote, "A river is a necessity of life that must be rationed among those who have power over it." What does this mean in terms of relationships among the states?

7. One writer has said, "Political parties are the most effective way of getting cooperation between units of government." In what sense was he right? In what sense was he wrong?

8. Some people feel that a federal divorce law should be enacted. Do you think such a law would be desirable? What objections might there be to such a law?

THINGS TO DO

1. Have committees determine the facts concerning each of the main problems discussed in this chapter as they affect your state and suggest a solution to each problem. The committees should be prepared to defend their solutions when they report to the entire class.

2. Prepare a chart showing the changes in total budget and number of state employees in your state over the past ten years. What state services have benefited by these conditions?

3. Interview five adult citizens to find out what state services they would like improved. What services do they think could be eliminated?

4. Present a plan developed by a committee of students for improving the relations of your state government with those of a neighboring state.

5. Write a radio script dramatizing one of the important relationships between two states.

6. Prepare a report on one of the interstate compacts. Consult the *Readers' Guide to Periodical Literature.*

7. Prepare a chart showing the grants-in-aid received by your state in recent years. Consult *The Book of the States* or the *Statistical Abstract of the United States.*

8. Draw a map showing whether regionalism is a problem for your state.

9. Report to the class on how an international regional problem has been treated. (States along the Canadian and Mexican borders have regional problems that are really international problems.)

10. Draw a cartoon illustrating one of the problems discussed in this chapter.

11. Write a newspaper editorial pleading for increased cooperation among neighboring states.

12. Report to the class on how Maine separated from Massachusetts to become a state or on the way West Virginia separated from Virginia.

13. Prepare a list of public buildings constructed or other projects developed in your community by federal aid.

14. Hold a panel discussion on this topic: "The government of any one of the states cannot be understood except in the framework of the federal system and in its relations to the national government and the other state governments."

FURTHER READINGS

Adrian, Charles R., STATE AND LOCAL GOVERNMENTS. McGraw-Hill Book Co., Inc., 1967.

THE BOOK OF THE STATES, 1972-1973. Council of State Governments, 1972.

Ferguson, John H., and McHenry, Dean E., THE AMERICAN SYSTEM OF GOVERNMENT. McGraw-Hill Book Co., Inc., 1967. Chapter 32.

Maddox, Russell W., and Fuquay, Robert F., STATE AND LOCAL GOVERNMENT. D. Van Nostrand Co., Inc., 1966.

Munger, Frank (ed.), AMERICAN STATE POLITICS. Thomas Y. Crowell Co., 1966.

Reuss, Henry S., REVENUE SHARING: CRUTCH OR CATALYST FOR STATE AND LOCAL GOVERNMENTS? Praeger Publishers, Inc., 1970.

Rockefeller, Nelson A., THE FUTURE OF FEDERALISM. Harvard University Press, 1962.

Ross, Russell M., and Millsap, Kenneth F., STATE AND LOCAL GOVERNMENT AND ADMINISTRATION. Ronald Press Co., 1966.

Snider, Clyde F., and Gove, S. K., AMERICAN STATE AND LOCAL GOVERNMENT. Appleton-Century-Crofts, Inc., 1966.

Civil Service

Employment in governmental positions can be viewed from many different points of view. At one extreme are those who consider governmental employment as political patronage—the chance to reward the political faithful with a soft, well-paying position. At the other extreme are those who think of government workers as faithful, loyal, hardworking persons who do not receive adequate rewards for their efficiency and devotion to duty.

The excerpts below provide quotations which give some opinions and facts about civil service—especially as related to states.

* * *

The prestige value associated with the public service has been, until rather recent times, singularly low. Traditionally, American society has looked upon government service with a certain amount of disdain. . . . It is believed that many capable persons currently in the public service took a governmental position in the absence of a better opening. . . .

[The first state civil service law] was steered through the lower house of the New York legislature by Republican Assemblyman Theodore Roosevelt and signed by Governor Grover Cleveland on May 4, 1883. Massachusetts, in 1884, became the next state to enact a civil service law. . . .

The year 1940 marks a turning point in state personnel practices, as an amendment to the federal Social Security Act became effective which required the states to place all employees in those departments receiving federal grants-in-aid under the merit system. Most vitally affected were the unemployment security, public assistance, and, in some in-stances, highway departments or commissions.

Eventually state employees concerned with child welfare, public employment, public health and vocational rehabilitation activities were placed under the state merit system. All of the states have a merit system in operation for those agencies working in the areas of employment, health and welfare. In addition, the campaign for complete state-wide coverage has continued. In 1936 Utah became the thirtieth state to adopt a state-wide merit system.

Nevertheless, in twenty states the distribution of some of the state jobs is still determined by a political patronage system. Particularly in some of the Southern and Western states there is a considerable turnover of personnel with the change of administration.[1]

* * *

Recent major policy developments include the addition of two new civil service systems in North Carolina and Idaho. Several states now permit the interchange of employees or the use of the registers of other states. Recruitment from minority groups is increasing. Better salaries, improved training programs, fringe benefits such as group insurance, and retirement programs, and provisions for collective bargaining have characterized the recent efforts by some states to improve civil service.

Another interesting development is the establishment by some states of "suggestion programs." This encourages employees to participate in discovering new and better procedures by rewarding them for making good suggestions.[2]

---

[1] Russell M. Ross and Kenneth F. Millsap, STATE AND LOCAL GOVERNMENT AND ADMINISTRATION Copyright © 1966 The Ronald Press Company, New York, pp. 385-387.
[2] See *The Book of the States, 1966-67*. Council of State Governments, 1966, pp. 155-164.

Assign each of these excerpts to individuals or committees and ask them to make valid generalizations about civil service. Compile the resulting generalizations and have a class discussion on the effectiveness of civil service.

GOVERNMENT EMPLOYMENT AND PAYROLLS: 1960 TO 1970

YEAR	EMPLOYEES (in thousands)				PAYROLL (in millions of dollars)			
	TOTAL	FEDERAL	STATE	LOCAL	TOTAL	FEDERAL	STATE	LOCAL
1960	8,808	2,421	1,527	4,860	3,333	1,118	524	1,691
1965	10,589	2,588	2,028	5,973	4,884	1,484	849	2,551
1970	13,028	2,881	2,755	7,392	8,334	2,428	1,611	4,294
BY FUNCTIONS								
National defense and international relations	1,200	1,200	—	—	965	965	—	—
Postal service	731	731	—	—	555	555	—	—
Education	5,316	19	1,182	4,115	3,186	16	630	2,539
Highways	612	5	302	305	347	6	193	149
Health and hospitals	1,202	193	501	508	690	161	283	246
Police protection	538	30	57	451	370	32	43	296
Natural resources	404	221	151	33	305	201	90	14
Financial administration	334	94	95	145	223	92	61	70
All other	2,691	390	467	1,835	1,693	401	311	981

Source: Department of Commerce.

* * *

In the American system of government, political patronage has been a unique and cherished coin of the realm with which those in power could reward their friends for past performance and encourage continuing good will. The recent growth of the Civil Service, however, has diminished the availability of patronage appointments, particularly in the federal government, while at the same time continuing prosperity has reduced their allure.

The members of the new elite corps of American Politics—the fund raisers, the intellectual counselors, "media coordinators," and leaders of the growing citizens' movements—are profitably employed already, with better pay and working conditions than government can offer. To them, the most appealing aspect of a public job is the prestige. . . .

Happily, political leaders have devised ways to bestow the status symbol of high office without the job itself. At Democratic national headquarters in Washington, where many such split-level appointments are routinely requisitioned and cleared, the new institution is known as "the honorary." Elsewhere it has been dubbed the patronage non-job, and it can range from nomination to a White House advisory committee to an invitation to be an honored member of an Air Force civic-inspection tour of California, arranged at the request of your local Congressman.[1]

* * *

A Model State Civil Service Law has been prepared by the National Civil Service League and the National Municipal League as a cooperative venture. The Model Law provides for a state personnel department with a director of personnel as the single administrative head who directs administrative and technical operations. A civil service commission of three members is provided. The governor appoints the commission members on a nonpartisan basis for overlapping terms and appoints the director of personnel upon recommendation of the commission. The commission is limited to rule-making, the formulation of

[1] Don Oberdorfer, "The New Political Non-Job." Copyright © 1965, by Harper's Magazine, Inc. Reprinted from the October, 1965 issue of Harper's Magazine by permission of the author.

general policy, and the hearing of appeals.[1]

* * *

In fact, no American institution is more deeply embedded in the tradition of the land than the National Guard. From the earliest days, military policy has been based on the old Anglo-Saxon distrust of standing armies as a menace to freedom. In their wisdom, the founding fathers wrote the idea in the Constitution: Congress shall "provide for calling forth the Militia" and for "organizing, arming, and disciplining the Militia, and for governing such Part of them as may be employed in the Service of the United States." Further, the Constitution reserves to the states "the Appointments of the Officers, and the Authority of training the Militia according to the discipline prescribed by Congress."

Thus, the real commanders of National Guard units are not the Pentagon generals but the state governors, who are free to hand out Guard officerships to qualified friends or political allies through the state adjutants general, who themselves are usually appointees of the governor. The opportunity for patronage can be seen.[2]

* * *

The biographer of Adlai Stevenson includes a few comments on his power over appointments when he became governor of Illinois in 1949. Among these are:[3]

That good government requires good people in government had been a cardinal point of Stevenson's campaign. He had promised to improve the quality of the state's personnel. And on no phase of his administration did he spend more

painstaking care than on the selection of personnel.

The problems the new governor faced, in this respect, were typical of American Government. For the most part they stemmed from the fact that the salaries paid key officials were pitifully small when measured against the responsibilities those officials must shoulder. . . .

It is a general rule of personnel management that if you pay less than the going wage you'll get, on the average, less than you pay for, whereas if you pay more, and can choose your employees from among many competing applicants, you're very likely to get more than you pay for. Failure to apply the general rule to public administration is by no means due wholly to popular ignorance. It is due also, and perhaps equally, to the fact that certain elements have a vested interest in corrupt, inefficient government. There are men who shout loudly for economy in government salaries, precisely because they profit personally from a system that virtually ensures mediocrity and venality among public servants. . . .

Occasionally the new governor could obtain a good man with little effort. On the day after his election, he received some 250 telegrams urging him to appoint one Leonard Schwartz of Edwardsville to be director of the Department of Conservation. This aroused suspicions of a political deal, but when Stevenson investigated he found that the wires came from sportsmen's clubs and that Schwartz was a nationally known writer for outdoor magazines, an organizer and former president of the Illinois Federation of Sportsmen's Clubs, and had helped to raise hundreds of quail and pheasant each year for Illinois hunt-

[1] See *A Model State Civil Service Law*. The National Civil Service League and the National Municipal League, 1953.

[2] "The National Guard—Time for a Change." *Time*, October 20, 1967. Copyright Time Inc. 1967.

[3] Reprinted by permission of G. P. Putnam's Sons from THE POLITICS OF HONOR: A BIOGRAPHY OF ADLAI E. STEVENSON by Kenneth S. Davis. Copyright © 1957, 1967 by Kenneth S. Davis.

ers. The appointment was made and Schwartz did an excellent job.

Generally, however, appointment making was an arduous process during which the governor drew heavily upon the advice and good will of his long-time friends. . . .

Another position for which the governor was particularly anxious to find an outstanding man was that of director of the Public Welfare Department, by far the largest of all departments in Illinois government. . . . (He appointed Fred Hoehler, executive director of the Chicago Community Fund, at a reduction in salary from $18,000 a year to $8,000 a year.)

The Welfare Department, with a biennial budget of some $125,000,000 and a payroll of nearly twelve thousand people, had in its jurisdiction children's hospitals, mental hospitals, correctional institutions, sanatoriums, schools for the deaf and blind—twenty-four institutions in all. These cared for some fifty thousand persons and had theretofore been staffed in many professional positions by political appointees. Hoehler changed this. He insisted that Public Welfare should be a career service staffed by professionals who were chosen and promoted on the basis of professional competence. Stevenson agreed and gave Hoehler full backing, despite loud protests by certain Democratic politicians who felt themselves robbed thereby of the fruits of party victory. . .

* * *

Governments are plagued with the problem of what to do for those who have served in the armed forces . . . every state operating under a state-wide merit system has established, usually by statute, some provision for veteran preference. Disabled veterans are usually granted ten additional points. . . .

After the applicants have been . . . subjected to a series of examinations the personnel agency . . . has the responsibility of preparing a list of eligible candidates. This register, which is a listing of the candidates who passed according to their relative standings as indicated by individual scores, is usually based on the following items: (1) scores on written and oral tests; (2) records of education and experience; (3) results from personal interviews or investigations; and (4) in some instances the addition of veterans' preference points. . . .

Appointments are then made from these lists of eligible candidates. In filling a position the department or agency having the vacancy on its staff forwards a requisition or request for certification to the central employment agency which maintains the eligible lists. Upon receiving a requisition the personnel agency then certifies to the appointing officers within the department or agency the names of eligibles from the register. The exact number that is certified depends upon the law or rule of the personnel system. A number of states follow the "rule of three" by which only the names of the three persons receiving the highest scores will be sent to the appointing authority. In some services the personnel agency is required to submit only the highest-ranking name on the list while others allow a larger group to be certified. Many of the jurisdictions permit an appointing authority to reject the first list of certified names "for cause" and to request another group of eligibles.[1]

● What are your views of the civil service?
● How does your state deal with these matters?

1 Russell M. Ross and Kenneth F. Millsap—STATE AND LOCAL GOVERNMENT AND ADMINISTRATION Copyright © 1966 The Ronald Press Company, New York, pp. 395-396.

5

LOCAL GOVERNMENT

City of Philadelphia

Mention that the study of local government can be very interesting today because there are so many changes and new approaches occurring at this level.

The picture on the opposite page is of Mayor Frank Rizzo of Philadelphia. Philadelphia is the fourth largest city in the U.S.

Local governments continue to be an important influence in the lives of all people. While state governments have become more important and powerful, and while the national government is assuming more and more direction of the lives of citizens through new and expanding programs, local governments have not become less important. Even though some local governments, such as townships and counties in some states, are being eliminated or are having their powers reduced, the over-all importance of local governments remains and is increasing.

Local government is much the same throughout the nation. The organization of local government differs, however, especially as one moves from one section of the country to another. There are counties, towns, townships, villages, boroughs, and cities. The names are not the same throughout the nation. But even where the names are the same, the form of government may vary.

Most states have counties. In New England the town is a chief unit of local government. The Middle West has townships. Everywhere there are cities and villages. Mayors, councilmen, selectmen, clerks, treasurers, assessors, supervisors, sheriffs, and still other officials carry out the functions of local government and provide its services for the millions of people.

Local governments are of many kinds and sizes. They vary from the crossroads hamlets of a few dozen inhabitants to New York City with its millions of people. Size somewhat but not completely determines the way in which a unit of local government is organized. Bigness also has nothing to do with the goodness of local government. Size by itself does not make local government either good or bad.

Local governments, especially in large cities and in metropolitan areas, are facing almost insurmountable problems. Chief among the causes are the inequities resulting from the extremes of poverty and wealth, the racial conflicts, the rapid urbanization, and the concentration of people. Many local governments are striving to meet these conditions and to solve their problems. At the same time they are turning to state and national governments for assistance. The inability of local governments to raise enough local tax money to carry on their programs makes this assistance necessary.

This unit deals with all types of local governments, their powers and duties, and problems facing them.

Chapter 19 describes the government of cities and gives the three types of city government.

Chapter 20 deals with county government, its organization, and suggestions for changes.

Chapter 21 treats the government of towns, townships, and villages.

Chapter 22 considers certain problems of local governments, especially those of cities and metropolitan areas.

407

CHARTER—a written document similar to a constitution; a statement of the rules and regulations and source of power under which a local government or a corporation operates.

COMMISSION—the group of persons elected to operate the city government and to make its laws under the commission form of government.

COUNCIL—the legislative branch of city government, especially in the mayor-council type of government.

ENVIRONMENT—conditions or circumstances surrounding a person or place.

HOME RULE—power granted by a state to its cities to write their own charters and to make changes in them without needing approval from the legislature.

LONG BALLOT—a ballot containing many offices, candidates, and issues.

ORDINANCE—a law or regulation passed by a city council or commission.

POLITICAL MACHINE—a political organization, usually within a political party, which has great influence over elected officials and in the selection of candidates.

STRONG MAYOR—designation given the chief executive in the mayor-council type of city government when the mayor has great power, when there are few other elected administrators, and when other officials are responsible to him.

URBANIZATION—the process of people moving from rural areas to or near large cities; the quality of taking on characteristics of a city.

WEAK MAYOR—opposite of the strong mayor; he has little power, there are many other elected officials who are not responsible to him.

THE LANGUAGE OF GOVERNMENT

19

The City

All persons in the United States, except residents of the District of Columbia, live under three systems of government: national, state, and local. One national government, fifty state governments, and thousands of local governments make up the structure of government. Of these three systems, the local governments are closest to the people. The county seat, the city hall, and the town hall are frequented by more citizens than are the state or national capitals. The local officials are usually better known.

NUMBER OF LOCAL GOVERNMENTS

The Bureau of the Census reports the following number of local government units in the country in a recent year:

Counties	3,049
Townships	17,105
Municipalities	18,048
School Districts	21,782
Special Districts	21,264
Total	81,248

This means an average of about 1,625 local governments for each of the states. Most students of government agree that this number is too large for the operation of good government. However, during the past several decades the number of local governments has been reduced considerably. In 1942, for example, the number was more than 155,000. The reduction to the present number has been brought about largely through the consolidation of school districts. This reduction in the number of school districts is continuing.

But running your own government is an American tradition, and people generally want to keep their small local units of government. Many people oppose any move to combine several small units into a larger one, even though the larger unit could give them better and more efficient services. They want to keep the small unit going, because it is close to home. They can see it carry on its daily operations.

Local governments are of many kinds.

They differ somewhat in various parts of the country. The relationships of the local units to the state government also vary from state to state. The type of local government which involves more people directly than any other is the city.

THE GROWTH
OF CITIES
The automobile, economic life, opportunities for employment, and cultural advantages are factors which have been bringing people closer together and concentrating population in large urban centers. Urbanization has created huge metropolitan areas with their large central cities and surrounding complex of suburbs.

Today more than 70 per cent of the people of the United States live in cities and urban areas. This is very different from the three out of every one hundred people who lived in cities at the beginning of our nation in 1789. The growth of American cities has come mainly since 1850 and has

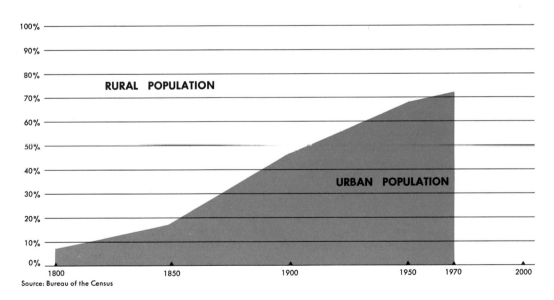

Source: Bureau of the Census

The graph shows the tremendous increase in the percentage of Americans living in urban areas. What are some of the reasons for this change?

Office buildings, stores, and factories seem to blend into each other in this aerial view of downtown Atlanta, Georgia. Why are urban areas growing? (Atlanta Chamber of Commerce)

been the result of several factors, including inventions, immigration, increased farm production, and the population explosion.

The many mechanical inventions and the growth of factories have made it possible for people to earn a living by producing goods in large quantities. Immigration from Europe during the nineteenth century and the first part of the twentieth brought to the United States many workers for these factories. Large numbers of them settled in the cities where they could find employment.

Because of new methods of farming and the invention of farm machinery, fewer people were needed to raise the necessary food for a growing population. Consequently many people from farm areas moved to the city. To these factors should

be added the population explosion. As the birth rate increased more people tended to live in urban areas.

All of these factors combined to bring about a rapid rise in the proportion of Americans living in cities. This rise is continuing as more and more people are crowding into the cities and suburbs.

CITY PROBLEMS   The growth of cities brought with it many problems. As more and more people moved into cities, the difficulties of living together became greater. From the beginning of time people have joined together to help solve common problems. By joining together they were able to provide needed protection and other services of

Invite a leader of the city government to discuss the problems of government in this community. Have students prepared to question and comment.

Mass production and assembly-line methods are used in the manufacture of many different products —from chocolate (left) to automobiles (right). How does this relate to the growth of cities? (Left, Hershey Foods Corporation; right, Ford Motor Company)

various kinds. As towns and cities developed, problems could be solved better and more rapidly through cooperative efforts.

But having many people live close together not only helps to solve common problems, it also creates some. The city of today is a place of great contrasts. It provides a fine life in many respects for many people. At the same time it is a poor living environment for many others. City government has the responsibility of improving the conditions of living for all people within its limits.

City government was once looked upon as the darkest spot in American political and governmental life. Dishonesty, inefficiency, and the worst kind of politics were common. In this century, however, reform movements were started. Tremendous gains were made in reforming city government. Today many American cities are well governed. The improvements in city government have taken place during the period when cities were growing very rapidly. In spite of the growth of cities, the quality of their governments became better.

But while they are better governed, cities have deteriorated in many other ways. The following quotation from "Crisis in the City" portrays the problem.

Streets choked with autos, trucks, and buses . . .

Aging buildings blackened by soot and exhaust fumes . . .

Slum districts jammed with low-income workers, immigrants, itinerants . . .

Shrinking tax funds and inadequate representation in Federal and state governments.

This is the picture of most of America's big cities. . . . It is not a happy picture—and it is one that may get worse before it gets better, as the U.S. population continues to *rise* and *shift*.[1]

The concentration of people in cities has also brought racial problems as well as conflicts among people of different nationalities. Today's cities are places of great wealth, but also of extreme poverty. Issues such as slum housing, unemployment, inadequate transportation, and crowded schools face them. Many of these have resulted

---

[1] From *Senior Scholastic*. © 1960 Scholastic Magazines, Inc.

Discuss the political machines that ran many of our cities in the past. (See Chapter 7, pages 138 and 139.)

This is an aerial view of Reston, Virginia, a new city near Washington, D.C. Reston was carefully planned to make the best and most orderly use of the available land. (Blue Ridge Aerial Surveys)

from the population explosion and the great influx of people. If our cities are to survive as decent places in which to live, they must solve these and similar problems that will be further discussed in Chapter 22.

SERVICES OF CITY GOVERNMENTS   Many of the services which people want for themselves can be better supplied by their city government than by individuals or by private businesses.

As cities grow larger and more crowded, the problem of waste disposal becomes more and more acute. How is such waste disposed of in your community? (Pennsylvania Dept. of Health)

Ask the student to consider what services his local government supplies.

Former Mayor Cavanagh (center) of Detroit, Michigan examines the design for the first of several urban renewal projects for low-income housing. Urban renewal has proved to be an important factor in efforts to revitalize our crowded cities. (City of Detroit)

This is the Port Authority Bus Terminal in New York City. Notice the provision for parking on the roof to help relieve congestion in nearby streets. (The Port of New York Authority)

These services have increased greatly over the years.

The services of city governments are of many kinds. They are services which the majority of people need and want. They are carried on by the city because they can be furnished more readily by people working together as a group than by having each person or family supply them.

Among these services are police and fire protection; rubbish and garbage disposal; traffic regulation; provision of sanitation facilities; street and sidewalk construction and maintenance; establishment of parks, boulevards, and recreation areas; inspection of food establishments and restaurants; regulation of weights and measures; control of communicable diseases; welfare aid; and establishment and maintenance of schools.

Each of these services would be too costly if each household had to supply it for itself. By cooperating under a city government, the cost of these services to each individual is reduced and more and better services can be supplied.

People living in small communities or in rural areas do not need as many services as do people crowded together in large cities. And it is not possible to furnish some services to rural communities. For example, a city pumps water to each home, while the farmer supplies his own water from a well dug on his land. Again, if the city dweller does not have a garbage grinder, he must have his garbage picked up regularly by a city department or this garbage becomes a health menace and a breeding place for insects and rats. The farmer buries his garbage in the ground.

It would be possible to indicate why the other city services are needed and why they are furnished through a city government. But these samples are perhaps enough to show the importance of good city government. That government is good which supplies needed and wanted services effectively and economically.

THE CITY CHARTER

The city operates under a *charter* granted by the state. The charter is to the city what a constitution is to a state or the nation. It sets forth the rules and regulations for the operation of the city government.

In some states an area must have at least 10,000 people to become a city; in others, as few as 200 are enough. The particular conditions and procedures vary with different states. When an area of the state has at least the minimum number of people, it can apply to the state to be incorporated as a city.

In some states all cities have charters which are very much alike. In other states special charters are granted to each city. In still other cases each city may write its own charter, including whatever it wishes as long as nothing conflicts with the state or national constitutions. Cities having this latter type of charter are called *home-rule cities*.

The form and the functions of the city government are described in the charter. The charter can be changed or revoked by the state, but this is rarely done. However, cities frequently find themselves in the situation of having to ask the state legislature for permission to do certain things and to carry on some activities not included in their charters. This has been irritating to some cities which feel that the state legislature has too much control over them.

As cities have grown in size and importance, they have tried to free themselves of a measure of the control exercised by the state. The result has been a growth in the number of home-rule cities. In the states where cities operate under home rule, each

Old and new city halls are contrasted here. At the right is Philadelphia's City Hall, an old landmark to residents of that city. In the left-hand photograph Boston's new City Hall is seen in the left foreground. (Right, Philadelphia Convention and Tourist Bureau; left, Boston Redevelopment Authority)

city writes its own charter. As has already been mentioned, in those states permitting them, the only requirement of a home-rule charter is that it contain no provisions which conflict with the state constitution. Two thirds of the states now grant home rule.

Citizens of our large cities have been especially pleased with the opportunity for home rule. This has freed them from the necessity of going to the legislature every time they wish to make a change in their city government not specifically stated in the charter. On the other hand, some people are opposed to complete home rule, maintaining that the state government should keep some control over the local governments within the state.

TYPES OF CITY GOVERNMENT

How are cities organized so that government serves the people well? We have seen that the national and state governments have three branches: executive, legislative, and judicial. The city governments too have these three branches, although they are not always as clearly defined as they are for the states and the nation.

Over the years city governments have experimented with different forms of organization in order to provide efficient and effective services. The problems of city government are many. As yet cities have not learned to solve all of them by any single type of government organization. The study and experimentation are still

Emphasize how experimentation has led to new forms of city government.

415

John Lindsay was elected mayor of New York City in 1965 at the age of 43. A Republican in a predominantly Democratic city, he succeeded Democrat Robert Wagner who had held the office for three terms. Lindsay had left his seat in Congress to take on the job which Mayor Wagner had called "the second most demanding public job in the nation."

The new mayor became interested in Republican politics in 1948. In 1952 he headed a group of young Republicans and helped to found "Youth for Eisenhower." In 1958 he was elected to Congress from New York's Seventeenth Congressional District, which is on the east side of Manhattan Island, and was re-elected four times. In Congress he had a reputation of being a liberal and often voted on the side of liberal Democrats.

As Mayor of New York, he worked to solve the city's problems, of which there were many. Some of the factors which confronted him were:

New York has a budget of about four billion dollars. But most of this money is legally earmarked for certain agencies or projects or is absolutely needed to carry on an orderly society.

The city has nearly 300,000 civil service employees. But there are only about 350 appointive positions, so the mayor must work through the established bureaucracy.

The city includes places of the greatest concentration of wealth (Wall Street, for example) and at the same time areas of deepest poverty (Harlem, for example).

There has been a large influx of people from low-income groups into the city and at the same time a corresponding exodus of middle-income families. Nearly a million middle-class persons left New York City in the past twenty years.

A thousand miles to the west, Mayor Richard Daley at age 69 was confronted with similar factors and was trying to solve the problems they create in the nation's second city, Chicago. Daley, a Democrat, was elected to his fifth term as mayor in 1971 by the biggest majority in his political life. His majority of more than 400,000 votes gave him another landside victory over a Republican opponent.

He was the recognized leader of the Democratic political organization of Chicago. As such he was sometimes called "the last of the big city bosses." As mayor and as party leader, Daley controlled some 30,000 patronage jobs in Chicago, providing him with many opportunities to appoint people to carry out his programs for Chicago and to reward political workers. In contrast, New York's mayor could appoint only a few hundred people. Much of Chicago's progress in public transportation, business development, expressway system construction, new skyscrapers, and civic development during the past decade has either been initiated by Daley and his administrators or has been effectively helped by them.

Daley began his political career at the local level, struggling over the years to advance from precinct worker to mayor. Along the way he was also a state senator and served as financial adviser to Adlai Stevenson when the latter was governor of Illinois.

These are two big city mayors—Lindsay and Daley. One, a former Republican turned Democrat, is a relative newcomer to municipal administration; the other, a Democrat, has spent a lifetime in municipal government. They are different in many ways, but both have stated similar goals, which they share with many other mayors across the nation—to improve living for the residents of our cities where so many of the nation's people are.

going on. Very few cities have a government structure exactly the same as that of another city. In general, however, the different types of city government can be classified in three ways: mayor-council, commission, and city manager.

THE MAYOR-COUNCIL TYPE. The form of city government which is most nearly like the national and state governments is the mayor-council type. It is also the oldest and most widely used type of city government. More than half of our

MAYOR-COUNCIL TYPE (weak mayor)

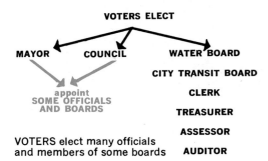

VOTERS ELECT

MAYOR   COUNCIL   WATER BOARD
CITY TRANSIT BOARD
appoint
SOME OFFICIALS
AND BOARDS
CLERK
TREASURER
ASSESSOR
VOTERS elect many officials
and members of some boards   AUDITOR

MAYOR-COUNCIL TYPE (strong mayor)

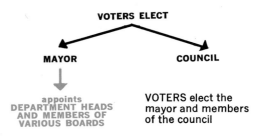

VOTERS ELECT

MAYOR   COUNCIL

appoints
DEPARTMENT HEADS
AND MEMBERS OF
VARIOUS BOARDS

VOTERS elect the
mayor and members
of the council

cities have this type of government. It has, however, a number of important defects. These are related primarily to the diffusion of administrative authority. Some cities have made progress in eliminating the defects of their mayor-council form of government by strengthening the power of the mayor.

THE MAYOR. The mayor is the chief executive, elected by the people for a two-to-four-year term. The extent of his power and duties depends upon whether the *weak-mayor* or the *strong-mayor* type of government is used. In the weak-mayor type he makes few appointments and has little power over the other administrative officials. In the strong-mayor type he appoints many officials, and the other administrators are responsible to him.

The position of the mayor in the weak-mayor type is somewhat like that of the governor in many state governments; the strong-mayor type is patterned after the relation of the President to his Cabinet and the executive departments.

The mayor has the power to sign or veto measures passed by the council. Usually the council may override the mayor's veto by a two-thirds vote. In a strong-mayor type of government the council will be more likely to accept suggestions from the mayor; the council members will also often ask advice

from the mayor and his administrative heads on issues being considered by the council. They will pay attention to his recommendations in setting the city budget, in voting on appropriation measures, and in passing city ordinances. This cooperation between mayor and council usually leads to good government giving fine services.

Sometimes, however, disagreements arise between the mayor and the council. These can lead to bitter conflicts in which the city services suffer and citizens may lose respect for their government. Such conflicts are often settled only when the voters at the next election choose a new mayor or council or both who will cooperate in providing good government.

In the weak-mayor type, on the other hand, the council may pay little or no attention to the mayor. Further, in the weak-mayor type other administrative officials feel little responsibility to the mayor and his program, since many of them are elected directly by the people in the same manner as the mayor. The weak-mayor type has often resulted in poor government and graft and corruption, because there is no single person responsible for administration in the government.

There has been a tendency for more cities to develop strong-mayor types of govern-

Indianapolis and Marion County, Indiana, have joined to form one city-county governmental unit. Here the twenty-nine-member city-county council meets. Twenty-five members are elected from single-member districts and four at-large. (Dennis Bogden/City of Indianapolis)

ment, so that responsibility can be concentrated in a single administrative head. The people then have a chance to give praise or blame for success or failure.

THE COUNCIL. The members of the council (sometimes called aldermen) are elected by the people for terms of from one to four years. Their number and their manner of election vary considerably from city to city. Some cities have a small council of from five to nine members, while others have as many as fifty members on their council. The smaller-sized councils seem to be gaining in popularity, because it is easier for the citizens to follow the actions of individual councilmen if there are only a few of them.

Some cities elect their councilmen at large, that is, from the city as a whole. Others elect them by districts, each ward or district electing its representative to the council. Both systems have advantages and disadvantages. When members are elected

at large, they usually feel a greater responsibility for the total city and that they are representing the whole city. They may be more inclined to work for the good of *all* people. On the other hand, areas of the city that do not have persons on the council from their areas sometimes believe they are not being represented.

In elections at large, also, there are frequently a great many candidates, making it difficult for the people to vote intelligently. For example, in a recent primary in a large city in which eighteen candidates were to be nominated for the council, there were nearly 300 names on the ballot.

> *Each local unit should have a single chief-executive, either elected by the people or appointed by the local legislative body, with all administrative agencies and personnel fully responsible to him; election of department heads should be halted.*
>
> —COMMITTEE FOR ECONOMIC DEVELOPMENT, *Modernizing Local Government*, 1966, p. 17.

On the other hand, in those cities where councilmen are elected by wards, there may be fewer candidates and the people may know them better. But the councilmen may too frequently be concerned only about their own wards. They seem to feel first responsibility to the people who elected them and may not act in the best interests of the whole city.

The council is usually a one-house legislature with a variety of duties. It appropriates money, votes on expenditures, sets up a budget (sometimes in cooperation with the mayor and his administrative heads), passes city ordinances, and fixes tax rates. Whatever it does must conform to the constitution and laws of the state as well as to the city charter.

Council members are frequently poorly paid, which leads to several shortcomings in the operation of the council. Serving on the council is often a part-time job, for members must earn a living doing other work. Frequently highly qualified persons do not run for the council.

This condition is being corrected, however, with the greater emphasis on the improvement of city government. More cities are paying their councilmen a larger salary in keeping with the importance of the job and are expecting better work from the council.

A DAY IN THE LIFE OF A COUNCILMAN

Being a councilman is a full-time job for members of the councils of our large cities. The following description condensed from a newspaper article of one of the big city papers tells this story:

The councilmen are up at 7, leave the house at 8, after receiving several telephone calls from taxpayers; they spend an hour or so touring various sections on their way to the city hall.

"I live in the far north section," one of the councilmen said, "and I get downtown by such devious routes as the extreme east side or the far west side.

"I have to keep posted on what is happening in the various sections of town, or visit projects pending before the council."

From 9 until council committee meeting time at 10:30, they answer correspondence and telephone calls.

A freshman councilman said that in that 90 minutes of his first day on the job, he answered 22 telephone calls and made 10 of his own to check up on matters brought to his attention by taxpayers.

Another said his telephone calls start at 7 A.M. and do not end until 12 midnight.

Morning council sessions seldom end before noon and often last until 1 P.M.

When the county board of supervisors is in session, councilmen go directly to the county sessions from the city hall meetings.

In addition, they must attend supervisors' committee meetings many afternoons.

For more than eight weeks of the year they sit all day studying the budget and as a board of review on tax assessments.

When these functions are not going on, they either answer telephone calls or mail, study matters pending before the council, or attend the many affairs with which all elected officials are plagued.

The council president said he spent 60 to 70 hours studying the new budget before it was discussed by the council.

Never an evening passes but they must

attend from one to three meetings of civic organizations which invite them.

"These organizations have the right to demand reports from city officials," said the president, "and we have an obligation to respond."

"I will admit that there is some politicking involved in this phase of the job," added another member, "but there also is an obligation. In addition, it gives us the opportunity to get out and meet with groups and learn what they want or need."[1]

CRITICISM. There has been much criticism of the mayor-council form of city government. However, the strong-mayor type with a small council is giving many cities an efficient and businesslike government. Under this system the criticisms of the mayor-council type of government are gradually becoming fewer. But the weak-mayor type, in which the mayor has little control over administrative heads, can lead to abuses and shortcomings in government.

The history of municipal government includes many instances of a political boss taking over control. Graft, poor management, and inefficient government have been the result; each citizen loses. Greater interest on the part of citizens in better municipal government has helped to correct these abuses in many cities.

Another serious fault of the mayor-council type of municipal government has been the so-called *long ballot* in which voters are asked to elect officials for many offices. Because voters cannot learn to know all candidates, they frequently choose poor officials.

Name candidates or candidates of political machines get control of city offices. A name candidate is a person having the same last name as that of a well-known person.

[1] Adapted from an article by Harold Schachern in the Detroit *News*.

COMMISSION TYPE

VOTERS ELECT the members of the commission

↓

COMMISSION—each commission member is the head of a department

↓

DEPARTMENTS

1 2 3 4 5

Voters often vote for the name because they have heard it frequently, even though the person on the ballot is not the same person whose name has been in the news.

A shortened ballot with fewer officials to be elected helps to improve the quality of the candidates. Voters can study the records of candidates and make more intelligent choices at the election. When fewer officials are elected, the mayor makes many appointments. The administrative heads are responsible to him, and the people hold him accountable for the operation of the government.

THE COMMISSION TYPE. In 1900 a tidal wave in the Gulf of Mexico drowned about one of every six people of the 37,000 living in Galveston, Texas. The city, under a mayor-council government, had been poorly managed. The new problems following the death and destruction from the tidal wave were too great for the city government, and the people demanded a new government to deal with the emergency. The state legislature gave Galveston a new charter which provided for a commission of five members with power to make the laws and to administer the government of the city.

From tragedy a new type of city government was born. It had been set up as a temporary government to deal with the emergency, but it worked so well that it was soon copied in other places. Among them was Des Moines, Iowa, which is given credit for improving the commission type of government by adding the initiative, referendum and recall, nonpartisan elections, and the merit system.

EXECUTIVE POWERS. The commission type of government has no single executive head. Instead there are usually five commissioners, one of whom is designated as mayor. He has, however, no more power than the other commissioners, except that he presides at the commission meetings and represents the city at official functions. The commissioners have both executive and legislative powers.

Each commissioner is made the administrative head of a department, such as public safety, parks and public property, finance, public health and welfare, and streets and public improvements. This is both an advantage and a disadvantage. On the one hand, the work of each commissioner can be readily judged in terms of the department which he administers. On the other hand, often a commissioner will be concerned with his department only and will try to improve and expand it at the expense of the other departments of the city government.

Sometimes, too, the election may result in having two commissioners elected who are well qualified to head the same department but not qualified to head another department. For example, both may be good administrators of public safety but not of finance. As a result there may be no commissioner who is well qualified to administer the department of finance.

LEGISLATIVE POWERS. The commissioners as a group are also the legislative body. They meet regularly to pass city laws, called *ordinances*. They prepare and approve the budget. They review assessments. They hold public hearings. They do the legislative work of a city council.

People who favor the commission type of government emphasize the facts that only a small number of people are elected, that citizens can more easily watch those in charge of city government, and that responsibility for good or bad government can be readily fixed. The commissioners are elected from the city at large. Since there are only a few of them, they can be paid higher salaries than could be paid if there were many elected officials plus a large council receiving smaller salaries. For this reason better people can be attracted to run for office.

Opponents of the commission type point out two important facts. First, the commissioner who is in charge of a certain department is not necessarily an expert in that field. As was noted before, a commissioner who might have been good at public safety may be poor at finance. But one of the commissioners must head the department of finance. This may lead to poor and costly administration.

Second, the same commissioners make laws and enforce them. They appropriate money and spend it. In our national and state governments and in many city governments, the legislative branch passes laws and appropriates the money, but the executive branch administers the laws and spends the money. In these systems of government, the executive cannot spend money unless the legislators vote money for a particular purpose. The commission type of city government does not have this check on the handling of money. The same persons do both.

THE CITY-MANAGER TYPE. The city-manager type of city government was started by the citizens of Staunton, Virginia, in 1907 when that city tried to make its government more efficient. The council appointed a manager to run the city government. He was placed in charge of administering the city; he could appoint and dismiss employees. He operated the city as

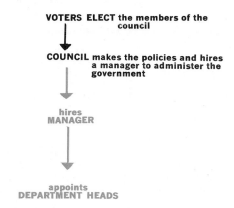

VOTERS ELECT the members of the council

COUNCIL makes the policies and hires a manager to administer the government

hires
MANAGER

appoints
DEPARTMENT HEADS

a business manager operates a business. He cut expenses and provided greater services. As a result, this type of government was soon copied by other cities. Des Moines adopted the city-manager system in 1949, as did Galveston in 1960. Today more than 2,000 cities and towns operate under some form of city-manager government.

In the city-manager cities there is usually a council or commission of three or five persons. One of them may be the mayor as in the commission type. Here again he conducts the meetings and represents the city in official capacities, but he has no more power than the other members.

The council acts as a kind of board of directors and sets the policies for the city government. It is the legislative branch. To carry out these policies, the council hires an expert, a city manager. This person has made city administration his career; he usually has had college training for his job.

Very often he is not a local person; the council hires the best man it can get to do the job. He has no stated term of office, but he may be removed by the council or by recall of the voters if the city charter has such a provision.

The city-manager type of government has

certain advantages over the commission type. The council makes the policies, and the city manager carries them out. The members of the council concern themselves with the whole city government not with just a single department, as each member does in the commission type.

The manager is trained and experienced in city administration and is usually better qualified to run the city government than are the commissioners. Responsibility for administration is centered in one person, and he can quickly be removed if he is doing an unsatisfactory job.

But the city manager differs from the mayor in the mayor-council type. He has no veto over the council's actions. If he disagrees with council policies, he has usually only two choices of action. He may try to change the members' ideas or he may resign and seek employment elsewhere. In the case of the strong mayor-council type, of city government, disagreements sometimes arise between mayor and council which are settled only by the voters at the next election.

The city-manager type, however, does not provide for this division of the executive and legislative branches. The voters do not elect the chief city executive. For this reason, some people prefer the strong mayor-council type over the city-manager type. This is especially true for very large cities; up to the present time, none of the large cities over 1,000,000 has hired a city manager.

JUDICIAL BRANCH   Throughout this chapter the discussion has emphasized the executive and legislative branches and activities. Since cities and other local governments are parts of states, judicial activities are the responsibility of the state court system. There are, however, separate municipal courts in most cities. (See Chapter 17.)

WASHINGTON, D. C.

In a special class by itself is the capital city of our nation, Washington, District of Columbia. It is unique in that while it is within the United States, it is not a part of any state. The seventy-four square miles of the District were given to the national government by the state of Maryland. It is also unique in that the Constitution provides that Congress has the exclusive power to legislate for the District (Article I, Section 8, Clause 17).

Under the President's authority to reorganize executive agencies of the federal government (see Chapter 13), President Johnson proposed a new form of government for the city of Washington in 1967. This proposal was accepted by the Congress and was put into effect that year. Washington now has a commissioner, vice-commissioner, and a council of nine members, all appointed by the President and confirmed by the Senate.

Before 1967 the administration of the District had been by a three-member commission, the commission also appointed by the President with Senate approval. Two members of the commission were civilians having three-year terms. The third was an engineer with a term of indefinite length. These three commissioners were the executives of the system. Congress, however, retained the main legislative functions.

This system had been in effect since 1878. Under it the citizens of the District had no vote and no voice in the operation of their city. While the new system does not yet give them the right to vote for the commissioner and the members of the council, it is a step in that direction. But much more needs to be done to give these citizens true citizenship.

One step toward giving residents of the District the vote was started in 1960 when

Three Negro mayors of major American cities met in 1967 with Robert Weaver, then Secretary of Housing and Urban Development. They are, from left to right: Weaver; Mayor Carl B. Stokes, of Cleveland; Mayor-Commissioner Walter Washington, of Washington, D.C.; and Mayor Richard G. Hatcher, of Gary, Indiana. (UPI photo)

Congress initiated a constitutional amendment allowing the District to choose three presidential electors. The amendment was ratified by the needed thirty-eight states in less than a year and became the Twenty-third Amendment to the Constitution. Eligible citizens of Washington, D. C., were then able to vote for President and Vice President in 1964 for the first time in history. But they do not vote for local officials.

This lack of complete voting rights has caused great controversy over the years. The nearly one million people in our capital city are denied the voting rights of citizens. This condition has not always been true in the area of local government. In the early years of the District the people elected a city council. Later they were allowed to elect a mayor. For fifty years, until 1871, the people elected the mayor and council. From 1871 to 1875 they elected a delegate to Congress.

But following the Civil War there was a period of inefficient government in the city which resulted in a great financial deficit. The conditions caused Congress first to set up a temporary government of commissioners. This was followed by the system which was in effect until 1967.

Proposals for a return to some form of home rule have been introduced in recent Congresses with the recommendation of the President. They have failed to pass apparently because of tax problems, the unwillingness of Southern congressmen to give the vote to the largely Negro population, and the feeling that the nation's capital should not be controlled by local politics.

The change in government of the District made in 1967 did not give it home rule, but in the words of the new commissioner it contains elements of "beginning the process of home rule." The first commissioner (mayor) is Walter E. Washington, a Negro housing expert. The capital thus became the first major city in the nation with a Negro mayor. The commissioner and assistant are appointed by the President with the consent of the Senate. The term of office is four years. Members of the council are appointed for staggered three-year terms. No more than six of the nine may be members of the same political party.

While the council has some legislative authority, general laws for the District continue to be made by Congress, which still also makes appropriations for the city. But the mayor has some authority regarding the distribution of funds. He is also in charge of the city departments.

The courts of the District consist of a federal court of appeals down through the usual courts to the police court. The judges are appointed by the President.

It is believed that the new form of government will provide greater efficiency and also a better avenue of communication between the growing Negro population of the city and its government. It is also hoped that the present system will eventually bring a return to the home rule enjoyed by the city before 1871. One such step was taken later in 1967 when Congress voted to permit the residents to elect the members of their school board. Before then members of the board were appointed by the federal district judges. Another step was taken in 1970 when Congress passed a bill that was signed by the President giving the District of Columbia a nonvoting delegate in the House of Representatives.

STUDY QUESTIONS

1. Why do many people wish to retain their small units of local government?

2. What factors account for the rapid rise of American cities?

3. What are some of the problems facing American cities?

CONCEPTS AND GENERALIZATIONS

1
The number of local governmental units has been greatly reduced during the past few decades.

2
Many units of local government survive because of the satisfaction many people get from operating a government close to home.

3
Factors which have contributed to the rapid growth of cities are immigration, inventions, increased farm production, and the population explosion.

4
The concentration of large numbers of people in urban areas has made possible improvement of services but has also created serious problems.

5
City governments provide a great variety of services.

6
Home rule gives cities opportunities to plan and provide services without interference from the state.

7
The three general types of city government are mayor-council, commission, and city manager.

8
In the mayor-council type of government the executive and legislative powers are generally separated, with the mayor having great power under the strong mayor type.

9
In the commission type the same persons have both executive and legislative powers.

10
In the city manager type the commission has legislative power and delegates executive power to a manager who is responsible to the commission.

11
The nation's capital, Washington, D.C., has a unique form of local government with a commissioner (somewhat like a city manager) and a council appointed by the President.

4. What are some of the important services of city government?

5. Why must the city government furnish certain services which are not furnished to persons in rural communities?

6. What is a city charter?

7. How does a community become a city?

8. Why do cities want home rule?

9. What are the three general types of city government?

10. What is the difference between the weak-mayor and the strong-mayor types of government?

11. What are the usual duties of city councils?

12. What helps to make the strong-mayor type of city government efficient?

13. How does the long ballot help political machines?

14. What are the strong points of the commission type of government?

15. Why is it generally unwise to have the same persons appropriate and disburse money?

16. How does the city-manager type of government differ from the commission type?

17. Why do some people prefer a strong mayor to a city manager?

18. How does Washington, D.C., differ from other cities in the United States?

19. What changes have been made in the government of Washington over the years?

20. Why has complete home rule not been given to the capital city of our nation?

IDEAS FOR DISCUSSION

1. Home rule leads to abuses on the part of some communities. Do you think that this is sufficient reason for doing away with home rule? Why?

2. Home rule allows a city to determine its own speed laws and other traffic regulations. This may cause some confusion because of different regulations in various cities. Should traffic laws be made uniform? Can this be achieved without eliminating home rule?

3. Discuss the advantages and disadvantages of electing councilmen (a) by districts and (b) at large.

4. How can citizens' interest in good government reduce graft and inefficiency?

5. There are some people who believe that in a strong-mayor government only the mayor should be elected in the executive branch; all other administrators, such as treasurer and clerk, should be appointed by him. Do you think that this arrangement would improve city government? Why?

6. "The commission type of government is not suited to large cities." Discuss this statement. Do you agree or disagree? Why?

7. One of the weaknesses of the commission type of government is that administrators sometimes head departments about which they have little knowledge. Do you think the manner of election should be changed to elect commissioners for special departments?

8. One of the chief differences between the operation of government in the United States and in some other countries is that we have fewer top administrators who have made a career of government work. Do you think we ought to have more career administrators? If so, should we encourage the spread of the city-manager type of government?

9. Full voting rights should not be denied any adult citizen of the United States. Do you agree? Discuss the statement as it applies to residents of the city of Washington, D.C.

THINGS TO DO

1. Use your state government manual to make a study of the number and kinds of local governments in your state.

2. What attempts have been made to reduce the number of local governments in your state? Make a chart or graph showing the number of local governments over a period of years.

3. Get a copy of a city charter. When was it adopted? What changes have been made since its adoption? Make a list of the important sections of the charter to determine its contents.

4. Study the type of government of cities in your state. Make a chart listing the cities in three columns: mayor-council, commission, city manager.

5. If you live in a city, have a committee of your class interview the mayor about changes he would like to make in the operation of your city government. Discuss these with your class.

6. Make a chart of the advantages and disadvantages of the several types of city government.

7. If your city or a neighboring city has a city manager, have a member of your class make an appointment to interview him about his position. Report to the class on the type of training and education needed by city managers.

8. Have members of the class assume the roles of city councilmen or city commissioners. Hold a mock council meeting in which you discuss an important issue of local government.

9. Prepare a bulletin board display of newspaper clippings dealing with the local issues being discussed and considered by the council and mayor or the city commission.

10. Make an appointment with your representative in Congress to get his views on granting home rule to the city of Washington and full voting rights to its citizens.

FURTHER READINGS

Adrian, Charles R., and Press, Charles, GOVERNING URBAN AMERICA. McGraw-Hill Book Co., 1972.

Gardiner, John A., THE POLITICS OF CORRUPTION. Basic Books, 1970.

Green, Constance McLaughlin, THE RISE OF URBAN AMERICA. Harper & Row, Publishers, Inc., 1965.

Jackson, Kenneth T., and Schultz, Stanley K., CITIES IN AMERICAN HISTORY. Random House, Inc., 1972. (Paperback edition)

Kotler, Milton, NEIGHBORHOOD GOVERNMENT: THE LOCAL FOUNDATIONS OF POLITICAL LIFE. Bobbs-Merrill, 1969.

Lavine, David, MAYOR AND THE CHANGING CITY. Random House, Inc., 1966.

Lowe, Jeanne, CITIES IN A RACE WITH TIME. Random House, Inc., 1967.

Matthews, Byron S., LOCAL GOVERNMENT. Nelson-Hall Co., 1970.

Robson, William C., and Regan, D. E., GREAT CITIES OF THE WORLD. Sage Publications, 1972.

Rogers, David, THE MANAGEMENT OF BIG CITIES: INTEREST GROUPS AND SOCIAL CHANGE STRATEGIES. Sage Publications, 1971.

Scientific American, CITIES. Alfred A. Knopf, Inc., 1965.

AUDIT—to examine and check accounts.

BOND—a contract by which a bonding or insurance agency guarantees that it will repay the city, county, or state for any financial loss because of dishonest or wrongful acts of an employee.

BOROUGH—a unit of local government; the term used for a county in Alaska.

CONSOLIDATION—the act of combining into one; the process of uniting several units of local government into one larger unit.

CORONER—county officer who investigates deaths under unusual or unnatural circumstances or where no doctor was in attendance.

COUNTY—a unit of local government; a subdivision of the state.

DEED—a document transferring ownership from one person to another.

INQUEST—an investigation or hearing, conducted by a coroner, into the circumstances of death from unnatural causes.

PARISH—the term used for a county in Louisiana.

REAL PROPERTY—land and buildings.

SHERIFF—county officer with specific court and jail duties; traditionally also the county law officer.

SHIRE—a British district similar to a county.

THE LANGUAGE
OF GOVERNMENT

20
The County

There is an important difference between counties and cities as units of local government. The city is a governmental unit established as the result of the request of the people living in the area to carry on the functions of local government. The county, on the other hand, is a geographical unit of land created by the state to carry on state governmental functions in the area. The county does, however, also serve in some ways as a local governmental unit. Especially for rural areas the county was, and in many places still is, the unit of government with which many people have their chief and greatest number of governmental contacts, both state and local.

HISTORICAL DEVELOPMENT
OF THE COUNTY
The county has an interesting historical development. Counties started in colonial days when colonies were subdivided into smaller units. The term itself was carried over from England, where this division of government existed.

In America the county became important in the South and, later, in the West. Here

Point out that much of American local government had its origin in England.

427

Many counties have rural areas like this one, where a county agricultural agent is helping a farmer look over his crop of oats. Why has county government been particularly important in rural areas? (USDA photo)

people lived far apart, and the large unit of government, the county, served them well. In New England, where people lived close together, the town was the important unit of local government. In the Middle States both the town and the county developed as local government units.

The names of several county officials are carried over from the early development of the counties of England. The county coroner gets his name from the "crowner" of England who represented the king (the crown) in the local area of government. The "shire-reeve" of England became the sheriff in America. The reeve was the overseer of the shire, the medieval name given to a piece of land, later called the county.

The purposes of the county divisions dif-

County government developed early in the western states. Shown here is the county courthouse at Independence, Missouri, in 1855. (Library of Congress)

fer considerably from state to state. In general, however, county officers are state agents who carry out state laws and functions. They bring the state services close to the people. In many states, counties also have powers and functions of local government.

In the state of Rhode Island the counties are not set up for local government; its five counties are solely judicial districts. Since 1959 Connecticut has had no county government; the governmental duties were turned over to the state, leaving the county as a geographic unit only. In Louisiana the counties are called *parishes*; in Alaska they are called *boroughs*.

The county government traditionally had several important functions and duties. It maintained law and order; it collected state and local taxes; it kept records of titles to land; it issued marriage licenses; it built and maintained roads; it provided health and welfare services; it administered justice; it conducted county, state, and national elections; it supervised schools; it took care of the property of persons who had died.

In some states, as the years have gone by, a number of these functions have been taken over by the state. Also, other units of local government now share some of these duties with counties. But in most counties today these traditional activities are still carried on by county officials.

In some cases purely local responsibilities have been given to county government. These include fire protection, land use planning and zoning, rubbish and sewage disposal, water supply, parks and recreation facilities, and libraries.

NUMBER AND SIZE
OF COUNTIES

There are more than 3,000 counties throughout the United States, which means an average of about sixty for each state. But there is little uniformity about them as to size and number. Some states have only a few counties, and others have many more than the average of sixty. Delaware has the fewest—3; and Texas has the most—254.

Counties also vary in size. The average county has almost 1,000 square miles. But some independent city-county areas in Virginia are only about one mile square, while San Bernardino County in California has more than 20,000 square miles and Alaska's are even larger.

Counties differ, too, in the number of people they contain. A few counties in the West have barely 200 people. Los Angeles County in California is the largest, having more than six million people.

But, large or small, counties as units of local government have some things in common. These include the officers and their governmental functions.

THE COUNTY
SEAT

The center of county government is the county seat, which is usually located in the central part of the county. This location was chosen so that it could easily be reached from all parts of the county. The county seat is to the county what the state capital is to the state.

Since counties developed during our horseback and horse-and-buggy stage, it was found desirable to lay out counties and to locate county seats in accord with those means of transportation. The county seat was usually a day's journey by horse from the farthest corner of the county.

At the county seat is located the county building or courthouse, which houses the county offices. Here are stored the county records. In this building the sessions of the county court are held. It may contain the county jail and sometimes living quarters

This is a view of the city of Dallas, Texas, which is also the county seat of Dallas County. Dallas recently built a modern County Government Center. Is county government important in this part of the country? (Dallas Chamber of Commerce)

for the sheriff or his deputy. Often, especially in rural areas, it is the most prominent building in the whole area and has become the symbol of local government.

THE COUNTY BOARD

The governing body of the county is the county board. It has different names in various sections of the nation. Common names are board of county supervisors, board of county commissioners, and county court. Altogether there are some twenty different titles used.

The duties of county boards vary too from state to state. Usually they levy taxes and appropriate money. Sometimes they are administrative boards and administer the affairs of the county.

The representatives in the state legislature from each county usually have control over legislation for the county, because the state legislature will usually pass laws affecting a particular county only if the legislators from that county approve it. Some county boards also have some limited legislative powers of their own given to them by the state legislature.

County boards are elected in different ways. In some counties the members of the board are elected at large; in others they are elected by districts, with each district having a representative on the board. The advantages and disadvantages of each method are similar to those in the election of city councilmen, discussed in Chapter 19. In a few states the township supervisors and

Jefferson County Courthouse in Louisville, Kentucky, is the center of county government and an impressive building built in 1859 in the Greek Revival style. (Louisville Chamber of Commerce)

In summary the Board adopts a budget, prescribes regulations for carrying out the county's duties, and often acts as administrator of county functions.

representatives from cities make up the county board; this accounts for the name board of supervisors.

In 1968 the U. S. Supreme Court ruled that local government units must have governing bodies elected on a one-man, one-vote basis. The effect of this decision may be to change the representation on county boards and also on boards or councils of other units of local government.

The term of office of members of county boards presently varies from two to eight years, with most boards having terms of four years. In Michigan for many years the term of office was the same as that of the township supervisors, who were also members of the county board of supervisors. In 1968 the state attorney general ruled that these individuals could not serve in dual roles. Persons elected to the county board had to give up any other local government office. In southern states the county judge, whose term of office is eight years, is also chairman of the county board.

The size of county boards varies too. Some boards have only one member, while a few have more than 100. The one-man boards exist in a number of counties in southern states where a judge is both judge and legislator for the county. The very large boards are in those counties in which the township supervisors form the county board. Both of these extremes are bad. A small number does not give representation to all parts of the county; a large number is not good for efficient operation of county affairs. About three-fourths of all counties have boards of three to seven members, which is a good size in the opinion of many political scientists.

State constitutions and laws or rules of the board itself determine how often a board meets. Many boards have monthly meetings. However, some small boards may meet regularly more frequently. On the other hand, some large boards meet only a few times each year and use committees to carry on the administration of the county.

COUNTY OFFICERS

The county does not have an executive head comparable to the President, the governor, or the mayor. Executive duties of the county are usually shared by many officials and boards. Some executive functions are performed by the county board. In addition, there are many officials, each of whom has a specialized executive job.

Some people feel that county government would be greatly improved if there were an executive who had the responsibility of administering the county government. This idea is growing, and a number of counties are experimenting with either elected or appointed executive heads. There are other people, however, who believe that the county does not need an executive and that the present practice of having several administrators carry on the many functions is good.

Altogether there are about twenty different elected administrative officials in different counties across the country. Most counties have at least six or more. Most of their duties are state functions which they carry out at the local level.

Often the county officials work independently of one another. This sometimes leads to difficulties and a lack of cooperation between county departments. That condition is especially likely to result if county officials of opposing parties are elected. County officers are ordinarily elected for two- or four-year terms, although there is some variation from state to state.

Most counties have similar duties to perform, but they are not always done by officials with the same titles. For example, in one state the county clerk issues marriage licenses, while in another state this same work is done by the clerk of the court. In another case the county auditor acts as secretary of the county board, although in most states this work is done by the county clerk. The paragraphs that follow will discuss the main county officials and their chief duties as found in many states.

THE SHERIFF. Most county sheriffs are elected by the people. In Rhode Island they are appointed. The work of the sheriff as the person who maintains peace and order has been popularly shown in "Western" movies and television shows. This may lead to wrong impressions, however, for many sheriffs have little to do with maintaining law and order. In cities and towns law enforcement is the duty of the local police departments and the constables. The sheriff's duty to keep peace and order is limited largely to the rural areas; even here it is gradually being reduced by the growth of state police departments.

The sheriff, however, has some other important duties in connection with the operation of the courts and in the supervision of the county jails. He carries out the orders of the court, notifies witnesses and members of the jury to appear in court, and maintains order in the courtroom. He is in charge of the county jail. He guards persons accused of crimes, brings them to court at the time of their trial, and carries out sentences imposed by judges.

The office of sheriff has been one of the most controversial government positions. There have been movements to abolish it because of the reduction in the sheriff's police duties. Some experts also think that the sheriff's court duties could be delegated to a person responsible to the county judge. His jail duties could be handled by a warden or an overseer.

Further opposition comes from the manner of paying the sheriff in many states—on a fee basis rather than a salary. This system is gradually being changed. The fees tended to become very large in the counties with large populations as sheriffs were paid for each order they carried out, for each meal served prisoners in jail, for each arrest made, and for the many other duties they performed. No one knew exactly how much money a sheriff earned, but there was a general feeling that the amount was large. This criticism of the sheriff's office has become weaker, however, as more and more states passed laws to pay the sheriff a salary rather than fees for his services.

THE COUNTY CLERK. About half of the states have county clerks. Among their common duties are to act as secretary of the county board, to keep county records and minutes of board meetings, to superintend the county buildings, to issue warrants on the treasurer, to receive and record claims against the county, to issue marriage licenses, to keep records of births and deaths, to assist in determining the county tax rate, to conduct local and state elections, and to issue various licenses in rural parts of the county. These are examples of the clerk's duties. However, a particular

---

County modernization should be pressed with special vigor, since counties—everywhere except in New England—have high but undeveloped potential for solving the problems of rural, urban, and most metropolitan communities.

Counties are less limited in area, population, and tax base than most local units, and consolidations could correct existing deficiencies in these respects. Their present legal powers are less adequate than those of municipalities, however. And county structural organizations and staffing powers are obsolete. If the nation is seriously concerned about stronger and better local government, as it should be, these weaknesses must be remedied to permit counties to play a major role.

—COMMITTEE FOR ECONOMIC DEVELOPMENT, *Modernizing Local Government*, 1966, p. 18.

A young couple has just kept an important appointment with the local county clerk. Marriage license in hand, they look forward to the wedding bells that soon will be ringing. (Alan Cliburn)

county clerk may not have all of these or he may have additional ones.

The county clerk is an important official and usually has a large staff of clerical workers to carry out the duties of his office. He is an elected person and as such he is independent of the county board, although he is often the secretary of the board. He must attend the board's meetings, but he has no vote. Because he is usually better informed than other officers on many county affairs, his suggestions are welcomed by county board members.

The work of the county clerk affects many persons, at least indirectly. In accordance with state laws, his office records their birth and, finally, their death. If they wish to marry, in many cases it is the county clerk who issues the license. The county clerk's office prepares the ballots for state and county elections and keeps a record of the returns in those elections.

THE CORONER. If a death occurs under unusual conditions or without the attendance of a doctor, it is the duty of the coroner to try to determine the cause. If there are mysterious circumstances, he is expected to begin an investigation at once. The purpose of the investigation is to determine whether a crime has been committed or whether there is suspicion of a crime. No one can compel him to make the investigation; others may urge him to do so, but he alone decides whether one is necessary.

If after his own preliminary investigation the coroner decides a fuller investigation is necessary, he holds an *inquest.* This is conducted by a coroner's jury, which usually consists of six persons. The inquest may be held either at the scene of the death, or in the coroner's office, or in the undertaker's establishment.

The coroner's jury listens to witnesses brought before it by the coroner. He cannot compel anyone to appear, but the jury listens to police officers and others who appear before it and who may know something about the circumstances of the person's death. The coroner himself is not a member of the jury, but he is in charge of the investigation.

The purpose of the inquest is to try to determine how the person died. The jury may make any one of a number of decisions: (1) The person's death was due to natural causes, an accident, or suicide. In this event the case is usually considered closed. (2) The person's death was the result of unnatural circumstances, such as poisoning, violence on the part of others, or foul play. If the jury has reason to suspect a particular individual or individuals, it names the person or persons. Arrest follows, and the prosecutor is expected to bring the accused to trial. (3) The person's death was due to some kind of foul play, but by an individual or individuals unknown to the jury. In this case the jury reports the facts, and urges the prosecutor and the police to continue a search for the guilty persons.

The coroner is elected by the people. Some political scientists think that his position should be abolished and his duties divided between the prosecutor and an appointed medical examiner. They base their conclusions on the fact that the coroner and the coroner's jury cannot acquit or convict anyone. The coroner or the jury merely suggests that a crime may have been committed. The prosecution must be done by the prosecutor in a court of law. In addition, the medical examiner would be better trained to undertake the necessary examinations into the causes of deaths.

Others believe that the office of the coroner should be retained but that the qualifications should be more exacting, so that he can become more effective in determining the cause of death. Many states are moving in this direction by requiring that the coroner be a licensed physician.

THE CLERK OF THE COURT. In some states the county clerk performs certain duties in connection with the courts. In nearly three-fourths of the states, however, a special person, the clerk of the court, is elected to take care of these duties.

The work of the clerk of the court is rather technical and specialized. He must keep a record of all court proceedings; either he or a member of his staff must make a complete stenographic record of all court sessions. He makes out the notices for witnesses and jurors which are delivered by the sheriff. He carries out the orders of the court, preparing necessary papers and documents.

The records of the clerk of the court contain information about all lawsuits brought before the court. This includes the decisions made by the juries and the sentences imposed by the judges.

In some states the clerk of the court issues the marriage licenses and keeps the record of births and deaths.

THE PROSECUTING ATTORNEY. Mention has already been made of the prosecuting attorney in connection with the duties of the coroner. The prosecuting attorney is charged with solving crimes and bringing criminals before the court. Nearly all states have county prosecuting attorneys, although they may have different names for them, such as district attorney and state's attorney.

Like other county officials, the prosecuting attorney is elected directly by the people and is not responsible to any other officials. Whether or not he prosecutes an individual is mainly up to him. No one can force him to do so, though public pressure is often an important factor in the decisions he makes.

The prosecuting attorney represents the people of the state in *criminal cases*. It is the duty of the prosecutor to bring the accused to court, to present the evidence against them, and to try to have them convicted. The prosecutor is a state official carrying out state duties for the county area in which he is elected.

The county attorney also provides legal advice to other county officials. Some counties may have a separate person provide this service, but in many counties the same attorney is both prosecutor and legal adviser. As legal adviser, the attorney defends the county in any lawsuits brought against it and handles legal documents and contracts involving the county.

THE RECORDER. If your family owns a home or a piece of vacant property, the deed to that property is recorded in the county building. Here a record is kept of the ownership of all land in the county. This is an important job done by an elected official usually called the recorder of deeds or the register of deeds.

A *deed* is a document received by a buyer showing that he is the owner of the piece of property. Before the person buys the property, he or his representative examines the records to make sure that the seller owns the property and has a right to sell it. This search of the records is made in the office of the recorder of deeds, where the files and record books show the names of all the previous owners of the property.

The work of the recorder must be accurate. His office must be exact in copying the information on the deed onto the permanent records so that no mistakes are made. The recorder usually also keeps a record of the mortgages held on the property in the county and any other information which is important in the sale and transfer of property.

THE TREASURER. The county treasurer has charge of the county funds. He collects tax money and spends it on orders issued by the county clerk or auditor according to the appropriations made by the county board. Especially in the large counties this is an important responsibility, for large sums of money are handled by him.

The treasurer is *bonded* to insure the return of money lost by the county due to any carelessness or dishonesty on his part. To be bonded means that the bonding company guarantees to repay the county for any loss.

In a few states the sheriff collects the taxes; in some other states special tax collectors take over that particular duty. Tax collectors throughout history have often been paid according to the amount of money collected. Some county treasurers are still paid that way—on a commission or fee basis; in most cases, however, the treasurer now receives a stated salary, which is considered to be a better system.

THE AUDITOR. In order to make sure that the county money is spent according to

A clerk in the office of the recorder of deeds in Philadelphia holds in her hand two tapes which will save space by preserving on microfilm the entire contents of the massive ledger held open. (City of Philadelphia, Office of City Representative)

the law, many counties have an auditor. It is his duty to check on the financial matters of the county. Very often he issues the orders on the treasurer for the payment of bills and salaries.

While the treasurer is the keeper of the county funds, the auditor is the guardian of these funds. The auditor makes regular *audits* of the books of the treasurer and other financial officers. His reports deal with such items as the legality of expenditures, the financial status of the county, and the probable future financial needs.

In some counties the auditor may have certain duties which have little or nothing to do with financial matters. For example, in a number of states he acts as county clerk and is in charge of the clerical records of the county. In still others he is also the assessor.

THE ASSESSOR. The chief sources of

One of the functions of government is to maintain accurate records of deeds and other documents. To save space, in Philadelphia records are microfilmed and read through these viewers. (City of Philadelphia, Office of City Representative)

money for operating the county government are the property taxes—real and personal. *Real property* refers to land and buildings; *personal property* includes such items as furniture, paintings, machinery, and diamonds.

If your family owns property, it pays a yearly tax on this property. The amount of the tax, however, may not be the same as that of your neighbor. The tax rate must be the same throughout the county, but the amount paid by each taxpayer may be different. (See Chapter 24.)

The person who has responsibility for determining the tax on each piece of property is the assessor. He sets a value on the property. This value is then multiplied by the tax rate to determine the amount of the tax.

The assessor uses a number of factors in setting the value of the property. Some of these are the size of the lot, the number of rooms in the house, the construction of the house (brick or frame), the type of heating, and the age of the house.

If the owner of the property is not satisfied with the assessment; that is, if he thinks his property is assessed too highly in comparison with other property in the county, he can appeal to the *board of review*. This board is set up to review the assessments and to make any corrections in cases where the members believe the assessor has not placed a fair value on the property.

In counties which do not have an assessor, the assessment of property is done by cities or townships. County taxes may then be collected by the city or township and turned over to the county treasurer.

THE COUNTY SUPERINTENDENT OF SCHOOLS. In most counties there is a superintendent of schools who often has supervision of the schools in the rural districts only. He gets his position in various ways, most often by election. In other cases he is appointed by the county school board, the state board of education, or the governor.

His duties are of many kinds. The ones most frequently mentioned are to help teachers with teaching problems, to issue emergency teaching certificates, to assist in the selection of teachers, to distribute state school funds to school districts of the county, to gather school statistics, to work for general improvement of the schools of the county, and to aid in consolidating small school districts into larger units.

OTHER OFFICIALS. There are a number of other county officers who have rather important positions in some counties or whose decisions and work become extremely important at times.

The *county surveyor* will survey your land for a fee, when requested to do so, in order to determine exact boundary lines. In the case of a court case over a disputed piece of property, he may be ordered by the court to make a survey to help to decide ownership.

In many sections of the country, a *county road* or *highway commissioner* has charge of the construction and maintenance of county roads. In some states this work is done by the *county engineer*. The engineer often does the surveying work for the county. He also has charge of the construction of bridges, drainage systems, and rubbish disposal plants.

The *county health officer* supervises the public health agencies of the county. The county may have a health clinic, home nursing service, or hospital facilities. In some counties these are under a board of health. County health activities ordinarily include school health service, maternity care, and control of contagious diseases.

There are county officials who are as-

A county assessor confers with a property owner to explain factors used in determining the value of her property. (International Association of Assessing Officers)

437

A road location is surveyed by Corpsmen in Ouachita, Arkansas National Forest. (Courtesy of Office of Economic Opportunity)

signed duties in connection with social and welfare work. The county poor farm or house was for a long time an institution in American life. But county welfare and social service work today include much more than operating these homes. People in need of assistance are helped in various ways and under many circumstances, not only in old age. Counties and other units of government cooperate with the state and national governments to aid the poor, the needy, the unemployed, the handicapped, and the disabled. This phase of government work will be discussed more fully in Chapter 31.

COUNTY EMPLOYEES

In this chapter, reference has often been made to the work done by a county official as though he himself performed each of these duties. The extent to which he does so depends on the size and the population of the county. In the smaller and less populous counties the elected or appointed official does all or most of the work himself. In the larger counties and especially in those with a large popula-

tion, each county official has a staff of employees to assist him. The size of his staff depends on the extent of his duties.

In many counties these employees are political appointees; that is, they are given their position partly because they are friends of the official, they are members of the same political party as the official, or they helped in the campaign to get the official elected to office.

Under this system many of the employees are replaced when a new official takes office. More and more counties are putting their employees under civil service, whereby employees receive their positions on a competitive merit basis and keep them as long as they give satisfactory service.

COUNTY GOVERNMENT REFORM

Throughout this chapter it has been apparent that there is no uniform pattern in which the more than 3,000 counties are governed. Such words as *many, most,* and *some* have been frequently used. Some states have one pattern of county organization; others have another; not all of them have the same county officials.

One trend in county reform has been toward the use of functional consolidation, such as city-county or bi-county health departments.

Even in instances where they have officials with the same title, the duties and responsibilities may differ.

This may seem confusing, but this variation can be one of the strengths of a democratic form of government. The people can make their local government what they want it to be, in keeping with their needs and desires. For this reason different systems of county government have developed in different places.

Much criticism, however, has been leveled at county government. There are political scientists who think that counties should be abolished; others believe very strongly that some changes in county government should be made.

Criticism has come mainly for four reasons: (1) the county has no chief executive; (2) the functions of the county overlap with those of the state and other local governments; (3) there is too much of the bad side of politics in county government; and (4) many counties do not have an adequate tax base to support an effective system of government.

THE COUNTY MANAGER. A number of counties are trying to overcome the lack of an executive head by hiring a county manager. The system is working

Government serves all members of the community. Here children browse through books in the county library. In some counties bookmobiles are used to bring the library to the children. (The Detroit News)

well where it has been tried. The county board hires an expert with experience to administer the affairs of the county. The department heads, as with a city manager, are responsible to the county manager, and he has authority to appoint people to these positions.

The board determines policies, and the manager, together with his department heads and subordinates, has the responsibility for putting policies into action. In this way most of the elected positions are eliminated, and the voters can more easily fix responsibility for good or bad government. This is one method by which some counties are trying to improve their government.

OVERLAPPING FUNCTIONS. Some functions of county government are also carried on by other units of government. In certain cases, functions which at one time were handled by the county have been taken over by the state or the national government. Taking care of the poor was at one time almost exclusively a county function. Since 1930 much of the welfare and

---

THE COUNTY OF THE FUTURE?

Political scientists generally agree that improvement in county government will result if county government is reorganized to include a responsible executive and a functioning legislative body. Onondaga County in New York took a first step in such reorganization when it adopted a new charter in 1961 which provides for an elected executive. Important statements from that charter are the following clauses:

"The executive branch of county government shall be administered by the county executive, who shall be elected from the county at large.

"The county executive shall:

Be the chief executive officer and administrative head of the county government.

Except as otherwise provided in this charter, and subject to confirmation where so provided, appoint to serve during his pleasure the head of every department and other administrative units of the county and the officers and employees of his own office.

Supervise and direct the internal organization and reorganization of each department or other administrative units, the head of which he has the power to appoint.

Perform such other duties and have such other powers as may be prescribed for him by law, administrative code, county ordinance or resolution."

The charter gives the details of other executive powers which make the county executive the true administrative head of the county.

A further step was taken by Onondaga County in 1966 when it approved a legislative plan which went into effect January 1, 1968. Under this plan the county has a twenty-four-member legislature, elected from twenty-four districts into which the county has been divided. The following statements from the legislative plan describe its organization and some of its duties:

"The legislative branch of the government of Onondaga County shall consist of an elective governing body which shall be known as the county legislature.

"The county legislature shall have power to enact local laws or rules fixing the dates and time of its sessions; governing the conduct of the members at such sessions and the manner of transacting business thereat. . . .

"The county legislature shall be the policy-determining body of the county and shall be vested with all the powers of the county.

"The county legislature shall have . . . the following powers and duties:

To make appropriations, levy taxes, incur indebtedness and adopt the budget.

To exercise all powers of local legislation in relation to enacting, amending or rescinding local laws, legalizing acts, ordinances or resolutions, subject to veto by the county executive in such instances as are specifically provided in this charter or by other applicable law. . . ."

social work has been done by states and the nation.

Road building and maintenance was at one time done locally. More and more, the highways are becoming a state and national concern. Some phases of education such as increased financial support and certification of teachers have become state obligations. With the rise of state police departments there is less need for the sheriff.

For these and similar reasons some people argue that the county should be abolished. On the other hand, some county services are increasing. For example, the number of county hospitals, libraries, and airports is growing. Some experts think the solution lies, not in doing away with the county, but in having it perform those services which can be done more effectively on a county level than on either a state or city level.

MERIT SYSTEMS. We have already mentioned the increasing trend in the selection of county employees on a merit basis. As the county civil service system improves and as purely political appointments become less of an influence in hiring workers, county government will improve. Any government can be no better and no more efficient than the people who do the work.

CONSOLIDATION. Counties with poor land and few or even no industries frequently have difficulty raising enough money to support their government. Income from taxes is too low to insure good government. Good government costs money, and without enough of it a county government cannot render good service.

In some states a few counties have solved this problem by *consolidation*, whereby several counties have united to form one county. By doing so they have increased the amount of money available by eliminating the duplication of some services. This movement has made slow progress, however.

About 90 per cent of all counties are in rural areas and most of them have small populations. Consolidating counties so that each would have at least 50,000 people would make more effective government possible. But population is only one of several factors which should be considered in reorganizing counties for greater effectiveness. The Committee for Economic Development summarizes the factors in this recommendation:

> . . . that the 2,700 counties outside metropolitan areas be consolidated into no more than 500 strong and effective units—using such criteria as minimum population, accessibility to the county seat, trading and communications patterns, revenue base, and geography.[1]

HOME RULE. The Committee for Economic Development recommends that counties be given a greater measure of home rule. This recommendation "rests on the concept that county governments . . . should be empowered to serve the interests of their people directly, and be organized along lines determined locally." Home rule would give counties more authority in local government and would reduce the amount of control by state legislatures.

County home rule is now possible in a few states, but only about twenty counties have adopted charters under home rule provisions. Most of these are in California, where county home rule has been permitted since 1911.

Since county government is close to the people, the quality of all government is sometimes judged by it. It could be improved through greater interest and participation of the people. It would become more effective through wide-spread use of such practices as administration by a chief

---

[1] COMMITTEE FOR ECONOMIC DEVELOPMENT, *Modernizing Local Government,* 1966.

executive or a county manager, a merit system, home rule, consolidation of neighboring counties, the elimination of duplication of state and city services, and the strengthening of county services.

*STUDY
QUESTIONS*

1. In what significant way is the county different from the city as a unit of local government?

2. Why did the county develop as an important unit of government in the South and the West?

3. What county officers get their titles from English officials?

4. What are the chief functions of county government?

5. What were some important considerations in the location of the county seat?

6. What are some general duties of county boards?

7. What are the duties of the county sheriff? What are some of the reasons given for the proposal to do away with the office of sheriff?

8. Why is the work of the county clerk important for most people?

9. Under what circumstances is an inquest held? What is its purpose?

10. What are the special duties of the clerk of the court?

11. Who is the representative of the people of a state in criminal cases?

12. Why is accuracy especially important in the work of the recorder?

13. Why is it considered better to pay treasurers a stated salary rather than a commission?

14. Why is the work of the county auditor important?

15. What are some of the factors used in determining the value of property for tax purposes?

16. Why is the county superintendent of schools an important official in rural areas?

17. Why do some people favor a county manager system? Why do others oppose it?

18. What are the chief areas of criticism of county government? Explain each.

1
The county is a geographical unit created by the state to carry out certain governmental functions.

2
The county is a carry-over of a similar unit of government in England.

3
There is considerable variation in area and population among the more than 3,000 counties in the nation.

4
The county seat with its county building may be considered the "capital" of the county.

5
The governing body of the county is a board, whose title and specific responsibilities differ from state to state.

6
The best-known county official is the sheriff, who has certain court duties and in some cases is responsible for maintaining law and order.

7
Common responsibilities of the county clerk, such as keeping records and issuing licenses, affect the lives of many people.

8
Other important county officials are coroner, clerk of the court, attorney, recorder, treasurer, auditor, assessor, and superintendent of schools.

9
County government usually improves as employees are put under civil service.

10
The use of a county manager helps to overcome the lack of a county executive.

11
County government efficiency may be improved by eliminating or reducing overlapping functions of city, county, and state, by home rule, and by consolidation of neighboring counties.

12
Counties need an adequate tax base to provide good government.

IDEAS FOR
DISCUSSION

1. Some political scientists think that county government should be reorganized with a single elected executive who would have power to appoint lesser officials. Do you think this is a good proposal? Do you see any disadvantages in making this change? Any advantages?

2. There are a number of large metropolitan areas in which the city or the city and its suburbs occupy the land of the entire county. Should county government be eliminated in these areas? Why? What additional governmental functions would need to be assumed by the cities in those cases?

3. The opinion is held that the coroner should be a licensed physician. How do you feel about this proposal?

4. Many people want to install merit systems for county employees where such systems are not now in operation. Do you think there are important values in the merit system? What advantages or disadvantages of the merit system can you list? Why?

5. Would it be wise to make county government more uniform throughout the nation?

6. One proposal for the improvement of county government is the consolidation of neighboring counties into larger units. What would be the effect of consolidation in your state?

7. Some people have proposed that the kind and number of governmental services of counties should be increased. Can you suggest any additional services which should be supplied by counties? Do you think that these would improve county government?

8. Read again the first sentence in the special box, "The County of the Future?" on page 440. What suggestions can you give for getting "a responsible executive and a functioning legislative body" for counties?

THINGS
TO DO

1. On an outline map of your state fill in the names of counties and county seats.

2. Make a study of the operation of the county board in your state. What are the duties of the board? How are its members chosen?

3. Visit your county courthouse. What offices are located there? What are the duties of each of the officials? Report your findings to the class.

4. Secure a blank form of a deed for real property. Read it to the class and explain the terminology.

5. Select a committee to interview your county assessor. Ask him about the assessments on various pieces of property in the county. How are assessments made?

6. Compare the county government in your state with the general discussion in this chapter. Make a chart showing the agreements and disagreements.

7. Prepare a bulletin board display of various blank forms and documents which you may secure from the courthouse. Some of these are licenses, tax bills and notices, and deeds. You may wish to include official notices, such as election notices, notices about the sale of property, and notices for bids on proposed purchases.

8. Interview your county sheriff to learn about his duties and responsibilities. Compare these to the sheriff you have learned to know from the "Westerns." In what ways are the two sheriffs alike? How are they different?

FURTHER
READINGS

Bureau of Social and Political Research, THE COUNTY BOARD OF SUPERVISORS: ITS POWERS AND DUTIES. Michigan State University Press, 1959.

Gove, Samuel K., "County Works for Cities," in STATE AND LOCAL GOVERNMENT (Herbert L. Marx, Jr., ed.). H. W. Wilson Co., 1962.

Kelliher, C. L., "The County's Problems," in STATE AND LOCAL GOVERNMENT (Herbert L. Marx, Jr., ed.). H. W. Wilson Co., 1962.

Lockard, Duane, THE POLITICS OF STATE AND LOCAL GOVERNMENT. Macmillan Co., 1963. Chapter 6.

Michener, James A., REPORT OF THE COUNTY CHAIRMAN. Random House, Inc., 1961.

Miller, Robert H., POLITICS IS PEOPLE. James H. Heineman, Inc., 1962.

Ross, Russell M. and Millsap, Kenneth F., STATE AND LOCAL GOVERNMENT AND ADMINISTRATION. Ronald Press Co., 1966. Chapter 4.

Superintendent of Documents, COUNTY AND CITY DATA BOOK, 1967. Washington, D. C.: Government Printing Office, 1967.

Wager, Paul W., COUNTY GOVERNMENT ACROSS THE NATION. University of North Carolina Press, 1950.

CAUCUS—meeting of members of a political party to nominate candidates or to agree on a position on an issue.

CONGRESSIONAL TOWNSHIP—a geographic subdivision of the county, usually thirty-six square miles in area.

CONSOLIDATION—combining of several smaller units into a larger one.

CONSTABLE—police officer of a town, township, or village.

INCORPORATE—to receive the right to carry on the functions of local government, such as levying taxes.

MODERATOR—presiding officer of a town meeting.

ORDINANCE—a law or regulation passed by a unit of local government.

SELECTMEN—chief officers of a New England town.

SUPERVISOR—township officer; member of the county board.

TOWNSHIP—a unit of local government; a geographic subdivision of a county, usually thirty-six square miles in area.

VILLAGE—a local unit of government, often incorporated to provide governmental services; a rural community.

WARRANT—a special notice indicating the items to be voted on in a town meeting.

THE LANGUAGE OF GOVERNMENT

444

21

The Town, Township, and Village

A map of almost any section of our country shows dozens of small dots. Each dot represents a community where people live and have organized some kind of government to help them live pleasantly and comfortably. Some of these places are large, with thousands of people; but many are small, with only a few inhabitants.

A cross-country trip by automobile formerly took the traveler through hundreds of these small communities. The roads of yesteryear brought people and business to them. Today's superhighways bypass them. Many of them have thus lost much of their contact with the outside world and have declined in population and importance. Others have met the challenge of highway bypasses by developing new industries and new local attractions and are luring businessmen and tourists to them. The result for such communities has been not only survival, but growth.

Typical of the New England villages is East Corinth, Vermont. In such small units it is possible for all villagers to meet together to decide on local issues. (Courtesy of the Vermont Development Department)

Wherever people live together—in a small rural crossroads community, in a growing town, or in a large metropolitan city—for an orderly life they need rules and regulations and officials to carry them out. For the nation the rules and regulations are the Constitution and our national laws; for the states they are constitutions and laws on the state level; for cities they are charters and local ordinances. To enforce these, we have national, state, and city units of government. The small community, too, needs the rules, the regulations, and the enforcement that come with organized government.

For millions of Americans the town, the township, or the village is local government close to home. It is government which they can see and watch; it is government operated by people whom they know personally and well.

The form of these local government units varies in different parts of the country. In general, however, each type of local government is organized to furnish certain services to the people of the local area. While these services may differ from one state to another, they generally include water supply, schools, fire and police protection, street lighting, rubbish collection, sewage disposal, and the building and maintenance of libraries, hospitals, parks, recreation areas, sidewalks, roads, and streets.

In this chapter we will look at three forms of local government to see how they operate and how they differ from one another: the New England town, the township, and the village.

THE NEW ENGLAND TOWN One of the characteristics of our democratic form of government is that people have a voice in the operation of their government. In most cases the people use this voice through representatives and executives whom they elect to operate the government for them as, for example, the President and the Congress of the United States or the state governors and legislatures.

With respect to the New England town discuss the terms "direct" and "indirect democracy," and "pure" and "representative democracy."

In smaller units, however, the people sometimes come together for annual meetings in which they make certain decisions and then elect officials to operate the government until the next annual meeting. Examples are the many small school districts and the villages. The best example, however, is the New England town.

The town in New England is not like a town in other parts of our country. It is more like the townships of many other states. It usually covers an area of from twenty to forty square miles and often includes one or more villages.

The town developed among early New Englanders as a convenient way of providing the governmental services they needed. Each town usually covered about the same territory as the church parish. The meetinghouse often served both as a church and as a place for the town meetings. It was here in the town hall that the people came together to make the laws that were to govern their town.

THE TOWN MEETING. At first, town meetings were held monthly, and the town tried to conduct all of its business at this meeting. It was soon found, however, that someone had to conduct the town affairs between meetings. Also, as the populations of the towns increased, it was more desirable to have less-frequent meetings. Today the meetings are usually held annually in the spring, and officials called *selectmen* conduct the town business between meetings.

The town meeting day is an important one for the townspeople. In the past most of the voters turned out for the meeting. This is still true in the smaller towns. In the larger towns, however, a smaller per-

Early in March every year the town of Lyman, New Hampshire, holds its annual meeting at which officers are elected and local issues discussed and voted upon. (State of New Hampshire photo by Stephen T. Whitney)

centage of the people attend the meeting. This emphasizes the need for a representative form of government as the population increases, but it also shows the need for having people remain concerned about their government regardless of community size. The town meeting gives people direct participation; representative government allows them indirect participation through their vote.

Two important tasks are taken care of by the voters at the town meeting: (1) By secret ballot they elect their officers for the next year. (2) They discuss and vote on such items as money for schools and highways, parking regulations, local legislation, zoning ordinances, street lighting, police protection, and park areas.

The town clerk is the secretary of the meeting and calls the meeting to order. The meeting begins with the election of the *moderator*, who is the presiding officer in charge. Then the nominations for the town's officers are made. Although the candidates are nominated from the floor, they may have been agreed upon by separate party meetings, or caucuses, several days earlier.

After the nominations have been made, the voting is done by secret ballot. Ordinarily the polls remain open several hours to give all voters an opportunity to cast their ballots.

The business session of the meeting is held in the afternoon or evening. The items to be voted upon have been previously announced to the townspeople in a special notice, called a *warrant*, which is posted some days or weeks before the meeting. This gives the voters an opportunity to discuss these items beforehand.

Many items are routine and are quickly passed. Others are discussed at some length and may be passed or voted down. Sometimes the debates become heated before a decision is reached. At other times certain issues are settled only after a stirring speech by one of the townspeople. The town meeting is a place where every adult citizen has a voice and a vote and where he has a chance to use them directly.

THE TOWN OFFICERS. The chief town officers are the *selectmen*. Usually there are three, though some towns have as many as nine. As a board they conduct the town affairs between the annual meetings.

The town has no executive head, and so the selectmen act as a group to carry on the administrative duties of the town government. Among their duties are these: controlling the town property, granting licenses, issuing warrants for the annual meeting and stating the subjects to be discussed, laying out drains, constructing and maintaining highways, arranging elections, writing orders on the treasurer for the payment of bills, and adjusting claims against the town. The selectmen have no power over town taxes. These are determined by the people themselves in the town meeting; at the same time, the people decide how to spend the money for the coming year.

A number of towns have engaged *town managers* who operate much like the city manager discussed in Chapter 19. A town manager carries on his work under the supervision of the selectmen.

Perhaps the most important single town official is the *town clerk*. His duties are similar to the duties of clerks in other units of government. It has already been mentioned that he is the secretary of the town meeting and calls the meeting to order. He also acts as secretary to the board of selectmen.

The town clerk has responsibility for keeping the town records. Marriages, births, and deaths are recorded by the clerk. He issues licenses and records land titles. He maintains an accurate list of the town's eli-

The town of Peterborough, New Hampshire, was the first in the United States to establish a tax supported, free public library. (State of New Hampshire photo by Eric Sanford)

gible voters and keeps the official record of the vote for county and state officers. As clerk he carries on the town's correspondence, issues the necessary legal notices, and arranges for the town printing. The clerk is elected at the annual meeting, but the same person is frequently reelected year after year.

The town also has other officers. The number depends on the land area and the population of the town. The treasurer collects the town money; he spends it according to the appropriations made at the town meeting and on orders of the selectmen. The tax assessor determines the property values and assesses the taxes.

The constable is the arresting officer and issues orders for the arrest of individuals suspected of committing crimes. The justice of the peace is the town judge.

The overseer of the poor takes care of the needy and the welfare cases. The school committee has control of the town schools. The highway or road commissioner has charge of the town roads; the park commis-

sioner, of the town parks; and the library board, of the town library.

There may also be a board of health, a fire brigade, pound keepers, fish wardens, and other similar officials.

Not every town has all of these officers, but a number of them are found in each town. They are either elected at the town meeting or appointed by the selectmen. Most of the offices are only part-time positions, and the officials receive only small fees for their services. Most officials hold other full-time jobs. For many of them the honor connected with the town job is the important part of their town pay.

CHANGES IN TOWN GOVERNMENT. New England town government is changing. As the towns have grown in size, there has been a movement to change from a town meeting in which all citizens participate to a *representative* town meeting. In this meeting the representatives of the town conduct the affairs for all. These representatives are elected from the various sections of the town.

Two factors have brought about this movement. One, the population of many towns has become too large for the town hall. So some method had to be found to hold a meeting and to carry on discussions of the town business. Also, many newcomers in the town, especially Europeans and French Canadians, were unfamiliar with the meeting procedures and were often confused. In order to give everyone representation and to continue the town-meeting type of government, the representative meeting was begun. Usually the number of representatives is rather large— 200 or more—so that the value of direct participation of many people is being carried on.

As towns have grown in size, some of the town business has become specialized. In addition to the town manager, some towns have also established finance committees to advise the town meeting regarding financial matters. This committee usually consists of a group of unpaid citizens who study the town's financial problems, prepare a proposed budget, and present their ideas to the townspeople assembled on the day of the meeting.

The Committee for Economic Development calls attention to the fact that only 10 per cent of all New England towns have as many as 10,000 inhabitants and that more than 1,200 of the 1,400 towns are outside of metropolitan areas. For these reasons the committee believes that there should be a drastic program of consolidation. But not all members agree. Three of them state ". . . proposals to consolidate these small towns into enlarged units, geared to the virtues of greater efficiency, would meet a great deal of resistance. A more realistic goal for New England might involve small rural communities banding together for the provision of common services, but with each retaining a measure of individuality and a direct relationship to its own electorate as well."[1]

THE TOWNSHIP   As our country grew and as New Englanders moved to the West, they carried with them the idea of town government. They tried to develop local governments close to the people and formed townships. But townships of the North Central States and other states differed from the New England town.

The New England town grew up around a settlement of people. The township in other parts of the country was mainly a geographic subdivision for the purpose of surveying and locating plots of land. In many instances the township was laid out before settlers occupied the land. In a few cases the township was laid out along natural boundaries such as rivers. For the most part it was laid out in thirty-six-square-mile areas called *congressional townships*. As the townships were settled, they became units for carrying on certain functions of local government.

While the township developed as an important unit of local government in states settled by people from New England and the Middle Atlantic States, the county became the important unit for states settled by people from the South. Some states, like Illinois and Missouri, received settlers from both. In these states some of the counties were divided into townships and some were not, reflecting the influence of the states from which the settlers had come.

DECLINE OF TOWNSHIP GOVERNMENT. The township as a unit of government has become less and less important over the years. Where a township still exists, it usually functions only in the rural

[1] COMMITTEE FOR ECONOMIC DEVELOPMENT, *Modernizing Local Government,* 1966, p. 65.

TREDYFFRIN TOWNSHIP
CHESTER COUNTY ⟶ PENNA.

HIGHWAY MAP

SCALE
IN FEET

ALVA L. ROGERS
CIVIL ENGINEER & SURVEYOR
WAYNE ⟶ PA.

Indicates State Highway

Several heavily populated townships may adjoin within an area of only a few square miles. This sometimes complicates the administrative and service functions of local government. (Map courtesy of Tredyffrin Township)

Local townships provide necessary bus transportation for individual or consolidated school districts. (Peter MacLaren)

areas outside cities or villages. Ordinarily, township areas in which many people live close together will form a village or a city for the purpose of carrying on the business of local government. But the area that remains outside the village or city continues to operate as a township.

As cities and villages have grown, and as their number has increased, the township as a unit of government has disappeared in many places. Another factor which has made the township less necessary as a governmental unit today than in former days is the ease of transportation and communication. Good roads, telephones, radio, and television have brought people much closer to the larger county and state units of government.

Many of the duties and services formerly supplied by the township have been turned over to the county and the state. One reason is that expensive equipment such as road scrapers and snowplows can be furnished more economically by larger units. Such equipment is often too costly for each township to buy.

TOWNSHIP GOVERNMENT TODAY.

In a few states such as Michigan, however, the township is still an important unit of government. In more than a dozen others some township functions are still carried on, township meetings are held, and township officials are elected.

The powers of townships differ somewhat from state to state. Townships conduct local business and are also agencies for carrying on state and county affairs. In general, the township has only such powers as are expressly given it by the state.

These may include assessing and collecting taxes; conducting national, state, and local elections; licensing various establishments, such as theaters and bowling alleys; controlling highways, schools, and welfare agencies; establishing libraries, parks, and cemeteries; and maintaining fire stations and hospitals. In some states township officers are also members of the county board, and so they have powers on the county level.

Some townships still hold meetings patterned after the New England town meet-

The table giving the number of local governments on page 408 shows that there are more than 21,000 special districts. These exist in both rural and urban areas of all fifty states. Each district has been created to provide a particular service or facility, such as parks, recreation, sewage-disposal plant, airport, soil conservation, water supply, or parking. The nearly 22,000 school districts should also be included among the special districts.

Special districts are independent units of local government, having their own taxing and bonding authority. They are usually set up because they can provide the special service more easily and effectively than can the conventional units of local government—county, municipality, or township. This is especially true in providing finances for the special services in those instances when the county or the municipality has reached its legal taxing and bonding limits. Another reason for creating special districts is to service areas greater than the existing units of local government. For example, a soil-conservation district may include land in several counties, and a park district may include a city and additional land in adjoining counties.

The governing body of a special district is usually a board of three to nine members. In some cases they are elected; in others they are appointed by state or county officials.

Most political scientists agree that special districts are desirable units for providing the services given. Some do point out, though, that the existence of these districts has some disadvantages. Since special districts are independent, board members may not always coordinate their functions with those of other governmental units. These additional governments may also require unnecessary duplication of certain personnel positions and equipment. They do have the advantage, however, that board members can concentrate their attention on the one service, or very few services, for which the district was created.

Among the well-known special districts are the following:

- *The Port of New York Authority, which has charge of port facilities in the New York-New Jersey area.*
- *The Chicago Sanitary District, which handles sewage disposal for Chicago and the surrounding area.*
- *The Metropolitan Water District of Southern California, which supplies water to the Los Angeles area from the Colorado River.*

ing. But ordinarily only a few people attend, and the business of the township is conducted by just a handful of voters, often by only the elected officials. In most states there are no township meetings. The business is carried on by the elected township board, and questions which must be decided by the citizens are submitted to them at the township election.

The chief township officer is the *supervisor* or *chairman*, who is assisted by a *township board*. In some states the township has no single executive head, but a board of supervisors or trustees is its ruling body. The board checks the township expenditures and audits the books of town-

ship officials. The township usually has a considerable number of officials. Their duties are similar to those of officials holding similar titles in other units of government. But, of course, their scope is very limited.

Besides the supervisor, a township may have an assessor, an overseer of the poor, a clerk, a highway commissioner, a treasurer, a justice of the peace, a constable, a tax collector, an election inspector, a pound keeper, a registrar, a health officer, a comptroller, policemen, firemen, a veterinarian, and members of various boards.

Just the listing, however, shows that many of these officials have duties which overlap

A burying ground in a small village of New Hampshire reveals on its aging markers how long ago the area was settled. (State of New Hampshire photo by Stephen T. Whitney)

with those of county and state officials. For that reason more and more political scientists are suggesting that the township as a unit of government be abolished. They say it has outlived its usefulness.

But a constitutional amendment is needed in most states to do away with the township, and such amendments are difficult to pass. There are people who feel that the township government should be continued. Among them are the thousands of township officials, but there are also others. They argue that too much government is far removed from the people, and they want local township government continued, for it is close to home. Here people can see government in operation and run it in their own way.

Nevertheless, the movement to abolish townships is growing and their functions are being taken over by county governments. The Committee for Economic Development believes that a township can function effectively if it has a large enough population and if it is given adequate authority. Lacking these requirements, it should be abolished.

THE VILLAGE   As you drive along the nation's highways, you pass through some villages and towns. The signs give the names and often the population of each. Sometimes they also tell whether or not a place is *incorporated*. An incorporated place has been given legal status by the state to do business. Its privileges include

A village differs from a city in these ways:

(1) A village is part of the surrounding township, whereas cities are separate from the township.

(2) Cities have their own representatives on the county board of supervisors. Villages are not represented separately, but must depend for their representation on the township supervisor.

(3) Many people believe that villages are smaller than cities. This may or may not be so. There are several villages with populations of over 10,000—larger than many cities in Michigan.

(4) Cities and villages are incorporated under different laws. Cities are given somewhat more power.

—Robert H. Pealy, Editor, *Study Kit on Michigan Local Government,* The University of Michigan Press. Copyright © by the University of Michigan 1958. Reprinted by permission.

Point out that in some states the village, or borough, is independent of the township in which it is located. Let the students discuss how this may result in overlapping functions.

453

Edward Mason, mayor of West Point, Kentucky, confers on matters of local interest with Police Judge Gladys Stackhouse. (Du Pont, Better Living Magazine)

having its own government, raising taxes, borrowing money, and bringing suit. An unincorporated place has none of these.

The incorporated places are known by different names in various parts of the country; village, town, and borough are the most common ones. When they are large enough, they are called cities. The United States Bureau of the Census classifies as a city any incorporated place which has 2,500 or more people. However, about half of the states allow cities to be formed with less than 2,500 inhabitants.

But an incorporated village may usually be formed with only about 200 to 300 people. Some states also require that these people must live within a certain area. In New York, for example, by popular vote 200 people living within an area of one square mile may become a village. In Illinois 300 people in an area of two square

miles many become a village; when the population reaches 1,000, the village may become a city.

Not all villages and towns are very small places, however. Many have more than 20,000 inhabitants. One of the largest— Oak Park, Illinois—is a suburb of Chicago. This village has a population of more than 60,000.

Village government, just as town government, is usually very simple. Only in the larger villages are there any full-time officials. A few of them have adopted a manager form of government in which one person spends full time carrying on the work usually done by several part-time officials.

The *village board* or *council* is the ruling body. Its members, usually five or seven, are elected by the village at large for terms of one or two years. They are called *trustees, aldermen, burgesses,* or *commis-sioners.* The village board has the authority to pass ordinances and regulations for the village. The extent of its authority varies from state to state. The usual powers are to provide police and fire protection; to license peddlers; to make special assessments; to operate water and sewer facilities; to pass health regulations; to maintain libraries and parks; to levy taxes and to control the village funds; to build sidewalks and streets; to license theaters and other amusement places; and to appoint various officials.

The chairman of the board is the *village president,* sometimes called the *mayor.* He usually has the right to vote at board meetings, although in some villages he votes only in case of a tie. He has the duty of enforcing the village ordinances.

Other common village officials are the clerk or recorder, the treasurer or collector, the marshal or constable, the street commissioner, and the assessor. The village may also have an overseer of the poor, a justice of the peace, an attorney, and school officers. In many states most of these officials are appointed by the village board; however, in some states, especially in the West, they are elected by the voters.

Village government, like that of the township and the New England town, is close to the people. Village ordinances and the work of village officials are often the chief topics of discussions and conversations in village gathering places. Some of these discussions lead to constructive results; others do not. But they are democracy in action, and most villagers consider them a rightful part of their village life.

Village government is another example of government of, by, and for the people. But having government close to the people does not necessarily make it good. Like other forms of local government it can be improved through the active participation of informed citizens.

Village government can ordinarily supply needed services only at higher costs than can larger units of government. This is especially true of the many small rural villages. For this reason the Committee for Economic Development recommends:

> Most—if not all—of the 11,000 non-metropolitan villages with fewer than 2,500 residents should disincorporate to permit strong county governments to administer their services on a special assessment basis, or they should contract with counties for such services.[1]

---

[1] COMMITTEE FOR ECONOMIC DEVELOPMENT, *Modernizing Local Government,* 1966, p. 42.

STUDY QUESTIONS

1. How has the nation's superhighway system affected many small communities?

2. Why is local government so important to millions of Americans?

3. What are the chief services of local governments?

4. Why is the New England town a good example of democratic government?

5. What business is conducted at the town meeting?

6. Why is the government of New England towns changing from direct to indirect participation?

7. Why is the warrant important for good democratic government?

8. Who are the chief town officials and what are their duties?

9. How does the township differ from the New England town?

10. What factors have combined to make the township less and less important?

CONCEPTS AND GENERALIZATIONS

1
All communities—large and small—need some form of organized government to provide services and to enforce rules and regulations.

2
Modern highway systems have caused the decline of many small communities.

3
The original government of the New England town is an example of pure democracy with widespread citizen participation.

4
As towns grew in population, the form of government gradually changed to a representative democracy.

5
The township originated as a geographic subdivision of the county.

6
Improvements in communication and transportation have made small units of local government less necessary.

7
Small units of local government tend to be costly to maintain.

8
The number of residents needed by an area to form a corporate government varies among the states.

9
The Bureau of the Census defines a city as any incorporated place having 2,500 or more people.

10
Political scientists and others who have studied the governments of small areas recommend consolidation into larger units or provision of local services by county government.

11
Small units of local government continue to exist in many places because their citizens wish to retain local control.

11. What are some common powers of townships?

12. Name the more important township officials and describe their duties.

13. What is the meaning of incorporation?

14. How do states and the federal government distinguish between villages and cities?

15. Who are the chief village officials and what are their duties?

IDEAS FOR DISCUSSION

1. Big cities do not have "town meetings"; they do not issue warrants, the special notices about "town business." How are these factors handled in large cities? Which procedure is more effective? Which is more democratic?

2. For many New England town officers the honor which their position brings them is reward enough for the work they do. Is this true of officials in other levels of government?

3. One of the factors which is helping to eliminate township government is the question of economy. Democratic government is not necessarily cheap; it costs money. Some people maintain that in spite of its cost township government should be continued because it is close to the people. How do you feel about this? Shall we continue to maintain township governments even though money could be saved by eliminating them?

4. The expression *vested interests* refers to people and agencies who have a personal interest in a particular function or service. Township officials may have a vested interest in the continuation of township government because of the positions they hold. Should the opinions of these officials be considered in reaching a decision about the continuation of township governments? Why?

5. "Villages offer more opportunities for participation in government than do big cities." This is one of the arguments advanced by village people in listing advantages of village life. Do you agree?

6. If you had been a member of the Committee for Economic Development, how would you have voted on the issue of consolidation of New England towns? (See page 449) Why?

7. Discuss the relative costs of services supplied by small and large units of local government. Should small units be retained even though their costs for services may be higher? Why?

THINGS TO DO

1. Make a chart of the rural and urban population of your state by decades. How has the percentage of each changed over the years?

2. The student council is a form of representative government. Compare its organization and operation with representative government in the larger New England towns.

3. Make a study of village government in your state. What are the state regulations about incorporation? Does your state have regulations about population and area?

4. If you live near a village, visit the mayor or president and talk with him about the values of village life.

5. Plan to attend a meeting of one of the following groups: selectmen of a New England town; a township board; a village council. Prepare a report of the items discussed and the nature of the business conducted.

6. There may be students in your class who have lived in both a small community and a large city. Plan a panel discussion in which these students discuss the advantages and disadvantages of living in large and small communities.

7. Color an outline map of the United States to indicate in different colors:

  a) States with town organization

  b) States with township organization

  c) States in which counties are not subdivided.

8. Make a study of the special districts in your state. Report to the class on the number of such districts and the services they supply.

FURTHER READINGS

Fuller, Wayne E., RFD: THE CHANGING FACE OF RURAL AMERICA. Indiana University Press, 1964.

Hoiberg, Otto G., EXPLORING THE SMALL COMMUNITY. University of Nebraska Press, 1955.

Ladd, Everett C., Jr., IDEOLOGY IN AMERICA: CHANGE AND RESPONSE IN A CITY, A SUBURB AND A SMALL TOWN. Cornell University Press, 1969.

Ross, Russell M., and Millsap, Kenneth F., STATE AND LOCAL GOVERNMENT AND ADMINISTRATION. Ronald Press Co., 1966. Chapter 5.

Snider, C. F., and Gove, S. K., LOCAL GOVERNMENT IN RURAL AMERICA. Appleton-Century-Crofts, Inc., 1957.

Superintendent of Documents, THE VICE PRESIDENT'S HANDBOOK FOR LOCAL OFFICIALS. Washington, D.C.: Government Printing Office, 1968.

Syed, Anwar H., THE POLITICAL THEORY OF AMERICAN LOCAL GOVERNMENT. Random House, Inc., 1966. (Paperback)

Vidich, Arthur J., and Bensman, J., SMALL TOWN IN MASS SOCIETY: CLASS, POWER, AND RELIGION IN A RURAL COMMUNITY. Doubleday & Co., Inc., 1960. (Paperback)

Woolley, David, TOWN HALL AND THE PROPERTY OWNER. Barnes & Noble, Inc., 1967.

AUTONOMOUS — independent; having self-government.

CONSOLIDATION—the process of forming one unit of government from two or more; merger.

CONSTITUTIONAL HOME RULE—home rule granted to local governments under the state constitution.

CURFEW—a time beyond which the civilian population or certain groups, such as children, may not be on the streets.

FLUORIDATION—the process of adding fluorides to the public water supply in an effort to reduce tooth decay.

GHETTO—a section of a city in which members of a minority racial, religious, or nationality group are forced to live because of social or economic pressures; usually a poor and depressed area.

GRANT-IN-AID—money provided by one unit of government to help another unit carry on some service; for example, by a state to its local units.

HOME RULE—power granted by a state to local units of government to write their own charters and to make changes in them without needing approval of the legislature.

LEGISLATIVE HOME RULE—home rule granted to local governments by the state legislature.

MEGALOPOLIS—an urban region consisting of metropolitan areas with their large cities and many towns and suburbs.

METROPOLITAN AREA—a central city and the surrounding suburban communities.

ZONING—a plan for the use of certain lands as commercial, industrial, or residential property; usually zoning describes the kinds of buildings that may be constructed in designated areas.

THE LANGUAGE
OF GOVERNMENT

22

Problems of
Local
Government

The legislature of a midwestern state was considering a law to set a maximum number of hours in the work week of municipal policemen and firemen. Several city councils sent resolutions to the legislature opposing this proposed law. They said that the bill interfered with home rule. A mayor said, "The bill would compel the city to pay overtime rates which the city cannot afford." A city manager said, "The proposal before the legislature would be all right if the state agreed to pay part of the expense."

This incident illustrates one of the problems of local government: relations with state government. Other problems arise in the relationships of one unit of local government with another; for example, counties and cities. Some problems arise because of the overlapping of services of village or city and township or county governments.

Special problems have come about because of the rapid growth of cities and

Ask the student to offer suggestions relative to the problems of the large metropolitan areas with which he is familiar. Evaluate these suggestions in a class discussion.

metropolitan areas. This rapid growth and urbanization have shown dramatically some shortcomings of our society. These center in civil rights, civil unrest and disturbances, and poverty—some of our most urgent and pressing problems. Still other problems arise when many similar units of local government are close together and people move freely from one to the other. This is especially true in the large metropolitan areas. The boundaries between the units of local government mean little to individual families, but they are important in the operation of government.

This chapter will discuss these problems and some of their suggested solutions. The problems are grouped for discussion under four headings:

1. Relations of state and local governments
2. Overlapping and duplication of services of various units of local government
3. Growing unrest in the cities
4. Cooperation in metropolitan areas.

RELATIONS OF STATE AND LOCAL GOVERNMENTS

The councilmen who objected to a state law setting hours of work for policemen and firemen said that this law was a violation of home rule. They believed that cities should run their affairs without interference from the state government, that each unit of local government should decide such issues for itself. There were others in the state, however, who held that the state legislature should make uniform rules which would apply to all local governments of the state. They believed that the same set of rules should apply to all local governments.

However, during the past one hundred years, more and more people have come to realize that not every section or community of a state can be operated in the same way. A large city has problems which are different from those of the small towns in the same state. Communities of the same size may not be alike at all. Even cities with similar problems may want to try different solutions.

A town in an agricultural area of the state may be in need of different treatment from one in an industrial area. People, too, are not the same in various parts of a state. They may not all want the same kind of local unit of government. They may wish to organize their governments differently.

SPECIAL LEGISLATION. Because of these differences states began to make various arrangements to allow local governments to have more to say about the operation of local affairs. One of the earliest methods was to have the state legislature pass *special legislation* which applied only to a specific city or town.

Since the time of the legislature is limited, it gradually became the practice to pass special local legislation without debating it if the representative from that locality was in favor of it. This led to some abuses. Local-interest groups had only to convince their representatives in the legislature of the value of a certain piece of legislation to have it passed. This sometimes led to bribery and the passage of legislation which benefited only a few individuals.

Frequently a law was passed which was not in the best interest of the majority of the people and which many people living in a locality did not want. A few examples in which special local legislation might be advantageous to a particular group are the location of a new highway, the formation of an election district, the granting of a franchise to a utility company.

Sometimes the extension of home rule to local areas by the state is referred to as state-local federalism.

In order to overcome these abuses of special legislation, different states have tried various other procedures. In some states constitutional amendments have been passed which forbid any special legislation that does not apply to all parts of the state. This is not always workable, because, as we have seen, different sections of a state may have different problems.

In other states the constitution provides that any special legislation must be accepted by the locality before it can be put into operation. Before a law which applies to local communities becomes effective in a particular city, either the local officials or the people themselves must vote to accept it. This seems like a defensible compromise. The legislature has the power to pass special legislation which affects only a single local area or a group of areas. But the legislation does not become effective until the people of the local area affected accept it.

HOME RULE. Another method to provide for differences among local units of government in the same state is a system known as *home rule.* This system operates in about two-thirds of the states, although the term itself has various interpretations. In general, it means what it says—the local people rule themselves. Home-rule cities and counties have charters which permit them to determine the form and powers of their local government with only a few restrictions. This frees the state legislature from the necessity of dealing with a large number of special local problems.

A distinction should be made between legislative and constitutional home rule. In *legislative home rule* the legislature grants permission to a local unit of government to pass its own laws. Under this type of home rule, however, the legislature may take such permission away. But in *constitutional home rule* only an amendment to the constitution can change the powers of the home-rule city or county.

There is much discussion and great difference of opinion about the degree to which a local community should rule itself. If it does so without regard to the welfare of the state and nation, this is not wise. Certainly the life and interests of the city, the state, and the nation are woven together. Each must be operated in such a way as to consider the best interests of the others. This is not always done. This factor, together with the reluctance of state legislatures to give up powers, accounts for the slow spread of home rule since its beginning nearly a hundred years ago.

Missouri in 1875 was the first state to allow constitutional home rule. The movement grew in the early 1900's when about a dozen states added home-rule provisions to their constitutions. In recent years several other states have been added to the list. Today over half of the states have some form of constitutional home rule, but in many of them it is limited to the larger cities.

STATE AID. In Chapter 18, "Problems of State Government," grants-in-aid from the federal government to the states were discussed. In much the same way states are granting money to local units of government to help them carry on their work. Most frequently these grants to local governments are for schools, roads, and health and welfare services. Usually they are earmarked for a specific service.

Many state-aid programs were begun during the depression years of the 1930's. During those years many units of local government had difficulty collecting enough tax money to provide necessary services. They turned to the states and to the national government for help. Since then, the amount of state aid has increased greatly.

Most state aid goes to school districts for education and to counties for welfare ser-

Funds from the federal and state governments help cities to solve a variety of urban problems, such as the erection of low-income housing projects. (The Detroit News)

vices. Only a small portion goes to cities, townships, and villages, although the states are helping all units of government more and more, especially in highway improvement and welfare assistance programs.

Three main reasons for grants-in-aid from states to local units of government are:

1. Local governments are usually more limited in their ability to tax than is the state. The state helps the local units by collecting taxes on a statewide basis and returning portions of the tax money to the local governments. Sales, income, gasoline, and automobile license taxes are the usual sources of state money for state aid to local governments. However, the state also uses much of this tax money to carry on state programs.

2. There is usually great variation in wealth between different parts of the state.

Without state help the poor sections cannot provide as many services as the wealthy sections, and the quality of the services is not always the same. The poor sections may have poor schools, poor highways, poor health facilities, poor libraries.

These differences between sections can be reduced through state aid. Part of the state-aid money is distributed according to need. The communities that need more help are given greater amounts. This helps to improve the services of the poorer communities, and tends to equalize opportunities and services throughout the state.

3. There are often new services which the state would like to have started in the state by local governments, such as aid to widows or aid to handicapped people. In order to get them started the state may make grants-in-aid to local governments. In this

As the life span of our population increases, care of our senior citizens becomes an important problem at all levels of government. Shown here is a man receiving therapy to give him increased use of his arthritic fingers. (City of Philadelphia, Office of the City Representative.)

way state aid helps to raise the level of services of local governments.

Not all people are in favor of state aid. There are people who feel that these grants-in-aid are making the local governments less independent. They say that the unit of government, in this case the state, which supplies the money also controls the service. This is sometimes true. The state usually places some condition on the acceptance of the money. For example, school districts may be required to provide certain minimum services before they are given state aid. The state may require a certain number of school days each year, a certain amount of training for teachers, or a minimum salary for teachers.

However, people who favor state aid say that our governmental services have become so involved that local governments cannot furnish them without this financial help from the state. The viewpoint of these people is prevailing. State aid has increased greatly in the past few decades and is growing each year. Unless local governments are given new sources of taxation, state aid will, and must, continue to increase.

POLICE SERVICES. Another area in which the state and the local units of government are brought close together is in police work. Cooperation between the two levels is important. Drivers' licenses are issued by the state, but the examinations for the licenses may be given by local authorities.

Some states are moving in the direction of having a central filing system for recording traffic violations of drivers. To make such a system effective it is important that local authorities make regular and accurate reports to the state. In this way the state helps the local communities by having complete records for their use. Under the lead-

Point out that where a metropolitan area extends beyond the boundaries of a single county, city-county consolidation cannot provide a single area government.

ership of the state the local governments work together to supply a necessary service of record-keeping. The automobile and the ease of movement from one community to another has made this necessary.

About half of the states have a state police force. Here again cooperation between the local and state police is important for the protection of life and property and for the apprehension of criminals. State and local governments in states with a state police force are cooperatively giving better service than either one of them could give alone.

OVERLAPPING AND DUPLICATION OF

SERVICES   There are many instances of duplication of services provided by various units of government. The citizen pays city and county taxes. Each unit may have its

own assessor and its own treasurer. A township has road equipment to take care of township roads; the county has similar equipment for county roads in the same township. These are a few examples to illustrate duplication.

Some of this overlapping and duplication of services may be necessary, but some of it can be eliminated. Where two units of government are supplying the same service for an area, duplication is costly and often unnecessary. Study and cooperation have done away with some of this duplication at a saving of tax money. Many people believe that much more duplication can be eliminated.

Many cities have grown so large that they occupy much of the land area of the counties in which they are located. Yet in many cases these counties continue to operate as they did when most of the area was rural. They elect the same officials as for-

An example of city-county cooperation is the City-County Building of Detroit and Wayne County. By having employees of both governments here, some duplicating of services is eliminated. (City of Detroit photo)

merly, while the city carries on most of the governmental functions.

A number of the larger cities, however, are trying to solve this problem through city-county consolidation, in which one government takes care of the duties of both governments. St. Louis, Philadelphia, Miami, and Boston are examples.

Some of the other city-county areas are trying to reduce duplication of services by having one official do the same work for both units. One treasurer may collect both city and county taxes; one assessor may assess property for both units of government; one purchasing agent may buy needed materials and equipment for both; and so on. This may gradually lead to more economical local government as further study shows other areas in which duplication is unnecessary.

A similar situation exists between township and county governments in the rural areas. We have already mentioned the maintenance and repair of roads. In areas where the township still services its own roads, the townships duplicate much of the county equipment and leave it idle much of the time. So, many counties are servicing completely all roads in the county, including township roads. In this way the county buys the needed expensive equipment and uses it fully.

Cooperation between townships and county saves money and often provides better service. Also, as in the case of city-county cooperation, some county officers are taking over the duties of township officials. The county treasurer, for example, may collect all the taxes for the county, including those for the townships.

The problem of duplication of services is by no means solved. There are individuals who feel that the services should be kept close to the people. They say that the township assessor should assess the local property and the township treasurer should collect the tax. In many cases the individual who may lose his job because of the elimination of duplicate services agrees with them.

For example, if one treasurer collects taxes for two governments, the services of two treasurers are no longer needed. One is enough. But the one who is to lose his job may try to find reasons to show why consolidation is bad. It may be only a selfish motive on his part. He places personal interests above the interests of the whole community.

Nevertheless, more and more people realize that much duplication can be eliminated. By doing so, money can be saved and service may be improved. Studies are constantly being made by governmental agencies and private groups to find ways and means of doing away with the duplication of services. This is often referred to as "streamlining" government.

GROWING UNREST IN THE CITIES

The 1960's saw the development of a series of urban disorders, especially in the North, that were an outgrowth of the struggle for the freedom and rights described in Chapter 4. In many cities there were riots and civil disturbances. Some Negroes were rebelling against the many years of injustice and deprivation. They were seeking equality of opportunity and equal rights before the law. They needed adequate housing, better schools, and more jobs. Real progress in all these important fields had been too long delayed.

Individuals and groups, both Negroes and white, pressed for faster action. Congress, state legislatures, and city councils were urged to pass laws and ordinances to ensure that all American citizens would enjoy the rights and opportunities that were too

Refer to the report of the President's National Advisory Commission on Civil Disorders, 1968.

often withheld from a large minority. These groups organized marches, picketed, carried signs, and held sit-ins to emphasize their demands. To some extent they were successful in their demands, but full civil equality was not achieved. Too many Negroes continued to be second-class citizens.

CIVIL DISTURBANCE. Upsurge of Negro pride, coupled with demands for economic, political, and social advances, gave emphasis to the growing discontent. During the long, hot summers—and the disturbances were not always confined to the summer months—it took only an incident to light the spark that set off a riot among some groups protesting the prevailing conditions. An arrest—a rumor about an imagined crime, or perhaps even an actual one—a story of real or alleged mistreatment —a traffic ticket—such were the sparks that ignited into riots and serious civil disturbances in a matter of hours, sometimes minutes. These occurred in Los Angeles, Chicago, New York, Detroit, Cleveland, Milwaukee, Newark, and many other cities. All were faced with civil uprisings that resulted in gunfire, injury, death, burning, looting, and fighting in the streets.

Local police were often unable to deal with the situation. They needed help from the state police and the national guard. States of emergency were declared. Curfews were imposed. People were ordered to stay in their homes. Businesses closed down. Travel was restricted. Theaters were closed. Sporting events were canceled. Sale of liquor was forbidden. Gradually order was restored with soldiers patrolling the streets.

But order without a change of the conditions that led to the uprising is not a solution. All that is done is to provide time to correct inequities, to change the conditions which create the unrest and bring on the riots. What are these conditions and what is being done to change them?

THE EFFECTS OF HISTORY. One of the basic factors behind the problems that face our cities today is history. Hundreds of years of the evils of slavery cannot be quickly erased. Slavery was presumably followed by freedom and equality after the Emancipation Proclamation and the adoption of Constitutional amendments 13, 14, and 15. But for the large majority of Negroes this equality was never achieved. So the history of several centuries of slavery and second-class citizenship provided the background for the unrest among a part of our population and the resulting uprisings and rebellion. Congress and the courts have taken several important steps to correct the effects of history, as was described in Chapter 4. But there is yet much more to be done.

GHETTOS AND SUBURBS. The population explosion and the mobility of the people have affected cities in many ways and have contributed to the unrest in the cities. Two important factors are the development of ghetto and slum conditions on the one hand and the movement to suburban areas on the other. Since World War II Negroes have migrated from the South to northern cities in large numbers. Thinking there were greater opportunities for education and employment, more and more Negroes joined the trek to the cities. Soon many cities had nonwhite populations that were 20, 30, 40 per cent, and even higher. But the opportunities Negroes sought and hoped for were often not there. Some jobs were open to them; but for many jobs they lacked the necessary education and training. Also, some employers would not hire them. Negroes who did find employment frequently did not stay employed very long. They were the first victims of changes in the economy. All too often they were "the last hired and the first fired."

Urban renewal programs provided for the transformation of this Detroit slum area into an attractive-looking neighborhood. (City of Detroit photo)

With respect to housing, often only the poorest homes were available to them; only the most depressed areas were places where they could live. Usually by agreement whites refused to sell or rent homes to Negroes in desirable areas, and most Negroes lacked money to buy into these areas in the first place. This is a vicious circle —lack of jobs, lack of money, poor homes and surroundings. As a result a number of Negroes live under slum and ghetto conditions. Often these areas also have fewer governmental services, older schools, and inadequate shopping areas. All of this adds up to a situation that kills initiative, develops discontent, and is a breeding place for crime.

At the same time that Negroes were moving into the city, many of the whites in middle and upper income groups were moving out of the city into the suburbs. The services of these individuals are usually no longer available to the city to help improve city conditions; neither are their tax dollars.

WORK ON THE PROBLEM. What is being done to try to correct the situation? The national, state, and local governments are working on many aspects of the problem. The national government has an extensive program to reduce poverty. State

A day-care center established by the Office of Economic Opportunity in Newburgh, New York, has served as a model for similar anti-poverty projects elsewhere in the United States. (Du Pont, Better Living Magazine)

and local governments are trying to eliminate slum and ghetto conditions. All units of government are providing improved educational opportunities for children and adults. Urban renewal programs are aimed at making better housing available. Government and private industry are cooperating to reduce unemployment and to provide training for the unemployed to make them employable. But there is so much to be done, and it takes time to catch up on the failures of past generations. Someone has said, "We are engaged in a race between achieving the goals of a good life for all people and catastrophe." Remedies must be achieved not only to avoid more riots in the future, but mainly to secure for all people the basic rights which are theirs as part of the human race.

COOPERATION IN METROPOLITAN
AREAS   Some of the most disturbing problems among local governments arise in the large metropolitan areas. The communities are so close together that what one does or does not do affects many others.

The metropolitan area includes the city and often dozens of suburban towns and cities, many of them located in neighboring counties.

In some cases the metropolitan area even includes land in more than one state. The metropolitan area of New York City, for example, includes land in New Jersey; "Chicagoland" reaches into Indiana and Wisconsin; metropolitan St. Louis crosses the Mississippi River into Illinois; Greater Detroit includes land in at least three counties in Michigan and has an important bearing on land across the international boundary of Canada. These are only samples. Similar conditions apply to most of our large cities.

Today areas even larger than a metropolitan area are developing. The increase in population and the urbanization of our society has brought about concentration of population, business, and industry in several geographic corridors. One of these is the land along the Atlantic coast from Boston through New York to Washington, D. C. Another is on the Pacific coast from San Francisco through Los Angeles to San Diego. In the Midwest there is the Chicago-

Members of the Louisville, Kentucky, Urban League board work together to promote such activities as job development and educational assistance. (Du Pont, Better Living Magazine)

Cleveland-Detroit-Pittsburgh corridor. *Megalopolis* is the name often given these areas.

What are some of the problems that arise? There are many. A few of the more general ones are: the many units of government, rubbish disposal, transportation and traffic, law enforcement, water supply, zoning, taxation, recreation facilities, and airports.

MANY UNITS OF GOVERNMENT. Because there are many communities that comprise a metropolitan area or a megalopolis, there are many units of local government. Each of them is *autonomous,* each is its "own boss." Each could, and sometimes does, pass regulations and ordinances which differ from those of the others. This can, and sometimes does, cause confusion.

Each of the various communities of the same metropolitan area has its own way of doing things, which can result in confusion and even serious disagreements. For example, schools may operate on different schedules; tax systems may vary; and traffic laws may not be the same. These differences be-

come greater as a metropolitan area grows and spills over into neighboring states.

DISPOSAL OF RUBBISH. All cities have large amounts of rubbish which they collect each day and week. They must dispose of this in one way or another. It was formerly the general custom for large cities to rent land outside of incorporated communities and to use it as a dumping place for its rubbish. Usually this was low land which needed filling. As cities have grown and as suburban areas have sprung up, these "dumps" were of necessity located farther and farther away from the city. The suburban towns did not want the city rubbish dumps near them.

Cities have turned to incinerators to help them dispose of their burnable rubbish. While this helps, there is still the ash to be hauled away and dumped. Then, too, the location of incinerators is a problem. No one seems to want the incinerator in his neighborhood. Rubbish disposal is a major problem for metropolitan areas.

TRANSPORTATION AND TRAFFIC. Many of the people who live in the subur-

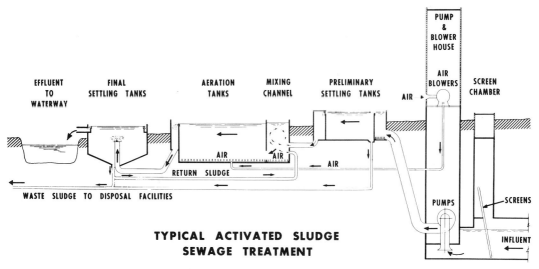

TYPICAL ACTIVATED SLUDGE SEWAGE TREATMENT

An effective method of sewage disposal used in Chicago is illustrated here. (Courtesy of the Metropolitan Sanitary District of Greater Chicago)

ban areas surrounding a large city work in the city. Each morning they go into the city and each evening they come home. The city has its own traffic problem. But this movement of people to and from the suburbs creates an even greater transportation and traffic problem.

Transportation systems—railroads, buses, subways—are needed to carry the people to and from the city. Who should provide and regulate the transportation system—the city where they work or the suburb where they live? Highways are needed for the buses and for the hundreds and thousands of private cars which go back and forth. Who should construct and maintain the highway—the city or the suburb? What responsibility should be assumed by the state governments? the national government?

The movement of many people creates traffic congestion. This traffic must be regulated as it moves throughout the whole metropolitan area. If the traffic ordinances differ from one community to the next, there is more confusion and greater congestion. Who makes the regulations? Who

controls the traffic, especially at intersections on the boundaries of neighboring communities?

Transportation and the regulation of traffic is truly a major problem in a metropolitan area. Anyone who has been a part of the five o'clock home-bound traffic jam in any of our large cities will agree.

LAW ENFORCEMENT. Regulation of traffic is only one part of law enforcement in metropolitan areas. Control of crime is of great importance, too. For this each community has its own police force. There is frequently great variation among the communities in the degree to which they enforce state laws. Sometimes one suburb will become notorious for its lack of law enforcement. There may be secret bargains between criminals and police officers. Some of the crime resulting from this lax enforcement may affect neighboring communities.

Another problem in metropolitan areas is created by gangs going from one community to another and causing trouble. Sometimes the local police may be satisfied merely to move the gang on, getting it beyond its own city limits. The traffic viola-

Helping to handle the enormous flow of traffic into New York City is the George Washington Bridge. (Port of New York Authority)

Large urban areas face the problem of providing an adequate water supply for vast numbers of people. The Spruce Run Reservoir near Clinton, New Jersey, helps meet the needs of its area. (Courtesy of New Jersey Dept. of Conservation and Economic Development)

tor who gets quickly from one suburb to another presents another problem for police officers. Law enforcement is a problem, and strict and uniform law enforcement in the many communities is a goal of metropolitan areas.

WATER SUPPLY. An adequate water supply is always a necessity for any community. But when as many as forty to fifty separate communities exist in a single area, supplying water becomes a real problem. Shall each community have its own source of water? Shall one community develop an adequate water system and then sell water to each of the others? In areas where this is done, it is usually the large city which supplies the water. When it does so, shall its regulations regarding the use of water be binding on the communities to which it supplies water?

For example, if it sets hours for lawn sprinkling during the summer, shall the other communities also observe these hours? Does this mean that one unit of local government is making rules for another? When the city makes a decision about *fluoridating* its water, this decision also affects the other

communities. Should it be permitted to do so without getting acceptance of its decision by the affected communities? These are some of the questions that arise in providing an adequate water supply for a metropolitan area.

ZONING. Often some local communities are successful in separating factory areas, business districts, residential sections, and other areas through good zoning ordinances. But some of the results of good zoning may be destroyed because neighboring communities may not have zoning laws. A small factory section or a row of ill-kept stores may grow up in one community across the boundary from a fine residential section of another.

There is little that one community can do by itself to avoid such conditions. But regional planning and zoning will help. Just as cities have learned that planning the growth of the city is important, so metropolitan areas are learning that planning for the whole area is important and necessary. The metropolitan areas of Boston, Cleveland, and Detroit are examples of areas doing regional planning.

A good project for this chapter is a land map of your city or community. Have students locate the residential, commercial, and industrial areas of your city. Ask for suggestions for improvements in zoning.

TAXATION. Suburban areas surrounding a large city often boast of their lower taxes. Real estate men use the claim of lower taxes as an inducement for getting people to buy suburban property. But large cities sometimes provide services not provided by the smaller communities. These additional services tend to make the city's tax rate higher.

In trying to coax industrial concerns from the cities to build factories in their areas, the smaller communities advertise lower taxes. Sometimes a community will even offer a factory free land. The factory means work for the people. It means business for the merchants. The tax from the factory means income for the local government.

This rivalry between city and surrounding communities may lead to disagreements and bitterness. Instead of cooperation there may be harmful competition.

Such rivalry may bring about unpleasant fights and arguments between the officials of the central city and those of other governments in the metropolitan area. This is especially true in state-aid payments.

The suburbs in many metropolitan areas are growing faster than the central city. The population of some cities is even declining. State-aid payments are usually made on the basis of the number of people in each community. The fast-growing communities want a census made more frequently than each ten years because this increases their state aid. A slower-growing place, usually the central city, may not be in favor of a new census, because its state aid might be reduced. The financial poli-

---

COG

A new word—more correctly, a new abbreviation—has come into the political and economic life of metropolitan areas. COG, which stands for council of governments, is a voluntary organization of local governments of a metropolitan area. Its purpose is cooperative planning and action on area-wide problems and issues.

There are today about one hundred councils throughout the United States. The largest is the Metropolitan Regional Council in the New York City area. The fifteen county and the twenty-two city governments of the area have a combined population of about sixteen million. Some councils have been organized in areas without large cities, but most of them are developing around the nation's larger cities.

The recognition of a need for the councils has come since about 1950 because of the rapid growth of metropolitan areas and the spread of urban living. Experience shows that to function effectively each local government in a metropolitan area cannot carry on its many activities without concern for the effect of its actions on other units. This becomes readily apparent when it is realized that the metropolitan areas of such cities as Chicago and Philadelphia each have about a thousand governmental units of various kinds.

But the council of governments idea is not accepted without reservation by all governments of a metropolitan area. Among some officials the organization of a council is a highly controversial issue. Some big-city officials feel that COG may not give the city as much representation as the size of its population deserves. Some small community officials are suspicious that COG may be dominated by the larger cities and that the smaller units may have no influence in its operation.

In spite of these concerns members of both groups realize that some form of cooperative arrangement is needed to provide more effective services of all kinds in metropolitan areas. There is a growing acceptance of the COG idea. It is very likely that the number of councils will of necessity continue to increase. As their influence grows, they may become effective in unifying the goals and programs of metropolitan areas.

cies of the communities of the metropolitan area are a sore problem which causes many headaches.

RECREATION FACILITIES. A small community in a large metropolitan area has a fine community park. To keep the park for its own residents and to keep out other people from the metropolitan area, it builds a fence around the park and issues passes to its own people. No one can get in without a pass. When we look at this action from the point of view of the people of the small community, we might agree that they should keep the park for their own use.

But in the same metropolitan area the large city maintains many parks and playgrounds. Who uses these? Obviously the city cannot issue a pass to each of its more than a million people. Even if it could, it would be very costly to police the parks to keep nonresidents out. So people from the whole metropolitan area use the city's parks and playgrounds.

The same is true of the city's zoos, libraries, art and other museums, bathing beaches, and the like. Shall the large city furnish such services for the whole area? These are some of the services which may make the city's tax rate higher. On the other hand, the smaller communities often raise questions about providing police and traffic services for city residents as they pass through the suburbs and smaller communities on their way to recreation areas.

In other cases, the central city locates some of its facilities, especially zoos and golf courses, in suburban areas. These are tax exempt. But the small community must furnish police service for the crowds who come from the city. The small community often complains about the cost of this service. This question of providing recreation facilities and services related to them is truly an area problem.

AIRPORTS. Bus and railroad depots are usually located in the center of the city. But air transportation has developed after most of the city has been built. Where shall the city locate an airport? Or shall it be a metropolitan area airport? Everyone agrees that metropolitan areas need airports with adequate facilities. But, like the rubbish dump, nobody seems to want an airport in his backyard.

Community recreation centers provide an opportunity for people to come together to enjoy their leisure hours. (City of Detroit photo)

If the airport is too far from the center of the metropolitan area, much of the value of air transportation is lost. Trying to locate it within a short driving distance from downtown creates difficulties with the neighboring communities. This is one of the more recent problems of metropolitan areas which few cities have solved satisfactorily.

POLLUTION. Air and water pollution are rapidly becoming major problems facing metropolitan areas. While the problem of pollution is not limited to metropolitan areas, it is especially acute there because of the concentration of people and industry.

The pollution of air results largely from the operation of internal combustion engines of motor vehicles, the operation of industrial plants, and the burning of coal and oil to generate electric power. The water of rivers and lakes is becoming polluted with sewage and industrial wastes.

Various levels of government are beginning to look for solutions to this problem of air and water pollution. For example, New York City passed a law in 1966 aimed at cleaning up the air of the city. About twenty years before that Los Angeles County established a board which had responsibility for working on the problem. In 1967 Congress passed a law requiring new automobiles to be equipped with devices to control pollution. Water pollution is being attacked by some governments and private industries through improved methods of sewage and waste disposal. The concern about water pollution is bringing about some anti-pollution laws and some voluntary efforts.

However, much more needs to be done if the air we breathe and the water we drink is to be made and kept pure. Metropolitan areas are learning that the free air and the almost free water can be very costly. This is largely a case of an advancing civilization creating its own problems.

SOLVING METROPOLITAN - AREA PROBLEMS. This section has called attention to some of the common problems of metropolitan areas. As more and more people move to the urban areas and as our population grows, these problems will become even greater. How are they being met? What is being done about them?

To a great extent the large city takes the leadership and the small surrounding communities follow her example. Metropolitan traffic laws are often patterned after those of the large city. Also in other specific instances the suburbs watch to see what the city does. The city provides the leadership; it sets the example. The smaller communities and the suburbs follow.

More and more, however, people are recognizing that this type of voluntary action does not always solve the problem. Sometimes the smaller communities may be

But Don't Take Off Your Gas Mask Yet!

Poinier in the Detroit News.

dissatisfied with the city's course of action. Sometimes they may be antagonistic toward the city and its leadership. Often the large city has no better solution to a problem than does the small community. A greater number of people are beginning to realize that if some of these problems of metropolitan areas are ever to be solved, it must be done by cooperative effort.

The number of metropolitan-area regional planning commissions throughout the United States is growing. These are cooperative efforts to solve common problems. Planning is being done on a regional basis rather than on a community basis. The cities, towns, and suburbs of a metropolitan area are getting together to tackle their common problems. Housing, traffic, airports, parks, recreation, police and fire protection, highways, hospitals, rubbish disposal, control of air and water pollution, and other services and facilities for the whole area are being studied by groups representing all communities. Raising money to pay for services is becoming an area concern. Taxation is more than a single-community problem; solutions are being sought on an area basis.

The area commission is composed of representatives from communities throughout the metropolitan area. Every community is represented. The task of the commission is to seek solutions which are in the best interests of the whole area. While much of this regional planning is still in the discussion stage, some of the results are encouraging. Successful programs are in operation with respect to highways, airports, water systems, sewage disposal plants, and recreation facilities.

Examples are the extensive expressway programs of several metropolitan areas, the disposal of sewage by the Chicago Sanitary District, and the parks and recreational facilities of the Huron-Clinton Metropolitan Authority (Detroit Area). Such regional planning helps to overcome some of the big problems of urban living in our metropolitan areas. In many cases national and state governments are also cooperating in the search for solutions to the problems facing these areas.

STUDY QUESTIONS

1. What are some of the problems confronting local government?

2. What are some reasons for allowing home rule for local governments?

3. How can the passing of special legislation lead to abuses?

4. How are these abuses corrected?

5. Distinguish between legislative and constitutional home rule.

6. For what services do states make grants of money to local governments?

7. Why are these grants-in-aid made?

8. What is a chief argument of people who oppose state aid?

9. How do state and local governments cooperate in carrying on police services?

10. What are some examples of duplication of services by two or more local governments? How could the duplication be eliminated?

11. What has been the chief cause of the unrest in the cities?

12. What has been the role of history in the racial problems facing the nation?

13. What are some of the features of the ghetto conditions in large cities?

14. Why has the movement to the suburbs been harmful to cities?

15. Why do large metropolitan areas present special problems?

16. Why has rubbish disposal become an especially vexing problem?

17. What problems of traffic regulation and enforcement face most metropolitan areas?

18. Why is the cooperation of law-enforcement officers of neighboring communities important?

CONCEPTS AND GENERALIZATIONS

1
Some of the chief problems between states and their local governments concern the extent of home rule.

2
One method of state legislatures in dealing with local problems is to pass special legislation which applies only to one community or to a limited number of communities.

3
Home rule for local governments may be either legislative or constitutional.

4
State grants-in-aid are made to assist local governments and to promote state programs.

5
State and local governments cooperate extensively in the area of police work.

6
Needless and costly duplication of services can be avoided by cooperative planning among local governments.

7
The basic cause for civil disturbances in the cities has been the long history of inequalities in the treatment of members of minority groups.

8
The migration of Negroes to the cities and the movement of middle-class whites to the suburbs have emphasized the racial problems of cities.

9
Governments and private groups are working to improve the realization of the basic rights of all people with respect to employment, housing, and education.

10
The growth of metropolitan areas has brought into sharp focus certain conditions and problems resulting from the concentration of people in limited geographic areas.

11
Cooperation among local governments in a metropolitan area or a megalopolis tends to improve living for all people in the area.

19. What is meant by regional planning and zoning?

20. Why is there sometimes disagreement between a large city and its suburbs regarding the need for a census?

21. Why are airports of most older large cities far from their central areas?

22. Why is regional planning important for metropolitan areas?

IDEAS FOR DISCUSSION

1. Some persons oppose state grants-in-aid to local governments on the basis that the local communities and the people tend to lose some of their independence. They fear that increased dependence on the state and the national government will tend to destroy our democratic way of life. Discuss this idea with your classmates.

2. State laws for the issuing of drivers' licenses are uniform throughout a state. But in some states when the examinations are given through local agencies, individual interpretations and requirements may make it easier to secure a license in one locality than in another. Should drivers' licenses be issued by state agencies to insure uniformity? Why?

3. The disposal of garbage is a major problem of metropolitan areas. Various proposals are being suggested to solve this problem. A number of communities are considering the idea of installing a garbage grinder in each residence and of having residents pay for the installation over a period of years. Discuss this proposal, considering especially cost and health factors.

4. Discuss the relative merits of cooperation and competition between a city and its suburbs.

5. Should the small community which borders a large city restrict the use of its park and playground to its own residents? Why?

6. Since the large city of any metropolitan area includes many more people than the neighboring communities, the latter should follow the lead of the city in policies and practices. Do you agree? Discuss the reasons for your reactions.

7. Discuss the importance and the effect of these data:

　　a) In 1910, 73 per cent of all Negroes lived on farms and in small communities.

　　b) In 1960, 73 per cent of all Negroes were living in urban areas.

c) Between 1920 and 1940 the number of Negroes in central cities increased by 83 per cent.

d) Between 1940 and 1960 the number again increased, this time by 123 per cent.

8. Discuss this situation:

The director of a metropolitan regional planning authority writes to the governor: "We need the state's help to carry out our progressive program for the entire region. City X has never sent a representative to any of our meetings, although it has been invited and urged to do so many times. Right now we are planning an expressway which must pass through City X. We cannot get that city to cooperate. The expressway will have little value if we must continue to use the narrow surface road through City X. We want the state to force City X to cooperate with the rest of the region."

THINGS TO DO

1. Make inquiries about the extent of home rule in your state. Report your findings to the class.

2. Find out how much state aid your local governments have received in the past year. Have committees of students visit county, city, and school offices to get this information. For what services was the money used?

3. Find out how the licensing of automobile drivers is handled in your state. Report to the class on any special requirements for young drivers and on conditions under which a license may be revoked.

4. Have a group of students write to the chambers of commerce in several large cities. Each student should request information about the size and boundaries of the county in which it is located. In some cases it will be possible to secure maps which will show graphically the territory covered by each. Discuss the implications of the information obtained.

5. Most of our large metropolitan areas are planning and building limited-access expressways. If you live near a large city, secure literature about its expressway plan. Study it, and show the class how it will help solve the traffic problem. You may also be able to build scale models to show the operation of the expressways.

6. Select a number of large cities, and make a study of the location of their airports. Find out especially how far the airport is from the center of the city and the driving time necessary to reach it. Find out how cities acquire land outside their boundaries for airports.

7. Hold a panel discussion on one of the major problems of metropolitan regions. Have members of the panel represent various interests of the area: the large city, the suburbs, and the rural community.

8. After the riots of the summer of 1967 President Johnson appointed the National Advisory Commission on Civil Disorders to make a thorough study of the causes of the riots and to make recommendations for remedying the causes and for preventing future riots. Its chairman was Governor Kerner of Illinois. Get a copy of the report and summarize the recommendations of what cities should do. Discuss the recommendations with your classmates.

9. Make a survey of the poor in a city ghetto area to find out about their problems, their frustrations, and their hopes.

FURTHER READINGS

Bollens, John C., and Schmandt, Henry J., THE METROPOLIS: ITS PEOPLE, POLITICS, AND ECONOMIC LIFE. Harper & Row, Publishers, Inc., 1970.

Farkas, Suzanne, URBAN LOBBYING: MAYORS IN THE FEDERAL AREA. New York University Press, 1971.

Herber, Lewis, CRISIS IN OUR CITIES. Prentice-Hall, Inc., 1965.

Lancaster, Lane W., GOVERNMENT IN RURAL AMERICA. D. Van Nostrand Co., Inc., 1952. Chapters 14 and 15.

Lineberry, Robert L., and Sharkansy, Ira, URBAN POLITICS AND PUBLIC POLICY. Harper and Row, Publishers, 1971.

Liston, Robert A., DOWNTOWN: OUR CHALLENGING URBAN PROBLEMS. Delacorte Press, 1968.

McQuade, Walter, ed., CITIES FIT TO LIVE IN. The Macmillan Co., 1971.

Mills, Edwin S., URBAN ECONOMICS. Scott, Foresman and Co., 1972.

Seashore, Stanley E., and McNeill, Robert J., MANAGEMENT OF THE URBAN CRISIS. Free Press, 1971.

Von Eckhardt, Wolf, CHALLENGE OF MEGALOPOLIS. Macmillan Co., 1964. (Paperback)

Wood, Robert C., SUBURBIA: ITS PEOPLE AND THEIR POLITICS. Houghton Mifflin Co., 1959.

Civil Disturbance and the Cities

In the spring and summer of 1967 racial disturbances and riots erupted in many cities of the nation. The listing of places and dates was headed a "Calendar of Violence" by one writer:[1]

City	Dates
Omaha (Neb.)	April 1-2
Nashville (Tenn.)	April 8-10
Jackson (Miss.)	May 10-13
Houston (Texas)	May 16-17
Chicago (Ill.)	May 21 and 30
Boston (Mass.)	June 2-5
Tampa (Fla.)	June 11
Prattville .(Ala.)	June 11
Cincinnati (Ohio)	June 12-16
	July 3-5
	July 26-27
Atlanta (Ga.)	June 19
Buffalo (N.Y.)	June 27-29
Des Moines (Iowa)	July 2 and 16
Kansas City (Mo.)	July 9
Waterloo (Iowa)	July 10
Erie (Pa.)	July 12-13
Hartford (Conn.)	July 12-13
Newark (N.J.)	July 13-17
Plainfield (N.J.)	July 17-19
New York City	July 23-26
Detroit (Mich.)	July 24-27
Cambridge (Md.)	July 24-25
Grand Rapids (Mich.)	Late July
Rochester (N.Y.)	July 24-25
Milwaukee (Wis.)	July 30-Aug. 2

* * *

In a speech in August of 1967 delivered before the Twenty-eighth Triennial Council Meeting of the United Chapters of Phi Beta Kappa, Senator Abraham Ribicoff, Democrat of Connecticut, described the situation in these words:

A century of neglect has turned America into a nation of defiant cities. The children and grandchildren of the Southern sharecroppers are an urban generation—and they have found that the promised land of the North is barren. They have not found jobs, decent housing, adequate education, good health, and regular police protection.

Nobody planned it that way. But the results of this neglect are as systematic and devastating as if it had been planned —every bit of it—down to the last detail.

. . . I do not have the whole answer. Nor does anyone else. But I do believe that any program of ending the slums and building the cities of tomorrow must include five basic elements:

1. Guaranteeing job opportunities for all;

2. Providing a decent home in a decent environment that includes personal security and public safety;

3. Offering the maximum encouragement to private investment in rebuilding our cities and the lives of our people;

4. Involving the individual in his own destiny and emphasizing neighborhood development;

5. Reorganizing our Federal government so that the new ideas of today will not wither on the bureaucratic vines of yesterday.[2]

* * *

As Detroit and some other cities began to return to some semblance of a peaceful way of life, President Johnson established the National Advisory Commission on Civil Disorders on July 28, 1967. In an address to the nation he said,

. . . The only genuine, long-range solution for what has happened lies in an attack—mounted at every level—upon the conditions that breed despair and

---

[1] From *American Observer*, published by Civic Education Service, Washington, D.C.

[2] From a condensed version of the speech in *The Key Reporter*, Autumn, 1967, pp. 3, 4.

violence. All of us know what those conditions are: ignorance, discrimination, slums, poverty, disease, not enough jobs. We should attack these conditions—not because we are frightened by conflict, but because we are fired by conscience. We should attack them because there is simply no other way to achieve a decent and orderly society in America. . . .

He appointed Governor Otto Kerner of Illinois, a Democrat, as chairman of the Commission and Mayor John Lindsay, a Republican, as vice chairman. Other members of the Commission were:

Senator Fred R. Harris of Oklahoma
Senator Edward W. Brooke of Mass.
Representative James C. Corman of Calif.
Representative William M. McCulloch of Ohio
I. W. Abel, President of the United Steelworkers of America
Charles B. Thornton, Chairman of the Board of Litton Industries
Roy Wilkins, Executive Director of the National Association for the Advancement of Colored People
Katherine Graham Peden, Commissioner of Commerce of the State of Kentucky
Herbert Jenkins, Chief of Police of Atlanta, Georgia

The President charged the Commission to answer three basic questions:

What happened?
Why did it happen?
What can be done to prevent it from happening again?

The Commission reported the results of its study and its recommendations to the President and to the nation in March of 1968. In summary, it stated in its report of more than 500 pages:

This is our basic conclusion: Our Nation is moving toward two societies, one black, one white—separate and unequal.

Reaction to last summer's disorders has quickened the movement and deepened the division. Discrimination and segregation have long permeated much of American life; they now threaten the future of every American.

This deepening racial division is not inevitable. The movement apart can be reversed. Choice is still possible. Our principal task is to define that choice and to press for a national resolution.

To pursue our present course will involve the continuing polarization of the American community and, ultimately, the destruction of basic democratic values.

The alternative is not blind repression or capitulation to lawlessness. It is the realization of common opportunities for all within a single society.

This alternative will require a commitment to national action—compassionate, massive and sustained, backed by the resources of the most powerful and the richest nation on this earth. From every American it will require new attitudes, new understanding, and, above all, new will.

The vital needs of the Nation must be met; hard choices must be made, and, if necessary, new taxes enacted.

Violence cannot build a better society. Disruption and disorder nourish repression, not justice. They strike at the freedom of every citizen. The community cannot—it will not—tolerate coercion and mob rule.

Violence and destruction must be ended—in the streets of the ghetto and in the lives of people.

Segregation and poverty have created in the racial ghetto a destructive environment totally unknown to most white Americans.

What white Americans have never fully understood—but what the Negro can never forget—is that white society is deeply implicated in the ghetto. White institutions created it, white institutions maintain it, and white society condones it.

It is time now to turn with all the purpose at our command to the major unfinished business of this Nation. It is time to adopt strategies for action that will produce quick and visible progress. It is time to make good the promises of American democracy to all citizens—urban and rural, white and black, Spanish-surname, American Indian, and every minority group.

Our recommendations embrace three basic principles:

- To mount programs on a scale equal to the dimension of the problems;

- To aim these programs for high impact in the immediate future in order to close the gap between promise and performance;

- To undertake new initiatives and experiments that can change the system of failure and frustration that now dominates the ghetto and weakens our society.

These programs will require unprecedented levels of funding and performance, but they neither probe deeper nor demand more than the problems which called them forth. There can be no higher priority for national action and no higher claim on the nation's conscience.[1]

The report details the conditions in our cities as the Commission learned to know them through extensive study. It is not a pleasant picture that the report portrays. But it is one the nation must face realistically if it is to survive and if it is to move forward.

In chapter after chapter the members make strong recommendations for action to these groups and in these areas:

Local governments
City government and police authorities
Control of disorder
The administration of justice under emergency conditions
Damages: Repair and compensation
National action in the areas of
   Employment
   Education
   The welfare system
   Housing

- Some members of the class may wish to report on the specific recommendations of the Commission given in each of these sections.

The Commission concludes its report with these words:

One of the first witnesses to be invited to appear before this Commission was Dr. Kenneth B. Clark, a distinguished and perceptive scholar. Referring to the reports of earlier riot commissions, he said:

"I read that report . . . of the 1919 riot in Chicago, and it is as if I were reading the report of the investigating committee on the Harlem riot of '35, the report of the McCone Commission on the Watts riot.

"I must again in candor say to you members of this Commission—it is a kind of Alice in Wonderland—with the same moving picture reshown over and over again, the same analysis, the same recommendations, and the same inaction."

These words come to our minds as we conclude this report.

We have provided an honest beginning. We have learned much. But we have uncovered no startling truths, no unique insights, no simple solutions. The destruction and the bitterness of racial disorder, the harsh polemics of black revolt and white repression have been seen and heard before in this country.

_____
[1] Report of the National Advisory Commission on Civil Disorders. Government Printing Office, 1968.

480

It is time now to end the destruction and the violence, not only in the streets of the ghetto but in the lives of people.

* * *

Then, soon after the publication of the Report, the nation was shocked and stunned by the wanton and senseless killing of the Rev. Dr. Martin Luther King. Dr. King was the civil rights leader who placed his faith in nonviolence. He had gone to Memphis, Tennessee, to lead a civil rights demonstration in support of a strike of the city's garbage and sanitation workers, most of whom were Negroes. A planned peaceful march erupted in violence led by a group of young Negroes. A few days later Dr. King returned to try the nonviolent approach again. He was the victim of an assassin's bullet as he stood on the balcony of the motel where he was staying.

In the wake of the slaying came both bad and good. On the one hand, there was a return to violence in more than 100 of the nation's cities and communities, notably in Chicago and Washington. On the other hand, there was a resolution on the part of most Americans that Dr. King should not have died in vain. They resolved that the ideals for which he lived and died must be put into practice and that the racism in our society must be eliminated. President Johnson declared an official day of mourning. He asked for speedy enactment of complete and full civil rights for all people. He called for new federal programs to eliminate the problems of the nation which tend to turn Americans against one another.

As you review and discuss the racial problems facing the nation, consider the following:

- The Commission's recommendations
- Agreements and differences between Senator Ribicoff's suggestions and the Commission's recommendations
- Changes effected by civil rights legislation
- The results of Dr. King's assassination
- Programs and plans of your community and state in securing the blessings of liberty for all people
- Your suggestions for improving life for all of the nation's minorities
- The changes in conditions since the Commission Report of 1968
- The situation today
- Are we moving toward unity or toward greater separation?
- Changes since the 1967 riots
- Nonviolence to achieve civil rights
- Militancy to achieve civil rights
- Discrimination toward other minority groups

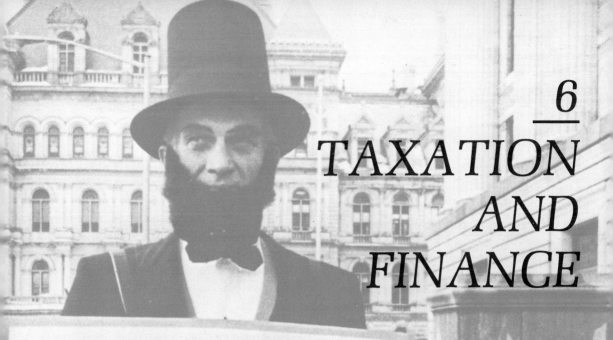

6
TAXATION AND FINANCE

NEEDED: ANOTHER ABE LINCOLN TO *FREE* NEW YORK STATE BUSINESSMEN FROM Sales Tax SLAVERY

Government is big business. During the past few decades it has become constantly bigger. As in any other business, the government operates by taking in money to provide the services it supplies. The money it receives it spends in various ways for such items as salaries and wages, equipment and supplies, and land and buildings.

The cost of government has risen very sharply as the cost of living has gone up. This rising cost of living is reflected in everything for which national, state, and local governments spend money. Wages are higher, materials cost more, construction of buildings and highways is more expensive.

Another reason for the rise in the cost of government is defense. Our nation has been involved in costly wars. We have been much concerned about national defense. As a result the expenditures of the federal government for defense have increased by many billions of dollars.

Still another reason is the demand for more services from governments. Examples of these services are social security on the part of the federal government, more highways built by state and federal govern-

ments, and improved school facilities required by local governments.

Governments get their money in several ways: loans, fees, licenses, toll charges, grants-in-aid, and taxes. Of these, taxation is the most important source. Taxes are most commonly levied on property, incomes, purchases, sales, profits, imports, and wages. As the cost of government has increased, more and more people have been affected by taxation and to a greater extent. Today, nearly everyone pays taxes in some form to all levels of government.

This unit discusses and analyzes the cost and the income of governments.

Chapter 23 describes in some detail the costs of national, state, and local governments. It explains the rise in the cost of government, gives examples of recent budgets and shows the controls which are placed on governmental expenditures.

Chapter 24 treats the income of the three levels of government. It describes the sources of government income and devotes extensive treatment to the various forms of taxation. A number of problems concerning taxation conclude the chapter.

ADMINISTRATIVE BUDGET—budget system used by the federal government until fiscal year 1968; it omitted trust funds from expenditures and receipts.

APPROPRIATION—amount of expenditures specifically designated by Congress for an agency or program.

AUTHORIZATION—amount of money stated in an act, all, part, or none of which may actually be appropriated for the program by Congress in later acts.

BID—the price at which a person or an organization will sell an item or service.

BUDGET—a plan showing the expected income and the proposed expenditures of government.

FISCAL YEAR—the year that the government uses for financial purposes; July 1 to June 30 is the fiscal year for the federal government.

GROSS NATIONAL PRODUCT—the dollar value of all goods and services produced in a country in a given year.

INFLATION—the increase in the cost of goods and services caused by the decreased purchasing power of the dollar.

SPECIFICATION—an exact description of a wanted item or service.

TRUST FUND—money that the government keeps separate from other receipts; money earmarked for specific purposes, such as social security receipts.

UNIFIED BUDGET — budget system adopted by the federal government in fiscal year 1969; budget includes both general funds and trust funds.

THE LANGUAGE OF GOVERNMENT

Make sure that the students understand the meaning of inflation and why it has been a U.S. phenomenon for many years.

23

The Cost of Government

More than one thousand dollars for every man, woman, and child in the United States was spent by the federal government in one recent year. It is almost impossible to understand or imagine the total amount for that year—246 billion dollars. It helps, however, if you realize that the federal government expenditures were equal to spending nearly eight thousand dollars every second, day and night, including Sundays and holidays, during that year.

Before World War I federal government expenses amounted to less than one billion dollars each year. In President Washington's time they were only five million dollars, about sixteen *cents* for each second compared to the present 8,000 *dollars* for each second. Many factors are responsible for this increase.

But federal government expenditures are only part of the picture. In addition there are the costs of the thousands of local governments and the fifty state governments. In recent years these governments have spent more than 100 billion dollars each year. For a long time in our history most of the governmental spending in this country was done by state and local governments. But depression and wars have drastically changed that picture. The table on this page shows that expenditures of all governments—federal, state, and local—have risen sharply since 1913.

GOVERNMENT

SERVICES   Throughout this book you have been studying the various governments which serve you. Many kinds of governmental services have been discussed. It costs money to supply those services—a great deal of money. Each person benefits either directly or indirectly from governmental services. Therefore all must help pay the cost in whatever manner and to whatever extent the people or their representatives decide. Governmental services must be paid for, just as we pay for the services of mechanics, doctors, lawyers, barbers, cleaners, bakers, taxi drivers, and so on.

Do governmental services reach you? Sometimes we meet governmental services each day, but they are so close to us that we more or less take them for granted. Often we forget that they are there and that they cost money. Let us review a few of the

EXPENDITURES OF STATE-LOCAL AND FEDERAL GOVERNMENTS FOR SELECTED YEARS, 1913 TO 1970

(in billions of dollars)

YEAR	STATE AND LOCAL	FEDERAL
1913	2.3	.7
1922	5.6	3.3
1932	8.4	4.7
1934	7.8	6.7
1940	11.2	9.1
1944	10.5	95.1
1948	21.3	33.1
1952	30.8	65.4
1954	34.2	68.8
1957	44.9	68.2
1959	48.9	75.3
1960	51.9	76.7
1962	59.7	89.0
1966	94.9	129.9
1968	116.2	166.4
1970	148.1	184.9

Source: U.S. Department of Commerce.

Spot checks are run on food products to make certain they measure up to government health and nutrition standards. Here government inspectors prepare to test a sample of hot dogs at a chemistry laboratory of the Department of Agriculture's Consumer and Marketing Service. (USDA photo)

services that affect almost all of us very often.

Police and fire protection is provided for all of us. The policeman walking his beat, the scout car, the traffic officer, the corner signal light, the stop sign are all part of this protection. The firemen who are sitting in the firehouse waiting for an alarm to ring are part of government. Even though we may never need to call them to put out a fire at our house, they are there for our protection. Besides, the fact that they are there helps to lower our fire insurance costs.

Garbage and rubbish collection and disposal are necessary, especially in towns and cities. What would we do with the garbage and rubbish that gathers in each household every day if collections were not made?

Construction and maintenance of streets and highways is an absolute necessity today. We want more and better roads. We want them kept in good repair. Seldom do we think about government when we are planning a vacation trip. We merely look at our highway map, lay out our route, get in the car, and go. Behind the trip is a government or a series of governments which build and maintain highways and make the trips possible.

Vacation trips take us to national and state parks. Local communities have parks and playgrounds. Governments supply recreation areas and facilities of many kinds. We look for them, we use them. As an example, millions of people each year visit parks like Yellowstone and the Grand Canyon. Here is a government service to help us with our leisure time and to make life more pleasant.

Near your town may be a radar installation for the detection of planes. There may be an army, naval, or air force base nearby. There may be an ordnance plant which makes defense and war materiels. All of these and many more activities are being carried on by the federal government for the defense of the nation. At the present time about one-third of the total of all federal government expenditures is for defense. The defense of the nation has become one of the most expensive services that we buy. It is one service of which most people are aware.

Local and county school districts and state governments support elementary and secondary schools for all children. The local and state governments are also providing college and university education for more people at public expense. Through a number of expanding programs the federal government is helping supply more and more educational service.

There are many other important services that could be added to this list of government activities. All of them cost money. Many of them are very expensive. But they would be much more expensive if each family had to supply them by and for itself. As a matter of fact many of them could not be provided on an individual basis. By a government supplying them not only is the cost reduced, but they are actually made possible.

THE RISE IN THE COST OF GOVERNMENT

How much does it cost to operate our governments? The unit introduction mentioned some of the costs. Let us examine them a little more closely. In recent years, about one of every four dollars spent in this country for all purposes has been spent by national, state, or local governments. In earlier days the proportion was much lower. Why the increase? There are a number of reasons, and each one helps to explain a part of the rising cost of government.

The many international problems have

When disasters such as floods and hurricanes occur, the federal government comes to the aid of the victims by supplying food from the Food and Nutrition Service of the Department of Agriculture. (USDA photo)

made it necessary to increase greatly the defense of our nation. This has been the chief single cause for the increased cost of government. Wars and defense have always been costly. But World War II was especially so for the United States; we were really involved in two wars at the same time —with Germany and Japan. The tremendous cost of this war is reflected in the graph on page 497. Note the jump in yearly expenditures from 1940 to 1944. The interest on the money borrowed by the federal government for that war still amounts to several billion dollars each year.

The appropriations for defense since 1945 continue to be high, and they are rising. The Korean and Vietnam wars are factors. However, even without them the threat of war in other places, national defense, and our commitments throughout the world cost many billions of dollars each year.

People have been demanding more services from the government; more services mean higher costs. Some of the increased services of governments are health and welfare facilities; mental hospitals; more and better schools; elimination of poverty and reduction of unemployment; urban renewal and lower-cost housing; improved highways, bridges, parks, and recreational facilities. Each time a new service is added or an old one is expanded, the cost of government is increased.

Another obvious reason for the rise in the cost of government is *inflation,* resulting in the steady increase in the cost of living in the United States and throughout the world. There have been large increases in wages and salaries and in the cost of goods throughout the nation. Things cost more than they did a quarter of a century ago. Government wages and the cost of government services have risen too. The price of everything government buys is higher now. This fact of inflation has added

ESTIMATED EXPENDITURES OF FEDERAL GOVERNMENT FOR FISCAL YEAR 1973—BY AGENCY

(in millions of dollars)

Legislative Branch	505
The Judiciary	189
Executive Office of the President	71
Funds appropriated to the President	4,131
Department of Agriculture	11,005
Department of Commerce	1,425
Department of Defense (Military)	75,900
Department of Defense (Civil)	1,822
Department of Health, Education, and Welfare	78,953
Department of Housing and Urban Development	4,214
Department of the Interior (Deduct)	−1,138
Department of Justice	1,476
Department of Labor	9,589
Department of State	576
Department of Transportation	8,155
Treasury Department	27,737
Atomic Energy Commission	2,422
Environmental Protection Agency	1,541
General Services Administration	110
National Aeronautics and Space Administration	3,191
Postal Service	1,409
Veterans Administration	11,715
Other Independent Agencies	8,572
Allowance for pay increases	775
Allowance for contingencies	500
Interfund transactions (Deduct)	−8,590
TOTAL	246,257

Source: *The Budget of the United States Government for the Fiscal Year Ending June 30, 1973.* U.S. Government Printing Office, 1972.

much to the overall cost of government.

In summary, governmental costs are high today because of (1) wars and military defense, (2) demands for additional governmental services, and (3) the general rise in the cost of living.

FEDERAL GOVERNMENT EXPENDITURES

We have been discussing government cost in rather general terms. Let us now look at some specific government expenditures. To do this we will examine federal, state, and local government costs for recent years. First to be

To maintain an efficient system of roads and highways across the country requires enormous outlays of federal funds. (U.S. Dept. of Transportation)

discussed is the federal government. For the *fiscal year* 1973, the United States government estimated that it would spend more than 246 billion dollars.

This total as given in the accompanying tables is very much greater than the corresponding totals for the years before 1969. Some of the increase is due to increases in the federal programs. However, much of it results from a difference in budget proce-

dures. Prior to 1969 the federal government used an *administrative budget* which did not include *trust funds*. These are now included in what is called the *unified budget.*

ESTIMATED EXPENDITURES OF FEDERAL GOVERNMENT FOR FISCAL YEAR 1973—BY FUNCTION
(in millions of dollars)

National defense	78,310
International affairs and finance	3,844
Space research and technology	3,191
Agriculture and rural development	6,891
Natural resources and environment	2,450
Commerce and transportation	11,550
Community development and housing	4,844
Education and manpower	11,281
Health	18,117
Income security	69,658
Veterans' benefits and services	11,745
Interest	21,161
General government	5,531
General revenue sharing	5,000
Allowance for pay increases	775
Allowance for contingencies	500
Interfund transactions (Deduct)	−8,590
TOTAL	246,257

Source: *The Budget of the United States Government for the Fiscal Year Ending June 30, 1973.* U.S. Government Printing Office, 1972.

THE BUDGET DOLLAR FOR 1973 —WHERE IT GOES

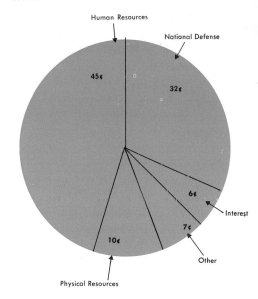

Source: Bureau of the Budget

Federal expenditures can be classified into five groups: human resources, national defense, physical resources, interest, and other expenses.

Trust funds include the money collected by the government for specific purposes and kept in trust for these accounts, such as social security and federal employees retirement funds. Money from these funds is expended as needed. For the 1973 fiscal year, about sixty-four billion dollars in trust funds are included in the tables.

The two tables on pages 488 and 489 tell the story of federal government expenditures, but they do it in different ways. The first shows how money is spent according to branches, departments, and agencies. The legislative and judicial branches together have 694 million dollars of expenditures, and the executive branch and its many agencies have the balance.

One of the greatest amounts—more than seventy-seven billion dollars—is for the Department of Defense. Some departments with smaller amounts are Commerce, Interior, Justice, and State; but even some of them had expenditures larger than the total federal budget before World War I. The Department of the Interior has income from various sources, such as oil leases. An unusually large income for 1973 accounts for the more than one billion dollar surplus over expenses of that department. "Allowance for contingencies" is money set aside for unforeseen expenses that may arise after Congress passes the budget. There is also an allowance set aside for pay increases for government personnel.

The second table gives the same information, but it lists the expenses according to function, that is, according to the kind of service the money buys. Similar functions are not limited to one department or agency. For example, the Department of Defense has the duty of providing national defense. But other agencies also provide some services which contribute to the defense of the nation. One of these is the Atomic Energy Commission.

Notice that in the second table the interest paid by the government is more than twenty-one billion dollars. This is more than the total federal expenses for any year until World War II. The interest is money paid on the national debt, which in 1972 amounted to more than 400 billion dollars. This means that the federal government owed an amount equal to about $2,000 for every person in the nation.

The rise in the national debt reflects again the increased costs of government during depression and war. In 1915 the debt was only slightly more than one billion dollars. The table below on this page shows how this sum has increased during the years. While the amount of the large national debt has been increasing steadily over the past years, in terms of the rise of the national economy it has been decreasing. For example, in 1960 the national debt was about 59 per cent of the *gross national product,* but in 1970 it was about 40 per cent.

The tables on pages 488-489 do not include all the expenditures of the federal government. They include only the amounts that must be raised by taxes, by borrowing, or by payments to trust funds. Additional

FEDERAL GOVERNMENT DEBT
(in billions of dollars)

AT END OF YEAR	AMOUNT
1900	1.3
1915	1.2
1920	24.3
1925	20.5
1930	16.2
1935	32.8
1940	48.5
1945	259.1
1950	257.4
1955	274.4
1960	290.9
1965	323.2
1970	382.6
1972	455.8 (est.)

A BILLION DOLLARS

*If you were to spend one dollar each minute every day, it would take you more than **1,900 years** to spend a billion dollars, not including interest.*

If you were to lay one-dollar bills end to end, a billion of them would go around the earth at the equator about four times.

If you were to lay one-dollar bills end to end, you would need about two and one-half billion to reach the moon.

billions are spent, but this is money that is received by the government directly for certain services and is spent to carry on these services.

For example, the gross expenditures of the Postal Service for the 1973 fiscal year were estimated at 10.6 billion dollars. But the Service expected to receive 9.2 billion dollars through the sale of stamps and other charges. So its estimated net expenditure is 1.4 billion dollars above revenue.

STATE GOVERNMENT
EXPENDITURES

State governments also carry on many activities and furnish many services for their citizens. To carry on this work they, too, make large expenditures. They do not spend as much money as the federal government does. But the amounts are large and, like federal expenditures, they have risen sharply in recent years. Again, the reasons for the increases have been mainly the demands for increased services and the rising general costs.

The total expenditures for all state governments in a recent year were 77,643 million dollars. The table on this page shows in some detail how these millions of dollars were spent. The amount for education includes the money which the states distributed to local school districts and the costs of state universities and colleges. The operating expenses of the executive, legislative, and judicial branches are included in "all other."

The expenditures vary widely among the states, depending on their size and wealth. Another factor which causes variation among states is the kinds and amounts of grants-in-aid to local governments. The range of state expenditures for one year, for example, varied from a low of 176 million dollars for Wyoming to a high of 8,561 million dollars for California. It must also be borne in mind that these figures are for state expenditures only; in some states local units of government bear more of the costs of these services than they do in other states.

The table on the next page tells the story of how one of the states spent money in its general fund in a recent year. This table does not include 2,112 million dollars over which the legislature and the governor have no control. These are restricted funds for which the state is really only a collection agency. This is money which was turned over to local units of government or had to be used for specific purposes according to the state constitution. The constitution

EXPENDITURES OF THE STATE GOVERNMENTS FOR A RECENT YEAR
(in millions of dollars)

Education	30,865
Highways	13,483
Public welfare	13,206
Health and hospitals	5,355
Natural resources	2,223
Housing and urban renewal	120
Air transportation	225
Social insurance administration	767
Interest on debt	1,499
All other	9,900
TOTAL	77,643

Source: U.S. Department of Commerce.

Point out the large percentage of expenditures that goes to education.

491

states that all motor vehicle gasoline tax money and all motor license money must be used for highway construction and maintenance. Also, two cents of the sales tax on each dollar of sales must be paid into the School Aid Fund for the use of local school districts. These two items are examples of the state's earmarked funds and are not included in the general fund expenditures.

The amounts given in the table were appropriated by the state legislature for the various branches and departments of the state government. The central operation of the government is reflected in the appropriations for the executive office and the legislative and judicial branches. The appro-

priations for the departments are made separately as is done in the federal budget.

The largest appropriation is for education. This included amounts for the operation of the department at the state level, for state universities and community colleges, and for supplementary school aid.

Large appropriations were also made for the departments of mental health and social services. These indicate increased state services and concerns in the whole area of social welfare. Similarly, the names of other departments and the appropriations for them give some idea of the services and duties carried on by state government. The large amount for the item called "Debt service, grants and transfers" is for the payment of principal and interest on debts, for additional money turned over to other units of government, and for the transfer of some funds from one department of the state government to another.

EXPENDITURES OF ONE STATE FOR A RECENT YEAR

(in millions of dollars)

Executive Office		8.0
Legislative		16.3
Judicial		12.6
Education		1,215.0
Department	166.8	
Higher Education	431.4	
School Aid	616.8	
Departments:		
Administration		19.1
Agriculture		16.2
Attorney General		6.0
Civil Rights		4.1
Civil Service		4.5
Commerce		30.3
Corrections		47.0
Labor		8.8
Licensing		3.9
Mental Health		249.0
Military Affairs		5.5
Natural Resources		49.3
Public Health		70.7
Social Services		1,172.6
State		32.5
State Police		50.9
Treasury		23.0
Debt service, grants and transfers		354.8
TOTAL		3,400.1

Source: State of Michigan budget.

LOCAL GOVERNMENT EXPENDITURES

Local governments make expenditures for services which are well known to most of us. We can usually see what local government money buys. Nevertheless, local governments do spend money for many activities and services which are not readily seen. As a matter of fact, one may not know about these activities unless local government expenditures are studied.

The table on page 493 tells the story of the expenditures of all local governments for a recent year. These include counties, cities, townships, and school and special districts. Nearly half of the total sum of 82,582 million dollars was spent for education. Other large expenditures were made for highways, police protection, sewers and sanitation, public welfare, and health and hospitals.

Providing an able and well-equipped fire department is the responsibility of local government officials. (Photo by De Lange)

One of our large cities spends annually about 625 million dollars in general expenditures. Some of these expenses are for fixed items and cannot be changed. Nearly twenty-seven million dollars is for debt retirement; it is money needed to pay debts which have been made in former years. The interest on these debts amounts to more than thirteen million dollars. A large amount is also included for the pension and retirement funds of policemen, firemen, and other city employees.

The largest amounts of general expenditures are for police and fire protection, public works, public welfare, public health, and public lighting. The department of public works includes such services as maintenance of public buildings, street maintenance and construction, city trucking and other transportation, and rubbish and waste disposal.

The public welfare department assists children without parents, old people no longer able to work, people who are out of work, and people who are mentally ill. The public health department operates hospitals and sanitariums, enforces public health ordinances, and carries on health education programs.

EXPENDITURES FOR ALL LOCAL GOVERNMENTS FOR A RECENT YEAR

(in millions of dollars)

Education	38,938
Highways	5,383
Public welfare	6,477
Health and hospitals	4,880
Police protection	3,806
Fire protection	2,024
Sewers and sanitation	3,413
Parks and recreation	1,888
Natural resources	574
Housing and urban renewal	2,115
Air and water transportation	1,062
Parking facilities	158
Correction	575
Libraries	646
Financial administration	1,007
General control	1,954
Public buildings	947
Interest	2,875
Other	3,860
TOTAL	**82,582**

Source: U.S. Department of Commerce.

Compare the services listed in the local government expenditures table in the text with the services which your local community provides.

Street lighting is the responsibility of the public lighting commission. Smaller amounts are spent for building inspections, city planning, civil defense, human relations problems, elections, historical commission, loyalty investigations, zoning, and the zoo.

Premiums for employees' hospitalization insurance, damage claims against the city, decorations for special observances, such as a Memorial Day parade and exhibits at the city hall, require funds too.

These 625 million dollars are not all of the money handled and spent by the city during a year. Altogether, its gross expenditures are over 800 million dollars. About 125 million are for services that pay for themselves; the largest amounts are forty-three million for the municipal transportation system paid by passenger fares, thirty-five million paid for water service, twenty million for sewage disposal, and twenty million for city-owned housing.

Not all local governments spend the millions of dollars that are spent by large cities. But even the small communities have expenditures amounting to many thousands of dollars. For example, a small suburban community of 4,000 people spends about $750,000 a year, and a rural community of 1,500 people has a budget of $200,000.

Other units of government also set up plans for expenditures to pay for their services. Included are counties, townships, special districts, and school districts.

KINDS OF COSTS   All levels of government have three main kinds of costs: salaries and wages, government purchases, and government contracts.

SALARIES AND WAGES. The services of government are provided by people. Therefore, salaries and wages are among the largest costs of government. In one

New highway construction is usually done by private companies given contracts by the government because they have submitted the lowest bid for a project. (Courtesy of the Pennsylvania Department of Highways)

Before the federal government can award contracts for defense expenditures, such as development of new aircraft, budget appropriations must get congressional approval. (North American Rockwell Corporation)

month of a recent year the various governments had over thirteen million employees, two million of them were part-time workers. They were paid a total of $8,911 million dollars each month. The table on page 496 shows how these employees were distributed among federal, state, and local governments.

GOVERNMENT PURCHASES. In carrying on their governmental work these employees need many kinds of materials, machines, and equipment. Most of the uniforms, automobiles, typewriters, guns, and hundreds of other items are purchased from private industries.

But most government buying differs from most personal buying in one important way. When the government wishes to buy something, it makes out *specifications* for the item and advertises for *bids*. The speci-

fications describe exactly what is wanted. Any person or business organization which can supply the item according to the specifications may bid on the item. The bid is the price at which the firm will sell the item to the government.

In advertising for bids the government sets the date and time by which all bids must be submitted. The bids are submitted in closed or sealed envelopes which are opened at the specified time. Anyone may attend the opening of bids.

The government has the right to reject all bids which do not meet specifications. But it must buy from the *lowest* bidder if that firm can meet the specifications. This system is used so that government employees cannot be induced to buy from friends or cannot be influenced by the promise of favors or bribes.

Make clear to the student the relationship between specifications and bids.

GOVERNMENT EMPLOYEES AND THEIR EARNINGS FOR ONE MONTH OF A RECENT YEAR

	NUMBER OF EMPLOYEES (in thousands)	EARNINGS (in millions of dollars)
Federal (civilian)	2,872	2,529
States	2,832	1,742
Counties	1,270	722
Municipalities	2,273	1,482
School districts	3,436	2,146
Townships	342	138
Special districts	291	152
TOTAL	13,316	8,911

Source: U.S. Department of Commerce.

GOVERNMENT CONTRACTS. Not all government services are provided by government employees. Very often the government has a specialized job to do which can be done more efficiently and effectively by private industry. A new courthouse is to be built, a highway is to be constructed, a road grade separation is needed, the army needs tanks or other equipment—all of these and many other projects are usually performed by private industry.

In awarding the jobs to the business concerns, the same system of bids according to specifications is used. The job always goes to the lowest bidder who can do the work according to the specifications. This insures getting the best job at the lowest possible price.

CONTROLLING GOVERNMENT EXPENDITURES

We have seen how the government spends money for various services, activities, and materials. But this expenditure of money is not automatic. Decisions have to be made by people. Who determines how much shall be spent? Should the police force be increased? Should there be weekly or twice-weekly rub-

bish and garbage collections? Should Fifth Avenue be paved? Should a new school be built? Should a particular project be carried out this year or should it be postponed?

BUDGETS. These and many more questions need to be answered before spending government money. A system of *budgeting* provides for planning expenditures in an orderly way and for systematic spending.

A *budget* is a statement of how the government proposes to raise and spend its money during the coming year. *Appropriations* are the items in the budget which set aside a specific amount of money for each service. The tables on pages 488-489 are from the federal budget for the fiscal year 1972-1973 and are an example of appropriations set aside for the various services. They list not only the proposed expenditures but also the expected income. (See page 505.)

We speak of *balancing* the budget, meaning that the receipts and the expenditures are equal, that they balance each other. Groups and individuals have budgets, just as governments do. You have a personal budget, and whether you call it that or not makes little difference. And even if you do not think so, you balance your budget. If your income is greater than your expenses, you balance your budget by saving the surplus. If it is the other way and your expenses are larger than your income, then you take one of several steps: you increase your income, you reduce your expenses, or you go into debt by borrowing money.

Governments operate the same way with their budgets. If income is greater than expenditures, a government can reduce its income or it can increase it services to balance the budget. But if the expenditures are greater, it can reduce services (cut expenses), or increase income.

For the government, increasing income is sometimes easier than it is for the individual. Raising the tax rate and issuing bonds

There are times, according to Keynesian economists, when it is not desirable to have a balanced budget; explain when this might be so.

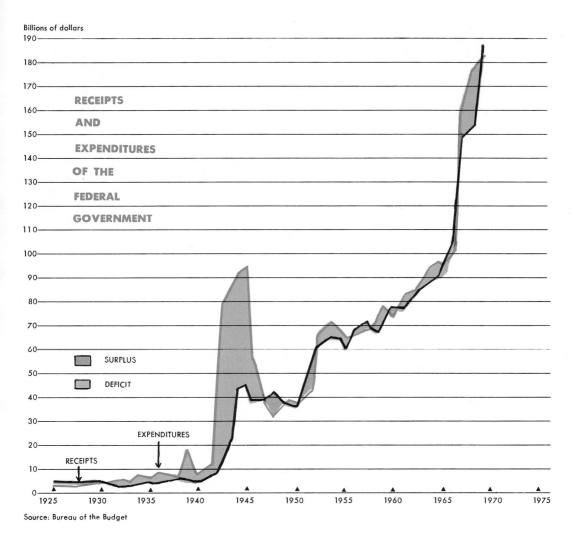

Billions of dollars

RECEIPTS AND EXPENDITURES OF THE FEDERAL GOVERNMENT

SURPLUS

DEFICIT

EXPENDITURES

RECEIPTS

Source: Bureau of the Budget

This graph shows the receipts and expenditures of the federal government since 1925. Deficits and surpluses are indicated. How often has there been a surplus?

are two common methods that governments use to get more income to balance their budgets. But this is not always easily done.

All government budgets—federal, state, local—are made in about the same way. The executive branch proposes how it will spend money during the coming year and asks the legislative branch to make the necessary appropriations: the budget.

PREPARING THE BUDGET. In preparing the budget the President, the governor, or the mayor asks each of the departments to estimate carefully how much money will be needed during the next year. The head of each department must state in detail how this money will be spent. The executive and his budget bureau then discuss the requests with department heads,

Have students plan and make an extensive bulletin board display of the state or national budget showing both income and expenditures.

497

In 1965 Congress passed an act known as the Elementary and Secondary Education Act (ESEA) of 1965. Officially it is Public Law 89-10 of the Eighty-Ninth Congress, H.R. 2362. Various amendments to the original act have been passed in succeeding years.

As part of the act Congress authorized the expenditure of specific amounts of money for certain educational programs named in the act. But these *authorizations* are only ceiling amounts which the government officials and agencies *could* spend if Congress appropriates the money. In a sense an act which contains authorizations says that Congress believes this to be a worthwhile activity and that it will look at the program from time to time, usually yearly, to decide how much money should actually be appropriated for it.

As an example of authorizations, the ESEA of 1965 contained the following section:

"Sec. 201. (b) For the purpose of making grants under this title, there is hereby authorized to be appropriated the sum of $100,000,000 for the fiscal year ending June 30, 1966; but for the fiscal year ending June 30, 1967, and the three succeeding fiscal years, only such sums may be appropriated as the Congress may hereafter authorize by law."

The act also contained other sections with additional authorizations. The amendments of 1967 to ESEA changed the foregoing section to read:

"Sec. 201. (b) For the purpose of making grants under this title, there are hereby authorized to be appropriated the sum of $100,000,000 for the fiscal year ending June 30, 1966, $125,000,000 for the fiscal year ending June 30, 1967, $150,000,000 for the fiscal year ending June 30, 1968, $175,000,000 for the fiscal year ending June 30, 1969, $200,-000,000 for the fiscal year ending June 30, 1970, and $225,000,000 for the fiscal year ending June 30, 1971."

Each year Congress then makes *appropriations* which are the amounts that the government officials and agencies can spend. The amount of the appropriation is determined by the total budget passed by Congress and by its opinion of the value of each particular program. Often the actual appropriation is less than the authorization given in the act. Sometimes Congress may even appropriate nothing for a program it has previously authorized.

As an example of the difference between authorization and appropriation, the total amount authorized for ESEA for fiscal year 1968 was 3,965 million dollars. However, only slightly more than 50 per cent, 2,042 million dollars, was appropriated. The following examples of authorizations and appropriations indicate these differences for various parts of ESEA.

	AUTHORIZATION	APPROPRIATION
	(in millions of dollars)	
Assistance for education of children of low-income families	2,563	1,191
School library resources, textbooks and other instructional materials	155	104
Education of handicapped children	159	18
Adult education programs	60	40

and often the amounts requested are reduced.

When the executive is satisfied that all requests can be justified, they are put together in a total budget and presented to the legislative branch—Congress, the state legislature, or the city council. This group then carefully studies the proposed budget. It adds and subtracts, it debates the various items, it makes changes. Finally, the legislature returns its revised budget to the executive for his approval or veto.

Justus in the Minneapolis Star.

Various government officials and agencies have the responsibility of checking continuously to see that expenditures are made according to budget appropriations. Commonly this is done by an auditor general or a budget bureau. Frequently this person or agency must decide whether a particular expenditure is permitted under the budget.

The budget bureau must at all times be able to determine how much unexpended money remains for a particular service. Records must be kept to see that no department or agency spends more than its appropriation. These individuals and agencies are the "watchdogs" of public money.

Beyond them are the people themselves. Part of the duty of citizens is to determine for themselves whether the government is spending money wisely. They keep informed by studying budget messages of executives, by paying attention to government reports, by watching appropriations made by the legislative branch.

Their wishes can be made known by personal contact, by telegrams, by letters. People sometimes control government spending by setting charter or constitutional limits on taxes and borrowing. Governments cannot go beyond these limits without a vote of the people.

Finally, people can approve the way in which government is spending money by returning government executives and legislators to office; they can also show their disapproval of unacceptable spending by voting certain people out of office.

We have seen that government is big business. The owners of the business must always ask themselves, "Are we getting our money's worth?" The owners, as citizens, have the opportunity to express their feelings at each election. They can, at least in part, make their wishes known by the way they vote.

For a school district the budget is prepared by the superintendent of schools and his staff. It is then presented to the board of education for approval, amendments, or revision.

The process of budget-making usually takes months, and there is a good deal of give and take before the final budget is set up. When completed, this budget becomes the law under which money is spent during the coming year.

It is the duty of the executive to see that the expenditures during the year do not go beyond the budget. If an emergency arises or if the appropriation is too small, he must go to the legislature for extra funds before he can exceed the budget.

Budget-making is democracy in action. The representatives of the people determine how money is to be spent. No single citizen or small group of citizens can do this. Only the elected representatives of the people can make appropriations for the spending of government money.

CONCEPTS AND GENERALIZATIONS

1
The cost of government has risen sharply since World War I, and especially since the depression and war years.

2
Government services touch the lives of all people in many ways.

3
The rise in the cost of government has been due mainly to wars and defense, additional and increased services, and increased cost of living.

4
National defense is the largest single item in the federal budget.

5
The national debt is about equal to one-half of the amount of the annual gross national product.

6
The largest single item in state budgets is education.

7
About one of every twenty persons is involved in some kind of government employment.

8
Government purchases and contracts are made on the basis of specifications, and materials are purchased from and contracts awarded to the lowest bidder.

9
Budget-making is the cooperative responsibility of the executive and legislative branches for all levels of government.

10
Checking the expenditures of government is the responsibility of a budget bureau or an auditor general and is finally in the hands of the people.

1. Give some examples to show the cost of services of the federal government.

2. Mention some of the common governmental services.

3. What three factors have combined to increase greatly the costs of governmental services?

4. Explain the difference in the two methods of listing government expenditures according to the tables on pages 488-489.

5. What are the big items in federal government expenditures?

6. How is the rise in the national debt related to war and depression?

7. Explain federal government expenditures from the budget dollar graph on page 489.

8. Compare the national debt for the current year with that of 1970 in terms of its percentage of the gross national product for each of those years.

9. Explain the items for which state governments spend money. (See the tables on pages 491 and 492.)

10. Why do state government expenditures vary widely?

11. Explain the expenditures of local governments. (See the table on page 493.)

12. What services of your local government pay for themselves?

13. About what percentage of government expenditures goes for salaries and wages? (See the tables on pages 489, 491, 493, and 496.)

14. In what important way does most government buying differ from personal buying?

15. Mention the various ways in which government spending is controlled.

16. Describe the steps in the making of a budget.

17. What is the responsibility of the auditor general or the budget bureau?

IDEAS FOR DISCUSSION

1. Study the table on page 485 and discuss the effects of war and depression on governmental expenditures.

2. Which table on pages 488-489 is a more meaningful way of listing governmental expenditures? Why?

3. Fiscal year refers to the financial year of business or government. It is often different from the calendar year. What reasons can you give for having governments operate on that basis?

4. The national debt is about 400 billion dollars. Some people say we should not be concerned about repaying this money since we owe it to ourselves. Other people say this large debt must be reduced or we will have financial troubles. Discuss the question of the reduction of the national debt.

5. Often there may be heated discussions at a budget session of the city council, the school board, or the county board about a particular item in the budget: should it be included, should it be reduced, or should it be eliminated? If your local government is considering a debatable item in its budget, discuss it in your class. If you were a councilman or a board member, how would you vote? Why?

6. Some financial experts say it is unwise to write limits on government spending into a constitution or a charter. They say that government may be hampered because of such limitations. How do you feel about this issue? Why?

7. Discuss the significance of the fact that while the national debt rose from 1960 to 1972, its percentage of the gross national product decreased.

THINGS
TO DO

1. Keep a record for a period of several weeks of the services of government with which you have some contact.

2. Use your class bulletin board for posting clippings of newspaper articles which involve (a) governmental services and (b) governmental expenditures.

3. Have a committee study the expenditures of the federal government for the current year and compare them with the tables on pages 488-489. Report on important differences.

4. Have another committee secure information about the expenditures of your state government and make comparisons with the information given in this chapter.

5. Have a third committee get a copy of the budget of your local government for the current year. Arrange a bulletin board display to show how the money is being spent.

6. Make a chart to show the number of employees and their earnings of the national, state, and local governments for a recent year.

7. Get a copy of purchase specifications from your city hall or county building to show to the class.

8. Find out when bids for some purchases will be opened by your city or county. Attend the opening-of-bids session, and report to your class on the proceedings.

9. Attend a budget session of your city council or the county board. Report to the class on the discussions in connection with the making of the budget.

10. Make a graph showing the increase in the national debt since 1900. Use the data in the table on page 490.

FURTHER
READINGS

Bureau of the Budget, THE FEDERAL BUDGET IN BRIEF. Washington, D.C.: Government Printing Office.

Galbraith, John Kenneth and Randhawa, M. S., THE NEW INDUSTRIAL STATE. Houghton Mifflin Co., 1967.

Groves, Harold M., FINANCING GOVERNMENT. Holt, Rinehart and Winston, Inc., 1964.

Harrod, Roy, DOLLAR. W. W. Norton Co., Inc., 1963. (Paperback)

Hazlitt, Henry, THE FAILURE OF THE NEW ECONOMICS: AN ANALYSIS OF THE KEYNESIAN FALLACIES. D. Van Nostrand Co., Inc., 1959.

Myrdal, Gunnar, BEYOND THE WELFARE STATE. Yale University Press, 1960.

Sayre, J. Woodrow and Stull, Edith, TAXATION. Franklin Watts, Inc., 1963.

Schick, Allen, BUGET INNOVATION IN THE STATES. The Brookings Institution, 1971.

Taylor, Philip E., THE ECONOMICS OF PUBLIC FINANCE. Macmillan Co., 1961.

ASSESSMENT—value placed on real and personal property for tax purposes.

DEDUCTION—amount allowed to be subtracted from income in figuring taxes.

DEFICIT—the difference between income and expenditures when the latter is larger.

EARMARK—to set aside for a specific purpose; for example, to require that the income from certain taxes be used for the construction of highways.

EXCISE TAX—a tax on the manufacture, sale, or use of an item.

EXEMPTION—in figuring taxes, the amount allowed to be subtracted from income for each dependent.

GRADUATED TAX RATE—a rate of taxation that increases as income increases.

INDIRECT TAX—a tax not paid directly to the government by the taxpayer.

RETURN—a completed statement giving required information and computation in figuring taxes.

SURTAX—an additional tax placed on something already taxed.

TAX DELINQUENCY—the nonpayment of taxes by the due date.

TAX LIMITATION—the ceiling or limit placed on tax rates by law or constitutional amendment.

TAX RATE—the amount or per cent of tax paid for each $1,000 of income or of value of property.

UNIFORM TAX—a tax rate that is the same for all income.

WITHHOLDING TAX—tax money withheld from wages and paid to the government for the worker by his employer.

THE LANGUAGE OF GOVERNMENT

24

The Income of Government

The statement of expenditures of national, state, and local governments is only half of the total picture of government finance. The other half—how these governments get their income—is just as important. A government is like any family. The bills for the home, food, clothing, and auto have to be paid from the family income. Usually father—and sometimes mother, brother, and sister—earn money to pay for these things.

How does a government earn money? Who pays the bills for the expenditures of government? In one sense the answer is simple because *we all do*. All of us help pay for our government in some way or other. But the answer is complex too. Governments spend such huge sums of money. Their sources of income are so varied. We do not always realize the many ways in which we are paying the cost of government.

A practical activity for this chapter is filling out an income tax return. A hypothetical case may be used to give a uniformity to the computations. Material may be obtained from the Internal Revenue Service.

SOURCES OF GOVERNMENT
INCOME

Most government income, or revenue, comes from *taxes*, but there are other important sources. Among these are loans, fees and licenses, fines, tolls and charges for services, and grants-in-aid. Most governments make *loans* at some time or other. Some loans are long-term loans to be repaid over a period of years, for example, a twenty-year bond issue to pay for a new courthouse. Other loans may be made for only a short period of time, for example, a three-month loan to pay current expenses until next year's taxes begin to be collected.

State and local governments get a share of their income from *fees* and *licenses*. Fees for certain services, such as for inspecting various industries and for recording deeds to property, are examples. Fees for automobile, marriage, and animal licenses are common. Some businesses, such as beauty parlors and places of recreation, need licenses, too.

While the individual *fines* are usually small, the amount of money collected in this way is rather substantial, especially in some municipalities. Fines are usually of the three-to-ten-dollar variety for minor traffic violations. But even these help to pay some of the cost of local governments.

Special sources of government income are *tolls* and *charges* for some types of businesses operated by the government. A major example is, of course, the postal service of the federal government. But there are many others.

Most local governments own the local waterworks, and some have plants to produce electricity. Municipal transportation systems are owned by some towns and cities. There are toll bridges and a number of toll roads which are operated by governments.

Toll charges bring money into the government treasury, mainly to pay for the construction, maintenance, and operation of the services. Sometimes, however, they return a profit to the government.

Finally, governments often receive money from the other governments as *grants-in-aid*. When one government, usually a higher

Turnpikes are one source of government revenue, although a large portion of the tolls helps to pay for the maintenance and operation of these highspeed highways. (Delaware State Highway Dept.)

503

level of government, gives money to another one to carry on a service, it is giving a grant-in-aid. We have already seen how the federal government makes grants-in-aid to state governments and also how these, in turn, make other grants to local governments.

TAXES. Even though governments get some money from all of these services, the chief source of government income is taxes. There are various ways which governments use to levy and collect tax money. The authority to tax is obtained from constitutions, charters, laws, and ordinances.

In Chapter 3 on the United States Constitution, it is pointed out that one of the weaknesses of the Articles of Confederation was that the government had no power to tax. The Constitution changed this and said that "the Congress shall have power to lay and collect taxes, duties, imposts, and excises, . . . but all duties, imposts, and excises shall be uniform throughout the United States."

One-Way Ride

Why have taxes increased over the years? (Buescher, King Features Syndicate)

In the same way, the power to tax has been written into state constitutions and charters of local governments. Until 1913 all taxes levied by the federal government had to be uniform, the same for everyone. With passage of the Sixteenth Amendment in that year income taxes could be levied on the basis of ability to pay. Not all people had to pay the same amount nor at the same rate.

The kind of tax which a government levies is usually determined by the principle of collecting the largest amount of money with the minimum effort on the part of government and the least opposition on the part of the taxpayers. But obtaining large amounts of money and getting little opposition do not always go hand in hand. So government must often make a choice as to which is more important and necessary—more tax money or less citizen opposition.

Frequently the choice is made on the basis of gaining public favor, as, for example, when taxes are reduced in an election year. On the other hand, patriotic appeals and informational programs often get people to accept large and unusual tax levies. Two examples are the large federal income taxes during World War II and the extra taxes for school construction in many communities during recent years.

METHODS OF TAXATION. There are three general ideas as to the method by which taxes should be levied. *First idea:* Taxes should be levied on the basis of benefits received; for example, a tax for a new pavement levied only against the property fronting on that street. *Second idea:* Taxes should be based on the same amount of tax for everyone; for example, head taxes levied in some states by which each person pays the same amount. *Third idea:* Taxes should be levied on the basis of ability to pay, of which the income tax levied by the federal government and also other units of government is an example.

The first method is widely used by local governments to pay for special projects which benefit small groups of people. The second method at one time was used widely as a method of determining who could vote, since only those people were permitted to vote who had paid their head or poll tax.

Most taxes of all governments are today levied according to the third method. The amount of property that a person owns, the size of his income, and the amount of money he spends are the usual ways of determining his ability to pay.

Ability to pay is also often reflected in setting tax rates. Two systems are in general use. A *uniform* tax rate is one that is applied equally to all income or property, for example, a 5 per cent tax on all incomes. But a *graduated* tax rate is one that applies a different rate as incomes increase, for example, a 5 per cent tax on the first thousand dollars of income and 10 per cent on all income above one thousand dollars.

CLASSIFYING TAXES. From another point of view all taxes may be classified as direct or indirect. A *direct tax* is one that the individual pays directly to the government. He knows that he is paying it, and he is well aware of the exact amount of the tax. An example is the real estate tax on a piece of property.

An *indirect tax* is one that is charged to a consumer and is paid to the government by someone else. For example, the tax on a gallon of gasoline is included in the price. Some drivers may not be aware of the tax when they buy gasoline, but they pay it nevertheless. For this reason indirect taxes are sometimes referred to as *hidden taxes*.

KINDS OF TAXES. The most common kinds of taxes are income, excise, employment, customs, estate and gift, property, sales and use, and gasoline taxes.

> *Taxes are what we pay for civilized society.*
> —JUSTICE OLIVER WENDELL HOLMES, JR.

In general, most of these are based on the principle of ability to pay. There is some criticism, however, of the sales tax from people who feel that it is unfair to the person of low income in that he must pay a greater proportion of his income in taxes than the large wage earner. The person of low income must usually spend all of his income, while the large wage owner may save at least a part of it.

FEDERAL TAXES The estimated expenditures of the federal government for the 1973 fiscal year were over 246 billion dollars. (See the table on page 488.) Where did the government get the money to meet these expenses? In setting up the budget for that year the Budget Bureau estimated that the net budget receipts would be 221 billion dollars. This meant an estimated *deficit* of over 25 billion dollars. The table below shows the sources of estimated receipts

ESTIMATED RECEIPTS OF FEDERAL GOVERNMENT FOR THE FISCAL YEAR 1973
(in millions of dollars)

Individual income taxes	93,900
Corporation income taxes	35,700
Social insurance taxes and contributions	63,683
Excise taxes	16,300
Estate and gift taxes	4,300
Customs duties	2,850
Other	4,052
TOTAL	220,785

Source: *The Budget of the United States Government for the Fiscal Year Ending June 30, 1973.* U.S. Government Printing Office, 1972.

Mention the tremendous growth of federal taxes just since 1939, a period of only one generation.

for the 1973 budget. Actually, however, the 1973 deficit may be more or less than the 25 billion dollars, depending upon the accuracy of the estimates of receipts and expenditures. Although highly unlikely, there may be a surplus.

When the government has a deficit, more money must be raised. This is done by borrowing, thus increasing the debt. To keep the debt from rising, either expenditures must be reduced or taxes must be raised.

Some of this money in the table of estimated receipts cannot be spent for general government, because it is collected by the government for special purposes and must be set aside to be used in that way. This is the money in trust funds. These trust fund receipts are the social insurance taxes and contributions. Part of the trust fund is money collected from federal employees for their retirement fund. The trust funds also include money for social security and an unemployment fund.

THE INCOME TAX. The table shows that the income tax is the chief source of income for the federal government. Many states and cities also levy an income tax.

Income taxes are generally levied as follows: There is a basic *exemption* for each person dependent on the income. For example, in a family with father, mother, and two children, there would be four dependents. Often there are also allowable *deductions* for contributions to churches and charities, for tax and interest payments, and for other special expenses.

The federal income tax is figured on the balance by means of a *graduated percentage.* Let us see how this tax works in the case of the federal income tax.

A person's income includes his wages, interest, rent, and any other income he receives. In 1972 the basic exemption was $750 for the wage earner and an additional $750 for each dependent. So a married man

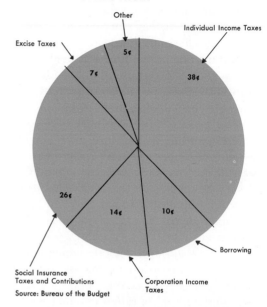

THE BUDGET DOLLAR FOR 1973 —WHERE IT COMES FROM

Other

Excise Taxes

Individual Income Taxes

5¢

7¢

38¢

26¢

14¢

10¢

Borrowing

Social Insurance Taxes and Contributions

Corporation Income Taxes

Source: Bureau of the Budget

How greatly does the federal budget depend on the income of individuals and corporations?

with two children was allowed a basic exemption of $3,000 for himself, his wife, and his two children.

He was also permitted certain deductions. These included contributions to charities, interest payments, taxes paid to state and local governments, fire and storm losses, some medical expenses, and dues and other expenses in connection with his work.

After subtracting his deductions and exemptions, he figured his income tax on the balance. On the first $1,000 he paid 14 per cent. The percentage gradually increased until it reached 70 per cent for any amounts over $200,000. These rates were set by the Revenue Act of 1964. Before then the rates had been considerably higher.

The *return*, a statement of the earnings, deductions, exemptions, and other facts, together with any money due the government, must be filed with the collector of internal revenue by April 15 of each year.

Discuss the relationship between raising taxes and reducing inflation.

Tax returns flood Internal Revenue offices as the deadline approaches. All levels of government depend on taxes as their chief source of income. (Southeast Region, Internal Revenue Service)

Tax returns are checked by the government for accuracy. Employers, banks, and other institutions are required to file reports with the Internal Revenue Service in which they state the payments they have made to individuals. Federal employees and computers check the tax returns to determine whether taxpayers have included all of their earnings and other taxable incomes.

Refunds are due some taxpayers because more money is withheld from their wages than they owe in taxes. The system of having employers *withhold taxes* was started during World War II. At that time taxes were greatly increased, and the withholding system eased the burden on the taxpayer. Before then taxpayers made their payments in one sum at the time of filing their returns.

Now each payday the employer withholds money from the pay of each employee and sends it directly to the government. At the end of the year the employer gives each employee a statement of the money withheld and paid to the government. The taxpayer uses this statement in filing the return. If too much has been paid, a refund is made; if not enough has been paid, the taxpayer pays the balance.

Farmers, professional people, and self-employed workers make their own payments according to regulations passed by Congress.

Corporations also pay income taxes. This is the second largest source of federal income. But the rates on corporation incomes are different from those on the incomes of individuals. All income tax rates are set by Congress and are raised or lowered from time to time, depending on the need for additional tax money. The corporation income-tax rate in 1970 was 22 per cent of income up to $25,000 of net income and 48 per cent of income above $25,000.

U S Department of the Treasury / Internal Revenue Service
Individual Income Tax Return
1971

For the year January 1–December 31, 1971, or other taxable year beginning ...., 1971, ending ...., 19 ....

First name and initial (If joint return, use first names and middle initials of both)	Last name	Your social security number

Present home address (Number and street, including apartment number, or rural route)		Spouse's social security number

City, town or post office, State and ZIP code	Occu-pation	Yours
		Spouse's

Filing Status—check only one:

1 ☐ Single

2 ☐ Married filing jointly (even if only one had income)

3 ☐ Married filing separately **and** spouse is also filing.
Give spouse's social security number in space above and enter first name here ►

4 ☐ Unmarried Head of Household

5 ☐ Surviving widow(er) with dependent child

6 ☐ Married filing separately and spouse is not filing

Exemptions Regular / 65 or over / Blind Enter number of boxes checked

7 Yourself . . . . ☐ ☐ ☐

8 Spouse (applies only if item 2 or 6 is checked) ☐ ☐ ☐

9 First names of your dependent children who lived with you _____

Enter number ►

10 Number of other dependents (from line 33) . . . ►

11 Total exemptions claimed . . . . ►

12 Wages, salaries, tips, etc. (Attach Forms W–2 to back. If unavailable, attach explanation) . | 12 |

(left margin, vertical text) Please print or type If Form W–2 to back

Parts of the front and back of the form for the individual federal income tax return for 1971 (Form 1040) are shown here.

PART V.—Credits

51 Retirement income credit (attach Schedule R)	51	
52 Investment credit (attach Form 3468)	52	
53 Foreign tax credit (attach Form 1116)	53	
54 **Total credits** (add lines 51, 52, and 53). **Enter here and on line 20** . . . ►	54	

PART VI.—Other Taxes

55 Self-employment tax (attach Schedule SE)	55	
56 Tax from recomputing prior-year investment credit (attach Form 4255)	56	
57 Minimum tax (see instructions on page 8). Check here ☐, if Form 4625 is attached	57	
58 Social security tax on unreported tip income (attach Form 4137)	58	
59 Uncollected employee social security tax on tips (from Forms W–2)	59	
60 **Total** (add lines 55, 56, 57, 58, and 59). **Enter here and on line 22** . . . . ►	60	

PART VII.—Other Payments

61 Excess FICA tax withheld (two or more employers—see instructions on page 8)	61	
62 Credit for Federal tax on special fuels, nonhighway gasoline and lubricating oil (attach Form 4136) .	62	
63 Regulated Investment Company Credit (attach Form 2439)	63	
64 **Total** (add lines 61, 62, and 63). **Enter here and on line 26** . . . . ►	64	

☆ U.S. GOVERNMENT PRINTING OFFICE:1971—O–418-133/418-134 EI - 52 - 07 - 33 - 972

To reduce the deficit in the federal budget and also to slow the rising inflation, President Johnson asked Congress in 1967 and 1968 for a 10 per cent surtax to be added to all income taxes. Congress passed the surtax as a temporary measure. The tax was discontinued in 1970. Further, the personal income tax exemption for each taxpayer and dependent was raised in a series of steps to $750 by 1972. (See the Case Study at the end of this unit.)

EXCISE TAXES. Another important source of federal income is the *excise tax.* This is a tax levied on the manufacture, sale, or use of certain commodities or services. Excise taxes are paid on many items, such as automobile tires, cigarettes, sugar, fishing equipment, telephone service, air tickets, and alcoholic beverages.

The tax is always paid by the consumer even though he may not realize it at times. Sometimes the tax is added to the purchase

Point out how difficult it is in our complex, affluent society to determine what a luxury item is.

MAGNETIC TAPE READING AND WRITING UNITS

CURRENT TAX DATA FROM ATLANTA

PROGRAM INSTRUCTION TAPE

UPDATED TAXPAYER MASTER RECORDS

TAX DATA FOR ATLANTA

By the use of computers, the Internal Revenue Service can check many more returns and do so more quickly and accurately. (Internal Revenue Service)

price, as in the case of automobile tires when the merchant figures the amount of the tax at the time of the sale. At other times the tax becomes a part of the selling price, as in the case of a package of cigarettes.

The excise tax has become an important source of government income, as shown in the table on page 505. While there is much opposition to the excise tax, its advocates believe it is a fair tax. The advocates say that the people who can afford these luxuries can also afford to pay the additional tax.

On the other hand, the people who are opposed to certain excise taxes say that the items taxed are not always luxuries. They mention automobile tires as an example of necessities. Some industries, such as telephone, gasoline, and liquor companies, and the airlines, object to taxes imposed on their charges and fares. They say that the tax harms their business.

Placing a tax on a specific item is never popular with the people whom it affects. Government has the task of getting its income in such a way that it benefits the greatest number of people and at the same time is fair to all of them. There are people who do not believe that the excise tax meets this condition.

EMPLOYMENT TAXES. Employment or *payroll* taxes are collected for special purposes. Much of this money is used, under social security laws, for old-age and survivors' insurance and Medicare. The

Refer to the discussion of social security in Chapter 31, pages 674-676.

employee and the employer pay equal amounts. At the present time (1973) both pay a 5.85 per cent tax on the employee's income up to $10,800. The rate will be raised to 6.05 in 1978 and to 7.3 by 2011. The rate is set by Congress. (See Chapter 12.)

The tax is commonly known as the social security tax. It is really a form of insurance whereby each worker pays into a trust fund from which the government will pay him or her an amount each month upon retirement. If the worker should die, certain monthly payments will be paid to surviving dependents. Social security differs from ordinary insurance in that the employee must pay the tax if he or she works at a job covered by social security. The worker has no choice.

There are additional employment taxes paid by employers having four or more employees to protect workers in times of unemployment. The collection of this tax and the payment of unemployment compensation is carried out on a cooperative basis by the federal government and the states.

ESTATE AND GIFT TAXES. Some money is collected by both the federal and state governments on estates and gifts. An *estate tax* is a tax placed on the estate of a person who has died. Some deductions are allowed for various expenses. *Gift taxes* are levied on large gifts made to individuals before one's death. States usually have a *tax on inheritance* after the money or property of a deceased person has been distributed among the heirs. The table on page 505 shows that the government expected more than four billion dollars in estate and gift taxes in 1973.

CUSTOMS. Customs are taxes on goods coming into the country. These taxes are

Travelers returning from outside the United States must pay a duty on items purchased abroad that exceed in value the amount permitted to be brought in duty-free. Shown here are travelers checking through the customs counters at the John F. Kennedy Airport in New York. (Bureau of Customs)

Refer to the successful Kennedy Round of GATT (General Agreement on Tariffs and Trade) negotiations, which lowered tariffs world wide.

also called *duties* or *tariffs*. The amount of the tax varies on different articles. Tariffs are placed on articles for either or both of two reasons, to get money for the federal treasury or to protect certain American industries. In general, the tax is lower when revenue is the goal and higher when protection is the goal.

When the tax is too high, certain goods are not imported at all, because the American manufacturer can sell his product cheaper than the cost of the foreign goods plus the tariff. Since the foreign product is not imported, this tax, of course, brings no money into the treasury. However, the American industry is protected against cheaper competition from foreign countries. In order to bring in revenue a tariff must be low enough so that when it is added to the foreign price, the total cost is not higher than people will pay and is still lower than the cost of production in this country.

Some merchandise comes into the country duty-free; that is, no tariff is placed on it. This merchandise usually consists of articles which are not grown or manufactured here. We also have certain reciprocal trade agreements with foreign nations in order to encourage trade. We lower the tariff on their goods coming here in return for a lower tariff on American goods going into their countries. These agreements with more than seventy foreign nations have helped to increase trade between countries.

STATE AND LOCAL
TAXES   To meet their increasing costs, state and local governments have several important sources of tax revenue.

PROPERTY TAXES. The federal government does not levy a property tax. But this tax is a chief source of income for most local governments and some state governments. The tax is levied on real and personal property. The larger amount comes from real property: land and buildings. Personal property includes such items as pianos, appliances, jewelry, equipment, stocks, bonds, and bank accounts. The amount of a person's tax is the assessed value multiplied by the *tax rate*. Let us see what these are and how they are determined.

In earlier chapters we learned about assessors and their duties. It is their job to determine the value of property in their city, town, or county. The value they place on each piece of property is called the *assessment*. This assessment is usually much less than the actual value of the property. Often it is only between 25 and 50 per cent of the real value. But everyone's property in a community is assessed at the same percentage of real value, making the assessment fair to everyone.

However, if a property owner believes that his assessment is too high in comparison to that of other people, he may appeal to a board of review or to a court of tax appeals.

After all property has been assessed, the total value of the property is divided into the amount of tax money needed to operate the government for a year. This answer is the tax rate.

In the previous chapter the total tax income needed by cities and states was discussed. One year it was $102,056,621 for one of our larger cities. The assessed valuation of all real and personal property in that city that year was $4,592,304,610.

By dividing the total tax income needed by the valuation, a tax rate of .022223 is obtained. This means that for every dollar of assessed valuation that year each taxpayer paid a tax of slightly more than 2 cents. The tax rate was then multiplied by 1,000 to get the rate for each thousand dollars of assessed valuation. The city tax

The general property tax for states has declined in importance proportionally since 1900.

511

Property records must be kept up to date for property tax assessments. What levels of government use the property tax as an important source of revenue? (International Association of Assessing Officers)

rate that year was $22.223. If a taxpayer's property was assessed at $5,000, the rate (22.223) was merely multiplied by five to find the amount of the tax.

$$22.223 \times 5 = \$111.12$$

This man's property tax for that year was $111.12. Every tax bill is figured in the same way.

A property-tax bill shows the assessed valuation, the tax rate for various agencies of government, and the amount of the tax. It also gives the date and method of payment.

Property taxes are ordinarily paid in one or two installments, although some cities are allowing payments to be spread throughout the year. Many people who are buying a home on time include their tax payments as part of each monthly payment on the loan. The loan company then pays the tax for them. This method has helped to reduce *tax delinquency*, a term used for nonpayment of taxes.

If the tax is not paid, the government has the right to sell the property for back taxes. When times are good, there is little tax de-

linquency. In times of much unemployment, however, such as in the depression of the 1930's, many pieces of property were sold by the government to collect the taxes due on them. If the selling price was more than the tax due plus interest, the balance went to the taxpayer. Tax delinquency during the 1930's, plus the belief of many people that property was paying too large a share of the taxes, caused many state and city governments to turn to other kinds of taxes, especially sales and income taxes.

SALES AND USE TAXES. A tax used by many states and some cities is the *general sales tax*. This is a tax of usually 2 to 5 per cent on all sales. The sales tax has the advantage of being easily collected. There is very little tax delinquency. The tax is paid in small amounts to the merchant at the time of each purchase. The merchants must make regular reports and turn the money over to the government.

In some cases the sales tax applies to all sales. In some states food and drugs are not taxed. This exception is made to overcome one objection to the sales tax. Some individuals and certain groups, especially

Describe why certain groups feel that sales taxes are unfair to small-income people.

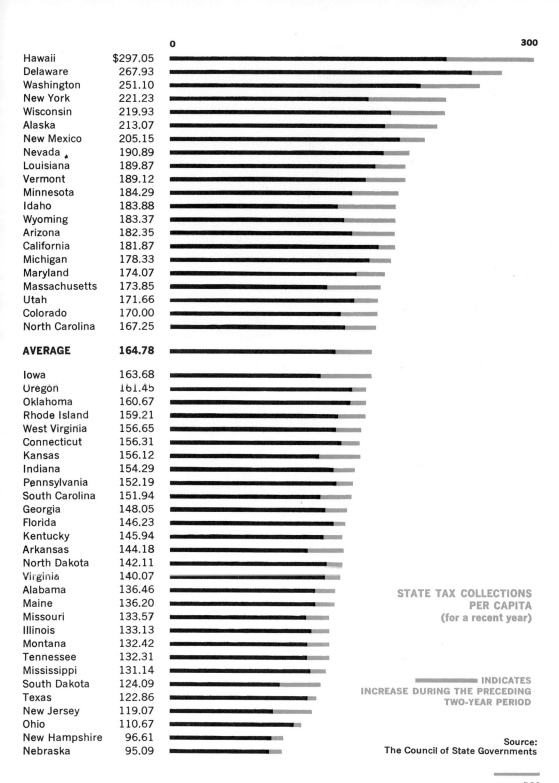

		0	300
Hawaii	$297.05		
Delaware	267.93		
Washington	251.10		
New York	221.23		
Wisconsin	219.93		
Alaska	213.07		
New Mexico	205.15		
Nevada	190.89		
Louisiana	189.87		
Vermont	189.12		
Minnesota	184.29		
Idaho	183.88		
Wyoming	183.37		
Arizona	182.35		
California	181.87		
Michigan	178.33		
Maryland	174.07		
Massachusetts	173.85		
Utah	171.66		
Colorado	170.00		
North Carolina	167.25		
AVERAGE	**164.78**		
Iowa	163.68		
Oregon	161.45		
Oklahoma	160.67		
Rhode Island	159.21		
West Virginia	156.65		
Connecticut	156.31		
Kansas	156.12		
Indiana	154.29		
Pennsylvania	152.19		
South Carolina	151.94		
Georgia	148.05		
Florida	146.23		
Kentucky	145.94		
Arkansas	144.18		
North Dakota	142.11		
Virginia	140.07		
Alabama	136.46		
Maine	136.20		
Missouri	133.57		
Illinois	133.13		
Montana	132.42		
Tennessee	132.31		
Mississippi	131.14		
South Dakota	124.09		
Texas	122.86		
New Jersey	119.07		
Ohio	110.67		
New Hampshire	96.61		
Nebraska	95.09		

STATE TAX COLLECTIONS
PER CAPITA
(for a recent year)

INDICATES
INCREASE DURING THE PRECEDING
TWO-YEAR PERIOD

Source:
The Council of State Governments

513

labor unions, object to the sales tax on the basis that it is unfair to families with small incomes. These individuals and groups who object feel that the sales tax is made more fair when food and drugs are exempted from the tax.

Small-income families must usually spend their entire income on necessities most of which are subject to the sales tax. Higher-income families can save some of their income or spend a good share of it for services and entertainment on which there is no sales tax in many states.

The *use tax* is a tax levied by a state on merchandise purchased in another state and brought into the state to be used there. The use tax came about in this way. Some people avoided paying the sales tax on large items or purchases by buying them in neighboring states.

In order to discourage this practice and also to collect the tax on such purchases, many states which have a sales tax have also passed a use-tax law. The law is enforced on automobiles, for example, by not granting a license for an automobile purchased in another state until the use tax has been paid.

GOLD

About thirty miles south of Louisville, Kentucky, is a military reservation, Fort Knox, which is much like other military reservations throughout the nation. But it is different in one important respect. Here, in heavily guarded vaults, is stored most of the nation's gold supply. This storage place was built in 1936 as part of a plan to get the gold reserves of the nation away from the coasts.

The world's supply of gold has always been limited. That is one of the reasons it is a precious metal and much sought after. Throughout the world's history a discovery of gold has always started an immediate "gold rush," as it did in California in 1849 and in the Klondike in 1897.

Scarcity has made gold an excellent medium for exchange of goods and services among people and nations. In the United States it ceased to be the backing for our money when the nation went off the gold standard in 1933. At that time the government recalled all gold coins and certificates. It became illegal to have them.

Gold is used in the world market, but our expanding foreign purchases of goods and services have developed a gold crisis for the nation.

At one time foreign trade worked in our favor. For more than a decade after the depression of the 1930's our sales abroad far exceeded our purchases. This brought gold —the medium of exchange—to the United States. By 1950 we had about twenty-four billion dollars worth of gold, almost three-fourths of the world supply.

Since 1950, however, the balance of trade has steadily been going the other way. So the gold reserves of the United States have been declining. By 1968 they were down to about twelve billion dollars, only about one-half of the reserves of two decades earlier.

The President, the Congress, and the nation generally have been concerned about reversing the trend in order to balance our trade with other nations, especially those of Europe. The situation at any given time is known as the *balance of payments,* in and out of the country. The balance is favorable if exports of goods and services are greater than imports. That means gold is flowing into the country. The balance is unfavorable if imports are greater or if we spend more abroad. In only one year from 1949 to 1967 has the balance been favorable to the United States.

In March, 1968 because of the drain on our gold supply and the devaluation of the British pound, the United States and six other nations stopped supplying gold to private buyers. Between governments, the price remained at $35 an ounce, but private buyers paid at the market price.

GASOLINE AND OTHER SPECIAL TAXES. All states have a tax on gasoline sold for the operation of motor vehicles. It varies from five to nine cents a gallon. There is also a four-cent federal tax on gasoline. At first all the gasoline-tax money collected by the states was used for the construction and maintenance of roads. Now, however, some states use it for other purposes as well.

States and local governments also have special taxes on cigarettes, alcoholic beverages, playing cards, amusement tickets, hotel charges, and the like which are similar to the excise taxes of the federal government.

SOME SPECIAL INCOME AND TAX ISSUES

In recent years there have been several important issues raised in regard to government income and taxes.

SPECIAL STATE PROVISIONS RE GARDING TAXES. During the past forty years two special provisions about taxes have been written into laws and even into constitutions in more and more states. The first provision concerns a *tax limitation.* We have already noted that during the depression days of the 1930's many people believed that property was paying too large a share of the taxes. In order to make sure that the property tax would not rise beyond certain limits, laws were passed and amendments made to constitutions stating that property could not be taxed beyond certain limits.

This provision has caused difficulty in many places. With increasing populations and with the rising costs of goods and services, many local governments have not been able to carry on necessary services within the limits set. As a result there have been many special propositions on local ballots asking voters to increase these limits for a period of time to pay for needed

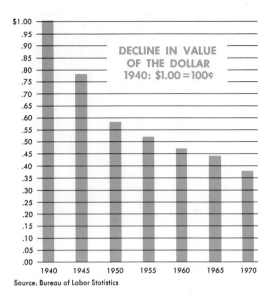

Source: Bureau of Labor Statistics

The graph shows the decline in the purchasing power of the dollar. How does this affect the tax revenues that governments require?

improvements and services. This procedure has been good from one point of view, however—governments have had to convince voters that the requested increases are necessary.

The other provision concerns the writing of statements into the constitution assigning money for certain purposes. For example, a constitutional amendment could be passed assigning one-third of the sales tax to schools or all the gasoline tax to highways. This procedure is usually called *earmarking funds,* and the money so earmarked must be spent for the designated purposes. Most earmarked funds have been for schools and public welfare and highways. (See page 493.)

These provisions have usually come about because certain groups have felt that the legislature did not appropriate enough money for these special purposes. Earmarking funds has the disadvantage of not permitting the legislature to determine what share of the state money should go to the various services. When a large portion of

Give some examples of earmarked funds in your state and local area.

515

Products that cannot be produced or grown in the United States may often be imported duty-free. Here, a cargo of bananas is being unloaded at a dock in Baltimore. (United Fruit Company)

the state income is earmarked, the legislature has little control over expenditures, and as new conditions arise certain parts of the state program may suffer.

TAXES NOT FOR REVENUE. Taxes are not always levied solely for the money they will bring into the government treasury. It has already been noted that some tariffs are placed on foreign goods to protect American industry. The government wants to keep the goods out and uses the tax to do so.

Sometimes a government will put a high tax on a business or an industry to regulate it or to make sure that no one engages in

that business. For example, the federal government has a tax of $300 a pound on making opium for smoking. This tax is so high that it keeps people out of this business. In order to achieve a similar result, a local community may place a high tax on some kinds of door-to-door salesmen or on undesirable amusement places.

LOANS OR PAY-AS-YOU-GO? In a preceding section, "Sources of Government Income," borrowing was mentioned as one source of government income. Governments borrow money for many reasons. Many state and local governments have sold bonds to pay for highways, schools,

Based on Keynesian economic theory, deficit spending is justified just so long as a country does not borrow from outside its borders; the vast percentage of the U.S. debt is owed to Americans.

office buildings, prisons, hospitals, bridges, airports, and similar projects.

In the previous chapter it was mentioned that the indebtedness of the federal government is more than 400 billion dollars, most of which was spent for defense and war equipment.

There is much difference of opinion regarding the wisdom of government borrowing to pay for projects. The policy of building only as much at any time as can be paid for is commonly known as *pay-as-you-go*.

The advantage of such a policy is the savings in interest on debts. The interest on the federal debt is over twenty-one billion dollars yearly. The total interest payments of state and local governments amount to hundreds of millions of dollars each year. People who want pay-as-you-go argue that this interest money could pay for large amounts of service.

There are many people, however, who believe that at least some government borrowing is necessary and desirable. A new highway is needed, a new dam is to be built, the schools are old and overcrowded and new ones are necessary, there is a lack of mental hospitals—these are some of the circumstances under which borrowing is justified, they argue.

They raise these questions: Shall we do the job now when we need it, or shall we build only what we can afford each year? To build now, shall we tax ourselves so heavily that it becomes a huge cost for everyone, or shall we spread a smaller tax over many years so that people who will benefit from this improvement in the future also help pay for it? They answer their own questions by saying, "If we really need it, let's build now. In order to spread the cost, borrow the money, and pay a part each year for ten, fifteen, or twenty years, or even longer."

So there are seemingly good reasons for both pay-as-you-go and for borrowing. Many students of government lean toward the idea of pay-as-you-go if you can because you get more for your money. However, if such a policy will prevent needed construction and improvements, then most people agree it is wise to borrow and to build. In this spirit many units of local government and state governments have passed bond issues. Often there are limits on the amount that may be borrowed. Also, there are definite provisions to repay the loans as quickly as possible to reduce the interest charges.

STUDY QUESTIONS

1. What are the chief sources of government income? Explain each source.

2. What sections of the Constitution of the United States refer to taxes?

3. Explain the three general ideas according to which taxes are levied.

4. What is the difference between uniform and graduated tax rates?

5. Why is there often less objection to an indirect tax than to a direct tax?

6. What are the four main sources of income of the federal government?

7. Why is the withholding-tax system a wise method for collecting income taxes?

8. Explain exemptions and deductions as they are used in an income tax program.

9. What are the two methods of collecting excise taxes?

10. Why does the federal government collect employment taxes?

11. Why are gift and estate taxes sometimes called "painless" taxes?

12. What are the two reasons for placing taxes on goods coming from foreign countries?

13. Explain how the property-tax rate is determined.

14. Under what conditions does tax delinquency increase?

Plan a class activity around the tax bill of the average family and the services received for this tax money.

517

CONCEPTS AND GENERALIZATIONS

1
The chief source of government income is taxes.

2
Other sources of government income are loans, fees, licenses, fines, tolls, service charges, and grants-in-aid.

3
The power to tax is given to governments by constitutions and laws.

4
Bases used in levying taxes are benefits received, equal taxation for all, and ability to pay.

5
Taxes are classified as direct—paid directly to the government—and indirect—paid to the government through another person or a business.

6
The chief sources of income for the federal government are individual and corporation income taxes.

7
The income tax is a graduated tax based on ability to pay.

8
Other important sources of federal income are excise and employment taxes and tariffs.

9
The property tax is a chief source of income for local governments and some state governments.

10
Sales and use taxes and income taxes are being used more and more by state and local governments as sources of revenue.

11
Two tax provisions that have been written into state constitutions during the past few decades are tax limitation and earmarking of funds.

12
Taxes are sometimes levied on a product or service to regulate business or keep the product from being manufactured.

13
Two opposing methods of providing money for needed buildings and construction are loans and pay-as-you-go.

15. Why do some groups object to a sales tax on food and drugs?

16. What difficulties arise from tax-limitation provisions?

17. What factors should help a city decide whether to borrow money or to operate only on a pay-as-you-go basis?

IDEAS FOR DISCUSSION

1. Discuss the statement of Justice Oliver Wendell Holmes given on page 505.

2. Discuss the fairness of the graduated income tax.

3. A number of the federal excise taxes were begun as war measures during World War II. Should they have been eliminated at the end of the war? Why?

4. An important consideration in a discussion of excise taxes is the classification of luxuries and necessities? Should excise taxes be limited to luxuries? Why?

5. Mr. A must frequently go to a neighboring state on business. A few years ago he bought an automobile in that state to avoid paying the sales tax in his own state. Now his state also levies a use tax which he maintains is unfair to him. What do you think?

6. There is a proposition on the ballot to amend the state constitution to earmark for highway construction certain income from gasoline taxes and automobile license fees. What factors would influence you to vote for the amendment? What factors would influence you to vote against the amendment?

7. A school district has always operated on a pay-as-you-go basis. Many new subdivisions have been developed in recent years, causing a serious shortage of school facilities. Should the district change its policy and borrow money for new buildings? If so, what suggestions do you have for "selling the idea" to the citizens?

8. Hold a general discussion on the advantages and disadvantages of the various kinds of taxes.

THINGS TO DO

1. Get information about the current expenditures of the federal government. Compare its items with the table on page 488.

2. The Internal Revenue Service is the collection agency for federal taxes paid by individuals and corporations within the United States. Secure a copy of an income-tax return from this office or from your local post office. Complete the return, using income and deductions of a fictitious family. Explain to your classmates how you computed the tax.

3. Find out whether your state or city has an income tax. If it has, report to your class on the important parts of the tax, such as rate, filing date, exemptions, and amount of money collected.

4. Some local governments are levying a payroll tax. Make a study of this tax for a report to the class.

5. Visit the office of your local assessor or treasurer. Ask him for information about needed tax income, assessed valuations, and tax rate. Also request a sample tax bill to show the class. Explain to the class how the tax rate is determined.

6. Report to the class on sales and use taxes in your state.

7. Find out whether your state constitution provides for (a) any tax limitations and (b) any earmarking of funds. If there are any, discuss their effects with local government or school officials. Report your discussions to the class.

8. Does your city have any taxes which are levied only to regulate a business or to keep a particular business from starting? Make a survey to find out whether the tax has achieved its purpose.

9. Make a chart to show the indebtedness of your city or school district. When were the loans made and for what purposes? Include in your chart information about the amounts of interest paid and the lengths of time needed to repay the loans. Draw some conclusions about the wisdom of particular loans.

FURTHER READINGS

Due, John F., STATE AND LOCAL SALES TAX: STRUCTURE AND ADMINISTRATION. Public Administration Service, 1971.

Groves, Harold M., FEDERAL TAX TREATMENT OF THE FAMILY. The Brookings Institution, 1963.

———, FINANCING GOVERNMENT. Holt, Rinehart and Winston, Inc., 1964.

Hellerstein, Jerome R., TAXES, LOOPHOLES AND MORALS. McGraw-Hill Book Co., Inc., 1963.

Lekachman, Robert, THE AGE OF KEYNES. Random House, Inc., 1966.

Mitchell, Bruce, A CITIZEN LOOKS AT TAXES. Vantage Press, Inc., 1965.

National Bureau of Economic Research, THE ROLE OF DIRECT AND INDIRECT TAXES IN THE FEDERAL REVENUE SYSTEM. Princeton University Press, 1964. (Paperback)

Oates, Wallace E., FISCAL FEDERALISM. Harcourt Brace Jovanovich, Inc., 1972.

Taxation and the Economy

Throughout this unit the discussion of taxation has been centered on taxes as the chief source of government income. That is the traditional and historic reason for levying taxes. Governments need money to carry on their services; their primary sources for getting this money are taxes. There is, however, another reason for taxation, and that is to regulate or control the economy of the nation. This is a relatively new idea. It was first widely advocated by John Maynard Keynes, an outstanding British economist. He set forth his ideas in a book, *The General Theory of Employment, Interest, and Money,* published in 1936. Some of his ideas were adopted by our government during the Great Depression.

Keynes believed that government had a vital role to play in the development of a stable and strong economy. In essence, he stated that in times of a decline of the private sector of the economy, the government should step in with a spending program to improve the economy. Then, as the private sector improved, government should decrease its spending to avoid inflation.

Taxation enters this picture in that taxes could be lowered when the economy is sagging to leave more money with the people to spend. Such spending, it was reasoned, would help to restore the health of the economy. In contrast, in a time of high prosperity taxes should be raised in order to withdraw money from the economy to prevent inflation and to reduce rising prices. The purpose behind government spending and taxation, from this point of view, is to provide stability and growth for the economy of the nation.

TRYING TO AVOID A RECESSION

President John F. Kennedy was greatly concerned about the possibility of a recession in the early days of his administration. He looked at the effects of government spending, of the federal budget, and of the federal tax program on the economy and conferred with his economic advisers about possible change and tax reform. The concerns of the President and his advisers together with the steps taken by them to get the 1963 tax cut bill through Congress are described by Theodore C. Sorensen in his book *Kennedy*, as follows:[1]

> . . . proposal considered in our May 29 meeting, which was considered throughout the balance of the summer . . . was a "quickie" income tax cut of $5-10 billion. It was to apply to both individuals and corporations, and last one year or even less. The Council of Economic Advisers was for it, unless the economy improved. Secretary Dillon was against it, unless the economy worsened. The President reserved judgment until he saw which way the economy moved. . . .
>
> For the President to assert that a "quickie" tax cut was essential to our economic health, and then have it rejected, might well worsen the climate of confidence, further depress the stock market and impair prospects for the 1963 tax bill. Even the supporters of a temporary tax cut in the Congress and business community could not agree on its size, scope, timing, nature or conditions. . . .
>
> . . . it was clear to Kennedy that, in the absence of overwhelming evidence that a tax reduction bill was needed to prevent a recession, the Congress . . . would not pass such a bill in that session. . . .

Finally, after a review of the figures for July showed no signs of a recession sufficiently strong to convince him or the Congress, he delivered on August 13 an economic report to the nation by television from the White House. He concluded that report by promising a permanent tax cut bill in 1963 and by rejecting a temporary tax cut unless subsequent events made it necessary to recall the Congress for that purpose. . . .

. . . that . . . speech . . . laid the groundwork for one of the boldest and most far-reaching domestic economic measures ever proposed—the $10 billion tax cut bill of 1963. . . .

The origins of that bill can be traced to the preinaugural task force on taxation. . . . That report, like the President's comprehensive Message on Taxation in April, 1961, recommended without details a sweeping, long-range tax reform bill. . . .

Meanwhile the President was rejecting Walter Heller's advocacy of a quickie tax cut in the spring of 1961 and the summer of 1962. But even as he rejected them . . . the President gave thought to a Heller favorite theme: namely, that the Federal tax rates, established in wartime to prevent inflation, were taking in so much money as the economy recovered that they were draining off the private funds needed for full growth. Heller wanted a quickie tax cut as a down payment on a permanent reduction. . . .

[Later in 1962] the President, seeking to give the nation more cause for confidence after the drop in the market and the pause in the economy, and seeking to answer public pressures for a tax cut that summer, included in his press conference review of the economy an almost hidden pledge:

". . . making effective as of January 1 of next year an across-the-board reduction in personal and corporate income tax rates which will not be wholly offset by other reforms—in other words, a net tax reduction. . . ."

Nevertheless the President remained unenthusiastic, if not skeptical, about tax reduction. He still thought in terms of tax reform more than a tax cut for 1963. He was committed to no figure. . . .

The President did not become fully enthusiastic until December, and it was the convincing effect of one of his own speeches that helped convince him. The speech, designed to unveil the basic tax and Budget outlines, was delivered to a conservative gathering of mostly Republican businessmen, the Economic Club of New York. . . .

But the man most concerned about the speech was the President. He worried less about the policy than the Economic Club audience, wondering how they would swallow a large tax cut at a time of increasing deficits, increasing expenditures and increasing prosperity. "If I can convince them," he said . . . , "I can convince anybody."

He did convince them. The speech . . . was well received. . . . The President's own enthusiasm grew. He began to look to the tax cut as his most potent weapon against the persistent unemployment still plaguing him. He began to concentrate on it in his conferences, his speeches, his Budget, his legislative program and his State of the Union Message; and tax cuts, rather than tax reform, dominated his talks about the bill. . . .

The Republicans called the tax cut the "biggest gamble in history" and predicted that unemployment would not decline. But having long talked about removing the heavy hand of government, they were unable to quarrel with the President's reasons for a tax cut and quarreled instead with the Budget. . . . The President calmly emphasized that the choice was not between a Budget deficit and a Budget surplus but between two kinds of deficits—one from "waste and weakness" as the result of slack growth and lagging taxable income and one "incurred as we build our future strength" on the way to a full-employment economy. With full employment, he said, we would have no deficit, but delaying a tax cut until expenditures could be equally cut meant waiting until our population stopped growing and the Communists stopped threatening. . . .

Dillon and Hodges had analyses showing the benefits of the bill to business—cuts in the top brackets and in corporation taxes, combined with the tax gains given business the previous year—and Heller and Secretary of Labor Wirtz had tables to show labor and liberals that the lower-income groups had the largest proportionate cut. Both were right. But the President emphasized that the usual class warfare jargon was inappropriate, that his effort was not how to divide the economic pie but how to enlarge it for everyone. Helping business profits led to more jobs. Helping consumer income led to more sales. . . .

. . . as the House prepared to vote, the President went on television once again. . . . Illustrations of how the bill would reduce the taxes of a typical family, and how their tax savings would be used to create more jobs, were inserted. So were the President's favorite statistics: ten thousand new jobs had to be created every day; recessions have occurred on the average every forty-four months since World War I; seven million more young people will come into the labor market in the sixties than in the fifties. Some of his own familiar phrases were included: "We need a tax cut to keep this present drive from running out of gas"; "this nation is the keystone of the arch."

This time the speech was a success, and so was the bill.

The Kennedy tax bill, as finally enacted with the help of his successor, and the unparalleled period of expansion both its anticipation and enactment helped bring to the American economy, stand as monuments to the economic wisdom and political tenacity of John Kennedy. They embody a repudiation of the most persistent fiscal myths and fears which have so long dominated this nation.

- How did the tax cut develop in the Kennedy mind?

- Analyze the strategy in getting the tax bill passed.

- What were the effects of the 1963 tax bill? How effective was it in stimulating the economy?

- What measures were taken during World War II which reflect the ideas in the opening paragraphs of this unit case study?

THE SITUATION IS REVERSED

During 1966 and the following years President Lyndon B. Johnson believed the economic state of the nation and the world to be the opposite of that of the early sixties. He and his advisers said that the economy was moving too rapidly, that it needed to be slowed down if we were to avoid runaway inflation. He used this as one of his arguments for requesting a tax increase.

At first the President was not specific as to the size of the increase needed, but he talked about a 6 per cent surcharge tax. It was his proposal that all individuals and corporations pay an additional 6 per cent on their computed income taxes. The request was later raised to 10 per cent. As the money situation and the gold problem worsened in 1968, the request for the tax increase grew. In some quarters the suggestion was made that all of the tax cuts which resulted from the 1963 bill be restored. But others, both in and out of Congress, felt that before taxes were raised, federal spending should be cut, the budget balanced, and the deficit reduced. At any rate, all of these should be done at the same time that taxes were raised.

The following quotations from a running coverage of *The Christian Science Monitor* describe some phases of the proposed tax increase and the opinions of individuals about it.[1]

(June 29, 1967) Administration officials this week erased all doubt about whether they will seek a tax increase. The administration wants Congress to vote a tax hike before it adjourns. . . .

The first clear call came from William McChesney Martin, Jr., chairman of the independent Federal Reserve Board. Viewing the mounting budget deficit and the prospect of climbing interest rates, Mr. Martin . . . declared himself "prepared now" to support an "even higher" tax hike than the 6 per cent President Johnson proposed months ago.

. . . Gardner Ackley, chairman of the President's Council of Economic Advisers, told Congress there is "no escape" from the need to raise taxes "in the near future." A renewed boom in the economy is just around the corner, he predicted, and he wants to be sure restraint is imposed through taxes and not through tight money. . . .

With an "appropriate" tax increase, he asserts, "we can look forward to continued high employment, progress toward price stability, and a smooth flow of credit."

Without a tax hike, he warns, the economy would be running so strong by the end of the year that prices and interest rates would head up again. . . .

. . . says the President's adviser, the

GNP [Gross National Product] could be mounting by $15 billion a quarter, or a rate of $60 billion a year, in the absence of a tax hike. That, he insists, is too much steam.

—Philip W. McKinsey

(August 4, 1967) President Johnson finally has tipped his fiscal-policy hand with his request for a temporary 10 percent surtax on both corporate and individual income taxes.

Yet not until there is a more accurate reading of congressional enthusiasm for the tax proposal is there likely to be any clear-cut response from businessmen, economists, or investors.

Certainly Congress won't buy the whole tax plan. What must be seen now is how much of the plan it will buy— and how quickly. . . .

If the tax plan should clear Congress unaltered, it would bring into the Treasury $3 billion more in revenue this year and another $10 billion or so more in 1968.

The impact of that big a tax jolt would be considerable.

For one thing, higher taxes would presumably so reduce the perils of inflation that while the Federal Reserve might not be able to keep credit as easy as it has indefinitely, neither would it have to swing as sharply toward monetary restraint as it did in 1966 when taxes weren't raised. . . .

Congress will approach the bill with care. . . .

The administration's rationale is clear enough. If defense spending and civilian spending both went unchecked, the result could be intolerable inflation. Since the administration can't, in its view, cut defense spending, then civilian spending must be cut—with White House policymakers banking on the highly stimulative federal budget, and generally easy money, to keep the economy moving.

—Philip W. McKinsey

August 4, 1967) First reaction, in loud tones from all sides: At last the blow has fallen. The mounting cost of the war in Vietnam has struck home. The strain of paying for both guns and butter has hit the American taxpayer. President Johnson is compelled to face economic realities now.

Second reaction, if and when the American public starts to think about it: How small is the blow, relatively speaking. How powerful is the American economy. . . .

[First congressional reaction to the tax proposal was cool. Although some Democratic leaders gave full support, others sided with the general Republican opposition to the recommended surcharge.

[Rep. Wilbur D. Mills (D) of Arkansas, who heads the tax-planning House Ways and Means Committee, declared himself "uncommitted" to the proposal. . . .

[Sen. William Proxmire (D) of Wisconsin, chairman of the Senate-House Economic Committee, opposed the presidential request on grounds that it would hamper business growth and generate little new revenue.

[And Sen. John J. Williams (R) of Delaware, senior Republican on the Senate Finance Committee, called for a cut in domestic spending as a condition for his approval of a tax increase.]
—Saville R. Davis

(September 23, 1967) In closed-door sessions of the House Ways and Means Committee Congress has been giving the administration blunt news: Cut spending substantially, or no tax hike.

And members are saying flatly they won't settle for any vague promises about how much the President must cut; they want detailed lists. . . .

Ways and Means chairman Wilbur D. Mills (D) of Arkansas, whose support for a tax hike is considered necessary if it is to pass, says Congress wants some advice on priorities. . . .

President Johnson has never before had to come up with any lists of budget cuts before Congress would act on taxes. But this year Representative Mills and his colleagues hold an ace. Since they are less convinced than the President that an inflationary boom is imminent if Congress fails to raise taxes, they figure they can play a waiting game.

The argument over whether to raise taxes has become more political than economic. The committee could not help but have been impressed at the near unanimity of economists who testified that a tax hike is necessary, even if not as large as the 10 per cent surtax Mr. Johnson seeks. Economic data to be released soon will strengthen the administration's argument that a dampener on the economy is needed.

But Mr. Mills has indicated that his price for support on a tax hike is a dollar of spending cut for every dollar of tax hike. That would mean about $5 billion. No tax hike will be temporary, he feels, unless spending cuts are made. He recalls that the Korean "war tax" lasted 13 years.

—Philip W. McKinsey

Congress did not pass a tax increase in 1967. President Johnson renewed the request in 1968. Again, an important person involved in the whole issue was Representative Wilbur D. Mills. *The New York Times Magazine* of February 25, 1968 featured him in its major article. Written by Julius Duscha, it is entitled, "The Most Important Man on Capitol Hill Today." The following quotations illustrate Mills' influence on the tax issue.

. . . With telephone calls, informal meetings and conferences designed to seek his advice, the President has lavished attention on Mills in recent weeks in an effort to get his support for the 10 per cent income tax surcharge originally proposed by Johnson last summer

But flattery seems to be getting the President nowhere.

Johnson has also built a strong case for a tax increase. He has argued that higher taxes are needed to prevent a serious inflation and to bring the budget more nearly into balance. His arguments have been buttressed by support for his position from highly respected economists.

Mills has, however, continued to argue that nondefense spending could be cut sufficiently to make a tax increase unnecessary. (He has refrained from saying exactly what expenditures should be reduced.) He has also expressed skepticism that inflation is as great a menace as the President contends. . . .

Mills has emphasized again and again that the primary reason for his opposition to a tax increase is his concern over rising Federal spending "We want to pause in this headlong rush toward ever bigger government.". . .

Mills' questioning of witnesses at Ways and Means Committee hearings clearly shows his skepticism over the arguments that higher taxes are needed to damp down an overheated economy, and the President's case on this point is open to considerable doubt. However, the fiscal arguments for a tax increase—in his budget message this year Johnson emphasized that the additional revenue would be used to reduce the deficit—appeal to the conservative Mills. . . .[1]

Congress approved President Johnson's request and passed the tax increase, a surcharge tax of 10 per cent. However, that is not the end of the story. The discussion about taxes and their effect on the economy continues. President Nixon had said during his campaign that he would work to eliminate the surcharge tax. But the tax was continued during the first part of his administration. It was reduced, and then finally eliminated July 1, 1970.

Many advisers and economists, both in and out of the administration, said that the tax should have been continued. There was growing concern that it should be levied again to halt inflation and also to help balance the federal budget.

The government made further efforts to increase the amount of money in the hands of consumers by additional tax reductions. In 1971 the excise tax on automobiles was eliminated. Also, the income tax exemption for each taxpayer and dependent was raised through a series of increases to $750 by 1972. While the increased exemptions reduced taxes for all taxpayers, they especially helped the persons with small incomes.

What the next steps of the President and the Congress will be in trying to halt inflation and to balance the federal budget remains to be seen. The search for a stable economy seems to be a never-ending one.

- What are the factors which should decide the issues raised by this case?
- Which statements in the many quotations are facts? Which are opinions?
- How can you determine whose judgment is right?
- What was the economic effect of the tax increase?
- What was the effect of the elimination of the tax increase?
- What were the effects of the elimination of the excise tax on automobiles?
- Was the raising of the income tax exemption a wise economic move?
- What is the political effect of raising, or lowering, taxes?
- What was the purpose of President Nixon's wage and price controls of 1971? What were the results?

[1] © 1967/1968 by The New York Times Company. Reprinted by permission.

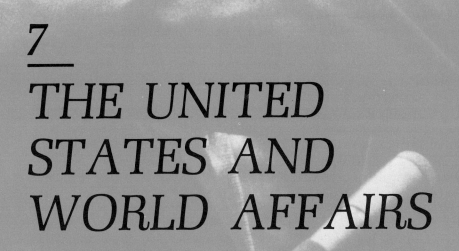

7
THE UNITED
STATES AND
WORLD AFFAIRS

Make it clear to the student that due to American reluctance and isolationism, the U.S. has only emerged as a great world power since World War II. We had the capacity for such a role earlier, but our historical tradition refuted it.

Slower readers sometimes learn readily from cartoons. Discuss and explain the cartoons in the text. Ask a small committee to collect cartoons pertaining to this unit and prepare a bulletin board display.

In the picture on the opposite page President Nixon is shown greeting President Luis Echeverria of Mexico on the latter's trip to the U.S. in 1972.

During this century the United States has become one of the great leaders in world affairs. The acts of our country affect the lives of people all over the world. But the activities of other nations change the lives of our citizens too, because all nations are part of one international community.

The international community has not been a peaceful one. Wars have troubled mankind throughout its history, but in this century two of the most destructive wars of all the ages have taken place. As a result, nations today maintain large military forces and spend a huge part of their national income for defense.

Because of the threat of communism the world has been divided into two armed camps. The period since the end of World War II has been called the Cold War. There has been actual fighting, as in Korea and Vietnam, but there has been more of an intense economic, social, and propaganda war in many parts of the world. Constantly the threat of complete destruc-

tion by the atom bomb or the hydrogen bomb has been in the minds of men.

In a period of such great uncertainty, the United States as a world leader has had to give the most serious attention to its international relations. The President, Congress, and political parties have given major attention to world problems. The American people have had to learn much about international matters.

From the broad range of international affairs, four important phases of governmental activity have been chosen for this unit.

Chapter 25 discusses the world leadership position of the United States including the making and conduct of foreign policy.

Chapter 26 describes the national defense policies and other efforts to provide national security.

Chapter 27 emphasizes the position of the United Nations among international organizations.

Chapter 28 contrasts the governments of other nations as an aid to fuller understanding of world affairs.

COLD WAR—the conflict between communist and non-communist nations carried on by propaganda, economic rivalry, spy activities, and political pressures without actually engaging in armed war.

COMMON MARKET—a group of western European nations organized to promote trade among themselves, especially by reducing tariff barriers.

CONTAINMENT—a foreign policy that attempts to keep communism within its present boundaries.

EXECUTIVE AGREEMENT—a formal agreement between the President and the heads of one or more nations which does not require approval by the Senate.

FOREIGN SERVICE—the agency of the State Department that includes the official representatives of the United States to other nations.

GUERRILLAS—fighters in an undeclared, irregular war who operate as more or less independent individuals or small groups.

IMPERIALISM—the policy of one nation's gaining control over other nations, including the acquiring of colonies or dependencies.

NEUTRALITY—the foreign policy of a nation which refuses to take sides or participate in conflicts between other nations.

OPEN DOOR—the policy of allowing all nations to engage in activities with other nations on equal terms; the policy of the United States toward China in the early part of this century.

PRAGMATIC—concerned with practical results or values.

RECOGNITION—the formal acknowledgment of the existence of a government of another nation, including the agreement to exchange diplomatic representatives.

SPHERE OF INFLUENCE—an area or region more or less dominated by a more powerful nation without having formal control of the region.

TREATY—a formal international agreement between two or more nations which has been adopted by the constitutional procedures of the participating nations.

THE LANGUAGE OF GOVERNMENT

25

International Relations

When historians of the future try to describe the major trends of the Twentieth Century, they will have a difficult time. Man's flights into outer space probably will be high on any list of trends. The recognition of the rights of non-white people may be very significant. Scientific advances in medicine, electronics, transportation could easily receive major attention. Concern for the poverty-stricken in our own country and the developing countries of Asia, Africa, and South America may also seem of great importance.

TWO MAJOR TRENDS Two trends might well lead the list, however. One is *war*; the other is the emergence of the United States and the Soviet Union as *leaders* of competing systems.

WAR. This century has been a century of war. As the century began, the Boer War (1899-1902) was being fought in South

This has been called a "Century of Total War"; discuss its meaning.

Africa. That war had been preceded by the Spanish-American War, which lasted for a few weeks in 1898. But these were small wars and did not stir or harm masses of the people.

Then came World War I (1914-18) fought between the great nations of the world. Although it was thought to be the war which would end all wars, it was followed by World War II (1939-45). These were devastating wars that destroyed not only nations, but resources, families, cities, alliances, and previous ways of living.

Before and after these great world wars lesser wars took place. The Korean War (1950-53) involved the United States in a part of the world that would have seemed remote before World War II. But the war in Vietnam further demonstrated that Asia was no longer remote, for by 1968 more American troops were involved than had been used in Korea. So, a program of assistance to Vietnam begun in 1954 to aid a small, newly created country evolved into a full-scale war of the twentieth century.

NEW WORLD LEADERS. At the start of this century the great world powers were the European nations of Great Britain, France, and Germany. Spain had deteriorated into a second-rate power. Italy was underdeveloped but rising in power. Russia was a powerful monarchy ripe for revolution. Japan was stirring and had made its influence felt in Asia. China was divided among internal factions, each struggling to gain power. The United States had arisen as the defender of the Americas, but remained aloof from European intrigue.

Today there are two giant world powers: the United States and the Union of Soviet Socialist Republics. Other nations have been so drained by the results of the wars of this century and by the resulting economic conditions that they have lost their positions of supremacy. In terms of indus-

trial capacity and military strength, including nuclear weapons, these two superpowers have dominated the affairs of the world.

Other nations have tended to divide into two camps around their differing ideologies, with the U.S. and U.S.S.R. as leaders, or to maintain neutral roles. A Cold War between the communist and noncommunist spheres developed and persisted. France flirted with the U.S.S.R. as De Gaulle tried to restore his country's former greatness. Communist China split away from the Russian brand of communism to break the solidarity of the communist camp.

In the postwar years, too, India gained freedom and tried to feed its great population while maintaining stability of government and neutrality. Japan regained its industrial strength. Germany was divided into East and West Germany, and the latter developed into one of the powerful industrial nations of the world. Former colonies of European nations in Asia and Africa gained freedom and the urge to have a higher standard of living.

So the United States, as a great world leader, has changed in this century of war from a nation almost removed from the mainstream of international affairs into one of the two powerful nations that can and do determine the whole future of mankind. As a result the United States has intimate, delicate, complex, and fateful relations with other nations. The choices to be made depend upon the goals of our foreign policy.

GOALS OF UNITED STATES FOREIGN POLICY

The development and conduct of foreign policy is the responsibility of the President working through the Department of State and with the Congress. The Secretary of State in the annual report, *United States Foreign Policy,* has stated our goals in these words:

As we develop our new relationship with the People's Republic of China, we will also be seeking to place our existing ties with the Soviet Union on an increasingly constructive basis.

As we and our allies embark on an effort of reconciliation of all Europe's nations, we will not forget that western Europe's strength and unity are the sound foundation upon which progress must be based.

As the character of our military and political involvement in East Asia continues to change, we will strengthen our ties with our major ally . . . Japan.

As we seek closer bonds with the world's larger powers, we will be making special efforts to respond to the concerns of the peoples of the western hemisphere.

As we adjust our role in foreign assistance to emphasize the primary responsibilities of developing countries and the larger capabilities of other donors, we will maintain our commitment to development.

As we negotiate a transformation of the postwar international economic system, we will endeavor to preserve the economic openness which made that system so successful for so long.[1]

PUBLIC OPINION AND FOREIGN POLICY

These goals were not thought up in a secluded conference room of the State Department. Rather, they represented then and do now a clear statement of the ideas of many of the people of the United States on foreign policy matters. The people can and do actively participate in accepting, rejecting, or amending these goals as well as the actions which are taken to achieve them.

In discussing his foreign policy before

[1] Department of State Publication 8634, 1972, pp. v-xi.

World War II, President Franklin D. Roosevelt pointed out that certain things he thought needed to be done could not be done because the American people were not ready for them. Other Presidents too have realized that basically American public opinion determines our international policies.

Public opinion on international matters is determined in much the same way that it is on any other public issue. Speeches are made. Editorials are written. Television and radio give time to an issue. One person talks with another. Interest groups present their views to public officials and their leaders engage in public debates. Letters and telegrams are sent to public officials. These are the usual devices for forming and changing all public opinion. Gradually the people come to some kind of decision.

This decision may be expressed by voting for or against a President or a member of Congress. It may be expressed through a public opinion poll. It may be reflected by a vote on a crucial issue in Congress or by a shift in policy by the President. On such an important issue as the conduct of the war in Vietnam, strategies originally used in the civil rights struggle were employed by opponents of the policies of Presidents Johnson and Nixon. There were demonstrations on college campuses and at public meetings in many cities. There were marches on Washington. There were some who burned draft cards in protest. These actions were designed to attract attention to dissent and focus public attention on the issue.

In rebuttal, the President, the Secretaries of State and of Defense, leaders in Congress, and prominent lay citizens had to explain and defend the policies. Others of equal prominence explained their opposition. Candidates for public office became involved in trying to explain, defend, criticize, or develop policies.

Define what so-called "trial balloons" are with respect to public opinion and foreign policy.

While in Moscow in 1972 President Richard Nixon and Communist Party Chief Leonid I. Brezhnev (right) signed and exchanged copies of a treaty to halt the nuclear arms race. Watching the historic occasion is Soviet President Nikolai V. Podgorny (center). (UPI photo)

These activities, carried on over many months, were evidence that the public is involved in determining foreign policy and can be very influential in setting policy.

BUILDING FOREIGN
POLICY   On this broad base of public opinion, the President tries to build the kind of foreign policy which he thinks is needed. Often he tries to change public opinion. When he desires, he may exert his great influence on public opinion by a *public speech*, a *press conference*, or a *message to Congress*.

THE PRESIDENT'S POWERS. In 1937 in Chicago President Franklin Roosevelt gave a famous speech called the "Quarantine Speech" in which he condemned nations which broke the peace and urged that they be "quarantined" by all other nations.

This speech was a deliberate effort to arouse the American people to the dangers of dictatorships.

In the midst of great tension between Communist China, Russia, and the United States, in 1955, a U. S. plane was shot down off the China coast. President Eisenhower, at his press conference the following day, exerted a calming influence on public opinion by his comments that the shooting was a local occurrence and not a matter of deliberate policy.

The famous Monroe Doctrine was first stated in a message to Congress in 1823. The effect of this message on our own people and on Europe was so great that this doctrine is still a basic part of our foreign policy. As recently as 1962, President Kennedy and members of Congress, in discussing the communist influence in Cuba, called attention to this doctrine that any

Debate the question as to whether or not the office of the President has over the years usurped the power of Congress to declare war.

threat upon a country of the Western Hemisphere would be regarded as an unfriendly act toward the United States.

President Johnson, in his first official trip outside the continental United States, flew to Hawaii in 1966 to meet with the Vietnamese Premier. There he announced the "Honolulu Declaration" to influence public opinion.

To emphasize ·the direction of foreign policy, President Nixon on June 1, 1972, spoke to a joint session of Congress after his return from Russia.

CONSTITUTIONAL POWERS. The President has the power to conduct international affairs. Under the Constitution the states are denied the power to make treaties or agreements with a foreign power (Article I, Section 10, Clauses 1 and 3).

The President has treaty-making power, the power to appoint ambassadors, ministers, and consuls (Article II, Section 2, Clause 2), and the power to give information and to recommend measures to Congress (Article II, Section 3). These powers together with Supreme Court decisions and past practices give the President the leadership and the power in foreign relations.

TREATIES. The President begins negotiations for treaties. While most of the activities are carried on by the Secretary of State, Presidents Nixon, Johnson, Kennedy, Eisenhower, Truman, and Roosevelt participated actively in these matters.

Once a treaty has been prepared, it must be submitted to the Senate for ratification, which requires a two-thirds vote in favor of the treaty. Senates have refused to confirm some treaties. Sometimes, too, Congress has refused to appropriate money to make a treaty effective.

EXECUTIVE AGREEMENTS. The political difficulties, plus the time consumed in getting treaties through the Senate, has led Presidents to handle many international matters by a device which avoids writing a treaty. This device is called the executive agreement. It is a kind of treaty without Senate approval. In a recent year the United States was a party to 947 treaties and 4,359 executive agreements.

These agreements have been upheld by the Supreme Court in those cases that have been heard by it. For the most part, the executive agreements deal with relatively small matters, for example, a financial claim of an American citizen against a foreign government or a strictly administrative matter such as the international postal regulations.

But some of these executive agreements have far-reaching effects: the obtaining of the Panama Canal Zone in 1904, the "gentlemen's agreement" with Japan on immigration in 1907, the use of British bases in the Atlantic in 1940, the Vietnam war-related activities in Laos, Cambodia, and Thailand in the sixties.

Under our system of checks and balances, what brake is there on the making of these executive agreements? Fear of political action by an aroused Senate is one chief factor that has kept Presidents from making greater use of such agreements. The Senate is jealous of its power to ratify treaties.

In order to defeat an executive agreement, Congress will sometimes not appropriate needed money to carry it out. An example is the agreement made by President Franklin D. Roosevelt with Canada in 1941 about the St. Lawrence Seaway. Congress refused to grant the necessary funds. Not until 1954 did Congress pass the legislation to make the seaway possible.

Critics of the use of executive agreements led a strong movement to amend the Constitution to provide that no provision of a treaty or other international agreement which conflicted with the Constitution should have any force or effect, as was discussed in Chapter 9. This so-called Bricker amendment was defeated in 1954—failing by one vote to get the necessary two-thirds majority. Since some agreements have been kept secret, Congress in 1972 passed a law requiring the secretary of state to transmit to Congress the text of any executive agreement. The vote in the Senate was 81 to 0 and the House approved by voice vote.

RECOGNITION. The power of recognition of another country is another important power in the President's role as international leader. One country "recognizes" another country when diplomatic relations are carried on directly through ambassadors or ministers. Hence, the power of a President to send an ambassador to another country or to call one home becomes a powerful tool in the building of our foreign policy.

When a foreign government by war or revolution changes its government, should the United States recognize the new government? In the past our government has usually recognized the new government when it seemed to be in actual control of the government machinery and able and willing to carry out its governmental obligations toward its people.

Recognition, in our earlier history, never meant that we approved the form or actions of the new government. We have recognized monarchies and dictatorships as well as democracies. But as the struggle between communism and democracy has gone on, our Presidents have sometimes been reluctant to give international recognition to tyrannical governments.

Between 1917 and 1934 our country did not recognize Russia. Since the communists gained control of China in 1949, we have not formally recognized the present government of the People's Republic. The visit by President Nixon in 1972, however, initiated a new relationship between the nations.

THE USE OF TROOPS. As commander in chief of the military forces, the President may think it is necessary to send troops to troubled spots outside the United States. When Congress has passed a formal declaration of war, no questions about the President's powers arise. But Presidents have repeatedly used the power to send troops—without a declaration of war. In 1900 President McKinley sent troops to China at the time of the Boxer Rebellion. Troops were sent to Mexico in 1914 and in 1916 by President Wilson when American lives and property were being destroyed. President Truman ordered military forces to Korea in 1950 in what he called a "police action." In 1965 President Johnson ordered marines to the Dominican Republic in the West Indies to protect American interests, which appeared to be in danger because of civil war. These examples show that a President can influence foreign policy by the manner in which he uses or fails to use our military forces.

In examples of the types listed above, the President will usually consult with congressional leaders and explain his actions to the people. Sometimes he goes beyond this by asking Congress for advance approval if he thinks he may need to send troops. President Eisenhower asked Congress to approve the use of force if necessary in 1955 if Formosa were attacked and again in 1957 in case of aggression in the Middle East. Similarly, President Johnson obtained from Congress, in August 1964, the "Gulf of Tonkin Resolution" that granted him power to "take all necessary measures to repel any armed attack against the United States and to prevent further aggression" in Vietnam. Basing his authority on this resolution, the President carried on the war in Vietnam. The Senate repealed the resolution in 1970; the House did not.

In terms of constitutional powers, such advance approvals by Congress are probably not necessary. The fact that such approval is desired does indicate that the Presidents view their powers to commit troops as needing the support of the Congress and the people.

THE POWERS OF CONGRESS. Thus, while the power of the President in making foreign policy is very great, the role of Congress is still an important one. Ratifying treaties, approving appointments of ambassadors and ministers, appropriating money, as well as having public debate of issues give Congress great power. Actually our international policy is most effective when there is real cooperation between the President and the Congress.

Most treaties are approved by the Senate —more than 90 per cent in fact. But the occasional treaty that is rejected becomes terribly important. The League of Nations was rejected by the Senate in 1920, and membership in the Court of International Justice was defeated in 1926 and 1935. Because one-third of the members present can reject a treaty, many have argued that this really gives control of our foreign policy to the minority in the Senate. Proposals to amend the treaty-making parts of the Constitution were described in Chapter 9.

Congress does have some direct methods which it can employ in foreign affairs. *Resolutions* can be passed which, while not compelling a President to act, give direction to our foreign policy. The Fulbright Resolution of the House and the Connally Resolution of the Senate in 1943 paved the way for United States participation in the United Nations. Texas and Hawaii were annexed as territories by joint resolutions, and World War I was officially ended by the same process.

In other words, Congress and the Presi-

dent can quarrel or they can work together. Each has weapons if they quarrel. Together they make an imposing foreign policy team.

Recent Presidents have tried to use the team concept effectively. Presidents have deliberately included key members of the Senate Foreign Relations Committee in their plans. Members of the House Committee on Foreign Affairs have been consulted too. Members of both political parties have been consulted. Frequently, crucial support has come from leaders of the minority party. Presidents and Secretaries of State have tried to conduct international affairs on a bipartisan basis, but the team concept works best when the leaders in Congress and the President are members of the same political party.

THE CONDUCT OF FOREIGN POLICY

The responsibility for the conduct of foreign policy lies with the Department of State. The organization and personnel of this department were described in Chapter 12. The Secretary of State is a person of tremendous influence, not only in the United States, but throughout the world. He is a central figure in most great international conferences.

THE DEPARTMENT OF STATE. For

---

*. . . in international relations we are dealing not with general terms—tribe, region, nation; or national, regional, international organizations; or political, economic, social ideological forces. We are dealing with **people**, with human beings who are born, live, and die; who rejoice and mourn; who triumph and suffer; who create and destroy both ideas and institutions; who respond to persuasion as well as bow to force.*

—MRS. VERA MICHELES DEAN, Professor of International Development, New York University, in *Political Science in the Social Studies*, 36th Yearbook of the National Council for the Social Studies, copyright 1966, page 85.

Our government officials know the importance of communicating with the people. Here, Dean Rusk, Secretary of State in the Johnson Administration, presents his views to an audience of young people at a news conference in Washington, D.C. (U.S. Dept. of State)

many years the work of the department was divided between the Departmental Service (employees who work only in Washington) and those who were in the *Foreign Service*. As a result there was criticism of this division because officials in the Foreign Service had not returned to the United States for regular tours of duty at home as is expected.

One man had only thirteen months of home duty out of forty-three years spent in the service. The fear was that such long absence from one's country would cause diplomats to lose touch with the real interests and ideals of the American people. As a result of this criticism, the Washington staff and those in foreign countries have been unified on a more workable basis.

FOREIGN SERVICE PERSONNEL. The importance of securing able persons for our Foreign Service cannot be overestimated. These people *are* the United States to many of the people in foreign lands. Their conduct symbolizes to others what we as a people are. They are our advance listening posts learning what is happening in the important spots around the world. They are our voices telling the world what we stand for. They must be loyal. If these officials are alert and accurate in their reports, the dangers of serious conflicts are reduced.

How can people of such high ability be recruited? Some argue that we need a West Point or an Annapolis just for training career diplomats. Others plead for a superscholarship program like the R.O.T.C. of the Navy.

Actually, obtaining a position as a junior officer in the Foreign Service is very difficult. The selective process is based on such high standards that only the unusually intelligent and able college graduate can pass the necessary examinations. The desired qualifications include the ability to read and speak another language; knowledge of geography, history, and economics; understanding of American government and governments of other countries; knowledge of international laws and politics; special study of some particular region of the world. Superior intellectual, personal, and health requirements are necessary too.

In a recent year the State Department received about 6,000 applications for the Foreign Service. Some 4,000 took the department's examinations, with about 1,000 passing them. Of these, approximately 200 finally received appointments, following an intensive oral interview.

These new junior officers are sent to Washington for training in the Foreign Service Institute and are then assigned to a low-ranking diplomatic post. From this first modest post, under a merit system, advancement is made through eight classifications to positions of greater and greater responsibility.

The Foreign Service Act of 1946 established the basis for this system. The desire was to develop a permanent group of trained experts as the backbone of our Foreign Service. This act also joined under one director the *consular service*, which handles business matters, and the *diplomatic service*, which handles political matters. The goal was to develop one great Foreign Service instead of the two groups as had been true in the past.

Employees selected for the Foreign Service need to be able to have contacts with people in all walks of life. Snobbery or aristocracy are damaging to the best interests of the United States. Until this century the diplomats of all nations traditionally associated chiefly with the "upper" classes. They lost contact with the poor and the middle classes.

With millions of poor people around the world seeking improvement in their ways of living, it is essential that our diplomats understand and know what the hopes of these people are.

The successful conduct of our foreign policy depends on having trained, intelligent, democratic diplomats at work throughout the world.

HISTORIC FUNDAMENTALS OF OUR FOREIGN POLICY

At any given moment it is difficult to describe American foreign policy. Today's headlines may require a shift or reappraisal of policy. Nevertheless, throughout our history there have been certain fundamentals that have provided keys to our foreign policy. These historic fundamentals have been: (1) isolation, (2) territorial expansion, (3) the open door policy in Asia, (4) the good neighbor policy, and (5) freedom of the seas.

ISOLATION. Our foreign policy for many years was a simple one. It could have been advertised by a "Keep Off" sign. We said to Europe, "Stay out of America." At the same time we tried to stay out of Europe.

This *isolation* policy began with George Washington's idea that the United States should not engage in permanent alliances with other nations. We kept Europe from this continent by the Louisiana Purchase in 1803 and the Florida Purchase in 1823.

The Monroe Doctrine in 1823 was a special statement of this policy. The policy fitted the times. It was successful because until 1914 Britain controlled the sea with the biggest navy in the world. It was successful because during those formative years we had not become a great world power. As was noted earlier in this chapter, the idea that this continent is not open to inroads by other nations still is part of our foreign policy.

Much of the nineteenth century was a century of territorial acquisition by the U.S.

At his inauguration in 1933, President Franklin Roosevelt stressed the importance of America's being a good neighbor to all. (Franklin D. Roosevelt Library photo, Hyde Park, N.Y.)

TERRITORIAL EXPANSION. From the time of the original thirteen colonies up to the present the United States has been willing to acquire territories. We acquired New Mexico and California in 1848 after a war with our neighbor, Mexico. We purchased Alaska from Russia in 1867. After the war with Spain in 1898 we acquired the Philippines, Guam, and Puerto Rico. Hawaii was annexed the same year and was made a territory in 1900. The Panama Canal Zone was acquired in 1904. The Virgin Islands were purchased from Denmark in the year 1917. Numerous small islands were taken as a result of the wars of this century.

The nineteenth century and the first half of the twentieth century was a period of imperialistic expansion by European powers. The United States was involved to some degree in this same expansion.

THE OPEN DOOR. In the Far East, our historic policy was based on the *open door.* By this policy we held that our citizens in other countries should have the right to equal economic opportunities with the citizens of any other country. Our citizens should be able to trade and make investments wherever this is done by citizens of other countries.

This became our policy because each European nation was trying to carve out special *spheres of influence,* especially in China, in order to have a monopoly of trade in that portion of China. We opposed this idea and tried to develop our relations with Asiatic nations on the basis of equal treatment for all nations.

THE GOOD NEIGHBOR. The good neighbor policy is usually thought of as a special policy developed during and since the 1930's to improve our relations with the Latin American countries.

This is true, but in his inaugural address in 1933 President Franklin D. Roosevelt included the whole world in our good neighbor policy. At that time he said: "In the field of world policy I would dedicate this nation to the policy of the good neighbor—the neighbor who resolutely respects himself and, because he does so, respects the rights of others—the neighbor who respects his obligations and respects the sanctity of his agreements in and with a world of neighbors."

In these words he was really putting the ideals of the American people into a world-wide international policy. He was building on the goodwill tours that President Hoover

The Open Door policy again coincided with British interests, as did the Monroe Doctrine.

had made in South America and on our many years of peace with Canada as examples of what we really desired in world affairs.

FREEDOM OF THE SEAS. Our country has always held that the oceans were highways that should be open to the vessels of all nations. We have been a nation of traders and have insisted that our ships be allowed to travel anywhere.

In part the War of 1812 was fought over this issue. Our entry into World War I was the direct result of President Wilson's insistence on American citizens having "the full enjoyment of their acknowledged rights on the high seas."

REMNANTS OF THE IMPERIALISTIC PERIOD

Scattered in the Atlantic and Pacific Oceans are peoples and places dependent on the United States. They are reminders of that period when nations were acquiring territories under imperialistic policies.

Puerto Rico is an island in the Caribbean Sea that was acquired in 1898 at the end of the war with Spain. Since 1952 Puerto Rico has had self-government under a commonwealth status by which it is associated with the United States in matters of immigration, tariff, and defense. Puerto Ricans are citizens of the United States, but they are not subject to federal income taxes.

The Virgin Islands are about 40 miles east of Puerto Rico. They were purchased by the United States from Denmark in 1917 for 25 million dollars. The islands are a natural protector of the Panama Canal Zone. The inhabitants are citizens of the United States. The Virgin Islands are a dependency of the United States. After 1954 the islands had self-government with a governor appointed by the President. Since 1970 the governor has been elected.

The Panama Canal Zone is a ten-mile wide strip, about fifty miles long, extending along both sides of the Panama Canal. The land was purchased from the Republic of Panama by treaty in 1904 for $10,000,000 and what is in effect an annual rental payment. The Zone has a governor, who is usually an army general, appointed by the President and responsible to the Secretary of the Army. Efforts have been made to negotiate a new treaty with Panama.

Guam, in the Pacific Ocean, was obtained in 1898 at the end of the war with Spain. It was ruled by the Navy until 1950, when the Department of the Interior took over the administration.

American Samoa consists of a small group of islands in the South Pacific which were obtained by a treaty with Great Britain and Germany in 1899. Though originally administered by the Navy, they have been under the jurisdiction of the Department of the Interior since 1951.

Wake Island and the *Midway Islands* are small islands in the Pacific obtained by right of discovery and occupation. They are important for naval operations and military and commercial air flights. Wake Island is administered by the Air Force, while the Midway Islands are administered by the Department of the Navy.

Other Pacific Islands administered by the Navy are *Johnston, Sand Islands,* and *Kingman Reef. Palmyra, Baker, Howland,* and *Jarvis Islands* are administered by the Department of the Interior. *Canton* and *Enderbury* are jointly administered by Great Britain and the United States Department of the Interior.

Under the trusteeship plan of the United Nations, several hundred small islands in the Pacific are administered by the United States. By the trusteeship plan a nation may administer a territory but cannot annex it. In 1947 the United States agreed to administer the Marianas, the Marshalls, and the Carolines as the *United States Trust Territory of the Pacific Islands.*

Some islands taken from Japan after World War II, including *Iwo Jima* and *Okinawa,* were controlled by the United States under the Japanese Peace Treaty. They were returned to Japan in 1968 and 1971 respectively.

The People's Republic of China was admitted to the UN on October 25, 1971. The leader of the first Chinese delegation, Huang Hua, is shown speaking to the Security Council. (United Nations)

APPRAISAL. These historic policies evolved to meet the conditions of the times which they served. As with all foreign policy they were based on our desire for national security, economic welfare, and peace. Some Americans wish that these historic policies could be in effect today. Certainly within our country there are important groups and individuals who now support each of these policies.

Most observers would say, however, that isolation has been replaced by international cooperation, that the United States today is no longer interested in territorial expansion, that the desirability of the open door still exists but that conditions in Asia have made this policy impractical. They would agree, too, that the good-neighbor policy and the freedom of the seas are still fundamentals of our foreign policy and would extend the idea of freedom of the seas to the air spaces beyond our planet.

In other words, our foreign policy is undergoing a constant re-examination because of world conditions and our position of world leadership. As a State Department bulletin says: "The foreign policy of the United States cannot be codified or given formal legal expression in any single official document. It does not lend itself to such treatment, for it must remain flexible and capable of adjustment to the changing circumstances of the times."

MODERN FUNDAMENTALS OF FOREIGN POLICY

In this constant re-examination and adjustment of foreign policy three fundamentals of foreign policy have emerged. They are: (1) international cooperation, (2) idealism, and (3) practical cooperation.

INTERNATIONAL COOPERATION. International cooperation during this century has replaced isolation as a fundamental in our foreign policy. This is a simple statement of fact. We are a member of the United Nations. We give foreign aid to many nations. We have treaties with other nations. We participate in international conferences. As a nation we are a world leader.

International cooperation as a policy was not adopted without strong opposition. In this century some newspapers and some political leaders opposed this policy, pre-

Evaluate the seeming demise of isolationism in the U.S. Discuss the relationship of the three modern fundamentals of foreign policy.

539

ferring our older policy of isolation. They wanted the United States to be a gigantic fortress, so strong that no one would dare attack us. With this strength they would then want the rest of the world to solve its own problems. We would leave them alone; they would leave us alone.

The events of this century, however, compelled our nation to abandon isolation and to cooperate with other nations in international affairs. In adopting this new policy some problems, of course, arose. One of these was our *inexperience* in the conduct of world affairs. In contrast to the British, for example, we did not have a long tradition of devoted service to international affairs, and we did not have the advantage of years and years of experience in dealing with these affairs in all parts of the world.

Another problem was the *reactions to our own great strength and power.* We had so much money, so many resources, so many arms that some people in other nations resented our great power. It seems to be a peculiar part of human nature that the small frequently resent the big. In sports, for example, the underdog frequently gets the greater support.

Communist propaganda makes clever use of this human characteristic and encourages "Hate America" and "Go Home, America" campaigns. Nevertheless, we find it necessary to cooperate even though some people in foreign nations dislike us. Fortunately we have many friends throughout the world—"a reservoir of good will" as the late Wendell Willkie, a one-time Republican candidate for President, once said.

IDEALISM. Modern foreign policy has been based on high ideals. As President Kennedy said in his inaugural address,

The world is very different now. For man holds in his mortal hands the power to abolish all forms of human poverty and all forms of human life. And yet the same revolutionary beliefs for which our forbears fought are still at issue around the globe—the belief that the rights of man come not from the generosity of the state, but from the hand of God.

We dare not forget today that we are the heirs of that first revolution. Let the word go forth from this time and place, to friend and foe alike, that the torch has been passed to a new generation of Americans—born in this century, tempered by war, disciplined by a hard and bitter peace, proud of our ancient heritage—and unwilling to witness or permit the slow undoing of those human rights to which this Nation has always been committed, and to which we are committed today at home and around the world.

In keeping with these ideals, we have favored disarmament and the outlawing of war. Attempts at *disarmament* have been one phase of our international cooperation for a long period of time. In 1899 and in 1907 we participated in the conferences at The Hague in the Netherlands. Our major interest in these conferences was in the arbitration of international disputes, but disarmament was discussed at each conference—without success.

The Washington Naval Conference was called by Secretary of State Hughes in 1921 and was followed by the London Naval Conference in 1930. Some limitations were placed on the size of navies of the great powers, but permanent results were not achieved.

In the League of Nations disarmament was discussed, and in the United Nations disarmament continues to be discussed. The U.S. Arms Control and Disarmament Agency develops disarmament plans. Efforts at disarmament have not been very successful, because one nation hesitates to give up

Mention the 1968 non-proliferation treaty of the U.S., Britain, and the Soviet Union concerning nuclear weapons.

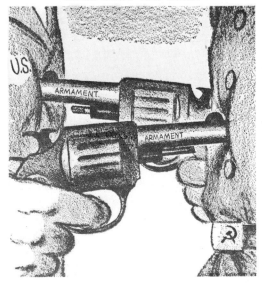

Don Hesse in the St. Louis Globe-Democrat.

powerful weapons until another nation has already given up its strong weapons.

Sometimes it is forgotten that the *outlawing of war* was another international effort in which we cooperated. A Republican Secretary of State, Kellogg, working with Briand, the French foreign minister, developed in the late 1920's a plan for outlawing war. Some sixty nations signed this treaty "renouncing war as an instrument of national policy." This has been called the period of "wishful thinking," for a decade later these nations were again at war.

The idealistic approach to foreign policy has continued. Since the development of the atomic bomb, there has been a continuous effort by the United States to control the use and spread of nuclear weapons. Although disarmament conferences have not been successful in controlling the production of atomic bombs, because of differences over methods of inspection, three significant steps have been taken.

In 1957, based on a plan submitted by President Eisenhower, the International Atomic Energy Agency was created. Over 100 nations have joined this agency which seeks to employ atomic energy for the peace, health, and prosperity of the world.

In 1963 under President Kennedy, a limited nuclear test ban treaty was signed with Great Britain and the Soviet Union. It was agreed not to conduct nuclear test explosions in the air, in outer space, or under water. Underground tests were permitted. More than 100 nations have joined this treaty. But France and Communist China have not signed and have continued to make tests.

Since 1969 the United States and the Soviet Union have engaged in the Strategic Arms Limitation Talks (SALT) aimed at halting or reducing nuclear weapons systems. While President Nixon was in Moscow in 1972, a treaty sharply limiting defensive antiballistic missile sites was agreed on. And an agreement was signed freezing offensive missiles at roughly current levels for five years.

PRACTICAL COOPERATION. Disarmament, outlawing of war, and attempts to control the atomic bomb can be looked upon as the idealistic attempts in international cooperation. But our country has been engaged in great practical cooperation.

As a people, we have learned to value the flexible, practical approach to the solution of problems. We tend to focus our energies and resources on a specific problem and attempt to reach a reasonable solution in a short time. In this sense we are a *pragmatic* people concerned with the practical results of a policy.

World War II was an example of practical international cooperation. In the years leading to our participation we had tried to avoid war by a policy of strict *neutrality*. We changed to a system by which the warring powers could purchase materials in our country. We next adopted a lend-lease program by which we supplied aid to Britain with no immediate provision for payment.

President Roosevelt and Prime Minister Churchill joined in a common statement of an eight-point peace program called the Atlantic Charter. With the bombing of Pearl Harbor we went to war. Each of these events was a recognition that for practical reasons we could not remain isolated.

In the years since the war, practical cooperation has been a major force behind our international policies. At the end of the war much of Europe and parts of Asia were devastated. Starvation and hunger faced millions of people. Factories and normal trade conditions had been destroyed. Our wartime ally, Russia, began a program of expansion.

The United States was forced into a position of world leadership. Our response was typically American; we did those practical things that seemed necessary for us to do.

PRAGMATIC FOREIGN POLICY SINCE WORLD WAR II

Faced with the Cold War, the United States has undertaken numerous practical policies designed to help other nations and to protect our own security. Regardless of the President's party affiliation, since World War II, there has been a consistent attempt to solve the problems which have arisen in various parts of the world. President Kennedy reflected this viewpoint in a speech on June 10, 1963, when he said, "Peace is a process—a way of solving problems."

THE UNITED NATIONS. The need for some type of effective international organization was recognized before the end of World War II. Although we had refused to join the League of Nations, we played a leading part in the development of the United Nations. This organization is so important that it will be discussed in detail in Chapter 27.

The United Nations was viewed as a desirable long-range policy, but until the UN could be strong enough to prevent wars, even among the great powers, the development of other appropriate policies was necessary.

CONTAINMENT. The central purpose of our foreign policy after the war was to hold the Soviet Union and its recently acquired countries within their present boundaries. *Containment* became the label that was applied to this general policy. It was an effort to prevent further communist expansion.

Military bases, some left over from World War II, were established around the rim of the Soviet empire in a series of closely related actions.

THE TRUMAN DOCTRINE. By 1947 communist *guerrillas* were fighting in northern Greece while at the same time Turkey was under pressure to give up control of the Dardanelles—the narrow sea-lane from the Black Sea. By these actions the Soviet Union was attempting to control the northeastern Mediterranean. If Greece and Turkey fell to communism, the road to the oil of the Middle East would be open to the Soviets.

On March 12, 1947, President Truman sent a message to Congress requesting 400 million dollars to help the Greek and Turkish governments get food, machinery, and military supplies plus technical industrial advice. This was the announcement of the *Truman Doctrine* which stated that the United States must "help free people to maintain their free institutions and their national integrity."

Great Britain had announced that it no longer could afford to assist Greece; the United Nations was not able to extend help

The C-47 planes in the squadron were part of the 1948 Berlin Airlift, carrying food and supplies into the city, which had been blockaded in a Soviet power move. (Official U.S. Air Force photo)

of the kind that was needed. Congress granted the money. As a result of the Truman Doctrine, Greece and Turkey remained independent.

THE BERLIN AIRLIFT. On June 24, 1948, the Soviets blocked all railroads, highways, and canals leading from West Germany to Berlin. Their hope was to force the Western powers out of Berlin. For the following eleven months, British and American airmen flew more than two million tons of food and supplies including coal into this city of over two million people. On one record day a plane landed every forty seconds. This famous *Berlin airlift* dramatized the containment policy by an air feat which the world had considered impossible. Al-

though the Soviets split the city and succeeded in establishing a municipal government over East Berlin, when they realized that the blockade was a failure they lifted it in May 1949.

THE KOREAN INTERVENTION. While the containment policy was being worked out in Europe, an event took place in Korea that caused all Americans to realize that the Soviet Union faced East as well as West. Korea had been dominated by Japan for nearly fifty years. Throughout that period it had longed for its former independence. After World War II, Soviet troops occupied the territory of North Korea above the thirty-eighth parallel, and United States troops occupied the territory to the south.

Discuss the railroad, highway, canal, and air routes into West Berlin from West Germany, including their origin.

543

Soldiers of the U.S. Eighth Army stand watch at a guard post in Korea for signs of North Korean military action. (U.S. Army photo)

After two years of this divided occupation, unification of the country seemed impossible, and separate governments were created for North and South Korea. Both Russia and the United States withdrew their armies.

Then early in the morning of June 25, 1950, North Korean soldiers invaded South Korea. To all the world this seemed to be an act of open aggression. The UN Security Council, with Russia absent, demanded withdrawal of the North Koreans and called for the military support of South Korea by the member-nations. Sixteen nations supplied troops, with the United States carrying the biggest share.

The North Korean invasion was being repulsed when Communist China entered the war in November. After a bitter struggle with neither side victorious, an armistice was signed on July 27, 1953. A buffer zone was set up where the battle lines had been when the truce was signed. The troops withdrew one and one-quarter miles from each side of this zone, which has remained the dividing line between North and South Korea.

The fighting in Korea was evidence that if communism was to be stopped, it would have to be on a global basis.

THE WAR IN VIETNAM. With a basic foreign policy goal of containing communism, the United States became involved in a costly, ruthless, devastating war in Vietnam. The effort attempted to prove to com-

Marines of the 5th Regiment, with an LVT in support, fire at fleeing Viet Cong during operations in the Vietnam War. (Defense Dept. photo)

Describe the role of the United Nations in the Korean War.

munists that guerrilla "wars of liberation" would not be allowed to succeed.

During World War II the Japanese had occupied the French colony of Indochina. At the end of the war, in 1945, the French returned to rule the country. They were resisted by nationalist forces under the leadership of a communist, Ho Chi Minh. For nine years the French fought an expensive war against guerrillas with the aid of anti-communist Vietnamese, but were never really able to gain control. After the French lost a key fortress to the communists in 1954, a conference was called at Geneva, Switzerland. Representatives of France, Communist China, the Soviet Union, Great Britain, and Indochina agreed to a division of the country. North of the seventeenth parallel was to be the communist nation of Vietnam, which became known as North Vietnam. The balance of the original country was divided into three noncommunist states—Laos, Cambodia, and South Vietnam. While the United States was not represented at the conference, we accepted the basic agreement.

Ho Chi Minh became the head of the North Vietnamese, and the French withdrew. Elections were to be held in two years to decide on a government for the whole country. These elections were not held, supposedly because North Vietnam would not guarantee free elections.

In South Vietnam, communist forces, called the Viet Cong, engaged in terrorism, subversion, and guerrilla warfare. Presidents Eisenhower, Kennedy, and Johnson each pledged to preserve the security of South Vietnam. At first only military advisers were sent but over the years, as the condition of the South Vietnamese worsened, more and more United States troops were sent—until by 1968 more of our military forces were there than had been involved in Korea. The brunt of the fighting was carried on by United States troops until President Nixon began a policy of withdrawal and a training program for South Vietnamese soldiers.

The North Vietnamese received military aid from Communist China and the Soviet Union, but the fighting was done by the Viet Cong and the North Vietnamese.

Some critics within the United States have called this "the most disliked war in United States history." Others have labeled it "the wrong war, at the wrong time, and the wrong place."

The United Nations, Presidents Johnson, Nixon, and other world statesmen struggled to work out a negotiated peace. The price the United States is willing to pay to contain communism at this spot in Southeast Asia is a great unknown. So is the ability of the North Vietnamese to withstand the horrible devastation. In April 1972 North Vietnam invaded the South. President Nixon ordered the mining of harbors and the bombing of North Vietnam. The President and his aide, Henry Kissinger, undertook new peace offensives.

CUBA. Another great threat to containment is represented by Cuba. In Cold War terms containment requires that communism be kept from breaking out in new parts of the world. Yet, a few minutes' flying time from Florida, a communist nation has developed under Fidel Castro.

Castro came to power in 1959. Leading a hardy group of guerrilla fighters in the hills of Cuba, Castro protested against the great gap between the rich and the poor in his country. On January 1, 1959, he succeeded in overthrowing the dictatorial President Batista. Shortly thereafter, it became clear that the new dictatorship of Castro was a communist regime. Properties of Americans were seized, mass killings of Cubans opposed to Castroism were held, and a propaganda campaign of hostility to

Point out how Communist Cuba can also be considered a violation of the U.S. Monroe Doctrine.

545

the United States was conducted—especially in Latin America.

In January 1961, the United States broke off diplomatic relations with Cuba. During the previous six months, President Eisenhower had reduced Cuba's sugar quota; the quota allowed Cuba to ship sugar to the United States at premium prices. Exports to Cuba were also stopped except for medical supplies and certain foodstuffs. This was, in effect, economic war.

When President Kennedy took office, a plan had been developing to aid Cuban exiles to attack Cuba by air and sea. Once a landing had been made the expectation was that Cuban citizens would join in overthrowing Castro. The new President approved the plan and on April 17, 1961, an ill-fated invasion began. Lacking air support, the invaders were destroyed by Castro's troops at the Bay of Pigs.

Apparently made bolder by the failure of the invasion, the Soviet Union increased shipments of military supplies and technical advisers to Cuba. The excuse was that Cuba needed to be protected from future invasion threats.

Then, in October 1962, United States aerial photographs revealed that missile installations were being built in Cuba capable of taking offensive action against the United States. Against the threat of the launching of nuclear missiles, President Kennedy acted forcefully. Recognizing that war between the two countries was very close, the President notified Soviet Premier Khrushchev that the missiles must be removed. He also declared a quarantine on shipment of offensive military equipment to the island. A tense world waited to see if Soviet ships en route to Cuba would turn back. They did. Shortly after, the missile bases in Cuba were dismantled and war was avoided.

Until the missile crisis, other Latin American countries had not taken the threat of communism too seriously. In the years since, however, some countries in the Southern Hemisphere have recognized that subversive activities directed from Cuba are a threat to their governments. While Cuba without nuclear missiles is not a direct menace to the United States, it is a hole in the dike of containment.

FOREIGN AID. Intermingled with the policy of containment and inseparable from it is the policy of aiding other countries by financial, technical, and military assistance. The Truman Doctrine preached more than containment; it provided aid to Greece and Turkey. Foreign aid became a central feature of foreign policy after World War II with the creation of the Marshall Plan.

THE MARSHALL PLAN. In a speech at Harvard University, in June 1947, Secretary of State George C. Marshall proposed a European Recovery Program. The purpose of this plan, which became known throughout the world as the *Marshall Plan*, was to help the democracies restore their economic life.

Beginning with seven billion dollars the first year and five billion the second year, a total of more than twenty billion dollars was spent under the Marshall Plan.

Originally the Economic Cooperation Administration was created to operate this program. It was replaced successively by the Mutual Security Agency, the Foreign Operations Administration, the International Cooperation Administration, and the Agency for International Development as aid for economic recovery was widened from Europe to all parts of the world.

Great Britain, when its economy was strong enough, requested that its aid be stopped. Other nations that needed help received our assistance. Our intent was to help the free nations aid themselves so that they could easily resist communism.

Give a short sketch of George C. Marshall.

Originating as a policy to help restore countries that had been weakened by World War II, foreign aid has been modified over the past two decades. Some has been direct economic aid; some has been military aid. The success of the Marshall Plan in restoring the economies of Western European nations caused the United States to extend foreign aid to underdeveloped countries in Asia, the Middle East, Africa, and Latin America.

TECHNICAL ASSISTANCE. Assisting countries with the expert knowledge that is required for modern industrial, agricultural, and medical systems is an important aspect of foreign aid. One program which captured the imagination of the people of the world was the *Point Four Program* announced by President Truman in his inaugural address of January, 1949. The plan was to make "the benefits of scientific advances and industrial progress available for the growth and improvement of underdeveloped areas" around the world.

This was not just a program aimed at the war-stricken countries. This was a bold idea to try to raise the standard of living around the world. Fundamentally it was an attempt to remove poverty, ignorance, and poor health as the breeding spots for communism.

The plan had two parts:

1. To provide technical knowledge to help countries solve their problems. Conservation experts have aided foreign countries with plans for building dams and improving forests. Public health experts have helped control disease. Farm experts have taught better use of soil. Educators have helped develop better schools.

2. To develop regional resources. Large investments by private business and smaller ones by government were desired. Our government guaranteed the private investor against loss.

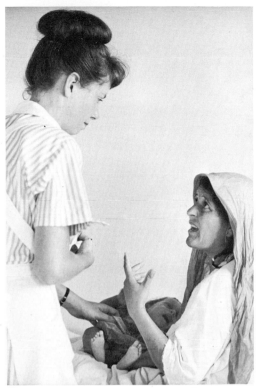

A young American Peace Corps worker serves as a volunteer nurse in a hospital in Sousse, Tunisia's third largest city. (Peace Corps photo)

From a modest beginning under Point Four programs, technical assistance has become an important method of assisting other nations. This type of help has great appeal to the developing nations.

In 1961 President Kennedy launched another program which has had great appeal in the United States and around the world. This was the *Peace Corps*, which provides skilled men and women who volunteer to live, work, and teach in countries that are on the threshold of modernizing their economies. This type of person-to-person assistance is now given to over fifty countries that have requested help. Peace Corps volunteers range in age from eighteen to over sixty-five, but most are young people in their twenties who desire to perform

Compare the value of technical assistance with that of military aid.

547

Military headquarters of the North Atlantic Treaty Organization are housed in this vast complex of buildings in Belgium. (NATO photo)

some useful service for others. They receive special training and serve for two years. Families are now recruited, too.

Peace Corps activities include teaching illiterates to read, developing water supplies, improving hospital care, training auto mechanics, improving agricultural methods, and digging ditches. Peace Corps volunteers receive no formal salaries from the United States, but get an allowance to pay their living costs. When they leave the service, they receive a separation payment which has accumulated at the rate of $75 a month.

Technical assistance has contributed human resources in addition to the billions of dollars of financial aid which has been given to other countries.

Many believe that the only way in which communism can finally be defeated is by aiding people all around the globe to improve their standard of living. One American, after serving several months in another country on one of these programs, stated, "I don't know how to teach democracy to starving people. After they get enough food, maybe, then it will be possible to interest them in a better way of life."

ALLIANCES AND TREATIES. Inter-

twining with and undergirding the practical policies of containment and foreign aid is a network of alliances and treaties of which the United States is a member. Our nation has entered into multilateral and bilateral treaty arrangements with more than forty countries on five continents.

THE NORTH ATLANTIC PACT. A defensive military alliance, called the North Atlantic Pact, was signed in Washington in April 1949. The nations bordering on the North Atlantic agreed by this treaty that in case of armed attack in Europe or North America against any member the attack should be considered to be against all the member nations. The original signers of the treaty were Belgium, Canada, Denmark, France, Great Britain, Iceland, Italy, Luxemburg, the Netherlands, Norway, Portugal, and the United States. Since then Greece, Turkey, and West Germany have joined.

To make this alliance effective the *North Atlantic Treaty Organization (NATO)* was established. Through this organization the United States offered military supplies to its allies. General Eisenhower, before he became a candidate for President in 1952, served as supreme commander of the NATO combined defense forces.

With respect to treaties and alliances compare the United States prior to World War II and since World War II. The North Atlantic Pact was the first U.S. peacetime alliance since the American Revolution.

France, under De Gaulle, became unhappy with the military arrangement under NATO with its highly integrated international military force. In the background, of course, United States nuclear power provided the ultimate support of NATO. France developed its own nuclear capacity and, in 1966, De Gaulle ordered the withdrawal of all NATO forces from France.

The military headquarters was moved from France to Belgium. But of more importance, conditions in Europe—including the devaluation of the pound, British admission to the Common Market, the invasion of Czechoslovakia, and new agreements on West Berlin—led to many questions concerning the future of this alliance.

THE ASIATIC TREATIES. Events in the Far East have led to a number of alliances and treaties with the nations concerned about trends in Asia. In 1951 the *Anzus pact* was signed. The United States, Australia, and New Zealand agreed to come to each other's aid if any of the three nations is attacked in the Pacific area.

In the same year a peace treaty was signed with Japan, together with a *mutual defense pact* by which we maintained military forces in and around Japan. This treaty was revised in 1960 into a Treaty of Mutual Cooperation and Security to develop closer cooperation in defense.

In 1951, also, a *Philippine pact* was signed, providing for mutual defense in the Pacific.

Because of the need to strengthen our policy in the Far East, a *Southeast Asia Treaty Organization (SEATO)* was formed, based on the example of NATO. Eight nations met at Manila in September, 1954, to join forces to halt the expansion of communism in Asia.

Australia, Great Britain, France, New Zealand, Pakistan, the Philippines, Thailand, and the United States met and signed a loose treaty of mutual assistance subject to the constitutional processes of each participating state. Notable among the absentees were Burma, Ceylon, India, and Indonesia, who declined to attend.

SEATO represented an effort to deal with the situation in Vietnam after the French withdrawal. As the war in Vietnam increased in intensity, three of the signers—Great Britain, France, and Pakistan—declined to participate in the war. Indeed, Pakistan signed an arms agreement with the Soviet Union and became friendly with Communist China, primarily to get support in disputes with India.

In addition to these Asiatic treaties, the United States has a mutual defense treaty signed with South Korea in 1953. A similar treaty was signed in 1954 with Nationalist China in case either country is attacked in the Formosa area.

MIDDLE EAST ALLIANCES. The United States has not been able to develop a strong regional pact in the Middle East. The complexities of oil-rich lands, the Cold War rivalries, and the struggles between Israel, Egypt, and other Arab nations have left chief reliance on the *Eisenhower Doctrine* and United Nations activities. Under the Doctrine the United States pledges support and assistance to any Middle Eastern nation which requests help when threatened by internal subversion or external aggression. The Doctrine was developed after the Suez Crisis in 1956 when Israel with the help of France and Great Britain was at war with Egypt. In 1958 United States troops were sent to Lebanon to quell an uprising.

Earlier in 1955, Turkey, Iraq, Iran, Pakistan, and Great Britain joined in a defensive alliance called the Baghdad Pact. Iraq withdrew in 1958, and the name was changed to the *Central Treaty Organization (CENTO)*. Although the United States was active in developing this alliance, it is

Point out that the Eisenhower Doctrine was actually designed to check overt aggression not covert infiltration.

549

Foreign Affairs ministers confer at a meeting of the Organization of American States (OAS) held in Washington, D.C. in 1964. (OAS photo)

The Pan American Union building in Washington, D.C. houses the central agency of the Organization of American States. (OAS photo)

not an official member but does participate actively on various committees. The United States did sign mutual defense agreements with Iran, Pakistan, and Turkey in 1959.

The continuous struggle between Israel and the Arab nations erupted in war in 1967 and was followed by military build-ups and guerilla warfare. The United Nations and the superpowers, fearing world war, tried to bring peace to the Middle East.

LATIN AMERICAN TREATIES. The basic treaty with Latin American countries is the *Rio Pact (The Inter-American Treaty of Reciprocal Assistance)* signed in 1947 in Rio de Janeiro, Brazil. The U.S. and nineteen Latin American countries agreed upon mutual defense against external attack, although each nation retained the right to decide whether to use armed forces.

The following year at Bogotá, Colombia, twenty-one nations formed the *Organization of American States (OAS)*, the first

Mention the long-standing interest that the United States has had in Latin America even during our isolation years.

regional agreement under the United Nations. The earlier Pan American Union continues as the central agency for the OAS. The members agree to ensure the peaceful settlement of disputes that may arise among the member states.

Three major events have indicated that the Rio Pact and the OAS are not entirely successful in settling hemisphere disputes. (1) In 1954 the president of Guatemala claimed that a successful effort to overthrow him was caused by neighbors, Nicaragua and Honduras, with the support of the United States. He refused to appeal to the OAS and appealed instead to the UN Security Council. (2) Again, the OAS, while supporting the United States during the Cuban missile crisis by expelling Cuba from the inter-American system, has not resolved the threat Cuba poses to other Latin American countries. (3) When President Johnson, because of his fear of a communist takeover, sent troops to the Dominican Republic in 1965 without consulting the OAS, the future of the organization was strained. The OAS did send a peace-keeping force until free elections were held and order was restored.

Considerable foreign aid has been given to Latin American countries through the United Nations and directly by the United States. But some of these countries, after comparing the aid that they received with that given European countries, have felt that they were badly neglected.

President Kennedy, therefore, developed a program that became the *Alliance for Progress*. Twenty nations meeting in Uruguay in 1961 signed an agreement which was designed to provide economic development through land reform, improvement of educational and health conditions, and elimination of poverty. This was not just a United States program of foreign aid, for each of the Latin American states pledged to devote an increasing part of its own resources to improve living conditions. Senator Robert Kennedy called the Alliance an effort "to do nothing less than to lift an entire continent into ·the modern age."[1] **Progress has been slow, partly because of the reluctance of military-dominated regimes to make changes. President Nixon made a firm commitment to help the hemisphere develop on a partnership basis in which the initiative of each Latin American nation would be respected.**

STUDY QUESTIONS

1. What nations are the world leaders today?

2. What are the major goals of the foreign policy of the United States?

3. Why must the foreign policy of a President, in the long run, represent the will of the people?

4. How does a President try to influence public opinion?

5. How are treaties adopted?

6. Why are executive agreements used?

7. How can a President influence foreign policy by his power of recognition? by his use of troops?

8. What powers does Congress have for the determination of foreign policy?

9. Do the President and Congress agree on international policy at the present time?

10. What is the role of the Department of State in foreign policy?

11. How are Foreign Service employees selected?

12. What are the historic fundamentals of our foreign policy?

13. What are the modern fundamentals of foreign policy?

14. How successful was the policy of containment?

15. Explain the following foreign policies of the United States: the Truman Doctrine, the Marshall Plan, the Point Four Program, the

---

[1] Robert F. Kennedy, *To Seek a Newer World*, Doubleday & Company, Inc. Copyright © 1967 by Robert F. Kennedy.

CONCEPTS AND GENERALIZATIONS

1
In this century of war, the United States and the Union of Soviet Socialist Republics have emerged as world leaders.

2
A Cold War has existed between these two great powers which has divided other nations into noncommunist, communist, and neutral groups.

3
The foreign policy of the United States is determined by the President, but he is influenced by the Department of State, the Congress, and public opinion.

4
The actual conduct of foreign policy under the President is carried on by the Department of State through the Foreign Service.

5
Historically, the foreign policy of the United States was based on isolation, territorial expansion, the open door in Asia, the good neighbor policy, and the freedom of the seas.

6
The historic policies have been modified by policies of international cooperation, idealism, and practical cooperation.

7
Practical cooperation has consisted of participating in the United Nations, containment of communism's expansion, the giving of foreign aid, and the development of a network of alliances and treaties.

Rio Treaty, the North Atlantic Pact, the Southeast Asia Treaty Organization, the Alliance for Progress, the Peace Corps.

16. What effects has the war in Vietnam had on foreign policy?

IDEAS FOR DISCUSSION

1. Under what circumstances should the United States refuse to recognize the government of another nation?

2. Do you favor isolation or international cooperation as the basis for our present foreign policy? Why?

3. President Nixon visited China and the USSR in 1972. What have been the effects of these visits on historic fundamentals of foreign policy? On pragmatic foreign policies?

4. To what extent has U. S. foreign policy been idealistic? To what extent has it been practical?

5. In what ways can you, or your class, influence foreign policy?

6. Why is the conduct of the members of our Foreign Service of great importance?

7. Former Defense Secretary Robert McNamara testifying before the House Armed Forces Committee in February 1965 stated, "Our foreign policy has been remarkably consistent over the years. We ourselves have no territorial ambitions anywhere in the world, and we insist that all nations respect the territorial integrity of their neighbors. We do not seek the economic exploitation of any nation. Indeed, since the end of World War II, we have given other nations more than 100 billion dollars of our wealth and substance—an effort unparalleled in the history of mankind. We do not seek to overthrow, overtly or covertly, the legitimate government of any nation, and we are opposed to such attempts by others. In short, we seek a world in which each neighbor is free to develop in its own way, unmolested by its neighbors, free of the fear of armed attack from the more powerful nations." Do you agree or disagree? Why?

8. The Department of State has an Assistant Secretary for Congressional Relations. He obtains, for the Secretary of State and other officials of the department, congressional views and advice on important foreign policy matters. He informs Congress about policies and plans of the department. Why is this Assistant Secretary an important agent of our foreign policy?

9. A writer says, "We have reached the ultimate in military proficiency: a bomb that outlaws itself. . . . Today, victory goes not to the country that can build the biggest bomb, but to the country that can devise the most attractive propaganda." Do you think this person is right? What meaning does the statement have for U. S. foreign policy?

Current U. S. policy toward the Soviet Union
Current U. S. policy toward Europe
Current U. S. policy toward China
Current U. S. policy toward Latin America
Current U. S. policy toward Africa
Foreign aid
Trade with other nations

THINGS TO DO

1. Make a survey of class members to determine how many have relatives living in foreign countries. Are they citizens of these countries, civilian employees of the United States, members of the military services, employees of business firms, or visitors? What impressions of foreign policy are gained from communicating with these persons?

2. Read, in newspapers, and news magazines, reports of the President's press conferences over a period of time. To what extent do the press conferences influence public opinion on international relations?

3. Investigate the career possibilities of the Foreign Service.

4. Prepare a report on "The United States and recognition of foreign countries."

5. Prepare a report on "The cost to the United States of the Vietnam War."

6. Prepare an imaginary front page of a newspaper featuring the announcement of the Monroe Doctrine.

7. Write an imaginary history of events since June 25, 1950, assuming that the United States had not resisted the communist aggression in Korea and Vietnam.

8. Prepare a "fact sheet" in which you emphasize the importance of the Peace Corps.

9. Have students represent India, Thailand, the Philippines, and Burma and discuss their views on SEATO.

10. On a world map, color those countries that belong to NATO, those that belong to SEATO, those that belong to the Organization of American States, and those that are in the CENTO group.

11. Have a committee keep a bulletin board display on international relations. Illustrate aspects of international affairs from current newspapers and magazines.

12. Report on one of the following aspects of our international relations:

FURTHER READINGS

Acheson, Dean, PRESENT AT THE CREATION: MY YEARS IN THE STATE DEPARTMENT. W. W. Norton, 1969.

Baker, Benjamin, and Friedelbaum, Stanley H., GOVERNMENT IN THE UNITED STATES. Houghton Mifflin Co., 1966. Chapter 24.

Blancke, W. Wendell, THE FOREIGN SERVICE OF THE UNITED STATES. Praeger Publishers, Inc., 1969.

Brandt, Heinz, SEARCH FOR A THIRD WAY. Doubleday and Co., Inc., 1970.

Ferguson, John H., and McHenry, Dean E., THE AMERICAN SYSTEM OF GOVERNMENT. McGraw-Hill Book Co., Inc., 1967. Chapter 19.

Kennedy, Robert F., TO SEEK A NEWER WORLD. Doubleday & Co., Inc., 1967.

Lent, Henry B., THE PEACE CORPS: AMBASSADORS OF GOOD WILL. Westminster Press, 1967.

Lisagor, Peter, and Higgins, Marguerite, OVERTIME IN HEAVEN: ADVENTURES IN THE FOREIGN SERVICE. Doubleday & Co., Inc., 1964.

Merk, Frederick, THE MONROE DOCTRINE AND AMERICAN EXPANSIONISM, 1843-1849. Alfred A. Knopf, Inc., 1967.

Myrdal, Gunnar, ASIAN DRAMA: AN INQUIRY INTO THE POVERTY OF NATIONS. Pantheon Books, Inc., 1972.

Pratt, Julius W., A HISTORY OF UNITED STATES FOREIGN POLICY. Prentice-Hall, 1972.

Shaw, Robert d'A., RETHINKING ECONOMIC DEVELOPMENT. Foreign Policy Association Headline Book, 1971. (Paperback book)

Shepherd, George W., Jr., RACIAL INFLUENCES ON AMERICAN FOREIGN POLICY. Bantam Books, Inc., 1970.

Stephansky, Ben S., LATIN AMERICA: TOWARD A NEW NATIONALISM. Foreign Policy Association Headline Book, 1972. (Paperback book)

Tully, Andrew, and Britten, Milton, WHERE DID YOUR MONEY GO—THE FOREIGN AID STORY. Simon and Schuster, Inc., 1964.

THE LANGUAGE OF GOVERNMENT

DEFERMENT—the official postponement of being drafted for military service.

DRAFT—to select for military service from the eligible group.

INDUCTION—the formal entry of a civilian into military service.

INFILTRATION—the gradual, and usually secret, entry into an organization or agency with the intention of gaining control.

INTERNAL SECURITY—freedom from danger, risk, or fear from within a country.

MILITARISM—the tendency to put affairs of the armed forces or of war ahead of other matters; a warlike spirit.

NATIONAL SECURITY—freedom from danger, risk, or fear from within or outside a country.

SELECTIVE SERVICE—the system of drafting persons for military service.

SELF-SUFFICIENT—the ability to supply one's own needs; to produce enough of a substance or product within a nation so that imports of the substance or product are not necessary.

STOCKPILING—building a reserve supply of an essential substance or product for use in the event of war.

SUBVERSIVE—tending to bring about the overthrow of a government by unlawful methods; a person who tries to overthrow or undermine the government.

26

National Security

The dual problem of the United States in this century has been how to operate within a framework for achieving peace and still provide for national security. The people of the United States, as do the people of other nations, want to live in peace —so the conduct of international relations is a constant struggle to find peaceful ways to solve problems. But, in a century dominated by war, one fundamental of foreign policy has been to keep the United States strong enough to exist as a prosperous, democratic nation.

The people of the United States desire peace, but regardless of the political party in power or who has been President, the nation has always tried to be prepared in case of war. National security is essential.

National security is a many-sided operation. There is no simple formula by which safety from aggression can be obtained. Instead many different approaches have to be used. Chief among these are (1) military defense—efforts that are made to protect us from any type of external aggression; (2)

internal security measures—plans that are made to protect our nation from dangers within our borders; (3) economic defense measures—plans that are developed to assure that our industrial system can operate at full strength if a war comes; (4) international relations—efforts to win allies and to develop effective international organizations.

Only the first three of these approaches will be discussed in this chapter since international relations were discussed in the preceding chapter.

MILITARY

DEFENSE   There is an old football slogan, "The best defense is a good offense." Similarly, in a world where peaceful settlement of international disputes has not yet been achieved there is a saying, "The best way to prevent war is to have such strong military forces that no one will dare attack you."

This has been the basis of United States military policy during the past several years. In effect our statesmen have been saying, "The only thing an aggressor nation understands is strength. If we keep strong military forces, no nation will be foolish enough to attack us."

DEFENSE AND THE CONSTITUTION. The men who wrote the Constitution were thoroughly familiar with war. Because of their experiences with military life and with tyrannical governments, they had strong beliefs about the proper relationships of government and defense.

The Constitution gives the national government responsibility for defense. It declares that the individual states are not permitted to maintain military forces or engage in war. The last sentence of Article I of the Constitution says, "No state shall, without the consent of Congress, . . . keep

troops or ships of war in time of peace, . . . or engage in war, unless actually invaded, or in such imminent danger as will not admit of delay."

The responsibility for national defense having been given to the national government rather than to the states, the powers of the Congress and the President relating to defense were described in the Constitution.

The *powers of Congress* are listed in Article I, Section 8. There are eighteen clauses describing these powers. Seven of the clauses deal with matters of defense. Congress, an elected body, has the power to declare war, the power to raise and support armies, and the power to provide and maintain a navy. The national guard, or state militia, comes under the congressional powers. The clear intent of the Constitu-

'Then It's Agreed---We'll Ban the Use of Spears in Battle'

Wallmeyer, Long Island (Calif.) Independent.

While Congress can check the President's military powers by refusing to appropriate his requested funds, how does party allegiance affect this power?

The largest office building in the world, the Pentagon in Arlington, Virginia, is headquarters for the Department of Defense. (U.S. Air Force photo)

tion is that civilians shall control the nation's military forces.

The *President's defense powers* show also this intent to have an elected civilian as the head of our military forces. Article II, Section 2, Clause 1 states, "The President shall be commander in chief of the army and navy of the United States, and of the militia of the several states, when called into the actual service of the United States. . . ."

As commander in chief, the President has tremendous powers. He may send troops, naval vessels, or airplanes wherever he thinks best. He can plan overall military strategy. He can give battle orders to generals if he so desires. He commissions the officers of the military forces.

In time of war these powers become almost unlimited. In time of peace by sending troops to, or withholding troops from, troubled spots in the world, the President can lead us to undeclared war and has done so.

These powers are so great that between World War I and World War II there was much discussion of amending the Constitution to provide that war could be declared only by vote of the people. With

the development of nuclear bombs not much was heard of this idea until the Vietnam war. But the fact that Congress had never declared war on North Vietnam raised serious problems about the use of military forces by the President.

In some quarters, moreover, there has been much discussion of the dangers of domination of our life by the military. In a divided world the need for strong military forces is generally recognized, and the need for secrecy in many military matters is accepted also.

But critics point out that never before in our history have so many citizens served in the military forces. The number of ex-military officers in key governmental positions is viewed with alarm by some. These dangers of *militarism* are new to the present generation. But they were known to the framers of the Constitution and they acted accordingly.

One remedy for militarism is civilian control of the national defense. This civilian control is achieved by the constitutional provisions just described and by the appointment of civilians to the key positions in the Department of Defense.

PLANNING FOR DEFENSE. Congress and the President cannot with their many other duties take direct interest in the *details* of national defense. This is the responsibility of the Department of Defense, which was described in Chapter 12. It is worth repeating here, however, that the Secretary of Defense and the Secretaries of the Army, the Navy, and the Air Force are traditionally civilians. They have responsibility for administering national defense policy.

The planning of this policy is certainly one of the most important matters for our nation. Do we need a new anti-ballistic missile system? Do we need both a large air force and a large navy? How many land troops should be in the army? Who makes these policy decisions? Who plans our defense? Basically the President is responsible for these decisions.

THE NATIONAL SECURITY COUNCIL. The final *planning* for defense is done by the National Security Council. This agency provides the President with the advice by which he makes major decisions on defense policy. The council consists of the President, the Vice President, the Secretary of State, the Secretary of Defense, and the Director of the Office of Emergency Preparedness, plus other officials invited by the President.

The President serves as chairman, but there is a civilian executive secretary who heads the council staff. Additional members may be appointed to the council with the consent of the Senate.

The Council studies the purposes, obligations, and risks of the United States in relation to our military power. It directs the activities of the Central Intelligence Agency, our super-spy organization. This agency collects and analyzes essential information on national security. Much information about foreign countries is kept secret.

OTHER MAJOR PLANNING GROUPS. The *Armed Forces Policy Council* and the *Joint Chiefs of Staff* are the two major planning groups immediately below the level of the President and the National Security Council. The Armed Forces Policy Council consists of the Secretary of Defense as chairman; the Secretaries of the Army, the Navy, and the Air Force; the Deputy

This Distant Early Warning station is atop a Greenland ice-cap. It is part of the DEW Line which stands guard to alert United States forces about impending air attack. (Western Electric Co.)

Secretary of Defense; the Director of Defense Research and Engineering, and the military staff heads of each of the three departments. The chairman of the Joint Chiefs of Staff is also a member. This council is the advisory group to the Secretary of Defense on all policies.

The Joint Chiefs of Staff are the principal military advisers to the President, the National Security Council, and the Secretary of Defense. The Chairman of the Joint Chiefs of Staff is the most important professional military man in this country. He is appointed by the President with the consent of the Senate. He is the highest-ranking officer in military service.

The Chief of Staff, United States Army; the Chief of Naval Operations; and the Chief of Staff, United States Air Force are the other members. These are the professional military leaders of our country. The Commandant of the Marines sits as an equal with the other members when they are considering marine corps matters.

They have expert knowledge about the resources of our military services. They prepare strategic plans, establish the unified commands, review requirements for personnel and material, and make the plans for training the military forces. They also provide the United States representation on the Military Staff Committee of the United Nations.

Within the Department of State is a *Bureau of Politico-Military Affairs* that advises the Secretary of State on long-range policy. Since foreign policy determines the general nature of our military requirements, the bureau director works closely with the other planning groups. The policies of the armed forces and of the State Department are unified through the National Security Council.

Congressional committees also play an important part in the development of the defense plans. Through the planning agen-

THE MILITARY-INDUSTRIAL COMPLEX

A vital element in keeping the peace is our military establishment. Our arms must be mighty, ready for instant action, so that no potential aggressor may be tempted to risk his own destruction. . . .

. . . we can no longer risk emergency improvisation of national defense; we have been compelled to create a permanent arms industry of vast proportions. Added to this, three and a half million men and women are directly engaged in the defense establishment. We annually spend on military security more than the net income of all United States corporations.

This conjunction of an immense military establishment and a large arms industry is new in the American experience. The total influence—economic, political, even spiritual —is felt in every city, every state house, every office of the federal government. We recog-

nize the imperative need for this development. Yet we must not fail to comprehend its grave implications. Our toil, resources, and livelihood are all involved; so is the very structure of our society.

In the councils of government we must guard against the acquisition of unwarranted influence, whether sought or unsought, by the military-industrial complex. The potential for the disastrous rise of misplaced power exists and will persist.

We must never let the weight of this combination endanger our liberties or democratic processes. We should take nothing for granted. Only an alert and knowledgeable citizenry can compel the proper meshing of the huge industrial and military machinery of defense with our peaceful methods and goals, so that security and liberty may prosper together.

—PRESIDENT DWIGHT D. EISENHOWER, Farewell Address, Jan. 17, 1961.

cies the President can develop plans and administer them. But any new laws which may be required, including the appropriation of necessary money to carry out the laws, must be made by the acts of Congress.

The Armed Services Committees of the House and of the Senate, therefore, are kept informed about plans, and they also conduct their own investigations. They frequently are given secret information that is not available to other congressmen. Through public or secret committee hearings they can question the Secretary of Defense or the Chiefs of Staff. As a result, the actions of these committees become crucial in the determination of our military policy.

The decisions made by these groups affect all of us in many important ways. The amount of taxes we pay goes up or down to meet military requirements. Some factories hum with activity or shut down depending on whether a defense contract is awarded. The lives of American youth are changed by the number of men and women needed by the armed services. The way in which persons are selected for military service, therefore, becomes one of the most important matters of governmental policy.

OBTAINING PERSONS FOR MILITARY SERVICE

There have been traditionally two methods used to get the needed persons for our military forces: enlisting and drafting. When the military requirements could not be met by voluntary enlistment, citizens were drafted for the armed forces.

Until the start of the Civil War in 1861 the enlistment system had always provided enough manpower. In that struggle both the federal and the confederate governments had to use a compulsory draft. The

system was not completely satisfactory, for men could avoid service by hiring substitutes. After the close of the war, our policy again was to have a small enlisted military force.

THE SELECTIVE SERVICE SYSTEM. This policy was changed in 1917. A month after our entry into World War I, a Selective Service Act was passed which made most men from ages twenty-one to thirty-one subject to draft. Later, the ages were changed to include all men from eighteen to forty-five. The draft was not popular but was accepted as a necessary evil of war. When peace came, the draft was abandoned in favor of the old policy of the small enlisted force.

Our first draft act in peacetime was passed in September, 1940. Never before in American history had it seemed neces-

President Woodrow Wilson asks the Congress of the United States to declare war on Germany on April 2, 1917. (Library of Congress)

Ask for student opinion concerning the pros and cons of the draft law.

559

The surprise attack on Pearl Harbor by the Japanese in 1941 was a serious blow to the American fleet. Shown burning is the USS Shaw. (Official U.S. Navy photo)

sary to draft citizens for military service when we were not at war. But Hitler had started a new world war on September 1, 1939. The dangers of our getting into the war were so great that the Selective Service Act was adopted for all men within the age limits of twenty-one to thirty-five. This act as later expanded continued through World War II and after the peace until 1947. Then it was abandoned for one year.

In 1948 continued threats to national security caused Congress to pass another peacetime selective service law. This law was passed again in 1951 and every four years thereafter including 1967.

In 1967 because of the many criticisms of the draft, Congress reviewed the entire system. The great increase in the number of draftees for the Vietnam War was the primary cause of this review. The protests against the war and the draft on college campuses, the burning of draft cards by some young men, and the plea of Mohammad Ali (Cassius Clay) to be classified as a conscientious objector dramatized the selective service system.

Some critics argued that the draft should be based on a lottery system rather than by the method of selecting men on the basis of their current activities, marriage, or student situation. There was criticism, too, that the approximately 4,000 local

draft boards had too much freedom to decide whom to draft. Examples were given to show that in almost identical cases the draft policies of a local board in one state would be different from those in another state. There were even differences in policies among boards in the same state.

The system was defended on the basis that the system worked, that the lottery system had been tried before and had produced undesirable results, and that it is desirable to keep control at the local level rather than in an office in Washington.

During the controversy, the then Defense Secretary, Robert S. McNamara, suggested a form of universal service for all American youth under which they would spend two years either in military service or in some peacetime activity, such as the Peace Corps. This idea, however, was not even debated in Congress.

Congress in 1969 changed the draft law to allow the President to establish **a draft lottery, the first in twenty-seven years. The new system made nineteen-year-olds principally liable for service** for one year, depending on when one's birthday is drawn in the lottery. Issues concerning student deferments, conscientious objectors, and a volunteer army were left for future debate.

MILITARY SERVICE. Under the present military service laws every qualified young man is liable for service with one of the armed forces when he reaches the age of eighteen and one-half years. The laws provide that every man under twenty-six who enters one of the armed forces—by enlistment, draft, or appointment—*automatically* acquires a six-year military service obligation. This service is divided into three phases:

First, there is full-time active duty in the armed forces.

Second, there is duty in the ready reserve. This duty consists annually of attending forty-eight weekly drills of two to four hours each, usually at night or on weekends, plus two weeks of active duty for training *or* thirty days of active duty for training.

Third, there is duty in the standby reserve, a pool of men who have completed their active and their ready reserve duty and take no further training. Men in the standby reserve may be called to active duty by Congress declaring a national emergency.

The time spent in each of these three phases of military service varies with the type of service chosen. The choices are so many and so complex that it may take careful individual study and investigation to decide which is best.

A young man, in general, has seven choices in planning for military service.

1. He can enlist in the regular branch of the service he prefers: two to four years of active duty, one to three years in ready reserve, one year in the standby reserve.

2. He can volunteer for a special four- to six-month period of active duty followed by seven and one-half years in the ready reserve.

3. He can enlist in the reserves for six years: two years active duty, three years in ready reserves, one year in the standby reserve.

4. He can wait to be drafted, usually into the army, but taking a chance he will be assigned to the service he prefers: normally two years active duty, three years in ready reserves, and one year in standby reserve.

5. He can enlist in the national guard: seven and one-half to eleven years of service similar to the ready reserve, plus full-time duty in emergencies.

6. He can, if in college, join an accredited officers' training program: six months to four years active duty plus the required time in the reserves.

7. He can ask for a specific deferment.

THE ARMY. At the age of seventeen, enlistment is possible in the army for periods ranging from two to six years. Physical, intellectual, and moral requirements must be met. Young men with parents' consent may enlist at seventeen; young women, at eighteen, but they must have parents' consent until they reach twenty-one. Women are now able to enlist in each of the armed services, except the coast guard, but they are not assigned to combat units.

The infantry, the artillery, and the armor make up the army combat units. Technical units include engineers, chemical corps, signal corps, ordnance, quartermaster, and transportation units.

An enlisted man can usually choose the specialized service he would like. Those with a high school diploma may qualify for special technical training. Approximately 150 courses are available for men; about twenty-six are open to women. Details about the requirements for enlisting and the types of positions are described in the *U.S. Army Occupational Handbook.*

THE NAVY. The ages and general requirements for enlistment in the navy are approximately the same as those for the army. Enlisted men may take specialized courses at navy service schools. More than

Emphasize the need for a young man to examine carefully all enlistment opportunities before joining the armed forces.

561

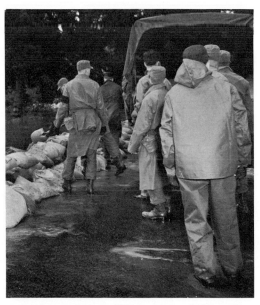

Serving in peace as well as in wartime, soldiers from Fort Ord, California, offer assistance during a Carmel Valley flood. (U.S. Army photo)

Positions aboard naval vessels are varied. Here two sailors man the air search radar aboard the USS Ticonderoga. (Official U.S. Navy photo)

Leathernecks of the 26th Marines board a helicopter to be lifted into battle against the North Vietnamese west of Khe Sanh in 1967 during the Vietnam War. (Defense Dept. photo)

Air Force mechanics and munitions men work together to position a mobile console and power unit on the flight line at Korat Air Base, Thailand. (U.S. Air Force photo)

twenty schools train men to serve in such positions as cooks, electricians, hospital corpsmen, mechanics, motion-picture technicians, radiomen, and torpedomen.

The combat ships include cruisers, aircraft carriers, destroyers, and submarines. Noncombat ships include ammunition ships, supply ships, transports, tankers, hospital ships, and tenders.

Details about the requirements for enlisting and the types of positions are described in the *U.S. Navy Occupational Handbook for Men* or the similar *Handbook for Women*.

THE MARINES. The marines are the land force for the navy. Enlistment requirements are similar to those for the army and the navy. Special opportunities exist in radar, antiaircraft, electronics, marine aviation, and many other specialized services.

THE COAST GUARD. In times of peace the United States Coast Guard is a part of the Transportation Department. In times of war or national emergency it operates under the direction of the United States Navy. Enlistment requirements are similar to those of the navy. Special training is possible in such fields as electricity, radar, gunnery, and radio.

THE AIR FORCE. The general requirements for enlistment in the air force are similar to those for the other services; but an airman qualifying examination must be taken to determine in which of four aptitude areas (mechanical, administration, general, or electronics) the man will serve. Many opportunities exist for a great variety of occupations. Some of the specialties include photo-mapping, air-traffic control, guided-missile systems, aircraft-engine maintenance, food service, and management methods.

ORGANIZED RESERVES. Each of the armed services maintains organized reserves in which, through summer training and training on certain evenings or weekends during the year, the required service in the ready reserves can be completed. The national guard, the air national guard, the officers' reserve corps, the army reserve, the naval reserve, the air force reserve, the marine reserve, the coast guard reserve, and the public health service reserve are the recognized reserve units.

Under the organized reserve plans the period of active duty is usually shorter. Most reserve training is done in the hometown. Openings in some of the organized reserve units are rare, waiting lists are long, and being on a waiting list does not give draft deferment.

Military authorities are agreed that graduation from high school before entering military service is the wisest policy.

OFFICERS' TRAINING. The need for trained officers has long been recognized. The United States Military Academy at West Point, N. Y., was founded in 1802; the United States Naval Academy at Annapolis, Maryland, was started in 1845; the Coast Guard Academy at New London, Connecticut, dates back to 1876; the Marine Corps School at Quantico, Virginia, was established in 1917. The new Air Force Academy was started at Colorado Springs in 1954.

Students are admitted to the military, naval, and air force academies on the recommendations of their senators and representatives. Frequently, this means winning a competitive examination. (Entrance to the Coast Guard Academy is by competitive examination only—no congressional recommendations—and the Marine Corps School receives its students from several sources, including graduates from the military and naval academies.) Some enlisted men of outstanding ability may also be appointed by the President and Vice President.

All candidates must meet age, physical, and scholastic requirements. The college officer-training programs also provide officers for the services.

THE DRAFT. According to present law each young man must register with his local draft board within sixty days of his eighteenth birthday. There is at least one local board for most counties and more for large cities. Each board is composed of three or more resident civilians. Men between the ages of eighteen and a half and twenty-six years are eligible to be drafted. Certain persons who are deferred remain liable for military service until age thirty-five.

The local board is responsible for the registration, examination, classification, selection, and delivery of the draftee for induction. The board must maintain records of the men registered. On the basis of the records, registrants are placed in one of the following five major classifications:

CLASS I-A: registrant available for military service.

CLASS II: registrant deferred because of civilian occupation.

CLASS III: registrant deferred because of dependents.

CLASS IV: registrant deferred by law or because unfit for military service.

CLASS V: registrant over the age of liability for military service.

Objections to classifications must be made within ten days from the date of the notice of classification. Appeals are first made to the local draft board, then to state appeal boards, and, finally, in certain cases to a national appeal board.

High school students are not drafted before graduation, or until they reach age twenty, if their scholastic record is satisfactory. Full-time college and university students who are doing satisfactory work are usually deferred until the end of a term.

Local boards are assigned the number of persons to be drafted by their state board. Draftees until 1970 were called for service in the sequence of their birth dates, beginning with age twenty-five and working

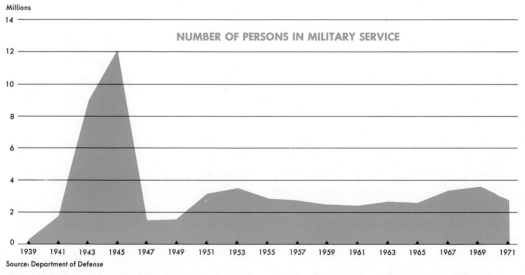

NUMBER OF PERSONS IN MILITARY SERVICE

Source: Department of Defense

The graph shows the number of persons in military service from 1939 to the present. Why were so many in the armed forces in 1945?

THE GREAT HOPE

Charles E. Merriam was one of the greatest of political scientists. Born in Iowa in 1874, he thought he would become a teacher or a lawyer. These combined interests led him to the field of political science, and he received his Doctor of Philosophy degree from Columbia University in 1900.

For over fifty years he taught at the University of Chicago. During those years, in addition to teaching and writing, he was a member of the city council in Chicago for six years and a candidate for mayor. He served on presidential commissions and as president of the American Political Science Association. He was a rare combination of scholar, practical politician, and statesman.

As he neared seventy, eleven former students, each a distinguished political scientist, wrote a book of essays to honor him, *The Future of Government in the United States*. One of the students remembered listening to him in the classroom by day and sitting in the council chamber at night while he battled corrupt politicians. Another recalled that on his desk calendar was a brief question and answer, "What is difficulty? A mere notice of the necessity for exertion."

In an essay about his life work, in the book, Merriam concluded with these words:

"No student of government is ignorant of the long years of slavery and caste; of brutality and exploitation; of prisons, dungeons, exiles, beatings, brandings, breakings on the wheel, the screams of tortured men, the cynical gloatings and squeakings of brutal little masters and keepers dressed in a little brief authority; of the annals of weakness, wickedness, vanity, corruption, treason, folly; of incompetence, futility, cowardice, fussiness in politics; of rascality and roguery; of the long series of rows of army trenches that mark for a little while through unending cemeteries, east and west, the flower of youth and manhood; or the slow-burning hatreds smoldering for centuries in millions of mankind.

"But I see also the emergence of law; the rise of order, the organization of justice, of common counsel; of rational discussions, of management, not merely humane, but human. I see the growth of liberty. . . .

"In a moment of cruel race antipathy and incredible brutality among civilized people, I seem to see the rising figure of the brotherhood of man. I seem to see that love is stronger than hate, strong as that dark passion may be, and that love will create more than hate destroys."

down into the lower brackets. Most of the older ages have been called or are exempt, and the present lottery system assigns first liability to the nineteen-year-old.

INTERNAL SECURITY

The nations after World War II were divided into two armed camps based on differing ideologies. The rivalry between these groups ebbed and flowed between a cold war and a hot war. This was an intense rivalry, a world struggle for survival of completely different systems.

In this struggle the communists became skilled at taking over countries by infiltration without war. Communists "seeped" into key positions in government, industry, and labor. Through propaganda they deceived people. Finally, they seized control of the government. Poland, China, Czechoslovakia, and Cuba are examples of successful infiltration.

In the United States the communists have tried to steal our military secrets. They have had some success. They have tried, too, to win American citizens over to their views. At this they have had very little success. Their ultimate aim is proclaimed as world domination by their ideas.

Describe the role of the Communist Party in the United States today.

It seems unbelievable that even a few American citizens would throw away their liberties and their system of popular elections for communist ideas. Yet the record of convictions in our courts of people who have betrayed their country has frightened many thoughtful citizens.

The record shows: Alger Hiss, a high State Department official, was convicted of perjury and sentenced to prison because the courts held that he lied about his communist connections. Morton Sobell, the Rosenbergs, Harry Gold, and others have been tried and convicted for stealing atomic energy information and giving it to communists. The Rosenbergs were put to death as traitors.

The Attorney General at one time listed 185 organizations as "communist-action, communist-front, or communist-infiltrated" organizations. But to protect their constitutional liberties the Supreme Court has ruled that individual members of these communist organizations cannot be forced to register as communists or communist sympathizers.

Against these attempts to infiltrate governmental departments and civilian organizations the government has taken several measures.

THE FEDERAL BUREAU OF INVESTIGATION. The FBI in the Justice Department has responsibility for investigating those violations of federal law not allocated to other agencies. It, therefore, has special responsibilities for guarding the internal security of the United States against espionage, treason, and sabotage. The FBI has become the first line of defense against communist infiltration and spying in this country.

FBI agents have been planted in communist organizations. They have been able to get evidence on communist activity. At one trial of communists, an FBI witness, the night before appearing in court to testify against the communist conspirators, participated as a communist with those

A fingerprint expert of the FBI is shown comparing prints in preparation for giving testimony in court. (Federal Bureau of Investigation)

defending the accused! By skilled police methods the FBI has been able to get advance evidence about communist **plans.**

CONGRESSIONAL INVESTIGATING COMMITTEES. Three congressional committees have carried on investigations to uncover subversive activities. These committees are the House Un-American Activities Committee, the Senate Judiciary Committee with its Subcommittee on Internal Security, and the Senate Committee on Government Operations with its Permanent Subcommittee on Investigations.

The House committee was first created in 1938 to investigate activities of the German Hitler movement in this country. In 1945 it was made a permanent committee and specialized for many years in communist investigations. The committees are usually called by the names of their chairmen. In the past, for example, the House committee has been known as the Velde Committee, the Walters Committee, the Willis Committee, and the Ichord Committee—depending on the current chairman. The Senate committees similarly have been labeled the Jenner Committee, the Kilgore Committee, the McCarthy Committee, the McClellan Committee, the Jackson Committee, and the Eastland Committee.

These committees have tried to search out persons who are communists or who have aided communists. They have held hearings in many parts of the country. These hearings have dramatized the workings of subversive groups.

The committees have been criticized for their methods. They have been accused of calling innocent people communists and giving these people no chance to defend themselves. Some claim they are trying to police the thoughts and ideas of U. S. citizens. The methods of the McCarthy Committee in particular were the subject of public scrutiny in the spring of 1954,

when the Army-McCarthy investigation was televised. In recent years the committees have enlarged their activities to include investigations of the Ku Klux Klan, sympathizers with the Viet Cong, militant groups, and riots in cities.

The House Un-American Activities Committee has had a stormy history. It has been severely criticized by some liberals for lack of concern for civil liberties, unfair procedures, and stifling of dissent. Since 1959 efforts have been made to abolish the committee. In 1969 the name was changed to the Committee on Internal Security.

In spite of all the criticisms, however, Congress has continued the committees because of the intense pressure to insure internal security. In recent years, however, the appropriations for the House Internal Security Committee have been reduced. The activities of these committees have raised this question: Can those who are disloyal to America be uncovered without destroying the basic liberties of the American people?

ANTISUBVERSION LAWS. Fear of subversive activities was so great in this country for more than a quarter of a century that many laws were passed to control those who might engage in such activities. From laws on loyalty oaths to those on treason there was great effort to legislate against the dangers of subversion —particularly communism.

THE SMITH ACT. In 1940 the Smith Act was passed. This act made it illegal to advocate or strive for the violent overthrow of the government of the United States—or to organize knowingly or to help organize any group for these purposes. Originally the Supreme Court in *Dennis* v. *United States* (1951) upheld the constitutionality of the law in a case involving the accusation that eleven top leaders of the American Communist Party conspired to advocate the violent overthrow of the government.

In later cases the Court severely limited the applications of the law. In *Yates* v. *United States* (1957) fourteen second-string communist party leaders were involved. In this case the Court held that abstract advocacy of violent overthrow of government was not prohibited by the Smith Act. Justice Harlan stated,

> That sort of advocacy even though uttered with the hope that it may ultimately lead to violent revolution, is too remote from concrete action to be regarded as the kind of indoctrination preparatory to action which was condemned in *Dennis*. The essential distinction is that those to whom the advocacy is addressed must be urged to *do* something, now or in the future, rather than merely to *believe* in something.

Later the Court clarified its position on the membership clause of the Smith Act in *Scales* v. *United States* (1961). In a 5-4 decision with Justice Harlan again writing the majority opinion the Court ruled that,

> A person who joins the Communist party, however active he may be, may not be prosecuted under the membership provisions unless there is proof that he joined with intent to bring about the overthrow of government as speedily as circumstances would permit.

Based on this decision the present situation seems to be that membership in the Communist Party is not held illegal; *active* **membership based on knowledge that the party acted to overthrow the government by force *is* illegal.**

THE INTERNAL SECURITY ACT. Commonly called the McCarran Act, the Internal Security Act of 1950 is a long, complicated law passed at a time when the Korean War had again aroused members of Congress to the dangers of communism. Among other things the law outlawed conspiracy to establish a dictatorship in the United States, made it more difficult for communist aliens to enter or leave the United States, increased requirements for alien registration, and prohibited communists from being employed by the federal government or from working in a defense plant.

To enforce the law a five-member Subversive Activities Control Board was created, with its members to be appointed by the President. This Board was to determine whether organizations were "communist-action, communist-front, or communist-infiltrated" organizations and whether individuals were members of such organizations. The law required communist organizations to register with the Attorney General.

When the law was passed, it was vetoed by President Truman who argued that it would help the Communist Party more than it would hurt it. But the law was passed over his veto. Some journalists have argued that the effect of the law has been to drive the party underground; others have argued that world events since 1950 have resulted in the gradual deterioration of the party in the United States.

The constitutionality of the various provisions have been the subject of long, slow court procedures. In 1961 the Supreme Court in *Communist Party* v. *Subversive Activities Control Board* by a 5-4 decision ruled that communist-action organizations must register when ordered to do so by the Subversive Activities Control Board. Then, in 1965, the Court took the teeth out of this earlier decision by an 8-0 ruling, in *Albertson* v. *Subversive Activities Control Board*, that the Communist Party *member* could not be required to register as this requirement violated the member's Fifth Amendment right not to incriminate himself. When this decision was announced,

Gus Hall, the longtime leader of the Communist Party in the United States declared that the party would again run candidates for public office, and it did. The Communist Party in the United States had not run a candidate for public office in ten years.

One other decision seemed to undermine the effectiveness of the Subversive Activities Control Board. In the case, *United States v. Robel* (1967), a worker in a shipyard—a defense industry—who was a member of the Communist Party was not required to leave his job as provided by the law because this violated his right of free association under the First Amendment. In a 6-2 decision Chief Justice Warren wrote the majority opinion.

These decisions leave many parts of the McCarran Act in doubt. Congress debated abolishing the SACB but continued its appropriation. Debate was held too on the writing of laws that would modify the Court decisions.

THE COMMUNIST CONTROL ACT OF 1954. The intent of the McCarran Act was to make communists known by giving them widespread publicity through registration. But at the height of the McCarthy era there was also great pressure on Congress to outlaw the Communist Party. The Communist Control Act of 1954 was passed as an attempt to deny the Communist Party any chance to participate in the election processes. The law deprived the party of "any of the rights, privileges, and immunities attendant upon legal bodies created under the laws of the United States" or of a state. Because the Party is a "clear, present, and continuing danger to the security of the United States" it has been denied the opportunity to engage in normal political activities.

The law has not been fully tested in the courts. As the Communist Party, in view of related decisions, nominates candidates for public office, future actions could be brought before the courts.

THE 1967 AND 1972 SACB ACTS. At the close of Congress in December 1967 a new law concerning the Subversive Activities Control Board was passed. In an attempt to "breathe some life" into the Board, a procedure was established by which SACB would hold quasi-judicial hearings on cases referred to it by the Justice Department and would decide whether the organizations or individuals were communists. But under the pressure of court decisions no important activities were attempted.

President Nixon in 1971 tried to revitalize SACB by giving it authority to investigate and compile a list of groups which it considered subversive. The House accepted this idea and voted to give it the new powers but renamed it the Federal Internal Security Board. The Senate, however, by a vote of forty-two to twenty-five refused to appropriate any money for the Board and in effect ended its authority. Civil liberty leaders hailed this as a great victory which they hoped "ended a useless relic of a frightened era."

LIBERTY V. SECURITY. The issue of whether disloyalty and subversion can be uncovered without destroying the liberties which have been basic to our system of government has faced our society since World War II. The dangers of disloyalty, subversion, and spying are real; the cold war is fought on many fronts. Yet, the purpose of the cold war on the part of the United States is to maintain our system of government, which is based on fundamental freedoms. The right to dissent, to present differing views, to hold ideas that are not held by the majority is necessary for the future of democratic government.

Faced with this dilemma Congress, the Presidents, and the courts are still struggling for a system that will provide sufficient internal security without sacrificing the essential liberties. Chief Justice Warren in the 1967 *Robel* case expressed the issue in these words, "It would indeed be ironic if, in the name of national defense, we would sanction the subversion of one of those liberties—the freedom of association—which makes the defense of the nation worthwhile."

Some political scientists and some congressional leaders believe that the issue of subversive activity has been overemphasized —especially in recent years. They hold that with the passing of years, there are new leaders of the Soviet Union who wish to get away from the party doctrine of world domination. These critics urge that efforts be centered on developing cooperative relationships with these new Russian leaders. They consider that the present control of the Soviet Union is no longer the solid, centralized, unified power that it was after World War II. In addition, these critics believe that the split between the Soviet Union and China will deepen and that the chances for better relationships with these nations will improve in the years ahead. Their hope is that improved relations will decrease the threats of subversion in this country. Similar ideas led President Nixon to visit Russia and China in 1972.

CIVILIAN DEFENSE. One other aspect of internal security—civilian defense—has received some, but not continued, attention from the American people. Some people believe that any future attack by an enemy of this nation will come as a surprise missile attack with nuclear bombs. The enemy would attempt to destroy our fighting potential concentrated in urban areas before the military forces could start a counterattack. To protect us from such attacks requires both military preparedness and a strong civilian defense organization.

The Federal Civil Defense Administra-

tion was established in 1950 as an independent agency to develop a national program of civil defense. This agency was an outgrowth of the civilian defense organization of World War II.

In 1958 civil defense was transferred to the White House Office and in 1961 to the Department of Defense, with some planning responsibility left with the Office of Emergency Planning. These officials have responsibility for developing and directing a national program of civil defense. They coordinate all civil defense of the national, state, and local governments.

Adequate protection of the civilian population in war emergencies is the goal of civil defense. Studies are undertaken for effective civil defense measures, such as shelter design, use of public buildings for fallout shelters, treatment of casualties, and standardization of equipment and facilities. Information is supplied to educate the public on civil defense protection. A thirteen-member Civil Defense Advisory Council advises the Office of Emergency Preparedness regarding civil defense policies.

Guidance is given states in the organizing and training of persons for specialized civil defense services. States are helped and encouraged to negotiate interstate compacts as a way of providing assistance to their civil defense programs.

The best known of the recent civilian defense activities are the enlisting of volunteers to serve as airplane spotters, the maintaining of bombproof communication centers in large cities, the development of plans for aiding metropolitan areas in the event of bombing, the plans for rushing first aid to such centers, and the nation-wide air-raid drills.

Since 1953 civil defense activities have also included assistance to state and local governments in major disasters. In order to ease damage, hardship, or suffering after

Point out that civilian defense organizations are also used in natural disasters.

Civil Defense organizations hold classes in radiological monitoring, where techniques are learned to detect amounts of fallout that might occur after nuclear attack. (Dept. of Defense photo)

a great disaster, the administrator is expected at the request of the President to use the available resources of federal agencies to supplement the local and state resources.

ECONOMIC DEFENSE
MEASURES   There is a third aspect of national security that is as important as internal security or national defense. This is the phase that deals with economic or industrial measures. Our vast industrial resources are one of our greatest defensive strengths.

Modern wars require tremendous amounts of raw materials that have to be manufactured into military supplies and equipment. The battle front is dependent on an effective industrial front. Steel, oil, textiles, foods, modern technology, and skilled workers are as essential to modern war as are guns, airplanes, missiles, and soldiers.

THE SUPPLY OF NATURAL RESOURCES. One economic question that has to be answered for national security is this: Does the United States have sufficient

natural resources to supply the raw materials for our industries? For generations we have thought of the United States as a land of unlimited resources. Only in the years since World War II have there been rumblings that our resources are being used up.

In the early 1950's headlines like "Metals Running Out" began to appear. The President's Material Policies Commission reported in 1952 that our country now uses considerably more raw materials than are produced within our borders. The Commission pointed out that we import substantial portions of the minerals and other substances which our factories require and that in this century we have consumed much of our own resources. In the future, they concluded, there will be serious problems in getting enough raw materials to feed our industries.

A report of the United States Bureau of Mines about the same time indicated that out of thirty-eight important industrial minerals, we are *self-sufficient* in only nine. For thirteen minerals we produce less than 60 per cent of our requirements. For another seven we are dependent on other countries for about 100 per cent of our needs. This increased dependence on foreign sources of supply has influenced our defense plans.

The publication of these findings led to discussion and plans for maintaining adequate supplies. *Stockpiling* of minerals and other critical materials has been carried on through annual appropriations by Congress to buy essential materials. Reserve supplies of tin, manganese, natural rubber, copper, and other items are stored to protect us against the time when we cannot import them. Currently, the supplies are so large that some are being sold by the government.

Searching for new sources of supply has been encouraged by awarding exploration-project contracts to those who will seek out new sources. The government pays a percentage of the costs of these explorations. If minerals are located, the money is repaid the government, without interest, from the resulting production.

New processes are encouraged. Synthetic rubber plants were developed during World War II, when our supplies of natural rubber from Malaya and Indonesia were cut off.

Less dramatized but of great importance are the new methods that have been developed to extract iron and copper from the poorer grades of ore. The development of the St. Lawrence waterway was stimulated in part because it was believed that our supplies of iron were being used up and that newer mines in Newfoundland might have to become our chief source of supply.

These and other activities have led Congress to study this question intensively. A congressional committee reported that "80 per cent of the nation's defense stockpile of strategic minerals has been imported." They noted that many of these materials are under the control of weak allies or potential enemies and urged: tax relief for mineral producers, changes in tariff policies, stockpilings, and closer cooperation among the nations of the western hemisphere.

The latter recommendation is based on the belief that the nations of North America and South America together are more nearly self-sufficient than any other part of the world.

INDUSTRIAL CAPACITY. If adequate raw materials can be assured, a second economic defense question that must be answered is this: Will industries be able to produce the supplies and equipment needed by the military? A nation's industrial capacity has definite limits. To increase that capacity takes time. An automobile factory can be changed to a tank factory or an airplane factory—but not overnight. The Office of Emergency Preparedness, an agency in the Executive Office of the President, therefore has the responsibility to study the industrial capacity of our country.

Various devices are used to increase our industrial capacity: (1) Certain industries are encouraged to build additional factories that may be needed in the event of war. To encourage this construction, certain income tax benefits are provided. (2) Defense contracts are awarded some industries to keep their operations up to date in essential processes and to keep employees skilled. (3) Some plants are asked to keep "standby" equipment ready for immediate operation. Under this system a factory may continue to produce its normal civilian product but will have a portion of the factory set aside and equipped to go into the immediate production of some military necessity.

POWER. A third economic question to answer is whether the United States has enough power resources. During World War II for example, it was necessary to ration the amount of gasoline civilians could use and to put many communities on daylight saving time the year around

UNITED STATES ENERGY SOURCES, 1940-1980 (in per cent)			
SOURCE	1940	1960	1980 (est.)
Coal	50	25	20
Natural gas and natural gas liquids	14	32	34
Oil	32	39	37
Water power	4	4	4
Nuclear	0	0	5
TOTAL	100	100	100

Adapted from *Resources,* June 1963, Resources for the Future, Inc.

in order to conserve gasoline and electricity. In recent years brownouts and blackouts in metropolitan areas have occurred.

The changes in our energy sources are shown in the above table. It should be remembered that all these sources are used to produce electricity. The table shows we are using less coal proportionately and are relying on oil and natural gas.

It is easy to find different opinions about our power resources. Some point out that while we produce over half the world's oil supply this is not enough to satisfy our needs, so we import about a million barrels of oil per day. Others show that the known oil reserves are huge and that in the past twenty years we have discovered more oil than we have consumed. Natural gas follows the pattern of the oil industry.

There is general agreement that running short of coal is not an immediate danger. Estimates are that we have enough coal to last several centuries.

Water power over the years has remained a minor source of power. Some people feel its use could be greatly expanded. Scientists talk a good deal about new sources of energy. Efforts are being made to harness the motion of the tides and to obtain power directly from the sun. But the potential new source of power seems to be atomic energy.

THE ENVIRONMENT. Development of new power sources has brought concern about what power plants do to health and environment. Ecologists argue that increased use of energy increases pollution.

In 1970 the Environmental Protection Agency was established to control pollution. The National Environmental Policy Act of 1969 was used to halt several projects designed to enlarge supplies of electricity. The Water Quality Improvement Act forced atomic energy plants to revise procedures.

Ecologists are determined that the push for more energy sources shall not come at the expense of the environment. The energy-environment dilemma is a real one. The Department of the Interior states that "coal, natural gas, and oil resources are not being developed to meet our projected energy demand." But environmentalists point out that spills from oil tankers and off-shore wells have polluted coastlines, strip mining of coal has ruined topsoil, and hot water and radioactive wastes from nuclear power plants may ruin surrounding water and underground facilities.

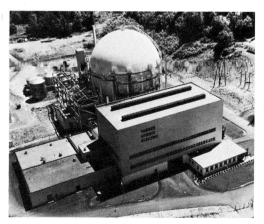

The production and use of atomic energy is one of the greatest U.S. enterprises. (Yankee Atomic Electric Co.)

ATOMIC ENERGY. The atom bomb and the hydrogen bomb are mankind's most destructive weapons. Yet the peacetime use of atomic energy represents one of man's greatest hopes for the future.

The atomic bomb was developed under the direction of the U. S. Army Corps of Engineers in cooperation with American, British, and Canadian scientists. This was a secret, emergency program. Once the public became aware of the bomb, a basic decision had to be made: Should the work on atomic energy remain with the military services, or should atomic activities be under the direction of a civilian group?

COMMISSIONS AND COMMITTEES. In keeping with our traditional concept of civilian control of military defense, Congress passed the Atomic Energy Act in 1946, creating a five-member civilian Atomic Energy Commission.

The five members are appointed for five-year, overlapping terms by the President with the consent of the Senate. One member is named chairman by the President. The commission has control of a huge industrial empire. In effect, it is one of America's largest corporations—bigger than General Motors or United States Steel.

It owns property about equal in size to Delaware and Rhode Island. The factories and laboratories are located at various points over the United States including: Oak Ridge, Tennessee; Los Alamos, New Mexico; Paducah, Kentucky; Aiken, South Carolina; Lemont, Illinois; Richland, Washington; Ames, Iowa; Livermore, California; Rochester, New York; and in university centers of more than half the states.

The commission appoints a general manager who is the executive responsible for the operations. Three permanent committees are created under the law to advise the commission. The General Advisory Committee consists of nine civilian members appointed by the President to advise on scientific and technical matters.

The Military Liaison Committee consists of representatives of the Department of Defense and at present has seven members. The committee consults with the commission on all atomic energy matters which relate to military applications.

The Congressional Joint Committee on Atomic Energy consists of nine senators and nine members of the House of Representatives. This committee continuously studies the activities and problems relating to atomic energy.

PEACETIME DEVELOPMENTS. The basic purpose of the development of atomic energy was stated in the Atomic Energy Act in these words:

> . . . *Subject at all times to the paramount objective of assuring the common defense and security, the development and utilization of atomic energy shall, so far as practicable, be directed toward improving the public welfare, increasing the standard of living, strengthening free competition in private enterprise, and promoting world peace.*

By 1954 two things were clear: (1) Russia had also developed atomic energy, and (2) the atom was about ready for wide use in peacetime activities. President Eisenhower in a dramatic speech proposed that all the nations pool their atomic information for peaceful uses.

Although Russia did not accept this proposal for over a year, Congress reconsidered the atomic energy program. The act was amended that year to provide for sharing our atomic information with other countries under certain conditions.

The act was also amended to give private business greater access to atomic information in order to develop peacetime uses.

This led to a famous congressional debate on atomic energy with continued public discussion of the important issues involved.

The lengthy debate centered around the ownership and control of atomic energy. The people of the United States have invested nearly nine billion dollars in atomic energy. No private corporation could have afforded this huge expenditure. But the production and control of atomic energy was a governmental monopoly.

Some felt that if private business could be given a greater part in producing atomic energy the peaceful uses and developments would be speeded up. Others feared that business might use this information for private gain, and the people would lose out on their great financial investment.

Some saw this as the great debate of this generation, because they believed that whoever gained control of atomic energy was gaining control of the energy sources of the future. The 1954 amendments were at best compromises. The basic issue of who is to control atomic energy was not settled. The issue is likely to be prominent in political discussions for years to come—especially so as atomic energy becomes an increased source of power as it is expected to by the end of the century.

SPACE PROGRAMS. The same issues are raised concerning the enormous expenditures for space programs. No private corporation or combination of corporations could afford the expenditures to launch rockets into space. Building launching facilities, developing liquid and solid fuels, devising tracking systems, inventing electronic devices, and developing spacecraft was beyond the capacity of any private enterprise. This responsibility was given to the *National Aeronautics and Space Administration,* an independent agency responsible to the President. The Administrator is appointed by the President with the consent

An astronaut collects rock samples on the moon using a lunar surface rake and tongs. Because space exploration is costly it is carried on by a federal agency, but through contracts with private industries. (NASA photo)

of the Senate. (See Chapter 13.) An advisory group, the National Aeronautics and Space Council, is in the Executive Office of the President.

There is a fundamental difference, however, in the operations of the space agency and the development of atomic energy. The latter was developed by an independent government corporation, the Atomic Energy Commission. In contrast the space-age activities have not been carried on by governmental employees of a governmental agency, but by contracts with private industries and with universities. As much as 80 per cent

Relate President Eisenhower's Farewell Address (page 558) concerning the military-industrial complex to the space program alone.

of the work of NASA is done under the private contract system. As many as 5,000 contracts were issued for the Gemini project alone. Over five billion dollars annually have been expended under this private contract system. An efficient system of government planning and management with specific contracts being given to industries and universities has developed. The government-owned and operated corporation versus the system of government planning under a contract system represents a new dimension in the old issues of ownership and control of these gigantic enterprises which are paid for by tax funds.

The economic consequences of space programs and the development of atomic energy go beyond the question of who owns and controls these enterprises. As a result of the huge expenditures and the inventiveness required, entire new industries have been developed, as for example in the case of electronics, satellites, and aeronautics. Places like Cape Kennedy, Florida, and Los Alamos, New Mexico, that were unknown a generation earlier are now known throughout the world. The location of a plant or the award of a contract may bring prosperity to one part of the country and loss of jobs to another part. As a result members of Congress compete with each other to get their state or district a share of the awards. As another example, the governors of the Great Lakes states combined their efforts to get more space contracts because they felt that the east and west coast areas were getting economic advantages in the awarding of contracts.

The struggle for national security is, thus, more than a contest between the noncommunists and communist nations. It is more than an issue of war and peace. The consequences of maintaining national security affect civil liberties, the economic system, and a vast range of political activities.

CONCEPTS AND GENERALIZATIONS

1
Political leaders have considered a strong military defense to be a necessity for national security.

2
Civilian control over military forces is part of the constitutional and traditional practice in the United States.

3
Only Congress has the right to declare war, but the activities of the President as Commander-in-chief may bring war without a formal declaration.

4
Under the President's direction, planning for military defense is the responsibility of the National Security Council, the Armed Forces Policy Council, and the Joint Chiefs of Staff; congressional committees are important in planning too.

5
Persons are obtained for military service through enlistment and the selective service.

6
Every man under twenty-six who enters the military service has at least a six-year obligation.

7
Efforts to locate subversive persons and to write laws to control their activities have been difficult, because in striving for security there is danger of destroying individual liberty.

8
Civilian defense, while important, has not received as much attention as other aspects of national security.

9
Adequate economic defense measures require having sufficient natural resources, industrial capacity, and power sources.

10
Atomic energy and space explorations were developed by different policies; the government corporation was used for atomic energy, while the contract with private groups was used for space projects.

1. What part of the United States Constitution deals with national defense?

2. How has civilian control of military defense been made a part of the historic policy of our country?

3. What is the purpose of the National Security Council? How does its work differ from that of the Armed Forces Policy Council? of the Joint Chiefs of Staff?

4. How does Congress get the necessary information to legislate on military matters?

5. What has been the history of draft acts in the United States?

6. What branches of the armed forces are open to young men? to young women?

7. How does the Selective Service System operate?

8. What choices are available in military service?

9. What measures has the government used for protection against communist infiltration?

10. Which congressional committees investigate communism?

11. Why have congressional investigations of communist activity been criticized?

12. How have Supreme Court decisions affected these efforts?

13. What is the present status of civilian defense in your community?

14. What are the chief economic measures that have been used to insure national security?

15. How do the Atomic Energy Commission and NASA operate?

16. What are the basic issues in the debate over control of atomic energy?

IDEAS FOR DISCUSSION

1. Do you agree that "strong military forces are our best defense against another war"?

2. Is the United States in danger of being dominated by the military?

3. A slogan of the military forces is "Stay in school as long as you can." Why do the military services want young men and women to graduate from high school?

4. Dr. John A. Hannah, former President of Michigan State University, served as Assistant Secretary of Defense in charge of Manpower and Personnel the first two years of the Eisenhower Administration. He wrote: "I think we would be foolish to stress the material benefits of military service, or to waste many tears on the time young men must spend away from their normal home environments. We should emphasize instead the moral obligation which rests upon each of us to perform his assigned task—and to do his best at it—in defending the privileges which have been defended by others in the past for our benefit, so that they may be passed on, unimpaired, to young men and women yet to come upon the scene." Do you agree? Would Vietnam dissenters agree? Why?

5. The draft is called "the democratic method of getting men to serve their country." What democratic principles are involved? Do you think the present draft law is needed? Is it fair? Should women be included under the provisions of the selective service law?

6. Are the traditional civil liberties of U. S. citizens in danger because of (a) communist infiltration, (b) congressional investigation, (c) the increased numbers who have had military service?

7. How do you answer this question: Can those who are disloyal to America be uncovered without destroying the basic liberties of the American people?

8. Which pattern of government operation of a large scale enterprise do you prefer: the Atomic Energy Commission model or the NASA model? Why?

9. Some critics have argued that Congress is no longer effective because the top policy making is done by the National Security Council, the Central Intelligence Agency, the Atomic Energy Commission, the National Aeronautics and Space Administration, and the Joint Chiefs of Staff. How influential are these agencies? What control does Congress have over them?

10. Some writers believe that stockpiling is no longer a matter of military necessity but has become a device to give aid to civilian producers of metals. Is it possible for military needs to be used to aid special segments of the economy? Is this desirable?

THINGS TO DO

1. Dramatize a meeting of the President's Cabinet in a session to discuss national security.

2. Prepare special reports on the following topics:

  Civilian defense
  Central Intelligence Agency
  Communist investigations
  Peacetime use of atomic energy
  Disarmament

3. Write a brief biography of one of the members of the Joint Chiefs of Staff.

4. Invite a member of a local draft board to speak before your class and answer questions.

5. Invite teachers who have had military service to come to the class and speak about experiences that will help high school students learn about military life.

6. Hold a debate on this topic: "*Resolved,* That the United States should have a military force made up entirely of volunteers."

7. Draw a chart showing the present organization of the military defense system.

8. Hold a panel discussion on the topic: "The industrial-military complex has become too powerful for the best interests of this country."

9. Conduct a public opinion survey of adult friends to determine their attitudes toward environmental pollution.

10. Draw a map showing installations under the control of the Atomic Energy Commission.

11. Prepare an exhibit to show other students the various aspects of national security.

12. Read one of the Supreme Court decisions on subversive activities and present your reactions to the class.

13. Invite a representative of the local electric power company to speak to the class on the energy-environment dilemma.

FURTHER READINGS

Abel, Elie, THE MISSILE CRISIS. J. B. Lippincott Company, 1966.

———, U.S. AIR FORCE ACADEMY. Lothrop, Lee & Shepard Co., Inc., 1959.

———, WEST POINT. Lothrop, Lee & Shepard Co., Inc., 1959.

Archer, Jules, TREASON IN AMERICA: DISLOYALTY VERSUS DISSENT. Hawthorn Books, Inc., 1971.

Blitz, Donald F., THE ROLE OF THE MILITARY PROFESSIONAL IN U.S. FOREIGN POLICY. Frederick A. Praeger, Inc., 1972.

Couper, J. M., LOTTERY IN LIVES. Houghton Mifflin Co., 1971.

Engeman, Jack, ANNAPOLIS. Lothrop, Lee & Shepard Co., Inc., 1965.

Englebardt, Stanley L., STRATEGIC DEFENSES. Thomas Y. Crowell Co., 1966.

Ferguson, John H., and McHenry, Dean E., THE AMERICAN SYSTEM OF GOVERNMENT. McGraw-Hill Book Co., Inc., 1967. Chapter 21.

Habenstreit, Barbara, ETERNAL VIGILANCE: THE AMERICAN CIVIL LIBERTIES UNION IN ACTION. Julian Messner, Publishers, 1971.

Howard, William E., and Baar, James, SPACECRAFT AND MISSILES OF THE WORLD. Harcourt, Brace & World, Inc., 1967.

Knoll, Erwin, and McFadden, Judy, eds., AMERICAN MILITARISM. Viking Press, 1970.

Lee, Irwin H., NEGRO MEDAL OF HONOR MEN. Dodd, Mead, and Co., 1969.

Liston, R., DISSENT IN AMERICA. McGraw-Hill Book Co., 1971.

Moskos, Charles C., Jr., THE AMERICAN ENLISTED MAN. Basic Books, 1970.

Polner, Murray, NO VICTORY PARADES: THE RETURN OF THE VIETNAM VETERAN. Holt, Rinehart and Winston, Inc., 1971.

Stein, M. L., FREEDOM OF THE PRESS: A CONTINUING STRUGGLE. Julian Messner, Inc., 1967.

Tully, Andrew, THE FBI'S MOST FAMOUS CASES. William Morrow and Co., 1965.

Von Braun, Wernher, SPACE FRONTIER. Holt, Rinehart and Winston, Inc., 1971.

Wise, David, and Ross, Thomas, THE INVISIBLE GOVERNMENT. Random House, Inc., 1964.

Zahn, Gordon C., WAR, CONSCIENCE AND DISSENT. Hawthorn Books, Inc., 1967.

ABSTAIN—to be present but not voting.

ARBITRATION—the process by which one or more persons settle a dispute.

BALANCE OF POWER—the distribution of power among nations so that no one nation or group of nations can dominate others.

INDICT—to accuse; to bring to trial in order to determine guilt or innocence.

JURISDICTION—to have control, power, or authority.

MEDIATOR—one who is selected to assist in settling a dispute by making suggestions and offering compromises.

ORGAN—one of the major branches of a governing organization, especially of the United Nations.

SANCTIONS—an action by one or more nations toward another nation designed to force that nation to obey international law.

SECRETARIAT—the executive branch of the United Nations, headed by the Secretary General.

SOVEREIGNTY—supreme power or authority.

TRUST TERRITORY—a non-self-governing land or area administered by a nation under the direction of the Trusteeship Council of the United Nations.

THE LANGUAGE OF GOVERNMENT

Refer to the Kellogg-Briand Pact of 1928.

27

International Organizations

Disputes within our nation are settled by a system of laws enforceable in courts. If a man steals or kills, he can be arrested, tried in a court, and sentenced to prison. In a civilized society police, laws, courts, and prisons represent forces which prevent individuals and groups from disrupting and destroying the society.

In disputes between nations similar forces do not exist. While some international law has been built up very slowly, no peaceful way has been discovered to compel a nation to obey an international law. The nation that steals or kills or threatens its neighbors must finally be stopped by war—at least so it has always been.

But war is not and never has been a satisfactory way to settle disputes. So today man yearns for a way to avoid war. In earlier times, too, men tried to find ways to prevent war. The search for ways to settle international disputes by peaceful means has been going on for centuries. No satisfactory solution has yet been found, so armies, navies, and air forces are a part of modern life.

We have learned to control the individual person who breaks a law, but we have not yet learned how to write the laws for nations.

Progress has been made, however. Over the years nations have learned much about getting along with each other. Just as most citizens are not thieves or murderers, so, too, most nations try to live harmoniously with other nations. Because a nation turns gangster does not mean that the search for peaceful settlement of international disputes is hopeless. Indeed the fact that there has been a war going on somewhere nearly every year of this century does not mean that war is inevitable. Twentieth-century wars have caused citizens in many nations to search harder for more effective ways to settle international disputes.

The United Nations was born out of this great desire to find some way to prevent another world war. While the United Nations is not a perfect organization, and has been unsuccessful in maintaining peace, it is another attempt to find some way to solve international problems without war. If the United Nations continues to be unable to prevent wars, people will have to try again to devise some method by which nations can live together in peace and harmony. At least in the past such efforts have always been made.

METHODS OF INTERNATIONAL COOPERATION
Over the centuries, in addition to the use of international organizations to keep the peace and resolve disputes, nations have relied on the balance of power, international agreements,

and the development of international law.

BALANCE OF POWER. The most common method by which nations have tried to gain peace has been by organizing one combination of nations strong enough to discourage any other combination of nations from starting war. Before World War I France had joined an alliance with Great Britain and Russia for mutual protection in a possible war with Germany. At the same time, Germany was allied with Italy and Austria-Hungary. One hundred years earlier Great Britain and Russia had joined in an alliance with Prussia and Austria against France. The present alliances are similar in nature.

This system of keeping peace by alliances results in a struggle for the *balance of power.* Peace comes because the members of each alliance are afraid of defeat if they attack the other powerful group.

Alliances have brought long periods of peace but not permanent peace because nations become suspicious of each other. Sometimes one nation does not trust another member of the alliance if that nation becomes too powerful. So membership of alliances changes over the years, and there is a constant struggle to keep some balance of power.

Some authorities on international affairs believe that we are now going through one of these great, historic shifts in balance of power as a result of the changes in strength among nations since World War II. The policies of the United States, Russia, China, or other nations may alter the alliances developed during the Cold War era.

INTERNATIONAL AGREEMENTS. In addition to the alliances developed around the great powers, there are all kinds of international agreements, ranging from formal treaties to informal agreements. Some treaties determine boundaries, establish conditions for trade, set up means for

The International Court of Justice hears counsel for the Federal Republic of Germany. The hearing concerned use of the continental shelf between Germany and the Netherlands. (United Nations)

control of radio or television, or regulate the use of canals.

Executive agreements are reached between nations. In addition, there are simple understandings between executives which have no formal basis whatever. The President of the United States in a White House conversation with the Japanese Prime Minister, for example, might reach a preliminary agreement on future policy which is known only to the two men and their advisors.

These different types of agreements have helped to maintain friendly relations between nations on many important matters. But the agreements can be broken, and there is no final way to enforce them. Disagreements may lead to war.

INTERNATIONAL LAW. Over the years a set of rules for the conduct of nations has gradually developed. These rules have grown up from custom, from court decisions, and from treaties. The United States Supreme Court has held that international law is a part of the law of the United States.

Some early writers held that international law should consist of the rules of correct conduct which nations *ought* to observe. Most modern writers hold that international law really consists of the rules that nations *actually* observe. What are these rules? They are of three types: laws of peace, laws of war, laws of neutrality.

The *international laws of peace* are concerned with the recognition of nations, proper treatment of ambassadors, the rights and duties of aliens, the use of the air space over nations, and the extradition of criminals.

The *war laws* deal with declarations of war, the exchange and treatment of prisoners, the treatment of civilians, and the custody of captured property.

The *laws of neutrality* are concerned with moving troops across neutral territory, the use of neutral ports, and the rights of neutral ships on the seas.

Needless to say, international laws are broken both in peace and in wartime. The mistreatment of U. S. soldiers in Korea who became Chinese prisoners of war was in

Discuss the role, if any, that international morality plays in international law.

581

direct violation of international law. Although the laws were broken, the law was not destroyed and continued to provide the basis of treatment of prisoners taken by both sides in the Vietnam war.

Unfortunately, there is no way at the present time to compel a nation to obey existing international laws. Nations, if they wish, may settle disputes by arbitration or by sending the disputes to an international court, but the *nations* make the choice. When disputes are over national security, national honor, or important foreign policy matters, the nations may not be willing to live by the rules of international law.

INTERNATIONAL ORGANIZATIONS. International organizations for specific purposes have had a successful history. For example, letters may be mailed from your home town to any part of the world under provisions of the Universal Postal Union, which was established in 1875. Under this union each nation honors the postage of the other nations.

The International Bureau of Weights and Measures, which was organized in 1875, established standards for weighing and measuring. The international use of telegraph, telephone, and radio has been regulated by an organization which originated in 1865. At the present time, the United States is a member of more than fifty international organizations.

But not all international organizations have been successful. Perhaps the biggest failure was the *League of Nations.* Fifty-nine nations joined the League, but the United States never became a member.

In several cases the League of Nations was successful. A war between Greece and Bulgaria was prevented in 1925. The control of contagious diseases, regulation of narcotic drugs, and improvements in labor conditions were important accomplishments.

But the most important task—keeping world peace—became too complicated a job; the members were not able to use effective measures against nations that refused to live by international agreements. The League of Nations could not prevent World War II, and with the start of that war the League of Nations died.

THE UNITED NATIONS

The search for a way to prevent war did not die, however. During World War II the United States, Great Britain, and Russia agreed to the establishment of "a general international organization . . . for the maintenance of international peace and security." Representatives of these and other nations reviewed the strengths and weaknesses of past international organizations and designed the United Nations.

In April 1945, as World War II was drawing to a close, 1,500 delegates from nations all over the world met in San Francisco to write a constitution for a new international organization. On June 26 the completed document, the charter of the United Nations, was signed by representatives of fifty nations. The next month, on July 28, 1945, the United States Senate ratified the charter by a vote of eighty-nine to two.

The UN is now twice its original size and has more than 120 members. Its headquarters are in New York City on land donated by John D. Rockefeller, Jr.

THE CHARTER. The "constitution" of the United Nations is a long document containing nineteen chapters and 111 articles. There is a preamble which states the reasons for the organization. The major chapters describe the membership, the six principal *organs*, and the ways of settling disputes.

The general organization of the UN re-

Make it clear that the UN has many functions besides its peacemaking role.

The European office of the United Nations is housed in the former League of Nations building in Geneva, Switzerland. (United Nations)

sembles a national government but does not create a world government.

The charter is more like the Articles of Confederation than the Constitution of the United States. The General Assembly, with one important exception, which will be mentioned later, does not have legislative powers. The power to legislate is strictly limited, but roughly the legislative branch is the Security Council. The executive branch is the Secretariat; the chief executive is the Secretary General. The International Court of Justice provides a judicial branch, but compared to the Supreme Court of the United States, the International Court has little power.

The Economic and Social Council and the Trusteeship Council are unique organs that can only be roughly compared to the executive departments and the independent agencies in the government of the United States. Each of these six organs will be described after a brief discussion of the purposes of the UN.

THE PURPOSES. The charter of the United Nations begins with these words:

We, the peoples of the United Nations, determined to save succeeding generations from the scourge of war, which twice in our lifetime has brought untold sorrow to mankind, . . . through representatives . . . do hereby establish an international organization to be known as the United Nations.[1]

Four purposes are named in the charter. They are:

- *To maintain international peace and security*
- *To develop friendly relations among nations*
- *To achieve international cooperation in solving international problems of an economic, social, cultural, or humanitarian character and in promoting respect for human rights*
- *To be a center for harmonizing the actions of nations in the attainment of these common ends.*

To achieve these purposes the charter provided for six chief organs.

THE GENERAL ASSEMBLY. Each member-nation of the United Nations is automatically a member of the General

[1] The complete preamble contains eight clauses of which only the first and last are quoted here.

Discuss how, just as the framers of our Constitution had to compromise between large and small states in the legislature, the UN handled this same problem between the Assembly and the Security Council.

Composed of representatives from each member-nation of the United Nations, the General Assembly (above) serves as a Town Meeting of the World. (Right) The representative from Uganda addresses a meeting of the General Assembly's Special Political Committee. (United Nations)

Assembly. Each member-nation may send up to five delegates to the Assembly meetings which are held annually beginning in September.

Regardless of the number of delegates sent, each nation, no matter what its size, has just one vote. Thus the United States has one vote and Zambia has one vote. Special sessions of the Assembly may be called at the request of the Security Council or of a majority of the members of the United Nations.

The Assembly is really a gigantic forum for discussion and propaganda. It has been nicknamed "The Town Meeting of the World." In the Assembly any nation can speak through a delegate, and the world will be able to listen. But the Assembly has little power; the real power was given to the Security Council. The planners of the UN thought that peace could be kept by the Great Powers and did not vision that

these powers would not remain on friendly terms.

Because of the differences that arose among the big nations, at the fifth annual general session in November, 1950, an important change was made that gave the Assembly one very important legislative

THE LANGUAGE BARRIER

When the leaders of fifty nations were meeting in San Francisco in 1945 to write a charter for the United Nations, World War II was almost ended. People everywhere were hoping for a lasting peace. Progress was being made on the writing of the charter, when the delegation of the Soviet Union refused to accept a provision which the United States wanted. For three days all work on the charter stopped. It looked as though the attempt to build a United Nations organization would fail.

During those three days Harold Stassen, a former governor of Minnesota and at one time a special assistant to the President on disarmament, was busy. As an official delegate of the United States, he spent his time going back and forth between the representatives of the Soviet Union and the United States representatives. He could not understand why the two groups could not agree on what seemed to be a simple matter. Finally, he made a discovery. In translating the English word *indict* into Russian, the interpreter was giving the Russians a wrong idea of what the United States wanted.

The English word *indict* means to accuse someone of being guilty. We use the word to mean that we think someone has done something wrong and we want to bring the person to trial to find out whether he is guilty. But the Russians were translating the word to mean, "You are guilty." Once they understood that the English word *indict* meant to accuse—with a trial coming later—they said that was all they had been asking. Agreement was reached, and a big stumbling block to the writing of the United Nations charter was removed.

The translation of one word almost prevented the writing of the UN charter.

---

power: *If the Security Council fails to act to keep the peace, the General Assembly is given the power to take action to keep or restore peace.* But the Assembly has not been able to use this power effectively.

The Assembly chooses members for other agencies and commissions of the UN. It approves the UN budget. It receives and debates the reports of the UN agencies. It can notify the Security Council of matters which it thinks are important.

Up to the present time the chief value of the General Assembly has been that debates on all kinds of international problems have been heard. Meeting together, listening to each other, trying to change public opinion have been the functions of this world assembly.

THE SECURITY COUNCIL. The United Nations was planned to give the control of international disputes to the Security Council. This Council now consists of fifteen members, although originally there were only eleven members. The addi-

tional members were added in 1966 to get a more representative and influential body. Five are permanent members: the United States, Great Britain, the Soviet Union, France, and China. (From 1950 to 1971 the Nationalist government of China which was established on the island of Formosa [Taiwan] had a permanent place on the Security Council. In 1971 Communist China was admitted to the UN and given this seat on the Security Council.) There are ten nonpermanent members elected for two-year terms by the General Assembly.

The Security Council may study any disputed matter between nations that might disturb international peace. Recommendations for a settlement can be made. But all actions on important matters require the approval of seven members, including *all* the permanent members. Thus each one of the "Big Five" permanent members has an actual *veto* over any act of the Security Council.

If one of the Big Five does not want

something done, it can refuse approval. The Soviet Union has been the chief user of the veto, preventing action on many matters. The UN was able to vote to resist the attack on South Korea in 1950 because the Soviet Union was not present. The United States used the veto for the first time in 1970.

The Security Council is organized so that it can be in continuous session if necessary. A president of the Council is chosen for each month on a rotation basis following the English alphabetical order.

Two important agencies report directly to the Security Council. They are the *Military Staff Committee,* which advises the council on military matters, and ,the *Disarmament Commission,* which studies ways to reduce armaments and to control atomic energy.

THE SECRETARIAT. The detailed work of the United Nations is carried on by hundreds of employees who form a kind of international civil service. These employees are under a chief administrative officer, the Secretary General, and are organized into departments and offices under his direction. This entire administrative organization is known as the Secretariat.

The Secretary General is elected for a five-year term by the General Assembly on the recommendation of the Security Council. The Secretary General makes an annual report and other reports to the General Assembly. He has the duty to bring to the attention of the Security Council any matter that is a threat to international peace. The first Secretary General was Trygve Lie of Norway, who held office from 1945 to 1953, being reelected in 1950. He was followed by Dag Hammarskjöld of Sweden, who died in a plane crash in 1961 while on UN business in the Congo. U Thant of Burma succeeded him. Kurt Waldheim of Austria took over the office in 1972.

The employees are selected on a worldwide basis, and nearly all countries of the world are represented among the employees. Although much of the work is routine office work, some employees are engaged in important studies and investigations and need highly specialized training.

THE INTERNATIONAL COURT OF JUSTICE. Fifteen justices, each selected from a different country, make up the International Court of Justice. The justices are selected for nine-year terms by the Security Council and the General Assembly and may be reelected. The court meets at The Hague in the Netherlands.

Members and nonmembers of the United Nations may have disputes settled by the court, but only nations—not individuals—can bring cases before the court. Disputes involving interpretations of treaties, executive agreements, or international law come

One of the six main organs of the United Nations, the International Court of Justice is located at The Hague in the Netherlands. (United Nations)

Drugs, clinic equipment, and other aid from the United Nations Children's Fund help set up health units, such as this in Burma, where a young girl receives a smallpox vaccination. (UNICEF)

before the court. Decisions are made by majority vote. Advisory opinions are given on matters requested by organs of the United Nations. Members of the United Nations do not have to refer disputes to the court unless they have agreed specifically to do so by a treaty.

The court has *jurisdiction* only in international affairs; the UN charter specifically excludes "domestic affairs" from the jurisdiction of the court. Some nations have agreed to allow the court to decide when an issue is domestic, but the United States by a Senate reservation retains the right to make this decision. Other nations have reserved this right, too. As a result the court has not played an important role in settling major disputes.

THE ECONOMIC AND SOCIAL COUNCIL. The framers of the United Nations charter believed that regions with poor economic and social conditions were the breeding places for war. They provided, therefore, for the Economic and Social Council, which was to be the organ to improve the standards of living and human welfare throughout the world. This

council consists of twenty-seven members elected for three-year terms by the General Assembly. Originally the membership was eighteen, but nine members were added in 1966 because of the increased membership of the UN. Nine members are elected each year.

The Economic and Social Council performs its work through special commissions. Among the subjects which have been studied are the status of women in the world, human rights, narcotic drugs, population, statistical information, financial information, transportation and communication, and broad social policy. There are also economic commissions for Europe, Asia and the Far East, Latin America, and Africa. These commissions are concerned with improving economic conditions in these regions.

The *specialized agencies* of the United Nations, as shown in the chart on page 589, work with and through the Economic and Social Council and the Secretariat. They do some of the most effective work of the UN.

The International Labor Organization

The United Nations Educational, Scientific and Cultural Organization (UNESCO), with headquarters in Paris, promotes the exchange of ideas between nations. (United Nations)

(ILO) strives to improve labor conditions and living standards. The Food and Agricultural Organization (FAO) tries to improve food production, distribution, and nutrition. The World Health Organization (WHO) provides medical and public health aids to nations making requests. The International Atomic Energy Agency (IAEA) is semi-independent, promoting peaceful uses of atomic energy.

The Universal Postal Union (UPU) deals with problems of postal service among the nations. The United Nations Educational, Scientific, and Cultural Organization (UNESCO) is concerned with the exchange of educational and cultural ideas. The International Telecommunication Union (ITU) deals with international problems of telephone, telegraph, radio, and television.

The International Civil Aviation Organization (ICAO) develops standards and regulations for civilian and commercial aircraft. The World Meteorological Organization (WMO) brings together and standardizes weather information.

The International Bank for Reconstruction and Development (World Bank) makes loans to countries or helps them get loans to improve their productivity. The International Monetary Fund tries to encourage international trade through stabilizing the value of the money of different countries. The International Finance Corporation (IFC) encourages economic development.

The Intergovernmental Maritime Consultative Organization (IMCO) gets governments to cooperate on technical international shipping problems. The International Development Association (IDA) aids development by loans, especially to underdeveloped nations.

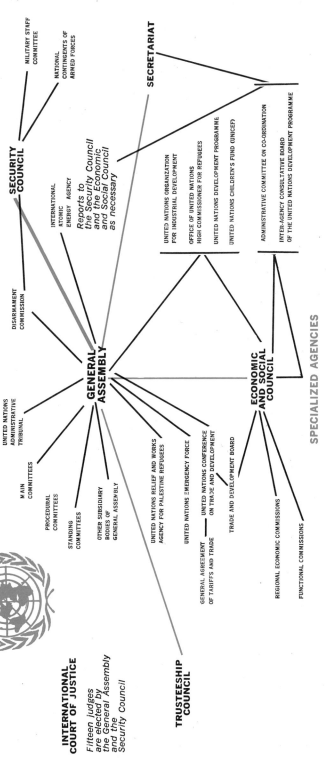

THE UNITED NATIONS AND SPECIALIZED AGENCIES

INTERNATIONAL COURT OF JUSTICE

Fifteen judges are elected by the General Assembly and the Security Council

TRUSTEESHIP COUNCIL

GENERAL ASSEMBLY

MAIN COMMITTEES

PROCEDURAL COMMITTEES

STANDING COMMITTEES

OTHER SUBSIDIARY BODIES OF GENERAL ASSEMBLY

UNITED NATIONS RELIEF AND WORKS AGENCY FOR PALESTINE REFUGEES

UNITED NATIONS EMERGENCY FORCE

GENERAL AGREEMENT ON TARIFFS AND TRADE

UNITED NATIONS CONFERENCE ON TRADE AND DEVELOPMENT

TRADE AND DEVELOPMENT BOARD

UNITED NATIONS ADMINISTRATIVE TRIBUNAL

DISARMAMENT COMMISSION

INTERNATIONAL ATOMIC ENERGY AGENCY

SECURITY COUNCIL

MILITARY STAFF COMMITTEE

NATIONAL CONTINGENTS OF ARMED FORCES

SECRETARIAT

Reports to the Security Council and the Economic and Social Council as necessary

ECONOMIC AND SOCIAL COUNCIL

REGIONAL ECONOMIC COMMISSIONS

FUNCTIONAL COMMISSIONS

UNITED NATIONS ORGANIZATION FOR INDUSTRIAL DEVELOPMENT

OFFICE OF UNITED NATIONS HIGH COMMISSIONER FOR REFUGEES

UNITED NATIONS DEVELOPMENT PROGRAMME

UNITED NATIONS CHILDREN'S FUND (UNICEF)

ADMINISTRATIVE COMMITTEE ON CO-ORDINATION

INTER-AGENCY CONSULTATIVE BOARD OF THE UNITED NATIONS DEVELOPMENT PROGRAMME

SPECIALIZED AGENCIES

FOOD AND AGRICULTURE ORGANIZATION OF THE UNITED NATIONS

INTER-GOVERNMENTAL MARITIME CONSULTATIVE ORGANIZATION

WORLD BANK — INTERNATIONAL BANK FOR RECONSTRUCTION AND DEVELOPMENT

INTERNATIONAL CIVIL AVIATION ORGANIZATION

IDA — INTERNATIONAL DEVELOPMENT ASSOCIATION

IFC — INTERNATIONAL FINANCE CORPORATION

ILO 1919-1969 — INTERNATIONAL LABOR ORGANIZATION

ITU — INTERNATIONAL TELECOMMUNICATION UNION

UNESCO — UNITED NATIONS EDUCATIONAL, SCIENTIFIC AND CULTURAL ORGANIZATION

INTERNATIONAL MONETARY FUND

WMO — WORLD METEOROLOGICAL ORGANIZATION

WORLD HEALTH ORGANIZATION

UNIVERSAL POSTAL UNION

Symbols courtesy the United Nations

589

THE TRUSTEESHIP COUNCIL. In Chapter 25 it was noted that some territories are ruled by nations under the direction of the United Nations. The government of these "trust territories" is supervised by the Trusteeship Council.

The Council is composed of one delegate from each of the Big Five nations plus one delegate from each other nation administering a trust territory. In addition, there is an equal number of delegates from countries not holding trusteeships.

The Council receives annual reports, visits the trust territories under certain conditions, and receives complaints or suggestions from the territories. At one time there were eleven territories supervised by the Council. This number has been reduced to two. The others, exercising the right of self-determination, have become or have joined independent nations.

HOW THE UNITED NATIONS TRIES TO SETTLE INTERNATIONAL DISPUTES

The people of the world hoped that the United Nations would be able to prevent war. Many people have not studied the six principal organs described above. They have been interested in just one thing: Why has the UN failed to prevent war? The ways in which the UN tries to settle and to prevent international disputes are described in the following eight steps.

1. DISPUTES ARE BROUGHT BEFORE THE SECURITY COUNCIL. The Secretary General, the General Assembly, or any nation may ask the Security Council to consider an international dispute. The nation making the request does not have to be a member of the United Nations. For example, in 1946 Thailand, a nonmember at the time, asked that a dispute with France be discussed by the Security Council.

2. THE SECURITY COUNCIL MAY ASK THAT THE DISPUTE BE REFERRED TO THE INTERNATIONAL COURT OF JUSTICE. If the dispute seems to be one that could be settled by court procedures, the case is referred to the International Court of Justice. For example, Great Britain complained that Albania had damaged British shipping by illegal mining of the waters of the Corfu channel. The Security Council referred the dispute to the Court, which awarded damages to Great Britain.

3. THE SECURITY COUNCIL MAY RECOMMEND THAT THE DISPUTE BE SETTLED BY NEGOTIATION OR ARBITRATION. The dispute may be one in which a UN commission or a UN representative might be able to adjust the differences between the parties. In such a case the Council may request *arbitration* or the use of a *mediator*. For example, Dr. Ralph J. Bunche, of the United States, was the mediator in the armistice negotiations between the Arab nations and Israel in 1949; Lester Pearson of Canada served in a similar role in 1957; and Gunnar Jarring of Sweden since 1967 has served as special envoy to try again to resolve the differences in the Middle East.

4. THE SECURITY COUNCIL MAY RECOMMEND ECONOMIC SANCTIONS. The framers of the UN charter believed that economic pressures might be used against a nation to prevent war. Provisions were made whereby the Security Council might cut off trade between other nations and an aggressor nation. For example, in a dispute between the Arab nations and Israel in 1948 the threat of economic sanctions helped to settle the dispute.

5. THE SECURITY COUNCIL MAY RECOMMEND MILITARY ACTION. The Security Council has the power to carry on military action against any nation

With respect to the bypassing of the Security Council, introduce and briefly describe the "Uniting for Peace Resolution" passed by the General Assembly in 1950.

that refuses to settle disputes by peaceful means. For example, the Security Council declared the invasion of Korea in 1950 a breach of the peace and asked the UN members to send troops to the aid of Korea. With the United States bearing the greatest burden, sixteen UN nations carried on the fight against the aggressors.

6. THE ACTION OF THE SECURITY COUNCIL MAY BE VETOED BY ONE OF THE BIG FIVE MEMBERS. Any of the actions to settle a dispute may be vetoed by one of the five permanent members of the Security Council. For example, the Soviet Union vetoed the use in Greece of a Security Council investigating commission which was trying to negotiate a Balkan dispute.

7. IN CASE OF A VETO THAT THREATENS THE PEACE, THE GENERAL ASSEMBLY MAY REQUEST MILITARY ACTION. The General Assembly is normally not allowed to act on matters that are before the Security Council. However, if in the Council a veto threatens the peace, the Assembly may by a two-thirds vote request nations to carry on military action against an aggressor nation. In the 1956 dispute over the Suez Canal small nations were asked to supply troops for a "police action." This United Nations Emergency Force continued to police the Egyptian-Israeli borders even after the six-day war in 1967. In addition United Nations Emergency Force (UNEF) soldiers have been used to stabilize conditions in the Congo, to act as buffers between Greeks and Turks in Cyprus, and to monitor the Kashmir cease-fire between India and Pakistan.

These seven steps may be employed whenever a dispute threatens the peace. They have not been used in the Vietnam War or in the India-Pakistan War of 1971 because the great powers disagreed.

8. DISCUSSIONS IN THE GENERAL ASSEMBLY AND THE ACTIVITIES OF THE ECONOMIC AND SOCIAL COUNCIL ARE USED TO PREVENT CONFLICTS FROM ARISING. Much of the work of the United Nations is directed toward preventing disputes from reaching a crisis stage. The two phases of the work of the UN which are most important here are (a) the discussions that take place in the meetings of the General Assembly and (b) the study and actions of the Economic and Social Council and the specialized agencies on social, educational, economic, and health problems.

In great regions of the world masses of people live in hunger and misery. UN agencies help them get food, fight tuberculosis and malaria, dig canals, build roads, and abolish illiteracy. These are the preventive measures which try to get rid of the causes of conflicts. Prevention of conditions that lead to war is an important part of keeping the peace.

IMPROVING THE UNITED NATIONS

The United Nations has been effective in many of its activities. Several threats to world peace have been handled in ways to avoid wars. In Syria, Lebanon, Iran, Greece, Kashmir, and Africa explosive situations were dealt with and possible wars were averted. The fighting by UN forces in Korea demonstrated that the UN could act forcefully against an aggressor nation when one of the five permanent members of the Security Council did not prevent action by using the veto.

Living standards in underdeveloped areas were raised by technical assistance programs. Ignorance, hunger, disease, and poverty were decreased in many parts of the world because of the effective work of the Economic and Social Council.

Make it clear that the United Nations can only be as effective as the permanent members of the Security Council permit it to be.

591

Kurt Waldheim of Austria became Secretary General of the United Nations on Jaunary 1, 1972. He succeeded U Thant of Burma who retired after ten years. (United Nations)

vetoes. Seven nations were excluded by the Western powers. In other words, the Soviet Union would not admit nations that were friendly to the West, and the West would not admit nations that were friendly to the Soviet Union. Finally, in 1955, a compromise was reached and sixteen new members were admitted. Four more, including Japan, were admitted in 1956. Ghana and the Federation of Malaya (now called Malaysia) were added in 1957. Then the admission of the new nations, mostly from Africa, increased the membership rapidly. There has been some alarm because these new members form an African-Asian bloc.

For twenty years the People's Republic of China had been denied membership. But on October 25, 1971, it was admitted and given a permanent seat on the Security

The territories which are not self-governing were administered fairly by the Trusteeship Council.

The rights of individuals and of religious, racial, national, and ethnic groups were strengthened by the reports of UN commissions.

WEAKNESSES. UN activities showed definite weaknesses, however. The large nations sometimes bypassed the UN and did not make use of its machinery when this served their convenience. In these cases, the influence of the UN declined. Important problems were dealt with in special international conferences and not through the UN organs. Friends of the United Nations pointed out that "the machinery of the UN was rusting because of idleness."

The veto power in the Security Council sometimes made action almost impossible. One example was especially dramatic. From 1950 to 1955, nations desiring to join the UN could not get admitted. Fourteen countries were kept out by the Soviet Union

The late Dr. Ralph J. Bunche, Under-Secretary for Special Political Affairs in the United Nations from 1955 to 1971, received the Nobel Peace Prize in 1950. (United Nations)

It is interesting to note that the United States in 1945 very strongly supported the veto idea.

Bastian in the San Francisco Chronicle.

United Nations. As stated earlier, the United Nations is a confederation of sovereign states, somewhat like the United States under the Articles of Confederation. These nation-states, especially the larger ones, have not been willing to give up sovereignty to the UN.

Aggressive war is outlawed under the UN charter, but member states may still legally engage in defensive war. Thus, in accepting membership in the UN, all nations except the five permanent members of the Security Council have accepted the principle that their sovereignty has been diminished by giving up the right to wage aggressive war. Since the five permanent members have a veto over any action of the Security Council, they did not give up any sovereignty. They and the other powers have not really given up this power because they can argue that any war in which they engage is defensive.

The issue of sovereignty, therefore, raises two questions about the UN: Should the use of the veto be eliminated? Can the UN devise means for deciding who is the aggressor in a war?

If these questions are answered affirma-

Council. At the same time, against the desire of the United States, Nationalist China was expelled from the UN.

The hydrogen and atom bombs were not brought under international control. Disarmament was discussed, but effective regulation of weapons failed. However, an encouraging step forward was taken when the General Assembly in June, 1968, voted in favor of a treaty to prevent the spread of nuclear weapons to other nations.

The inability to make peace in Vietnam, in the Middle East between Israel and the Arab nations, or in the India-Pakistan War caused some international experts to realize that the United Nations might suffer the fate of the League of Nations.

SOVEREIGNTY. Fundamental to the future of the United Nations is the issue of sovereignty. At present the supreme authority over the acts of a nation remains with the individual nation and not with the

> . . . if the United Nations is to grow into a really effective instrument for maintaining the rule of law, the first step must be the willingness of the member states to give up the concept of the absolute sovereign state in the same manner as we individuals give up our absolute right to do just as we please, as an essential condition of living in an organized society. . . . It seems to me that the United Nations must develop in the same manner as every sovereign state has done. If the United Nations is to have a future, it must assume some of the attributes of a state. It must have the right, the power, and the means to keep the peace.
>
> —U THANT, Secretary General of the United Nations, in a speech in Sweden, May 1962. Reprinted from *Vital Speeches*, Vol. XXVIII, No. 8, July 1, 1962.

tively, the UN would be a world govern ment instead of a limited international or- ganization. In discussions on amending the UN charter the United States has favored the abolition of the veto in specific matters —such as, the admission of new members and the peaceful settlement of disputes— but has not been willing to give up the veto on the right to overrule decisions on making war.[1]

FINANCE. The future of the United Nations is troubled, too, because of finan- cial problems. The UN has no power to tax. Money needed for its operations is raised by an assessment placed on each member. The annual regular budget amounts to approximately $200 million —about the same as Vermont or New Hampshire would spend in a year for gen- eral expenditures. After the General As- sembly has approved the budget, individual assessments for each nation are made by a formula using four factors: total national income, per capita income, economic condi- tions caused by war, and ability to acquire foreign currency. In the early years of the UN the assessment for the United States came to nearly half of the total budget; but it seemed unwise to permit any nation to contribute such a large portion of the total, and the decision was reached that no nation should pay more than one-third of the total cost. In recent years the United States assess- ment has been about 32 per cent of the budget. Russia has paid about 15 per cent, Great Britain about 7 per cent, India about 2 per cent. The minimum assessment for the small nations has been about $80,000.

If a member fails to pay an assessment,

it can be denied a vote in the General Assembly.

In addition to the regular budget, money is required to pay the costs of the peace- keeping efforts that have been attempted by the United Nations Emergency Force. For these expenses *special* assessments are made. The Soviet Union, France, and ten other nations have refused to pay some of these special assessments because they did not approve the actions in the Congo, Egypt, Lebanon, or other places. As a re- sult the United Nations is heavily in debt— having sold bonds to finance these opera- tions. The debt was over $170 million including the $50 million dating back to the 1957 conflict over the Suez Canal.

In 1965 an effort was made to deny the vote to those nations which had not paid their assessments. The International Court of Justice had ruled in a nine-to-five deci- sion that special assessments were the re- sponsibility of the entire membership. After a yearlong struggle in which the UN was close to coming to an end, the United States gave up its fight in the General Assem- bly to force members to pay or to lose the vote. The majority of the members seemed to fear that if the UN charter provision were enforced, the Soviet Union and its supporters would withdraw from the UN.

VOTING. The voting provisions in the United Nations represent an area of the greatest difficulty, with three distinct prob- lems. First, in the Security Council each of the five permanent members has the right to veto any action on the original theory of the planners that in the Council the great powers would work together and keep final control. This has not happened, result- ing often in the inability of the UN to act. Moreover, if the veto is proper for some nations, should this power be denied to such important nations as West **Germany**, Japan, and India?

---

[1] The charter provides that amendments may be proposed by a two-thirds vote of the General Assem- bly and ratified by two-thirds of the members in- cluding all permanent Council members. In addi- tion, a conference to review the charter may be called by a two-thirds vote of the Assembly and nine Council members.

Summarize by describing how the world conditions of 1945 are still reflected in the present United Nations organization.

Second, in the General Assembly the policy of *one-nation, one-vote* has been under severe attack. The policy indicates that all nations are equal when actually the members are very unequal. For example, the forty-member-nations from Africa have a combined population of about 340 million and have forty times as many votes as India with its population of over 540 million. Tiny ministates like Botswana, Lesotho, Gambia, or Yemen have the same vote as the United States or any other great power. Very small states now possess more than one-third of the total votes.

Third, it is worthy of note that granting the weaknesses in the one-nation, one-vote system, a method of voting has evolved so that one feature is unique. In most lawmaking bodies majority rule is the practice with members being either for or against a proposition. In the General Assembly, however, there is in reality a three-fold voting system: those for, those against, and those abstaining. *Abstaining* from voting is recorded and is interpreted as an effort by some nations either to avoid taking a stand or a deliberate effort to express a preference for a different policy.

THE FUTURE   The difficulties of the United Nations, particularly its inability to prevent wars involving the major powers, have caused a return to the old balance of power system and an increase in the independent action of the individual nations. The complexities of world problems and the weaknesses of present international or-

> *If we are going to have peace in the world we will have to find machinery to draw us together and we have got to find a way by which we can actually attack the problems before they reach the point where people will want to go to war about them.*
> —ELEANOR ROOSEVELT, Speech, Jan. 19, 1938

ganizations are resulting in a rethinking of the place of the United States in world affairs. Some people would have the United States develop a new kind of isolation. Others want the United States to take leadership for some form of world government with police power.

ISOLATION.   The isolationists look upon the billions spent in foreign aid as "water down the drain." They resent the fact that some allies do not have the will to resist and that we have weakened our financial resources by giving aid to those who do not help us in Vietnam. They believe in military might. They are doubtful that the United Nations can be an effective international organization and are suspicious that the weaknesses in the voting system mean that the United States will increasingly be at a disadvantage.

Opponents of the new isolationists ridicule these claims as "eighteenth-century thinking." They feel a return to isolation would mean that communists would overrun Europe and Asia and we would be so alone that we would eventually be defeated. Their slogan is "We cannot survive alone."

WORLD GOVERNMENT.   At the opposite extreme from the isolationists are the believers in world government. There are variations among these advocates, but basically they think that the ills of the world will be solved only by greater cooperation among nations who are willing to give up sovereignty. They are disappointed in the United Nations. They want a stronger, more powerful form of international government.

They point out that just as the thirteen original colonies gave up the Articles of Confederation in favor of the United States Constitution, it is time for the nations of the world to give up sovereign rights and establish a world government. They say that if some nations will not join, then the other nations should join together and leave the door open for others to come in later.

Opponents of world government argue that the world has become more nationalistic in the past ten years and that nations are less likely than ever to give up power to a superstate.

They point out the difficulties of representation in such a world government: Are the numbers of people to be the basis for representation? Regardless of education? Or of previous experience with democracy? Are power, wealth, industrial potential to be considered? Wouldn't one nation really come to dominate a world parliament? Would this be China, the Soviet Union, or the United States?

They stress the defects of the League of Nations and the United Nations to show the difficulties of world government. These opponents do not want the United States to give up any power to any kind of world government.

THE HOPE. These alternatives for international organizations will change. New ones will be advocated. Old policies may be restored.

Republicans and Democrats, regardless of which party is in control, cannot escape the difficulties of world leadership. The price of our strength, our past successes, and the present condition of the United Nations is that, right or wrong, our attitudes toward international organizations will affect the life of each of us in the United States and in the world.

The hopes and doubts of all mankind were expressed by Pope Paul VI when he addressed the General Assembly of the United Nations on October 4, 1965. He asked in his speech,

"Will the world ever succeed in changing that selfish and bellicose mentality which, up to now, has been interwoven into so much of its history?" He answered in these wise words,

"This is hard to foresee; but it is easy to affirm that we must resolutely take the road towards a new history, a peaceful history, one that will be truly and fully human, the very history God promised to men of good will."

This is the spirit in which international organizations must be developed. It is easy to scoff at mistakes, to say "I told you so" when an ally acts differently from the way we would, when a nation uses force instead of persuasion, or when the UN fails.

It may be pleasant to read the sports news, the movie gossip, or the comics and to skip the foreign news, but we cannot hide our heads in the sand on international affairs. The final test is: Will we, the American people, measure up to the important place we now hold in world affairs?

STUDY QUESTIONS

1. What is the present world balance of power?

2. What are examples of formal international agreements? of informal agreements?

3. How effective is international law?

4. Why have international organizations for specific purposes been successful?

5. In what ways was the League of Nations a success? Why did it fail?

6. Compare the executive, legislative, and judicial branches of the United Nations charter with those of the United States Constitution.

7. Who are members of the General Assembly? What powers does the General Assembly have?

8. Who are members of the Security Council? What powers does the Security Council have?

CONCEPTS AND GENERALIZATIONS

1
The most common method for trying to maintain peace has been by the balance of power strategy.

2
International agreements and international law have helped to maintain peaceful relations among nations, but they have not been enforceable if a nation wished to violate them.

3
International organizations with a specific purpose—such as the Universal Postal Union—have been successful.

4
The United Nations was designed to keep the peace by giving power in the Security Council to the great nations, who were expected to work together.

5
The General Assembly, in which each nation has one vote, provides a forum where the propaganda and discussion of views of any nation may be heard.

6
The executive branch of the United Nations is the Secretariat, headed by the Secretary General.

7
The International Court of Justice settles disputes submitted to it by members and nonmembers of the United Nations.

8
The Economic and Social Council of the United Nations through specialized agencies tries to prevent war by assisting in the solution of health, education, and economic problems of developing nations.

9
The issues of sovereignty, finance, and voting are serious obstacles to the effectiveness of the United Nations.

10
While the United Nations has demonstrated great usefulness, its weaknesses are causing some people to examine the alternatives of a new isolation policy or of a world government organization.

9. What are the duties of the Secretary General?

10. How does the International Court of Justice function?

11. Why was the trusteeship system made a part of the United Nations?

12. How does the United Nations try to settle international disputes?

13. How can the United Nations charter be changed?

14. How has the admission of new members changed the voting strength in the General Assembly?

15. What are the strengths and weaknesses of the United Nations?

16. What are the alternatives to the United Nations?

IDEAS FOR DISCUSSION

1. Is war inevitable? Is human nature such that wars are necessary?

2. How does international law compare with criminal law?

3. Is a balance-of-power system a necessary part of international organization?

4. How does the preamble to the United States Constitution compare with the preamble to the United Nations charter?

5. Which organ of the UN has the real power —the Security Council; the General Assembly; the Secretariat; the specialized agencies?

6. At the tenth anniversary of the beginning of the United Nations in San Francisco, President Eisenhower made a speech in which he tried to show that peace could be obtained by:

a) recognizing that mankind has individual rights, divinely bestowed and limited only by the obligation to avoid infringement upon the rights of others;

b) assuming that all people have the inherent right to the kind of government under which they choose to live;

c) having access to knowledge and education;

d) accepting the conviction that no nation has the right to employ force aggressively against any other.

How far has the world moved toward these ideals?

7. Do you favor abolishing the veto power in the Security Council? Why? How could this be done?

8. How could the International Court of Justice be made more effective?

9. A Washington newspaper correspondent, commenting on the criticisms of the UN in this country, wrote, ". . . some forty new members were admitted to full and equal voting rights in the General Assembly. Our old majority was swamped by the new nations. . . . Thus far we have been able to win satisfactory majorities on most questions. But we are afloat in the turbulent sea of the new UN parliamentary diplomacy." Has the admission of new members changed the position of the United States in the UN? Does the United States have less influence in the UN?

10. Should the United States give up some of its sovereignty to the United Nations?

11. What improvements for financing the United Nations do you consider desirable? practical?

12. Where do you place yourself on the isolation–world government scale? Why?

13. The constitution of the United Nations Educational, Scientific, and Cultural Organization (UNESCO) begins with these words: "Since wars begin in the minds of men, it is in the minds of men that the defenses of peace must be constructed." Some people have objected to this statement on the basis that wars do not begin in the minds of men. Do you agree or disagree with the UNESCO statement?

THINGS TO DO

1. Write a short play or story based on the Rip Van Winkle theme in which a man falls asleep after the creation of the League of Nations and wakes up this year. Describe his reactions to our present ideas of war and peace.

2. Prepare a special report on one special international organization. Examples are the Universal Postal Union, the International Bureau of Weights and Measures, the International Red Cross, the Organization of American States, the World Meteorological Organization, the World Health Organization.

3. Hold a panel discussion on the topic, "The League of Nations would have succeeded if the United States had been a member."

4. Prepare a special report on the failure of some nations to pay assessments to the United Nations.

5. Organize special committees to study and report on the special organs and agencies of the United Nations.

6. Prepare a report on Trygve Lie, Dag Hammarskjöld, or U Thant, each of whom has been Secretary General of the UN.

7. Interview citizens in your community who belong to organizations that are opposed to the UN. Interview citizens who belong to organizations that want some stronger international organization than the UN. In addition, members of these organizations might be interviewed: the American Legion, the American Bar Association, the local council of churches, the Daughters of the American Revolution, the League of Women Voters. Report your interviews to the class.

8. Hold a mock meeting of the UN Security Council.

9. Draw a cartoon illustrating the way in which the veto has been used in the Security Council.

10. Investigate the Universal Declaration of Human Rights to determine the basic arguments of those in our country who advocate it and those who oppose it.

11. Draw a replica of the UN flag and explain the meanings of the symbols.

12. Prepare a special report on the withdrawal of Indonesia from the United Nations.

13. Design a pattern for voting in the General Assembly which you consider superior to the present one-nation, one-vote system.

FURTHER READINGS

Barnett, A. Doak, and Reischauer, Edwin A., THE UNITED STATES AND CHINA. Praeger Publishers, Inc., 1970.

Bingham, June, U THANT: THE SEARCH FOR PEACE. Alfred A. Knopf, Inc., 1966.

Boyd, Andrew, UNITED NATIONS: PIETY, MYTH, AND TRUTH. Penguin Books, Inc., 1963. (Paperback edition)

Carr, Albert Z., A MATTER OF LIFE AND DEATH: HOW WARS GET STARTED—OR ARE PREVENTED. Viking Press, 1967. (Paperback edition)

Cox, Robert W., ed., THE POLITICS OF INTERNATIONAL ORGANIZATIONS: STUDIES IN MULTILATERAL SOCIAL AND ECONOMIC AGENCIES. Praeger Publishers, Inc., 1970.

Davis, K. S., THE POLITICS OF HONOR: THE LIFE OF ADLAI E. STEVENSON. G. P. Putnam's Sons, 1967.

Ferguson, John H., and McHenry, Dean E., THE AMERICAN SYSTEM OF GOVERNMENT. McGraw-Hill Book Co., Inc., 1967. Chapter 20.

Fisher, Roger, INTERNATIONAL CONFLICT FOR BEGINNERS. Harper and Row, Publishers, 1969.

Hammarskjold, Dag, MARKINGS. Alfred A. Knopf, Inc., 1964.

Holcombe, Arthur N., A STRATEGY OF PEACE IN A CHANGING WORLD. Harvard University Press, 1967.

Lash, Joseph P., DAG HAMMARSKJOLD. Doubleday & Co., Inc., 1961.

Lodge, George C., ENGINES OF CHANGE. Alfred A. Knopf, Inc., 1970.

MacVane, John, THE HOUSE THAT PEACE BUILT—THE UNITED NATIONS. Public Affairs Pamphlet, 1967.

Settel, T. S., ed., THE LIGHT AND THE ROCK: THE VISION OF DAG HAMMARSKJOLD. E. P. Dutton & Co., 1966.

Szulc, Tad, LATIN AMERICA. Atheneum Publishers, 1966.

Tavares, Hernane de Sá, THE PLAY WITHIN THE PLAY: THE INSIDE STORY OF THE UN. Alfred A. Knopf, Inc., 1966.

Ward, Barbara, FIVE IDEAS THAT CHANGED THE WORLD. W. W. Norton Co., Inc., 1959.

THE LANGUAGE OF GOVERNMENT

AUTHORITARIANISM — governmental system in which the people are forced to give unquestioned obedience to the person or group in power.

CAPITALISM—economic system based on the private ownership of the means of production and distribution.

COMMON LAW—the unwritten laws of a nation based on court decisions and custom; the law and decisions of the courts in England.

COMMUNISM—system of government in which the state has supremacy over the rights of the individual; economic system in which the government owns the means of production and distribution.

DEMOCRACY—government by direct or indirect participation of the people.

ELITISM—system in which one individual or small group is superior to the other people, or assumes this superiority.

LAISSEZ FAIRE—system in which the government does not interfere with the operation of business in any way; to do as one pleases.

PARLIAMENTARY—system of democratic government which does not have separation of powers but places the power in the legislature.

REPUBLIC—government by the people through elected representatives.

SOCIALISM—economic system in which government owns and operates the major industries.

TOTALITARIANISM—system of government in which the total life of the individual is under the control of the government; total dictatorship.

VOTE OF CONFIDENCE—the vote in a parliament on an issue to determine whether the prime minister shall continue in office or be required to call an election.

WELFARE STATE—system of government in which government has taken over responsibility for protecting citizens against economic and social hazards, such as unemployment and sickness.

THE LANGUAGE OF GOVERNMENT

Point out that a study of comparative governments is actually a study of comparative political systems because a government is only part of a political system.

28

Comparative Government

Nationalism has been the predominant force in international affairs for years. The nation-state has been the building block of international relations. While international organizations like the United Nations have had some success, the major impact on world affairs has been the conduct of the nations themselves. Since nations are governed in different ways, it is necessary to know something about their varied forms of government in order to understand better the subtleties of international relations.

The basic idea of the democratic form of government in the United States is that men can govern themselves. Four fundamental ingredients make up this self-government, as was pointed out in Chapter 1. These are liberty, concern for the general welfare, majority rule, and respect for the rights of minorities. The degree to which these ideas can be made to function effectively for all citizens determines the effectiveness of our system of government in achieving democracy.

Not all governments subscribe to these basic ideas. Some deny them; others uphold them. Ours is not the only country that has a democratic system of government. Many nations are democracies. There are also nations which call themselves democracies but are that in name only. Among the democracies and nondemocracies there are systems of government which differ markedly from our own. An understanding of these governments helps provide a fuller understanding of our own system and of the differences between our government and others.

Chief among other contrasting systems of government are the *parliamentary* democracies and the communist *authoritarian* systems. An example of an important parliamentary system is the government of Great Britain. Examples of communist governments are those of the Soviet Union, China, and Cuba.

THE GOVERNMENT OF BRITAIN

The parliamentary system of Great Britain is a democracy. In some respects it is like our own in that it has a legislative branch of two houses, the House of Commons and the House of Lords, and in that the government reflects the will and voice of the people through popular elections. The government is based upon law, as is our own.

But the differences between our form of government and that of Great Britain are many. The titular head of the British government is a king or a queen (this person is head in name only). The king has little power in the actual operation of the government. He is the ruler largely for ceremonial purposes. However, the figure and image of the monarch provide a unifying factor for the United Kingdom.

The real power of the British government rests in the House of Commons, the Cabinet, and the Prime Minister. The members of the House of Commons are

As head of the British Commonwealth of Nations, Queen Elizabeth II pays a visit to the Canadian capital of Ottawa in 1967. (Canadian National Film Board photo)

elected by the people, with each member elected by a district. The member need not be, and often is not, a resident of the district from which he is elected; thus, a member is not considered a representative of a district. Rather his constituency is the whole nation.

Great Britain has a strong two-party political system. Currently the Labour and Conservative Parties are in control, although at times a strong third party has gained power, as in the case of the Liberal Party. The Prime Minister is the leader of the majority party in the House of Commons. He is appointed by the monarch, but his appointment is a formality, since the monarch appoints the person who is the recognized leader of the majority party and who can get the support of the majority in Parliament.

After his appointment, the Prime Minister forms a Ministry, or Cabinet, of some twenty members, who operate the government according to laws and policies determined by Parliament. Great Britain does not have a written constitution, but operates under *common law*, an unwritten body of law which comprises the judicial precedents and customs that have developed over the centuries.

The length of the term of a Parliament is five years or less. It is less than its full length when the Prime Minister asks the monarch to dissolve the Parliament to call for an election. This happens when the House of Commons fails to give the Prime Minister a *vote of confidence* by defeating a measure which he proposes. Then he either resigns or calls for a new election. When a new election is called, the Prime Minister, in a sense, goes to the people to determine whether they wish to send to Parliament individuals who support his program. He retains or loses his position according to the vote of the people.

The House of Lords, which is the upper house of Parliament, has little legislative authority. While at one time it was the ruling body, its power was gradually taken away by the House of Commons. Its members are not elected. They get their seats in the House of Lords by inheritance or because of their positions as knights or as leaders in the Church of England.

The parliamentary system of government does not have the separation of powers among the three branches of government as we know it in the United States. The British Cabinet system combines the executive and legislative branches largely in the Prime Minister, the Ministry, and the Parliament. The judicial branch is separate, although the House of Lords may serve as a court of appeals in certain cases.

Many other nations have parliamentary systems of government similar to that of Great Britain. While they may differ in some details, their operation is similar to the British system in that power usually rests in the legislative body and the prime minister. But there are also important differences among them. For example, France has a parliamentary form of government, but it has a president and a multiparty system. Its constitution of 1958 gives vast powers to the president.

THE GOVERNMENT OF THE SOVIET UNION

In an authoritarian system the power of government is concentrated in one individual or in a small group of people. This individual or small group exercises complete executive power. It also has complete control over legislative and judicial powers. If there is a legislature, its members are dominated by the executive and pass legislation which the executive directs. The courts, too, are controlled by the executive. They interpret

A nation such as the present Soviet Union, which is run by a relatively small group of people, is sometimes referred to as an oligarchy.

Soviet leaders address the World Conference of Communist Parties in Moscow in 1969. The men are, left to right, Soviet Premier Alexei Kosygin, Soviet Communist Party Leader Leonid Brezhnev, and Soviet President Nikolai Podgorny. In his speech, Brezhnev accused Red China of planning war against the Soviet Union. (UPI cablephoto)

laws and pass judgments according to his wishes. Elections, if held, are also controlled, and only candidates approved by the executive appear on the ballot. Usually there is also a one-party system with the control of the party and of the government in the hands of the same individual or small group.

Past examples of such authoritarian systems were the governments of Nazi Germany under Adolf Hitler and Fascist Italy under Benito Mussolini. Today the communist governments of the Soviet Union and Communist China are outstanding examples of authoritarian governments.

The authoritarianism of the Soviet Union is based on the economic and political ideas of Karl Marx. The present Soviet government was established during World War I through a revolution against the despotic and authoritarian rule of the Russian czars. But the government that developed after the revolution has been as authoritarian as that of the czars.

The government of the Soviet Union, actually the Union of Soviet Socialist Republics, is generally called communistic because of its basis in Marx's communism and because of its control by the Communist Party. The system is a one-party system with the party in control of all aspects of economic, social, and political life.

The party in Russia operates differently from political parties in the United States and Great Britain. The Communist Party in Russia does not seek members as do parties in our country. It is a privilege and a distinction to get into it. Admittance to the Party means acceptance into the power structure of the Soviet Union.

Elections are held, but these differ from ours. There is only one party—the Communist Party—on the ballot, and only approved names appear on the ballot. Elections are a formality, for voters have no choice between opposing candidates of different parties.

The governmental control is in the Presidium of the Supreme Soviet. Its members are the top officials of the central government and of the political subdivisions. Heading the government is the premier, who is often in control of the party. His is a position of great power, and he retains it as long as he can control all aspects of the government and of the party. Force, intrigue, and intimidation have frequently been used to gain and keep this power. Not only the executive departments, but also the legislature and the courts are dominated by the power of the premier and party leader.

In recent years the power of the premier has been reduced. Other officials have a voice, and the government has become somewhat more responsive to the pressures of outspoken critics. Still, institutions, legislative bodies, and courts make their decisions and render their verdicts in keeping with the wishes of the dictatorship. Governmental operation and administration in Russia and in the other authoritarian nations is very different from that which we know in a democratic system.

Having now had this brief background of parliamentary governments, as in Great Britain, and of authoritarian governments, as in the Soviet Union, following an extensive study of our own democratic system, our discussion and study of government will examine a philosophical and theoretical analysis of government.

THE BASIC CLASSIFICATION OF GOVERNMENTS
The basic way to classify all governments is to divide them into two types:

1. Those that adhere to the idea that people can govern themselves: *democratic* governments.

2. Those who believe that people cannot govern themselves: *authoritarian* governments. These hold that individuals must obey an authority over which the people have no control. This higher authority, be it a king or a dictator, is not chosen by the people.

The difference between these types is not necessarily always sharp and clear. Each may contain elements of the other.

DEMOCRATIC GOVERNMENTS. Democracies can be divided into two major types:

1. *Direct democracy* (often called pure democracy). Direct democracy can be seen in the town meeting. Here people participate directly in government. They are individually involved in making decisions about their government. They decide issues and determine procedures.

2. *Indirect* or *representative democracy.* In an indirect or representative democracy, representatives elected by the people make decisions for them. Such a democracy is also called a *republic.*

Which of the above types of democracy exists in any given place depends largely on the size and complexity of the community. Thus, direct democracy could be practiced in the small city-state of ancient Athens because each citizen could attend the lawmaking assembly and make his opinions heard. He voted on the proposed laws for his community. This kind of direct democracy can be found today in some small New England communities where all citizens can come together in a town meeting to make or change the laws of the community. The citizen directly controls the government.

When the community becomes too large, it becomes too difficult for each citizen to participate personally in the operation of the government. Instead, the people elect representatives to govern in their place, creating a representative democracy or a republic. Our large cities, as well as our state and national governments, use the representative form of democratic government.

AUTHORITARIAN GOVERNMENTS. There are all degrees of authoritarianism in government. A government may have a great deal of authority, such as our

Mention that the word "democracy" means "people rule," from the Greek word *demos* meaning "the people."

A BRITISH STATESMAN BECOMES AN AMERICAN CITIZEN

"I cannot help reflecting that if my father had been an American and my mother British, instead of the other way round, I might have got here on my own."

So spoke Winston Churchill as he addressed the members of the Congress of the United States when he recalled for them the circumstance of birth which made him British and not American. He was the son of a British lord and an American beauty. Had it been the other way around, he might well have become the President of the United States instead of the Prime Minister of Great Britain.

Born in 1874, Winston Churchill lived for more than ninety years to help shape the destiny of a nation and the world. During those long years he lived a rich and eventful life, serving his country as Prime Minister on several occasions. He was a member of Parliament for much of his adult life. Besides being Prime Minister, at one time or another he was home secretary, first lord of the admiralty, secretary of state for war and air, chancellor of the exchequer, first lord of the treasury, and minister of defense.

Among his chief interests were naval service and writing. As first lord of the admiralty he prepared the British navy for World War I. As a writer he achieved fame and wealth and was awarded the Nobel prize for literature in 1953. Among his chief writings are six volumes on *The Second World War* and *A History of the English-Speaking Peoples* in four volumes.

Churchill's greatest service to his country and the world came during the dark days of World War II. As Prime Minister he told the British people, "I have nothing to offer but blood, toil, tears, and sweat." But he never lost courage, confident that Great Britain and her allies would gain the final victory. His optimism heartened his countrymen, and his "V for Victory" became their rallying cry. The successful end of the war justified this optimism.

His life was not all success and victory, however. He was defeated in his first try for a seat in Parliament. He resigned his admiralty position under criticism during World War I. His party was defeated in 1945, and he lost the prime ministership. Always, however, he came back from defeat with greater accomplishments and service.

Churchill's fame and friendships were not limited to England. He also had many friends and admirers on this side of the Atlantic. Two of his warmest friends were Presidents Franklin D. Roosevelt and Dwight D. Eisenhower. Congressmen and senators looked on him as one of the great leaders of this century. By a congressional act in 1963 they made him an honorary citizen of the United States.

national government, and still be democratic so long as the people are directly or indirectly in control of that government. When the authority of the government is no longer under the control of the people, there is no longer a democracy but an authoritarian form of government.

The most extreme form of authoritarianism is *totalitarianism*—a total dictatorship. This form of government is the exact opposite of direct or pure democracy. Complete totalitarianism has probably never been achieved, although some recent dictatorships, such as Germany under Adolf Hitler, the Soviet Union under Joseph Stalin, and China under Mao Tse-tung, have come very close to being totalitarian dictatorships. Under totalitarianism the total life of an individual is under the control of the government. The government is not merely satisfied to control the actions of its citizens, it seeks to control even their thoughts. No self-government is permitted; the dictator seeks to eliminate any individuality that citizens may possess. Each person must behave and think as the dictator tells him.

Include in your discussion some of the more famous dictatorships in Latin America such as those of Juan Perón of Argentina and Rafael Trujillo of the Dominican Republic.

The U.S.S.R. today is still authoritarian and still a dictatorship, but it is less authoritarian than it was under the harsh dictatorship of Stalin. The dictatorship in Yugoslavia is *less* authoritarian than that of the U.S.S.R., while the dictatorship of China is *more* authoritarian than that of the U.S.S.R. All of these governments, whether more or less authoritarian, are, nevertheless, authoritarian rather than democratic, because *most* of the control of the political power is centered in a small group of communist leaders rather than in the people. Some dictatorships may someday become democracies if the control of power shifts to the people. Some writers think that this shift may be taking place in such countries as Spain and Yugoslavia.

Most of the governments of the world have been and still are authoritarian. Occasionally democracy has existed at certain times and in certain places. Democracy is not easily established. However, when a democracy is firmly established and nourished for a long period of time, it becomes a hardy organism able to withstand attacks by those who would destroy it. But even under these favorable conditions, democratic government must not be taken for granted.

The question is often asked, "Will our increasingly complex American civilization, which has led to a greater amount of government control or regulation, end up with an authoritarian government and, perhaps, even a dictatorship?" It is hard for experts to see how the authority of our government will decrease; it will, they predict, almost certainly increase. However, even though governmental authority or control over our lives increases, as it apparently must, our government will remain democratic so long as the government is under the control of and responsive to the wishes of the people.

CLASSIFICATION OF GOVERNMENTS ACCORDING TO HOW THE POLITICAL POWER IS DISTRIBUTED

Most of us are citizens of several governments. We may be citizens of various local govern-

The 482 elected deputies of the French National Assembly hold their legislative sessions in this former palace in Paris. (French Govt. Tourist Office)

ments: township, village, town, city, county. We may be citizens of a certain state, and all of us are citizens of a certain nation. A political system can be classified according to how the political power is distributed among the various governments within its jurisdiction. There are three types of government determined by how the power is distributed:

1. UNITARY GOVERNMENT. Here the political power is concentrated in a central government. For example, Great Britain and France have unitary governments. In Great Britain the local governments were created by Parliament, and they cannot overstep the authority given them by Parliament. Thus, the power is primarily in the hands of the central or national government.

2. CONFEDERATE GOVERNMENT. This is the opposite of a unitary government. Here the power is located in the various state or local governments. Our country began with a confederate government which put most of the power in the hands of the thirteen states and gave very little power to the central or national government. This was one of the major weaknesses during the critical period when the Articles of Confederation were in effect. The thirteen states could not be held together, and there was great danger that the new nation known as the United States of America would fall apart and become thirteen separate nations. The United Nations, a loose confederation, is today in a somewhat similar critical situation.

3. FEDERAL GOVERNMENT. Federalism does not give the bulk of power either to the national government or to the state governments. Instead, there is a division of power between the two levels. Most federal systems of government require a written constitution to specify clearly the different areas of power between the two

The Gothic-style Parliament Buildings in Ottawa are the seat of the Canadian government. (Canadian Govt. Travel Bureau photo)

governments. Great Britain, a unitary government, does not have a written constitution, but France, another unitary government, does have one.

It is important to keep in mind that the classification of governments into unitary, confederate, or federal does not tell whether or not they are democratic or authoritarian. It is true that most authoritarian governments, such as an absolute monarchy or a dictatorship, are also unitary governments. However, some unitary governments, such as Great Britain and France, are democracies. On the other hand, although most federal governments, such as the United States, Canada, Switzerland, and Australia, are democracies, the Soviet Union is set up by its 1936 constitution in the form of a federal government, even though in reality it concentrates most of the power in the central government.

CLASSIFICATION OF
GOVERNMENTS ACCORDING
TO THE ROLE THEY PLAY IN
THE ECONOMIC LIFE OF THE
COUNTRY   Because communism, socialism, and capitalism involve government in
certain relationships, differences in governments according to the role they play in the
economic life of the country must be considered. The extent to which the government is involved in the economic life determines its place on this spectrum. On one
extreme is *laissez-faire* capitalism, in which
the government permits complete economic
freedom without interference in business
activity. Diametrically opposed to *laissez-
faire* capitalism is *communism*, in which
there is little or no private ownership.
Since the government owns just about
everything, there is little or no free enterprise, thus, little or no competition. Prices
are determined by the government, not by
the open market.

MIXED ECONOMIES. Between these
two extremes are all shades of differences
which are often referred to as *mixed economies. Socialism* is a mixed economic system in that the government owns the major
industries, such as steel, coal, the railroads,
and the airlines. The rest of the economy
is generally permitted to have private ownership, free enterprise, and competition in
the market place.

CAPITALISM. Capitalism is an economic system in which the means of production and distribution, capital, are *privately
owned.* These means include factories,
transportation systems, businesses, industries, as well as wholesale and retail stores.
Each business seeks to make a *profit,* to
receive more money for its product than
it cost to manufacture, to transport, and
to sell the product. The business is in *competition* with other businesses making similar products or providing similar services.

The *price* is determined by the market
place and the operation of the *law of supply
and demand.* Under the law of supply and
demand, as the demand for a product goes
up, as people want more of a certain product, the price tends to go up. But as the
price increases, the demand tends to go
down. This decrease in demand tends to
lower prices, and lowered prices again tend
to increase demand. Supply and demand
vary with increase and decrease of prices.
Eventually, supply and demand balance,
creating a market price.

An important feature of capitalism is
free enterprise, the freedom to start and
operate a business subject to certain legal
restrictions and regulations. The business
is generally free to operate as it wishes,
to gain the largest possible profit through
competition with other businesses in the
same industry.

Laissez-faire capitalism simply means capitalism which is free from any governmental
interference. Our present economy in the
United States is certainly not one of *laissez-
faire* capitalism. Based on the writings of
Adam Smith, who is regarded as the father
of *laissez-faire* capitalism, early *laissez-faire*
capitalists argued that the public was the
ultimate benefactor of *laissez-faire* capitalism, since competition tended to drive
prices of goods downward. In other words,
"private greed led to public good." Unfortunately, many producers decided that
while competition benefited the public by
keeping prices down, it hurt the producer
because it also kept profits down. Hence,
there developed pools, trusts, and other
forms of monopoly in order to eliminate
competition and keep prices, and thus
profits, high. The public was hurt, while
monopolistic capitalists reaped enormous
profits. Because we are a political democracy, many citizens put pressure on Congress to pass laws to protect the consumer.

The capitalist could hardly argue that with monopolies the public good was benefiting from private greed.

As a result of pressure by the Populists and later by the *muckrakers*, many laws were passed which transformed our economic system. For example, there are the Sherman Antitrust Law, the Clayton Act, the Pure Food and Drug Act, as well as the Sixteenth (or Income Tax) Amendment. Under the New Deal of the 1930's, the second phase of the transformation took place with laws concerning collective bargaining, child labor, minimum wages, and social security.

Today, there are not many who would claim that we have *laissez-faire* capitalism in the United States. The government is now an integral part of our economy. For example, the government is expected to prevent depressions. Even recessions and moderate unemployment are matters in which the government is expected to act. Today, as in the case of TVA, government is in the electric power business. It is also the largest participant in scientific research and technological development. It is the principal purchaser of missiles and aircraft. In short, *laissez-faire* capitalism does not exist in present day America.

COMMUNISM. Karl Marx (1818-1883) saw the effects of nineteenth-century *laissez-faire* capitalism upon the factory workers in Germany, France, and especially England where the industrial revolution had started and was, therefore, most advanced. He wrote his chief work *Das Kapital* (which is the German word for capital or capitalism) as a criticism of nineteenth-century *laissez-faire* capitalism. From his writing and thinking, as well as that of others, developed communism.

Under communism there is public ownership of business. Since the government owns all businesses, there is, of course, no

Because the government owns all businesses under communism, these Russian factory workers are the employees of the state. (TASS from SOVFOTO)

competition, nor are prices set by the market; instead, the government determines the prices on all items. Free enterprise, that is the right to start and run a business as one sees fit, is not possible under communism, since it is the government that decides which businesses shall be allowed to exist and how they shall be run. Under communism, the business of government is business.

SOCIALISM. Somewhere between capitalism and communism is socialism. Under socialism the government is an active participant in the economy because it owns the *major industries* of a nation. Since the government of the United States has not entered into the ownership of the major industries, it can be said that we do not have socialism in our country. Some economists argue, however, that it is not public ownership that makes an economy socialistic, but rather the degree of government regulation. In this sense, they argue, our economy is socialistic, since the amount of government regulation is enormous and growing.

CLASSIFICATION OF GOVERNMENTS BY THEIR CONCERN FOR THE WELFARE OF THE PEOPLE

Yet another way of classifying governments is according to the degree to which they concern themselves with the welfare of the people. Our government has always been concerned with the welfare of the people, for one of the goals stated in the Preamble to the Constitution is "to promote the general welfare."

In many ways our government has aided various segments of our country. Schools, canals, railroads, rural electrification, farm price supports, collective bargaining, subsidies, flood control, social security, urban renewal, and the war on poverty are all examples of how our government has increasingly tried to improve the general welfare of our people. Today, our government is doing so much for the welfare of the people that critics have called our country a *welfare state*, just as England, France, and the Scandinavian countries are often referred to as welfare states.

Both socialism and communism endorsed the welfare state idea. The essential difference is that most socialistic countries are democratic, both politically and economically, while most communist countries are authoritarian dictatorships, both politically and economically. Thus, under socialism the citizens have a large voice in what governments do for them, and this is also true in our own modern *non-laissez-faire* capitalistic system.

Most governments today are operating in varying degrees as welfare states. Under modern *(non-laissez-faire)* capitalism and socialism, the people are regarded by the government as being capable of judging what kind of welfare state is best for them. Under communism the people are told

On a kibbutz, or collective farm in Israel, children are cared for, in groups, while their parents are busy working. (Israel Information Services)

what is best for them and have little voice in their own welfare. In the last few years the Soviet government has been working out "new" economic ideas to make its system more responsive to the desires and needs of the Soviet people. In this sense it may be said that the Soviet economy is becoming less authoritarian. However, it remains authoritarian enough to continue to be called a dictatorship.

President Nixon is greeted by Mao Tse-tung, Chairman of the Chinese Communist Party. (UPI photo)

CLASSIFICATION OF GOVERNMENTS ACCORDING TO THEIR VIEWS OF HUMAN NATURE

Governments can be classified according to their optimistic or pessimistic views of human nature. Democratic governments are generally optimistic about human nature. This is to be expected, since democratic government is based upon a fundamental belief in the ability of people to rule themselves. To those who believe in democracy, individuals are, on the whole, good and capable of governing themselves. They recognize, however, that while *most* people are good and will do the right thing even when a policeman is not watching, there are some people who, for various reasons, are a danger to society and must be controlled by laws and enforcement officials.

Authoritarian governments are generally pessimistic about human nature. The average person is seen as being weak-willed and incapable of ruling himself. Indeed, the average person is seen as not truly knowing what is good for him. Thus, most authoritarian governments are based upon the principle of *elitism*; that is, there must be leaders who are superior—physically, intellectually, or morally—and the people must for their own good faithfully follow the leadership of the superior elite. During most of man's history, and even today, the pessimistic view of human nature was the one most commonly held. Therefore, it is not surprising that most governments have been aristocracies, monarchies, dictatorships, or some other form of authoritarian government.

The first quarter of the twentieth century saw the rejection of the monarchy as an effective form of authoritarian government. Fascism and communism rose as new threats to the democratic conception of government. Both fascism and communism are extreme forms of authoritarian government. Germany under Hitler, the Soviet Union under Stalin, and China under Mao Tse-tung are examples of authoritarian governments approaching totalitarianism.

There is an important difference between fascism and communism and, oddly enough, it has to do with a difference in the way human nature is conceived. The communists profess to have an optimistic view of human nature. They say that human nature is basically good and that government can either reinforce or distort that goodness. Government under capitalism, they say, has miseducated the people to be greedy and to exploit their fellowman. Merely doing away with the government will not be enough, they say, because the capitalists will continue to seek profits at the expense of the other members of society. The "poisons" of capitalism must be thoroughly removed from the people by a rigid system of education. This will require a period of dictatorship, a *dictatorship of the proletariat*, the workers.

When the entire world has become communistic, when all the people of the world have been educated to the virtues of communism so that no one will take advantage of anyone else, then the dictatorship will wither away and the people will live happily forever. In short, the communists believe that man has the capacity for being good, but to make that capacity come true he must be educated properly. They believe they know how to do it; and they believe that this education must be given by an intellectual elite, the Communist Party and its leaders, under an authoritarian government.

Fascism takes a pessimistic view of human nature. One example was the Nazi Party in Germany, *Nazi* being an abbreviation for National Socialist Party. It was not socialistic, except in name, but it was nationalistic and elitist. It was an authoritarian and dictatorial type of government founded upon a pessimistic view that the average man is unable to know what is best for him. It maintained that man needs a leader to show him what to do, and this is, of course, why dictators like Hitler and Mussolini were felt to be necessary.

Nazism or fascism is thus based upon the elite or leadership principle. Hitler carried this leadership principle further by bringing in racial superiority. He argued that the Germans needed a leader like himself to direct them. The Germans were told by Hitler that they were superior to the other people of the world and, thus, were destined to be the leaders of the other races.

Unlike communists, the Nazis never claimed that each person could be educated **or trained to rule himself. Most people, the Nazis claimed, are born weak and there is little that they could do to change matters. Not only that, but certain unfortunate people were declared to be so inferior that they should be liquidated and removed from the earth.** This led to the almost unbelievable horror of the Nazi concentration camps where millions of Jews, Poles, Russians, and others were cremated in gas ovens. Because of this, nazism never was and never could become a world movement like communism is. Few people will follow a movement that declares them to be inferior.

WHAT LIES AHEAD? Today, the struggle is between modern capitalism and democracy on the one hand and communism and authoritarianism on the other hand. Communism is optimistic. It claims that history is on its side and that the whole world will someday become communist. It offers hope to underdeveloped people to share in a better life more quickly through revolutions which will wipe out the traditional *status quo* social and economic systems, which the masses of people feel are holding them down. Communism, thus, has enormous appeal to the people that fascism never had.

Communist revolution does lead to social change, and it may even improve the standard of living of some persons. But, as in all revolutions, the cost in lives is usually staggering as force is used to gain and maintain control. Examples of this are the purges that have taken place in the Soviet

With respect to the struggle for men's minds, describe the somewhat unusual approach of the Alliance for Progress.

Prime Minister Indira Gandhi of India (left) is greeted by U Thant, Secretary General of the United Nations, during a visit to the United Nations in 1966. (Wide World photo)

Union and Red China. Equally terrible are the extreme political and economic restrictions imposed by the communist dictatorship upon the people whom it conquers.

What is often forgotten, however, is that people in most underdeveloped countries do not now have democratic governments or a democratic tradition. What they see, instead, is a choice between an existing authoritarian government, which is not changing rapidly enough to meet their rising expectations, and an authoritarian communistic government, which will radically change things.

Communism seeks to wipe out the privileged classes and to make all people equal, but it does so at the price of freedom. The equality of communism is the equality one finds in a prison, even though the jailers may claim to be working for the good of the prisoners and that no prisoner or group of prisoners will be given special privileges. The fact remains that the communist state is a prison, even though the promise exists that freedom from prison will come eventually.

CURRENT FRUSTRATIONS. It is frustrating for Americans to see communism win dominance in certain areas of the world. We see many corrupt and inefficient governments in underdeveloped countries, governments which are not meeting the needs of the majority of the people. The only thing that can be said in favor of some of these governments is that they are anti-communist. We would like to accelerate change in these countries, but we face the danger of either touching off a revolution which may benefit the communists, or being

There are at the present time two great nations in the world, which started from different points, but seem to tend toward the same end. I allude to the Russians and the Americans. Both of them have grown up unnoticed; and while the attention of mankind was directed elsewhere, they have suddenly placed themselves in the front rank among the nations, and the world learned their existence and their greatness at almost the same time.

. . . The American struggles against the obstacles that nature opposes to him; the adversaries of the Russian are men. The former combats the wilderness and savage life; the latter combats civilization with all its arms. . . . The American relies on personal interest to accomplish his ends and gives free scope to the unguided strength and common sense of the people; the Russian centers all the authority of society in a single arm. The principal instrument of the American is freedom; of the Russian, servitude. Their starting point is different and their courses are not the same; yet each of them seems marked out by the will of heaven to sway the destinies of half the globe.

—Written in 1835 by ALEXIS DE TOCQUEVILLE in *Democracy in America.*

accused of interfering in the internal affairs of another country.

It is frustrating for Americans to hear communists proclaim the superiority of their system in the face of our ever-increasing economic gains. Actually, the communist countries are suffering serious food shortages. They are unable to supply their people with goods which in this country are regarded as everyday necessities rather than the luxuries they are in communist countries.

It is frustrating for Americans to hear communists promise underdeveloped countries rapid economic development when after years of communist rule, the Soviet Union and Red China are still far behind the United States in economic development. In China poverty continues to be widespread. The lot of the average Russian may be improving, but one cannot help wondering if it might not have improved more rapidly under a democratic system, as it did in the United States and in Western Europe, without the loss of personal freedom required by communism.

It is frustrating for Americans to help other countries with sums of money unheard of in the past history of nations, only to hear that we are without real friends or reliable allies.

It is frustrating to hear the former colonial powers criticize our actions in trying to straighten out the bad situations left by them when they were forced out of their colonies. Their opportunity to create modern self-sufficient friendly nations had been shunted aside by their greed for exploitation. The United States now is trying to do in a short time and under communist pressure what the former colonial powers should have done years ago.

These things are frustrating, but it is the penalty the United States must pay for being one of the great powers in the world in the twentieth century. We must keep trying to do our best. The role that we are playing is a recent one for us, and we are not quite accustomed to the frustrations that attend our position in the world. We must accept the role and its frustrations or give up our leadership of the noncommunist nations of the world.

Because our economic system has worked production miracles, because we are working to clear up the pockets of poverty in our own country in order to give the good life to all Americans, because we seek the betterment of all the people of the world, because we have, above all, preserved and expanded the freedom and dignity of the individual, we must not lose hope or begrudge the sacrifices necessary to preserve and improve the gains we have made.

STUDY QUESTIONS

1. What has been the predominant force in international relations?

2. What is the basic idea behind our democratic form of government? What four fundamental ideas are essential for democratic government?

3. What are some important features of the British parliamentary system of government?

4. What is meant by common law?

5. What are some important features of the government of the Soviet Union?

6. What is the difference between democratic governments and authoritarian governments?

7. Explain what totalitarianism means.

8. Explain the difference between the unitary, confederate, and federal systems of government.

CONCEPTS AND GENERALIZATIONS

1
Not all governments accept our basic ingredients of government: liberty, concern for the general welfare, majority rule, and respect for the rights of minorities.

2
The government of Great Britain is an example of a parliamentary democracy.

3
A fundamental difference between the governments of Great Britain and the United States is the lack of the separation of powers in the former.

4
The government of the Soviet Union is an example of an authoritarian system, with power in the hands of an individual or a small group.

5
Basically governments may be classified as democratic or authoritarian.

6
Democracies are either direct or representative.

7
In a totalitarian system the whole life of the individual is controlled by the government.

8
When viewed in terms of their role in economic life, governments may be classified as communistic, socialistic, or capitalistic.

9
Free enterprise is a basic feature of the capitalistic system.

10
A government which provides many economic and social benefits for its citizens is said by some to be a welfare state.

11
When viewed in terms of their ideas about human nature, governments may be classified as optimistic or pessimistic.

12
Today's world is largely divided into nations which are democratic and, to some degree, capitalistic and those which are authoritarian, whether they have a communist or other form of government.

9. Why is *laissez-faire* capitalism the opposite of communism?

10. What are some of the most important characteristics of capitalism?

11. What is an important feature of socialism?

12. What is meant by the welfare state? What are the differences among welfare states under capitalism, under socialism, and under communism?

13. How is the view of human nature held by a person who believes in democracy similar to that held by a communist? How is it different?

14. What is the view of human nature held by the Nazis?

15. What are some of the problems faced by the United States in the second half of the twentieth century?

IDEAS FOR DISCUSSION

1. What is the difference between a right and a responsibility? What are the four fundamental beliefs related to the basic idea of democracy? Can you see how these ideas are tied together into two complementary pairs, each of which combines a right and a responsibility?

2. It is said that "the optimist sees the doughnut but the pessimist sees the hole." What is meant by this? Give some illustrations showing the difference between an optimist and a pessimist.

3. Why is the Nazi view of the average man called pessimistic? Why is the communist view called optimistic? What belief does communism share with democracy? What belief does communism share with fascism or nazism?

4. Why does fascism or nazism have so little appeal to the people of underdeveloped countries? Why is communism, on the other hand, so often appealing to people in underdeveloped countries?

5. Abraham Lincoln said our government was "of the people, by the people, and for the people." What does this mean? How is this different from the view of nazism or fascism? How is this different from the view of communism?

6. As our way of life becomes more and more complex, the authority of the government to regulate our lives increases. As a result, some thinkers claim that someday we may find ourselves living under an authoritarian government. Do you agree or disagree? Explain.

7. When the initiative, referendum, and recall were introduced into state government, they were said to be examples of *direct democracy* being injected into indirect democracy. Explain.

THINGS TO DO

1. Make a display poster showing the differences between the democratic and the authoritarian forms of government.

2. Construct charts which show:

a) The various degrees between the extremes of democracy and authoritarianism.

b) The various degrees of capitalism, socialism, and communism.

3. Write a research paper showing what the words "democracy" and "equality" meant to Jefferson, Lincoln, Hitler, Mussolini, Lenin, and Stalin.

4. Prepare a report for the class which traces the breakdown of the unity between the Soviet Union and Red China and the reasons for the internal turmoil in China today.

5. Develop a file of newspaper and magazine clippings which illustrate how the various civil rights which are enunciated in our Bill of Rights are violated by authoritarian governments.

6. Form a discussion panel of four students to discuss whether or not our federal system of government is becoming a unitary system and whether or not this poses a danger to our democracy.

7. Read George Orwell's *Animal Farm,* and then read a short account of the history of communism in the Soviet Union. Has Orwell's book, which was published in 1945, reflected or prophesied much of what has happened in the Soviet Union of today?

8. Prepare a bulletin board display of newspaper clippings, showing "Great Britain and the Soviet Union in Today's News."

FURTHER READINGS

Armstrong, John A., THE SOVIET UNION: TOWARD CONFRONTATION OR COEXISTENCE. Foreign Policy Association Headline Book, 1971. (Paperback edition)

Blondel, Jean, AN INTRODUCTION TO COMPARATIVE GOVERNMENT. Praeger Publishers, Inc., 1970.

Brumberg, Abraham, ed., IN QUEST OF JUSTICE: PROTEST AND DISSENT IN THE SOVIET UNION. Praeger Publishers, Inc., 1970.

Churchill, Randolph S., WINSTON S. CHURCHILL: YOUTH, 1874-1900. Houghton Mifflin Co., 1966.

Crankshaw, Edward, KHRUSHCHEV: A CAREER. Avon Book Div., Hearst Co., 1967. (Paperback)

Ebenstein, William, TODAY'S ISMS: COMMUNISM, FASCISM, SOCIALISM, CAPITALISM. Prentice-Hall, Inc., 1967.

———, TWO WAYS OF LIFE. Holt, Rinehart and Winston, Inc., 1964.

Goldston, Robert, THE RUSSIAN REVOLUTION. Bobbs-Merrill Company, Inc., 1966.

Hook, Sidney, MARX AND THE MARXISTS. D. Van Nostrand Co., Inc., 1955.

Jacobs, Dan N., ed., THE NEW COMMUNIST MANIFESTO AND RELATED DOCUMENTS. Harper & Row, Publishers, Inc., 1964.

Huntington, Samuel P., and Moore, Clement H., eds., AUTHORITARIAN POLITICS IN MODERN SOCIETY. Basic Books, 1970.

Ketchum, Richard M., WHAT IS COMMUNISM? E. P. Dutton & Co., 1955.

Lee, Baldwin, CAPITALISM AND OTHER ECONOMIC SYSTEMS. McGraw-Hill Book Co., Inc., 1959.

Lovenstein, Meno, CAPITALISM, COMMUNISM, SOCIALISM. Scott, Foresman and Co., 1962.

Michener, James A., THE BRIDGE AT ANDAU. Random House, Inc., 1957.

Miller, W. J., and others, THE MEANING OF COMMUNISM. Simon and Schuster, Inc., 1963.

Richards, Kenneth G., SIR WINSTON CHURCHILL. Childrens Press, Inc., 1968.

Rieber, Alfred J., and Nelson, Robert C., STUDY OF THE USSR AND COMMUNISM. G. P. Putnam's Sons, 1964.

Robottom, John, MODERN RUSSIA. McGraw-Hill Book Co., Inc., 1971.

Scholastic Magazines, editors, WHAT YOU SHOULD KNOW ABOUT COMMUNISM AND WHY. McGraw-Hill Book Co., Inc., 1965.

Shulman, Colette, WE THE RUSSIANS: VOICES FROM RUSSIA. Praeger Publishers, Inc., 1971.

Swearingen, Rodger, THE WORLD OF COMMUNISM. Houghton Mifflin Co., 1962.

Swisher, Earl, CHINA. Ginn and Co., 1964.

Walker, Patrick G., THE BRITISH CABINET. Basic Books, 1970.

The Pueblo *Incident*

On January 22, 1968, shortly before midnight Eastern Standard Time, the *Pueblo,* a United States intelligence ship was seized by four small North Korean boats and forced into the harbor at Wonsan, North Korea. The entire crew of eighty-three men was captured. The extent to which electronic gear and secret codes of the spy ship were captured was not known. This was the first time in over a hundred years that a U.S. Navy ship was taken on the high seas without a fight.

President Johnson was awakened at 1:45 A.M. and notified of this hijacking of the tiny ship, which was one of many similar ships used by the United States and the Soviet Union for purposes of espionage. The capture of the *Pueblo* followed an attempt by North Korean guerrillas earlier in the week to assassinate the president of South Korea.

The following log summarizes the events of this affair as they were reported by newspapers, radio, and television to the American people for five weeks.

Jan. 23—North Korea reported that the *Pueblo* had violated her territorial waters by entering inside the twelve-mile territorial limit.

The United States reported that the *Pueblo* was not inside the twelve-mile limit. Secretary of State Dean Rusk reported that the capture "was a matter of the utmost gravity" and advised the North Koreans "to cool it."

The Navy ordered the nuclear-powered aircraft carrier *Enterprise* to move into the Sea of Japan in the direction of North Korea. (Several other warships were reported being moved in the same direction. A Japanese newspaper released a picture which showed a Russian spy ship, similar in type to the *Pueblo* trailing the *Enterprise*.)

Jan. 24—President Johnson conferred with the National Security Council and appointed a special Planning Committee to deal with the crisis. He also met with key congressional committees.

A special meeting of the Korean Military Armistice Commission was held at Panmunjom, Korea, to consider the incident but resulted only in angry arguments between the American and North Korean representatives.

Jan. 25—Announcement was made that 14,787 air force and navy reservists were being called to active duty, and that a plea would be made to the United Nations.

The North Korean radio broadcast a supposed confession by Captain Bucher of the *Pueblo* which his wife and friends thought could not be his voice or his manner of expression.

Ambassador Thompson in Moscow, on Washington's instructions, urged the Soviet Union leaders "to convey our request" to North Korea for the immediate release of the American prisoners.

Jan. 26—In a short nationwide television broadcast to the American people, President Johnson said, "We shall continue to use every means available to find a prompt and peaceful solution." But he added, "This is a wanton and aggressive act and clearly cannot be accepted."

Ambassador Goldberg called on the UN Security Council "to act with the greatest urgency" and not force the United States to use "other courses which the UN charter reserves to member states." With charts he showed that the *Pueblo* had not entered North Korean territorial waters. Soviet Delegate Morozov requested the Council not to consider the issue, but was voted down twelve to three—with only Hungary and Algeria supporting Russia.

Jan. 26—North Korea declared, according to an Associated Press (AP) dispatch from Tokyo, that it would not recognize any Security Council resolution on the seizure of the *Pueblo* that covered up United States aggression. It said the nation was prepared for combat and could deliver the United States "an exterminatory blow." The statement contended that the UN had no right to discuss the *Pueblo's* seizure.

Idaho Senator Frank Church (D) called the seizure "an act of war, the ship must be returned at once, with all Americans aboard. Our national honor is at stake." Massachusetts Congressman William Bates (R) of the House Armed Services Committee called the incident, "a dastardly act of piracy." Kentucky Senator Thruston Morton (R) on a television program argued that the President had been unwise in announcing publicly that he had asked for Russia's help, "because this made it diplomatically impossible for Russia to come to our aid." Senate Majority Leader Mike Mansfield (D) of Montana warned, "We ought to keep our shirts on and not go off half-cocked until we know more."

Jan. 27—The Defense Department indicated that the *Pueblo* was seized twenty-five miles from the mainland of Korea and fifteen miles from Wonsan Harbor. The State Department insisted that the *Pueblo* was not engaged in any hostile action and had a right to be on the high seas off North Korea.

The Security Council adjourned for a weekend of private talks. Ethiopia suggested that North Korea be invited to tell her side of the story to the Council, since North Korea is not a member of the UN. Canada informally suggested that it serve as an intermediary "to exercise good offices"

between the United States and North Korea.

The United Press International (UPI) reported that the United States was soliciting a large number of countries for whatever aid they could provide for the release of the *Pueblo*, but administration spokesmen declined to say what diplomatic channels were being used.

Senator John Sparkman (D), Alabama, the second ranking member of the Senate Foreign Relations Committee, stated that the North Koreans might give up the *Pueblo* and its crew just as suddenly as they had seized it. "The Communists don't think like we do," said Sparkman. "Neither do many Asians."

Former Vice President Nixon, a Republican presidential candidate, declared that not protecting the *Pueblo* was a great blunder.

Jan. 28—A report from Tokyo on Red China's reaction, breaking a five-day silence, reported that Peking in its first formal comment on the *Pueblo* affair gave a usual denunciation, charging the United States with an "utterly naked war threat against the Korean people." The basic problem in Peking's view was "U. S. aggression in Vietnam."

Ambassador Goldberg and Soviet Ambassador Morozov met for the first time in an informal talk, which Russia declared to be routine.

Soviet Premier Kosygin, speaking in India, said there was no doubt that the *Pueblo* had intruded into North Korean waters and that the United States and North Korea must settle the matter themselves.

An official North Korean statement indicated that the country was antagonistic to any UN role in a settlement of the incident. "It is the sacred right of each independent state to defend its security and sovereignty from the encroachment of the enemy; this is an internal affair in which no one can interfere."

Senate Republican leader Everett Dirksen of Illinois said, "We are going to have to put our foot down" in Korea if diplomatic efforts failed to free the *Pueblo* and its crew, but he supported President Johnson's efforts to solve the dispute through diplomacy. Two leading Democratic Senators, Fulbright of Arkansas and Long of Louisiana, expressed pleasure that force was not being used, but Long indicated that if diplomacy was not successful force should be used. He suggested, "The United States might start sinking North Korean gunboats and holding merchant ships as hostages." Senator Stennis of Mississippi (D) mentioned the possibility of a blockade of North Korea.

Jan. 29—The Security Council did not meet in order to give more time for private talks.

The AP reported that congressional leaders were growing restless over the failure to gain the release of the crew of the *Pueblo*.

Jan. 30—California Republican governor, Ronald Reagan, often mentioned as a presidential candidate, reported that he was "deeply ashamed of the way we have failed to take a position." He said, "The full power of the government should have taken action." He maintained that the United States should have entered the North Korean port and freed the seized ship and its crew.

The UN Security Council canceled indefinitely its meeting on the *Pueblo* crisis.

Jan. 31—A bloc of Afro-Asian nations suggested that the United States meet with North Korea in Geneva to discuss solution of the *Pueblo* incident.

The White House press secretary, according to UPI, indicated that the government had succeeded in opening indirect communication with North Korea. He reported

that Washington had received word that the crew members were being properly treated and given medical aid.

Feb. 1—*The New York Times* reported that the United States was preparing a new direct approach to North Korea through the Military Armistice Commission, which meets at Panmunjom in the demilitarized zone between North and South Korea.

The AP reported that a North Korean leader hinted that the crew of the *Pueblo* might be released if the United States apologized and admitted that it had violated territorial waters. Earlier Senator Mansfield had stated that he would make such an admission even if it were not true in order to get the release of the crew.

Feb. 2—A State Department spokesman announced that the United States would soon hold another meeting with North Korean representatives of the Armistice Commission.

Time magazine stated, "No sooner was the capture of the U.S.S. *Pueblo* reported last week than high-placed and usually accommodating news sources became tight-lipped or inaccessible. From Washington to Tokyo, no one in the know was talking—at least not for the record."[1]

Feb. 3—President Johnson confirmed that there had been meetings between North Korean and United States representatives at Panmunjom. He said also that the experts he had talked with believed there was a definite connection between the uprising of Vietnamese communists and the seizing of the *Pueblo*. He indicated no optimism about an early release of the crewmen.

Feb. 4—Secretaries Rusk and McNamara reported on a television interview that it was possible, but not probable, that the

---

[1] By permission from TIME, The Weekly Newsmagazine; Copyright Time Inc. 1968.

Pueblo had been in North Korean waters. Secretary McNamara stated, "This could not really be known until the crew was released."

Late evening broadcasts reported that three meetings had been held at Panmunjom since Friday, February 2.

Feb. 5—An AP story stated, "Seoul officials expressed suspicion that the United States was getting ready to issue an apology to North Korea over the incident in order to get the *Pueblo* crewmen back. . . .

"South Korean officials generally feel that the U. S. government is so preoccupied with the plight of the *Pueblo* and its crew that it is not paying sufficient attention to what they consider the main Communist threat —increased infiltration across the demilitarized zone and the recent invasion of Seoul by a team of commandos bent on assassinating President Park."[1]

The State Department reported that talks were continuing at Panmunjom.

Michigan's Governor Romney, then a Republican presidential hopeful, cited the *Pueblo* incident as another example of the "credibility gap." He stated, "What this country needs is a President who will give the public the truth no matter whether the news is good or bad."

Feb. 6—The Senate Foreign Relations Committee asked for a full report on the *Pueblo* seizure, including details of all United States spy ship operations.

Feb. 7—The White House announced the name of the sailor killed in the capture of the *Pueblo* and the names of three injured men. The names had been provided by the North Korean representatives at a conference in Panmunjom.

Feb. 8—Premier Kim of North Korea told his army it should prepare to meet an invasion. He accused the United States of

trying to solve the *Pueblo* crisis "by means of threat and blackmail."

Feb. 9—Special presidential assistant Cyrus Vance was sent by President Johnson to Seoul to confer with President Park of South Korea. Because of increased activity in the Vietnam War, South Korean officials were fearful that the threats from North Korea were not recognized by the United States.

Feb. 10-11—Over the weekend the Harris and Gallup polls showed that a large majority of the people approved the use of diplomacy in the *Pueblo* case. Only a small minority favored the use of force to get the release of the ship and crew.

Senator Mansfield proposed that the *Pueblo* dispute be submitted to the International Court of Justice.

Feb. 12—Six secret meetings had now been held at Panmunjom.

An AP report stated that so far nothing had been produced by the meetings except an aggravation in relations between South Korea and America.

The report added that the fiercest fighting of the Vietnam War took place in the past week, with Saigon and other cities being attacked.

Feb. 16—Special envoy Cyrus Vance returned from South Korea and reported that his talks with officials were cordial. Measures were being taken to strengthen South Korean and American forces in case of emergencies.

Feb. 19—A CBS radio bulletin from Seoul, Korea, reported that there had been a blackout on news from Panmunjom for the past week.

Feb. 22—An AP story stated, "President Johnson is quietly confident that diplomacy eventually will win release of the captured *Pueblo's* crew. In the face of a new North Korean threat to try the 82 surviving crew members, Johnson is said to believe a way

---

[1] Reprinted by permission from AP Newsfeatures.

will be found to reach a settlement after the other side has had its day of blustering."[1]

Feb. 23—The aircraft carrier *Enterprise* was returned to duty in North Vietnam waters.

For the next ten months frustrating negotiations were held at Panmunjom between the United States and North Korean diplomatic teams. Finally an unusual agreement was reached. On December 21, 1968 Major General Gilbert H. Woodward, the head negotiator for the United States, signed a confession that the *Pueblo* had been engaged in espionage. At the same time he agreed in writing to an apology and promised that spying would cease.

Immediately, and with the approval of the North Koreans, he declared that his "confession" was false and not really an official admission of guilt. General Woodward emphasized that he signed the document only "to free the crew. . . . My signature," he said, "will not and cannot alter the facts."

Captain Lloyd M. Bucher and the eighty-two surviving members were released the next day. In the next few days Captain Bucher reported that he and his crew had been brutally treated and that he finally signed a false confession because the Communists threatened to kill his crew.

A Naval Court of Inquiry, under the direction of Vice Admiral Harold S. Bowen, was created to investigate the *Pueblo* case. Starting January 2, 1969 the commander and crew spent eighty days testifying before this court. At the end of this period, the court recommended a court-martial for Captain Bucher for failing to defend his ship and for Lieutenant Stephen R. Harris, who was in charge of the ship's intelligence records, for failure to destroy these secret materials. Reprimands were also given to their superior officers who were in charge of naval operations in Japan and the Pacific.

The Secretary of the Navy, John H. Chafee, in May 1969 overruled the Court of Inquiry. He stated, "I have decided that no disciplinary action will be taken against any of the personnel involved in the *Pueblo* incident. . . . They have suffered enough and further punishment would not be justified." Secretary Chafee's final action clearly meant that the Navy, too, had been on trial and that the captain and his crew should not be punished for actions that were the result of higher orders and changes in the historic concepts of sovereign ships and territorial waters.

A further inquiry was made by the House Armed Services Subcommittee, which reported in July 1969 that serious deficiencies existed in the command structure of the Department of Defense—particularly in dealing with emergency situations. The Subcommittee also recommended a study of the Code of Conduct, which governs the behavior of captured prisoners. The *Pueblo* affair seemed to have ended.

Several books have been written about the affair. One is by the Commander, *Bucher: My Story;* another by an officer, Lieutenant E. R. Murphy, *Second in Command;* others include *Matter of Accountability* by Trevor Armbrister and *Last Voyage of the USS Pueblo* by Edward Brandt.

- What principles of international relations were illustrated by the *Pueblo* incident?
- What conclusions do you reach concerning the role of the United Nations?
- Is the information gained by such missions as the *Pueblo*'s worth the cost?
- Was a false confession good diplomacy? Why or why not?
- Were the actions of the Defense Department proper? Why or why not?

---

[1] Reprinted by permission from AP Newsfeatures.

Pictorial Parade/Editorial Photocolor Archives

FARM LABOR
INFORMATION

8

GOVERNMENT AND THE LIFE OF OUR PEOPLE

Compare the needs which our government supplies to its citizens today with the needs yet to be provided and contrast all of this with an earlier era in our national history when needs were supplied by other means.

Role-playing is an effective device for helping students see other viewpoints. This unit presents many opportunities in connection with such topics as management and labor disputes, compulsory health insurance, federal aid to education, public ownership of power projects, and bonding versus pay-as-you-go. Use some of these areas to create situations in which students play the role of "the other person" to develop greater insights.

The young man shown on the opposite page is being counselled by an agency of the Farm Labor and Rural Manpower Service.

Much of life for all people revolves around the physical needs of food, clothing, and shelter and the psychological need of being an accepted member of society. These needs have become so much a part of life that frequently they are taken for granted. People think little about them and assume them to be part of their basic rights. Usually only as the needs are not adequately met do they become subjects for discussion and action. The satisfaction of these needs for all people has become an increasing concern of government.

In a simple society it was comparatively easy to meet these needs for most people. But in our complex industrial society it is often much more difficult. Meeting these needs for all people calls for extra effort and help on the part of many individuals and groups. For government it involves adequate and effective programs in agriculture, conservation, and business and labor relations. It includes provisions for the education, the welfare, and the health of the people. It involves a real concern for adequate housing facilities and for a life free from the disturbing effects of crime and accidents.

Some of these issues in the achievement of a rich and full life for our people have been part of government's program for many years, a few since the founding of our nation. Others have become the concern of government only recently. But all are now accepted by most of the people as part of the work and function of our government.

The manner in which these problems of life together for a democratic people are being met and resolved is the subject of study for this final unit. The four chapters give an account of the governmental activities carried on in a number of important areas of life.

Chapter 29 discusses agriculture in the United States and the extensive conservation programs of government.

Chapter 30 deals with the areas of business and labor and describes the role of government in these important economic aspects of living.

Chapter 31 treats significant aspects for the general welfare of the people; it discusses the activities of government in education, social welfare, and health.

Chapter 32 shows how government affects the life of the people through programs in the field of housing and through attempts to protect life and property against crime and accidents.

This unit presents many opportunities for bringing in speakers to discuss certain topics or issues with the class.

623

CONSERVATION—the preservation and wise use of the nation's natural resources.

CONTOUR PLOWING — plowing across the slope of the land to create furrows for prevention of erosion.

CROP ROTATION — changing of crops from year to year to preserve the chemical balance of the soil.

EROSION—the wearing away and loss of soil.

FLOOD CONTROL — system of keeping water in the river basin to prevent flooding of land and destruction of property.

PARITY — equality; a system whereby a farmer receives a price for his products which gives him the same purchasing power he would have had in a base year or years.

PRICE SUPPORT—basic price set by the government for a certain crop or commodity.

RECLAMATION—restoring wasteland or arid land to a state of productive usefulness.

RESOURCE—a natural asset of a nation which can be converted to a good use.

SOIL CONSERVATION DISTRICT — a group of farms or ranches organized to promote good conservation practices.

STRIP FARMING—the process of planting alternate strips of land with different crops as a conservation measure.

TERRACING—farming in a series of steps to prevent erosion from heavy rainfall.

THE LANGUAGE
OF GOVERNMENT

Make it clear that in the field of agriculture, as opposed to education, housing, and health, the national government has had a long interest stretching back into the last century.

29
Agriculture,
Conservation,
and Government

More than 70 per cent of the population of the United States lives in urban areas. It is estimated that by the year 2000 this figure will be about 90 per cent. But this large per cent of the people lives on only a small per cent of the land of the United States. Some of the land outside of the urban areas is desert, mountainous, or wasteland. But most of it is devoted to agriculture, mining, conservation projects, or is covered by forests. Observation on a trip across the country by automobile, bus, or train shows the uses to which Americans have put much of the more than three and a half million square miles of land of the nation.

The land and the riches that come from the land have helped to make the United States great. Corn, cotton, wheat . . . beef and pork . . . tobacco . . . vegetables . . . oranges . . ..these are products of our fertile soil. Oil and gasoline . . . coal . . . lumber . . . minerals of all kinds . . . these are riches that come from our land.

As a nation we have been blessed with a wealth of natural resources. Our strength, our prosperity, our means of earning a living have been dependent on our land.

The combination of great *resources* plus an intelligent, ambitious people has helped make the standard of living high in the United States. But our resources are not unlimited; there is need for wise conservation. And the farmer faces many problems which need solution.

AGRICULTURE   Once we were a nation of farmers. At the time our Constitution was written nine out of ten families earned their living by farming.

CHANGES IN FARM CONDITIONS. Today less than one family in ten lives on a farm. Today there are only 30 per cent

as many people living on farms as there were in 1920. This trend away from the farm is continuing. In 1960 more than fifteen million persons still lived on farms, but by 1970 the number had declined to less than ten million, less than 5 per cent of the total population. Annually 500,000 to 600,000 persons migrate from the farms to the city. Now we are an industrial nation, but the millions who work in factories or stores or garages depend for their food on our farms.

While the farm population has been decreasing, a second change has taken place: the productivity of the farmer has greatly increased. Today the output for each farmworker is more than double what it was sixty years ago. The Industrial Revolution brought the tractor, truck, and automobile to the farm. The modern farm is a mecha-

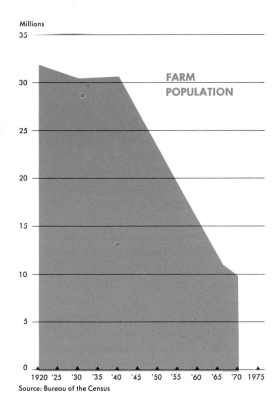

Millions

FARM POPULATION

Source: Bureau of the Census

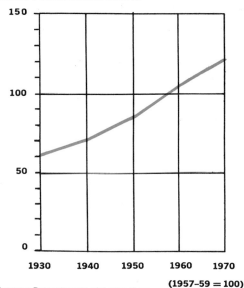

FARM PRODUCTION INDEX

Source: Department of Agriculture

(1957–59 = 100)

The graphs show that farm population has decreased while farm production has increased. What is the reason for this apparent paradox?

Ask how our agricultural production capacity could be greatly increased if needed.

Farmers are able to fill large granaries like this one all across our country. What has caused the tremendous increase in farm production over the past hundred years? (USDA photo)

nized, electrified farm. The modern farmer is a combination of businessman, mechanic, and chemist, as well as a grower of crops.

A third change is the trend toward big, factory-type farms. The number of single-family farms has been decreasing steadily, while the huge industrial-type farms have increased greatly. This change is shown by the fact that in 1935 the United States had nearly seven million farms with a total area of slightly more than a billion acres. Today there are only about three million farms with 1.1 billion acres. During these years the number of farms has been reduced by more than 50 per cent, but the amount of land being farmed has increased slightly. The farms are getting larger each year. On these big farms, especially in the West, machines and migratory workers do much of the work. The assembly-line technique has been moved to the farm.

Change in farm income is a fourth important agricultural change. In 1929, agriculture accounted for 6.5 per cent of our national income. By 1939 this figure was reduced to 6.2 per cent. In 1949 it had decreased to 5.9 per cent. Today it is estimated to be only about 3 per cent. The farmer complains that he is not getting his fair share of the national income.

THE FARMER AND POLITICS. The farmer has always been very influential in politics. As farm conditions changed, the farmers used their votes to get government help with their problems. As has been noted in earlier chapters the rural areas controlled many state legislatures and had a powerful voice in Congress. The farm lobbies—the Grange, the Farmers Union, the American Farm Bureau Federation—are among the most powerful in the nation.

In many states farmers are the most effective political group. Although in terms of national politics, there are fewer farm voters than urban voters, the strategic position of the farmer can determine the results of elections. For example, when labor and management favor different candidates, farm support to one candidate often decides the election.

Because the problems of the farmer are important to the whole nation and because the farmer has great political power, government always has been active in agricultural matters. This concern for the needs and wants of the farmer has been demonstrated in the programs of agricultural education, agricultural research, farm credit, rural electrification, price supports, and soil conservation. Each of these programs to aid the farmer will be discussed briefly in the following pages.

AGRICULTURAL EDUCATION. Until the middle of the nineteenth century, knowledge about farming was passed along from father to son. For generations farm methods changed little. Then science began to influence farming as it did all other human activities. Farm leaders began to see the importance of developing ways to keep farmers up to date.

A few states had pioneered in agricultural education, but the big developments started after 1862 when Congress passed the Morrill Act. By this law land was given to the states. The income from this land was used to establish colleges, called land-grant colleges, for the teaching of agriculture and mechanical arts. As the programs of these colleges developed, agricultural education was placed on a firm basis.

In 1887 a law was passed which provided funds to create agricultural experiment stations at these land-grant colleges. Research and education were combined so that new findings were made available to agriculture students.

By 1914 demands were made to have such services brought to those farmers who could not get to a college. As a result a system of county farm agents was developed. Today, there are more than 3,000 county agricultural agents working through extension services in farm communities.

The county agent is primarily a teacher of farmers. He holds meetings, demonstrates new methods, gives talks, writes for local papers, tests soils. He knows the new varieties of seeds, the latest conservation practices, the best fertilizer for a farmer's

A 4-H leader demonstrates the correct way to load a camera to beginners in a 4-H photography project. (Courtesy, National 4-H Service Committee)

Point out that many state universities today were originally land-grant colleges created by the Morrill Act of 1862.

soil. He cannot require a farmer to follow any of his suggestions; he can teach what he knows. Each farmer decides whether to follow the teachings.

In most counties, too, there are 4-H Club agents and home-demonstration agents. About two million young people participate in the 4-H Clubs. In these clubs they are learning to be good farmers and good citizens. The 4-H agent helps the members with their problems of raising their own cattle, hogs, or chickens. Help is given too on ways of preserving food, on personal development, on child care, and on personal grooming.

The home-demonstration agent makes information available to homemakers. Family menus, home furnishings, clothing, and nutrition are the general areas in which help is given.

These agents work through the extension services of the Department of Agriculture in cooperation with agricultural colleges and county governments.

AGRICULTURAL RESEARCH. Research has always been one of the chief activities of the Department of Agriculture.

At present all research activities of the Department are organized under the Agricultural Research Service.

Much research is done at the 12,000-acre research farm at Beltsville, Maryland. Other projects are carried out in other states and in foreign countries.

Research programs are designed for the study of plant diseases and insects which injure crops. Quarantine regulations are established and enforced to prevent the spread of diseases and harmful insects.

Livestock regulation programs are part of the Research Service. Animal diseases are studied, quarantines are established, and meat is inspected. All meat slaughtered and sold in interstate commerce is inspected to insure freedom from disease and decay.

Crop research is undertaken to determine the best means of weed control, to develop plants that are more resistant to disease, and to investigate new uses for agricultural products.

Seed companies, fertilizer suppliers, feed companies, the veterinary profession, and private laboratories have contributed much original research. In addition, they have

The Department of Agriculture carries on much of its research at the research farm at Beltsville. This is an aerial view of the dairy buildings at Beltsville. (USDA photo)

helped government agencies put the results of research into practical use.

The American farmer carries on a continuous battle against corn borers, flies, boll weevils, rabies, cholera, hoof-and-mouth disease, and other pests and diseases. He searches constantly for ways to improve the yield from his acres, to get more milk from his cows and more eggs from his chickens. He is aided by the research efforts of the agricultural scientists.

FARM CREDIT. Farming requires a large investment in land and machinery. Seed, fertilizer, and livestock are costly. Yet the farmer's income does not come in steadily week after week. It comes in when a crop is harvested or cattle are sold. If wind, rain, or hail should cause damage, or other disaster should occur, the farmer can lose his cash resources in a hurry.

Because of these financial hazards the government has made it relatively easy for the farmer to borrow money to buy land, to repair buildings, to buy machinery, to pay medical bills, and to provide for any other expenses of farming. This financial assistance is given through the Farm Credit Administration, an independent agency, and through the Farmers Home Administration of the Department of Agriculture.

The Farm Credit Administration divides the nation into twelve farm-credit districts. In each district there are four types of farm-credit institutions:

1. The federal land banks, which make long-term mortgage loans to farmers and ranchers at low interest rates. This bank system is a cooperative, farmer-owned system.

2. Intermediate-credit banks, which are "bankers' banks." They do not lend directly to farmers but take over the loans made by other banks and credit institutions.

3. Production credit corporations, which are owned by farmers on a cooperative basis. These organizations supply short-term credit for all types of farm and ranch operations. They are supervised by the government. The government originally supplied the money for capital, but most of this money has now been repaid.

4. A central bank for cooperatives, which provides a permanent source of credit to farmers' cooperatives.

The *Farmers Home Administration* helps the small family-type farmer. Loans are made to help these independent farmers over periods of distress and to aid tenants, farm laborers, sharecroppers, and veterans to purchase small farms. It is important to help farmers of this type in order to decrease the number of farm tenants.

In 1930 about 42 per cent of the farms in the United States were rented. Today only about 25 per cent are rented. This decrease in renting has been caused, in part, by the ease with which the farmworker can borrow to buy his own farm.

Operating loans of not more than $35,000 are made to buy livestock, seed, fertilizer, and other farm necessities. Loans may be made for family living needs, including medical care. Special loans are made for providing water facilities, for emergencies in disaster areas, and for raising livestock.

Ownership loans are made for the purchase of family-type farms. These loans may also be used to construct or repair buildings, to improve the land, to develop water resources, and for other farm-related costs. The combined total of all loans may not exceed $100,000. Veterans are given special privileges on these loans. The loans are repayable over periods ranging from 33 to 50 years.

All loans are made through local offices, usually at the county seat. A county committee of three, at least two of them farmers, must review all applications. Whether or not a loan is allowed depends on their

The wheat crop being harvested here looks like a large one, but some years it may not reach this size. How does this relate to the necessity of providing means for the farmer to borrow money? (Kansas Dept. of Economic Development)

This is one of many power lines constructed with the aid of funds supplied by the Rural Electrification Administration. The REA has helped to bring telephones as well as electricity to farms. (USDA photo)

opinion of the applicant, his farm, and his record of repaying debts.

In a typical year farmers and their cooperatives will borrow around two billion dollars from these credit institutions. These institutions, together with regular banking facilities, have eased many of the farmers' problems of borrowing.

RURAL ELECTRIFICATION. Forty years ago, nine farms out of ten did not have electricity. Today the exact opposite is true; nine out of ten farms do have electricity. The farmer needs electricity to operate milking machines, to grind feed, to pump water, to freeze foods and meats, and to run many other laborsaving devices.

He uses electricity for the TV set, the radio, the washing machine, the refrigerator, and the air conditioner. Electricity makes his life more efficient, more pleasant, and more comfortable.

Getting electricity for the farmer was not

Mention the development of the TVA during the same period with respect to rural electrification.

casy. The cost of transmission lines was very high. Private companies found it very risky to invest money in these miles of lines, because they were not sure how large the rural market for electricity would be. Finally during the depression, in 1935, the government established the Rural Electrification Administration to get electricity to the farms.

The REA lends money to local government units and farmers' cooperatives and to individuals, associations, and corporations for the construction of rural electrical facilities. One hundred per cent of the cost of a project will be lent. The interest rate is only 2 per cent, and the loan can be paid off over as long a time as thirty-five years.

The intent of the REA was not to compete with private power companies but to get electricity into farm areas where population is thinly distributed and where private companies might not be likely to provide service. The program has been very successful. This is shown by the steady increase in the number of farms with electricity. More than three billion dollars has been lent through REA. Over 1,000 REA-financed power systems are in operation, serving about five million consumers.

Families, too, may borrow money from REA at low interest rates over a period of five years for wiring homes and farm buildings, for buying appliances, or for plumbing.

Since 1949 the REA has also had funds and authority to lend money to local telephone companies for the improvement of telephone service in rural areas. In 1949 fewer than four out of ten farms had telephones. Under the REA program telephones on farms are becoming as common as electricity.

PRICE SUPPORTS. Farming is an uncertain business. One year the sun may shine and the rains may come at just the proper times. The result: a bumper crop.

But when the farmer wants to sell, he may find so much has been grown that prices have fallen, and he may not get enough for his total product to pay for his expenses and time.

Or this year the city dweller may want to eat chickens, but next year turkeys may be more popular—with prices changing because of the shifts in demand. Can these hazards of farming be reduced so that farmers can be assured of a fair income?

Government and agriculture leaders have searched for an answer to this question for many years. In 1933 the *Agricultural Adjustment Act* was passed in an attempt to get farm income in balance with other types of income.

The method of this first AAA was to pay farmers a bonus for planting fewer acres and for decreasing the number of farm animals raised. The money for the bonus was obtained by placing a tax on those who processed the farm products. For example, the companies that ground wheat into flour had to pay the special tax. The decrease in production resulted in increased prices because supply and demand became about equal.

The system worked for the farmer, but it was never liked by some people in the cities. Unemployed, hungry people did not understand why food should be destroyed and less raised when they were desperate to find something to eat. Finally the Supreme Court ruled that the law was unconstitutional because of the tax device used to pay the bonuses to the farmers.

In 1938 Congress passed a new Agricultural Adjustment Act which kept the bonus provisions of the first act but paid farmers for good soil-conservation practices and eliminated the earlier special tax.

The chief new feature of this second AAA was the *ever-normal granary.* In the years when bumper crops were raised, the

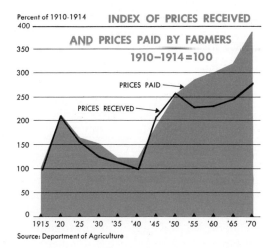

Percent of 1910-1914

INDEX OF PRICES RECEIVED AND PRICES PAID BY FARMERS

1910–1914=100

PRICES PAID

PRICES RECEIVED

400
350
300
250
200
150
100
50
0

1915 '20 '25 '30 '35 '40 '45 '50 '55 '60 '65 '70

Source: Department of Agriculture

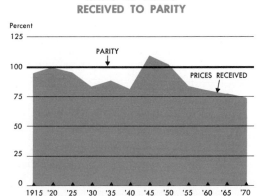

RATIO OF PRICES RECEIVED TO PARITY

Percent

PARITY

PRICES RECEIVED

125
100
75
50
25
0

1915 '20 '25 '30 '35 '40 '45 '50 '55 '60 '65 '70

The parity ratio drops when the prices farmers receive fall below the prices they must pay.

surplus was to be stored for use during years of low production. Farmers storing crops under this program were to be lent money until the crops were sold. The government was to help build storage facilities to aid in carrying over crops from one year to another.

Some surplus farm products were to be purchased by the government for distribution to the unemployed and for a free-lunch program in schools. The chief agent of this program was the Commodity Credit Corporation. This program was beginning to raise farm income when World War II started.

During the war the demand for food exceeded the supply. All food was rationed, and farmers were urged to produce more and more food. Acres and acres of land that had not been used for crop farming were put into wheat, corn, cotton, rice, and other crops.

Long hours of work, better types of seed, and more efficient farm methods caused a tremendous increase in production. Prices rose because production never caught up with demand. To prevent prices from getting too high for consumers, price ceilings were set. Thus the farmers were *not* able to sell their products for as high prices as they might otherwise have obtained.

To the farmers this seemed unfair. At the same time, farmers were worried that at the end of the war, prices would drop because so much was being produced. For example, they remembered that after World War I wheat fell from two dollars to forty cents a bushel.

To try to give the farmer fair payment for his work, a device was created to keep farm prices at about the level of 1914 plus any increase in the farmer's cost of living since that time. This device was called *parity.* In other words, parity is the price which a farmer must receive on a commodity today to give him the same purchasing power he would have had on the average during the years 1910–1914.

For example, if the average price of wheat was 90 cents a bushel from 1910–1914, and if the cost of living has increased an estimated $1.50 a bushel since then, the parity price of wheat would be determined by adding 90 cents to $1.50 to equal $2.40. In terms of this example a farmer needed to receive $2.40 a bushel if his purchasing

Define the concept of parity carefully; encourage examples other than those in the textbook.

power now is to be equal to what it was in 1910–1914.

Each year economists, by a complicated system, determine what this parity price should be for the year's farm products.[1] Then Congress decides how much of the parity price the government will guarantee to the farmer. One year the guarantee on wheat was 90 per cent of parity. Another year it might be 75 per cent of parity. If the actual selling price falls below the guarantee price, the government pays the farmer the difference.

The effect of the use of parity price is to guarantee the farmer a minimum price for his crop. Altogether, 166 crops have come under this type of price control.

In addition to the parity payments and the ever-normal granary, there are three other features of the present government price-support program: control of crop production, crop insurance, and cash awards for soil conservation.

Control of crop production is attempted by limiting the number of acres that a farmer may plant to a specific crop. Marketing quotas are also used to control production. To keep supply in line with demand for such crops as cotton, peanuts, rice, tobacco, and wheat, both acreage allotments and marketing quotas may be used. These restrictions are determined by the Department of Agriculture but go into effect only when two-thirds of the growers of that crop vote in favor of limiting the number of acres that can be planted.

Crop insurance has been attempted to protect farmers against crop losses that are beyond normal control. Bad weather, insects, and diseases are the common dangers. The Federal Crop Insurance Corporation was created to administer the program.

---

[1] Consult the current *Economic Almanac* for a description of determining parity prices.

This corporation enables farmers in a county to pay a premium and be insured against loss. For the program to operate in any county, at least 200 farms, or one-third of the farmers producing the crop, must take out the insurance.

Cash awards for soil conservation are used to encourage practices to save the soil. They are linked here with price supports because farmers using the conservation practices receive cash awards, and thus their total income is increased. Under the *soil bank* program, cotton, wheat, corn, rice, and tobacco growers can collect cash payments by putting cropland into grass, trees, ponds, or game refuges.

This plan increases the farmer's income, cuts down production, and conserves the soil.

The price-support program is the subject of much controversy. The Democrats have favored a high price support at full parity levels. The Republicans have favored flexible price supports fitted to specific commodities. Individual political leaders have argued for 100 per cent parity payments. The government spends about one and a half billion dollars for this program each year.

Some farmers object when they are required to reduce acreage in order to get benefits. The huge quantities of commodities that have been stored over the years have made some people wonder if we would ever be able to dispose of our surplus farm products. That time may have come, as we are using some of the surplus to feed hungry people in other countries. We may be moving from a period of large surpluses to one of scarcity.

SOIL CONSERVATION. Farmers are faced not only with the immediate problems of getting enough income, as described above, but also with a long-range problem of great importance: Can our soil be kept

This is a scene in the "Dust Bowl" during one of the severe dust storms of the 1930's. Poor farming practices had damaged or destroyed the plant cover that would have protected the soil during the severe drought. (Library of Congress)

fertile enough to produce the foods that our country will need in the future?

Two facts are important: (1) The population explosion in the United States and throughout the world is adding millions of people to the population each year. (2) Estimates are that 40 per cent of the fertile topsoil of the United States has been destroyed. Are we to be faced with a problem of feeding more people from a soil that is less fertile?

Topsoil is destroyed by *erosion*. Wind blows the soil away; water washes it away. When land was plentiful, some farmers paid little attention to erosion. For several centuries after the establishment of settlements in the Americas farming practices were very destructive of the topsoil. Land clearance, methods of farming, and certain crops, such as tobacco and corn, destroyed much topsoil. The result is that 35 million acres were ruined. Another 225 million acres lost so much topsoil that fertility decreased to a danger point.

If all of these worn-out acres could be assembled in one area, they would cover the states of Kentucky, Illinois, Indiana, Iowa, Michigan, Minnesota, Nebraska, Ohio, and Wisconsin.

The causes of this soil destruction include:

- *Plowing in straight rows directly uphill and downhill*
- *Cutting too many trees and destroying forests*
- *Failing to rotate crops or raising only one crop*
- *Allowing cattle to graze too long in one pasture*
- *Permitting water to run off the land too rapidly.*

The Soil Conservation Service of the Department of Agriculture has demonstrated that each of these bad practices can be cured. Several thousand soil-conservation districts were formed to reclaim land and to show farmers how to conserve soil. These districts include demonstration projects to illustrate methods of grazing and crop rotation. Farmers are helped to follow these improved practices:

CONTOUR PLOWING. Instead of going uphill and downhill, the plowing is done across the slope of the land. The furrows become little dams to hold back the water instead of channels that speed the flow.

STRIP FARMING. Strips of land are planted

Contour plowing is an important means of soil conservation. What other methods are used to conserve soil? (International Harvester Company)

alternately with different crops. By this method, air currents and the rush of water are broken up.

THE USE OF GRASS WATERWAYS. Gullies which have been dug by the rush of water are seeded to grass and allowed to stay as permanent grass areas. The grass holds more water and slows the speed of flowing water.

TERRACING. Planting on the "steps" of a terrace prevents most of the washing from heavy rains.

THE USE OF WINDBREAKS. Trees and shrubs planted at strategic places slow down the force of the wind and help prevent wind erosion and the running off of water.

The Soil Conservation Service carries on its work through soil-conservation dis-

Strip farming helps to prevent erosion of valuable soil. Notice also how trees are used as windbreaks on this farm. (USDA photo)

tricts. Districts are organized by a vote of the farmers or ranchers. After a district is organized, an acre-by-acre survey is made of a farm or a ranch. Then a conservation plan is developed. Finally a soil conservationist helps the farmer start and maintain good conservation practices.

CONSERVATION   But conservation is concerned with more than the preservation and wise use of agricultural land, important as that is. Conservation has come to have a broad meaning. Conservation is concerned with reclaiming desert lands, controlling floods, restocking lakes and streams for better fishing, and restoring and protecting forests and woodlands.

It is concerned with wildlife refuges, irrigation projects, national parks, mines, and oil wells. It is concerned with the best use of our human resources. All the natural assets of our country have become the concern of the conservation movement.

This is a twentieth-century movement. Our forefathers believed our resources were unlimited. They were wasteful and took advantage of the fact that the United States was so richly blessed. Then, in 1908, President Theodore Roosevelt began to dramatize the importance of conservation. A conference was held at the White House. A national conservation movement was started.

Presidents and governors since that time have continued to emphasize the need for conserving our natural resources. The government conservation activities have been chiefly in the following major areas: water and flood control, reclamation, forests, fish and wildlife, parks, and minerals.

WATER AND FLOOD CONTROL. Citizens living in areas where water is plentiful have little realization of how important water is to all sections of the United States. Large cities such as New York and Los Angeles can exist only if they get adequate amounts of water. The prosperity of the arid and mountainous western states depends upon controlling the sources and the distribution of water.

In other parts of our country, floods have made citizens realize that the waters pouring down the Ohio, the Mississippi, and the Missouri rivers can be among man's most destructive enemies.

The fact that there is not enough water in some places and too much water in others has created a new engineering science to control water. This science is chiefly concerned with three goals: (1) the building of dams to control flood waters; (2) the restoration of forests and vegetation along tributary streams; and (3) the movement of water to places of greatest need.

The building of dams has become one of the great enterprises of modern governments. In all parts of the world, governments have built and are building dams to hold back water. The water is then released for irrigation, flood control, water supply, or to make electric power.

The United States has been one of the leaders in this movement. More than 150 dams which are 200 feet high or higher have been built in this country. Some of these dams are as well-known as famous people. They are a tourist attraction.

Oroville Dam in California, 770 feet high, is the highest dam in this country. The first water deliveries from the dam were made in 1962 to the San Francisco Bay Area through the Feather and Sacramento River channels. By 1972 water from the dam traveled as far as 650 miles to homes, farms, and industries in the central, southern, and coastal areas of California. The system includes the 444-mile-long California Aqueduct, which supplies water for the Los Angeles area.

AMERICA, THE MORE BEAUTIFUL

From sea to shining sea, we take pride in the scenic riches of our land and sing of its beauties. We rightly expect this beauty—the forests, mountains, the leaves, and flowers—to be part of our daily experience.

The sad fact is that this beauty is floating away on a swift tide of cement, polluted water, and dirty air.

The amount of air pollution spewed from American automobiles every day equals the weight of a line of cars stretched bumper-to-bumper from New York to Chicago. Our national parks are jammed throughout the summer, and even our hillsides hold side-by-side subdivisions.

Our eyes, our senses, and our health have been offended. Our wisdom tells us, "This need not be so!"

Congress senses our conservation crisis and has passed many measures to protect our national parks, wilderness areas, recreation areas, and seashores. It is also helping cities and states pay for recreation sites, open spaces, urban design, waterfront rehabilitation, and preservation of historic sites.

Other challenges have a measurable price tag—for removing the stain of pollution from our rivers, for removing smog from our air. But who can say that the resulting public health and happiness will not be worth the cost?

Once the American people want to fight for a life-giving environment and are willing to pay whatever is necessary to win that fight—the battle will really begin.

Stewart L. Udall, U.S. Secretary of the Interior, Special Message.
Special permission granted by *Current Events* published by American Education Publications, Columbus, Ohio. (Vol. LXV, Issue No. 28, April 20, 1966.)

Hoover Dam, across the Colorado River, is the second highest. Completed in 1936, this 726-foot dam is in the states of Arizona and Nevada. The waters held back have made an artificial lake, Lake Mead, one of the world's largest reservoirs. The waters are used for both irrigation and production of electricity. It is also a recreation area.

Shasta Dam, across the Sacramento River in California, is 602 feet high. Hungry Horse Dam, across the South Fork of the Flathead River in Montana, is 564 feet high. Grand Coulee Dam, across the Columbia River in Washington, is 550 feet high.

Not so large, but equally famous, is Norris Dam, across the Clinch River in Tennessee. This dam was completed in 1936 as part of the *Tennessee Valley Authority* project, which has been the subject of political discussions for more than a quarter of a century. (See Chapter 13.)

The Tennessee Valley Authority was a dramatic effort to control the waters of an entire region. In 1920 the federal government had created the Federal Power Commission and given exclusive control of all power sites on navigable waters to the federal government.

In 1935 this control was increased by giving the commission the right to regulate rates and equipment. In addition, the commission also regulates the issuing of securities by companies engaged in the interstate transmission of electric power.

During these same years the TVA was coming into being. By an act of Congress in 1933 the TVA, a government corporation, was created. This corporation had a three-man board of directors appointed by the President. The TVA was given authority to improve navigability and to provide for flood control, reforestation, and the agricultural and industrial development of the Tennessee Valley.

Our nation's soil supports many different kinds of agricultural products, including cotton (left) and wheat (right). Have we always used the land wisely? (Left, Louisiana Department of Commerce; right, North Dakota State Highway Department)

With this broad grant of power, the TVA built dams, carried on soil-conservation programs, helped control floods, developed recreational areas, and increased commercial water traffic. It also sold the electric power generated at the dams. This resulted in a head-on collision with those citizens who believed that electric power should be sold by private companies under a free-enterprise system.

This controversy still exists. There are citizens who believe that government should build the dams, construct the electric generators, and sell power. There are other citizens who believe that this is not the proper function of government. The TVA became the focus for this type of public discussion.

Other similar projects continue to raise this same fundamental question. The Missouri River Basin Project, the St. Lawrence

Power Project, and the Bonneville Power Administration, in different parts of the country, have raised this issue of public vs. private power. We seem to have reached

Cattle raising is an important part of our nation's agriculture. Sometimes land that cannot support crops has proved valuable as pasture. Shown are cattle grazing in North Dakota. (North Dakota State Highway Department)

To rule the mountain is to rule the river.

—Ancient Chinese proverb.

Arrowrock Dam, on the Boise River in Idaho, is one of the largest of the Bureau of Reclamation's irrigation projects. Why have we been concerned with irrigating so many acres of our western lands? (Idaho Department of Commerce and Development)

agreement on the conservation values but have not reached agreement on the proper roles of government and business in controlling water.

RECLAMATION. In the arid and semi-arid lands of the West, water can change desert land into highly productive farmland. Consequently, since 1902, when the Bureau of Reclamation was established, many irrigation projects have been developed. The law authorizes the government to construct irrigation works and to charge for the use of the water.

More than seven million acres of western land are now served by these irrigation projects—an area slightly smaller than Massachusetts and Connecticut combined. Congress has usually recognized that the arid states of the West have the first rights to use water controlled by dams.

For miles around Bonneville Dam, for example, one can drive through green farmlands that would again become deserts if the water were not available. At crossroads, villages have developed where none existed just a short time ago. The possibilities of reclaiming wasteland by irrigation have been demonstrated. If the time

comes that our country needs more land for raising food, cheap water power and irrigation might help to supply our needs.

FORESTS. Once the United States was heavily covered with forests so thick they were considered a handicap by some settlers. Trees were so abundant that no one thought of saving them. Actually many trees were obstacles for the pioneers. Much of the back-breaking work of their time was put into clearing the land of trees to make farmland and roads.

Later, in the nineteenth century, with the coming of industrialization, fortunes were made in the lumber business. Lumber was needed, but trees were cut wastefully and recklessly.

Our generation has had to learn new methods of forest preservation. We now understand that trees because of their large root system hold water on hills, preventing soil erosion and stopping floods at the places where they start. We know, too, that our forests are not unlimited. We either preserve them or go without the hundreds of items made from wood.

Since 1891 Congress has given the national government increasing power over

Discuss some of the important products which are derived from the forests.

639

forests. In that year the President was authorized to establish national forests on lands owned by the government. In 1911 Congress approved a law that permits the government to buy land along navigable streams for forest development. In the 1930's unemployed young men worked in Civilian Conservation Corps camps planting trees and protecting the forests.

These and other activities have been carried on chiefly by the Forest Service in the Department of Agriculture. The service cares for more than 150 national forests— about 190 million acres located throughout the states and in the Commonwealth of Puerto Rico.

Various methods are used to protect the forests from fire, insects, and disease. New trees are planted. The cutting of trees and grazing are regulated by scientific methods. The sale of the timber and the grazing fees help pay the cost of the Forest Service.

Forest conservation is complicated by the fact that most forests are privately owned. State and national government agencies have tried to teach good forestry methods to these private owners and have helped with fire prevention and fire fighting. Yet for many years more trees were cut down than were replaced. In addition, forest fires, chiefly caused by carelessness, destroy about fifteen million acres of trees each year.

Many private lumbering companies are aware of the need for conservation and have adopted modern forestry practices, including the planting of a new tree for each tree that is cut down.

These practices are beginning to produce results. If they are continued, we may be able to repair much of the damage that has been done to our land.

FISH AND WILDLIFE. The movement of people westward, the increasing population, and the industrialization of our country destroyed animals, birds, and fish as well as forests. Some species were destroyed by too much hunting. Others were killed because their natural homes were destroyed by floods, by the draining of swamps, or by the cutting of trees.

Citizens, however, have come to realize the importance of conserving animal life on the land, in the sea, and in the air. Animals are important sources of food and clothing. They help, too, in keeping a balance among nature's forces.

State laws regulate hunting and fishing as a conservation measure. States have developed fish hatcheries and wildlife refuges. Sportsmen's associations have helped develop a public opinion to support these activities.

The Fish and Wildlife Service of the Department of the Interior carries on similar conservation activities and cooperates with the state governments. Funds appropriated by Congress to assist states with their programs are administered by the service. The commercial fisheries of Alaska and inland fisheries are also supervised by it. Waterfowl are protected in their migrations by cooperative action with Canada and Mexico.

PARKS. Local, state, and national governments operate parks. One purpose of these parks is to provide outdoor recreation. Another purpose is to preserve a few great areas in their natural state, unchanged for all generations. Each of these purposes fits the goals of the conservation movement.

Our national parks are best known for their preservation of scenery and natural life, but some state and local parks have also preserved important areas. In a typical year one out of three persons in the United States will visit one of our national parks.

Miracles of erosion are seen at the Grand Canyon, Bryce Canyon, and Zion Canyon.

Stress the need for more local, state, and national parks.

The giant redwoods grow in California. Waterfalls, geysers, and other scenic beauties are waiting for the traveler in the West at Yellowstone, Yosemite, Mount Rainier, and Grand Teton National Parks. Shenandoah National Park and Great Smokies National Park are attractions in the East.

The National Park Service is responsible for the preservation of the parks and of historical sites and buildings. Its program includes constructing roads and trails, maintaining campsites and picnic grounds, supervising overnight accommodations, and providing lecture and guide service. The service is faced with a twofold problem: (1) keeping areas in their natural state, and (2) providing enough places to eat and sleep so that people can enjoy the natural wonders without undue commercialization.

MINERALS. Modern industry has a huge appetite for raw materials. Since 1900 our use of minerals has increased more than six times, while our total use of agricultural products has increased less than three times. During World War II industry gobbled up raw materials at a terrific rate. This demand for raw materials has continued and is growing. As a result, people have come to realize that the United States does not have inexhaustible resources.

Here is one example: Iron ore from the mines of Wisconsin and Minnesota has been plentiful. Yet one of the arguments for building the St. Lawrence Seaway was that these vast mines are about worn out and that most iron for the future would have to be shipped in from Newfoundland.

The President's Materials Policy Commission, reporting in 1952, stated that by 1975 we shall face serious problems in supplying raw materials to feed our industries. The commission feared that our basic materials would become harder and more expensive to obtain, because the richest deposits will be used up.

Some raw materials, of course, are not found in the United States. There were twenty-seven minerals needed during World War II for which there was no supply within the United States.

Since most mineral resources are privately owned, the government is limited in what can be done about the wise use of these resources. Information on the importance of conservation can be supplied, and a program of education can be carried on. Research to learn more efficient practices can be conducted.

Surveys to locate new sources of supply can be made, and subsidies can be given to encourage prospectors to search for new sources. In the Department of the Interior, the Bureau of Mines and the Geological Survey are responsible for these activities.

The mineral rights on all public lands, such as national parks, are leased by the Department of the Interior's Bureau of Land Management. Mining operations on these lands are supervised and regulated by the Geological Survey.

Optimists and pessimists can be found among the experts on mineral supplies. The optimist points out that the supply of coal is so great that there is no foreseeable danger of running short of coal. He says that we have discovered more oil since 1938 than we have used. He usually concludes by saying that scientists will find new ways to replace minerals that run short.

The pessimist says that American industry must constantly expand and will need more and more raw materials. He looks at the growth in population rates and observes that more people will use up materials at a faster rate. He looks at worn-out coal, iron, and copper mines and decides that we had better learn to be less wasteful. He respects the scientist but expresses doubts that even science can get something from nothing.

Emphasize again that the United States is far from being completely self-sufficient.

Crater Lake National Park in Oregon is one of many locations whose natural beauty is preserved by the National Park Service. How does preserving our national parks relate to the idea of conservation? (Oregon State Highway Department)

This is an aerial view of a copper mine in Nevada, a state rich in minerals. Why have we become increasingly concerned about the more efficient mining and wiser use of our mineral resources? (The Anaconda Company)

What does the typical citizen do? He looks at our past history and says to himself, "Grandpa and great-grandpa and great-great-grandpa could have saved us a lot of trouble if they had learned to conserve. I wonder what our grandchildren will say about us."

STUDY QUESTIONS

1. What four major changes in farming have taken place in the United States?

2. Why has the farmer been active in politics?

3. How has government aided the education of the farmers?

4. How does the Department of Agriculture aid the farmers through research activities?

5. What does the Farm Credit Administration do?

6. How does the Farmers Home Administration help the small farmer?

CONCEPTS AND GENERALIZATIONS

1
The land of the United States and its riches have contributed much to the nation's high standard of living.

2
Industry and urban areas have replaced agriculture and rural areas in central economic importance.

3
The farmer continues to be an important person in the political and economic life of the nation.

4
Agricultural education and research have combined to change farming methods and to increase crop production.

5
Various government agencies and programs have helped the farmer overcome some • of his economic, production, and marketing problems.

6
Parity tries to keep the farmers' income in line with that of persons in other vocations.

7
Conservation of all our resources has become an important goal of the United States in the twentieth century.

8
Some of our largest engineering projects are the result of the concern for an adequate water supply and the necessity to control water.

9
The nation's conservation programs involve water, forests, soil, fish and wildlife, and minerals.

10
Pollution and the depletion of natural resources have become major problems in this century.

7. Why was the Rural Electrification Administration established?

8. What plans have been used to support the prices paid farmers for their crops?

9. What are the common causes of erosion?

10. What practices help to reduce and to prevent erosion?

11. How and when did the conservation movement come into national prominence?

12. What are the three phases of water and flood control?

13. How has the TVA operated?

14. What is the work of each of the following services: the Bureau of Reclamation, the Forest Service, the Fish and Wildlife Service, the National Park Service?

15. Why are our mineral resources no longer considered inexhaustible?

IDEAS FOR DISCUSSION

1. The statement has been made that "farmers hold the balance of power in American politics." Why do you agree or disagree with this statement?

2. Should commercial banks and privately owned utilities take over the work of farm credit and rural electrification?

3. Farmers are considered to be highly individualistic and the backbone of our free, competitive enterpise system. Yet farmers have been aided by plans which some citizens call socialistic. How do you account for this apparent conflict in basic philosophy?

4. Should price supports be linked to good soil-conservation practices? Why?

5. Should the government continue to build dams and generate electricity, or should electricity be produced exclusively by private companies? Why?

6. What should government do about the conditions reported by the President's Materials Policy Commission? What should private business do? Do the facts show that the prediction made by the Commission in 1952 was correct?

7. Scholars who have made careful studies of the conservation movement now write about "resource-use education" rather than "conservation education." Why are they shifting their emphasis from conservation to wise use of resources?

8. When the twelve-man Hoover Commission made a report to Congress recommending the transfer of many federal lending and guarantee services to private enterprises, two Republican and three Democratic members of the Commission did not agree with the majority. One said, "The recommendations if carried out would make it harder for American citizens to buy homes or get loans for their farms or businesses." In view of this minority criticism, why did the majority make its recommendation? Do you agree with this majority point of view?

9. An agricultural economist wrote, "Price supports for the farmers are of the same order as unemployment compensation for wage-workers. Unemployment is the wage-worker's difficulty, and inadequate prices are the farmer's." Do you think this comparison is justified?

10. In the old days lumbermen had a tough motto: "Cut and get out." Today, lumbermen talk about "tree farming." In what ways is this change a symbol of a new era for conservation?

THINGS TO DO

1. Hold a socio-drama with students representing United States senators. Have senators from Illinois and Iowa oppose irrigation projects, while senators from Montana and Utah plead for them.

2. Prepare a chart showing the changes in the farmers' portion of the national income. For data, consult the latest edition of the *World Almanac* or the *Survey of Current Business* (annual number) published by the Department of Commerce.

3. Investigate which of the "aids to farmers" discussed in this chapter have offices in your county. Have individuals or committees visit these offices and report on their activities.

4. Prepare a special report on the surplus crops that are now in storage in the United States.

5. Prepare an exhibit to show the common causes of erosion and ways of preventing erosion.

6. Draw a chart to show the federal government agencies that are engaged in some type of conservation activity.

7. Write a series of "Believe-it-or-nots" illustrating changes that have taken place in agricultural life during this century.

8. Conduct a public opinion poll among farmers to determine their attitudes toward price supports, rural electrification, soil conservation, and the farmer in politics.

9. Prepare a special report on "Vocational Opportunities in Farming."

10. Write a radio or TV skit to emphasize an aspect of conservation that is important to your community.

11. Make a list of common minerals used in the industries of your state. By investigation in the library, determine which are not available in the United States and how long there will be supplies available of the U.S. minerals.

12. Arrange to visit farms and other places to see good and poor conservation practices.

13. Organize a special committee to find out what your state government does for conservation.

FURTHER READINGS

Bixby, William, A WORLD YOU CAN LIVE IN. David McKay Co., Inc., 1971.

Carr, Donald E., DEATH OF THE SWEET WATERS. W. W. Norton Co., Inc., 1966.

Day, Albert M., MAKING A LIVING IN CONSERVATION. Stackpole Books, 1971.

Douglas, William O., A WILDERNESS BILL OF RIGHTS. Little, Brown and Co., 1965.

Fisher, James, WILDLIFE IN DANGER. Viking Press, 1969.

Graham, Frank Jr., MAN'S DOMINION: THE STORY OF CONSERVATION IN AMERICA. M. Evans & Co., Inc., 1971.

Halacy, D. S., NOW OR NEVER. TODAY'S POLLUTION, TOMORROW'S TRAGEDY. Four Winds Press, 1971.

Hollon, W. Eugene, THE GREAT AMERICAN DESERT THEN AND NOW. Oxford University Press, 1966.

National Geographic Society, AS WE LIVE AND BREATHE: THE CHALLENGE OF OUR ENVIRONMENT. National Geographic Society, 1971.

Reische, Diana L., ed., U.S. AGRICULTURAL POLICY. H. W. Wilson Co., 1966.

Superintendent of Documents, MAN . . . AN ENDANGERED SPECIES? Washington, D.C.: Government Printing Office, 1968.

Terrell, John Upton, THE UNITED STATES DEPARTMENT OF AGRICULTURE: A STORY OF FOOD, FARMS, AND FORESTS. Meredith Press, 1966.

COLLECTIVE BARGAINING—the process by which labor and management representatives work out agreements.

COPYRIGHT—the exclusive right of author, composer, or artist to publish, reproduce, and sell books, pamphlets, and other written, musical, and artistic works.

CORPORATION—a group of individuals who have a charter granting them permission to operate a business, with privileges and liabilities as a group and not as individuals.

INJUNCTION—a court order forbidding certain activities, such as a strike or a violation of a contract.

MEDIATOR—a person or a group who makes suggestions or offers compromises to settle a dispute; for example, a labor dispute between a union and an industrial concern.

MONOPOLY—complete control of a service or of the production of a commodity.

PATENT—the exclusive right of an inventor to manufacture and sell the invention.

PUBLIC UTILITY—a private company that provides service to the public without competition and subject to government regulation.

STRIKE—the refusal of employees to work, usually because of a dispute involving wages, other benefits, or working conditions.

SUBSIDY—a grant of money from one government to another or to a private enterprise which is providing a public service.

TARIFF—a tax on imported goods; also called duty.

TRADEMARK—a distinctive word or symbol to identify a particular product or company.

TRUST—a combination of companies organized to eliminate competition and control prices.

WORKMEN'S COMPENSATION—money paid to an employee injured in the course of his work; compensation insurance; accident insurance.

THE LANGUAGE OF GOVERNMENT

Describe how the national government is able to regulate business and labor through the rather broad interpretation of the interstate commerce clause in the Constitution.

30
Business, Labor, and Government

In the fall of 1966 Congress made some changes in the minimum wage law. New minimums were established under which five million low-wage workers received pay increases. Eight million additional workers were brought under the law. For the first time some agricultural workers were affected by the minimum wage law. An additional 37,000 grocery stores were covered.

The President hailed the increases and the new coverages as a step forward in getting larger incomes for low-income families. George Meany, president of the AFL-CIO, called them "the most potent single weapon in the war on poverty." Many businessmen agreed with these views, but some said the new minimums could lead to further inflation.

Business, labor, government—all three were involved in these and later amendments to the minimum wage law. Business had to pay the higher wages to workers affected by the law. Labor benefited from the new rates. Government was concerned with

The automobile industry is one of the largest in America. It employs many, many workers who are dependent on its existence for their livelihood. Shown here is an exterior view (left) and a portion of an assembly line (right) of an American Motors plant. Why has it been found necessary to have a certain amount of government regulation of labor? Why has it been necessary to have a certain amount of government regulation of industry? (American Motors Corporation)

raising the level of income of workers and, at the same time, with keeping income rates in line with what business could afford to pay. This is an example of government as the maker of the rules under which business and labor operate.

GOVERNMENT AS THE RULES-MAKER   There are three ideas about the position government should take

on the proper rules for business and labor. Position 1 is that government should stay out of all of these affairs. This has become known as the *laissez-faire* system. The term is French and means "to let alone." Under this system government does not make rules. Business and labor are "let alone"; they do as they please.

Position 2 is that government should aid and regulate business and labor only insofar as this is good for the general welfare.

Ask for student opinion relative to the three stated positions.

Under position 2, government does not let business or labor alone; it makes rules when they are needed and gives special help if the necessity arises.

Position 3 is that government completely takes over business and labor. The government owns business and industry. It controls the lives, wages, and hours of work of the laborers. Government is no longer the servant of business and labor but the master.

Which of these positions do we have in the United States? Examples can be found in which our government has taken each of these positions, but, in general, we have held to position 2. The minimum wage law is one example.

As was discussed in Chapter 1, we believe in the basic idea that our government is concerned with both liberty and the general welfare. Because we believe in liberty we have encouraged the free-enterprise system. We have held to the right of individuals and groups to own private property and have had faith that competition was the best regulator of business.

But we have also believed that business and labor need the help of government and that at times they need to be regulated. While our governments have owned and operated some businesses, we have not adopted the practice that labor and business should be completely controlled by the government.

GOVERNMENT AIDS TO BUSINESS

From its beginning our government has given assistance to business. Alexander Hamilton and, later, Henry Clay have been among the most famous supporters of government aid to business.

The Constitution gives the federal government the right to regulate and control interstate and foreign commerce. Coining money, establishing currency, granting copyrights and patents, and regulating bankruptcy are other constitutional powers that have been used to help business. As a result of our past history, the constitutional powers, and the present needs, the chief governmental aids to business today are the Department of Commerce, tariffs, loans, subsidies, copyrights, patents, trademarks, weather reports, and standards for weights and measures.

THE DEPARTMENT OF COMMERCE. The businessman's department in Washington is the Department of Commerce. As described in Chapter 12, the department carries on a great variety of activities. The department was originally created in 1903 as the Department of Commerce and Labor, but separate departments were made in 1913.

The Department of Commerce promotes foreign and domestic commerce; foreign travel to the United States; and the mining, manufacturing, shipping, and fishing industries. Information essential to businessmen is brought together and published. The department's monthly magazine, *Survey of Current Business,* is well known among businessmen and economists for reports on economic conditions.

TARIFFS. A tax placed upon an import from a foreign country is a *tariff.* Throughout our history such taxes have been used to help businesses. If it costs more to produce an article in the United States than it does in another country, the foreign product could be shipped here and sold for less than the U. S. product. The result would be that the U.S. businessman would have to reduce his costs or go out of business. When our country was young, it seemed necessary to protect business from this type of foreign competition. So a tax was placed on the import to raise the cost of the foreign product above the cost of the U.S. product.

Describe the difference between a protective tariff and a revenue tariff.

647

For many years the tariff was considered to be one of the best ways to give aid to businessmen. In recent years there have been differences of opinion over this type of aid to business. After World War I and again in the depression year of 1930, Congress increased tariff rates. These actions decreased the imports coming into our country, but they also decreased our exports. When we did not buy the products of other countries, they did not buy our products.

As a result of these experiences and the great growth of our economic and political power in world affairs, there have been many efforts to change our tariff policy. A basic change was made by the Reciprocal Tariff Act of 1934, a law which was renewed with minor changes until 1962. By this law the President was given the authority to negotiate trade agreements with foreign countries on the basis that if they would lower their tariffs we would lower our tariffs too.

The Trade Expansion Act of 1962 gave the President the broadest powers ever to regulate tariffs. It contained an adjustment-assistance provision to aid businesses and workers who are hard hit by losses because of lowered tariffs.

The State Department, the Department of Commerce, and special commissions have made studies of tariff problems. Their reports have met with varied reactions by differing groups. Some businessmen would like to move toward complete free trade. Other businessmen favor a return to a high-tariff policy. Congressmen finally have to decide. Recent Congresses have favored lowering tariffs.

Tariff treaties are actually made by the State Department for the President. In addition the President relies on the United States Tariff Commission, an independent agency, for facts and information. Before 1934 the Tariff Commission was influential in raising or lowering tariff rates, but since that time it has become primarily a research and reporting agency. The Special Representative for Trade Negotiations in the Executive Office of the President also advises the President on matters related to international trade agreements.

LOANS AND SUBSIDIES. Government has helped many types of business by lending money or by gifts of money called *subsidies.* From 1932 to 1954 the Reconstruction Finance Corporation (RFC) was the giant of banking institutions in this country. RFC was a government corporation that lent money to banks, to railroads, to industries, and to many governmental agencies.

The RFC was abolished because Congress felt that it was no longer needed. The war and depression conditions which had brought about the need for government loans to business had disappeared.

Subsidies have been used to help many types of business. A subsidy is a grant or gift; it is not a loan. In the early history of railroads, public land was given to railroads to help them expand across the country. In recent years the merchant marine and commercial aviation have been aided because of their importance to our defense and to our economic life.

COPYRIGHTS, PATENTS, AND TRADEMARKS. The Constitution states (Article I, Section 8) that Congress has the power "to promote the progress of science and useful arts by securing for limited times to authors and inventors the exclusive right to their respective writings and discoveries." Under laws passed by Congress, these exclusive rights are granted through copyrights, patents, and trademarks.

The *copyright* gives to the author, artist, or publisher the exclusive right to sell a

Ask the students to think of some common trademarks.

The Patent Office Public Search Room in Washington, D.C. contains descriptions of more than 3,300,000 patents by subject category. (Patent Office, U.S. Dept. of Commerce)

writing or a work of art. Books, magazines, pamphlets, songs, cartoons, maps, motion pictures, and lectures can be copyrighted. Copyrights last for twenty-eight years and may be renewed. Copyrights are granted by the Library of Congress through the Register of Copyrights.

The *patent* grants the inventor or the owner of an invention the exclusive right to manufacture and sell the invention. Under the terms of the present law, a new process or a new variety of living plant is treated in the same manner as an invention.

The patent lasts for seventeen years. It is granted by the Patent Office in the Department of Commerce. Before the patent is granted, a careful search is made to be sure that the invention is really a new one.

Patents have helped build many of our largest industries; among them are the electronics, chemical, and automotive industries. It is interesting to note, however, that the automobile companies have voluntarily agreed to make any patent available to other companies after a period of one year. As a result, such items as automatic transmissions and wrap-around windshields quickly became common on all makes of cars.

The *trademark* is a distinctive word or symbol that is used on some product sold in interstate commerce. The registration of a trademark lasts for twenty years and may be renewed as often as desired.

The Supreme Court has held that the power to register trademarks comes from the interstate commerce clause, so only products sold in interstate commerce are eligible. Trademarks are promoted by modern advertising and can be sold along with the business. They are registered by the Patent Office.

OTHER AIDS. A few other aids to business deserve special mention. The National Weather Service of the Department of Commerce gives important aid not only to business but to the rest of us, too. Airlines, railroads, truckers, fruit growers, fishing companies, and other businesses dependent on weather conditions are especially interested in the regular weather reports.

The National Bureau of Standards in the Department of Commerce, in accordance with the Constitution, fixes the standards for weights and measures. In addition, research activities are carried on to detemine quality and performance of products used by federal agencies. Some of this research is done also for private business.

The National Ocean Survey of the Department of Commerce and the Coast Guard of the Transportation Department give much help to commercial shipping and to fishing fleets.

REGULATION OF
BUSINESS   The American people believe in American business, and they want it to thrive. The happiness and welfare of each of us is dependent in part upon the success of business enterprises. At the same time, we recognize that competition causes some people to do unfair things. Most athletes are good sportsmen, but now and then in the heat of athletic competition someone will take advantage of the rules.

The same is true of businessmen. Most of them are honest and believe that "what is best for the customer is best for them." But there are businessmen who are unfair and even dishonest. Some operate according to the code of "let the buyer beware." Business is so important in all of our lives that the rules for competition have to be made and enforced because of those who take unfair advantages.

MONOPOLIES. In a free-enterprise system built on the values of competition, to destroy competition is to destroy our economic system. Consequently, government tries very hard to prevent one person or one company from getting complete control of any product. Such exclusive control is called a *monopoly* and ends competition.

When businesses were small and owned by one person or by partners, there was little danger of monopoly. But with the growth of modern industry, the cost of factories and machines has become very great. As a result, the *corporation* developed as a method of owning business. As corporations grew in size, their control of the manufacture of certain products also grew.

With their large investments and their vast ability to produce, it was perhaps inevitable that some corporations tried to protect their profits by eliminating competition. Sometimes this was done by gaining control of all other competing companies. Other times, it was done by reaching agreements to fix prices and to fix territories where sales could be made.

Toward the end of the nineteenth century the evils of these types of business arrangements became apparent, and in 1890 Congress passed the *Sherman Antitrust Act.* This act was aimed at one specific type of monopolistic practice—the *trust.* A trust exists when one company buys the controlling stock of a number of separate companies. The persons who own the trust

It is interesting to note that the Sherman Antitrust Act of 1890 was so loosely worded that for ten years no large corporation was convicted.

then can control each of the companies.

In making this type of organization illegal, the Sherman Act used very broad language. The act states that "every contract, combination in the form of trust, . . . or conspiracy, in restraint of trade or commerce among the several states, or with foreign countries" is illegal. Thus the position of the government against monopoly was made clear. The enforcement of the law has, however, been difficult. The courts must decide whether a combination is in restraint of trade.

In cases brought before the Supreme Court various interpretations of the act have been made. Two general policies have been used to settle disputes: (1) The Supreme Court has held that agreements between companies to fix prices are destructive of competition and are not legal. (2) The Court has also held that bigness alone is not destructive of competition.

Therefore, when two or more companies join or merge into one company, the "rule of reason" must apply. If the joining seems to be for the purpose of destroying competition, the merger is illegal. If the purpose of the merger is not monopolistic, it is legal. The effects of these decisions have been to encourage some businesses to combine.

In 1914 the national government made two other attempts to prevent the curbing of competition. Within one month the Federal Trade Commission was established and the Clayton Antitrust Act was passed.

The *Federal Trade Commission* is an enforcement agency, designed to prevent "unfair competition in interstate commerce." As in so many public matters, Congress had learned that laws are not effective unless there is an enforcement agency. The commission consists of five members, appointed for seven-year terms. No more than three members can belong to the same political party.

The commission investigates unfair business practices that tend to destroy competition. Penalties and "cease and desist" orders can be applied. Failure to obey the commission's orders results in appeal to a federal court of appeals for appropriate court action.

The *Clayton Antitrust Act* is an extension of the Sherman Antitrust Act. Two features are important: (1) Organized labor and nonprofit agricultural organizations are specifically exempted from the provisions of the act. (2) Instead of general provisions against unfair competition, the act condemns specific practices. For example, these practices were made illegal: price cutting to drive out competition; false advertising; interlocking directorates; different prices for different purchasers.

Since 1914 the story of monopoly and unfair competition has been one of enforcement rather than one of legislation. The Antitrust Division of the Department of Justice is the chief agency to prosecute monopoly. The Federal Trade Commission investigates specific unfair trade practices.

Consolidated Edison Company's power plant, which serves New York City and some adjacent areas, is the largest privately owned power plant in the United States. Why are public utilities under careful government regulation? (Courtesy Consolidated Edison Company, N.Y.)

One important feature of the commission's work has been the conferences on trade practices. Business representatives of specific industries are brought together, and fair and unfair practices are demonstrated and explained. Few American businessmen violate the law willfully. Their complaints have been that they were not sure what was legal and what was illegal. The conferences have helped honest businessmen to obey the laws.

The issue of "bigness" still remains before the American people. The complicated industrial processes plus the mechanization of industry have tended to bring about larger and larger companies. No other nation has ever tried to insist upon free competition as we have done.

Are there dangers in steel companies, automobile companies, grocery companies getting too big? If big companies can sell better products at lower prices, is this what the people want? Can a free-enterprise system survive if control of the chief industries is in the hands of a few companies?

PUBLIC UTILITIES. Some businesses are so important to the general welfare that government gives them special privileges. Telephone, gas, electricity, and transportation companies are typical. It does not seem wise to have several telephone companies serving one community. Nor does it seem wise to have several gas or electric companies putting mains or wires around the same town.

Businesses of this type are given exclusive rights and then are carefully regulated. These "legal" monopolies are usually called *public utilities.*

Public utilities may be regulated by local, state, or national governments. The regulation usually takes four forms: prices have to be approved, minimum standards of service have to be maintained, the bookkeeping or accounting system has to be approved, and sale of stocks or bonds or any borrowing must be approved. In other words, public utilities are privately owned companies over which the government maintains a great deal of control.

Gas and electric utilities are regulated by state public utility commissions. The Federal Power Commission, an independent agency, regulates the sale of electricity and natural gas across state lines. It also regulates companies that produce electricity from water power.

The Federal Railroad Administration in the Department of Transportation regulates the railroads, interstate motor trucking and bus lines, and the pipelines that transport petroleum and petroleum products. The commercial airlines are regulated on matters of safety and traffic by the Federal Aviation Administration in the same department.

The Federal Communications Commission regulates the telephone, telegraph, and cable services and the radio and television companies. Most states also regulate the telephone and telegraph companies within their boundaries. Radio and television companies are not restricted on profits, since they are not strictly public utilities and there is competition between companies. But the number of air channels is limited, so the government has placed their regulation under the FCC.

REGULATION OF OTHER BUSINESSES. Government now regulates the sale of stocks and bonds; the sale of insurance; and the sale of foods, drugs, and cosmetics.

Stocks and bonds are owned by many people. The number of persons owning stocks and bonds has increased greatly in the past two decades. Any person can buy a share in some business.

As a result of the stock market crash in 1929, the federal government passed laws establishing the *Securities and Exchange Commission* (SEC). The law requires that before a company may issue and sell stocks or bonds all necessary information must be registered with the SEC. Companies are also required to publish complete annual reports. The accuracy of the information is checked by the commission, and there are penalties for companies that make false claims.

Insurance companies are the largest single group of investors in the nation. They have huge resources to invest. They have come to be one of the fundamental supports of our economic system. States, through state insurance commissions, have been the chief regulators of the insurance companies.

From 1868 to 1944 the Supreme Court held that regulation of insurance was outside federal control, because it was "not a transaction of commerce." However, in 1944 the Court decided that insurance was subject to federal regulation under the commerce clause. The insurance companies are now subject to the federal antitrust laws.

Foods, drugs, and cosmetics are regulated by several state and federal agencies. The chief federal agencies include the **Food and Drug Administration** in the Department of Health, Education, and Welfare, which tries to prevent the misbranding or adulteration of foods, drugs, and cosmetics; the Federal Trade Commission, an independent agency, which investigates false and misleading advertising; and the animal inspection service of the Department of Agriculture. States have similar agencies to protect the buying public.

As the great "rules-maker," government has aided business when this seemed desirable and has regulated business when this seemed necessary. But in this century a new force has become powerful in American life. This new force is organized labor.

Government has found it essential to be rules-maker for labor just as it has for business.

GOVERNMENT AIDS TO LABOR

The position of labor in American life has changed greatly in the past hundred years. Once an employer could make any kind of job arrangement with an employee. He could hire young children. He could hire women. His employees could work long hours under unsanitary conditions. He could pay the workers as little as they would accept.

Workers in earlier periods could not organize because the courts held that unions interfered with the employer's right to determine his rightful share of profits. Such conditions have gradually changed until today labor holds a powerful place in political and economic life. The chief governmental aids to labor are the Department of Labor, recognition of unions and collective bargaining, unemployment assistance, help in settling labor-management disputes, and anti-injunction legislation.

THE DEPARTMENT OF LABOR. Labor was not strong enough politically to get a separate department until 1913. The Department of Labor, as described in Chapter 12, is concerned with fair labor standards, safety for the worker in industry, workmen's compensation, and the welfare of the woman worker.

Information on unemployment, wages, and working conditions is gathered. One of the department's publications, the *Monthly Labor Review*, is a standard source of information on such matters. Another source is a second monthly publication of the department, *Employment and Earnings and Monthly Report on the Labor Force*. The department is one of the smaller ones, but many activities helpful to labor are also

The first woman Cabinet member, Frances Perkins, was Secretary of Labor under Franklin Roosevelt. She championed Negro labor rights.

Secretary of Labor James D. Hodgson meets with railroad officials in August 1970 to discuss new and better collective bargaining methods in the railroad industry. (U.S. Dept. of Labor)

carried on by other departments and independent agencies.

UNIONS AND COLLECTIVE BARGAINING. The chief aid that government has given to labor is the right to organize unions and the right to collective bargaining. As long as courts held that unions were "criminal conspiracies," labor's advances were very slow. Then in 1935 Congress passed the National Labor Relations Act, often called the Wagner Act. Labor leaders have called this law the "Great Charter" for the labor movement.

Later amendments have changed some of the provisions of the original law. The chief amendments were made by the Taft-Hartley Act of 1947 and the Landrum-Griffin Act of 1959.

The Wagner Act and its later amendments established the National Labor Relations Board (NLRB), with five members appointed by the President for five-year

terms. The NLRB has two chief tasks: (1) to promote collective bargaining and (2) to prevent unfair labor practices.

Collective bargaining means that negotiations on wages, hours, or working conditions are carried on between the representatives of a labor union and the employer, rather than between the individual employee and the employer. Who should be the employee's representative?

It is at this point that NLRB comes into action. The board holds an election among employees to decide whether a majority wants a particular union to represent them. When one union gets a majority vote, the employer is required to bargain collectively with that union's representatives.

Unfair labor practices of employers are defined in the law. Among these are interference by the employer with the right to organize unions, discrimination against employees because of union activity, domina-

Make sure that the student understands such terms as "collective bargaining," "right-to-work laws," "union shop," "arbitration," etc.

COLLECTIVE BARGAINING AGREEMENT

ARTICLE I—RECOGNITION

The Company recognizes the Union as the exclusive representative of the employer's production and maintenance employees for the purpose of determining wages, hours, and all other conditions of employment. . . .

ARTICLE II—MANAGEMENT RIGHTS

The management of the Plant and the direction of the working force, except as otherwise qualified herein, are the exclusive functions of the Company.

ARTICLE III—UNION MEMBERS REQUIREMENTS AND CHECKOFF

SECTION 1. All present employees who are members of the Union shall, as a condition of employment, maintain their membership in the Union during the life of this Agreement through regular payments of dues to the Union. The Company may hire new employees from whatever source it desires, but all new employees and all present employees who are not members of the Union shall, as a condition of continued employment, join the Union within thirty (30) days after the date of employment. . . .

SECTION 2. New employees with less than thirty (30) days of service may be discharged at the sole discretion of the Company without appeal by the Union. . . .

ARTICLE IX—GRIEVANCES AND ARBITRATION

SECTION 1. All differences, disputes, and grievances that may arise between the Union and the Company under the terms of this Agreement shall be handled in the following steps:

a. By the aggrieved employee with or without the Union Section Steward on the one hand and the Section Foreman on the other hand. If no satisfactory settlement is reached within forty-eight (48) hours, the matter shall be referred to:

b. The Union Shop Committee on the one hand and the Department Head or Superintendent on the other hand. If no satisfactory settlement is reached within forty-eight (48) hours, the matter shall be referred to:

c. The Union Shop Committee and Representatives of the National Union on the one hand and the Company's Representatives on the other hand. If no satisfactory settlement is reached between them within five (5) days, the matter shall be submitted to arbitration as hereinafter provided.

SECTION 2. All differences, disputes, and grievances that may arise between the Union and the Company with regard to the interpretation or application of the provisions of the Agreement, which have not been satisfactorily settled after following the procedure hereinabove set forth, shall, at the request of either party, be submitted to arbitration by a Board of Arbitration. The Board of Arbitration shall consist of one member selected by the Union, one member selected by the Company, and a third impartial member selected by the two. If no agreement shall be reached on the third arbitrator within five (5) days, a third arbitrator shall be appointed by the American Arbitration Association. The decision of the Board shall be by majority vote and in each case the decision shall be final and binding upon each of the parties. . . .

—Excerpts from a fictitious agreement, quoted in full in: Robert E. Doherty, *Labor Relations Primer,* Ithaca, New York: New York State School of Industrial and Labor Relations, 1965.

tion of the union by the employer, and refusal to bargain with the representatives chosen by the employees. The board is required to prevent such practices.

Labor organizations, by this law, are forbidden to use certain practices, including charging excessive initiation fees to join a union, forcing employers to pay money for services not performed, and keeping employees from organizing or bargaining collectively.

The act applies only to employers engaged in interstate commerce, but most of the industrial states have passed similar laws. These laws have been declared constitutional by the Supreme Court. The effect on the growth of labor unions has been great. In 1935 union membership was about three million. Today it is estimated to be around nineteen million. The AFL-CIO, the federation of unions combined from the old American Federation of Labor and the Congress of Industrial Organizations, is the largest labor organization. There are about fifty smaller unions.

Section 14 (b) of the Taft-Hartley Act has been the subject of much controversy. Under the provisions of this section, states are allowed to forbid employers and unions to make union shop agreements in shops where the federal government has jurisdiction. As a result, a number of states have passed laws known as *right-to-work* laws. In these states union membership is not a condition for employment or for retaining a job.

The controversy is between unions and union leaders, on the one hand, who want the section repealed and some individuals and groups, on the other hand, who want it retained and even strengthened. The unions oppose the right-to-work laws and favor a union shop in which each worker must join the union in order to stay on the job. They maintain that all who benefit from union activity should support the union by membership. Opponents of the union shop state that the employee should be free to join or not to join a union as he wishes.

Congress has had bills on both sides of the issue before it. It has not acted either to repeal or to strengthen Section 14 (b).

UNEMPLOYMENT ASSISTANCE. When a worker is unemployed he may need two types of assistance: some money to help until he gets regular work, and aid in locating a new job.

Financial assistance is given through unemployment compensation, a part of the social security system. Unemployment compensation is a feature of the 1935 Social Security Act, but a national system was not established. Each state makes its own unemployment laws, but the federal government has supervision over the programs.

The payments are made from funds collected by the states taxing employers of four or more persons; in some cases, even smaller employers. The rate averages about 2 per cent of the total payroll, excluding the earnings above a certain amount per year for any worker. The limit varies with states; it may be as low as $3,000 and as high as $7,200. The money collected is placed in an unemployment trust fund kept

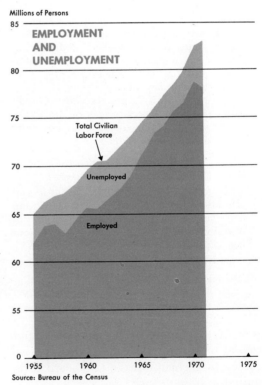

Millions of Persons

EMPLOYMENT AND UNEMPLOYMENT

Total Civilian Labor Force

Unemployed

Employed

Source: Bureau of the Census

The graph compares the total labor force with the actual number of persons employed. What are some effects of unemployment?

Discuss the question whether or not a person should collect unemployment if he is out on strike.

in the United States Treasury, but money is returned to the states as they need it for payments to the unemployed. The payment to the individual worker is made only in accordance with state law, and, consequently, there are great variations from one state to another.

The average weekly benefit paid is about forty to fifty dollars. Payments are made only to those registered for a job with the United States Employment Service and in nearly all states after a waiting period of one week. Payments may be drawn for periods of twenty-six weeks.

Aid in locating a job is obtained from state employment agencies and the United States Employment Service. This service administers funds of the federal government which are given to the state employment agencies subject to certain restrictions. One restriction is that the state agencies must cooperate with each other. As a result, an unemployed person in one state can learn about available jobs in another state. Another restriction is that federal funds must be matched by state funds in every instance.

ASSISTANCE IN SETTLING DISPUTES. When employers and employees cannot agree on wages or working conditions, a *strike* is the usual outcome. A strike is labor's most powerful weapon. The right to strike has been held legal by the courts, although some specific strike actions have been ruled illegal.

Strikes cause hardship for many workers because the loss of income during a strike is the same as when they are unemployed. Some unions keep large sums of money in reserves, "strike funds," to help strikers during periods of a prolonged strike.

Strikes cause difficulties for workers, employers, and the general public. The government, without interfering with the right to strike, tries to help bring industrial disputes to an end. The Federal Mediation and Conciliation Service has agents in seven regional offices and in most of the large industrial centers.

These agents, called *mediators*, try to bring the representatives of employers and employees together in conferences to reach agreements on disputed matters. Experience in other disputes, skill in keeping discussion going, and good will developed over the years have helped the mediators in the solution of many difficult labor-management problems. The service has no law-enforcement powers. Any success in settling disputes must come about through persuasion.

The service has found that, by encouraging better day-to-day relations between labor and management, most disputes do not reach the strike stage. The service is available only to industries engaged in

---

In his veto message[1] of the Taft-Hartley Act President Truman stated:

Our basic national policy has always been to establish by law standards of fair dealing and then to leave the working of the economic system to the free choice of individuals. . . . I find that this bill is completely contrary to that national policy of economic freedom. It would require the Government, in effect, to become an unwanted participant at every bargaining table. . . . The National Labor Relations Act would be converted from an instrument with the major purpose of protecting the right of workers to organize and bargain collectively into a maze of pitfalls and complex procedures.

Senator Taft answered President Truman in a radio address. Among other things he said:

The bill in no way interferes with the rights of the parties to bargain, in no way limits the right to strike if they fail to agree, except in the case of a nation-wide strike for a period of eighty days until an election can be held.[2]

[1]The bill was later passed over the President's veto.

[2]Robert A. Taft, radio address quoted in the *New York Times,* June 21, 1947. © 1947 by the New York Times Company. Reprinted by permission.

Members of a Detroit auto union listen to a speech by their co-director informing them of new gains obtained by the union in contract talks with management. (AFL-CIO News photo)

interstate commerce, but most industrial states have similar agencies for helping to settle disputes in industries which do not cross state lines.

The National Mediation Board performs similar services for the railroads, express companies, and airlines. Employers and employees of these companies are regulated by the Railway Labor Act rather than by the National Labor Relations Act.

ANTI-INJUNCTION LEGISLATION. An *injunction* is a court order forcing someone to do something or to stop doing something. For years labor unions were suspicious of courts because they would issue injunctions forcing strikers back to work. Labor leaders saw this use of the injunction as a threat to the labor movement.

In 1932 Congress passed the Norris-LaGuardia Act which denied courts the use of the injunction in cases involving refusal to work, joining a union, paying union dues, or peaceful assembly. Labor considered this act a great victory. Several states enacted similar laws.

For fifteen years, these uses of injunctions were illegal. Then in 1947 the Taft-Hartley Act made injunctions legal again in cases of labor disputes under certain conditions. The National Labor Relations Board may go to court to get an injunction against any unfair labor practice.

The law also provides that the President may ask the Attorney General to get an injunction forbidding a strike for eighty days if the strike might "imperil the national health and safety." The intent was to provide a cooling-off period of eighty days for very serious strikes. Labor has not liked this renewed legality of the use of injunctions.

LABOR REGULATIONS It is hard today for people to realize what working conditions were even a few decades ago. Long hours, low pay, poor working conditions were typical. Leisure time was rare. Vacations with pay for workers were practically unknown. In poor families, children and mothers worked as long and as hard as

Refer to the famous Pullman Strike of 1894, when President Cleveland obtained an injunction against interference with the mails and interstate commerce.

fathers. Accidents in industry were considered a normal risk of employment. Well-lighted, well-ventilated, sanitary factories were practically unknown. "Sweatshop" was the common term of scorn applied to the place where one worked.

These conditions have changed greatly, partly because employers have recognized that well-paid, healthy workers produce more and buy more and partly because of agreements reached by employers and interest groups led by unions. But many of these changes came about because sympathetic people and labor unions insisted that laws be passed to regulate and improve working conditions. The health and welfare of workers and their wages and hours of work became the subject of much federal and state legislation.

CHILDREN. As late as 1910, nearly one out of every five children between the ages of ten and fifteen in this country was at work. Today children of this age group are in school. This is one of the great social gains of this century. The change was brought about by a combination of child labor laws and compulsory school attendance laws.

Every state has laws dealing with child labor. The difficulty with state control is that one state hestitates to make its laws too severe for fear that industry will move to another state. Federal legislation, therefore, was urged. However, attempts to get a national child labor law were declared unconstitutional by the Supreme Court. In 1924 Congress passed a child labor amendment to the Constitution, but as yet not enough states have ratified it.

In 1941 the Supreme Court reversed its former policy and ruled that the Fair Labor Standards Act was constitutional. This act forbids employment of children under sixteen, or under eighteen in hazardous occupations, in interstate commerce, manufac-

Before the passage of child labor laws, young boys worked long hours, as seen here in an Indiana glassworks at midnight, 1908. (Library of Congress photo)

turing, mining, and transportation. Exceptions are made for child actors and for work on farms. The Office of Child Development in the Department of Health, Education, and Welfare is the chief agency concerned with children's welfare.

WOMEN. Women today are employed in far greater numbers than ever before in our history. The slogan of the woman worker is "Equal pay for equal work." By civil rights laws this is the policy of government and business. A woman cannot be discriminated against on the basis of her sex.

Most states have passed laws dealing with the woman worker. These laws restrict night work, prohibit employment in certain dangerous occupations, limit the hours of work, and set a minimum wage. The Women's Bureau of the Department of Labor in the federal government studies and reports on the problems of the woman worker, but it cannot enforce any laws.

HOURS AND WAGES. Today the federal government and most states have laws that fix the maximum hours a person may work and the minimum wage that must

Make it clear that the federal laws only apply to women and children in interstate commerce.

659

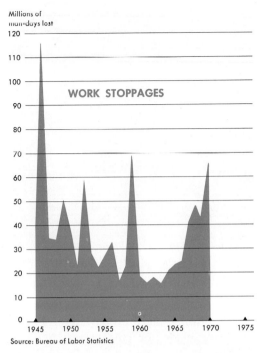

Millions of
man-days lost

WORK STOPPAGES

Source: Bureau of Labor Statistics

The graph shows the number of man-days lost through work stoppages from 1945 to the present. Note that the largest number of man-days lost was in 1946. What effects do these stoppages have on production, earnings, and profits?

be paid. For a long time the courts held that such laws were unconstitutional, since it was claimed that they interfered with the freedom of the employer and the employee. The maximum hours and minimum wage laws represent a great victory for labor.

The Federal Fair Labor Standards Act was passed by Congress in 1938. This is the law to which reference was made in the opening paragraphs of this chapter. The act now provides that any employee engaged in interstate commerce or in the production of goods for interstate commerce must be paid at the rate of not less than $1.60 an hour and time and a half for overtime worked beyond a forty-hour work week.

The original minimum hourly rate was 25 cents an hour. This was raised to 40

cents during World War II, to 75 cents in 1949, to $1.00 in 1956, to $1.25 in 1964, and to $1.40 in 1967. Since February, 1968, the rate has been $1.60 an hour.

The forty-hour maximum work week has been the rule since the Fair Labor Standards Act was adopted. If industry becomes more efficient and a surplus of employees develops, however, Congress might reduce the number of hours to be worked. The provision for paying time and a half for overtime has operated since the act went into effect, but some groups of employees are not included in the overtime provision.

Certain industries were originally exempted from the provisions of the act. However, as the law was amended over the years, more and more industries and employees were included. The basic idea of a "floor under wages and a ceiling over hours" seems now to be an accepted part of our economic system.

The enforcement of this and other wage acts is done by the Office of Wage and Compensation Programs in the Department of Labor. It has ten regional offices and many field offices to which investigators report.

WORKMEN'S COMPENSATION. The rise of the factory system with its increased use of machinery brought with it many hazards for workers. Accidents and industrial disease increased. In a recent year there were two million industrial accidents resulting in 15,000 deaths.

Who should pay for these accidents? Should the worker who has a hand cut off in a machine have to pay for his medical expenses? Or should the employer pay? The worker says the machine was at fault; the employer says the worker was careless.

What about the worker's family? Will he be able to earn as much after the accident? Will the children be supported as well? What if the worker develops a skin disease because of some process used in tanning leather? Or a lung disease because of dust from a grinding process?

For many years a worker had to sue the employer to prove that conditions beyond the worker's control caused the accident or the disease. This was a costly and usually losing legal battle. Then, in the early part of this century, several states pioneered with laws that placed the costs of accidents as a charge against the employer rather than as a personal claim of the employee.

Today all states have such laws. The federal government has similar laws for federal employees, railroad workers, and some others not protected by state laws.

These workmen's compensation laws are patterned after insurance policies. The employer pays a certain sum each year to protect his employees in cases involving industrial accidents and diseases. If an employee has an accident or becomes seriously ill because of his work, he is paid according to a schedule that is part of the system.

The state laws are administered by state workmen's compensation commissions; the federal law, by the Employment Standards Administration in the Department of Labor.

In addition, there are laws which give state departments of labor power to enforce safety regulations and sanitary conditions. These laws are enforced by official state inspectors. Most employers also have introduced effective safety campaigns. The public, the employer, and the worker have found that it pays to prevent accidents and to reduce sickness.

THE FUTURE. During the past few decades the working conditions in all occupations have been improved greatly. It is likely that the years ahead will see further government regulation of working conditions. State and federal laws together with additional worker benefits written into labor-management contracts will provide even better conditions, with more leisure and higher wages for all workers.

STUDY QUESTIONS

1. As rules-maker, what positions can government take toward business and labor?

2. What parts of the Constitution affect business?

3. What does the Department of Commerce do for business?

4. How are tariff rates determined?

5. Why has government given and lent money to business?

6. Why are copyrights, patents, and trademarks important aids to business?

7. How do the National Weather Service, the National Bureau of Standards, the National Ocean Survey, and the coast guard help business?

8. What are the chief antitrust laws? Why are they necessary?

9. How does the Federal Trade Commission influence business?

10. What are the chief federal agencies for the regulation of public utilities? What are their duties?

11. Name other government agencies that regulate business and give the duties of each.

12. What does the Department of Labor do for labor?

13. Why did labor unions develop slowly until the passage of the National Labor Relations Act?

14. How does collective bargaining work?

15. Explain the controversy over section 14(b) of the Taft-Hartley Act.

16. What help is given to the unemployed?

17. How do mediators help settle disputes between employers and employees?

18. Why do labor leaders oppose the use of injunctions in disputes between employers and employees?

19. How has child labor been regulated?

20. How have employment conditions for women been regulated?

CONCEPTS AND GENERALIZATIONS

1

The three possible positions of government in relation to business and labor are no control, control only for the general welfare, and complete control.

2

The traditional position of the United States with regard to business and labor is to make only those regulations which are necessary for the general welfare.

3

Government aids to business include providing services of the Department of Commerce and of government agencies; enacting tariff and trade laws; making loans and subsidies; and granting copyrights, patents, and trademarks.

4

Government regulations in regard to business are concerned with protecting the consumer and the general public and with ensuring competition in the free enterprise system.

5

Government aids to labor include providing services of the Department of Labor and of government agencies, enacting laws to promote collective bargaining and to prevent unfair labor practices, giving assistance to unemployed workers, and helping to settle labor-management disputes.

6

Government regulations, together with the work of individuals and groups, have greatly improved working conditions during the past few decades.

7

Among improved working conditions are those affecting women and children, hours and wages, and workmen's compensation.

21. What are the present provisions of the minimum wage law?

22. How are workers protected against industrial accidents and diseases?

IDEAS FOR DISCUSSION

1. How do Democrats and Republicans differ in their ideas about government as the rulesmaker?

2. Do you favor a high or a low tariff policy? Why?

3. Has the federal government gone too far in the regulation of American business? Not far enough? Why?

4. Why do labor unions call strikes?

5. Are the interests of employers and employees similar or quite different?

6. The Taft-Hartley Act has been vigorously supported and as vigorously opposed. Why has this law caused controversy?

7. Should business and labor be active in politics?

8. Discuss "right-to-work" laws, which prohibit union shop contracts. Who would favor such laws? Who would oppose them? Which types of states have adopted these laws?

9. A number of states have passed fair employment practices acts, commonly called FEPC laws. The purpose of the laws is to make certain that religion, race, or nationality are not factors in employment within the state. FEPC laws are patterned after fair employment practices of the federal government. Beginning during World War II the federal government has had a series of committees to carry out its nondiscrimination policy in employing persons. This work is now the responsibility of the Department of Labor. What is your opinion of these laws and committees? Are they necessary? Should they be continued?

10. The Committee for Economic Development, an organization of businessmen, has stated that "a major aim of American foreign policy is to strengthen the political and economic health of friendly countries. . . . Our foreign economic policy and our tariff policy are intimately involved in this task. . . . It is in the national interest of the United States to continue a policy of gradual and selective tariff reduction." How is tariff policy related to foreign policy? Do the actions of U.S. business and labor leaders affect other parts of the world?

11. What problems of business, labor, and government do you anticipate in the next ten years?

THINGS
TO DO

1. Interview adults to determine their attitudes toward government regulation of business and labor.

2. Invite a local business person to your class to discuss the effects of tariffs.

3. Hold a panel discussion on the topic "Modern advertising has harmed American business because it has taught young people not to trust the claims that are made for products."

4. Make a collection of trademarks for display on a classroom bulletin board.

5. The *World Almanac* lists the following facts on strikes in the United States:

Year	Number of strikes	Workers involved	Man days idle
1953	5,091	2,400,000	28,300,000
1954	3,468	1,530,000	22,600,000
1955	4,320	2,650,000	28,200,000
1956	3,825	1,900,000	33,100,000
1957	3,673	1,390,000	16,500,000
1958	3,694	2,060,000	23,900,000
1959	3,708	1,880,000	69,000,000
1960	3,333	1,320,000	19,100,000
1961	3,367	1,450,000	16,300,000
1962	3,614	1,230,000	18,600,000
1963	3,362	941,000	16,100,000
1964	3,655	1,640,000	22,900,000
1965	3,963	1,550,000	23,300,000
1966	4,115	1,791,700	25,105,000
1967	4,595	2,870,000	42,100,000
1968	5,045	2,649,000	49,018,000
1969	5,700	2,481,000	42,869,000
1970	5,716	3,305,000	66,414,000

From a recent *World Almanac* or the Bureau of Labor Statistics publication *Monthly Labor Review*, bring the figures up to date. Prepare a graph based on these facts. What conclusions do you draw from these facts?

6. Have individuals or committees prepare special reports on the work of the Department of Commerce, the Federal Trade Commission, the Federal Tariff Commission, the Coast Guard, the Federal Power Commission, the Federal Communications Commission, the Securities and Exchange Commission, the Interstate Commerce Commission, the Food and Drug Administration, the National Labor Relations Board, the Federal Mediation and Conciliation Service, the Employment Standards Administration, or the Patent Office.

7. Invite a representative of a labor union to your class to discuss the effects of collective bargaining in your community.

8. Interview a representative of a profit-sharing organization in your community and report on the ways in which this system operates.

9. Participate in a socio-drama in which an employer and a labor union representative have a collective-bargaining session. Both parties are in agreement on all issues except a union shop. If they are not able to agree, have a mediator attempt to adjust this difference.

10. Prepare a booklet entitled "Who's Who in Business and Labor." Include brief biographies of prominent business and labor leaders.

11. Make a study of current tariff rates. Which tariffs are primarily for income? Which are for protection?

12. Visit a credit union office and interview the manager about government regulation of his organization. Give a report to the class.

FURTHER
READINGS

Bernstein, Irving, TURBULENT YEARS: A HISTORY OF THE AMERICAN WORKER, 1933-1941. Houghton Mifflin Co., 1970.

Clark, John O., COMPUTERS AT WORK. Grosset & Dunlap, Inc., 1971.

Cook, Roy, LEADERS OF LABOR. J. B. Lippincott Company, 1966.

Coombs, Charles I., WHEELS, WINGS, AND WATER: THE STORY OF CARGO TRANSPORT. World Publishing Co., 1963.

Dulles, Foster Rhea, LABOR IN AMERICA. Thomas Y. Crowell Co., 1961.

Fanning, Leonard M., TITANS OF BUSINESS. J. B. Lippincott Company, 1964.

Galenson, Walter, A PRIMER ON EMPLOYMENT AND WAGES. Random House, Inc., 1966.

Jones, Edward H., BLACKS IN BUSINESS: PROBLEMS AND PROSPECTS. Holt, Rinehart and Winston, 1971.

Marx, Herbert L., AMERICAN LABOR TODAY. H. W. Wilson Co., 1965.

Paradis, Adrian A., BUSINESS IN ACTION. Julian Messner, 1962.

Terrell, John Upton, UNITED STATES DEPARTMENT OF COMMERCE: A STORY OF INDUSTRY, SCIENCE AND TRADE. Meredith Press, 1966.

Werstein, Irving, THE GREAT STRUGGLE: LABOR IN AMERICA. Charles Scribner's Sons, 1965.

CATEGORICAL AID—help for a specially designated group or classification.

COMMUNITY COLLEGE—a college or junior college sponsored by a local area and fitting its offerings to the community's needs.

CONSOLIDATED — combined into one; merged.

DE FACTO SEGREGATION—actual separation of the races, as by residential patterns.

DE JURE SEGREGATION—separation of the races by law, by legal means.

DISADVANTAGED—persons who are now living, or have lived, under unfavorable conditions.

LAND-GRANT COLLEGE—a college established with the help of a gift of land by the federal government to encourage the study of agriculture and the mechanical arts.

LIBERAL ARTS—subjects of the college curriculum which are designed to provide a general knowledge rather than training for a specific profession or occupation.

MEDICARE—medical care program of the federal government for the aged.

SUPERINTENDENT OF SCHOOLS—person employed by the board of education to administer the schools.

VITAL STATISTICS—information and records regarding births, deaths, and marriages.

WELFARE—the well-being of people; help given to people in need.

THE LANGUAGE
OF GOVERNMENT

Ask the students what they think the writers of the Constitution had in mind in 1787 when they wrote the general welfare clause.

31

Education, Social Welfare, Health, and Government

"To promote the general welfare"—the writers of the Constitution stated this as one of the purposes of our government. They believed that one of the reasons for establishing the government of the United States was to provide services which would benefit all of the people.

What those writers of nearly two hundred years ago specifically had in mind when they wrote that phrase may have been quite different, however, from what we do today in promoting the general welfare. Today local, state, and national governments provide many services which are concerned with the improvement of living for people throughout the nation. They are services for the general welfare of the people.

About 30 per cent of the people in the United States attend some kind of school, ranging from elementary schools, such as this one in Philadelphia, to universities. (City of Philadelphia, Office of the City Representative)

GENERAL WELFARE

As our nation has grown, the general welfare has become increasingly a most important objective. As local communities, as individual states, and as a nation we have tried to realize this objective in a variety of ways. We now provide many services which contribute to the general welfare, for the young and the old, for the rich and the poor, for both urban and rural people, for people in all walks of life.

But not all the problems of providing for the general welfare have been solved, nor has the nation fully reached the objective. Not everyone agrees that what has been done is enough and that what is being done is always well done. Nevertheless, the governmental programs and activities for the general welfare are many and their number is growing almost every year. Previous chapters have described many of them. These final chapters will describe and summarize some special areas of concern with regard to the general welfare.

The governments of the United States

(1) maintain educational systems; (2) look after the security of the disabled, the poor, the aged, the unemployed, the widowed, and the orphaned; (3) provide health services and housing facilities; and (4) protect the life and property of its citizens. Each of these services is important for the development of our nation. Each is concerned with the well-being of our people.

EDUCATION

In the United States we have come to take education for granted. Nearly everybody goes to school for a number of years. Going to school is compulsory. There are parts of the world where this is not so. And it has not always been so in our country. As you know, Abraham Lincoln and most of his generation attended school for only a short time.

Today, going to school is the job of America's children and young people. In addition, thousands of adults attend special schools, colleges, universities, trade schools, and evening schools.

Emphasize the fact that the United States is unique in that it has been educating the masses through public education for many years.

A STATE AND LOCAL FUNCTION.
The Constitution does not include encouraging education as a power of Congress. Our educational systems developed as functions of state and local governments.

In colonial times many people believed that everyone should be educated enough to read the Bible and participate in the affairs of the colonies. But schools were private and many persons could not afford the tuition.

Soon after the Revolutionary War, however, state and local governments began to establish public schools. By the time of the Civil War, most states were providing an elementary education for children at public expense. This later included secondary education. However, educational opportunity was not extended to all people. In some states it was illegal to teach Negroes to read and write.

It is estimated that today there are about sixty million persons enrolled in the more than 150,000 schools and colleges of all kinds in the United States. This means that more than 30 per cent of the people in the United States are going to school. Most of them attend the nation's public elementary and secondary schools, and public colleges and universities. There are also many private and church-supported facilities.

FINANCING PUBLIC EDUCATION.
Local and state governments spend more money for the schools of the nation than they do for any other governmental service. Money also comes from the national government. In recent years the total amount spent for education has been more than fifty billion dollars annually. Although this is a large amount of money, it does not appear so large when compared to the amount citizens spend for transportation, alcoholic drinks, or entertainment.

Much of the money for schools comes from local property taxes. For many years that was almost the only source of school income. During the Depression in the 1930's, however, many communities found it impossible to support their schools from local property taxes alone. They turned to the states for help. As a result the majority of states now make grants-in-aid for educational purposes to local communities.

These state funds are derived in a number of ways but chiefly from sales or income taxes. The typical school district now receives almost half its money from the state. The state also helps local school districts by financial assistance in establishing various special school services, such as schools for the blind, visiting teacher programs, and vocational schools.

Recent court decisions have raised serious questions about the legality of the property tax for financing public education. They have held that the property tax discriminates against poor districts which cannot raise as much money as districts with high property valuations. Many individuals and groups have suggested that the property tax be reduced, even eliminated, in favor of other means of taxation. The Supreme Court may soon decide the issue. As a result the next few years may bring about a completely new program for financing schools.

While education is a state and local function, the national government also provides increasing financial support for schools. Throughout our history the national government has given education financial help. The 1787 Ordinance for the Northwest Territory gave each township one section of land for school purposes. The money from the sale or rental of this land went to support public education.

Later Congress passed several measures to aid education in special ways. The Morrill Act of 1862 gave public land to the states to start agricultural and mechanical arts colleges, known as *land-grant* colleges. The Smith-Hughes Act of 1917 appropriated money for vocational education. This money helps states in teaching industrial subjects and home economics.

In more recent years Congress has provided educational funds for veterans of World War II, the Korean War, and the Vietnam War, aiding them to attend schools and colleges. Congress has also set aside some money to help the rapidly growing school districts build schools for children of workers in defense industries. The national government is now giving financial aid to districts which have children of certain types of federal government employees.

In 1958 Congress passed the National Defense Education Act (NDEA). The act provides loan funds for college students and financial support for elementary and secondary schools to improve guidance programs and the teaching of science, foreign languages, and mathematics. Amendments to the act have added history, geography, civics, reading, English, economics, and vocational education.

In 1965 Congress passed the Elementary and Secondary Education Act (ESEA) to provide money for various programs in elementary and secondary schools. Much of this money is for schools in *disadvantaged* areas. The purpose is to make available extra educational opportunities and materials for children and young people in the "war on poverty."

The financial aid under the earlier acts of Congress and under NDEA and ESEA is *categorical* aid. The money is appropriated for specific subject areas, such as vocational education, or for special groups, for example, the disadvantaged. There are many people who feel, however, that the national government should do more than help with these special or categorical funds. They believe that there should be general federal aid to education for all schools.

Money, they say, should be distributed to states on a population basis without reference to special areas or categories. All schools and all children should share in the federal money for education.

Another factor in the consideration of federal aid to education is the fact that educational opportunities are not equal throughout the United States. Those who are in favor of more federal aid to education say that the national government should make up for this difference in educational opportunity. They want the national government to equalize education among the states.

On the question of federal aid to education there are wide differences of opinion among the people. Some who oppose federal aid say that if the federal government supports the schools, it will also control them. They want local control, not control from Washington. Those who favor federal aid say that this federal control need not necessarily follow. They, too, want local control. But the opponents of federal aid believe we cannot have local control if we have federal support.

Controversy regarding federal aid also comes from the thinking on the part of some groups that federal aid should be given to all schools, private as well as public. Until now all attempts to pass a general federal-aid bill have been defeated, but the Elementary and Secondary Education Act comes closer to it.

PUBLIC SCHOOL SYSTEMS. The number of public school districts in the United States has been decreasing rapidly in recent years. There are, however, still more than 21,000 districts, but about 10 per cent of them do not actually operate a school of their own. Their children are sent to neighboring school districts on a tuition basis. The districts that do have schools vary in size from that of New York

Refer to Chapter 19, page 409, for a brief explanation of why school districts have been declining in number.

667

Teachers use many materials and techniques to help children and young people understand and appreciate their heritage. A special report by a pupil, the bulletin board display, and pictures tell these fifth-graders about famous Americans. (Photo courtesy Detroit Public Schools)

City, which has over one million pupils and about 55,000 teachers in 900 buildings, to those with one-room, one-teacher schools.

For each district there is a school board or board of education in charge. This may be a district, township, county, or city board of education. Its members are usually elected by the people, but in some cities they are appointed by other city officials, such as the mayor.

In each case the board operates the schools through persons employed by it. In most districts the board appoints a *superintendent* who employs the necessary teachers and other persons to help him in his work. Some of the other employees are

---

. . . schools and the means of education shall be forever encouraged.

—Northwest Ordinance of 1787.

principals, supervisors, secretaries, custodians, engineers, and bus drivers. In one-room districts and in other small districts the teachers are usually hired directly by the board.

The board of education has almost complete control in making decisions for the schools of its district. State laws may regulate training and certification of teachers, length of the school term, and compulsory age of school attendance, which varies from fourteen to eighteen years.

There are few state regulations as to what subjects a school must teach or how they must be taught. States with subject requirements for all schools usually limit these requirements to such courses as American history and government.

Most counties have a county superintendent who has supervision of the schools of the county, outside the cities.

All states have a state superintendent, and most of them have a state board of education to carry out the state laws with regard to education.

KINDS OF SCHOOLS AND CURRICULUMS. It is safe to say that almost anyone who wants to go to school in the United States can find a school to meet his special needs and abilities. The largest number of schools are, of course, *elementary schools.* Most of them have a kindergarten and continue through either the sixth or eighth grade. In a few districts there are nursery schools for children below the kindergarten age. A growing number of districts have middle schools that may cover grades 5 through 8.

More and more districts are supplying school services for handicapped children. There are teachers for the blind, the deaf,

A growing number of public schools are providing services for handicapped children, such as this school for the blind. (Courtesy Houston-Harris County Lighthouse for the Blind, Texas)

the hard-of-hearing, and the mentally retarded. There are special rooms for children in poor health and for crippled children. In some districts these special services are housed in separate buildings; in others there are rooms for them in the regular school buildings.

A number of school districts also provide teachers for home-bound or hospitalized children. These teachers go to the homes or hospitals once a week or oftener to give instruction to children who are bed-ridden for a long period of time.

The *secondary schools* usually include some of the grades from 7 to 14. In some places there are junior high schools with grades 7 to 9, senior high schools with grades 10 to 12, and community colleges with grades 13 and 14. In other places there will be a senior high school with grades 9 through 12. Especially in smaller communities, grades 7 to 12 may be housed in one secondary school.

The kinds of courses offered by a particular high school depend on its size and location. The student in a large secondary school has a choice of several programs: college preparatory, commercial, vocational, general, technical, and perhaps others. There are some courses in various subject areas—English, social studies, science, and mathematics—which all students must take. But each student may also elect other subjects in many fields: languages, mathematics, art, music, homemaking, science, social studies, retailing, business, crafts, shop, physical education, and others.

The student in the small secondary school often has very little choice beyond the required courses. Because of the small number of teachers, the number of subjects offered is necessarily limited.

The location of a school may determine its curriculum, at least in part. A school in an industrial area usually has many

Teaching the handicapped can be a challenging vocation. This young lady and her hard-of-hearing pupil are both gaining invaluable experiences. (From Careers in Special Education, *published by The Council for Exceptional Children)*

shop and vocational courses. A school in a rural community often has special agricultural courses.

Beyond high school there are schools, colleges, and universities of almost every description. Many of them offer a general college education, which is called *liberal arts.* But there are also many special schools which train doctors, lawyers, teachers, clergymen, engineers, technicians, nurses, accountants, business administrators, plumbers, beauty operators, and other specialized workers. For every profession and occupation, there are colleges and schools to supply the education or training.

In addition, more communities are establishing *community* or junior colleges and supporting them from local and state taxes, thus adding grades 13 and 14 to educational opportunities. This is one of the most rapidly growing areas of education. New community colleges are being opened in many states each year.

⬤ *FEDERAL GOVERNMENT AND EDUCATION.* We have already noted that the control of the schools is in the hands of the states and the local communities but that the federal government supplies some financial aid.

There are three other activities of the federal government in the field of education which should be mentioned. One is the work of the United States Office of Education in the Department of Health, Education, and Welfare, which was described in Chapter 12.

Another is the control of education by the federal government in the District of Columbia, in the territories, and on the Indian reservations. The schools in these places are supported by federal funds. The teachers and administrators of these schools are employees of the federal government.

The third is the educational program growing out of our recent wars and our position of world leadership. This program warrants special attention.

One aspect is the educational aid for veterans of World War II, the Korean War, and the Vietnam War. Another aspect is that the federal government maintains schools in many parts of the world for the children of United States armed forces and civilian personnel stationed there. For example, there are such schools in Germany, Austria, and Japan.

Another important aspect is that the

Discuss in more detail the large number of schools that the United States government maintains abroad for its overseas personnel.

federal government also supplies funds for bringing to the United States educational leaders from foreign countries to acquaint them with our schools, our country, our system of government, and our way of life. There have been various programs of this type under the Department of State, the Office of Education, and the Department of Defense.

Another part of this program makes it possible for teachers from our country to visit and teach in schools and colleges of foreign nations. The purpose of this whole program is to improve our relations with these countries through an understanding of their educational systems.

EDUCATIONAL PROBLEMS

One of the chief problems facing the schools resulted from mounting school enrollments after World War II. The school population increased greatly in the years after 1945. This meant that the schools needed more buildings, more teachers, more books, more supplies, more money, more of everything. Supplying these was not easy.

The federal government provides funds for the education of children on Indian reservations throughout the United States. (Bureau of Indian Affairs, Dept. of the Interior)

MORE BUILDINGS. This situation was made worse by the fact that very little school construction was done during the depression years of the 1930's and the war years of the 1940's. Many new schools have been built since the close of World War II. But many more are needed.

Most people recognized this important problem and were willing to do something about it initially. Many communities voted to increase their school taxes for a period of years to supply the necessary school buildings and needed equipment. In recent years, however, many school districts have had difficulty getting voter approval of bond issues.

MORE TEACHERS. Buildings alone are not enough. More teachers, too, were needed. Improved salaries helped. In the past few years the supply of teachers has been greater than the demand, even though some areas, such as mathematics and vocational education, still have a shortage. Nevertheless, the demand for good teachers continues.

Teaching positions in many communities are attractive enough to induce many of the finest and most capable young people to choose teaching as a career. The United States needs them to do the best possible job for our children and our young people.

A good salary is only one factor in choosing one's work. Young people considering future careers should also consider these advantages of the teaching profession: respected professional standing, relative permanence of position, opportunity for promotion, extended periods of time for travel and additional study, special local benefits such as sick leave, sabbatical leave, and exchange teaching.

EQUAL EDUCATIONAL OPPORTUNITY. Another educational problem of long standing is the difference in educational opportunity throughout the nation.

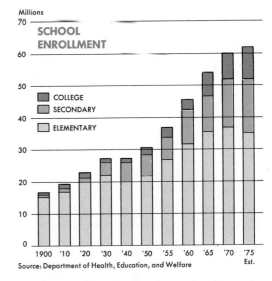

Millions

SCHOOL ENROLLMENT

COLLEGE
SECONDARY
ELEMENTARY

1900 '10 '20 '30 '40 '50 '55 '60 '65 '70 '75 Est.

Source: Department of Health, Education, and Welfare

Enrollment in our schools continues to rise. What problems does this create in regard to teachers, buildings, and taxes?

Some communities and states cannot afford to spend as much for their schools as others. Others choose not to do so even though they could afford more. In a recent year, for example, one state spent more than $1,400 for the education of each pupil, while another state spent only about $500.

In education, as in other areas, you usually get what you pay for. Around the question of amount spent on education and ability to pay centers much of the argument regarding federal aid to education. People ask, can states which spend little on education afford to spend more or are they spending as much as they can afford? Part of the answer to that question is that some states have more taxable wealth than others, and so the former can give their children a better education.

Even within the same state, educational opportunities are not always equal. City children often have better educational facilities than rural children. Wealthier suburbs have more money for education than does the central city. These inequali-

 Refer to the discussion concerning consolidation (page 673) as a possible answer for this problem.

ties have become especially important since so many people now move from one community to another and from one state to another. The quality of education in any part of the country is affected by the quality in others.

The problem of equal educational opportunity is especially real where separate schools have been provided for children of different races. The minority group often suffers because its schools are inferior.

In 1954 the United States Supreme Court stated that separate schools for Negro children are unconstitutional. (See Chapter 4.) This decision changed the pattern in much of the nation. But the change came slowly; southern states resisted the desegregation of their schools. This resistance brought about the use of federal troops to protect Negro pupils in some newly integrated public schools. In some places public schools were closed by local and state officials in defiance of federal court orders to integrate them. Private academies were opened to educate white children.

Since 1954 schools in the South have been integrated either voluntarily or by court order. Equal education in integrated schools for all children has been hastened by civil rights legislation and court orders. However, the problems related to school integration are not limited to the South. Northern cities are faced with *de facto* segregation largely because of housing patterns. Here, too, court orders are changing school attendance patterns to achieve integrated education.

Some courts have also held that segregation in some places resulted from the effects of laws. This is called *de jure* segregation. To achieve integration, courts have ordered busing programs within individual school districts and, also, across district boundaries. These decisions have resulted in widespread controversy, legislative debates and actions, and further lawsuits. The issue of busing as one means to achieve integration is not settled. In the next few years, the courts, Congress, state legislatures, and a proposed Constitutional amendment may possibly resolve the dilemma of busing. The issues of integrated schools and equal quality education are fundamental ones for a democratic society.

CONSOLIDATION. Directly related to this problem of educational opportunity is the large number of small schools. To make something big does not necessarily make it better. But, as has already been seen, the small schools are limited in the kinds and numbers of courses which they can offer to students.

In order to overcome their disadvantages, many small schools have joined with others to form *consolidated schools*. This movement is growing and is helping both to equalize educational opportunities and to offer rural children many of the advantages of city and suburban schools.

The increase in consolidated schools has brought with it the need to transport pupils. Fleets of buses—as many as forty to fifty for one school—bring pupils to consolidated schools each morning and take them home each afternoon.

IMPROVED TEACHING. A problem which teachers face continuously is the improvement of educational methods and materials. Educators across the nation are engaged in many research projects looking for answers to the question, "What methods and techniques help children to learn more effectively?" Just as other fields, such as medicine and engineering, are constantly in search of improved materials and techniques, so too is education.

The methods used by teachers are

constantly being changed in the light of what researchers find out about how people learn. Today's textbooks are greatly improved from those your parents used. Today's schools also use volunteer aides, many audio-visual materials, field trips, radio, television, a variety of books and pamphlets, and other materials to help students learn.

PUBLIC UNDERSTANDING. A part of all these problems is the necessity of keeping people of the community informed about the schools and their problems. Educators have learned that most Americans will support a good school program. Citizens want their schools to be the best that they can be. They have been willing to vote more money for them. But they must also understand what the schools are doing. In turn, their concerns and ideas about schools and their programs must be considered in developing educational programs.

So the problem of explaining the schools to all citizens and of involving them in school planning has become an important one. If this problem is not met successfully, the problems of inadequate buildings, of insufficient teaching materials, of unequal educational opportunities will continue. Where the schools have developed good community relations, these problems are beginning to be reduced. And where the schools are good, the level of living is better.

● SOCIAL
WELFARE   Closely related to the problem of providing an education for all of America's children and young people is the problem of taking care of people who are disabled in one way or another.

PRIVATE CHARITY. Until recent years this has largely been thought of as being charity. The orphanages took care of the children whose parents had died. The old folks' home was a place for old people who had no one to look after them. The poorhouse or poor farm took in those who were without work or money. Many acts of charity were done by churches and charitable organizations.

There is still much charitable work done by private and church organizations. Contributions of money for charity grow larger each year. In many communities the annual United Fund, Community Chest, Torch Fund, or Red Feather Drive raises millions of dollars. The orphanage, the old folks' home, the poor farm are still homes for those in need of help. But the concept of help for the needy has · changed among Americans. Charity is not enough. Security and welfare are the goals of our people.

SOCIAL AND REHABILITATION SERVICE. In 1967 the Department of Health, Education, and Welfare was reorganized to bring together under one administrator many of the social welfare services of the national government. These are now in the Social and Rehabilitation Service.

The unit includes the following agencies: Aging, Assistance Payments, Community Services, Medical Services, Rehabilitation Services, and Youth Development and Delinquency Prevention. In cooperation with the states, assistance is given to dependent children; to aged, disabled, and blind persons; and to programs for delinquents. States are given grants-in-aid to carry on these assistance programs if they are operated according to federal standards.

SOCIAL SECURITY. While a small part of the federal welfare program has been carried on for many years, most of it was begun during the 1930's when millions of people were out of work and could find no

It is interesting to note that in the 1930's many Americans were very concerned that this new welfare legislation was going to make a socialized America. Ask the students if they think this has come to pass.

A social worker calls on an elderly recipient of welfare benefits to learn if he is getting along satisfactorily. (Social and Rehabilitation Service, U.S. Dept. of Health, Education, and Welfare)

jobs. This is the social security program, most of which is administered by the Social Security Administration. The program now includes old-age and survivors benefits, disability insurance, and medical care for the aged, *Medicare.*

The practice of the American people with regard to welfare and security has changed since 1935. The first social security act of the federal government was passed that year. It has been amended several times since then. The amendments have increased the amounts of benefits and the number of workers covered by the act. Today about nine of every ten workers are covered by its provisions. See Chapter 12 for a discussion of social security taxes and of the benefits paid under the program.

There has not been complete agreement on the part that the federal government should take in providing security for all people. Soon after the original act was passed, it was challenged by some people. They said that the Constitution did not give the federal government the right to pay old-age pensions and to tax workers to pay these pensions. But in 1937 the Supreme Court declared the social security act constitutional.

The most common reasons given for social security on the federal level are:

1. In an industrial society most people cannot save enough in a lifetime to take care of their families in the event of the wage earner's death.

2. Industrial workers often have no control over periods of employment and unemployment; some provision should be made for times when they are unemployed through no fault of their own.

3. Throughout much of the history of our nation unemployed workers could always go to the frontier and start life over again; today there is no frontier left.

4. The benefits of social security should be assured to workers as part of the return for their work; these benefits should not be looked upon as charity for which a person in need must ask.

5. Social security benefits are good for the economic life of the nation; the unemployed persons and the old people have money to spend, which helps to keep the economy prosperous.

More than 600 district offices throughout the United States and its territories provide a full range of social security services—from account numbers to benefits. (Social Security Administration)

6. Many people who are able to save for their own future needs do not do so; social security, in a sense, forces them to save by taxing their wages.

7. Only the federal government can provide for all people; since there is so much movement from one state to another, social security should be a federal government function. It should not be left to private or local agencies.

Some of the arguments which have been advanced against federal social security are:

1. It is un-American to force people to pay a tax for their future security; every American should be allowed to decide for himself how he wishes to spend his money now and how he wishes to provide for himself in the future.

2. Not all people are covered by the present law; some people who may need help badly are not eligible for benefits, because they are not covered.

3. Many people believe that social security benefits are guaranteed to them; this is not so, for Congress could change the act at any time.

4. To receive benefits a person does not have to prove that he is in need; some peo-

ple who do not need help also receive benefit payments.

5. If a person does not qualify for benefits after reaching retirement age or if he dies before then without dependents, he loses all the money he has paid in social security taxes, and his heirs get only a fraction of it.

The issue of the extent of federal social security is not completely settled, but the idea is now generally accepted by most people. Both major political parties advocate its extension to more groups. Over the years members of both parties in Congress have voted to include more people.

There are still, however, some welfare areas about which there are sharp differences of opinion and which are hotly debated. One of these is general medical care for all people. Also, before its passage, the issue of whether the Medicare program should be financed through the social security tax was strongly debated in Congress.

HEALTH SERVICES

The problem of maintaining and improving health has become an

Compare our national health service with that of a country such as Great Britain, where they have what is commonly referred to as socialized medicine.

important part of the general welfare. Health services are provided on every level of government—national, state, and local.

NATIONAL HEALTH SERVICE. The health of the people has always been a chief concern of the national government. As early as 1798 Congress passed a bill establishing a marine hospital for merchant seamen. One hundred and fifty years later a report stated that forty-four separate agencies of the federal government were providing some form of health service.

The armed forces, for example, have several hundred hospitals and other medical facilities to care for the men and women in uniform. The Veterans Administration has more than a hundred hospitals and many out-patient clinics for the disabled veterans. There are special hospitals for lepers, for mental patients, and for narcotics addicts. These are some examples of the health services provided by federal agencies.

The chief health services of the federal

At the National Cancer Institute, part of the Public Health Service, a scientist uses an electron microscope in research. (National Institutes of Health)

government, however, are performed by the Public Health Service, which grew from the original marine hospital voted by Congress in 1798. The Public Health Service is now a branch of the Department of Health, Education, and Welfare. It is directed by the Surgeon General, who is appointed by the President with the consent of the Senate.

Since 1798 the purpose of the Public Health Service has been greatly expanded, so that today it has great responsibility for protecting and improving the health of the nation. To do this millions of dollars are spent yearly and thousands of professional health workers—doctors, nurses, sanitary experts, and researchers—are hired. They are charged with controlling the spread of diseases. They inspect shipments of goods from foreign countries; they check the health of immigrants; they examine steamships and airplanes as possible germ carriers. These examples illustrate their huge job of keeping communicable diseases from foreign countries from spreading to the United States.

The Public Health Service carries on research to determine the causes of sicknesses and to search for cures and preventives. It maintains many hospitals. Grants of money are made to university hospitals and medical schools to carry on needed research.

Drugs and serums are checked to determine their value and to make sure that they are not dangerous. The Public Health Service studies sources of drinking water to prevent and correct pollution. It cooperates with states in carrying out state health activities to improve the level of public health.

A large part of the federal health program is also carried on in cooperation with states and local communities. The federal government makes grants-in-aid to states for prenatal care and child health, for help in controlling tuberculosis and other dis-

The federal government has numerous agencies and bureaus which have responsibility for protecting the health and welfare of the people. One of these is the Food and Drug Administration (FDA). (See Chapter 12.)

The activities of the FDA, according to the *U.S. Government Organization Manual,* "are directed mainly toward promoting purity, standard potency, and truthful and informative labeling of consumer products. . . ."

To carry out this responsibility the FDA is engaged in continual testing and research of food and health products. When its study indicates that a product involved in interstate commerce is injurious to health or is falsely labeled or advertised, it takes action to have the product taken off the market or to have needed corrections made in the product, its labeling, or advertising. Sometimes it must go to court for a decision on its findings.

One such case involved an article known as Micro-Dynameter. This was an electrical device which, according to the company that manufactured and marketed it, was useful in the diagnosis of diseases. The FDA alleged that the company maintained that the device was effective in diagnosis of practically all disease conditions. The list of diseases and diseased conditions numbered more than fifty. Some typical ones were chronic appendix, insanity, heart trouble, tuberculosis, cancer, and tooth infection.

The government maintained that the device could not make such diagnoses, and that the electrical impulses registered by it were due to "the amount of perspiration on the skin and other similar factors."

The case was taken to a U.S. District Court with the United States as plaintiff and the company and its officers as defendants. The ruling of the court was in favor of the FDA. Among other conclusions the court decision stated,

"The defendants . . . are hereby perpetually enjoined and restrained . . . from directly or indirectly doing any of the following acts:

. . . introducing or causing to be introduced and delivering or causing to be delivered for introduction into interstate commerce the device designated as the "Micro-Dynameter" or the same device by any other designation or any similar device, bearing or accompanied by any written, printed, or graphic matter which states, represents, suggests or implies that said device is adequate and effective for diagnosing diseases as heretofore described. . . ."

The case was appealed to a U.S. Court of Appeals which sustained the ruling of the lower court.

The work of the FDA is an example of the activities carried on by government agencies in the interest of the health of the people.

eases, and especially for the construction of hospitals.

STATE AND LOCAL HEALTH SERVICES. States, too, carry on many functions to protect the health of the people. State boards of health and various other state agencies carry on a variety of activities in the interest of health. States control the private health practitioners by issuing licenses to medical doctors, osteopaths, chiropractors, dentists, pharmacists, and people in similar or related professions.

Through this means they try to prevent unqualified people from becoming health practitioners.

State legislatures have passed many laws regarding sanitation, water supply, and foods and drugs. They employ inspectors to see that these laws are enforced. Inspectors check water to make sure it is safe for drinking and swimming; they inspect meat, milk, and other foods to see that these are not contaminated and that they meet state standards; they inspect restaurants and other establishments where unsanitary conditions might lead to epidemics.

The state board of health enforces the state laws on quarantine for communicable diseases. There are many state hospitals for tuberculosis and other communicable diseases, besides general state hospitals for the poor and the needy who need hospital care. For the disease-control program the states supply vaccines and serums. They have laboratory facilities for making blood tests and other tests for diagnosing diseases.

An important part of the state health program is the collection and analysis of *vital statistics*, the essential facts about human beings. States keep complete records of births and deaths. These records are important for many reasons: for example, to provide legal proof of place and date of a person's birth; to predict school enrollments for years ahead based on number of births; to determine the chief causes of death and to note changes in causes over a period of years; to pinpoint areas where many people die of a particular disease; and to show the number of people living at various ages.

Local health officers carry on the state program in their communities as well as their own special local programs. Where many people live close together, as they do particularly in our large cities, it is important that health and sanitary regulations be strictly enforced. That is the chief function of the local health unit. It enforces quarantines, food and drug standards, and sanitary regulations.

Members of the health staff have the responsibility to see that proper methods are used for the disposal of garbage and sewage, that water is pure, that rats and insects are controlled, that people with communicable diseases are quarantined if necessary, and that similar health measures are obeyed.

PROBLEMS OF HEALTH

Private and public health services have made great progress in controlling disease and in improving the health of the people. Epidemics, such as those of the Middle Ages which killed as many as half of the people of a community, today seem unlikely. Smallpox cases are very rare. There are few deaths from pneumonia and diphtheria. Health measures plus new drugs and serums have brought these and other one-time killers under control. Transplants of vital organs, such as kidneys and hearts, are helping some people to live longer and to enjoy better health.

RESEARCH. There are other health problems which are today commanding the attention of medical and health researchers: cancer, tuberculosis, heart diseases, multiple sclerosis, and others. Health workers continue their search for causes and for cures.

One of the most stubborn ailments is the common cold. It strikes most people one or more times during the course of each year. It not only causes physical discomforts but it is costly in terms of time and manpower, causing absenteeism from both school and work. Progress is being made in its control, but it is one of the big unsolved problems of health.

COSTS. The cost of adequate medical care has been a big hurdle in our attempt to improve the health conditions of all people. Sometimes those who are most in need of health attention can afford it least. There are good reasons why good health care is expensive.

A person must spend many years, at great expense, to become a physician or surgeon. Many doctors start their careers heavily in debt; they had borrowed the money to pay their way through school. Then they must buy expensive equipment to begin their practice. It often takes years to build a good practice. On the other hand, most

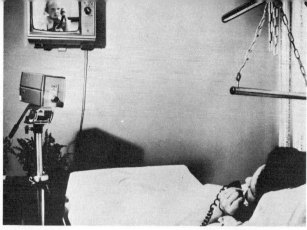

The patient is able to see and hear her granddaughter via closed circuit television. Services like this help cheer the patient. Many persons have found health insurance to be indispensable. Hospitalization claims are being processed in the Blue Cross office at the left. (Right, RCA; left, Blue Cross of Greater Philadelphia)

successful doctors have more than adequate financial returns and get great personal satisfaction from the service they render to their patients.

Other reasons for the high cost of health care are research for new drugs and medicines; expensive equipment needed for X rays, for cardiograms, and for making other diagnoses; specialist and nursing care; and the large hospital staffs.

Various methods are being tried to make health services available to all people when they need them. State and local health units have clinics for those who are unable to pay for medical service or have very limited incomes. Doctors sometimes set fees for their services on the basis of the patient's ability to pay.

In some areas doctors and hospitals have arranged prepayment plans whereby persons who join the plan pay a certain amount each month. The doctors and hospitals agree to supply services as needed to the subscribers.

HEALTH INSURANCE. There are also numerous health and hospitalization insurance plans. Insured persons pay monthly or quarterly premiums which entitle them to certain hospital, surgical, and medical benefits when needed. Sometimes the benefits do not cover the complete charges, but they pay for a share of the costs of the service depending upon the type of insurance carried. These insurance plans are voluntary; a person may join them if he chooses.

There are interest groups, however, who believe that health insurance should be made compulsory. They believe that the federal government should pass a law creating compulsory health insurance for all people to be paid for through taxes.

Proposals of this kind have been made from time to time with certain stipulations. These are (1) groups could be excluded if they chose to be, (2) doctors would be free to participate or not to participate in the program, (3) a small fee could be charged for each service, and (4) the service would apply only to people over a certain age.

There have been many arguments on both sides of the question as to whether such compulsory health insurance, sometimes called socialized medicine, would be good or bad. People who favor it say:

1. The health level of the nation would be raised, since all people would be able to get health services when needed.

2. The cost of health care would be spread more fairly among all people.

3. Persons who need little medical attention would pay their share for "stand-by" service which would be available to them when they need it.

4. Doctors and other health workers would be certain of being paid for services rendered.

5. The number of doctors and other health workers would be adequate, for the supply could be controlled.

6. Rural areas with few people and the poorer states would be given better health service than they can now afford.

7. Special equipment, costly drugs and medications, and the service of specialists would be available to all people.

Those who oppose compulsory health insurance say:

1. It is un-American to force a person to join an insurance plan, he should be free to decide for himself whether or not he wants insurance.

2. Health service will become poorer, for under the plan doctors and others will be paid anyway and there will be little incentive to improve their work.

3. Private groups can carry on an insurance program more efficiently than can the government.

4. Many people will take advantage of the plan by asking for health care when they do not need it.

5. The cost of health service will rise, because the program will have administrative costs for carrying on the insurance plan and these will need to be paid out of charges.

6. Many brilliant people who might enter private health work will be lost to the profession, because freedom of enterprise will be destroyed.

Until the present time Congress has not passed a general compulsory health insurance law, but in 1965 it passed a bill creating a medical care plan, often called Medicare, for persons age 65 and over. The plan has two parts. One is *hospital insurance,* which is financed through additions to the social security tax. The other is *medical insurance,* which is a voluntary program. It is financed by monthly payments of a fixed amount by each participant; these payments are matched by the federal government.

The money for both programs is kept in trust funds, the Federal Hospital Insurance Trust Fund and the Federal Supplementary Medical Insurance Trust Fund. The Medicare program has been in operation since July, 1966. Experience will indicate how effective it is in bringing better health service to the aged. It does not cover all medical expenses for them, but it does provide for payment of many of the health costs which older people have. A related program, *Medicaid,* is a joint federal-state program to provide basic medical care to the poor.

STUDY QUESTIONS

1. Why did education develop as a function of state and local governments?

2. What factor brought about the state grants-in-aid to local school districts?

3. How has the federal government provided financial support for education?

4. What are the purposes of the NDEA and the ESEA?

5. What are the arguments on both sides of the issue of federal aid to education?

6. What are some of the many kinds of schools and courses available to children and young people?

7. What are three special educational activities of the federal government?

8. How has our growing population created problems for schools?

CONCEPTS AND GENERALIZATIONS

1
The general welfare of the people has become an increasingly greater concern of government as our nation has grown.

2
Important governmental concerns in the area of general welfare are education, security, health, and safety.

3
Education has traditionally been the responsibility of local and state governments in the United States.

4
Federal support for education has been given as categorical aid and for special programs; opinion regarding general federal aid is sharply divided.

5
Authority for education at the local level is vested in a board of education, whose members are elected or appointed.

6
A chief problem of education concerns providing equal educational opportunities for all children and young people.

7
The depression of the 1930's was the main cause of the start of the social security program in the United States.

8
Over the years social security has grown with respect to programs, persons covered, benefits, and taxes.

9
The idea of the federal social security program is now generally accepted throughout the nation, but there are still individuals and groups who oppose it, especially some features, such as health insurance.

10
All levels of government provide some health services for the people.

11
Research to control disease and to improve health conditions is an important public health service.

12
Compulsory health insurance is still an unresolved issue in the broad area of general welfare.

9. Why has the movement to integrate schools been slow?

10. In what ways have consolidated schools improved educational opportunity?

11. How are today's schools different from earlier schools?

12. What is the role of citizens in public education?

13. What does the federal welfare program include?

14. What are the arguments for and against federal social security?

15. What are some of the health services of the federal government?

16. What are the duties of the United States Public Health Service?

17. What are some of the health services carried on by states?

18. Why is it important to keep accurate vital statistics?

19. Why is it especially necessary to enforce health and sanitary regulations in cities?

20. List diseases which are currently commanding the attention of medical and health research workers.

21. What are some of the reasons for the high cost of good health care?

22. What are some methods for making health services available to people?

23. What are the arguments for and against compulsory insurance plans?

24. What are the provisions of the Medicare program?

IDEAS FOR DISCUSSION

1. One of the controversies in connection with federal aid to education centers around this question: "Shall such aid be given to parochial and private schools, or shall it be given to public schools only?" What do you think about this?

2. "Federal aid always means federal control." Do you agree with this statement? Does it apply to education?

3. "The larger the school, the better it is." Do you agree? Under what conditions does making a school larger make it better? Can a school become too large?

4. Many people believe that the level of living is directly related to educational opportunity. Do you agree with this? What does it mean for educational planning?

5. "The problem of segregation in schools is limited to the southern states." Do you agree with this statement? Distinguish between fact and opinion in the ideas on this statement.

6. "Since Negroes and other minority groups have been deprived of adequate education for so many years, they should be given added educational opportunities and a larger proportion of tax money for schools in their areas." Do you agree with this proposal, which is known as *compensatory education*? Why?

7. Social security tax payments differ from many insurance premiums in that the funds cannot be withdrawn. Should this condition be changed to make social security more like regular insurance? What would be the effect of such a change?

8. Improving the health of the nation has created some other problems. More people live longer. Working with and helping people for their later years is called *geriatrics*. The specialists in old-age problems have discovered that more people need to develop satisfying activities for their later years. What are some other results and problems of longer life for more people?

9. Hold a class discussion on the desirability of a compulsory health insurance law.

THINGS TO DO

1. Make a study of the early history of education in your state. Report your findings to the class.

2. Have a committee interview your county superintendent of schools or high school principal and ask about your state regulations and laws with regard to education. Make a report to the class.

3. Use a bulletin board for newspaper clippings concerned with education. Use some of these clippings for a discussion about the current problems of schools.

4. Report to the class on any recent news items related to the question of school integration.

5. Have a committee collect information about school enrollments in your district. Make a chart to show how enrollments have increased. Make some predictions about the number of additional schools and classrooms required.

6. Study the recent amendments to the Social Security Act. Tell the class how these amendments have changed social security benefits and taxes.

7. Make a listing of the various health services provided by your state and community. Check those which are used by all people even though they may not know it.

8. Talk to your family doctor about health insurance plans. Report his views on compulsory insurance to the class.

9. Visit a nongovernmental agency which provides welfare services. Report to the class on its activities and the kinds of services which are available at the agency.

10. Make a study of the Torch Fund (Red Feather) program in your community. Study such items as amount of money contributed, agencies included in the program, services provided by the agencies, and number of persons receiving assistance.

FURTHER READINGS

Altmeyer, Arthur J., FORMATIVE YEARS OF SOCIAL SECURITY. University of Wisconsin Press, 1966.

Anderson, Margaret, THE CHILDREN OF THE SOUTH. Dell Publishing Company, Inc., 1967. (Paperback)

Burt, Olive, BORN TO TEACH. Julian Messner, Inc., 1967.

Eddy, Elizabeth M., BECOMING A TEACHER: THE PASSAGE TO PROFESSIONAL STATUS. Teachers College Press, 1971.

Gelinas, Paul J., SO YOU WANT TO BE A TEACHER. Harper & Row, Publishers, Inc., 1965.

Keppel, Francis, THE NECESSARY REVOLUTION IN AMERICAN EDUCATION. Harper & Row, Publishers, Inc., 1966.

Koestler, Frances A., CAREERS IN SOCIAL WORK. Henry Z. Walck, Inc., 1965.

Perlman, Helen H., SO YOU WANT TO BE A SOCIAL WORKER. Harper & Row, Publishers, Inc., 1962.

Superintendent of Documents, WHAT THIRTEEN LOCAL HEALTH DEPARTMENTS ARE DOING IN MEDICAL CARE. Washington, D.C.: Government Printing Office, 1967.

Terrell, John Upton, THE UNITED STATES DEPARTMENT OF HEALTH, EDUCATION, AND WELFARE: A STORY OF PROTECTING AND PRESERVING HUMAN RESOURCES. Meredith Press, 1965.

BLIGHTED AREA—a neighborhood that is run-down, dirty, and gradually being destroyed; slum.

COMMON CARRIER a transportation company carrying passengers for a fee.

CRIMINOLOGIST—person who makes a scientific study of crimes and criminals.

OPEN HOUSING—situation in which the sale and rental of houses is available to people of all groups, in which there is no discrimination in regard to race, religion, or nationality.

PASSENGER MILES — the total of all miles traveled by all passengers; a means for comparing related travel data.

PROBATION—procedure whereby a convicted person remains free and is not sent to prison if he follows the conditions set down by the court.

RESTRICTIONS—in housing, the conditions under which a person may buy, build, or rent; declared illegal with reference to race, religion, or nationality.

SUBSTANDARD — inferior; not up to standard set by law; in housing, not meeting building and sanitation codes.

URBAN RENEWAL—process of rebuilding slum areas, especially blighted central portions of the city.

THE LANGUAGE OF GOVERNMENT

Point out that many topics covered in this chapter are relatively new areas of concern for the national government.

32

Housing, Crime, Accidents, and Government

Much of man's history can be written in terms of his search and his struggle for greater fulfillment of the three basic physical needs—food, clothing, and shelter. To satisfy these needs, man has moved from place to place on the face of the earth. Wars have been fought to take away from other people the materials to fill these needs. To supply his daily wants, man works and toils.

The degree to which different people and nations can fulfill these basic physical needs varies greatly because of human and social factors and geographic conditions. Nowhere in the world is there as great an opportunity for all people to supply these needs so fully as in the United States. However, in spite of our abundance, our natural resources, our wealth, our economic system, and our advanced knowledge, there are some people in our country who do not have adequate food, clothing, and shelter.

There are still many problems connected with supplying everyone with enough means to fill these basic physical needs.

Some of these problems have been at least partly solved through expanding social security and welfare programs, which were discussed in the previous chapter. In this chapter we shall study the special problems of housing and the attempts to improve the shelter of all people. We shall also study the work being done to protect the life and property of citizens and the problems raised by crime and accidents.

HOUSING   A house to come home to —a place to live with the members of the family—a place to eat and sleep—a place to be together with loved ones—a place to have the companionship and fellowship of others—a place to get away from the cold or the heat, the snow or the rain—a place to spend the hours of darkness—a place of joy and sorrow—a place for rest and relaxation. Home may be for you all of these things and many more—or it may be only a place for shelter.

A house may be large or small, old or new, brick or frame, urban or rural, elaborate or modest. All of these may have little to do with how people feel about a house. The characteristics of a house do not necessarily make it a home; it is the people who live there who make it a home.

But the appearance and condition of a house can affect the people who live in it. A run-down building may make the people who live in it feel like the building—run-down, despised, unwanted. It may be a breeding place of sickness, crime, insects, pests.

A well-kept home in cheery surroundings is more likely to have the opposite effect. Its people are more likely to be optimistic, cheerful, and contented. There is less likelihood of crime and infectious disease. These statements are not true in every case, but studies show that the crime and disease rates are higher in slum areas than they are in suburban communities. The topic of housing is discussed under two headings: (1) the individual and his home and (2) government and the housing problem.

THE INDIVIDUAL AND HIS HOME. One of the basic freedoms of a citizen of the United States is the right to choose his

A lack of municipal services such as paved roads and streetlights adds to the problems of some of our poor and points up the need for more good housing units. (Los Angeles Times *photo*)

place to live. He may choose the country or the city. He may decide to live near the center of town or in the suburbs. He may select an apartment in a large project or a single-family home.

He may want a large home, a small mobile home, or something between the two extremes. He may decide to buy his own home, or he may wish to rent one. There are many factors which determine his choice, but if he has the money and if the homes are available, the choice should be his.

Which of these choices shall he make? Each person and each family needs to determine what the choice will be. There may be both favorable and unfavorable factors in any choice of a place to live. Owning a home usually involves both advantages and disadvantages. So does living in the city. So does renting an apartment. The same is true of each of the other choices mentioned. The important point, however, for the United States citizen is that he should be able to make the choice. But this is not completely true for all of our people.

THERE ARE RESTRICTIONS ON HOMES FOR SOME PEOPLE. Members of some races, religions, and nationalities find that some communities are closed to them. They cannot live wherever they wish. Certain communities have placed restrictions on the kinds of people who may move into the community.

Our courts have decided that such restrictions or restrictive agreements are illegal. They are unconstitutional. But they continue to exist, often not as written agreements but as "gentlemen's agreements," whereby individuals agree not to sell property to people of certain races, religions, or nationalities.

This is one of the areas where the practice of democracy is not perfect. Some

The Federal Housing Administration (FHA) helps people to buy homes of their own, regardless of race, creed, or color. (U.S. Dept. of Housing and Urban Development)

progress is being made. Some places where minority groups—Negroes, Jews, Mexicans, Chinese, for example—were formerly banned are now unrestricted. But the movement is slow.

Some cities are passing fair- or open-housing ordinances. States are passing or considering laws to make restrictions illegal. A federal open housing law was passed by Congress in 1968. The purpose of this legislation is to open all residential areas to all people, to remove all restrictions in the sale and rental of property. But to get such laws or ordinances passed has not been simple. There are still too many people who wish to maintain restrictions. Their reasons are many, but these chiefly relate to mistrust, misunderstanding, or fear of other racial, religious, or nationality groups. So these people resist both voluntary and legal efforts to achieve open housing.

Among these people are some who are opposed to any and all integrated housing. They want restrictive agreements, whether legal or illegal, to be used to keep members of some groups out of certain residential areas. Among them also are others who, while opposed to immediate open housing, are in favor of gradual removal of restrictions. They give as a reason for their opposition the intense feelings of people toward others whom they do not understand.

This latter group says that the feelings of people cannot be changed quickly. An order of a court does not change feelings. These citizens believe that changes in restrictions should be made gradually, that people should be given a chance to change their feelings over a long period of time. They say that forcing people to accept other groups merely intensifies any ill feelings toward members of these groups.

However, more and more people of all races and religions are becoming concerned that we are not moving fast enough to remove housing restrictions of whatever nature. We are making a mockery of democracy by restricting the rights of some individuals and groups. Every person should be permitted to live where he wants to live and where he can afford to live regardless of his race, nationality, or religion. Each individual should be treated with respect and should be given the rights and privileges which are accorded any other person. That is the American way. That is democracy. People who believe this do not want to wait for gradual changes. The Constitution guarantees all people fair and equal treatment; the courts have declared restrictions on housing illegal; Congress has made open housing the law of the land. The right to housing should be the practice of the nation as a right of the individual and for the benefit of the nation.

The issue has been debated in Congress, in state legislatures, and in city councils. Proponents of civil rights have pressed for open housing, making all houses and areas open to all people and allowing everyone to live wherever he can afford to live. With the passage of such legislation on all levels and with its actual practice, the nation will have taken a major step forward in giving equal and fair treatment to all persons.

In April 1968, following the death of Dr. Martin Luther King, Congress took an important step in providing open housing. It passed another civil rights act which was quickly signed by President Johnson. The act includes an open housing provision. According to the law, by now nearly all housing is to be sold or rented without regard to race. There are only two exceptions. These are: (1) rental housing with up to four units, one of which is occupied by the owner and (2) single-family houses sold by the owner-occupant without the help of a real estate agent and without the mention of any racial preference in advertising.

THERE ARE NOT ENOUGH HOMES. One of the factors which has intensified the restrictions for minority groups is the shortage of homes. There are not enough homes in the cities and communities where there are jobs for people. A number of factors have combined to cause our serious housing shortage: growth of cities, depression, World War II, returning veterans, years of great prosperity, and increased population.

The rapid industrialization of our society brought many people to our cities. Here there was work for them to do. In Chapter 29 we noted that proportionately fewer and fewer workers were needed on the farm. The workers were needed for our large industrial output. They flocked to the cities and the metropolitan areas. All of them wanted and needed a place to live.

The depression of the 1930's reversed this trend for a time. The factories closed their doors. There was no work. Some people left the cities. Other families joined together to live in one home. Houses in many cities became plentiful. Few new homes and apartments were built; additional housing was not needed. There was little demand for new housing.

Then came World War II. With it came the greatest demand for industrial output our nation had ever experienced. The industrial areas were flooded with workers, and thousands and thousands of homes were needed. But building materials and labor were scarce. Both were going into war production. The nation's answer to the great need for housing during the war was temporary homes, built to last only a few years. But there was little permanent home building.

After the war the returning veterans wanted homes. During and after the war they had married in large numbers. They wanted homes, and the demand for housing grew. New subdivisions were opened in most cities and metropolitan areas. The one thing that all of these areas had in common after 1945 was that they were growing. The growth in housing could not equal the demand. This condition has continued since then during years of prosperity and great economic growth. Even though thousands and thousands of new houses and other living units have been built, the demand has always been greater than the supply.

To all of the factors which have contributed to the housing shortage must be added the rapid increase in the nation's population. More people means an even greater demand for homes. This increased population has helped to give our nation its largest building boom.

MANY HOMES ARE SUBSTANDARD. The shortage of homes has caused people to accept any place as a place to live. This situation has developed what may be looked upon as a vicious circle: shortage of homes —high prices—live anywhere—high rents even for poor homes—keep all places for homes regardless of their condition. This has created one of the important problems of our generation: much substandard housing in an age of plenty and prosperity.

Many families live in buildings which are unfit for human habitation. Because there is a widespread shortage of dwelling places, even the worst flats and tenements can be rented. Because they can be rented, many owners do not make necessary repairs and improvements. Some owners feel they cannot afford to modernize their properties because of the high cost of materials and labor. But others deliberately do nothing about their poor rental units, getting as much rent as they can and putting only as much back into their rental property as they must.

This combination of factors has increased the slum housing conditions in many communities, where families live in cramped quarters which are firetraps, rat-infested, and unsanitary. The buildings lack adequate plumbing and lighting and are badly in need of repairs. Sometimes government will step in to force a landlord to make needed repairs to his property to get it into a safe, sanitary, and livable condition. A local government may condemn substandard housing and not permit it to be used as a dwelling place until building and sanitation codes are met.

The lack of adequate housing is one of the important problems of our urban industrial society. Various attacks are being

A modern high-rise apartment building offering low-cost housing to the elderly was built on the site of this rundown area. (Minneapolis Housing and Redevelopment Authority)

made on the problem, both to relieve the housing shortage and to remove the substandard homes as places to live.

Much is being done by private builders, as may be seen by a trip through any metropolitan area. New subdivisions of hundreds and hundreds of homes are springing up everywhere. Many new apartment house projects too are being built with private funds.

GOVERNMENT AND THE HOUSING PROBLEM. The government too has been active in many aspects of the housing problem. The federal government entered the housing field with full force, as it did many other economic and social areas, during the depression of the 1930's. The hardships caused by the depression were many.

The widespread unemployment of these years resulted in a situation in which thousands of homeowners could not meet the principal and interest payments on the mortgages on their homes. Many lost their homes through mortgage foreclosures. Banks did not have sufficient funds to finance new construction. Many lending institutions were afraid of making new loans. They did not want more homes on their hands which they might have to take over if people were unable to make continued mortgage payments.

So, starting in 1932, the government set up a number of agencies to help eliminate some of the housing problems caused by both the economic depression and the shortage of sufficient housing. Among these are: (1) the Federal Home Loan Bank System, (2) the Home Owners' Loan Corporation, (3) the Federal Housing Administration, (4) the Public Housing Administration, and (5) the Housing and Home Finance Agency.

The *Federal Home Loan Bank System* was established to provide money for home mortgages. It makes loans to various agencies—savings and loan associations, building and loan associations, savings banks,

Select two or three major cities in the United States and describe their renovation and rebuilding programs.

and insurance companies—so that they may in turn make loans to individuals for the construction of homes. This was especially necessary during the 1930's when little money was available for building homes.

The system helped to fight the depression in another way by providing jobs in the construction of the homes which were financed through it. An incentive for individuals to invest money in savings and loan associations was provided by insuring all deposit accounts (now up to $20,000) by a specially created government corporation, the Federal Savings and Loan Insurance Corporation.

The *Home Owners' Loan Corporation* (HOLC) was strictly a depression agency, operating only from 1933 to 1936. During those years millions of homeowners were unable to make the payments on their mortgages and to pay the taxes on their property. The HOLC was established by the federal government to lend money on homes during the emergency.

As a result many Americans were able to make their payments and to keep their homes. Nearly 100 per cent of all the loans made by the HOLC have been repaid in full with interest.

The *Federal Housing Administration* (FHA) was established in 1934 to help people buy homes and to improve the standards for homes. The FHA builds no homes and it makes no loans. It is an insurance and inspection agency. Loans for homes are made by banks and other lending institutions. (See Chapter 12.)

A person desiring an FHA loan is thoroughly investigated by the FHA with regard to income, ability to pay, and credit rating. If approved, the loan is insured by the FHA, which means that the FHA guarantees the lending institution that the loan will be repaid.

Homes insured by the FHA are inspected during construction and upon completion to make certain that they meet the standards set up by the agency. Thus the bank is guaranteed repayment of its loan, and the owner is guaranteed a well-constructed home.

The *Public Housing Administration* (PHA) deals with low-rent public housing programs and public war-housing programs. The PHA replaced the United States Housing Authority (USHA), which was created in 1937 to deal directly with the problem of providing decent housing for many low-income families.

Other depression agencies helped many people to finance and build their own homes, but they did little to improve the living of families with very small incomes. The USHA was created to fill this gap. It was authorized by Congress to help states and communities construct dwelling places to do away with the slum conditions under which many poorer families lived. World War II interfered with carrying out the full program of this agency.

Under the reorganization plan of 1947, the PHA (successor to USHA) was incorporated in the *Housing and Home Finance Agency*, which brought together many of the housing activities of the federal government into one independent agency. The various bureaus of this agency are now included in the Department of Housing and Urban Development (HUD).

In 1944 the federal government gave further help in solving the housing problem through a special provision in the Servicemen's Readjustment Act, the so-called GI Bill of Rights. Various states also helped in carrying out the program under this act. Veterans were given certain advantages in the purchase of homes with reference to guaranteed loans, small down payments, and lower interest rates.

The program of rebuilding the centers of many of our large cities is also related to this topic of government and housing. Most of our big cities are "rotting at the core." Around the central business district has grown up a circle of tenement and slum districts, a *blighted* area.

Most private builders find that it is cheaper to build new homes on vacant property than it is to buy run-down buildings and replace them with new ones. For that reason little was done to rid our cities of these blighted areas.

City planners have recognized the need for renovation and rebuilding the inner core of cities. With the help of the former Housing and Home Finance Agency, now part of HUD, many cities have condemned large tracts of land in these blighted areas. They are replacing slums with housing projects. Some of the housing projects are government projects; others are developed by private firms.

With the help of the federal government many cities are replacing slum dwellings with rental units for low-income families. Hundreds of cities have established local housing authorities and are erecting apartment buildings and houses to help solve the housing shortage. These projects and the building programs of private concerns have made some progress in overcoming the housing shortage.

Civic and art centers, parking areas, and expressways are also part of the overall planning in this rehabilitation program in various cities. *Urban renewal* is the name given to this whole program in many cities. As a result many of our large cities are changing their faces, and the centers of these cities are becoming more desirable places to live.

The Housing and Home Finance Agency provided impetus for this program. It has been carried forward by its successor, HUD.

The national concern for improved housing and living conditions has led to the establishment of this new department. It is significant that its first secretary, Robert C. Weaver, had been director of the Housing and Home Finance Agency. (See Chapter 12.)

The department encourages action by state and local governments and by private business to seek solutions to the problems of housing and urban development. Its aim is to have a major share of the action carried on by the private home building and mortgage lending industries.

PUBLIC PROTECTION

Man has always had to face hazards. Among them are fire, acts of nature, wild animals, severe weather conditions, criminals, bacteria, and accidents. These present a constant challenge to man in the struggle to live. Through the ages man has sought ways to protect himself against them and to reduce the hazards of life.

Early man fought wild animals with clubs. Early settlers in America built stockades as a protection against unfriendly Indians. Today man locks his doors and puts his money into banks for safekeeping.

But protection against the many hazards of life requires more than a locked door or a bank. There is continuous study and search for protective measures to reduce the hazards of living. Some of these measures are supplied by government, which has as one of its functions the protection of citizens against some of the many dangers that they face daily.

Throughout this book you have learned of government agencies and departments that are established for the protection of people. A chief one, of course, is the Department of Defense, whose primary respon-

Stress the increasing role of local, state, and national government as viewed historically with respect to crime and accident prevention.

sibility is to protect the nation from foreign enemies.

The previous chapter discussed in some detail the measures which are taken to protect the health of the nation. The Securities and Exchange Commission and the Federal Deposit Insurance Corporation were set up to safeguard the investments and savings of the people. The Department of Justice has as one of its duties the protection of the nation against individuals and groups who wish to overthrow our form of government.

The various law enforcement agencies have the special responsibility of protecting the life and property of citizens. Some special problems of this protection will now be discussed: (1) crime and its prevention and (2) accidents and their prevention.

CRIME AND ITS PREVENTION

Nearly six million major crimes are committed in the United States each year, one about every five seconds. In an average day, the following crimes take place: over 6,000 robberies and burglaries, over 2,000 murders and assaults, and 2,500 car thefts. About every minute and a half there is a crime of murder, manslaughter, or assault. Crime is increasing. The FBI reported that in 1970 all crimes were up 11 per cent over the previous year.

Crime has become one of the greatest

Behind the story of every community blighted by crime and racketeers is a longer tale of civic indifference and individual neglect. The citizen who condones gambling, who winks at dishonesty, and who shrugs off his community responsibilities, is at the base of the pyramid, which supports political corruption, vice, and crime.

—J. EDGAR HOOVER in THE ROTARIAN. Reprinted with permission of THE ROTARIAN.

problems of American cities. But while most crimes are committed in the large metropolitan areas, few areas are free from crime. Crime has increased everywhere, in rural as well as in urban areas. What are the causes of these crimes? Why do people commit them?

CAUSES OF CRIME. No single cause can be given as the major reason for the large number of crimes committed. There are many factors which contribute to this big problem. In the case of any individual who commits a crime there is often more than one cause which has led him to a life of crime or to commit a single great offense against society.

A list of the many causes certainly includes the following: breakdown of moral training in home, school, and church; rapid industrialization of our society; lack of adequate housing; unrest because of wars and war tension; poor mental and physical health; comics, radio, television, and movies which stress crime and horror; corruption of officials; inadequate law enforcement; sale of weapons; crowded prisons; lack of sufficient police, prosecutors, judges, probation officers; mistreatment of minorities; school dropouts; broken homes; high-speed automobiles; and increase in the use of narcotic drugs and alcohol.

The degree to which each of these is responsible for a share of the crime is difficult to determine. But the combination of these many factors operating together has brought about the problem which is becoming greater each year. There are people who believe that one or another is the chief cause, but there is little agreement as to which is the chief cause.

Some people say that the crime and mystery programs shown on television are mainly responsible. It may certainly be true that some individuals get ideas for crimes from such programs, but many

Evaluate some of the mentioned causes of crime as to their importance.

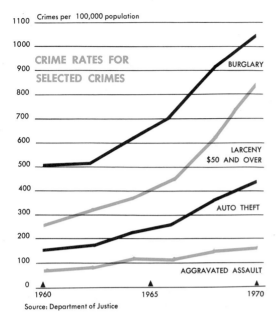

CRIME RATES FOR SELECTED CRIMES

Crimes per 100,000 population

BURGLARY
LARCENY $50 AND OVER
AUTO THEFT
AGGRAVATED ASSAULT

1960   1965   1970

Source: Department of Justice

The graph shows the increase in rate in recent years for four types of crime. What is being done to reverse this trend?

crimes were also committed before the days of television.

There are other people who maintain that some of the comic books children and young people read lead many of them into crime. Comic-book publishers themselves recognize this as part of the problem and are trying to place some controls on the content of these books.

Other people point to the large number in our population who do not attend church or synagogue and say that lack of religion is the cause of crime. Churches of all denominations are making real efforts to increase their memberships and to improve the influence of religion in the lives of more people.

Still other people say that parents pay too little attention to their children; they are too much concerned with making a living and with social obligations and do not know, and sometimes do not care, what

their children are doing. While this is true in some homes, the statement is an over-generalization and certainly does not apply to most parents.

In the same way we could go on examining the other items in the list of causes. With each one we would need to conclude that while it contributes to the total crime picture it is neither the only nor the chief cause. How can we then handle the situation and do something about it? Four approaches to the problem are important: (1) enforcement, (2) prosecution, (3) punishment, and (4) prevention.

ENFORCEMENT. A crime is a violation of a law; it involves doing something that the law forbids. So one of the important ways of decreasing crime is to force people to obey the law. To enforce the laws, all governments establish agencies and hire officers. These include constables, sheriffs, city policemen, state militiamen and police, marshals, Secret Service men, coast guardsmen, and FBI men.

Their job is a twofold one: the prevention of crime and the apprehension of criminals. The better they do the first job, the fewer criminals they need to arrest.

Law enforcement has become a technical job in the past few decades. At one time height and muscle were the chief qualifications of a police officer. While these are still valuable, he needs a thorough knowledge of law, technical information about crime prevention and detection, understanding of psychology and sociology, and complete honesty.

An adequate police force must be free from corruption and dishonesty. Most police officers are honest, but they are in positions where organized criminals try to undermine them. In a recent Senate investigation, evidence was presented that in some cities there was a direct link between criminals, politicians, and some police offi-

Discuss the use of police radio as an aid both in law enforcement and in crime prevention.

cials. Under such conditions crime finds its best breeding place.

A common complaint of police officials on local, state, and national levels is that they are understaffed. They need more help. A general observation in police work is that the better and larger the police force, the lower the crime rate. It follows that, when everything else is equal, if the force has more officers it will be better able to enforce obedience of the law.

The would-be criminal hesitates to commit a crime when a policeman is in the immediate neighborhood. Therefore, one of the first attacks on the crime problem is an adequate and well-trained police force on the local, state, and national levels to carry out necessary enforcement.

PROSECUTION. A basic concept of our system of law is that a person is innocent until proved guilty. This is to prevent the punishment of the innocent person. But this means also that in order to convict the guilty person, sufficient evidence must be well presented in court to prove that the person committed a crime.

Governments on all levels have prosecuting attorneys whose duty it is to present the evidence in court against a person accused of a crime. If this is well done, it tends to reduce crime, for the would-be criminal recognizes that if he is caught he will very likely be convicted.

On the other hand, if evidence is poorly presented by a prosecutor's office which is understaffed, inefficient, or dishonest, the criminal knows that he may not be convicted. Then the crime rate rises.

So an urgent need is for sufficient prosecutors who know how to gather evidence and how to present this evidence effectively in court. The need is for men who are honest and who cannot be bribed or **intimidated** into dropping a case against an accused person.

A second attack, then, on the crime problem is an adequate staff of prosecutors.

PUNISHMENT. After conviction, what? There are fines and prison sentences, sometimes the death penalty. For some individuals the fear of punishment keeps them from committing a crime, and for some convicted criminals a prison sentence or a fine keeps them from committing another crime. But other criminals come out of prison ready to continue a life of crime. Even some first offenders leave prison ready and equipped to commit crimes which they learned about in prison. For them prison was a school but of the wrong kind.

Criminologists and *penal experts,* who study crime and prisons, agree that prison reform is needed. Prisons should not be places of punishment only; they should be places where lives are made over. Prisoners should be separated according to crimes committed. First offenders should not be housed with hardened criminals.

More prisons are needed to reduce overcrowding. Special institutions are needed for the criminally insane and the feeble-minded. Treatment of prisoners should be humane, not cruel or sadistic. Persons in prison should be helped to learn a trade or a profession, to become contributing members of society. The aim should be to have people leave prison with a real desire to lead useful lives and not to return to a life of crime. Punishment and imprisonment should be used to protect society and to meet the needs of the offender.

Probation is being used instead of prison sentences in some cases. Before sentencing a convicted person, many judges ask for a report from a probation department. The report gives information about the person's previous record, his family, his job, his education, and his abilities. On the basis of this report the judge may suspend the sentence and place the person on probation.

Relate the story concerning the so-called "birdman of Alcatraz."

One of the most tragic crimes of recent years was the murder of Senator Robert Kennedy while he was campaigning for the 1968 presidency. In this picture is a portion of the huge crowd that lined the streets in New York for his funeral. (Photo courtesy The New York Times)

This means that the guilty person will not be sent to prison, but he will be set free and closely supervised by a probation officer, to whom he must report regularly. He is told the conditions of his probation and knows that if he does not follow them, he will be sent to prison.

Probation is being widely used in some states for youthful and first offenders. It helps married men whose families might suffer hardships if the wage earner were sent to prison. Probation is an attempt to have punishment fit the case and to help the offender to lead a useful life.

The third approach to the crime problem is, therefore, a review of the whole area of punishment.

PREVENTION. The best solution, of course, to the crime problem is its prevention. A reduction in the number of crimes means less prosecution, less punishment, and less of everything connected with crime —prisons, judges, courts, and so on. From a cost point of view alone, crime prevention

is to be desired. But there are many other desirable results in terms of better living for all, including the potential criminal and his family.

Many factors can help in crime prevention. The chief among them are elimination or reduction of the many causes mentioned earlier. Better housing, improved recreation, finer schools, more wholesome family life, more social work, better public officials—all these and more are parts of the big job of crime prevention.

The elimination of the conditions that breed crime, the breaking up of groups of people who thrive on crime, and a thorough educational program showing the cost of crime in money and broken lives will help to solve this problem.

This fourth approach to the crime problem is perhaps the most important, for prevention is more important than punishment or prosecution.

ACCIDENTS AND THEIR PREVENTION

Over 110,000 persons meet accidental death in the United States each year. Many more are seriously injured. Accidents bring suffering not only to those directly involved but to family members and friends. Many programs are being carried on to reduce accidents. The safety campaigns of private groups, our laws to provide safe conditions, and the enforcement of safety regulations by government agencies are designed to save lives. Accidents of all kinds and the circumstances surrounding them are thoroughly investigated by both public and private groups to determine causes and to prevent repetition.

The prevention of accidents rightly continues to be one of the chief concerns of government. Many of its activities are directed at the reduction of accidents and the enforcement of safety laws. The work of government in relation to safety regulations in industry was discussed in Chapter 30. Here we will study government's activities in two additional areas: (1) common carriers and (2) highway traffic.

COMMON CARRIERS. Railroads, buses, ships, and planes are *common carriers*. Safety regulations similar to those that apply to factories and mines are enforced in the case of the common carriers. Both state and federal governments are concerned that people who use these means of transportation shall travel safely. They have passed laws to provide for safe conditions and make inspections periodically to see that the laws are obeyed.

The Department of Transportation is in charge of enforcing the federal laws which pertain to interstate trains, buses, and trucks. For railroads there are such requirements as automatic train stops and warning devices.

For buses and trucks there are regulations about the qualifications of drivers and about the safety equipment on the vehicles. For example, a bus driver is not permitted to work more than sixty hours a week; the vehicle must be equipped with flares to be used as warning signals if it breaks down.

The Federal Aviation Administration in the Department of Transportation enforces safety regulations for air travel. Its responsibilities include examination of pilots, inspection of airplanes, and management of air traffic. The agency integrates and regulates civilian and military air travel.

The railroads, bus companies, and airlines have generally been very cooperative in putting the safety regulations into effect. They too want their carriers to be safe. Safety means public confidence, and public confidence means greater use.

How effective are the programs of the government and the carriers in making travel safe? In 1907 nearly 12,000 persons were killed in railroad accidents. Now the number, including highway grade-crossing accidents, is about 2,500 each year.

As a group the drivers of buses and trucks have a much better safety record than drivers of private cars. Highway bus travel is comparatively safe. In a recent year there were 2.2 passenger deaths (including drivers) in automobile accidents for each 100 million passenger miles. For buses the figure was only 0.2. Scheduled domestic air travel has an excellent safety record. The rate of accidental deaths has decreased greatly since the early days of commercial aviation. The average is now much less than one death (0.13) per 100 million passenger miles for domestic airlines. It is safer to travel in any common carrier than in a private automobile.

HIGHWAY TRAFFIC. The number of highway traffic deaths is now about 55,000 each year. This average of more than 150 deaths each day is far too many, and the number has been about the same for several years. It must be recognized that the record, when looked at in terms of the number of miles driven, has gotten somewhat better over the years.

There are many more cars now on the streets and highways than in former years, and most cars are being driven more miles. The improvement in the driving record on the basis of miles driven is shown by the fact that in 1935 there were sixteen deaths for each 100 million miles of driving. By 1970 this number had been reduced to five, less than one-third of the 1935 rate.

There are three factors in the traffic safety program: car, road, and driver. Attempts to reduce accidents must deal with each. A traffic expert has said that the car is safer than the road, and the road is safer than the driver. New safety features are added to new models each year. Highways cannot be changed readily; once built they are used for years. Drivers are difficult to change; their attitudes and habits become fixed.

Federal, state, and local governments are cooperating to improve traffic and highway conditions. Planning and construction of highways have been changed drastically in the past few years. The system of turnpikes and expressways has speeded travel and has helped to make it safer. The death rate for each 100 million passenger miles on turnpikes is about half the rate for all automobile travel.

Manufacturers of cars and accessories carry on continuous research to make cars and equipment safer. The federal government has entered this part of the safety

Driving on a crowded expressway requires maximum alertness as well as caution at all times to avoid accidents. (American Airlines)

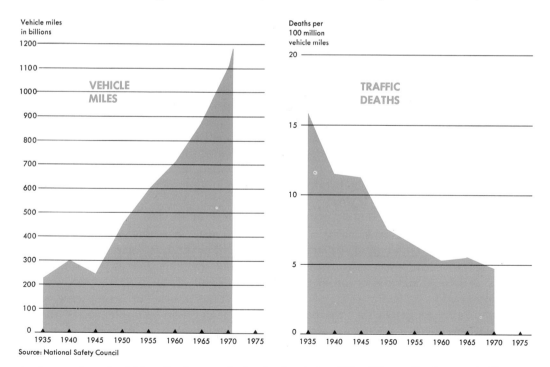

Source: National Safety Council

As the number of vehicle miles increased, the death rate per 100 million miles decreased. However, the number of persons killed in highway accidents each year is still a major problem. What efforts are being made to reduce this toll?

The Flint Journal, *Booth Newspapers, Inc.*

program by requiring various safety features on new motor cars. Many private groups, such as automobile clubs, are also working on the problem of safety.

GOVERNMENT PROGRAMS. The work of governments in relation to highway and automobile safety may be summarized as follows: enforcement of laws, changes in traffic regulations, elimination of traffic hazards, improved highway construction, licensing of drivers, and inspection of cars and trucks.

It is generally recognized that the number of traffic accidents is related to *enforcement;* as enforcement goes up, accidents go down. Other factors, such as weather and road conditions, also affect the number of accidents. Police and courts cooperate in

such programs as "Drunk drivers go to jail" and "The pedestrian has the right of way." Enforcement has been one way of solving the accident problem.

Changes in *traffic regulations* are used. Examples of such changes are lower speed limits under certain conditions, regulations on making turns, and designating certain streets as one-way streets. *Elimination* of traffic hazards may take such forms as the building of a railroad overpass or the leveling of a steep hill. Improved *highway construction* in the form of turnpikes and freeways makes allowance for more cars on the road traveling at higher speeds. The new roads have no intersecting roads, and the points of access are kept at a minimum.

But improved roads and changed traffic regulations have shown the need for improving drivers too. *Licensing* of drivers helps to keep unfit drivers off the road. Periodic *inspection* does the same for cars and trucks. Cars with unsafe equipment must either be made safe or not be permitted on streets and highways.

All levels of government—local, state, and federal—are involved in the safety program. The federal government has taken a more active role in helping to promote safety since the passage of the highway and traffic safety acts and the creation of the National Transportation Safety Board in 1966.

OTHER PROGRAMS. Manufacturers are continuously searching for improvements that will make cars safer. Puncture-proof tires and hydraulic brakes are examples of the outcome of this research. Occasionally the public is slow to accept new safety equipment. For example, even though safety belts and shoulder harnesses are now required on all new cars, not all people use them.

Many private groups add to traffic safety with programs of their own. A traffic safety

With respect to automobile safety, discuss Mr. Ralph Nader and his book *Unsafe at Any Speed* (1965).

THE AMERICAN POLITICAL SCIENCE ASSOCIATION

Throughout this book reference has been made to political scientists and the work they do. Many of them belong to the American Political Science Association which was founded in 1903. The association is "the major professional organization in the United States devoted to the development of the art and science of government."

The organization has about 18,000 members. Over the years many outstanding individuals in government and in political life have belonged to it. Among its past presidents are Woodrow Wilson, Charles A. Beard, and Ralph J. Bunche.

The association is engaged in a variety of activities dealing with political science. These are designed to bring together theory and practice in the broad field of government. The association conducts educational programs for professors of political science, teachers of government courses, and government officials. Its work is supported by membership fees and grants from several private foundations.

Among the association's activities are cooperative research, congressional fellowships, regional seminars, congressional awards, and an annual meeting. Examples of research projects are a study of the organization of Congress which led to the Legislative Reorganization Act of 1946 and a study of the selection of delegates to the 1952 political conventions. Under the congressional fellowships program outstanding young persons are given the opportunity to spend a year as assistants to members of Congress. The regional seminars bring together persons with political science interests on a regional basis. Congressional awards are made to a distinguished Democrat and Republican in both the House and the Senate for each session of Congress. The annual meeting provides an opportunity for the presentation of ideas in the broad field of political science and for a discussion of current issues.

The official publication of the association is *The American Political Science Review,* which is published four times a year. This quarterly contains articles on political science developments and reports on activities in the field. Significantly, the headquarters office of the association is in Washington, D.C.

---

association, for example, uses slogans or billboards to call the driver's attention to particular laws or violations. Some other group works with schools to emphasize to children the dangers of jaywalking. The efforts of these agencies and groups have combined to reduce traffic accidents.

In spite of all that has been done, traffic safety continues to be one of the nation's big headaches. The problem is a group problem, but it is also an individual one. The group can pass good laws and enforce them. It can improve the highways and build safer cars, but it is only the individual driver who can make highways and cars safer for himself and others.

It is the individual's concern for others, his feeling of responsibility, his attitude toward his fellowmen which will make the statistics go up or down. In a democracy, driving a car, like so many other acts, is a privilege which carries with it a responsibility. Government can offer public protection through laws and regulations, but each citizen needs to cooperate to make this protection effective. Each citizen must carry out his responsibility. This is especially important in the use of an automobile, because its use is so universal.

STUDY QUESTIONS

1. What are the basic human needs which are common to all people?

2. What makes a house a home?

CONCEPTS AND
GENERALIZATIONS

1
The research and struggle to satisfy the basic physical needs of food, clothing, and shelter have dominated much of man's history.

2
The shortage of adequate housing in the United States has resulted from a number of factors related to wars, economics, and population growth.

3
Housing restrictions with regard to race, religion, and nationality are gradually being eliminated by law, court orders, and improved human relations.

4
Government on all levels and private industry are working to eliminate slum conditions and to provide adequate housing for all people.

5
The federal government has been very active in the housing field since the depression years of the 1930's.

6
Crime is a major problem of the nation, and all levels of government are giving it increasing attention.

7
Solutions to the crime problem are being approached through enforcement, prosecution, punishment, and prevention.

8
The aim in the treatment of offenders should be to make them useful members of society.

9
Various governmental agencies and private groups are involved in programs to provide safer travel and to prevent accidents.

10
Accidents involving automobiles are chief contributors to the rising number of accidental deaths and injuries.

11
Safety programs are directed toward safer automobiles, improved highways, and more responsible drivers.

3. How does the kind of house influence the lives of people in it?

4. What are some of the possible choices a person must make in the selection of a home?

5. What is meant by restrictions on homes?

6. What progress has been made in doing away with restrictions?

7. What are the factors which have caused the housing shortage?

8. Why do many families live in substandard homes?

9. How did the depression of the 1930's affect home-ownership?

10. Explain the work of the housing agencies of the federal government.

11. What is meant by the statement that our big cities are rotting at the core?

12. What are cities doing to eliminate slum conditions?

13. Mention some of the government agencies and departments which have been established to protect people.

14. What are the commonly mentioned causes of crime? Show that any one of these is not the only cause.

15. What are four important approaches to the reduction of crime?

16. Why is more than strength necessary as a qualification for a police officer?

17. Why is an effective staff of prosecutors needed for the reduction of crime?

18. What purposes should prisons serve?

19. Why is probation sometimes used instead of a prison sentence?

20. What are some factors which can help in the prevention of crime?

21. Why is the safety record of common carriers better than that of private autos?

22. What are the three important factors in the highway safety program?

23. What are governments doing to improve traffic safety?

IDEAS FOR DISCUSSION

1. "Living near the center of the city has many advantages over suburban living." Do you agree? From your discussion make a list of the advantages of both city living and suburban living.

2. Some communities and subdivisions have restrictions on homes which deal with the size and kind of house a person may build. Are these restrictions good? Would you put such restrictions in the same classification with restrictions about persons who may live in the subdivision?

3. It is usually cheaper to buy vacant land for new houses than to buy land with buildings on it, clear the land, and rebuild it with new houses. This is one of the reasons for slow progress in slum clearance. Do you have any suggestions as to how this difficulty may be overcome?

4. Many people believe that the greatest help for home ownership has been the FHA. Do you agree? Why?

5. Should government stop its work in the housing field, leaving all housing to private business? What is your opinion on this question, and what facts do you have to support your opinion?

6. Gutenberg, the inventor of the printing press, is reported to have said that if he thought the bad effects of the printing press would be greater than the good, he would destroy his invention. Some crime may be due to the printing press. How? Should Gutenberg have destroyed his invention?

7. "The accident toll could be greatly reduced if all that is known about safety were used in designing and constructing cars and if all safety regulations were followed." What is your opinion of this statement?

8. Some cities and states have adopted open- or fair-housing legislation. What is the situation in your community and state with regard to this issue? Is further legislation needed?

9. Discuss the crime situation in your community. What steps do you suggest should be taken to reduce crime in your area?

THINGS TO DO

1. Have committees report on some phase of housing in your community by selecting one of the following topics and interviewing an official at the city or township hall.
  a) Building restrictions
  b) Building permits issued each year during the past twenty-five years
  c) Substandard houses
  d) Shortage of homes
  e) Public housing developments
  f) Fair-housing legislation

2. If you live in a large city, make a study of the slum clearance and urban renewal work being done. Interview someone at the city hall to get information on the city's plans. Also visit an urban renewal project to get first-hand information.

3. Collect data on the increase (or decrease) of crime in your state or community over the past thirty years. Make a series of charts for a bulletin board display of your information.

4. Make a study of a recent criminal case from newspaper accounts. Report on the effectiveness of the prosecutor's work.

5. Interview a local judge or prosecutor to learn what steps are being taken by your community in the prevention of crime. Use pictures and drawings of some of the activities for a bulletin board display.

6. Prepare a report on the accident and safety records of your community.

7. If your community has a community or human relations commission, interview one of the staff members about the effect of housing on relations between people of different racial or nationality groups.

8. Make a study of the effect of daylight and darkness on (a) crime or (b) accidents. Report your study to the class.

FURTHER READINGS

Committee for Economic Development, REDUCING CRIME AND ASSURING JUSTICE. The Committee, 1972.

Committee for Economic Development, IMPROVING THE PUBLIC WELFARE SYSTEM. The Committee, 1970.

Fried, Joseph P., HOUSING CRISIS IN THE U.S.A. Praeger Publishers, Inc., 1971.

Glaser, Daniel, CRIME IN THE CITY. Harper & Row, Publishers, 1970.

Hanna, John Paul, TEENAGERS AND THE LAW. Ginn and Co., 1967.

Kearney, Paul, HIGHWAY HOMOCIDE. Thomas Y. Crowell Co., 1966.

Liston, Robert A., YOUR CAREER IN LAW ENFORCEMENT. Julian Messner, Inc., 1965.

President's Commission on Law Enforcement and Administration of Justice. THE CHALLENGE OF CRIME IN A FREE SOCIETY—A REPORT. E. P. Dutton & Co., Inc., 1969.

Interpreting Data

This final unit has discussed various aspects of the life of the people. It concludes with a series of informational statements and several tables and charts of statistical data. These deal primarily with population, agriculture, and welfare. The information is significant in shaping the life of the people of the nation (and of the world). It will have a direct influence on the goodness of life in the United States in the decades ahead. Data such as these are being studied, analyzed, and interpreted in trying to project the future living conditions and of trying to improve them for all people.

As you study and discuss the following statements and data, try to determine what they mean for our country. Raise such questions as these:

- What do the data mean?
- What is the relationship of the population data to the information about agriculture?
- What generalizations can you draw from the information given?
- What predictions can you make about the future?
- What additional information and data would you like to have?
- What actions do you propose for the United States, your state, your community in the light of the data?
- In the light of the data, what should be the role of government in agriculture?
- What other facts would you like to know about welfare?

POPULATION

Much has been written in recent years about trends in population change and the

POPULATION OF THE UNITED STATES, 1870-1970
(in thousands)

YEAR	RURAL	URBAN
1870	28,656	9,902
1880	36,026	14,130
1890	40,841	22,106
1900	45,835	30,160
1910	49,973	41,999
1920	51,553	54,158
1930	53,820	68,955
1940	57,246	74,424
1950	54,479	96,847
1960	54,054	125,269
1970	53,887	149,325

Source: *Statistical Abstract of the United States, 1971.*

PROJECTIONS OF TOTAL POPULATION OF THE UNITED STATES, 1975-2000
(in millions)

YEAR	POPULATION
1975	218
1980	232
1985	249
1990	266
1995	283
2000	301

Source: *Statistical Abstract of the United States, 1971.*

"population explosion." The tables and charts that follow show several different trends in the population of the United States.

In making the projection estimates in the table above, the population of the United States in 1969, 203 million, was taken as a base. Other population projections for the year 2000 range from a low of 266 million to a high of 321 million.

The graphs on the next page show two significant trends in population change: (1) the increasing concentration of our population in urban areas, which was discussed in connection with the problems of local governments (Chapter 22) and the problems of the farmer (Chapter 29); (2) the decrease in the median age of our population in recent years.

THE TREND TO URBANIZATION

More and more people live in and about metropolitan areas (central-core cities and their suburbs,.as defined by the Government). Particularly dramatic have been the increase in the suburban population and the decline in the percentage of people living on farms, as distinguished from those living in what the Government defines as nonfarm rural areas.

	CENTRAL CORE	SUBURBS	FARM	NONFARM
1915	31%	16%	32%	21%
1949	34%	24%	17.5%	24.5%
1967	30%	34%	6%	30%

Redrawn by permission from *The National Observer*.

MORE YOUNG PEOPLE

The median age of Americans rose steadily because of increased longevity, but since the 1950's it has headed downward again as young people, products of the postwar "baby boom," become a greater part of the population.

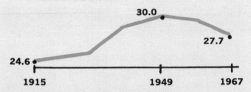

30.0

27.7

24.6

1915   1949   1967

Redrawn by permission from *The National Observer*.

Both of the foregoing charts are from *The National Observer*, November 20, 1967. The year 1915 is taken as a base, because from 1915 to 1967 the population of the United States doubled from 100 million to 200 million.

AGRICULTURE

Threshing machines, steel plows, seed drills, mowers, rakes, cultivators, and reapers significantly increased the farmer's efficiency. With these machines he could cultivate much larger acreages than was possible with the primitive hand tools that had historically been his lot. The mechanization of the American farm was widespread by 1915 and, in addition, the development of the gasoline engine had solved the age-old problem of the limitations imposed by animal power. Some of the steam-operated farm machines of the late nineteenth century had become so large that 40 horses were necessary to move them. The advent of the gasoline-powered farm tractor in the early years of the twentieth century cut the last bond that tied man to the relatively puny resources of animal power, and the farmer's capability literally soared. . . .

In summary, we can conclude that the rise in real farm output during the past 90 years has been phenomenal. The index of farm output compiled by the Department of Agriculture indicates that real output increased about six-fold in the period 1870-1960. But, even more important for our purposes, during the period 1889-1960 farm output per man-hour increased about 4 times.[1]

* * *

The . . . characteristic of modern agriculture is the rapid technical and economic changes that have occurred in the United States during the last 30 years and that are continuing, making possible the steady increase in output without increasing the amount of land, labor, or other items used in production. New machines, new varieties of crops, fertilizers, and insecticides, improved breeds of animals, and new management techniques have rapidly increased farm output. Each of these innovations was profitable and when adopted on a wholesale basis resulted in increased farm output. . . .

For the first time in our history, nonfarm people are in a position to adopt

[1] Thomas J. Hailstones and others, *Contemporary Economic Problems and Issues*. South-Western Publishing Co., 1966, pp. 96-97.

FARM EMPLOYMENT AND OUTPUT PER MAN-HOUR
1947-1971

YEAR	EMPLOYMENT (in thousands)	OUTPUT PER MAN-HOUR (1967 = 100)
1947	7,891	29.2
1950	7,160	37.7
1955	6,449	49.5
1960	5,458	64.9
1965	4,361	86.9
1967	3,844	100.0
1970	3,462	115.6
1971	3,387	125.6

Source: *Economic Report of the President, 1972.*

OUTPUT PER ACRE FOR SELECTED CROPS
1935-39 AND 1965-69

CROP	1935-39 YIELD PER ACRE	1965-69 YIELD PER ACRE
Wheat	13.2 bu.	27.5 bu.
Corn	26.1 bu.	77.4 bu.
Hay	1.24 tons	1.94 tons
Potatoes	70.3 cwt.	212.3 cwt.
Cotton	226 lbs.	485 lbs.
Tobacco	886 lbs.	1,957 lbs.

Source: *Statistical Abstract of the United States, 1971.*

almost any kind of a farm program they believe we should have. In the past, urban people have been rightly indignant over some of the economic waste and political excesses that were a part of our farm programs. It is hoped that as the political power over the determination of farm policy swings to urban people, they will exercise that power carefully, recognizing the contributions as well as the problems of modern agriculture in a modern economy.[1]

[1] Dale E. Hathaway, "The U. S. Farm Problem," *Vital Issues* Volume XIV, No. 4. Center for Information on America, Washington, Connecticut, copyright 1964.

The following item is an example of similar situations in other countries of the world. The statement is an excerpt from an article by Robert Trumbull in *The New York Times* of March 21, 1968.

At first it may seem that the statement about Japan does not belong in a discussion about population and agriculture in the United States. But think about it.

● Why is the article pertinent to the foregoing discussion?
● How is the growing industrialization of Japan and other countries affecting the United States?

Japan Worried by Growing Flight from Farms

How are you going to keep them down on the farm after they've seen Tokyo? Or Osaka or Nagoya or Nagasaki or any of Japan's throbbing, brightly lighted cities?

The question is causing deep concern among Japanese economists and fiscal officials, as the hope of national self-sufficiency in food production rapidly recedes with the trek from farm to the city growing in volume yearly.

With the young men moving away from the countryside in large numbers, the cities have become overwhelmingly attractive for the farmer's daughter, too. . . .

According to the latest figures, the number of Japanese tilling the soil has dropped to fewer than 10 million, or just under 20 per cent of the national labor force. Twenty years ago, 47.3 per cent of the population was employed in agriculture.

While there has been some satisfaction that Japan is taking on more of the appearance of a thoroughly modern industrial nation, . . . the exodus to the cities is also a serious national problem.

Food production dropped from 82 per cent of the nation's requirements in 1965 to less than 75 per cent in 1967. . . .

Authorities point out that the move to the cities is leaving the rural areas without the kind of labor necessary to implement plans for the official encouragement of wholesale farm mechanization, a step urged for the improvement of output.[1]

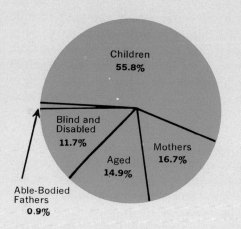

Source: *Bulletin of the Department of Health, Education, and Welfare, 1972.*

WELFARE

Government has taken an increasing role in providing welfare services. State and lo-cal governments and the federal government join in supporting people in need. In one month of a recent year there were 13,600,000 persons on welfare rolls receiving aid in federally-assisted programs. Among these were 126,000 able-bodied males, less than 1 per cent of the total. The chart on the left shows how the more than 13 million people are distributed.

The largest public assistance program is Aid to Families with Dependent Children. One of the statements sometimes made is that once a family gets on welfare it stays there. How do you view this statement in light of these data?

LENGTH OF TIME ON WELFARE

Less than six months	17.4%
Six months to one year	17.8%
One to two years	20.8%
Two to three years	12.2%
Three to five years	13.7%
Five to ten years	11.6%
Ten years or more	6.1%

Source: *Bulletin of the Department of Health, Education, and Welfare, 1972.*

- Each chapter of this book was con-cluded with a series of statements called "Concepts and Generalizations." What concepts and generalizations can you write as a result of your study of this final Discovery Episode, "Inter-preting Data"? Discuss these with your teacher and classmates.

---

[1] © 1968 by The New York Times Company. Reprinted by permission.

33
Unfinished Business

Our American Government is revised and brought up to date every two years to coincide with the election of a new Congress. A few last-minute changes can be made after the November elections, but most of the changes have to be made during the summer and early autumn. At the time of going to press, there are always unsettled matters as well as new ideas and issues emerging. This final chapter brings to your attention some of these last-minute, unresolved topics. These ideas may deserve special attention during the next two years.

In the fall of 1972 the presidential election was the predominant issue before the American people. The Olympic games in Munich, with the tragic killing of Israeli athletes in a ransom attempt by Palestinian guerrillas, had come to a sad end. The United Nations convened its Twenty-sixth General Assembly in New York. The Vietnam war was still making headlines.

Congress was in its annual struggle to adjourn. Senators and representatives were eager to get back home to their own political campaigns. But bills that had long been debated still awaited passage. Finally on October 18, 1972, the Ninety-second Congress came to an end.

As the election approached, television, newspapers, and magazines gave renewed emphasis to the issues that were so important for the future of the United States and the world. In international affairs the Vietnam war, the situation in the Middle East, the new approaches to China and the Soviet Union, the world money system, and the needs of developing nations received much attention.

In domestic affairs the headlines dealt with poverty, the welfare system, drug us-age, pollution, women's rights, busing, economic conditions, the rights of minority groups, and problems of urban living. There was indeed much unfinished business.

The voices of dissent were muted, less shrill than they had been. After a few years of violence and revolutionary talk there seemed to be a return to rationality and order. Critics, in their efforts to bring change, were emphasizing reform of the political process.

POLITICAL REFORMS

Approaches to refining and improving political institutions and procedures took many forms. Some had been underway for many years; some were relatively new. Several vital ones are discussed below.

ELECTION CAMPAIGN REFORMS. The November 1972 election was closely watched to determine if the new Federal Election Campaign Act made any real differences in the conduct of the election—particularly in the financing of campaigns. (See pages 142-143.)

Common Cause, a nonpartisan watchdog

organization, argued that the press should cover campaign spending "as regularly as it does the weather." In spot checks around the nation Common Cause found that the law was widely ignored. In Ohio, for example, of the eighty-two candidates for Congress only thirteen filed reports of contributors. In Pennsylvania only sixteen of eighty-six filed.

John Gardner, head of Common Cause, stated, "Clearly, many Congressmen just don't want the public to know where they get their campaign money."

Efforts were also made to pressure President Nixon into revealing the names and amounts of contributions received before April 7, 1972, when the new law became effective. The President and his chief fund raiser, Maurice Stans, argued that they did not have to report contributions given before that date. Gardner filed a lawsuit under the old Corrupt Practices Act of 1925 to try to force the Committee to Re-Elect the President to reveal the information. The Committee chose to make public a partial list of contributors.

In the months following the election, the cost and regulation of campaigns could again become an issue before Congress.

POLITICAL PARTY REFORMS. The 1972 presidential nominating conventions set the stage for efforts to reform the political process within the two major political parties.

At the August convention of the Republican party, leaders from the large industrial states tried to introduce a new system for the future selection of delegates. The intent was to select more blacks, Chicanos, Indians, young people, and women. It was a plea to open the system. The smaller southern and western states opposed the changes arguing that this would distort the traditional pattern of Republican representation. They pointed out that the percent-

ages of youth, women, and minorities were increased in the 1972 convention over previous conventions and that the increases would undoubtedly continue. They opposed any quota system.

On a related issue the reformers wanted bonus votes given to states electing Republican governors and Republican members of Congress. At present, bonus votes are given only for states in which a Republican presidential candidate wins the electors.

On both issues the smaller states won before the Rules Committee, and no floor fight developed. The struggle for more delegates for the industrial states will undoubtedly continue. As one delegate pointed out, "A delegate from Alaska represents a handful of Republicans, while a delegate from New York represents a huge number." A court fight may result. One definite change is that the 1976 convention will have at least 600 more delegates than the 1,347 at the 1972 convention.

The Democrats had changed the system of selecting delegates to the 1972 convention based on rules developed by the McGovern Commission. The result was a convention of many delegates (3,016) with more rank-and-file members and fewer professional politicians. State delegations had to include women, young people, and minority group members in approximate proportions to their populations within the state. Delegations that did not meet these guidelines were successfully challenged before the Credentials Committee.

The Democratic reform commissions had also proposed a national Democratic Party charter. The original proposal had highlighted three features: 1. enrolling party members and requiring payment of dues by those able to pay; 2. increasing the size of the Democratic National Committee from 110 members to 344 members; 3. holding a National Policy Conference in even-

As late as 1972, some states prohibited women from sitting on juries.

numbered years in which there is not a presidential election.

At the Democratic convention, however, on July 13, 1972, it was voted overwhelmingly to delay consideration of these proposals for two years. Instead the convention voted to establish a commission to recommend an overhaul of the party structure at a special conference to be held in 1974 and to enlarge the National Committee to 303 members.

EQUAL RIGHTS FOR WOMEN. Fortynine years after first being introduced, a proposed constitutional amendment concerning equal rights for women passed Congress and was sent to the states for ratification. The proposed amendment was adopted by the Senate on March 22, 1972, by a vote of 84 to 8. Earlier, on October 12, 1971, the House had passed the amendment by a vote of 354 to 23. If ratified by three-fourths (38) of the states within the seven-year limitation, this would become the Twenty-seventh Amendment to the Constitution.

The proposed amendment reads: "Equality of rights under the law shall not be denied or abridged by the United States or by any state on account of sex. The Congress shall have the power to enforce, by appropriate legislation, the provisions of this article. This amendment shall take effect two years after the date of ratification."

Many women, individually and in groups, have struggled for this amendment for nearly half a century. In 1923, three years after women won the right to vote, the first "equal rights" amendment was proposed in Congress. Twice the Senate passed the amendment—in 1950 and again in 1953. The House also passed it twice—in 1970 and in 1971. But it had never been approved by both houses in one Congress until the action by the Ninety-second Congress.

Over the years women's liberation groups

Women are 53 per cent of the population in this country. Yet we are served by a U.S. House of Representatives with only fourteen women members and a Senate with no women. Our representation at state and local levels is not much better. To change that, we need power, political power.

—National Women's Political Caucus

have argued that sex discrimination is a fact in the United States. The Civil Rights Act of 1964 struck at this type of prejudice since it prohibited employers from hiring, firing, or in any other way discriminating against any individual for reasons of race, color, religion, or sex. (See pages 103, 169-175, 266, 291.)

Martha Griffiths, the Congresswoman from Michigan who sponsored the Twenty-seventh Amendment, believes the amendment is necessary because the Supreme Court "has held for ninety-eight years that women, as a class, are not entitled to equal protection of the laws. They are not 'persons' within the meaning of the Constitution."

Sponsors of the amendment hope for the end of laws and practices that treat women unfairly in matters of property, divorce, inheritance, and pensions.

Hawaii became the first state to ratify—acting less than two hours after the Senate vote. In the next seven months twenty-one states had ratified. Backers of the amendment expect ratification to be completed in 1973 or 1974. One group of women, however, has organized to oppose ratification because their leaders claim the amendment makes women eligible for the military draft and tends to destroy the family as a unit. Some opposition by labor unions has also appeared.

THE EIGHTEEN-YEAR-OLD VOTE. Both political parties wooed the youth vote

Ralph Nader, the consumer advocate and critic of Congress' inefficiency, appears before a Senate Committee. (Camera 5—Steve Northup)

in the days leading up to the November election. Symptomatic of this concern was the election of young delegates to the national conventions. Of the 3,016 delegates at the Democratic convention in July 1972, 683 were under age thirty—22.6 per cent. In 1968 only 4 per cent of the delegates had been in this age group. At the 1972 Republican convention, 101 of 1,347 delegates were under age thirty—7.5 per cent contrasted with 1 per cent in 1968.

McGovern forces claimed they would receive a large percentage of the youth vote. The Nixon camp with its *Young Voters for Nixon* campaign made similar claims.

Observers were eager to study the results of the election, not only to learn for whom the youth voted, but to determine the percentage of youth who availed themselves of their new voting opportunity.

NADER'S CONGRESS PROJECT. The largest project yet to be attempted by Ralph Nader and his "raiders" is a mammoth study of Congress as an American institution. (See page 289.) Some 1,000

graduate students, lawyers, professors, and members of the League of Women Voters are employed by the "Congress Project."

Nader has declared that Congress is "a continuous underachiever" and that it is "under the domination of the White House and relentless special interests."

Work on the study of Congress began in the summer of 1971 when some dozen staff members made preliminary analyses of possible areas of study. From September 1971 to February 1972, a permanent staff of fifteen prepared general plans and recruited the hundreds of investigators needed for the intensive work in the summer and fall of 1972. Expenses, estimated to run from $100,000 to $150,000, will be paid from the fees and royalties of Nader speeches and reports.

The Congress study has three major parts. First, before the November 1972 election, profiles of members of Congress were compiled and published to assist voters in their assessment of their senators and representatives. These profiles gave

The books that result from this Project make interesting additions to a bibliography on government.

accounts of how members voted, what they did in committee and what they neglected, and how their service affected their districts. The facts were assembled from written replies to questionnaires, interviews, and voting records. Members of Congress reported that answering the 633 questions required ten to twelve hours of time.

Second, Nader proposed a "topic study" to analyze the Congressional process. Twelve topics were selected for this study by teams of experts. Included in the topics were: rules of Congress, apportionment, the appropriations process, campaign financing, history of Congress, and similar matters. It was planned to publish the reports in the early months of 1973.

Third, there was to be a study of Congressional committees, which was expected to result in a book of twelve chapters. Each chapter was to be written by an expert with the aid of several assistants. Each chapter would deal with the activities, successes, and failures of one or more Congressional committees. The report was scheduled for publication in 1973.

Three minor studies were also planned. One dealt with Congressional press relations, another with establishing a permanent data bank by putting information about members of Congress into a computer, and a third with producing a *Handbook for Citizens* to assist voters in their apraisal of, and their dealings with, members of Congress.

When announcing the project Ralph Nader asked, "What does the public know of Congress?" He answered the question in these words, "Not much at all." He hoped for a different answer after completion of the "Congress Project."

1. *What have been the results of political reforms?*
2. *Is the Federal Election Campaign Act successful?*
3. *Do you prefer the Democratic or Republican approach to party reform? Why?*
4. *What has happened to the proposed Equal Rights Amendment?*
5. *What effect did the new youth vote have in the 1972 election?*
6. *How effective is the Nader "Congress Project"?*

INTERNATIONAL AFFAIRS

The prolonged Vietnam war continued to emphasize the great differences in opinion on international affairs that existed among the American people. There were differences over the right to declare war, defense needs, and the role of the United States in international trade.

UNDECLARED WARS. The issue of the part Congress should take in declaring war loomed large in 1972. The Constitution states in Article 1, Section 8, Paragraph 11, "The Congress shall have power . . . to declare war. . . ." But from the earliest days of the nation, the United States has engaged in hostilities with foreign nations without a Congressional declaration of war. Since World War II the role of Congress with respect to this issue has deteriorated.

Presidents on their own have committed the United States to war or actions that might have led to war in Korea, Lebanon, the Dominican Republic, and Indochina. The escalation of the war in Vietnam by successive presidents pushed into the limelight the issue of who has the right to make war. Congressional leaders have become especially sensitive to the criticism that they have given up their power to declare war and have become subservient to the President.

To restore the balance between the executive and legislative branches, the Senate in April 1972 passed a bill defining the constitutional war powers. During hearings before the Senate Foreign Relations Committee, Senator Jacob K. Javits, Republican of New York, said, "We live in an age of undeclared war, which has meant presidential war. Presidential war has created a most dangerous imbalance in our constitutional system of checks and balances."

The Senate bill tried to deal realistically with present conditions. It recognized that, in an age of nuclear war and guerrilla fighting, formal declarations of war might be too slow and might endanger our ability to defend ourselves or our allies. The bill limited unilateral action by the President to specifically defined instances where the United States or its armed forces have been attacked. The President could also use military force to protect American lives or to uphold terms of treaties or executive agreements approved by Congress. The crucial feature of the bill was a provision setting a limit of thirty days during which military forces could be used by the President in these specified cases. For use beyond thirty days, Congress would have to pass specific legislation authorizing continued use. Thus Congress would have thirty days for debate as to whether any military action was justified.

The bill passed the Senate by a 68 to 16 roll-call vote. Similar bills were defeated in the House in 1970 and 1971, and the present bill was weakened by the House. No action was taken in conference committee before the adjournment of Congress in 1972.

The judicial branch became prominent in the issue when Supreme Court Justice William O. Douglas stated on a Columbia Broadcasting System interview on September 4, 1972, that he thought the Vietnam War might be unconstitutional because it had not been formally declared by Congress. In contrast Justice William H. Rehnquist, when he was Assistant Attorney General, defended the 1970 invasion of Cambodia as constitutional since earlier Presidents, Congresses, and the Supreme Court had recognized such actions as a rightful use of presidential power. On October 16, 1972, the Supreme Court by a 7 to 2 vote refused to hear a case on the legality of Vietnam war.

ANTI-BALLISTIC MISSILE SITES. The Strategic Arms Limitation Treaty (SALT) with the Soviet Union was signed in May 1972 and approved by the necessary two-thirds vote of the Senate on August 3, 1972. (See page 541.) The treaty provided that each nation could build two defensive anti-ballistic missile sites—one to protect the capital of the country and one to protect a retaliatory offensive missile site.

The House approved both ABM sites, but the Senate on the recommendation of the Armed Services Committee refused to appropriate funds for the Washington, D.C., site. The Senate committee decided it did not have enough information on the

This is a section of the Grand Forks Safeguard anti-ballistic missile site in North Dakota. (Wide World photo)

worth and functioning of the Washington, D.C., site to justify going ahead with it. Accordingly only one ABM site is being constructed—at Grand Forks, North Dakota.

The Grand Forks ABM site is a huge self-contained complex with seven-foot-thick steel-reinforced concrete walls. Six large generators are housed in an underground power plant. There are 150 intercontinental ballistic missiles (ICBM's) aimed at the Soviet Union and China. The electronic equipment is exceedingly complex. One observer commented, "Compared with this missile-site radar, an aircraft carrier is a junior-high-school toy."

LIMITING OFFENSIVE NUCLEAR WEAPONS. The anti-ballistic sites treaty was one of two formal agreements reached by President Nixon on his visit to Moscow in May 1972. The other was a U.S.-Soviet interim agreement limiting offensive nuclear weapons. (See page 541.)

It was agreed that for five years neither power would start construction of additional fixed land-based intercontinental ballistic missile launchers. Nor would either power convert present launchers for lighter missiles into launchers for heavier missiles. It was also agreed to limit submarine missile launchers to numbers already operational or under construction.

This executive agreement under provisions of a 1961 law on disarmament required the approval of both the Senate and the House. By a 329 to 7 roll-call vote the House approved the agreement on August 18, 1972. The Senate on September 14, 1972, approved the agreement by an 88 to 2 vote after a month's debate. Senator Henry M. Jackson had proposed a controversial amendment. The amendment urged that in any future agreement the levels of strategic forces must not leave the United States in an "inferior" position. The White House finally agreed to this amendment. Cloture

was adopted by a 76 to 15 vote, and the amendment was accepted by a 56 to 35 vote. (See page 211.) The agreement was expected to lead to Phase II of the Strategic Arms Limitation Talks.

THE MILITARY DRAFT. At the end of August 1972 Defense Secretary Melvin Laird released a fifty-one-page report calling for the end of military conscription. The Secretary wrote, "Every effort will be made to minimize draft calls, if not avoid them entirely, between January and July 1973 when the current induction authority expires." President Nixon approved the report, since he had pledged to end the draft by July 1973. Whether Congress will approve was uncertain and might depend on world conditions and the makeup of the Ninety-third Congress.

INTERNATIONAL TRADE. The United States depends on trade with other nations. This trade takes many forms: foreign travel, exchange of goods and products, foreign aid, overseas investment, defense spending. For two decades, however, the flow of dollars to other nations has not been matched by a returning flow of dollars to the United States. The result has been continued deficits in the United States balance of payments. (See page 514.)

The failure to balance our imports and exports caused a reduction in U.S. gold stocks from 23.4 billion dollars to 10.1 billion dollars over a twenty-year period. At the same time the value of the dollar, the currency most widely used in international trade, became increasingly unstable. Finally, the President asked Congress to devalue the dollar by raising the price of gold to $38 from the $35-an-ounce price that had been in effect since 1934. Congress approved this action on March 21, 1972.

Gold devaluation was essentially a defensive measure, however. Offensive action was also necessary. This was and is being taken.

Two examples illustrate situations that warrant careful watching in the future. These are new trade agreements with the Soviet Union and Japan.

During President Nixon's visit to Moscow in May 1972, trade was a central issue for discussion. Within a few weeks a historic three-year agreement had been reached that provided that the United States sell 750 million dollars worth of corn, wheat, oats, barley, or sorghum to Russia. This was termed the largest single grain transaction that had ever occurred. Shipping began in late July. The general satisfaction over the agreement was marred when accusations were made in September 1972 that grain exporters received advance information on the deal from government officials and profited at the expense of farmers. Various investigations were begun, but the entire affair is very complex.

The agreement, however, was believed to be just the beginning of increased trade relations between the two giant nations. The Soviet Union wants our machinery and equipment as well as grains. They need help in such industries as air-conditioning, construction, data processing, and automotive parts. In return we need fuels such as natural gas, and raw materials such as chrome, copper, nickel, and platinum.

On August 31 and September 1, 1972, President Nixon met in Hawaii with Japan's new Prime Minister, Kakuei Tanaka for summit talks. Again trade was prominent in the discussions. For many years, Japanese trade barriers had prevented the import of large quantities of goods from the United States. The annual deficit grew to more than 3.8 billion dollars, as Japanese exports to the United States continued to exceed their imports. Devaluation of the dollar alleviated the situation somewhat, particularly since it reduced the import of small Japanese automobiles. The real need, however, was for the reduction in Japanese tariff barriers to encourage an increase in the flow of goods from the United States to Japan.

At the end of the meeting, a joint statement was issued announcing an emergency trade agreement by which Japan would buy 1.2 billion dollars' worth of aircraft, agricultural, forestry, and fishery products plus "uranium enrichment services." Premier Tanaka stated, "It was the intention of the government of Japan to reduce the imbalance to a more reasonable size within a reasonable period of time." There was no indication that major concessions on trade barriers had been made.

Another major change in international trade will take place in 1973 with the anticipated entry of Great Britain, Denmark, and Ireland into the Common Market. The Common Market is officially known as the European Economic Community. (See page 549.) It was organized in 1958 by six countries—Belgium, France, Italy, Luxembourg, Netherlands, and West Germany. The members have tried to remove all barriers to trade among themselves and to standardize tariffs between themselves and nonmember nations.

With its expansion to nine members, the Common Market's total population will exceed that of the United States. As an economic unit the Market is comparable to the United States. The enlargement and strengthening of the Common Market will have an impact on economic interests of the United States. The United States has regularly sold more to the Common Market community than it has purchased in return. This has resulted in a large trade surplus favoring the United States. Agricultural support prices and possible preferential trade arrangements among the Common Market nations are of concern to the US since they might reduce our trade surplus.

It appears that a new set of world economic relationships may develop in the future.

1. *Who should have the responsibility of deciding to declare war? Congress? the President? the people? Why?*
2. *Has any additional progress been made toward arms limitation?*
3. *What is the present status of the military draft?*
4. *Has the world monetary system been stabilized? What has happened to the value of the dollar?*
5. *Is the balance of trade now favorable to the United States?*
6. *Why are new world economic relationships needed?*

NATIONAL

AFFAIRS   The nation, too, was faced with unfinished business that was waiting for action. Questions had arisen from the results of the 1970 census. The system for selecting the President and the Vice President were being criticized. Busing, taxation, inflation, economic conditions, and urban transportation were topics for which discussion was turning into action.

WE, THE AMERICANS. In 1970 the federal government took a census of the people, as it has done every ten years since 1790. (See pages 268-269.) Beginning in 1972 the Census Bureau issued a series of publications for teen-agers reporting the results of that census.[1]

At the time of the 1970 census there were 203,235,298 Americans living in the United States. If all the military and other government employees and their families living abroad are counted, the total would be 204,816,296. Of the total population, 73.5 per cent was classified as urban, yet these people lived on less than 2 per cent of the total land area of the nation.

All regions increased in population during the decade of the sixties, but the largest percentage increase was in the West. There the gain was almost 25 per cent, from 28 million to nearly 35 million. The state with the largest increase was California, with a gain of 4.2 million people between 1960 and 1970. Other large increases occurred in Florida, 1.8 million; Texas, 1.6 million; and New York, 1.5 million. One of the smallest states on the basis of population, Nevada, had the largest percentage gain. Its population increased 71.3 per cent between 1960 and 1970.

There are now six cities with a population of more than one million: New York, Chicago, Los Angeles, Philadelphia, Detroit, and Houston. However, some of these, as well as other large cities, declined in population as the move to the suburbs continued. The suburbs had 75.6 million people while the inner cities had only 63.8 million. The other 63.8 million lived in nonmetropolitan areas.

The United States had an average of 58 persons per square mile in 1970, 7 more than in 1960. The average for the world is 68. The most densely populated state was New Jersey with 953 persons per square mile.

The 1970 population included 22,580,289 blacks and 792,730 American Indians. During the 1960's both of these groups had a greater percentage increase than the national average. The gain for the black population was 20 per cent and for American Indians, 51 per cent.

Women and girls outnumbered men and boys in 1970, 104.3 million to 98.9 million. According to age, 10 per cent of the population is 65 years of age or older. About

---

[1] The information in this item is adapted from *We, the Americans—Who We Are*, a publication of the Social and Economic Statistics Administration, Bureau of the Census, U.S. Department of Commerce.

one-third of the total population is between 5 and 21, the school and college years.

The population of the United States is on the move, from the farm to the city, from the city to the suburbs, from one part of the country to another. Each year about 20 per cent of all residents change their addresses. This migration is the most important factor in the differing growth rates of states and regions. It has a significant effect on changing racial characteristics, political alignments, economic conditions, and the average age of the population of cities, states, and regions.

THE VICE PRESIDENCY. On July 13, 1972, Senator George McGovern, the presidential nominee of the Democratic Party, chose Senator Thomas F. Eagleton as his running mate. According to custom the party convention then nominated Eagleton as its choice for Vice President. Eagleton joined McGovern in making acceptance speeches to the convention and in planning their campaign to win the November election.

A few short weeks later Eagleton withdrew his name and resigned from the ticket. Why? What had happened?

The fact that Eagleton had suffered from, and was treated for, an emotional problem became front-page news. Some people, both in and out of the Democratic party, felt that public ignorance about mental problems threatened the Democratic chances for victory in November. The result was Eagleton's withdrawal as a candidate for the vice presidency. Critics felt that this decision was made as a matter of political expediency at the insistence of McGovern and Democratic leadership.

Could this entire situation have been avoided? Could a more careful screening of possible nominees for Vice President have prevented the resulting embarrassment?

Probably yes. However, the present method of nominating persons for the two highest offices makes a deliberate choice difficult. Those people wanting to be President campaign vigorously for many months and even years for the nomination. When the successful campaigner finally gets his party's nomination for the top spot, he must choose his running mate, usually in less than a day. The vice-presidential nominee must be acceptable both to the presidential nominee and to the party. Both major parties have this problem except when the incumbent President seeks re-election with his current Vice President. This was the case with President Nixon and Vice President Agnew in 1972.

Is there a better way? Can vice-presidential nominees be selected with less haste and with fuller knowledge about possible candidates? It has been said on more than one occasion that "the Vice President is only a heartbeat away from the presidency." Since this has been demonstrated many times in the nation's history, the Vice President ought to be selected with the same care and thought as in choosing the President.

The writers of the Constitution were concerned about this. (See pages 236-238, 735.) Their plan was to have the electors vote for two persons. The person receiving the highest number of votes was to be President, and the person receiving the second highest number, Vice President. However, this plan had not envisioned political parties, and it was changed by the Twelfth Amendment after the 1800 election resulted in a tie vote for Thomas Jefferson and Aaron Burr. (See pages 237-241.) The present practice is that candidates for President and Vice President of each party run as a team and are elected together.

Several plans have been proposed on the selection of a vice-presidential candidate. Among the proposals are the following:

• Presidential and vice-presidential candidates run as teams of two to get the nomination of their party.

• Party conventions nominate only a candidate for President. The presidential nominee would then have a period of time (two to four weeks) to select a running mate. The nomination would be made by the national committee of the party, which would meet within a month after the close of the convention.

• Nominations for both President and Vice President be made by each party in national primary elections.

• The party's two leading candidates at the convention become its nominees for President and Vice President, respectively. Thus, the runner-up in convention voting would automatically become the party's vice-presidential nominee.

Which of these proposals, if any, has merit? Which has a chance of being adopted? What are their relative strengths and weaknesses?

In this same connection, attention should be called to the fact that the whole method of election by means of the electoral college is still being questioned. (See pages 240-242.) The concern for changing the electoral college system was dramatized in the election of 1968. There was an indication that the third-party candidate, George Wallace of Alabama, might receive enough electoral votes to keep either candidate of the two major parties from getting the necessary majority of electoral votes. This did not happen.

During the 1972 nominating campaign Wallace was shot, and his resulting poor health prevented his accepting the nomination of the American Party. Political observers thought that otherwise he might have prevented either McGovern or Nixon from getting the necessary majority in 1972.

Several plans for changing the electoral college have been considered. One is that

the election be decided by direct popular vote. In 1969 the House of Representatives passed a proposed amendment to the Constitution calling for the direct election of the President. Action on this proposal was stalled in the Senate. Will future elections again bring this issue to the public's attention?

THE BUSING ISSUE. The Deep South first faced the busing issue when court decisions ordering desegregation led to busing. By the late 1960's dramatic changes in the segregation patterns of the region were taking place. The dual system of education, one for whites and one for blacks, was being effectively destroyed. (See page 673.)

During the same period inner city schools in the North and the West became even more predominantly black as the movement of whites to the outskirts of the city and to the suburbs accelerated. Then federal district courts began to order the end of school segregation in these regions, too. Denver, Colorado; Richmond, Virginia; and Detroit, Michigan, were ordered by federal district judges to desegregate their schools. This moved the issue of busing farther North and to the West.

The issue was debated on the local, state, and national levels. Both major political parties included busing in their 1972 platforms. (See pages 128-129.) The Republicans favored strong anti-busing action and, if necessary, an appropriate amendment to the Constitution. The Democrats stated that busing is one means of desegregation and it must continue to be available for use according to Supreme Court decisions.

During the summer of 1972 Congress passed a bill requiring the postponement of a court order if it involves transfer or transportation of pupils for the purpose of achieving a balance among students with respect to race. The postponement is in effect until all court appeals have been ex-

Review with the students "The Beliefs of Supreme Court Members" on page 311.

THE BURGER COURT

Warren E. Burger was appointed Chief Justice of the United States Supreme Court by President Nixon in May 1969. Prior to service on the Court, he had served for thirteen years on the United States Court of Appeals in the District of Columbia—sometimes called the "second highest court in the land."

Burger's first year as Chief Justice began with the October 1969 term of the Supreme Court. The year was one of transition. The Warren Court had been a liberal court. (See page 307.) But the new Chief Justice established himself as the leader of the Court's conservative group, as President Nixon continued to appoint to the Court new members who reflected his political thought. In 1970 Harry A. Blackmun was appointed. He had served for eleven years on the Eighth Circuit Court of Appeals. Prior to that time he had been in private law practice in Minnesota. The Senate confirmed his nomination less than a week after rejecting the nomination of G. Harrold Carswell of South Carolina. Earlier Clement F. Haynsworth, Jr., of Florida had also been rejected.

In December 1971, two more nominations from President Nixon were confirmed by the Senate: Lewis F. Powell, Jr., of Richmond, Virginia, and William H. Rehnquist of Phoenix, Arizona. Justice Powell had been in the private practice of law and was a former president of the American Bar Association. Justice Rehnquist had served as Assistant Attorney General, Office of Legal Counsel. Neither had previous judicial experience, but President Nixon said they upheld his judicial philosophy that the Court should not "twist or bend" the Constitution.

The Court, with these appointments, tended to divide into three groups. There were the four conservatives appointed by President Nixon, three liberals (Brennan, Douglas, and Marshall), and two "swing" justices (Stewart and White).

The court was unusually hard-working. The 1971-72 session was one of the longest in history, and the workload the greatest in many years.

Twenty-seven cases were settled by majorities of one vote. President Nixon pronounced that the Court was "as balanced as I have had the opportunity to make it." The differences of opinion on the Court were so great that there was a tendency for the Justices to write individual opinions.

Decisions on the stopping of suspects by police, the answering of questions by reporters before grand juries, the providing of lawyers for poor people facing jail sentences, capital punishment, and residency requirements for voting left the ultimate direction of the Court unclear. The shifting of one vote would have changed some decisions and might still change some in the future if similar cases are heard. Future appointments will probably determine the final appraisal of the Burger Court.

hausted. President Nixon signed the bill into law. Its proponents thought it would effectively halt all court-ordered busing until January 1974.

However, before the opening of school in September 1972, Supreme Court Justice Lewis F. Powell, Jr., refused to delay a desegregation plan involving busing in the Augusta, Georgia, schools. He was acting as the responsible justice for the Fifth Circuit Court of Appeals while the Supreme Court was in summer recess. Justice Powell said that the anti-busing law does not require a moratorium on all busing to achieve desegregation, but a moratorium on busing ordered "for the purpose of achieving a racial balance among students with respect to race." He therefore ordered the Augusta plan for desegregation be put into effect. Whether a majority of the Supreme Court Justices agree with Justice Powell may be determined in the 1972-73 term of the Court when it hears this appeal and other appeals from other courts.

DRIVING OLD DOBBIN ON THE FREEWAY.

Detroit News

Congress continues to debate the issue and is considering further legislation. A possible Constitutional amendment is also being discussed.

THE PROPERTY TAX. Courts in Arizona, California, Minnesota, New Jersey, and Texas have ruled that the method of financing public elementary and secondary education by means of the local property tax is unconstitutional. Similar cases are before the courts in a number of other states. The individuals and groups who have brought the issue of the property tax before the courts point out that education is a state function. As such, they say income for schools should be uniform throughout the state. They argue that differences in wealth among school districts penalize children and young people attending schools in poorer districts.

The Texas case has been appealed to the United States Supreme Court, and the Court has agreed to hear the case during its 1972-73 term. The case involves fifteen parents and children of the Edgewood Independent School District who claim that basing education on property values results in unequal education. The court ruled in their favor and noted that the value of property for tax purposes for each student in Edgewood was only 5,429 dollars. That was the lowest for the San Antonio area; the highest was in Alamo Heights, which has a value of 45,095 dollars for each of its students.

The courts in the five states did not rule that the local property tax is unconstitutional, but that it is unconstitutional for purposes of financing a state function—education. It is conceivable that a similar ruling might be made for other state functions, for example, welfare.

A tax on real and personal property has been a traditional source of income for states and local governments. (See pages 511-512.) It now brings in more than 40 billion dollars a year. While other forms of taxes, especially sales and income taxes, are increasingly being used, the income from the property tax continues to grow at the rate of about 10 per cent a year. (See pages 506, 512-514.)

The arguments in the court cases challenging the property tax center on assessments, tax rates, and wealth of districts. (See page 436.) Property assessment practices vary widely among the states, from 5 per cent of actual value for one state to almost 100 per cent for another. There are also differences among districts within a single state. Some states are trying to correct this practice by establishing uniform statewide assessment practices. Michigan, for example, equalizes assessments at 50 per cent of market value.

Tax rates vary widely, too. So does wealth. This results in the spending of unequal amounts for education by the dis-

Peterson, The Vancouver Sun

tricts of any given state. (See pages 672-673.) It is these factors that have brought about the decisions in a number of states that the local property tax is unconstitutional for a state function. Similar court cases are pending in other states.

Several remedies have been suggested. One is that all financing of public schools be done at the state level. This would insure uniform assessments and rates and equal distribution of tax money throughout the state. Money could be obtained through a state tax on income and/or property. Another proposal is to have the federal government provide grants to states and local governments in order to reduce the reliance of these units on the property tax. Grants would be contingent on elimination or reduction of the property tax. One idea under discussion is a value-added tax (VAT) at the national level. This is essentially a national sales tax, a tax on the increased value of an item as it moves from producer to consumer. While this tax has many proponents, it also has many opponents, especially among labor and low-

income groups. They oppose it because the tax would tend to raise prices and the increased burden would fall, proportionately, most heavily on persons with low income. Whether its advocates succeed in passing such a tax and whether, if passed, it will provide a means for equal education remain to be seen.

WAGE AND PRICE CONTROLS. In a surprising television appearance on August 15, 1971, President Nixon announced a program of wage and price controls to slacken inflation. Prior to this announcement he had been opposed to government controls. However, he yielded to the pressure to do something about rising prices, unemployment, and the general weakening of economic conditions. (See pages 520-525.) Earlier, Congress had passed legislation giving the President power to impose controls. At the present time President Nixon favors such presidential power and will very likely ask Congress to extend the controls after their current termination date, April 30, 1973.

What has been the effect of a year of

wage and price controls? The answers to the question differ, depending on the person asked. Some criticize the program and its effects; others praise it.

Criticisms are generally made about the lack of controls on food prices and only limited controls on profits. Critics also feel that the program has been more effective in controlling wages than prices.

Praise for the program is given for holding down wage increases, for reducing the unemployment rate somewhat, and for slowing down the rise in the cost-of-living index. (See pages 269-270.) Economists do not agree on whether these effects have resulted from the wage and price controls or are due to other factors. There is general agreement, however, that the state of the economy has improved since August 1971.

One facet of the economy is a particularly troublesome one for persons in all walks of life. That is the cost of food. Agricultural products are not in the control program, and food prices continue to rise. In recent months, they account for nearly two-thirds of the rise in the cost-of-living index. Any effective program to halt inflation may need to deal more thoroughly with agricultural products. The next few months may give some indication of how government will deal with prices, wages, profits, employment, interest rates, and other economic factors in attempts to bolster the economy and to reduce inflation.

URBAN TRANSPORTATION. Bay Area Rapid Transit (BART) began operating in September 1972. This is the rapid transit system for the San Francisco Bay area. The system has seventy-five miles of track and serves thirty communities. Its construction took about ten years at a cost of nearly 1.5 billion dollars.

The system is operated by computers, and trains are fully automated. Fares are paid by computerized credit cards. Starting, running, stopping, and spacing of trains are also done by computers. Trains have a maximum speed of eighty miles per hour and an average of forty-five miles per hour including station stops.

The BART system will be closely watched by other crowded metropolitan areas across the country. In these areas people are on the move almost continuously, both within the city and in and out of the city. The urban areas are beset by massive traffic congestion, by obsolete transportation equipment, by rapidly expanding suburbs, and by a need for rapid transit systems. (See pages 469-470.)

It is hoped that rapid transit systems will help to rebuild the cities of the nation, stop the movement of people and industry out of the cities, and relieve traffic congestion. The promoters of BART claim that it has already begun to do this for the San Francisco Bay area. They say that BART is responsible for the many new office buildings, hotels, and theaters being built in San Francisco. Similar center city construction is going forward nearby in Oakland and Berkeley.

Another aspect which will be carefully watched is whether people will use the system. BART can carry peak loads of about 29,000 passengers per hour per track. Will it be used? If there are enough riders, the system should be able to meet its operating costs and will take many automobiles off the streets and highways, especially during rush hours.

Among metropolitan areas studying BART and planning or projecting rapid transit systems to improve their urban transportation are Atlanta, Baltimore, Buffalo, Detroit, Los Angeles, and St. Louis. If BART is successful, it is likely that these and other areas will be building new transit systems during the next two decades.

Help in the planning and construction

of these systems is now available from the federal government. Two-thirds of the capital costs can be paid with federal funds. However, these federal grants will be made only after state and local governments provide their own one-third share. President Nixon plans federal government expenditures of 10 billion dollars for urban transportation projects over the next ten years. Secretary of Transportation John Volpe sees an even larger need, however. In his 1972 report he projected a need for 63 billion dollars for urban public transportation for the seventies and eighties.

MINIMUM WAGE. During 1972 both houses of Congress passed bills to increase the minimum wage. (See page 660.) The Senate bill would raise the minimum wage to $2.00 per hour on January 1973, and increase it to $2.20 in January 1975. The House bill would raise it to $1.80 per hour starting in January 1973 and to $2.00 one year later, but it would retain the $1.60 minimum for workers under age eighteen.

Since there are differences in the two bills, compromise was needed for passage. On two occasions a vote by the House of Representatives to send the bills to a House-Senate conference committee was defeated by conservative members of the House. Their negative votes were based on the lack of assurance from the Senate that it would scale down the minimums in the Senate bill and keep the $1.60 minimum for workers under eighteen. Some House members maintain that a higher minimum for school dropouts will close jobs to them, increase unemployment among teen-agers, and result in increased crime. The stalemate was not resolved in the 1972 session.

1. *What are the political and economic implications of the 1970 census?*
2. *What effects did the Eagleton affair have on the McGovern-Nixon campaign?*
3. *Should a person be disqualified from seeking political office because of a previous mental health problem?*
4. *How should the President and Vice President of the United States be chosen?*
5. *What are the recent developments on busing and desegregation of schools? court decisions? actions of Congress? state legislatures? local boards of education?*
6. *Is the local property tax being challenged and debated in your state?*
7. *What factors are now influencing the economy? Has inflation been curtailed?*
8. *What is being done in your state to improve urban transportation?*
9. *What is the current status of the minimum wage?*

NEWS
BRIEFS   In a world of fast-breaking news, some events take place that cannot be fitted into the text of *Our American Government* quickly as the book goes to the printer. Among these late-developing items are the following:

SECOND WOMAN SENATOR. Elaine S. Edwards of Louisiana was appointed to the United States Senate on August 1, 1972, by her husband who is governor of the state. The appointment was made to fill the vacancy caused by the death of Allen J. Ellender, who had served thirty-six years in the Senate. Governor Edwards, in making the appointment, stated that it would be a temporary appointment until a new senator could be elected in November 1972. Mrs. Edwards became the second woman senator in the Ninety-second Congress, joining Margaret Chase Smith of Maine.

REVENUE SHARING. The House and the Senate passed bills to share federal revenues with states and local governments. (See page 399.) The bills provide about five billion dollars annually for a period of five years to be spent as state and local government officials see fit.

The House and the Senate bills differed as to how the money should be distributed. The disagreement centered on whether to favor the small rural states or the large urban industrial states. The Senate favored a distribution formula giving major consideration to the little states. The House granted more funds to the states with large urban populations.

In conference committee a compromise was developed for the 30 billion dollar five-year plan. The compromise gave each state the opportunity of selecting whichever formula, House or Senate, was most favorable to it. Half of the first year's allocation, 2.65 billion dollars, was to be distributed during October 1972.

COURT ENFORCEMENT OF EQUAL OPPORTUNITIES. After a seven-year struggle by civil rights groups, Congress gave enforcement powers to the Equal Employment Opportunity Commission (EEOC) in 1972. EEOC is a five-member commission created by the Civil Rights Act of 1964. The Commission was charged to end discrimination based on race, color, religion, sex, or national origin in hiring, promoting, firing, wages, testing, and all other conditions of employment.

The Commission previously had only the power to conciliate job discrimination problems. The enforcement powers were granted only after five weeks of filibuster ending with a successful cloture vote. (See page 211.) The Commission can now take to court any employer charged with discrimination.

The new law provides that business or labor organizations with fifteen or more employees or members are subject to the law. Also, state and local government employees and employees of educational institutions are covered.

The law established for the Commission an independent general counsel, appointed by the President with the consent of the Senate, for a four-year term. The counsel after an investigation and hearings can bring a civil suit against an employer found to be discriminatory. The court is authorized to halt such practices and to provide remedies for past actions.

Civil rights advocates had wanted "cease and desist" powers but the court-enforcement approach, first suggested by the Nixon administration, was viewed as a major step forward.

NEW DEPARTMENT. In May 1972 the Government Operations Committee of the House of Representatives approved legislation authorizing a proposed Department of Community Development. This new department would replace the present Department of Housing and Urban Development. It would also include several bureaus and agencies from the Department of Agriculture. At this writing no further action has been taken either by the House or by the Senate. Also, no Congressional action has been taken on the other departmental reorganizations proposed by President Nixon.

THE GREAT LAKES AND POLLUTION. Pollution of the Great Lakes has been a growing problem of the United States and Canada and of the states and provinces bordering the lakes. Individuals and groups concerned about the problem have given the pollution wide publicity. Attempts have been made to stop the pollution and to introduce some corrective measures.

In 1972 a large-scale, united effort to cope with the issue was started. United States and Canadian officials announced a new international treaty and the creation of an international policing board. The officials maintain that the Great Lakes will be cleaned up "within our lifetime." The commission to carry out the program will have headquarters in both Washington and Ottawa.

Advising the commission and the two governments is a board with eighteen members, nine from each nation. The board will establish rigid standards for water purity and set a timetable for states, provinces, and industry to meet the standards. Plans include studies of land use and industrial development in the Great Lakes basin, dredging operations, and disposal systems. These will provide bases for action.

LOWER UN FEES? The United States launched a new campaign in the fall of 1972 for a reduction in its fees to the United Nations. The United States in 1972 paid 64 million dollars, 31.5 per cent of the total United Nations budget. This is the highest amount paid by any UN member. The US requested a reduction of the assessment so it will be no more than 25 per cent of the regular UN budget.

Since 1946 the United States position and that of many other states has been that "it is unhealthy for a worldwide organization to be excessively dependent upon the financial contribution of any one member state." In a document explaining its position, the US government expressed the hope that the reduction could be accomplished through the admission of new members and increases in the assessments of a few members that would reflect "their comparative economic growth."

In addition to the budget assessment, the United States pays large sums in voluntary contributions to UN activities.

CHINA'S FIRST VETO IN UN. At the end of August 1972, ten months after admission to the United Nations, China cast its first veto in the Security Council. The Chinese Ambassador Huang Hua's veto barred Bangladesh from UN membership. Once the eastern half of Pakistan, Bangla-

desh broke away in a short war in December 1971. India with help from the Soviet Union had supported Bangladesh, but China had backed Pakistan. The independence of Bangladesh had been recognized by eighty-five nations.

China charged that Bangladesh violated two UN resolutions. One demanded the return of all prisoners of war. China claimed that more than 90,000 civilian and military prisoners were still held by India. The other resolution required removal of all foreign troops from Bangladesh, which China also claimed had not been accomplished.

China first attempted to delay the vote on Bangladesh until the two resolutions had been obeyed. This failed. On the crucial Security Council vote on admission, eleven members, including the United States, the Soviet Union, and India favored admission. Three abstained; only China opposed.

China, while defending UN principles, may have lost status with the small developing nations. But in the power-politics struggle, China retained a foothold in the Indian subcontinent by siding with Pakistan.

RAILROAD FIREMEN. Since 1937 the nation's railroads and the United Transportation Union have been involved in a labor dispute over firemen on diesel locomotives. On the old steam locomotives, firemen shoveled coal. On the diesel-powered trains, they have been used as lookouts. The railroads claim they are not needed. The union does not agree, maintaining that the firemen are needed as a safety measure to assist the engineer in watching the tracks ahead. The disagreement has led to repeated strikes and strike threats during the past thirty-five years.

In July 1972, railroad management and the union announced settlement of the long-standing dispute. Under the agreement the fireman will be kept as a third man on engines of passenger trains. The other two are the engineer and the brakeman. Firemen will also be kept on some freight trains to provide for promotions as engineer positions become vacant.

The firemen now on the job will have job security until age sixty-five. Also, some laid-off firemen will be rehired. Gradually, however, the number of firemen will be reduced from the 16,000 now working on the nation's railroads.

APPELLATE COURT SYSTEM STUDY. A Commission on Revision of the Federal Court Appellate System of the United States was created by a joint House and Senate resolution in July 1972.

The Senate Judiciary Committee reported that the US appellate court system "faces an overwhelming caseload"—with crisis conditions in the 5th and 9th circuits. The number of courts-of-appeals judges was increased from 68 in 1960 to 97 in 1970. But the number of cases increased from 3,899 to 12,788 in that decade. The Supreme Court caseload increased from 2,313 in 1960 to 4,212 in 1970.

The commission of twelve members will study conditions for two years and make recommendations to the Supreme Court, Congress, and the President. Alternatives to be considered are adding additional judges, changing boundaries of circuit courts, and eliminating boundaries.

IMPROVING STATE COURTS. A National Center for State Courts began operation in 1972. Created at the urging of Chief Justice Burger, the American Bar Association, and other judicial organizations, the Center is guided by two bodies, a Board of Trustees and an Advisory Council. Judge Winslow Christian of the California Court of Appeals was selected as the first Executive Director.

Judge Christian and his staff are charged to assist state judicial officers in modernizing and reforming their court systems. The Center will serve as a clearinghouse for information on court procedures. Research projects, experimental programs, and the exchange of ideas will be undertaken.

METRIC SYSTEM FOR THE UNITED STATES? The Senate by a voice vote passed a bill to bring about the voluntary conversion of the United States to the metric system over a ten-year period. The bill had been recommended by the Department of Commerce after a three-year study. The system would replace yards, pounds, and quarts with meters, kilograms, and liters. The bill now goes to the House.

The United States is one of ten countries not on the metric system. The bill would establish an eleven-member national metric board to plan over the next eighteen months for the change to the metric system. The federal government would change to the metric system and encourage the voluntary change on the part of industry. It is expected that the metric system would become the predominant, but not exclusive, system of measurement in the United States.

MASTER CLOCKS. On June 30, 1972, one second was added to the world's master clocks in the United States and in other countries. This was done to correct an error in the clocks because of changes in the earth's rotation. The error was discovered in 1958 with the development of atomic clocks. Since then corrections amounting to eleven seconds have been made by international agreement. Future corrections, if any, will be determined by the earth's rotation. The master clocks use the earth's rotation for measuring time, while atomic clocks use the vibrations of atoms. The latter are so accurate that it would take 50,000 years for one to gain or lose a second.

ELECTION RESULTS—1972

Although Richard M. Nixon, a Republican, was returned to the Presidency, he did not sweep Republicans into office with him. President Nixon won an estimated 61% of the popular vote and 521 of the 538 electoral votes. The Republicans, however, lost one governorship and two Senate seats, while gaining only thirteen House seats. Democrats retained control of both houses of Congress.

The Election by Party

STATE	GOVERNORSHIP 1972	GOVERNORSHIP 1968, 1970	SENATE 1972	SENATE 1966	HOUSE 1972	HOUSE 1970
Alabama			*D		4-D 3-R	5-D† 3-R
Alaska			*R		1-D	1-D
Arizona					1-D 3-R	1-D† 2-R
Arkansas	*D		*D		3-D 1-R	3-D 1-R
California					23-D 21-R	20-D† 18-R
Colorado			D	R	3-D 2-R	2-D† 2-R
Connecticut					3-D 3-R	4-D 2-R
Delaware	D	R	D	R	1-R	1-R
Florida					11-D 4-R	9-D† 3-R
Georgia			D	D	9-D 1-R	8-D 2-R
Hawaii					2-D	2-D
Idaho			R	R	2-R	2-R
Illinois	D	R	*R		10-D 14-R	12-D 12-R
Indiana	R	R			4-D 7-R	5-D 6-R
Iowa	*R		D	R	3-D 3-R	2-D† 5-R
Kansas	*D		*R		1-D 4-R	1-D 4-R
Kentucky			D	R	5-D 2-R	5-D 2-R
Louisiana			D	D	7-D 1-R	8-D
Maine			D	R	1-D 1-R	2-D
Maryland					4-D 4-R	5-D 3-R
Massachusetts			*R		8-D 3-R 1-Other	8-D 4-R
Michigan			*R		7-D 12-R	7-D 12-R
Minnesota			*D		4-D 4-R	4-D 4-R
Mississippi			*D		3-D 2-R	5-D

STATE	GOVERNORSHIP 1972	GOVERNORSHIP 1968, 1970	SENATE 1972	SENATE 1966	HOUSE 1972	HOUSE 1970
Missouri	R	D			9-D 1-R	9-D 1-R
Montana	D	D	*D		1-D 1-R	1-D 1-R
Nebraska			*R		3-R	3-R
Nevada					1-R	1-D
New Hampshire	R	R	*D		2-R	2-R
New Jersey			*R		8-D 7-R	9-D 6-R
New Mexico			R	D	1-D 1-R	1-D 1-R
New York					22-D 17-R	24-D† 17-R
North Carolina			R	D	7-D 4-R	7-D 4-R
North Dakota	D	D			1-R 1-Other	1-R†
Ohio					7-D 16-R	7-D† 17-R
Oklahoma			R	D	5-D 1-R	4-D 2-R
Oregon			*R		2-D 2-R	2-D 2-R
Pennsylvania					13-D 12-R	14-D† 12-R 1-Vacant
Rhode Island	D	D	*D		2-D	2-D
South Carolina			*R		4-D 2-R	5-D 1-R
South Dakota	*D		D	R	1-D 1-R	2-D
Tennessee			*R		3-D 5-R	5-D† 4-R
Texas	D	D	*R		20-D 4-R	20-D† 3-R
Utah	*D				2-D	1-D 1-R
Vermont	D	R			1-R	1-R
Virginia			R	D	3-D 7-R	4-D 6-R
Washington	*R				7-D	6-D 1-R
West Virginia	*R		*D		4-D 1-R	5-D
Wisconsin					5-D 4-R	5-D† 5-R
Wyoming			*R		1-D	1-D

* Indicates incumbent.

† Reapportionment after the 1970 Census changed the number of representatives in certain states.

- Why do you think voters split their tickets?
- What do you think this shows about voters?
- How does ticket-splitting affect the party system?
- Will the party system continue?

Voter Turnout

ESTIMATED ELIGIBLE VOTERS	THOSE VOTING	ESTIMATED % VOTING
139.6 million	75.4 million	56%

- What do these figures show you about voter turnout?
- Why do you think the percentage of people voting was not higher?

- Would you have voted if you had been eligible? Why? Why not?
- Do you think voter turnout is higher or lower in off-year elections?

Black Members of Congress

Forty-four blacks ran for national office in 1972 and many more ran on the state and local levels. Only one of the three black senatorial candidates was successful. However, sixteen candidates for the House were elected including thirteen incumbents. This is the highest number of blacks ever to serve in Congress. Three of the seventeen blacks are women.

SENATE
Massachusetts	Edward Brooke, R.

HOUSE
California	Yvonne Brathwaite Burke, D.
California	*Ronald V. Dellums, D.
California	*Augustus T. Hawkins, D.
District of Columbia	*Walter Fauntroy, D.
Georgia	Andrew Young, D.
Illinois	*George W. Collins, D.
Illinois	*Ralph Metcalfe, D.
Maryland	*Parren Mitchell, D.
Michigan	*John Conyers, Jr., D.
Michigan	*Charles C. Diggs, Jr., D.
Missouri	*William L. Clay, D.
New York	*Shirley Chisholm, D.
New York	*Charles B. Rangel, D.
Pennsylvania	*Robert N. C. Nix, D.
Texas	Barbara Jordan, D.

* Indicates incumbent.

Congresswomen

Many women ran for national, state, and local offices in 1972. On the national level, fourteen women were elected to the House of Representatives, but all senatorial candidates were defeated. Margaret Chase Smith, the four-term Senator from Maine, lost to a younger man who had waged a very active campaign.

HOUSE
California	Yvonne Brathwaite Burke, D.
Colorado	Pat Schroeder, D.
Connecticut	*Ella Grasso, D.
Hawaii	*Patsy Mink, D.
Maryland	Marjorie Holt, R.
Massachusetts	*Margaret Heckler, D.
Michigan	*Martha Griffiths, D.
Missouri	*Leonor Sullivan, D.
New York	*Bella Abzug, D.
New York	*Shirley Chisholm, D.
New York	Elizabeth Holtzman, D.
Oregon	*Edith Starrett Green, D.
Texas	Barbara Jordan, D.
Washington	*Julia Butler Hansen, D.

* Indicates incumbent.

Congressmen of Spanish-Descent

Of the number of Americans of Spanish-descent who ran for national office in 1972, only the incumbents were elected. They rejoined the one Mexican-American Senator in Congress, Joseph Montoya of New Mexico.

HOUSE
New Mexico	*Manuel Lujan, Jr., R.
New York	*Herman Badillo, D. L.
Texas	*Eligio de la Garza, D.
Texas	*Henry B. Gonzalez, D.

* Indicates incumbent.

- Were any blacks, women, or members of other minorities running for national office from your state? for state office? for local office?

APPENDIX

DECLARATION OF INDEPENDENCE

In Congress, July 4, 1776

The Unanimous Declaration of the Thirteen United States of America

When, in the course of human events, it becomes necessary for one people to dissolve the political bands which have connected them with another, and to assume, among the powers of the earth, the separate and equal station to which the laws of nature and of nature's God entitle them, a decent respect to the opinions of mankind requires that they should declare the causes which impel them to the separation.

We hold these truths to be self-evident: That all men are created equal; that they are endowed by their Creator with certain unalienable rights; that among these are life, liberty, and the pursuit of happiness. That, to secure these rights, governments are instituted among men, deriving their just powers from the consent of the governed; that, whenever any form of government becomes destructive of these ends, it is the right of the people to alter or to abolish it, and to institute new government, laying its foundation on such principles, and organizing its powers in such form, as to them shall seem most likely to effect their safety and happiness. Prudence, indeed, will dictate that governments long established should not be changed for light and transient causes; and accordingly all experience hath shown that mankind are more disposed to suffer while evils are sufferable, than to right themselves by abolishing the forms to which they are accustomed. But when a long train of abuses and usurpations, pursuing invariably the same object, evinces a design to reduce them under absolute despotism, it is their right, it is their duty, to throw off such government, and to provide new guards for their future security. Such has been the patient sufferance of these colonies; and such is now the necessity which constrains them to alter their former systems of government. The history of the present King of Great Britain is a history of repeated injuries and usurpations, all having in direct object the establishment of an absolute tyranny over these states. To prove this, let facts be submitted to a candid world.

He has refused his assent to laws the most wholesome and necessary for the public good.

He has forbidden his governors to pass laws of immediate and pressing importance, unless suspended in their operation till his assent should be obtained; and, when so suspended, he has utterly neglected to attend to them.

He has refused to pass other laws for the accommodation of large districts of people, unless those people would relinquish the right of representation in the legislature,—a right inestimable to them, and formidable to tyrants only.

He has called together legislative bodies at places unusual, uncomfortable, and distant from the depository of their public records, for the sole purpose of fatiguing them into compliance with his measures.

He has dissolved representative houses repeatedly, for opposing with, manly firmness, his invasions on the rights of the people.

He has refused, for a long time after such dissolutions, to cause others to be elected, whereby the legislative powers, incapable of annihilation, have returned to the people at large for their exercise; the state remaining, in the mean time, exposed to all the dangers of invasions from without and convulsions within.

He has endeavored to prevent the population of these states; for that purpose obstructing the laws for the naturalization of foreigners, refusing to pass others to encourage their migration hither, and raising the conditions of new appropriations of lands.

He has obstructed the administration of justice, by refusing his assent to laws for establishing judiciary powers.

He has made judges dependent on his will alone for the tenure of their offices, and the amount and payment of their salaries.

He has erected a multitude of new offices, and sent hither swarms of officers to harass our people and eat out their substance.

He has kept among us, in times of peace, standing armies without the consent of our legislatures.

He has affected to render the military independent of, and superior to, the civil power.

He has combined with others to subject us to

a jurisdiction foreign to our constitutions, and unacknowledged by our laws; giving his assent to their acts of pretended legislation:

For quartering large bodies of armed troops among us;

For protecting them, by a mock trial, from punishment for any murders which they should commit on the inhabitants of these states;

For cutting off our trade with all parts of the world;

For imposing taxes on us without our consent;

For depriving us, in many cases, of the benefits of trial by jury;

For transporting us beyond seas to be tried for pretended offenses;

For abolishing the free system of English laws in a neighboring province, establishing therein an arbitrary government, and enlarging its boundaries, so as to render it at once an example and fit instrument for introducing the same absolute rule into these colonies;

For taking away our charters, abolishing our most valuable laws, and altering fundamentally, the forms of our governments;

For suspending our own legislatures, and declaring themselves invested with power to legislate for us in all cases whatsoever.

He has abdicated government here, by declaring us out of his protection and waging war against us.

He has plundered our seas, ravaged our coasts, burned our towns, and destroyed the lives of our people.

He is at this time transporting large armies of foreign mercenaries to complete the works of death, desolation, and tyranny already begun with circumstances of cruelty and perfidy scarcely paralleled in the most barbarous ages, and totally unworthy the head of a civilized nation.

He has constrained our fellow-citizens, taken captive on the high seas, to bear arms against their country, to become the executioners of their friends and brethren, or to fall themselves by their hands.

He has excited domestic insurrection among us, and has endeavored to bring on the inhabitants of our frontiers the merciless Indian savages, whose known rule of warfare is an undistinguished destruction of all ages, sexes, and conditions.

In every stage of these oppressions we have petitioned for redress in the most humble terms; our repeated petitions have been answered only by repeated injury.

A prince whose character is thus marked by every act which may define a tyrant is unfit to be the ruler of a free people.

Nor have we been wanting in our attentions to our British brethren. We have warned them, from time to time, of attempts by their legislature to extend an unwarrantable jurisdiction over us. We have reminded them of the circumstances of our emigration and settlement here. We have appealed to their native justice and magnanimity; and we have conjured them by the ties of our common kindred to disavow these usurpations, which would inevitably interrupt our connections and correspondence. They, too, have been deaf to the voice of justice and consanguinity. We must, therefore, acquiesce in the necessity which denounces our separation, and hold them, as we hold the rest of mankind, enemies in war, in peace friends.

We, therefore, the representatives of the United States of America, in General Congress assembled, appealing to the Supreme Judge of the world for the rectitude of our intentions, do, in the name and by the authority of the good people of these colonies, solemnly publish and declare, That these united colonies are, and of right ought to be, free and independent states; that they are absolved from all allegiance to the British crown, and that all political connection between them and the state of Great Britain is, and ought to be, totally dissolved; and that, as free and independent states, they have full power to levy war, conclude peace, contract alliances, establish commerce, and do all other acts and things which independent states may of right do. And, for the support of this declaration, with a firm reliance on the protection of Divine Providence, we mutually pledge to each other our lives, our fortunes, and our sacred honor.

ARTICLES OF CONFEDERATION, MARCH 1, 1781

Reprinted from *Documents Illustrative of the Formation of the Union of the American States,* published by the Library of Congress with spelling, capitalization, and punctuation as in the original.

To all to whom these Presents shall come, we the under signed Delegates of the States affixed to our Names, send greeting.

Whereas the Delegates of the United States of America, in Congress assembled, did, on the 15th day of November, in the Year of Our Lord One thousand Seven Hundred and Seventy seven, and in the Second Year of the Independence of America, agree to certain articles of Confederation and perpetual Union between the States of Newhampshire, Massachusetts-bay, Rhodeisland and Providence Plantations, Connecticut, New York, New Jersey, Pennsylvania, Delaware, Maryland, Virginia, North-Carolina, South-Carolina, and Georgia in the words following, viz. "Articles of Confederation and perpetual Union between the states of New-hampshire, Massachusetts-bay, Rhodeisland and Providence Plantations, Connecticut, New-York, New-Jersey, Pennsylvania, Delaware, Maryland, Virginia, North-Carolina, South-Carolina, and Georgia."

Article I. The Stile of this confederacy shall be "The United States of America."

Article II. Each state retains its sovereignty, freedom, and independence, and every Power, Jurisdiction and right, which is not by this confederation expressly delegated to the United States, in Congress assembled.

Article III. The said states hereby severally enter into a firm league of friendship with each other, for their common defence, the security of their Liberties, and their mutual and general welfare, binding themselves to assist each other, against all force offered to, or attacks made upon them, or any of them, on account of religion, sovereignty, trade, or any other pretence whatever.

Article IV. The better to secure and perpetuate mutual friendship and intercourse among the people of the different states in this union, the free inhabitants of each of these states, paupers, vagabonds and fugitives from justice excepted, shall be entitled to all privileges and immunities of free citizens in the several states; and the people of each state shall have free ingress and regress to and from any other state, and shall enjoy therein all the privileges of trade and commerce, subject to the same duties, impositions and restrictions as the inhabitants thereof respectively, provided that such restriction shall not extend so far as to prevent the removal of property imported into any state, to any other state, of which the Owner is an inhabitant; provided also that no imposition, duties or restriction shall be laid by any state, on the property of the united states, or either of them.

If any Person guilty of, or charged with treason, felony, or other high misdemeanor in any state, shall flee from Justice, and be found in any of the united states, he shall, upon demand of the Governor or executive power, of the state from which he fled, be delivered up and removed to the state having jurisdiction of his offence.

Full faith and credit shall be given in each of these states to the records, acts and judicial proceedings of the courts and magistrates of every other state.

Article V. For the more convenient management of the general interests of the united states, delegates shall be annually appointed in such manner as the legislature of each state shall direct, to meet in Congress on the first Monday in November, in every year, with a power reserved to each state, to recal its delegates, or any of them, at any time within the year, and to send others in their stead, for the remainder of the Year.

No state shall be represented in Congress by less than two, nor by more than seven Members; and no person shall be capable of being a delegate for more than three years in any term of six years; nor shall any person, being a delegate, be capable of holding any office under the united states, for which he, or another for his benefit receives any salary, fees or emolument of any kind.

Each state shall maintain its own delegates in a meeting of the states, and while they act as members of the committee of the states.

In determining questions in the united states in Congress assembled, each state shall have one vote.

Freedom of speech and debate in Congress shall not be impeached or questioned in any Court, or place out of Congress, and the members of congress shall be protected in their persons from arrests and imprisonments, during the time of their going to and from, and attendance on congress, except for treason, felony, or breach of the peace.

Article VI. No state, without the Consent of the united states in congress assembled, shall send any embassy to, or receive any embassy from, or enter into any conference, agreement, alliance or treaty with any King prince or state; nor shall any person holding any office of profit or trust under the united states, or any of them, accept of any present, emolument, office or title of any kind whatever from any king, prince or foreign state; nor shall the united states in congress assembled, or any of them, grant any title of nobility.

No two or more states shall enter into any treaty, confederation or alliance whatever between them, without the consent of the united states in congress assembled, specifying accurately the purposes for which the same is to be entered into, and how long it shall continue.

No state shall lay any imposts or duties, which may interfere with any stipulations in treaties, entered into by the united states in congress assembled, with any king, prince or state, in pursuance of any treaties already proposed by congress, to the courts of France and Spain.

No vessels of war shall be kept up in time of peace by any state, except such number only, as shall be deemed necessary by the united states in congress assembled, for the defense of such state, or its trade; nor shall any body of forces be kept up by any state, in time of peace, except such number only, as in the judgment of the united states, in congress assembled, shall be deemed requisite to garrison the forts necessary for the defence of such state; but every state shall always keep up a well regulated and disciplined militia, sufficiently armed and accoutred, and shall provide and constantly have ready for use, in public stores, a due number of field pieces and tents, and a proper quantity of arms, ammunition, and camp equipage.

No state shall engage in any war without the consent of the united states in congress assembled, unless such state be actually invaded by enemies, or shall have received certain advice of a resolution being formed by some nation of Indians to invade such state, and the danger is so imminent as not to admit of a delay till the united states in congress asssembled can be consulted: nor shall any state grant commissions to any ships or vessels of wars, nor letters of marque or reprisal, except it be after a declaration of war by the united states in congress assembled, and then only against the kingdom or state and the subjects thereof, against which war has been so declared, and under such regulations as shall be established by the united states in congress assembled, unless such state be infested by pirates, in which case vessels of war may be fitted out for that occasion, and kept so long as the danger shall continue, or until the united states in congress assembled, shall determine otherwise.

Article VII. When land-forces are raised by any state for the common defence, all officers of or under the rank of colonel, shall be appointed by the legislature of each state respectively, by whom such forces shall be raised, or in such manner as such state shall direct, and all vacancies shall be filled up by the State which first made the appointment.

Article VIII. All charges of war, and all other expences that shall be incurred for the common defence or general welfare, and allowed by the united states in congress assembled, shall be defrayed out of a common treasury, which shall be supplied by the several states in proportion to the value of all land within each state, granted to or surveyed for any Person, as such land and the buildings and improvements thereon shall be estimated according to such mode as the united states in congress assembled, shall from time to time direct and appoint.

The taxes for paying that proportion shall be laid and levied by the authority and direction of the legislatures of the several states within the time agreed upon by the united states in congress assembled.

Article IX. The united states in congress assembled, shall have the sole and exclusive right and power of determining on peace and war, except in the cases mentioned in the sixth article—of sending and receiving ambassadors—entering into treaties and alliances, provided that no treaty of commerce shall be made whereby the legislative power of the respective states shall be restrained from imposing such imposts and duties on foreigners as their own people are subjected to, or from prohibiting the exportation or importation of any species of goods or commodities, whatsoever—of establishing rules for deciding in all cases, what captures on land or water shall be legal, and in what manner prizes taken by land or naval forces in the service of the united states shall be divided or appropriated—of granting letters of marque and reprisal in times of peace—appointing courts for the trial of piracies and felonies committed on the high seas and establishing courts for receiving and determining finally appeals in all cases of captures, provided that no member of congress shall be appointed a judge of any of the said courts.

The united states in congress assembled shall also be the last resort on appeal in all disputes and differences now subsisting or that hereafter may arise between two or more states concerning boundary, jurisdiction or any other cause whatever; which authority shall always be exercised in the manner following. Whenever the legislative or executive authority or lawful agent of any state in controversy with another shall present a petition to congress stating the matter in question and praying for a hearing, notice thereof shall be given by order of congress to the legislative or executive authority of the other state in controversy, and a day assigned for the appearance of the parties by their lawful agents, who shall then be directed to appoint by joint consent, commissioners or judges to constitute a court for hearing and determining the matter in question: but if they cannot agree, congress shall name three persons out of each of the united states, and from the list of such persons each party shall alternately strike out one, the petitioners beginning, until the number shall be reduced to thirteen; and from that number not less than seven, nor more than nine names as congress shall direct, shall in the presence of congress be drawn out by lot, and the persons whose names shall be so drawn or any five of them, shall be commissioners or judges, to hear and finally determine the controversy, so always as a major part of the judges who shall hear the cause shall agree in the determination: and if either party shall neglect to attend at the day appointed, without showing reasons, which congress shall judge sufficient, or being present shall refuse to strike, the congress shall proceed to nominate three persons out of

each state, and the secretary of congress shall strike in behalf of such party absent or refusing; and the judgment and sentence of the court to be appointed, in the manner before prescribed, shall be final and conclusive; and if any of the parties shall refuse to submit to the authority of such court, or to appear or defend their claim or cause, the court shall nevertheless proceed to pronounce sentence, or judgment, which shall in like manner be final and decisive, the judgment or sentence and other proceedings being in either case transmitted to congress, and lodged among the acts of congress for the security of the parties concerned: provided that every commissioner, before he sits in judgment, shall take an oath to be administered by one of the judges of the supreme or superior court of the state, where the cause shall be tried, "well and truly to hear and determine the matter in question, according to the best of his judgment, without favour, affection or hope of reward:" provided also, that no state shall be deprived of territory for the benefit of the united states.

All controversies concerning the private right of soil claimed under different grants of two or more states, whose jurisdictions as they may respect such lands, and the states which passed such grants are adjusted, the said grants or either of them being at the same time claimed to have originated antecedent to such settlement of jurisdiction, shall on the petition of either party to the congress of the united states, be finally determined as near as may be in the same manner as is before prescribed for deciding disputes respecting territorial jurisdiction between different states.

The united states in congress assembled shall also have the sole and exclusive right and power of regulating the alloy and value of coin struck by their own authority, or by that of the respective states—fixing the standard of weights and measures throughout the united states—regulating the trade and managing all affairs with the Indians, not members of any of the states, provided that the legislative right of any state within its own limits be not infringed or violated—establishing or regulating post-offices from one state to another, throughout all the united states, and exacting such postage on the papers passing thro' the same as may be requisite to defray the expences of the said office—appointing all officers of the land forces, in the service of the united states, excepting regimental officers—appointing all the officers of the naval forces, and commissioning all officers whatever in the service of the united states—making rules for the government and regulation of the said land and naval forces, and directing their operations.

The united states in congress assembled shall have authority to appoint a committee, to sit in the recess of congress, to be denominated "A Committee of the States," and to consist of one delegate from each state; and to appoint such other committees and civil officers as may be necessary for managing the general affairs of the united states under their direction—to appoint one of their number to preside, provided that no person be allowed to serve in the office of president more than one year in any term of three years; to ascertain the necessary sums of money to be raised for the service of the united states, and to appropriate and apply the same for defraying the public expences—to borrow money, or emit bills on the credit of the united states, transmitting every half year to the respective states an account of the sums of money so borrowed or emitted,—to build and equip a navy—to agree upon the number of land forces, and to make requisitions from each state for its quota, in proportion to the number of white inhabitants in such state; which requisition shall be binding, and thereupon the legislature of each state shall appoint the regimental officers, raise the men and cloath, arm and equip them in a soldier like manner, at the expence of the united states; and the officers and men so cloathed, armed and equipped shall march to the place appointed, and within the time agreed on by the united states in congress assembled: But if the united states in congress assembled shall, on consideration of circumstances judge proper that any state should not raise men, or should raise a smaller number than its quota, and that any other state should raise a greater number of men than the quota thereof, such extra number shall be raised, officered, cloathed, armed and equipped in the same manner as the quota of such state, unless the legislature of such state shall judge that such extra number cannot be safely spared out of the same, in which case they shall raise officer, cloath, arm and equip as many of such extra number as they judge can be safely spared. And the officers and men so cloathed, armed and equipped, shall march to the place appointed, and within the time agreed on by the united states in congress assembled.

The united states in congress assembled shall never engage in a war, nor grant letters of marque and reprisal in time of peace, nor enter into any treaties or alliances, nor coin money, nor regulate the value thereof, nor ascertain the sums and expences necessary for the defence and welfare of the united states, or any of them, nor emit bills, nor borrow money on the credit of the united states, nor appropriate money, nor agree upon the number of vessels of war, to be built or purchased, or the number of land or sea forces to be raised, nor appoint a commander in chief of the army or navy, unless nine states assent to the same: nor shall a question on any other point, except for adjourning from day to day be determined, unless by the votes of a majority of the united states in congress assembled.

The congress of the united states shall have power to adjourn to any time within the year, and to any place within the united states, so that no period of adjournment be for a longer duration than the space of six Months, and shall publish the Journal of their proceedings monthly, except such parts thereof relating to treaties, alliances or military operations, as in their judgment require secrecy; and the yeas and nays of the delegates of each state on any question shall be entered on the Journal, when it is desired by any delegate; and the delegates of a state, or any of them, at his or their request shall be furnished with a transcript of the said Journal, except such parts as are above excepted, to lay before the legislatures of the several states.

Article X. The committee of the states, or any nine of them, shall be authorized to execute, in the recess of congress, such of the powers of congress as the united states in congress assembled, by the consent of nine states, shall from time to time think expedient to vest them with; provided that no power be delegated to the said committee, for the exercise of which, by the articles of confederation, the voice of nine states in the congress of the united states assembled is requisite.

Article XI. Canada acceding to this confederation, and joining in the measures of the united states, shall be admitted into, and entitled to all the advantages of this union: but no other colony shall be admitted into the same, unless such admission be agreed to by nine states.

Article XII. All bills of credit emitted, monies borrowed and debts contracted by, or under the authority of congress, before the assembling of the united states, in pursuance of the present confederation, shall be deemed and considered as a charge against the united states, for payment and satisfaction whereof the said united states, and the public faith are hereby solemnly pledged.

Article XIII. Every state shall abide by the determinations of the united states in congress assembled, on all questions which by this confederation are submitted to them. And the Articles of this confederation shall be inviolably observed by every state, and the union shall be perpetual; nor shall any alteration at any time hereafter be made in any of them; unless such alteration be agreed to in a congress of the united states, and be afterwards confirmed by the legislatures of every state.

And Whereas it hath pleased the Great Governor of the World to incline the hearts of the legislatures we respectively represent in congress, to approve of, and to authorize us to ratify the said articles of confederation and perpetual union. Know Ye that we the under-signed delegates, by virtue of the power and authority to us given for that purpose, do by these presents, in the name and in behalf of our respective constituents, fully and entirely ratify and confirm each and every of the said articles of confederation and perpetual union, and all and singular the matters and things therein contained: And we do further solemnly plight and engage the faith of our respective constituents, that they shall abide by the determinations of the united states in congress assembled, on all questions, which by the said confederation are submitted to them. And that the articles thereof shall be inviolably observed by the states we respectively represent, and that the union shall be perpetual. In Witness whereof we have hereunto set our hands in Congress. Done at Philadelphia in the state of Pennsylvania the ninth day of July, in the Year of our Lord one Thousand seven Hundred and Seventy-eight, and in the third year of the independence of America.

Constitution of the United States

PREAMBLE

We the people of the United States, in order to form a more perfect union, establish justice, insure domestic tranquility, provide for the common defense, promote the general welfare, and secure the blessings of liberty to ourselves and our posterity, do ordain and establish this Constitution for the United States of America.

—— The preamble sets forth the reasons for writing the Constitution. (See pages 36-37.)

Article I

LEGISLATIVE DEPARTMENT

Section 1

CONGRESS

Legislative powers vested. All legislative powers herein granted shall be vested in a Congress of the United States, which shall consist of a Senate and House of Representatives.

—— Only the Congress has the power to make laws for the United States. A Congress of two houses was one of the great compromises of the Constitutional Convention. (See pages 44-45.)

Section 2

HOUSE OF REPRESENTATIVES

1. *Election.* The House of Representatives shall be composed of members chosen every second year by the people of the several States, and the electors in each State shall have the qualifications requisite for electors of the most numerous branch of the State legislature.

—— There has been much discussion in recent years to change the term of office of members of the House of Representatives from two years to four years. In 1966 President Johnson proposed that Congress initiate an amendment to make this change. The "electors" are the voters who are eligible to vote according to state and federal laws. (See Chapter 9.)

2. *Qualifications.* No person shall be a representative who shall not have attained to the age of twenty-five years, and been seven years a citizen of the United States, and who shall not, when elected, be an inhabitant of that State in which he shall be chosen.

—— The Constitution gives some basic qualifications for the elected federal officials. Compare the qualifications of members of the House of Representatives with those of senators (Article I, Section 3) and of President (Article II, Section 1).

3. *Apportionment.* Representatives and direct taxes shall be apportioned among the several States which may be included within this Union, according to their respective numbers, which shall be determined by adding to the whole number of free persons, including those bound to service for a term of years, and excluding Indians not taxed, three fifths of all other persons. The actual enumeration shall be made within three years after the first meeting of the Congress of the United States, and within every subsequent term of ten years, in such manner as they shall by law direct. The number of representatives shall not exceed one for every thirty thousand, but each State shall have at least one representative; and until such enumeration shall be made, the State of New Hampshire shall be entitled to choose three, Massachusetts eight, Rhode Island and Providence Plantations one, Connecticut five, New York six, New Jersey four, Pennsylvania eight, Delaware one, Maryland six, Virginia ten, North Carolina five, South Carolina five, and Georgia three.

—— This clause contains another of the great compromises; slaves (all other persons) were counted three-fifths for both representation and taxation. (See page 46.) This was changed by the Fourteenth Amendment. The provision that taxes must be apportioned to the states on the basis of "their respective members" (population) was changed by the Sixteenth Amendment. The first enumeration (census) was made in 1790; it has been repeated every ten years.

4. *Vacancies.* When vacancies happen in the representation from any State, the executive authority thereof shall issue writs of election to fill such vacancies.

—— When a vacancy occurs, the governor must call a special election to fill it unless a regularly scheduled election is to be held soon.

5. *Officers; impeachment.* The House of Representatives shall choose their speaker and other officers, and shall have the sole power of impeachment.

— See the discussion of congressional officers in Chapter 10. To impeach means to indict, to bring charges; only the House of Representatives can impeach federal officials.

Section 3

SENATE

1. *Election.* The Senate of the United States shall be composed of two senators from each State, chosen [by the legislature thereof] for six years; and each senator shall have one vote.

— The provision that senators were to be chosen by state legislatures was changed in 1913 by the Seventeenth Amendment.

2. *Classification.* Immediately after they shall be assembled in consequence of the first election, they shall be divided as equally as may be into three classes. The seats of the senators of the first class shall be vacated at the expiration of the second year, of the second class at the expiration of the fourth year, and of the third class at the expiration of the sixth year, so that one third may be chosen every second year; [and if vacancies happen by resignation, or otherwise during the recess of the legislature of any State, the executive thereof may make temporary appointments until the next meeting of the legislature, which shall then fill such vacancies.]

— Since the term of senators is six years, only about one-third of them are elected at each congressional election. Two-thirds of them are holdovers; so the Senate is referred to as a continuing body. Vacancies are now filled by election of the people, not by state legislatures, but some state legislatures have given the governor the power to make a temporary appointment until an election is held. (See Amendment 17, page 730.)

3. *Qualifications.* No person shall be a senator who shall not have attained to the age of thirty years, and been nine years a citizen of the United States, and who shall not, when elected, be an inhabitant of that State for which he shall be chosen.

— Note the older age and longer citizenship requirements than those of members of the House of Representatives.

4. *President of Senate.* The Vice-President of the United States shall be President of the Senate, but shall have no vote, unless they be equally divided.

— This is the only duty given the Vice President by the Constitution. As president of the Senate he may vote only in case of tie votes.

5. *Other officers.* The Senate shall choose their other officers, and also a president *pro tempore,* in the absence of the Vice-President, or when he shall exercise the office of President of the United States.

— See discussion of congressional officers in Chapter 10. *Pro tempore* means for the time being, temporary.

6. *Trial of impeachments.* The Senate shall have the sole power to try all impeachments. When sitting for that purpose, they shall be on oath or affirmation. When the President of the United States is tried, the chief justice shall preside: and no person shall be convicted without the concurrence of two thirds of the members present.

— The Senate has the power to try impeachment cases. The Vice President presides except in a trial of a President when the chief justice of the Supreme Court presides. This exception was made because the Vice President may be influenced by the fact that he would succeed the President if the latter were found guilty.

7. *Judgment in case of conviction.* Judgment in cases of impeachment shall not extend further than to removal from office, and disqualification to hold and enjoy any office of honor, trust, or profit under the United States: but the party convicted shall nevertheless be liable and subject to indictment, trial, judgment, and punishment, according to law.

— If an impeached person is found guilty, he can only be removed from office and be forbidden ever to hold federal office again. No other punishment can be imposed by the Senate, but the person may also be tried in the regular courts and, if convicted, punished.

Section 4

ELECTION AND MEETINGS

1. *Election.* The times, places, and manner of holding elections for senators and representatives, shall be prescribed in each State by

the legislature thereof; but the Congress may at any time by law make or alter such regulations, except as to the places of choosing senators.

— Congress has set the first Tuesday after the first Monday in November of even-numbered years as the day for congressional elections. Since the passage of the Seventeenth Amendment the last phrase of this clause no longer applies.

2. *Meetings.* The Congress shall assemble at least once in every year, [and such meeting shall be on the first Monday in December, unless they shall by law appoint a different day.]·

— The requirement that Congress should meet at least once each year was put into the Constitution, so that no President could get complete control of the government. The meeting date of Congress was changed to January 3 by the Twentieth Amendment.

Section 5

ORGANIZATION OF CONGRESS

1. *Organization.* Each House shall be the judge of the elections, returns, and qualifications of its own members, and a majority of each shall constitute a quorum to do business; but a smaller number may adjourn from day to day, and may be authorized to compel the attendance of absent members, in such manner, and under such penalties as each House may provide.

— Each house is the sole judge of the qualifications of its members; by majority vote it may refuse to seat a newly elected member. There is no appeal from such ruling. Only rarely, however, has a house refused to seat a member. One more than half of the members of each house is needed for a quorum to conduct business. But if no one asks for a count of the members present, business may be conducted with less than a quorum, which is the practice in both houses.

2. *Rules.* Each House may determine the rules of its proceedings, punish its members for disorderly behavior, and, with the concurrence of two thirds, expel a member.

— Each house makes its own elaborate rules for carrying on its work. For certain items a two-thirds vote is required; one of these is to expel a member—which is seldom done. Others are impeachment trials and passage of a bill over a presidential veto.

3. *Journal.* Each House shall keep a journal of its proceedings, and from time to time publish the same, excepting such parts as may in their judgment require secrecy; and the yeas and nays of the members of either House on any question shall, at the desire of one fifth of those present, be entered on the journal.

— The proceedings of Congress are published in the *Congressional Record.* However, a house may vote to keep certain proceedings secret. These secret meetings are called "executive sessions."

4. *Adjournment.* Neither House, during the session of Congress, shall, without the consent of the other, adjourn for more than three days, nor to any other place than that in which the two Houses shall be sitting.

— Both houses of Congress must stay in session until they can agree on an adjournment date.

Section 6

PRIVILEGES AND RESTRICTIONS

1. *Pay and privileges.* The senators and representatives shall receive a compensation for their services, to be ascertained by law, and paid out of the Treasury of the United States. They shall in all cases, except treason, felony, and breach of the peace, be privileged from arrest during their attendance at the session of their respective Houses, and in going to and returning from the same; and for any speech or debate in either House, they shall not be questioned in any other place.

— Congressmen are paid by the United States, not by the individual states from which they are elected. They have been given the privileges mentioned in this clause, so that they may speak freely and so that they may not be prevented from attending congressional sessions. (See Chapter 9 for salaries and other benefits.)

2. *Prohibitions on members.* No senator or representative shall, during the time for which he was elected, be appointed to any civil office under the authority of the United States, which shall have been created, or the emoluments thereof shall have been increased during such time; and no person holding any office under the United States shall be a member of either House during his continuance in office.

— This clause was included in the Constitution to prevent corruption, to keep the President from

having undue influence on congressmen by offering them appointments to political offices, to
keep the branches of government separate.

Section 7

METHOD OF PASSING LAWS

1. *Revenue bills.* All bills for raising revenue
shall originate in the House of Representatives;
but the Senate may propose or concur with
amendments as on other bills.

— The constitutional convention discussed this issue
at length. It was felt that money bills should originate in the House of Representatives in order to
keep the spending of money close to the people.
In practice the Senate has equal influence on
these bills.

2. *How bills become laws.* Every bill which
shall have passed the House of Representatives
and the Senate, shall, before it become a law,
be presented to the President of the United
States; if he approve he shall sign it, but if not
he shall return it, with his objections to that
House in which it shall have originated, who
shall enter the objections at large on their journal, and proceed to reconsider it. If after such
reconsideration two thirds of that House shall
agree to pass the bill, it shall be sent, together
with the objections, to the other House, by
which it shall likewise be reconsidered, and if
approved by two thirds of that House, it shall
become a law. But in all such cases the votes of
both Houses shall be determined by yeas and
nays, and the names of the persons voting for
and against the bill shall be entered on the
journal of each House respectively. If any bill
shall not be returned by the President within
ten days (Sundays excepted) after it shall have
been presented to him, the same shall be a law,
in like manner as if he had signed it, unless
the Congress by their adjournment prevent its
return, in which case it shall not be a law.

— For a full discussion of how a bill becomes a law
see Chapter 10.

3. *The President's veto power.* Every order,
resolution, or vote to which the concurrence of
the Senate and House of Representatives may
be necessary (except on a question of adjournment) shall be presented to the President of
the United States; and before the same shall
take effect, shall be approved by him, or being
disapproved by him, shall be repassed by two
thirds of the Senate and House of Representatives, according to the rules and limitations
prescribed in the case of a bill.

— Bills passed by Congress must be approved by the
President before they become laws. However,
Congress may pass a law over the President's
veto by a two-thirds vote of each house.

Section 8

POWERS GRANTED TO CONGRESS

— This section lists the many powers granted to
Congress. (See pages 193-198.) The first seventeen clauses deal with specific powers; these
are commonly called the enumerated powers.

1–17. *Enumerated powers.* 1. The Congress
shall have power to lay and collect taxes, duties,
imposts, and excises, to pay the debts and provide for the common defense and general welfare of the United States; but all duties, imposts, and excises shall be uniform throughout
the United States;

— One of the difficulties of the government under
the Articles of Confederation was its inability to
force the states to pay their taxes to the national
government. The Constitution gives Congress the
power to collect taxes directly from the people.
These taxes were to be uniform throughout the
United States; this was changed by the Sixteenth
Amendment.

2. To borrow money on the credit of the
United States;

— Under this power the United States has incurred
its debt of more than 350 billion dollars.

3. To regulate commerce with foreign nations, and among the several States, and with
the Indian tribes;

— The need for regulating commerce among the
states was one of the reasons for calling the
Constitutional Convention.

4. To establish an uniform rule of naturalization, and uniform laws on the subject of
bankruptcies through the United States;

— See Chapter 5 for a discussion of naturalization.
Laws regarding bankruptcies must be the same
throughout the United States.

5. To coin money, regulate the value thereof, and of foreign coin, and fix the standard of weights and measures;

— Only the national government can mint and print money. Congress also fixes the standards for weights and measures, such as an ounce and a mile.

6. To provide for the punishment of counterfeiting the securities and current coin of the United States;

— Congress determines the punishment for counterfeiting.

7. To establish post offices and post roads;

— Post offices and the postal system are established by the Congress.

8. To promote the progress of science and useful arts by securing for limited times to authors and inventors the exclusive right to their respective writings and discoveries;

— Congress passes laws regarding patents and copyrights to protect inventors and authors.

9. To constitute tribunals inferior to the Supreme Court;

— Under this power Congress has established our federal court system. (See Chapter 14.)

10. To define and punish piracies and felonies committed on the high seas, and offenses against the law of nations;

— The "law of nations" is now known as international law. (See pages 581-582.)

11. To declare war, grant letters of marque and reprisal, and make rules concerning captures on land and water;

— Only Congress can declare war. However, the President as commander in chief has engaged the United States in wars without a declaration by Congress. The Korean and Vietnam wars are recent examples, but there have been other cases even in our early history; for example, the war with Tripoli under President Jefferson. Letters of marque and reprisal are no longer used; they were permits granted to private citizens to capture enemy ships.

12. To raise and support armies, but no appropriation of money to that use shall be for a longer term than two years;

13. To provide and maintain a navy;

14. To make rules for the government and regulation of the land and naval forces;

— The military forces of the United States are established by Congress. Money can be appropriated for only two years at a time.

15. To provide for calling forth the militia to execute the laws of the Union, suppress insurrections, and repel invasions;

16. To provide for organizing, arming, and disciplining the militia, and for governing such part of them as may be employed in the service of the United States, reserving to the States respectively the appointment of the officers, and the authority of training the militia according to the discipline prescribed by Congress;

— The states have authority to establish militias. (See pages 352 and 561.) These may be called for service by the federal government; at such times the President is also commander in chief of state militias, now called National Guard. (See Article II, Section 2.)

17. To exercise exclusive legislation in all cases whatsoever, over such district (not exceeding ten miles square) as may, by cession of particular States and the acceptance of Congress, become the seat of the government of the United States, and to exercise like authority over all places purchased by the consent of the legislature of the State in which the same shall be, for the erection of forts, magazines, arsenals, dockyards, and other needful buildings; and

— Under this clause Congress had the power to establish the District of Columbia. It has power to govern the District and has authority over other property of the federal government.

18. *Implied powers.* To make all laws which shall be necessary and proper for carrying into execution the foregoing powers, and all other powers vested by this Constitution in the government of the United States, or in any department or officer thereof.

— Clause 18 deals with the implied powers of Congress; it is known as the "elastic clause." Under it Congress has passed many laws not otherwise possible under the enumerated powers. (See pages 195-196.)

Section 9

POWERS FORBIDDEN TO CONGRESS

1. The migration or importation of such persons as any of the States now existing shall think proper to admit, shall not be prohibited by the Congress prior to the year one thousand eight hundred and eight, but a tax or duty may be imposed on such importation, not exceeding ten dollars for each person.

— Congress could not stop the importation of slaves until 1808.

2. The privilege of the writ of *habeas corpus* shall not be suspended, unless when in cases of rebellion or invasion the public safety may require it.

3. No bill of attainder or *ex post facto* law shall be passed.

— Congress was forbidden to pass these laws which interfered with personal freedom. (See The Language of Government of Chapter 3 for a definition of terms.)

4. No capitation, or other direct, tax shall be laid, unless in proportion to the census or enumeration herein before directed to be taken.

— The Sixteenth Amendment was passed to modify this requirement and permit an income tax.

5. No tax or duty shall be laid on articles exported from any State.

— Congress cannot place a tax on exports.

6. No preference shall be given by any regulation of commerce or revenue to the ports of one State over those of another: nor shall vessels bound to, or from, one State be obliged to enter, clear, or pay duties in another.

— Congress may not pass laws affecting commerce which would favor one state over others.

7. No money shall be drawn from the treasury, but in consequence of appropriations made by law; and a regular statement and account of the receipts and expenditures of all public money shall be published from time to time.

— Money cannot be paid from the federal treasury without the consent of Congress. Financial statements must be issued from time to time.

8. No title of nobility shall be granted by the United States: and no person holding any office of profit or trust under them, shall, without the consent of the Congress, accept of any present, emolument, office, or title of any kind whatever, from any king, prince, or foreign State.

— The United States cannot give anyone a title of nobility. To prevent the bribery of federal officials by a foreign government, this clause provides that no official may accept any honor or consideration from a foreign government without the consent of Congress.

Section 10

POWERS FORBIDDEN TO STATES

1. No State shall enter into any treaty, alliance, or confederation; grant letters of marque and reprisal; coin money; emit bills of credit; make anything but gold and silver coin a tender in payment of debts; pass any bill of attainder, *ex post facto* law, or law impairing the obligation of contracts, or grant any title of nobility.

— Much of this clause prohibits the states from exercising powers which were granted to Congress in Section 8; also some of the powers which were forbidden to the federal government are forbidden to the states.

2. No State shall, without the consent of the Congress, lay any imposts or duties on imports or exports, except what may be absolutely necessary for executing its inspection laws: and the net produce of all duties and imposts laid by any State on imports or exports, shall be for the use of the treasury of the United States; and all such laws shall be subject to the revision and control of the Congress.

— Congress is again given authority over foreign and interstate commerce.

3. No State shall, without the consent of Congress, lay any duty of tonnage, keep troops, or ships of war in time of peace, enter into any agreement or compact with another State, or with a foreign power, or engage in war, unless actually invaded, or in such imminent danger as will not admit of delay.

— The making of foreign policy and the carrying out of national defense measures are reserved for the federal government.

Article II

EXECUTIVE DEPARTMENT

Section 1

PRESIDENT AND VICE-PRESIDENT

1. *Term.* The executive power shall be vested in a President of the United States of America. He shall hold his office during the term of four years, and, together with the Vice-President, chosen for the same term, be elected as follows:

— The executive of the United States is the President. He and the Vice President are elected for four-year terms. The Constitution placed no limit on the number of times the President may be re-elected, but this was changed by the Twenty-second Amendment.

2. *Electors.* Each State shall appoint, in such manner as the legislature thereof may direct, a number of electors, equal to the whole number of senators and representatives to which the State may be entitled in the Congress: but no senator or representative, or person holding an office of trust or profit under the United States, shall be appointed an elector.

— The President and Vice President are elected by the electoral college, which is fully explained in Chapter 11. Members of Congress and other officials of the United States government may not be electors.

Former method of election. [The electors shall meet in their respective States, and vote by ballot for two persons, of whom one at least shall not be an inhabitant of the same State with themselves. And they shall make a list of all the persons voted for, and of the number of votes for each; which list they shall sign and certify, and transmit sealed to the seat of the government of the United States, directed to the president of the Senate. The president of the Senate shall, in the presence of the Senate and House of Representatives, open all the certificates, and the votes shall then be counted. The person having the greatest number of votes shall be the President, if such number be a majority of the whole number of electors appointed; and if there be more than one who have such majority, and have an equal number of votes, then the House of Representatives shall immediately choose by ballot one of them for President; and if no person have a majority,

then from the five highest on the list the said house shall in like manner choose the President. But in choosing the President, the votes shall be taken by States, the representation from each State having one vote; a quorum for this purpose shall consist of a member or members from two thirds of the States, and a majority of all the States shall be necessary to a choice. In every case, after the choice of the President, the person having the greatest number of votes of the electors shall be the Vice-President. But if there should remain two or more who have equal votes, the Senate shall choose from them by ballot the Vice-President.]

— The method of election set forth in this paragraph was changed by the adoption of the Twelfth Amendment. (See Chapter 11 for discussion of the method and of the reasons for the change.)

3. *Time of choosing electors.* The Congress may determine the time of choosing the electors, and the day on which they shall give their votes; which day shall be the same throughout the United States.

— The election is held every four years in years divisible by four on the first Tuesday after the first Monday in November; the electors meet in their respective state capitals in December to cast their votes. These votes are opened and counted in a joint session of Congress in January.

4. *Qualifications of the President.* No person except a natural born citizen, or a citizen of the United States, at the time of the adoption of this Constitution, shall be eligible to the office of President; neither shall any person be eligible to that office who shall not have attained to the age of thirty-five years, and been fourteen years a resident within the United States.

— The Constitution gives the basic qualifications for the President. See the discussion about "natural born" in Chapter 11.

5. *Vacancy.* In case of the removal of the President from office, or of his death, resignation, or inability to discharge the powers and duties of the said office, the same shall devolve on the Vice-President, and the Congress may by law provide for the case of removal, death, resignation, or inability, both of the President and Vice-President, declaring what officer shall then act as President, and such officer shall act

accordingly, until the disability be removed, or a President shall be elected.

— The Vice President becomes President on the death, resignation, or removal from office of the President. By a law passed in 1947 the persons next in line are the Speaker of the House and the President pro tempore of the Senate. The Twenty-fifth Amendment sets up a procedure for filling the office of Vice President if it becomes vacant and for carrying on the Presidency if the President becomes disabled.

6. *Salary.* The President shall, at stated times, receive for his services a compensation, which shall neither be increased nor diminished during the period for which he shall have been elected, and he shall not receive within that period any other emolument from the United States, or any of them.

— The President is paid by the United States; his salary cannot be raised or lowered during his term of office. He can receive no payments from any state. (See Chapter 11 for information about his salary and other benefits.)

7. *Oath.* Before he enter on the execution of his office, he shall take the following oath or affirmation:—"I do solemnly swear (or affirm) that I will faithfully execute the office of President of the United States, and will to the best of my ability, preserve, protect, and defend the Constitution of the United States."

— The President takes this oath on inauguration day —January 20 after his election.

Section 2

POWERS OF THE PRESIDENT

1. *Military powers; reprieves and pardons.* The President shall be commander in chief of the army and navy of the United States, and of the militia of the several States, when called into the actual service of the United States; he may require the opinion, in writing, of the principal officer in each of the executive departments, upon any subject relating to the duties of their respective offices, and he shall have power to grant reprieves and pardons for offenses against the United States, except in cases of impeachment.

— The commander in chief of the armed forces is a civilian, the President. The words, "principal officers in each of the executive departments," give

the idea of a President's Cabinet, but Cabinet is not mentioned in the Constitution. (See Chapter 12.) The President also has certain judicial powers. (See Chapter 11 for a discussion of presidential powers.)

2. *Treaties; appointments.* He shall have power, by and with the advice and consent of the Senate, to make treaties, provided two thirds of the senators present concur; and he shall nominate, and by and with the advice and consent of the Senate, shall appoint ambassadors, other public ministers and consuls, judges of the Supreme Court, and all other officers of the United States, whose appointments are not herein otherwise provided for, and which shall be established by law: but the Congress may by law vest the appointment of such inferior officers, as they think proper, in the President alone, in the courts of law, or in the heads of departments.

— The President has the power to make treaties and to appoint various officials of the government, but he must do so with the advice and consent of the Senate. (See Chapter 9.)

3. *Filling of vacancies.* The President shall have power to fill up all vacancies that may happen during the recess of the Senate, by granting commissions which shall expire at the end of their next session.

— If the Senate is not in session, the President may make appointments without its consent. But these appointments expire at the close of the next Senate session unless they get Senate approval.

Section 3

DUTIES OF THE PRESIDENT

He shall from time to time give to the Congress information of the state of the Union, and recommend to their consideration such measures as he shall judge necessary and expedient; he may, on extraordinary occasions, convene both Houses, or either of them, and in case of disagreement between them with respect to the time of adjournment, he may adjourn them to such time as he shall think proper; he shall receive ambassadors and other public ministers; he shall take care that the laws be faithfully executed, and shall commission all the officers of the United States.

— One of the duties of the President is the annual "State of the Union" message. By means of it and other special messages to the Congress, the President indicates the kind of legislation he believes necessary. The President also has the authority to call special sessions of Congress. The President receives representatives of other nations and carries on our relations with these nations. He must administer the laws passed by Congress.

Section 4

IMPEACHMENT

The President, Vice-President, and all civil officers of the United States, shall be removed from office on impeachment for, and conviction of, treason, bribery, or other high crimes and misdemeanors.

— The President and other officers of the national government may be removed from office for reasons mentioned in this clause. Powers of impeachment and trial are given to the House and Senate, respectively. (See Chapters 9 and 11.)

Article III

JUDICIAL DEPARTMENT

Section 1

FEDERAL COURTS

The judicial power of the United States shall be vested in one Supreme Court, and in such inferior courts as the Congress may from time to time ordain and establish. The judges, both of the Supreme and inferior courts, shall hold their offices during good behavior, and shall, at stated times, receive for their services, a compensation which shall not be diminished during their continuance in office.

— Congress has the power to control important aspects of the Supreme Court. Congress has varied the number of judges from six in 1789, to five in 1801, to six in 1802, to seven in 1807, to nine in 1837, to ten in 1863, to six in 1866, and again to nine in 1869.
— The main inferior courts established are the federal district courts and the courts of appeal.
— The principle of virtual life tenure is established by the Constitution.
— Congress can and does change the salaries of judges.

Section 2

JURISDICTION OF FEDERAL COURTS

1. *Federal courts in general.* The judicial power shall extend to all cases, in law and equity, arising under this Constitution, the laws of the United States, and treaties made, or which shall be made, under their authority;—to all cases affecting ambassadors, other public ministers and consuls;—to all cases of admiralty and maritime jurisdiction;—to controversies to which the United States shall be a party;—to controversies between two or more States;—between a State and citizens of another State;—between citizens of different States,—between citizens of the same State claiming lands under grants of different States, and between a State, or the citizens thereof, and foreign States, citizens or subjects.

— The Constitution, federal laws, and treaties are the supreme law of the land. The two general types of cases to come before federal courts are determined by: the nature of the case, or the parties involved. (See Chapter 14.)
— The provision concerning controversies between "a state and citizens of another state" was restricted by the Eleventh Amendment to suits by a state against citizens of another state.

2. *Supreme Court.* In all cases affecting ambassadors, other public ministers and consuls, and those in which a State shall be party, the Supreme Court shall have original jurisdiction. In all the other cases before mentioned, the Supreme Court shall have appellate jurisdiction, both as to law and fact, with such exceptions, and under such regulations, as the Congress shall make.

— The cases mentioned here start and end in the Supreme Court because here original jurisdiction is also final jurisdiction.
— Congress has limited the appeals that can be made to the Supreme Court and that court does not accept all cases that are appealed. Hence, the Courts of Appeals are the final courts for most cases that are appealed. (Court terms are defined in the Glossary, and in the Language of Government section of Chapter 14.)

3. *Trials.* The trial of all crimes, except in cases of impeachment, shall be by jury; and such trial shall be held in the State where the said crimes shall have been committed; but when not committed within any State, the trial shall be at such place or places as the Congress may by law have directed.

— The right of trial by jury, inherited from longtime English practice, is guaranteed here. The Fifth, Sixth, and Seventh Amendments add to this provision. Impeachment is excluded from trial by jury because of the provisions for these cases in Articles I and II.

Section 3

TREASON

1. *Definition.* Treason against the United States, shall consist only in levying war against them, or in adhering to their enemies, giving them aid and comfort. No person shall be convicted of treason unless on the testimony of two witnesses to the same overt act, or on confession in open court.

— Definitions of treason under English kings had varied. Here a definite and clear definition is provided. An "overt act" requires some kind of action; talking, threatening, or thinking are thus not treason. Since treason is such a serious crime, two witnesses are required, or a "confession in open court"—meaning, of course, that torture or brutality cannot have been used.

2. *Punishment.* The Congress shall have power to declare the punishment of treason, but no attainder of treason shall work corruption of blood, or forfeiture except during the life of the person attainted.

— Congress provides for a death penalty or imprisonment for five years and a fine of not less than $10,000 for treason. "Attainder of treason" means to be convicted of treason; "corruption of blood" means that a person cannot inherit or transmit this guilt. The effect is that punishment of treason cannot be passed on to descendants.

Article IV
RELATIONS OF THE STATES
Section 1

PUBLIC RECORDS

Full faith and credit shall be given in each State to the public acts, records, and judicial proceedings of every other State. And the Congress may by general laws prescribe the manner in which such acts, records, and proceedings shall be proved, and the effect thereof.

— The acts of one state must be accepted by another state under "the full faith and credit" provision. (See Chapter 18.)
— Congress has passed laws stating that laws carrying the seal of the state or court decrees carrying the signature of the court clerk are considered legal.

Section 2

PRIVILEGES OF CITIZENS

1. *Privileges of citizens.* The citizens of each State shall be entitled to all privileges and immunities of citizens in the several States.

— For example, a citizen of Florida traveling in New York has all the privileges of a New York citizen.

2. *Fugitives from justice.* A person charged in any State with treason, felony, or other crime, who shall flee from justice, and be found in another State, shall on demand of the executive authority of the State from which he fled, be delivered up to be removed to the State having jurisdiction of the crime.

— This clause provides the basis for extradition. As noted in Chapter 16, a governor does not have to surrender a person accused of a crime.

3. *Fugitive slaves.* No person held to service or labor in one State, under the laws thereof, escaping into another, shall, in consequence of any law or regulation therein, be discharged from such service or labor, but shall be delivered up on claim of the party to whom such service or labor may be due.

— This clause was for all practical purposes replaced by the Thirteenth Amendment. It is now obsolete.

Section 3

NEW STATES AND TERRITORIES

1. *New states.* New States may be admitted by the Congress into this Union; but no new State shall be formed or erected within the jurisdiction of any other State; nor any State be formed by the junction of two or more States, or parts of States, without the consent of the legislatures of the States concerned as well as of the Congress.

— Congress accepted the plan of admitting new states from territories as described in Chapter 15.
— Note that a state cannot be divided into two or more states without its consent. Kentucky was originally part of Virginia; Tennessee was part of North Carolina; Maine was part of Massachusetts. West Virginia split from Virginia during the Civil War, and Congress accepted the new state on the basis that Virginia had rebelled.

2. *Territory and property.* The Congress shall have power to dispose of and make all needful rules and regulations respecting the territory or other property belonging to the

United States; and nothing in this Constitution shall be so construed as to prejudice any claims of the United States, or of any particular State.

— This clause was originally adopted to adjust the conflicting claims of six states to the Northwest Territory but provided the basis for future territorial governments.

Section 4

PROTECTION OF THE STATES

The United States shall guarantee to every State in this Union a republican form of government, and shall protect each of them against invasion; and on application of the legislature, or of the executive (when the legislature cannot be convened), against domestic violence.

— This clause can be enforced in two ways: Congress could refuse to admit representatives and senators from the state, and the President could send troops to the state to assure a republican form of government.
— The federal government assumes responsibility for any types of invasion.
— In case of riots, for example, the federal government can intervene. The President has intervened, as in the Illinois Pullman strike in 1894, against the desires of the governor.

Article V

AMENDMENTS

The Congress, whenever two thirds of both Houses shall deem it necessary, shall propose amendments to this Constitution, or, on the application of the legislatures of two thirds of the several States, shall call a convention for proposing amendments, which, in either case, shall be valid to all intents and purposes, as part of this Constitution, when ratified by the legislatures of three fourths of the several States, or by conventions in three fourths thereof, as the one or the other mode of ratification may be proposed by the Congress; Provided that no amendment which may be made prior to the year one thousand eight hundred and eight shall in any manner affect the first and fourth clauses in the ninth section of the first article; and that no State, without its consent, shall be deprived of its equal suffrage in the Senate.

— Of the methods for amending the Constitution, only the method of proposing amendments by Congress has been used. Ratification by state legislatures has been used in all cases except for the Twenty-first Amendment.
— The last clause of this article reinforces the Great Compromise of the Constitutional Convention by which the small states with two senators had an equal voice in the Senate with the large states.

Article VI

THE SUPREME LAW OF THE LAND

1. *Public debt.* All debts contracted and engagements entered into, before the adoption of this Constitution, shall be as valid against the United States under this Constitution, as under the Confederation.

— A principle of international law that a new state shall assume the debts of its predecessors was recognized here. Hamilton insisted, not only that the debts of the Confederation should be assumed, but those of the individual states too.

2. *Supreme law of the land.* This Constitution, and the laws of the United States which shall be made in pursuance thereof; and all treaties made, or which shall be made, under the authority of the United States, shall be the supreme law of the land; and the judges in every State shall be bound thereby, anything in the Constitution or laws of any State to the contrary notwithstanding.

— The "supreme law of the land" is defined as: the Constitution, the federal laws, and the treaties. The Constitution does not indicate who is to decide whether a law or treaty is in accordance with the Constitution, but Chief Justice John Marshall decided that the Supreme Court had this right of judicial review.
— Federal and state judges are obliged to abide by "the supreme law of the land." The right of the federal courts to declare an act of a state legislature unconstitutional derives from this clause.

3. *Oath.* The senators and representatives before mentioned, and the members of the several State legislatures, and all executive and judicial officers, both of the United States, and of the several States, shall be bound by oath or affirmation to support this Constitution; but no religious test shall ever be required as a qualification to any office or public trust under the United States.

- Public officials are required to take an oath of loyalty to the Constitution.
- Any kind of religious test for holding federal office is forbidden.

Article VII
RATIFICATION OF THE CONSTITUTION

The ratification of the conventions of nine States shall be sufficient for the establishment of this Constitution between the States so ratifying the same.

Done in Convention by the unanimous consent of the States present the seventeenth day of September in the year of our Lord one thousand seven hundred and eighty-seven, and of the independence of the United States of America the twelfth. In witness whereof we have hereunto subscribed our names,

Gº: Washington—
Presd.ᵗ and Deputy from Virginia.

(Signed also by thirty-eight other delegates, from twelve states.)

- The Articles of Confederation required a unanimous vote of the state legislatures for ratification. This revolutionary proposal for ratification by nine states enabled the Constitution to be put into effect.

Amendments to the Constitution

Article I
FREEDOM OF RELIGION, SPEECH, AND PRESS

Congress shall make no law respecting an establishment of religion, or prohibiting the free exercise thereof; or abridging the freedom of speech, or of the press; or the right of the people peaceably to assemble, and to petition the government for a redress of grievances.

- (1791) The first ten amendments are called the Bill of Rights. They were adopted because some states refused to ratify the Constitution unless they were added. They protect the individual from unjust acts of government.
- This first amendment is a clear statement of the citizen's absolute rights.

Article II
RIGHT TO BEAR ARMS

A well regulated militia, being necessary to the security of a free State, the right of the people to keep and bear arms, shall not be infringed.

- (1791) The right to bear arms is granted here only to a "well-regulated" group "necessary to the security of a free state." The right to regulate the sale and use of guns is not involved.

Article III
QUARTERING OF SOLDIERS

No soldier shall, in time of peace, be quartered in any house, without the consent of the owner, nor in time of war, but in a manner to be prescribed by law.

- (1791) Troops cannot be assigned to live in private homes except in war-time and, then, only in accordance with the law.

Article IV
SEARCH WARRANTS

The right of the people to be secure in their persons, houses, papers, and effects, against unreasonable searches and seizures, shall not be violated, and no warrants shall issue, but upon probable cause, supported by oath or affirmation, and particularly describing the place to be searched, and the persons or things to be seized.

- (1791) This is a protection against "unreasonable searches and seizures." For search or arrest, ordinarily a legal warrant is necessary.

Article V
RIGHTS IN CRIMINAL CASES

No person shall be held to answer for a capital, or otherwise infamous, crime, unless on a presentment or indictment of a grand jury, except in cases arising in the land or naval forces, or in the militia, when in actual service in time of war or public danger; nor shall any person be subject for the same offense to be twice put in jeopardy of life or limb; nor shall be compelled in any criminal case to be a witness against himself, nor be deprived of life, liberty, or property, without due process of law; nor shall private property be taken for public use without just compensation.

— (1791) A capital crime is one punishable by death; an infamous crime is one punishable by death or being placed in prison. A grand jury determines if there is enough evidence to hold a person for trial. (See Chapter 17.)
— Military courts handle those cases involving persons in the armed forces.
— A person may not be tried twice for the same offense, but if a jury cannot agree on a verdict a mistrial is ordered and a new trial is possible.
— The present interpretation holds that a person cannot be forced to testify against himself by any agency of government including congressional investigating committees.
— The "due process of law" clause is one of the most important safeguards of liberty.
— The right of government to take property for public use is called "eminent domain." Without right to take property for public use, highways, schools, airports, and other public facilities might not be built in desirable locations.

Article VI

RIGHTS IN CRIMINAL CASES

In all criminal prosecutions, the accused shall enjoy the right to a speedy and public trial, by an impartial jury of the State and district wherein the crime shall have been committed, which district shall have been previously ascertained by law, and to be informed of the nature and cause of the accusation; to be confronted with the witnesses against him; to have compulsory process for obtaining witnesses in his favor, and to have the assistance of counsel for his defense.

— (1791) Many recent decisions of the Supreme Court are based on these rights to a fair trial, to know the accusation, to confront witnesses, to be able to compel witnesses to attend, and to have the right to a lawyer.

Article VII

RIGHT OF TRIAL BY JURY

In suits at common law, where the value in controversy shall exceed twenty dollars, the right of trial by jury shall be preserved, and no fact tried by a jury shall be otherwise re-examined in any court of the United States, than according to the rules of the common law.

— (1791) The right to a jury trial is here extended to civil cases, but a jury is not compulsory.

— On appeals, the court cannot re-examine the facts, only questions of errors of law.

Article VIII

BAIL, FINES, PUNISHMENT

Excessive bail shall not be required, nor excessive fines imposed, nor cruel and unusual punishments inflicted.

— (1791) The excessive bail provision comes from the English Bill of Rights. The intent is to prevent fixing the bail so high that the accused cannot reasonably pay it, but high enough so that he will not run away. The court has to determine what bail is excessive, and it has to determine whether fines are excessive and punishments cruel and unusual.

Article IX

RIGHTS RESERVED BY THE PEOPLE

The enumeration in the Constitution of certain rights shall not be construed to deny or disparage others retained by the people.

— (1791) This amendment was added because the people are sovereign and, although the major freedoms were listed in the first eight amendments, this provided an insurance clause that rights not listed were still retained.

Article X

POWERS RESERVED TO THE STATES

The powers not delegated to the United States by the Constitution, nor prohibited by it to the States, are reserved to the States respectively, or to the people.

— (1791) This amendment provides the basis for much of the "states' rights" arguments. Actually the federal government through its stated and implied powers has been able to do those things that are "necessary and proper."

Article XI

SUITS AGAINST STATES

(Amendment to Article III, Section 2, Clause 1)

The judicial power of the United States shall not be construed to extend to any suit in law or equity, commenced or prosecuted against one of the United States, by citizens of another State, or by citizens or subjects of any foreign State.

(1798) Shortly after the adoption of the Constitution, in *Chisholm* v. *Georgia* (1793) a man from South Carolina brought suit against the state of Georgia over an inheritance. Georgia refused to be sued but the Supreme Court ruled that it could. Georgia then led a movement to amend the Constitution and succeeded. Now the only way a citizen of another state or foreign nation can sue a state is by gaining permission to do so.

Article XII

ELECTION OF PRESIDENT AND VICE-PRESIDENT

(Amendment to Article II, Section I, Clause 2)

The electors shall meet in their respective States, and vote by ballot for President and Vice-President, one of whom, at least, shall not be an inhabitant of the same State with themselves; they shall name in their ballots the person voted for as President, and in distinct ballots the person voted for as Vice-President, and they shall make distinct lists of all persons voted for as President and of all persons voted for as Vice-President, and of the number of votes for each, which lists they shall sign and certify, and transmit sealed to the seat of government of the United States, directed to the president of the Senate;—The president of the Senate shall, in the presence of the Senate and House of Representatives, open all the certificates and the votes shall then be counted;— The person having the greatest number of votes for President shall be the President, if such number be a majority of the whole number of electors appointed; and if no person have such majority, then from the persons having the highest numbers not exceeding three on the list of those voted for as President, the House of Representatives shall choose immediately, by ballot, the President. But in choosing the President, the votes shall be taken by States, the representation from each State having one vote; a quorum for this purpose shall consist of a member or members from two thirds of the States, and a majority of all the States shall be necessary to a choice. And if the House of Representatives shall not choose a President whenever the right of choice shall devolve upon them, [before the fourth day of March next following,] then the Vice-President

shall act as President, as in the case of the death or other constitutional disability of the President. The person having the greatest number of votes as Vice-President shall be the Vice-President, if such number be a majority of the whole number of electors appointed, and if no person have a majority, then from the two highest numbers on the list, the Senate shall choose the Vice-President; a quorum for the purpose shall consist of two thirds of the whole number of senators, and a majority of the whole number shall be necessary to a choice. But no person constitutionally ineligible to the office of President shall be eligible to that of Vice-President of the United States.

— (1804) The major change made by this amendment was to provide for separate ballots in the electoral college vote for President and Vice President. In 1800 Jefferson and Burr had received the same number of votes, throwing the election to the House of Representatives—which almost resulted in Burr's election (see Chapter 11). To correct the defect this amendment was passed.

— The amendment also corrected an omission from the original Constitution by providing that the Vice President should have the same qualifications as the President.

— The March 4 date for the inauguration was changed to January 20 by the Twentieth Amendment.

Article XIII

ABOLITION OF SLAVERY

Section 1

Neither slavery nor involuntary servitude, except as a punishment for crime whereof the party shall have been duly convicted, shall exist within the United States, or any place subject to their jurisdiction.

— (1865) This is the first of the Civil War amendments. The language eliminating slavery in the United States was adapted from the Northwest Ordinance of 1787.

Section 2

Congress shall have power to enforce this article by appropriate legislation.

— Although this section gives power to the Congress, the Supreme Court had declared parts of the Civil Rights Act of 1875 unconstitutional. In 1954 the Supreme Court changed its position.

Article XIV
CIVIL RIGHTS
Section 1

Protection of political privileges. All persons born or naturalized in the United States, and subject to the jurisdiction thereof, are citizens of the United States and of the State wherein they reside. No State shall make or enforce any law which shall abridge the privileges or immunities of citizens of the United States; nor shall any State deprive any person of life, liberty, or property, without due process of law; nor deny to any person within its jurisdiction the equal protection of the laws.

— (1868) After passage by Congress this amendment was rejected by the Confederate states. Then Congress passed the Reconstruction Act of 1867 which established provisional governments until the amendment was ratified.

— This section provides the only definition of citizenship in the Constitution. It gave citizenship to Negroes but now is more widely applied.

— The last sentence provides the basis for some Supreme Court decisions on segregation. Since a corporation is viewed legally as a person, the sentence also has been used to protect corporations from having property taken without due process of law.

Section 2

Apportionment of representatives. Representatives shall be apportioned among the several States according to their respective numbers, counting the whole number of persons in each State, excluding Indians not taxed. But when the right to vote at any election for the choice of electors for President and Vice-President of the United States, representatives in Congress, the executive and judicial officers of a State, or the members of the legislature thereof, is denied to any of the male inhabitants of such State, being twenty-one years of age, and citizens of the United States, or in any way abridged, except for participation in rebellion, or other crime, the basis of representation therein shall be reduced in the proportion which the number of such male citizens shall bear to the whole number of male citizens twenty-one years of age in such State.

— This section provided the penalty for not permitting Negroes to vote, but the terms have never been enforced.

Section 3

Loss of political privileges. No person shall be a senator or representative in Congress, or elector of President and Vice-President, or hold any office, civil or military, under the United States, or under any State, who, having previously taken an oath, as a member of Congress, or as an officer of the United States, or as a member of any State legislature, or as an executive or judicial officer of any State, to support the Constitution of the United States, shall have engaged in insurrection or rebellion against the same, or given aid or comfort to the enemies thereof. But Congress may by a vote of two thirds of each House, remove such disability.

— The intent of this section was to prevent leaders of the Confederacy from holding public offices.

Section 4

Public debt. The validity of the public debt of the United States, authorized by law, including debts incurred for payment of pensions and bounties for services in suppressing insurrection or rebellion, shall not be questioned. But neither the United States nor any State shall assume or pay any debt or obligation incurred in aid of insurrection or rebellion against the United States, or any claim for the loss or emancipation of any slave; but all such debts, obligations, and claims shall be held illegal and void.

— This section insured that the debts of the United States would be paid. But the debts of the Confederate states were not to be paid. Thus holders of bonds and money of the Confederacy lost these amounts. Former slave owners were not paid for the slaves who were freed.

Section 5

Enforcement. The Congress shall have power to enforce, by appropriate legislation, the provisions of this article.

— The effects of this section were similar to those of Section 2 of the Thirteenth Amendment.

Article XV
NEGRO SUFFRAGE
Section 1

Right to vote. The right of citizens of the

United States to vote shall not be denied or abridged by the United States or by any State on account of race, color, or previous condition of servitude.

— (1870) The right to vote is guaranteed Negroes by this amendment.

Section 2

Enforcement. The Congress shall have power to enforce this article by appropriate legislation.

— For many years the amendment was not enforced in southern states, but recent acts of Congress and decisions of the Supreme Court are expected to change this situation. (See Chapter 4.)

Article XVI

INCOME TAXES

The Congress shall have power to lay and collect taxes on incomes, from whatever source derived, without apportionment among the several States, and without regard to any census or enumeration.

— (1913) In 1894 Congress passed an income tax law which the Supreme Court declared unconstitutional. This amendment was passed by Congress in 1909 and with its ratification legalized the income tax, which has become the federal government's largest source of revenue.

Article XVII

DIRECT ELECTION OF SENATORS

(Amendment to Article I, Section 3, Clauses 1 and 2)

The Senate of the United States shall be composed of two senators from each State, elected by the people thereof, for six years; and each senator shall have one vote. The electors in each State shall have the qualifications requisite for electors of the most numerous branch of the State legislatures.

When vacancies happen in the representation of any State in the Senate, the executive authority of such State shall issue writs of election to fill such vacancies: *Provided,* That the legislature of any State may empower the executive thereof to make temporary appointments until the people fill the vacancies by election as the legislature may direct.

— (1913) The system of election of senators by the state legislatures had been abused. Five times the House of Representatives passed this amendment before it was accepted by the Senate. After both the Democratic and Republican parties favored the amendment it was passed by the Senate and ratified by the states.

Article XVIII

PROHIBITION OF LIQUOR

Section 1

After one year from the ratification of this article the manufacture, sale, or transportation of intoxicating liquors within, the importation thereof into, or the exportation thereof from the United States and all territory subject to the jurisdiction thereof for beverage purposes is hereby prohibited.

Section 2

The Congress and the several States shall have concurrent power to enforce this article by appropriate legislation.

Section 3

This article shall be inoperative unless it shall have been ratified as an amendment to the Constitution by the legislatures of the several States, as provided in the Constitution, within seven years from the date of the submission hereof to the States by the Congress.

— (1919) This amendment was repealed by the Twenty-first Amendment. Section 3 is the first use of a time limit for ratification.

Article XIX

WOMAN SUFFRAGE

Section 1

The right of citizens of the United States to vote shall not be denied or abridged by the United States or by any State on account of sex.

Section 2

Congress shall have power, by appropriate legislation, to enforce the provisions of this article.

— (1920) After years of agitation and with many states allowing women to vote, this amendment passed Congress in 1919 and was ratified within fifteen months.

Article XX

TERMS OF PRESIDENT AND CONGRESS

Section 1

The terms of the President and Vice-President shall end at noon on the 20th day of January, and the terms of senators and representatives at noon on the 3d day of January, of the years in which such terms would have ended if this article had not been ratified; and the terms of their successors shall then begin.

Section 2

The Congress shall assemble at least once in every year, and such meeting shall begin at noon on the 3d day of January, unless they shall by law appoint a different day.

Section 3

If, at the time fixed for the beginning of the term of the President, the President-elect shall have died, the Vice-President-elect shall become President. If a President shall not have been chosen before the time fixed for the beginning of his term, or if the President-elect shall have failed to qualify, then the Vice-President-elect shall act as President until a President shall have qualified; and the Congress may by law provide for the case wherein neither a President-elect nor a Vice-President-elect shall have qualified, declaring who shall then act as President, or the manner in which one who is to act shall be selected, and such persons shall act accordingly until a President or Vice-President shall have qualified.

Section 4

The Congress may by law provide for the case of the death of any of the persons from whom the House of Representatives may choose a President whenever the right of choice shall have devolved upon them, and for the case of the death of any of the persons from whom the Senate may choose a Vice-President whenever the right of choice shall have devolved upon them.

Section 5

Sections 1 and 2 shall take effect on the 15th day of October following the ratification of this article.

Section 6

This article shall be inoperative unless it shall have been ratified as an amendment to the Constitution by the legislatures of three fourths of the several States within seven years from the date of its submission.

— (1933) This is the "lame duck" amendment. Prior to its adoption members of Congress could continue to serve after they had been defeated. New members did not take office until thirteen months after their election. Improved transportation and communication made such a long delay unnecessary. The old March 4 date for the beginning of presidential and congressional terms was changed to January 20 and January 3, respectively.

— Sections 3 and 4 take care of the possible death or disqualification of the President-elect or Vice President-elect (or the candidates if the election goes to the House of Representatives).

Article XXI

REPEAL OF PROHIBITION OF LIQUOR

Section 1

The eighteenth article of amendment to the Constitution of the United States is hereby repealed.

Section 2

The transportation or importation into any State, Territory, or possession of the United States for delivery or use therein of intoxicating liquors, in violation of the laws thereof, is hereby prohibited.

Section 3

This article shall be inoperative unless it shall have been ratified as an amendment to the Constitution by conventions in the several States, as provided in the Constitution, within seven years from the date of submission hereof to the States by the Congress.

— (1933) Experience with the Eighteenth Amendment had been unsatisfactory to so many citizens that the amendment was repealed, although Section 2 protects local and state prohibitions of the use of intoxicating liquors. Section 3 was the first time that ratification by conventions was required.

Article XXII

PRESIDENT LIMITED TO TWO TERMS OF OFFICE

(Amendment to Article II, Section 1, Clause 1)

Section 1

No person shall be elected to the office of the

President more than twice, and no person who has held the office of President, or acted as President, for more than two years of a term to which some other person was elected President shall be elected to the office of the President more than once. But this article shall not apply to any person holding the office of President when this article was proposed by the Congress, and shall not prevent any person who may be holding the office of President, or acting as President, during the term within which this article becomes operative from holding the office of President or acting as President during the remainder of such term.

Section 2

This article shall be inoperative unless it shall have been ratified as an amendment to the Constitution by the legislatures of three fourths of the several States within seven years from the date of its submission to the States by the Congress.

— (1951) The momentum for this amendment came from those who had opposed President Franklin Roosevelt's violation of the "no third term" tradition, which had been established by Washington and Jefferson. President Eisenhower was the first to be affected by the amendment. President Johnson was eligible for a third term because he served less than two years of President Kennedy's term.

Article XXIII
SUFFRAGE FOR DISTRICT OF COLUMBIA IN ELECTION OF PRESIDENT AND VICE PRESIDENT

(Amendment to Article II, Section 1)

Section 1

The District constituting the seat of Government of the United States shall appoint in such manner as the Congress may direct:

A number of electors of President and Vice President equal to the whole number of senators and representatives in Congress to which the District would be entitled if it were a State, but in no event more than the least populous State; they shall be in addition to those appointed by the States, but they shall be considered, for the purposes of the election of President and Vice President, to be electors appointed by a State; and they shall meet in the District and perform such duties as provided by the twelfth article of amendment.

Section 2

The Congress shall have power to enforce this article by appropriate legislation.

— (1961) By this amendment citizens of the District of Columbia may vote in presidential elections. They still cannot vote for members of Congress or for local officials.

Article XXIV
POLL TAX

Section 1

The right of citizens of the United States to vote in any primary or other election for President or Vice President, for electors for President or Vice President, or for senator or representative in Congress, shall not be denied or abridged by the United States or any state by reason of failure to pay any poll tax or other tax.

Section 2

The Congress shall have the power to enforce this article by appropriate legislation.

— (1964) This Civil Rights amendment prevents the use of the poll tax to deny a citizen the right to vote in national elections.

Article XXV
PRESIDENTIAL DISABILITY AND SUCCESSION

(Amendment to Article II, Section 1, Clause 5)

Section 1

In case of the removal of the President from office or his death or resignation, the Vice President shall become President.

Section 2

Whenever there is a vacancy in the office of the Vice President, the President shall nominate a Vice President who shall take the office upon confirmation by a majority vote of both houses of Congress.

Section 3

Whenever the President transmits to the President pro tempore of the Senate and the Speaker of the House of Representatives his written declaration that he is unable to discharge the powers and duties of his office, and until he transmits to them a written declaration to the contrary, such powers and duties shall be discharged by the Vice President as Acting President.

Section 4

Whenever the Vice President and a majority of either the principal officers of the executive departments or of such other body as Congress may by law provide, transmit to the President pro tempore of the Senate and the Speaker of the House of Representatives their written declaration that the President is unable to discharge the powers and duties of his office, the Vice President shall immediately assume the powers and duties of the office as Acting President.

Thereafter, when the President transmits to the President pro tempore of the Senate and the Speaker of the House of Representatives his written declaration that no inability exists, he shall resume the powers and duties of his office unless the Vice President and a majority of either the principal officers of the executive department, or of such other body as Congress may by law provide, transmit within four days to the President pro tempore of the Senate and the Speaker of the House of Representatives their written declaration that the President is unable to discharge the powers and duties of his office. Thereupon Congress shall decide the issue, assembling within 48 hours for that purpose if not in session. If the Congress, within 21 days after receipt of the latter written declaration, or, if Congress is not in session, within 21 days after Congress is required to assemble, determines by two-thirds vote of both houses that the President is unable to discharge the powers and duties of his office, the Vice Presi-

dent shall continue to discharge the same as Acting President; otherwise, the President shall resume the powers and duties of his office.

—— (1967) Two possibilities that have been of concern to thoughtful citizens have been cared for by this amendment. One provides for the filling of a vacancy in the Vice Presidency. The other takes care of a situation involving a disabling illness of the President. Woodrow Wilson's long illness and the fact that Presidents Eisenhower and Johnson had been victims of heart attacks provided the impetus for the amendment.

Article XXVI
SUFFRAGE GRANTED TO 18-YEAR-OLDS
Section 1

The right of citizens of the United States, who are eighteen years of age or older, to vote shall not be denied or abridged by the United States or any state on account of age.

Section 2

The Congress shall have the power to enforce this article by appropriate legislation.

—— (1971) Congress in 1970 passed a law to permit voting at age eighteen in all federal, state, and local elections. The Supreme Court by a five to four vote in *Oregon* v. *Mitchell* upheld the law for federal elections but ruled the change unconstitutional for state and local elections. Faced with the confusion of differing age standards for elections commonly held at the same time, Congress on March 23, 1971, quickly proposed this amendment. Ratification was completed June 30, 1971—the shortest time elapsed for any amendment.

Table 1 Voting Requirements for State Elections[1]

STATE	RESIDENCE			REGISTRATION	
	STATE	COUNTY	PRECINCT	PERMANENT	PERIODIC
Alabama	30 days	30 days	30 days	x	
Alaska	75 days		30 days	x	
Arizona	50 days	30 days		x	
Arkansas				x	
California	30 days	30 days	30 days	x	
Colorado[2]	3 months		32 days	x	
Connecticut[3]				x	
Delaware				x	
District of Columbia				x	
Florida	60 days	60 days		x	
Georgia				x	
Hawaii				x	
Idaho	6 months	30 days		x	
Illinois	6 months		30 days	x	
Indiana	6 months	60 days	30 days	x	
Iowa	30 days	30 days	30 days	x[4]	x
Kansas	20 days	20 days	20 days	x	
Kentucky	30 days	30 days	30 days	x	
Louisiana				x	
Maine[5]	1-9 days		1-9 days (municipality)	x	
Maryland	29 days	29 days	29 days	x	
Massachusetts				x	
Michigan[6]				x	
Minnesota			30 days	x	
Mississippi	30 days	30 days	30 days	x	
Missouri	1 year	60 days	60 days	x[4]	x
Montana				x	
Nebraska				x	
Nevada	30 days	30 days	30 days	x	
New Hampshire	6 months	6 months	6 months	x	
New Jersey	40 days	40 days		x	
New Mexico[7]	42 days	42 days	42 days	x	
New York	30 days	30 days	11 days	x	
North Carolina	1 year[8]		30 days	x	
North Dakota	30 days	30 days	30 days	x	
Ohio		30 days	30 days	x[4]	
Oklahoma[9]	6 months	2 months	20 days	x	
Oregon	30 days			x	
Pennsylvania	30 days		30 days	x	
Rhode Island	30 days		30 days (municipality)	x	
South Carolina	6 months	3 months	30 days		x
South Dakota	180 days	90 days	30 days	x	
Tennessee				x	
Texas	30 days	30 days		x	
Utah	6 months	60 days		x	
Vermont	90 days	3 months	3 months	x	
Virginia				x	
Washington	30 days	30 days	30 days	x	
West Virginia	30 days	30 days	30 days	x	
Wisconsin	10 days		10 days	x[4]	
Wyoming	30 days	30 days	10 days	x	

Source: The Secretaries of State and State Boards of Elections

1 The Supreme Court ruled in March 1972 that lengthy state and local residency requirements are unconstitutional. Thirty days was suggested as an adequate time limit. State courts and legislatures were in the process of adjusting to this decision when this table was compiled.

2 A Colorado Supreme Court decision was pending in late fall of 1972 that would make 32 days the uniform residency requirement in the state.

3 A person must be a *bona fide* resident of the town in which he applies to become a voter.

4 Only in some areas of the state.

5 Ninety-day requirement if moving from within the state.

6 A voter must be a resident of Michigan and the city or township in which he is voting on or before the fifth Friday prior to any election; qualified voters may still vote if they move to another city or township in the 30 days before an election.

7 The present requirement is the result of a legislative ruling that may be tested.

8 Thirty days for President and Vice President.

9 Subject to review.

Table 2 The Presidency and the Congress

CANDIDATES	POPULAR VOTE	ELECTORAL VOTE	CONGRESS	MAJORITY PARTY	MINORITY PARTIES
1789 GEORGE WASHINGTON	—[1]	69	1st Senate	AD–17	OP–9
to *John Adams*	—	34	House	AD–38	OP–26
1792 John Jay	—	9	2nd Senate	F–16	DR–13
R. H. Harrison	—	6	House	F–37	DR–33
John Rutledge	—	6			
John Hancock	—	4			
George Clinton	·	3			
Samuel Huntington	—	2			
John Milton	—	2			
James Armstrong	—	1			
Benjamin Lincoln	—	1			
Edward Telfair	—	1			
(Not voted)	—	12			
1792 GEORGE WASHINGTON (F)	—	132	3rd Senate	F–17	DR–13
to *John Adams* (F)	—	77	House	DR–57	F–48
1796 George Clinton (DR)	—	50	4th Senate	F–19	DR–13
Thomas Jefferson	—	4	House	F–54	DR–52
Aaron Burr	—	1			
1796 JOHN ADAMS (F)	—	71	5th Senate	F–20	DR–12
to *Thomas Jefferson* (DR)	—	68	House	F–58	DR–48
1800 Thomas Pinckney (F)	—	59	6th Senate	F–19	DR–13
Aaron Burr (AF)	—	30	House	F–64	DR–42
Samuel Adams (DR)	—	15			
Oliver Ellsworth (F)	—	11			
George Clinton (DR)	—	7			
John Jay (IF)	—	5			
James Iredell (F)	—	3			
George Washington (F)	—	2			
John Henry (I)	—	2			
S. Johnston (IF)	—	2			
C. C. Pinckney (IF)	—	1			
1800 THOMAS JEFFERSON (DR)	—	73[2]	7th Senate	DR–18	F–13
to *Aaron Burr* (DR)	—	73	House	DR–69	F–36
1804 John Adams (F)	—	65	8th Senate	DR–25	F–9
C. C. Pinckney (F)	—	64	House	DR–102	F–39
John Jay (F)	—	1			
1804 THOMAS JEFFERSON (DR)	—	162	9th Senate	DR–27	F–7
to *George Clinton*[3]*			House	DR–116	F–25
1808 C. C. Pinckney (F)	—	14	10th Senate	DR–28	F–6
			House	DR–118	F–24
1808 JAMES MADISON (DR)	—	122	11th Senate	DR–28	F–6
to *George Clinton*	—	6	House	DR–94	F–48
1812 C. C. Pinckney (F)	—	47	12th Senate	DR–30	F–6
(Not voted)	—	1	House	DR–108	F–36
1812 JAMES MADISON (DR)	—	128	13th Senate	DR–27	F–9
to *Elbridge Gerry*			House	DR–112	F–68
1816 DeWitt Clinton (Fusion)	—	89	14th Senate	DR–25	F–11
(Not voted)	—	1	House	DR–117	F–65

AD–Administration   AF–Anti-Federalist   DR–Democratic Republican   F–Federalist   I–Independent   IF–Independent Federalist   OP–Opposition   President–capital letters   Vice President–*italics*

[1] In our earliest elections, the electors were chosen by the state legislatures.

[2] Election was decided in the House of Representatives.

[3] Because of the 12th Amendment, the Vice President was the President's running mate from here on.

* Clinton received 6 electoral votes for President while a vice-presidential candidate on the DR ticket.

	CANDIDATES	POPULAR VOTE	ELECTORAL VOTE	CONGRESS	MAJORITY PARTY	MINORITY PARTIES
1816 to 1820	JAMES MONROE (DR) *Daniel D. Tompkins*	—	183	15th Senate House	DR–34 DR–141	F–10 F–42
	Rufus King (F) (Not voted)	— —	34 4	16th Senate House	DR–35 DR–156	F–7 F–27
1820 to 1824	JAMES MONROE (DR) *Daniel D. Tompkins*	—	231	17th Senate House	DR–44 DR–158	F–4 F–25
	John Q. Adams (IR) (Not voted)	— —	1 3	18th Senate House	DR–44 DR–187	F–4 F–26
1824 to 1828	JOHN Q. ADAMS[4] *John C. Calhoun*	108,740	84[5]	19th Senate House	AD–26 AD–105	J–20 J–97
	Andrew Jackson Henry Clay W. H. Crawford	153,544 47,136 46,618	99 37 41	20th Senate House	J–28 J–119	AD–20 AD–94
1828 to 1832	ANDREW JACKSON (D) *John C. Calhoun*	647,286	178	21st Senate House	D–26 D–139	NR–22 NR–74
	John Q. Adams (NR)	508,064	83	22nd Senate House	D–25 D–141	NR–21; Other–2 NR–58; Other–14
1832 to 1836	ANDREW JACKSON (D) *Martin Van Buren*	687,502	219	23rd Senate House	D–20 D–147	NR–20; Other–8 AM–53; Other–60
	Henry Clay (NR) William Wirt (AM) John Floyd (NUL) (Not voted)	530,189 — — —	49 7 11 2	24th Senate House	D–27 D–145	W–25 W–98
1836 to 1840	MARTIN VAN BUREN (D) *Richard M. Johnson*	765,483	170	25th Senate House	D–30 D–108	W–18; Other–4 W–107; Other–24
	William H. Harrison (W) } Hugh L. White (W) } Daniel Webster (W) } W. P. Mangum (AJ) }	739,795[6]	73 26 14 11	26th Senate House	D–28 D–124	W–22 W–118
1840 to 1844	WILLIAM H. HARRISON[7] (W) *John Tyler*	1,274,624	234	27th Senate House	W–28 W–133	D–22; Other–2 D–102; Other–6
	Martin Van Buren (D)	1,127,781	60	28th Senate House	W–28 D–142	D–25; Other–1 W–79; Other–1
1844 to 1848	JAMES K. POLK (D) *George M. Dallas*	1,338,464	170	29th Senate House	D–31 D–143	W–25 W–77; Other–6
	Henry Clay (W) James G. Birney (L)	1,300,097 62,300	105 —	30th Senate House	D–36 W–115	W–21; Other–1 D–108; Other–4
1848 to 1852	ZACHARY TAYLOR[8] (W) *Millard Fillmore*	1,360,967	163	31st Senate House	D–35 D–112	W–25; Other–2 W–109; Other–9
	Lewis Cass (D) Martin Van Buren (FS)	1,222,342 291,263	127 —	32nd Senate House	D–35 D–140	W–24; Other–3 W–88; Other–5
1852 to 1856	FRANKLIN PIERCE (D) *William R. King*	1,601,117	254	33rd Senate House	D–38 D–159	W–22; Other–2 W–71; Other–4
	Winfield Scott (W) John P. Hale (FS)	1,385,453 155,825	42 —	34th Senate House	D–40 R–108	R–15; Other–5 D–83; Other–43

AD–Administration AJ–Anti-Jackson AM–Anti-Masonic D–Democratic DR–Democratic Republican
F–Federalist FS–Free Soil IR–Independent-Republican J–Jackson L–Liberty NR–National Republican
NUL—Nullifiers W—Whig R—Republican

[4] No distinct party designations. [5] No electoral majority; election decided in House of Representatives.

[6] Whig tickets were pledged to various candidates in various states.

[7] W. H. Harrison died in office and John Tyler became President 1840-1844.

[8] Taylor died in office and Millard Fillmore became President 1850-1852.

	CANDIDATES	POPULAR VOTE	ELECTORAL VOTE	CONGRESS	MAJORITY PARTY	MINORITY PARTIES
1856 to 1860	JAMES BUCHANAN (D) *John C. Breckinridge*	1,832,955	174	35th Senate House	D–36 D–118	R–20; Other–8 R–92; Other–26
	John C. Fremont (R) Millard Fillmore (A)	1,339,932 871,731	114 8	36th Senate House	D–36 R–114	R–26; Other–4 D–92; Other–31
1860 to 1864	ABRAHAM LINCOLN (R) *Hannibal Hamlin*	1,865,593	180	37th Senate House	R–31 R–105	D–10; Other–8 D–43; Other–30
	J. C. Breckinridge (D-S) Stephen A. Douglas (D) John Bell (CU)	848,356 1,382,713 592,906	72 12 39	38th Senate House	R–36 R–102	D–9; Other–5 D–75; Other–9
1864 to 1868	ABRAHAM LINCOLN⁹ (R) *Andrew Johnson*	2,206,938	212	39th Senate House	U–42 U–149	D–10 D–42
	George B. McClellan (D) (Not voted)	1,803,787 -	21 81	40th Senate House	R–42 R–143	D–11 D–49
1868 to 1872	ULYSSES S. GRANT (R) *Schuyler Colfax*	3,013,421	214	41st Senate House	R–56 R–149	D–11 D–63
	Horatio Seymour (D) (Not voted)	2,706,829 —	80 23	42nd Senate House	R–52 R–134	D–17; Other–5 D–104; Other–5
1872 to 1876	ULYSSES S. GRANT (R) *Henry Wilson*	3,596,745	286	43rd Senate House	R–49 R–194	D–19; Other–5 D–92; Other–14
	Horace Greeley (D) Charles O'Connor (SD) Thomas A. Hendricks (ID) B. Gratz Brown (D) Charles J. Jenkins (D) David Davis (D) (Not voted)	2,843,446 29,489 — — — — —	—¹⁰ — 42 18 2 1 17	44th Senate House	R–45 D–169	D–29; Other–2 R–109; Other–14
1876 to 1880	RUTHERFORD B. HAYES (R) *William A. Wheeler*	4,036,572	185	45th Senate House	R–39 D–153	D–36; Other–1 R–140
	Samuel J. Tilden (D) Peter Cooper (G)	4,284,020 81,737	184 —	46th Senate House	D–42 D–149	R–33; Other–1 R–130; Other–14
1880 to 1884	JAMES A. GARFIELD¹¹ (R) *Chester A. Arthur*	4,453,295	214	47th Senate House	R–37 R–147	D–37; Other–1 D–135; Other–11
	Winfield S. Hancock (D) James B. Weaver (GL) Neal Dow (Proh.)	4,414,082 308,578 10,305	155 — —	48th Senate House	R–38 D–197	D–36; Other–2 R–118; Other–10
1884 to 1888	GROVER CLEVELAND (D) *Thomas A. Hendricks*	4,879,507	219	49th Senate House	R–43 D–183	D–34 R–140; Other–2
	James G. Blaine (R) Benjamin F. Butler (GL) John P. St. John (Proh.)	4,850,293 175,370 150,369	182 — —	50th Senate House	R–39 D–169	D–37 R–152; Other–4
1888 to 1892	BENJAMIN HARRISON (R) *Levi P. Morton*	5,447,129	233	51st Senate House	R–39 R–166	D–37 D–159
	Grover Cleveland (D) Clinton B. Fisk (Proh.) Anson J. Streeter (UL)	5,537,857 249,506 146,935	168 — —	52nd Senate House	R–47 D–235	D–39; Other–2 R–88; Other–9
1892 to 1896	GROVER CLEVELAND (D) *Adlai E. Stevenson*	5,555,426	277	53rd Senate House	D–44 D–218	R–38; Other–3 R–127; Other–11
	Benjamin Harrison (R) James B. Weaver (P) John Bidwell (Proh.) Simon Wing (SL)	5,182,690 1,029,846 264,133 21,164	145 22 — —	54th Senate House	R–43 R–244	D–39; Other–6 D–105; Other–7

A–American   CU–Constitutional Union   D–Democratic   D-S–Democratic-Southern   G–Greenback   GL–Greenback Labor   ID–Independent Democratic   P–People's   Proh.–Prohibition   R–Republican   SD–Straight Democratic   SL–Socialist Labor   U–Unionist   UL–Union Labor

⁹ Lincoln was assassinated and Andrew Johnson became President 1865-1868.

¹⁰ Greeley died shortly after the election and the electors supporting him cast their votes as shown.

¹¹ Garfield was assassinated in office and Chester Arthur became President 1881-1884.

	CANDIDATES	POPULAR VOTE	ELECTORAL VOTE	CONGRESS	MAJORITY PARTY	MINORITY PARTIES
1896 to 1900	WILLIAM McKINLEY (R) *Garret A. Hobart*	7,102,246	271	55th Senate / House	R–47 / R–204	D–34; Other–7 / D–113; Other–40
	William J. Bryan (D)	6,492,559	176	56th Senate / House	R–53 / R–185	D–26; Other–8 / D–163; Other–9
	John M. Palmer (ND)	133,148	—			
	Joshua Levering (Proh.)	132,007	—			
	Charles H. Matchett (SL)	36,274	—			
	Charles E. Bentley (N)	13,969	—			
1900 to 1904	WILLIAM McKINLEY[12] (R) *Theodore Roosevelt*	7,218,491	292	57th Senate / House	R–55 / R–197	D–31; Other–4 / D–151; Other–9
	William J. Bryan (D)	6,356,734	155	58th Senate / House	R–57 / R–208	D–33 / D–178
	John C. Wooley (Proh.)	208,914	—			
	Eugene V. Debs (S)	87,814	—			
	Wharton Barker (P)	50,373	—			
	Jos. F. Malloney (SL)	39,739	—			
1904 to 1908	THEODORE ROOSEVELT (R) *Charles W. Fairbanks*	7,628,461	336	59th Senate / House	R–57 / R–250	D–33 / D–136
	Alton B. Parker (D)	5,084,223	140	60th Senate / House	R–61 / R–222	D–31 / D–164
	Eugene V. Debs (S)	402,283	—			
	Silas C. Swallow (Proh.)	258,536	—			
	Thomas E. Watson (P)	117,183	—			
	Charles H. Corregan (SL)	31,249	—			
1908 to 1912	WILLIAM H. TAFT (R) *James S. Sherman*	7,675,320	321	61st Senate / House	R–61 / R–219	D–32 / D–172
	William J. Bryan (D)	6,412,294	162	62nd Senate / House	R–51 / D–228	D–41 / R–161; Other–1
	Eugene V. Debs (S)	420,793	—			
	Eugene W. Chafin (Proh.)	253,840	—			
	Thomas L. Hisgen (I)	82,872	—			
	Thomas E. Watson (P)	29,100	—			
	August Gillhaus (SL)	14,021	—			
1912 to 1916	WOODROW WILSON (D) *Thomas R. Marshall*	6,296,547	435	63rd Senate / House	D–51 / D–291	R–44; Other–1 / R–127; Other–17
	Theodore Roosevelt (Prog.)	4,118,571	88	64th Senate / House	D–56 / D–230	R–40 / R–196; Other–9
	William H. Taft (R)	3,486,720	8			
	Eugene V. Debs (S)	900,672	—			
	Eugene W. Chafin (Proh.)	206,275	—			
	Arthur E. Reimer (SL)	28,750	—			
1916 to 1920	WOODROW WILSON (D) *Thomas R. Marshall*	9,127,695	277	65th Senate / House	D–53 / D–216	R–42 / R–210; Other–6
	Charles E. Hughes (R)	8,533,507	254	66th Senate / House	R–49 / R–240	D–47 / D–190; Other–3
	A. L. Benson (S)	585,113	—			
	J. Frank Hanly (Proh.)	220,506	—			
	Arthur E. Reimer (SL)	13,403	—			
1920 to 1924	WARREN G. HARDING[13] (R) *Calvin Coolidge*	16,143,407	404	67th Senate / House	R–59 / R–301	D–37 / D–131; Other–1
	James M. Cox (D)	9,130,328	127	68th Senate / House	R–51 / R–225	D–43; Other–2 / D–205; Other–5
	Eugene V. Debs (S)	919,799	—			
	P. P. Christensen (FL)	265,411	—			
	Aaron S. Watkins (Proh.)	189,408	—			
	James E. Ferguson (A)	48,000	—			
	W. W. Cox (SL)	31,715	—			

A–American   D–Democratic   FL–Farmer-Labor   I–Independence   N–Nationalist   ND–National Democratic
P–People's   Prog.–Progressive   Proh.–Prohibition   R–Republican   S–Socialist   SL–Socialist Labor

[12] McKinley was assassinated and Theodore Roosevelt became President 1901-1904.

[13] Harding died in office and Calvin Coolidge became President 1923-1924.

	CANDIDATES	POPULAR VOTE	ELECTORAL VOTE	CONGRESS	MAJORITY PARTY	MINORITY PARTIES
1924 to 1928	CALVIN COOLIDGE (R)	15,718,211	382	69th Senate	R–56	D–39; Other–1
	Charles G. Dawes			House	R–247	D 183; Other–4
	John W. Davis (D)	8,385,283	136	70th Senate	R–49	D–46; Other–1
	Robert M. LaFollette (Prog.)	4,831,289	13	House	R–237	D–195; Other–3
	Herman P. Faris (Proh.)	57,520	—			
	Frank T. Johns (SL)	36,428	—			
	William Z. Foster (W)	36,386	—			
	Gilbert O. Nations (A)	23,967	—			
1928 to 1932	HERBERT C. HOOVER (R)	21,391,993	444	71st Senate	R–56	D–39; Other–1
	Charles Curtis			House	R–267	D–167; Other–1
	Alfred E. Smith (D)	15,016,169	87	72nd Senate	R–48	D–47; Other–1
	Norman Thomas (S)	267,835	—	House	D–220	R–214; Other–1
	Verne L. Reynolds (SL)	21,603	—			
	William Z. Foster (W)	21,181	—			
	William F. Varney (Proh.)	20,106	—			
1932 to 1936	FRANKLIN D. ROOSEVELT (D)	22,809,638	472	73rd Senate	D–60	R–35; Other–1
	John N. Garner			House	D–310	R–117; Other–5
	Herbert C. Hoover (R)	15,758,901	59	74th Senate	D–69	R–25; Other–2
	Norman Thomas (S)	881,951	—	House	D–319	R–103; Other–10
	William Z. Foster (Comm.)	102,785	—			
	William D. Upshaw (Proh.)	81,869	—			
	William H. Harvey (L)	53,425	—			
	Verne L. Reynolds (SL)	33,276	—			
1936 to 1940	FRANKLIN D. ROOSEVELT (D)	27,752,869	523	75th Senate	D–76	R–16; Other–4
	John N. Garner			House	D–331	R–89; Other–13
	Alfred M. Landon (R)	16,674,665	8	76th Senate	D–69	R–23; Other–4
	William Lemke (U)	882,479	—	House	D–261	R–164; Other–4
	Norman Thomas (S)	187,720	—			
	Earl Browder (Comm.)	80,159	—			
	D. Leigh Colvin (Proh.)	37,847	—			
	John W. Aiken (SL)	12,777	—			
1940 to 1944	FRANKLIN D. ROOSEVELT (D)	27,307,819	449	77th Senate	D–66	R–28; Other–2
	Henry A. Wallace			House	D–268	R–162; Other–5
	Wendell L. Willkie (R)	22,321,018	82	78th Senate	D–58	R–37; Other–1
	Norman Thomas (S)	99,557	—	House	D–218	R–208; Other–4
	Roger Q. Babson (Proh.)	57,812	—			
	Earl Browder (Comm.)	46,251	—			
	John W. Aiken (SL)	14,892	—			
1944 to 1948	FRANKLIN D. ROOSEVELT[14] (D)	25,606,585	432	79th Senate	D–56	R–38; Other–1
	Harry S. Truman			House	D–242	R–190; Other–2
	Thomas E. Dewey (R)	22,014,745	99	80th Senate	R–51	D–45
	Norman Thomas (S)	80,518	—	House	R–245	D–188; Other–1
	Claude A. Watson (Proh.)	74,758	—			
	Edward A. Teichert (SL)	45,336	—			
1948 to 1952	HARRY S. TRUMAN (D)	24,105,812	303	81st Senate	D 54	R–42
	Alben W. Barkley			House	D–263	R–171; Other–1
	Thomas E. Dewey (R)	21,970,065	189	82nd Senate	D–49	R–47
	Strom Thurmond (SR)	1,169,063	39	House	D–234	R–199; Other–1
	Henry Wallace (Prog.)	1,157,172	—			
	Norman Thomas (S)	139,414	—			
	Claude A. Watson (Proh.)	103,224	—			
	Edward A. Teichert (SL)	29,244	—			
	Farrell Dobbs (SW)	13,613	—			

A–American   Comm.–Communist   D–Democratic   L–Liberty   Prog.–Progressive   Proh.–Prohibition
R–Republican   S–Socialist   SL–Socialist Labor   SR–States' Rights   SW–Socialist Workers   U–Union   W–Workers
[14] Franklin D. Roosevelt died in office and Harry S. Truman became President 1945-1948.

	CANDIDATES	POPULAR VOTE	ELECTORAL VOTE	CONGRESS	MAJORITY PARTY	MINORITY PARTIES
1952 to 1956	DWIGHT D. EISENHOWER (R)	33,936,234	442	83rd Senate House	R–48 R–221	D–47; Other–1 D–211; Other–1
	Richard M. Nixon			84th Senate House	D–48 D–232	R–47; Other–1 R–203
	Adlai E. Stevenson (D)	27,314,992	89			
	Vincent Hallinan (Prog.)	140,023	—			
	Stuart Hamblen (Proh.)	72,949	—			
	Eric Hass (SL)	30,267	—			
	Darlington Hoopes (S)	20,203	—			
	Douglas A. MacArthur (Const.)	17,205	—			
	Farrell Dobbs (SW)	10,312	—			
1956 to 1960	DWIGHT D. EISENHOWER (R)	35,590,472	457	85th Senate House	D–49 D–233	R–47 R–200
	Richard M. Nixon			86th Senate House	D–64 D–283	R–34 R–153
	Adlai E. Stevenson (D)	26,022,752	73			
	T. Coleman Andrews (SR)	107,929	—			
	Eric Hass (SL)	44,300	—			
	Enoch A. Holtwick (Proh.)	41,937	—			
1960 to 1964	JOHN F. KENNEDY[15] (D)	34,227,000	303	87th Senate House	D–65 D–263	R–35 R–174
	Lyndon B. Johnson			88th Senate House	D–67 D–258	R–33 R–177
	Richard M. Nixon (R)	34,108,000	219			
	Eric Hass (SL)	46,560	—			
	Rutherford Decker (Proh.)	46,203	—			
	Orville Faubus (SR)	44,977	—			
	Farrell Dobbs (SW)	39,541	—			
1964 to 1968	LYNDON B. JOHNSON (D)	43,129,000	486	89th Senate House	D–68 D–295	R–32 R–140
	Hubert H. Humphrey			90th Senate House	D–64 D–246	R–36 R–187
	Barry Goldwater (R)	27,178,000	52			
	Eric Hass (SL)	45,186	—			
	Clifton DeBerry (SW)	32,705	—			
	E. Harold Munn (Proh.)	23,267	—			
1968 to 1972	RICHARD M. NIXON (R)	31,785,480	301	91st Senate House	D–57 D–243	R–43 R–192
	Spiro T. Agnew			92nd Senate	D–54	R–44
	Hubert H. Humphrey (D)	31,275,166	191		C–1	I–1
	George C. Wallace (AI)	9,906,473	46	House	D–255	R–179
	Henning A. Blomen (SL)	52,588	—		V–1	
	Dick Gregory (NP)	47,133	—			
	Fred Halstead (SW)	41,389	—			
	Eldridge Cleaver (PAF)	36,385	—			
	Eugene McCarthy	26,553	—			
	E. Harold Munn (Proh.)	15,123	—			
1972 to 1976	RICHARD M. NIXON (R)	45,287,197	521	93rd Senate House	D–57 D–241	R–43 R–192
	Spiro T. Agnew				I–1	PAF–1
	George S. McGovern (D)	28,160,419	17			
	John Schmitz (A)	1,064,159	—			
	Benjamin Spock (P)	74,014	—			

A–American   AI–American Independent   C–Conservative   Const.–Constitution   D–Democratic
I–Independent   NP–New Party   NPol–New Politics   P–Peoples   PAF–Peace and Freedom
Prog.–Progressive   Proh.–Prohibition   R–Republican   S–Socialist   SL–Socialist Labor
SR–States' Rights   SW–Socialist Workers   V–Vacancy
[15]John F. Kennedy assassinated and Lyndon B. Johnson became President 1963-1964.

Table 3 State Legislatures

STATE	YEARS IN WHICH SESSIONS ARE HELD	LIMIT ON LENGTH OF SESSION	NUMBER IN SENATE	NUMBER IN HOUSE	TERM OF SENATORS (YEARS)	TERM OF REPRE-SENTATIVES (YEARS)	SALARY OF MEMBERS (DOLLARS)
Alabama	odd	36 days	35	106	4	4	300 per month[1]
Alaska	annual	none	20	40	4	2	6,000 annual[2]
Arizona	annual	none	30	60	2	2	6,000 annual[3]
Arkansas	odd	60 days	35	100	4	2	1,200 annual[4]
California	annual	none	40	80	4	2	19,200 annual[5]
Colorado	annual	none	35	65	4	2	7,600 annual
Connecticut	annual	150 days (odd years) 90 days (even years)	36[6]	177	2	2	3,250 biennial[7]
Delaware	annual	180 days	21	41	4	2	6,000 annual
Florida	annual	60 days	40	120	4	2	12,000 annual[3]
Georgia	annual	45 days (odd years) 40 days (even years)	56	180	2	2	4,200 annual[8]
Hawaii	annual	60 days	25	51	4	2	12,000 annual[9]
Idaho	annual	60 days	35	70	2	2	10 per day[2]
Illinois	annual	no limit	59	177	4	2	17,500 annual
Indiana	annual	none	50	100	4	2	6,000 annual
Iowa	annual	none	50	100	4	2	40 per day[10]
Kansas	annual	90 days (odd years) 60 days (even years)	40	125	4	2	10 per day[11]
Kentucky	even	60 days	38	100	4	2	25 per day[12]
Louisiana	annual	30 days (odd years) 60 days (even years)	39	105	4	4	50 per day[13]
Maine	odd	none	33	151	2	2	2,500[14]
Maryland	annual	90 days	43[15]	142	4	4	11,000 annual
Massachusetts	annual	none	40	240	2	2	11,400 annual[16]
Michigan	annual	none	38	110	4	2	15,000 annual[17]
Minnesota	odd	120 days	67	134	4	2	4,800 annual
Mississippi	annual	125 days (every 4th year) 90 days (others)	52	122	4	4	5,000 annual[18]
Missouri	odd	180 days	34	163	4	2	8,400 annual
Montana	odd[19]	60 days	50	100	4	2	20 per day[8]
Nebraska	annual	60 days (even years) 90 days (odd years)	49-member unicameral			4	400 per month
Nevada	odd	60 days	20	40	4	2	40 per day[8]
New Hampshire	odd	90 days or July 1	24	400	2	2	200 biennial[20]
New Jersey	annual	none	40	80	4	2	10,000 annual
New Mexico	annual	60 days (odd years) 30 days (even years)	42	70	4	2	40 per day
New York	annual	none	60	150	2	2	15,000 annual

STATE	YEARS IN WHICH SESSIONS ARE HELD	LIMIT ON LENGTH OF SESSION	NUMBER IN SENATE	NUMBER IN HOUSE	TERM OF SENATORS (YEARS)	TERM OF REPRESENTATIVES (YEARS)	SALARY OF MEMBERS (DOLLARS)
North Carolina	odd	none	50	120	2	2	2,400 annual[21]
North Dakota	odd	60 days	51	102	4	2	5 per day[22]
Ohio	annual	none	33	99	4	2	12,750 annual
Oklahoma	annual	90 days	48	101	4	2	8,400 annual
Oregon	odd	none	30	60	4	2	275 per month[23]
Pennsylvania	annual	continuous	50	203	4	2	7,200 annual[24]
Rhode Island	annual	60 days[25]	50	100	2	2	5 per day[20]
South Carolina	annual	none	46	124	4	2	4,000 annual[26]
South Dakota	annual	30 days (even years) 45 days (odd years)	35	70	2	2	3,000 biennial
Tennessee	odd	90 days	33	99	4	2	3,600 annual[27]
Texas	odd	140 days	31	150	4	2	4,800 annual[28]
Utah	odd[29]	60 days	29	75	4	2	25 per day[26]
Vermont	odd	none	30	150	2	2	150 per week[30]
Virginia	annual	60 days[31] (even years) 30 days (odd years)	40	100	4	2	5,475 annual
Washington	odd	60 days	49	98	4	2	3,600 annual[8]
West Virginia	annual	60 days	34	100	4	2	3,300 annual[32]
Wisconsin	odd	none	33	99	4	2	8,900 annual
Wyoming	odd	40 days	30	62	4	2	15 per day[5]

Source: The Secretaries of State and State Boards of Elections

NOTES FOR TABLE 3

[1] Plus $30 per day while in session.
[2] Plus $35 per day while in session.
[3] Expense allowance regulated by statute. (Florida: legislative pay may be regulated by statute.)
[4] Reimbursable interim expense account which for 1972-1973 could not exceed $1,200 per member.
[5] Plus $26 per day travel and expense allowance while in session. ($25 for Wyoming)
[6] Number of senators and representatives in litigation in late 1972.
[7] Salaries changed with the election of new members in 1972.
[8] Plus $25 per day while in session; $40 for Washington while in session.
[9] Plus $750 annual allowance; plus $20 per day for non-Oahu legislators.
[10] Compensation and expense allowance may be established by statute.
[11] Plus $35 per day expenses while in session; $200 per month while not in session; mileage allowance.
[12] Plus $300 monthly expense account when not in session; $25 per day when in session.
[13] Plus $6,000 annually for expenses.
[14] In first year of biennium; $1,000 in second year.
[15] Constitutional amendment pending to change the number of members in both houses.
[16] Plus expenses.
[17] Plus $3,000 expense allowance.
[18] Plus $100 per month when not in session; $12.50 expense allowance per day for 90 legislative days.
[19] New constitution with a provision for annual sessions being considered in late 1972.
[20] Plus mileage allowance.
[21] $600 expense allowance plus $25 per day when in session.
[22] Plus $20 per day for first 60 days of session; $35 per month thereafter.
[23] Plus $20 per day while in session; $100 per month when not in session.
[24] Plus $4,800 per year for clerical help.
[25] Session may be continued beyond this time without pay.
[26] Plus $15 per day expenses while in session. (South Carolina: not to exceed 45 days.)
[27] Plus $30 per day while in session and mileage between home and capital for one round trip.
[28] Plus $12 per day for first 120 days of regular session and 30 days of special session plus mileage.
[29] In even years the budget session lasts 20 days.
[30] Plus expenses and mileage not to exceed $4,500 for a regular session.
[31] Session may be continued for an additional 30 days.
[32] $25 per day plus one round trip between home and capital per week; an additional $35 per day for extraordinary sessions.

Table 4 The Use of Initiative and Referendum in the Making of State Laws

STATES USING	INITIATIVE*		REFERENDUM			
	VOTERS' SIGNATURES FOR PETITIONS	VOTE REQUIRED FOR ENACTMENT	SUBMISSION BY		VOTERS' SIGNATURES FOR PETITIONS	VOTE REQUIRED FOR ENACTMENT
			PETITION	LEGISLATURE		
Alaska	10%[1]	majority	x		10%	majority
Arizona	10%[2]	majority	x	x	5%	majority
Arkansas	8%[3]	majority	x		6%	majority
California	5%[3]	majority	x		5%	majority
Colorado	8%[3]	majority	x	x	5%	majority
Hawaii	Does not use			x		majority
Idaho	10%	majority	x	x	10%	majority
Kentucky	Does not use			x		majority
Maine	10%	plurality	x	x	10%	plurality
Maryland	Does not use		x		3%	majority
Massachusetts	3%	majority + 30% of total votes cast at election	x		1½-2%	majority
Michigan	8%	majority	x	x	5%	majority
Missouri	5%[4]	⅔ of congressional districts	x	x	8%	majority
Montana	8%[5]	majority	x	x	5%	majority
Nebraska	7%[6]	majority	x		5%[7]	majority
Nevada	10%	majority	x		10%	majority
New Hampshire	Does not use			x		majority[8]
New Jersey	Does not use			x		majority
New Mexico	Does not use				10%	majority
North Dakota	10,000[9]	majority	x		7,000	majority
Ohio	6%[10]	majority	x		6%	majority
Oklahoma	8%[2]	majority	x	x	5%	majority
Oregon	6%[3]	majority	x	x	4%	majority
South Dakota	5%	majority	x		5%	majority
Texas	Does not use		To be proposed in party platform			
Utah	10%	majority	x		10%	majority
Washington	8%	majority	x	x	4%	majority
Wisconsin			May be placed on ballot by legislature			
Wyoming	15%	majority	x		15%	majority

Source: The Secretaries of State and the State Boards of Elections

* Fifteen states have procedures for constitutional amendment by initiative: Arizona, Arkansas, California, Colorado, Florida, Illinois, Massachusetts, Michigan, Missouri, Nebraska, Nevada, North Dakota, Ohio, Oklahoma, Oregon.

[1] Actually 10% of those who voted in the preceding general election and resident in at least ⅔ of the election districts in the state.

[2] 15% for amendments to the constitution.

[3] 8% for amendments to the constitution. (Colorado: 8% of those who voted for the Secretary of State.)

[4] Constitutional change pending adoption would change the figure to 8% of the legal voters in each of ⅔ of congressional districts for initiative and 5% for referendum. Constitutional amendment by initiative would be allowed.

[5] Constitutional change pending adoption would change the figures to 5% from ⅓ of the legislative districts for both.

[6] This 7% figure must also include the distribution factor of at least 5% of the electors of each of ⅖ of the counties of the state. Petitions for constitutional amendment require 10% of the voters and the same distribution factor as above. The whole number of votes cast for Governor at the general election next preceding the filing of an initiative or referendum petition shall be the basis on which the number of signatures to such petition shall be computed.

[7] If the purpose of the referendum is to suspend the enactment of a law prior to the voting upon such referendum, the petitions must contain the number of signatures equal to 10% of the votes cast for governor at the last preceding general election. The distribution factor remains the same as in the case of initiative petitions.

[8] ⅔ of the votes cast for constitutional amendments.

[9] 20,000 for constitutional amendment.

[10] 10% for constitutional amendment.

Table 5 Term of Office and Pay of Governors

STATE	TERM IN YEARS[1]	ANNUAL SALARY	OFFICIAL RESIDENCE	STATE	TERM IN YEARS[1]	ANNUAL SALARY	OFFICIAL RESIDENCE
Alabama	4	$25,000	Yes	Montana	4	25,000	Yes
Alaska	4 (2)	40,000	Yes	Nebraska	4 (2)	25,000	Yes
Arizona	4	35,000	No	Nevada	4	25,000	Yes
Arkansas	2	10,000	Yes	New Hampshire	2	30,000	Yes
California	4	49,100	Yes	New Jersey	4 (2)	50,000	Yes
Colorado	4	40,000	Yes	New Mexico	4 (2)	26,000	Yes
Connecticut	4	35,000	Yes	New York	4	85,000	Yes
Delaware	4 (2)[3]	35,000	Yes	North Carolina	4[2]	35,000	Yes
Florida	4 (2)	36,000	Yes	North Dakota	4	18,000	Yes
Georgia	4[2]	42,500	Yes	Ohio	4 (2)	40,000	Yes
Hawaii	4	42,000	Yes	Oklahoma	4	35,000	Yes
Idaho	4	30,000	Yes	Oregon	4 (2)	29,500[4]	No
Illinois	4	45,000	Yes	Pennsylvania	4 (2)	45,000	Yes
Indiana	4	36,000	Yes	Rhode Island	2	30,000	No
Iowa	2	30,000	Yes	South Carolina	4[2]	35,000	Yes
Kansas	2	20,000	Yes	South Dakota	2 (2)	25,000	Yes
Kentucky	4[2]	30,000	Yes	Tennessee	4[2]	30,000	Yes
Louisiana	4 (2)	26,374	Yes	Texas	2	63,000	Yes
Maine	4 (2)	20,000	Yes	Utah	4	30,000	Yes
Maryland	4 (2)	25,000	Yes	Vermont	2	30,000	No
Massachusetts	4	40,000	No	Virginia	4[2]	35,000	Yes
Michigan	4	40,000	Yes	Washington	4	32,500[5]	Yes
Minnesota	4	35,000	Yes	West Virginia	4[2]	25,000	Yes
Mississippi	4[2]	35,000	Yes	Wisconsin	4	25,000	Yes
Missouri	4 (2)[3]	37,500	Yes	Wyoming	4	25,000	Yes

Source: The Secretaries of State and the State Boards of Elections

[1] Numbers in parentheses indicate the maximum number of consecutive terms permitted; states without numbers have no restrictions on the number of terms the governor may serve.
[2] Governor may not serve an immediate successive term.
[3] Governor limited to an absolute total of two terms, which may or may not be consecutive.
[4] Plus $1,000 monthly for expenses.
[5] Plus $16,500 for mansion expenses.

GLOSSARY

absentee voting—a system by which a person who cannot be present at his regular voting place on election day may vote beforehand or by mail.

abstain—to be present but not voting.

acquittal—the act of setting free by declaring a person not guilty.

activist—a person emphasizing vigorous political action.

administrative budget—budget system used by the federal government until fiscal year 1968; it omitted trust funds from expenditures and receipts.

admiralty—dealing with affairs of the sea and ships; referring to the law of the sea and ships.

alien—a person who is not a citizen of the country in which he lives.

all deliberate speed—a phrase from a Supreme Court decision indicating that integration of schools should proceed without undue delay.

ambassador—the highest official representative of one country to another.

amendment—a change or alteration; a formal addition to a constitution, making a change in the structure or operation of government.

anarchist—a person who believes in a society without government or laws and who sometimes tries to overthrow established governments.

annuity—regular monthly or yearly payments to an individual from a fund to which the individual has made prior payments.

appeal—a request to have a law case taken to a higher court to be heard again.

appellate jurisdiction—the right of a court to hear cases that have been appealed.

apportion—to divide into proportional shares; to distribute the 435 memberships in the House of Representatives among the states.

appropriation—amount of expenditures specifically designated by Congress for an agency or program.

arbitration—the process by which one or more persons settle a dispute.

arson—the crime of purposely setting fire to property.

assessment—value placed on real and personal property for tax purposes.

audit—to examine and check accounts.

auditor—officer who authorizes the expenditure of state funds according to law and audits state accounts.

authoritarianism—governmental system in which the people are forced to give unquestioned obedience to the person or group in power.

authorization—amount of money stated in an act, all, part, or none of which may actually be appropriated for the program by Congress in later acts.

autonomous—independent; having self-government.

balance of power—the distribution of power among nations so that no one nation or group of nations can dominate others.

balanced legislature—a lawmaking body in which members of the lower house are selected by population apportionment but those in the upper house are selected from geographic areas.

bankruptcy—the condition of being unable to pay one's debts.

bicameral—a legislature with two branches or houses.

bid—the price at which a person or an organization will sell an item or service.

bill of attainder—a law passed to punish a person without giving him a judicial trial.

bipartisan—representing two political parties.

blighted area—a neighborhood that is run-down, dirty, and gradually being destroyed; a slum.

bond—a contract by which a bonding or insurance agency guarantees that it will repay the city, county, or state for any financial loss because of dishonest or wrongful acts of an employee.

borough—a unit of local government; the term used for a county in Alaska.

boss—a leader of a political party who controls the organization of the party for personal gain.

boycott—to join together with others to stop buying the products of a certain business; an attempt by a labor group to force an employer to meet its requests by joint agreement not to buy the company's products.

budget—a plan showing the expected income and the proposed expenditures of government.

bureau—an office; a division of a governmental agency.

bureaucrat—an official, usually appointed, who administers an agency or bureau of the government.

capitalism—economic system based on the private ownership of the means of production and distribution.

categorical aid—help for a specially designated group or classification.

caucus—meeting of members of a political party to nominate candidates or to agree on a position on an issue.

census—an official counting of the people, farms, business places, children of school age, or other groupings of a nation, state, or community.

challenge—the right of a lawyer to object to the qualifications of a prospective juror.

charge—the instructions the judge gives to a jury.

charter—a written document similar to a constitution; a statement of the rules and regulations and source of power under which a local government or a corporation operates.

check and balance—a system by which each branch of government has influence over other branches.

citizen—a person who is a member of a state or nation, owing it allegiance and entitled to full civil rights.

civil case—a legal dispute involving two or more citizens.

clearing house—an agency for collecting, classifying, and distributing information.

cloture—a system by which debate in the United States Senate can be ended by vote of two-thirds of the senators present and voting.

coalition—a joining together into a combination or alliance.

Cold War—the conflict between communist and noncommunist nations carried on by propaganda, economic rivalry, spy activities, and political pressures without actually engaging in armed war.

collective bargaining—the process by which labor and management representatives work out agreements.

commission—the group of persons elected to operate the city government and to make its laws under the commission form of government.

common carrier—a transportation company carrying passengers for a fee.

common law—the unwritten laws of a nation based on court decisions and custom; the law and decisions of the courts in England.

Common Market—a group of western European nations organized to promote trade among themselves, especially by reducing tariff barriers.

communism—system of government in which the state has supremacy over the rights of the individual, and the government owns the means of production and distribution.

community college—a college or junior college sponsored by a local area and fitting its offerings to the community's needs.

commutation—a change of a court sentence to one that is less severe, usually from a death sentence to life imprisonment.

compact—an agreement between two or more parties.

compromise—a settlement in which each side in a dispute makes concessions, each giving up some of its demands.

concurrent jurisdiction—the right of two or more courts to hear a legal case.

confederation—a joining of independent nations or states by a treaty or alliance for joint action (as for common defense). In a confederation each nation or state retains sovereign power; in a federation the nations or states give up some power to the new union.

conference committee—a special joint committee from both houses of a legislature that attempts to make bills alike.

Congressional Record—the official publication containing a complete daily account of all the business conducted by Congress.

congressional township—a geographic subdivision of a county, usually thirty-six square miles in area.

conservation—the preservation and wise use of the nation's natural resources.

consolidation—combining into one; the uniting of several units of local government into one larger unit; merger.

constable—police officer of a town, township, or village.

constitution—the system of fundamental laws or principles under which a government operates.

constitutional home rule—home rule granted to local governments under the state constitution.

constitutionality—the quality or state of being in accord with or consistent with a constitution.

consul—a member of the Foreign Service who assists American citizens and businesses in foreign countries in matters affecting their business and commercial interests.

containment—a foreign policy that attempts to keep communism within its present boundaries.

contiguous—in close contact; touching; near.

copyright—the exclusive right of author, composer, or artist to publish, reproduce, and sell books, pamphlets, and other written, musical, and artistic works.

coroner—county officer who investigates deaths under unusual or unnatural circumstances or where no doctor was in attendance.

corporation—a group of individuals who have a charter granting them permission to operate a business with privileges and liabilities as a group and not as individuals.

corrupt practice—a dishonest act; a morally weak act; an improper political or legal act.

council—the legislative branch of city government, especially in the mayor-council type of government.

county—a unit of local government; a subdivision of a state.

courts-martial—courts made up of military officers to try those accused of violating military law.

creative federalism—a working partnership among federal, state, and local governments.

criminal case—a court action in which a person is accused of breaking a law; one in which a wrong has been done against the whole community.

criminologist—person who makes a scientific study of crimes and criminals.

crop rotation—changing of crops from year to year to preserve the chemical balance of the soil.

cross-examination—the questioning of a witness of the opposite side in a lawsuit.

curfew—a time beyond which the civilian population or certain groups, such as children, may not be on the streets.

dark horse—a person unexpectedly nominated for a public office; one who has had only a slight chance of being nominated to public office.

deduction—amount allowed to be subtracted from income in figuring taxes.

deed—a document transferring ownership from one person to another.

de facto segregation—actual separation of the races, as by residential patterns.

de jure segregation—separation of the races by law, by legal means.

defendant—the party being accused; the person on trial.

deferment—the official postponement of being drafted for military service.

deficit—the difference between income and expenditures when the latter is larger.

democracy—government by direct participation of the people.

direct primary—the first election, to decide which of several persons will run for an office.

disadvantaged—persons who are now living, or have lived, under unfavorable conditions.

dissenting opinion—a statement written by a judge or justice who disagrees with the opinion of the majority.

disarmament—the reduction or limitation of military equipment and forces.

docket—a list of court cases.

draft—to select for military service from the eligible group.

earmark—to set aside for a specific purpose; for example, to require that the income from certain taxes be used for the construction of highways.

elastic clause—the "necessary and proper" clause of the Constitution.

electoral college—group of electors from each state who choose the President and Vice President in December after the popular election.

elitism—system in which one individual or small group is superior to the other people, or assumes this superiority.

embassy—the official office or residence of an ambassador in a foreign country.

en banc—all judges of a court are present to hear a case. (A word from the French meaning "on the bench.")

environment—conditions or circumstances surrounding a person or place.

erosion—the wearing away and loss of soil.

excise tax—a tax on the manufacture, sale, or use of an item.

executive—the branch or part of the government which enforces the law and carries out or performs governmental activities.

executive agreement—a formal agreement between the President and the heads of one or more nations which does not require approval by the Senate.

exemption—amount allowed to be subtracted from income for each person dependent on the income in figuring taxes.

ex post facto—a law passed to punish a person for acts that were not illegal before the passage of the law.

expressed power—a specific power given to Congress by the Constitution; an enumerated power.

extradition—the process of turning over a criminal or a person accused of a crime from one state to another; interstate rendition.

federal system—a union of nations or states under a central government; a federation.

felony—a serious crime such as murder, kidnapping, or theft.

filibuster—a scheme whereby one senator, or a small group of senators, may talk against a bill for so long that all business of the Senate is stopped.

fiscal year—the year that a government uses for financial purposes; July 1 to June 30 for the federal government.

flood control—system of keeping water in the river basin to prevent flooding of land and destruction of property.

foreign service—the agency of the State Department that includes the official representatives of the United States to other nations.

franking—the privilege of sending mail without cost.

free enterprise—the economic system in which first reliance is placed on private business operating in competitive markets.

full faith and credit—the principle that the acts, records, and judicial proceedings of one state shall be honored in another state.

general welfare—the state of well-being of the public as a whole; the common good.

gerrymander—an unfair division of legislative districts to give one political party greater power.

ghetto—a section of a city in which members of a minority racial, religious, or nationality group are forced to live because of social or economic pressures; usually a poor and depressed area.

graduated tax rate—a rate of taxation that increases as income increases.

grand jury—a jury that decides whether or not there is enough evidence to think that an accused person might be guilty.

grandfather clause—a voting eligibility provision requiring high standards of reading and ownership of considerable property except for descendants of men voting before 1867.

grant-in-aid—money provided by one unit of government to help another unit to carry on some service.

gross national product—the dollar value of all goods and services produced in a country in a given year.

gubernatorial—relating to the governor or his office.

guerrillas—fighters in an undeclared, irregular war who operate as more or less independent individuals or small groups.

habeas corpus—an order of the court requiring that an imprisoned person be brought before the court to determine whether his imprisonment is legal.

home rule—power granted by a state to its cities to write their own charters and to change them without approval from the legislature.

honest graft—taking money or accepting a favor, which is legally right but morally wrong, by a person in a political position.

hung jury—one in which the jurors cannot agree upon a decision.

immigrant—a person who leaves one nation to reside in another.

immunity—freedom; to be free from arrest for a crime.

impeach—to make an official accusation against a public official for improper conduct.

imperialism—the policy of one nation's gaining control over other nations, including the acquiring of colonies or dependencies.

implied power—a power that is not directly specified; a power derived from the "necessary and proper" clause.

inauguration—a formal ceremony at which an elected official takes office.

incorporate—to receive the right to carry on the functions of local government, such as levying taxes.

indict—to accuse; to bring to trial in order to determine guilt or innocence.

indictment—a statement formally accusing a person of a crime.

indirect tax—a tax not paid directly to the government by the taxpayer.

induction—the formal entry of a civilian into military service.

infiltration—the gradual, and usually secret, entry into an organization or agency with the intention of gaining control.

inflation—the increase in the cost of goods and services caused by the decreased purchasing power of the dollar.

initiative—the method by which citizens, outside the legislature, can propose a law or amendment.

injunction—a court order forbidding certain activities, such as a strike or a violation of a contract.

inquest—an investigation or hearing, conducted by a coroner, into the circumstances of death from unnatural causes.

interest group—an organization of persons who have some common interest; a pressure group.

internal revenue—income of the government from domestic, not foreign, sources.

internal security—freedom from danger, risk, or fear of individuals or organizations within a country.

interstate compact—a written agreement between two or more states that has been approved by Congress.

isolation—a foreign policy advocating that the United States stay out of conflicts between other nations; nonparticipation in international affairs.

item veto—the power of an executive to refuse to approve parts of a bill.

Jim Crow law—measure designed to prevent Negroes and whites from intermingling in public places.

judicial—the branch or part of the government which interprets laws and administers justice.

judicial review—the right of a court to determine whether a law or an act is constitutional.

junkets—pleasure trips; disguised vacations.

jurisdiction—the control, power, or authority to apply the law.

kangaroo court—an irregularly conducted court which disregards legal procedures.

keynote address—the first major speech at a national political convention stating the policies of the party.

laissez-faire—system in which the government does not interfere with the operation of business in any way; to do as one pleases.

lame duck—a person defeated or not running for public office but completing the balance of his term.

land-grant college—a college established with the help of a federal land grant to encourage the study of agriculture and mechanical arts.

law of supply and demand—condition under which the market operates in the free enterprise system.

legislative—the lawmaking branch of government.

legislative council—a permanent research committee of a legislature which meets continuously even when the legislature is not in session.

legislative home rule—home rule granted to local governments by the state legislature.

legislator—a member of a lawmaking body.

liberal arts—subjects of the college curriculum which are not part of the professional or technical curriculum.

liberty—freedom from arbitrary or despotic choice.

limited monarchy—a form of government in which the supreme power of a hereditary ruler is limited by laws or a constitution.

lobbying—efforts to influence the members of a legislature.

lobbyist—the paid agent of an interest group.

lockout—refusal of an industry to permit employees to come into its buildings to work until they agree to its terms.

logrolling—a legislative practice of trading votes; an informal agreement between two legislators to vote for each other's bills.

long ballot—a ballot containing many offices, candidates, and issues.

majority opinion—a statement written by a judge or justice expressing the opinion of the majority.

majority rule—the political principle that the greater number (usually one more than 50 per cent) shall have the power to make decisions.

mandamus—a court order compelling a person to do something.

matching fund—a grant which requires the receiver to pay a certain percentage of the total amount.

mediation—the process by which one or more persons, selected to assist in settling a dispute, make suggestions or offer compromises, as for example, in a labor dispute.

mediator—a person or a group who makes suggestions or offers compromises to settle a dispute; for example, a labor dispute between a union and an industrial concern.

Medicare—medical care program of the federal government.

megalopolis—an urban region consisting of metropolitan areas with their large cities and many towns and suburbs.

metropolitan area—a central city and the surrounding suburban communities.

militarism—the tendency to put affairs of the armed forces or of war ahead of other matters; a warlike spirit.

minority—less than half; a group that is a small but important portion of the total population.

misdemeanor—a minor crime.

moderator—presiding officer of a town meeting.

monarchy—system of government with a hereditary chief of state—usually king, queen, or emperor.

monopoly—complete control of a service or the production of a commodity.

national security—freedom from danger, risk, or fear from within or outside a country.

naturalization—a process by which an alien becomes a citizen.

neutrality—the foreign policy of a nation which refuses to take sides or participate in conflicts between other nations.

nominate—to select a person to be a candidate for a public office.

nonpartisan—not associated with political parties; no party affiliation.

nonviolence—refraining from the use of violence as a matter of principle.

office-column ballot—the arrangement of candidates on a ballot by the offices for which they are running.

open door—the policy of allowing all nations to engage in activities with other nations on equal terms; the policy of the United States toward China in the early part of this century.

open housing—situation in which the sale and rental of houses is available to people of all groups, in which there is no discrimination in regard to race, religion, or nationality.

ordinance—a law or regulation passed by a unit of local government.

organ—one of the major branches of a governing organization, especially of the United Nations.

original jurisdiction—the right to hear a case for the first time.

panel—the group of persons who have been called for jury service.

pardon—release from punishment for a crime; forgiveness.

parish—the term used for a county in Louisiana.

parity—equality; a system whereby a farmer receives a price for his products which gives him the same purchasing power he would have had in a base year or years.

parliamentarian—an expert in the rules and customs of a legislative body.

parliamentary—system of democratic government which does not have separation of powers but places the power in the legislature.

party-column ballot—the arrangement of candidates on a ballot by parties.

passport—a document issued by the government giving a citizen permission to travel in foreign countries.

patent—the exclusive right of an inventor to manufacture and sell the invention.

patronage—the jobs or favors which are given by a person in politics.

persona grata—a person who is welcome in a foreign country as an official representative of his country.

persona non grata—a person who is unwelcome in a foreign country; an official representative of a country who is to be recalled by his government at the request of the foreign government.

petit jury—a jury that determines the guilt or innocence in a criminal case or the right or wrong in a civil case; a petty jury.

pigeonholing—a method of defeating a bill by keeping it in a committee.

plaintiff—the party making the complaint in a civil case; the opposite of the defendant.

plank—an idea or belief for which a political party stands, as stated in its official platform.

pocket veto—the defeating of a bill by the executive refusing to sign it at the end of a legislative session.

political machine—a political organization, usually within a political party, which has great influence over elected officials and in the selection of candidates.

pragmatic—concerned with practical results or values.

preamble—an introduction which gives reasons or purposes for writing the constitution.

precedent—an act that serves as an example for later action.

precinct—a district or area containing one place to vote.

presidential preference primary—a primary election held in some states to determine who shall be the state's preferred presidential nominee of a political party at a national convention.

pressure group—an interest group that tries to influence governmental processes.

price support—basic price set by the government for a certain crop or commodity.

primary—the first election to decide which of several persons will be chosen to run for office.

pro tempore—temporary; for the time being.

probation—procedure whereby a convicted person remains free and is not sent to prison if he follows the conditions set down by the court.

proletariat—workers, especially industrial workers.

propaganda—efforts to influence public opinion.

proprietor—the owner; the one who has the final right or title to something.

public opinion—the attitude of a particular group of people at a given time on a socially significant issue; majority opinion.

public utility—a private company that provides service to the public without competition and subject to government regulation.

qualification—quality or characteristic needed to be eligible for an elective or appointive office.

quasi-judicial—to some extent like a court; an agency having power to interpret laws or settle disputes in a way similar to a court.

quasi-legislative—to some extent like a legislature; an agency having power to make rules and regulations with the force of laws.

quota—the portion or share of a total number; the number of immigrants permitted to enter the United States from a particular country.

ratification—a vote for approval; the act of approving a constitution or a constitutional amendment.

real property—land and buildings.

reapportionment—the act of apportioning again, the process of dividing the legislature on the basis of population changes after each census.

reclamation—restoring waste or arid land to a state of productive usefulness.

recognition—the formal acknowledgment of the existence of a government of another nation, including the agreement to exchange diplomatic representatives.

referendum—the submitting of a bill, a constitution, or a constitutional amendment to the direct vote of the citizens.

referral—the passing along or forwarding of something; the sending of a bill by the presiding officer to a committee.

regionalism—the administration of a governmental unit by the federal government and the states without regard to state boundaries.

register—the list of eligible candidates for a civil service position.

registration—the act of getting one's name on the list of those eligible to vote.

representative government—the system in which elected officials are chosen to rule.

reprieve—postponement of punishment for a crime.

republic—government by the people through elected representatives.

resource—a natural asset of a nation which can be converted to good use or to manufactured products.

restrictions—in housing, the conditions under which a person may buy, build, or rent; declared illegal with reference to race, religion, or nationality.

return—a completed statement giving required information and computation in figuring taxes.

revenue—the income of government.

rider—an amendment which might not pass by itself attached to a bill which is sure to pass.

rural—relating to predominantly agricultural areas outside of cities and towns.

sample—the cross-section of people to be interviewed in a public opinion poll or survey.

sanctions—an action by one or more nations toward another nation designed to force that nation to obey international law.

secondary boycott—the boycott of a second company which is doing business with a company involved in a labor dispute.

Secretariat—the executive branch of the United Nations, headed by the Secretary General.

security—a legal document showing ownership of a company; stock or bond certificate.

selective service—the system of drafting persons for military service.

selectmen—chief officers of a New England town.

self-sufficient—the ability to supply one's own needs; to produce enough of a substance or product within a nation so that imports of the substance or product are not necessary.

senatorial courtesy—a custom under which senators have agreed that they will not approve an appointment by the President to a position in a particular state, if it is opposed by a senator from that state who is a member of the same party as the President.

seniority—a system of choosing committee chairmen and members on the basis of length of service.

separate-but-equal—a phrase from an 1896 Supreme Court decision holding that segregation is acceptable if Negroes and whites have equal facilities.

session—a yearly meeting of Congress.

shared revenue—monies collected by one unit of government which are returned to another unit of government.

sheriff—county officer with specific court and jail duties; traditionally also the county law officer.

shire—a British district similar to a county.

social class—a broad group of people with similar economic, cultural, or political behavior.

socialism—economic system in which government owns and operates the major industries.

soil conservation district—a group of farms or ranches organized to promote good conservation practices.

sovereignty—supreme power or authority.

Speaker—the presiding officer of the House of Representatives.

specification—an exact description of a wanted item or service.

sphere of influence—an area made up of countries dominated by a more powerful nation.

split-ticket voting—voting for candidates of more than one party.

status quo—present or existing condition.

stockpiling—building a reserve supply of an essential substance or product for use in the event of war.

straight-ticket voting—voting only for the members of one political party.

strike—the refusal of employees to work, usually because of a dispute involving wages, other benefits, or working conditions.

strong mayor—designation given the chief executive in the mayor-council type of city government when the mayor has great power, when there are few other elected administrators, and when other officials are responsible to him.

subpoena—an order to appear in court.

subsidy—a grant of money from one government to another or to a private enterprise which is providing a public service.

substandard—inferior; not up to standard set by law; in housing, not meeting building and sanitation codes.

subversive—tending to bring about the overthrow of a government by unlawful methods; a person who tries to overthrow or undermine the government.

suffrage—the right to vote.

superintendent of schools—person employed by the board of education to administer the schools.

supervisor—township officer; member of the county board.

surtax—an additional tax placed on something already taxed.

tariff—a tax on imported goods; also called duty.

tax delinquency—the nonpayment of taxes by the due date.

tax limitation—the ceiling or limit placed on tax rates by law or constitutional amendment.

tax rate—the amount or per cent of tax paid for each $1,000 of income or of value of property.

term—the time or period during which something lasts; the two sessions of Congress from one election to the next.

territory—a part of the nation that does not have the status of a state; it has its own elected legislature but an appointed governor.

totalitarianism—system of government in which the total life of the individual is under the control of the government; total dictatorship.

township—a unit of local government; a geographic subdivision of a county, usually thirty-six square miles in area.

trademark—a distinctive word or symbol to identify a particular product or company.

treaty—a formal international agreement between two or more nations which has been ratified by the constitutional procedures of the participating nations.

trial court—a lower court in which a jury may be used.

trust—a combination of companies organized to eliminate competition and control prices.

trust fund—money kept separate from other government receipts, earmarked for specific purposes, such as social security.

trust territory—a non-self-governing land or area administered by a nation under the direction of the Trusteeship Council of the United Nations.

unalienable—cannot be taken away; belongs to each human being by right of birth; inalienable.

unicameral—a legislature with one branch or house.

unified budget—budget system adopted by the federal government in fiscal year 1969; budget includes both general funds and trust funds.

uniform state law—a model law prepared by an organization for possible adoption by all states.

uniform tax—a tax rate that is the same for all income.

urban—relating to cities and towns.

urban renewal—process of rebuilding slum areas, especially blighted central cities.

urbanization—the process of people moving from rural areas to or near large cities; the quality of taking on characteristics of a city.

verdict—the decision of a jury; a decision.

veto—the action of the President, governor, or mayor in not approving an act passed by Congress, a state legislature, or a city council.

village—a local unit of government, often incorporated to provide governmental services; a rural community.

visa—a special document or an endorsement on a passport giving a person permission to enter a foreign country.

vital statistics—information and records regarding births, deaths, and marriages.

vote of confidence—the vote in a parliament on an issue to determine whether the prime minister shall continue in office or be required to call an election.

voting examiners—officials appointed by the United States Civil Service Commission to determine if eligible voters are denied the right to register and vote in a state and to make provisions for their registration.

warrant—1. a special notice indicating the items to be voted on in a town meeting. 2. a written order authorizing an act; a court order permitting an arrest, the taking of property, or a search.

weak mayor—opposite of the strong mayor; he has little power; there are many other elected officials who are not responsible to him.

welfare—the well-being of people; help given to people in need.

welfare state—system of government in which government has taken over responsibility for protecting citizens against economic and social hazards, such as unemployment and sickness.

whip—a leader of a party in Congress or other legislature who has responsibility for getting members to vote.

withholding tax—tax money withheld from wages and paid to the government for the worker by his employer.

workmen's compensation—money paid to an employee injured in the course of his work; compensation insurance; accident insurance.

zoning—a plan for the use of certain lands as commercial, industrial, or residential property; usually zoning describes the kinds of buildings that may be constructed in designated areas.

INDEX

Figures in italics indicate pages
upon which illustrations or tables
appear.

Brotherhood of Locomotive Firemen and Enginemen, 160
Brotherhood of Sleeping Car Porters, 62, 69
Brown, H. "Rap," 69
Brown v. Board of Education, 62-63, 297
Brownell, Herbert, 139, 336
Bryan, William J., 257
Bryce, James, quoted, 36
Bryce Canyon, 640
Buddha, 18
budget: administrative, 484, 489; defined, 346, 484, 496; democratic controls, 499; government, *495*, 496-497; preparation of, 497-498; school district, 499; state, 353, 355; unified, 484, 489; United Nations, 594
buffer zone, 542
Bulgaria, 582
Bunche, Ralph J., 590, *592*, 699
bureau, defined, 231
Bureau of the Budget, 228, 248, 399
Bureau of the Census, 183, 268-269, 408, 454; reports, 714
Bureau of Domestic Commerce, 269
Bureau of Engraving and Printing, 262
Bureau of Indian Affairs, 267
Bureau of International Commerce, 269
Bureau of Labor Statistics, 270
Bureau of Land Management, 267, 641
Bureau of Mines, 267, 571, 641
Bureau of the Mint, *47*, 262
Bureau of Narcotics, 266
Bureau of Politico-Military Affairs, 558
Bureau of Prisons, 265
Bureau of Reclamation, 268, *287*, 639
bureaucracy, 257
bureaucrats, 123, 274
Burger Court, 717
Burger, Warren E., *307*, 717
burgess, village, 455
Burke, Edmund, quoted, 337
Burma, 549, *587*
Burr, Aaron, 237, 715
business: government aids to, 647-650; government as rules maker, 646-647; government regulation of, 650-653; groups and public opinion, 156; state regulation of, 387
busing issue, 63, 72, 673, 716-717
Byrd, Sen. Harry F., *182*, 242
Byrnes, James F., quoted, 256

C

Cabinet, Great Britain, 602
Cabinet, President's: advisory functions of, 255-256; establishment of, 255, 256; executive departments under, 255; members, appointment of, 256; under George Washington, 255
Cahill, Gov. Wm., *383*
Calendar of Bills, 219
calendars, congressional, 219-220
California, 183, 184, 342, 537, 636; Central Valley Project, *392*; constitution, 330; constitutional amendments, 330; cross-filing system, 117; government data, 332, 337, *762-765*; voting requirements, *754*
California Aqueduct, 636
California Court of Appeals, *366*
Cambodia, 532, 545
Camp Kilmer, New Jersey, *9, 72*
campaigns, *125*, 126-131, 136, 139-140, *142*, 161-163, 236; reforms, 706-707
Canada, 538, 548; form of government, 607; visit by Queen Elizabeth II, *601*
cancer research, 158
candidates, selection of, 115-120
Cannon, Joseph G., 205
Canton Island, 538
Cape Kennedy, 576
capitalism, 600, 608-609, 612
Capitol, The, 178, 231
card-stacking, 162
Carmel Valley, California, *562*
Carmichael, Stokely, 69
Caroline Islands, 538
carpetbagger, 188, 190
Carswell, G. Harrold, 717
case studies, 76-77, 316-321, 478-481, 520-525, 617-621
Castro, Fidel, 545, 546
categorical aid, 664
caucus: defined, 97, 144; nomination by, 115-116; party in Congress, 204, 209; in town meeting, 447
Cavanagh, Mayor Jerome, *413*
censorship, 155
census, defined, 178, 254
Census of the United States: Constitution requires, 268; purpose of, 269; and reapportionment, 183; 1970, 183, 185, 714
Center for the Study of Responsive Law, 289
Central Arizona Project Association, 160
Central High School, Little Rock, 396
Central Intelligence Agency, 250
Central Treaty Organization (CENTO), 549-550
Central Valley Project, *392*
Ceylon, 549

challenges, jury, 364, 376
charge, 264
charity, private, 674
charter: city, 414-415; colonial, 25; defined, 17; home rule, 414, 460; United Nations, 582
charter colonies, 25
Chavez, Cesar, *85*
checks-and-balances system, 12-13, 35, 48-50
Chicago, 419
Chicago Sanitary District, 452, *469*, 475
Chicanos, 73. See also Spanish-speaking Americans.
Chief Justice, U.S. Supreme Court, 243, 302, 305, *307*, 717
Chief of Naval Operations, 558
Chiefs of Staff, Armed Forces, 558, 559
child labor amendment, 659
children, aid to, 271
Children's Fund, United Nations, *587*
China, 529, 533; immigration quotas, 92; open-door policy, 528, 537
China, Communist, 533, 549, 565, 570, 614, 723; government of, 603, 605; and United Nations, 585, 592-593; and Vietnam War, 544-545
China, Nationalist, 533, 549; and United Nations, 585, 593
Chinatown, San Francisco, *14*
Chinese Exclusion Act, 91
Chinese in U.S., *14*, 73. See also American Orientals.
Chisholm, Shirley, *176*
Christ Church, Philadelphia, *39*
Christian, Judge Winslow, 724
Christianity, 18
Churchill, Winston, 244, 542, 605
Church of England, 602
circuit courts, 367-368
cities: growth of, 409-410; problems of, 410-412; representation in state legislature, 334; population of, 714; size to determine, 454; unrest in, 464-468; and zoning, 471
citizens: classifications of, 83-85; defined, 80; participation of, 81, 83; as political groups, 138; and propaganda, 162-163; and public opinion, 147-155; rights of, 4
citizenship: in ancient Athens, 18; by birth, 86-87; loss of, 90; and marriage, 87; naturalization, 87-90; responsibilities of, 93-94; and suffrage, 101; in territories, 86, 87; and voting, 98-100; and Warren Court, 311
city council, *416*, 417-420
City-County Building, Detroit, Michigan, *463*

city government: charters, 414-415; city hall, 408, *415*; city-manager, 421-422; commission, 420-421; councils, 417-420; and county consolidation, *463*, 464; expenditures of, 492-494; home rule, 414; mayor, 416-417, 419; mayor-council, 416-420; planning, *412*, 691; and political bosses, 138-139; responsibility of, 411; revenue sources, 511-512; services of, 412-414; taxes, 511-512; types of, 415-422; wards, 417-418
city hall, 408, *415*
city-manager form of government, 421-422
city organization, political, 137
city planning, *412*, 691
city-states, 398
civil cases, *373*; defined, 297, 364; full faith and credit, 391-392; settlement of, 372; trial of, 373-374
Civil Defense Advisory Council, 570
civil disturbances, 68-69, 465, 567
Civil Disturbances and the Cities (case study), 478-481
Civil Division, Department of Justice, 265
Civil Liberties Unit, 62
civil rights: of aliens, 89; and colonial charters, 25; under Bill of Rights and Constitution, 59-60; and Declaration of Independence, 28-29; and education, 673; of Englishmen, 20-23; federal aid, 266; and housing, 686-687; legislation, *59*, 64, 67, 102; Negroes' struggle for, 56-73; of non-black minorities, 72-73; and right to vote, 102-105; to trial by jury, 4, 364-365, 378
Civil Rights: *Passage of the Civil Rights Act of 1964* (case study), 169-175
Civil Rights Act (1957), 64, 102
Civil Rights Act (1960), 64, 102
Civil Rights Act (1964), 103, 169-175, 266, 291, 708, 722
Civil Rights Act (1968), 68
Civil Rights Commission, 102
Civil Rights Division, Department of Justice, 265
civil service: county, 441; federal, 279-280
Civil Service (discovery episode), 402-405
Civil Service Commission, U.S. 52, 279-280
Civil War, 309, 559
Civilian Conservation Corps, 640
civilian defense, 570-571
civilizations, ancient, 18-20

Clark, Champ, 205; quoted, 214
Clark, Dr. Kenneth B., 63, 71, 479
Clay, Cassius (Muhammad Ali), 300, 560
Clay, Henry, 205, 257, 647
Clayton Antitrust Act, 609, 651
clearing house, 383
clerk, town, 447-448
clerk of the court, 434
Clerk of the House, 142, *221*
Cleveland, Grover, 132, 237, 241; quoted, 108
Cleveland, Ohio, *71*, *423*
Clinton, New Jersey, *470*
closed primary, 118-119
cloture, 56, 67, 201, 210-211, 712, 722
coalitions: defined, 80, 123; political, 124-125
coast guard, 273, 563, 650
Coast Guard Academy, 563
COG, 472
coins and coinage, *42*, *47*, 262
Cold War, 528, 529, 542, 545, 580
Coleman Vote Tally System, 113
collective bargaining, 645, 654; agreement, 655
colleges, kinds of, 669
colonial agreements, 24-25
colonial government in America, 24-28
colonies: charter, 25; original, 24; proprietary, 25; royal, 24-25
Colorado: constitutional amendments, 330; Game, Fish and Parks Department, *358*; government data, 337, *762-765*; voting requirements, *754*
Colorado River, 267, 637
Columbia River, 396, 399
commander in chief, 263, 533, 556
commerce: in the Confederation, 40; and Congress, 195; Federal regulation of, 650-653; Interstate Commerce Commission, 286-287; interstate regulation of, 394; and open-door policy, 537
Commerce, Department of, 268-269, 488, 647
commission, defined, 408
Commission on Interstate Cooperation, 394
Commission on Organization of the Executive Branch of Government, 294
Commission on Registration and Voting Participation, 100, 104, 105
Commission on Revision of Federal Court Appellate System, 724
commission type of government, 420-421

commissioner: congressional, 187, 326; federal, 303; village, 455
Committee for Economic Development, 331, 333, 337, 346, 366, 394, 417, 432, 441, 449, 453, 455
Committee of the Whole, 220
Committee on Appropriations, 204
Committee on Committees, 212-213
Committee on Fair Employment Practices, 62
Committee on Public Education, 140
committeeman, 137
committees, congressional: campaign, 136; chairmen, 208; conference, 221, 227-228; hearings, 218; importance of, 211; investigating, 567; joint, 221, 226-228; membership, 212-214; number of, 211; party representation, 213, 214; regular, 211-212; reports, 218; seniority, 213-214
committees, national convention, 239-246
committees, state legislative, 339
Committees of Correspondence, 28
commodities, surplus, 632
Commodity Credit Corporation, 268, 632
common carriers, *287*, 684, 696
Common Cause, 142, 158, 706, 707
common defense, *35*, 37
common law, 600, 602
Common Market, European, 528, 549, 713
communications, federal regulation of, 288
communications industry. *See* magazines; newspapers; radio; television.
communications satellite bill, 211
communism: in Asia, 533, 544, 549, 565; authoritarian system of, 602-604; bipartisan front against, 534; containment of, 542-543; in Cuba, 545-546; defined, 600; and foreign policy, 530; in governments, 565, 603, 609; and human nature, 611-612; and immigration, 92; internal security against, 567-568; life under, 612-613; minorities under, 13; nations threatened by, 546-547; propaganda, 540; spread of, 565; theory of, 609
Communist Control Act, 569
Communist Party, 135, 567-569, 603, 612; and Warren Court, 311
Communist Party v. *Subversive Activities Control Board*, 568
Community Chest, 674

community college, 664, 670
Community Relations Service, 266
Community Services Administration, 674
commutation, 346, 355-356
Compact on Education, 394
compacts, colonial, 23-24; defined, 17, 383; interstate, 392-393
compensation, federal employees, 270
compromise, 35, 44-46
Comptroller of Currency, 263, 292
computer-printer, *336*
concurrent jurisdiction, 297
confederate government, 607
confederation, 17
conference committees, 201, 221, 227-228, 558-559
conflict of law, 392
Congo, 591, 594
Congress: adjournment, 191-192; aids to legislation, 214-215; black members of, *727*; budget appropriations, *495*; calendars, 219-220; caucuses, 204; checks and balances, 48-50; committees, 208, 211-214, 218-219, 221, 226-227, 558-559; composition of, 1789-1972, *756-761*; Constitutional provisions, 209, 504; debate, 201-202; and defense, 555-556, 558; District of Columbia governed by, 187; ethical conduct, 225; may expel members, 190; expert help for, 214-216; expressed powers, 178, 194-195; filibustering, 201-202; floor leaders, 208; foreign policy role, 534; gerrymandering, 184-185; impeachment powers, 196; implied powers, 195-196; interstate compacts, 392-393; investigations, 223-225; Joint Committee on Atomic Energy, 574; joint committees, 226-227; journals, 218, 221; judicial powers, 297-298; lame duck, 192; lawmaking procedure, 217-222; leaders, 203-208; legislative council, 215, 226; letters to, 151-152; lobbying, 216-217; meetings, 180; minority party in, 209; opening date, 180, 192; parliamentarian, 204-205; party control of, 209; party membership on committees, 212; party whips, 208; pensions, 190-191; powers, 192-198; President's messages to, 247; President's relations with, 227; privileges of members, 191; problems of, 202-203; and public opinion, 151; qualifications of members, 180, 188-191; reapportionment,

183-184; reforms, 225-228; reorganization, 213; representation in, 44, 185; riders, 222; rules, 209-210; and selective service, 559-560; seniority rule, 213; sessions, 191-192; special powers, 180, 196-198; special sessions, 192; study of, 709-710; and Supreme Court, 309-311; terms, 180, 191-192, 225; territorial representation, 187; and treaties, 534; vacancies, 187-188; veto, 49, 247; and Vice President, 205-206; visitors to, 178-179; voting, 220-221; whips, 208; women in, 181, 203, *727*; work of, 201-228
Congress of the Confederation, 39-40
Congress of Industrial Organizations, 140, 157, 645, 656
Congress of Racial Equality, 69
congressional campaign committees, 136
congressional committees, study of, 710
congressional district, 183; map, *184*
congressional investigating committees, 567
congressional law, unconstitutional, 308-309
Congressional Quarterly, 217
Congressional Record, 173-175, *189,* 191, 199, 201, 211, 217, 218, 221
Congressional Research Service, 215, 227
congressional township, 444, 449
congressmen: black, *727*; choosing, 183-188; and Constitution, 183, 191; and freedom of speech, 191; new, 181; offices of, 181; previous experience, 181; privileged from arrest, 191; qualifications, 188-191; salaries of, 190-191; terms of office, 183, 186; of Spanish Descent, *727*
Congressmen of Spanish Descent, *727*
Congresswomen, *727*
Connally, Gov. John, *353*
Connally Resolution, 534
Connecticut: as charter colony, 25; constitution, 328; government data, 339, 429, *762-765*; voting requirements, 754
Connecticut Compromise, 44
Consent Calendar, 219
conservation: and Department of the Interior, 268, 640-641; defined, 624; fish, 640-641; forests, 639-640; minerals, 641-642; parks, 640; reclamation and irrigation, 639; soil, 633-636;

water and flood control, 636-639; wildlife, 640-641
Conservative party, 602
Consolidated Edison Company, *651*
consolidated schools, 673
consolidation: defined, 427, 444, 458; of local governments, 441, 464; of school districts, 409
constable, town, 444, 448
constitution, defined, 35
Constitution of the United States: amendment of, 50-51; amendments to, 4, 38; and Articles of Confederation, 31, 38-41; and branches of government, 48-50; changing, 50-52; checks and balances in, 12-13, 48-50; compromises, 44-46; and congressional privileges, 191; and congressional representation, 44, 186; and control of commerce, 44-46; and defense, 555-556; defines citizens, 86; division of powers, 46-48; elastic clause, 52-53, 178, 195-196; and election of President, 237-241; and foreign policy, 532; and general welfare, 9; history of, 31, 36; interpretation of, 52; interstate agreements, 392; Preamble, 4, 9, 36-37, 610; and the President, 46, 232, 243, 260, 532; and qualifications of congressmen, 188-190; ratification, 38; regulation of business, 44-46, 647; relation of states, 391-392; rights of Congress, 209; safeguards civil rights, 59-60; and self-government, 4; signing, *38*; and slavery, 46, 47; states restricted by, 48; steps leading to, 31; and suffrage, 98-99; tax power of, 504; territories and, 326-327; text, 735-753; Twenty-seventh Amendment, proposed, 708; "unwritten," 237; writing of, 41-46
Constitutional Convention, *39,* 41-46
constitutional conventions, state, 328, *329*
constitutional home rule, 458, 460
constitutional law, 300
constitutionality, defined, 35
constitutions, state: age of, 328; amendment and revision of, 328-330; characteristics, 327-332; early, 29; future of, 331-332; length, 327-328; parts of, 327; ratification, 330-331
consular service, 536
consuls, foreign, 259, 260
containment, 528, 542-543
Continental Congress, 29, 30

continental notes, *42*
contracts, government, 496
contributions, political, 140
contour plowing, 624, 634
convention system, 116-117
conventions: city, 116; constitutional, 328, *329*; county, 116; national, 116-117, 238-240, 707-708; nominating, 52; state, 116
conviction, court, 372
Coolidge, Calvin, 231
cooperatives, farmers', 629
copyright, 645, 648-649
Corfu channel, 590
coroner, county, 427, 428
coroner's jury, 433
corporations: defined, 277, 645; government, 291-292; income taxes, 507-508; state regulation of, 386-387
Corps of Engineers, 264, 574
Corrupt Practices Act of 1925, 141, 707
corrupt practices acts: defined, 123; national, 141, 143; state, 141
cost-of-living index, 270, 720
costs of government: controlling, 496-499; federal, 488-491; kinds of, 494-496; local, 492-494; state, 491-492
council: city, 416-420; defined, 408; legislative, 341; village, 454
Council for a Livable World, 160
Council of Economic Advisers, 248
Council of Governments, 472
Council of State Governments, 342-343, 394-395
Council on Environmental Quality, *249*-250
Council on International Economic Policy, *249*, 250
counties, number of, 408, 429
county: defined, 427; of the future, 440
county agricultural agent, *428*, 628
county assessor, 435-436
county auditor, 435
county board, 430-431
county clerk, 432-433
county committee, 137
county coroner, 428, 433
county courthouse, *428*, 429-430
county courts, 367
county engineer, 437
county government: consolidation, 464; election duties, 433; employees, 438; functions of, 440-441; historical development of, 427-429; home rule, 442; number of, 408, 429; officers, 431-438; overlapping services, 464; reform, 438-442; size of, 429
county health officer, 437-438
county highway commissioner, 437
county manager, 439-440

county recorder, 434-435
county road commissioner, 437
county seat, 408, 429-430
county sheriff, 428, 432
county superintendent of schools, 437, 668
county surveyor, 437
county treasurer, 435
court interpretation, 52
Court of Claims, 312
Court of Customs and Patent Appeals, 312
Court of International Justice, 534
court systems, relationship of, 298
courts of appeal, 303-305
courts, city, 367
courts, county, 367
courts, federal: appeals, 303-305; cases, 298-301; district, 303; established by Congress, 303; handle state disputes, 387-390; judges, 301-303; judicial review, 307-310; jurisdiction, 299, 305; kinds of, 303-307; officials, 265, 303; special 311-313; and state courts, 298-299; Supreme Court, 305-307; territorial, 312-313
courts, state: appellate, 368; centralized organization, 380; city, 367; civil cases, 373-374; criminal cases, 374-376; district, county and circuit, 367; domestic relations, 372; and federal courts, 298-299; general trial, 367-368; improvement of, 376-380; judges, 367; judicial council, 380; justice of the peace, 365; juvenile, 371; lower, 365-367; magistrate, 366-367; municipal, 365, 367; police, 366, 367; pretrial conference, 379; probate, 371; procedure, 372-376; small claims, 371, 374; special, 371-372; supreme, 368, 370; traffic, 372; trial, 367
courts-martial, 297
Crater Lake National Park, *642*
creative federalism, 383, 399
credit unions, 272
crime and criminals: causes, 692-693; extradition, 336; felonies and misdemeanors, 374-375; increase in, *693*; pardons, 247, 355; parole, 356; prevention, 695; prosecution, 694; punishment, 694-695; rate of, 719; trial of, 375-376; and voting privilege, 106; and Warren Court, 311
criminal cases: defined, 297, 364, 372; federal, 300; and prosecuting attorney, 434; trial of, 375-376
Criminal Division, Department of Justice, 265
criminologist, 684

Cromwell, Oliver, 22
crop rotation, 624
crops: insurance, 633; production, 633; surplus, 632
cross-examination, 364, 374
cross-filing, in primaries, 117
Crossley poll, 151
Crump political machine, 139
Cuba: Communist influence in, 531-532, 545-546, 565; missile crisis, 546, 551
Cubans in U.S., 73; refugees, 92. *See also* Spanish-speaking Americans.
cultural pluralism, 96
curfew, 458
currency, *42*, 261, *262*
custom, and Constitutional change, 51-52
customs, 510-511; inspector, *312*
Customs, Bureau of, 262
Customs Court, 312
Cyprus, 591
Czechoslovakia, 565

D

Daley, Mayor Richard, 116, 139, 416
Dallas, Texas, *430*
dams, 636-637
dark-horse candidate, 231, 240
Dartmouth College case, 310
Das Kapital, 609
data, interpreting (discovery episode), 702-705
Daughters of the American Revolution, 158
Davis Mountain, Texas, *391*
Day Care and Community Action Programs, 248
Dean, Vera Micheles, quoted, 534
debate, freedom of, 202
debt, national, 263, 490
Declaration of Independence, *30*; and equality, 10; history of, 28-29; and liberty, 4; text, 728-729
Declaration of Rights and Grievances, 28
deduction, 502
deed, 427, 435
de facto segregation, 56, 63, 664, 673
defendant, 297, 373
Defense, Department of, 255, 263-264, 488, 570, 574, 671, 691
defense, military, 555-565
defense pacts, 548-550
deficit, 502; federal, 505
DeGaulle, 529, 549
de jure segregation, 664, 673
Delaware: constitutional amendments, 330-331; government data, 335, 337, *762-765*; as pro-

"grass roots" expressions, 151
Great Britain, 529, 532, 541-542, 545, 549, 550, 580; documents of liberty, 20-23; government of, 601-602, 607, 610; NATO membership, 548; in UN, 585, 590, 594
Great Charter (Magna Carta), 20-21, 378
Great Lakes, 722-723
Great Seal of the United States, 257, *258*
Great Smokies National Park, 641
Greece: ancient, 18 10; modern, 543, 548, 562, 591
Greensboro, North Carolina, 65
Griffiths, Martha, *182*, 708
Grodzins, Morton, quoted, 397
gross national product, 484, 490
Guam, 538; acquisition, 537; and citizenship, 86, 87; congressional delegate, 187, 326; courts, 312
Guatemala, 551
gubernatorial, defined, 346
guerilla: defined, 528; warfare, 542, 544
Gulf of Tonkin Resolution, 533
Gulf States Marine Fisheries Compact, 393

H

habeas corpus, writ of, 35, 47
Hague, The, Netherlands, 540, *581*, 586
Hague political machine, 139
Hall, Gus, 569
Hamilton, Alexander, 41, 43, 647
Hammarskjöld, Dag, 586
Hancock, John, *3*, 28, 43
Hand, Learned, quoted, 8
Handbook for Citizens, 710
handicapped, schools for, *669*, 670
Handlin, Oscar, quoted, 81
Hanna, Mark, 139
Harding, Warren G., 240
Harlan, Justice John M., 568
Harlem, New York City, 68
Harper v. *Virginia State Board of Education,* 102
Harris poll, 151, 320
Harrison, Benjamin, 241
Harrison, William H., *232*
Hatch Acts, 141
Hatcher, Mayor Richard G., *423*
Hawaii: capitol, *326*; citizenship, 87; constitution, 328; government data, 337, *762-765*; as territory, 327, 534, 537; voting requirements, 99, *754*
Haynsworth, Clement F., Jr., 717
head tax, 505
health: costs, 679-680; federal programs, 677; inspection, 678; insurance, 680-681; licensing, 678; local programs, 678-679; problems of, 679-681; public, 677, 678; research, 679; state responsibilities, 385-386, 678-679; World Health Organization, 588
health, board of, *359*, 678, 679
Health, Education, and Welfare, Department of, 255, 270-272, 653, 659, 670, 674, 677
Hearst newspapers, 153
Henry, Patrick, 4, 43
hidden government, 137
hidden taxes, 505
high court, 365
highways: construction and maintenance, *387*, *489*, *494*; safety programs, 273; state responsibility, 385; and traffic, 696
highways, commissioner of: county, 437; town, 448
Hiroshima, 285
Hiss, Alger, 566
Hitler, Adolph, 6, 559, 605, 611, 612
Ho Chi Minh, 545
Hodgson, James D., *654*
holding companies, 289
Holmes, Justice Oliver Wendell, 306, 307, 310; quoted, 302, 505
home demonstration agent, county, 628
Home Owners' Loan Corporation, 690
home rule: cities, 414; constitutional, 460; defined, 408, 458; legislative, 460; local, 460; Washington, D.C., 423-424
Honduras, 551
honest graft, 132, 139
Honolulu, Hawaii, *326*
Honolulu Declaration, 532
Hoover, Herbert, 234, 235, 366
Hoover, J. Edgar, quoted, 692
Hoover Commission, 266
Hoover Dam, *267*
"horse trading," political, 240
hospital insurance, 681
hospitals, military, 677
House Calendar, 219
House Committee on Education and Labor, 204
House Committee on Foreign Affairs, 534
House of Burgesses, 25-26, *27*
House of Commons, 601-602
house of delegates, state, 333
House of Lords, 601-602
House of Representatives, *207*; action on bills, 220-221; Armed Services Committee, 558, 560; calendars, 219-220; Committee of the Whole, 220; Committee on Appropriations, 204; Committee on Committees, 213; Committee on Foreign Affairs, 213, 534; committees, 204, 211-212, 227, 228; congressional campaign committee, 136; congressional districts, 183-185; debate, freedom of, 191; Democratic committee, 213; and election, 180, 190; elects President in case of tie, 196, 236; established, 44; foreign relations activities, 534; gerrymandering, 184-186; impeachment powers, 196, *197*; joint committees, 226-227; Judiciary Committee, *99*, 301; leaders, 203-208; legislative procedure, 217-222; meetings, 180; membership apportionment, 183; Negroes in, 181, *727*; party control, 209; pensions, 190-191; presiding officer, 180; qualifications, 180, 188-191; reapportionment, 183; Republican committee, 213; rules, 209-210; Rules Committee, 220; salary, 180, 190-191; seating arrangement, 209; Speaker, 204-*205*; special powers, 180, 196-197; special privileges, 191; term of office, 180, 183; Internal Security Committee, 567; vacancies, 187; Ways and Means Committee, 204, 213; women in, 181, *727*
house of representatives, state, 333
housing: and civil rights, 686-687; for elderly, 688; Federal Housing Administration, 272, *686*, 690; ghetto, 467; and government, 689-690; Home Owners' Loan Corporation, 690; low income, *461*; open, 687; public housing laws, 299; redevelopment, 467-468; restrictions, 686; shortage, 687-688; substandard, 467, 684, 688-689
Housing and Home Finance Agency, 689, 690, 691
Housing and Urban Development, Department of, 255, 272, 488, 690
Houston County, Alabama, *375*
How They Became Governor, 350
Howland Island, 538
Huang Hua, Ambassador, *539*, 723
Hughes, Charles E., 257, 307, 381
Hull, Cordell, 257
Human Rights Party, 135
Humphrey, Hubert, 71, *195*, 237, 321
hung jury, 364, 376
Hungry Horse Dam, 637
hunting, regulation of, 640
Huron-Clinton Metropolitan Authority, 475

hydroelectric power, 288, 292, 636, 638
hydrogen bomb, 285, 593

I

IBM Votomatic, *112,* 113
ICBM's, 712
Iceland, 548
Idaho, *639;* constitutional amendments, 330; government data, *762-765;* voting requirements, *754*
ideas of government, fundamental, 1-15, 17-32
Illinois: constitutional amendment, 330; court system, 367-368; governmental data, 183, *762-765;* voting requirements, *754*
immigrant, defined, 80
immigration, *81, 91;* preference system, 92-93; quotas, 91-92, 93; restrictions, 91-92; temporary, 93; U.S. policies and laws, 91-93; violations, 265-266
Immigration and Nationality Act, 87
Immigration and Naturalization Service, 88-89, 265-266
immunity, congressional, 201, 224-225
impeachment: of federal judges, 302; powers of House and Senate, 196, *197;* presidential, 242-243
imperialism, 528
imports, 262
In the Matter of Gault, 371
inauguration, presidential, 242
income, government: sources of, 502-505; special issues, 515-517
income tax: corporation, 507; deduction, 506; exemptions, 506; federal, *50,* 506 508; individual, 261, 506, *508;* return, 506; state, 506
incorporate, defined, 444
incorporated place, 454
Independence, Missouri, *428*
Independence Hall, *4, 30*
independent government agencies, 277-294; expenditures of, 488
India, 92, 549, 594, 595, 723; American Embassy, *259;* War with Pakistan, 591, 593
Indian Affairs, Bureau of, 267, 667
Indiana: government data, *762-765;* Indianapolis City-County Council, *418;* voting requirements, *754*
Indians, American, 57; and Bill of

Rights, 69; citizenship given, 87; education of, 670, *671. See also* American Indians.
indict, defined, 579
indictment, 364, 375
indirect democracy, 4, 604
indirect initiative, 341
indirect tax, 502, 505
individual: concern for, *6, 7;* and liberty, 6
Indochina, 545
Indonesia, 549, 572
industry: capacity of, 572; defense measures, 571-576; federal aid and regulation of, 648-661; power for, 572
infiltration, 554
inflation, 484, 488, 720
inheritance tax, 510
intiative: amending state constitutions, 330; direct, 324; indirect, 341; use of, *764*
injunction, 645, 658
inquest, 426, 433
Institute for Propaganda Analysis, 161
insurance: health, 681; hospital, 680-681; regulation of, 653; unemployment, 270, 656-657
Inter-American Affairs, Bureau of, 260
Inter-American Treaty of Reciprocal Assistance, 550
interest groups: classification by, 84-85; contributions by, 140-141; defined, 146; nature of, 156; private, 156-158; public, 158-159; and public opinion, 155-159; range of, 156; strategies of, 159-163
interest on national debt, 489, 490, 517
Intergovernmental Maritime Consultative Organization, UN, 588
interim appointments, 246
Interior, Department of, 267-268, 488, 640-641
intermediate credit banks, 629
internal revenue: court cases, 300; defined, 254, 261
Internal Revenue Service, 261-262, *507, 509*
internal security, 554, 565-571
Internal Security Act, 567
Internal Security Division, 265
international agreements, 580-581
International Atomic Energy Agency, 541, 588
International Bank for Reconstruction and Development, UN, 588
International Brotherhood of Teamsters, 157, 160
International Bureau of Weights and Measures, 582

International Civil Aviation Organization, UN, 588
international cooperation, methods of, 539-540, 580-582
International Cooperation Administration, 546
International Court of Justice, UN, *581,* 583, 586-587, 594
International Development Association, 588
International Finance Corporation, UN, 588
International Labor Organization, 587-588
international law, 581-582
International Monetary Fund, 588
international relations: alliances, 548-551; arbitration of disputes, 590-591; Asiatic pacts, 549; Congress and 534; containment policy, 542-543; executive agreements, 532-533; freedom of seas, 538; good-neighbor policy, 537-538; and idealism, 540-541; and international cooperation, 539-540; isolation, 536-537; Latin American treaties, 550-551; Marshall Plan, 546-547; Monroe Doctrine, 531, 536; NATO, 548-549; open-door policy, 537; Point-Four program, 547; President's role, 529-532; and public opinion, 530-531; reciprocal trade agreements, 648; SEATO, 549; treaties, 548-551; trends, 528-529; Truman Doctrine, 542-543, 546; world government, 595-596
international trade, 712
International Telecommunication Union, UN, 588
Interpreting Data (discovery episode), 702-705
Interstate Commerce Commission, 286-287
interstate compacts, 383, 392-393
Interstate Compact for the Supervision of Parolees and Probationers, 393
Interstate Compact on Education, 395
Interstate Compact on Mental Health, 394
Interstate Oil Compact, 393
interstate relations, 387-400
interstate rendition, 356
investigations, congressional, 223-225
Invisible Presidency, The, 244
Iowa: government data, *762-765;* voting requirements, *754*
Iran, 549-550, 591
Iraq, 549
irrigation, 268, 637
isolation, 536-537, 595

Israel, 549-550, 590, 591, 593, *610*
Italy, 529, 548
item veto, 226, 346, 355
Iwo Jima, 538

J

Jackson, Andrew, 132, 279
Jackson, Senator Henry M., 712
Jackson, Reverend Jesse, *116*
Jamestown, Virginia, 22, 23, 24
Japan, 529, 532, 538, 543, 549, 592; trade with, 713
Japanese in U.S., 73
Jarring, Gunnar, 590
Jarvis Island, 538
Javits, Senator Jacob K., 711
Jefferson, Thomas, *3, 29, 30,* 43, 131, 197, 210, 237, 257, 309
Jefferson County Courthouse, Kentucky, *430*
Jefferson-Jackson Day dinners, 140
Jefferson Memorial, 178
Jenner Committee, 567
Jesus, 18
Jewish religion, 18
Jim Crow laws, 56, 60, 61
Job Corps, *9, 72,* 248
John F. Kennedy Airport, *510*
Johnson, Andrew, *197,* 242-243
Johnson, Lady Bird, *243*
Johnson, Lyndon B., 124, 132, 141, 229, 231, 237, 242, 507, 533; and civil rights, 64, *65,* 67-68, *105*; and Dominican Republic, 244, 551; economic policy, 522-525; State-of-the-Union address, 225-226, 399; and Vietnam, 213-214, 395, *531,* 532, 545
Johnson, Richard M., 197
Johnson Island, 538
Joint Chiefs of Staff, 264, 557-558
Joint Committee on Atomic Energy, 574
joint committees: congressional, 226-227; state legislative, 339
Joint Senate-House Economic Committee, *212*
Joliet, Illinois penitentiary, *390*
Jones v. *Mayer,* 69
Jordan, Vernon E., Jr., 62
journals, congressional, 218, 221
Judge Advocates General, 313
judges: federal, *88,* 301-302; impeachment of, 302; justices of the peace, 365-366; salaries and benefits, 302; state, 376-377
judicial branch: checks and balances, 48-50; defined, 35
judicial circuits, 304
judicial council, 380
judicial power: of Congress, 195;

of governor, 355, 356; of President, 246-247
judicial review, 297, 307-311
Judiciary Committee, *99,* 301
junior college, 671
junkets: congressional, 224
jurisdiction: appellate, 305, 367, 368; concurrent, 297; defined, 579; original, 305, 367, 368
jury, *93*; challenges to, 376; colonial, 26-27; coroner's, 433; criticisms of, 378; grand, 375; hung, 376; improvements, 378-380; Negroes and, *375*; panel, 375; petit, 375; selection of members, 375-376, 378-379; trial by, 365, 373, 375-376
jus sanguinis, 87
jus soli, 87
Justice, Department of, 264-266, 303, 488, 651, 692
justice, equal, 11, 36
justice of the peace, 488; courts, 365, 366
Justices, U.S. Supreme Court, 63, 105, 214, 216, 306, 307, 348, 569, 570
juvenile courts, 371

K

kangaroo court, 364
Kansas, 99, 342; government data, 337, 341, *762-765*; voting requirements, 754
Kashmir, 591
"Keep America Beautiful" campaign, *243*
Kefauver, Sen. Estes, 223, 226
Kellogg-Briand Treaty, 541
Kelly machine, 139
Kennedy, Jacqueline, *243*
Kennedy, John F., 132, 231, 244, 301, 532; Alliance for Progress, 551; and civil rights, 58, *61,* 64-67; and Cuba, 531-532, 546; economic policy, 520-522; grave of, 178; inaugural address, 540; and nuclear test ban, *246,* 541; and Peace Corps, 548; and public opinion, 151, 153; quoted, 58, 139, 232, 542; and voter participation, 100, 104
Kennedy, Joseph P., 81
Kennedy, Robert, 188-190; assassination of, *695*; and civil rights, 64; quoted, 551
Kennedy family, 81-82, 139
Kentucky, 99; government data, *762-765*; voting requirements, *754*
Kerner, Gov. Otto, 68, 479
Kerner report, 478-481
Keynes, John Maynard, 520-525
keynote address, 231, 239

Khe Sanh, Vietnam, *562*
Khrushchev, Soviet Premier, 546
kibbutz, *610*
Kilgore Committee, 567
King, Dr. Martin Luther, Jr., *103*; assassination of, 68, 69, 481, 687; doctrine of nonviolence, 69; march on Selma, 57; march on Washington, *65*; and Nobel Peace Prize, *61*; quoted, 58-59, 67, 467; and Southern Christian Leadership Conference, 69; and voting rights bill, *105*
Kingman Reef, 538
Kirkpatrick v. *Preisler,* 186
Kissinger, Henry, 545
Koenig, Louis W., 244
Korat Air Base, Thailand, *564*
Korea, 263, 533, 586, 591; North, 617-621; South, 549
Korean War, 308, 529, 543-544, 568
Kosygin, Alexei, *603,* 618
Kremlin, 258
Ku Klux Klan, 224, 567

L

labor: child, *659*; collective bargaining, 654; federal regulations, 658-661; government aids to, 653-658; hours and wages, 659-660; organizations, 157; state regulation of, 386-387, 659-661; and women workers, 659; workmen's compensation, 660
Labor, Department of, 269-270, 488, 653, *654,* 659-661
labor relations cases, 300
Labor Standards, Bureau of, 270
Labor Statistics, Bureau of, 270
labor unions, 62, 654-656
Labour party, Great Britain, 602
LaFollette, Robert, 133
laissez-faire, 600, 608-609, 646
Lake Mead, 267, 637
lame duck, 178, 192
Land and Natural Resources Division, 265
land-grant colleges, 627, 664, 666
Land Management, Bureau of, 267, 641
Landon, Alfred M., 150
Landrum-Griffin Act, 290, 654
language barriers, 585
Laos, 532, 545
Lasswell, Prof. Harold D., 132
Latin American treaties, 550-551
law: citizenship, 87; civil, 373-374; criminal, 300, 374-376; enforcement, 195, 470-471, 693; how passed, 217-222; international, 581-582; of neutrality, 581-582; of peace, 581; safeguards on, 339-340; strategy of making, 222; of supply and demand,

608; Supreme Court interprets, 309-311; of war, 581
Law and the Court, 302
Lawrence machine, 139
Lazarus, Emma, quoted, 91
Leadership Training School, Republican, *138*
League of Nations, 49, 197, 534, 540, 542, 582, 593
League of Women Voters, *101,* 158, 163
Leavenworth federal prison, 266
Lebanon, 549, 591, 594
legal aid bureaus, 374
legislative assistance, 215-216
legislative branch: checks and balances, 48-49; duties of President, 247-248; expenditures of government, 488
legislative council, 324, 341
legislative home rule, 458, 460
Legislative Reference Bureau, 338
Legislative Reference Service, 227
Legislative Reorganization Act, 211, 216, 226-228
legislator, 324
legislature: bicameral, 333; colonial, 25-26; Congress, 217-222; Continental Congress, 29; state, 333, 343, *762-763;* unicameral, 333
lend-lease programs, 541-542
Lesotho, 595
Lewis, John, *65*
Lexington, Massachusetts, 28
liberal arts college, 664, 670
Liberal Party, 134
Liberal Party, Great Britain, 602
liberty: American documents of, 23-28; and Bill of Rights, 4; British documents of, 23-28; and free enterprise, 7; and individual, 6; limitations of, 7-8
library board, town, 448
Library of Congress, 178, *214,* 215, 649
licenses, 385, 387
Lie, Trygve, 586
lieutenant governor, 339, 346, 357
Lillie, Judge Mildred L., *366*
limitations, tax, 515
limited monarchy, 17, 21-22
Lincoln, Abraham, 8, 132; quoted, 3, 31
Lincoln, Nebraska, *328*
Lincoln Day dinners, 140
Lincoln Memorial, *59, 178*
Lindsay, Mayor John, *365,* 416, 479
literacy tests, 104, 105, 121
Literary Digest, 150
Little Rock, Arkansas, 63-64, *396*
Livermore, California, 574
Livingston, William, 43
loans: to business, 648; to farmers, 629-630; under FHA, 272,

689-690; government, 515-516; government regulation of, 287; v. pay-as-you-go, 516; under RFC, 291, 648
lobbying: in Congress, 216-217; defined, 56, 146; of farm organizations, 626; by interest groups, 159-161; in state legislatures, 340-341
lobbyists: defined, 140; registration of, 216-217; state, 344
local government: chartered by states, 414-415; city, 408-424; county, 427-442; and education, 666; expenditures of, 485, 492-494; forms of, 414-423, 427-429, 444, 455; grants-in-aid to, 460; home rule, 460; New England town, 445-449; number of, 408; overlapping services, 463-464; problems of, 458-475; relation with state and federal governments, 459-463; taxes, 511-515; town, 445-449; township, 449-453; village, 453-455
lockout, 277
logrolling, 201, 222
London Naval Conference, 540
long ballot, 408, 420
Longworth, Nicholas, 205
Los Alamos, N.M., 574, 576
Los Angeles, 137; county, 429, 471; Watts area, 68
Louisiana, *638;* constitution, 330; government data, 337, 429, *762-765;* voting requirements, *754*
Louisiana Purchase, 536
Louisville, Kentucky, *430, 468*
low income, 270
lunar surface rake and tongs, *575*
Luxemburg, 548
Lyman, New Hampshire, 446

M

MacArthur, Gen. Douglas, 263
McCarran Act, 568
McCarthy, Sen. Joseph, 225
McCarthy Committee, 567
McClelland Committee, 567
McCulloch v. *Maryland,* 194
McGovern, George S., 124, *133,* 148, 237, 715
machine, political, 138-139
McKissick, Floyd B., 69
McNamara, Robert S., 552, 560, 619
Madison, James, 41, 43, 309
magazines, 266; and public opinion, 152-154
magistrate courts, 366-367
Magna Carta (Great Charter), 20-21, 378

mail: franking privilege of Congress, 190; Post Office Department, 266-267, 491; Universal Postal Union, 582, 588
Maine, 339; government data, *762-765;* voting requirements, *754*
majority opinion, 297
majority rule: dangers of, 12; defined, 2; and education, 11-12; and equality, 10-11; and representative government, 10
Malaysia, 572, 592
Malcolm X, 70
manager: city, 421-422; county, 439-440; town, 447
mandamus, writ of, 297, 309
mandatory referendum, 341
Manpower Administration, 270
Mansfield, Sen. Mike, *215*
Manual of Parliamentary Procedure, 210
Mao Tse-tung, 6, 605, *611*
Marbury v. *Madison,* 309
march on Washington, *65*
Marianas Islands, 538
marine corps, 264, *562,* 563
Marine Corps School, 563
Maritime Administration, 273
marriage, 387
marshal, district, 265, 303
Marshall, George C., 257, 546
Marshall, John, 257, *302,* 306, 309
Marshall, Justice Thurgood, 214, 306, *307,* 717
Marshall Islands, 538
Marshall Plan, 546-547
Martin, Joseph W., 205
Marx, Karl, 603, 609
Maryland: government data, 33, 335, 337, *762-765;* as proprietary colony, 25; voting requirements, *754*
Mason, Mayor Edward, *454*
Massachusetts: as charter colony, 25; constitutional amendments, 330; constitutional convention, 327; government data, 337, 339, *762-765;* voting requirements, *754*
Massachusetts Bay colony, 28
master clocks, 724
matching fund, 383
Material Policies Commission, 571, 641
Mayflower Compact, *23-24*
mayor, 416-420, 455; big city, 416
mayor-council government, 416-420
Mead, Lake, 267, 637
Meany, George, 645
mediation, 592, 657; defined, 383
mediator, 579, 645
medical care, costs of, 679-680
medical insurance, 681

Medical Services Administration, 674
Medicare, 271, 664, 675, 676, 681
Medicaid, 681
megalopolis, 458, 469
melting pot theory, 96
Memphis, Tennessee, 69
mentally ill and suffrage, 106
Meredith, James H., 6-7
merger, 651; railroad, *268*
merit system, county, 441
Merriam, Charles E., 565
metric system, 724
metropolitan areas; airports, *473*; defined, 458; law enforcement, 470-471; and pollution, 474; recreation facilities, 473; rubbish disposal, 469; solving problems, 474-475; taxation, 472-473; transportation and traffic, 469-470; water supply, 471; and zoning, 471
Metropolitan Regional Council, New York, 472
Metropolitan Water District of Southern California, 452
Mexican Americans, 73. *See also* Spanish-speaking Americans.
Mexico, 533, 537; President Echeverria, *526*
Miami, Florida, 464
Michigan, 183, 341; budget, 492; constitution, 328, 330, 331; government data, 337, 431, *762-765*; voting requirements, 99, *754*
Micro-Dynameter, 678
Middle Ages, 19-20
Middle East alliances, 549
Midway Islands, 538
militarism, 554, 556
military academies, 563-564
Military Appeals, U.S. Court of, 313
military defense, 555-565
military-industrial complex, 558
Military Liaison Committee, 574
military reserve program, 563-564
military service, 559-564
Military Staff Committee, UN, 558, 586
militia, state, 352, 555
Mills, C. Wright, quoted, 83-84
minerals, conservation of, 268, 641
Mines, Bureau of, 267, 571, 641
minimum wage, 721; laws, 660
ministers, U.S. foreign, 260, 532
Minneapolis, Minnesota, 388
Minnesota, 154, 333; government data, *762-765*; voting requirements, *754*
minor political parties, 132-135
minority group members, 57, 60, 72, 73
minority party in Congress, 209
minority rights, *12*, 13-15

Mint, Bureau of, *47*, 262
misdemeanor, 364, 374
Mississippi; and civil rights, 66; government data, *762-765*; and poll tax, 102; voting requirements, *754*
Mississippi, University of, 6-7
Missouri, constitution of, 328, 330; government data, *762-765*; voting requirements, *754*
Missouri Compromise, 309
Missouri Plan, 377
Missouri River, 396
Missouri River Basin Project, 638
mixed economic government system, 608
model, defined, 86
moderator, 444
Model Civil Service Law, 403-404
Modernizing Local Government, 441, 449, 455
Modernizing State Government, 331-338, 343, 346, 361, 366, 377, 380, 394
Mohammed, 18
monarchy, 611
money: coinage of, 47, *262*; paper, *42*, 261; printing, 262; Treasury Department, 228, 261, 263
monopolies, 288, 300, 650, 652; defined, 277, 645
Monroe, James, 132
Monroe Doctrine, 531, 536
Montana: government data, *762-765*; voting requirements, *754*
Montgomery, Alabama, 65
Monthly Labor Review, 653
Morison, Samuel Eliot, 23-24
Morrill Act, 666
mortgages, home, 272, 689-690
Morven, *349*
Mount Rainier National Park, 267, 641
Mount Vernon, 178
movies, and public opinion, 155
muckrakers, 609
Muhammad, Elija, *70*
Muhammad Ali (Cassius Clay), 300, 560
multiparty system, 602
municipal courts, 365-367
municipalities, number of, 408
Murphy, George, 190
Muscle Shoals, Alabama, 292
Muskie, Edmund, 321
Mussolini, Benito, 6, 603, 612
mutual defense pacts, 549-550
Mutual Security Agency, 546

N.

Nader, Ralph, 289, *709*, 710
Nader's Raiders, 289, 709

Nagasaki, 285
name-calling, political, 161-162
Narcotics, Bureau of, 263
Nash political machine, 139
Nation, The, 72
national, defined, 87
National Advisory Committee on Civil Disorders, 478-481
National Aeronautics and Space Administration, *283*, 284, 488, 575-576
National Aeronautics and Space Council, *250*, *575*
National Archives Building, *281*
National Archives and Record Service, 277, 281
National Association for the Advancement of Colored People, 61, 69, 158, 306
National Association of Electric Companies, 157
National Association of Home Builders of the United States, 160
National Association of Manufacturers, 156
National Association of Real Estate Boards, 157, 160
National Bureau of Standards, 269
National Cancer Institute, *677*
National Catholic Welfare Conference, 158-159
National Center for State Courts, 724
national chairman, 135-*136*, 256
national committees, 136
National Conference of Christians and Jews, 158
National Conference of Commissioners on Uniform State Laws, 395
national conventions, 116-117, 238-240
National Cotton Council, 158
National Council of Churches, 159
National Credit Union Administration, 272
National Dairy Council, 158
national debt, 263
national defense: and Congress, 195; expenditures, 489. *See also* national security.
National Defense Education Act, 272, 667
National Education Association, 158, 160
National Environmental Policy Act of 1969, 573
National Environmental Satellite Service, 269
National Farmers Organization, *159*
National Farmers Union, 157-158, 160

National Federation of Federal Employees, 157
National Federation of Independent Business, 160
national government. *See* federal government.
National Grange, *157*-158, 626
national guard, 352, 555, 561
National Highway Traffic Safety Administration, 273
National Labor Relations Act, 654, 658
National Labor Relations Board, 290-291, 654, 658
National Marine Fisheries Service, 269
National Mediation Board, 290-291, 658
National Milk Producers Federation, 158
National Municipal League, 403-404
National Oceanic and Atmospheric Administration, 269
National Ocean Survey, 269, 650
National Park Service, 268, 641
National Peoples Party, 135
National Railroad Passenger Corporation, 283
National Republican Party, 132
National Science Foundation, 285
national security: defined, 554; economic defense measures, 571-575; and internal security, 565-570; and military defense, 555-565; and space program, 575-576
National Security Act, 263-264
National Security Council, 248, 557-558
National Transportation Safety Board, 273, 698
National Urban League, 61-62, 69
National Weather Service, 269, 650
National Women's Political Caucus, quoted, 708
nationalism, 600
Nationalist China, 533, 549, 585
Nationality Act, 87
natural resources: government responsibility for, 265; state responsibility for, 386; supply of, 571-572
naturalization, *88*; Congress and, 195; defined, 80; group, 87; individual, 87-88; petition for, 88-89; requirements, 88-89
navy: enlistment opportunities, 561-563; responsibilities of, 264
Navy, Department of, 264; Secretary of, 264
Nazi party, 603, 612
nazism, 612
Near v. Minnesota, 154

Near Eastern and South Asian Affairs, Bureau of, 260
Nebraska: capitol, *332*; constitutional amendments, 330; unicameral legislature, *332*, 333; government data, *762-765*; voting requirements, *754*
necessary and proper powers, 196
Negroes: case studies, 76-77, 478-481; and civil rights, 56-73, 384, 465; and the Constitution, 60; and desegregated classes, 68; discrimination against, 102-105; and education, 60-61, 672-673; and jury panels, *375*; list of distinguished, 70-71; mayors, *423*; and voter registration, 67. *See also* Afro-Americans, blacks.
Netherlands, 548, *586*
neutrality, laws of, 528, 581-582
Nevada, *642*; constitution, 330; government data, 333, *762-765*; voting requirements, *754*
New Deal administration, 609
New England Confederation, 27-28
New England towns, 445-449
New England Welfare Compact, 394
New Hampshire, *443*; constitution, 327; government data, 333, 334, *762-765*; as royal colony, 25, 28; voting requirements, *754*
New Jersey: constitution, 328, 330; government data, 333, 337, *762-765*; governor's mansion, *349*; as royal colony, 25; veterans, *338*; voting requirements, *754*
New Jersey Plan, 44, 45
New Mexico, 327, 537; government data, 337, *762-765*; voting requirements, *754*
New Politics party, 135
New York, 183; administrative departments, 360; assembly, *340*; constitutional convention, *329*; government data, 333, 337, *762-765*; governor, *356*; literacy test, 106; as royal colony, 25; voting requirements, *754*
New York City, *413*, 416, 474, 582
New York Times, 72
New Zealand, 572
Newark, New Jersey, 68
Newfoundland, 572
newspapers, and public opinion, 152-154
Nicaragua, 244, 551
Niebuhr, Reinhold, quoted, 368
Nineteenth Amendment, 51, 98, 106
Nixon, Pat, *243*

Nixon, Richard M., 68, 124, 132-133, *134*, 148, 234, 237, 242, *245*, 316-321, 399, 525, *531*, *611*, 618; visit to China, 533; visit to Moscow, 541, 712, 713; with Mexican President, *526*
Nobel Peace Prize, *61*, 71, *592*
nomination of candidates: caucus, 115-116; convention, 52; 116-117; defined, 97, 115, 231; direct primary, 117-119; petition, 115; for Presidency, 238-240; self-announcement, 115
nonpartisan, defined, 97
nonpartisan ballot, 377
nonpartisan election, 107, 108
nonpartisan primary, 119-120
nonviolence, 56, 69
nonvoting, 164-165
Norris, Sen. George W., 229, 292
Norris Act, 292, 399
Norris Dam, 637
Norris-LaGuardia Act, 658
North Atlantic Pact, 548
North Atlantic Treaty Organization, 548-549
North Carolina: congressional district maps, *187*; government data, 339, 354, *762-765*; as royal colony, 25, 28; voting requirements, *754*
North Dakota, 342, *638*; constitutional amendments, 330; government data, *762-765*; voting requirements, *754*
North Korea, 263, 533, 586, 591, 617-621
Northwest Ordinance, 326, 666, 668
Norway, 548
Nuclear Test Ban Treaty, *246*, 541
nuclear weapons, 570, 593, 712

O

Oahu, Hawaii, *101*
Oak Park, Illinois, 454
Oak Ridge, Tennessee, 574
obscenity and Warren Court, 311
Occupational Safety and Health Administration, 270
Office of Consumer Affairs, *249*, 250
Office of Economic Opportunity, 248, *467*
Office of Education, 271-272, 670
Office of Emergency Preparedness, 248, 557, 570, 572
Office of Intergovernmental Relations, *249*, 250
Office of Management and Budget, 248, 399
Office of Saline Water, 268
Office of Science and Technology, 248, 250
Office of the Special Representative for Trade Negotiations, 250

Office of Telecommunications Policy, *249*, 250
Office of the Treasurer of the United States, 261
Office of Wage and Compensation Programs, 270, 660
office-column ballot, 97, 108, *109*
officers' training, 563-564
Ohio, 183; constitutional amendments, 330; government data, *762-765*; voting requirements, *754*
Ohio River Valley Water Sanitation Compact, 393
Okinawa, 538
Oklahoma: constitutional amendments, 330; government data, 337, *762-765*; voting requirements, *754*
Olav V, King of Norway, *61*
old-age retirement benefits, 271, 675
Old-Age Survivors and Disability Insurance, 271
one-party system, USSR, 602-603
Onondaga County, New York, 440
open-door policy, 528, 537
Open Housing-Civil Rights Act, 211
open housing legislation, 68, 684
open primary, 117-118
opinion polls, 133, 148-151
opium, 516
Opportunities Industrialization Center, *66*
opportunity, equality of, 11
optional referendum, 342
ordinances, 408, 421
Oregon, 342, *642*; constitutional amendments, 330; government data, *762-765*; voting requirements, *754*
Organization of American States, *550*, 551
organs, UN, defined, 579
original jurisdiction, 297, 305, 367-368
Oroville Dam, 636
Ottawa, Canada, *601, 607*
overseer of the poor, county, 448

P

Pacific islands under U.S. control, 268, 538
Pacific Marine Fisheries Compact, 393
Pacific Pact, 549
Paducah, Kentucky, 574
page: congressional, 215, *221*; state legislature, *334*
Pakistan, 549-550, 591, 723; war with India, 591, 593
Palmyra Island, 538

Pan American Building, Washington, D.C., *550*
Pan American Union, 551
Panama Canal Zone, 264, 291, 312, 532, 537, 538
panel, jury, 364, 375
Panmunjon, 619
paper money, U.S., *42*, 261, *262*
parcel post system, 266
pardon: defined, 231, 346; by governor, 355-356; by President, 247
Paris, France, *588*
Paris peace talks, 709
parish (county), 427, 429
parity programs, 624, 632
park commissioner: state, *391*; town, 448
parks, national, 640-641
Parliament, Great Britain, 601-602
Parliament Building, *22*
parliamentarian, 201, 204-205
parliamentary democracy, 600, 601
parliamentary system, 601-603
parole, 356
party-column ballot, 97, 108, *109*
party nominating convention, 116-117, 238-240
party whip, 208
passenger miles, 684
passport, 254, 259
Patent Office, U.S., 269, 649
patents, 269, 645, 649; typical legal case, 300
patronage, 123, 139
Paul VI, Pope, 596
pauper, 106
pay-as-you-go policy, 516
payroll tax, 509
Peace and Freedom Party, 135
Peace Corps, 260, 547-548
Pealy, Robert H., quoted, 453
Pearl Harbor, 542, *560*
Pearson, Lester, 590
Pendergast machine, 139
penitentiary, state, *390*
Penn, William, 25, *26*, 28
Penn Central Railroad, *286*
"Penn's Treaty with the Indians," *26*
Pennsylvania, 183; computer-printer, *336*; government data, 337, *762-765*; as proprietary colony, 25; reapportionment, 184; voting requirements, *754*
pensions: congressional, 190-191; old-age, 271, 675
Pentagon, 264, *556*
People's Republic of China. *See* China, Communist.
Percy, Sen. Charles, *127*
perfect union, 36
permanent registration, 101
Permanent Subcommittee on Investigations, 567
persona grata, 254, 259

persona non grata, 254, 260
personal income tax, 261, 506
personal property, 436
Petersborough, New Hampshire, *448*
petit jury, 364, 375
petition: for naturalization, 88-89, for nomination, 115
Petition of Right, 20, 21
Philadelphia, Mississippi, 66
Philadelphia, Pennsylvania, *406, 415, 435, 436*, 464, *665*
"Philadelphia Plan," 72
Philippine Islands, 537
Philippine Pact, 549
pigeonholing bills, 201, 218, 339
Pilgrims, 23-24
plaintiff, 364, 373
plank, platform, 123, 127
Planned Parenthood Association, 158
platforms: major party, 127, 128-129; at national conventions, 239
Plato, 19, 20
Pledge of Allegiance, 4
Plessy v. *Ferguson*, 60
pluralistic group model, 86
Plymouth, Massachusetts, 22-24
pocket veto, 201, 222, 247
Podgorny, Nikolai, *531*, 603
Point-Four Program, 547
Poland, 565
police: and law enforcement, 470-471, 693; local, 352, 462, 486; state, 352, 353, 462; state-local cooperation, 462-463
police court, 366-367
political bosses, 138-139
political clubs, 138
political machines, 138-139, 408
political parties, foreign: France, 602; Great Britain, 602; splinter-party, 131; USSR, 602-603
political parties, U.S.: assessments, 140; bosses, 138-139; campaigns, 126-131; clarify issues, 127-128; coalitions, 124-125; committees, 212-213, 239; congressional campaign committees, 136; contributions, 140; control Congress, 209; convention system, 238-240; cross party lines, 209; defined, 124; finances, 139-141; gifts, 140; and interest groups, 156; local level, 137; machines, 138-139, 408; membership, 125-126; minor, 132-135; national chairman, 135-136; national committee, 136; nature of, 124-126; organization, 135-139; platforms, 127, 239; responsibilities, 130; select candidates, 126-127; services, 126-131; social functions, 140; state central committee,

estate, 510; evasion and fraud, 262; excise, 502, 508-509; federal, 261, 505-511; gasoline, 515; gift, 510; head, 505; hidden, 505; income, 504, 506-508; indirect, 502, 505; inheritance, 510; local, 435, 511-515; payroll, 509-510; poll, 51, 102, 105; property, 511-512, 666, 718-719; sales, 512-514; social security, 509-510, 515; special, 515; state, 511-515; uniform, 502, 505; use, 512-514; value added, 719; withholding, 261, 502, 507

teachers, *668*; certification of, 440; improving methods, 673; shortage of, 672

Teapot Dome scandal, 223

technical assistance, foreign, 547-548

television: campaigning, *127*; and Congressional investigations, 223; federal regulation of, 155, 288; and public opinion, 154-155

teller, vote counting by, 220

Ten Commandments, 18

Tennessee, 60; constitutional amendments, 330; government data, 334, *762-765*; reapportionment, 335; voting requirements, *754*

Tennessee River, 396, 399

Tennessee Valley Authority, 292, 398-399, 609, 637-638

Tenth Amendment, 48, 192

term: of Congress, 101; defined, 178; of representatives, 180, 183; of senators, 180, 186

terracing, 624, 635

territories: administered by UN, 590, 592; and citizenship, 86, 87; and Congress, 187, *194*, 195; courts, 312-313; defined, 324; and expansion, 592

testimonial, 162

Texas, 183, 534; government data, *762-765*; and poll tax, 102; voting requirements, *754*

Thailand, 549, *564*, 590

Thames River, *22*

theory of government, 1

Thirteenth Amendment, 51, 60, 465

Thurmond, Sen. J. Strom, 133-134, 197, *202*

Ticonderoga, USS, *562*

tie votes, 196, 206, 236, 237

time, measurement of, 724

Tocqueville, Alexis de, 193; quoted, *613*

Torch Fund, 674

totalitarianism, 600-605

town clerk, 447-448

town hall, 408

town manager, 447

town meeting, 10, 446-449

Town Meeting of the World, *584*

township, 449-453; congressional, 444; number of, 408

Toy Manufacturers of the U.S.A., 157

trade agreements, 250

trade associations, 156-157

Trade Expansion Act, 648

trade, international, 712

trademarks, 301, 645, 649-650

traffic, 273; fatalities, *697*; safety, 696-697; and state responsibility, 385

traffic court, *365*, 373

transfer, device, 162

transportation: ICC regulation of, 286-287; in metropolitan areas, 469-470, 720-721

Transportation, Department of, 254, 255, *257*, 272, 273, 286, 488, 563, 650, 652, 696; Secretary of, *257*, 273

treasurer: county, 435; state, 357-358; town, 448

Treasurer of the United States, 261

Treasury, Department of the, 261-263

treaties: and Bricker Amendment, 432; defined, 528; making of, *246*; President negotiates, 532; Senate's role, 532; states forbidden to make, 48

Treaty of Mutual Cooperation and Security, 549

trial, 365, 373, 375-376

trial by jury, right to, 4, 364-365, 378

trial courts, 367; defined, 364

troops, use of, 533

Truman, Harry S., 132, 151, 168, 197, 235, 244, 532, 542; and civil rights, 62; and communism, 568; election, *150*; Point-Four Program, 547; quoted, 231; and steel strike, 308

Truman Doctrine, 542-543, 546

trust, 645

trust funds, 484, 489-490

trust territories, 579, 590, 592

trustee, village, 455

Trusteeship Council, 583, 590-592

trusts, federal actions against, 651

Turkey, 542-543, 548

turnpikes, *503*

Tuskegee Institute, 60

Twelfth Amendment, 38, 51, 197, 232, 237, 240, 715

Twenty-fifth Amendment, 51, 236

Twenty-first Amendment, 38, 51

Twenty-fourth Amendment, 51, 236

Twenty-second Amendment, 51, 237, 250

Twenty-sixth Amendment, 51, 99, 106

Twenty-third Amendment, 51, 98, 100, 424

Twenty-seventh Amendment, proposed, 708

two-party system, Great Britain, 602

two-party system, United States, 131-135

U

U Thant, 586, *613*; quoted, 593

Udall, Stewart L., quoted, 637

Un-American Activities Committee, 567

Uncertain Tradition, An, 256

undeclared wars, 710

Under-Secretary of State for Special Political Affairs, *592*

unemployment and federal government, 269, 715

unemployment compensation, 270, 656-657

unicameral legislature, 333; defined, 324

unified budget, 484, 489

uniform state law, 383

uniform tax, 502, 505

Union Calendar, 219

Union of Soviet Socialist Republics, 529, 533, 541-543, 545, 546, 570, 574, 585, 592, 723; government of, 602-604, *609*

unions, 62, 654-656

unitary government, 607

United Automobile Workers, 147, 157

United Electrical, Radio, and Machine Workers of America, 157

United Federation of Postal Clerks, 160

United Fund, 674

United Kingdom. *See* Great Britain.

United Nations: admission of new nations, 592; Big Five, 585-586; budget, 594; charter, 582-583; disputes, settling, 590-591; Economic and Social Council, 583, 587-588, 591; economic sanctions, 590; European office, *583*; finances, 594; future of, 595, 596; General Assembly, 583-585, 590-595; headquarters, *539*, 582; International Court of Justice, *581*, 583, 586-587, 594; and Korean intervention, 591; Military Staff Committee, 558, 586; purposes of, 583; Secretariat, 583, 586; Secretary-General, 583, 586, *592, 613*; Security Council,

weights and measures, 269
welfare, 664, *705*; social, 674-676
Welfare administration, 271, 674
welfare state, 600, 610
Wesberry v. *Sanders*, 186
West, Benjamin, *26*
West Germany, 548
West Indies, 533
West Point, Kentucky, *454*
West Virginia, 333, 337; government data, *762-765*; voting requirements, *754*
Whig party, 132
whip, party, 201, 208
whip check, 208
whip notice, 208
White, Justice Byron R., 306, *307*, 717
White, Walter, 61
White Citizens Council, 63
White House, *98*, 178, *233*
White House Conference on Civil Rights, 67, 72
White House Conference on Equal Employment Opportunity, 71
White House Office, 248, 258
white primary, 102
Wickersham Commission, 366
wildlife conservation, 640
Wilkins, Roy, 61, *65*, 69
William and Mary, monarchs of England, 22
William the Conqueror, 20
Williamsburg, Virginia, *26, 27*
Williams, G. Mennen, quoted, 361
Willis Committee, 567

Willkie, Wendell, 540
Wilson, Woodrow, 3, 132, 133, 195, 197, 244, 533, 538, 699; as governor, 347; and League of Nations, 49; and World War I, *559*
windbreaks, 635
Wisconsin: electric voting machine, 325; government data, *762-765*; state assembly, 334; supreme court, *370*; voting requirements, *754*
withholding tax, 261, 502, 507
women: in Congress, 181, *203*, *727*; equal opportunity for, 659, 708; labor regulations for, 659; in military service, 561; suffrage for, *98, 99*, 106
Women's Bureau, 270, 659
women's liberation groups, 708
women's rights, constitutional amendment for, 708
work experience programs, 248
workmen's compensation, 301, 645, 660-661
world affairs, U.S. and, 528-551
World Court, 211
world government, 595-596
World Health Organization, 588
World Meteorological Organization, 588
World War I, 529, 534, 538, 559
World War II: Atlantic Charter, 542; bipartisan cabinet, 256; international cooperation, 541-542; and selective service, 559-560
writ of: *habeas corpus*, 35, 47;

injunction, 297, 309, 645, 658; mandamus, 297, 309
write-in vote, *107*
Wyoming, 99, 183; government data, 337, *762-765*; voting requirements, *754*

Y

Yates v. *United States*, 568
Yellin v. *United States*, 225
Yellowstone National Park, 268, 641
Yellowstone River Compact, 393
Yemen, 595
Yorty, Mayor Sam, *366*
Yosemite National Park, 641
Young, Whitney, 62, *65*, 75
Young Democrats clubs, 138
Young Republican National Federation, *138*
Young Republicans clubs, 138
Youth Development and Delinquency Prevention Administration, 674
youth vote, 708-709; college students registering, *111*
Yugoslavia, 606

Z

Zambia, 584
Zenger, John Peter, 27
Zion Canyon, 640
zoning: metropolitan, 458, 471